P9-AFY-885

WITHDRAWN

Contemporary Literary Criticism Yearbook 1994

Guide to Gale Literary Criticism Series

For criticism on	Consult these Gale series
Authors now living or who died after December 31, 1959	*CONTEMPORARY LITERARY CRITICISM (CLC)*
Authors who died between 1900 and 1959	*TWENTIETH-CENTURY LITERARY CRITICISM (TCLC)*
Authors who died between 1800 and 1899	*NINETEENTH-CENTURY LITERATURE CRITICISM (NCLC)*
Authors who died between 1400 and 1799	*LITERATURE CRITICISM FROM 1400 TO 1800 (LC)* *SHAKESPEAREAN CRITICISM (SC)*
Authors who died before 1400	*CLASSICAL AND MEDIEVAL LITERATURE CRITICISM (CMLC)*
Black writers of the past two hundred years	*BLACK LITERATURE CRITICISM (BLC)*
Authors of books for children and young adults	*CHILDREN'S LITERATURE REVIEW (CLR)*
Dramatists	*DRAMA CRITICISM (DC)*
Hispanic writers of the late nineteenth and twentieth centuries	*HISPANIC LITERATURE CRITICISM (HLC)*
Native North American writers and orators of the eighteenth, nineteenth, and twentieth centuries	*NATIVE NORTH AMERICAN LITERATURE (NNAL)*
Poets	*POETRY CRITICISM (PC)*
Short story writers	*SHORT STORY CRITICISM (SSC)*
Major authors from the Renaissance to the present	*WORLD LITERATURE CRITICISM, 1500 TO THE PRESENT (WLC)*

ISSN 0091-3421

Volume 86

Contemporary Literary Criticism

Yearbook 1994

The Year in Fiction, Poetry, Drama, and World Literature and the Year's New Authors, Prizewinners, Obituaries, and Outstanding Literary Events

Christopher Giroux
EDITOR

Jeff Chapman
ASSOCIATE EDITOR
CLC YEARBOOK

Pamela S. Dear
John D. Jorgenson
Matt McDonough
Brigham Narins
Deborah A. Stanley
Aarti D. Stephens
Polly A. Vedder
Thomas Wiloch
Kathleen Wilson
Janet Witalec
ASSOCIATE EDITORS

An International Thomson Publishing Company

NEW YORK • LONDON • BONN • BOSTON • DETROIT • MADRID
MELBOURNE • MEXICO CITY • PARIS • SINGAPORE • TOKYO
TORONTO • WASHINGTON • ALBANY NY • BELMONT CA • CINCINNATI OH

STAFF

Christopher Giroux, *Editor*

Jeff Chapman, Pamela S. Dear, John D. Jorgenson, Matt McDonough, Brigham Narins,
Deborah A. Stanley, Aarti D. Stephens, Polly A. Vedder, Thomas Wiloch,
Kathleen Wilson, Janet Witalec, *Associate Editors*
George H. Blair, *Assistant Editor*

Marlene H. Lasky, *Permissions Manager*
Margaret A. Chamberlain, Linda M. Pugliese, *Permissions Specialists*
Susan Brohman, Diane Cooper, Maria Franklin, Pamela A. Hayes, Arlene Johnson, Josephine M. Keene, Michele Lonoconus, Maureen Puhl, Shalice Shah, Kimberly F. Smilay, Barbara A. Wallace, *Permissions Associates*
Edna Hedblad, Tyra Y. Phillips, *Permissions Assistants*

Victoria B. Cariappa, *Research Manager*
Frank Vincent Castronova, Eva M. Felts, Mary Beth McElmeel, Donna Melnychenko, Tamara C. Nott,
Tracie A. Richardson, Norma Sawaya, *Research Associates*
Shirley Gates, Michele P. Pica, Laurel D. Sprague, Amy Terese Steel, *Research Assistants*

Mary Beth Trimper, *Production Director*
Shanna Heilveil, *Production Assistant*

Cynthia Baldwin, *Product Design Manager*
Barbara J. Yarrow, *Graphic Services Supervisor*
Sherrell Hobbs, *Macintosh Artist*
Willie F. Mathis, *Camera Operator*
Pamela A. Hayes, *Photography Coordinator*

Library of Congress Catalog Card Number 76-38938
ISBN 0-8103-4996-5
ISSN 0091-3421

Printed in the United States of America

10 9 8 7 6 5 4 3 2 1

I(T)P™ Gale Research Inc., an International Thomson Publishing Company.
ITP logo is a trademark under license.

Contents

IN MEMORIAM

TOPICS IN LITERATURE: 1994

Preface

A Comprehensive Information Source on Contemporary Literature

Scope of the *Yearbook*

Contemporary Literary Criticism Yearbook is a part of the ongoing *Contemporary Literary Criticism (CLC)* series. *CLC* provides a comprehensive survey of modern literature by presenting excerpted criticism on the works of novelists, poets, playwrights, short story writers, scriptwriters, and other creative writers now living or who died after December 31, 1959. A strong emphasis is placed on including criticism of works by established authors who frequently appear on syllabuses of high school and college literature courses.

To complement this broad coverage, the *Yearbook* focuses more specifically on a given year's literary activities and features a larger number of currently noteworthy authors than is possible in standard *CLC* volumes. *CLC Yearbook* provides students, teachers, librarians, researchers, and general readers with information and commentary on the outstanding literary works and events of a given year.

Format of the Book

CLC, Volume 86: *Yearbook 1994,* which includes excerpted criticism on more than twenty authors and comprehensive coverage of three key issues in contemporary literature, is divided into five sections—"The Year in Review," "New Authors," "Prizewinners," "In Memoriam," and "Topics in Literature: 1994."

- **The Year in Review**—This section consists of specially commissioned essays by prominent writers who survey the year's works in their respective fields. Bruce Allen discusses "The Year in Fiction," Allen Hoey "The Year in Poetry," Julius Novick "The Year in Drama," and William Riggan "The Year in World Literature." For introductions to the essayists, please see the Notes on Contributors.

- **New Authors**—This section introduces eight writers who received significant critical recognition for their first major work of fiction in 1994 or whose work was translated into English or published in the United States for the first time. Authors were selected for inclusion if their work was reviewed in several prominent literary periodicals.

- **Prizewinners**—This section begins with a list of literary prizes and honors announced in 1994, citing the award, award criteria, the recipient, and the title of the prizewinning work. Following the listing of prizewinners is a presentation of eleven entries on individual award winners, representing a mixture of genres and nationalities as well as established prizes and those more recently introduced.

- **In Memoriam**—This section consists of reminiscences, tributes, retrospective articles, and obituary notices on six authors who died in 1994. In addition, an Obituary section provides information on other recently deceased literary figures.

- **Topics in Literature**—This section focuses on literary issues and events of considerable public interest, including Electronic "Books," Graphic Narratives, and Sylvia Plath and the Nature of Biography.

Features

With the exception of the four essays in "The Year in Review" section, which were written specifically for this publication, the *Yearbook* consists of excerpted criticism drawn from literary reviews, general magazines, newspapers, books, and scholarly journals. *Yearbook* entries variously contain the following items:

- An **Author Heading** in the "New Authors" and "Prizewinners" sections cites the name under which the author publishes and the title of the work discussed in the entry; the "In Memoriam" section includes the author's name and birth and death dates. The author's full name, pseudonyms (if any) under which the author has published, nationality, and principal genres are listed on the first line of the author entry.

- The **Subject Heading** defines the theme of each entry in "The Year in Review" and "Topics in Literature" sections.

- A brief **Biographical and Critical Introduction** to the author and his or her work precedes excerpted criticism in the "New Authors," "Prizewinners," and "In Memoriam" sections; the subjects, authors, and works in the "Topics in Literature" section are introduced in a similar manner.

- A listing of **Principal Works** is included for all entries in the "Prizewinners" and "In Memoriam" sections.

- A **Portrait** of the author is included in the "New Authors," "Prizewinners," and "In Memoriam" sections, and an **Excerpt from the Author's Work,** if available or applicable, is also provided. Whenever possible, a recent, previously unpublished **Author Interview** also accompanies each entry.

- The **Excerpted Criticism,** included in all entries except those in the "Year in Review" section, represents essays selected by editors to reflect the spectrum of opinion about a specific work or about an author's writing in general. The excerpts are typically arranged chronologically, adding a useful perspective to the entry. In the "Year in Review," "New Authors," "Prizewinners," and "In Memoriam" sections, all titles by the author being discussed are printed in boldface type, enabling the reader to more easily identify the author's work.

- A complete **Bibliographical Citation,** designed to help the user find the original essay or book, precedes each excerpt.

- **Cross-references** have been included in the "New Authors," "Prizewinners," and "In Memoriam" sections to direct readers to other useful sources published by Gale Research. Previous volumes of *CLC* in which the author has been featured are also listed.

Other Features

The *Yearbook* also includes the following features:

- An **Acknowledgments** section lists the copyright holders who have granted permission to reprint material in this volume of *CLC*. It does not, however, list every book or periodical reprinted or consulted during the preparation of this volume.

- A **Cumulative Author Index** lists all the authors who have appeared in the Literary Criticism Series published by Gale Research, with cross-references to Gale's Biographical and Autobiographical Series. A full listing of series referenced in the index appears at the beginning of the index. Readers will welcome this cumulated author index as a useful tool for locating an author within the various series. The index, which lists birth and death dates when available, is particularly valuable for locating references to those authors whose careers span two periods. For example, Ernest Hemingway is found in *CLC,* yet a writer often associated with him, F. Scott Fitzgerald, is found in *Twentieth-Century Literary Criticism.*

- Beginning with *CLC,* Vol. 65, each *Yearbook* contains a **Cumulative Topic Index,** which lists all literary topics treated in *CLC* as well as the topic volumes of *Twentieth-Century Literary Criticism, Nineteenth-Century Literature Criticism,* and *Literature Criticism from 1400 to 1800.*

- A **Cumulative Nationality Index** alphabetically lists all authors featured in *CLC* by nationality, followed by numbers corresponding to the volumes in which the authors appear.

- A **Title Index** alphabetically lists all titles reviewed in the current volume of *CLC.* Listings are followed by the author's name and the corresponding page numbers where the titles are discussed. English translations of foreign titles and variations of titles are cross-referenced to the title under which a work was originally published. Titles of novels, novellas, dramas, films, record albums, and poetry, short story, and essay collections are printed in italics, while all individual poems, short stories, essays, and songs are printed in roman type within quotation marks. When published separately, the titles of long poems (e.g., T. S. Eliot's *The Waste Land*) are printed in italics.

Citing *Contemporary Literary Criticism*

When writing papers, students who quote directly from any volume in the Literary Criticism Series may use the following general forms to footnote reprinted criticism. The first example is for material drawn from periodicals, the second for material reprinted from books:

[1]Alfred Cismaru, "Making the Best of It," *The New Republic,* 207, No. 24, (December 7, 1992), 30, 32; excerpted and reprinted in *Contemporary Literary Criticism,* Vol. 85, ed. Christopher Giroux (Detroit: Gale Research Inc., 1995), pp. 73-4.

[2]Yvor Winters, *The Post-Symbolist Methods* (Allan Swallow, 1967); excerpted and reprinted in *Contemporary Literary Criticism,* Vol. 85, ed. Christopher Giroux (Detroit: Gale Research Inc., 1995), pp. 223-26.

Suggestions Are Welcome

The editor hopes that readers will find *CLC Yearbook* a useful reference tool and welcomes comments about the work. Send comments and suggestions to: Editor, *Contemporary Literary Criticism,* Gale Research Inc., 835 Penobscot Building, Detroit, MI 48226-4094.

Acknowledgments

The editors wish to thank the copyright holders of the excerpted criticism included in this volume and the permissions managers of many book and magazine publishing companies for assisting us in securing reprint rights. We are also grateful to the staffs of the Detroit Public Library, the Library of Congress, the University of Detroit Mercy Library, Wayne State University Purdy/Kresge Library Complex, and the University of Michigan Libraries for making their resources available to us. Following is a list of the copyright holders who have granted us permission to reprint material in this volume of ***CLC.*** Every effort has been made to trace copyright, but if omissions have been made, please let us know.

COPYRIGHTED EXCERPTS IN *CLC,* VOLUME 86, WERE REPRINTED FROM THE FOLLOWING PERIODICALS:

The American Book Review, v. 14, February-March, 1993. © 1993 by *The American Book Review.* Reprinted by permission of the publisher.—***Analog Science Fiction/Science Fact,*** v. CXI, January, 1991. © 1991 by Davis Publications, Inc. Reprinted by permission of the publisher.—***The Atlantic Monthly,*** v. 274, September, 1994 for "The End of the Book?" by D. T. Max. Copyright 1994 by The Atlantic Monthly Company, Boston, MA. Reprinted by permission of the author.—***Book World—Chicago Tribune,*** April 17, 1994. © copyrighted 1994, Chicago Tribune Company. All rights reserved. Used with permission.—***Book World—The Washington Post,*** March 28, 1993; January 23, 1994. February 6, 1994. © 1993, 1994, *The Washington Post.* All reprinted with permission of the publisher.—***Booklist,*** v. 90, October 1, 1993; v. 90, October 15, 1993. Copyright © 1993 by the American Library Association. Both reprinted by permission of the publisher.—***Books in Canada,*** v. XXI, September, 1992 for "Gritty Terrain" by Douglas Hill; v. XXII, April, 1993 for "Memorable Images" by Sandra Birdsell, Douglas Glover, and Jack Hodgins. Both reprinted by permission of the respective authors.—***The Boston Globe,*** January 30, 1994. © 1994 Globe Newspaper Co. Reprinted courtesy of *The Boston Globe.*—***Boston Review,*** v. XIX, February-March, 1994 for a review of *Remembering Babylon* by Harvey Blume. Copyright © 1994 by the Boston Critic, Inc. Reprinted by permission of the author.—***Chicago,*** v. 43, January, 1994. Reprinted by permission of the publisher.—***Chicago Tribune—Books,*** May 9, 1993 for "End as a Man" by Charles R. Larson; April 3, 1994 for "From Canada: A Portentous, Symbol-laden Tale of Forgetting and Identity" by Anne Whitehouse. © copyrighted 1993, 1994, Chicago Tribune Company. All rights reserved. Both reprinted by permission of the respective authors.—***The Chronicle of Higher Education,*** v. XL, May 11, 1994. Copyright © 1994 *The Chronicle of Higher Education.* Reprinted with permission of the publisher.—***CLA Journal,*** v. XX, June, 1977. Copyright, 1977 by The College Language Association. Used by permission of The College Language Association.—***Commonweal,*** v. CXIX, February 28, 1992. Copyright © 1992 Commonweal Foundation. Reprinted by permission of Commonweal Foundation.—***Communication Research,*** v. 16, August, 1989. © 1989 Sage Publications, Inc. Reprinted by permission of the publisher.—***Comparative Literature Studies,*** v. 22, Spring, 1985. Copyright © 1985 by The Pennsylvania State University. Reproduced by permission of The Pennsylvania State University Press.—***The Dalhousie Review,*** v. 68, Winter, 1988-89 for "Potterland" by Paul Delany. Reprinted by permission of the publisher and the author.—***Detroit Free Press,*** s. G, May 22, 1994 for "Inspired by War" by Kevin Walker. Reprinted by permission of the author./June 6, 1994. Reprinted by permission of the publisher.—***Entertainment Weekly,*** n. 212, March 4, 1994. © 1994 Entertainment Weekly Inc. All rights reserved. Reprinted by permission of the publisher.—***The Hudson Review,*** v. XLVI, Autumn, 1993; v. XLVI, Winter, 1994. Copyright © 1993, 1994 by The Hudson Review, Inc. Both reprinted by permission of the publisher.—***Hungry Mind Review,*** n. 28, Winter 1993; n. 29, Spring, 1994. Both reprinted by permission of the publisher.—***The Journal of Japanese Studies,*** v. 7, Winter, 1981. © 1981 Society for Japanese Studies. Reprinted by permission of the publisher.—***Kirkus Reviews,*** v. LXI, February 15, 1993; v. LXI, October 15, 1993; v. LXII, February 15, 1994. Copyright © 1993, 1994 The Kirkus Service, Inc. All rights reserved. All reprinted by permission of the publisher.—***Library Journal,*** v. 115, March 15, 1990 for "Picture This: Graphic Novels in Libraries" by Keith R. A. DeCandido; v. 117, February 1, 1992 for "The Print Prison" by Eldred Smith; v. 118, March 15, 1993 for a review of *Neon Vernacular: New and Selected Poems* by Lenard D. Moore; v. 113, April 15, 1993 for a review of *Theory of War* by Scott H. Silverman. Copyright © 1990, 1992, 1993 by Reed Publishing, USA, Division of Reed Holdings, Inc. All reprinted from *Library Journal,* published by R. R. Bowker, Co., Division of Reed Publishing, USA, by permission of the publisher and the respective authors.—***London Review of Books,*** v. 15, May 13, 1993 for "Nicely! Nicely!" by Jenny Turner; v. 15, August 5, 1993 for "Small Bodies" by Wendy Brandmark; v. 16, May 12, 1994 for "So Sue Me" by Michael Wood; v. 16, May 26, 1994 for "The Paranoid Sublime" by Andrew O'Hagan. All appear here by permission of the *London Review of Books* and the respective authors.—***Los Angeles Times,*** July 11, 1993; June 12, 1994. Copyright, 1993, 1994, *Los Angeles Times*. Both reprinted by permission of the publisher.—***Los Angeles Times Book Review,*** November 8, 1992; March 7, 1993; May 30, 1993; October 31, 1993; February 20, 1994; May 29, 1994; October 30, 1994; November 13, 1994. Copyright 1992, *Los Angeles Times*. All reprinted by permission of the publisher.—***Meanjin,*** v. 52, September, 1993 for "Forgetting Colonialism" by Peter Otto. Reprinted by permission of the author.—***The Nation,*** New York, v. 250, March 19, 1990; v. 258, March 14, 1994; v. 258, April 25, 1994; v. 259, October 24, 1994. Copyright 1990, 1994 *The Nation* magazine/The Nation Company, Inc. All reprinted by permission of the publisher.—***The New Leader,*** v. LXXVII, January 17-31, 1994; v. LXXVII, February 14-28, 1994; v. LXXVII, March 14-28, 1994. © 1994 by The American Labor Conference on International Affairs, Inc. All reprinted by permission of the publisher.—***The New Republic,*** v. 198, February 15, 1988; v. 202, January 8-15, 1990; v. 208, April 5, 1993; v. 210, February 7, 1994; v. 210, April 4, 1994; v. 210, May 2, 1994; v. 210, May 9, 1994. © 1994 The New Republic, Inc. All reprinted by permission of *The New Republic*.—***New Statesman & Society,*** v. 1, July 29, 1988; v. 7, March 18, 1994. © 1988, 1994 Statesman & Nation Publishing Company Limited. Both reprinted by permission of the publisher.—***New Statesman,*** v. 114, December 12-25, 1987-January 1, 1988. © 1988 The Statesman & Nation Publishing Co. Ltd. Reprinted by permission of the publisher.—***The New York Review of Books,*** v. XXXIV, May 7, 1987; v. XXXVIII, March 7, 1991; v. XL, April 22, 1993; v. XL, December 20, 1993; v. XLI, February 17, 1994. Copyright © 1987, 1991, 1993, 1994 Nyrev, Inc. All reprinted with permission from *The New York Review of Books*.—***The New York Times,*** June 12, 1994 for an interview between Dennis Potter and Melvyn Bragg by John Rockwell. Reprinted by permission of Robert Cornfield Literary Agency./October 19, 1993; January 4, 1994; February 14, 1994; February 25, 1994; March 29, 1994; April 10, 1994; April 13, 1994; May 2, 1994; May 12, 1994; August 19, 1994; October 14, 1994; November 6, 1994; November 29, 1994; December 16, 1994. Copyright © 1993, 1994 by The New York Times. All reprinted by permission of the publisher.—***The New York Times Book Review,*** November 15, 1987; August 8, 1993; December 19, 1993; January 9, 1994; January 16, 1994; February 27, 1994; March 6, 1994; March 20, 1994; April 3, 1994; August 14, 1994; October 9, 1994. Copyright © 1994 by The New York Times Company. All reprinted by permission of the publisher.—***New York*** Magazine, v. 26, December 13, 1993; v. 27, January 10, 1994; v. 27, January 31, 1994; v. 27, April 4, 1994. Copyright © 1994 K-III Magazine Corporation. All rights reserved. All reprinted with the permission of *New York* Magazine.—***The New Yorker,*** v. LXX, March 7, 1994 for "Bad Influence" by Henry Louis Gates, Jr.; v. LXX, April 11, 1994 for "Eugène Ionesco" by John Lahr; v. LXX, May 16, 1994 for "Sons and Mothers" by John Lahr. © 1994 by the authors. All reprinted by the respective authors./v. LXIX, March 15, 1993 for "Recruiting Raw Nerves" by John Updike; v. LXX, March 14, 1994 for "Visible Man" by David Remnick. © 1993, 1994 by the authors. All reprinted by permission of the publisher./v. LXX, March 28, 1994. © 1994 by The New Yorker Magazine, Inc. Reprinted by permission of the publisher.—***Newsday,*** March 24, 1994. © Newsday, Inc. 1994. Reprinted by permission.—***Newsweek,*** v. CXXIII, January 17, 1994; v. CXXIII, February 28, 1994; v. CXXIII, April 11, 1994; v. CXXIV, September 5, 1994. © 1994, Newsweek, Inc. All rights reserved. All reprinted by permission of the publisher.—***The Observer,*** January 17, 1993; February 6, 1994; June 12, 1994; August 14, 1994;. All reprinted by permission of The Observer Limited, London.—***The Progressive,*** v. 56, November, 1992; v. 58, May, 1994. Copyright © 1992, 1994, The Progressive, Inc. Both reprinted by permission from *The Progressive,* 409 East Main Street, Madison, WI 53703.—***Publishers Weekly,*** v. 235, February 17, 1989; v. 236, November 24, 1989; v. 237, July 27, 1990; v. 240, May 24, 1993; v. 240, August 30, 1993; v. 240, September 6, 1993; v. 241, January 31, 1994; v. 241, July 18, 1994; v. 241, August 8, 1994; v. 241, August 22, 1994; v. 241, August 29, 1994; v. 241, September 19, 1994; v. 241, October 24, 1994. Copyright 1989, 1990, 1993, 1994 by Reed Publishing USA. All reprinted from *Publishers Weekly,* published by the Bowker Magazine Group of Cahners Publishing Co., a division of Reed Publishing USA.—***Quardrant,*** v. XXXVIII, January-February, 1994 for "Artful" by Cynthia Blanche.

Reprinted by permission of *Quadrant,* Sydney, Australia and the author.—***Quill & Quire,*** v. 58, May, 1992 for a review of *Amnesia* by Daniel Jones. Reprinted by permission of *Quill & Quire* and the author.—***Rolling Stone,*** i. 578, May 17, 1990. © by Straight Arrow Publishers, Inc. All rights reserved. Reprinted by permission of the publisher.—***The Sewanee Review,*** v. C, Spring, 1992 for "Well Wrought Facts" by Michael L. Hall. © 1992 by The University of the South. Reprinted with the permission of the editor of *The Sewanee Review* and the author.—***The Spectator,*** v. 272, April 2, 1994. © 1994 by *The Spectator.* Reprinted by permission of *The Spectator.*—***Theatre Journal,*** v. 44, May, 1992. © 1992, University of College Theatre Association of the American Theatre Association. Reprinted by permission of the publisher.—***The Threepenny Review,*** v. XV, Summer, 1994. © copyright 1994 by *The Threepenny Review.* Reprinted by permission of the publisher.—***The Times Literary Supplement,*** n. 4375, February 6, 1987; n. 4437, April 15-21, 1988; n. 4669, September 25, 1992; n. 4691, February 26, 1993; n. 4748, April 1, 1994; n. 4757, June 3, 1994. © The Times Supplements Limited 1987, 1988, 1992, 1993, 1994. All reproduced from *The Times Literary Supplement* by permission.—***The Times,*** London, May 16, 1994; August 19, 1994. © Times Newspapers Limited 1994. Both reproduced from *The Times,* London by permission.—***Utne Reader,*** n. 62, March-April, 1994. Copyright © 1994 by LENS Publishing Co. All rights reserved. Reprinted by permission of the publisher.—***Vanity Fair,*** v. 57, April, 1994. Copyright © 1994 by The Condé Nast Publications Inc. Courtesy *Vanity Fair.*—***The Village Voice,*** v. XXXIV, March 1, 1994 for "Albeecentric" by Michael Feingold; v. XXXIX, March 15, 1994 for "Full Disclosure" by Karen Houppert; v. XXXIX, April 5, 1994 for "Twilight's First Gleaming" by Michael Feingold. Copyright © 1994 by The Village Voice, Inc., 1994. All reprinted by permission of *The Village Voice* and the author.—***Vogue,*** v. 184, March, 1994 for "Stolen Kisses," by Orville Schnell. Copyright © 1994 by The Condé Nast Publications Inc. Reprinted by permission of the author.—***The Wall Street Journal,*** July 26, 1993 for "Race, Justice and Integrity in the Old South" by Bruce Bawer. © 1993 Dow Jones & Company, Inc. All rights reserved Worldwide. Reprinted by permission of the author./ February 13, 1992; July 12, 1994. © 1992, 1994 Dow Jones & Company, Inc. All rights reserved Worldwide. Both reprinted by permission of *The Wall Street Journal.*—***The Washington Post,*** April 18, 1994, for "The Singular Vision of Ralph Ellison by Charles Johnson." © 1994, Washington Post Co. Reprinted by permission of Georges Borchardt, Inc.—***The Women's Review of Books,*** v. XI, July, 1994 for "Haunted Household" by Barbara Rich; v. XI, July, 1994 for "The Workings of Chance and Memory" by Sue Russell; v. XI, September, 1994 for "A Piece of the Past" by Jewelle Gomez. Copyright © 1994. All rights reserved. All reprinted by permission of the respective authors.—***World Literature Today,*** v. 52, Spring, 1978; v. 56, Winter, 1982; v. 58, Summer, 1984; v. 61, Spring, 1987; v. 62, Summer, 1988; v. 65, Spring, 1991. Copyright 1978, 1982, 1984, 1988, 1991 by the University of Oklahoma Press. All reprinted by permission of the publisher.

COPYRIGHTED EXCERPTS IN *CLC,* VOLUME 86, WERE REPRINTED FROM THE FOLLOWING BOOKS:

Andrews, Carol M. From "Cleanth Brooks on Faulkner: Yoknapatawpha and the Vanderbilt Tradition," in ***The Vanderbilt Tradition: Essays in Honor of Thomas Daniel Young.*** Edited by Mark Royden Winchell. Louisiana State University Press, 1991. Copyright © 1991 by Louisiana State University Press. All rights reserved. Reprinted by permission of the publisher.—Berendt, John. From ***Midnight in the Garden of Good and Evil: A Savannah Story.*** Random House, 1994. Copyright © 1994 by John Berendt. All right reserved.—Bolter, Jay David. From ***Writing Space: The Computer, Hypertext, and the History of Writing.*** Erlbaum, 1991. Copyright © 1991 by Lawrence Erlbaum Associates, Inc. All rights reserved. Reprinted by permission of the publisher.—Brady, Joan. From ***Theory of War.*** Alfred A. Knopf, 1993. Copyright © 1993 by Joan Brady. All rights reserved.—Brown-Guillory, Elizabeth. From ***Their Place on Stage: Black Women Playwrights in America.*** Greenwood Press, 1988. Copyright © 1988 by Elizabeth Brown-Guillory. All rights reserved. Reprinted by permission of Greenwood Publishing Group, Inc., Westport, CT.—Childress, Alice. From ***A Hero Ain't Nothin' but a Sandwich.*** Coward, McCann & Geoghegan, 1973. Copyright © 1973 by Alice Childress. All rights reserved.—Childress, Alice. From an interview in ***Interviews with Contemporary Women Playwrights.*** Edited by Kathleen Betsko and Rachel Koenig. Beech Tree Books, 1987. Copyright © 1987 by Kathleen Betsko and Rachel Koenig. All rights reserved. Reprinted by permission of Beech Tree Books, a division of William Morrow and Company, Inc.—Cooper, Douglas. From ***Amnesia: A Novel.*** Hyperion, 1994. Copyright © 1994 Douglas Cooper.

All rights reserved.—French, Albert. From ***Billy.*** Viking Penguin, 1993. Copyright © Albert French, 1993. All rights reserved.—Gaddis, William. From ***A Frolic of His Own.*** Poseidon Press, 1994. Copyright © 1994 by William Gaddis. All rights reserved.—Hamilton, Ian. From ***Keepers of the Flame: Literary Estates and the Rise of Biography.*** Hutchinson, 1992. Copyright © Ian Hamilton 1992. All rights reserved. Reprinted by permission of the publisher.—Killens, John O. From "The Literary Genius of Alice Childress," in ***Black Women Writers (1950-1980): A Critical Evaluation.*** Edited by Mari Evans. Anchor Press/Doubleday, 1984. Copyright © 1983 by Mari Evans. All rights reserved. Used by permission of Doubleday, a division of Bantam Doubleday Dell Publishing Group, Inc.—Landow, George P. From "Changing Texts, Changing Readers: Hypertext, Literary Education, Criticism, and Scholarship," in ***Reorientations: Critical Theories and Pedagogies.*** Edited by Bruce Henricksen and Thais E. Morgan. University of Illinois Press, 1990. © 1990 by the Board of Trustees of the University of Illinois. Reprinted by permission of the publisher and the author.—Lee, Helen Elaine. From ***The Serpent's Gift.*** Atheneum, 1994. Copyright © 1994 by Helen Elaine Lee. All rights reserved.—Malcolm, Janet. From ***The Silent Woman: Sylvia Plath and Ted Hughes.*** Knopf, 1994. Copyright © 1993 by Janet Malcolm. All rights reserved. Reprinted by permission of Alfred A. Knopf, Inc.—Malouf, David. From ***Remembering Babylon.*** Pantheon Books, 1993. Copyright © 1993 by David Malouf. All rights reserved.—McCall, Nathan. From ***Makes Me Wanna Holler: A Young Black Man in America.*** Random House, 1994. Copyright © 1994 by Nathan McCall. All rights reserved.—Min, Anchee. From ***Red Azalea.*** Pantheon Books, 1994. Copyright © 1994 by Anchee Min. All rights reserved.—Ōe, Kenzaburo. From ***The Silent Cry.*** Translated by John Bester. Kodansha International, 1974. Copyright © 1974 by Kodansha International Ltd. All rights reserved. Reprinted by permission of the publisher.—Roth, Philip. From ***Operation Shylock: A Confession.*** Simon & Schuster, 1993. Copyright © 1993 by Philip Roth. All rights reserved.—Shea, Lisa. From ***Hula: A Novel.*** W. W. Norton & Company, 1994. Copyright © 1994 by Lisa Shea. All rights reserved.—Slatin, John. From "Reading Hypertext: Order and Coherence in a New Medium," in ***Hypermedia and Literary Studies.*** Edited by Paul Delany and George P. Landow. The MIT Press, 1991. © 1991 Massachusetts Institute of Technology. All rights reserved. Reprinted by permission of The MIT Press, Cambridge, MA.

PHOTOGRAPHS AND ILLUSTRATIONS APPEARING IN *CLC*, VOLUME 86, WERE RECEIVED FROM THE FOLLOWING SOURCES:

AP/Wide World Photos: **pp. 33, 328;** Photograph by Andrew Semel/OUTLINE: **p. 41;** Jacket of ***The Alienist***, by Caleb Carr. Copyright © 1994 by Random House, Inc. Jacket design by Andy Carpenter. Jacket photograph: "The Street" by Alfred Stieglitz, from Camera Work, July 1903, courtesy of The Library of Congress. Reprinted by permission of Random House, Inc: **p. 46;** Photograph © Normand Blouin: **p. 50;** Photograph by Kelly Case: **p. 61;** Cover of ***Billy,*** by Albert French. Copyright © 1993 by Albert French. Cover photograph reprinted by permission from the Doris Ulmann Collection, #5790, Special Collections, University of Oregon Library. Cover design reprinted by permission of Viking Penguin, a division of Penguin Books USA Inc: **p. 66;** Photograph by Keith Jenkins: **p. 68;** Photograph by Anthony Barboza: **p. 73;** Photograph by Joan Chen: **p. 82;** Photograph by Bill Hayward: **p. 98;** Photograph by Alix Jeffry, courtesy of Edward Albee: **p. 117;** © Jerry Bauer: **pp. 129, 291, 304;** © Nancy Crampton: **pp. 137, 146, 170, 195, 247, 317, 451;** Photograph by Alan Wylie: **p. 180;** Photograph by Mandy Sayer: **p. 190;** Cover of ***Neon Vernacular: New and Selected Poems,*** by Yusef Komunyakaa. Copyright © 1993 by Yusef Komunyakaa. Cover art: "Uptown Looking Downtown" by Romare Bearden. Reprinted by permission of the estate of Romare Bearden: **p. 193;** Reuter/Bettmann: **p. 221;** Photograph by Mary Ann Halpin Photography, courtesy of The Tantleff Office: **p. 265;** Photograph by Jay Thompson: **p. 271;** Photograph courtesy of the Estate of Cleanth Brooks: **p. 277;** Archive Photos/London Daily Express: **p. 330;** Photograph by Sarah Potter, courtesy of the Estate of Dennis Potter: **p. 342;** Cartoon from ***From Hell,*** by Alan Moore. Copyright © 1994 by Alan Moore and Eddie Campbell, published by Kitchen Sink Press Northampton MA: **p. 413;** Illustration from ***Church And State Volume 1,*** by Dave Sim. Art by Dave Sim and Gerhard. Reprinted by permission of Aardvark-Vanheim, Inc: **p. 427;** Photograph © Rollie McKenna: **p. 439;** Aurelia Schober Plath: **p. 456.**

The Year in Review

The Year in Fiction

by Bruce Allen

The most significant publication of 1994, to my mind, was that of a curious and remarkable novel at long last rediscovered, only to go virtually unremarked by review media and readers alike—a cruel echo of the fate it suffered when originally written, almost a half-century ago.

John Cowper Powy's ***Porius: A Romance of the Dark Ages*** was completed in 1949 after seven years' labor. But despite its author's high reputation, both the length of its typescript (1,589 pages) and the effects of a postwar paper shortage forced Powys to abridge the novel drastically and publish, in 1951, a truncated version of it some three hundred pages shorter than the original.

Now we have the restored text (heroically edited by Professor Wilbur Albrecht of Colgate), and what emerges is another flawed masterpiece deserving of comparison with such weighty volumes as Powys's other major historical novel *Owen Glendower* (1938) and the most celebrated of his "modern" novels *A Glastonbury Romance* (1932).

Like them, ***Porius*** mingles the rich fruits of exhaustive research, keen psychological perception expressed with plangent lyricism, and soaring, swelling, empurpled rhetorical rant to tell a simple story made intriguingly, frustratingly complex by the number of discrete individual destinies woven into its fabric. Its action occurs during a week in the year 499 A.D. as the legendary King Arthur, then of Wales, plots his defense of Britain against approaching Saxon invaders. Members of Arthur's family and court, including the wizard Myrddin (Merlin), figure importantly, as do various noblemen, priests, poets, and mercenaries—not to mention assorted Druids and "aboriginal giants"—and the novel's title character, son of an admired prince and himself a bold adventurer whose journey to manhood reflects and parallels the exploits of his heroes and mentors.

Powys, who lived from 1872 to 1963 and wrote until nearly the end, may always be an acquired taste, for even his greatest work is flawed by garrulous digressiveness and archaic fustian. But in his grasp of historical process as psychic experience and his sympathetic fascination with larger-than-life characters who struggle to remake and understand themselves, he rivals Melville and Dostoevsky as fiction makers who embrace as their province the whole universe and all of time.

The Classical Novels restores to us the historical fiction of Mary Butts (1890-1937), a Bohemian British expatriate once highly esteemed for her presumably autobiographical "Taverner Novels" and for a limpid memoir of her childhood, *The Crystal Cabinet*. Both *The Macedonian* (1933), a witty portrayal of Alexander the Great as a likable megalomaniac, and the revisionist *Scenes from the Life of Cleopatra* (1935) explore the hearts and minds of grand and grandiose figures with disarming forthrightness. Modernist irony enlivens Butt's otherwise plain prose, yet her pictures of these ancient worlds glow with conviction.

The Armstrong Trilogy collects in a single volume Guyanese novelist Roy Heath's vivid and touching chronicle of a star-crossed family striving and failing to overcome the constrictions of colonialism, poverty, and their own flawed natures. *From the Heat of the Day* (1979) describes the hopeful union of class opposites Sonny and Gladys Armstrong and their painfully combative years of marriage. *One Generation* and *Genetha* (both 1981) trace the sexual confusions and psychological instability that doom their promising son Rohan and timid daughter Genetha to fates no less devastating. The trilogy comprises a superb psychological novel whose combination of pictorial detail and emotional intensity will remind many readers of Hardy and Lawrence.

Trinidadian-born V. S. Naipaul continues the elegant analysis of his own ethnic and cultural heritage begun in *The Enigma of Arrival* (1987) with ***A Way in the World,*** a gorgeously written meditation on the exploration and exploitation of South America and the Caribbean. The examination of psychic aggression and the causes of lingering social trauma may be too discursive to make for fully satisfying fiction, but the book is nevertheless every bit as challenging and compelling as any of its author's more conventional narratives.

South Africa's J.M. Coetzee has chosen for his new novel, ***The Master of Petersburg,*** an innately dramatic subject: the great Russian novelist Fyodor Dostoevsky, here depicted as a grieving survivor investigating the death of his stepson Pavel, a reputed suicide who, the novelist suspects, may have been misled by and sacrificed to a mysterious anarchist organization. Coetzee's portrayal of Dostoevsky's mercurial emotionalism rings true, but the novel's sluggish plot adumbrates rather too conveniently motifs and characters from novels we know he would subsequently write. It all feels more than a little labored.

Nadine Gordimer adds to her impressive fictional portrait of her embattled homeland ***None to Accompany Me,*** a tense account of South Africa's troubled transition to black majority rule expressed in a series of balancing and conflicting characterizations. The figures of Didymus and Sibongile Maquoma (to some degree ironic refractions of Nelson and Winnie Mandela), and especially the complex, driven liberal lawyer Vera Stark are stunningly credible, and the novel's millenarian fervor, virtuosically limned in vivid realistic detail, make this one of the recent Nobel Prize-winner's strongest books in years.

Other cultures and their colorful citizens are expertly delineated in two novels published here last year by Louis de Bernières, a British-born writer whose varied travel and career experiences have inspired no fewer than *four* of the liveliest and funniest books of very recent vintage. ***The Troublesome Offspring of Cardinal Guzman*** describes with magical-realist *brio* a battle for the soul of a scruffy South American village between a flinty, deranged cleric and a host of cheerfully unregenerate lay persons. And in ***Corelli's Mandolin,*** de Bernières offers a vast, emotionally shaded picture of life on a Greek Island inundated by foreign soldiers during World War II. De Bernières effortlessly creates large canvasses filled with brawling characters, and explores tensions between chauvinist myopia and polyglot eclecticism with displays of narrative ingenuity and verbal wit that make him the most remarkable writer to have emerged thus far in the 1990's.

Another brilliantly accomplished British writer, Pat Barker, amplifies the story told in her highly acclaimed novel *Regeneration* (1992) with its sequel ***The Eye in the Door.*** Again writing of the psychic casualties of World War I, Barker revisits the hospital where poet-soldier Siegfried Sassoon and neurologist W. H. R. Rivers (both real historical figures) so memorably matched wits and shared feelings—and expands her vision to include other victims and heroes, chief among them a lower-class officer unsure of both his status and his allegiances. Even more successfully than its superb predecessor, this moving novel embraces both a fascinating meditation on the concepts of loyalty and belonging, and a sequence of heartening images of human resourcefulness and courage.

Dreams of Dead Women's Handbags collects twenty years' worth of short stories by Shena Mackay, a droll observer of urban complacency and genteel hysteria whose oddly shaped tales at their best resemble the imperturbable nightmares patented and perfected by Muriel Spark. Another enjoyable collection, ***Ten Tales Tall & True*** showcases the quirky talents of Scotland's Alasdair Gray, a deadpan chronicler of Glaswegian *angst* whose clever stories of common people assailed by surrealist mischance and fantasy (accompanied by Gray's own eerie drawings) link him with such offbeat comic masters as Flann O'Brien and Donald Barthelme.

More mainstream fiction from Scotland included Jeff Torrington's ***Swing Hammer Swing!***, a wonderfully written first novel set in Glasgow's tenement district and focussed on a besieged young householder—a kind of Scottish "Ginger Man"—whose efforts to keep body and soul, not to mention home and family, together are described with intense empathy and in prose so rhythmic and muscular it all but vibrates on the page.

And, in James Kelman's Booker Prize-winning ***How Late It Was, How Late,*** a blunt piece of naturalism that might have been titled "Down and Out in Glasgow," life in this grim industrial inferno is encapsulated in the limited viewpoint of Sammy, a scrounger and thief imprisoned, brutalized by police, and incapacitated by his own despairing drunkenness. The novel is, as its detractors have alleged, sordid and monotonous, yet its picture of a defiant human wreck who doesn't give a damn for others' standards or opinions has real authority, and merits recognition. There is in Kelman's rude, profane idiom a little of James Hanley's belligerent immersion in the rawness of real life, and even a trace of Charles Bukowski. The minority Booker judges who rued the awarding of their Prize to James Kelman deplored it as the filthiest book of the year, but seem not to have noticed that it's also one of the funniest.

I also found myself laughing aloud throughout ***The Consequence,*** a first novel by Ireland's Colbert Kearney in which a first novelist named Fintan Kearney discovers he has unwittingly maligned persons both near and dear to him—including, most troublesomely, the late Brendan Behan. Fintan's scrambling attempts to undo done damage and explain himself to his outraged readership exfoliate into an ever-deepening maze of a novel (reminiscent of and perhaps inspired by Nabokov's *Pale Fire* [1962], as well as the aforementioned Flann O'Brien's *At Swim-Two-Birds*, 1939) that's a continuous delight.

Veteran novelist Beryl Bainbridge switched gears to brilliant effect in ***The Birthday Boys,*** a swift, elegantly economical narrative of the ill-fated expedition led by Robert Falcon Scott to Antarctica in 1912. Bainbridge tells the story from the viewpoints of Scott and his four-man crew, and there emerges from her restrained portrayal of their passive stoicism a powerful indictment of the phlegmatic "courage" soon thereafter to take such disastrous form on the battlefields of Europe. One scarcely knows which to admire more: Bainbridge's frighteningly vivid imagining of what her protagonists may have experienced; or her ability to present them simultaneously as examples of a national ethos and as individually distinctive, admirable characters. In every way, this is the best novel she has yet written.

The same perhaps cannot be said for Iris Murdoch's ***The Green Knight,*** the twenty-fourth of her agreeably convoluted explorations of the conflicts between individuals and their communities, the willfully solipsistic ego and the stubborn social fact of contingency.

Both the biblical story of Cain and Abel and the medieval tale of "Sir Gawain and the Green Knight" underlie Murdoch's dense narrative, in which temperamentally opposed half-brothers exchange views of "the good" and of the world; in which a presumably murdered man is recalled to life and assumes extraordinary importance to the circle that closes around him; and where lovers of all sorts and conditions learn that imperfect happiness is, after all, happiness, and very much worth having.

As always occurs in Murdoch, the characters brood and fret and *talk*, exhaustively, and a large cast of characters is indifferently manipulated by a sometimes wavering hand (it isn't always clear who is sleeping with or pursuing or fixated on whom).

But once you're drawn into one of her novels, you're hooked, and ***The Green Knight*** is typically rich in suggestive, seductive incident and imagery, not to mention thumping good melodrama. What one values most in Murdoch's novels is their affectionate tolerance for human folly and their serene insistence that, fools though we be, everything we do is interesting to observe, and, in spite of all, we matter.

American-born Carol Shields, who now lives in Canada, take a quantum leap beyond her previous fiction with ***The Stone Diaries,*** a beautifully composed chronicle of the life of an ordinary woman, Daisy Goodwill, from her childhood in smalltown Manitoba through marriages, childbearing, career, and an old age in which she grows more and more a stranger to herself. Shields's delicate understanding of the confusing (*and* intriguing) stages of advancing age gives her feisty heroine great depth as a character and turns this multifaceted self-portrait into one of the most engaging examinations of woman's fate in contemporary fiction.

Ontario's Alice Munro ranks high on everybody's list of the finest living short story writers, and her standing is emphatically confirmed by ***Open Secrets,*** a collection of eight ambitious stories about women's lives set in the rural western Ontario territory she has made triumphantly her own.

Often displaying the length or scope of novellas, these stories offer extended glimpses into the essentials of our own and others' lives that we think we know (thus, they're "open secrets"), which become increasingly complex and ambiguous as we grow older, live and learn, accept our limitations, and lament the passing of opportunities to comprehend ourselves and our lives.

The stories are made of incident and reflection, shifting time frames and interpolated sub-stories, letters and flashbacks and other extrapolations and correctives to stories that always turn out to contain more than we had anticipated.

The marvelous story "Open Secrets" confronts a complacent married woman with echoes of mysterious accidents and disappearances remembered from her girlhood, and afflicts her with intimations of "another life that she is leading, a life just as long and complicated and dull and strange as this one." In "A Wilderness Station," Munro transforms the tale of a luckless orphan's blighted marriage into a harsh, haunting Canadian *Rashomon* (Akira Kurosawa, 1950). And in the stunning "Carried Away"—a story James Joyce might have conceived—a young librarian's inchoate "relationship" with a wounded soldier reshapes her entire life and becomes both the despair and the comfort of her old age. This is, simultaneously, her best story and an unarguable demonstration of the increasing technical dexterity and sympathetic understanding of her people that have made Munro one of the world's very best writers. And she's getting better and better.

Last year's foreign-language fiction included a number of significant works first appearing in English translation. Prominent among them was ***The Silent Angel,*** written in 1951 by Nobel laureate Heinrich Böll but denied publication, undoubtedly because of its frank contemplation of a stunted and disillusioned postwar Germany. This was Böll's first novel, and it abounds with faults that would weaken even his more fully achieved fiction—chiefly, lumbering exposition and stagy symbolism. But its portrayal of an embittered war veteran determined to wrest a new life out of the war's rubble is affecting, and the novel should be warmly welcomed by Böll's many admirers.

Welcome new or less familiar voices included that of Johannes Bobrowski (1917-1965), the German poet whose ***Darkness and a Little Light*** memorializes in spare, simply written stories the character of life in rural Sarmartia (eastern Prussia), and its passing under the impact of war and modern life in general. And Wolfgang Koeppen's ***Death in Rome,*** a 1954 novel only now available in English, adroitly combines a *Buddenbrooks*-like portrayal of a self-satisfied German family in the postwar years with a stinging indictment of the attitudes and prejudices that made the war inevitable. It's a bleak, ugly novel, powered by a disenchantment that shades over frequently into loathing—and it lingers in the mind uncomfortably.

The Collected Novellas of Arno Schmidt (1914-1979) initiates a projected four-volume edition of the early fiction of a demanding modernist writer whose labyrinthine later books reveal affinities with the polyphonic novels of his countrymen Hermann Broch, Alfred Döblin, and Robert Musil, and also with the deranged structure and fiendish wordplay Joyce's modernist touchstones *Ulysses* (1922) and *Finnegans Wake* (1939).

Schmidt's novellas, rife with digressions and expostulations, second thoughts and outrageous puns, are probably best viewed as impudent sendups of received ideas and traditional images (*his* witty revisionist look at "Alexander" the Great and his comic dystopia "Republica Intelligentsia" are splendid examples). They're very entertaining when read aloud—though I don't doubt they must be read several times if one is to ferret out what's really going on in them. All honor to Schmidt's translator John E. Woods and to his American publishers for this important undertaking.

Three pungent, disturbing works by the great Japanese novelist Junichirō Tanizaki (1886-1965) appeared in English translation last year. ***Quicksand,*** completed in 1930, delineates a vindictive amorous triangle involving a deceptively subservient wife, her unemotional husband, and an avaricious art student who, with nearly contemptuous ease, overpowers them both. Tanizaki's urbane anatomies of such *ménages* are the Eastern literary equivalent of *film noir*.

Its companion volume, ***"The Reed Cutter" and "Captain Shigemoto's Mother,"*** includes two of this very sophisticated craftsmen's best short novels. Both study protagonists whose views of themselves and their families are forever influenced by stories emerging from the past—which are perhaps true, perhaps fabricated. Each offers an eloquent demonstration of a theme that surfaces frequently in Tanizaki's fiction: the buried lives we disavow or repress, and the power of these to impinge upon and threaten our outward, public selves.

Two classic Scandinavian authors are represented by retrospective collections of some of their finest work. ***A Sud-***

den Liberating Thought displays the Norwegian Kjell Askildsen's icy, sardonic portraits—written between 1966 and 1991—of dispossessed and alienated souls variously at odds with the limiting, judging culture from which they struggle to free themselves. The most memorable of them is a loner ("Carl Lange") accused of sexual misconduct who cannot escape the character others assume him to possess. Askildsen has been compared to Beckett and Kafka, but his trademark concentration on protagonists who can't help but be "different" reminds me of his great countryman and predecessor Knut Hamsun.

Denmark's Jens Peter Jacobsen (1847-1885) was a superb poet who, in his short working life, also produced fiction of startling originality and clarity. Ford Press, which previously published a new English version of Jacobsen's masterly *bildungsroman Niels Lyhne* (1880), now offers a first English translation of his ***Mogens, and Other Stories*** (1882). With one hair-raising exception—the Kafkaesque parable "The Plague at Bergamo"—these are delicate, sensuous evocations of village life circumscribed and defined by the surrounding natural world. And the title novella "Mogens" is a lyrically accomplished love story that rivals the best such work of Turgenev.

There were also new translations of the Polish modernist Witold Gombrowicz's 1953 novel ***Trans-Atlantyk***—a mordant satire on dullwitted nationalism re-creating its author's own lengthy exile in Argentina during World War II in a racy seventeenth-century idiom that reads like an unholy (and hilarious) combination of Samuel Pepys and Samuel Beckett—and of ***Tales from Two Pockets,*** a full collection of the distaff "mystery stories" written in the late 1920s by the great Czech writer Karel Čapek (1890-1938). These comically subversive fictions ring varied and provocative changes on the famous lesson of Poe's "The Purloined Letter": that the inexplicable often proves annoyingly obvious, and that everyday encounters and relationships are riddled with unanswerable questions. The stories are modestly conceived, and quietly presented, but their lingering open-endedness creates a persuasive, pervasive impression of the bullheaded complexity of ordinary life.

Among new fiction from Europe, I especially liked: ***Peace on Earth,*** in which Polish science-fiction master Stanislaw Lem sends his recurring explorer character Ijon Tichy to the moon, with the result that the world is both saved from imminent destruction and exposed to unanticipated new dangers; ***The Following Story*** by Dutch novelist Cees Nooteboom, a brief, painfully funny *récit* about a middle-aged former teacher whose unruly dream life propels him into a transformative metaphysical adventure; and ***Under the Frog,*** Hungarian-born Tibor Fischer's captious, irreverent peek at his homeland's postwar experiences, seen through the raffish misadventures of the members of Hungary's traveling state basketball team. Though written in English, and by a second-generation Hungarian born in Britain, this is, in all essential respects, a European novel—and an engagingly funny one.

Other distinguished fiction from Europe includes two novels which eerily mirror each other: ***Nightfather,*** Dutch novelist Carl Friedman's harrowing, dreamlike portrayal of a family forced to share the memories, and the trauma, compulsively relived by its father, a survivor of the Nazi camps; and Jean Rouaud's ***Of Illustrious Men,*** a bereaved young boy's imaginative reconstruction of the life of his self-effacing father, a former hero of the French Resistance. These are remarkably moving works from new writers who promise to become two of Europe's finest.

Professor Martens' Departure marks the second appearance in English of Estonian novelist Jaan Kross (whose *The Czar's Madman*, published here in 1993, is one of the best recent historical novels). This is the story of a career diplomat who realizes too late that his "useful" talents for compromise and accommodation have helped sustain a tyrannical government—that of Czarist Russia in the latter nineteenth century. Its subtle portrait of a decent man increasingly unacquainted with and frightened by the stranger he has become quietly gathers overpowering momentum. This is an important work by a novelist from whom we must hear more.

A generally less successful year for Latin American fiction nevertheless saw the publication of Mexican Carlos Fuentes's ***The Orange Tree,*** which is comprised of five calculatedly exuberant novellas that reimagine, in the manner of his major novel *Terra Nostra* (1975), the history of this region and the sensibilities of its explorers and colonizers, among others. We also have ***The Assault,*** a sluggish, argumentative finale to the five-volume autobiographical "quintet" completed shortly before the death (in 1990) of the renegade Cuban novelist Reinaldo Arenas.

These were bettered in quality by ***The Tree of the Seventh Heaven,*** Brazilian novelist Milton Hatoum's ambitious picture of an immigrant Lebanese family relocated in a city on the Amazon, offered in alternating voices by its many members as expressions of culture shock and grudging acclimatization; and by ***The House on the Beach,*** a compelling 1966 novel by Mexico's Juan García Ponce in which the interactions of four friends sharing a "vacation" provoke a questioning and redefinition of several identities—particularly for the story's protagonist, a self-possessed woman lawyer whose convictions are eroded as if by waves battering a coastline. This is a tense, claustrophobic novel which, in its best moments, reads like a Harold Pinter play.

Two novels from Israel revisit territories with which their respective authors have become firmly identified. Aharon Appelfeld's ***Unto the Soul,*** the tenth of his closely related fictional explorations of the emotional legacy of the Holocaust, tells the taut troubling story of a brother and sister who are transformed in unexpected ways when they are made caretakers of a Jewish cemetery in an unnamed Eastern European country. Like such distinguished previous books as *Badenheim 1939* (1980) and *To the Land of the Cattails* (1986), this novel shimmers with Appelfeld's passionate concentration on the ambiguities of memory, sympathy, and survival, elevating his simple narrative to the level of profound and resonant statement.

Appelfeld's younger countryman David Grossman has produced in ***The Book of Intimate Grammar*** a brilliant counterpart to his highly praised *See Under: Love* (1986).

Like that earlier novel (and, in part, like Günter Grass's *The Tin Drum*, 1959), this is an imaginative portrayal of adolescence *in extremis*. In the story of prepubescent Aron Kleinfeld, a dreamy kid whose body mysteriously refuses to mature as his Jerusalem neighborhood absorbs information about the forthcoming Six-Day War (of 1967), Grossman has devised a dazzling metaphor for the individual's sense of displacement and alienation from a world that's changing faster that he can grow. A stunning performance.

From Egypt's Nobel laureate Naguib Mahfouz there appeared ***The Harafish,*** a 1977 novel whose interlocking stories relate the history of a Cairo neighborhood as experienced and observed by its "rabble" (harafish) under the rule of successive "clan chiefs" and their assorted offspring, lovers, and co-conspirators. It's a vigorous, colorful work, though of uneven quality, which forms a fascinating pendant to such thematically similar works as its author's celebrated "Cairo Trilogy."

Sutra & Other Stories offers six replete, satisfyingly detailed stories of life in her native Iran by Simin Daneshvar, whose 1969 novel *Savushun* marked the watershed appearance of a forthright criticism of that country's poverty and injustice by—of all things—a woman writer. Daneshvar is one of the world's most interesting and powerful writers: a clear-eyed analyst of traditional folk culture in transition, and a courageous spokesperson for her country's various underclasses.

From Russia there arrived two meticulously crafted new novels. Ludmilla Petrushevskaya's ***That Time: Night*** presents the first-person story of Anna Andrianovna, a rapidly aging would-be poet whose yearning to dedicate herself to art is compromised by the necessity of earning her living and of shouldering burdens imposed by her incompetent children and elderly mother. It's a surprisingly comical and lively portrait of the artist, and a most enjoyable character study.

Vassily Aksyonov's ***Generations of Winter,*** a conscious evocation, if not imitation, of Tolstoy's *War and Peace* (1869), survey's Russia's Stalinist years (1925-1945) through the prism of experiences undergone by an aristocratic family of the intelligentsia, the Gradovs, and others whose lives intersect, often disastrously, with theirs.

Adapting the method of John Dos Passos's *U.S.A.* (his trilogy of novels published in 1930, 1932, and 1936), Aksyonov alternates vivid scenes showing his characters' increasing misfortune and disillusionment with "Intermissions," in which newspaper items and similar announcements or scraps of information convey the menacing character of the times they live through.

It's a masterfully controlled panorama, yet most readers will remember longest the novel's hauntingly vivid characters: patriarch Boris Nikitovich Gradov, an eminent surgeon who meekly consents to do the Kremlin's bidding; his eldest son, Nikita, a career army officer whose victimization by the cause to which he has committed himself destroys both his happy marriage and his strong character; his sister Nina, a free-spirited beauty reminiscent of Tolstoy's Natasha Rostov; and many others, equally sharply delineated. Of all the foreign language fiction I read in 1994, ***Generations of Winter*** impressed me most.

In American fiction, the year's most noteworthy event was the re-emergence, after a sixty-year silence, of Henry Roth (b. 1906), whose *Call It Sleep* (1934) has long been recognized as *the* classic fictional study of the immigrant experience in America. In old age, Roth has completed and is now beginning to publish *Mercy of a Rude Stream,* an autobiographical novel in six volumes, of which the first, ***A Star Shines Over St. Morris Park,*** has now appeared.

It is, patently, a continuation of *Call It Sleep*, although the protagonist is here renamed Ira Stigman, and the narrative of his family's struggle to survive in New York City throughout the World War I years is juxtaposed with the comments of the aged Ira, "talking" to the computer on which he composes his life story.

Here and there, we catch flashes of the earlier Henry Roth's tangy ethnic *argot*—but, sad to say, this initial volume reads more like *précis* than fully imagined and shaped fiction. One senses that Roth has returned at last to deeply personal material with which he knows he hasn't finished; but he seems to only circle around it, hinting at the complexities and depths in the Stigman's common experience, failing, or refusing to fully explore them. We'll have to see much more of this extended work before it will be possible to say whether it compares favorably with its author's one great novel.

The posthumous publication of the late Isaac Bashevis Singer's formerly serialized novels continues with ***Meshugah,*** a colorfully written and vividly populated story (from 1981-1983) of Jewish immigrants in New York in the 1950s that reaches back to its characters' experiences in the concentration camps. The novel's amorous entanglements closely recall those of Singer's *Enemies: A Love Story* (1966) but in its protagonist, journalist Aaron Greidinger, Singer has created both an amusing self-portrait and a striking image of the writer as explorer, memorialist, and ombudsman. This is a gem: one of its author's very best books.

Another eagerly awaited reappearance takes form in Joseph Heller's ***Closing Time,*** a sequel to his masterpiece *Catch-22* (1961) set fifty years following the latter book's wartime action. Once again Heller's focus is on his protagonist ("hero" isn't quite the word) Yossarian, perversely blessed with good health while enervated by his pessimistic conviction that the world around him is going to hell at an ever accelerating pace.

There really isn't anything wrong with ***Closing Time,*** which is smoothly written and amusing enough—but it feels like commentary: a gloss on *Catch-22* rather than a recapturing of the antic spirit that made that novel something abrasively new in our fiction. I read it with pleasure, and ended up admiring it; but it didn't make me crazy, and I don't love it the way I've always loved Heller's incomparable original. Maybe you really can't go home again.

Three writers whom we haven't heard from in many years returned with worthy new books. ***Moses Supposes*** collects the curious stories that Ellen Currie has been publishing in magazines for some thirty years. They're sardonic, knowing portraits of feisty, quarrelsome Irish American family members who, against all odds, seem to thrive on their own avarice and spitefulness. They're nasty people, more often than not, but they're great fun to hang out with.

I also enjoyed James Buechler's ***In That Heaven There Should be a Place for Me,*** ten gritty, unsentimental "Stories of the Mohawk Valley," likewise written over a period of many years, and concerned with dramatic crises in the lives of the ethnically mixed populace of their upstate New York locale. "The Proud Suitor" and "John Sobieski Runs" are the standout stories, but all will reward close attention.

And Eugene Mirabelli, whose *No Resting Place* (1972) was one of the best coming-of-age novels of the 1970s, has now written ***The World at Noon,*** a big and big-hearted chronicle of a New England Italian-American family whose members live in their common memories and myths of past generations as well as in the embattled present, and a loving character portrayal of its protagonist, Nicolo, a middle-aged youth who, in his earlier years, would have made fine company for Joseph Heller's Yossarian.

Several established writers of significant reputation published new novels last year. Peter Taylor's ***In the Tennessee Country*** reworks this author's familiar theme of a romantic, charismatic figure's effect on the timid relative who admires, but cannot emulate, his daring. It's very talky, and lacks both the vigor of Taylor's late short stories and the concision and intensity of his fine previous novel *A Summons to Memphis* (1986).

John Barth's ***Once Upon a Time***—a title which, now that I think of it, I'm amazed he hasn't used before—is another erudite commingling of the themes of storytelling, sailing, and romantic love, as beautifully written and agreeably frisky as, though not sufficiently distinguishable from, earlier books in which the accomplished Barth has played the same hand.

E. L. Doctorow's ***The Waterworks,*** which expands an earlier short story into a metaphysical melodrama set in post-Civil War New York City, leaves a terrific promise—the existence of a subterranean city that parallels and mocks the "real" one—frustratingly only half-developed.

The End of the Hunt impressively concludes Thomas Flanagan's fictional trilogy surveying Ireland's troubled history. Its province is "the Troubles" of 1919, and its host of characters, real and fictional alike, is dominated by a heroine who finds herself drawn, against her will, deeply into the struggle for Irish independence.

Two other well-known novelists achieved, in my opinion, only mixed success. Tim O'Brien's ***In the Lake of the Woods*** broods unproductively on the guilt that shadows a Viet Nam veteran, and finds its objective correlative in a mysterious crisis in his domestic life. The novel feels unfinished. And John Irving's ***A Son of the Circus*** blends together the world of medicine, the culture of India, and the traumatic aftereffects of a murder in an energetic mishmash that aims at Dickensian depth and manages little more than surface cacophony. Oddly, though, its protagonist Dr. Farrokh Daruwalla emerges as one of Irving's most fully realized characters.

I found little of interest, I'm sorry to say, in new books by veteran novelists Thomas Berger (***Robert Crews***), Jayne Anne Phillips (***Shelter***), Paul Auster (***Mr. Vertigo***), and Ellen Glasgow (***Starcarbon***). But I did admire the vivid account of an unconventional adolescent friendship in Lorrie Moore's ***Who Will Run the Frog Hospital?;*** the clever reworking of familiar fairy-tale material in Alice Hoffman's ***Second Nature;*** and the amusing unexpected twist in the ongoing adventures of serial protagonist Peter Leroy in Eric Kraft's (nicely titled) ***What a Piece of Work I Am.***

Several writers of more recent vintage produced interesting new work. Howard Norman's ***The Bird Artist,*** a flavorful tale of illicit love, murder, and painfully acquired maturity set in 1911 coastal Newfoundland, provides many of the pleasures nostalgically associated with traditional realistic fiction—and also happens to be superbly written. The same can be said for Deirdre McNamer's ***One Sweet Quarrel,*** an ambitious tale of a scattered Montana family variously drawn to and affected by a heavyweight championship fight held in their state in 1923.

Jane Hamilton's ***A Man of the World*** movingly details the effect on a young Wisconsin farm wife of a terrible accident for which her neglect was responsible—but the story's moral thrust is blurred by its spillover into unsuccessfully integrated melodrama. Andrew Bergman's ***Sleepless Nights*** expertly reshapes the unlikely materials of Holocaust survival and incest into a charming comedy of growing up absurd. David Guterson's ***Snow Falling on Cedars,*** set in Puget Sound, fashions from the trial for murder of a Japanese-American fisherman a complex portrait of complicity, prejudice, and moral courage among members of the island community variously touched by the event. Guterson's prose is a bit stiff, but his ambitious reach and empathy with his novel's impressive range of characters make it one of the year's most commendable efforts.

Louise Erdrich's ongoing picture of Native American life continues with ***The Bingo Palace,*** another tale of the collision of traditional folkways with contemporary business priorities. It doesn't tell us much that wasn't more vigorously presented in Erdrich's justly celebrated first novel *Love Medicine* (1984). William T. Vollmann's seven-volume work in progress "A Book of North American Landscapes" has now reached (albeit out of sequence) volume six. ***The Rifles*** is an unfortunately flaccid reimagining of Sir John Franklin's doomed expedition to the Arctic in the 1840s and its lingering effect on that region's indigenous culture. But Susan Straight, a white author who writes with great understanding of black family life, achieves her third consecutive unqualified success with ***Blacker Than a Thousand Midnights,*** the emotional story of a young husband and father determined to raise himself and his family above their inhibiting environment. It's a lovely performance.

The year's work in short stories included retrospective collections from Stephen Dixon (***Stories***), the gutsy and fluent Grace Paley (***Collected Stories***), and most notably, Louis Auchincloss (also titled ***Collected Stories***), whose sophisticated, varied tales may surprise those who pigeonhole him as a sober celebrant of the social lives of wealthy professional people.

I also recommend to you the excellent work to be found in Ethan Canin's ***The Palace Thief,*** Richard Bausch's ***Rare & Endangered Species,*** and in three excellent first books of stories: Tom Perrotta's ***Bad Haircut,*** Ann Packer's ***Mendocino,*** and Michael Parker's ***The Geographical Cure.***

Among a number of fine first novels, I especially liked: Tom Drury's ***The End of Vandalism,*** a piecemeal portrayal of the eccentric denizens of Grouse County, a genial midwestern hell on earth that has some of the goofy charm of Garrison Keillor's Lake Woebegon; Maxine Clair's ***Rattlebone,*** a vivid novel-in-stories about a black midwest community in the 1950s filled with dyspeptic, long-suffering yet life-affirming, fully credible people; and Robert Hellenga's ***The Sixteen Pleasures,*** a worldly and charming novel about the adventures, aesthetic and otherwise, of an idealistic young woman who travels to Florence to help preserve the city's art objects from water damage caused by flooding. From its offbeat premise through its surprising and satisfying conclusion, this is a work of smooth sophistication, containing many more pleasures than sixteen.

The year's best first novel was Alan Isler's ***The Prince of West End Avenue,*** a lyrically written story set in a retirement home where resident Otto Korner recalls his complicated life in World War II Germany and thereafter in America. When he stages a production of *Hamlet,* enacted by his fellow retirees, he is stimulated to relive painful occasions and memories he had believed were safely buried. Isler skillfully reveals his protagonist from a variety of viewpoints, and the result is one of the most thorough characterizations in contemporary fiction.

Finally, some words about the best fiction produced in 1994 by several of our best writers.

Vermont's Howard Mosher has written brilliantly of life in the remote Northeast Kingdom of his home state since the appearance of his first novel *Disappearances* (1973), in my opinion a neglected classic which blends regional mythifying with a knowing portrait of a lively, truculent rural clan. Mosher's new book ***Northern Borders,*** his best one since, offers an episodic reminiscence of the life of Austen Kittredge, a motherless twelve-year-old whose widowed father sends him to live with his cantankerous grandparents in a remote township of Vermont's "Kingdom County," near the Canadian border.

Young Austen's captive status as an unwilling enlistee in his grandparents' "Forty Years' Domestic War" is presented in delicious serio-comic tall-tales worthy of Dickens or Twain, expressed in beautiful, image-filled, long looping sentences. This captivating novel memorializes a vanishing way of life with minimal sentimentality and refreshing dignity; it's a pastoral varied and shaded by meticulous detail and exhilarating sheer cussedness.

Reading Maine's Carolyn Chute, I'm reminded of Grandma Moses and Woody Guthrie: folk artists whose spare, unfussy creations contain whole worlds full of local specificity, and speak in plain strong voices of troubles we all know we've all seen.

Chute's ***Merrymen*** returns to the backwoods town of her famous first novel *The Beans of Egypt, Maine* (1985) and weaves in and out of the life stories, over thirty-plus years, of four protagonists and their lovers and kin, all of whom variously feel the crippling social effects of technological advancement and commercial "incorporation." It's a heartfelt paean to the survival instincts and innate decency of "the people," marred by occasional stridency yet distinguished as much by the quality of its partisan fury as by the beauty of its style and conception.

The productive powerhouse that is Joyce Carol Oates weighed in with two new books. ***Haunted*** collects sixteen examples of her "grotesque" fiction. They're alternately convincingly eerie and lamely shrill, ingenious and derivative—but at least two ("The Premonition" and "Thanksgiving") rank among her best stories. Her ambitious new novel ***What I Lived For*** returns to the manner of such realist successes as *them* (1969) and *You Must Remember This* (1987), to study in clinical Dreiserian detail the career, family life, and inner torment of Jerome "Corky" Corcoran, a bantamlike businessman whose urgent acquisitiveness is persuasively linked with his family's violent history and his own compulsive sexuality. It's an R-rated *Babbitt* (1922), an uncompromisingly rough trek into the male psyche that shows Oates at her most imaginative and challenging.

I also admired Rhoda Lerman's ***Animal Acts,*** an extravagantly funny narrative that moves swiftly and surely beyond comedy to tell the story of Linda Morris, a bored suburban housewife who, while fleeing from her unsatisfactory husband *and* lover, inadvertently kidnaps a carnival gorilla—and discovers that her new animal companion, named Moses, is far and away the most interesting male she knows. This is a dazzlingly risky and exuberant book, both feminist romance and murderous satire on marriage and other atrocities. It also has the year's best dust jacket illustration.

One of our finest writers produced two books of very different aim—*and* accomplishment. John Updike's ***Brazil*** reinvents the story of Tristan and Isolde as a heavy-breathing tale of an amorous mixed couple in flight from disapproving family and other authorities. It seems to me lubricous and no more than self-consciously clever. But ***The Afterlife,*** a collection of twenty-one recent stories that explore the culture and psychology of middle and old age, contains some of Updike's most gorgeous writing: sympathetic comprehension of survivors and loners stunned by the changes time and experience have wrought in themselves and their loved ones, expressed in imagery of haunting spareness and clarity. "A Sandstone Farmhouse," "Farrell's Caddie," and "Grandparenting," to name only the three most appealing, suggest that here may be one of our few important contemporaries whose best work is yet to come.

Another may be Cormac McCarthy, whose "Border Trilogy" was initiated by *All the Pretty Horses* (1992), the most highly acclaimed American novel of the past ten years. Its successor ***The Crossing*** recounts with brooding lyric power the ordeals suffered by teenaged brothers Billy and Boyd Parham in southwestern New Mexico and (across the border) Mexico in the years spanning America's entry into World War I.

The novel focusses on a sequence of tasks and searches undertaken in pursuit of manhood and in deference to a stoic code of conduct that forces these boys to engage "a world provisional, contingent, deeply suspect" that challenges their will to persevere at every "crossing" they encounter.

Chaos and loss lie at the ends of their several journeys, but the impression left is of anything but futility. McCarthy's characters hauntingly embody the proposition that man and nature are inextricably part of one another and that each survives in, and as, the other. And in the book's extended opening episode—the tale of Billy Parham's determination to return a captured she-wolf to the distant mountains whence it came—McCarthy has produced a set-piece of unrivalled magnificence, as good as anything his great exemplar William Faulkner ever wrote.

But the best new novel published in 1994 was William Gaddis's ***A Frolic of His Own,*** a bleakly funny satire on the profession of law and the American passion for litigation. Like Gaddis's previous novels, this is a lavish display of vernacular rhetoric, an ingeniously orchestrated cacophony of passionate declamatory conflicting voices.

Not that there isn't a plot—it's a beauty. Beginning with college teacher Oscar Crease's lawsuits—against the insurance company that withholds coverage when he's run over by his own car, and against the Hollywood sleazemaster who blandly appropriates Oscar's Civil War play as the basis for a lascivious bloodsoaked epic—the novel exfoliates into a chain of mad legal actions and counteractions which are argued at Olympian and hilarious length. In boardrooms and hospital rooms and bedrooms as well as courtrooms, said arguments are supported by invented legal documents and, in successive chunks, the text of Oscar's play *Once at Antietam*. The whole confabulation mushrooms into a vision of universal bickering and disharmony of which Pope or Ben Jonson would have approved. It's a staggeringly brilliant performance; you read it shaking your head in admiration and disbelief.

More accessible than such wintry jeremiads as Gaddis's *JR* (1975) and *Carpenter's Gothic* (1985), this splendid work belongs on the same shelf as its author's classic first novel *The Recognitions* (1955). For me, it's not just the book of the year, but the best thus far of this parlous and peculiar decade, an outpouring of the blackest pessimism shaped with the most accomplished artfulness. We may indeed be slouching toward Armageddon, exactly as ***Frolic*** seems to forecast, but I see a few contrary hopeful signs. Any year that brought us novels by John Cowper Powys and William Gaddis was, in spite of all else, a good one.

The Year in Poetry

by Allen Hoey

The best news of 1994, the publication of ***The Great Fires,*** Jack Gilbert's third collection issued over the past 32 years, is genuine cause for celebration. Gilbert's poems are as spare as his output, written in a style he has refined since *Views of Jeopardy* (1962), on through *Monolithos* (1982), trimming back the few excesses the early poems allowed, tempering them and remaining constant to his earliest influences, poems from The Greek Anthology and Waley's Chinese translations.

Typically, his poems begin in the middle of things and establish situation by accretion, so that it may be necessary to reread them immediately to get the fullest sense. The opening of "Measuring the Tyger" serves as an example:

> Barrels of chains. Sides of beef stacked in vans.
> Water buffalo dragging logs of teak in the river mud
> outside Mandalay. Pantocrater in the Byzantium dome.
> The mammoth overhead crane bringing slabs of steel
> through the dingy light and roar to the giant sheer
> that cuts adamantine three-quarter-inch plates
> and they flop down.

Details—absolutely specific but apparently unrelated either temporally or geographically, linked in the poet's mind through their scale, yet the action is not merely external, for, by extension, "The weight of the mind fractures / the girders and piers of the spirit, spilling out / the heart's melt." All of the noise and incandescence a figure for the vastness of loss within—in this case, as throughout the book, the death of the poet's wife. He rebuffs those who would comfort him, suggesting that in time he "will / love again"; all that remains is "[d]ay after day of the everyday. / What they call real life, made of eighth-inch gauge"—paltry when compared to "three-quarter-inch plates." What he wants is something other than newness, "[i]rony, neatness and rhyme pretending to be poetry," something stricter:

> I want to go back to that time after Michiko's death
> when I cried every day among the trees. To the real.
> To the magnitude of pain, of being that much alive.

Yet the point is neither grief nor pain, nor mindless pleasure, but the awareness of being alive; not even ecstasy, for Gilbert "does not want / to know rapture by standing outside himself. / He wants to know delight as the native land he is" ("Thinking about Ecstasy").

Although Gilbert has spent most of his adult life living abroad, the poems do not read like the travelogue of an academic's Guggenheim year, in part because he has preferred isolation and subsistence. Like the monks in "On Stone," Gilbert seems to have "petition[ed] to live the harder way," seeking a "scraped life" that includes "pull-[ing] water up / hand over hand from thirty feet of stone." Yet poverty is not a martyr's badge; if he must "scrape the burned soup from [his] only pan / with a spoon after midnight by lamplight" ("The Lives of Famous Men"), he also remembers, in "Man at a Window,"

> the cold and hunger as he walked
> the alleys all night that winter down by the docks
> of Genoa until each dawn, when he held the hot bowls
> of tripe in his numb hands, the steam rising into his face
> as he drank, the tears mixing with happiness.

We find no self-pity in these poems; Gilbert seeks a life apart that he might be able to find "a base line / of the Lord" ("The White Heart of God"), because "[t]he discomfort of living this way / . . . makes / death and the world visible. Not the harshness / but the way this world can be known by pushing / against it." He has reached an age where, as he writes in "Me and Capablanca," "There is not / enough time left to use it for dissatisfaction."

At the heart of the collection is the death of the poet's wife, commemorated directly in such poems as "Married," "Michiko Nogami (1946-1982)," and "Michiko Dead." Among the more striking is "Alone," which begins:

> I never thought Michiko would come back
> after she died. But if she did, I knew
> it would be as a lady in a long white dress.
> It is strange that she has returned
> as somebody's dalmatian.

Characteristically, from this almost surreal premise, Gilbert develops a moving poem that seems not merely credible but necessary:

> If nobody
> is around, I sit on the grass. When she
> finally quiets, she puts her head in my lap
> and we watch each other's eyes as I whisper
> in her soft ears. She cares nothing about
> the mystery. She likes it best when
> I touch her head and tell her small
> things about my days and our friends.
> That makes her happy the way it always did.

Rather than strain to convince us of his sincerity by attempting to explain "the mystery," Gilbert concentrates on the details, keeping his language simple and his voice low, trusting the "real nouns" to do the hard work. (See Jack Gilbert, "Real Nouns," in *19 New American Poets of the Golden Gate*, edited by Philip Dow (San Diego: Harcourt, 1984), pp. 3-8. If this essay served as a primer in creative writing classes, most of the problems associated with contemporary American poetry would be eradicated.) The poems in this collection push past easy surfaces, getting to the heart, seeing the suffering and madness, and saying, as he does at the end of "A Stubborn Ode," "nevertheless." The publication of ***The Great Fires*** confirms that Jack Gilbert is one of the very few absolutely essential poets writing today.

Although Louise Glück does not mention Jack Gilbert in any of the essays in ***Proofs & Theories,*** much of "Disruption, Hesitation, Silence," in which she specifically addresses a poem of George Oppen's, might as well apply to Gilbert's work. Like Oppen's work, Gilbert's is "fiercely economical. . . . Each turn is distilled, each movement essential." This might as easily refer to Glück's own approach in these essays. She wastes little time, compressing considerable intellection and analysis in a short space, a method that demands the reader approach the essays with full "attentiveness to the path of thought" ("The Best American Poetry 1993") and "receptivity, which begins with the self's effacement" ("Disinterestedness"). If we retort before we understand, forming opinions before working through the fullest implications of her ideas, we likely miss her point entirely.

Glück admits that she is not by temperament drawn to the essay form; in "Death and Absence," she writes, "I don't trust my prose, except in letters." Yet these essays do not have the feel of being pulled from her like impacted teeth, though many were written for specific occasions. Perhaps because she lacks the comfort of facility, she is more able to bring to these pieces rigor of thought and unstinting honesty. And such scrupulous examination begins with herself; discussing an early poem, she notes that it "has ferocity without depth" and that "it reads . . . now as the degeneration of a set of discoveries into a set of mannerisms." One can think of few of Glück's contemporaries capable of noting such flaws in their early work, much less confessing them in terms so devoid of apology.

Taken in sum, ***Proofs & Theories*** serves as a place to begin assessing the shortfalls and liabilities of contemporary poetry. She explores such pernicious problems as the emphasis on "sincerity" as opposed to authenticity, the valorizing of obsession as "courage" in the critical lexicon, the promulgation of the subjective, and, as she writes in "Invitation and Exclusion," "the proprietary obsessiveness of much contemporary poetry which stakes out territorial claims based on personal history: my father, my pain, my persistent memory." Of these, the notion of "sincerity," of telling the truth—or at least seeming to—perhaps most pervades discussion of contemporary poetry; one strives to affect a sincere tone, to modulate one's voice such that the sincerity cannot be called into question. In "Against Sincerity," Glück notes the "gap between truth and actuality" and argues, "The artist's task . . . involves the transformation of the actual to the true." And, further, that "the ability to achieve such transformations . . . depends on conscious willingness to distinguish truth from honesty or sincerity." Equally "unnerv-[ing]" is "the thought that authenticity, in the poem, is not produced by sincerity." Here, she posits a careful distinction; that which leaves the aftertaste of authenticity—that which strikes us as credible, reliable, as *true*—may not be voiced in the saccharine tones of excessive sincerity. David Dooley has expressed much the same distinction when he noted that a particular poet "employs a rhetoric of sincerity, which leads to quite different results than if he had employed a rhetoric of plausibility" (see David Dooley, "The Contemporary Workshop Aesthetic," in *The Hudson Review* XLIII, No. 2, p. 272). The failure is as much a failure of character, or at least of imagination, for, as Glück posits, "the processes by which experience is charged—heightened, distilled, made memorable—have nothing to do with sincerity. The truth, on the page, need not have been lived. It is, instead, all that can be imagined." While this might well be addressed to any number of working poets, and to quite a few herein reviewed, Dooley's remarks are directed toward a poem by Stephen Dunn, "The Routine Things around the House," which Dunn esteemed enough to include in his volume of selected poems.

New and Selected Poems 1974-1994 gathers poems—gathers them generously—from each of Dunn's eight previously published collections, along with a goodly number of new poems. Most of the poems are marked by the rhetoric of sincerity; Dunn wants to convince us that he is a decent man, a thoughtful man, the kind of man, as he writes in "Beyond Hammonton," "on whom nothing is lost." Yet that is the kind of someone, in the poem, the speaker merely wishes he were. In fact, much seems lost on the speaker whose voice drones through this tome, perhaps because he is, instead, the kind of man who believes that "mood invents landscape" ("Round Trip"), who finds "comfort in [his] own noise" ("Sympathetic Magic"), who feels "so importantly sorry for [him]self" ("Night Truths"), and who asserts that "honesty [is] the open yawn / the unimaginative love / more than truth" ("Mon Semblable"). This last is interesting in light of Glück's suggestion that honesty—sincerity—is a trope of failed vision.

Dunn also believes that mice bed down at nightfall ("A Petty Thing"), apparently unaware that they are, by and large, nocturnal rodents. He begins another poem, "I place a dead butterfly on the page, / this is called starting / with an image from real life." I presume we are supposed to find this witty, charming, yet little in the book convinces me that he knows any better how to start "with an image from real life." After all, in "Midnight" he admits that "[o]n TV the other night / the South Bronx had no life / I could recognize," and few of us, I dare say, could imagine much in the United States that reeks more of "real life." In much the same vein, Dunn asks in "Loves," "Aren't facts / essentially loose, dull?. . . / It's the personal makes things count, / steadies a fact into importance."

Other people fare little better. In "Truck Stop: Minnesota," Dunn complains that a waitress "looks at [his] face as if it were a small tip," but, instead of "com[ing] back at her / with *java*," he "say[s] *coffee*, politely." The poem seems to want us to credit the speaker for his restraint, yet what compassion does he show for a woman laboring at a thankless task, for minimum wages, who faces each night truckers calling her "Sweetheart. . . . / Honey. Doll." If, as the speaker asserts, "[s]he is the America [he] would like to love," what stops him? Failed empathy? Self-absorption and self-pity that would pass themselves off as introspection? "[T]here's an advantage to limitation," Dunn writes in "Moralists," "as long as one doesn't make a career of it." He seems not to have taken his own advice. At nearly 300 pages, this collection displays any number of limitations at greater length than it would profit most to read.

While Dunn, particularly in early poems, occasionally mugged for the neo-surrealist camera, James Tate, in ***Worshipful Company of Fletchers,*** his twelfth collection, demonstrates that a career can be made of this limitation. No introspection here, no pretense at facts, no distracting forays into the actual. Instead, we hear "endless palaver, the well-wishing / like a blue smoke circling," and we realize, with Tate's speaker, that this "wasn't a stage [he] was going through" ("50 Views of Tokyo"). I refer both here and in reviewing Dunn to the "speaker" of the poems, but in both cases tonality and what is called "voice," the rhetorical attitude toward both poetic material and subject, vary little from poem to poem, insignificantly enough that the distinction between poet and speaker is smudged for the reader. So much so, the unkind reader is inclined to take almost as an ars poetica, at the least a badge of pride, this passage from "Becoming a Scout":

> My mind is drifting, as if on a leaf, on a wave,
> a warm current is pulling my brains out, away,
> away from me.
> Therefore I must proceed in a thoughtless, indeed brainless,
> fashion, which could prove painful,
> though I shall barely notice.

And that reader barely suppresses the urge to wonder, painful to whom?

In general, neo-surrealism, with its unusual phrases and bizarre juxtapositions, seems too facile a way to achieve "poetic effects." Reality—the lives we lead quite apart from pages in books, where we get up and go to work and return home and quarrel with our spouses or suffer and rejoice at the lack of them, albeit a concept anathema to some strains of critical theory—can be strange enough that we hardly need, if we observe, synthesize, present clearly what goes on around us, to ornament or augment its strangeness with rhetorical parlor tricks. Surrealism, at its purest, uses the unlikely to illuminate this quality of life, but we seldom encounter surrealism at its purest in post-Deep Image poetry. Instead, tropes exist for their own sake or in order that we might admire the imagination and skill of the poet.

In his best work, John Ashbery appreciates this distinction, employing his enviable craft, surety of line, and frequent command of tone, for purposes of illumination. He describes this quite well in "Bromeliads":

> It's as if the people
> who brought you up were to abandon you in your best interests
> so as to bring on a crisis of enlightenment—
> and then jump up from behind furniture and out of closets
> screaming, "Surprise! Surprise!"

Everything familiar, yet nothing familiar, and Ashbery tries to render the shock of waking to the surprise of the ordinary in poems that achieve

> the
> openness
> of the dream turned inside out, exploded
> into pieces of meaning by its own unasked questions,
> beyond the calculations of heaven.
>
> ("The Improvement")

Alas, in ***And the Stars Were Shining,*** his sixteenth collection of poems—his third in four years—Ashbery rarely manages this high level. Instead, the poems seem retreads of those in *April Galleons*, *Hotel Lautréamont*, or any of his books since *Houseboat Days*, enough that readers might well experience the sensation described in "Till the Bus Starts": "It seems strange I read this page before, no, / this whole short story."

The possibilities of Ashbery's poetic task—and, as I argued concerning *Flow Chart* in *CLC-70* (1991), he has one—are constrained by the endeavor's limits: "the systematic probing and undermining of our accepted notions of how syntax and semantics wed to make easy sense." By its nature, this pursuit will tend toward the abstruse and lend itself to the mandarin. Having explored this through at least half a dozen volumes since *Self-Portrait in a Convex Mirror*, Ashbery seems to have declined from mandarin to camp, a habit of mind that distances from the material; the one who winks is never entirely engaged. One too often feels, reading ***And the Stars Were Shining,*** that these lines from the title poem too accurately describe Ashbery's current mode of composition: "Rummaging through some old poems / for ideas—surely I must have had some / once?" The urge to explore and exceed the limits of language to express cognition seems too often reduced, as he writes in "The Mandrill on the Turnpike"—one of the more amusing poems in the collection—to a mere "what if ": "well, *you* know, what I call the subjunctive creeps back in, / sits up, begs for a vision, or a cookie." How sad, given such mastery, to settle for a cookie.

Problems of stance—the poet's attitude toward the poem, its material, and, by extension, the reader—also mar Edward Hirsch's achievement in ***Earthly Measures,*** his fourth collection. In "Earthly Light," he describes an epiphany when he "turned away // from the God or gods I had wanted / so long and so much to believe in," culminating in the realization that

> this world, too, needs our unmixed
> attention, because it is not heaven

but earth that needs us, because
it is only earth—limited, sensuous
earth that is so fleeting, so real.

Effectively crafted lines articulating an understanding that has produced much of the best poetry in the Romantic tradition. Yet this urge must be coupled with a capability to shuck the constraints of the self, to immerse the self, Whitman-like, in the mundane, promiscuously, with abandon, to exult as Wordsworth did. Instead, Hirsch seems distanced, overly conscious of the higher enterprise; if not quite mandarin, immersed more in erudition than the actual (as three packed pages of notes, providing source material and background, on half the poems in the book, bear witness), closer kin to Henry James, as Hirsch imagines him, young and in Rome, in "The Italian Muse," than Hirsch might care to recognize:

Where else were one's prodigious walks in line
With the perpetually transcendent attention—
Call it taste, fancy, perceptive emotion—
Of St. Ivo and St. John Lateran?

Hirsch leaves it to the reader to experience either the chummy glow of the erudite or the blush of the dunce, according to whether they understand this reference or not.

As well, Hirsch seems prey to the current notion that "real" poems abound with metaphors. As Jonathan Holden writes in *The Fate of American Poetry*:

When the traditional, metrical, sonic means of foregrounding the verbal surface of verse is not available, a poet will turn, instinctively almost, to semantic means: stock lines with metaphors and similes, as if to compensate in the domain of "sense" what he has given up in the domain of sound.

And stock Hirsch does. He demonstrates a clear taste for personification: "the bridge unlocking its steel shoulders" ("Orpheus: The Descent"); "the shattered spine of a bridge" and "the ruined breath . . . of a factory" ("In the Midwest"); the thoroughly original opening, "Once more the clock tolls like a heartbeat" ("In the Midnight Hour"); "the swollen eyelids of daybreak" ("Roman Fall"); "the skulls of churches" and "the lungs of a tunnel" ("The Watcher"). Such overwrought and trite metaphors blur the focus, because they are so imprecise. Yet precision seems to be what Hirsch's "ars poetica" demands, as articulated at the end of "Sortes Virgilianae":

". . . If you want to become more than a shadow
Among shadows, you must carry back the memory
Of your father disintegrating in your arms,

You must bring words that will console others,
You must believe in stairs leading upward
To summer's resplendent, celestial blues."

Such words must bear weight—not the weight of scholarly apparatus or figurative afflatus or fancy: the weight of the world seen, touched, lived, embodied, and envisioned.

Fancy and afflatus describe too often the work of the late Amy Clampitt, as much in earlier works as in her fifth volume, ***A Silence Opens.*** Clampitt describes her mode astutely in "Syrinx," the first poem, tracing the evolution of vocal expression:

Syntax comes last, there can be
no doubt of it: came last,
can be thought of (is
thought of by some) as a
higher form of expression:
is, in extremity, first to
be jettisoned: as the diva
onstage, all soaring
pectoral breathwork,
takes off, pure vowel
breaking free of the dry,
the merely fricative
husk of the particular, rises
past saying anything, any
more than the wind in
the trees, waves breaking. . .

In this, she seems one of those writers not by nature inclined toward syntax, who, Glück observes, find it "stultifying . . . a language of rules, of order. Its opposite is music, that quality of language which is felt to persist in the absence of rule" ("Education of the Poet"). The "danger," as Glück observes in "Disruption, Hesitation, Silence," is that "the expansive poet is prone to premature linguistic satiation, by which I mean that the sense of something's having been made comes into existence too readily. The ratio of words to meaning favors words. The poem exists in its adornments." Too often, one feels that Clampitt's logophilia becomes something less pleasant, devolving, as she describes in the ten-page "Matoaka," into an "interminable, / fatiguing catalog."

In the course of her rhetorical arias, the real world, the seen world, becomes blurred, her observations imprecise. In "White," for instance, Clampitt evokes a ravine in language that seems, in its use of geometric terms and biological nomenclature, exact:

interspersing glooms
of conifers the far
side of the pass with
mazily hexagonal

lopsided falling things
or substances   or stuffs

Stuffs? If she intends to enshroud the seen world with mystery, Glück's reminder in "On George Oppen" serves as a rigorous corrective: "precision is not the opposite of mystery." Poets too much in thrall to blurry evocation of "mood" should blaze this motto on their foreheads.

As a creative writing teacher, Philip Booth stressed the maxim, "Sequence must lead to consequence." Whatever details are gathered should function clearly and precisely as means to an end, rather than as an end to themselves. If "consequence" gets lost in Clampitt's "tendency to ramble / and run on" ("Paumanok"), Andrew Hudgins, in ***The Glass Hammer,*** seems to lose a sense of consequence in the rush of confessional purgation. These poems, weaker and flatter than any published in his three previous collections, take as their subject Hudgins' Southern childhood. We read of racial tensions, brotherly disputes, class consciousness, and family skeletons: "Which uncles drank and where they hid the bottle. / Which cousin lost a child or had to marry" ("Mending Socks"). Many of the details establish place and time strikingly, like the "black thread pilfered from the mill" that steers "skeeter kites" in the poem of that title, or, in "Blemishes," the mother "lift[ing] / the lukewarm rag and popp[ing] [the speaker's] zits / between her red thumbnails." Yet, like this last image, many details seem designed to shock or titillate, the frequent profanities in the closing line or two of a poem too often gratuitous. Here, for instance, are the last lines of "The Social Order," a poem about his family's racism: "I love some of these people. / Let Jesus love them all. Let Jesus / love every fucking one of us." Or the conclusion of "My Father's Rage":

> But now his crazy anger's gone
> to whole days watching teevee, watching
> golf, football, weather—gone to whole days
> watching the fucking all-news channel.
> And I, goddamn him, I want it back.

Glück, once more, provides incisive commentary: "When we speak of honesty, in relation to poems, we mean the degree to which and the power with which the generating impulse has been transcribed. Transcribed, not transformed. Any attempt to evaluate the honesty of a text must always lead away from that text, and toward intention" ("Against Sincerity"). Hudgins in "Afterword," provides insight into his intent; "As a child, I swore I'd tell my story / while I was still angry," he begins:

> Now, having told, my story, said my piece,
> I'm not as angry as I was,
> but tired. And guilty. All telling's betrayal,
> I've learned again: selection, rounding off,
> interpretation. . .

From the poet of *Saints and Strangers*, we might have expected much more acute "selection" and "rounding off," interpretation of a life rather than airing of dirty laundry.

Selection and interpretation make James McMichael's ***Each in a Place Apart,*** his fourth collection, a wonderfully concise and moving narrative. This book-length poem, gathered in untitled sections, chronicles the author's second marriagc, from its beginnings as an adulterous affair between a married man and a significantly younger woman, a member of the church youth group he sponsored, through the dissolution of his first marriage, their marriage, and the slow dissolving of their relationship. The details are carefully sifted, presented in muted, balanced tones, with full awareness of tone and irony. McMichael restrains whatever anger he might feel—toward her, toward himself, toward fate or circumstance—and gives us the simple facts of their life. One section begins:

> Except when there's fog,
> we can see from our long front window the huge
> supertankers and the half-day boats. There are
> California
> gray whales in the winter. I'm through writing
> by
> lunchtime usually if I've gotten a good start,
> and on afternoons I'm not at school, there's
> reading to do. When I'm at my best with it,
> its phrases as much in league as I want
> things for us to be. When I follow to the letter
> first
> this phrase, this one, and now this and this,
> they feel looked back on from a time so ample
> that whatever has been hoped for is made whole.
> I'm not
> married now. Linda's not alone.

No straining to enlist our belief in his sincerity; the sincerity is plain from the low tones of a man recounting only, but completely, a life lived, considered, and finally revealed.

Although less systematic and unified than ***Each in a Place Apart, What the Body Remembers,*** Adèle Slaughter's first collection, presents a life story through these relatively spare, well-crafted lyrics. The book's analytical, rather than exclusively purgative, bent is signalled by the section epigraphs, two from psycho-analytical texts and the third from Rilke's *Letters to a Young Poet.* Grounded in details, the poems evoke the experience of growing up as an army brat with an abusive, alcoholic father, yet Slaughter does not revel in self-pity or excoriate her family; instead, the poems attempt to make discriminations, to separate the essence, as she writes of eating Concord grapes from her grandfather's unkept vines, "gather[ing] the seeds with lips, tongue and teeth, / trying to separate the thick mucous from seed" ("American Summer"). Experience is refined and distilled through memory, which heightens the flavor, like "the taste of spaghetti, better the next day" ("Body Memory"), but the aim is to find a myth to accommodate the details, to weave them into a whole which will allow greater sense to be made of the parts. She remains alert, however, to the pitfalls of such mythologizing, as she writes in the seventh section of "Marriage":

> But what is the story here? I hide behind my-
> self
> giving you images—dominos, flies,
> bell-shaped flowers, milk-fed veal and dolphins.
>
> I become a little i and twist my rings
> denying them, a whole life doesn't exist.
> Little i wants ten thousand lovers;
>
> The little i buries her left hand deep inside her
> pocket.
> The married i relies on dreaming hands
> to hold the way of dreaming.

"But stories do not end in dreams," she begins the next section, a clear-headed recognition. This volume announces the presence of a careful, capable poet.

For Linda Gregg in ***Chosen by the Lion,*** her fourth collection, the myth seems compounded from the Attic, the Gnostic, and the Christian. The poems take as their subject a failed adulterous affair but conceive of that affair as emblematic of the failed Eden of a passionate life. "The gods," she writes in "The Ninth Dawn," the opening poem, "want the honey in the hive, are willing to have / the lovers destroyed. There is a grand design / pulsing around their perishing." In these poems, Gregg attempts piece by piece to delineate what she can of that design. The body of the abandoned lover is, in a reversal of the orthodox figure, like the body of the dead Christ: "The body without / God inside. The spirit exited, Jesus all body now" ("The Spirit and What Is Left Behind (After Giotto)"). Pure and earthy, grand and ordinary, Gregg's vision of love seeks to reconcile these opposites. On the one hand, she "want[s] the world to be made / out of passion and grace" ("Official Love Story") and argues, "The form / of love was purity. An art. An architecture" ("Looking for Each of Us"), yet the "one delicate thing," she also writes, "is found / in life's rudeness. The design of beings married together" ("The Delicate Thing"). Further, she "wanted [love] made of actual things. Dirt / and corpses even." The difficulty of her task is reflected in two facing poems, slightly more than halfway through the book. "The City of God" begins,

What thou lovest well is felt violently.
Stays on in us. I know Paradise is not
the cypress tree God showed me as his heart.
Is not the country, is not beautiful.
It is the city streets in bad weather.
Small dirty shops with custard pastries
and coffee and steam-covered windows.
I do not speak the language of that paradise.

For all its ordinariness, this paradise is reachable, unlike the paradise in "Sometimes," which "is always the impossible / grown in the heart. / Until, fully formed, it escapes / as pictures on wooden panels / or on the plastered ceiling." Reading these poems, one never doubts Gregg's earnestness or the depth of her loss; comparing her poems with those of Jack Gilbert, her mentor, one sees the remnant of indulgence, a hive plundered before the honey was quite ripe.

The ordinary world fascinates Jane Hirshfield, as it does Gregg, not because it is a template for a lost paradise but because in "this visible world . . . all is transformed" ("The Wedding"). The poems in ***The October Palace,*** her second full-length collection, celebrate that world through references thrown even wider than those of Gregg and with what seems considerably greater erudition. Hirshfield's net gathers Zen monks, Cycladic figures, Modernist painters, Praxilla, Grant's *Common Birds and How To Know Them,* and a car named Big Mama Tomato. Her knowledge never seems donned like a valedictory robe, however, but serves to illuminate recesses of thought, not resting on elegant surfaces, for, as she begins " 'Perceptibility Is a Kind of Attentiveness' ":

It is not enough
to see only the beauty,
this light
that pools aluminum
in the winter branches of apple—
it is only a sign
of the tree looking out
from the tree,
of the light looking
back at the light,
the long-called attention.

But the things of this world do not serve only to "distract / in their sweetness and rustling"; the body is also a "net": "The one / we willingly give ourselves to. . . / each knot so carefully made, the curved / plate of the sternum tied to the shape of breath, / the perfect hinge of knee. . ." ("Of the Body"). The real world, the made world, "reveals itself in iron" of raised nails in flooring, "to be pounded down again, for what we've declared / the beautiful to be" ("Floor"). What Hirshfield hopes to help us see through these poems is a way, as she titles one poem, of "Meeting the Light Completely." The goal of Zen practice is to see the world as it is, just as it is, not other than an ideal world of enlightened experience, not quite the same: "Not one, not two," a Zen saying insists. But in the details, banal as "the chipped lip / of a blue-glazed cup" (and pause just a moment to reflect on the sensual beauty of those lines as verbal music), we see the beauty of "the found world," which surprises as profoundly as being able, in those odd moments when we are truly present, to recognize the former "unrecognized stranger" in "the long beloved," leading us to say with "all lovers," " 'What fools we were, not to have seen.' "

What Carolyn Forché wishes us to see in ***The Angel of History*** is less the spiritual underpinning of the ordinary world than the inherent political dialectic. This third collection represents a dramatic departure from the relatively short-lined lyrics of her earlier books; instead, her lines reach and fracture across the page in their effort to contain history, to record the voices of the dispossessed, whose "ordinary world" means "bootprints in clay, / the persistence of tracked field. // What was here before imperfectly erased / and memory a reliquary in a wall of silence." In "The Notebook of Uprising," she returns to the Czech Republic and traces the experiences of her maternal grandmother during World War II and the subsequent Communist occupation, including dislocation and terrorization. In one section, one of her relatives speaks:

Put into question others, put into question God.
Whatever can be taken away is taken
to allow suffering to remain.

Autumn. That autumn. Other autumns.
It was as if we'd been given to walk through a
world to come.

That world, we take it, is our world, full of terror and uncertainty. God is no longer sure, leaving us, as she suggests in "Elegy," nothing to cling to, even "[t]he page is a charred field the dead would have written." In these poems, the personal and historical are collapsed, history seen not in terms of troop movements, military strategies, economic curves, or abstract body-counts but in the lives those remains once lived. History at its best, recorded by Walter Benjamin's angel, provides a sense of "how incomplete a moment is human life," as she notes in "Book Codes: II," "though," she cautions, "this is not a fairy tale explained in advance." These poems challenge our expectations of poetry, bearing closer resemblance to the recent work of Jorie Graham than to Forché's earlier poems, especially in embedding fragments of other texts in the tissue of the poems. Unlike Graham's work, however, Forché is deeply concerned with the human beyond what we usually take to mean the "ordinary": a world of suburban luxury; instead, she attempts to sink her poems in the ordinary brutality of our century, even though her sheer erudition at times distances from the pathos.

However much satisfaction readers of poetry experience

from repeated readings of favorite poems, they, too, can become as impatient and anxious for a new volume by a favorite poet as any other member of our consumer society. So I await each of Galway Kinnell's new books, savoring whatever information I garner regarding its movement toward print. Frequently, however, what we await most impatiently cannot satisfy our expectations. The poems in ***Imperfect Thirst,*** Kinnell's twelfth collection, do not instantly grab me, shake me up, make chills run up and down my spine, take off the top of my head. And Emily Dickinson's visceral criteria have always seemed best, since the ways a poem moves each individual reader, the depth and breadth, is the truest measure of its having tapped the source. Except in moments, these new poems do not affect me in ways that a good half dozen in *The Past* do, increasingly on repeated readings. Still, if even two or three poems in a collection have that effect on me, I consider it solid, and this new collection exceeds that requisite minimum.

First, to complain: too many of the poems seem derivative—of Kinnell himself—exercises in familiar modes, like the long-lined "The Pen," "Proem" to the volume, which lacks the vitality of "The Road Between Here and There," for instance, or, from *When One Has Lived a Long Time Alone*, the movingly humorous "Oatmeal." Similarly, the longer ode-like poems in section V, particularly "Holy Shit" and "Flies," seem more concerned with revelling in surfaces than grappling with depth, mere poetic parlor games; "Holy Shit" begins with three pages of epigraphs before getting to the poem, which occupies only slightly more space. This is not particularly different from other volumes; Kinnell is not always the best judge of his work upon initial book publication, which is why his work benefits from such revisiting as last year's *Three Books.*

On the plus side, however, when Kinnell nails it, the satisfactions are enormous. In this volume, "Trees," "Rapture," and "Neverland" score highest marks. In "Rapture" the description of waking, making love, drowsing, and waking again to watch the lover dress poignantly evokes the eros of the ordinary:

> She takes a piece of silken cloth
> from the drawer and stands up. Under the falls
> of hair her face has become quiet and downcast,
> as if she will be, all day among strangers,
> looking down inside herself at our rapture.

Even more, "Neverland," an elegy for the poet's sister, explores the uncomfortable territory of watching a loved one die, knowing, as life fades, that one "could take off right now, climb the pure forms / that surmount time and death" to "hurtle" into the arms of a lover and "taste . . . the actual honey of paradise." Instead, he stays, watching and waiting. By the end, "as they ratchet the box holding / her body into the earth," he hears

> her voice,
> calling back across the region she passes through,
> in prolonged, even notes, which swell and diminish,
> a far landscape I seem to see as if from above,
> much light, much darkness, tumbling clouds,
> sounding back to us from its farthest edge.
> Now her voice comes from under the horizon,
> and now it grows faint, and now I cannot hear it.

Poems like this can fill what, in "The Striped Snake and the Goldfinch," Kinnell calls the "unfillableness in us," providing the satisfactions that lead us to poems in the first place.

Readers familiar with the work of William Everson, who also published under the name Brother Antoninus, from a few scattered anthology pieces will be gratified by the depth and range of the work gathered in ***The Blood of the Poet: Selected Poems.*** Albert Gelpi has gleaned from the extent of Everson's career, organizing the book in three sections that correlate with the three volumes of Everson's collected poems: "The Residual Years," "The Veritable Years," and "The Integral Years." Gelpi's "Afterword" also provides a clear history of Everson and his work, including his relationship with Catholicism, particularly of interest given his stint as both lay brother and ordained monk. Like Rexroth, with whom Everson was associated in the Fifties, and Robinson Jeffers, whose imprimatur is plain in these poems, Everson is a poet of nature, particularly the hills of California. From the earliest lyrics to the recent meditations, Everson cannot regard nature without seeing God or consider God without incarnating Him in fields, rivers, bears, or deer. His eye is not judgmental; he seeks not to discriminate good from evil in the natural world but to see the fullness of God's grandeur:

> And the strong weed
> Seeds, and the weak weed
> Scatters, and I see in them each
> A glory of God. . .

In these lines from "The Falling of the Grain," I hear a resonance with Kit Smart, another "renegade" influence along with Lawrence, Whitman, Blake, and Jeffers. The volume includes very recent work which shows no diminution of poetic power or vision; the details remain sharp, reaching beyond the literal to embrace the inherent Incarnation:

> Suddenly a kingfisher swoops between.
> In midflight he sees us, veers sharply,
> Utters a sudden electrifying screech,
> The ineluctable tension cruxed at the heart of things
> Splitting his beak, the mystery
> Out of which life springs and from which it passes.
>
> ("Stone Face Falls")

Though not a major poet, Everson stands as an accomplished journeyman, the sort of poet whose service consolidates in order to extend and expand the possibilities of the art.

W. H. Auden, in his introduction to *19th Century British Minor Poets*, established five criteria for being major, of which a candidate must satisfy at least three and a half. The poet must be prolific, demonstrate "wide range in subject matter and treatment," evidence "originality of vision and style," show mastery of verse technique, and continue maturing as a poet until death. Hayden Carruth meets all these conditions, as his ***Collected Longer Poems*** demonstrates by itself; taken together with his *Collected Shorter Poems* (1992), it marks Carruth as a preeminent master. The poems were composed between 1957 and 1983 and have been published in various collections, only one previously unavailable except in a fine-press edition. Three are written in Carruth's trade-mark "paragraphs," rhymed, variably metered fifteen-line stanzas, including *The Sleeping Beauty*, the heart of Carruth's oeuvre to date. Other poems in the collection are written in sprawling Whitmanesque lines, tercets, free-verse lyrics, and loosened blank verse, the chosen form answering the demands of the subject matter. Few, if any, of Carruth's contemporaries—or immediate predecessors or followers—have demonstrated such extensive mastery.

Carruth's mastery, scope, and development can be shown by comparing passages from the three poems in "paragraphs," beginning with the first poem in the book, "The Asylum":

> And is not the whole earth
> Asylum? Is mankind
> In refuge? Here is where we fled in birth.
> Yet what we fled from we shall find,
> It fills us now. And we shall search the air,
> Turning drained eyes along the wind, as blind
> Men do, but never find asylum here.
>
> (Section 11)

The variable iambic lines, elevated and stiff as the diction may be, are flexible and fluid, varying the caesura, alternating end-stopped and enjambed lines to affect pace and phrasing, positioning inversions to intensify the signal as well as vary the beat. The rhymes are clear and clean but unobtrusive. For all that, the poem never entirely rises free of period style. Compare this with a passage from "The Moon," in *Contra Mortem* (1966):

> Reflected light reflected again on snow
> but beauty is lonely beauty The snowsurface
> is hard gleaming vitrescent blue
> without crest or crevice
> extending beyond anywhere for long ago
> the horizon crumbled in an indeterminate glow
> and the night has stillness

Carruth's extensive vocabulary is again evident, but his treatment of the form markedly differs: lines more frequently enjambed, rhymes more slant, the meter considerably loosened, losing in some places entirely the iambic pulse, then reasserting it subtly. Here, however, the style is less period academic and more reminiscent of the "other" school of American poetry, resembling the work of such post-Poundians as Denise Levertov and Robert Creeley. Finally, this passage from section 94 of *The Sleeping Beauty*:

> The poem moves.
> After fierce intention,
> The exalting, reaching and thrusting through lust,
> Through densities of image, to explode transcendence
> From a broken language, to touch
> Everyone's wordlessness, to crush what was meant
> Till it dances clear of language like forestfire bent
> And flaring in the wind—
> Snow dances
> Like fire sometimes, windblown.

Flexibility of line, including caesura and enjambment, emphasis and phrasing—in both poetic and musical senses—remain constant. Yet, around a consistent armature, Carruth alters the way he handles the poetic clay.

If such diversity puzzles a readership obsessed with a poet's one "true voice," Glück again offers insight: "for the writer, thinking and writing (like thinking and feeling) are synonyms. Style changes when one has got to the end, willingly or not, of a train of thought" ("The Idea of Courage"). Carruth's fundamental concern with the tough issues of being is clear enough from the passages quoted, yet they are issues in plural, a life's work to ponder and puzzle, to grapple with again and again. Madness, the riddle of being, the paradoxically ennobling and damaging Romantic myth—"An aspect of relentless intelligence," Glück writes in "On Hugh Seidman," "is that it finds no resting place. . . ." Certainly, for Carruth, "the poem keeps moving," fluid, flexible, bearing witness. His ***Collected Longer Poems*** finishes gathering his past work, though, as the last section of the *Collected Shorter Poems* indicates, the body of his work continues to grow.

The Year in Drama

by Julius Novick

1994 was not an auspicious year for American drama. *Angels in America* by Tony Kushner, still by a wide margin the most important American play of the 1990s, opened in Los Angeles in 1992 and on Broadway in 1993; in 1994 it closed on Broadway at a reported loss of $660,000. (It will, however, be produced in Chicago, San Francisco, and elsewhere.) As I write, in January, 1995, *not one* American non-musical play is being performed on Broadway, which is dominated more than ever by a very few, very expensive musicals. The great network of nonprofit professional theaters, established in this country over the last fifty years as an alternative to Broadway, continues to function, but has been hard-hit by the diminution of government funding. Those who train young theater artists are talking about how to deal with the fact that playwrights, directors, and actors can no longer realistically expect to make a living in the professional theater, which more and more has become a sort of farm system, or an expensive hobby, for workers in film and television. ("If I do a couple of films, I'll be able to afford to do a play.")

And yet, stubbornly, quixotically, talented American men and women continue to bring their work to the stage—including, in 1994, two eminent elder playwrights: Arthur Miller (born 1915) and Edward Albee (born 1928). Neither has regained his midseason form, but both, perhaps, displayed their best work since their great days.

Albee's return was particularly triumphant. The off-off-Broadway Signature Theater, which devotes itself to a different playwright every year, gave a whole season of his more esoteric work. Meanwhile, his ***Three Tall Women*** opened in New York at the nonprofit Vineyard Theater, transferred to a commercial off-Broadway house for a long run, and won the Pulitzer Prize. Albee maintains that no previous play of his has had such a favorable response from the New York critics.

The protagonist of ***Three Tall Women*** is a very rich, very difficult, very old lady: imperious, self-centered, incontinent, reminiscent, forgetful, given to sudden bursts of anger and of weeping. In Act I, she passes the time with her middle-aged companion (the second tall woman), as the third tall woman, a young lawyer, tries to get her to put her affairs in order. At the end of the act, she has a stroke. In Act II, the three actresses play the protagonist at different ages, her three selves considering her life from their varying perspectives, as her son sits silently at her bedside. The play is generally understood to be the author's *homage* to his adoptive mother.

Three Tall Women has the elegant prose and the desiccated, distanced quality characteristic of Albee's late work. As a reverie on one character's past and present, it has, like other Albee plays, a clear debt to Beckett. The ending is Beckettian: the old lady says, "I was talking about. . . what: coming to the end of it; yes. So. There it is. You asked, after all. That's the happiest moment. . . . When it's all done. When we stop. When we can stop."

For me, however, this evening of reminiscences failed to fuse into significance; I found it fine-spun but very thin. Still, it is livelier and funnier than most late Albee, and it leaps into intensity when the silent son appears, and the two older selves of the protagonist recall with bitterness the day he "went away, took his life and one bag and went off." A veteran actress named Myra Carter made a deserved hit as the old lady in both acts, but I was taken even more by the compelling angularity of Marian Seldes as the companion in Act I and the middle-aged protagonist in Act II.

Arthur Miller's new play, ***Broken Glass,*** was less successful with the critics and the public. After a troubled tryout at the Long Wharf Theater in New Haven, it came to Broadway, received mixed reviews, and closed in short order. But it is a play of substance. Its title comes from *kristallnacht,* when the Nazis smashed the windows of Jewish stores, foreshadowing the persecutions to come. In Brooklyn, in 1938, a Jewish housewife named Sylvia Gellburg becomes obsessed with the Nazi threat, and mysteriously loses the use of her legs. A doctor, searching for psychological causes, makes disquieting discoveries about the Gellburg marriage: once again a Miller play probes into the past to see how it has shaped the present.

Broken Glass has its murky aspects: the relation between the terrors of history and the private sorrows of the Gellburgs is not clearly and convincingly established, and it is not clear what we are supposed to make of the Jewish doctor who rides horseback every day on Ocean Parkway, has fond memories of his student days in Germany, and is attracted to Sylvia. But my attention was held by the search for the secret of Sylvia's disability. John Tillinger staged the play with dignity and grace, and it was finely acted by Amy Irving as Sylvia, David Dukes as the doctor, and especially by Ron Rifkin as Sylvia's husband Phillip. (Rifkin's performance is climaxed by a terrifically graphic heart attack.)

Above all I was fascinated by Phillip, whose relation to his own Jewishness is so exquisitely complex and exquisitely painful. He is desperate to distance himself from other Jews, pathetically proud to be "the only Jew ever worked for Brooklyn Guarantee in their whole history," the only Jew ever to set foot on the deck of his boss's yacht. He glories in the fact that his only son is an army officer: "I wanted people to see that a Jew doesn't have to be a lawyer or a doctor or a businessman." His hatred of himself as a Jew is related to his sexual impotence and to his wife's paralysis. He is so divided against himself that his heart attack is like a bursting apart, after a lifetime of holding himself ever-so-tightly together. A number of recent American plays—by Neil Simon, Herb Gardner, Donald Margulies, Jon Robin Baitz, Wendy Wasserstein, and others—have wrestled with the vexed question of what it means to be an American Jew; ***Broken Glass*** is a notable contribution to that ongoing discussion.

If ***Broken Glass*** is this year's play about being Jewish, ***Love! Valour! Compassion!*** by Terrence McNally is this year's play about being homosexual. Its setting is an idyllic country house not far from New York, where eight gay men foregather to eat, talk, bond, court, and skinny-dip. (The skinny-dipping caused some raised eyebrows among the more straitlaced subscribers at the Manhattan Theater Club.)

The house is owned by a generous dancer-choreographer named Gregory, whose lover, Bobby, is a sweet, curly-haired, blind young man, not only blind but so spiritual that immediately upon arrival he goes out to say "Thank you, God" for the house and grounds. But Bobby is not too spiritual to be seduced by Ramon, a hunky young Puerto Rican dancer, who is the lover, for the moment at least, of John, a sharp-tongued, malicious Brit. When Gregory finds out about Bobby and Ramon he is furious, but when he realizes he is too old to dance the brilliant new solo he has created, he nobly resigns it to Ramon. Meanwhile, John's brother James turns up, and turns out to be as nice as John is nasty. Pudgy Buzz ("Love me, love my love-handles") falls in love with James, who reciprocates. The remaining houseguests are Arthur and Perry, who have been together for fourteen years. "We're role models," says Perry wryly. "It's very stressful."

As any play about contemporary gay life must do, ***Love! Valour! Compassion!*** acknowledges the shadow of AIDS. Buzz and James are both HIV-positive; Buzz has a long (too long) speech of complaint about it, and James collapses as he and his friends, in tutus, dance an excerpt from *Swan Lake*. In a sense, this is a play *about* AIDS. But it does not harrow us with death-throes; as the title implies, its spirit is gentle, sentimental, affirmative. Nathan Lane as Buzz gets the best of the playwright's abundant laugh-lines, and makes the most of them, while not neglecting the human being behind the class-clown antics. John Glover does a spectacular turn as both John and James, transforming himself instantaneously by just a twist of body language. Randy Becker lets us see that Ramon is using his truculent sexual glamor as a shield against men who are older, better educated, and more firmly established in the world than he. But the play is an ensemble piece, impeccably acted by all concerned under Joe Mantello's sensitive direction, offering a deliberately unreal, wishful, sometimes cloying, but generally disarming image of the gay world as ultimately a band of brothers, somehow united by the scourge that threatens them. A hit at the Manhattan Theater Club, ***Love! Valour! Compassion!*** transferred to Broadway.

Like Terrence McNally, Sam Shepard has had a thirty-year career as a playwright (with time out, in Shepard's case, to write, direct, and act in movies). Shepard's new play, ***Simpatico,*** which played a limited engagement at the New York Shakespeare Festival's Public Theater, revolves around a fraught relationship between Carter, who is rich and smooth, and Vinnie, who is poor and unkempt. (The two have reminded many observers of the respectable brother and the outlaw brother in Shepard's *True West*.) Many years ago they were involved in framing a horse-racing official; then Carter took Vinnie's wife and his Buick; now Carter supports Vinnie, who has a cardboard box full of photos that could incriminate his erstwhile partner.

Shepard is a maker of American dreamscapes, not particularly a storyteller; he has loaded this play with more plot than he is able to articulate clearly. In spite of impressive acting by Ed Harris and Fred Ward as Carter and Vinnie, James Gammon as the man they framed, and Beverly D'Angelo as Carter's wife, ***Simpatico*** is full of dull confrontations, with much beating around the bush, culminating in revelations that fail to reveal anything of consequence.

Tony Kushner, arguably at this moment our country's leading playwright, was represented this year by a minor work. ***Slavs! (Thinking About the Longstanding Problems of Virtue and Happiness),*** which came from the Actors Theater of Louisville to the New York Theater Workshop, is an 80-minute piece that recycles material Kushner originally wrote for *Perestroika*, the second part of *Angels in America*. Like *Angels*, ***Slavs!*** buzzes with intellectual energy, viewing politics and private life through a combination of realism, fantasy, and satire.

There is a beautiful, complex moment at the end of it, when a little Siberian girl, born mute and sickly as a result of prenatal exposure to radiation from a Soviet nuclear device, and now dead, appears in the afterlife, suddenly able to speak. She meets two high-ranking Soviet apparatchiks, also deceased, playing cards in the snow. "The socialist experiment in the Soviet Union has failed, grandfathers," she tells them gravely. ***Slavs!*** is a tragicomic elegy—not for Stalinism, for which Kushner has no sympathy whatever—but for the hopes and the sufferings invested so vainly in "the Soviet experiment."

Unfortunately, the earlier parts of ***Slavs!,*** in which Kushner parodies Marxist rhetoric, and then shows us a foolish apparatchik in love with the lesbian custodian of the storage-room where the brains of deceased Bolsheviks are kept, have a dangerously high ratio of words to action, and are performed with execrable heavy-footedness under Lisa Peterson's direction. The sloppy Russian accents are a disgrace throughout.

Another American playwright interested in history is Suzan-Lori Parks, author of a work modestly entitled ***The America Play.*** Its protagonist is an African-American grave-digger called "The Foundling Father" or "the Lesser Known," who impersonates Abraham Lincoln in a fake beard, and gets assassinated over and over and over again. This play has its admirers. It was commissioned and developed by Theater for a New Audience, workshopped at Arena Stage (Washington, D. C.) and Dallas Theater Center, and performed in New Haven and New York as a co-production of the Yale Repertory Theater and the New York Shakespeare Festival. It seemed to me an endless evening of tricky, fiddly, empty conceits. A play's power and meaning must be rooted in a dramatic action, or, nine times out of ten, it will have no power and no meaning.

This year's most striking playwriting debut was made by David Ives, the author of an evening of six oddly intriguing comic playlets presented off-Broadway under the title, ***All in the Timing.*** In "Sure Thing," the first of them, a nice young man tries to pick up a nice young woman in a cafe. Every time the conversation goes offtrack, a bell rings, and they try again until they get it right; the result is a gentle, perceptive satire on dating rituals and small talk. In "Words, Words, Words," three monkeys named Milton, Swift, and Kafka try to type *Hamlet*, without knowing what *Hamlet* is. In "The Universal Language," a new and pleasantly cockeyed invented language, "Unamunda," becomes an occasion for romantic comedy, as teacher and student fall in love. "Philip Glass Buys a Loaf of Bread" is a parody, set in a bakery, of Glass's operas and their monotonous repetitions. In "The Philadelphia," cities give their names to states of being. Mark is "in a Philadelphia," which means that "no matter what you ask for, you can't get it," while Al "woke up in a Los Angeles. And life is beautiful"—no matter what happens. "Variations on the Death of Trotsky" begins with "Trotsky sitting at his desk, writing furiously. The handle of a mountain-climber's axe is sticking out of the back of his head."

These are slight pieces, skits really, and some of them go on too long. But David Ives is a truly original comic mind. Under the direction of Jason McConnell Buzas, his work gets the kind of light-touch revue acting it needs.

Three works this year rendered with particular precision aspects of contemporary American life. Eric Bogosian, the performance artist (his *Pounding Nails in the Floor with My Forehead* was reviewed in this space last year), has written a full-fledged play in which he does not appear. In his solo pieces, Bogosian is a scathing satirist; in this play he is a sober realist. Entitled ***Suburbia,*** it is set in a fictional but all-too-real town called "Burnfield—pizza and puke capital of the world." It presents us with a group of young men and women—not kids any more, but unable to grow up—whose main activity in life is hanging out by the 7-11, drinking beer and throwing fast food on the pavement. There is a plot—a minor rock-and-roll star comes home to Burnfield to look up his old buddies, and the result is sexual rivalry and death—but what is most convincing—and terrifying—is the aimlessness of the lives we see. "It's the end of the world, man, no hope, no ideas, no future, fuckin' apocalypse." Robert Falls's finely naturalistic staging of ***Suburbia*** for the Lincoln Center Theater is full of galvanic youthful energy, which only intensifies the pervading sense of bitterness and frustration, waste and loss.

There are bitterness and frustration, waste and loss to burn in ***Twilight Los Angeles, 1992,*** which came from the Mark Taper Forum in Los Angeles, to the McCarter Theater in Princeton, New Jersey, to the Public Theater in New York, and on to Broadway. But there is something healing in this work's very existence. ***Twilight,*** about the racially-fueled riots in Los Angeles, is the latest one-woman performance piece by Anna Deavere Smith, who also created *Fires in the Mirror: Crown Heights, Brooklyn, and Other Identities*, about a previous instance of racial strife. These two works are part of a series she calls *On the Road: A Search for American Character*. "Each *On the Road* performance," she writes, "evolves from interviews I conduct with individuals directly or indirectly involved in the event I intend to explore. Basing my scripts entirely on this interview material, I perform the interviewees on the stage using their own words."

Smith is slender, light-skinned, African-American; her characters are black, white, Asian, Latino, male, female, young, old, rich, poor, dignified, fatuous, militant, peaceful: dozens of them, emerging one after the other through the voice and body of this one woman. She presents them all with scrupulous fairness. The result is a compelling collage, showing no demons, just a lot of people acting according to the logic of their own feelings and assumptions. Everybody, it seems, wants "justice." But what is that? Anna Deavere Smith honors with seriousness and skill the function of the theater as "the abstract and brief chronicles of the time."

Another work that manages the astonishing feat of dealing evenhandedly with a fiercely contentious issue is ***Keely and Du*** by the reclusive Kentucky playwright Jane Martin. (So closely is her identity guarded that many people suspect that "Jane Martin" is a pseudonym.) Martin begins with a compelling premise: a group of anti-abortion activists who call themselves "our Lord's underground" have kidnapped a pregnant woman who was seeking an abortion, have handcuffed her to a bed in a basement, and propose to keep her there until she has her baby.

There are, of course, heated arguments pro and con, but Martin never loses sight of the immediate emotional realities of the situation—which serves to increase both the urgency and the cogency of the arguments. The two main characters—Keely, the pregnant woman, and Du, the kindly but fanatical woman who guards her—have strikingly individual voices: both are working class, but Keely is abrasive, slangy, contemporary, while Du is old-fashioned, straitlaced, warm and homey. Predictably, the two women begin to bond together—but Martin keeps their relationship firmly this side of sentimentality. Neither retreats from her beliefs and demands, but they form a kind of women's alliance against pompous, patriarchal Walter, who descends periodically to lecture Keely on what the Lord has in mind for her. (The playwright takes no side—or rather, both sides—in the abortion debate, but the men in her play do not come off well.) At the end, Martin finds a way to resolve the dramatic situation without diminishing our respect for both Keely and Du and for what they stand for.

Keely and Du was first presented at the Actors Theater of Louisville in 1993; according to *American Theater* magazine, it was the most popular play of the 1994-95 season at the nation's resident theaters, with 14 productions scheduled. Strangely, no plans have been announced to produce it in New York City. Like ***Twilight Los Angeles, 1992, Keely and Du*** has probably not changed many minds, but though the former is fact and the latter is fiction, both have the power to give people valuable insight into the minds of those who disagree with them.

1994 was not a year when new foreign plays made a great impression. From London to Lincoln Center (in a new American production) came ***Hapgood*** by Tom Stoppard, partly a spy movie for the stage, partly a parody of a spy movie; it is also a high comedy, and includes a rueful love story, a tough, noirish sex story, and extensive reflections on the similarity between spying and particle physics, grounded on the essential unknowability of reality. Stockard Channing, one of our finest actresses, plays the eponymous Hapgood, a high-ranking British Intelligence operative, with an admirable balance of crispness and warmth, and also gets to impersonate Hapgood's blowsy twin sister. (Twinship is one of the themes of the play.) She is beautifully supported by David Strathairn as a thoughtful Russian physicist, Josef Sommer as a senior Intelligence officer, and David Lansbury as a thuggish agent. Jack O'Brien's staging is brisk, smooth, elegant.

But in this play Stoppard's celebrated cleverness gets the better of him. Right from the first scene—an intricate pantomime of ducking into cubicles, handing off briefcases, picking up towels, set in the locker room of a public swimming pool—the action moves faster than the audience can take it in. It is hard to avoid the feeling that Stoppard is deliberately teasing us. ***Hapgood*** is written in enjoyably neat and cultivated prose; when Hapgood's young son is in danger, the plot does begin to grip; but it remains tantalizing rather than satisfying. When the thuggish agent, trying to puzzle out what has happened, says wryly, "Give me a minute—I'm slow," he speaks for the audience as well.

Three Birds Alighting on a Field by Timberlake Wertenbaker is a London art-world satire that gets off some shrewd hits: "Here come some rich people. Tell 'em how art makes being rich all right." Originally produced at the Royal Court Theater in London, it came to the Manhattan Theater Club with its original director, Max Stafford-Clark, and its original leading actress, Harriet Walter, who gives a remarkable performance as a Candide-like youngish woman learning the ways of this esoteric world. But the play wanders off in too many directions to be very effective.

More interesting than this year's new imported British plays were the revivals by British directors. In a production that began at the Royal National Theater in London, Stephen Daldry has radically rethought ***An Inspector Calls,*** an old chestnut of provincial English rep written in 1946 by J. B. Priestley, a popular novelist, playwright and pundit now largely forgotten. The time of the action is before World War I, during the heyday of British capitalism. An inspector knocks at the door of Arthur Birling, a prosperous manufacturer. A young woman, formerly employed in Birling's factory, has just killed herself. By the time the inspector has finished his inquiries, every member of the Birling family is shown to bear some responsibility in her death—and it becomes apparent that the inspector is not a police inspector at all, but a mysterious, presumably supernatural emissary of social justice, come to show these complacent plutocrats their sins.

Daldry and his designer Ian MacNeil have broken the play out of its deceptively cozy domestic interior and set it on a rain-swept, darkling plain, in the midst of which is an isolated miniature house on stilts, just large enough to contain the actors who play the Birlings. In a stunning *coup de théâtre*, the house opens up, exposing its inmates literally as the inspector exposes them metaphorically. Later, a chorus of silent, sober figures appears at one side of the stage, watching accusingly. Still later, the house becomes a gaping wreck, tilted all askew. When the Birlings regain confidence, the house, astonishingly, rights itself and closes once again—and opens again, to reveal the accusing chorus *inside*.

All these and many other wonders are accompanied by four live musicians playing Stephen Warbeck's melodramatic incidental music. Yet the bold, powerful acting of Daldry's cast—Philip Bosco as Arthur Birling, a sleek, self-satisfied walrus, Rosemary Harris sashaying regally as Mrs. Birling—holds its own against the spectacle and the music. "Revisionist" directors, who stage plays in ways their authors never could have imagined, usually work their wills on the classics of the stage, often with dire results. But ***An Inspector Calls*** is nobody's classic. Daldry has taken Priestley's rather stuffy socialist parable and shaken it into new life, made it an explosive, hallucinatory indictment of Britain in the Thatcher Era, not without implications for Americans.

From the little Almeida Theater in London came the ***Medea*** of Euripides, staged by Jonathan Kent as a star turn for Diana Rigg as a witty and polished, rather than a primitive and elemental, Medea. At the end, in a *coup de théâtre* not unlike those in ***An Inspector Calls,*** and perhaps even more powerful, the great rusted steel plates that form Peter J. Davison's setting fall away clangorously, revealing Medea outlined triumphantly against the sky.

While ***An Inspector Calls*** and ***Medea*** were booked into commercial Broadway houses, Nicholas Hytner's production of ***Carousel,*** from the Royal National Theater, came to the Vivian Beaumont Theater in Lincoln Center. With expressionistic sets by Bob Crowley, and a beautiful Act II ballet choreographed by the late Sir Kenneth MacMillan, Hytner's somber production de-emphasizes the homogenized heartiness and New England charm that many people associate with this Rodgers and Hammerstein classic, and focusses instead on the somber story of a star-crossed young couple and their unhappy daughter. Some people complained about the interracial casting in a show set in a small town in Maine—where in real life one would expect to find few African-Americans—but Hytner pointed out that in his production the ocean was represented by blue linoleum, so that "real life" was somewhat beside the point.

It was good to have ***Carousel*** back in New York after many years. But what has the world come to when the

British are reinterpreting our classic musicals for us? On the other hand, there were revivals of musicals by American directors as well. From the Old Globe Theater in San Diego came ***Damn Yankees,*** originally produced in 1955: the one about the middle-aged Washington Senators fan who makes a deal with the devil to become a baseball star and help the Senators to a pennant. Revised and staged by Jack O'Brien, artistic director of the Old Globe, who provided a new, gently satirical take on the Formica paradise of 1950's suburban domesticity, and sporting zestful, sometimes hilarious dances choreographed by Rob Marshall, it made excellent light entertainment.

Assisting O'Brien on the revisions was George Abbott, the show's original coauthor and director. It was the last project for "Mr. Abbott," as he was universally known; he died on January 31, 1995, at the age of 107, after an astonishing eight decades in the theater as an actor, playwright, librettist, producer, and above all as a director, famous for fast-moving, meticulously staged, *funny* musicals and farces.

Somewhat more substantial was ***Show Boat,*** the 1927 classic with book and lyrics by Oscar Hammerstein and music by Jerome Kern. It came to Broadway from Toronto in a big, festive, strongly-cast production staged by Harold Prince. ***Show Boat*** has a reputation as a pioneer "serious" musical: it deals with racial persecution and marital desertion, among other things. The Prince production pays some rather self-conscious attention to oppressed African-Americans, but it is not a revisionist staging; it does full justice to ***Show Boat***'s old-fashioned, sentimental heart. Rebecca Luker as Magnolia Hawks, the showboat captain's daughter, ages convincingly from an innocent girl to a strong woman, and Mark Jacoby is handsome, though not particularly dashing, as Gaylord Ravenal, the gambler whom Magnolia marries. Kern's melodies are beautifully sung (though the sound man turns up the volume noticeably for big climaxes). Even at a top price of $75—a new high for Broadway—***Show Boat*** is a big hit.

New musicals? There were some off-Broadway. ***Hello Again*** at Lincoln Center was inspired by Schnitzler's *La Ronde,* in which A sleeps with B, who sleeps with C, and so on until someone finally sleeps with A again, completing the circle. But the copulations in *La Ronde* take place in a small span of time and space, while in ***Hello Again*** they range back and forth over the decades from the turn of the century to the present. Michael John LaChiusa, who wrote the words and music, was rumored to be an important new musical-theater talent, but ***Hello Again*** seemed to me chilly, uninviting, and without much point, though it was staged with exquisite smoothness by Graciela Daniele, and impeccably performed by the entire ensemble.

I preferred another, less publicized off-Broadway musical, ***Christina Alberta's Father*** at the Vineyard Theater, with words and music by Polly Pen, based on an obscure novel of the same name by H. G. Wells. Set in England early in this century, it went all out for offbeat charm, and often achieved it. (Father to heroine: "I hope, my dear, among all these artists and people, you are not getting . . . ramshackle.") Polly Pen will, I hope, be heard from again.

New Broadway musicals? *Sunset Boulevard* (which of course is originally from London), was reviewed here last year; in 1994 it moved from Los Angeles to Broadway, with Glenn Close still starring flamboyantly: at only $70 for the best seats, it rivaled ***Show Boat*** in the big-hit category. So did ***Beauty and the Beast,*** a ponderous stage version of the Disney cartoon film, notable mainly as the beginning of what promises to be a long-term Disney involvement with Broadway.

Passion, the newest work by Stephen Sondheim (music and lyrics) and James Lapine (book and direction) was not a big hit: it opened on Broadway in May, and closed the following January. It was, however, the most controversial production of the year, much loved and much loathed. From a little-known Italian film, and an even less-known nineteenth-century novel, comes its strange story of obsessive love. It begins with two lovers in bed, singing rapturously of their joys. But Giorgio, an army officer, is ordered away to a remote provincial town, and his beautiful Clara (who is married to someone else) is left behind in Milan. As Giorgio and Clara write to each other of their mutual longing, he is stalked by Fosca—the cousin of his commanding officer—an ugly, sickly woman, sunk deep in resentment and self-pity, given to hysterical seizures, who has fallen desperately in love with him, and *demands* that he love her in return.

"Is this what you call love," he asks her, "this endless and insatiable smothering pursuit of me? . . . This is not love, just a need for possession." "Loving you is not a choice," she replies. ". . . You are why I live." An ugly woman in love with a man who doesn't care for her is often a figure of fun, but Donna Murphy plays Fosca with fierce dignity and strength. Finally Giorgio realizes that "No one has truly loved me as you have, Fosca"—and realizes, moreover, that he loves her.

There is something deeply disquieting in Fosca's implacable pursuit of Giorgio, in her use of her sickness, her unhappiness, her very ugliness, to enforce her demand on him; in real life it would be an intolerable campaign of emotional blackmail. But ***Passion*** insists, romantically, on the transcendent value of emotional intensity. Yet it does not depend on big gestures, big outbursts, big avowals; the passion of ***Passion*** is more intense for the restraint with which it is expressed. Lapine's staging, in uncluttered sets by Adrianne Lobel, with subdued lighting by Beverly Emmons, is beautifully austere. Sondheim's music avoids catchy tunes and turn-up-the-volume climaxes; his score weaves recurring themes and fragments into a spellbinding web.

Passion is really a chamber opera, and it is a work of great distinction. The wonder is that it ran as long as it did. Sondheim and Lapine have succeeded in using the Broadway apparatus to do their own admirable work. Even on Broadway, the art of the theater is still possible.

The Year in World Literature

by William Riggan

The two biggest literary events of 1994 outside the Anglo-American orbit both occurred in France and both involved posthumous publications.

The first came in April with the much-belated release of Albert Camus's final, incomplete novel, ***Le premier homme*** (The First Man), thirty-four years after the Nobel Prize-winning author's death in a car crash. Long withheld from publication by his family both because the manuscript was unfinished and because of the strong opposition it surely would have aroused among staunch Gaullists and ardent supporters of Algerian independence alike, the novel interweaves three basic story lines: the Algiers childhood of one Jean Cormier, a figure closely resembling the young Camus; the adult Cormier's quest to learn about his father, killed at the Battle of the Bulge when the boy was only ten; and the history of French Algeria, at the point now when it was about to vanish. (The vast majority of *pieds-noirs* or French Algerians fled to France in 1962 upon the triumph of the Front de Libération Nationale and the onset of negotiations between the FLN and the French government that led to Algerian independence.) A complex, ambitious, and ambiguous work, the novel has occasioned endless and heated debate in France ever since its springtime release and has racked up astronomic sales figures as well (50,000 hardback copies sold the first *week*). Originally, ***Le premier homme*** would likely have been issued at approximately the time of the *pieds-noirs*' flight; in a large irony of history, it now appears as Algeria is again slipping almost ineluctably into sociopolitical chaos, fueled by—among other factors—FLN decline and Muslim fundamentalism and aggravated by a virulent strain of hostility toward North African immigrants among the more nationalistic elements in France. The novel is a marvelous evocation of childhood, of a particular time and place, and of the *pieds-noirs*' right to be heard; it may also help to some degree toward an understanding of how the present troubles came about.

Even more remarkable perhaps than the publication of Camus's manuscript was the discovery and release of Jules Verne's long-lost 1863 novel ***Paris au XXe siècle*** (Paris in the Twentieth Century). The work is nothing less than astonishing in its clairvoyance, as Verne envisions a Paris brimming with electric railways, "gaz-cabs" that jam streets lit with electricity, air pollution from industrial discharges, recorded music blaring from loudspeakers, urban flight and concomitant suburban boom, and a general dominance by "machines and money," including faxes and computers—all of it much too familiar in the latter half of our century but more than prescient 130 years ago. The book's narrative, which follows a teenage orphan and would-be poet's unsuccessful efforts to integrate himself into the new society of no-nonsense business and assembly-line culture while continuing to preserve his artistic integrity and his love of classical literature, music, and painting, is minimalist, clearly serving only as a vehicle for the author's speculative description of what Paris in the 1960s would look like and feel like. It is a cold and cruel place, where naked ambition and avarice have killed all sensations of the heart, just as the city and society literally—if melodramatically—kill the sensitive young poet.

Aside from the Camus and Verne works, "La Francophonie"—the French-speaking world outside France proper—dominated French letters in 1994. The poet and essayist Edouard Glissant of Martinique brought out his second novel, a huge and ambitious effort titled, appropriately, ***Tout-Monde*** (All the World). The "world" or universe it depicts is one marked by *créolité*, a creolization of peoples, language, genres—of all facets of human life and endeavor, a commingling amply reflected in the very nature and structure of this massive, all-encompassing opus, which takes the reader on a world tour and international cultural adventure starting with the author's native island. Glissant's elder countryman Aimé Césaire, a cofounder of the famed Negritude movement of the 1930s and 1940s, celebrated sixty years of literary creativity with the definitive collected edition of his verse, simply titled ***La poésie*** (The Poetry). The younger Martinican prose writer Raphaël Confiant, a leader (with Patrick Chamoiseau) of the emergent Creole movement sparked by Glissant, brought out a new novel titled ***Commandeur du sucre*** ("Sugar Commander," i.e. an overseer on a sugarcane plantation), set during the cane-harvesting season of 1936 and evoking the entire world of plantation-era Martinique, from the lowest field hands and mill laborers to the powerful administrators and distant owners. The fine Franco-Lebanese writer Amin Maalouf produced his fifth novel, ***Le rocher de Tanios*** (also issued in English late in 1994 as ***The Rock of Tanios***), a sensuous and lyrical fleshing out of two Mediterranean myths concerning the murder of a Levantine patriarch and the disappearance of an ill-fated youth from the large rock on the Cypriot coast where he often sat in contemplation. And Tahar Ben Jelloun of Morocco, like Chamoiseau one of the few non-French ever awarded the coveted Goncourt Prize, weighed in with ***L'homme rompu*** (The Broken Man), a seriocomic novel about a minor civil servant who, in a society where corruption is pandemic, goes totally against the norm by refusing to take bribes, with disastrous consequences for all, especially his daughter and himself.

German writers are still attempting to come to terms with

reunification and all its attendant ills, including the ugly resurgence of violent nationalism, the discovery of tainted pasts among even the seemingly most noble and long-suffering citizens, and the enormous social and fiscal costs of melding two wholly divergent cultures and states. Wolfgang Hilbig's ***"Ich"*** ("I") tells the tale of one Cambert, a would-be writer who in the 1980s reluctantly became an "unofficial collaborator" of the dreaded Stasi (the East German Ministry for State Security), reporting principally and—he believes—benignly on "Reader," a leading member of Berlin's dissident literary underground in the final years of the Democratic Republic. Just how pernicious and widespread such collaboration actually is dawns all too slowly on Cambert, until virtually everyone in the East, even "Reader" and his ilk, is implicated and "everybody reports on everybody."

Siegfried Lenz takes a more fable-like approach to changing times in ***Die Auflehnung*** (The Rebellion), which focuses on the mundane lives and intertwined fates of two very different brothers, the fish rancher Frank and the recently retired tea taster Willy. Minor rebellions of all kinds abound, by wives and offspring and neighbors as well as by Willy and Frank, in reaction to various provocations and alterations in circumstances. The ultimate "lesson" (from the famous author of *The German Lesson*) seems to be that we must recognize when to accept reality, when to rebel against it, and when simply to move on.

The Austrian author Peter Handke, in contrast, continued marching to his own private drummer with the 700-page "fairy tale from modern times," ***Mein Jahr in der Niemandsbucht*** (My Year in No-Man's Bay). Alongside the chronicle of one year in the life of the fiftyish writer Gregor Keuschnig, divorced and living alone in a remote suburb of Paris, are contained the fantastic and fabulistic travel reports by seven of Keuschnig's friends detailing adventures and fantasy-filled journeys through Japan, Greece, the Scottish highlands, and other exotic realms. The point of it all is to learn to see the world and oneself anew and, if necessary, to transform and improve both in the process.

From Russia came a handful of important new works in 1994. ***Tiur'ma i mir*** (Prison and Peace) completed Vassily Aksyonov's much-heralded Moscow Saga, a monumental trilogy begun a year earlier with *Pokolenie zimy* (now available in English as *Generations of Winter*) and *Voina i tiur'ma* (War and Prison). A masterful Tolstoyan epic (down to the allusive titles of volumes 2 and 3), the chronicle follows the fictional Gradov family from the late 1920s, through the horrors of the 1930s purges and pogroms, to the destruction of World War II, down to the death of Stalin in 1953. The mix of actual characters (Stalin, Beria, the minor theoretician Bazarov) and events with fictional ones, the frequent and whimsical leaps in time and space, and the periodic intervention of the sly, garrulous narrator all serve to keep the reader perpetually off-guard and even fearful at times, as the work's capricious unpredictability echoes the pervasive anxiety and dread inspired in the Gradovs by the ever-increasing and increasingly pointless cruelty of the Soviet state. Comparisons are already being made to such earlier trailblazing efforts as Solzhenitsyn's *One Day in the Life of Ivan Denisovich* and Varlam Shalamov's horrifying *Kolyma Tales*.

Ludmilla Petrushevskaya's novel ***Vremia: Noch'*** (now in English as ***The Time: Night***), on the other hand, focuses on the gritty, day-to-day life of ordinary contemporary Russians: the aging minor poet Anna, her feckless daughter Alyona, and her ex-convict son Andrei. The story is relentlessly depressing yet laced with considerable sympathy, insight, and the author's characteristic black humor. Evgeny Popov's novel ***The Soul of a Patriot*** tracks a maverick literary dropout on his drunken meanderings through the streets of Moscow as he tries to circumvent the militia and police and get to Red Square, where funeral services for Brezhnev are taking place. And Andrei Bitov's first novel in nearly a decade, ***The Monkey Link,*** follows a talkative, philosophical poet as he traverses Russia from the Baltics to the Caucasus in the waning years of the Soviet empire and ends up witnessing the August 1991 coup in Moscow.

Translations of several notable new works from Eastern Europe appeared in 1994. In ***Moving House and Other Stories*** the acclaimed Polish novelist Pawel Huelle offers a witty, humane collection of tales filtered mostly through the consciousness of a child and evoking both the richness of his nation's past and the impoverishment of its embittered national memory. The Czech author Pavel Kohout's novel ***I Am Snowing*** presents itself as "The Confessions of a Woman of Prague" but overlays its putative old-fashioned first-person narrative with all manner of post-modernist devices designed, it would seem, to convey the confusion and banality that have marked the recent socio-political transitions in Eastern Europe. A complex and engaging effort, to be sure; whether it will be a lasting success is less certain. The Estonian novelist and perennial Nobel candidate Jaan Kross weighed in with another superb historical novel, ***Professor Martens' Departure,*** mingling the eponymous Martens' personal reminiscences of past affairs and family difficulties with an account of his service to Czar Nicholas as a privy counsellor and advisor in international law during delicate treaty negotiations with Kaiser Wilhelm in 1909.

Mexico's stellar fiction writer, Carlos Fuentes, brought out ***El naranjo*** (available in English as ***The Orange Tree***), a novel comprising five novellas, the first two of which focused on the unexpectedly tragic figure of the conquistador Hernán Cortés, as depicted by his willfully unreliable translator Jerónimo de Aguilar and by his two sons, both named Martín. The collective effect of the five novellas is the suggestion of a new world, the possibility of Otherness, of multiple lives and eternal recurrences, of cyclical and perpetual renewal—much as Cortés's discovery of the New World shattered Spain's sense of itself and overturned all assumptions as to how things were and could be.

With ***Del amor y otros demónios*** (already available in English as ***Love and Other Demons***) Colombia's Gabriel García Márquez continued the trend established in his two previous novels of writing on specific historical periods in northern Latin America, this time focusing on the eighteenth-century colonial era and exploring how that epoch's cultural and religious values restrain and deform the love between a cleric and the young daughter of a marquis. A slighter work than *The General in His Labyrinth* and *Love in the Time of Cholera,* the novelette dwells heavily on the magical and the supernatural, particularly the miraculous continued growth of the heroine's hair for twenty years after her untimely death from rabies and its preservation in pristine condition for over two centuries.

South Africa's J. M. Coetzee delved into the life and work of Fyodor Dostoevsky to produce his newest novel, ***The Master of Petersburg,*** a pastiche of images, motifs, and ideas traceable principally to Dostoevsky's 1872 novel *The Possessed* and to the infamous Nechaev case (the murder of a student by his fellow terrorist conspirators over a disagreement on tactics and as a test of loyalty to their cause) on which that book was based. Here the celebrated Russian author's stepson Pavel has disappeared under suspicious circumstances, and the father has returned to Petersburg incognito to retrace the youth's final weeks and days, recover his papers and effects, and possibly shed some light on his demise as well as effect a reconciliation of sorts with the young man's memory and spirit as atonement for the neglect with which he was treated for much of his life by his famous stepfather. Parallels between the political situation in 1869 Russia and the South Africa of today give the work a strong whiff of parable that was doubtless intentional.

Nadine Gordimer set her passionate new novel, ***None to Accompany Me,*** in the period immediately prior to the first nonracial election and the beginning of majority rule in South Africa. The dissolution of the old regime and the official demise of apartheid bring disruption and significant change in the lives of individuals as well, including Gordimer's protagonist, the lawyer Vera Stark, and the black couple Didymus and Sibongile and their daughter. Two other notable 1994 novels from Africa were ***Kehinde,*** a study of transculturation and adaptation by Nigeria's Buchi Emecheta; and ***Paradise,*** an absorbing exploration of the intricate and slowly vanishing culture of East Africa by Tanzania's Abdulrazak Gurnah.

Three of Israel's finest prose writers saw new or very recent novels issued in English translation in 1994. ***The Way to the Cats*** by Yehoshua Kenaz presents an unremittingly bleak view of old age and human decline in its portrait of a grotesque, narcissistic, and thoroughly unlikable woman during her nine-month stay in a hospital while recovering from a broken leg. David Grossman, in ***The Book of Intimate Grammar,*** chronicles a lonely, sensitive young boy's fears, anguish, and emotional breakdown against the backdrop of his country's own imminent coming of age in the violent Six-Day War. And in ***Unto the Soul*** Aharon Appelfeld tells the solemn and disturbing story of a brother and sister who serve as caretakers of a cemetery for Jewish martyrs in turn-of-the-century Eastern Europe. Appelfeld also brought out a new novel in Hebrew, ***Laish*** (Lion), a livelier but still typically spare tale of a long, arduous pilgrimage from Central Europe to Jerusalem by six wagonloads of Jewish widows, orphans, pogrom survivors, and holy men. The passing years, the rigors of the road, the perfidy of merchants and thieves en route, and the vicissitudes of weather and disease exact a high toll on the travelers, including the youthful chronicler Laish, and fewer than half of the Bergman-like company reach their journey's end. Even there, no paradise awaits them, only an uncertain future with little likelihood of their ever being able to return to their European homelands.

Another novel by Egypt's 1988 Nobel laureate Naguib Mahfouz made its long-overdue debut in translation in 1994. ***The Harafish*** (the title means "The Common People"), from 1977, is a vastly entertaining, colorful epic tale about a lowly cart driver turned clan chieftain and populist ruler who is succeeded by ever more decadent and thuggish types given over solely to luxury and extortion. Turkey's Bilge Karasu made his English debut with ***Night,*** a determinedly postmodernist assemblage of diary entries, fragmentary jottings, and footnote glosses which together tell a disturbing tale of political terror and repression in a totalitarian Everycity modeled on Istanbul of the early 1970s.

The biggest single literary *cause célèbre* in Asia in 1994 was the banning of Taslima Nasrin's novel ***Lajja/Shame*** by authorities in Bangladesh and the death threat issued against the Bengali author by Islamic extremists for what they perceived to be her blasphemous demands for revision of the Koran. However deplorable that circumstance, the book that is at the center of the controversy in this case—unlike Salman Rushdie's *Satanic Verses,* which was a vibrantly imaginative and wonderfully entertaining piece of postmodern narrative—is a dense mixture of polemic and harangue tacked onto the thinnest and most programmatic of story lines and will greatly disappoint readers expecting a better-written work of fiction around which they can rally on the beleaguered author's behalf. Far more competent and compelling was the superb Urdu writer Qurratulain Hyder's novel ***Fireflies in the Mist,*** which appeared in English fifteen years after its original publication. Here four decades (1939-79) and a multiplicity of themes, characters, and events leading up to and following from the India-Pakistan-Bangladesh partition are seamlessly woven into a postnationalist epic of significant and moving proportions. Rushdie himself was vigorously in evidence in ***East, West,*** a scintillating collection of short stories, ironic fables, and grown-up fairy tales overflowing with linguistic exuberance and multicultural references of every conceivable stripe.

Four important new books from Chinese authors reached Western audiences in 1994. The supremely talented Wang Meng, the former Minister of Culture who resigned his post in 1989 rather than parrot the party line on the Tiananmen Square events, brought out ***The Stubborn Porridge, and Other Stories,*** a collection of wonderfully subtle and satiric pieces that skewer a variety of targets, from individual politicians and cultural figures to broad social experiments and government policies. ***The Remote Country of Women*** by the dissident screenwriter and novelist Bai Hua blends the harshly satiric tale of a political prisoner's escape and refuge with a poetic folktale-like narrative of earthy and harmonious life among the Mosuo people of China's mountainous southwest. Liu Sola followed up the success of her 1993 story collection *Blue Sky Green*

Sea with the highly imaginative and experimental novella ***Chaos and All That,*** an amalgam of scenes and songs which blend in slightly disjointed postmodern fashion to recount the experiences of the female protagonist Huang Haha as she grew up amid the deadly, mindless din of the Red Guard era in mainland China. In ***Grass Soup*** Zhang Xianliang presents a fictionalized account of his harrowing labor-camp confinement in 1958-61 during Mao's disastrous Great Leap Forward campaign, aimed at pushing the nation into communism but instead exacting a terrible toll (thirty to forty million dead by some estimates) from famine and official brutality. Zhang takes himself and other intellectuals to task as well for their compromises, complicity, and general passivity during that difficult period of Chinese history, but his allusive, low-key account of the material and spiritual privations suffered by all mainland Chinese under the Great Leap Forward is extremely effective in reminding readers that the full story of this historical tragedy remains to be told.

Japan's popular and talented young novelist Haruki Murakami brought out ***Dance Dance Dance*** in 1994, the long-awaited sequel to his acclaimed *Wild Sheep Chase* of 1989. Here the same ordinary protagonist's extraordinary journey continues, taking him on a spiritual quest to northern Hokkaido and yet another mysterious encounter with the sage old Sheep Man. As before, the narrative takes on aspects of an allegorical game strewn with indirect commentary on the glitzy postmodern world of an advanced capitalist culture that seems to preclude setting down roots and to foster perpetual motion and constant activity—such as the protagonist's continual effort to keep dancing. That he does at last drop anchor and settle down, after a fashion, with a Sapporo receptionist would seem to be positive development.

From the fine older writer Shusaku Endo came an impressive new collection of short fiction, ***The Final Martyrs,*** gathering stories written over the course of some thirty years. Their themes are much akin to those of Endo's well-known novels: the martyrdom of Roman Catholics in Japan, the fear and nostalgia that accompany old age, the incongruous experiences of Japanese travelers in Europe, spiritual doubts and sexual yearnings, and the author's own difficult childhood in a contentious household. Translations of two earlier novels, ***The Girl I Left Behind*** and ***Deep River,*** were less impressive but added nevertheless to the rich array of Endo's works (more than a dozen now) available to readers in the West.

Endo's coeval and colleague/rival Kenzaburo Ōe garnered the world's highest literary accolade in 1994 with his receipt of the Nobel Prize and continued his prolific career with the publication of ***Yureugoku*** (Vacillation), the second installment of his monumental "Burning Green Tree" trilogy—which he claims will be his final work of fiction. Set in an idyllic village of the author's native Shikoku, the trilogy takes as its topic nothing less than the fate of humanity and the universe, replete with folkloric healers, mystical forest dwellers, transmigrating spirits of the dead, animist forces of the natural world, and messianic visionaries intent on reinvigorating and perpetuating the archetypal Tree of Life to ensure the continued survival of humankind and the cosmos. The project, to be completed in 1995, is characteristic of Ōe's entire oeuvre: marvelously imaginative yet also maddeningly complex and certain to appeal only to the most ardent and diligent of readers. More accessible is ***The Pinch-Runner Memorandum,*** his 1976 novel which made its first-ever appearance in English in 1994, recounting in a lively double-layered narrative the involvement of a typically Ōe-like father and his retarded son in the violent 1960s demonstrations against the Mutual Security Treaty between the U.S. and Japan. Along with such now-classic novels as *A Private Matter* and *The Silent Cry,* this work would provide an excellent introduction for readers curious to learn more about the world's newest Nobel laureate in literature.

A rich, eventful literary year by any standard.

Notes on Contributors

Bruce Allen is a frequent contributor of reviews to the *Chicago Tribune*, *The New York Times Book Review*, the *Philadelphia Inquirer*, and Monitor Radio. He is currently at work on a critical history of the American short story.

Allen Hoey is the author of *A Fire in the Cold House of Being*, a verse collection chosen by Galway Kinnell for the 1985 Camden Poetry Award. An Associate Professor in the Department of Language and Literature at Bucks County Community College outside of Philadelphia, Hoey has contributed poems and essays to such journals as the *Georgia Review*, the *Hudson Review*, the *Ohio Review*, *Poetry*, *Southern Humanities Review*, and the *Southern Review*. He holds an M.A. and a D.A. from the English Department of Syracuse University. *What Persists*, his most recent collection of poetry, was published in 1992.

Julius Novick is Professor of Literature and Drama Studies at Purchase College of the State University of New York. The author of *Beyond Broadway: The Quest for Permanent Theaters*, Novick is the theater critic for *The Threepenny Review* and a winner of the George Jean Nathan Award for Dramatic Criticism.

William Riggan is Associate Editor of *World Literature Today* and an expert on Third World, Slavic, Anglo-American, and smaller European literatures. The author of *Picaros, Madmen, Naïfs, and Clowns: The Unreliable First-Person Narrator*, Riggan has written extensively on the history of both the Nobel and the Neustadt International Prizes in Literature. He also regularly reviews new foreign poetry and fiction for several journals and newspapers.

New Authors

John Berendt
Midnight in the Garden of Good and Evil: A Savannah Story

Born in 1939, Berendt is an American nonfiction writer and journalist.

INTRODUCTION

Midnight in the Garden of Good and Evil (1994), a combination travel book and true-crime narrative, begins as a tour of Savannah, Georgia, a city Berendt describes as "an isolated environment with its own rules, where each person you meet is stranger than the next." Drawing on his familiarity with Savannah's population—he lived there for a seven-year period—Berendt introduces such colorful and unique characters as a voodoo queen, a black transvestite, a con man who squats in mansions when their owners are out of town, and a local inventor who threatens to poison the city's water supply. A major figure in *Midnight in the Garden of Good and Evil* is Jim Williams, an antiques dealer, gun buff, and owner of one of the largest houses in the city. When Williams is accused of murdering his male lover, the book enters the true-crime genre, and in recounting the four subsequent murder trials involving Williams, Berendt examines the effects of the trials on Savannah society. Critics have generally praised *Midnight in the Garden of Good and Evil,* especially for the way Berendt captures Savannah's eccentric—and yet genteel—residents and history. Glenna Whitley has observed that Berendt's account may be "the first true-crime book that makes the reader want to call a travel agent . . . for an extended weekend at the scene of the crime."

CRITICISM

Martha Schoolman (review date 15 October 1993)

SOURCE: A review of *Midnight in the Garden of Good and Evil,* in *Booklist,* Vol. 90, No. 4, October 15, 1993, pp. 413-14.

[*In the following review, Schoolman offers a positive assessment of* Midnight in the Garden of Good and Evil.]

[John Berendt's ***Midnight in the Garden of Good and Evil: A Savannah Story***] is a wonderfully subtle and well-told story of life in Savannah, Georgia, during the eight years the New York-based *Esquire* magazine columnist spent there as an "experiment in bi-urban living." It is an old saw that the Deep South is populated exclusively by faded beauty queens, con men, eccentric socialites, and a skeleton in every closet, but Berendt manages to tread on the edges of the stereotype without caricature or condescension. "Always stick around for one more drink," one of the local characters advises him early in the book. "That's when things happen. That's when you find out everything you want to know." Berendt not only takes the drink but is game for every half-baked errand he is asked to perform, always with excellent narrative results. Perhaps one of the things that make this nonfiction work unique is that its plot centers on a murder, but Berendt takes his sweet time getting around to that fact, allowing the reader to be as surprised as he must have been watching the events unfold. ***Midnight*** is a solidly rewarding read.

Kirkus Reviews (review date 15 October 1993)

SOURCE: A review of *Midnight in the Garden of Good and Evil,* in *Kirkus Reviews,* Vol. LXI, No. 20, October 15, 1993, p. 1300.

[*In the following review, the critic offers praise for* Midnight in the Garden of Good and Evil.]

Steamy Savannah—and the almost unbelievable assortment of colorful eccentrics that the city seems to nurture—are minutely and wittily observed [in John Berendt's ***Midnight in the Garden of Good and Evil: A Savannah Story***].

In the early 1980's, Berendt (former editor of *New York Magazine*) realized that for the price of a nouvelle cuisine meal, he could fly to just about any city in the US that intrigued him. In the course of these travels, he fell under the spell of Savannah, and moved there for a few years. Central to his story here is his acquaintance with Jim Williams, a Gatsby-like, newly moneyed antiques dealer, and Williams's sometime lover Danny Hansford, a "walking streak of sex"—a volatile, dangerous young hustler whose fatal shooting by Williams obsesses the city. Other notable characters include Chablis, a show-stealing black drag queen; Joe Odom, cheerfully amoral impresario and restaurateur; Luther Driggers, inventor of the flea collar, who likes it to be known that he has a supply of poison so lethal that he could wipe out every person in the city if he chose to slip it into the water supply; and Minerva, a black occultist who works with roots and whom Williams hires to help deal with what the antiques dealer believes to be Hansford's vengeful ghost. Showing a talent for penetrating any social barrier, Berendt gets himself invited to the tony Married Women's Club; the rigidly proper Black Debutantes' Ball (which Chablis crashes); the inner sanctum of power-lawyer Sonny Seiler; and one of Williams's fabled Christmas parties (the one for a mixed group; the author opts out of the following evening's "bachelors only" fête). The imprisonment and trial of Williams, and his surprising fate, form the narrative thread that stitches together this crazy quilt of oddballs, poseurs, snobs, sorceresses, and outlaws.

Stylish, brilliant, hilarious, and coolhearted.

Rhoda Koenig (review date 10 January 1994)

SOURCE: "That's What We Like about the South," in *New York* Magazine, Vol. 27, No. 2, January 10, 1994, pp. 57-8.

[*In the following review, Koenig discusses the colorful and eccentric characters in* Midnight in the Garden of Good and Evil.]

When John Berendt, a former editor of this magazine [*New York*], decided to spend some time in Savannah, he thought he could write a book about this decayed but elegant one-time capital of the cotton kingdom, a city so hospitable that it provides a marble mausoleum for any visitors who happen to die there. After a while, though, his research started to wander from the restoration of the Victorian district, or anecdotes about such past Savannahians as Conrad Aiken and Johnny Mercer. "We do our best to set you on the straight and narrow," a neighbor of Berendt's complained, "and look what happens. First you take up with folks like Luther Driggers, whose main claim to fame is he's gettin' ready to poison us all. Then you drive around in an automobile that ain't fit to take a hog to market in, and now you tell us you're hangin' out with a nigger drag queen. I mean, really!" Some might think, though, that the neighbor is not one to talk: He moves from place to place, tapping other people's utility lines, writing bad checks, and opening whatever house he is living in—including one in which he is illegally squatting—to bogus historic tours, at times while occupied with one of his lady friends. "Beyond this door lies the mansion's master bedroom," his loyal guide will say, "and today the editors of *Southern Accents* magazine are photographing it for publication, and we cannot disturb them."

The rather somber title of ***Midnight in the Garden of Good and Evil*** doesn't suggest the stream of rococo personalities within, expressing themselves uninhibitedly in this city that is, as one grande dame puts it, "gloriously isolated" and likes it like that. Here old-fashioned formality ("This is a town where gentlemen own their own white tie and tails") is allied with an eccentricity so marked that the whole place seems to be in a permanent state of tilt. Besides Chablis (the transvestite who revenges herself on respectable black society by crashing the black debutante ball) and Luther (who is thought to be plotting to poison the water supply, and walks flies attached to colored strings), there are William Simon Glover, who, for a very good reason, walks an imaginary dog, and Harry Cram, a remittance man who punishes latecomers by shooting the hood ornaments off their cars as they come up the drive. With characters like these, you don't need writing that draws attention to itself, as Berendt realizes: Though his purpose is intrusiveness, his prose is impeccably restrained. The one exception is a chapter about a girl's sexual encounter with a psychopath; by adopting the girl's voice and thoughts, the writing occasionally becomes as lurid as its subject.

The evil, the equivocal, and the scary in ***Midnight*** are represented by that psychopath and a cool, courtly antiques dealer called Jim Williams, who lives in one of the grandest mansions in town and whose annual Christmas party makes uninvited socialites want to cut their throats. At the party Berendt attends, in a house filled with Fabergé boxes, Sargent portraits, and imperial silver, a Nazi historian asks an heiress if she recognizes the make of revolver he is carrying. "Of course I do," she says. "My late husband blew his brains out with one of those." Another one chimes in, "Oh! So did mine! I'll never forget it." The talk of gunplay is more than usually unsettling in view of the fact that the host is under indictment for murder. A few months before, Williams killed a young handyman who, he said, had shot at him and missed. The man's record of vandalism and violence was so long that the coroner remarked, "Mr. Williams probably did his civic duty shooting this sonofabitch." But Williams, it seems, had been paying the dead man for some decidedly odd jobs.

Considering the shooting a lovers' quarrel, the district attorney has Williams tried three times (two convictions are overturned on appeal, and a third jury fails to reach a verdict) before a fourth trial decides his fate. In the process, the enforcers of Savannah law show that their ideas of correct behavior are as relaxed as those of its partygoers. Offi-

In deftly mingling the frivolous and sinister, Berendt has created an immensely entertaining portrait of Savannah high and low.

—Rhoda Koenig

cial reports are given to the defense with crucial statements removed or whited out by the D.A.'s office; Williams is allowed, while awaiting trial and after being convicted, to travel to Europe and New York for purchases and parties. But in assuming that the jurors will extend their tolerance of sexual irregularity to those whom one courtroom observer calls "hermaphrodites," Williams makes the Oscar Wilde mistake of excessive urbanity. "We'd had sex a few times," he says of the dead man. " 'I had my girlfriend, and he had his. It was just an occasional, natural thing that happened.' The expressions on the jurors' faces suggest they do not find this arrangement natural at all."

As the Williams case shows, behind the traditions and grace of Savannah can lurk something quite unnerving—as Berendt also saw when the St. Patrick's Day parade passed, with its Confederate marchers accompanied by a horse-drawn wagon. From the street the wagon looked empty, but from a rooftop he could see that it held the bloody corpse of a Yankee. In deftly mingling the frivolous and sinister, he has created an immensely entertaining portrait of Savannah high and low.

Lee Lescaze (review date 4 February 1994)

SOURCE: "Sin and Hurt Mixed with Charm Down South," in *The Wall Street Journal,* February 4, 1994, p. A8.

[*In the following excerpt, Lescaze praises Berendt's memorable characters in* Midnight in the Garden of Good and Evil *but laments the book's excessive focus on the Williams' trials and questions his blending of fact and fiction in a nonfiction work.*]

Joe Odom, a genial rogue who calls himself the host of Savannah and specializes in freeloading, round-the-clock parties and passing bad checks, says Savannah has three basic rules:

—Always stick around for one more drink.

—Never go south of Gaston Street.

—Observe the high holidays—St. Patrick's Day and the day of the Georgia-Florida football game.

Not all Savannahians play by Mr. Odom's rules, of course, but his dedication to drinking, partying and a snobbery that ignores certain sections of the city is shared by most of the dozens of exotics who feature in John Berendt's entertaining account of good times, serious crime and raffish behavior, ***Midnight in the Garden of Good and Evil.*** I don't know what this book will do for Savannah tourism overall, but it is certain to attract anyone with a taste for old houses and enduring vices.

One Savannahian who had both was Jim Williams, a controversial and flamboyant antiques dealer. How does it feel to be nouveau riche, Williams was asked. "It's the riche that counts," he replied. Of the old-money social elite, Williams told Mr. Berendt that if they share a single trait, "it's their love of money and their unwillingness to spend it."

Some members of old families fought with or snubbed Williams. But Williams was famous for his Christmas party in his home, the largest private residence in the city. The grandeur of his house, the beauty of its furnishings, his clever manipulation of his guest list and his lavish spending turned Williams's gala into Savannah's party of the year.

From Williams, Mr. Berendt got an introduction to Savannah's darker side. "You mustn't be taken in by the moonlight and magnolias. There's more to Savannah than that. Things can get very murky," Williams said while describing a series of murders among the rich that had been swept under the rug.

Soon, murk descended on Williams himself. In his study, he shot and killed a 21-year-old hustler named Danny Hansford who had been his lover and also worked in his furniture-restoration shop.

Hansford's fame for sexual ability had been spreading. Prentiss Crowe, an old-money Savannahian, reacted to the killing with confidence that Savannah justice would once again shield a rich man caught in an exposed position, but with equal certainty that some men and women would be resentful. He explained: "Hansford was known as a good time . . . but a good time not yet had by all."

In keeping with the elite's attitude toward the less fortunate dead, Williams was cool when asked in court about the appropriateness of his relationship with Hansford given their ages. "I was 52-years-old, but he had 52 years' worth of mileage on him," he replied.

New York-based Mr. Berendt fell for Savannah's sinful ways and old-fashioned charms in the early 1980s and decided to take up bi-city living. He wasn't there long before he saw a book before his eyes.

Midnight is at its best when it is sketching the nature of the city and introducing characters such as the black transvestite Chablis; Col. Jim Atwood, owner of Hitler's silverware; and Luther Driggers, a man who may or may not have a vial of deadly poison, but is more immediately determined to make goldfish glow in the dark.

The Williams murder trials—there were three of them—became the core story of ***Midnight in the Garden of Good and Evil.*** Mr. Berendt is a skillful narrator, but interesting as the Williams case is, it doesn't remain fascinating over all the pages Mr. Berendt gives it.

All the main characters are memorable, though, at least until the reader reaches the book's last page and finds an author's note revealing that a number of pseudonyms have been used and, what's more, Mr. Berendt has altered descriptions of some people to protect their privacy. "Though this is a work of nonfiction, I have taken certain storytelling liberties, particularly having to do with the timing of events," Mr. Berendt adds. Altered how? Was Danny Hansford really Danielle Hansford? And what storytelling liberties allow a nonfiction writer to alter chronology? Faction is an unlikable hybrid.

Jonathan Yardley (review date 6 February 1994)

SOURCE: "Even in the Best of Cities," in *Book World—The Washington Post,* February 6, 1994, p. 3.

[*Yardley is an American critic and biographer. In the following review, he praises Berendt's elegant prose and sharp eye in* Midnight in the Garden of Good and Evil.]

Herewith one of the most unusual books to come this way in a long time, and one of the best. Indeed it is two fine books for the price of one. The first is a portrait of Savannah, "a rare vestige of the Old South," a "hushed and secluded bower of a city on the Georgia coast." The second is a true-crime account of the murder of a young male hustler named Danny Hansford and the four murder trials undergone by his sometime employer and lover, Jim Williams, "a successful dealer in antiques and a restorer of old houses." No doubt it is this second to which most readers will be attracted, inasmuch as the case offers everything from sex to violence to voodoo, but *caveat emptor:* the first story will blow your mind.

Being a reader neither of *New York* magazine, of which John Berendt was once editor, nor of *Esquire,* for which he writes a column, I confess to being caught totally off guard by ***Midnight in the Garden of Good and Evil.*** The reader ignorant of Berendt's skills is in for equal (which is to say ample) measures of surprise and delight, for his prose is both elegant and seamless while his eye is as sharp as a stiletto. He can make you laugh out loud and he can bring you up short, a splendid one-two punch all too rarely encountered in what passes for writing these days.

Berendt, a New Yorker, first visited Savannah in the early 1980s on what began as a lark but rapidly became an infatuation. He was drawn to the city by "the beauty of the name itself: Savannah" and by certain romantic images it quickly formed in his mind: "rum-drinking pirates, strong-willed women, courtly manners, eccentric behavior, gentle words and lovely music." In substantial measure those images were shaped by two people: the aforementioned Jim Williams, with whom Berendt speaks in a masterly opening chapter, and Mary Harty, an elderly member of the city's aristocracy who, in the second chapter, helps Berendt bring Savannah into focus. To wit:

> "We may be standoffish," she said, "but we're not hostile. We're famously hospitable, in fact, even by Southern standards. Savannah's called the 'Hostess City of the South,' you know. That's because we've always been a party town. We love company. We always have. I suppose that comes from being a port city and having played host to people from faraway places for so long. Life in Savannah was always easier than it was out on the plantations. Savannah was a city of rich cotton traders, who lived in elegant houses within strolling distance of one another. Parties became a way of life, and it's made a difference. We're not at all like the rest of Georgia. We have a saying: If you go to Atlanta, the first question people ask you is, 'What's your business?' In Macon they ask, 'Where do you go to church?' In Augusta they ask your grandmother's maiden name. But in Savannah the first question people ask you is 'What would you like to drink?' "

A party town and a drinking town but not, by any stretch of the imagination, a wild town: "Savannah was a place of manners and decorum, first and foremost." Even so rakish a fellow as the singularly engaging Joe Odom, self-described as "a tax lawyer and a real estate broker and a piano player," a layabout whose goal in life is to "mix business and pleasure in whatever proportion I wanted," plays according to his own version of Savannah's rules of decorum. The city is sufficiently tolerant and easy-going to embrace eccentricity in a wide variety of guises, but always within the parameters of a courtly decorousness such as one might expect to find within the lyrics of a song by Savannah's favorite son, Johnny Mercer, whose music is distinguished by what Mary Harty calls "a buoyancy and a freshness."

All of this being so, it need scarcely be said that Savannah was shocked to the quick when word got out in May, 1981, about the killing of Danny Hansford by Jim Williams, a case that quickly disclosed "a plot involving sodomy, murder and theft." Once they got over the initial impact of the news, most people in the elite circles traveled by Williams assumed that he would be let off on the grounds that he had fired at Hansford in self-defense, but the prosecution chose to argue that "the shooting of Danny Hansford was neither self-defense nor a crime of passion but a carefully planned murder"—a contention accepted by all members of two juries and all but one of a third before finally being rejected by a fourth once the case was at last moved out of town and away from the various technicalities that caused previous verdicts to be overturned.

Berendt followed these developments closely and describes them with clarity and wit, but without strained efforts to turn them into a morality play. This is consistent not merely with the highly uncertain facts of the case but also with the worldly temper of old Savannah; the city may have been troubled by the case but not so as to let its distasteful details cloud the prevailing local calm. "We happen to like things just the way they are!" is how Mary Harty had characterized that mood in her conversation with Berendt, a judgment that in the end he is not inclined to dispute, as his concluding paragraph so handsomely declares:

> For me, Savannah's resistance to change was its saving grace. The city looked inward, sealed off from the noises and distractions of the world at large. It *grew* inward, too, and in such a way that its people flourished like hothouse plants tended by an indulgent gardener. The ordinary became extraordinary. Eccentrics thrived. Every nuance and quirk of personality achieved greater bril-

> liance in that lush enclosure than would have been possible anywhere else in the world.

It's difficult to imagine that another writer could more faithfully or more keenly portray both the lush enclosure and its inhabitants. Some characters have Berendt's attention from first page to last while others make only brief appearances, but all are drawn with care and wry sympathy. Though his focus is primarily on the white upper crust, Berendt is attuned to the complexities of black life in a city that may have been described by Martin Luther King Jr. in 1964 as "the most desegregated city in the South" but that in the 1980s was beset by black "anguish and despair." He takes equal delight in Jim Williams's lavish annual Christmas party and in the lush mysteries of Bonaventure Cemetery, just as he is equally comfortable raising a glass at Joe Odom's round-the-clock bacchanal and sipping tea with a grande dame of high society.

The objection can be raised that the clarity with which Berendt claims to recall long stretches of dialogue is suspect, but he covers this with a disclaimer: "Though this is a work of nonfiction, I have taken certain storytelling liberties . . ." His intention, he says, "has been to remain faithful to the characters and to the essential drift of events as they really happened." There seems no reason to doubt him; certainly there is every reason to celebrate his surprising, wonderful book.

Malcolm Jones, Jr. (review date 28 February 1994)

SOURCE: "Drag Queens, Death and Dixie," in *Newsweek,* Vol. CXXIII, No. 9, February 28, 1994, p. 62.

[*In the following review, Jones describes* Midnight in the Garden of Good and Evil *as an affectionate portrait of Savannah, noting its popularity with Georgia audiences.*]

Yankees have always been beguiled by Savannah. When Gen. William T. Sherman cut his incendiary swath through the South in 1864, he spared Savannah and presented it to President Lincoln as a Christmas present. A century later, *Esquire* columnist John Berendt showed up for a long weekend, wound up living there off and on for eight years and concluded his stay with a book-length bread-and-butter note, ***Midnight in the Garden of Good and Evil.***

At first glance, Berendt's nonfiction portrait of Georgia's oldest city looks like anything but a proper thank-you. The characters he celebrates include a drag queen, a piano-playing deadbeat, a man who walks an imaginary dog and another fellow who's said to possess enough poison to spike Savannah's entire water supply. Those are the warm-up acts. At the heart of the book lies a celebrated murder case in which Jim Williams, a socially prominent and autocratic antique dealer, was accused of shooting his young male lover. Savannahians still rehash this decade-old case, and small wonder. No Gothic novelist could concoct a riper tale: the suave but sinister Williams went on trial four times before he won acquittal, while the dead boyfriend was eulogized by local wags as "a walking streak of sex." With all this, Berendt has fashioned a Baedeker to Savannah that, while it flirts with condescension, is always contagiously affectionate. Few cities have been introduced more seductively.

The characters Berendt celebrates include a drag queen, a piano-playing deadbeat, a man who walks an imaginary dog and another fellow who's said to possess enough poison to spike Savannah's entire water supply. Those are the warm-up acts.

—Malcolm Jones, Jr.

But how does Savannah feel about it? Berendt's book full of anecdotes proves that Savannahians love to talk about their city, but they're not too keen on faint praise from outsiders. In 1946, when Lady Astor came to call, the old downtown was a shambles. She called the city "a beautiful woman with a dirty face." People still bring that up.

Judging by the action downtown at the E. Shaver bookshop one recent afternoon, Savannah is in no mood to quarrel. While Berendt autographed more than 1,200 books, the mood inside and on the sidewalk out front was convivial and gossipy. Matrons in Mercedeses and lawyers from old white-shoe firms hailed their chums with "Are you in the book?" Those who were had the odd habit of volunteering the page number on which they appeared, as though it were a title, or an honorary degree. One nattily coiffed man introduced himself as "Jimmy Taglioli, page 181." He was Jim Williams's barber and he had nothing but praise for Berendt. "He got those people to a T." He would not speak ill of Williams (who died of a heart attack soon after his acquittal). "He was a very nice man. He was just confused about some things."

Williams left Savannah confused about a few things as well. Before the murder, his homosexuality was neither disparaged nor endorsed. But when Williams's open secret hit the front page, the city was forced to reassess the rules and rigging of its social structure. Berendt used the Williams case like a crowbar to get inside Savannah's psyche. He found an inward-looking city determined to keep things "just the way they are." (A list of major exports reads like a bill of lading from colonial times: tobacco, cotton, sugar, clay—clay!—and wood pulp.) Ironically, Berendt discovered, it's this aversion to progress that's preserved the city's character while so much of the country has coasted toward blandness: "Savannah's resistance to change was its saving grace."

A number of the natives are quick to dispute Berendt's conclusions. "He makes too much of Savannah society being closed to outsiders," one said. "Hell, anybody can come here and get into society if they've got the money, the inclination and they're white." Sometimes the reaction is more personal. In a restaurant, Berendt went to say hello to one of the few figures who comes off looking bad in the book. The man drew back: "Don't come near me."

Not all the locals are so riled. The best review comes from Gloria Daniels ("I'm on page 259"), housekeeper for Joe Odum, the book's convivial Greek chorus who was infamous around town for conducting historic tours through homes he didn't own. Daniels praises the book and then says fervently, "I got to get Mr. John's address. I want him to do my obituary before I die." No writer could ask for a greater vote of confidence.

Mr. Berendt's writing is elegant and wickedly funny, and his eye for telling details is superb.

—Glenna Whitley

Glenna Whitley (review date 20 March 1994)

SOURCE: "Voodoo Justice," in *The New York Times Book Review,* March 20, 1994, p. 12.

[*In the following review, Whitley discusses* Midnight in the Garden of Good and Evil *as a unique combination of true-crime story and travel book.*]

The voodoo priestess looked across the table at her wealthy client, a man on trial for murder: "Now, you know how dead time works. Dead time lasts for one hour—from half an hour before midnight to half an hour after midnight. The half-hour before midnight is for doin' good. The half-hour after midnight is for doin' evil. . . . Seems like we need a little of both tonight."

When he began living part of the year in Savannah, Ga., John Berendt, a columnist for *Esquire* and a former editor of *New York* magazine, was looking for—what? Respite from the big city? A charming little Southern town dripping with humidity and history to observe as fodder for a novel? What he found was a cultured but isolated backwater, a town where who your great-grandparents were still matters, where anti-Yankee resentments are never far from the surface and where writers from New York are invited to midnight voodoo ceremonies in graveyards.

The book he has written based on his eight years of living part-time in Savannah is a peculiar combination of true crime and travelogue. The first half of ***Midnight in the Garden of Good and Evil*** is about the people Mr. Berendt encountered: Joe Odom, a ne'er-do-well lawyer, piano player and tour guide, who drags antiques and an entourage of eccentrics to reside in one historic house after another from eviction to eviction; the Lady Chablis, a radiant black drag queen who uses the author as a convenient chauffeur to drive her home after her hormone shots; Serena Dawes, whom Cecil Beaton once called "one of the most perfect natural beauties I've ever photographed," now in middle age and given to boas, chiffon and dark green nail polish. And there's her lover, Luther Driggers, an inventor who discovered that a certain pesticide could pass through plastic, making flea collars and no-pest strips possible. After failing to capitalize on his find, he has become a town character who "walks" flies by gluing threads to their backs, and keeps the people of Savannah tense with threats to poison the water supply.

The second half of the book is the story of Jim Williams, a rich antiques dealer and restorer of Mercer House, one of the city's most beautiful historic homes and the site of the Christmas party Savannah's social elite "lived for." Six months after Mr. Berendt arrived, Williams was charged in the 1981 shooting of Danny Hansford, a tempestuous young man known as "a walking streak of sex" to both men and women in town.

Williams, Hansford's employer and sometime lover, pleaded self-defense. The evidence was far from clear-cut. It appeared that Williams may have staged the shooting, moving crucial pieces of evidence to make it look as if he fired his gun only after Hansford tried to kill him. Convicted, he quickly won a new trial when evidence of prosecutorial misconduct was sent anonymously to his attorney.

Before his second trial, besides engaging expensive criminal lawyers to represent him in the courtroom, Williams hired Minerva, the voodoo priestess, to put a curse on the prosecutor. Mr. Berendt makes it clear where Williams thought the better value for the dollar was.

Despite Minerva's ministrations, the second trial also ended in conviction. While Jim Williams ran his antiques business and wrote letters to *Architectural Digest* from jail, his lawyers managed to persuade the Georgia Supreme Court to overturn the verdict and order yet another trial. Again Minerva went to work, throwing graveyard dirt on the steps of Williams's enemies' homes. After the third trial ended in a mistrial, Williams was retried yet again and became the only person in Georgia history ever tried for the same murder four times. Seven months after finally being acquitted, Williams died, in January 1990.

Mr. Berendt's writing is elegant and wickedly funny, and his eye for telling details is superb. In recounting the tale of Williams's trials, he frequently veers off and includes overheard conversations, funny vignettes and bits of historical and architectural data—a method that a lesser observer might have botched but that works wonderfully here. ***Midnight in the Garden of Good and Evil*** might be the first true-crime book that makes the reader want to call a travel agent and book a bed and breakfast for an extended weekend at the scene of the crime.

The New Yorker **(review date 28 March 1994)**

SOURCE: A review of *Midnight in the Garden of Good and Evil,* in *The New Yorker,* Vol. LXX, No. 6, March 28, 1994, p. 115.

[*In the following review, the critic offers a laudatory assessment of* Midnight in the Garden of Good and Evil.]

Two stories make up [John Berendt's ***Midnight in the Garden of Good and Evil: A Savannah Story***]: the detailed account of a 1981 murder case involving Jim Williams, a prominent citizen of Savannah, and Danny Hansford, a young hustler who died in the study of Williams's antique-laden mansion; and a quirky travelogue devoted to the history, architecture, and citizenry of Savannah, where Berendt lived off and on during the nineteen-eighties. Although the twin narratives are not always seamlessly joined, and the prose suffers occasionally from overripeness, there is plenty of local color here to keep the reader up at night. An inscrutable voodoo practitioner, a bubba-boosting defense attorney, and a cadging piano-bar owner are memorable, but it is in the chapters given over to Chablis, a tough, sassy transvestite performer, that Berendt transforms his book from an amusing document into a work of art. Summing up her burgeoning stage career, Chablis tells the author, "The South is one big drag show, honey, and they all know The Lady. They all know The Doll." Thanks to Berendt, the rest of the country can now know her, too.

An excerpt from *Midnight in the Garden of Good and Evil: A Savannah Story*

Under the banner headline WILLIAMS CHARGED IN SLAYING, the story was very brief. It said that at 3:00 A.M., police had been summoned to Mercer House, where they found Danny Hansford, twenty-one, lying dead on the floor in the study, his blood pouring out onto an oriental carpet. He had been shot in the head and chest. There were two pistols at the scene. Several objects in the house had been broken. Williams had been taken into custody, charged with murder, and held on $25,000 bond. Fifteen minutes later, a friend of Williams had arrived at police headquarters with a paper bag containing 250 one-hundred-dollar bills, and Williams was released. That was all the newspaper said about the shooting. Williams was identified as an antiques dealer, a restorer of historic houses, and a giver of elegant parties at his "showplace" home, which Jacqueline Onassis had visited and offered to buy for $2 million. About Danny Hansford, the paper gave no information other than his age.

The next day's newspaper carried a more detailed account of the shooting. According to Williams, he had shot Danny Hansford in self-defense. He and Danny had attended a drive-in movie, he said, and returned to Mercer House after midnight. Back at the house, Hansford suddenly went wild, just as Williams said he had done a month earlier. He stomped a video game, broke a chair, smashed an eighteenth-century English grandfather clock. Then—just as he had done before—he grabbed one of Williams's German Lugers. But this time he did not fire it into the floor or out into Monterey Square. This time he aimed it directly at Williams, who was sitting behind his desk. He fired three shots. All three missed. When he pulled the trigger to fire again, the gun jammed. That was when Williams reached into his desk drawer and took out another Luger. Danny was struggling to unjam his gun when Williams shot him.

John Berendt, in his Midnight in the Garden of Good and Evil: A Savannah Story, *Random House, 1994.*

Valentine Cunningham (review date 14 August 1994)

SOURCE: "A Down-Home Twin Peaks," in *The Observer,* August 14, 1994, p. 16.

[*In the following positive review, Cunningham argues that Berendt's* Midnight in the Garden of Good and Evil *is as exuberant and entertaining as most fiction set in the American South.*]

John Berendt's first book, ***Midnight in the Garden of Good and Evil,*** is American travel-writing at its fictional-factional best. It's a bowl-you-over, enthralled-appalled trawl in the magical depths of Savannah, Georgia, the prettiest surviving corner of the Old South.

An editor and columnist from New York, Berendt knew the Savannah mixture by repute—as most of us do. On the one hand, the lovely old squares and homes that General Sherman did not burn down in the Civil War, the town where the poet Conrad Aiken, a friend of T S Eliot's, is buried and Johnny ('Moon River') Mercer came from. On the other hand, the place where murderous old Cap'n Flint handed Billy Bones the map of Treasure Island before he died shouting for more rum, and where Hard-Hearted Hannah, the Vamp of Savannah, did her dire worst down on the seashore with a watering can (she was pouring water on a drowning man).

Berendt dropped in for a short visit and got utterly hooked on the vivid contrasts of tone that still mark the place, the farcical striations of class and style and morals that comprise modern Savannah, GA.

The freaky acquaintance Berendt strikes up is as richly eccentric a bunch of gargoyles as any you'll find peopling a Dickens novel. There's Joe Odom, attorney, cheque-bouncer, piano-player and proprietor of the Sweet Georgia Brown bar, who turns his clutch of rented houses into illegal tourist attractions; his friend Mandy, crowned Miss Big Beautiful Woman (BBW) of Vegas; the black drag-queen The Lady Chablis, so free with cross-dressing advice and with Berendt's motorcar.

Then there's the glum chemist, who made no money from inventing the flea-collar and is said to own a jar of poison enough to kill off the whole town; the lovely Baptist pianist and singer whom Johnny Mercer called the 'Lady of 6,000 Songs' and who never turns down a gig; the gung-ho lawyer who owns the University of Georgia bulldog football-mascot named UGA the Fourth; the voodoo priestess; the snobby old trouts of the rule-corseted Married Woman Card Club; and many more.

Berendt and his story move easily along and across the social divides. An old-fashioned Southern darkness is not unknown among the antiques-buying, down-town-renovating, black-tie-owning rich folks Berendt gets to know. Anti-Semitism is the foundation of the exclusive Oglethorpe Club. The love of antiques extends with suspicious relish to Nazi relics. But still, money does immunise rather against the city's really seamier stuff. Until, that is, the Jim Williams scandal burst on to the scene.

Wealthy bachelor Williams is one of the chief restorers of Savannah's glorious antebellum housing, and a collector of Fabergé. He gives legendary Christmas parties top socialites would kill to get invited to. And one night in 1981 he shoots his wildly sexy male assistant to death. It's a rich shock to the town's rich. He pleads threats to his life and self-defence. Amidst a great swirl of homosexual scandal, he's found guilty. Four lengthy trials later, each one severely denting the DA's reputation for probity and mightily enriching the doggy-mascot lover and the voodoo priestess, both of whom are enlisted in Williams's cause, this verdict is overturned. But that's in nearby Augusta. There, it seems, juries are less appalled at learning about male hustlers plying the posh South's leafiest squares. Owning antiques in Savannah will never look the same again.

Some of the more enthusiastic American reviewers are hailing [***Midnight in the Garden of Good and Evil: A Savannah Story***] as a re-run of *In Cold Blood.* It's not that. Berendt's criminal proceedings stand to Capote's like a muggy-day Dixieland shuffle does to hard-stepping bebop. But these wonderfully fat helpings of murk and malignancy are certainly as satisfying as anything you can find in Deep South fiction and, for that matter, they're as juicily prurient as those superb photo forays into American darkness that *Granta* magazine goes in for so tellingly.

Caleb Carr
The Alienist

Born in 1955(?), Carr is an American novelist and nonfiction writer.

INTRODUCTION

Set primarily in New York City during the spring of 1896, *The Alienist* (1994) details the efforts of a select and unorthodox group of investigators to track down a serial killer with a predilection for adolescent male prostitutes. Assembled at the behest of Theodore Roosevelt, the city's reform-minded police commissioner, the team includes John Schuyler Moore, a crime-reporter for the *New York Times* who also acts as the story's narrator; Laszlo Kreizler, a psychologist, or alienist in the language of the day; Sara Howard, a secretary who hopes to become the city's first female police officer; and Lucius and Marcas Isaacson, a pair of detectives with specialties in forensic medicine and various state-of-the-art techniques in criminal science. Under Kreizler's direction, the investigators gather and interpret evidence from the various crime scenes to formulate a hypothetical model of the killer. Their musings focus on the murderer's background, particularly his childhood, as Kreizler's theory of "context" posits that early experiences play a decisive role in an individual's later attitudes, idiosyncracies, and obsessions. The team's efforts are hampered by prominent citizens who consider Kreizler's psychological theories a threat to traditional social values and by members of New York's criminal underworld who hope to incite unrest among the city's immigrant population by convincing them that the police have no interest in pursuing a murderer of poor immigrant children. Reaction to *The Alienist* has been mixed. While some commentators considered Carr's explanation for the killer's actions overly sympathetic to the murderer, others noted that it highlights issues concerning free will and psychological determinism, and provides insight into the nature of evil. Although reviewers generally praised the plot as compelling, some found the narrative tedious and faulted Carr for using hackneyed elements from the thriller genre. Critics agree, however, that Carr succeeds in vividly evoking the place and mood of New York in the 1890s. As John Katzenbach argued, "what [Carr] does best is capture the excitement of a world on the verge of change, where invention was the stuff of daily miracle."

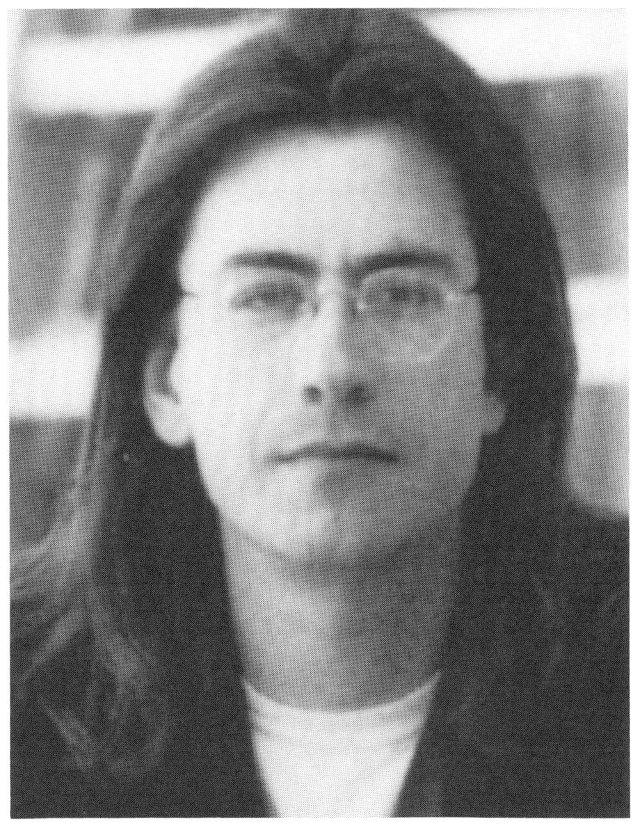

CRITICISM

Christopher Lehmann-Haupt (review date 29 March 1994)

SOURCE: "Of an Erudite Sleuth Tracking a Madman," in *The New York Times,* March 29, 1994, p. C17.

[*Lehmann-Haupt is a Scottish-born American critic and novelist. In the review below, he remarks on the themes of* The Alienist.]

You can practically hear the clip-clop of horses' hooves echoing down old Broadway in Caleb Carr's richly atmospheric new crime thriller, ***The Alienist,*** set in 19th-century New York City. You can taste the good food at Delmonico's. You can smell the fear in the air.

The year is 1896. On a March night so cold that horse waste has frozen in the streets, John Schuyler Moore, a police reporter for *The New York Times,* is awakened in his grandmother's house at 19 Washington Square North and summoned to the site of the newly begun Williamsburg Bridge, on the East River. There he encounters the new Police Commissioner, Theodore Roosevelt, so grim-visaged that his huge teeth are for a change not snapping. Inside the bridge's tower, Roosevelt shows Moore the multilated corpse of yet another boy from the brothels of lower Manhattan. A seemingly insane killer has struck once again.

The task of tracking this madman has been assigned to Moore's and Roosevelt's old friend from their Harvard days, Dr. Laszlo Kreizler, who is an alienist, or an expert on mental pathologies (minds that are alienated from themselves), as the novel's epigraph explains.

These three men became acquainted during their Harvard undergraduate years, when Kreizler debated William James on determinism, James having argued for free will, Kreizler having sided with psychological causation. The dredging up of this argument takes us to the philosophical heart of ***The Alienist,*** which explores the causes of insanity and criminality, and ultimately the nature of evil.

Having been secretly put in charge of the investigation, Kreizler begins asking questions about the crimes. Why do they always occur in a high place near water? What explains the sexual mutilation? Why are all the victims' eyes gouged out? What happened to the killer in his or her childhood, that would provoke such violence?

Kreizler also gains the services of two brilliant forensic specialists, the Isaacson brothers, Lucius and Marcus, whom Roosevelt has hired onto his more progressive police force. Over a sumptuous multi-course dinner at Delmonico's, the Isaacsons introduce Kreizler to new investigative techniques like anthropometry, the measurement of body parts, and dactyloscopy, the science of fingerprinting. The Isaacsons also believe that dead retinas retain the final images impressed on them. They wonder if this explains why the killer gouges his (or her) victims' eyes out.

Yet Kreizler and his colleagues are not free to investigate these conundrums in a vacuum. Unhappily, the mad killer works on a schedule apparently dictated by religious holidays and there is an abundance of those coming up. As a voice keeps whispering in the back of Moore's mind, "Hurry up or a child will die!" Moreover, certain forces are working to thwart Kreizler's investigation.

When J. P. Morgan gathers a group of powerful citizens to confront Kreizler and Moore, Anthony Comstock, "the notorious censor of the U.S. Post Office," expresses his outrage on behalf of respectable society. " 'Rank determinism!' Comstock declared, unable to contain himself. 'The idea that every man's behavior is decisively patterned in infancy and youth—it speaks against freedom, against responsibility! Yes, I say it is un-American!' "

Mr. Carr is by and large successful in bringing to life his period thriller. An editor at *MHQ: The Quarterly Journal of Military History* and the author of ***The Devil Soldier,*** a biography of the American mercenary Frederick Townsend Ward, among other books, Mr. Carr has lovingly evoked not only a physical sense of old New York but the spirit of the time as well, when the powers in charge were worried about unrest among the masses of cheap immigrant labor.

The only real weakness of the book lies in the stringent rationality of Kreizler's investigation. The more his logic makes sense the less threatening his quarry seems, at least to the reader. For if the murderer is purely the product of negative conditioning, then he or she is somehow drained of evil. As Moore sums up:

> Kreizler emphasized that no good would come of conceiving of this person as a monster, because he was most assuredly a man (or a woman); and that man or woman had once been a child. First and foremost, we must get to know that child, and to know his parents, his siblings, his complete world. It was pointless to talk about evil and barbarity and madness; none of these concepts would lead us any closer to him. But if we could capture the human child in our imaginations—then we could capture the man in fact.

True, the narrator of ***The Alienist*** later distances himself somewhat from this outlook by lightly mocking Kreizler's radical determinism. Still, the story's fatalism grows tedious. You begin to long for a touch, say, of bad old Hannibal Lecter. Nor does it help that throughout most of the story none of the major characters are directly threatened by the killer. Of course, it is deplorable that children are being murdered. But none of them figure strongly enough in the story to arouse the reader's visceral identification.

Still, despite the absence of a truly evil threat and despite the somewhat musty quality of the narrative—with its pseudo-Victorian prose, its mustache-twirling villains and its cliff-hanging chapter endings—***The Alienist*** does keep its philosophical questions simmering. And by the time these are resolved we have been caught up in the resolution of the action. If Mr. Carr's novel remains somewhat mechanical, its parts are intricate enough to keep us entertained with a simulacrum of the past.

Bret Easton Ellis (review date April 1994)

SOURCE: "Victorian Vice," in *Vanity Fair,* Vol. 57, No. 4, April, 1994, p. 108.

[*An American novelist, Ellis is best known for such novels as* Less than Zero *(1985) and* American Psycho *(1990). In the review below, he provides a mixed assessment of* The Alienist.]

Manhattan, 1896. A serial killer haunts the city, mutilating boy prostitutes. In order to solve the case, Theodore Roosevelt, as New York City's police commissioner, brings together John Moore, a police reporter for *The New York Times,* Sara Howard, a police secretary, and Dr. Laszlo Kreizler, an old school chum who is now a brilliant "alienist" (in the 19th century, the mentally ill were called "alienated," and psychologists were thus labeled "alienists"), whose theories on child-parent relations pre-date Freud and provide insight into the mind of ***The Alienist's*** warped monster-cannibal.

What makes this novel so potentially fascinating is that these three are not detectives, and in the face of a skeptical pre-forensics society, they solve this mystery not by matching fibers and semen samples but by amassing a psychological profile of the killer. ***The Alienist*** is a large, commercial mixture of solid, impersonal craftsmanship and gothic horror; it's also a historical novel of New York manners dressed up in a garishly lurid thriller plot. It's prissy *and* ghoulish.

The writer, Caleb Carr, a contributing editor to *Military History Quarterly* and the author of a biography of soldier of fortune Frederick Townsend Ward, uses his formidable skills as a historian to good effect, but attached to a pulpy, middlebrow thriller, they ultimately (at least for the first three-quarters of the book) help sink it. The case under investigation is as gruesome as anything out of James Ellroy, but it feels as if it had been rewritten by James Michener. Paramount Pictures has already staked $500,000 on Carr's story for producer Scott Rudin, but whether the studio is going to be willing to spend the additional $60 million it will take to re-create turn-of-the-century Manhattan for *Cruising*-Meets-Edith Wharton is another, altogether more immediate mystery.

***The Alienist* is a large, commercial mixture of solid, impersonal craftsmanship and gothic horror; it's also a historical novel of New York manners dressed up in a garishly lurid thriller plot. It's prissy *and* ghoulish.**

—Bret Easton Ellis

The book's narrator is John Moore, the *Times* reporter, who is, unfortunately, the least interesting character. Since he's a journalist and *not* a novelist, we get long, impressively detailed descriptions of Delmonico's, the Metropolitan Opera, what 10th and Broadway might have looked like on a foggy spring morning 100 years ago. This is all *un*-leavened by dialogue that is almost completely expository—huge blocks of info bereft of drama. For all its elegance, ***The Alienist*** lacks the nasty, prankish fun—the dirty kick—we expect from a thriller. It's a stodgy, plodding *Masterpiece Theatre*-style thriller, so genteel that one can almost hear the ghost of Alastair Cooke narrating in the background, until you realize the ghost of Alastair Cooke *is* narrating in the background. It's a "literary" humanist-liberal story with an anachronistic smattering of P.C. elements that seems pandering: the wildly independent career woman, the noble black bodyguard, a fairly contemporary concern with gay prostitution and psychology.

As a historian, Carr knows more about 1896 New York than any writer under 40, but as a novelist he's smart in all the wrong ways. His fusion of a murder mystery with the politics of the historical moment provides enticement, but ***The Alienist*** is only sporadically suspenseful and often stylistically moribund. There's no point of view here, no attitude, nothing suggestive or elliptical or ambiguous. Our narrator is a straightforward, spotless good guy. For all its historical data and abundance of arcane exotica, as a novel it's a chore to read because it veers toward the mechanical and the clichéd. Its only real concern (and attribute) is to be an entertainment.

And as far as entertainments go, it is a big and busy one, and protracted as it is (500 pages), it's technically accomplished. Talent and taste (sometimes too much) are evident. Almost every chapter ends with a cliff-hanger, and at its core is a killer with some genuinely creepy tics. The action picks up in the last 100 pages as a showdown nears in the bowels of the Croton Reservoir, and these elements help make Carr's book a cinematic tome—but imagine Merchant-Ivory remaking a 1950s Hammer horror flick and you'll get the idea.

Stephen Dobyns (review date 3 April 1994)

SOURCE: "New York Was a Heck of a Town," in *The New York Times Book Review,* April 3, 1994, p. 19.

[*Dobyns is an American poet, novelist, and critic. In the following mixed review, he faults the narrative voice of* The Alienist *as inappropriate.*]

The word "light"—often spelled "lite"—has come to signify a laudable quality in our society: light beer, light cigarettes, light hot dogs. As a qualifier for "reading," however, "light" has been replaced by the word "page-turner." One may read at a breakneck pace in order to discover what happens, or one may be turning the pages faster in a frantic search for substance. ***The Alienist,*** by the historian Caleb Carr, fits neatly into both categories.

Told by a turn-of-the-century *New York Times* reporter, John Schuyler Moore, the novel deals with the gruesome murders of a number of boy prostitutes in Manhattan in 1896. Alienist, a note tells us, is an outdated term for an expert in mental pathology. (A mentally ill person was considered alienated from his true nature and from society.)

The alienist hero is Dr. Laszlo Kreizler, who holds the newfangled beliefs that a person's actions can be understood by the context of his life and that those actions even suggest the context. For these ideas he is held up to much scorn. Still, Dr. Kreizler has been engaged by his old friend, New York City's Police Commissioner Theodore Roosevelt, to find the killer. Kreizler then engages John Schuyler Moore for his knowledge of the city, as well as two eccentric New York police detectives who believe in such pioneering techniques as fingerprinting. The fifth member of the group is Sara Howard, a derringer-toting young police secretary. She happens to be the first female to be hired by the New York Police Department. Together they begin their quest for the murderer, who operates by dropping down from rooftops and snatching boy prostitutes through the windows of their brothels.

Mr. Carr has done his research. This is both a curse and a blessing, for although the novel's ostensible subject is who-is-killing-these-children, the real subject is New York City in the 1890's.

Our team of detectives eats at Delmonico's, attends the opera and visits the new American Museum of Natural History. The murders occur at famous landmarks: Bartholdi's statue of Lady Liberty, the towers of the still-under-construction Williamsburg Bridge. The low life of lower Manhattan is carefully sifted: Five Points, the Dead Rabbit gang, Shang Draper's bawdy house on the corner of Sixth Avenue and 24th Street. And famous people make their appearances: the journalist Lincoln Steffens, the gang leader Paul Kelly, the anti-vice crusader Anthony Comstock, the financier J. P. Morgan.

It is possible to love one's research too much. At times in ***The Alienist*** the reader may feel that an event is occurring only because Mr. Carr has found a nice place for it to happen. At times, too, the author is simply touching a historical base, as in "we passed the graveyard at Trinity Church—where the father of the American economic system, Alexander Hamilton, lay buried." This is a long and complicated novel, and Mr. Carr's historical asides occasionally become so much chaff.

A slightly more serious problem is the novel's first-person point of view. John Schuyler Moore is a charming character, but the consequence of his charm is that the changes the narration into chat. We are presented with dreadful mutilations—eyeballs gouged out, genitals removed—and chat seems an inappropriate tone for such material.

Added to this are the bromides with which Moore energizes his narrative. These aren't quite clichés, but one has a sense of over-familiarity. When Paul Kelly appears with his "chiseled, Black-Irish features" the air suddenly becomes "charged with oppressive threat." At another point Roosevelt asks, "Do you have any evidence to support such a theory?" Dr. Kreizler responds, "None, of the kind you mean. I have only a lifetime of studying similar characters. And the intuition it has given me." About one of the murder victims, Moore says, "Whatever Ernst Lohmann's way of making a living, whatever his error in trusting a stranger, the penalty was too severe, the price too abominably high." After the death of a friend, Moore thinks, "Every human being must find his way to cope with such severe loss."

We find many such examples. It may be argued that a page-turner requires this sort of familiar writing: getting into such a book is like pulling on a pair of well-worn and comfortable blue jeans. "Bully!" says Roosevelt. "This is what I like—a scientific approach!"

And to be sure ***The Alienist*** is a pleasing entertainment. The plot moves forward without much struggle and the events are diverting. It is like an agreeable train ride: a pleasant destination and gratifying scenes to look at through the windows. Mr. Carr knows his history and the details are interesting. But perhaps it would have been a stronger book if written in the third person. John Schuyler Moore, for all of his turn-of-the-century trappings, is basically a contemporary voice. His values and cultural background are of the 1990's more than the 1890's. He is our representative through the world that Mr. Carr creates,

An excerpt from *The Alienist*

[Roosevelt] slammed another fist into an open hand. "By thunder, Doctor, I know of a pair of detectives that would suit your purpose down to the ground! But tell me—where would you begin?"

"For the answer to that," Kreizler replied, pointing over to me, "I must thank Moore. It was something he sent me long ago that sparked the idea."

"Something *I* sent you?" For a moment egotism made me put aside my trepidation at this dangerous proposal.

Laszlo approached the window and raised the shade altogether so that he could look outside. "You will remember, John, that some years ago you found yourself in London, during the Ripper killings."

"Certainly I remember," I answered with a grunt. It had not been one of my more successful holidays: three months in London in 1888, when a bloodthirsty ghoul had taken to accosting random prostitutes in the East End and disemboweling them.

"I asked you for information, and for local press reports. You very decently obliged and included in one pouch some statements made by the younger Forbes Winslow."

I raked my memory of the time. Forbes Winslow, whose similarly named father had been an eminent British alienist and an early influence on Kreizler, had set himself up as an asylum superintendent during the 1880s by trading on his father's achievements. The younger Winslow was a conceited fool, for my money, but when the Jack the Ripper killings began he was sufficiently well known to be able to inject himself into the investigation; indeed, he'd claimed that his participation had caused the murders (still unsolved at the time of this writing) to come to an end.

"Don't tell me Winslow's pointed the way for you," I said in astonishment.

"Only inadvertently. In one of his absurd treatises on the Ripper he discussed a particular suspect in the case, saying that if he had created an 'imaginary man'—that was his phrase, 'imaginary man'—to fit the known traits of the murderer, he could not have devised a better one. Well, of course the suspect he favored was proved innocent. But the expression lodged itself in my head." Kreizler turned back to us. "We know nothing of the person we seek, and are unlikely ever to find witnesses who know any more than we do. Circumstantial evidence will be sparse, at best—he has been at work for years, after all, and has had more than enough time to perfect his technique. What we must do—the only thing that *can* be done—is to paint an imaginary picture of the sort of person that *might* commit such acts. If we had such a picture, the significance of what little evidence we collected would be dramatically magnified. We might reduce the haystack in which our needle hides to something more like a—a pile of straw, if you will."

Caleb Carr, in his The Alienist, *Random House, 1994.*

but because of Moore's limitations—the chat, the hipness—he also becomes an obstruction. This is primarily a problem of tone: it is difficult for a novel in which children are killed to function as a comedy.

Stephen J. Dubner (essay date 4 April 1994)

SOURCE: "Serial Killing for Fun and Profit," in *New York* Magazine, Vol. 27, No. 14, April 4, 1994, pp. 58-62.

[*In the following article, based on a conversation with Carr, Dubner discusses the writing and reception of* The Alienist *as well as Carr's childhood and career.*]

Caleb Carr is not above deception. Two years ago, for instance, it was time for the writer to start his next book. Although he had written a coming-of-age novel in 1980, Carr, 38, had been a nonfiction man ever since: politics and history mainly, military history especially. And that's what his publisher—and his readership, small though it was—expected of him.

He gave his editor and his agent a twenty-page proposal for the new book. It would examine a serial killer who roamed New York City in 1896, preying on young male prostitutes, and the three men who united to stop him: John Schuyler Moore, a New York *Times* reporter; Dr. Laszlo Kreizler, an "alienist," as psychiatrists were then called; and Theodore Roosevelt, New York's police commissioner at the time. The book would also explore one of the first cases in which forensic psychiatry was used to catch a killer; just as important, it would capitalize on the boom in serial-killer lit.

Suzanne Gluck, Carr's agent at ICM, and Ann Godoff, his editor at Random House, loved the proposal. Yes, it was crowded with historical detail—Carr's writing always was—but it read *just like a novel.*

Guess what, Carr told them. It *is* a novel. Roosevelt may indeed have been police commissioner at the time, but Kreizler, Moore, and the killer existed only in Carr's imagination. "I didn't think you would entertain fiction from me," he explained, "without my presenting it in some unorthodox way." Godoff was calm for the first fifteen minutes, then slammed her hand on the table. "Well," she said, "let's see what we can do."

Carr got a $65,000 advance for ***The Alienist.*** Last spring, he turned in a 700-page manuscript, which immediately began a well-hyped orbit around Hollywood.

Suddenly . . . Mike Nichols is looking at the Caleb Carr manuscript! Kathleen Kennedy is looking at the Caleb Carr manuscript! *Scott Rudin* is looking at the Caleb Carr manuscript!

Carr's phone would not stop ringing. He had never had this problem, and the pressure became a bit much. So, on the morning of June 25, 1993, a Friday, he put on his black Converse high-tops, shouldered his golf clubs, stepped outside his East Village apartment, and headed for Van Cortlandt Park in the Bronx.

Rudin, meanwhile, had decided he *had* to buy the rights to Carr's book. Immediately. He offered Carr's agent $400,000—good only until 3 P.M. Hollywood time.

Carr, of course, couldn't hear his phone ringing from the eighth-hole dogleg. Rudin bumped the price up to $450,000. Carr, on the fourteenth hole, was oblivious.

By the time Carr was ready for cocktails—having shot a respectable 88—Rudin had offered half a million dollars. When he got back to town, Carr called Rudin to accept the offer. "You know," he said, "I used to read books in your development office for 50 bucks a pop."

"Well," said Rudin, "I guess the price has gone up."

Last week, ***The Alienist*** finally arrived in bookstores. Only now will Carr discover if his greatest feat of deception has succeeded: While his novel might strike some as little more than a baroque murder mystery (*Silence of the Lambs* meets *Ragtime* is how Random House is hawking it), in truth, ***The Alienist*** is practically a blueprint for the very sharp mind of Caleb Carr, revealing just how strangely and personally well versed he is in New York history, psychology, child abuse—even murder.

"I remember being here for Son of Sam the summer of '77," Carr is saying, "which was the most cool-bizarre experience. It was the great spectator sport that summer. Every day was 'Hey, did he get somebody last night? Did *they* get *him?* Did he send another letter?' I remember shooting pool in a bar on 13th Street, which isn't there anymore, the night they caught him, and it was total goose-bump time." Carr leans forward in his living-room chair, fervent, as if he's about to share a secret, gory detail. "And when you saw a picture of him, all of a sudden he was a real guy, just this poor schnook being led away by the cops."

Carr lives alone in a cautiously comfortable one-bedroom walk-up on 2nd Street just east of First Avenue (if it were half a block farther east, ICM's messengers would refuse to visit). While writing ***The Alienist,*** he turned the apartment into a sort of war room, papering the walls with period maps of police precincts and political wards, schematics of the human brain, and a blizzard of typed notes charting each fictional movement of Carr's monstrous serial killer and his team of pursuers.

Carr's most prized possessions are his grandmother's Tiffany lamp, its periwinkle shade decorated with swirly gold lily pads, and a framed print of *Heroes of the Republic,* which portrays Ulysses S. Grant and a raft of ruddy-faced Union officers on horseback, triumphant.

Carr has a sort of nineteenth-century face himself. He is handsome in a rakish way, with straight hair that hangs to his shoulders, deep-set green eyes behind rimless glasses, and a mouthful of crooked teeth. He is an uneasy hybrid of bohemianism, which his parents embraced, and aristocracy, which runs deep in his family (an ancestor, Dabney Carr, was Thomas Jefferson's favorite brother-in-law). There is a constant edge to Carr's voice—as if he's a kid who's already been suspended by the principal and knows he can take a few more shots without further penalty.

Sitting back after his Son of Sam story, Carr mulls a connection. "Frankly, what interested me about serial killers," he says, "was that if I had gone four or five steps in another direction, I could have been one of these guys—the anger they had, the way they chose to embody it."

Carr's friends, when they hear this quote, can't believe he actually said it. Yes, he is irascible sometimes, and distrustful, and morose. But all agree: No one paints Caleb Carr darker than Caleb Carr himself.

He'll say this, for instance: "I'm the only kid in my family who never tried to kill himself; I kind of figured somebody else was going to kill me anyway." But he'll cackle after saying it, and start talking about the huge games of Capture the Flag he still organizes at his family's country house in upstate New York; or about how Dylan is the sole beacon of morality on *Beverly Hills 90210;* or about what a great father Teddy Roosevelt was.

The subject of fatherhood comes up often in conversations with Carr, usually in anger. Lucien Carr, 69, now lives in Washington, D.C. He retired last September after 47 years at UPI, ending his run as chief of the world desk. In 1944, he was a sophomore at Columbia, a very handsome, talented, and troubled young writer. He was also the center of a circle that included Jack Kerouac, Allen Ginsberg, and William Burroughs—none of whom had yet written anything of note.

Carr might have made more cultural noise than any of them had he not killed a man that summer. The man's name was David Kammerer, and he had been Lucien Carr's scoutmaster back in St. Louis. Kammerer was clearly infatuated with the boy, following him to each prep school and college that Carr was admitted to and then kicked out of. In New York, as always, he insinuated himself into Carr's life. Late one summer night, in the tall grass of Riverside Park, Kammerer did something to Carr—kissed him, perhaps—that made Carr pull out his Boy Scout knife and ram it into Kammerer's chest. He rolled the body into the Hudson and, with Kerouac's help, got rid of Kammerer's eyeglasses and the knife.

Kerouac spent a few days in jail as an accomplice; Carr, who was able to convince the court that he had been defending himself against an unwanted homosexual advance, was out in two years.

A family friend got Lucien Carr a job at UPI in New York. He married a reporter there, Francesca von Hartz, and had three sons: Simon, Caleb, and Ethan. Lucien gave up writing anything other than newspaper articles, but, living with his family on Horatio Street, he remained a magnet for Kerouac, Ginsberg, and Burroughs.

"They were nice enough guys," says Caleb, "but they were really weird. To be a young child, particularly a young male child, around people like Allen and Burroughs was a little unnerving. I became a writer *despite* them, basically. It never occurred to me that they would be brought up in the story of *my* success. And, to a certain extent, it infuriates me that they are."

Carr's childhood was, by all accounts, a rough one, and in an early interview, he flatly declares the period off-limits. But, little by little, the stories spill out—sad, bitter details about neglect and drunkenness and beatings in the middle of the night.

Lucien and Caleb Carr's relationship today is distant, at best. Lucien won't talk about the long-ago violence: "I think it's something that, if it did exist, Caleb would remember far better than I."

Caleb's parents divorced when he was 8. His mother, a sweet woman with bad luck in men, married John Speicher, an editor and novelist who, according to Caleb, was as good a drinker as her first husband. He brought along three daughters from another marriage to create what Caleb calls "the dark Brady Bunch."

"It was a difficult situation, and we all spun pretty fast," says Simon Carr, 40, a painter who lives in the West Village. (Ethan Carr, 35, is a Parks Department landscape architect in Washington, D.C.)

The political scholar and former *Times* editor James Chace, 62, was friendly with John Speicher and has known Caleb since he was 9. "He's survived a lot, Caleb has," says Chace. "He had not-such-perfect role models." Still, says Chace, as chaotic as the house was, it was also full of learning. "The thing is, most people tend to be narrow," he says. "But all the Carrs knew music incredibly

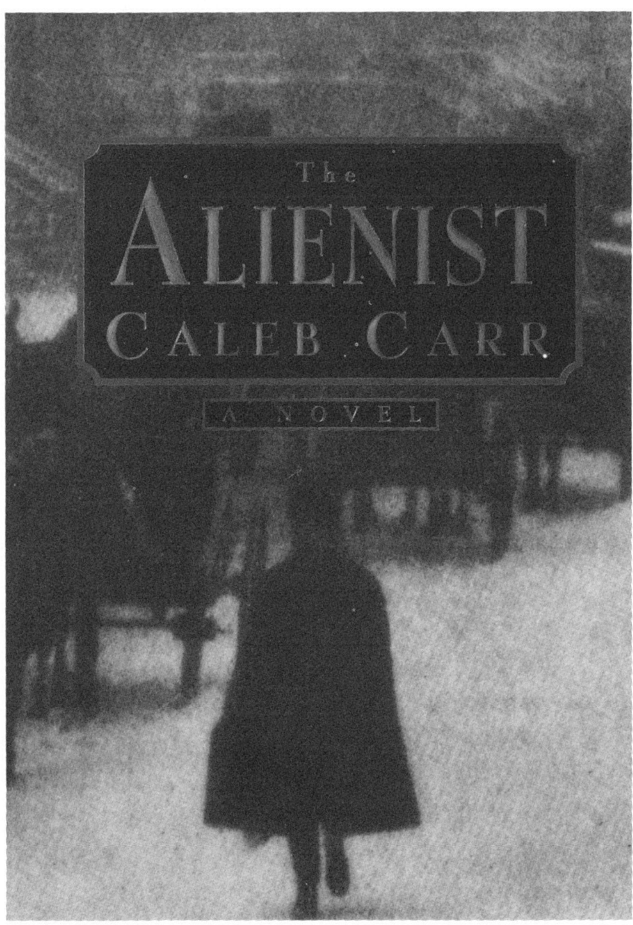

Dust jacket for The Alienist.

well, history, literature—they're extraordinarily remarkable."

The family moved from the genteel West Village to a loft on the nastiest stretch of 14th Street, between Second and Third Avenues. Caleb spent as much time out of the house as he could. Central Park, the Metropolitan Museum, and the movies, especially war movies—the more heroic, the better. By 12, Caleb was already a military buff, hanging battle-axes and coats of arms in his bedroom. "There's no question that I have a lifelong fascination with violence," he says. "Part of it was a desire to find violence that was, in the first place, directed toward some sort of purposeful end, and second, governed by a definable ethical code. And I think it's fairly obvious why I would want to do that." In the swirl of a bohemian, jug wine household, Carr looked toward British colonialism and Hamiltonian aristocracy.

Since there was little money in the family, Caleb's grandmother Marion Carr paid for the boys' education. Caleb went to high school at Friends Seminary, on East 16th Street. As a devoted fan of warfare at a Quaker school, he stood out. There were other reasons, too: spontaneously reciting Schiller's "Ode to Joy" (in the ninth grade, in German), swimming across the mucky seal pond in Central Park Zoo (on a $40 dare), and devouring everything from *Star Trek* to Wagner to medieval history. "He had a kind of sophisticated, far-flung interest without any pretense or affectation," says Oren Jacoby, an old friend. "*Puncturing* affectation was what Caleb cared most passionately about."

Not everyone saw it that way. Despite excellent grades, he didn't get into Harvard, and settled for Kenyon College, in Ohio. He later found out why: His Friends transcript was marked SOCIALLY UNDESIRABLE. "I was fucking stunned," he says. "We had guys in our school who dealt pure opium and cocaine out of their fucking lockers, and the teacher would take *them* aside and have *conversations.* But *me,* because I was blowing things up, just making general mayhem—that kind of thing got no sympathy."

After two claustrophobic years at Kenyon, Carr moved back to New York and worked as a researcher at *Foreign Affairs,* where James Chace was the managing editor. *Foreign Affairs* is the house organ of the Council on Foreign Relations, and, therefore, the locus of Establishment politics. The Council was not amused, then, with Carr's first published work: a New York *Times* letter to the editor in October 1974 that skewered Secretary of State Henry Kissinger's vision of diplomacy. Carr was 19.

He went back to school, at NYU, studying military and diplomatic history. Not long after graduation, he published a highly autobiographical novel called ***Casing the Promised Land.*** It's a classic Bildungsroman, full of starry-eyed philosophizing and rock and roll (for several years, Carr played guitar in a punkish pop band called Hell and High Water). ***Casing*** is also classic Caleb Carr: very bighearted, very cynical.

Carr has pretty much written for a living—albeit a meager one—ever since: articles for the *Times* op-ed page (**"Security Precedes Credibility"**) and *MHQ: The Quarterly Journal of Military History* (**"The Troubled Genius of Oliver Cromwell"**), as well as the occasional play and screenplay. In 1988, Carr and James Chace co-wrote ***America Invulnerable,*** a history of American national-security policy. Carr's next book was ***The Devil Soldier*** (1992), an enthusiastically received biography of an American soldier of fortune named Frederick Townsend Ward, who became a national hero in China. One sentence early in the book, although written about its subject, captures its author as well: "Ward was neither an idealist nor a philosopher but an adventurous realist who sought to carve out a place in what had consistently been, for him, a hostile and violent world."

Carr has plenty of friends his own age, but he has also accumulated a number of father figures, Chace chief among them. On the other hand, some of Carr's closest friends can't vote yet. ***The Alienist*** is dedicated to the five teenagers who acted in ***Bad Attitudes,*** a Fox-TV movie Carr wrote in 1991. The production itself was nightmarish—to keep one particular line in the film, Carr threatened to burn down the studio—but he and the actors became good friends. "Caleb is constantly trying to realize that childhood isn't necessarily a horrible thing," says Ellen Blain, 17, "and I think the five of us helped him believe that."

But ***The Alienist*** seems to show that Carr is not fully convinced. The murder victims are children like Georgio Santorelli, a Lower East Side urchin who, beaten by his father, winds up working the skin trade. The book opens as Georgio's mutilated body is discovered on the Williamsburg Bridge.

Still, Carr was determined to write a historical novel, not a child-abuse screed. "Your job as a writer is to take what's important to you and make it into something imaginative," he says. "Every book Charles Dickens wrote was the same goddamn autobiography, but he put in the details that made them interesting, you know?"

For fourteen months, Carr lived ***The Alienist.*** He read dozens of books on serial killers and huddled with Dr. David Abrahamsen, a dean of forensic psychiatry. Friends would bump into Carr at odd hours, in odd parts of town, trying to track down addresses that had long disappeared. One ex-girlfriend recalls that during touch-football games, he'd talk brain dissection.

Sometimes, ***The Alienist*** falls into a beguiling, neo-Conan Doyle groove, mixing sharp deduction with a sort of let's-put-on-a-mystery zeal. At other times, Carr's homework intrudes. Bret Easton Ellis, who trumpeted his own serial-killer lust in *American Psycho,* just reviewed ***The Alienist*** for *Vanity Fair.* As a historian, Ellis wrote, "Carr knows more about 1896 New York than any writer under 40, but as a novelist, he's smart in all the wrong ways."

"There are some people in this world by whom it is honorable to be held in contempt," says Carr, "and he is one of them."

Carr has tried hard to be extravagant since Scott Rudin and Paramount Pictures gave him that half-million. He has taken lots of friends to Petrossian, and although he won't admit it, he has been exceedingly philanthropic. Two weeks ago, Carr took a vacation, his very first, in St. Kitts.

James Chace, who now edits *World Policy Journal* and teaches international relations at Bard, wonders, in all seriousness, if Carr might not end up working at the National Security Council one day.

Maybe, if he's not seduced by Hollywood first. The moment Rudin bought ***The Alienist,*** Carr was flown to Los Angeles and offered dozens of writing projects. "You'd go in to some very famous person's company," he recalls, "and you'd go, Oh my fucking God, that is the stupidest thing I have ever heard in my life. How do I get out of this room without insulting anybody?"

Things worked out nicely with Universal, though. Carr is adapting the *Green Hornet* radio serial for the studio; he's even more enthusiastic about a Universal TV show he's working on. "Basically," he says excitedly, "it's teens in space—*Beverly Hills 90210* meets *Star Trek.*"

Still, his motivation for writing ***The Alienist*** is never out of his mind. "I always think of Chuck Jones, the Warner Bros. cartoon guy," he says. "And I always remember an interview where the reporter said, 'Your cartoons are amazing because kids think they're so funny, *and* adults think they're so funny. Who were you making them for?' And Jones said, 'We were making them for *ourselves. We* thought they were funny.' " Carr stops himself, wondering if he's worthy of the comparison.

"If I had known that nothing would have come out of this book other than the advance, I still would have written it exactly the same," he continues. "But if you were to ask me to trade in this book, this whole career, and have my childhood be different, I probably would."

Paul Levine (review date 17 April 1994)

SOURCE: "Psychology Yesterday," in *Book World—Chicago Tribune,* April 17, 1994, p. 4.

[*Levine is an American novelist and critic. In the review of* The Alienist *below, he praises Carr's attention to historical detail.*]

Eight years after Jack the Ripper terrorized the East End of London, an equally vicious killer was loose in the slums of lower Manhattan, preying on young male prostitutes. The murderer in ***The Alienist,*** Caleb Carr's elegant historical novel, is fictional, but the portrait of the Lower East Side with its "disorderly houses," undercover "fly cops" and gangsters called "rabbits" rings true.

The "alienist" is Dr. Lazlo Kreizler, who treats the mentally ill, then thought to be merely alienated from their true natures. Part Sigmund Freud, part Sherlock Holmes, Kreizler constantly challenges the medical (and political) establishment with his radical theories that childhood experiences can influence an adult's actions.

Kreizler's doctrine of "context" appalls both the "free will" theorists, who believe that sheer force of willpower could overcome psychic ailments, and the physicians, who believe that psychopaths have organically diseased brains. When a sadistic murderer begins killing and disemboweling young male prostitutes, Kreizler is ridiculed for his idea that "no adult's personality can be truly understood without first comprehending the facts of his individual experience."

Enter new York City Police Commissioner Theodore Roosevelt, who secretly appoints the doctor to investigate the murders, exclaiming "Bully, bully" and "By thunder" at the slightest provocation. Kreizler is aided by John Schuyler Moore, an aristocratic *New York Times* "scribbler," or police reporter, and Sara, a spunky secretary who yearns to be the city's first female cop.

Moore narrates the tale with reverence for the doctor's modern ways:

> Kreizler emphasized that no good would come of conceiving of this person as a monster, because he was most assuredly a man (or a woman); and that man or woman had once been a child. First and foremost, we must get to know that child, and to know his parents, his siblings, his complete world. It was pointless to talk about evil and barbarity and madness; none of these concepts would lead us any closer to him. But if we could capture the human child in our imaginations—then we could capture the man in fact.

In classic feats of investigative deduction drawn against the backdrop of the city's roiling slums, the trio constructs the first psychological profile of a murderer, one that would do the FBI's behavioral science unit proud. Assisting this team of modernists are the brothers Marcus and Lucius Issacson, two young detectives trained in handwriting analysis and dactyloscopy, known now as fingerprinting.

When they're not debating whether a mother's mistreatment can cause a boy's mental illness, the investigators consume gluttonous midnight dinners at Delmonico's, Luchow's and Brubacher's. Carr's fine eye for period detail includes his description of sumptuous meals of turtle soup au clair, Creole eggs, broiled squab, saddle of lamb a la Colbert and "a liter of smooth, dark Wurzburger [beer] that had a head as thick as whipped cream."

In the style of E.L. Doctorow's *Ragtime* and other novels that mix fact and fiction, Carr peppers his languidly told tale with real characters. Juxtaposed to the crusading Roosevelt are millionaire J.P. Morgan and U.S. postal censor Anthony Comstock, who scheme to cover up the lurid crimes lest the masses become agitated. Journalists Lincoln Steffens and Jacob Riis play cameo roles.

In effect, this 1896 murder mystery doubles as a painless history lesson. The descriptions of time and place are dead-on perfect: The characters dash around New York in horse-drawn hansoms, doctors carry Gladstone bags and there are enough newspapers for real circulation wars. It was an era when the *New York Times* would not print the facts, much less the details, of gruesome crimes, and silk-stocking bishops conspired with politicians to keep the immigrant rabble from knowing that a murderer stalked their children.

The stark contrasts between Morgan's opulent Black Library and the teeming tenements where police dare not enter are reminders that crime and class distinction are hardly new. Neither is drug abuse, as gangsters snort cocaine or ingest morphine, and everyday citizens become addicted to chlorohydrate.

A historian by background, Carr clearly knows the difference between a hansom and a calash, a landau and a barouche. The dialogue is larded with expressions of the times, as Sara demands not to be "mollycoddled" by the men, who are given to exclaiming "Hell's Bells!" in outrage. Stale-beer joints in the Tenderloin (serving the flat, tasteless dregs from kegs sold elsewhere) and utterly repulsive child brothels are described with seeming accuracy.

It is the attention to period detail and the modernistic psychological investigation that sets apart what would otherwise be a fairly conventional murder mystery. The long story never becomes tedious, and at the end the reader thirsts for another tale of Dr. Lazlo Kreizler, and another stein of Wurzburger as well.

Douglas Cooper
Amnesia

Born in 1960, Cooper is a Canadian novelist.

INTRODUCTION

Set in present-day Toronto, Canada, *Amnesia* (1992) concerns an unnamed narrator who, hours before his wedding, is confronted in his office by Izzy Darlow, a stranger who commences to relate his life story to the narrator. The narrator, a municipal archivist in charge of overseeing the collection of plans for the city, suffers from amnesia caused by the shock of a past event. He never attends his wedding, but through Izzy's stories pieces together the events of his life which, he discovers, is intimately connected to those of Izzy, his family, and a mental patient named Katie. Like the narrator, Izzy and Katie suffer from identity crises: Izzy's personality was split in two, with one half of himself transformed into a monster, after being caught in a machine one of his brothers built in order to resurrect dead animals, while Katie lost all memory of her past after undergoing electric shock therapy in the asylum to which she was committed following her rape and subsequent nervous breakdown. As with the narrator, Katie rediscovered her past through the stories Izzy told her while he was an employee at the asylum. Structured around a quote from Sigmund Freud—"The mind is like a city"—*Amnesia* contains explicit references to such works as Mary Shelley's *Frankenstein* (1818), William Shakespeare's *Hamlet* (1600-01), Samuel Taylor Coleridge's *The Rime of the Ancient Mariner* (1798), and Anton Chekhov's *The Seagull* (1896), and addresses such themes as storytelling, memory, insanity, and the nature of identity. Critical reaction to *Amnesia,* which was originally published in the United Kingdom and Canada in 1992, has been mixed. While some consider the novel's plot and structure confusing, others describe it as unified and tightly integrated, praising Cooper's use of interrelated symbols and images. Noting the novel's dark and troubling tone, Douglas Hill has written that "[Cooper's] imagery is scary and erotic; his prose is low-keyed but suggestive. In the end, it's his imagination of the borders between the real and the magical, the sane and the psychotic, that gives the novel its considerable power to unsettle."

CRITICISM

Daniel Jones (review date May 1992)

SOURCE: A review of *Amnesia,* in *Quill and Quire,* Vol. 58, No. 5, May, 1992, p. 19.

[*Jones is a novelist. Below, he favorably reviews* Amnesia.]

An archivist, who suffers from amnesia, sits in his office. He is to be married in four hours. A stranger, Izzy Darlow, enters the office and, for the next several hours, relates his life story to the archivist. The archivist subsequently misses his own wedding.

This is, ostensibly, the plot of Douglas Cooper's first novel, ***Amnesia.*** Through Izzy's story, however, Cooper explores a bewildering variety of themes and subjects: storytelling and its relation to memory, obsession, and madness, and the landscape of Toronto, to name a few.

Izzy's story is centred on his dysfunctional family. Physically isolated from one another by the very design of their labyrinthine house in Toronto's Annex neighbourhood, the family members are free to develop their eccentricities. Izzy's brother, Aaron, conducts elaborate experiments designed to reanimate the dead; Josh, the youngest brother, wanders the streets at night and meets a violent death; the father, a developer, grows more and more estranged from his family.

In his late teens Izzy finds companionship with a young woman, Katie, whom he meets in the hospital where he volunteers. Katie has been driven to madness by an incident in her childhood—which may or may not have been instigated by Izzy—and now is suffering from amnesia, a result of shock therapy.

Izzy's inability to admit, or to remember, his complicity in Katie's madness is paralleled by the archivist's own amnesia and hesitation about his marriage. But Izzy's "amnesia" has darker origins. As a child, reading accounts of the Holocaust, he was forced to come to terms with his own complicity in the horrors perpetrated by men and women against one another.

For Cooper, as for the eccentric characters who populate this novel, the telling of stories becomes both a means of restoring a lost history and a moral imperative, a necessary act of memory in a world where it is easier to forget. While ***Amnesia*** explores a variety of large and interconnected issues, it is remarkable for the lucidity and power of its prose. Cooper has written an engaging first novel. For its evocation of Toronto, both past and present, ***Amnesia*** deserves to be shelved between *Cat's Eye* and *In the Skin of the Lion.*

Douglas Hill (review date September 1992)

SOURCE: "Gritty Terrain," in *Books in Canada,* Vol. XXI, No. 6, September, 1992, pp. 48-9.

[*Hill is a Canadian nonfiction writer, fiction writer, poet, and critic. In the following excerpt, he presents a positive assessment of Amnesia.*]

Douglas Cooper's ***Amnesia*** is a dark and troubling story . . . with an . . . important thematic centre. A series of narrative meditations on memory and forgetting, the novel finds its energy source in domestic disintegration; around the tale's specific events lurks the enormous memory-shadow of the Holocaust, modern history's most infamous example of family destruction. We forget what we can no longer bear to remember, Cooper suggests, personally and collectively. Either way is trauma; either way we suffer.

The novel is set in Toronto, in the present and the recent past. It opens with the narrator, a municipal archivist sitting in his office just before he is to be married, confronted by a spellbinding stranger named Izzy Darlow. Izzy, like the Ancient Mariner, talks; the archivist, unlike the Wedding Guest, never gets to the wedding. What Izzy talks *about* is his city, his family, his friends, his love, his obsessions. Gradually Izzy's story takes over the archivist's; narrative consciousness begins to merge, memories over-

An excerpt from *Amnesia*

Katie sat despondently at the window that was his door and stared at the sky. The relentless cloud showed no sign of diminishing. Across the city she could hear a siren, the sound strangely muffled. She waited.

There was another sound down in the shadows of the ravine, as if bones were cracking, and then a loud tearing. For the first time, Katie noticed that his eyes were gold. Not brown, but gold: the color of a lion's skin. Of a lion's eyes. Only one dye was poured into the substance that made the lion, and it is a calm, fathomless gold; to stare into the eyes of a lion is to swim in the presence of a cool and impenetrable soul whose windows are gold.

Then again, she could never be sure that he was not in fact canine, or human.

For the first time, Katie was frightened.

He picked her up as if she were a piece of thread and carried her up against the wall, where he pressed himself against her so that their hearts beat together, and she understood then that his heart beat far too slowly.

Desire can take fear and bend it until it is an ornament. Katie no longer knew why she was breathing so quickly, merely that she was. She put out her arms for the first time to touch him.

Every time he breathed, her face would cloud over with mist. There was another tearing noise, less horrible than the sound in the ravine, and she realized that he was tearing her gown. In strips. Strip by strip. Until she was clothed only in thin tatters of cloth.

And then, for the first time, he kissed her.

If a moment could be expanded to articulate its parts—and for the next year of her life she would try to do this in her mind—the sequence of that moment would unfold slowly like this: she felt his lips against hers, and closed her eyes to be for a moment almost alone in her happiness; and her happiness swelled into a brief delirium.

And then she felt a hand between her legs, a cold, vicious hand, and then unspeakable agony as if something sharp had been driven through her, through her sex and up into her chest, and then the cold when her heart froze into white petals and then she screamed as the flower shattered under the hammer of his chest and she opened her eyes as wide as she could but they were still not wide enough to encompass those golden eyes. She realized, as she fell to the floor sobbing pitifully, that those eyes were mocking her. Laughing at her innocence, enjoying her pain. And then he was gone.

When she could at last lift herself from the tears and blood on the floor, she pulled herself still doubled over and crying to the night table, and as she stared at it she felt herself dying, and then dying again, and then dying again.

This time, he had left nothing.

Douglas Cooper, in his Amnesia, *Hyperion, 1994.*

lap, events slide together, elements of the supernatural transform the temporal and local.

A reader may occasionally protest that the author is indulging in too much self-conscious mystification, too much self-conscious profundity. The novel seems to unfold rather slowly at the beginning, and shut the door rather quickly at the end. But on the whole Cooper controls his material successfully. His imagery is scary and erotic; his prose is low-keyed but suggestive. In the end, it's his imagination of the borders between the real and the magical, the sane and the psychotic, that gives the novel its considerable power to unsettle. If we still ask of fiction that it create a world whole, and wholly believable, on its own terms, then ***Amnesia*** does the job with convincing skill. The questions Cooper raises are serious, and the disturbing implications of the story will stay with a reader; one blackly funny scene—which gives new resonance to the phrase "broken home"—should win the Magic Realism Award for 1992.

Sandra Birdsell, Douglas Glover, and Jack Hodgins (essay date April 1993)

SOURCE: "Memorable Images," in *Books in Canada,* Vol. XXII, No. 3, April, 1993, pp. 8-13.

[*Birdsell is a Canadian novelist, short story writer, and critic. Glover is a Canadian novelist, short story writer, and critic. Hodgins is a Canadian novelist, short story writer, educator, and critic. In the following excerpt, these three judges for the Smith Books/*Books in Canada *First Novel Award for 1992 present their varied appraisals of* Amnesia, *which was nominated for the prize.*]

[Sandra Birdsell]: I found Douglas Cooper's ***Amnesia*** confusing and difficult to follow. It beings at the city archives in the office of an archival librarian. He is the keeper of memories and of history, but cannot recall his own. It has been taken from him by an event he can't remember. One fall day, several hours before he's to be married, the archivist is in his office when a man called Izzy walks in and begins to tell him a story. Hours pass and so does the time for the wedding.

The archivist has a framed quotation by Freud sitting on his desk: "The mind is like a city." Izzy seizes upon it and says that although Freud rejected the idea, "the analogy is important. It is the clue to everything." Aha! I thought, the structure of this novel must also be like a city. It's a place where the past and present, good and evil, exist simultaneously. I took that to be a clue as to how to read the book, and looked for a kind of organic structure whose parts would exist as separate entities but together form a larger, complete story. But the "whole" kept collapsing in on the "parts."

Cooper continually backs away from the "parts" and avoids shaping his material. By using the "let me tell you what happened to me" storytelling method, he doesn't ever grapple with the lives of the people he's telling us about, and therefore they are flat, mere puppets, saying what he's set out for them to say. There's no sense of discovery in this book.

Whenever Izzy the storyteller was gracious enough to step aside and allow the curtain to open and the players to play, the novel was in danger of becoming interesting. In the instance of the story of Izzy's family, for example. There are some great moments there with little brother Josh, who stutters, but can sing beautifully; who walks through the city during the night and sees houses deconstruct as he passes by; who knows Izzy's crime. There's a hilarious scene in which Aaron, the oldest brother, builds a machine that is supposed to bring back to life a dead half-wolf pup. Wonderful. But just as the parents want to become intriguing, Izzy dismisses them as being for the most part "unfathomable." Katie, a central character, never rises above the stature of a pathetic victim; and when 13-year-old Izzy rejects Margaret, his girlfriend, she becomes suicidal. We meet the elusive Campbell briefly and then he disappears and reappears at the end of the book in a way that feels contrived. All the characters have the same voice—Izzy's. And all the events that occur are given equal emotional value. It's just too much caviar and not enough bread.

Izzy warns us early in the novel that it's "a dangerous kind of story that finds its way into your life, like a spore, and grows." The story did grow and did find its way into the archivist's life, enabling him to remember the event he'd forgotten, but by the time we emerge from this labyrinth of a novel, the event the archivist couldn't remember seems almost trivial considering what we've been through to arrive at that place. . . .

[Douglas Glover]: [Douglas Cooper's ***Amnesia***] is an oddly (for an experimental book) moralizing melodrama about a broken family (whose house explodes) and a boy who drives a mentally frail girl insane with his careless sexual advances. ***Amnesia*** has harsh things to say about all the safe targets—Toronto, Sigmund Freud (it holds him personally responsible for electro-shock therapy), modern technology (the Frankenstein myth), and teenage boys. It is restless and relentless in its patterning of images, structured mainly like a dream (or nightmare), with multiple shifts of point of view and narrative leaps that work by association or puns or image repetition. Near the end, the author cuts in a lengthy discourse on the ancient Greek art of memory that is meant to explain form and function (when Izzy, the protagonist, returns to his ravine-side home, he begins to remember the awful things he did to Katie, the girl he destroyed). . . .

[Jack Hodgins]: Douglas Cooper's ***Amnesia*** uses an intriguing variation on the Ancient Mariner technique to grab the reader by the lapel; then, in wonderfully controlled prose, it weaves an intelligent and moving story through a complex network of related symbols. It is probably the most tightly unified and integrated novel on the list. [The other novels under consideration were Carole Corbeil's *Voice-over,* Kenneth J. Harvey's *Brud,* Greg Hollingshead's *Spin Dry,* and John Steffler's *The Afterlife of George Cartwright.*] It is also quite unsettling. "I occupied another realm," says the narrator looking at his family, and you begin to wonder if this writer could make your own family and your own home appear as alien and threatening as he does the ravine. I suspect I'll never see Toronto in quite the same way again!

Michiko Kakutani (review date 25 February 1994)

SOURCE: "An Ancient Mariner Tells a Haunting Modern Tale," in *The New York Times,* February 25, 1994, p. C29.

[*In the following review, Kakutani provides a thematic analysis of* Amnesia.]

Amnesia, Douglas Cooper's chilly, chilling first novel, is one of those books that immediately make you think of dozens of other books. Its allusive narrative is filled with explicit references to *Frankenstein, The Sea Gull, Hamlet* and the writings of Freud and Nietzsche, while its elliptical narrative style recalls works by D.M. Thomas, Paul Auster, Sam Shepard and Vladimir Nabokov. The framing story is borrowed from Coleridge's *Rime of the Ancient Mariner.* As in that famous poem, a man on his way to a wedding (in this case, the groom himself) is buttonholed by a stranger, who has a bizarre tale to tell; the tale will become both a private act of expiation and a public means of communicating (and transferring) his pain.

Indeed storytelling, and the bond of complicity between writer and reader, lies at the heart of this novel. Storytelling, Mr. Cooper suggests, is a way of shaping and mastering reality. For Mr. Cooper's characters, there is nothing passive about the power of stories; they learn, in fact, that stories possess the ability to change people's lives, the power to infect or redeem their souls.

The main storyteller in ***Amnesia***—the Ancient Mariner, in a sense—is a strange, haunted, man named Izzy Darlow, who turns up one day in a librarian's office. The librarian—an unnamed man, who has lost his earlier life to amnesia—is on his way to his wedding; he is supposed to marry a woman he does not love. He will never get to the wedding; indeed, he will find his life transformed by Izzy's story.

Izzy's story, we soon learn, is a surreal mixture of truth and imagination, facts, metaphors, rationalizations and omissions. Izzy, it seems, is the middle son of a Toronto real-estate developer and his neurasthenic wife. His older brother, Aaron, is an aspiring Dr. Frankenstein: he builds strange machines in his bedroom, machines designed to bring the dead back to life. Izzy's younger brother, Josh, is a secretive artist who fills his journals with eerily prophetic tales and who wanders the city at night, singing mysterious songs.

Although Izzy has ostensibly been the normal brother in this anomalous family, an accident involving one of Aaron's machines will irrevocably alter his fate. It will turn him, a part of him anyway, into a monster.

In relating this peculiar tale, Izzy juxtaposes his life with the life of a girl named Katie: a beautiful, fragile girl, who plays the part of Mr. Cooper's Ophelia. Like Izzy, Katie suffers from bizarre visions and hallucinations, and she confides her dreams to a raggedy doll she has found in the ravine outside her house. One night, a stranger comes in Katie's window and rapes her. The event will land her in a mental institution, where Izzy finds her traumatized, feverish and mute.

Shock treatments administered by the hospital's doctors destroy Katie's memory: they not only erase her memory of the rape; they erase her entire past, too. Into this psychic vacuum, Izzy pours his elaborate stories. He tells Katie who she is and what their relationship has been. "I had always wanted nothing more than to mean everything to Katie," he tells the librarian, "and now that was literally true: without me to reconstruct the continuity of her life, there was no meaning."

Are the stories Izzy tells Katie really true? Has he misrepresented his own role in her life? Are hurtful events better forgotten or remembered? Can people truly reinvent themselves, or do they lose something essential in trying to shed their pasts? Is storytelling a tool of memory or a means of subverting its hold?

Mr. Cooper raises such questions both directly and indirectly. Sometimes, his characters simply make portentous statements that italicize his message. Sometimes, his narrative elliptically loops around the twin themes of memory and storytelling, leaving behind assorted poetic exfoliations. A building supported by human hands, collapsing from its own weight; a house architecturally designed to recapitulate the entire history of the site; a subway station built underground and then permanently abandoned; a predatory bird that snatches children from the cradle and drops them from the sky: such disturbing images cannot help but command the reader's attention, and yet they often feel gratuitous and contrived. The reader can feel Mr. Cooper *writing,* earnestly hammering out sentences and scenes.

Although this self-conscious quality never entirely lifts, one gradually comes to appreciate Mr. Cooper's copious gifts: his ability to manufacture odd, cinematic images; his talent for creating a musically patterned narrative out of repeated symbols and motifs; his willingness to tackle ambitious intellectual themes. The result is a highly cerebral novel, a novel that appeals more to the head than the heart, a novel one admires more than likes.

James Polk (review date 6 March 1994)

SOURCE: "Izzy's Own Story," in *The New York Times Book Review,* March 6, 1994, p. 17.

[*Polk is an educator. In the review below, he comments on Cooper's treatment of memory and characterization in* Amnesia.]

Douglas Cooper's ***Amnesia,*** a dense, absorbing first novel, locates prominent features in the landscapes of mind and memory. The geography it maps out is rich and challenging, filled with provocations.

Without forewarning, Izzy Darlow begins reciting a strange narrative to an archival librarian who is to be married in four hours. At first, this seems to be Izzy's own story. But is it? "Something . . . makes it want to replicate, breed inwardly like cancer. . . . The smallest part of this tale contains within it, like a hologram, the beginning, middle and end."

The story's characters lurch after meaning; as they do, individuals become multiples and boundaries blur. Struggling to uncover a personal context, each character assumes the shadows of all, and all become symbols in the memories of each.

Gradually, the entranced librarian realizes that he will never get to the wedding and will never marry. It doesn't matter. What matters is that he begins to hear, startlingly, elements of his own lost story. It is mixed in with those of Izzy's brother Josh; a woman named Margaret, whom everyone takes for granted; and a young woman named Katie, who then becomes the central figure against whom others are measured.

Driven by her demons to a mental institution, Katie loses her past to electric shock and enters the country of the featureless, whose "personal storyteller had died, or perhaps gone away, leaving their days listless and similar and white." They have become "perfect citizens of the modern city: clinging to life, and nothing else."

But Izzy, now in full retreat from a disintegrating family and consumed by guilts real and imagined (many of which somehow involve Katie), works at the hospital and can remake the young woman's yesterdays. "I had always wanted nothing more than to mean everything to Katie," he says, "and now that was literally true: without me to reconstruct the continuity of her life, there was no meaning."

If there is a lesson to be derived from *Amnesia,* it comes from the ancient Greek poet Simonides. The inventor of a system of mnemonics, he is called here "the Father of Memory"—and memory, according to Mr. Cooper, is both the gift and the curse of the human condition.

—James Polk

Lacking continuity, past, present and future disconnect and drift. In the background is the physical shape of the author's native Toronto, a city that splits apart in the nightmares of its inhabitants, the metaphor behind all the other metaphors. It symbolizes the modern world, where "nothing . . . is thought worthy of preservation, and growth is almost a religion," and where it is probably impossible to have a past.

But without a past, it's difficult to have a present, to say nothing of a future. If there is a lesson to be derived from ***Amnesia,*** it comes from the ancient Greek poet Simonides. The inventor of a system of mnemonics that tied events in the outer world to an inner architecture, he is called here "the Father of Memory"—and memory, according to Mr. Cooper, is both the gift and the curse of the human condition.

If our memories are taken from us, as are Katie's, then we cannot hope to have a context, and without a context what chance is there for meaning? In posing such a question, ***Amnesia*** affords a dark, unsettling view of the chaotic dislocation that comes when we allow ourselves to forget.

Anne Whitehouse (review date 3 April 1994)

SOURCE: "From Canada: A Portentous, Symbol-laden Tale of Forgetting and Identity," in *Chicago Tribune—Books,* April 3, 1994, pp. 3, 9.

[*In the following, which is a revised version, submitted by the critic, of a review that originally appeared in the* Chicago Tribune, *Whitehouse remarks on* Amnesia*'s intricate structure and Cooper's use of myriad symbols and images to discuss human consciousness.*]

As Canadian writer Douglas Cooper's first novel ***Amnesia*** begins, the nameless narrator, an archival librarian in Toronto, is surprised by a visitor to his office on the morning he is to be married. The visitor, disreputably dressed and carelessly groomed, introduces himself as Izzy Darlow, and proceeds to tell the story of his life, his troubled family, and his many crimes. Izzy alternates his life story with the story of a mentally disturbed young woman named Katie.

As the narrator listens to Izzy's confession, he realizes that he will never marry. The fiancée conveniently disposed of, the novel focuses on the tormented Izzy and hapless Katie. Yet we cannot help but wonder why the narrator lets Izzy ramble on, and what is the meaning of Izzy's enigmatic and portentous pronouncements. Soon after he enters the narrator's office, Izzy comments on a quote from Freud the narrator has framed on his desk: "The mind is like a city." "The analogy is important," Izzy says. "It is the clue to everything." "The smallest part of this tale," Izzy claims, "contains within it, like a hologram, the beginning, middle, and end."

It gradually becomes apparent that the novel is a carefully constructed puzzle based upon Freud's analogy as elaborately developed by Mr. Cooper, and that Izzy Darlow is none other than the youthful version of the narrator himself. Izzy is clearly described as the narrator's reflection: "Izzy sat facing me, in a chair that was the mirror image of mine . . . My hair, however, was parted on the left and Izzy's on the right. Viewed in plan, the room was symmetrical about the axis that divided the desk between us."

The narrator suffers from amnesia, presumably because of trauma: "I underwent something, which left me with an emotional burden too great for the conscious mind to bear." In other words, on the morning of his wedding, the narrator is surprised by his younger self, who brings him, in fragments, the lost memories of his past, which he must piece together.

Izzy is the middle son of three born to a secular Jewish family. His father, a real estate developer, is "a paragon of openness and civic loyalty." His mother, on the other hand, is "unfathomable." His older brother Aaron is a renegade and a tyrant, a teen-aged Dr. Frankenstein who, in the laboratory of his room, builds a machine with which he plans to bring a dead puppy back to life. Instead, Izzy gets trapped in the circuitry and suffers a shock which seems to split him in two.

The youngest brother Josh is described as an angelic innocent, eloquent in spite of a disfiguring lisp, who sings of prophetic visions of destruction and can intuit his brothers' dark deeds and desires. He takes solitary nocturnal walks through the city, and Izzy, who follows him on his circular route, hears him speak of a mysterious Katie.

The Darlows live above a chaotic ravine where dogs mate with wolves, and thieves wander at large. Katie's family lives in a house built right into the ravine so that her room cantilevers out over it. As an adolescent she is visited by a mysterious stranger, who leaves her bits of green plants and violates her despite her trust in him. As a result of this rape, she loses the ability to read and to speak and becomes hysterical. Eventually she is confined to the mental ward of the Jewish hospital.

Izzy has nothing but contempt for the safe, acceptable Judaism practiced by Toronto's bourgeoisie. Nevertheless, he accedes to his maternal grandfather's wish and agrees to study Hebrew and have a bar mitzvah, the Jewish ceremony in which a boy of thirteen leads the Sabbath service and assumes the religious obligations of a man. While he is preparing for his bar mitzvah, he begins his career as a thief. He steals not for gain, but for the thrill of committing a crime. He falls in with a gang of law-breaking hoodlums, who ironically call themselves the Friends.

Izzy is a self-styled young Nietzschean contemptuous of his fellow citizens, who despises the quality of niceness. "It is the barrier between a society and heroism," he proclaims. His bar mitzvah is a travesty that ends in tragedy and death. In his role as accessory in the Friends' biggest crime, he unknowingly robs himself of his inheritance.

Izzy's relationship with his fellow student Margaret is a battle of will and subjugation, which ends in her suicide attempt. It resembles his later relationship with the damaged Katie, whom he meets at the hospital and rejects when she desperately needs him. The mysterious perpetrator who raped Katie, it is implied, was that part of Izzy who was split off in Aaron's experiment.

The "hologram" which holds the meaning of the story seems to be the reductive version of Shakespeare's *Hamlet,* retitled *Ophelia,* which Izzy observes being performed in an abandoned subway station and takes part in. Both Katie and Margaret represent aspects of Ophelia, the girl who goes mad and the suicide. Izzy represents Hamlet, the confused, tormented, bookish philosophy student, incapable of love, who seeks "the unravelling of the maternal secret." Yet, in fact, Izzy is a caricature of Hamlet, without Hamlet's appeal, nobility, or morality. He has no murdered father to avenge or usurper to destroy.

"Something about this story makes it want to replicate, breed inwardly like cancer," Izzy proclaims, not once but twice. In this solipsistic novel, symbols and images constantly suggest themselves. The city is like the mind: the unmapped ravine is the unconscious, and the changing skyline and multiplying streets represent consciousness. The Darlows' duplex house, never entirely joined and made whole, is another image of the mind. The three brothers seem like split-off aspects of a single, damaged man.

Other symbols will suggest themselves to the reader. Mr. Cooper has constructed an intricate novel. Yet the sensibility which permeates it is so unpleasant and the symbolism so heavy-handed that the novel becomes both tiring and tiresome to read. The story disintegrates under the weight of the meaning it must bear. Mr. Cooper demonstrates that the difference between the portentous and the pretentious may be very slight indeed.

Douglas Cooper with Jeff Chapman, *CLC Yearbook* (interview date 16 January 1995)

[*In the following interview, Cooper discusses the themes and characters from* Amnesia, *his literary influences, and his views on Canadian literature.*]

[*Chapman*]: *What was the inspiration for* **Amnesia?**

[Cooper]: The inspiration was multiple. It's almost impossible to trace any large work back to a single inspiration, but I suppose I could trace it back to a single image: a boy trying to bring a kitten back to life by wrapping a wire around it's neck then trailing the wire up the television aerial, in homage to Doctor Frankenstein. I'm not sure if that was the very first image, but it was an extremely early one that gave rise to the entire project.

In the novel the animal is a puppy. Why did you change it from a cat to a dog?

I'm not precisely sure. It had something to with the dialogue between the feline and the canine, which is in some ways analogous to the dialogue between the masculine and the feminine, although I wouldn't say they map precisely. There was a relationship to that. The creative process you're asking me to talk about is seven years old, so it's hard to dredge up some of this.

Did you do any type of research?

Only the research that I'm always doing. Whenever I'm making anything based on a certain set of themes I'll find my reading tends to revolve around those themes. For the most part I drew on what I already knew. I've had to do much more research for the book I'm working on now because it involves knowing about areas that I don't actually know an awful lot about. You might say that every course I ever took in university prepared me for ***Amnesia.*** I studied philosophy; I studied architecture. I used everything I knew in my first novel.

Could you describe the relationship between memory, man-made structures, and narrative in **Amnesia?**

They're linked very explicitly according to an architectural model that I take from Dame Frances Yates' *The Art of Memory,* which she takes from various early rhetorical texts. Briefly put the model is this: the human mind can be conceived as a series of rooms and the memory can be partitioned architecturally in this way. You can imagine the remembering of a sequence of events as analogous to walking through a series of rooms and picking up pieces of narrative as you go along. That metaphor is at the very heart of memory theory. You find it in Cicero, you find it in *Ad Herennium* (a text that was thought to be Cicero's but in fact it's not) and all the handbooks of rhetoric. I think it actually goes back to Aristotle, who wrote the first explicit handbook of rhetoric, and it's traced back to myths about the poet Simonides, which I tell in my novel. I take this metaphor and make it even more explicit by having the architecture, the structures within the novel, not simply represent but contain memory in much the same way as this memory theory puts forward.

What is the significance of Izzy's brother Josh in the novel?

It's reductive to limit any character to a single symbolic role, and I wouldn't say that my processes are so rational that I could do that. Things aren't really capable of categorization in this way, but I would say that Josh, in a sense, represents the remembered, and his task is similar to the task of the Old Testament prophets, in particular Isaiah, the prophet of the destruction of the city. In fact, some of the rhetorical patterns of the passages in which Josh figures are taken explicitly from Isaiah. Josh is in a city which essentially represents amnesia. That is what Toronto does in this novel and, to my mind, in life. Josh is a ghost of the old world. He is the attempt to link nothingness to history.

What was the creature that raped Katie supposed to represent?

That's as difficult to answer as the canine versus feline question. I can give you answers that other people have given me. It's funny. Critics often make more sense of your book than you do. Some people have seen it as the emerging force of sexuality; some have seen it as the primordial and the bestial in the human persona: the archetypal rapist; Nietzsche's notion that there is a primitive but persistent impulse in men to commit rape. The lion may be in some respects a personification of that.

But I wouldn't really want to say. That would reduce the mystery of the novel. Specifically that one image; a lot of what makes this novel mysterious is the question regarding what precisely happened to Katie: whether it's related to Izzy, whether it really happened, whether both their accounts of what happened are accounts of the same event. All of that is very interesting and I would hate to simplify it.

You make numerous references throughout the novel to other literary works, such as Anton Chekhov's The Seagull *and Mary Shelley's* Frankenstein. *What were you hoping to accomplish with these and other references?*

It's a form of poetry in my mind to rhyme themes and stories. To my mind for instance, the albatross in *The Rime of the Ancient Mariner* rhymes with the image of the seagull in Chekhov's *The Seagull.* They are both bird images representing a moment of transgression and regret. In a similar way the narrative of *The Seagull* explicitly rhymes with the narrative of *Hamlet.* It's a peculiar use of the word "rhyme," but in so far as a novelist can commit rhyme, he does it in this way, by arranging notions or scenes or references that rhyme with each other. I think this is how Nabokov worked to an extent.

Some reviewers have suggested similarities between **Amnesia** *and* The Rime of the Ancient Mariner. *Did you have Coleridge's poem in mind when you were writing* **Amnesia?**

Very much so. Certainly for the opening. There's a certain kind of story—I don't know if I want to call it archetypal because that sounds crass and Jungian, but I guess I do believe, more in the sense of Northrop Frye than Jung, in the archetypal narrative—in which the everyday world is forced to deviate from its path through the entrance of a harrowing narrator. *The Rime of the Ancient Mariner* is one of the most famous of these, where someone comes in and ruins your day and insists that you listen to his story, as a result of which everything changes. I make it even more explicit than that by bringing in a wedding, which is of course crucial to *The Rime of the Ancient Mariner* as well. I like this kind of archetypal narrative because it stands for the power of storytelling itself: that a story can be so powerful that it can deform the ordinariness of your day, make you not go through with something very important because you're compelled to sit down and listen.

Many reviewers have commented on the quote from Freud—"The mind is like a city"—introduced in the first pages of the novel. Did you intend for this to be a key to the novel's structure and meaning?

It is one of the keys. This metaphor, the relationship between the mind and the city, is old. It recurs in Freud, but it goes back at least as far as Plato. I thought that Freud phrased it very concisely and with an interesting twist. In Freud you find this ghostly cohabitation of space by various buildings. You have all the buildings coexisting on the same site that were ever built on that site. You have this subversion of rational architectural space, through an image that is quite literally impossible for the human mind to grasp, even though it's supposed to be an image that represents the human mind. I find that interesting.

There are aspects of Freud that are fascinating. Nabokov used to call Freud a mystic, and I think that's probably quite true. What's interesting about Freud is that he's so far from science, not that he is, as some people think, the greatest scientist of the age. He's interesting because he's closer to David Koresh.

Two of the characters, Katie and the narrator, suffer from a loss of identity. What were you hoping to convey about the nature of identity?

They are the ones who suffer the most from this. Almost every character suffers from a loss of identity in some respect or another. One of the crucial themes of the novel is how the human persona is bound up through memory. How human identity is bound up by memory with the personal story; when you lose the personal story, what happens to the identity of the individual? This is an old philosophical theme: if you remove someone's personal story, through amnesia, what do you do to that person as a person? Does he still exist?

I wasn't consciously thinking about this when I was writing the novel, but it's one of the great themes of modernity. You find it from Conrad on down—the worry that we are somehow not whole, or one, that we are somehow capable of bleeding into the other. You find it a lot in contemporary French writing. You find it in Paul Auster. In Sam Shepard—the question of identity and memory loss.

A number of supernatural events occur within **Amnesia**—*the splitting of Izzy's personality and the meetings Katie has in her bedroom with the creature stand out. What do you see as the role of the supernatural in* **Amnesia?**

For awhile when critics had nothing to say they called ***Amnesia*** magic realism, which I think is lazy. The fairy tale is one of the oldest narrative forms, perhaps the oldest narrative form. Certainly the *Odyssey* can be considered to an extent a fairy tale as can aspects of the Bible or *The Epic of Gilgamesh.* Clearly it's something very important in the cycle of human storytelling. To banish the supernatural is trendy in writing programs, seems to go hand in hand with minimalism. To return to coincidence or the preternatural is simply to return to the roots of storytelling.

All this to say I don't plead guilty to the charge of magic realism. Not that I'm not impressed with certain forms of magic realism, it's simply not what I do. If anything I'm using traditional aspects of the fairy tale to highlight certain metaphysical notions. This is something Bulgakov does in *The Master and Margarita.* It's something closer to the tradition of the European metaphysical novel. I have read García Márquez's *One Hundred Years of Solitude,* but I hadn't read it at the time I wrote ***Amnesia.*** I had read Borges, but I think I associated magic realism with Allende's *The House of the Spirits,* a highly derivative, lesser version of what García Márquez was doing. So I didn't know the best of the tradition when I was writing ***Amnesia,*** and I'd rather not have it associated with the movement.

Almost every character in *Amnesia* suffers from a loss of identity in some respect or another. One of the crucial themes of the novel is how the human persona is bound up through memory. How human identity is bound up by memory with the personal story.

-Douglas Cooper

The hold many of the characters have on their pasts, even material objects from their past in the case of the watches belonging to Izzy's grandfather, is very tenuous. What were you trying to say about the nature of history?

That metaphor concerning the watches and Izzy's grandfather characterizes the modern, new world man's relationship to his own history and tradition. Izzy finds ironically that he has to steal elements of the tradition that by rights he should inherit. So inheritance is corrupted until it becomes literally a form of theft. This just highlights the difference between the true and the modern self and what should naturally be part of that self.

How does the Holocaust fit into your ideas on history and memory as expressed in the novel?

It's difficult to write about the Holocaust and it's difficult to talk about. Being two or three generations removed, I really wonder about my right to deal with this theme at all. On the other hand, in a certain sense, any serious piece of work after the Second World War that doesn't deal with this theme is blind. It's been pointed out for instance that the name of one of the characters from Beckett's *Waiting for Godot* was originally "Levi," or some derivation of that. Every major work since the war deals with this theme. There is no historical moment that defines my generation and the one immediately proceeding and following the way the Holocaust has. In a sense you could say that if you magnified to infinite powers what the earthquake in Lisbon did to the Enlightenment, you would approach what the Holocaust did to my generation, whether people know it or not. I mean most religious encounters, unless they're incredibly naive, are negative encounters these days. They're the encounter with radical evil. If you have a sense that there is anything beyond the merely mundane, it's a sense that there is something evil, not that there is something good. That to me is just a given. It's part of the modern landscape.

There's something extra-historical about the Holocaust. I studied with Rabbi Fackenheim and I agree with him that in a sense it's a theological event. In the same way that the Babylonian exile was a theological event. There are certain stories that are so important that they cease to become mere history. They become part of race memory; they transcend history.

Almost all the characters in **Amnesia** *suffer some sort of loss, either emotional or material. For instance, Izzy's family loses their house, his family breaks apart, and his brother and grandfather are killed. What were you trying to say about the nature of loss?*

That it's primary. Going back to what you asked about the Holocaust, when you encounter it—you encounter the Holocaust very young, especially in North America, you tend to be eight to twelve or thirteen or in my case younger—you are told this story of a people very similar to your people who live precisely the way you live at the same sort of level of material existence and who had everything taken away from them, unexpectedly and irrevocably. I don't know how a child is supposed to assimilate this knowledge except by thinking: alright, then everything I have could be taken away from me at anytime. That's the conclusion I came to and that conclusion is dramatized in the novel.

Two of the characters, Izzy's father and his brother Aaron, are in a sense creators of structures. Both are characterized unfavorably by Izzy. Why is that?

They're not so much architects as engineers, and in the father's case, he's a developer. I associate modern development at its most crass with engineering as opposed to architecture. It's much easier to get an engineer to design a box than to think hard about how you're changing the urban landscape. There is an impulse—which is the opposite impulse to nihilism—which is to build and to make things, but as soon as that impulse itself becomes corrupted by nihilism, you end up making things that are almost worse than having nothing, and I think that's what's happened. Late modernism is this horrendous rush to build the banal as quickly and as monstrously as possible. If there is a central motif in the book and in all of my work—it's in my next novel as well—it's the unthinking need to make large and meaningless structures. That's what forgetting is all about. That's what amnesia is. It seems that mankind has only been capable of building in this way and on this scale in the last hundred years. Shepherds putting up stone fences in Spain had an infinitely more profound sense of their architectural position than does your average shopping mall architect today. This is a serious problem.

At least two of the characters, Izzy and Josh, are involved in telling stories and constructing the pasts of others. In what ways did you intend **Amnesia** *to comment on the purpose of literature or to be metafictional?*

The telling of stories becomes a positive substitute for the building of banal structure. I see the creation of narrative structure as precisely analogous to the creation of architectural structure. They look the same. They work in the same way. They lead the human body and mind through the work in the same way. The storytelling that happens in ***Amnesia*** makes up for the architecture that happens or ceases to happen or is destroyed. Buildings are made poorly or decay in the novel; stories replace them and become in a sense the more important structure.

In a review from The New York Times, *Michiko Kakutani stated that* **Amnesia** *"is a highly cerebral novel, a novel that appeals more to the head than the heart." How do you react to that?*

I was amused actually. It's a tremendous compliment coming from her. Michiko Kakutani is a highly cerebral critic, a critic who appeals to the mind more than the heart. She is one of the smart ones out there. You have a sense that she has read everything, that no reference escapes her, so much so that you sometimes wonder to what extent she has engaged viscerally with the text. I just thought it was deeply ironic that she said mine is a text with which one does not engage viscerally. I don't mind that. I seem to be caught in the same critical limbo that Peter Greenway finds himself in: half the world seems to think that all you're producing is difficult thought, and that this is not art; while the other half of your audience seems to look at the work primarily as an emotional experience and not necessarily to think about it at all. I've had seventeen-year-old readers come up to me and tell me that the book deeply moved them, but they're clearly unable to tell me precisely what it's about.

If I really thought it was just an arid exercise in mental gymnastics, I would probably believe that I had failed as an artist, but I don't think that is the case. I engage in mental gymnastics to a certain extent, probably not to the same extent that say Nabokov does. There are some very self-consciously clever writers out there and I don't think I'm quite guilty of that. Very, very clever writers are often shallow. Clever minds are often facile. When you meet people whose minds work too quickly—Salinger used to call them high IQ show offs—there's a tendency for them not to have to work very hard and to produce glib, immediately impressive, vapid thought. I prefer the slow, deep mind. I prefer Dostoyevsky to Nabokov for that matter. I'm not saying Dostoyevsky wasn't clever—he's clearly not a stupid man—but he strikes me as having a deep mind that battled and wrestled things, as opposed to Bertrand Russell, for instance, who had a quick and facile mind that I don't particularly respect.

When you're young and at university, all that matters is that you be taken seriously as an intellectual and that people think you're smart and respect your ideas. But now I'm in this perverse situation of finding that people respect my ideas too much, and I'd much rather they engaged with my work on a different level. I'm not an academic, and I really don't care whether I have intellectual credibility at the moment. Artistic credibility strikes me as a much higher pursuit, at least in my field.

A number of critics commented on the frequent point of view shifts. Some even found the novel difficult to follow. What were you trying to accomplish with such shifts?

It's simply the way I work. Most authors talk about finding their voice; I found many voices. I recognized very early on that the way I write prose is an attempt to be polyphonic, or theatrical, or "dialogical," as Bakhtin called it. The way in which I write is dialogical, it's conversational, it involves many points of view and voices interacting to produce a fragmented whole. In this sense, perhaps, it's more Platonic than Aristotelian. Even though Plato's work finally points to a unified metaphysical whole, he felt that the only way to achieve that was through this conversational back and forth. I started out as a playwright. Part of it is my own personal history. I came out of fragmented media.

It's not a stylistic move. It's not something that I could do otherwise. All of my serious work is marked by this. Possibly it's an attribute of the age. People call me postmodern—I don't really like that word—but there seems to be a way of telling stories in the last ten or twenty years that looks a little bit like what I do, so maybe I've inherited that.

Who was your favorite character in the novel?

You have to be deeply in love with whichever character you're writing about at any given time. People assume that I am Izzy—some have noted that my Hebrew name is Israel—but I'm no more Izzy than Kafka is K. I use him to personify some of the most ugly aspects of Everyman, the way K. does. But nobody seems to be able to make the leap to the analogy between me and Katie. Everyone assumes that I wouldn't personify myself as the female protagonist.

What question or questions would you want readers to think about as they're reading **Amnesia?**

I'd like to think that all those questions are asked by the novel itself. That to me is partially the definition of a successful work of art. It's one that states its interrogative intentions, perhaps not clearly, but strongly, so that you're aware of the questions the novel raises while you're reading it. I hope the novel asks its questions in a profound way.

Could you describe your writing process?

Too slow. I felt vindicated by Beckett's biography when I discovered that he had nothing but contempt for those who write easily. I don't write very easily. In fact if you asked me at any given time whether I was writing well, I would say I'm blocked. I've always felt blocked. I felt blocked while I was writing ***Amnesia.*** I feel blocked while I'm in the midst of this next novel. I'm one of these people who constantly feels as if he's producing nothing. I always feel as if I should have produced so much more at this stage in my life.

Do you spend a lot of time revising?

Yes. Interestingly though, some things come out fully formed. I may rewrite one passage twelve times and not touch another passage. I'm not rigorous or neurotic about my rewriting habits. I have a sense of when something works, and when it works, I leave it alone, and until it works, I don't leave it alone. I push things around and vary them until they're right. It's rare that something is right the first time.

Do you have any type of ideal reader in mind when you write?

I tend to refer to Martin Amis's response because it's better than anything I've come up with. He says something to the effect that his ideal reader is that seventeen-year-old in the long black coat wandering through the library stacks looking for the book that will tell him or her how it is. That's my ideal reader. People are affected by books differently over time. It becomes much more self-conscious in later life, but teenagers—if they're not being ruined by drugs and bad music as to an extent I was—are affected by books very deeply. They are defining themselves in opposition or in response to what they're reading. Clearly you want to be part of that process as a writer. That's why I think Salinger is a great writer. I can't think of a single popular writer who has shaped the adolescent psyche the way that Salinger's books have. Your first encounter with *Nine Short Stories*—for some people it's *The Catcher in the Rye,* but for me it was *Nine Short Stories*—changes you, and that to me is successful writing.

Who are your primary literary influences and how have they informed your writing?

You often forget who your influences are. Stylistically I think I owe so much to so many different sources that I can't really be reduced to any one of them. In terms of narrative technique, I owe a great deal to Bulgakov—the alternation between the burlesque and the metaphysical. I owe something to Michel Tournier. I'm sure I owe something to Dostoyevsky. I would like to think that I owe something to Dostoyevsky. If there's a novelist of ideas who strikes me as truly successful it's Dostoyevsky. There's a strategy of careful fragmentation in T. S. Eliot that appeals to me. Not Joyce. A lot of people would argue that everybody owes something to *Ulysses* and I suppose I do–the great age of experimentation was set in motion by that book–but I haven't been greatly moved by Joyce. It's impossible not to respect him, but *Ulysses* was not a seminal text in my life. Yeats was very important early on. I can tell you what I read. It's hard to tell if these are direct influences. Dickens. Edgar Allen Poe, specifically the split house narrative. A lot of my influences are not literary. I take as much from dance or experimental theatre or painting. Beacon's screaming pope is as much of an influence on ***Amnesia*** as is say Bataille and the theology of horror. A lot of the influences would have to be extra-literary. Auselm Kiefer is very important to me.

How do you see your work fitting into the tradition of Canadian literature?

I define myself very much in opposition to Canada, but there are those who would insist that Canadian literature is a question of defining yourself in opposition to Canada: simply wrestling with identity makes you so Canadian that, whether or not you're a booster, you're part of that field. Certainly my techniques are very un-Canadian. If there's something that's typically Canadian, it's relatively naturalistic, tends to be short—Canadians are masters of the short story. To put it simply, I don't think there are many people in Canada doing what I'm doing. My book was greeted with a sort of sigh of relief. I think people were really quite pleased to see somebody creating Toronto in this way as opposed to the tried and true shopworn way of delivering up Toronto in literature. Of the people whom I don't consider entirely alien to what I'm doing, Michael Ondaatje would be one; Judith Thompson would be another. In so far as I have anything in common with those two, it's because they have nothing in common with what's happening in the rest of Canada.

Canadian literature is at an interesting and important stage. I really do think that Toronto is as interesting a capital of world literature as any at the moment. I'm contributing to that in the way that the exiles from Dublin contributed to the Irish Renaissance. I'm doing it from abroad in a highly critical manner, but I'm still part of it. I was actually called to task today for identifying myself as Canadian. Of course I'm Canadian. I'll never be able to lose that, and I tend to set most of my work in Canada. It's the country that made me who I am. It doesn't mean I have to be positive about it.

Do you have any works in progress or about to be published?

I have a work that is in the process of being published. My second novel, *Delirium,* is the first novel to be serialized on the World Wide WEB, and the third installment is going out into cyberspace tomorrow. There are about twenty or thirty pages out already. It's not finished. I'm serializing it in a nineteenth-century way: I'm publishing it as I write. It will ultimately appear as a book, but this is an experiment, an attempt to use a new architecture, in this case the architecture of cyberspace, to give a new kind of form to the novel. It's connected to ***Amnesia.*** I really want ultimately to write one book, and this is the next part.

Were you trying to attack any Canadian stereotypes in **Amnesia?**

I was trying to subvert them. The Canadian stereotype of the emotionless, frigid, northern persona begs its opposite. It's clear that any nation founded on that myth will give birth to a particular kind of northern decadence. You find this in Munch and Strindberg. (It's very, very important to note Strindberg and Munch and that whole circle among my conscious influences.) It's a particular artistic response to frigidity, to embrace the dark, violent, gothic, subliminal aspects of society, civilization's complement if you like, what it is that gets excluded by that kind of rigid civilizing impulse. And Toronto—which is seen as the nice, the clean, the good—is naturally going to give rise to its opposite. And did. That's what I encountered there. I encountered the perverse, the sexually malignant, the mystical, everything that's not supposed to be there, and it's there precisely because it's not supposed to be there.

Albert French
Billy

Born in 1943, French is an American novelist.

INTRODUCTION

Inspired by an actual event, *Billy* (1993) is the story of a black youth's victimization in rural 1930s Mississippi. Ten-year-old Billy Lee Turner is bold and reckless, not yet aware of the invisible social barrier between blacks and whites. When he impulsively leads his friend Gumpy to the outskirts of the white community, the foray results in double tragedy: the boys are attacked by two white teenage girls for trespassing on private property, and Billy fatally stabs one. Although he is young and acted in self-defense, he is tried as an adult for first-degree murder. The jury, eager to avenge a white girl's death at the hands of a "nigger," finds him guilty in a one-day trial, sending him to jail and the electric chair. Telling his story in the vivid dialect of an omniscient lower-class narrator, French earned praise for the authenticity of his narrative voice and his incorporation of powerful details of setting and character. Many of those details, French has revealed, came from his experiences as a Marine in the Vietnam War—*Billy*'s intense visions of death and fear and loss echo the horrors of war. Although some critics have argued that the narrative seems melodramatic at times and the voice inconsistent, many maintain that the novel nevertheless brings racism into painfully sharp focus. Nicci Gerrard called *Billy* a "devastating" tale about "monstrous racial injustice . . . a horror story played out to sweet music."

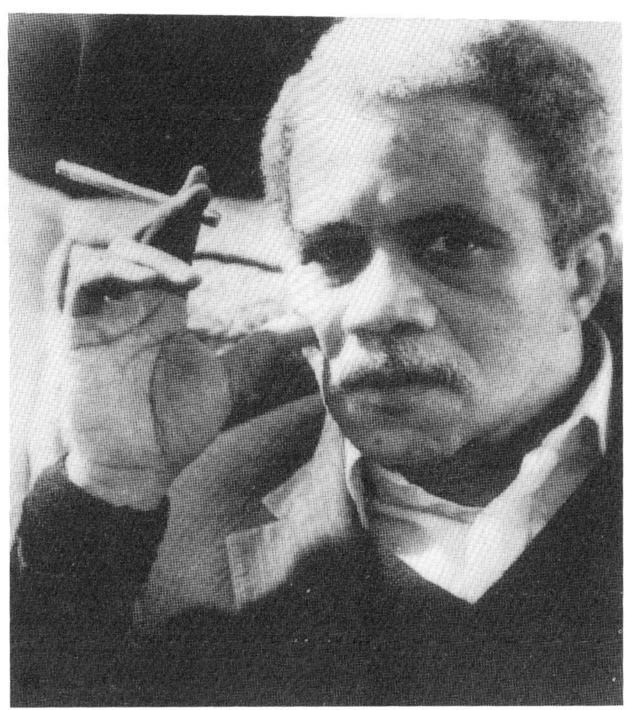

CRITICISM

Publishers Weekly (review date 30 August 1993)

SOURCE: A review of *Billy,* in *Publishers Weekly,* Vol. 240, No. 35, August 30, 1993, p. 73.

[*In the following review, the critic praises* Billy *for its intensity.*]

A talented writer makes his debut in this stark, harrowing novel [***Billy***] of a young black boy's death. Forcefully told, though sometimes veering into melodrama, the story vivifies the consequences of racial hatred. In 1937, in the small town of Banes, Miss., 10-year-old Billy Lee Turner lives with his mother in one of the miserable shanties of the black ghetto called the Patch. Headstrong Billy convinces another youngster to enter the white area of town, where they are attacked by teenaged cousins who are enraged to see black boys in "their" pond. Seeking to escape, Billy impulsively stabs one of the girls; she dies, and the white community works itself into a paroxysm of rage and violence. Though Billy is too young to comprehend what he has done, he is sentenced to the electric chair. The insistent voice of the narrator—convincingly rural, unlettered, and lower class—propels the narrative at a frantic pace, and the characters are delineated through vernacular dialogue that reproduces the unvarnished racism of most of the white community and the routinely profane interchanges of the uneducated blacks. Though nearly every scene is rendered with high-glare intensity, the closing episodes set in the Death House are especially searing. If in his need to sustain a feverish atmosphere French scants subtleties, the novel pulses with its unnerving vision of inhumanity legalized under the name of justice.

Donna Seaman (review date 1 October 1993)

SOURCE: A review of *Billy,* in *Booklist,* Vol. 90, No. 3, October 1, 1993, p. 254.

[*In the review below, Seaman hails* Billy *for its power and strong narrative voice.*]

This stunning first novel [***Billy***] seems to have sprung full-blown from the red dirt of the land it portrays, hot and dusty rural Mississippi circa 1937. It's a blazing summer Saturday, and the black folks in Banes are happy not to be laboring in the fields. Billy Lee Turner, 10 years old and as mysterious and independent as his beautifully golden and regal mother Cinder, convinces his friend Gumpy to cross the railroad bridge that separates the black neighborhood from the homes of the whites. The boys can't resist wading in the cool pond on the Pasko property and are terrified when Lori, 15, red-haired, mean, and powerful, and her friend Jenny sneak up on them and beat them up. Gumpy escapes, but Lori has hurt Billy badly. When she finally lets him go, he stabs her in the chest. Lori's death is like a match to kindling. The sheriff can barely contain the mob of whites intent on revenge. The frightened boys are tried as adults in a trial based not on justice, but on blatant racism. This is an American tragedy, stark and resonant, told in a voice as unwavering as the August sun and as timeless as sorrow.

Rhoda Koenig (review date 13 December 1993)

SOURCE: A review of *Billy,* in *New York* Magazine, Vol. 26, No. 49, December 13, 1993, p. 90.

[*In the following review, Koenig presents a mixed assessment of* Billy.]

On a hot afternoon in 1937, two black boys in a Mississippi town stray too far from home. They are attacked and beaten, and one of them, Billy Lee Turner, pulls out a knife in panic and sticks it between the ribs of the white teenage girl who has clawed at his face. In a short time, she bleeds to death. This kind of thing has not happened before, but the sheriff knows just what to do. He makes his way straight to LeRoy's bar and says to LeRoy,

> "I reckon it's about four-thirty, five o'clock abouts. I want them two boys fore that sun goes down. I don't get em, I'm not even gonna be askin why. Ya hear me? Ya want ta f— again, ya think about it." Sheriff Tom mumbled, but LeRoy heard him.

From then on, the plot moves with a grim inevitability for anyone who has read such a story before. The usual events are not altered by Billy's being inarticulate, not very bright, and 10 years old.

Albert French's novel [***Billy***] is told in the voice of an anonymous, omniscient narrator whose tough, earthy dialect vividly paints this ugly little place where both pleasure and fear are hot and quick. Billy is the fatherless son of Cinder, a beauty of rare self-possession: "Other girls her age kept away from her, but the boys be sniffin at her skirts like coon dogs. If one of them get too close, teased her at all, she look at em with them eyes and stare em down to their knees." Against the white world, however, Cinder has no powers. Real coon dogs howl, sniff her out, and

An excerpt from *Billy*

Coon dogs howl.

"Billy, run."

Shouts and yells near.

Lights bouncing up and down.

Coon dogs howl.

"Billy, run, run."

Coon dogs howl.

"Mama, Mama, they git us."

Thorn bushes bite.

"Over there. See em, Sheriff?"

"Run, Billy, come on."

"See em? Over there, see em?"

Silence.

"They up in there, hear em? Right in there."

Night-lights sway and point into the darkness.

Dark bulging bushes flash gray, green, then go black again.

Coon dogs howl.

Water splashes.

"There they are, Sheriff."

Billy slows and trembles.

Cinder drags him on.

Lights flash in her darkness.

"Mama, Mama."

Coon dogs nip and sniff at her feet.

Lights come into her face.

She grabs Billy.

Hands reach and snatch at her.

She jerks away.

Her hair is grabbed, yanked, and held.

"Ah got her. Sheriff, got em."

Albert French, in his Billy, *Viking, 1993.*

drag her down when she tries to hide Billy. The townspeople, jumpy with rage, go on a spree of violence, treating the incident as a tiny rebellion that has to be stamped down and burned out before it spreads.

While French's writing is undeniably powerful, it begs certain questions. When the dialogue needs to reproduce the accents of the educated characters, the narrator manages perfectly, although he or she otherwise uses an idiom full of grammatical mistakes and random misspellings ("hankerchiff," "hafe" for "half"); at other times, the voice changes to majestic-literary: "Time is no friend, it has turned its back and will not help. . . . Where it has given moments so freely and with abundances, it now gives eternity."

These shifts make the novel hard to trust, but what is even more unconvincing about ***Billy*** is its very "authenticity." If the details of action, character, and setting seem real, it is because they are so familiar from many other similar novels and films. Indeed, this book often sounds as if it has been *written* in 1937. The story—of a frightened, confused boy and an ineffectual liberal lawyer helpless before a brutal mob—is more a sad case history than a fictional drama, and one wonders why the author is presenting it to us if he has nothing to add. Though at first ***Billy***'s ambitions seem to be tragic, it ends up as something that is merely mimetic.

Michael Dorris (review date 19 December 1993)

SOURCE: "No Place for a Black Boy to Swim," in *The New York Times Book Review,* December 19, 1993, p. 7.

[*Dorris is an American poet, novelist, educator, and cultural anthropologist of Modoc Indian descent. In the review of* Billy *that follows, he examines the tragic consequences of racism.*]

In rural Mississippi in 1937, there existed a line described entirely by race that could be fatally dangerous for anyone, even a child, to cross. The memory of slavery, the hardship of poverty and the tunnel vision of ignorance combined with a one-sided system of justice to divide communities as acutely as the stab of a sharp knife. Communication between the two sides was like a shout heard through mud: frightening, indistinct, annoying, poorly comprehended.

Billy, Albert French's wrenching first novel, deals with the violence that ripples out from a single incident: a pair of teen-age girls take umbrage when two little boys swim in a pond situated on what, for them, is the wrong side of the tracks. Why the girls mind so much, and the brutal, bullying way in which they react, are the legacy of social attitudes and history, for they are white and the boys are black. Billy Turner, the younger of the two boys, defends himself with a pocket knife—instead of simply enduring a beating and then running away—because at age 10 he hasn't yet understood, much less internalized, the hierarchical rules of class and privilege that govern his world. In a moment of terror, Billy still believes he has a right to resist.

Of course, he's wrong. When, by freak chance, his blade fatally nips the tip of 15-year-old Lori Pasko's aorta, he activates a chain of events that neither common sense nor normal compassion can break. The (at least partly) self-provoked "accident" of Lori's death casts nearly every adult and child in the state into rigid roles. People who have long been amicably acquainted, if not friendly, suddenly perceive only the color of one another's skin. The principals are not merely victims trapped by the crush of circumstance, they are also high-voltage archetypes—black male, white female.

For the most part, Mr. French recounts events chronologically, in an economical, straightforward prose, and locates the drama in a place untouched by change:

> Ten years came, ten long slow times. Things ain't looked no different, Patch Road still dusty, Patch shacks still there, maybe leanin a little more. Things were no different, couldn't tell if they were, just like another wrinkle line on some old face, couldn't tell it from the other lines time left.

***Billy* is tragedy in the classical mode, mythic in the sense that instead of the surprise, the twists of plot we might discover in a more typical contemporary novel, here we are confirmed in our worst dreads as destiny immutably and shockingly unfolds.**

—Michael Dorris

The story, once in motion, gathers momentum like a landslide: at first a few pebbles disturb the quiet and then, inexorably, the earth itself seems to collapse into catastrophe; it's as if the very force of gravity were overpowering the personality of individual characters. ***Billy*** is tragedy in the classical mode, mythic in the sense that instead of the surprise, the twists of plot we might discover in a more typical contemporary novel, here we are confirmed in our worst dreads as destiny immutably and shockingly unfolds. Specific blame (or innocence) is as difficult to fix as the ultimate origin of the crime itself, but everywhere there is a pervading sense of waste, of helplessness and outrage.

Cinder, Billy's passionate, fierce mother, is the novel's most vivid character. Uneducated but deeply insightful, she braves the wrath of sheriff and posse to flee with her young son, to hide with him in a bleak and muddy wilderness until, before dawn, they are hunted down:

> She sees the lights swinging and flashing across the field, but they just seem to be there, maybe been there all the time, just swinging and swaying back and forth, not for her or of her, just there in the distant dark of her mind. They are still there, they won't go away, and she cannot turn from them; she watches them sway back

> and forth in the night. She shudders and feels the chill of a cold wind, then stills herself and sinks deeper into her darkness and peers through the thick leaves and branches of the bush. The lights still come. She turns and looks behind her and into the swells of shifting grays and blacks, then trembles and turns back to the lights. Her hand moves quickly but gently, she places her hand over Billy's mouth, then leans and whispers in his ear, "Billy, Billy, wake up, baby."

But Billy cannot wake up from his nightmare, cannot find ever again the sweet oblivion of childhood, cannot—even with the evidence of his fragile young body—wake up those who choose to view him as an adult and a murderer, those who finally kill him and call it justice.

Nicci Gerrard (essay date 6 February 1994)

SOURCE: "Flowing Fast and True from Vietnam," in *The Observer,* February 6, 1994, p. 18.

[*In the following essay, based on an interview with French, Gerrard explores how the author's Vietnam War experiences shaped* Billy.]

Once upon a time in America, an 11-year-old black boy was sent to the electric chair. His name is not remembered; records have been lost: it was a long time ago, before the war. Fifty years later, a sad man in search of a life was flicking TV channels and came across a panel discussing capital punishment, in which they mentioned the boy. His attention was caught, and four years later he started to write a book that would bring that little boy back to life, and send him to his death all over again.

Billy has taken America by storm. The tale of 10-year-old Billy Lee Turner, a black boy convicted of the murder of a white girl in Mississippi in 1937, is devastating in its close-up intensity, its unblinking focus on grief. Billy's mother, Cinder; his victim, the teenage white girl Lori; his friends and tormentors all loom out of the darkness of tragedy. Billy is about monstrous racial injustice, but it's also about how a young boy and his mother face his impending death. The novel is written in the rich, sing-song patois of the deep South: the progress to the ghastly denouement with the electric chair is a horror story played out to sweet music. I finished the book at one sitting, wishing I had never started it. I was enchanted, appalled and in tears.

Albert French, Billy's 50-year-old creator, is a rumble-voiced, courteous man (he calls me ma'am); both garrulous and shy. He has grizzled hair, a small moustache, a pouchy face, light brown skin and deep liquid-brown eyes. A bumpy scar runs down from his ear to his Adam's apple: he had been shot through the throat in Vietnam.

He's an unlikely writer for such an apparently artful book: he was always 'pretty bad' at school, doesn't read much, admits that his spelling is 'atrocious', doesn't understand sentence structure, has never come to grips with punctuation. The plot consisted of 12 to 13 numbered headings, with a two-word blurb by each number. Far from the dialect being difficult, it was 'natural'—the 'second language' of his childhood in Pittsburgh. His sentences can drift down the page like a lazy stream, picking up adjectives and rhythms, until a comma marks the place where French picked up a cigarette. Or they are short, because he stopped to think or have a coffee.

Billy is about racism in America, but it would never have been written without the war in Vietnam. Vietnam was the war where black soldiers were killed while white politicians talked about the cause and tapped maps with their pointing sticks. French went because he was sent. He was just 19, fresh from a boyhood of girlfriends, parties, football, happy families. When French talks about Vietnam, words pour from him in torrents: the dead bodies; the flies; the rain, the twitching of eyes all around him; the suddenness of death ('when that's that; that's IT').

***Billy* is about racism in America, but it would never have been written without the war in Vietnam.**

—Nicci Gerrard

He remembers his friends (he chants their names like a litany; tells me where to look for them on the Vietnam Veterans' Memorial in Washington). He remembers how they died, their last words, the blood, the mud, the terror. He remembers how he lay through a day and night with his throat shot away, listening to the sound of a little girl wailing, dying ('we were on edge, ma'am, if Jesus had walked past us that night we would have shot his head off'). When I asked him if he nearly died, he laughed mirthlessly: 'Well, a better way of saying that would be that I nearly lived, yeah, I nearly lived.' He won't talk about his guilt ('I haven't got to that part of the therapy yet').

The excruciating pain of ***Billy*** comes from Vietnam. When one of the characters looks at Lori's lifeless body, he thinks that 'only her hair has the colour of life'. This image comes from Vietnam, where French gazed at his dead friend Glipman and thought only his hair had life. When Cinder runs with her son through the dark, trying to flee from their invisible pursuers, 'I've done that a thousand times'. When she thinks of death ('not the death of a faceless child, but the death of feeling, of being, death of colour, death of night and day, but mostly the death of time'), then, 'that's me in Vietnam'. The loss, the horror, the monstrous fear—those are Vietnam too.

And perhaps Billy—the bright spark of black life who was snuffed out—is also the French who died in Vietnam. He went there young, he returned six months later an old man who'd seen too much ('and there weren't no yellow ribbons waiting for us'). He tried to re-enter the innocent life he'd left. But if a bulb exploded at a party, he'd be under the table howling. The smoke that belched from the steel mills where he worked reminded him of napalm. He drifted: from college ('they tried to get me to write on Martians'), to the mill ('I was surrounded by flames all day; I couldn't'); to a job as a janitor; a freelance photographer; a self-employed business man running a magazine. 'I wanted to fit in; God knows I tried. But I kept running into Vietnam.'

Then, in the mid-Eighties, his business folded and so did he. Vietnam—that great demolisher of men's lives—had caught up. He spent three years locked into his apartment, going out only to buy cigarettes: 'I had no identity, no dignity, no self-esteem, no nothing anymore. My life was a shambles. I guess the magazine had been a chance to do something with my life, and the chance died.' Finally he started to write. *Patches of Fire* was his first (unpublished) book—about Vietnam; ***Billy*** his first attempt at a novel. He wrote it in six weeks, on a rollercoaster of despair and hope. '***Billy*** permits me to believe that nothing is impossible; that one grows in the darkest of times. If it hadn't been for Vietnam, I wouldn't be able to see what I can now see, write what I write. ***Billy*** will be here long after I'm gone. That's my contribution. That's mine. That makes my life count.'

French lives on his own ('Just me, ma'am—although once I had a dog'). He loves children; he loves seeing people 'having fun'; but he gives off an air of acute loneliness. He's quietly delighted by the success of his novel, which is to be made into a film, and is working on a second, *Holly*. ***Billy*** has allowed him to see his life differently at last: 'This is important, ma'am. It's not me as an individual that counts, it's where I have been to. It's like climbing a mountain—I was lost and in the dark and I thought I was just going up a hill. Now people say, 'Were you really up there?' and I'm exhilarated but also I'm a little frightened, because I know that I have to go back.'

Albert French with Polly Vedder, *CLC Yearbook* (interview date 4 January 1995)

[*In the interview below, French discusses his writings, experiences that shaped his writing, and the writing process.*]

[*Vedder*]: *Racism is central to* **Billy;** *what kind of personal experience have you had with that issue?*

[French]: Well, the racism in ***Billy,*** quite honestly, is a backdrop. It's been written that it lights up the face of American racism; ***Billy*** was not meant to be that. My feeling about writing ***Billy*** was to get the feelings of Billy himself, Cinder, his mother, her feelings, Lori Pasko, Ginger Pasko, these people involved. It wasn't to light up the face of racism.

So it was character that was really interesting to you.

Right. Without racism the book would not have occurred, so it was a vital part of the book, but not my main focus when I started writing. I wasn't thinking "let's go attack racism." If I wanted to attack racism, I could probably have started out with Pittsburgh.

Billy *takes place in Mississippi, and many critics remarked on the authenticity of the setting. Where did that come from? Did you visit Mississippi?*

Never been there.

How did you capture it so well?

I've been to North Carolina, South Carolina, spent some time. The authenticity. . . that was relatively simple, in that I knew that they had a red clay or a reddish color to the clay dirt, but outside of that, it's a little bit of North Carolina, little of South Carolina. The South has its own personality and structure that is very distinct. Years ago, when I was in the South with the military, some of the signs were still up—"Black Only," "White Only," that kind of thing. One could be refused service in restaurants and what have you. I went down about '63, and that was around the time when you had many of the civil rights demonstrations emerging—Martin Luther King—things were going on, and you'd see the Klan.

Tell me about that.

The very first time was—these were not confrontations, I just used to see them—we used to go to a station in Lejeune, which is right outside of Jacksonville, North Carolina, and we used to go into town, into Wilmington. Jacksonville was a place—and I think there might be a little of Patch, a little bit of Banes County in it—was the place, in '63, that had paved streets, stores, and one main street, and on the main street you had clubs where the white marines used to go. When you crossed the tracks, the road became dirt—the pavement ended, the lights ended, the structure of the town ended. And you were into the black section of town, which was completely the opposite of the other side of the tracks. There were no paved roads, no nothing. There was that contrast: on one side of the tracks, on the black side of the tracks you could go back where you see the lights, you see all the activity on the other side of the tracks.

Very much two different worlds.

Exactly. So getting back to the Klan.... We were going into Wilmington, because it was a lot bigger and it's about fifty miles away. There was a place off to the left side of the road that I used to look at all the time because there was a barn that had horses, and I like horses so I'd always look over that way. As I looked going into town I saw the Klan burning a cross—the light caught my eye and I looked because there was something going on and I saw the cross up there burning. There were something like fifty people there.

So this was when you were in the Marines?

Right, which was 1963 to 1967.

How much of that time were you in Vietnam?

Not long—about six months.

You got injured....

Yeah. That was in '65.

The Observer *critic noticed that your Vietnam experience seemed to be expressed in* **Billy.**

Well, that's true, that's really true. I guess what I did was I transferred the emotions from different aspects of my life, mostly Vietnam. That's documented. Emotions are much the same, really. There's a part in ***Billy*** where Lori has passed away and the minister comes to pray over Lori's body, and he goes into the back room and pulls the blanket from Lori's face, and that's the line where "only her hair had the color of life." I remember writing that, and when I got to that point—I remember not really knowing what came next—it wasn't "I can't wait to get to this part"—when he pulled the blanket back, the first thing that popped into my mind was in Vietnam when the helicopters came down for the dead and wounded they blew ponchos off the bodies, and I looked down and there was a friend of mine right in front of me that I didn't know had died. When they blew the poncho off, only his hair had the color of life. There was no creativity in that sense, as it was a memory, or an association. When he pulled that blanket off it triggered that memory in my mind. That's how I remembered it.

You spoke briefly about not really knowing what's coming up next—you don't work from any kind of an outline?

You want the outline?

Sure.

It's right here—a bare outline, about a page on the inside cover of a book, and I think I wrote it down after I started the book. But basically what you have here—outside of telephone numbers, coffee stains—is ***Billy*** in chapters. Chapter One: intro to events. Two: background. Three: Billy and friend. Four: the crime. Five: the chase. Capture, jail, trial, death row, the execution.

Very much to the point. Did you work straight through it, from start to finish?

Yeah.

Is it pretty much as you submitted it to the publisher?

For the most part, the manuscript that was turned in to Viking and what was printed is almost verbatim. Changes were very minimal.

How did you find your publisher? Did you have an agent?

Yes—well, my cousin is a writer, John Edgar Wideman, and I gave it to him—not ***Billy,*** but *Patches of Fire.*

The one about Vietnam.

Right. Because that was the first one I wrote. I gave it to him to see what he thought of it, and he liked it, and he had already sent it to his agent, and I was very excited about that. I was just writing for myself and sent it on to him to read. I think to tell you the truth on one of the pages that I gave him, page one hundred or something, there was a cigarette burn on the page—that's what the actual manuscript looked like. So they gave it to his agent, and six weeks/two months later I got a call from my cousin's wife because the agency didn't have my number, but they read it and really liked it and gave it to these publishing houses—with holes in it! But it was copied by now, it showed up as a mark on the paper when what it was was a cigarette burn. *Patches of Fire* came back—my plan was when one would come out I'd send out another one. When ***Billy*** went out and while it was making the rounds I did *Holly.*

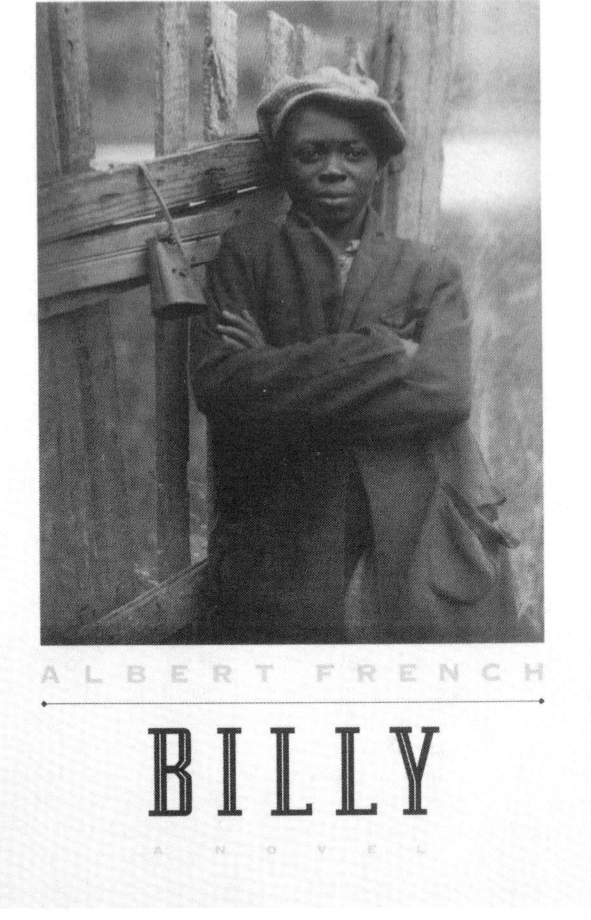

Book jacket for Billy.

Tell me about Holly.

Holly is a story about North Carolina, a little town called Supply on the south side of Wilmington. I once met a girl who said she was from Supply and I always remembered it because it's a military term. *Holly* is about an interracial relationship that occurred in North Carolina in 1954. Holly is a young white girl, nineteen years old, who inadvertently, reluctantly falls in love with a young black kid from the other side of the street. His name is Elias, and they begin a relationship which is doomed from the beginning.

You seem to have this continuous stream of ideas....

Well, I don't know. I've got to finish *Patches of Fire,* get *Holly* done.... *Patches of Fire* is not contracted yet—the original *Patches of Fire* has been redone and added on to. It's an autobiographical book; basically it's about me. What it is is the experiences that I had, the different things I saw. It's nonfiction, but I don't want to title it that way, or call it that way. It's not accurate in that I can't remember names, dates. When I think of nonfiction I think of something that's accurate, something that there are dates on. But I don't remember names—I remember faces, I remember first names—but I'm not sure if it was June, July, or August, so it's not accurate in that sense.

So it's like a memoir rather than history.

Correct. I think that's what they're going to call it, anyway, a memoir. A lot of names are made up. The situations occurring are not made up, they're actually what happened—with rough dates. It's a very interesting story, and I think to look back on events—from obscurity, this guy that basically locked up and didn't come out of his apartment for three years....

Literally?

Literally—well, except for cigarettes or something like that—and to write a book that ended up in the London *Times*—I feel good about that. A man from obscurity writing out of this depression is basically what it came down to. And to think of this kid that went into the service and what happened there, and what happened in Vietnam.... And so I guess in that sense the story is very interesting for someone. Writing the story you can always pop in and look at how things happen, but living the story you can't know what's going to happen.

How did you break that depression cycle and hit on writing?

I had nothing to do, there was no hope in my life or anything, and what I started to do is to—and I don't remember why—but I started writing different stories—short stories about Vietnam. I wasn't actually writing about battles and such, not in the *Rambo* sense, just some of the strange activities that occurred. I wrote one called "Lantern" first, and that was essentially a story about a man who one night came by with a lantern and I did not shoot. I remembered the lantern in the night, in the woods, and we did not shoot. I didn't know whether or not he was out looking for their cat—I figured anyone with any military bearing wouldn't walk around with a lantern like that, so.... These kinds of things play in your head. That's the first one I wrote, but I started writing, and I wrote that; I wrote another thing that occurred; wrote another incident that occurred, another incident that occurred, and so I guess before I knew it I had something like a hundred and some pages of stories, which became *Patches of Fire.*

The title "Patches of Fire" was from maybe December 10, 1965, and that describes just after the day that I was wounded, the night or that day or that evening—I guess it was about nine or ten in the morning when I was shot. I was in that rice paddy and it was getting toward dark and we were intending to get out of there. I remember standing out there, in shock or whatever with the situation, and in water all day long, and I was really weak. And I stood up and I looked back to the front of the battle—I was actually looking for a friend of mine, and I wasn't certain that he'd made it—there was burning up the hill. I remember the way I saw it was with the fog, there were patches of fire here and there, burning. So that's *Patches of Fire.*

What are your writing habits like?

I don't have a structure or anything about writing. What I do is, I have a desk here that I'm sitting at, a coffee cup, ashtray, white-out, typewriter, and junk. Not a lot of organization here. I use a typewriter, and I write the story. How I write is when the story comes. If I don't get it like that I don't do anything. I have to be there, with these people, who are real—they *are* real. I'm there and I just write down what I see. I really can't say *I* made them do things.

So it's like writing down a movie that you're watching.

Exactly.

That's interesting.

More so than a movie—I mean a movie—you have to walk out of the theater, but as a writer, you can't leave till the story's over. It was something to do at that time in my life, and I wanted to see if I could do it. I started it, and all up until the point that Lori dies—at that point the book became real. The Paskos definitely were, Lori . . . I liked her, I liked her personally, she was really spontaneous—and when she died that was when I felt pain. And I remember the night she died, it was about three in the morning, my time, and the book wasn't fun anymore, it wasn't at all. It became something, like a dream, and I was there. I was there, and the book I think took a life of its own, and there was no turning back. I knew at that point that Billy was doomed; I knew at that point that there was no question of the outcome. So at that point the book just kind of pulled me into it. Rather than *writing* the book, especially writing a novel.... A novel will reach out and pull you into it. In that respect you aren't writing so much as you are observing.

Helen Elaine Lee
The Serpent's Gift

Born in 1959(?), Lee is an American novelist.

INTRODUCTION

The Serpent's Gift (1994) centers on an African-American woman named Vesta Smalls and the survival, memories, loves, and losses of her extended family. The novel opens with Vesta as a child, her younger brother LaRue, and her mother moving in with their neighbors, the Staples, after the death of Vesta's abusive father. In their search for stability and happiness, Vesta and the other members of the Smalls-Staples clan pursue different means of coping over the years: LaRue weaves fantastic tales concerning characters named Miss Snake and Tennessee Jones; Vesta attempts to continually protect herself by repressing her memories of her father and his death, and by trying to emotionally isolate herself from others; and their "sister" Ouida Staples eventually finds fulfillment in a lesbian affair. Spanning over sixty years of Vesta's life and using such historic events as the Depression, World War II, and the Civil Rights movement as backdrops, *The Serpent's Gift* has been praised for its moving characterizations and its portrait of a woman continually fearful of that "slight lapse in judgment or balance that could send you hurtling through the air." Lauding Lee's focus on storytelling and her use of dialogue and lyrical language, reviewers have additionally stressed the mystical and mythical qualities of LaRue's tales, comparing the resourceful and unstoppable Miss Snake to such heroes of American folklore as Br'er Rabbit and Anansi the Spider.

CRITICISM

Kirkus Reviews **(review date 15 February 1994)**

SOURCE: A review of *The Serpent's Gift,* in *Kirkus Reviews,* Vol. LXII, No. 4, February 15, 1994, p. 166.

[*In the following review, the critic relates the plot of* The Serpent's Gift.]

[Helen Elaine Lee's ***The Serpent's Gift*** is a] richly textured first novel that begins with lyrical evocations of loss and love in two intertwined African-American families, but which later becomes more synopsis than saga.

In a nameless midwestern city, in 1910, the already fragile marriage of Eula and Ontario Smalls ends with Ontario's fatal fall while cleaning windows. Eula, with children Vesta and baby LaRue, is taken in by neighbors Ruby and Polaris Staples. The families had first met when Eula, badly beaten by Ontario, had fled with her two children and Ruby had been the only neighbor on the street willing to take her in. The two families now begin to live together with remarkable ease. Young Vesta is treated by Ouida, the Staples' only daughter, as the sister she'd always wanted; little LaRue and Ruby share a common delight in stories and creating beautiful things; and Eula, though scarred, finds solace in her work and in the affectionate security the Staples home provides. But as the story moves forward, the pace of events both personal and public accelerates, shortchanging plot and character along the way. Only LaRue's "famous" stories about Miss Snake, although they too lose much of their early charm as they multiply, seem to slow down the apparent rush to be done with the story. Vesta, forever affected by her family's past, lives a life of rigid order, only slightly relieved by the joy of raising the child during whose birth Ruby dies; Ouida, after a few failed affairs, finds true love with another woman; and LaRue, Ruby's male alter ego, becomes the family's nurturer and chronicler, who offers himself as the serpent's gift, the doorway "to the things that had happened before, to the things that had happened between them—to their history."

The seismic changes in race relations are perceptively noted, as are the realities of African-American lives, but the cursory treatment that results from the sprint to get it all down mars what could have been a magnificent African-American saga.

Paula L. Woods (review date 29 May 1994)

SOURCE: "Tell Your Friends," in *Los Angeles Times Book Review,* May 29, 1994, pp. 3, 13.

[*In the review below, Woods offers high praise for* The Serpent's Gift, *lauding Lee's characterizations and focus on storytelling, family, and love.*]

As a former member of corporate America who eventually turned to writing, I was extremely intrigued by this novel [***The Serpent's Gift***] written by Washington attorney Helen Elaine Lee. How many people have I met, fueled by the success of John Grisham or Michael Crichton, who report slaving away at their portable computers, trying to write the next *Pelican Brief* or *Disclosure?* Was Lee, I wondered, another one of these misguided souls who'd be better off writing legal briefs than literature? Should she be given that sage advice, "Honey, don't quit your day job"?

But after a marathon reading of ***The Serpent's Gift*** while I should have been enjoying the scenery on vacation, I wanted to advise Lee to start writing that resignation letter. For ***The Serpent's Gift*** marks the debut of an important new voice on the fictional landscape.

Although there's nary a lawyer or murder weapon in sight, Lee has nevertheless created an emotional, suspenseful page-turner. Her terrain is the human heart; the first two pages of the book alone contain one of the most haunting deaths in recent memory. This passing deeply affects young Vesta Smalls, creating in her a fear of making a critical misstep, of yielding to "the power of the small deed to rip the sky apart, and return it to seamless blue." And as the novel fast-forwards to an aged Vesta, now encased in tattered scarves and surrounded by plastic-covered furniture, you sense that she's paid some terrible price for a misstep, an accident long ago.

There's a saying that goes, "When one door closes, another opens." For Lee's character, the closing off represented by the accident and the violence leading up to it are a new beginning, an opening that propels the 8-year-old Vesta, her mother Eula and younger brother LaRue to the loving and colorful home of Ruby and Polaris Staples. There Eula finds a peaceful place in the basement in which to recede and muse on the nature of her love for Ontario Smalls, a love whose most visible remnant is a serpentine facial scar, which her rescuer and friend Ruby calls "angry healing flesh."

It is there that Vesta and LaRue find a sister in the Staples' daughter Ouida, an imaginative, confident child, and a ready-made mother in Ruby. And while Ruby's stories, told in stoop-sitting sessions with the neighbors, are too uncontrolled for the rigid vigil Vesta must keep over her life and emotions, young LaRue is drawn to this other mother, absorbing stories while sitting in a rocker in Ruby's kitchen. These stories ignite his imagination, allowing him to create his own make-believe character, Miss Snake, "who got in and out of fixes each time she appeared, who started out with purple spots but changed each time she shed her skin."

The creation of the Miss Snake stories, as well as the later tales of Tennessee Coal & Iron Company Jones, are Lee's masterstroke, completely rooted in the African American oral traditions of Br'er Rabbit and Anansi the spider. The stories, themselves deserving of their own book, act here to illuminate the narrative and give it a lyrical magic that both captivate and enlighten the characters. In young LaRue's mouth, the stories also represent a connectedness to African American culture and identity; they delight Ruby and Ouida, but dismay Vesta and Eula, who consider them "lies." For Eula and Vesta, the stories threaten to initiate an internal battle with secrets and dreams, long hidden but recurring as closed-off spaces that keep them from knowing peace. And until they understand the gift the Miss Snake stories have to offer, that peace remains elusive, just beyond their reach.

Lee has written in the siblings LaRue, Vesta, Ouida and December (who appear near the end of Part I) a quartet of unforgettable characters whose personalities run counter to expectation. LaRue is a sensitive, intuitive man with a spirit that cannot be crushed; a man who, when recognizing his love for Olive Winters, fights against his impulse to pull away; a man who marks the changes in his world from after the Great War through the 1960s with wonder, a great love for his people and a moving grace. His sister, Vesta, is rigid and frightened, a woman whose retreat from the pain of early disappointments drains the vitality from her life. Ouida supposedly has everything to be desired among black folk of the time—fair skin, vivacious wit, imagination—yet she makes a radical decision to embrace an unconventional love. Then there is December, Ruby and Polaris' daughter, whose arrival at the winter equinox signals birth out of death, but who, under Vesta's excruciatingly restrictive love, becomes a colorless cipher of a Detroit housewife, more concerned with the correctness of her peanut butter selection than the quality of her life.

Lee's novel also displays an adept use of color, light and space as indicators of vitality, of memory, of love and loss. Images appear in unexpected ways: The skin of an orange that stimulates the elderly Vesta's memories; her youthful retreat from the tumult of color into a seemingly serene world represented by an all-white wardrobe and meticulously cross-stitched homilies; the cobalt blue lovemaking of LaRue and Olive. While there are moments in which I wished Lee's style were a little more restrained, or conversely displayed more emotion, these are small quibbles about a book that is so richly imagined.

LaRue Smalls finishes many stories in ***The Serpent's Gift*** with, "I've told my friends, now you tell yours." The phrase is most apropos in celebrating the arrival of Helen

Elaine Lee and ***The Serpent's Gift,*** a book whose colors will linger behind the eyes long after you read the final page.

Sandra D. Davis (essay date 6 June 1994)

SOURCE: "The Storyteller's Gift," in *Detroit Free Press,* Sec. E, June 6, 1994, pp. E1, E3.

[*In the essay below, Davis favorably assesses* The Serpent's Gift *and relates Lee's upbringing and education, her influences, and the novel's publication history.*]

Helen Elaine Lee casts her spells mostly with blues. She invents seamless blue skies and small water-blue wildflowers. She defines comfort as cerulean and passion as cobalt.

After she works her magic with the tranquil-seductive-scorching hues of blue, she conjures up some mighty tall tales about a snake who finds renewal in the shedding of her skin and two African-American families who learn to pull light from darkness.

Lee, who grew up in Detroit, is the author of ***The Serpent's Gift,*** a novel that chronicles the intertwined lives of two families from before World War I through the early 1970s. Released in April, it has garnered rave reviews around the country and seems destined to end the law career of the Harvard-trained Lee.

Lee describes ***The Serpent's Gift*** as a story about risk-taking and renewal. It's also about family, so it's appropriate that her six-city tour, a welcome but all-too-rare vote of support by a publisher for a first-time author, brings her to Detroit, where family members get to show her off, and she gets to share the spotlight with those who nurtured her creative spark from early on.

Slender, with long hair with soft springy curls, Lee, who is single, had her mother, Dorothy Lee, and brother, George, at her side as she juggled interviews and appointments. Later this summer, the three of them will load a car with her books and take their own jaunt through the Midwest to cities this tour will miss.

"We are a very close family," George Lee says. "We actually talk to one another. Boost one another. We've always been like that. We're more like friends than family."

It's that kind of family closeness, Helen Lee says, that inspired ***The Serpent's Gift.***

Set in the Midwestern community of Black Oak, ***The Serpent's Gift*** is the story of Eula Smalls and her two children, LaRue and Vesta, sent by domestic violence and tragedy into the home of Ruby, Polaris and Ouida Staples. Times are hard. Cotton is still king in the south, and in cities such as Detroit, Chicago and St. Louis, blacks and whites are adjusting as throngs of African Americans migrate north in search of jobs and prosperity.

Sensitive, loving and a keen observer, LaRue is the storyteller, weaving great lies that amuse and sometimes help the combined household cope during some pretty dark times. LaRue's most fascinating stories are about his mythical alter ego, the colorful Miss Snake.

Vesta's early disappointments rape her of spirit and devour the modicum of confidence she starts out with. As she succumbs, she disposes of all her colorful attire and chooses to wear only white, starched whites, because "white has no history." And the beautiful winsome Ouida finds love in the arms of another woman.

"These are much like people in my family, in all families," Lee says. "This is about how families get along, how they protect their members, or in some cases fail them. No one here is perfect. I think that's what makes these characters so real."

Lee weaves these families' stories together with astonishing lyricism. The tempo is subtle, yet arresting. It is a summer breeze lightly whipping a clothesline full of white sheets on a cloudless summer day.

Wrote a *Washington Post* reviewer: "Beautifully crafted and profoundly insightful, this staggeringly accomplished first novel redeems the adjective 'heartwarming' from cliche."

I just want to write. I love language and storytelling. That's what I want to do. That's what makes me feel alive.

—Helen Elaine Lee

The Los Angeles Times declared that Lee's novel "marks the debut of an important new voice on the fictional landscape."

Says her mother, proudly, watching readers respond so positively to her daughter's work, "I didn't even know my daughter had all those funny stories in her!"

It is probably not surprising that Lee, 35, is a success: It's the family way. Dorothy Lee, who has a doctorate from Harvard, taught comparative literature for more than 40 years in the Detroit area, retiring in December after 20 years at the University of Michigan-Dearborn. Helen's late father, George E. Lee, earned his law degree at Harvard and had a long, distinguished career as a Detroit trial lawyer. He died two years ago of respiratory disease. Her brother, George V. Lee, is a Detroit graphic designer.

Home was a four-bedroom English Tudor on Fullerton Street in northwest Detroit's Russell Woods neighborhood. Trees lined the streets, and the park across the street offered a sense of privacy and a perfect place for George Lee to take the children sledding in winter, Dorothy Lee says.

On the blackboard in the kitchen, everyone added a new word every day and made a point to use the word at least three times that day. Word games and reading aloud were regular family activities. Gwendolyn Brooks, Emily Dickinson and many more authors were not just names but regular companions.

Says Dorothy Lee, "We valued creativity, my husband and I, as well as the analytical life."

That is one of the reasons the Lees sent both children to the Roeper School for gifted students in Bloomfield Hills. "There was respect for creativity and individuality," says Helen of her elementary through junior high years there.

Lee graduated from Cass Tech High School, then earned an undergraduate and law degree from Harvard.

She chose law mostly because her father loved it so much. Later it would become a necessary evil—the real job that paid the bills while she worked on the book.

"I thought it was what I wanted to do," Lee says. "I thought it was the way I wanted to participate in life, but it wasn't my gift."

So for four years, Lee practiced law and wrote fiction. At the halfway point, her father died. Then her close friends Eduardo and Andrew died, felled by AIDS. "It was very difficult to keep going," recalls Lee. "It was a very tough time for me."

She sent a half-completed manuscript to publishers. No one bit. But when she completed the book, Atheneum signed her on.

Atheneum publisher Lee Goerner says that stores already are requesting reorders and that "she has done extremely well in Washington," where she lives. "We are very pleased and very proud of what she has been able to do."

One thing she has been able to do is quit what she hopes was her last law job.

"I just want to write. I love language and storytelling. That's what I want to do. That's what makes me feel alive."

An excerpt from *The Serpent's Gift*

"Well, after some further discussion, they agreed on an elaborate plan to grab Miss Snake behind the head. Fox would get her attention, so that Goat would have time to create a whole mess of commotion and signal Lion to jump down from a tree and clamp his big old lion teeth right behind her head. They all clarified their roles, and at the agreed time went to the appointed place to wait for Miss Snake to amble by.

"The next day, Miss Snake set out for her morning constitutional, and they were all waiting. She wore her finest rattle, and skin of checkered orange and red. She had no idea that they were waiting for her, but Miss Snake was always prepared. They underestimated her, because she was as aware as they were of where her vulnerability lay. When she got to the appointed place, the other animals started to act their roles, and she heard all manner of carrying on.

"As things got louder and more confusing, Miss Snake realized that she was being ambushed. She looked up and saw Lion perched above her in the branches of a tree, and she thought that if she coiled around herself and moved in a circle, they wouldn't be able to find her head. Miss Snake flew into a circle, so quickly she surprised herself . . . she was looking, that day, like a ring of fire . . . it was something to see!

"Her attackers leaped back, in shock, afraid and confused, and some, like Deer and Rabbit, took off in a flash, thinking there was a forest fire taking shape. Miss Snake was an unbroken circle, and Lion didn't have the vaguest idea how to find her head. And if he couldn't find her beginning or her end, he couldn't catch her, could he, Olive?" He waited for her response. "Could he?" he said as he laughed. "I swear on high, this tale is true . . . if not for me, for sure for you."

Helen Elaine Lee, in her The Serpent's Gift, *Atheneum, 1994.*

Jewelle Gomez (review date September 1994)

SOURCE: "A Piece of the Past," in *The Women's Review of Books,* Vol. XI, No. 12, September, 1994, p. 25.

[*Gomez is an American poet, novelist, and essayist. In the following, she provides a thematic discussion of* The Serpent's Gift, *lauding Lee's focus on African-American history, the past, family, and personal relationships.*]

"This all reminds me," says LaRue Smalls towards the end of ***The Serpent's Gift,*** "of a story I need to tell you. It's the history of the world, from the beginning to the present." At some point in Helen Elaine Lee's first novel it becomes clear that this is indeed what she herself is doing: she's sliced us a thick wedge of history. The story begins with a young mother fleeing the violence of a drunken husband in Detroit after the turn of the century, and ends two generations later. The layers of life—birth, anxiety, triumph, love, death, trouble and survival—define a Black family here, but in essence are the history of us all.

When Eula Smalls escapes with her two children she is taken in by neighbors, Ruby and Polaris Staples. They move into the basement apartment and become part of the Staples family. Over time the children—Vesta and LaRue Smalls, Ouida and Dessie Staples—grow to regard each other as siblings: the adults share responsibility for them and each other. Each character struggles to cope with the change that is a part of life. Many ideas and themes are woven through the story, but change and the need to belong are two of the strongest.

The book opens with Vesta, the older Smalls child and the one most resistant to change. Fear of a "misstep" restrains her, keeps her from growing and moving forward:

> It was the single misstep that Vesta Smalls believed in. That slight lapse in judgment or balance that could send you hurtling through the air.
>
> Her father had given her this, and she held on

> to it, sensing that it gave her a certain edge on things, understanding the power of the small deed to rip the sky apart, and return it to seamless blue.

Throughout the book Vesta stays stuck in the memories of her dead father:

> Learning the sounds of nascent violence, Vesta could hear anger in his footsteps . . . the scraping of a chair . . . a falling fork. Her body tightened when she heard him at the door and relaxed only when he slept, and on the nights when there wasn't sleep, she lay awake and heard the little bits of killing that were delivered from his long graceful hands.

Her fears hold her at a distance from her siblings and from life. She fills her time with compulsive fruit-canning and cleaning, as if attention to detail will keep her memories at bay.

Lee's writing is fluid, elegant and lyrical; it is also lively and conversational, set squarely within the African American oral tradition. These two qualities, of language and of cadence, blend nicely ("It was during one of Vesta's cleaning frenzies that the heart attack knocked her flat. She went down in a cloud of Roman cleanser that dusted her white dress blue"). Lee reinforces the oral quality of the novel by making Vesta's brother LaRue a compulsive storyteller. LaRue resists isolation and stasis by creating elaborate tales, almost daily, like a television soap opera. Over the years he develops two mythical characters: Tennessee Jones, a stalwart adventurer who keeps the family informed about social and political developments, and Miss Snake. "The snake has been around since the beginning of time," says LaRue. "It is what you call grounded, living as it does in absolute intimacy with the earth . . . when it gets finished with the skin it's wearing, it sheds it, crawling on out of the past and into the future."

LaRue embroiders their stories for the family, and his inventions become the tour guides through a labyrinth of lessons and adventures that frame the "real life" passages. He wields his parables like a baton, using them to interrupt family disagreements, to dig his way through things he doesn't understand, and to woo the girl he finally marries.

LaRue finds kinship with Ouida who, unlike Vesta, is open to the tales he spins. Early in the novel Ouida follows the expected path—marriage—and then divorces. Vesta, more disappointed at this outcome than Ouida herself, asks what her husband did wrong; Ouida responds, "It's nothing he did, Vesta. It's who he is." This is the first articulation of the missing sense of connection in her marriage. But in the summer of 1926 Ouida meets a person who does make her feel connected: "Her kisses were like nighttime secrets, and Ouida swore that her laugh, like rain, made things grow. Zella Bridgeforth touched her somewhere timeless, held her, compelled her with her rhythms, and Ouida answered her call."

Their relationship blossoms in spite of the intolerance that surrounds them. No one openly disapproves, but neither is anyone quite able to look Zella in the eye. Lee presents Vesta's intolerance not as vicious, but as just another aspect of her inability to grow beyond the brutality of the past: "Her fear and mistrust had built up, layer upon layer, until she chose a path that would never bend back and meet itself, and something in her folded like a fan." Vesta repeatedly chooses isolation over connection, shielding herself from painful change but also from the warmth and sense of belonging that human intimacy bestows.

The climate surrounding Ouida and Zella as they set up house together remains cool; they do not deny the word "bulldagger" when it is hurled at them. "Brutal words for brutal people," Zella says. But they refuse to withdraw from the world or the Smalls-Staples family, even though LaRue is the only one who can truly embrace their union.

The narrative sweeps through history in broad strokes, incorporating events that necessarily affect the lives of the Smalls-Staples family: the Depression, Black urban migration, the Civil Rights movement. Lee offers an epic vision of the life of a Black family, something that has rarely been explored in this country's literature. We are able to see Black people managing their own lives within the frame of historical events, like the Depression, that are usually symbolized only by white characters. We see social phenomena like changing neighborhoods from the perspective of stable Black families rather than that of fleeing white families.

But Lee does not sacrifice the individual emotional upheavals to the tumultuous historical events that form the backdrop. She lets us marvel at Ouida's blossoming joy in physical desire without losing touch with how shocking that desire will seem to others. We feel triumphant when LaRue's talents find a use with the WPA and then in the growing Black newspaper field. Lee deftly weaves together deeply personal and sociopolitical developments, keeping each in its proper relationship to the other, as most of us must do in order to go on with life.

By giving Black characters a place in history, Lee makes the literary field seem so much more open than it ever has been. It makes us realize the inadequacy of the familiar stock characters, and that most of the stories of people of color—their observations and experiences through all of the twists and turns of our nation—have yet to be told. Each of them, passed down through generations, is an emotional building block, paving the road for Black writers and providing them with a sense of the familiar to come home to.

Near the end of ***The Serpent's Gift,*** Vesta sifts through the things that have accumulated in the family home over the years. She ships a box of items to each remaining family member. Ouida calls her to ask what all the boxes are: "The past," Vesta responds; "If you've got a use for it, it's yours." This is what Helen Elaine Lee has delivered to us—an invaluable piece of the past, a different world that has its practical use for us all.

Nathan McCall
Makes Me Wanna Holler: A Young Black Man in America

Born in 1955(?), McCall is an American journalist and autobiographer.

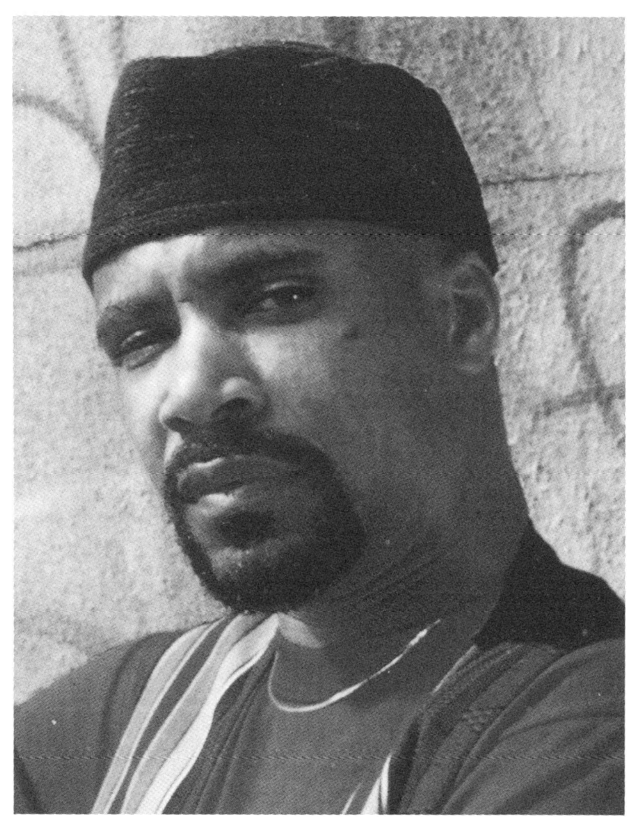

INTRODUCTION

Taking its title from a Marvin Gaye song, *Makes Me Wanna Holler* (1994) is McCall's shocking autobiography about growing up black in twentieth-century America. In praising the work, critics have cited McCall's honest attempt at understanding his own life as well as the lack of hope and self-esteem he sees within many sectors of the African-American community. McCall, who was raised in an established, working-class suburb in Portsmouth, Virginia, and later spent three years in prison for armed robbery, argues that white domination is responsible for many of the problems in black society. Although contested by some critics, McCall asserts that racism is ultimately to blame for what he describes as black self-hatred. This self-hatred, he claims, can lead to everything from random violence and widespread drug addiction to poor communication and failed relationships between black men and women. In an interview with Enrica Gadler, McCall explains: "If you're walking around with all this anger on your chest, you're going to release it somewhere. If most of the anger is about being black and about being rejected, then over time you can begin to hate blacks. . . . So the thing to do if you have all this hatred in you, and all this self-hatred, is to inflict it on someone else, someone else who is black—which, if you think about it, is a form of suicide."

CRITICISM

Paul Ruffins (review date 6 February 1994)

SOURCE: "The Crucible of Violence," in *Book World—The Washington Post,* February 6, 1994, p. 2.

[*In the following review, Ruffins praises McCall's autobiography for its honest attempt at helping other African-American men with similar backgrounds and beliefs to understand their own rational and emotional needs.*]

I've-been-to-prison books are always bridges. Some, like *Monster* by gangsta' celebrity Monster Kody Scott, span the gulf between the reader's world and life in the deadliest gangs or toughest prisons. But in more important works such as Nathan McCall's ***Makes Me Wanna Holler,*** prison is the midpoint in the writer's journey between crime and enlightenment.

In *Autobiography of Malcolm X,* Eldridge Cleaver's *Soul on Ice* or George Jackson's *Soledad Brother,* it is the stature of the author that lends significance to the memoir; the junkie/convict evolves into the revolutionary hero or martyred saint. Why then, is ***Holler*** a real contribution to this honorable genre, since McCall, a *Washington Post* reporter who once served time for armed robbery, is not a true gangster, revolutionary or saint? Because McCall's evolution from angry thug to edgy black professional is much more relevant to most people's lives. He not only constitutes a bridge from *Manchild in the Promised Land* to *The Rage of the Privileged Class,* but in the process he helps answer some important questions: What was he thinking about when he shot that guy? How come so many black men don't live with their children? Why do so many black professionals have ulcers?

Though McCall, 39, grew up in a pleasant section of

Portsmouth, Va., he deeply experienced the internalized wounds of race. Seeing a photograph of their grandmother warmly and sincerely smiling at the two white boys she cared for as a domestic, McCall and his brothers were pierced by the realization that she never seemed that loving when she was with them.

From McCall's adolescent perspective none of the honest, overworked older black people got any respect, only hustlers got respect. A good student traumatized by a racist school, he captures the aching to be cool that enslaves so many teens to peer pressure. "Alone I was afraid of the world and insecure," he writes. "But I felt cockier and surer of myself when hanging with my boys . . . We did things in groups that we'd never try alone. The group also gave me a sense of belonging that I'd never known before. With those guys I could hide in the crowd and feel like the accepted norm. There was no fear of standing out, feeling vulnerable, exiled and exposed. That was a comfort even my family couldn't provide."

McCall's world was ruled by the impulses of young men as if there was no option but to participate in gang fights, burglaries or running "trains" on girls—gang rapes. He barely survived a nightmare beating:

> I fell and felt the number and force of the blows multiply . . . I felt myself fading and remember thinking that I *had* to hold on, that eventually they would have to stop. But it seemed that an eternity passed and the beating went on. Then my fear turned to horror; the horror that comes the instant you realize that they have no way of knowing when they've gone too far; they don't know how many blows to the head will bring permanent damage or death.

In the hospital, McCall realizes he's not a great brawler but his solution isn't to stop fighting; it's to get a gun. Soon he deliberately shoots a man at point-blank range and learns that the courts value black lives as lightly as he does. The attempted murder gets him probation and four weekends in jail; robbing a McDonalds brings him 12 years.

Malcolm X, Eldridge Cleaver and George Jackson all discovered religion or revolution, extraordinary truths that transformed their lives. In prison McCall finds his salvation in smaller ideas like, "Work hard," and "Think before you act." Reading Malcolm X doesn't convert McCall to Islam, but to thinking.

> Up to that point, I'd often wanted to think of myself as a bad nigger, and as a result, I'd tried to act like one. After reading about Malcolm X, I worked to get rid of that notion and replace it with a positive image of what I wanted to become. I walked around silently repeating to myself, "You are an intelligent-thinking human being; you are an intelligent-thinking human being."

A model prisoner, McCall makes parole after three years, goes back to Norfolk State University and learns to write. After graduating he gets a break at his hometown paper, the *Virginian Pilot/Ledger Star* where his story was already known. Later he gets a job at the *Atlanta Journal-Constitution.*

As a reporter in Atlanta McCall discovers the same racism and frustrations confronting most minority journalists. The paper prints a Pulitzer prize-winning story about white bankers who reject far more black applicants, although statistics showed that whites defaulted at higher rates. Yet inside the newsroom, black reporters suffer the stereotypes that they aren't aggressive, can't write well or handle complicated stories. One editor hounds a black reporter, Michael, for making a number of mistakes over several years; then, when McCall and another reporter run a computer check of all the corrections printed as a result of white business reporters' errors, they find a pattern that was "no surprise" to them—"Some reporters had required numerous corrections in a single year—more than Michael had in his entire stay at the paper."

McCall faces the common stresses of black professionals, but with much heavier baggage than black yuppies ever bear. On job applications he fears the question, "Have you ever been convicted of a felony?" Not admitting that the three lost years on his resume were spent in jail ends up costing him his first shot at *The Washington Post.* Several years later, when the *Post* calls him back and he arrives at "The big time," he finds success, but little peace and even less love. He finds dating problematic, as he rejects uneducated women as ambitionless but experiences many professional sisters as status-mad or desperate.

One thing McCall shares with the notoriously violent Monster Kody is that his greatest guilt isn't over shooting men or assaulting women, but about living away from his children, as his own father did. With two divorces and three or possibly four children, by two or possibly three women, McCall is struggling to establish a relationship with his eldest son, 20-year-old Monroe, who now lives with him.

McCall's great fear is that Monroe might also head for trouble or fall victim to the streets. But reading ***Holler*** should help Monroe and thousands of other young black men in America to avoid—or recover from—the self-destructive cycle by teaching them the value of thinking, and of voicing the emotions they may feel but can't express. Without indulging in exhibitionism, McCall here strips himself naked in an honest confession. He may have a past he regrets, but ***Holler*** is a strong downpayment on his redemption.

Adam Hochschild (review date 27 February 1994)

SOURCE: "A Furious Man," in *The New York Times Book Review,* February 27, 1994, pp. 11-12.

[*Hochschild is an American writer, critic, and editor. In the following review, he contends that McCall's anger towards racial inequality and prejudice has negatively affected the focus and tone of his autobiography.*]

The social crisis in this country's black community is so catastrophic that we listen urgently to any new voice for

An excerpt from *Makes Me Wanna Holler: A Young Black Man in America*

One night, shortly after Liz's run-in with Plaz, she and I took Monroe to a carnival near Cavalier Manor. We were walking along, pushing him in a stroller, when Plaz and three of his boys walked up and confronted us. His eyes blazing, Plaz got within an inch of Liz's face, shook his finger at her, and said, "The next time you flash your middle finger at me, I'm gonna break it off. You hear me?!" Then he scowled at me, looked me up and down as if daring me to say something, and turned and walked away.

I just stood there thinking, *This niggah is gonna make me do something I didn't come here to do.* Not only had he disrespected me again, but he'd done it in *front* of my lady. I *had* to do something. That's when I decided to shoot him.

I told Liz, "Take the baby, put him in the car, and you two go on home."

She got scared. "Where are you going?"

"I'm gonna fuck that niggah up."

She pleaded, "Come on, Nate. We don't have to pay attention to him."

I didn't look at her. "Go on home!"

Liz turned and hurriedly pushed the stroller away.

As I walked in the direction Plaz and his boys had headed, I steeled my nerves. Whenever I wanted to do something really crazy like that, something I didn't have the natural heart to do, I had to run a head-game on myself. I had to shut down my mind. I had to block off all thoughts flowing through my brain to prevent me from talking myself out of it. That's the only way I'd be able to go through with it. That's what I did that night. I decided to shoot Plaz and I didn't want to change my mind. I couldn't allow that.

I had a shoulder pouch that I carried with me. In it were some drugs and a .22 pistol. I spotted Plaz and his boys milling around, talking with some other dudes they'd run into. I walked over to the crowd and said to him, "Yo, man. I wanna talk to you."

Flanked by his boys, Plaz really got loud then. He pointed a finger at me and said, "Niggah, you better get outta my face 'fore I stomp your ass! I'm tired a' you and that bitch. . ."

While he talked, I kept my hand inside the pouch, gripping the trigger. Sensing that a rumble was about to jump off, people started crowding around. I saw my buddy Greg in the crowd, looking nervously at Plaz's boys, counting heads. I knew he would go down with me if it came to that.

Moving close enough for me to smell his breath, Plaz poked a finger in my chest and kept on selling wolf tickets. "I'll kick your ass . . . !"

In one swift motion, I drew the gun, aimed it point-blank at his chest, and fired. *Bam!*

Nathan McCall, in his Makes Me Wanna Holler: A Young Black Man in America, *Random House, 1994.*

explanations. Nathan McCall's angry memoir, which takes its name from a song by Marvin Gaye, does not directly offer any. But obliquely it is a chilling commentary on where the problem is usually located: in aging, job-poor inner cities, filled with single mothers and abandoned by the black middle class. For in Portsmouth, Va., Mr. McCall grew up in an intact, stable family with a stepfather who always had a job, in precisely the kind of neighborhood of lawns and single-family homes that better-off inner-city blacks have moved to. At the time the McCalls moved there in 1964, when Nathan was 9 years old, it was the kind of close-knit community where one's parents and schoolteachers went to the same church. Why, even here, did Mr. McCall and most of his male friends end up in a maelstrom of drugs, gangs and jail? This is the question implicitly posed but not really answered by ***Makes Me Wanna Holler: A Young Black Man in America.***

Mr. McCall's adolescence was filled with macho posturing, street crime and the beating of white people unlucky enough to wander into the neighborhood. Then in 1975 he landed in a Virginia prison, where he served three years for the armed robbery of a McDonald's. Earlier, in a grudge shoot-out, he had almost killed someone, although for that he drew only a few days' jail time. ("I guess it's an indication of how they felt about the value of black life that I wasn't even required to post bond.")

The most painful parts of the book to read are Mr. McCall's accounts of the many gang rapes of black teenage girls that he took part in. With these, as with the fratricidal gang fighting, he makes clear that the driving force was group membership: "Alone, I was afraid of the world and insecure. But I felt cockier and surer of myself when hanging with my boys. . . . We did things in groups that we'd never try alone."

The reader of ***Makes Me Wanna Holler*** is torn by three conflicting feelings. One is a horrified fascination at being taken, with uncompromising candor, inside the head of just the kind of violent criminal everyone fears most. Another is respect for the enormous willpower it took for Mr. McCall to climb out of that life: after prison, he worked his way through college and up the job ladder to become a reporter at *The Virginian-Pilot and Ledger-Star, The Atlanta Journal-Constitution* and, since 1989, *The Washington Post.* The third feeling is a mounting exasperation at the way Mr. McCall blames the white world for almost everything he suffers.

Granted: he was beaten and cruelly taunted when he was at an almost all-white junior high school. Granted: growing up as a black man in the South means daily humiliations, large and small. Granted: racism is everywhere, even at a liberal big-city newspaper. But Mr. McCall's fury overflows all these targets. And this fury becomes a substitute for any real analysis of why his early life turned out as it did, and of what can be done to save a generation of young black men from the same fate. Black rage by itself, deeply justified though it is, is no longer news. Mr. McCall declares again and again that blacks in America have every right to be angry. At one point, he says, "I felt that any black person who had no anger was defeated." True. But then what?

At the three newspapers Mr. McCall has worked at, in the endless clashes with white colleagues or bosses that he describes, he is always in the right, and the problem is always the other person's racism: "Some white people are whiter than others. . . . They have a world view that sees whiteness as *the* standard and everything else as abnormal. I could spot such people in a stadium crowd. I could feel their overwhelming whiteness in my interactions with them."

If a white person wrote of spotting "overwhelming blackness" in somebody in a stadium crowd, what would Mr. McCall think?

He does grant that some white people are O.K. and, quite movingly, tells the story of his first close interracial friendship, with a white reporter in Atlanta. But Mr. McCall's anger goes far beyond race, for he seldom gives a shred of credence to the point of view of anyone else, white or black. In a furious description of his divorce, for example, he attacks his lawyer, his ex-wife, his former in-laws, the whole family court system.

Mr. McCall also sweepingly condemns Washington's black middle class ("some of the most bourgeois, pretentious, snooty black folks I've seen anywhere," people who "tell lies and put on airs") and other black reporters (who "talked white and thought white and even dressed goofy like the man: blue sport coats, high-water khakis and penny loafers"). In one of many passages about his difficulties with women, he rejects one working-class girlfriend because "she had no sense of her potential to grow and expand" and, a few paragraphs later, spurns a black professional woman because "she talked about her career all the time, like that was all there was to life. People like her convinced me more of how thoroughly brainwashed some blacks were." Mr. McCall does not sound like an easy person to live or work with.

Only rarely does he seem to wonder what the consequences of his anger have been for others, especially those he attacked in his street days. In the book's final pages, to his great credit, he seeks out one of his victims, a woman injured while escaping from an attempted gang rape long ago. "She was warm and cordial. I wondered how she could bring herself to forgive me for what I'd done to her." The woman has a teen-age daughter whom Mr. McCall may have fathered during a brief encounter a month before the attempted rape. At last, he fumblingly tries to take some responsibility for the girl's life. "I didn't know whether to hug her, kiss her or shake her hand." This sounds a deeper and less familiar note, different from what we have heard throughout the book; it is Mr. McCall's first attempt to move beyond anger to empathy and healing. If he had waited a bit longer to write ***Makes Me Wanna Holler,*** I suspect, there would be more such tries—and they would have made this a wiser, more original story.

Gene Lyons (review date 4 March 1994)

SOURCE: "In Living Color," in *Entertainment Weekly,* No. 212, March 4, 1994, pp. 56-57.

[*Lyons is an American essayist, reviewer, and nonfiction writer. In the following review, he argues that McCall's autobiography, although valid and moving, is ultimately dissatisfactory in its examination of McCall and its other black characters.*]

Many are the perils of autobiography. Seemingly the simplest form of storytelling, it tempts the unwary author with that most seductive narcotic: the first-person singular. Tricky enough in the hands of a literary sophisticate like James Baldwin or Philip Roth, the urge to turn one's life into narrative can easily lead less gifted authors into revelations very different from those they intended.

So it is with Nathan McCall's ***Makes Me Wanna Holler: A Young Black Man In America,*** the often remarkable, often remarkably obtuse saga of its author's seemingly improbable journey from a Virginia penitentiary for armed robbery to a career as a *Washington Post* reporter. McCall certainly has a story to tell, and a plainspoken journalistic style in which to tell it. Already optioned to *Boyz N the Hood* director John Singleton, ***Makes Me Wanna Holler*** is the episodic tale of a young black man's troubled coming-of-age in a world he sees as utterly dominated by white racism to the point where hatred and mad violence seem the only possible response—violence against white and black alike, and against black women in particular.

That McCall survived his adolescence at all—much less emerged as a white-collar suburbanite bitterly insulted by whites who lock their car doors when they see him coming, but fearful and resentful of black street gangs, too—is truly remarkable. To hear him tell it, random beatings, muggings, drug deals, shootings, stabbings, burglaries, armed stickups and appalling gang rapes were his youthful rites of passage—all explained, if not quite excused, to McCall's way of thinking, by feelings of powerlessness and self-loathing. "The guys on the street who got the most respect," he writes, "were those who had reps as crazy niggers. A crazy nigger was someone who had an explosive temper, someone who took flak from no one—man, woman or child. . . . We regarded craziness as an esteemed quality, something to be admired, like white people admire courage. In fact, to our way of thinking, craziness and courage were one and the same."

Oddly enough, McCall didn't grow up in a slum, nor in the kind of fatherless home so often blamed for social alienation. His family, of which he says remarkably little of real psychological interest, lived in Cavalier Manor, a middle-class black neighborhood in Portsmouth, Va., where his stepfather worked in a naval shipyard. Both parents preached the gospel of education, hard work, and self-denial.

Much affected by the civil rights turmoil of the '60s, however, McCall and his homeys drew their own conclusions. A painful experience as one of a handful of black sixth graders in a newly integrated school began the process. Watching his stepfather cringe over racial slights on the job and being treated like a groveling darky by whites for whom he did weekend landscaping left him angry. "A two-parent home," he says, "is no better off than a single-parent one if the father is f—ed up in the head and beaten down. There's nothing more dangerous and destructive in a household than a frustrated, oppressed black man."

So far so good. Sociology and racial polemics, however, can take a writer only so far—and in McCall's case, it's not far enough. After all, millions of black Americans have experienced racial indignities without allowing rage to consume their lives. Where McCall falters is not merely in the all-too-familiar the-white-man-made-me-do-it casuistry that pervades the book, nor in his constant demeaning references to "tweedy, pencil-head white men" and "flour-faced, blue-haired" white women—offensive though they are. The truth is that he doesn't do a whole lot more persuasive job with the book's one-dimensional black characters, beginning, unfortunately, with himself.

One needn't, for example, question the sincerity of McCall's regret for his violent past to wonder why he would characterize the manager of a McDonald's restaurant whom he threatened to shoot during a stickup as "an Uncle Tom, one of those head-scratching niggers, willing to put his devalued life on the line to protect the white man's property." But shouldn't a man with a confessed history of gang rape think twice before writing an account of the breakup of his second marriage that's so patently one-sided many readers will wish they could hear the ex-wife's story?

A troubling, compelling polemic all the same.

Henry Louis Gates, Jr. (review date 7 March 1994)

SOURCE: "Bad Influence," in *The New Yorker,* Vol. LXX, No. 3, March 7, 1994, pp. 94-8.

[*Gates is an American reviewer, editor, and educator known for his many contributions to the study of black literature. In the following review, he explores the place of McCall's autobiography in the existing canon of African-American literature.*]

In the course of a spectacularly uneven career, Richard Wright, the first black writer to earn a living by his pen, created two indelible characters. The first was Bigger Thomas, thc protagonist of *Native Son.* Young, black, and poor—and victimized by a series of events beyond his control or comprehension—Bigger ends up killing both a white heiress and his own girlfriend before being captured and sentenced to death. His rapid descent, detailed by Wright with unapologetic naturalism, reveals the hopelessness of a life where free will is merely an illusion, where any glimmering of real freedom is blotted out by the cruel collusion of racism and capitalism. Bigger was an archetypal vessel of what cultural commentators like to call "the rage of the black male."

The second of Richard Wright's enduring creations was Richard Wright. Most memorably set forth in the pages of his memoir, *Black Boy,* the character of Richard Wright is another study in black rage, as a Southern child discovers the oppressions of family, race, and region. But where the novel follows a downward spiral, the memoir is in some measure a narrative of transcendence. At least its narrator survived to write the tale.

There is larger significance in the fact that so often the first book published by a black American writer (though this was not true in Wright's case) has been autobiography; it's as if the tradition of the slave narrative had never been fully dislodged by post-emancipation history. My point is not about content so much as classification: many first novels are autobiographical, but they are not submitted for our consideration *as* autobiography. Say you grew up pale and Presbyterian in Poughkeepsie, attended Haverford College, experienced your first grand passion, and—well, you know the drill. Such is the stuff of the First Novel: the coming-of-age of a sensitive, misunderstood young man or woman who happens to bear an uncanny resemblance to the author. But it is the birthright of the black writer that his experiences, however personal, are also automatically historical. In the same way that Shelley saw all poems as fragments of one vast ur-poem, we see the black memoirist's tale as part of a larger, subsuming saga—an entry in the vast, multivolume project of Narrating the Negro.

The fact that McCall did not grow up surrounded by the stereotypical black urban mayhem is what makes his history of violence—mostly directed against other black men and women—so profoundly depressing.

—Henry Louis Gates, Jr.

Like most birthrights, this one is both a blessing and a burden. For one thing, it means that your tale is never completely your own—that the particularity of your tale is subordinated to an overarching narrative. If the goal of autobiography is the assertion of individuality, as has conventionally been understood, the typical black memoir is assigned the contrary task: that of being representative. (One of W. E. B. Du Bois's memoirs bears the portentous subtitle *An Essay Toward an Autobiography of a Race Concept.*) What's exceptional is not the tale you have to tell but the fact that you survived to tell it. As Whitman said, "I am the man, I suffer'd, I was there."

Two of the best-known works in the genre, Claude Brown's 1965 *Manchild in the Promised Land* and Eldridge Cleaver's 1968 *Soul on Ice,* self-consciously drew upon Wright in conjuring up the allure of the so-called Bad Nigger and the disastrous effects of ghetto life on the black male consciousness. At times, these books read like real-life versions of Bigger Thomas's story. Yet it's easy to forget that the social landscape they recorded was a veritable church picnic compared with the bullet-pocked desolation of the inner city now.

Today, advocacy groups declare the black man "an endangered species," and this is supported by reams of numbing statistics. But crisis requires narrative, not simply numbers: sooner or later, every generation must find its voice.

It may be that ours belongs to Nathan McCall, whose memoir is, finally, a stirring tale of transformation: Bigger Thomas becoming Richard Wright. (When I was shown the manuscript of this book last year, I was moved to offer a comment on its place in the canon of African-American literature for the book jacket.) McCall, a Washington *Post* reporter who, as a young man, served prison time for armed robbery, writes affectingly about his first encounter with his fictional alter ego, which comes at the center of his book, amid a harrowing description of prison life. While he is working as the inmate librarian, he picks up a copy of *Native Son* and finds himself unable to put it down:

> I identified strongly with Bigger and the book's narrative. He was twenty, the same age as me. He felt the things I felt, and, like me, he wound up in prison. The book's portrait of Bigger captured all those conflicting feelings—restless anger, hopelessness, a tough façade among blacks and a deep-seated fear of whites—that I'd sensed in myself but was unable to express. Often, during my teenage years, I'd felt like Bigger—headed down a road toward a destruction I couldn't ward off, beaten by forces so large and amorphous that I had no idea how to fight back. I was surprised that somebody had written a book that so closely reflected my experiences and feelings.

When McCall finished reading *Native Son,* he "broke down and sobbed like a baby." More to the point, his encounter with Wright led him to a "fascination with the power of words." He writes, "It blew my mind to think that somebody could take words that described exactly how I felt and put them together in a story like that."

This is a skill that McCall himself came to master. He is a mesmerizing storyteller, whose prose is richly inflected with the vernacular of his time and place. In fact, his colloquial style is so unshowy and unforced that his mastery is easy to overlook. There are no traces here of the anxious autodidact—no labored sentences, no straining for deep thoughts. He doesn't use "urinous" when "pissy" is the right word. He's not just a man with a story to tell; he's a writer.

Among Wright's papers are his notes for *Native Son,* including a sheet bearing the typed heading "Poetic Motifs To Be Woven Into Final Scene." With all due respect, I've always wondered if Wright's need to be "literary" wasn't itself a literary failure; a failure, at least, of nerve. Those "poetic motifs"—hidden like Easter eggs, more for the enjoyment of foraging literary critics than for the enlightenment of readers—seem too transparent a bribe. Is it so wrong to want our naturalism au naturel?

In this respect, McCall's discipline as a newspaperman has served him well. And his sense of pacing is nearly cinematic; scenes flash by as if projected on a screen. He can introduce new characters in a sentence or two and make them come alive. But most impressive are McCall's unflagging powers of retrieval and reconstruction: he never succumbs to the temptation to endow his earlier self with a consciousness beyond his years. The world view of the seventeen-year-old Nathan comes to us unretouched and unvarnished, or so it seems. And again, when he describes how, a few years later, he shot a friend who had insulted his girlfriend, he spares us the high-flown anguish, instead telling us, with disarming directness, "I felt like God. I felt so good and powerful that I wanted to do it again. I felt like I could pull that trigger, and keep on pulling it until I emptied the gun."

Is Nate McCall another Bigger Thomas? In some respects, I'd venture that the young McCall was closer to Bigger Thomas than Richard Wright was. The first part of ***Makes Me Wanna Holler*** gives us a portrait of the artist as serial rapist, stickup artist, drug dealer, gunman, brawler, and burglar. It's no surprise that the earth moved for McCall when he read *Native Son.* And black rage is in plentiful supply in his memoir. "After we reached the ninth grade . . . we fucked up white boys more than we went to class," McCall writes. He recalls one memorable afternoon:

> . . . we double-banked a guy standing at his locker in the area where the wood-shop classes were held. We walked as if we were going to pass him, then Lep hauled off and punched him in the face. Then I popped him in the mouth. He fell back and slammed his head into the lockers. Before I could hit him again, somebody else hit him with a barrage of punches that sent him crashing to the floor. We kicked him in the face and stomped him until blood squirted everywhere. After we finished, we ran out a side door and went home.
>
> I saw that white boy in school about a week later. Walking down the hall, Lep nudged me and pointed him out. He had his arm in a sling and bandages taped to the bridge of his nose. I snickered and told Lep, "We fucked him up *good.*"

Bigger Thomas, by his maker's stipulation, was the product of his environment: the slum, in all its desolation. Bigger competes for floor space with rats in a tenement on Chicago's South Side. But McCall was raised in a world that was working class by mainstream standards and middle class by black standards—a world which bore less resemblance to Richard Wright's soul-destroying South Side than to Gloria Naylor's Linden Hills. His family moved to Cavalier Manor, a black suburb of Portsmouth, Virginia, when he was nine:

> The streets had names such as Belafonte Drive, Basie Crescent, Eckstine Drive, and Horne Avenue. To add to the sense of optimism that the neighborhood was supposed to reflect, they even named one street Freedom Avenue. . . . Our eyes and mouths flew wide open. We saw impressive homes with freshly sprouted lawns, broad side-walks, and newly paved streets. On each side of the street that led to our section of the community were two sets of stately white brick pillars with black cast-iron bars flowing regally through their tops.

Driveways, garages, lawns: this was the sort of place where most black folks could only dream of living. Nor, as he points out, do the clichés about broken families apply to him. His parents were supportive of him and strict with him; his stepfather held two jobs and saved enough to insure that one of the family's two cars was always a late-model Cadillac. Indeed, the stepfather was everything John Calvin envisioned: "My old man had a serious thing about work. My brothers and I would wake up on a Saturday morning and he'd have a *long* list of things for us to do: rake the yard, cut the grass, wash the car, clean the gutters, sweep the walk. . . ." As a kid, McCall was constantly assured that "if you work hard, you can get anything you want in life."

Nevertheless, he spent his adolescence "training" girls (gang-raping them, that is), stomping on street kids, and ripping off stores. And still a bright future awaited him: he was named homecoming king of his high school, and was admitted to Howard University. At his high-school graduation, other black kids in his class walked off with prizes and scholarships—those students traipsing through the hallways with armloads of books, whom McCall had scorned as "no name lame" Negroes. But they clearly represent for him the road not taken. McCall was ultimately bound for success as a journalist, but not before his criminal pursuits resulted in his serving almost three years of a twelve-year prison sentence for armed robbery.

McCall's account of prison life is unsparing, but it seems to be a rare example of how a stint in a correctional facility actually corrected. Being behind bars "forced me to go deep, real deep, within and tap a well I didn't even know I had," McCall writes. "Through that painful trip, I'd found meaning. No longer was life a thing of bewilderment. . . . I knew that there was purpose and design in creation and that my life was somehow part of that grand scheme."

"Purpose and design," of course, are what any memoirist must discover within or impose upon his material. "Post hoc, ergo propter hoc" may be a logical fallacy, but it is the very lifeblood of narrative. And so an age-old problem arises. If telling stories is a way of assigning a chain of causation to acts and events—thus, revealing their "purpose and design"—how does a writer leave room for his character's free choice? *Native Son* veers from rigidly behaviorist to wildly existentialist models of human action: the Communist lawyer, Mr. Max, regards Bigger not as a man but as a type, a walking symptom of an American disease, while Bigger himself, even as he awaits execution, insists with twisted Cartesian certainty, "What I killed for, I *am!*" Nor, in subsequent works, did Wright succeed in resolving his warring intuitions on the subject. McCall knows better than to try.

This tension runs through public-policy discourse as well: Is black America ailing as a result of behavioral or structural causes? (Did you screw up, or did the system screw you?) When McCall theorizes about the problems of black America, he makes much of "the system." When he thinks about his own errancy, however, his mind runs on a different track. As a squad car takes him to the police station—he has just knocked over a hamburger joint—he's not thinking Mr. Max-like thoughts about environmental determinism. He's thinking that he should have listened to his mother. And he's thinking back to his third-grade spelling bee:

> I was an honor student then and felt so full of promise. I had made it to the competition finals but was eliminated after misspelling a word; I think it was "bicycle." *If I could go back to that night on that school stage,* I thought, *I would spell that word right and straighten out all the other things in life that had since gone wrong.*

McCall's reverie of self-recrimination suggests that, just as there are no atheists in the foxhole, there are no behaviorists in the holding cell. In other words, a bad environment might make someone else out there bad, but when it comes to me that explanation never seems quite convincing. Only at the price of relinquishing my own sense of humanity can I believe that I had no hand in my own fate.

And while the character Nathan McCall may display an occasional weakness for early-seventies-style racial Manichaeanism, the writer Nathan McCall is capable of revealing far more complexity and nuance. The old dialectic between fate and will, between social structure and individual agency—a dialectic that has been the shared preoccupation of naturalist fiction and sociological analysis—is rendered in this memoir as a tug-of-war between the two McCalls. Even the protagonist of *Native Son* outwitted his creator's announced desire to present a marionette of external social forces as he took on a dark life force of his own: Bigger Thomas as Coppélia. Somewhere, out there, the Black Boy and the Native Son are still having it out.

After his release from prison, McCall comes to realize both that the deck is stacked against him and that it is up to him to play the cards he has been dealt. He studies journalism at Norfolk State College; joins, then leaves, the American Muslim Mission; and, on graduation, takes a position at the *Virginian Pilot-Ledger Star,* his home-town newspaper. A writer is born:

> The first time I wrote a story as a full-fledged reporter, I stared at my byline a long time. There it was, just below the headline: Nathan McCall. It felt good seeing my name in the newspaper associated with something other than crime. It gave me a rush seeing that name on a document that was read by thousands of people. Sometimes, if I had a front-page story in the paper, I'd stop by newsstands on the street just to stare at my byline. I'd wonder how many people in the region would see that name.

The book's final section traces McCall's journalistic career, which leads him to the Atlanta *Journal-Constitution* and, finally, to the Washington *Post;* we see his attempts to deal with both the racism he perceives among his white colleagues and the difficulties attendant on his own upward mobility, the "crazy high-wire act" of living in "three conflicting worlds—among whites, working-class blacks, and bourgeois Negroes." There's an inevitable slackening of energy—and, perhaps, of perspective—in the book's final stretch, as McCall makes his ascent from b-boy to buppie. Still, the honesty of his self-examination remains unrelenting and often startling. A chapter entitled

"Hell," for example, isn't about coping with racism but about his marriage to Debbie, the woman he married so their son and daughter would have a legal father. McCall is now a successful journalist at a distinguished newspaper, and yet he can still experience a rage so profound that it threatens to demolish the life he has made for himself. In the midst of an unpleasant divorce, McCall finds himself watching Debbie speak and yet unable to hear her, so loud is his fury:

> That familiar tightness formed in my chest, that fight-or-flight feeling that used to come over me in the old days on the streets. I felt it rising, like vomit just before it convulses you and forces its way out of your mouth. I felt myself about to leap up and punch her in the face. I felt it coming over me, and I got scared. I knew that if I got up from that couch and took one swing—*one swing*—it would get *good* to me and I wouldn't stop. I wouldn't stop until I was completely exhausted or until my ex-wife was stone cold dead. As I sat there, mute, the voices of divorce veterans kept whispering, competing for control: *Knock that bitch's front teeth out. No, take the high road.*

Instead of taking a swing, McCall gets counselling, and comes to understand that "none of my domestic problems related directly to my race—divorce is a universal hell." When Debbie states before the divorce judge that she is afraid of her husband—a man who had, after all, been jailed for a violent crime—McCall is outraged. Yet he tells us that if it hadn't been for the calming words of a counsellor he probably would have killed her. McCall could easily have ended up like his former running partners, whom he reflects on toward the end of his book, as he takes a cruise through his old neighborhood:

> There was Steve and his brother, who both committed suicide, and Charlene, whose husband murdered her. Charlene had taught me how to hand-dance. And there was Jack, who blew his old man away with a shotgun blast. Ronald Bailey and Gibbs had gotten killed. The list of those dead was far too long for guys our age. Worse still was the list of those brothers who were drug zombies. They were breathing, but were more dead than alive. Teeth missing from their mouths. Skin pallid and ashen. Eyes vacant, and hearts cold as ice in winter.

What went wrong? That plaintive question fairly bleats through the pages. The fact that McCall did not grow up surrounded by the stereotypical black urban mayhem is what makes his history of violence—mostly directed against other black men and women—so profoundly depressing. As he recognizes, no social program, no Marshall Plan for the cities, would have saved a Nathan McCall, since he already had all the things whose lack is said to cause black suffering—the caring, stable two-parent family, the role models, the basic financial stability.

After Claude Brown's *Manchild in the Promised Land* was published, one reviewer wrote that his "miraculous autobiography suffers from a canker: the miracle of his salvation is presented brilliantly, but the causes for it remain vague." I suspect some will upbraid McCall for the opposite omission. He has a ready explanation for why he got back on track when most of his fellow-inmates returned to their old ways: he had that stable and supportive family; he was aware that "even when I chose the gutter, I'd always had a frame of reference for a better life." But why did he choose the gutter in the first place?

I read ***Makes Me Wanna Holler*** with a sense of both recognition and consternation. McCall and I are only a few years apart in age, so I share his cultural references; my old man, like his, was an unskilled worker who held two jobs. The warm-bath intimacy of the all-black world that McCall grew up in is familiar to me. But as for how a Bigger Thomas emerged from all this, McCall ultimately doesn't have a clue, and neither do I.

This isn't necessarily a failing. Instead, I think, McCall's refusal to reach for easy solutions is a sign of the fierce honesty that infuses the entire book; he's willing to address the question without pretending to have an answer to it. He can readily supply the proximate cause: bad influences of a subculture in which recreational gang rape was a fun alternative to stickball, and to shoot somebody for dissing you was the quickest way to establish your credibility as a real man. But what of those who emerged unscathed, those "no name lame" Negroes from school? McCall had been among their number before he succumbed to the romance of the street, and two of his brothers grew up to be decent, hardworking men without a detour.

One explanation that McCall flirts with amplifies something Mr. Max told Bigger Thomas: "You're trying to believe in yourself. And every time you try to find a way to live, your own mind stands in the way. You know why that is? It's because others have said you were bad and they made you live in bad conditions." When McCall encountered this passage, he "wept uncontrollably." Black people, he comes to believe, suffer poor self-esteem, even self-hatred, as the result of internalized oppression; these demons hound them even when those "bad conditions" are absent. And the tinselly notion of self-esteem is repeatedly invoked throughout the book. (At one point, he posits poor self-esteem as the real source of Southern white racism as well.)

The only trouble with this notion is that it explains too much. The world is full of well-behaved men and women who spend their sessions at the therapist discussing their lack of self-esteem; a self-esteem problem is just about the only difficulty that Bigger Thomas and the white heiress he kills would have had in common. Is bloodshed in Bed-Stuy to be assigned the same root cause as bulimia in Brookline? "All of America needs to be on the couch," McCall has said. But we know that in the age of Prozac the couch has an increasingly tenuous role; and while the temptation to reduce politics to psychology is not a new one, it may be more hazardous than ever. (I don't think I exaggerate: a recent article in *Newsweek* tells us that studies have connected violence to low serotonin levels in the brain, leading some clinicians to speculate about the usefulness of serotonin-boosters like Prozac in addressing the problem.)

McCall's final words on the subject of where he and his friends went wrong are curiously tentative. He sees that "the problems among us are more complex than something we can throw jobs, social programs, or more policemen at," and suggests that the trouble may have something to do with the way we perceive our life chances. Although "the reality may well have been that possibilities for us were abundant," he writes, "we perceived our choices as being somewhat limited." Again, there's something to this, but it doesn't quite measure up to the explanatory task at hand: it doesn't make comprehensible the bullets, the rapes, the robberies, and the sheer terrorism that McCall and his friends wreaked upon their community.

In his classic essay "How Bigger Was Born," Richard Wright wrestled with the same question. Emphasizing the point that Bigger is a type rather than an individual, he writes, "I'd better indicate more precisely the nature of the environment that produced these men, or the reader will be left with the impression that they were essentially and organically bad." He goes on to identify two factors that were always "psychologically dominant": first, Bigger had become "estranged from the religion and the folk culture of his race"; and, second, he was "trying to react to and answer the call of the dominant civilization whose glitter came to him through the newspapers, magazines, radios, movies, and the mere imposing sight and sound of daily American life." No doubt these are half-truths—Wright had no real answers, either—but half-truths in such matters may be the best we can hope for. Perhaps McCall cannot tell us why he made the choices he did, but at least he can bear witness to the results: I am the man, I suffer'd, I was there.

The Negro, Wright famously averred, was "America's metaphor." But he had more specific ambitions for his own creation; Bigger Thomas, he believed, would prove "a symbolic figure of American life, a figure who would hold within him the prophecy of our future." ***Makes Me Wanna Holler*** is about the unfolding of that dire prophecy, no more and no less. Fifty years later, Bigger lives on.

Anchee Min
Red Azalea

Born in 1957, Min is a Chinese-born memoirist now living in the United States.

INTRODUCTION

Recounting Min's coming of age and sexual awakening in Communist China during the 1960s and 1970s, *Red Azalea* (1994) details how the private lives of individuals were affected by the political indoctrination that permeated Chinese society under the regime of Chairman Mao Tse-tung. A series of vignettes related through Min's precise and sparse language, *Red Azalea* begins with Min as a child; she cares for younger siblings in a dilapidated, multi-family dwelling, while her parents work long hours in a factory. Min also works diligently at school, becoming one of the best students in her class. However, her faith in Mao's vision for China is severely tested when she is forced to denounce one of her favorite teachers. In 1974 she is sent to a youth camp, an assignment that separates her from her family and introduces her to a life of intense, regimented labor in which individual needs are sacrificed for the sake of the Revolution. Despite threats of punishment, including execution, Min develops an attraction for one of her female comrades. Sustained through the hardships at the camp by her love of Revolutionary operas, Min is unexpectedly selected as an actress for the government's musical productions and propaganda films. Apparently destined for a leading role in the Cultural Revolution, she engages in a surreptitious affair with a man known as the "Supervisor," who helps her attain the leading role in *Red Azalea,* a film about the life of Mao's wife, Comrade Jiang Qing. Min's harsh but upwardly mobile path collapses with the death of Mao in 1976, and she is immediately demoted to a custodial position in the studio where she had recently been a leading actress. In 1984, nearly penniless and able to speak little English, Min came to the United States under the sponsorship of a fellow actress who had previously immigrated. She began writing *Red Azalea* as an assignment for an English class, and over the course of seven years she worked through the painful psychological toll of her experiences in Communist China. Critics have applauded the book as an important case study of the Cultural Revolution's impact on average citizens. Although some reviewers disliked her short, sharp sentences and her use of anglicized Chinese names, others praised the stark bluntness of Min's story and the power of its language. As Laura Shapiro and Karen Springen have argued, "much of [*Red Azalea*'s] strength lies in [Min's] prose, as delicate and evocative as a traditional Chinese brush painting."

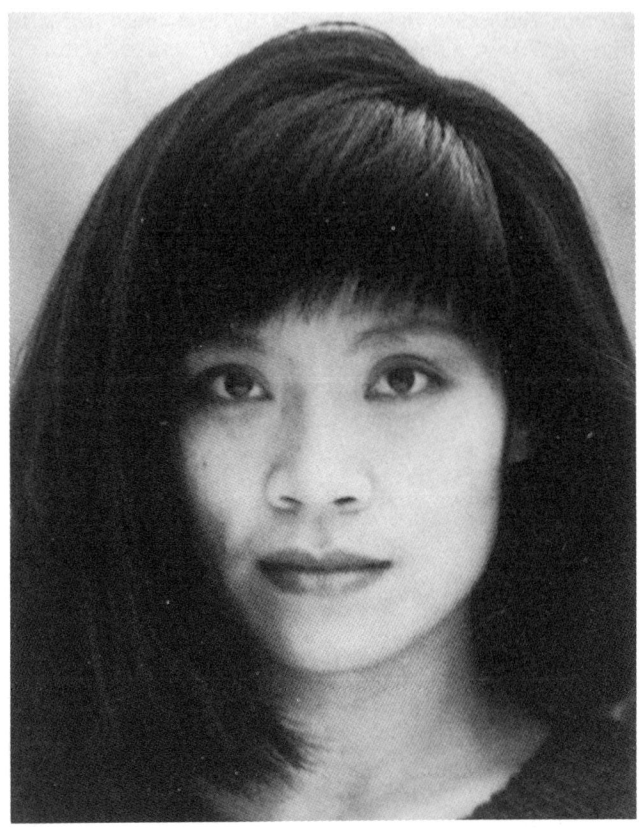

CRITICISM

Penelope Mesic (review date January 1994)

SOURCE: "Freedom Writer," in *Chicago,* Vol. 43, January, 1994, pp. 55-7, 112-14.

[*In the following review, based in part on a conversation with Min, Mesic discusses Min's first years in the United States and her struggle to deal with the brutality she endured in China.*]

Nine years ago a young woman named Anchee Min left mainland China to come to Chicago. She was 26 years old, had never flown before, spoke no English, and was weak from being compelled to do menial work despite recurrent, untreated bouts of pneumonia—an informal punishment for wanting to emigrate. Yet as the plane began its descent, the lights along the lake were so dazzling—"In Chinese cities there are not lights like these at night," she explains—that she thought of her father's passion for astronomy and his fantasy of flying to the stars. "Is this heaven?" she wondered. "Is this a different planet?"

In fact, the distance between her old life and the new is so great that the answer could almost be yes. Min grew up in extreme poverty amid the turmoil and repression of the Cultural Revolution, then at 17 was sent to a grim communal farm for three years of backbreaking labor. A rare chance—being chosen to play the lead in a film biography of Jiang Qing, the wife of Mao Tse-tung—turned sour when Mao died and his widow was jailed by her political rivals. Min abruptly fell from favor.

A friend, the actress Joan Chen, interceded, and Min was accepted as a student at the School of the Art Institute of Chicago. After learning English, she put her old experiences and her new freedom to use and wrote a powerful true account of her life in China. The agent who handled Amy Tan's blockbuster *The Joy Luck Club* agreed to represent Min and sold the story to Pantheon Books, which will publish ***Red Azalea*** in February. Min's editor at Pantheon considers it "our biggest book of the season" and a potential bestseller. The memoir has been chosen as a featured selection by two book clubs, the film rights have been optioned, and Min is scheduled to make a ten-city promotional tour. Recalling the past, Min seems almost stunned by her present success and prosperity.

On a bright afternoon last October, Min was dressed in the thoroughly American costume of oversize yellow sweater and black leggings. She had spent the morning in the equally American pastime of planning her daughter Lauryan's second birthday party. In China, Min says, she had lived with her family in a two-room apartment where three families shared a single toilet. Here she and her husband own a late-Victorian brick apartment building in Bridgeport that they have rehabbed together.

Min now exercises her artistic freedom not only as a writer but also as a painter and a photographer At last she can affirm the value of private feelings over the crushingly impersonal interests of the state. And she stands to gain enormously from her honesty. ***Red Azalea*** was published in England last fall, where a reviewer for the London *Times* wrote that it was "as simple as a young girl's diary and as evocative as the most skilled poetry." That praise doesn't really convey the book's urgency and power, for it reveals the human cost of political intrigue, sexual repression, and draconian punishment for anyone showing signs of the grave crime of "bourgeois individualism."

The one constant amid so much change is Anchee Min herself. The same qualities—intelligence, discipline, keen powers of observation, determination—that made her a leader of the Little Red Guard in grade school have helped her here. Overcoming the obstacles of a new language and a different culture, she has risen overnight (before ***Red Azalea*** she had published only two brief articles) to the top of a crowded and competitive field. But as her book makes clear, the New York publishing industry has nothing—in terms of crowds and competition—to compare with an underdeveloped country of one billion where cutthroat clandestine rivalries flourish.

Min grew up in Shanghai, a waterfront city always in the forefront of political and artistic movements. She was born in 1957 and from the age of five cared for two younger sisters and a younger brother, while her parents—prevented by policies of the Cultural Revolution from working at jobs commensurate with their education—struggled to earn enough to keep them alive. Min's brother was so thin, so raggedly dressed in hand-me-downs, that the neighbors called him "Flea."

Yet there were others so poor that they envied even the Mins. Below them was a family of 11, forced to live in one room, who coveted the Mins' four-room apartment. They tried to drive the Mins out by emptying their chamberpots onto the Mins' bedding. Next, an elder daughter, feigning madness, slashed Anchee's mother with a pair of scissors and threatened the children with an ax. The local shapers of the Cultural Revolution, having abolished the police in Shanghai as "a revisionist mechanism," had basically abandoned the city to chaos. The Mins believed they had no recourse but to put up notices asking to exchange their apartment for someone else's. The next day a burly man and his four grown sons arrived with their belongings in a truck, administered a preemptive beating to the neighbors' "mad" daughter, and forced the Mins out—to a much worse two-room apartment over a welding-equipment factory, where Anchee's parents live to the present day. While Anchee Min, ten at the time, speaks of the incident without a word of criticism for her parents' gentle inability to prevail, it is evident that it was a bitterly formative experience.

And yet as a child, she innocently espoused the system under which she lived. At one point she even considered denouncing her father, who was sometimes less than enthusiastic about government policies and encouraged her to think for herself. At another time, she recalls, "I was looking for a chance to save somebody and die, like one 12-year-old girl who had saved three children from a railroad track. The train ran over her legs and she got to see Mao and be a national hero." Min laughs. "One day a tricycle went in the street and I pulled the child out of the way, but no one reported my good deed, and I didn't die. I was so disappointed."

When the party introduced a new humanitarian campaign, she embraced the cause wholeheartedly. "They showed us pictures like starving Somalis and told us they were children in the United States. We didn't know not to believe. 'What do you do?' was the big slogan. So I led my class to collect papers for recycling, for which we got seven cents a pound to donate." In 1972, Min remembers, estrangement from the United States took a different form: fear of an air attack. "We practiced air-raid drills at midnight, dug foxholes—we were so scared of Americans."

Xian-Ming Yuan has known Min since 1970, when the two girls were Little Red Guard leaders together, and is now a computer expert in Massachusetts. "In the beginning we truly, truly, truly believed, and loved to see the party's slogans everywhere," she says. "As leaders we put the slogans up in classrooms. But after a while we were tired of that. The words seemed funny and meaningless"—an opinion that the girls, whose thoughts turned to foreign literature, drawing, and astronomy, could never openly express.

But before this period of doubt, when Min's belief was most fervent, an excruciating conflict arose. A teacher whose name means "Autumn Leaves" in English was Min's favorite. After studying in the United States, she had returned to China to teach. Affectionate and dedicated, she added enthralling fairy tales from the West to the curriculum. Perhaps because those qualities made her stand out—"In China you're promoted up, up, and then to jail," Min says, not joking—the young Anchee was encouraged by the local party secretary to denounce the woman as a "secret agent of the imperialists." The child struggled to decide whether the accusation was true. "One day when it was raining hard, the teacher gave students her raincoat, rainshoes, and umbrella as they went home. She went home wet," Min remembers. But the party secretary was relentless in his arguments; Min was won over, and Autumn Leaves was brought before a crowd of 2,000 people, including her own students and colleagues.

A nightmarish scene followed. Two men twisted the teacher's arm to compel a confession. She was kicked and manhandled. Her eyeglasses fell off. As the crowd roared threats at the teacher, Min, dizzy, her hands shaking, read the denunciation. Unexpectedly, the teacher squatted on her heels and confronted the child seriously, kindly, exactly as if seeking to explain a problem in math. "My heart felt like a boiling teapot," Min writes in ***Red Azalea***. Unable to back down, hating the beloved teacher precisely because her remembered kindness made the task of denunciation more difficult, she screamed a final accusation. When her parents found out what she had done, her mother, unworldly but principled, herself a teacher, locked the child out of the house for six hours and threatened to disown her. The teacher, lucky to escape imprisonment, was exiled from China for 11 years. When she returned, and by chance encountered Min, the teacher pretended not to recognize her. "I was not forgiven," Min writes with horrible finality.

In conversation, Min points out that this coercive process was tragic but unremarkable—there were countless public denunciations all over the country. "The party encouraged you to do things to show you were a revolutionary." Those things were *meant* to be painful. The pain was proof of one's selfless commitment. "Kids denounced their parents," says Min. She adds that it was hard to write about the episode with her teacher, but necessary because it was a lack of self-examination—of one's motives and responsibilities—that had led to the Cultural Revolution in the first place. Defiantly she adds, "I'm not afraid. If people read this about me and say, 'Anchee Min, you're such a terrible person,' I say, 'So? Who's not?' "

Her editor at Pantheon, Dan Frank, points to the passage as one that convinced him of the truthfulness of Anchee Min's account. "Her portrayal of herself is not necessarily a flattering one," he says. "You could accuse her of being manipulative or cold. It's such unflinching honesty."

Min is equally frank about what might be regarded as the book's central episode, when, at the age of 17, she was sent to Red Fire Farm. "Because the cities were so crowded," she explains, "one child from each family had to go to the countryside." It was a leveling policy that deliberately denied a college education to many of the brightest students, including Min. A truck carried the young people from Shanghai—Min didn't ride in a car until she was 20—to a uniquely unpromising stretch of land by the East China Sea. "The land was salt; everything did poorly there," she says. "The cotton we raised was nearly too poor in quality to use. We could not feed ourselves on what we grew."

In a particularly vivid passage she describes the stiff native reeds, which pushed back up despite every effort to eradicate them, not only competing with the crops but poking through the dirt floor of the bedroom she shared with seven other young women and penetrating her thin mattress. Clearly, for Min, they came to symbolize the inhospitable nature of the place. Later, looking at a photograph of one of her paintings, she indicates some bending vertical lines. "Look, those reeds have even gotten in here," she says, smiling faintly. The heat and insects, the heavy agricultural work done with few modern implements, the poverty and the hunger—"We dug up sweet potatoes at night and ate them raw," she remembers—made the life harsh. The rivalries, denunciations, and lack of prospects made it intolerable.

Some of the 13,000 workers sought dangerous consolation with one another. In ***Red Azalea,*** Min describes a barbarous event arising from that impulse. A beautiful young girl named Little Green, delicate, cheerful, well groomed, the grand-daughter of a Chinese opera singer, met secretly—but not secretly enough—with a thin, bespectacled young man. Led by the company commander, Yan Sheng, an energetic, broad-shouldered woman with glossy pigtails, a group of workers armed with flashlights and rifles crept up on the couple and caught them in the act. Min participated in the ambush, experiencing a horrible sense of disloyalty to her friend. She later explained the official position: "A good female comrade was supposed to devote all her energy, her youth, to the Revolution; she was not permitted to think about a man until she reached her late 20s." Four days of "intensive mind rebrushing" compelled Little Green to describe the encounter as a rape. In an impromptu trial in the cafeteria, her lover was sentenced to death. Little Green went mad. Later, the company commander, Yan, came to blame herself bitterly.

The incident chilled Min's revolutionary fervor. She came to regard the ambush and its aftermath as a fundamental outrage against the most necessary human need for intimacy. "The culture since Confucius encourages sacrificing your own self for the community. But the basic human desires cannot be repressed," she says. "They come out in other forms, often evil ones."

Despite the obvious risks, she had a love affair while at Red Fire Farm, and one potentially even more dangerous. Her partner was Yan, the camp commander. The two women fell into conversation one evening when the dashing commander, whom Min clearly hero-worshiped, was playing her erh-hu (a stringed instrument) in the commune's abandoned brickyard. Soon they were taking every opportunity to meet privately, at first only for companionship. Yan made Min a platoon leader, assigning her to sleep in the bunk above her own. For greater privacy from the other six women sleeping in the room, they left the mosquito nets around their bed unwashed and, within their dusty folds, embraced one another.

Asked if it had been embarrassing to write so frankly about their relationship, Min says, "I never thought of the question in this way. I thought I'd better be honest from head to toe. If I can't be true to myself, it's meaningless. Someone did research on modern Chinese women and found they are ashamed of sex, think it's an animal thing, disgusting. In America, on *Oprah Winfrey,* women are able to speak the unspeakable." She regards the relationship between herself and Yan as entirely natural. "It's not my point to write eroticism. It's about loving, being human in an inhuman environment. I'm lucky I had it. It's not man and woman or woman and woman; it's another person, another mind—that's the love affair."

Sexual repression, Min thinks, is merely one aspect of a larger problem. "My Chinese friends say: 'You are talking about things that have never been said in China.' It's against the Chinese nature to examine the inner world of feelings. We are trained to neglect our emotional needs."

Because their relationship was their only solace, Yan and Min continued to creep into each other's beds at night, although there was an added element of danger. Lu, a platoon leader jealous of Yan's command, began spying on them. An additional complication was that what can only be called government talent scouts had come to the farm in search of a promising young woman to play the lead in *Red Azalea,* a film version of the life of Jiang Qing, the wife of Mao Tse-tung. Min was being considered as the farm's candidate for the role, to compete against girls from all over China. It was a unique opportunity to return to the far easier life of the city, and she seized it with both hands. On the farm, she says, "people died like cockroaches. You think how to come out of this death pit. People chop off their fingers to go back to the city." Shrewdly, to convey an appropriate look of revolutionary dedication, she wore Yan's old military uniform, washed until it was faded to white, to what we would call the auditions. "A healthy look, a peasant quality," she says, was her greatest asset.

But Lu's insinuations about irregular relations between Yan and Min were beginning to jeopardize her chances. To play Jiang Qing, an actress had to exemplify revolutionary qualities, among them sexual purity. Ironically, Min later learned from an intimate of Jiang that she and China's leader had particularly enjoyed the danger of making love during enemy shelling. To remove suspicion from Anchee Min, the company commander pretended that she and Lu—the accuser—had in fact been lovers. Her selfless act doomed her to a demotion, but freed Min to go to Shanghai, one of five actresses who would train for a year before vying for the part of Jiang.

The five women, fierce rivals, lived together in a tumbledown cottage—luxurious compared with Red Fire Farm—on the grounds of the movie studio. The older actress responsible for their training, spiteful because she herself had no opportunity for the role, singled out another girl, a sly but talented beauty named Cheering Spear, as her favorite. When the filming began, Min had the job of set clerk—a position that covered the important tasks usually handled by an assistant director and menial jobs such as sweeping the floor. But well into shooting, the project mysteriously evoked official disfavor. In the shakeup that followed, Min replaced the first actress as Jiang. Going through a few stills from the production, she indicates one that shows her fending off an unidentified enemy of the people, and says, laughing, "That's me. Always with a gun."

With her new, more important role, Min was brought into intimate contact—and began a love affair—with a shadowy, androgynous high party official who was serving as the film's director. In ***Red Azalea*** this figure is identified only as "The Supervisor." He lived in spacious, elegantly furnished surroundings, smoked four packs of cigarettes a day at a time when smoking was regarded as a wasteful personal indulgence, and spoke with a reckless lack of political correctness. When Min objected that people would laugh at some artificial-sounding lines of dialogue, he answered, "Who do you think people are? They are walking corpses. The only thing they know is fear. That is why they need authority. They need a wise emperor. It's been that way for 5,000 years."

But just as Min was being initiated into the cynical honesty of real power, disaster struck. On September 9, 1976, Mao died. With his death, the authority of his wife drained away. Min puts it so vividly in ***Red Azalea:*** "The gossip grew fat, greasy, like a dish of pork neck," that Mao had been murdered by his wife. Within days, she was in jail, and crowds, dancing in the street "like boiling dumplings," called for her torture and death. The Supervisor, one of Jiang Qing's chief supporters, was clearly doomed. His best chance, he thought, was to get his name put on a list of mental patients, rather than one of traitors to the state. He had just enough time to pull strings at the studio, countermanding Min's banishment back to Red Fire Farm, before he disappeared.

The next six years were desolate. "I was forced to work as a set clerk again despite illness," Min says. "If I do not go to work, I lose my city permit"—which would essentially constitute exile to the countryside. Her applications to attend a university were denied unless, officials said, she was accepted at a foreign university. "That's like saying you can go to the moon if you want to," Min explains. But unexpectedly, in 1983, an actress whom she had met at the Shanghai film studio, Joan Chen, wrote and offered help. Chen had left Shanghai to appear in international productions, among them *The Last Emperor,* and she volunteered to find a school in the United States that would accept Min without test results demonstrating a knowledge of English.

"I had to do some tricks to get here. I wanted this so hard," Min says. "The studio finally let me go because I convinced them I wouldn't denounce my country." Meanwhile, Chen had found a place that required no proof of competency in English, the School of the Art Institute of Chicago. Min was accepted.

"I had my toughest job as an actress making my application to the American consulate," Min remembers. "I had a friend who wrote up what I had to say in English, and I memorized it. I was dressed in my mother's clothes, a green skirt and an old lady's blouse, and went into the consul general's office. She had these bright-green cat's eyes"—she points to her own eyes and opens them wide—"and it was the closest I had ever been to a Western person. It scared me, but I said my words right into her face. And then I kept showing her my paintings, explaining them so she couldn't ask me questions, because how would I know what she's asking? Finally I heard her say about the only English word I knew: 'OK.' And I go to myself, 'OK.' That's good, right? That means yes?

"I went to the next office and the translator there says, 'It's amazing. The consul general must be in a good mood today. She said she is giving you a visa because you are *just so determined.*' " With a proud, fierce look, she repeats it. " 'So determined.' "

And yet Min almost didn't make it into the country. A customs agent in San Francisco asked her a question. When she didn't answer, he held her back, surprised that a foreign student had no knowledge of the language. A translator conveyed his suspicions. Min took a bold course. "I said, 'It's true. But if I don't learn the language in half a year, I'll deport myself.' The translator lied for me and told the customs guy I was just nervous."

Once in Chicago, she lived for a few months with a cousin she had never met before coming to this country, who nevertheless treated her generously and made sure that she received treatment to cure her lingering pneumonia. Then, living on her own, she applied the resolute self-discipline she had summoned to survive on Red Fire Farm. "So I would learn the language, I did not allow myself to see any Chinese. I ate no Chinese food. I worked as a waitress, delivery messenger, in a fabric-painting shop, and babysitting."

Her friend Xien-Ming Yuan, who came to this country several years later, describes something that made coming to the United States particularly hard. "We had been told America was a terrible place, full of monsters. Gradually we were thinking surely the United States couldn't be the same as we were told." But what was it like? "It was a blank. Scary. Very shocking. We had made the choice to come here and spiritually to fulfill ourselves. But I don't know how many times I cried—and Anchee, too."

One of Min's earliest American friends was Michelle Smith, a fellow student at the School of the Art Institute. "This was her first or second semester," Smith, who now owns an antique shop, recalls. "We had a teacher who was a nice guy but overbearing. I was shy and she was in alien territory, and it was very horrible. We talked a lot together about art, political things, the social structure, and she always said she was glad I didn't ask about her past in China—the same questions everyone asked."

In 1988, Min met another student who didn't need to ask the same old questions. Newly arrived from Shanghai, Qigu Jiang was, like Min, a painter and a freethinker, whose exhibition had been shut down by the government. "It was a very dangerous time," Jiang recalls. At their first meeting he and Min had only their dislike for each other in common. "I thought she was no good; she thought, This is not the kind of man I like," Jiang says, laughing. But realizing how much they shared, they were married in a hasty civil ceremony, which Jiang recalls rather wistfully: "No family was there. When the judge says, 'Kiss the bride,' it wasn't even a kiss, just her hair brushing my cheek."

And yet, as Min established a life here, her thoughts returned to her past life in China. She wrote about Red Fire Farm for a writing course at the Art Institute. "The teacher said, 'Interesting, but you're a poor writer,' " she recalls. "I showed it to Joan Chen and she sent it to a friend, Mark Sulzman, who wrote *Iron and Silk,*" who in turn sent it to his agent. Eventually Min sent the story to the prestigious literary magazine *Granta.* "I didn't put return postage because I couldn't afford it," Min says. "Six months later I get a call from an editor there, Kim Addams. 'We're going to publish it. You'll be with a lot of great writers like Salman Rushdie,' she told me. And I said, 'Who's Salman Rushdie?' "

On the basis of the *Granta* article, which appeared in spring of 1992, Sandy Dijkstra, Amy Tan's agent, sold what was to become ***Red Azalea*** to Pantheon for a $75,000 advance. With her usual iron self-discipline, Min put the money in the bank and didn't touch it: "In case they don't want the book and I have to give the money back." She completed the manuscript on Christmas Day, 1992. "I was vomiting, my whole body was shaking after a year of living my past life and having to face myself." In a single sentence she describes her powerful, conflicting feelings: "I was so driven and so glad to be given the opportunity."

She says she doesn't know if she will write another book, feeling drained after the first one, "like I give birth to myself." But her editor, Dan Frank, feels sure that she will write more, saying that she has a writer's memory for detail and that not speaking English like a native has produced a startling freshness of language. "She doesn't know the common clichés—she has to invent her own way of saying things. I've tried to change what she's written as little as possible." A marvelously vivid example of what Frank is talking about occurs in an exchange between the grown-up Anchee and her mother: "My mother said she didn't believe evilness should rule. 'It's ruling,' I said." The word "evilness" has a quirky, awkward sharpness, which contrasts with the speed of Min's slightly unidiomatic rejoinder. In two lines she captures her mother's wistful naïveté and her own brisk realism. Her powers of description, her way with dialogue, her faithfulness to the story all confirm Frank's opinion that Min should write other books.

Since writing ***Red Azalea,*** Min has returned to her native city for an exhibition of her artwork and five evenings of readings at the Shanghai Municipal Center, a posh, modern glass-and-brick structure that reflects China's new prosperity under something closer to a free-enterprise system. "They allow me back because they think I brought the country honor and respect—that's before they read the book," Min says, laughing. She looks at snapshots taken at the readings—of her mother, the mayor of Shanghai, and old friends, among crowds of more than 1,000. Her editor says that these public readings before so many people in a position to know whether Min's story is true are further proof, if any were needed, of her veracity. They are also proof of her popularity, for as Min says, she is now treated as something of a hero for daring to speak honestly about the system. Yet the book will not appear in China, and Min's father tries to avoid danger by telling neighbors he hasn't read it and doesn't know what it is about.

Min still writes to friends in Shanghai. "We use a kind of code," she says. But she has never again seen the mysteriously elegant Supervisor or learned his fate, nor has she seen her lover Yan Sheng. "It would be like eating in front of a starving child," she says. The differences in their circumstances are simply too great.

All of Min's siblings have left China. "Her brother is in Japan; her sister Blooming lives here in Chicago with her husband and child; her sister Carol has moved to Austria," says her husband, Qigu Jiang. "They're quite an international family."

Min's parents have come to the United States for visits. "I want to have them here, but my mother has had a stroke," she says. "It's so cruel. By the time I can give her the chance to enjoy herself, her mind is gone." But Min's father, now the director of the Shanghai Children's Palace Planetarium, enjoyed his last visit, particularly meetings with officials of the Adler Planetarium, with whom he could discuss his beloved astronomy. "He knew in English the name of every constellation, every scientific word," Min says. "But when they said, 'Let's eat,' he needed a translation."

Min still feels, in her father's words, as if she has journeyed to the stars. "I wake up in the night and cannot believe I am here, cannot believe I drive a car. I'm so used to American freedom to say what I think now. I've become American," Min says. "I don't think my daughter, raised here, will ever have my appreciation of America."

Margo Jefferson (review date 26 January 1994)

SOURCE: "Growing Up amid the Conflicts of Ideology and Life," in *The New York Times,* January 26, 1994, p. C19.

[*In the following review, Jefferson provides a positive assessment of* Red Azalea.]

In a movie theater recently, when *Farewell My Concubine* ended, the man behind me turned to his companion and announced, "Well, it might not be the most sophisticated *film* I've ever seen, but what it shows us about life in China. . . ."

I found it a very sophisticated film, and one that showed much more than a social realist view of repression in imperial nationalist and Communist China. *Farewell My Concubine* also explored questions dear to postmodern Westerners: questions of sexual impulse and identity, of the treacherous balance of power between lovers, or friends, or teachers and students, and of the process by which a soul is patched together then broken apart by public ideology and private longing.

Red Azalea, Anchee Min's memoir of her life in Communist China, has this same reach. Part of it reads like raw testimony; part of it reads like epic drama, and part of it reads like poetic incantation.

Anchee Min was born in Shanghai in 1957 and reared on the teachings of Chairman Mao and the operas of Madame Mao, "Comrade Jiang Qing." Her parents were teachers who had to struggle to support four children, and Anchee, the oldest, was a tough-minded babysitter by the age of 5. She was smart, too, and when the Cultural Revolution got under way she became a leader in her school's Little Red Guard. By the age of 13 she was a little tyrant in the making, able to denounce a favorite teacher to the political authorities and able to draft a cunningly worded speech that protected her mother from the same fate. "We were fighting for the final peace of the planet," she writes. "Not for a day did I not feel heroic. I was the opera."

That heroism underwent severe stress when she was removed from school at 17 and sent to Red Fire Farm, a vast labor collective on the China Sea, to be placed, in her vice principal's words, "in the category of becoming a peasant."

At Red Fire Farm Ms. Min worked in the rice fields from 5 in the morning to 9 at night. Her best friend was a spirited young woman named Little Green, who dared to tie her braids with brightly colored string when everyone else tied theirs with mud-brown rubber bands. Still, she did not speak out when Little Green was caught making love with a young man and, after being forced into "intensive mind rebrushing," went mad.

One day, when Ms. Min was alone in the brick factory, she heard someone playing a song from a banned opera on a two-stringed banjo. The opera was about a pair of doomed lovers; the woman playing the forbidden song was the company's force leader, Yan. And at this point the story becomes a subversive opera in the making. To be its heroine, Anchee must learn to disdain every rule she has ever been taught.

The first transgression is that of friendship: she and Yan, always meeting in secret, tell each other their life stories, mock the "Little Red Book" and exchange fumbling inquiries about sex. The next transgression is that of romance, for through a series of elaborate, even courtly twists, the women become lovers. Danger abounds—will they be caught? how will they be punished?—when the deus ex machina arrives in true Hollywood fashion. Jiang Qing is reforming China's film industry, and her associates are scouring the country for suitably valiant-looking peasants and workers who can be trained to act.

At this point, Ms. Min's story becomes a movie, full of uneasy but gripping shifts between George Cukor melodrama and Ingmar Bergman expressionism.

Ms. Min finds herself in a Shanghai film studio competing

with a small claque of desperate starlets for the lead role in *Red Azalea,* the triumphant saga of Comrade Jiang Qing's life. She loses the part to a rival (a scenery-chewing "big tear machine"), and is reduced to scrubbing the set floors until the film's director, an elegant, faintly sinister man known only as the supervisor, notices her. Again, the affair begins with that most erotic of encounters: a furtively honest exchange. "The Supervisor asked me if he could have a cigarette. I lit the cigarette. His fingers were fine and smooth like a woman's. I lit the cigarette and gave it to him. The smoke we exhaled joined in the air."

We cut to frantic rehearsals, to fraught secret meetings with Yan, and to a park with the Supervisor, a park where Shanghai citizens come nightly to meet and mate, or to watch and masturbate, risking their reputations as patrolmen scan the bushes with flashlights, shouting, "Beware of reactionary activities!" The Supervisor deposes Ms. Min's rival and gives her the role of Red Azalea. "If it was love I shared with Yan," she writes, "it was ambition I shared with the Supervisor, to exceed ourselves, our time, to reach beyond our spoiled minds." And when feuds over the script's political content spoil that dream, the bottom line remains. "I paid a price at Red Fire Farm to get to play the role," Ms. Min says starkly. "I no longer cared whether other people would enjoy Comrade Jiang Qing's opera heroines. Red Azalea had become my life."

That life ended in 1976, when Chairman Mao died and Comrade Jiang Qing was arrested and denounced. In serious danger himself, the Supervisor stopped her from being deported to the farm, but could not stop her from being demoted to a menial studio job.

Ms. Min scrubbed floors for six years, sick with tuberculosis, fearful, "a stone, deaf to passion." She omits the details of how she managed to leave China, except for noting that her departure was set in motion by a letter from the actress Joan Chen, who had been in film training with her: At first, she writes, "the idea was as foreign to me as being asked to live on the moon, the moon as my father described it—icy, airless and soundless. Yet my despair made me fearless . . . I fought for my way and I arrived in America on Sept. 1, 1984."

That is the way Ms. Min talks. "My despair made me fearless." "The Supervisor had charged me with his lust the night before. I was like a bullet lying in the chamber of a gun." "She asked me to feel her heart. I wished I was the blood in that chamber." It was passion and despair that made her fearless; it was fearlessness that made her a writer.

Rhoda Koenig (review date 31 January 1994)

SOURCE: A review of *Red Azalea,* in *New York* Magazine, Vol. 27, No. 5, January 31, 1994, p. 63.

[*Below, Koenig favorably reviews* Red Azalea.]

An agricultural worker who was selected from the rice fields for movie stardom, Anchee Min has a marvelous story to tell, but her account of her own career is less fantastic than her portrait of everyday life in China during the Cultural Revolution. The Maoists did all they could to promote cooperation, and produced a society riven with envy and hatred; they tried to drive out such inefficient emotions as lust and love, and created a country of perverts and hysterics. In 1967, when Min was 10 years old, the neighbors, angry because her family had a bigger apartment than theirs, poured the contents of their chamber pots over the Mins' furnishings and threatened them with an ax. ("There were no police. The police station was called a revisionist mechanism and had been shut down by the revolutionaries.") They were forced to move to a two-room apartment shared by two other families, with one toilet for all fourteen people. Several years later, Min goes to the public park at night with her first boyfriend. Passing the bulletin board with pictures of couples caught making love in the park, and evading the flashlights of the sex guards, they find a quiet place in the bushes. They begin caressing, and almost at once are surrounded by a "forest of masturbators." Her lover whispers, "They know they will be shot if caught—so do we. . . . The fright sweetens the mood. We are so near to death as well as to heaven."

Red Azalea is written almost entirely in simple declarative sentences, a style that suits the brutality of Min's story as well as her own childlike frankness and ferocity. When a rival steals her movie role, "I ate my rice cake in the dark in the smoking room. I felt like an animal who ate its own intestine. I could not eat any more." Her forthright manner also counterpoints the relentless hail of lies and insanity under which she lives: the boys and girls, so hungry they gobble fruit peels from trash cans, told to collect pennies for "the starving children in America"; a teacher warning her never to read a novel that "corrupted and destroyed" another girl ("I immediately wanted to read the book *Jane Eyre,* although this was the first time I had ever heard of it").

Despite the efforts of their government, some Chinese manage to keep alive a sense of humor, bravery, tenderness. Min's most poignant and dramatic story is that of her affair with another woman, a company commander on the farm where she has been sent to labor from five in the morning till nine at night. At first forbiddingly righteous and heroic, Yan turns out to have a need for love as great as Min's; expressing it puts them both in danger, which Yan meets, ironically, with a great soldier's craftiness and self-sacrifice. Her friend's book is a fitting tribute, as well as an ungrieving obituary for a loathsome time:

> It was September 9, 1976. The reddest sun dropped from the sky of the Middle Kingdom. Mao passed away. Overnight the country became an ocean of white paper flowers. Mourners beat their heads against the door, on grocery-store counters and on walls. . . . The studio people gathered in the main meeting hall to moan. The sound of sobbing stretched like a hand-cranked gramophone at its spring's end. I had no tears. I cupped my face with my hands to hide my face.

Richard Eder (review date 20 February 1994)

SOURCE: "Life in a Chinese Opera," in *Los Angeles Times Book Review,* February 20, 1994, pp. 3, 7.

[*Eder is an American critic who has won a citation for excellence in reviewing from the National Book Critics Circle as well as a Pulitzer Prize for Criticism. In the following excerpt, he provides a favorable review of* Red Azalea.]

At home, Anchee Min's family was squeezed into two rooms shared with two other Shanghai families. From the age of 5, Min writes, she had to be an adult, tending her three younger siblings, Blooming, Coral and Space Conqueror—her father combined a private passion for astronomy with a public regard for Maoist oratory—until her parents got home late at night. Min's mother would arrive in a near-faint from her grueling factory job, and the four little children had to revive her with wet cloths and back rubs.

It was the early 1960s. Min's formerly middle-class family struggled in poverty amid the din and watchfulness of the Cultural Revolution. Her mother tended to misstep. As a teacher she was had up by her colleagues for using the wrong ideogram in a poster and turning its message from "Long Long Life to Mao" to "No No Life for Mao." Her apology was accepted, but she was banished to factory work when one of the squares of newspaper she used at stool was vigilantly found to contain a photograph of the leader.

As for Min, like many bright and nervy children she flew like the sparks, upward. If you were a brilliant student, assiduously applied yourself to the slogans and parables of Maoism, and were anxious to shine, you would. "I was raised on the teachings of Mao and on the operas of Madam Mao, Comrade Jiang Ching," Min writes at the start of her memoir.

Opera—Jiang Ching's were ideological epics—is the key to Min's memory of growing up, as well as to the distinctive style and tone of her book. "We were sure that we were making red dots on the world's map," she writes in a phrase comically reminiscent of George Bush's points of light. "Not for a day did I not feel heroic. I was the opera." Her part was to be a little Red Guard and a polished apple to her political teachers.

As with operatic arias, the important thing was to sing well. Then Min discovered that the arias contained real words and that words could kill. Her most-loved teacher—she recited classical poetry and demonstrated the meaning of infinity by holding out her arms, cross-like—was denounced as a spy. Min was named to take part in the public denunciation. Her description of the persuasion and pressures put on a 13-year-old girl is agonizing. When the teacher is kicked and abused, refuses to confess and gently questions Min, the distraught child screams: "Mama, Papa, where are you?" A moment later, hysterical, she shrieks out her assigned accusation. Years afterward, she apologizes to the old woman, who denies remembering her.

Min's book is in three parts. The first, brief and stunning, tells of her life until she is 17. The second, written more roughly but with great effect, describes her arduous assignment to work on a collective farm on the southeast coast. In the third, she is taken from the farm to compete as one of five finalists for a film role tailored to fit new ideological lines set out by Jiang Ching. Mao's wife, herself a former actress, was at the head of a hard-line faction jockeying for power, and the film was to be one of her weapons.

Here, Min lets her writing puff up into the operatic style that serves as her image of China in the '70s. The book's last part is by far its weakest. At the film school, Min is soon relegated to menial chores by officials who favor another candidate. Sitting in a dark stairwell after mopping the stage, she is approached by a sinuously beautiful man who comforts her and gives her egg rolls. He turns out to be a supremely powerful figure—known only as the Supervisor—who is Jiang Ching's right-hand man for the arts, and perhaps her lover.

He treats Min with alternating tenderness and coldness, makes love to her, has her brought to his magnificent mansion in Peking and gives her the coveted role of Red Azalea in a film that is intended to represent Jiang Ching's life. However, Mao dies, Jiang Ching and the Supervisor fall, and Min is back to mopping floors. The book ends there; years later she will emigrate to the United States.

Presumably the story is true but the telling is garishly unconvincing, an uneasy mix of "Cinderella" and *The Story of O.* "Pleasure swept over our flesh," Min writes steamily. The Supervisor stares into her eyes and demands to see in them "1,000,000 bulls rushing downhill with their tails on fire."

Min has written the book in English, and even in the first two parts the style can be awkward. Mostly she writes long strings of short declarative sentences—a rhythm, perhaps, brought over from Chinese—and this produces a cumulative small hammering. Yet time and again she makes a stranger's discovery, a glowing image or phrase that no native English-speaker would think of.

Such phrases light up the strangely affecting world of the Red Fire Farm, where 200,000 workers brought from the cities work 16-hour days, undergo constant haranguing by the cadres and sleep packed together in earth-floored huts, their only privacy the space under their mosquito netting: "a grave with a little spoiled air."

Min conveys the hardship and claustrophobia, but also the passions. She charts the unpredictable workings of exhilaration, exhaustion and despair. There is a splendid portrait of Yan, the section leader: big, fierce and vulnerable. Min and she become lovers; later Yan timidly confesses her liking for a male cadre, and Min helps her write steamy love letters that end up arousing them both. There is the fanatical, humorless Lu who covets Yan's job, yet Min writes of her in a way that captures our understanding if not sympathy. Through the horror of Maoism she is able to suggest the awful previous hopelessness that made so many Chinese welcome and administer it. She can give fanaticism a human face, which is not the same as embellishing it.

Despite her unworkable final section, Min's is a distinct and moving voice speaking out of a caldron of history. When, full of zeal, she goes to cancel her Shanghai residency before being trucked off to the farm, she has a premonition of the chill abstraction that lies beyond the fervor: "That afternoon I felt like a bare egg laid on a rock." Her family come down to see her off; she sits in the truck with the other conscripts. The cadres organize a sing-along, trying for exultation.

"My family stood in front of me, as if taking a dull picture," Min writes. "It was a picture of sadness, a picture of never the same. I was out of the picture. . . . We began to sing with Lu. Our voices were dry and weak like old sick farm cows. Lu waved her arms hard, trying to speed up the singing. People paid no attention to her. It was a moment when memory takes root. The moment youth began to fade. I stared at my parents who stood like frosted eggplants—with heads hanging weakly in front of their chests. My tears welled up. I sang loudly."

Judith Shapiro (review date 27 February 1994)

SOURCE: "Counterrevolutionary Sex," in *The New York Times Book Review,* February 27, 1994, p. 11.

[*In the following review, Shapiro concentrates on the sexual relationships in* Red Azalea.]

Even in today's comparatively freewheeling China of discos and dating, Anchee Min's steamy memoir of two love affairs—one with another woman, the other with a man—would be unprintable "spiritual pollution." But during Ms. Min's coming of age in China during the Cultural Revolution, nonmarital sex could be punishable by death and homosexual love was an unthinkable counterrevolutionary crime. This memoir of sexual freedom is thus a powerful political as well as literary statement.

In some ways, the story Ms. Min tells in ***Red Azalea*** is typical. Born in Shanghai in 1957, she was "raised on the teachings of Mao and on the operas of Madame Mao, Comrade Jiang Qing." She won contests in reciting from the little red book and denounced her teacher at a political meeting. When the call came for young people to "volunteer" for work in the barren countryside, she was assigned to the Red Fire Farm, a 13,000-member collective near the East China Sea.

And here her story acquires its dramatic complexities, with her introduction to her future lover, Party Secretary Yan, a charismatic woman with "the shoulders of an ancient warlord." Under Yan's leadership, Ms. Min fights sharp reeds and leeches to bring wormy cotton from the salty earth. Farm life is desolate and regimented, filled with political competition and rigid surveillance.

Only one delicate woman, Little Green, provides color and grace. So fastidious that she spreads pig manure "as if she were organizing jewelry," Little Green cannot survive the tyranny of sexual repression. Comrade Lu, a vicious creature who sleeps nose-to-nose with a skull, which she claims belongs to a Red Army martyr, ferrets out Little Green's romance with a man from a neighboring company. One night Ms. Min and her comrades are summoned to bring their guns and flashlights, and the couple are found together, half-naked, in the fields. When the man is executed for rape, Little Green goes mad.

As if to atone for her failure to prevent Comrade Lu's persecution of Little Green, Party Secretary Yan stays close to this sad creature: "They were like two lost boats drifting over the sea in a dense fog." Yan's compassionate nature begins to warm Anchee Min's desolate world. When she discovers Yan playing forbidden tunes on a two-stringed banjo in an abandoned brickworks, a secret friendship blooms. Yan confides that like Little Green, she too is in love with a man—and Anchee Min writes love letters on her behalf, stirring up her own erotic longings as well as Yan's. Soon the two women are sleeping in one bunk in a crowded room, their nakedness hidden by a mosquito net adorned with Mao buttons, while Lu studies the quotations of Mao nearby. Simple metaphors convey this dangerous passion: "A wild horse broke off its reins. . . . She was melting snow. I did not know what role I was playing anymore: her imagined man or myself. . . . I went where the sun rose. . . . My senses cheered frantically in a raging fire."

Their passionate and tender affair is interrupted when, in an extraordinary turn of events, Ms. Min is spotted by talent scouts from a Shanghai film studio. She is one of five women selected to compete for the title role in *Red Azalea,* a film about the life of Jiang Qing.

In Shanghai, Ms. Min is caught up in competition as vicious and hypocritical as any Hollywood intrigue. ("Firewood's singing was like a rooster under a blunt knife," she writes of one of her rivals.) And the political intrigues in the studio are only complicated further when she begins an affair with a mysterious, androgynous figure, close to Jiang Qing, who is known only as the Supervisor. This liaison puts her at the heart of a political plot typical of those in the "wild histories," a Chinese genre featuring embroidered exposés of the scandalous doings of top party leaders. The film is part of Jiang Qing's attempt to take power from a dying Mao by casting herself as a savior of the Chinese masses. "It must happen her way, for the people," the Supervisor tells Ms. Min. "Mao is over 83. The mud is reaching his neck."

In a macabre scene that conveys the connection between sexual and political repression that runs throughout Ms. Min's book, her affair with the Supervisor is consummated in a park that is near a crematorium. Dark and quiet, its groves are filled with lovers defying the "criminal-control patrols" that regularly sweep through with their flashlights. "The passion they had for the Great Helmsman has been betrayed," says the Supervisor, gloating over the couples rustling around them. "Oh, how grand a scene! I wish our greatest Chairman could see it. He would be shocked but impotent."

Ms. Min's fortunes are entwined with those of the Red Azalea she has never met, and her roller-coaster ride through Chinese art and politics is derailed by the downfall of Jiang Qing and the other members of the Gang of Four. Her entertaining, provocative and unusual account of those times concludes abruptly as she returns, with little but memories of Yan and the Supervisor to comfort her, to a drab and mundane life. In 1984, under circumstances she chooses not to describe, she found her way to the United States, gaining the freedom to write this extraordinary story.

An excerpt from *Red Azalea*

Lu's full name was Ice Lu. She was the daughter of a revolutionary martyr. Her father was killed by the Nationalists in Taiwan. He was murdered when carrying out a secret assignment. Her mother suffered this loss to her death. She died three days after giving birth. It was a terrible winter. Strong wind, like scissors, cut through the skin. She named her baby Ice. Ice was raised under the Party's special care. She grew up in an orphanage funded by the Party leaders. Like Yan, she was also a founder of the Red Guards. She had gone to visit Mao's hometown in Hunan, where she had eaten leaves from the same tree Mao had eaten when besieged and pinned down in the valley by the Nationalists some thirty years ago.

Lu showed me a skull she had discovered in the backyard of a house in Hunan. She said it was a Red Army martyr's skull. She pointed to a hole on the forehead of the skull and told me that it was a bullet hole. She fondled the skull with her fingers, going in and out of the eyeholes, touching its jaws. The strange expression on her face caught my breath. She told me that an old village lady buried the martyr secretly. Twenty years later the skull had risen above the soil. The old lady dug it out and gave it to Lu when she learned that her father had been a martyr too. Lu often thought it could have been her own father's skull.

I stared at the skull, trying to comprehend its attractiveness to Lu. Maybe the threatening spirit? Maybe the coldness that only death could carry? Lu had a look that matched her name. Her look was chilly. Her enthusiasm did not feel warm. She spoke slowly, pronouncing each syllable clearly. She had a long face, the shape of a peanut. Her expression was determined and judgmental. Her features were located evenly on her face. Slanting eyes, icy, like a painted ancient beauty. But her beauty was ruined by her forever-correctness. Her half-moon-shaped eyes were no longer warm and sweet to the soldiers. Our respect for her was that of mice for a cat.

Lu liked action. She did not know hesitation. She attacked and invaded. It was her style to catch and chop. Stand by, aim and shoot, as she always like to say. But that did not impress me. On the contrary, it distanced me. She had a fixed mind. A mind full of dead thoughts. She observed me. In coldness. In suspicion. It started the moment I moved in. Her smile carried warnings. She gave me a copy of her Mao study notes. Her handwriting was extremely square. I wished my calligraphy was like hers, but her writing bored me. Her mind was a propaganda machine. It had no engine of its own.

Anchee Min, in her Red Azalea, *Pantheon Books, 1994.*

Orville Schell (review date March 1994)

SOURCE: "Stolen Kisses," in *Vogue,* Vol. 184, No. 3, March, 1994, pp. 278, 281-82.

[*Schell is an American journalist, nonfiction writer, and critic who has written extensively on modern China. In the following review, based in part on a conversation with Min, he discusses* Red Azalea *and how Min came to write it.*]

> "Falling in love is so powerful that it makes you forget about almost everything else, even making revolution. Instead of wanting to struggle and destroy things, you want to find peace and to celebrate living. Because the Party knows that people in love are no longer completely under its control, its leaders have always been deeply fearful of love."
>
> —Anchee Min, Chicago, 1993

Anchee Min learned about the politically subversive power of love in the People's Republic of China during the Cultural Revolution in a place where neither she nor the Party expected her to find it, with another woman, who was Party secretary and commander of her work company at a forced-labor camp. Her wrenching new book, ***Red Azalea,*** chronicles two simultaneous odysseys: from Shanghai to Chicago, through the travails of both brute physical labor in the countryside and work as a janitor at the Shanghai Film Studio; and from the suffocating confinement of puritanical Maoism to sexual awakening.

Like other members of her generation, Min grew up believing that the self must always be sacrificed to the commonweal and that any deviation from wholehearted service to "the people" was tantamount to opposing Mao's revolutionary line. She lived in constant fear of being "murdered by bourgeois evil spirits," which Mao warned "were everywhere, hiding, waiting for the right time to get us."

Born in 1957, Min struggled diligently as a young girl to become a model student and Red Guard, but at thirteen she was forced to denounce one of her favorite teachers as a U.S. spy. "It was at that meeting I learned the meaning of the word *betrayal* as well as *punishment,*" she writes. The Party's kafkaesque response was always the same: "Our Party never accuses anyone who is innocent." The incident left Min wracked with a sense of guilt that not even an apology delivered 20 years later was able to erase.

In 1974 she was shipped off to do manual labor on Red Fire Farm, where any manifestations of individualism, much less physical intimacy, were enough to get inmates denounced. In one of the most evocative sections of her book, Min describes the irresistible physical attraction of an artistic and sensual young woman, Little Green, who dared to violate this code of militant puritanism. Even as they derided her, "the half-man, half-monkey male soldiers stared at her as she passed," writes Min of Little Green's sexual magnetism. "The good-for-nothings could not take their eyes off her, of that creature full of bourgeois allure. . . . I envied and adored her. In June she dared to go without a bra. I hated my bra when I saw her, saw her walking toward me, bosoms bouncing. She made me feel withered without ever having bloomed."

But like everyone who resisted surrendering the self, Little Green's fate was nightmarish. One night after being tipped off by a spiteful camp informer, a squad of camp "militia" caught Little Green making love in a wheat field. "About thirty other flashlights, including mine, were switched on at the same time," writes Min. "Little Green screamed. It broke the night. She was in her favorite shirt—the one embroidered with pink plum flowers. The lights shone on her naked buttocks. Her scream pierced me to the core. . . . It was as if a bomb exploded next to me."

Just as Min had been forced to denounce her teacher as a spy, Little Green was forced to condemn her lover as a rapist. After a hasty mock trial he was executed, and Little Green went mad with grief. "She took a pair of scissors and cut [her underwear] into strips. She chopped off her long braids and stopped combing her hair. Mucus dripped from her lips." She was finally taken to the hospital, held by four camp mates "as if carrying an animal to a slaughterer's shop," writes Min. "We strangled her into madness."

In spite of knowing that as a proletarian she did not "belong" to herself and that yielding to the temptations of the flesh meant almost certain damnation, Min increasingly felt herself "invaded" by "a nameless anxiety." "It felt like a sweating summer afternoon. Irritatingly hot. The air felt creamy. It was the ripeness of the body." Like Little Green's, Min's body "demanded to break away from its ruler, the mind." Despite being "chewed by shame," she was so starved for human contact and affection that she fell in love with Yan, the commander of her work team. Behind a flimsy mosquito net in their crowded bunk room, they sought furtive comfort in each other's arms.

But always under the scrutiny of others, particularly their politically correct and vindictive bunkmate, comrade Lu, who "sensed my intimacy with Yan immediately, like a dog to a smell," Min and Yan knew they could be destroyed by a single "ambiguous word" dropped into their dossiers.

Far from being a brief for homosexuality or hedonism, ***Red Azalea*** is an impassioned plea for privacy, for oases where intimacy and human closeness are allowed to exist uninvaded by politics. It is also a testament to how, even when "castrated" by an ideology as constricting and defoliating as Maoism, the human urge to love still somehow manages to express itself.

After two years laboring on Red Fire Farm, Min was unexpectedly chosen to try out for a role in one of Madame Mao's "revolutionary model operas," *Red Azalea.* "I knew nothing of acting but was made an actress," writes Min. At the Shanghai Film Studio, one of China's most famous filmmaking centers, she finds the attentions of the supervisor, an enigmatic but powerful cultural czar from Beijing, directed toward her. "Romantic love does not exist among proletarians," the supervisor insists. "It is a bourgeois fantasy." But Min soon discovers that the supervisor is not only penetrated by sadness but also possessed by an irrepressible appetite for intimacy. Despite the danger of being found out, he arranges a rendezvous with her one night at Peace Park, one of the few trysting places in Mao's China with any modicum of privacy. There, behind a public toilet, the supervisor and Min consummate their twisted quest to banish loneliness. All around them are other "moaners," who "masturbate and ejaculate their passion with a criminal guilt . . . their fronts and rears exposed like animals in mating season begging for penetration . . ." as patrols of police shout, "Beware of reactionary activities!" and rake the bushes with flashlights.

No Chinese, much less a Chinese woman, has written more honestly and poignantly than Anchee Min about the desert of solitude and human alienation at the center of the Chinese Communist revolution. Although others have written about the scars left by all the Party's campaigns of political persecution, Min is the first to plumb the depths of this benighted revolution's sexually repressive side. "I tried to stop my desire, [but] my lust was irresistible," she unabashedly writes of watching from behind a curtain as her ex-lover Yan finally gave herself to a man.

By daring to break the long-standing Chinese taboo against discussing sexual feelings in explicit terms and by delving so fearlessly into the ways the Party has intruded upon private life and destroyed the emotional basis of human relations, Min has given the frontiers of Chinese literature a giant push forward. But by imbuing her characters with an erotic as well as a political dimension, she has also created one of the few works of contemporary Chinese fiction that has truly universal relevance and appeal.

Red Azalea was written by Min in English, which she began learning in 1984, and as a result her language is sometimes imprecise and confusing. Although such roughness conveys a certain authentic rawness, one nonetheless wishes that her editors had been more helpful in smoothing out some of the clunky phrases and sentences that keep appearing. However, despite this shortcoming, the book sings. It is a small masterpiece that tells as much about the Chinese revolution as volumes of other political accounts.

Curious to know more about this spirited and resourceful young woman, I went to Chicago, where Min lives with her painter husband and two-year-old daughter. I was met at the door of a ramshackle South Side duplex by a woman in her late thirties whose broad, striking features and jet black hair make her look as much like an American Indian as a Chinese. Dressed in faded Levi's, a gray sweater, and socks with holes in the heels, she settled herself on a bedspread-covered couch that looked as if it had come from a thrift shop and began telling me about her life.

"As a girl in Shanghai, I hated how crowded it was, how we had to wait for the other families to use the toilet," she told me. "My biggest dream was to work hard and someday have a room of my own." It was with great pleasure that she later showed me around her new abode, a once burned-out building she and her husband have renovated, doing the plumbing and carpentry themselves.

Her dream of owning her own house did not come easily. After the production of the opera *Red Azalea* was canceled following the arrest of Jiang Qing and the Gang of Four, Min was demoted from an actress to a janitor and forced to mop floors. Only when film star Joan Chen (whom Min had met at the Shanghai Film Studio before falling from favor) helped enroll her in the Art Institute of Chicago was she able to get a passport and a visa. But upon arrival in Chicago, because she was unable to speak English, she was promptly kicked out of the school. For several years she worked at menial jobs, including stints as a waitress, a messenger, a baby-sitter, and hand painting Chinese peonies on women's underwear. At the same time she studied art, photography, and English. As a project for one language class, she began writing about her experiences in China. The first essay was about denouncing her old teacher. "From there I just kept going, laying out my story as straight as I could," she explained. It took her eight years. "The hardest thing was to face myself honestly," she said. "In China everything is so repressed that for a Chinese to overcome this inborn sense of shame is very difficult. The last thing I wanted to do, however, was to portray myself simply as a victim."

Despite her painful experiences growing up in China, it is with *tristesse* rather than bitterness that Min now looks back on her past life, "We were taught to sacrifice everything in order to serve others. It became a kind of an addiction. As a little girl I used to go down to the street corner hoping for an accident so that I could rescue someone and then maybe go and see Chairman Mao. We thought that if we were hard enough on ourselves we could even save the world." She paused reflectively. "I know it's good to share and serve others, but I wanted to sacrifice and die not because of selflessness but because of my own vanity."

When I asked Min how her mother, a retired teacher, and her father, an astronomer who organized exhibitions at the Shanghai Planetarium, took to her Maoist zealousness, she laughed sardonically. "At one point I almost disowned my father for not allowing me to have a Maoist study session in our home. At the time I actually thought he might be a reactionary."

Are the years of the Cultural Revolution still having an effect on her generation in this new Deng era of high-speed economic reform? She weighed my question for a moment and then said, "The same people who made the Cultural Revolution are now launching the Four Modernizations. They have forgotten what we did to each other. There is not much difference between the Red Guards, who thought that making revolution meant doing whatever they wanted, and the money worshipers of today, who feel so disillusioned that all they want to do is to get rich. They don't care about each other. When one generation is abused, it is easy for that generation to abuse the next."

At one point Min mentioned that her school in Shanghai had once collected pennies to donate to the "starving children of America." When I noted the irony of her now living here, she laughed. "Left in China I would have killed myself, turned into a mental patient, or become a self-hating person able to do nothing for anyone. America saved my life. Even when I was struggling to learn English and working three jobs at once for $3 an hour, I felt happy here. Why? Because I was working for myself and, at least, I could quit if I wanted."

As we picked up her daughter at the day-care center, I asked how she reconciles her residual guilty feelings about the past with her new life. "America makes me forgive myself by allowing me to believe that I can improve my life," she said. "I love it here because I have human dignity and the choice of being moral. In China, no one wants to talk about morality now, just money."

However, when I agreed that commercial culture has indeed become a Faustian wager in Deng's New China, she protestingly interrupted. "But I am still very Chinese! My father believes China can't be changed, but I think it can. The Chinese government may not want to hear it, but I'd like to be a kind of missionary, someone who reminds Chinese of their past as a way of saying that one does not have to live in such darkness forever."

Despite all her disillusionment, Min still retains more than a little of that old Maoist conviction that every person must find some way to serve society. Even though the Translation Publishing House in Shanghai has rejected ***Red Azalea*** as a "bad influence" and "too controversial" for publication in China, Min has not only been able to return to Shanghai to hold shows of her artwork and photography and to appear on television but to buy an apartment. In fact, she intends to spend part of each year there. "I want to do what I can for China, to give it my best," she says passionately. "***Red Azalea*** is an attempt to confront my own guilt and also to remind us all of our past and that in the future we have the choice to be moral."

Laura Shapiro and Karen Springen (review date 11 April 1994)

SOURCE: "This Girl's Life," in *Newsweek,* Vol. CXXIII, No. 15, April 11, 1994, pp. 76, 79.

[*In the following review, Shapiro and Springen comment on* Red Azalea *and Min's life after she left China.*]

Harrowing tales of life under totalitarianism have been published before, but Anchee Min's ***Red Azalea***—the story of a young girl coming of age in thrall to Maoism—ranks as one of the most memorable. Much of its strength lies in her prose, as delicate and evocative as a traditional Chinese brush painting.

Growing up in Shanghai in the 1960s, Min was the best student in her class, a junior Red Guard who memorized the revolutionary operas of Mao's wife, Jiang Qing, and sang them all day. But her faith was tested when she was told to denounce a beloved teacher, who had been accused of spying. Sobbing, Min spat criticisms into a microphone. She still feels the agonizing guilt.

At 17 Min was ordered to the countryside to work at a collective farm, and although she tried to muster the appropriate zeal, she and her family grieved as she boarded the truck. "My family stood in front of me, as if taking a dull picture," she writes. "It was a picture of sadness, a picture of never the same." Red Fire Farm was a desolate place, but Min was quickly drawn to the commander of her unit, Yan. "She had weather-beaten skin [and] a full mouth, in the shape of a water chestnut . . . She burned me with the sun in her eyes. I felt bare." Eventually the two shared a bed, although four other women slept in the room. "I told her not to wash the mosquito net because the dirt made it less transparent," writes Min.

On the basis of her looks and political reliability, Min was plucked from the farm to star in a movie called *Red Azalea,* one of Madame Mao's projects. At the film studio she fell in love with a mysterious man she calls "the Supervisor," a powerful ally of Madame Mao's. But before the movie was finished, Mao died, his wife was denounced and the Supervisor's fortunes collapsed. Min spent the next six years washing the studio's floors. In 1983 she received a letter from a friend in the United States, the actress Joan Chen. Would Min like to leave? "My despair made me fearless," she writes. The book ends with her arrival in Chicago in 1984.

Today the harsh scenes of China that Min conjures so vividly seem distant indeed. Min, 37, lives with her Chinese émigré husband and their 2-year-old daughter in Chicago, where she and her husband paint and Min writes. During her first years in this country she worked at numerous jobs—waitressing, fixing toilets, painting fabrics—while studying English and art. "I didn't even bother to take off my clothes at night," she says. ***Red Azalea*** began as an assignment for her English class; the book has 40,000 copies in print, and Min is at work on a sequel. That's happy news for readers who turned the last page of ***Red Azalea*** slowly—longing to know what happened next.

Anchee Min with Kathleen Wilson, *CLC Yearbook* (interview date 14 November 1994)

[In the following interview, Min discusses how the events of the Cultural Revolution affected her formative years and later prompted her to write Red Azalea.*]*

[*Wilson*]: *One of the most noticeable things about* **Red Azalea** *is that it was written without direct dialogue. Was there a reason for this?*

[Min]: It sounds more Chinese.

Is that how a Chinese novel would be written?

I'd say yes. Classic Chinese literature is very close to how lyrics are written. It's more about "Qi"—the breath of the piece, the music of the writing.

Do you think that if you had written a novel in Chinese it would have had the same tone and style?

My only experience in writing Chinese was writing essays on Mao studies and the Cultural Revolution. I'm a product of that period, so I think subconsciously that influenced me. I'd say that my writing in Chinese wouldn't be too different because I can't escape my character and memory even if I want to.

Did you find it difficult to find the right English translation for certain ideas, or were there concepts you tried to express that had no English equivalent?

It's not a matter of translation. When I was writing, I was emotional. Sometimes I had no way to express things. I tried to sound precise. For example, when I described my parents' relationship, in English I would say, "Although we were poor, my parents loved each other." But that's not precise; the picture didn't come alive. This book took me eight years to complete, and most of the time I spent trying to be precise. Finally, I came up with an equivalent description; I said, "My parents lived like a pair of chopsticks—one cannot function without the other." As chopsticks, they are in conflict and incorporated at the same time. Both chopsticks have to work against each other in order to pick things up. To me that's precise. This kind of task carried me throughout the book.

The Revolution claimed that what was good for the people wasn't necessarily the same thing that was good for individuals or families. Did this idea originate with communism in China, or did it have its roots in Chinese culture?

Yes, it had its roots in the culture. It formed the mentality. The Confucian influence was deep—"Young generations must obey the elder"—people were taught to obey the system. It was not about good or bad, but the "father figure"—it's about obeying—respect suppression. The communist idea was to beat the feudalists but they ended up doing the same thing. Mao was the "father figure." He got what he wanted under the heroic political projection "saving the world."

Did you have any desire to be a writer before you began **Red Azalea?**

No. In China it's not the way of thinking. I never thought that I would be anything, because I didn't belong to myself. You just don't think that you belong to yourself. It's not the right question to even ask yourself: "What would I like to do?" The school constantly convinced the children that we were "screws" fixed on the giant communist machine. We lived to serve the Party. I wrote ***Red Azalea*** because I had to express myself. Writing was a way to escape the pain.

Does the Red Fire Farm still exist?

Yes. It's a wasteland.

Are there still as many people on it?

No. In China there were 200,000 sent to those farms from 1966 to 1976. Now most of the people are back in the cities, except the ones who got married. A lot of sad stories.

The farm almost seemed to be a military-style outpost. Why were you armed with rifles?

It's a kind of system that Chairman Mao set up to control the youth. It's called *jun-keng-nong-chang.* It's a military-system camp. (*Nong-chang* is a regular farm). We all wanted to be soldiers. At that time, to be accepted as a soldier was the highest honor. If you got lucky, you would get sent to Vietnam to fight with Americans; you would really be considered honored. So in our high school, we all wanted to be selected by the army people, but only probably one or two out of fifty high school students in the class would be sent. When it came down to the farm, we liked to be militarily trained. It was an honor—an honorable thing to have the skill and be able to fight.

So you weren't part of the army. Did you have guns because you thought you were going to be invaded?

We thought we were going to be invaded all the time. Every five years, there would be something; either we were having problems with the Russian border in the northern part of China, or we were having emergency assignments. Even in the schools, at midnight the school would call an "emergency gathering." We'd get up and go to school together and do military exercises. The whole school—two thousand people. When we came to the farm, we were "on" all the time. We were afraid of American attacks. So Mao had this famous teaching: "Dig hole deep, collect the rice, and not be aggressors." We were mentally prepared for war at anytime.

In the early 1970s, every family was assigned to make bricks with mud. The government would come in to collect these dried mud bricks and bake them. There was no play time for children, or for parents and family. No, you just continue and keep up with the government's assignments. And to answer your question before, when you asked me if I wanted to be a writer—I never thought my story was ever special. My story is so ordinary. And lots of Chinese students in America wrote me after they read ***Red Azalea*** and said "It's my story. It's our story."

You spent three years at Red Fire Farm before you were discovered by the movie studio executives. What happened to the other peasants? Did people frequently find ways out of the farm or did most end up staying there indefinitely?

Most people stayed there until Mao died in 1976. The current leader, Deng Xio Ping, established a national examination test where one can apply for school. Another way was to get one's parents to retire; you could go back to the city to replace them [in the workforce]. My little sister, who was assigned to the farm after me, was one of the final people to get on the "last train." She wrote home and said, "Mom, you must retire, or I will end up in Red Fire Farm forever." Her body was deteriorating. Many of the people in the farm were very sick. My mother had high blood pressure, but she couldn't get sick enough to have the doctor write a proof that she was definitely, permanently damaged and had to retire. So my mother would go out and run and do dangerous things and just faint, so she could be sent "emergency" and get the letter from the doctor saying she couldn't work anymore. My little sister finally got off the farm by "replacing" mother.

Once a parent retired a child could come home?

Yes, but if the family had three children at the farm the parents had to make a choice to desert one. The one that's left feels very abandoned.

It seems that the Cultural Revolution did not discriminate against women. They were expected to work as hard as the men and suffer just as many physical hardships. Did you sometimes feel that women actually suffered more than the men and received less respect, or was it a fairly equal system?

Fairly equal system. That's probably the only positive thing about the Cultural Revolution. In mainland China, women nowadays are in economic power. My generation was raised to be equal; we never thought that we were less than men. Of course, we have to work harder to physically compete with men.

You wrote about how dangerous it was to become involved in a sexual relationship at both the farm and in the city. But what about friendship? Was friendship also discouraged, or was it dangerous?

We don't talk about friendship; it's comradeship. I don't know—that's a very good question. From my own experience, I didn't really have friends. I grew up seeing sons and daughters denounce their parents, so that basic trust was destroyed among people. I witnessed how terrible my mother was treated by being kind and honest. I basically thought that people were pretty evil, and I was scared of people.

Do you still think people are evil?

Not today in America. In the past we [in China] were not properly educated. From when I was eight years old until I was twenty years old, children were encouraged to denounce their parents. You lived only to love Mao. It was a good lesson; Chinese people paid a high price to learn about themselves.

You had some guilt when you were forced to denounce your teacher in elementary school. That affected you greatly; I imagine that other people also had experiences in which they felt bad about what they were forced to do.

My guilt made me suffer; in pain I learned shame. Knowing shame taught me to be a good person. I credit my mother, although she's considered a "society idiot." She basically believes in kindness, and it's very, very different from Mao's teaching. In a way I was torn in between; I admire my mother because she would rather stick to her principles than to denounce anybody—"to smell her party secretary's fart"—according to her little saying. But her whole life is a "failure" according to my revolutionary standards. My mother is always assigned to the worst jobs. I didn't want to be her; I went the opposite way. I wanted to be the head of the Red Guards. I wanted capital respect. But I'm my mother's daughter. So it's a conscious act—you just don't be a bad person. My mother beat that into my head. Home and society carried very different rules. It was mixed messages in education.

Everything you say about growing up during the Cultural Revolution suggests that it was dehumanizing. Were there any positive aspects at all?

Yes. It's so odd that the result is dehumanizing, but we were taught the basic slogan: "Sacrifice yourself for the people with heart and soul." You just forget about your own vacation and think about taking care of America's starving children. We spent all our holidays on the streets collecting pennies. I felt good when I was doing something for other people—and for children I didn't even know.

When I knew I was helping them, I felt good. So that's part of the thing in our generation that's so ironic.

You renounced your teacher when you were in elementary school, and then you were forced to ambush Little Green in the middle of the night at Red Fire Farm. Was it a compilation of all these things that made you turn against communism and Chairman Mao, or was there one particular moment that really stands out?

Both. In those circumstances, I guess falling in love changed me. We had no choice. Love is so beautiful, and it made you stop hating. But, of course, the accumulation of these events that you pointed out, with my teacher, with Little Green, I hated to see my best friends destroyed. The torture, the distortion—deep down I knew that it didn't feel right.

So you changed when you learned what love was?

Right. It made me think: "This feels right, feels good, and this is what I want. No more, no more slogans. No more Mao teachings." But these changes were bit by bit and yet so powerful because it's so secretive. My affair [with Yan]—we shared part of the guilt; it felt criminal.

At the film studio, you were accused by Soviet Wong of being a bourgeois individualist. At the time did you agree with her—did you think you were an individualist?

I don't even think Soviet Wong understands what "bourgeois individual" means. All she had was the anger, because she was a beauty and she was in her thirties. She had quite a bit of former education in filmmaking, and she didn't get to be what she wanted to be. So she had anger she had to shed on somebody else—she just could not see a younger person selected. It's like jealousy between concubines. The empress picks the new concubine, and the old concubine is deserted if she doesn't poison her. So Soviet Wong had to "poison" me, put me to death. I only had to raise her anger to give her a little chance. That's a life and death thing. If there wasn't the title of "capitalist" or "bourgeois," she would have invented something else. The meaning of the words was really not important.

Did you have a sense that you were different from other people because you wanted to be your own person?

I didn't know how other people thought in order to know that I was different. Even with Yan—she's savage, she's a warlord. We were from different family backgrounds. We didn't discuss private subjects much because it would be dangerous. At that time anybody could report anybody else to get promoted or to be considered a revolutionary activist, or to be accepted as a party member. That's how Mao controlled and programmed the Chinese people. You can't really trust each other to share these secret thoughts. You can only share your belief in communism. What made me different was that I acted. I refused to stay in the dark. I constantly search for light, for air.

How did you develop your talents in photography and art while you lived in China?

My painting was basically brush painting, because brush painting was a very regular thing. I started at six years old, and every week I had a calligraphy class. We learned the nature of brush painting, and because in school I was in charge of the large blackboard, I had to paint really big posters. In America you have Jackson Pollock and de Kooning and all these big, giant paintings. But for me it was very natural, so I painted in a big size and my strokes were firm and determined. Photography, I started in America.

The school you found here, the Art Institute of Chicago, didn't have an English language requirement. Is that more or less why you started studying art seriously?

I couldn't express myself except through art. You don't really have to speak regular English; if there's an assignment, you just show your photography or your paintings and it tells all about you. I had a lot of anger when I came, also a lot of passion toward life, so I produced things that had strong statements. They were really the screams of a wounded soul.

There's one scene in the book where you go to a Buddhist temple. Was religion tolerated under Chairman Mao?

No. There's no religion, but people did it secretly anyway. Temples in China now that weren't destroyed by the Red Guard in the Cultural Revolution weren't destroyed for a reason. For example, a hundred-year-old temple in Shanghai was taken as a headquarters of peasant rebels, thus it had a "revolutionary meaning." The one I mention in the book was built in 960 A.D. and had stone statues. The good guy was a patriotic general who later was murdered by a traitor. Behind that temple is a statue of these two figures. To learn patriotism from that hero was the reason that temple was preserved. Also the bad guy's statue was put in front of the hero in a cage so everyone can go there and spit—literally spit—on the statue to learn that you're going to be spit on for thousands and thousands of years if you betray the country.

So the temples that existed were only for communist purposes and had nothing to do with religion?

In remote places, in southwest China, the temples are so high you have to walk the whole day to get there. The Red Guards could not even reach there, so it carried on its activities. But the religion remains in the people's hearts. One just didn't talk about it. When you talk about it—you say the opposite. For example, you say: "Oh, I go there to criticize religion, to criticize all these people who created these statues."

Towards the end of the book, you write that being asked to come to America was like being asked to live on the moon. Was this because you didn't know much about the country, or because you were told that it was an unbearable place to live?

I was taught to shoot the Americans. I didn't start using a rifle at the farm, I started when I was fourteen years old. I was one of the activists sent to the army to learn how to shoot, so when we came back we could teach our fellow teenagers and tell them about combat. It's called "spreading revolution." The target we used to practice aiming was always a U.S. soldier's head, with the blue/brown eyes. But I thought if communism was a lie, those pictures I was shown of America could be a lie too. So I decided to take a chance.

The foundation of your education during the Cultural Revolution was Mao's Little Red Book. *Is it still taught in China today?*

No. The Communist Party doesn't want anybody to remember the revolution. They simply "shut the lid." The party collected the Mao buttons, Mao books, and nobody mentions it anymore. And people feel good about it nowadays, they use Mao as kind of a superstitious figure, and they play with him. The taxi drivers will put Mao pictures on the driver's seat and say, "nobody would dare hit Mao, so I'll be safe." You get to play with your "god" a little bit and put him down. Put him in a car. Make fun of him a bit. Kind of Chinese revenge in a little way.

What's taken the place of all that?

Speeding up of capitalism. People are convinced that communism doesn't work. Unless you get rich, you won't have a better life. People in China right now believe nothing except material stuff. You go to China, first thing people would ask is, "Are you from America? Are you interested in doing business with me?"

How has the push towards the free enterprise system changed the lives of ordinary citizens in China?

What I can see is that they're divided into two groups. One's called "survival of the fittest"—people that are capable of following the change. And the other group is people who have spent all their lives obeying one order and they are lost in the change. In America, you have a company, for example, you're in computers, and then tomorrow the company's no longer in business and the computer is replaced by something else. Then you're willing to go back to school, to learn, to change, to survive. But Chinese people don't know what to do. So they get angry; they are in a very poor situation. It's not just the skill, it's a way of thinking. For thirty or forty years, you're not used to change, and all of a sudden you must change or you are abandoned and your family goes starving. Especially in northern parts of China where there are miners and peasants. These people are not educated. They stick to their land. So that's the potential turmoil that the government's facing—people's inability to cope with change.

Would you say that the people who are adapting the best are the younger people?

Yes. People like me who went to the farm, and have seen the worst and know that if you don't move, you're going to freeze to death in winter. You better get moving, get exercise, buy some coats, and warm yourself up and survive. We try everything. If the way were to go to the moon, we'd go.

In another interview, you mentioned that "lack of self-examination led to the Cultural Revolution." As China becomes less isolated in the world community, are people starting to become more self-aware?

Yes. In China part of the news is international news. We see a lot about America in China, more than you see here about China. You don't see much about China here at all. But China sees the world. You know, we just jumped to the opposite. It's like a love affair; your parents say, "Don't date that boy." And you just go nuts for him. So China's like that. All those years the communists say Americans are dangerous. Now people have fallen in love with America.

Are people starting to develop a better sense of themselves and more individuality?

I think so, yes. When you have all this information, you learn how things work outside of China and you start to think, "Hey—what about my life?" You start to pay attention to your existence. You think, life is short—you start to think about how to live a beautiful life.

How did your parents react when you told them you were going to the United States?

Oh, they just said it's impossible. They were scared, although they wanted me to leave badly.

They didn't think you'd be able to get here?

No. They secretly prayed for me. It's a miracle. I'm glad I was young enough to have the guts. Now I think, "God, I made it that far." It's unthinkable.

Would you like **Red Azalea** *to be published in China?*

Yes. I tried, but it was rejected.

You said earlier that your story is more or less typical—it wasn't extraordinary at all, so it's not like the book would be any revelation to people.

The only revelation about it is the way I wrote it. I'm in America, and I consider myself American-educated. By that I mean that I was able to look at myself in a humanistic way. So I was not afraid of the "Chinese shame," and I think the contribution the book would make to China is that I am honest to the core. I'm opening something that the Chinese would feel too shameful to expose, because I think it's important to examine ourselves in an honest way. It's very painful but necessary. It's very simple. To re-learn to love each other. People see themselves in my book, in me. It's the process of admitting one's faults that becomes a way of enlightening. It's the education we should have had but didn't.

Can you say anything about your next book?

It will be out in June 1995. It's called *Katherine.* If ***Red Azalea*** is about how the Chinese minds were constructed and deconstructed, the new book is about the reconstruction of the minds. It has two major elements. One is China's flirtation with the West. And the second is the turning inward toward the ancient school of thought with a modern twist. It's like cooking, like fried rice, it's got all these different ingredients and you're trying to make a dish with what you have available. China's psyche is very interesting at this moment. It's a novel, but all the events are based in real life.

Lisa Shea
Hula

Born in 1953, Shea is an American novelist, editor, journalist, and poet.

INTRODUCTION

Hula (1994) is a moving account of survival, child abuse, sibling rivalry, male-female relationships, and the disintegration of a family. Centering on a war veteran, his passive wife, and their two daughters, the episodic *Hula* is told from the perspective of the youngest child and details over the course of two summers the sisters' entrance into adolescence, their growing interest in sex, and the demise of their parents' marriage. Subjected to their alcoholic father's random acts of violence and cruelty—he exhibits a penchant for arson, often destroys the girls' playthings, and in one scene tries to kidnap them at gunpoint—the narrator and her sister attempt to escape their situation by devoting their affections to their dog and by creating a fantasy world. Their bond of interdependence, however, remains irrevocably threatened by their fights with each other and by the older girl's relationships with the neighborhood boys. Earning Shea a 1993 Whiting Writers' Award, *Hula* has been generally well received. Although occasionally faulted for its one-dimensional portraits of the parents, *Hula* is noted for its psychological acuity and factual recounting of disturbing events in a voice that is devoid of artifice and emotion. Cynthia Dockrell observed: "Shea establishes a tension that builds almost unbearably as the novel progresses. She achieves this in part through the oddly distant first-person telling of the story; the girl's blunt, childlike recording of horrific events, interspersed with her descriptions of the pent-up, overheated atmosphere, pulls her back from the action while drawing us closer to it. Shea's taut prose further adds to the story's power as she paints vivid pictures stripped of all but the barest essentials."

CRITICISM

Kirkus Reviews (review date 15 October 1993)

SOURCE: A review of *Hula,* in *Kirkus Reviews,* Vol. LXI, No. 20, October 15, 1993, p. 1291.

[*In the following favorable review, written prior to the publication of* Hula, *the critic relates the plot of the novel.*]

[Lisa Shea's ***Hula*** is a tiny], lucid first novel about two

girls who navigate the shoals of puberty—and escape the dangers of a terrible, mean, cruel father.

In a wry but deadpan voice, the younger of two sisters (the older is getting breasts) narrates the events of the summers of 1964 and 1965, when the girls' parents at last split up. Mother teaches dance at a local studio, and father, with a shiny metal plate in the back of his head ("My mother says something happened to our father in the war but my sister says he is just mean"), hangs around the house and yard in a state of barely suppressed rage, often being cruel, sometimes drinking too much (this makes him prone to shoot his pistol), and on occasion (as at the end, when he attempts to kidnap his daughters) flying into real, wild violence. As the storm of their repressive father's irrationality slowly brews, the girls live their own carefully guarded, small, private lives, sneaking swims in a neighbor's above-ground pool (it has slugs in it), quarreling endlessly (along with scratches and punches), escaping on pretend-journeys in the burned-out car on the lawn (where their father sometimes sleeps, his feet sticking out the window), and stealing away at night to meet up with local boys. There's a small dog that adds a droll and often touching humor, an eerie episode of a sheep (father kills and then burns it), and a once-pet rabbit that lost its tail and now keeps to itself, though never going far from the yard ("Lily is wild but she is still ours"). Father's kidnap attempt, with car and gun and bullets and daughters, is, like everything else here, skillfully understated and vividly told.

Small, spare pleasures aplenty, albeit in a tale as worn and familiar as a soft old glove.

Gary Krist (review date 16 January 1994)

SOURCE: "Sins of the Father," in *The New York Times Book Review,* January 16, 1994, p. 11.

[*Krist is a prizewinning American short story writer. In the mixed review below, he praises Shea's focus on child abuse and survival in* Hula, *but faults her use of a child as a narrator.*]

Children, like many other small, apparently fragile creatures of nature, are actually great geniuses of survival. Forced to live in a world dominated by larger and more powerful animals, they learn to retreat to the inconspicuous corners of an unfriendly situation—accommodating the whims of the reigning bully, cultivating unobtrusiveness, vanishing when danger threatens only to re-emerge when the blustering of giants is past. Circumstances that would paralyze the average adult with despondency won't necessarily defeat a child, who doesn't labor under the same expectations of what life should be. As a result, children can thrive in the most unlikely places—even in that most noxious of environments, the traditional nuclear family.

Certainly the two nameless young girls at the center of ***Hula,*** Lisa Shea's terse, meticulously observed first novel, have ample opportunity to refine such psychological survival skills. The controlling figure in their 1960's Virginia household—their father, a menacing, periodically hospitalized veteran of precarious sanity—is not exactly what most child psychologists would consider an ideal parent. A man with "a bomb in his head that keeps going off," he is given to bizarre and arbitrary forms of discipline, subjecting his daughters to mock executions, burning their playthings, making the older girl strip naked on the porch and then throwing her clothes into the yard. The girls' mother, meanwhile, provides at best an ineffectual buffer against this abusive behavior, spending much of the book in bed with various ambiguous ailments. It's no wonder the two sisters learn to be invisible.

Invisible to adults, yes, but to each other they have vivid substance, sharing a private life that in its intensity and physicality verges on the erotic. Left largely to their own devices, the two form a kind of grudging alliance, like animals of the same species in the zoo, always snapping at each other in the close quarters of their cage but united by blood against all other species. Together, they manage to invest their joyless surroundings—the oozing sump pump, the forever-burning garbage barrel, the overflowing sewer pipe—with an aura of significance, transforming this suburban bleakness into something rich in possibility, endlessly fascinating and even, in a perverse way, alluring.

Ms. Shea, a widely published freelance writer, renders this closed, ritualistic world with great precision. Few novelists have written more convincingly about the sheer strangeness of the preadolescent mind, how artfully it sublimates abuse and early sexual feelings, incorporating them into the realm of play. To her credit, she doesn't dwell on obvious, overfamiliar escape fantasies, showing instead how dreams of flight are only one part of the girls' unconscious strategy for salvaging a normal childhood from such unpromising wreckage.

But her novel suffers, I believe, from a lack of authorial stance. Ms. Shea clings so insistently to the limited perspective of her narrator, the younger sister, that too much of the action plays out as raw image and impression, presented without the intellectual penetration required for readers to see beneath the surface of all these carefully hewn details. As a result, many of the secondary characters seem opaque or merely undeveloped: the mother a cipher, the father little more than a blur of indiscriminate malevolence. The reality of these and other characters doesn't seem to extend beyond the younger sister's narrow perceptions.

Ms. Shea has set a difficult challenge for herself: to remain loyal to the consciousness of a narrator too young and inexperienced to appreciate, even remotely, what is happening to her. Other writers—Deborah Eisenberg, Pat Barker, Kaye Gibbons—have managed to pull off the trick, filtering a story through the restricted vision of a child while at the same time conveying the sense of a more complex drama underneath. But Ms. Shea, I feel, hasn't succeeded at suggesting a novel's worth of depth below her book's graphic particulars.

And so ***Hula*** never becomes anything more than a series of fragments, vignettes. The inevitable, confrontation between the girls' father and mother—the culminating moment of the novel—lacks impact, not only because it is a collision between two such sketchy figures but also because the narrator and the author both seem to accept it all so passively, without judgment or reflection. By the epilogue, I found myself wishing Ms. Shea had dug deeper to provide more of a context in which her own insight and outrage could inform the story. As it is, ***Hula*** reveals her to be a strikingly gifted writer, but one whose talents deserve a larger, more ambitious showcase.

Cynthia Dockrell (review date 30 January 1994)

SOURCE: "Dancing in the Shadows of a Fearful Childhood," in *The Boston Globe,* January 30, 1994, p. A15.

[*In the following, Dockrell offers praise for* Hula, *discussing Shea's focus on victimization, abuse, and male-female relationships.*]

"Nothing will catch you. Nothing will let you go." So Lisa Shea warns us as she quotes Jorie Graham's *Tennessee June* in the epigraph to her first novel, ***Hula.*** Appropriate as it is, this signpost only hints at the netherworld that lies ahead, a limbo-like place where hiding becomes a high-stakes game of survival. It is a world of stark contrasts—light and darkness, flowers and ash, innocence and loss. It is a fear-filled place where fantasy is not just the stuff of childhood but a bridge to safety. It is sensuous, harrowing and mesmerizing.

In this slim volume, two sisters come of age in mid-1960s Virginia in the prison that is their back yard. Over the course of two steamy summers, the younger sister narrates as she and her sibling try to stay one step ahead of their war-damaged father and his unpredictable rages, while their shadowy mother, a former dance teacher, drifts ever further into the background.

To the narrator, who remains nameless, as do the others in the family, the father is an alien: "In the back of his head is a hole where no hair grows. Where no hair grows there is a metal plate attached to his head. In the sun, light strikes the metal plate like signals from a flying saucer." Indeed, he is unknowable and dangerous, punching his head with his fists, shooting up the back yard after a drink-filled day with a war buddy, donning a gorilla head and hands before driving off in the car. He metes out severe punishments for his daughters' smallest crimes, whipping them with a rope belt, burning the hula skirts in which they try to dance as their mother once did.

Faced with such horrendous abuse, the younger sister escapes into make-believe as she hides in the forsythia bushes, or on top of the garage, or in the ditch where her father burns everything from trash to the corpse of a puppy hit by a car. While in the shadows, she sets the world right, bravely transforming her parents into the king and queen or imagining great escapes in the burnt-out car at the end of the driveway. Her sister is both accomplice and enemy: In her emerging sexuality, she straddles the worlds of children and women, content with girls' games one day, contemptuous of them the next. Full of the false confidence of early adolescence, she teases her sexually innocent sister to the point of torment.

The only unwavering ally left to the narrator is the family dog, Mitelin, who literally protects the child as she pulls the dog's warm, scent-filled body on top of her, a shield. Mother of the dead puppy, Mitelin becomes something of a stand-in parent, patiently "dancing" in the girl's hula skirt and enduring the stifling heat of the car as they make their fanciful getaways. Mitelin is beloved in all her simplicity: "I smooth the fur on Mitelin's leg and put my hand in between the top of her haunch and her ribs. It is my favorite part of her except for the bump at the top of her head." There is an intimacy and poignancy to this relationship that makes the parents' wrongs all the more devastating.

Besides the wounded father, the other men in the novel are equally malevolent or deficient in some way. There is Ed Riley, a simple man who comes to mow the lawn and stutters when asked about the mother he reputedly never had; there is John Guidry, a tubercular alcoholic who passes out after drinking all day in the back yard; there is a chain gang of convicts who come to repair the road as the sisters watch transfixed; there are Frankie Blackmore and Duane Shields, neighborhood teen-agers who alternately lure and menace the girls with their aggressive sexuality. As the narrator says, "If you don't do what boys want, they can make you do it anyway."

This dark force of male power and inadequacy further imprisons the girls; nowhere is there a strong woman to help set them free. Only when faced with life-threatening violence does the mother mobilize herself enough to remove the children to their ultimate hiding place.

Shea's story can be taken as a parable about the price women have had to pay to coexist with men, but it is bigger than that, an exploration of the dangers inherent in growing up and what we must do to stay alive. The author's sensitive protagonist learns that this gets no simpler as we get older, that sex complicates things exponentially. Eavesdropping on a conversation between her mother and a friend, she observes: "I think [Mrs. Palmer] is a bad influence, not because she taught our mother how to smoke and dye her hair or because she wants her to leave our father. . . . I think Mrs. Palmer is a bad influence because she makes leaving seem like it is easy."

From the beginning, Shea establishes a tension that builds almost unbearably as the novel progresses. She achieves this in part through the oddly distant first-person telling of the story; the girl's blunt, childlike recording of horrific events, interspersed with her descriptions of the pent-up, overheated atmosphere, pulls her back from the action while drawing us closer to it. Shea's taut prose further adds to the story's power as she paints vivid pictures stripped of all but the barest essentials. The chapters are numerous and episodic: Each is a self-contained entity, with no conventional transitions; instead the narrative is held together by a string of significant events that the younger sister recalls repeatedly. At times this approach is jarring, but mostly it works. This is how children see the world.

The emotional chaos and pain-filled terrain of ***Hula*** continue to linger in this reader's memory, in no small part because Shea so deftly captures the inchoate and irreparable damage of wars large and small. All are victims here, even the man whose tyranny is not quite of this world: "When our father comes near me, I slide down under the table, but he pulls me back up by his hairy rubber hands. I don't say anything. He likes being the gorilla. After dinner, when he takes off the mask and hands, his face will be flushed and there will be tears in his eyes."

Karen Houppert (review date 15 March 1994)

SOURCE: "Full Disclosure," in *The Village Voice,* Vol. XXXIX, No. 11, March 15, 1994, p. 57.

[*Here, Houppert provides a favorable assessment of* Hula.]

Two girls sit on the front steps of their house watching the arrival of a storm while their parents fight inside, angry voices clearly audible. Their father's voice is "the thunder getting closer," their mother's "the wind shaking the

An excerpt from *Hula*

My mother says something happened to our father in the war but my sister says he is just mean. In the back of his head is a hole where no hair grows. Where no hair grows there is a metal plate attached to his head. In the sun, light strikes the metal plate like signals from a flying saucer.

Sometimes, our father hits his head with his fists. Once, my sister and I hit our heads and we both saw stars.

Other times he chases us up the stairs with his rope belt. By the time we get to the top, our legs are burning hot.

Our mother used to be a dancer. She taught the conga, tango, rumba, mambo, and cha-cha. She also taught the hula, the limbo, the dance of the seven veils. Now she works in a room above the studio, making costumes for the shows they put on.

When she met our father, she was dressed like a hula girl at a luau party and he was in charge of roasting the pig. She says our father's eyes were angry and blue and when he watched her hula, that was the end of her. She moves around in a little circle in the kitchen, doing one of the dances with the funny-sounding names. We watch, and my sister whacks the refrigerator over and over with the flyswatter until the handle breaks off.

When no one is home, we practice dancing in the living room. So far, my sister has taught me the twist, the hitchhiker, the watusi, and the swim. Sometimes we just bend and jump and twirl our bodies around. We call it the dance with no name because it can be anything.

Now we climb in through the punched-out windows of our father's burned-up car, parked on cinder blocks beside the driveway. Tall grass sticks up out of the engine. It pokes through the giant holes in the floorboards. My sister says our father blew the car up in an accident.

I tell her it might have burned up coming from outer space. She tells me to shut up about outer space.

From the backseat, we watch the sun go down. Birds fly off the telephone wires into the purple-and-orange sky. Our father pulls into the driveway in his new used car with the tied-on tailpipe that scrapes the ground. At night when he races down the driveway, we watch the sparks. Now he gets out of his car and walks past us toward the house. His shadow shoots up over the roof.

I ask my sister again if she thinks he's from outer space and she says No, but you are.

We stay in the backseat until it is almost dark and then we climb out of the car and walk up the driveway to our house. Slowly our shadows rise off the ground until they are smack against the bricks. Our shadows come up at us and then my sister pushes open the door and we go in.

Lisa Shea, in her Hula, *W. W. Norton & Company, 1994.*

pointy leaves of the mimosa tree." The narrator, a girl of about 10, has no shirt on because her volatile father has chased her suddenly from the house. Her older sister—12?—looks at the girl's bare chest. "Cover yourself," she says. The narrator answers: "I don't have anything."

So opens Lisa Shea's harrowing novel, ***Hula.*** Truly this young narrator has nothing to hide behind; the shame implied in covering up remains for her an adult convention. And while she doesn't shy from baring her stark world—isn't everyone's family just like mine?—it is her and her sister's skill at concealment that protects them from their father's wrath. Camouflaged beneath the mimosa branches, flat against the garage roof, beneath the porch, the two pubescent girls peer out at their world.

This short first novel takes place over two summers, during which the sisters are largely confined to the backyard. Their mother, trapped in a bad marriage, is depressed and distant. Their father, a severely disturbed veteran with a penchant for bonfires, is constantly burning whatever he finds disagreeable, from the dog's chew-bones to the girls' hula skirts to one of their puppies, Jupiter, killed by a passing car. The narrator and her sister crawl beneath the forsythia bushes or hide in the drainage ditch, fearful that the ashes coating everything might be Jupiter.

> My sister picks up a handful and sifts it through her fingers.
>
> "Jupiter," I tell her.
>
> "Jupiter is in the ground," my sister says.
>
> "He might be in the air."
>
> "He went down," she says.
>
> She throws the ash away. I close my eyes so a speck won't fly in. It might be Jupiter.

The sisters gravitate toward and away from each other in a painfully genuine leave-me-alone/where-are-you? relationship. And yet the narrator, frightened by her own, but mostly by her older sister's, emerging sexuality, clings to her one and only ally. Ordered to the car by their mother—domestic disputes often end with fast getaways—the girls sit.

> "How long do we have to wait?" I ask my sister.
>
> "Until," says my sister.
>
> "Until when?" I want to know.
>
> "Until you shut up!" she yells. . . . After a while, I reach for my sister's blond ponytail and hold it. She doesn't tell me to let go, so I keep holding it while the night comes down around the house and the trees and bushes and the car.

Sometimes cruelty makes its way into their games. They whip each other with forsythia branches, play "torture" by hanging naked from the branches of a tree where they pretend to be beaten until their "pinks" rise. From a second-story window they aim a real gun at their father's head. (" 'That's a sin.' 'Not when it's a war,' says my sister.") While their story is one of near misses, they never really stand a chance.

Shea exquisitely captures the straightforward voice of this young girl; ***Hula*** draws its power from this nonjudgmental immediacy. No narrator translates from the relative safety of middle age. No one gives distance. There is only the voice of one 10-year-old in the backyard, her playground and battlefield.

Lisa Shea on being called a new novelist:

I like the whole idea of first things—first novel, first poetry, first short story collections—because they're more transparent works and you can see what the writer was up to. Besides being called a first novelist, I can be called a failed poet. I think inside I feel much more like a failed poet than a first-time novelist.

Lisa Shea, in an interview with Elizabeth Manus, in The San Francisco Review of Books, *June-July, 1994.*

Barbara Rich (review date July 1994)

SOURCE: "Haunted Household," in *The Women's Review of Books,* Vol. XI, Nos. 10-11, July, 1994, p. 47.

[*Rich is an American critic and fiction writer. In the review below, she praises the thematic focus and stylistic features of* Hula.]

Lisa Shea is a freelance writer whose work has appeared in several prominent publications; she is the recipient of a 1993 Whiting Writers' Award. There are rumors that ***Hula*** is autobiographical, in the way so many first novels are. If this is the case, there's a strong temptation to offer up paeans yet again to the ability of human beings to survive.

The narrator of ***Hula*** and her older sister live in a rundown suburb in Virginia; the time is the mid-sixties. The children's mother, who used to be a dancer, and who taught the hula to the girls, is now a passive witness to their abuse, and to the disintegration of her marriage to a man who is, periodically, mad.

One of the telling symptoms of the narrator's separation from any sense of self is that no family names are provided. The children's animals have names: Mitelin, the dog; Max, her puppy; Lily, the mysteriously tailless rabbit. Neighbors, too, have names, but it's "our mother," "our father," "my sister" and "me."

> Our father walks down the hill, holding the scythe high above the grass . . . "What's he doing?" I ask again. My sister pinches me hard on the arm, which means shut up. Now our father is standing in front of the ditch, looking up at the house with the handle of the scythe lifted onto his shoulder. Our mother says our father has a bomb in his head that keeps going off. He has been taken to the hospital a few times but he keeps coming back.

The "bomb" is a metal plate, result of a war wound, that causes the father to commit random—and not so random—acts of abusive violence. The mother, while aware of this, cannot be roused from her beaten-down depression. So the children, one ten and the other pre-adolescent, engage in games: some violent, others self-protective. They watch a chain gang, and choose their "favorite" prisoner to fantasize about. The narrator observes her sister's precocious sexuality, and is torn between fear and jealousy. And they both try to be "invisible" when their father is around; but the narrator succeeds at this better than her sister, remarking at a crucial point, "She'll stick out like she usually does."

One chapter, "Blizzard," takes place during the summer of 1965. It is six pages of inner terror, wrapped up in a game of "pretend." The sisters and Mitelin are on a "journey" in the thick of an imaginary snowstorm, while the heat inside their father's burned-out car, parked on cinder blocks in the yard, grows more intense every minute.

> "Where are we going?" I ask my sister. Her arms are crossed and she is staring straight through the space between the dashboard and the steering wheel.
>
> "Away," she says.
>
> "Where?"
>
> "I'll think of a place."

The bogus blizzard reminds the narrator of a real snowstorm, when their mother took them to visit their father during one of his hospitalizations. He refused to see them, and Mitelin ate the entire cake they brought, including the box.

Hula is full of these childish yet old-beyond-their-years revelations, of events that shift from the present to the pitifully recent past. It is Shea's skill in showing chilling happenings so matter-of-factly that infuses and informs this brave, oddly mysterious novel. Which brings one quibble to mind: I wish Shea had been—at selective times—less elliptical, particularly in depicting the mother. Not necessarily a full portrait, but a somewhat clearer sketch . . .

As I was writing this review, my first visceral reaction to ***Hula*** came back, and I was struck by the power of its continuing impact. There is much about it to admire, even down to the cover design—a rear view of two small girls in hula skirts.

Hula is dedicated: "For my sisters." I choose to believe this is more than familial, that Lisa Shea wrote the book for women everywhere whose early years were marked by episodes of bewildering fear and pain, and who remain haunted by them.

Lisa Shea with Christopher Giroux, *CLC Yearbook* (interview date 2 December 1994)

[*In the interview below, Shea discusses various aspects of* Hula, *including its composition, her new work, and her literary influences.*]

[*Giroux*]: *Numerous critics have praised* **Hula's** *emotional honesty, noting that the book is dedicated "to my sisters." To what extent is* **Hula** *autobiographical?*

[Shea]: Like a lot of first novels it is and it isn't autobiographical. I think that the feelings that inform the book and the sensibility of the younger sister are very close to my sensibility and to my feelings. What I did was create a fictional story to get those feelings across. The impetus, I think, is always from your life. I think that the story itself is invented.

So did you do any sort of additional research for the book then?

No, I just lived (*laughs*). . . . There's wasn't anything that I had to go and look up that I can recall.

Another way to answer that question would be to say that I identify with all of the characters in the book. I feel that I could really be any and all of them. I have felt all those feelings and had some of those experiences, not as they are set down in the book, but similar ones. You know, there's that answer too, that I am all of those characters and not just one of them.

Is that part of the reason why the characters are never named?

Well, I don't know how much of a conscious choice that was. I think that I just felt comfortable not giving the two girls working names. I like in the book, just at the level of language, the repetition of "my sister," "our father," and "our mother." I thought that it was rather prayerful and intimate, so I didn't feel that names were necessary to this particular story or to these particular characters.

It's a very effective device. . . . I noticed, when I was reading the book, that the first part of the book includes more scenes with the father, and the second half places greater emphasis on the sisters, their relationship with each other, and their developing sexual awareness. But then at the very, very end, the father reappears. Were you consciously trying to split up your focus like that? And how is that splitting up of those sections and their respective themes related?

Well, there is a kind of split. Again, I think when you write a novel a lot happens at an unconscious level and then it's only your readers who point things out to you and you say "oh yes, I might have been doing that," but you didn't have an awareness of that at the time.

One thing that is key is that the book does take place over two summers. The book is split that way, 1964 and 1965, so when the book opens the narrator is ten; her older sister is twelve. Now the second summer, the narrator would be eleven and the older sister would be thirteen, and I think that, as in life itself, in the book that time from ten to eleven and twelve to thirteen is pivotal. Pivotal changes take place. So it may have been that there was more of an emphasis on the girls' relationship to the father over that first summer and then more of an emphasis on their sexual awakening in the second summer just because they were that one key year older. It certainly wasn't something that I was conscious of doing, although I see how it could be seen that way. But I think it's just that their sexual awareness became that much more heightened over the course of the year.

In *Hula* I really only wanted the reader to be privy to the narrator's thoughts and her observations and her feelings. I purposely didn't want the story to open up into an adult, or explaining, world.

—Lisa Shea

I also think that no matter how you write a novel, you have to have establishing scenes that let the reader know who the characters are. That's the reason for having scenes with the father at the beginning—to establish his presence. I think that more than a character in the book, he is a presence, as is the mother a presence, who exerts pressure on the girls rather than a character interacting with them scene after scene. He's at a remove, but he's such a menace that he feels a lot closer, a lot bigger, I suppose, in the story than his actual character.

That makes sense.

He sort of hovers. He and the mother kind of hover over the story and over the girls.

You've won the Whiting Writers' Award, and time and again critics praised your use of a child as a narrator, but there were some critics who faulted your reliance on this technique. How do you respond to that?

Well, one review I remember was in the *New York Times* where Gary Krist said something like "One wishes Ms. Shea hadn't clung so persistently to the narrator's limited point of view or voice," and I thought that's rather absurd. I mean how would I have written the story if I hadn't clung persistently to her view which is, perforce, by definition, limited as is the voice of every narrator. How else do stories get told except by what limits them? In the case of ***Hula*** the narrator is a ten- and eleven-year-old. This is her story coming from her very strangely cloistered, and at the same time, violent world. So I thought, well, there are always critics who would have written the book differently, but I was so certain—if there was *anything* I was certain of in writing that book—that I didn't want there to be any psychology going on, nothing explaining what the girls were up to. And I think one reason that it took me almost six years to write the book was the difficulty of staying in that little girl's voice. I really only wanted the reader to be privy to her thoughts and her observations and her feelings. I purposely didn't want the story to open up into an adult, or explaining, world.

You said the book took six years to write. I also read, in a press release, that it was written in a closet while you were trying to sort out your own feelings regarding your divorce. Is that true?

Well, the sequence of events was that my first husband and I separated, and I was living on my own here in New York with a roommate, an old friend from college, who was kind enough to let me move in with her until I could find my own place. In her house, which was huge, there was a walk-in closet, and it was during that first year of being separated that I began to work on the book. I didn't have my belongings with me. I had just a few clothes, my books and typewriter and so forth. So I was cut off from a lot of my possessions and belongings, and it eventually turned out to be a wonderful environment to let my imagination take up all the room that all these other things might have. So, I would say that for the first ten months I did work in that closet; it became a world apart where I could sit and confront some of the feelings I had about my own separation and then also reflect back on why my parents' marriage had ended so long ago. The book really began with a couple of photos that I had brought along with me. One was of a dog that we had, a dog that my sisters—I have two sisters—that my sisters and I had as children and whom we dressed in a hula skirt. I think of the dog as being another sister to the girls in the book and almost more than a sister, a mother and a handmaiden. I had a picture of this dog and I taped it up on the wall and I just went into that picture. It was one of these square Kodaks with the frilly edges, and it was taken in 1964. It gave me a place to go in.

The fact that the dog is a character—one that even has a name—reinforces what you said about the parents being more of a presence rather than characters.

Right, they're presences—

While the dog is someone the girls actually interact with all the time.

The bond of the girls and the dog is quite intimate, quite close. I think the little girl, the younger sister, actually goes and lies down in the spot in the ground where the dog likes to lie down in the bushes. There's that kind of closeness.

Hula was a spiritual and literary investigation of a time and a place warped by memory and fed by memory.

—Lisa Shea

Is it accurate to say that your goal in writing **Hula** *was therapeutic on your own part?*

It was investigatory. I prefer that word. It was a spiritual and literary investigation of a time and a place warped by memory and fed by memory.

I've read interviews where you've described yourself as a "failed poet," and I know that you've worked as an editor, too. Now, with a novel out, what do you consider your goals as a writer in general?

Just to be a better writer. I'm working on a second novel now and I don't know whether it is that we go after the things we want to write about or that those things come toward us and we just have to reach out and try to capture them and set them down on the page. I would say that my goals are so very fundamental, very basic—to hope that I find the story that I need to write. And/or the poems that I need to write.

Do you prefer writing poems to novels?

I think they're different activities. I love language and so when I write poetry I feel very freed into the play of language. To me it's a joyous exercise. Fiction writing seems more arduous, it's much slower. The rewards are different. It's not as enjoyable in the day to day, but it has a kind of cumulative power, a kind of seductiveness that pulls you along. I think it's harder to get in and out of fiction writing. If I have three hours in the morning to write and I use those three hours to write fiction, when it's time for me to go and pick up my little boy at preschool, I'm in a trance. I have to say "where's the school, where am I?" I find that fiction takes me very, very far away and I have to struggle back to reality. Poetry is easier to get in and out of.

You mentioned that you're working on a second novel. Can you talk about that at all? Does it continue themes that were developed in **Hula?**

It's a different story, called *The Free World.* I guess I'm thinking of it as a kind of female resurrection story. ***Hula*** was about a certain time and place. This book has more of a grounding in religion and politics. It's sort of a liturgy of one life set down over a period of six weeks, a very Catholic book, and perverse in its way. I suppose all my writing is about sex, and death. Isn't everybody's?

Do you have any idea when that book will be out?

Well, I just keep hoping that it won't be six years (*laughs*).

You mentioned that you write in the mornings—in a three-hour block—before you have to pick up your son. Can you describe your writing process more fully? Is that your time to write?

It is. It's a new schedule for me because my son just started school. I now have three new hours in my day, Monday through Friday, and I have found that since I wake up early anyway, the morning is the time when I can think and then the rest of the day gives over to a kind of chaos. So between nine and noon, I just try to be very diligent about using that time and working on the novel.

I write longhand, at my desk. I try to stay away from any kind of machinery that's noisy or makes me work too fast. I think computers speed things along somewhat treacherously. I like to go slow, so I just write on pads of paper. And if I write one to three pages each morning, I'm *very* happy about it.

When you write do you have a specific audience in mind?

No. When I was an undergraduate and wrote poetry, I remember that my friends and I revelled in the idea of being really obscure. We just thought that the more obscure our work was, the better it was. I would say that all these years later I probably think the reverse of that—which is that no matter what story you're telling, you have to tell it in a clear and convincing way. You can come in on a story sideways and backwards and upside down and make it clear. I'm not saying it has to be linear. You can tell it any way you want to, but you do have to bear in mind that there are readers out there. So I would say I don't write for a particular audience or readership, but I place a great value on clarity and lucidness however you do that.

Could you talk about who you consider your primary literary influences?

Well, the writers I love—you may see no bearing whatsoever in my own work, so I won't try to make that connection—but these are writers whose work I just love: James Joyce, Samuel Beckett, Charlotte Brontë, Emily Brontë, . . . Kafka, . . . George Eliot, . . . Faulkner, . . . I want to not forget the writer who had all the peacocks on her farm—Flannery O'Connor. I could go on with the list and maybe get more contemporary. There are so many poets whose work has influenced my prose, like John Ashbery, and some of the French surrealist poets. I love Baudelaire and Mallarmé and those fellows (*laughs*). I've been influenced by the surrealists, by the Irish writers, and by some of the American Southern writers.

You just noted that you didn't mention a lot of real contemporary writers, but how do you perceive yourself in relation to the larger picture of contemporary literature? Where do you place yourself?

Well, it's hard to say with one book. And my poetry is really more baroque and fanciful and. . . what other word could I use. . . . more language-drenched than ***Hula*** was. But I guess I feel you use the language that is appropriate to the story you're telling. If you're lucky, that language lends itself and is powerful enough to be able to tell all the stories you want to tell. I don't know. . . I think I'm still experimenting with that. Someone called ***Hula*** a "tour de force in the use of voice." I kind of agree that it's a voice novel, because it's not a novel of plot, certainly. But where do I place myself? Do you mean by that who am I like or who do I identify with who's contemporary?

Well. . . where do you see yourself fitting into what is popular nowadays?

That's hard to answer because I think every book is so different. I guess I instinctually feel that each book has its own voice, and style, and life.

Prizewinners

Literary Prizes and Honors
Announced in 1994

Academy of American Poets Awards

Fellowship of the Academy of American Poets
Awarded annually to recognize the distinguished achievement by an American poet.

David Ferry

The Lamont Poetry Selection
Established in 1952 to reward and encourage promising writers by supporting the publication of an American poet's second book.

Brigit Pegeen Kelly
Song

Peter I. B. Lavan Younger Poets Award
Established in 1983 to annually recognize three accomplished American poets under the age of forty.

Peter Grizzi (selected by John Ashbery)
Li-Young Lee (selected by David Wagoner)
Cynthia Zarin (selected by Richard Wilbur)

Walt Whitman Award
Secures the publication of the first book of a living American poet.

Jan Richman
Because the Brain Can Be Talked Into Anything

American Academy and Institute of Arts and Letters Awards

Academy Awards in Literature
Given annually to encourage creative achievement in literature.

Jon Robin Baitz, Marvin Bell, Stuart Dybek, Adrienne Kennedy, Tony Kushner, Mary Lee Settle, Chase Twichell, Geoffrey Wolff

Witter Bynner Foundation Prize for Poetry
Established in 1979 and awarded annually to recognize an outstanding younger poet.

Rosanna Warren

Sue Kaufman Prize for First Fiction

Awarded annually to the author of the best first fiction published during the preceding year.

Emile Capouya
In the Sparrow Hills

Richard and Hilda Rosenthal Foundation Award

Awards given annually for accomplishments in art and literature. The literature award recognizes a work of fiction published in the preceding year which, while not a "commercial success," is considered a literary achievement.

Janet Peery
Alligator Dance

James Tait Black Memorial Book Prize

Sponsored by the University of Edinburgh and awarded annually for the best work of fiction published during the previous year.

Caryl Phillips
Crossing the River

Booker Prize for Fiction

Britain's major literary prize awarded annually in recognition of a full-length novel.

James Kelman
How Late It Was, How Late
(see entry below)

Georg Büchner Prize

Awarded annually and considered Germany's most prestigious literary award.

Adolf Muschg

Commonwealth Writers Prize

Awarded annually to promote new Commonwealth fiction of merit outside the author's country of origin.

Vikram Seth
A Suitable Boy

Goncourt Prize

Awarded annually in France by the Académie Goncourt to recognize a prose work published during the preceding year.

Didier van Cauwelaert
Un aller simple

Governor General's Literary Awards

Honors writing that achieves literary excellence without sacrificing popular appeal. Officially known as the Canadian Authors Association (CAA) Literary Awards, these awards are given annually for works written in both English and French in the categories of fiction, nonfiction, poetry, and drama.

Robert Lalonde
Le Petit aigle à tête blanche
(fiction)

Rudy Wiebe
A Discovery of Strangers
(fiction)

Fulvio Caccia
Aknos
(poetry)

Robert Hilles
Cantos from a Small Room
(poetry)

Michel Ouellette
French Town
(drama)

Morris Panych
The Ends of the Earth
(drama)

Guggenheim Fellowships

Awarded annually to recognize unusually distinguished literary achievement in the past and exceptional promise for future accomplishment.

Mark Doty, Eamon Grennan, Brenda Hillman,
Karl Kirchway, Elizabeth Macklin, James McManus

Hugo Awards

Established in 1953 to recognize notable science fiction works in several categories.

Kim Stanley Robinson
Green Mars
(novel)

Harry Turtledove
Down in the Bottomlands
(novella)

Charles Sheffield
Georgia on My Mind
(novelette)

Connie Willis
"Death on the Nile"
(short story)

Ruth Lilly Poetry Prize

Awarded annually to an outstanding American poet.

Donald Hall

Los Angeles Times Book Awards

Honors technique and vision in various categories

Carolyn Forché
The Angel of History
(poetry)
(see entry below; see also *CLC*, Volume 83)

David Malouf
Remembering Babylon
(fiction)
(see entry below)

Martin M. Simecka
The Year of the Frog
(Art Seidenbaum Award for first fiction)

Lenore Marshall/*Nation* Poetry Prize

Established in 1974 to honor the author of the year's outstanding collection of poems published in the United States.

W. S. Merwin
Travels

National Book Awards

Established in 1950 to honor and promote American books of literary distinction in various categories.

William Gaddis
A Frolic of His Own
(fiction)
(see entry below)

James Tate
Worshipful Company
(poetry)

Sherwin B. Nuland
How We Die: Reflecting on Life's Final Chapters
(nonfiction)

Gwendolyn Brooks
(distinguished contribution to American letters)

National Book Critics Circle Awards

Founded in 1974 to recognize superior literary quality in American literature in several categories.

Ernest J. Gaines
A Lesson before Dying
(see entry below)

Mark Rudman
Rider

Nebula Awards

Established in 1965 to honor significant works in several categories of science fiction published in the United States.

Kim Stanley Robinson
Green Mars
(novel)

Jack Cady
The Night We Buried Road Dog
(novella)

Charles Sheffield
Georgia on My Mind
(novelette)

Joe Haldeman
"Graves"
(short story)

Neustadt International Prize for Literature

Awarded every two years by the University of Oklahoma for outstanding achievement in literature.

Edward Kamau Brathwaite

New York Drama Critics Circle Award

Presented annually in several categories to encourage excellence in playwriting.

Edward Albee
Three Tall Women
(see entry below)

Nobel Prize in Literature

Awarded annually to recognize the most distinguished body of literary work of an idealistic nature.

Kenzaburo Ōe
(see entry below)

Obie Awards

Given annually to recognize excellence in off-Broadway and off-off-Broadway theater productions in various categories.

Anna Deavere Smith
Twilight: Los Angeles, 1992
(best play)
(see entry below)

Eric Bogosian
Pounding Nails in the Floor with My Forehead
(playwriting)

Edward Albee
(sustained achievement)
(see entry below)

PEN American Center Awards

Faulkner Award for Fiction

Annually recognizes the most distinguished book-length work of fiction by an American writer published during the calendar year.

Philip Roth
Operation Shylock: A Confession
(see entry below)

Edgar Allan Poe Award

Presented annually for outstanding achievement in mystery writing.

Minette Walters
The Sculptress
(novel)

Laurie King
A Grave Talent
(first novel by an American)

Lawrence Block
"Keller's Therapy"
(short story)

Lawrence Block
(Grand Master)

Pulitzer Prizes

Awarded in recognition of outstanding accomplishments by American authors in various categories within the fields of journalism, literature, music, and drama. Literary awards usually recognize excellence in works that concern American life.

E. Annie Proulx
The Shipping News
(fiction)
(see *CLC,* Volume 81)

Yusef Komunyakaa
Neon Vernacular: New and Selected Poems
(poetry)
(see entry below)

Edward Albee
Three Tall Women
(drama)
(see entry below)

Rea Award

Presented annually to recognize outstanding achievement in the short story genre.

Tillie Olsen

Tanning Prize

Established in 1994, the Tanning Prize is the largest prize for poetry in the United States.

W. S. Merwin

Tony Awards

Officially titled the American Theatre Wing's Antoinette Perry Awards, prizes are presented in recognition of outstanding achievement on Broadway.

Tony Kushner
Perestroika
(see *CLC,* Volume 81)

United States Poet Laureate

Created in 1986 by an act of Congress to honor the career achievement of an American poet.

Rita Dove
(see *CLC,* Volume 81)

Whitbread Literary Awards

Awarded annually in several categories to encourage and promote English literature.

Joan Brady
Theory of War
(novel)
(see entry below)

Carol Ann Duffy
Mean Time
(poetry)

Rachel Cusk
Saving Agnes
(first novel)

Edward Albee
Three Tall Women

Award: Pulitzer Prize for Drama and New York Drama Critics Circle Award

(Full name Edward Franklin Albee III) Born in 1928, Albee is an American playwright, scriptwriter, poet, and short story writer.

For further information on Albee's life and works, see *CLC,* Volumes 1, 2, 3, 5, 9, 11, 13, 25, and 53.

INTRODUCTION

Three Tall Women (1991), Albee's third work to win a Pulitzer Prize, begins with a meeting between an elderly woman in her nineties known as A, her middle-aged caretaker B, and a young lawyer named C who has come to help A settle her affairs. As the three women interact, each becomes aware of and impatient with the others' shortcomings: the narrow-minded A, lamenting her advancing years, is in poor health and feels betrayed by family members; B is frustrated by her employer's numerous demands; and C, somewhat naive and temperamental, is shocked by what she considers the older women's vulgarity, prejudices, and lack of tolerance. The first act ends as A suffers a stroke, and in subsequent scenes Albee departs from a strictly linear plot, having all three characters appear as various manifestations of A at different times during her life. Through this use of multiple perspectives, Albee addresses various stereotypes associated with youth, middle age, and old age, and meditates on such issues as the evolving nature of personal identity, the emotional and intellectual ramifications of the aging process, and the relationship between past, present, and future. Familial ties are also central to *Three Tall Women,* which focuses in part on A's turbulent relationship with her homosexual son, and the play, described by Albee as a form of "exorcism," is considered largely autobiographical—the character A was based on Albee's mother and the relationship between parent and playwright mirrors that of A and her son. Critical reaction to *Three Tall Women* has been generally positive. Although commentators have consistently identified C as the weakest character in the play, they have lauded A and B as well-defined portraits and praised Albee's focus on universal concerns. Many critics have additionally asserted that *Three Tall Women* is the most successful work Albee has written in years, rivalling such classics as *The Zoo Story* (1959), *Who's Afraid of Virginia Woolf?* (1962), and *Seascape* (1975); they also note that due to its autobiographical content *Three Tall Women* offers invaluable insights into Albee's life and career. John Lahr observed: "Far from being an act of revenge or special pleading, the play is a wary act of reconciliation, whose pathos and poetry are a testament to the bond, however attenuated, between child and parent. *Three Tall Women* bears witness to the son's sad wish to be loved, but with this liberating difference: the child is now finally in control of the parent's destiny, instead of the parent's being in control of the child's."

PRINCIPAL WORKS

The Zoo Story (drama) 1959
The Death of Bessie Smith (drama) 1960
Fam and Yam (drama) 1960
The Sandbox (drama) 1960
The American Dream (drama) 1961
Bartleby [adaptor; from the short story "Bartleby, the Scrivener: A Story of Wall-Street" by Herman Melville] (opera) 1961
Who's Afraid of Virginia Woolf? (drama) 1962

The Ballad of the Sad Café [adaptor; from the novella by Carson McCullers] (drama) 1963
Tiny Alice (drama) 1964
A Delicate Balance (drama) 1966
Malcolm [adaptor; from the novel by James Purdy] (drama) 1966
Everything in the Garden [adaptor; from the drama by Giles Cooper] (drama) 1967
Box (drama) 1968
Quotations from Chairman Mao Tse-Tung (drama) 1968
All Over (drama) 1971
Seascape (drama) 1975
Counting the Ways: A Vaudeville (drama) 1977
**Listening: A Chamber Play* (drama) 1977
The Lady from Dubuque (drama) 1980
Lolita [adaptor; from the novel by Vladimir Nabokov] (drama) 1981
Finding the Sun (drama) 1983
The Man Who Had Three Arms (drama) 1983
Marriage Play (drama) 1987
Three Tall Women (drama) 1991
Fragments: A Concerto Grosso (drama) 1993

*This work was first produced as a radio play.

CRITICISM

Jeane Luere (review date May 1992)

SOURCE: A review of *Three Tall Women,* in *Theatre Journal,* Vol. 44, No. 2, May, 1992, pp. 251-52.

[*In the following review of a production of* Three Tall Women *directed by Albee, Luere offers praise for the play, comparing it to Albee's previous works and noting his focus on family, guilt, love, and identity.*]

Receptive audiences at Vienna's English Theatre, which in the past has been host to Tennessee Williams, Harold Pinter, Lanford Wilson, are hailing the new Edward Albee offering [***Three Tall Women***], giving the play's three-in-one heroine emotional precedence over men and women in his previous dramas. In stirring anecdotes, the eldest third of Albee's strong composite heroine, a ninety-year-old with a prodigal son, divulges her prejudices, her attitudes and insights on the lack of substance in the upper crust into which she has married. The two other onstage characters, materializations of her self before childbirth and at middle age, hear the older component bemoan her husband's and friends' lack of backbone or moral fibre. Regrettably, her disillusion has led her to replace the legendary milkman or back seat of a car with the family's groom and stable.

As in previous plays, the author is more concerned with characters and situations than with problems and their trite resolution. Albee's power to generate real characters is legendary; and his delicate drawing of this newest one, a tall mother whose indiscretions alienate her son, may show the author's intellectual sympathy for her, quelling critics' sporadic hints at anti-female strains in earlier work. However, Albee's mother-image in ***Three Tall Women,*** drawn with wit and truth, is itself more palatable than the insight into life which the play dramatizes. Albee's new work warns that in a land where the populace is obsessed with self-fulfillment and determined to be happy, what must cease at once is our perpetuation of our offsprings' notion that in life we get what we want, that parents and the world at large are perfect caregivers—or even caregivers at all. Rather, in the words of Albee's aged mother-composite, we must prepare the world's young for the actualities of a life in which "surcease or a series of surceases" is our only joy. Truth is our only salvation. So long as we hide from our children the sad truth of our imperfections and our mutability, we must expect the tragic splits that rend mothers and children.

Officiously, critics in the 1970s and 1980s often chided Edward Albee for drawing homosexual characters, like those in his ***Tiny Alice,*** too subtly, forming them implicitly rather than explicitly. With ***Three Tall Women,*** the upbraiders may be silenced. Albee's newest male character, a defiant son who, in his forties, returns to kiss his bedfast mother's hands and face—and who materializes on the stage as the youth who had packed his "attitudes" and left twenty years earlier—is strikingly portrayed by Howard Weatherall. The nature of the son evolves in frank phrases from the lips of his mother, delivered with chagrin by Myra Carter, who refers to her son and his friends as "he and his boys" and who laments, "He doesn't love me, he loves those boys he has!" Yet, in the mother's dotage, the son brings special gifts of candied orange peel and freesia and sees to happy outings for her.

New York critics who in 1983 misinterpreted the talentless former freak in Albee's ***Man Who Had Three Arms*** as an intimate revelation of the author's self may infer the present drama to be another little masochistic exercise, making amends for his "attitudes" as a teenager. If the play's authorial intention is a coming to terms with self, Weatherall's sincerity in the role of the son makes viewers long for their own second chance to reconcile with an aged parent as honestly as this character does.

The play's form is as convoluted as one expects from Albee. Here he intrigues us with the work's structure, forces us to figure out which of two worlds he is drawing us into—the totally naturalistic world of Act One, whose three tall women are a law clerk, a ninety-year-old mother and her nurse, or the presentationally-staged world of act two where a maternal, mystical identity falls to each actress.

The playwright's penchant for puzzles unsettles even deeply-moved audiences who crowd the sold-out theatre. Rapt viewers may lose the beauty and tension of Albee's language for those precious minutes they need to solve the problem of which world confronts them on stage. Yet critics' complaints about structure are not so indicative of a play's merit as the sentiment (as opposed to sentimentality) that an audience credits in the play. Albee's long-time obsession with the orchestration of emotions and with theatrical effectiveness culminates here. Audiences applaud how effectively the playwright has rendered the mother's guilt for infidelities and for failing to remain the pedestal-figure her son perceived her to be in his babyhood. Even so, the play's structure may need a touch of the author's clever directorial hand before moving from Vienna—a site Albee has called "off-off-Broadway"—to New York.

The cast's delivery of the emotion in Albee's language and in his subtext is cuttingly valid, particularly in act 2 when the actresses unfold the life of the mother at ages 26, 52, and 90. Carter is an electric presence on stage as the oldest maternal figure, and voices each bit of Albee's dialogue so piquantly that what might have been, with a lesser actress, rambly and senile chatter about a lecherous father-in-law, a frigid sister, and deceased friends, instead etches the mother's character just as finely as brush strokes create an amorphous WOLS leaf. Thus we feel the tension of the mother-character who suffers from her own infirmities. She won't admit that she can no longer manage her finances, or that she is partner to her son's long disaffection. Her resentment of male infidelity, her isolation by friends' deaths, her guilt at indiscretions—each is a theme from earlier Albee works like his miniature American tragedy, ***The Sandbox,*** or his Pulitzer prize drama ***Delicate Balance,*** themes broadened and surging with life in ***Three Tall Women.***

Representing the demanding and expectant youth of the mother, Cynthia Bassham is at once innocent and sophisticated. Bassham, who last year made indelible the naivete of Honey in ***Who's Afraid of Virginia Woolf?,*** sashays in a sleek gown as a Bergdorf-Goodman fashion model who climbs the social ladder when she marries into wealth. Later, Bassham's character, with haunted voice and mein, recoils at the prospect of living her life without joy. The actress's expressive face is proud and stubborn in act 2 as she innocently balks at hints of what may be slated for her life; and her face is livid in act 2 when she sees the actualities descend upon her.

Kathleen Butler, who triumphed in Albee's 1987's ***Marriage Play*** as a disenchanted wife who would rather be hit than left, now creates a more put-upon figure as the shrewder, middle span of Albee's composite mother. With humour the actress conveys the play's authorial discernments on the sad consistency of life—that with a doctor's firm slap and a hard first breath a baby comes in, and at the end, with a harder breath goes out. With strength and gravity, Butler demonstrates that a son's sulks and attitudes may freeze mother-love for a spell no matter how desperately she wants to forgive him. Later, with conviction, Butler shines as her mid-life character announces that, though her life has been crammed with hurt, she has now climbed the hill from which one can look back halfway and ahead halfway—in Albee's phrase, "the only time we have a three hundred and sixty degree view!"

After a painful search for serenity with the materialized components of her selves, Albee's ultimate mother-image realizes that joy lies not in the events of our lives but in surcease when each of her conflicts ends. Alone, at the mercy of caregivers and her own infirmities, she rejoices in the surcease of anxiety over real or imagined results of her actions or misjudgments of the past. In ***Three Tall Women*** Albee moves from his demons toward joy, surcease, and death; perhaps now he will write for us of love instead of disillusion.

Ben Brantley (review date 14 February 1994)

SOURCE: "Edward Albee Conjures Up Three Ages of Women," in *The New York Times,* February 14, 1994, pp. C13, C16.

[*In the following excerpt, Brantley comments on Albee's treatment of life, death, aging, identity, and personal experience in* Three Tall Women.]

The woman identified simply as A in Edward Albee's ***Three Tall Women,*** the startlingly personal work that is receiving its New York premiere at the Vineyard Theater, shares many of the linguistic and psychological traits common to characters in Mr. Albee's more abstract plays. She is given to questing reiteration of certain phrases that take on different shadings in the repetition; she shifts disjunctively between arrogant complacency and fearful disorientation; and her memory slides and stumbles like a neophyte skater. "I can't remember what I can't remember," she says.

But A is a woman whose speech patterns are not merely stylized representations of Mr. Albee's enduring obsessions with the elusiveness of personality and its self-deceptions. There is a purely naturalistic reason for her behavior. Played with virtuosic reversals of mood by the superb Myra Carter, A is a 92-year-old woman (or is it 91, as she insists?) who is on the threshold of death. And the way she talks is rooted in the very familiar struggle of the aged with encroaching senility.

Her presence reinforces what has always been implicit in the playwright's works: life must be defined by the inescapable proximity of death. As one character states, children should be made "aware they're dying from the moment they're born."

Three Tall Women, which is basically an anatomy of one life, is by no means an entirely, successful play. Cleanly directed by Lawrence Sacharow, it makes its points so blatantly and repeats them so often that one perversely longs for a bit more of the cryptic obliquity that is Mr. Albee's signature.

But it is often a truly moving work. Mr. Albee has admitted in interviews that it was directly inspired by his own adoptive mother, a domineering, Amazonian woman. And the details of A's life, including her ambitious marriage to a wealthy man and her warring relationship with her recalcitrant son, seem to tally with what we know of Mr. Albee's family history. He has described the writing of the play as "an exorcism." And one can see in A the roots of the controlling women who abound in the rest of his oeuvre.

The members of the play's speaking cast are indeed three tall women, whose roles, if not necessarily their functions, change in the play's two acts. (There is, very significantly, an additional wordless part, that of the prodigal son, played by Michael Rhodes, who arrives in the second act after his mother has a stroke.) Set in a bedroom (designed by James Noone) whose conventional but lavish appointments bespeak an insulating affluence, the play devotes its first half to dialogue among the aged A; B, her 52-year-old acerbic but empathetic caretaker (Marian Seldes), and C (Jordan Baker), a brashly confident 26-year-old from A's lawyer's office who has come to discuss finances.

Mr. Albee baldly sets these characters up as representatives of three ages of woman. C embodies all the intolerance and the conviction of immortality of youth, and is impatient with the old woman's meanderings. The caretaker, in turn, is impatient with C's impatience and given to sharp-tongued reminders that A represents C's future. (In this sense, she is a sort of stand-in for Mr. Albee, as playwright, not as son.) And throughout all this, A fades between past and present.

In the second act, a body with an oxygen mask, representing A, is found lying on the bed. The three actresses return, now as A at different phases in her life. Although this allows Mr. Albee to create a more complete and reflective biography of A, particularly involving her thorny relationship with her son, the symbolic triangle remains much the same, with the youngest woman shouting at the oldest, "I will not become you!"

There are some eloquently made statements in this act about the vantage points afforded by different ages, particularly on the subject of sexuality. Unfortunately, the revelations built around the reasons for A's son's leaving home have less than their intended dramatic impact. . . .

Ultimately, it appears that in working through autobiographical material, Mr. Albee has felt the need to be as carefully lucid and precise as possible. Though it seems unfair to accuse a playwright of excessive obviousness when he has so often been critically browbeaten for just the opposite, the play does suffer from didacticism and overstatement.

Nonetheless, ***Three Tall Women*** remains essential viewing for anyone interested in the forces that have shaped this influential writer.

Stefan Kanfer (review date 14-28 February 1994)

SOURCE: "Time—and Again," in *The New Leader,* Vol. LXXVII, No. 2, February 14-28, 1994, pp. 22-3.

[*Kanfer is an American novelist, playwright, short story writer, essayist, scriptwriter, and critic. In the excerpt below, he offers a mixed review of* Three Tall Women, *arguing that "this elegant minor effort gives very little reason to cheer" and lacks the qualities that characterize Albee's best works.*]

Whatever happened to Edward Albee? *The* young playwright of the early '60s, he began his career with small but auspicious Off-Broadway efforts like ***The American Dream*** and ***The Sandbox,*** both about the sorrow and bitterness of old age. His first full-length work, ***Who's Afraid of Virginia Woolf?*** (1963), focused on ambition and self-deception, dazzled Broadway audiences, won critics' awards, and announced the arrival of a major talent. Albee went on to earn two Pulitzer prizes (for ***A Delicate Balance*** and ***Seascape***) and to write many original plays, plus adaptations of other people's writings (including Carson McCullers' ***The Ballad of the Sad Café,*** and Vladimir Nabokov's ***Lolita***).

His reward for all this industry has been a latter-day neglect. Too many of Albee's major works have failed on the main stem, and lesser plays have not prospered Off-Broadway. Who remembers ***The Lady from Dubuque, The Man Who Had Three Arms, Finding the Sun?*** Although they are included in some anthologies of the American theater, an entire generation now regards the 65-year-old playwright as a supernova, a star that burned out long ago. The production of ***Three Tall Women*** at the Vineyard Theater may help to correct that impression—but just barely.

Here again is the once-famous amalgam of bitchiness and poignance. A rich and self-centered nonagenarian (Myra Carter) is failing rapidly. Known only as A, she is attended by B (Marian Seldes), a grim middle-aged factotum, and by C (Jordan Baker), an attractive young lawyer who is there to straighten the old lady's tangled finances. Act I concerns A's infirmities and incontinence, as she rails against her weak bones and failing memory. B variously prods and pampers her, while C is the observer. Shocked and horrified at the trials of senescence, she wonders whether A is being mistreated or merely handled with the firmness she deserves.

For A is a collection of resentments and prejudices. Blacks are niggers. Jews are to be used but never trusted. Homosexuals, including her son ("He just packed up his attitude and left me"), are referred to contemptuously. Through the years, she suspected every servant of pilfering. Without any evidence, B is included in that disgraceful company.

Like her two listeners, A was a tall woman (although age has made her bones shrink a little). Her late husband was a small man with a glass eye and a lot of money. He is fondly recalled—but not as fondly as the horse trainer who seduced her and, of course, had to be fired after a month of furtive adultery. "I had a good deal," she explains. "I couldn't endanger my situation." A's testimony is more than C can bear. There is no way, she vows, that she will come to *this* sort of end. But she has spoken too soon and too late.

In Act II, as A lies on her deathbed, B and C are revealed as something far different from their first appearances. They are not individuals after all; they are, rather, the former selves of A, at the ages of 52 and 26. Time is annihilated, and the three tall women interact. The young one, C, is full of romantic expectations, whirling on a dance floor, speculating about a series of beaux, planning a vibrant and happy life. B is the older and wiser one, having compromised her dreams for decades of imprisoning security. A is a kind of Queen Lear, having outlived her friends and become estranged from her only child. When he returns, The Boy (Michael Rhodes) can simply sit wordlessly at her bedside, his body language pronouncing the elegy for the mother he can neither leave nor love.

Under Lawrence Sacharow's subtle direction, the trio of actresses find every possible nuance in the text. Baker moves easily from terror to radiance and back again; Seldes gives the play its *gravitas;* and Carter manages to be querulous and comic in the same short breath, dropping her voice an octave to confide a secret, then rising to an eerie cackle as she recalls her husband's indiscretions and her own sexual misadventures. James Noone's bedroom set is merely functional, but Muriel Stockdale's costumes amount to a fifth character, commenting on the passages of time and the alterations of personality.

If this were 1962, ***Three Tall Women*** would herald the arrival of a playwright as promising as David Ives. One could hardly wait to see his next production. But we have been through all that with Albee, and this elegant minor effort gives very little reason to cheer. After years of commercial and esthetic disappointments, Edward Albee is once again Off-Off-Broadway. Like so many of his characters through the decades, he is going out the way he came in.

What Albee has wrestled down [in *Three Tall Women*] is his self-contradictory tendency toward attitudinizing and lowdown nastiness; to the extent that rudiments of both are still there, they have been polished and domesticated: There is no longer the freakish feel of a keyboard being played only at its two extremities.

—John Simon, in his "Trifurcating Mom," New York, ***28 February 1994.***

Michael Feingold (review date 1 March 1994)

SOURCE: "Albeecentric," in *The Village Voice,* Vol. XXXIX, No. 9, March 1, 1994, pp. 83, 86.

[*Feingold is an American critic and translator. In the following excerpt, he assesses the strengths and weaknesses of* Three Tall Women.]

Every writer knows that the hardest task in writing is to find your center. Once you're there, words, thoughts, events, characters, ideas, whatever, will flow freely. And the results, after some contemplation, will be far easier to shape and polish than if you had forced them. The hard part is getting to that sacred place at the core of your being from which all literary blessings flow.

On this count, the renaissance of Edward Albee is one of the happiest events in the history of American playwriting. After the era of forced writing that brought us treats like ***Counting the Ways*** and ***The Man Who Had Three Arms,*** and the era of self-imposed exile when he no longer cared to face the critical attacks such plays provoked, we have two newish Albee plays [being produced this season], one 11 years old (***Finding the Sun***) and one written within the last four (***Three Tall Women***). Both are alive, peopled, fresh, funny, a little harrowing, and tangibly authentic—the good qualities of Albee's exciting early plays. They come from the center; far from offering critical analysis or captious reservations, the press should probably sponsor parades. . . .

[Perfect] in its fairness is the full-length ***Three Tall Women,*** clearly Albee's all-out attempt to do justice to Mommy. [Like his 1960 work, ***The Sandbox,*** this too] is a death scene: The ailing, cantankerous heroine is flanked by her weary, stooped, middle-aged companion and a blankly helpless young newcomer from her lawyer's office. Power games, medical details, and recriminations ensue, leading to an apparent stroke. In Act II, the women appear as three aspects of the stroke victim, now helpless under an oxygen mask: her young, middle-aged, and old selves. The handsome Young Man, suffering mutely at her bedside, is no cartooned Angel of Death, but her son as he looked the day he left the house for good.

In this act, the middle-aged self dominates: Marian Seldes, who's had self-effacing, galumphing fun as the first act's humble companion, comes into her own, commanding the stage, head high, with fierce, grand-manner gestures, flanked—and sometimes outflanked—by Myra Carter's slyly stagy, astringent undercutting as the old woman. The staginess is in the character; you see how Albee might have gotten his theatrical instinct from this woman, with her calculated tantrums and high-handed tyrannizing.

The mother's story, as the three women relay it to each other, not without dispute, is the story of a tall beauty brought low—by her need to succeed in a society where women are ancillary, by the contrast between her modest upbringing and her married wealth, by rivalry with her prettier but less stable sister, by increasing frustration with husband and family, by failure to overcome inhibitions taught in an earlier age, finally by old age and illness. The author's love and hate, denial and acceptance, of this complex woman whirl around the room, almost visibly, while his mute spokesman onstage sits motionless, holding the hand of her almost-corpse.

Three Tall Women's fullness as writing makes it a big achievement, with only one minor flaw: The first act, which is really a prologue to the substantive second, goes on slightly too long, and should probably lose some of its repetitions.

Tim Appelo (review date 14 March 1994)

SOURCE: A review of *Three Tall Women,* in *The Nation,* New York, Vol. 258, No. 10, March 14, 1994, pp. 355-56.

[*Appelo frequently writes for* Entertainment Weekly. *In the review below, he favorably assesses* Three Tall Women *and discusses the insight it gives into Albee's life and works.*]

Photos reveal Edward Albee to be stricken with the Dick Clark Syndrome: an inexplicable imperviousness to physical decay. Instead, time has taken its toll on his festering reputation.

But I'm thrilled to report that Albee the artist lives. The

Vineyard Theater production of his 1991 play ***Three Tall Women,*** his first big New York premiere in over a decade, should help reverse his audience's exodus. No more the noisy young shockmeister pop star, now Albee plays unplugged, still singing, softly, his bitter old themes of domestic-*cum*-cosmic discord. Rod Stewart unplugged is a lazy disgrace, Clapton a drab craftsman, but Albee is more like Neil Young: chastened by age, sad where once he soared, yet still quavering on.

Three Tall Women is largely a portrait of Albee's late, very estranged adoptive mother at 92, though the character querulously insists she's 91. (In a 1966 *Paris Review* interview, Albee querulously insisted he was 37; the interviewer reminded him he'd be 38 when the piece was published.) James Noone's set neatly conveys the old woman's luxe past and funeral future: A central floral painting is flanked by floral wallpaper, floral prints, floral lace curtains, a bed with floral pillows and a blighted floral rug worn down to atoms.

So is the wraithlike heroine, but there's a death dance of semisenescent reminiscence left in the old gal yet. Myra Carter is, as the young people say, *awesome* in the role of A, the nonagenarian mom. Her phrasing of Albee's half-naturalistic, wholly calculated incipient-Alzheimer's talk is impeccable; her voice dwindles to an Edith Evans warble, ascends to a helium keening, erupts abruptly into lacerating sobs as required. Her moods, too, are musical—her memories lark and plunge. We're eager and grateful for each vivid bit of that past recaptured: her debutante milieu; her runty, randy groom; horseback riding; riding her horse's groom in the stables as she screams in sexual triumph. (Some of these memories are voiced by other actors, whom I'll introduce shortly.) ***Three Tall Women*** cops a bit of the puckish bleakness of Beckett (the sole dramatist Albee has claimed utterly to admire), and a bit of *Long Day's Journey Into Night,* but the grief and affection seem distant, glimpsed through the wrong end of a telescope. It's O'Neill without guilt, and with much less galumphing verbal rhythms. "Eventually he lets me talk about when he was a little boy," says A of her son's visits—Michael Rhodes plays the wordless role well enough—"but he never has an opinion on that; he doesn't seem to have an opinion on much of anything that has to do with us, with me." Creepily remote, Albee has predicted that he won't think much about his mom now that he's devoted a play to explicating her life. But I'll bet he didn't keep mum with Ma in real life: This is the guy of whom Richard Burton wrote, "A week with him would be a lifetime."

Old A is reproved by young C (Jordan Baker), a B-school type trying to get A's finances in order. The role is as thin as the pinstripes on C's suit, and Baker is way the hell the spindliest actor in the show. Twenty-six-year-old C is reproved by B (Marian Seldes), A's 52-year-old caretaker. As dazzling a talent as Carter, Seldes is earthy and spectral, not by turns but at once. Hunched like a sardonic question mark, she moderates the conflict between the old and young women, but she's openly on the old bat's side. She's like Mrs. Danvers on Prozac—still mean and weird, but detached, sourly entertained by life as if watching it from beyond, a well-adjusted shade. Her sly arched-brow amusement reminds me of Ian McKellen; her marvelously odd hand gestures remind me of Thai opera, except that I can't comprehend Thai opera, while her gestures clearly underline the dialogue. Many lovely ensemble moments seem centered on her hands, as if she were conducting. (Though Lawrence Sacharow's direction must have been superb, Ingmar Bergman was probably right to say that Albee's best plays can do without a director, just as chamber music doesn't require a dictatorial baton. The man is a composer, just as he wanted to be at age 11.)

Albee has this little problem as a dramatist: He abhors plots. But just as one realizes, with mounting irritation, that A's colorful fragmented vignettes will never cohere into a single structured picture—nobody cracks Albee's mosaic code—the author saves the play with a big switch in the second act. The three actresses fuse into one contrapuntally evoked character, A through the ages. It's played wonderfully (even Baker gets better), like a close basketball game going down to the wire. While the finale is a characteristic letdown (Albee favors inconclusive conclusions), by then the play has wandered around A's life long enough to give us a satisfying sense of her.

Mysteriously, we get very little sense of her relationship with her son, just a sketchy recounted encounter or two. I wanted more on this relationship, and fewer of the life lessons the play overbearingly urges upon us: "It's downhill from 16 on for all of us . . . stroke, cancer . . . walking off a curb into a 60-mile-an-hour wall . . . slit your throat. . . . All that blood on the Chinese rug. My, my." You can get deeper philosophical insights from Dionne Warwick's Psychic Friends Network. Yet even when Albee says something stupid, he says it in cadences of great and practiced beauty. The wisdom that eludes him in platitudes ("[Women] cheat because we're lonely; men cheat because they're men") he expresses better in drama: the anecdote of the pricey bracelet A's fellatio-craving husband proffers upon his angry penis is funny and scary, a lightning glimpse of a nightmare marriage.

I freely admit that much of the value of ***Three Tall Women*** is the light it sheds on Albee's life and other work. He has described ***TTW*** as an "exorcism." The original title of ***Who's Afraid of Virginia Woolf?*** was *The Exorcism,* which was retained as the title of the third act, and ***TTW*** makes me wonder whether critics haven't been misinterpreting his masterpiece all these years, focusing on George and Martha as archetypal man and wife (or, in a popular interpretation that infuriates Albee, as a gay couple in hetero drag. I don't see what difference it makes, nor why Albee sternly forbids all-male productions of the show). What gets exorcised—killed off—in ***Woolf*** is the imaginary kid. In ***TTW,*** the kid kills off the memory of his mom. What if George and Martha are "really" Edward and his ever-bickering mother, who needled him cruelly about his adoption and never forgave his desertion? In any case, the heroine A of ***TTW*** is a kind of combination of the Liz Taylor and Sandy Dennis characters in ***Woolf***: alternately a snarly and simpering, sickly fake mother, yet admirably defiant of the unmitigated insult of old age. From the first-act debate about a classic actress (Bette

Davis in the case of ***Woolf,*** Norma Shearer in ***TTW***) to the last act's rather heavy-handed stripping away of bourgeois illusions (who has them anymore?), the plays seem parallel, sister dramas reaching out to each other across the intervening wastes and oases of Albee's career.

Why is such a self-conscious iconoclast so annoyingly moralistic? Albee is the third-generation namesake of a top vaudeville impresario who got started with a revolting attraction: a twenty-four-ounce preemie advertised as "small enough to fit in a milk bottle." The child's name was Baby Alice. Does this have something to do with his reviled abstract play ***Tiny Alice?*** Edward Albee I ran a theatrical enterprise so bluenosed it blacklisted the actors it ruthlessly enslaved if they so much as uttered the words "son of a gun" on any of its nationwide stages. Having authored five "son of a bitch's" in ***Woolf*** alone, Edward Albee III was the Tom Paine of the dirty-speech movement in American theater, though he was more besides. Maybe there's an in-joke in his ***Alice,*** and a secret triumph in its commercial oblivion: the horribly lowest-common-denominator entertainment answered by a work of arrogant mandarin incomprehensibility, spurned by the ignorant masses.

With the entirely intelligible ***Three Tall Women,*** Albee is evidently mature enough not to crave our hatred. Maybe he doesn't even hate his mother anymore. What's more, he's back in tune with his times. In the three tall women's last-ditch attempt to define the nature of happiness, Seldes's B muses that her position at 52 is ideal: "Enough shit gone through to have a sense of the shit that's ahead, but way past sitting and *playing* in it. This *has* to be the happiest time." Shit happens—in a day when the nation's leading dramatic characters are Beavis and Butthead, what moral could be more modish than that?

Robert Brustein (review date 4 April 1994)

SOURCE: "The Rehabilitation of Edward Albee," in *The New Republic,* Vol. 210, No. 14, April 4, 1994, pp. 26, 28.

[*Brustein is an American educator, critic, and actor who frequently writes about drama. In the highly positive review below, he discusses Albee's focus on the past and present in* Three Tall Women, *praising it as "a mature piece of writing."*]

A number of years ago, while praising Edward Albee's much reviled stage adaptation of ***Lolita,*** I commented on the startling reverses in the fortunes of this once ionized American dramatist: "The crunching noises the press pack makes while savaging his recent plays are in startling contrast to the slavering sounds they once made in licking his earlier ones. . . . If each man kills the thing he loves, then each critic kills the thing he hypes . . . brutalizing the very celebrity he has created."

I was generalizing not only from Albee's career, but from that of Miller, Williams and Inge, for although I had often depreciated works by these playwrights myself, it struck me as unseemly that mainstream reviewers were displaying such fickleness toward their favorite Broadway icons. This may sound territorial, but it's not. Readers expect more intellectual critics to express dissent about an overinflated dramatic work, but it is an entirely different matter when those with the power to close a show become so savage and dismissive in their judgments. If it is a function of the weekly critic to try to correct taste, it is the function of the daily critic to guide theatergoers, not to trash careers or demolish reputations.

Fortunately, Albee's stubborn streak has kept him writing in the face of continual disappointment, a persistence he shares with a number of other artists battered by the New York press (Arthur Miller, David Rabe, Arthur Kopit, Christopher Durang, Philip Glass, etc.). I call this fortunate because Albee has a vein of genuine talent buried in the fool's gold, and there was always a hope, provided he was not discouraged from playwriting, that this would appear again in a work of some consequence. That work has now arrived in ***Three Tall Women,*** and I am happy to join his other former detractors in saluting Albee's accomplishment.

Three Tall Women is a mature piece of writing, clearly autobiographical, in which Albee seems to be coming to terms not only with a socialite foster parent he once satirized in past plays, but with his own advancing age. Three women are discovered in a sumptuously appointed bedroom decorated with Louis Quatorze furniture, a rare carpet and a parquet floor. They are called A, B and C, which suggests a Beckett influence, though on the surface the play appears to be a drawing-room comedy in the style of A. R. Gurney. The oldest of the women (known as A) is an imperious, rich invalid who appears hobbling on a cane, her left arm in a sling. She is attended by a middle-aged companion (B), who is an angular woman with a caustic tongue and a humped back, and a young, politically correct lawyer (C), who has come to discuss A's business affairs.

The first of the two acts examines some scratchy transactions among this symbiotic trio, consisting of A's recollections (clearly not in tranquility) and the shocked reactions of her companions. A has turned sour and abrupt in old age, and there are traces of Albee's celebrated talent for invective in her rage against life. Her spine has collapsed, she has broken her arm in a fall and now the bone has disintegrated around the pins. Likely to wet herself when she rises from a chair ("A sort of greeting to the day—the cortex out of sync with the sphincter"), she is inordinately preoccupied with the aging process—"downhill from 16 on for all of us." She even wants to indoctrinate children with the awareness that they're dying from the moment they're born, and that anyone who thinks she's healthy, as C does, had better just wait.

In short, A is an entirely vicious old wretch, with a volatile tongue and a narrow mind, but it is a tribute to the writing and the acting that she gradually wins our affections. Although prejudiced against "kikes," "niggers," "wops" and "fairies" (among them her own son), she is a model of vitality and directness when compared with the humor-impaired liberal C, who protests her intolerance. A remembers a past of supreme emptiness, of horse shows, dances and loveless affairs, and she remembers the time her husband advanced upon her with a bracelet dangling from his erect penis ("I can't do that," she said, "and his peepee got soft, and the bracelet fell into my lap"). That arid marriage, and the son who brings her chocolates but doesn't love her ("He loves his boys"), represent memories that can bring A to tears. They also bring her to a stroke at the end of the first act, as she freezes in midsentence describing her deepest family secrets.

The second act begins with A lying in bed under an oxygen mask. By this time B has been transformed from a sardonic, hunchbacked factotum, slouching toward Bethlehem like Igor or Richard III, into a stately matron in pearls, while C has become an elegant debutante in pink chiffon. Before long they are surprisingly joined by A, newly rejuvenated (the figure in the bed is a dummy), and the play shifts gears into a story of one woman at three different moments in time (A at 90, B at 52 and C at 26). Just as B has shed her hump and C her primness, A has lost her feebleness. All three share the same history, the same child, the same sexual experiences, but A and B are united against C in their hatred of illusions. They warn C that her future will be one of deception and infidelity: "Men cheat a lot. We cheat less, but we cheat because we're lonely. Men cheat because they're men."

Three Tall Women **is a mature piece of writing, clearly autobiographical, in which Albee seems to be coming to terms not only with a socialite foster parent, but with his own advancing age.**

—Robert Brustein

The prodigal child, now a young man carrying flowers, returns to sit by the bedside of his dying mother ("his dry lips on my dry cheeks"), silent and forlorn. None of the women will forgive him, nor will they forgive each other. A dislikes C and C refuses to become A, while B bursts out bitterly against "parents, teachers, all of you, you lie, you never tell us things change." The inevitability of change is responsible for the obscenities of sickness, pain, old age and death, but A, having accepted her fate, affirms that "the happiest moment is coming to the end of it." Taking a deep breath, she allows the action and her life to stop.

Beckett was the first dramatist to condense the past and present lives of a character into a single dramatic action, and *Krapp's Last Tape* is a play to which ***Three Tall Women*** owes a deep spiritual debt. (It was also the companion piece to Albee's first New York production, ***The Zoo Story,*** in 1960.) Beckett compressed youth and age through the device of a tape recorder, Albee uses doppelgängers; but both plays evoke the same kind of existential poignance. . . .

Most of us have encountered horrible old women like A, fuming over their pain and helplessness. It is Albee's personal and professional triumph to have made such a woman fully human. His late career is beginning to resemble O'Neill's, another dramatist who wrote his greatest plays after having been rejected and abandoned by the culture. Happily, unlike O'Neill, he may not have to wait for death to rehabilitate him.

David Richards (essay date 13 April 1994)

SOURCE: "Critical Winds Shift for Albee, A Master of the Steady Course," in *The New York Times,* April 13, 1994, pp. C15, C19.

[*In the article below, based in part on a conversation with Albee, Richards provides a brief overview of Albee's career, relates the playwright's reaction to winning the Pulitzer, and discusses the autobiographical basis of* Three Tall Women.]

For Edward Albee, the long exile is over.

Hailed more than 30 years ago for ***Who's Afraid of Virginia Woolf?*** but dismissed in the 1970's and 80's for what was perceived as his increasingly abstract style, he won a third Pulitzer Prize yesterday, for ***Three Tall Women,*** and reclaimed his position as one of America's leading dramatists.

"I suppose I will be very warm and cuddly and pleased with myself for a while," he said by telephone from Texas, where he is teaching a course in play writing at the University of Houston. "I never counted on it. I think you should always be surprised by awards and prizes, since you're always surprised when you don't get them."

Until recently, Mr. Albee had not had a new play produced in New York since ***The Man Who Had Three Arms*** was clobbered by the critics in 1983. The last of his dramas to receive a generally favorable reception was ***Seascape*** in 1975. Also a recipient of the Pulitzer, it nonetheless closed after 65 performances. While Europe has continued to pay him homage over the years—***Three Tall Women*** had its premiere at the American Theater in Vienna in 1991—only academia and a few regional theaters have offered him respect and a refuge in the United States.

"You can't let that eat at you," Mr. Albee said. "If you really thought that you were old-fashioned, you could get glum about it. But there is not always a great relationship between popularity and excellence. If you know that, you can never be owned by public opinion or critical response. You just have to make the assumption you're doing good work and go on doing it. Of course, there are the little dolls you stick pins in privately."

Even if Broadway remains aloof, it has been a turnabout year for the 66-year-old playwright, who won his first Pulitzer in 1967 for ***A Delicate Balance.*** Off Off Broadway, the Signature Theater Company, which devotes its entire season to the works of a single author, has given New York premieres to five Albee plays, among them ***Marriage Play,*** a 1987 drama; ***Finding the Sun,*** a long 1983 one-act, and ***Fragments,*** his latest work. And in February, the Vineyard Theater Company, an Off Broadway group, staged ***Three Tall Women.*** Reviewers were so enthusiastic and business so brisk that the production moved earlier this month to the Promenade Theater.

Overtly biographical, ***Three Tall Women*** deals with the death of Mr. Albee's mother, a one-time department-store mannequin named Frances Cotter, who married Reed Albee, heir to the Keith-Albee chain of vaudeville houses. The playwright, an adopted child, had a stormy relationship with the striking but headstrong woman before she threw him out of the family's Westchester County home when he was 18.

In the first act, she appears as a senile 92-year-old dowager, attended by her 52-year-old secretary and her 26-year-old lawyer. Failing fast, she suffers a severe stroke. In the second act, even though an inert body lies on the bed, the elderly woman is back on her feet. Lively and coherent, she enters into a three-way conversation with the lawyer and the secretary, who now embody her at 26 and 52. This way, Mr. Albee explained in an interview with *The New York Times* in 1991, she gets to do something not afforded the rest of us: talk with herself at different stages of her life and explore her own evolution.

"The play is a kind of exorcism," he said, "I didn't end up any more fond of the woman after I finished it than when I started. But it allowed me to come to terms with the long unpleasant life she led and develop a little respect for her independence. She was destructive, but she had lots of reasons to be. It's there on the stage, all the good stuff and the bad stuff. I just tried to examine it, sort it out, be objective about it. I couldn't have written the play while she was alive."

Asked what she might have thought of ***Three Tall Women,*** Mr. Albee said: "She probably would have claimed she didn't know what it was about. She went to see ***The American Dream*** and pretended she had no idea it was about the way she treated my grandmother. She had such misplaced pride. I think she was slowly going broke at the end. Stuff kept disappearing. Jewelry. Things, I think she was selling it, unless people were stealing her blind. But she wouldn't tell anyone."

"When she died, she cut me out of her will," he continued. "The church she never went to, the hospital and some other charities got her money. She left me change, as we say. She could never come to terms with my nature, my sexuality, wouldn't think of discussing it with me. We never reconciled."

Yet, as he chronicles in the play, he regularly brought bouquets of freesia, her favorite flower, to her bedside while she lay in a coma. "Sometimes she would smile," he said, "Sometimes she didn't."

If the difficult and domineering woman has inspired one of Mr. Albee's strongest plays in decades, she may also have given him the resilience to bear up under the years of critical disfavor. "Well, she was a tough old bird and you learn at your parents' knees," he admitted. "One thing I don't do is go around feeling sorry for myself. Maybe because I was an orphan and didn't fit in, I had to create my own identity. As an orphan, you don't have forebears. You're the first person who ever lived, in a way."

Mr. Albee said the low points over the last two decades have had less to do with the chilly reception of his plays than with the deaths of his longtime producers, Richard Barr and Charles Woodward; the director Alan Schneider, and the set designer William Ritman. "Here I am, only 66, and everybody I started out working with is dead," he said, "They were all mentors."

Although the jurors proposed ***Who's Afraid of Virginia Woolf?,*** still Mr. Albee's best-known work, for the 1963 Pulitzer, the board ignored the recommendation and refused to grant the prize at all that year. The vituperative play about marital infighting was thought shocking at the time and contributed to the enduring misconception that Mr. Albee was an American Strindberg.

"I guess I was mostly bemused by the fact that you could have the award taken away from you," Mr. Albee said, "I wasn't irritated. But I didn't like it four years later when ***A Delicate Balance*** got the award and people said it was nothing but a sop to make up for ***Virginia Woolf.*** There are always types like that. Anyway, I thought ***The Man Who Had Three Arms*** was a worthy play. So what do I know?"

His Pulitzer yesterday put Mr. Albee in the rarefied company of Robert E. Sherwood, also a three-time winner, and Eugene O'Neill, who still heads the pack with four, although the fourth award was bestowed on him posthumously for *Long Day's Journey Into Night.*

Reminded that he had already bettered Tennessee Williams, who was the recipient of two Pulitzers, Mr. Albee thought for a while and then said graciously, "Maybe Tennessee didn't get as many Pulitzers as he deserved."

Greg Evans on Albee's use of characterization in *Three Tall Women*:

[In *Three Tall Women* Albee provides] each "character" with all the dignity and indignity of their respective ages. Youth is both charmingly dreamy and maddeningly disdainful; the 52-year-old, while boasting that middle age is "the only time you get a 360-degree view," doesn't like what she sees on either side: and the old woman is by terms resigned to and anguished by her disintegration.

Greg Evans, in a review of Three Tall Women, *in* Variety, *14 February 1994.*

John Lahr (review date 16 May 1994)

SOURCE: "Sons and Mothers," in *The New Yorker,* Vol. LXX, No. 13, May 16, 1994, pp. 102-05.

[Lahr is an award-winning American critic, nonfiction writer, playwright, novelist, biographer, and editor. In the following excerpt, he lauds Three Tall Women *as "a wary act of reconciliation, whose pathos and poetry are a testament*

to the bond, however attenuated, between child and parent."]

For one terrible moment at the beginning of ***Three Tall Women,*** the pretension that has sunk so many of Edward Albee's theatrical vehicles in his middle years looms menacingly on the horizon. "It's downhill from sixteen on," says one of the women, a middle-aged character called B, who takes care of a rich, imperious, senile old bird called A and is herself a connoisseur of collapse. She goes on, "I'd like to see children learn it—have a six-year-old say 'I'm dying' and know what it means." But then, as we and the old lady settle into the demented fog of her remembering and forgetting, it becomes apparent that Albee has found his way back to the sour and passionate straight talking of his early, best plays.

The last great gift a parent gives to a child is his or her own death, and the energy underneath ***Three Tall Women*** is the exhilaration of a writer calling it quits with the past—specifically, the rueful standoff between Albee and his mother, the late Frances Cotter Albee, who adopted him only to kick him out of the family home, at eighteen, for his homosexual shenanigans and later to cut him out of her sizable will. The play has earned Albee, who is sixty-six, his third (and most deserved) Pulitzer Prize, but the writer's real victory is a psychological one—honoring the ambiguity of "the long unpleasant life she led" while keeping her memory vividly alive. Far from being an act of revenge or special pleading, the play is a wary act of reconciliation, whose pathos and poetry are a testament to the bond, however attenuated, between child and parent. ***Three Tall Women*** bears witness to the son's sad wish to be loved, but with this liberating difference: the child is now finally in control of the parent's destiny, instead of the parent's being in control of the child's. Here, in a set whose Empire furniture, mahogany parquet, flocked blue bedroom wallpaper, and resplendent silver tea service emphasize the iconography of privilege, and not the clutter of decline, sits the ninety-two-year-old A, a fragile, white-haired replica of Albee's mother. A is a spoiled, petulant, demanding, bigoted, manipulative old bat. "*I'll* fix him" she says of her absent son, her quicksilver emotions veering suddenly from tears to a hatred that includes B and a twenty-something female lawyer, C. "I'll fix *all* of 'em. They all think they can treat me like this. You all think you can get away with anything." A's transparent impotence makes the once horrible hectoring now merely laughable. But she is still a potent amalgam of dyspepsia and decrepitude. A former beauty (Albee's mother was briefly a model), A was protected first by the fortune of a face and then by a fortune. Her narcissism and her isolation are spectacular. "You take people as friends and you spend time at it, you put effort in, and it doesn't matter if you don't like them anymore—who likes anybody anymore?—you've put in all that time, and what right do they have to . . . to. . ." she says, her thoughts, like her life, evaporating disconcertingly before her eyes.

Act I paints the landscape of A's old age—the humiliations of incontinence, memory loss, confusion, and regret—and is dominated by the huge, heroic performance of Myra Carter. Ms. Carter, who is sixty-four and is new to me, gives one of the finest performance I've ever seen on the New York stage—an enormous feat of memory, energy, and observation. "I've shrunk!" she says, overwhelmed by the confusions, real and imagined, that beset her. "I'm not tall! I used to be so tall! Why have I shrunk?" Carter hits every vowel and consonant of Albee's words, filling each one with lucid thought and wonderful music. She growls, squawks, cackles, whimpers, rages through the torrent of emotion and memory that's called out of her by the two interlocutors. A's life turns out to have been a series of punishing losses: a sister who became a drunk; a mother who, when she moved into her daughter's home, became an enemy; a son who became a stranger; a husband who became first a philanderer and then a victim of cancer. Carter's face is still beautiful, and it lights up intermittently with childlike delight, even sweetness, which reminds us of the charm that A's former good looks exerted on the world, and mitigates the emptiness of the frivolous life she describes. "I was . . . well, I was naked; I didn't have a stitch, except I had on all my jewelry. I hadn't taken off my jewelry," A says, giggling, about a crucial episode of her early marriage, when "his pee-pee was all hard, and . . . and hanging on it was a new bracelet." Her husband wants a sexual favor that the well-mannered A can't and won't perform. She continues, "Well, it started to go soft, and the bracelet slid off, and it fell into my lap. I was naked; deep into my lap. 'Keep it,' he said and he turned and he walked out of my dressing room." She weeps at the memory, which sounds the first note of her husband's emotional retreat.

The ballast to A's dementia is provided by B, the droll and delightful Marian Seldes, who moves like a slow loris around the stage, her shoulders hunched as if lumbered with the weight of both her own and A's boredom with old age. "And so it goes" is her recurring catchphrase, which announces the giddy zone of resignation and detachment that she inhabits. "In the morning, when she wakes up she wets—a kind of greeting to the day, I suppose," she tells C, translating her irritation into little dollops of snideness to make it bearable. "The sphincter and the cortex not in synch. Never during the *night,* but *as* she wakes." B exists to register the old woman's existential anguish; and the inflexible C is there to broadcast moral horror. Albee is less successful with C, who is meant to be callow but—in the first act, at least—is just a poorly written prig. A lawyer sorting out A's unpaid bills, C (played by Jordan Baker) behaves more like an intemperate and insensitive teen-ager than like an employee. A, who is full of antique phrases like "Don't you get fresh," is also full of the ancient bigotries of her class. These draw implausible reactions from C. A's recollection of Irving Thalberg as "a real smart little Jew" prompts C's dopey outrage: "I'm a democrat." And, later, when A talks about "colored help" knowing their place ("none of those uppity niggers, the city ones"), C explodes in dismay, "Oh, Jesus Christ!" Her tone soon becomes predictable, and the character loses a purchase on the audience's imagination, which is focussed on A and on what she sees, at the end of Act I, as her inheritance of hate. "I think they all hated me, because I was strong, because I *had* to be," A says, rationalizing her self-involvement. "Sis hated me; Ma hated me; all those others, *they* hated me." She goes strangely silent after the speech. And Albee brings the curtain down with B and C realizing that their employer has had a stroke.

In Act II, by an ingenious coup de théâtre, ***Three Tall Women*** expands from a parental cameo to a vista of decline. At curtain rise, A is still collapsed in bed but now has an oxygen mask over her face. B and C seem to have dressed up for their bedside vigil in period high fashion—B in pearls and an elegant gray frock with a full, pleated fifties skirt, and C in a layered ankle-length cream chiffon dress that evokes the twenties. Then, as B and C bicker about death, and the conversation drifts to the absence of a living will and why A didn't write one, A herself, in an elegant lavender dress, walks in from the wings. "I was going to but then I forgot, or it slipped my mind, or something," she says. The moment is electrifying. The body in the bed turns out to be a mannequin. In this theatrical filip, Albee goes from a familiar external reality to a bold interior one. B and C are now projections of A, who speaks rationally for the duration of the play, responding from different stages of her life. Albee's wonderful invention allows him both to incarnate A's narcissism and to lift the play from characterization to meditation. What we get is a kind of Cubist stage picture, where the characters are fragments of a single self. The device is at its most eloquent when the son appears, in preppy clothes and clasping freesias, to sit by his comatose mother in a dumb show of devotion. The characters circle him:

> C (*Wonder*): I have children?
>
> B (*None too pleasant*): We have one; we have a boy.
>
> A (*Same*): Yes, we do. I have a son.
>
> B (*Seeing him, sneering*): Well, fancy seeing you again. (*Sudden, and enraged, into his face*) Get out of my house!

In this terrifying and terrible moment, the son doesn't react. In fact, he never speaks. B, the voice the son heard when he was growing up, berates him as "filthy," but A, from the distance of her dotage, begs for tolerance. "He came back; he never loved me, he never loved us, but he came back. Let him alone," she says, adding later, "Twenty-plus years? That's a long enough sulk—on both sides." Lawrence Sacharow, the director, stages these lines impeccably and with awful authenticity. The boy's muteness is a metaphor for the inconsolable gap between parent and child. It's also another of Albee's brilliant dramatic maneuvers: the child is forever outside the narcissistic parental embrace—seen but not heard.

The son's leave-taking ("He packed up his attitudes and he *left,*" B says) is just one of a litany of losses that A and her former selves pick over in this fugue of hope and hurt. Inevitably, the play becomes a dance of A's defensiveness, as her psyche struggles to idealize itself. "I . . . will . . . not . . . become . . . you. I will *not.* I . . . I deny *you,*" C says to A, who, in turn, is unrepentant and rejects their versions of life: "I'm *here,* and I deny you *all;* I deny every *one* of you." In this landscape of loneliness and heartache, C, at the finale, asks about the happy times. "I *know* my best times—what is it? happiest? —haven't happened yet. They're to *come,*" she says. "Aren't they? Please?" B can't agree, preferring her own middle age: "It's the only time you get a three-hundred-and-sixty-degree view—see in all directions. Wow! What a view!" But A has the final say, which is pitched, sardonically, like the happy ending of a Restoration play, with the characters joining hands to face the audience. With B and C on either side of her, A speaks her notion of the happiest moment in life. "When we stop. When we can stop," she says, and, as they together breathe and exhale for the last time, the lights fade to black. At the beginning of this gorgeous final speech, A catches herself lying about her age—a sweet vanity that Albee pays off with a joke. "Give a girl a break," she says to B. And that, finally, is what Albee's ***Three Tall Women*** does for his mother. The mute young man in the play can now, in his own middle age, give her the gift of his words, and make something beautiful and enduring about both her privilege and her neglect.

FURTHER READING

Criticism

Henry, William A., III. "Albee Is Back." *Time* 143, No. 8 (21 February 1994): 64.

Highly laudatory review of *Three Tall Women.* Henry asserts: "Out of the simplest and most familiar material—a woman of 90-plus years coping with the infirmities and confusions of the moment and looking back on a life of gothic excess—Albee fashions a spellbinder."

Kroll, Jack. "Trinity of Women." *Newsweek* CXXIII, No. 8 (21 February 1994): 62.

Offers a favorable assessment of *Three Tall Women,* calling it one of Albee's best works.

Weber, Bruce. "On Stage, and Off." *The New York Times* (15 April 1994): C2.

Relates events surrounding the decision to award Albee the Pulitzer Prize for Drama and the merits of the other nominees.

Additional coverage of Albee's life and career is contained in the following sources published by Gale Research: *Authors in the News,* Vol. 1; *Concise Dictionary of American Literary Biography, 1941-1968; Contemporary Authors,* Vols. 5-8 (rev. ed.); *Contemporary Authors Bibliographical Series,* Vol. 3; *Contemporary Authors New Revision Series,* Vol. 8; *Contemporary Literary Criticism,* Vols. 1, 2, 3, 5, 9, 11, 13, 25, 53; *DISCovering Authors; Dictionary of Literary Biography,* Vol. 7; *Major 20th-Century Writers;* and *World Literature Criticism.*

Joan Brady
Theory of War

Award: Whitbread Award

Born in 1939, Brady is an American novelist living in England.

INTRODUCTION

Initially set in post-Civil War America and spanning over 100 years of history, *Theory of War* (1993) concerns a white child, Jonathan Carrick, who at the age of four was sold by his family to a farmer to use as he willed until the boy turned twenty-one. Delineating the disturbing physical and psychological effects of slavery on the slave, the slave owner, and their descendants, *Theory of War* blends fictional events with factual information about the illegal act of buying children and about Brady's grandfather who was sold into slavery as a child. The narrator of *Theory of War,* Jonathan's granddaughter Malory, reveals her grandfather's story as she decodes his cryptic diaries and interviews her alcoholic Uncle Atlas, Jonathan's only surviving child. Malory relates the brutal treatment Jonathan experienced as a "boughten child": he was tormented and mocked by his owner's son, tethered like an animal and beaten for escape attempts, and, on one occasion, forcibly restrained by his owner while a travelling salesman pulled out his teeth. Jonathan, in turn, resorts to violence and represses his feelings as a means of surviving these atrocities. Although he eventually gains an education, escapes his bondage, and becomes a minister, he remains haunted by his past. He is unable to have intimate relationships with others, has trouble expressing his emotions and feelings, especially anger, and struggles with issues of theology, spirituality, and morality. These debilitating behavior patterns also impact the lives of Jonathan's five children—four commit suicide and the sole survivor, Atlas, succumbs to alcohol. Malory's own physical ailments—a crippling spinal growth—serve as a symbol of Jonathan's suppressed rage being passed on to yet another generation. Some critics have found Brady's presentation of a white slave unconvincing and faulted the work for weak connections between fact and fiction. Others have observed Brady's fitting use of military strategist Karl von Clausewitz's philosophy of war—"a battle between nations was not unlike a battle between two people"—as a simile for Jonathan's methods of survival. Critics have also praised *Theory of War* as a moving account of a childhood personality irrevocably damaged by abuse and brutality. Wendy Brandmark commented: "When we read about the little boy whose charming spirit is destroyed, we cannot help but think of generations of black slaves whose stories Jonathan's repeats. In her opening quotes Joan Brady suggests that slavery, like disability, is an 'allegory of all life in society . . . but with slavery the metaphor's so much a part of the language nobody pays attention to it anymore.' Through Jonathan the reader may feel what it means to lose one's bearings, to be made less than human."

PRINCIPAL WORKS

The Imposter (novel) 1979
**The Unmaking of a Dancer* (autobiography) 1982
Theory of War (novel) 1993

*This title was published in England as *Prologue.*

CRITICISM

Ruth Pavey (review date 17 January 1993)

SOURCE: "Grandfather's Footsteps," in *The Observer,* January 17, 1993, p. 49.

[*In the following excerpt, Pavey discusses Brady's focus on anger and faults her blending of fact and fiction in* Theory of War.]

Soon after the end of the American Civil War a ragged soldier leads a white child into a Mid-West general store, sells him, then disappears. This startling act, occupying only two pages of Joan Brady's ***Theory of War,*** is the source of her whole novel, a story of damage inherited as well as of damage direct.

The meaning of being 'boughten' soon becomes clear to the boy. He climbs cheerfully into his master's farm wagon, but Alvah Stoke is not used to blithe, infantile chatter. Fearing he may have bought an idiot, Alvah tries a clout. The chatter stops. Thus Jonathan Carrick, aged four, is initiated into a childhood of slavery, and a lifetime of anger. Indeed it is the start of generations of anger.

Jonathan's story is told by a now adult granddaughter, born after his death. From her uncle's memories and her grandfather's diaries she reconstructs a life of mythic harshness, intelligence and resilience, lived first as a slave on a faltering Kansas tobacco farm, then as a runaway on the railroads. Though he often has to submit, Jonathan is never submissive. Anger, aimed chiefly at George, Alvah's loathsome son, is his weapon. In the boys' power struggle it stands him in good stead. But later, it finds less deserving targets.

The ways in which this anger taints Jonathan's adult life make up Joan Brady's theme. In a postscript she notes that the book is indeed based on her own grandfather, and what she interprets as the legacy of his horrific childhood; four suicides among his children, for instance. While this is convincing beyond the context of the novel, it is only partially so within it. Brady interpolates it into the narrative as a moralist might clog up a good fable. The story of the grandfather is so exceptional that it might have stood better alone.

Kirkus Reviews (review date 15 February 1993)

SOURCE: A review of *Theory of War,* in *Kirkus Reviews,* Vol. LXI, No. 4, February 15, 1993, p. 163.

[*In the following review, the critic offers a mixed assessment of* Theory of War.]

A white slave in post-Civil War America: that's the hook for this semi-autobiographical fiction [***Theory of War***]. Brady has already written a novel (***The Impostor,*** 1979) and an autobiography (***The Unmaking of a Dancer,*** 1982); here, she reconstructs a life of her grandfather, the slave.

Jonathan Carrick was a so-called "boughten boy," purchased at age four for farmwork; he ran away at 16; four of his children would commit suicide. What interests

An excerpt from *Theory of War*

Atlas and I didn't agree about what happened next. Oh, not the facts. It's the heart of the matter, the truth, you might call it. But who can trust Atlas? Doctors spend so much time playing God themselves that they make lousy witnesses when it comes to the heart of things. Atlas wasn't even a very good doctor; he told me himself that he had to pay ten thousand dollars for his license to practice in Washington because he failed the exam. "I'm a yard bird," he said, back from his emergency call. "If it's lying there, I'll pick it up. If not, to hell with it."

"People like Dad, people with backgrounds like that, slavery, violence of one kind or another," he went on, "these people usually have minds as brute-like as their pasts. Usually they're inarticulate, confused, slow to everything but blows. That's what's amazing about Dad. How could anybody so enraged accept a God? Or any other abstract concept?" My attempts to explain away Jonathan's conversion to Christianity annoyed Atlas. "Truth? Don't give me that crap. He didn't want truth. He wanted judgment: revenge. Just like you. What'd you major in philosophy for? A waste of time, if you ask me. You should have gone into law. You belong on the bench of the Inquisition—"

"Let's get back to Jonathan," I said, annoyed myself.

"Okay. Okay. Now, look, his conversion embarrasses you. Why? One way or another it was almost inevitable. Slavery destroys the soul. It's a narcotic: it does what narcotic addiction does, kills pride, subtlety, initiative—"

"Yes, yes," I said, still annoyed.

"So here's a guy who never had anything that belonged to him, no home, no mother, father sold him—a piece of human shit—not even his own socks. Think of him there in that goddamned place, doilies and fish forks and roses on the crapper—Christ almighty, how does a slave go about learning to live on equal terms with people like that? What right has he even to attempt such a thing? The effrontery—Jesus, the arrogance of it. That's what's marvelous. Not the dull detail of a conversion. Anyhow, he wants to do this impossible thing—more than that—he's *going* to do this impossible thing, and obviously he can't do it all on his own. So he finds himself a God to help him. It's as simple as that."

This is how it happened:

In the middle of one frozen February night Jonathan, my grandfather, woke abruptly. "Sleepest thou?" a voice said to him. "Couldest thou not watch one hour?"

Hearing these words come to him out of the darkness, he did not for one minute doubt that the voice he heard was the voice of Jesus Christ Himself.

Joan Brady, in her Theory of War, *Alfred A. Knopf, 1993.*

Brady is identity. How is it formed if you are a solitary slave-child? Mulling over the question are narrator/granddaughter Malory Carrick and her uncle Atlas, a son of slave Jonathan. Sequences from Jonathan's life (slaving on a Kansas tobacco farm; riding the railroads, free at last, as a brakeman) are interrupted by discussions between niece and uncle (Atlas has his memories; Malory has been reading the coded diaries) about the meaning of Jonathan's life (the reader becomes a student at an offbeat seminar). Malory sees her grandfather's life fueled (and corroded) by hatred, not for slavemaster Alvah Stoke so much as for Stoke's son George, Jonathan's vicious tormentor. The slave is a model soldier in his war against George, striking opportunely, beating him until he is surely dead, then escaping. Twenty years later, a newly ordained minister, he will lose his religious faith when he discovers that George is alive and flourishing, a US senator; it's war again. Jonathan does get a life (he marries, has children, becomes a successful farmer, albeit a lousy husband and father), but his rage never subsides, returning him to the battlefield for a final confrontation with the Senator when both are old men.

There are problems here: awkward format, awkward fact/fiction straddle, overworked war analogy, hokey showdown. Yet this deliberately rough-edged work does command respect for its blistering anger at the poison of slavery in the bloodstream of the Carricks . . . and America.

Valentine Cunningham (review date 26 February 1993)

SOURCE: "Handing on Hate," in *The Times Literary Supplement,* No. 4691, February 26, 1993, p. 20.

[*In the following excerpt, Cunningham faults Brady's presentation of a white child as a slave during the post-Civil War era as unconvincing and historically inaccurate.*]

Theory of War is the grim story of how one Irish-American, called Jonathan Carrick, became morally and spiritually deformed, as he wrestled for mere survival in awful pioneering circumstances in the period after the American Civil War, and how he came to pass on his deformities to his descendants.

In the hands of Carrick's narrating granddaughter—who researches her family history from what is, for this fiction, a characteristically portentous wheelchair—the violence of his struggles is an allegory of human existence in general, but more feelingly of American humanity in particular.

The most momentous thing about young Carrick is that he is sold into what his narrator thinks of as slavery. A raw midwestern farmer called Stoke, on the lookout for cheap labour, pays the boy's father, who is down on his post-Civil War uppers, fifteen dollars to bind the boy in an apprenticeship that will last until he is twenty-one. Carrick cannot wait for this agreed manumission time. After beatings, being staked down to prevent escape, terrible drudgeries (on this farm even the wife pulls the plough), a foul kip in a damp sod shack, above all, the taunting of the son of the family, George, a fat boy sent out as a salesman in a frock-coat, Carrick runs away and he never stops hating the Stokes.

His Irish name gets him a job in a rail-yard. Soon he is a switch-man, then a brake-man, jobs involving nimbleness around the wheels of moving trains. It is a life without amenity or grace, in which awful brutality and living like beasts in physical danger and terrible filth are normal. But still Carrick gets on, fired by his hatred, stirred to seriousness by the surreal preaching of a saloon-bar whiskey priest. He goes to Bible College, fetches up as a Methodist minister, turns farmer, sires a family, lies to avenge himself on fat George, transmits his sorrows to his suicidal sons and confesses everything in coded diaries which his paralysed granddaughter reads.

This tale of the deprived little brother and his heritage of hate and revenge is folkish, something by the Grimms or out of the Old Testament, with Steinbeckian trimmings. Humour lightens its desperations at only a few points, and then only in hard satirical farcing—as when the narrator's uncle Atlas, the main source of family oral history, an aged medic slowly killing himself with the drink, pitchforks *croûte* across the napery at one of his latest wife's French evenings during a low tale about his daddy, a pitchfork and a bull.

Allegory keeps pressing in on Carrick's history. The smallest item can assume allegorical flesh. The frock-coats George wears which Carrick craves, the unsafe link-and-pin couplings on trains. They are the metaphorical bits that will colour up the grand metaphor, the human-American warfare that Carrick's life is offered as comprising. This is endorsed by the narrator's zest for violent events and framed throughout by reference to Clausewitz's theories.

Joan Brady isn't willing to stop there. She goes on to take in the likes of her grandfather, sold like Carrick into "slavery". It's time, this author thinks, to speak up once more about the American way of *white* slavery. The frequently heard case of the Native American and the African-American needs supplementing with that of the Irish or white American. As the Author's Note declares, "My grandfather was white. . . . And he was sold into slavery . . . in the United States." This is not a reminder which the exponents of special Native or African-American sufferings are perhaps quite ready for. Brady's persuasions will lack force for those—like me—who need more to make us believe that child apprentices were really the equivalent of slaves.

Scott H. Silverman (review date 15 April 1993)

SOURCE: A review of *Theory of War,* in *Library Journal,* Vol. 113, No. 7, April 15, 1993, pp. 124-25.

[*In the following review, Silverman lauds Brady for her powerful descriptions of anger and her strong storyline in* Theory of War.]

In 1865, a Civil War veteran indentures his four-year-old son to a vicious Kansas tobacco farmer. The boy, who is white and Brady's grandfather, is fictionalized in a remarkably compelling tale [***Theory of War***] that essentially draws its power from depicting unembellished brutality. Brady's narrative cuts between protagonist Jonathan Carrick's doomed attempts at love and normalcy and those of a son and granddaughter, reminiscing survivors who can only be termed "adult children of slaves." In the 60 years the protagonist's story spans, Johnny, intense and generally enraged, circuits the country, murdering, praying, drinking, and blaspheming, often simultaneously. The characters in this dark tale, cynics every one, alternately ponder the biggest of questions and submit, inarticulately, to unbearable pain. This graphic, ugly-beautiful novel, as eloquent for its articulation of obsessive rage as for its avoidance of melodrama and cliché, is recommended for libraries collecting serious contemporary fiction.

Wendy Brandmark (review date 5 August 1993)

SOURCE: "Small Bodies," in *London Review of Books,* Vol. 15, No. 15, August 5, 1993, p. 16.

[*In the following excerpt, Brandmark offers a thematic discussion of* Theory of War.]

In ***Theory of War,*** Joan Brady reveals a little-known piece of American history that has dominated her own life. In the chaos after the Civil War, white children, the sons and daughters of impoverished widows, of ragged soldiers, were sold into virtual slavery. Black slaves—who had been expensive—had just been liberated. These white children, 'a crop of kids nobody wanted', could be bought cheaply, with few questions asked. Jonathan Carrick is probably not more than four years old, a chatty, active, bright-eyed little boy, when he is sold to Alvah Stokes, a struggling tobacco farmer, a man brutal but shrewd. Alvah beats him into silence, denies him an education and forces him to work from dawn to dusk in the tobacco fields. When Jonathan tries to escape, the local shopkeeper who had arranged the sale gives him some advice: 'Grow up fast.' No one in the town can do anything to stop the family's abuse of the boy. To Alvah's son George, Jonathan is no better than a cow or a shipment of tobacco: 'You ain't even human. Never will be. Your pa sold you. My pa bought you. You're a commodity.'

When Jonathan finally escapes he can't speak: all his teeth have been removed (the remedy Alvah finds for a fever following one of his beatings). He never forgives George Stokes, his bullying 'brother', the boy who read the books and wore the frock coat he coveted, who won his trust for a moment and then abetted his destruction. Even after Jonathan is educated, becomes a successful preacher and marries a woman he adores, the thought of George's existence still poisons him. He murders George, then starves himself to death—as if the hatred were so much a part of him that killing the source of it was like killing himself.

Jonathan's story is pieced together by his unnamed granddaughter, who flies to Washington from England to speak with her uncle, the only remaining witness. Like her grandfather, she feels an outsider; she is a 'resident alien in England', an 'untouchable' disabled woman. Jonathan had rarely spoken of his enslavement, even to his family, and he wrote his diary in code: the benign tumour growing in the granddaughter's spine is perhaps too obvious a metaphor for her grandfather's suppressed rage.

A philosophy student, she uses the language of war to describe her grandfather's progression from rebellious child to murderous adult. Her commentary, with its observations on philosophies of war, its search for some Platonic truth in the face of her teachers' belief in the certainties of the material world, tries to make sense of her grandfather's enslavement. Her father committed suicide, her uncle is poisoning himself with alcohol, and she will never walk again. Decoding her grandfather's diary, breaking his silence, is not enough; she must move beyond despair. Her uncle berates her for seeking 'some consistency, some meaning': 'Life's not like that . . . It's a whirlpool . . . what's important is the rotating centre. Where's your sense of wonder? The pattern is alive. Infinitely complex.'

She refuses to accept this vision of a world without past or future, this strange marriage of American optimism and Zen Buddhism, this dream of forever becoming. Even after he lost his faith, Jonathan could not forget that Jesus had come to him once like a lost father. We are left with the granddaughter's (and Jonathan's) agnosticism; she cannot give up the search for 'eternal permanence' neither can she believe in it.

Theory of War is not without humour. The granddaughter, for example, describes her uncle's fourth wife as someone who

> had one of those faces that are purely American. Even at whatever ancient age she'd reached . . . there was nothing in the skin, nothing in the eyes, nothing around the mouth to betray a single thought or a single experience; all was as hygienic as an unwrapped roll of toilet paper, no hint whatever that anybody had ever lived there: a safe house rather than a face.

Joan Brady must counter this terrifying blankness, this banality. She is always contrasting the weight of tragedy with its denial; those who have been scarred by history with those (like 'he-man' Alvah Stokes) who are so devoid of humanity that they cannot be touched. Alvah is as empty as the featureless plains where he labours, as unthinking as the tobacco worms he crushes between his fingers. Not so much corrupt as amoral, he is the unacceptable face of the American Dream: 'take away Hollywood's sanitised version and this much loved hero was as brutish a creature as the pit of hell ever spewed forth.'

Theory of War is written with such passion and righteous anger that we are not surprised to discover it is based on the true story of the enslavement of Joan Brady's grandfather. His children, four of whom committed suicide, and his grandchildren inherited his fury and his despair. But when we read about the little boy whose charming spirit is dest·oyed, we cannot help but think of generations of black slaves whose stories Jonathan's repeats. In her opening quotes Joan Brady suggests that slavery, like disability, is an 'allegory of all life in society . . . but with slavery the metaphor's so much a part of the language nobody pays attention to it anymore.' Through Jonathan the reader may feel what it means to lose one's bearings, to be made less than human.

Helen Dudar (essay date 12 July 1994)

SOURCE:"A Novelist Imagines Grandpa's Boyhood in Bondage," in *The Wall Street Journal,* July 12, 1994, p. A13.

[*Dudar is a writer from New York City. In the following essay, in which she offers a favorable review of* Theory of War, *Dudar relates the volume's biographical influences, its composition, its critical reception, and its impact on Brady's writing career.*]

Now and then, more out of carelessness than conspiracy, a really first-rate book nearly dies of the reviewing community's neglect. Consider Joan Brady's novel ***Theory of War.*** It appeared in early 1993 and sank like a stone. Reviews were scanty, sales scarcely visible. Ms. Brady calculates that Knopf sold fewer than 7,000 copies.

Now, it is here in trade paperback and, after a glittering success abroad, may have a brighter future. So far, the book has been acquired for publication in seven other languages, including Korean, and Hollywood seems to be hungering to transform it into a film. Most significantly, it wears the prestige of the 1993 Whitbread award, an annual British honor never before conferred on a woman or an American, and one that also brought Ms. Brady the equivalent of $31,000, plus acres of media attention and, of course, serious sales in England.

Ms. Brady, who has lived in the postcard-pretty Devon town of Totnes for more than 20 years, was in the U.S. not long ago on the obligatory multicity visit designed to persuade American readers that her novel was worth their time. It surely is: a finely wrought, ironic and haunting tale of a forgotten piece of Americana. In the ferociously hard days just after the Civil War, Ms. Brady's grandfather, a four-year-old white boy, was sold for $15 to a hard-up Kansas farmer. For lack of documentary material, his granddaughter has imagined his cruel boyhood in bondage and its searing effects on virtually everyone he touched in later life.

A sunny, loquacious woman, Ms. Brady is an enviably brave one as well: At 54 years of age, she offers to public view a handsome face entirely innocent of makeup. She is also conspicuously multitalented. She began her working life as teenage ballerina in San Francisco and moved on to George Balanchine's troupe in New York. Then she gave up dancing to take a degree in philosophy, with Phi Beta Kappa honors, at Columbia University.

The impulse to set words to paper arrived only after she had been a wife and mother for some years. She had married Dexter Masters, a writer who had been director of the Consumers Union, and they produced a son; in the mid-1960s they decided they wanted to live in the English countryside and moved abroad. Her first book, ***The Imposter,*** a novel published in 1979, left the critics unimpressed. Her second, ***The Unmaking of a Dancer,*** an autobiographical work, found a better reception but failed to sell.

Undaunted, in the early '80s Ms. Brady began to think about her grandfather's history. When she was growing up in Berkeley, Calif., where her father was a professor of economics, Grandpa Brady was part of a repertoire of bedtime stories, "the boogie man, the scary figure of childhood." The meaning of a child's cruel servitude did not register on a small girl. What she chiefly remembered was the intensity of her father's feelings about his father. "You could hear the dislike, the resentment, the hatred," she says now.

But as an adult she began to understand how the experience must have poisoned Alexander Brady's life. He had escaped at 16, worked on the new frontier railroads, gone to school to become a preacher, developed a fruit farm in Washington State, married and produced seven children. Four of them, including Ms. Brady's father, were suicides; a fifth became alcoholic. When she talked to a surviving aunt and uncle, they confirmed what she already sensed: "He was a cold, distant man. You couldn't get close to him."

Indeed, while working at her computer, Ms. Brady would find herself in a sour state of irritation at her chief character. "Why the hell couldn't he be nicer?" she would ask herself. "I was forgetting what had happened to him. I set him up and could not keep in mind how deeply damaged he was." Ms. Brady actually had intended to write a history but soon learned there were no sources to be mined, no recorded facts, no figures. All she knew was that in the aftermath of the Civil War, some destitute parents or guardians sold very young children to be "bounden out" labor until they turned 21. "They were valuable weeding machines," she realized. The practice was not indenture, which had some legal safeguards; it was illegal and, for that reason, probably so clandestine that few written records were left.

When Ms. Brady found that all the details she knew about the practice covered no more than two pages, she began to think about fiction. Her acknowledgements include thanks to her late husband, the author of a successful novel, *The Accident.* He "taught me all I know about writing," she wrote, and supplied "the best line in the book."

Early in the narrative, Ms. Brady was having trouble with a scene in which a Kansas farmer set out to find a child for sale. Dexter Masters's suggestion ignited the narrative: As casually as he might order a sack of flour, the farmer drops into the town general store and tells the owner, "I want to buy a boy."

In 1986, work on ***Theory of War*** was suspended. Mr. Masters, many years his wife's senior, was stricken with a series of devastating illnesses; for four years he was almost helpless. Without funds for nursing assistance, all her attention went into his care. Her way of coping with difficulties under those circumstances was to focus on an orderly, undemanding subject. She spent spare moments working on problems in advanced algebra.

After Masters died in 1989, Ms. Brady went back to the novel. She stumbled on her title while reading Karl von Clausewitz on military strategy. She was writing about the near-fatal antagonism between the slave boy and the farmer's mean-spirited son when she came across a Clausewitz passage proposing that "a battle between nations was not unlike a battle between two people." Clausewitzian theory became her metaphor for the sometimes savage defensive war the slave boy waged in order to survive.

Before her trip here, Ms. Brady had just completed a visit to the Netherlands, where her book was greeted with abundant enthusiasm. She was bemused to find that the European view of its failure in the U.S. is that Americans, already burdened with the grievous history of black slavery, don't want to confront a "skeleton in the cupboard." A conspicuously non-paranoid person, she is inclined to think the neglect was just "bad luck."

The Whitbread money, meanwhile, has been more than an incentive to treat herself to baubles and bubble gum. Lacking both income and pension, Ms. Brady counts herself lucky to have a tenant paying rent on the garage apartment at her Totnes property. So far, the only want she has indulged is trading in a small, old German car for a small, slightly younger used French car.

Meanwhile, profitably work-obsessed, she has planned a writing schedule that should keep her busy for a while. She had written a book on an aspect of American medicine which she is now turning to a novel; she is taking physics courses so that she can proceed with another novel about a scientist. And oh yes, her algebra exercises: They led to the discovery of Evariste Galois, a French genius who died before his 21st birthday in a duel after inventing an entire subbranch of mathematics that now bears his name. He is to be the subject of a nonfiction work when she is done with her physicist.

Joan Brady with Pamela S. Dear, *CLC Yearbook* (interview date 26 January 1995)

[*In the following interview, Brady discusses the Whitbread Award,* Theory of War, *and her writing process.*]

[*Dear*]: *As the 1993 Whitbread Award winner for* **Theory of War** *you hold two special distinctions: you are the first woman and the first American to receive this honor. How did this feel?*

[Brady]: I didn't really expect to win. In the literary world here, the Whitbread now carries more weight than the Booker. I just couldn't see a middle-aged, American-sounding woman getting such a thing. Especially when the leading contender was a man—a poet, an establishment figure, very attractive—who had written a biography of Philip Larkin, another British poet, very eminent and newly dead. When the winner was announced, I was just plain shocked—and scared. I hadn't even prepared a speech. My agent had insisted I put on a "frock" for the event. I hadn't worn a dress in years, so I'd borrowed one and bought a pair of shoes that were a size too large. I'd stuffed the shoes with lamb's wool and tissue paper; they were half off when the announcement came. I wasn't at all sure I'd make it to the podium—a joke of a situation. But there's so much money involved, and money is so wonderful. And the publicity for the book, of course.

What exactly was the scary part of receiving the award? Was it that you had not anticipated the award?

The Whitbread Book of the Year Award is an elegant dinner held in a vast room for five hundred eminent people—literary and theatrical figures. Members of Parliament—a black tie affair, a time to sport the jewelry from the bank. The five contenders eat and wait, spaced out among the five hundred; the winner isn't announced until the dinner is over—rather like the Academy Awards—by which time all five are in an agony of anticipation that has been going on for more than two months. In my case, there was also the unaccustomed dress, the outsized shoes, no prepared speech. More important, for some contenders—certainly for me—winning means a change overnight from nonentity to celebrity, from poor sales and poor contracts to best-seller lists and big advances. The moment the announcement came, I knew I'd entered a whole new way of life.

What motivated you to write **Theory of War?**

It was such a good story. I had known a little about my grandfather's life from the time I was small, but I hadn't thought of him as a subject until I had written a first novel [***The Imposter***] and an autobiography [***The Unmaking of a Dancer***] and was casting around for something else to work on. All of a sudden, there it was; this marvelous story.

When you are talking about the idea of the story are you referring to the fact that your grandfather was sold?

The sale wasn't the idea that caught my attention. What interested me was the fact that my grandfather's children—my father, my aunts and uncle—hated him throughout their whole lives long. Most kids go through periods when they hate their parents, but such periods rarely persist. And there was the queer pattern of suicides—four out of his seven children ended up this way—and I was sure that the suicides, the slavery, and the hatred were all linked together.

Critics have praised your sense of detail, noting the powerful images you were able to create in **Theory of War.** *I am thinking, in particular, of the scene in which Jonathan had his teeth pulled out by his owner Alvah Stokes and the travelling salesman. Also, there are the scenes in which you describe Jonathan's first time sleeping in a bed with sheets and when you depict his admiration of the ornamental porcelain toilet. Where did the ideas and imagery for these scenes come from? Was there any research involved?*

The bed and the sheets and the porcelain toilet are pure invention. The teeth were a little different. A travelling salesman came to visit a dentist I went to in a nearby town and left him a book about false teeth, which the dentist gave to me. It was in this book that I read about the tooth drawers who waited on the edge of the battlefields during the Civil War; when the battle ended—and the living retired back to base camp for the night—the tooth drawers yanked their way through the mouths of dead soldiers for teeth that sold for $2 apiece on the London market. I was so struck by this queer kind of corruption that I decided my own character would lose his teeth—and his childhood supremacy of spirit—in much the same way.

I have never heard of this part of Civil War history.

Well, I can tell you this, they are in the books the dentists receive. You do find things in the damnedest places.

What other parts of the book did you research?

I did a lot of research on the period here in Totnes. There's a national library system in Britain, and the local librarians were very, very helpful. I also went to one of the University of London libraries. The selection of material itself is interesting because the English see Americans differently than Americans see themselves; what emerges is a picture unwashed by Hollywood and unfiltered by national pride. I also spent quite a lot of time talking to people about how to teach somebody who is illiterate to read, although almost none of this work ended up in the book. Then I had an aunt and an uncle who talked to me on tape, particularly about farming in the Northwest in the early part of the century but also about their father; they remembered far less than I'd hoped they might.

Judith Dunford noted that **Theory of War** *"occupies a place on the blurring line between fact and fiction." Some critics have faulted your work for this blending of fact and fiction—one recommending the book would have been better written as nonfiction. How do you respond to this?*

Virtually all novels have something of fact in them, some more than others; ***Theory of War*** has relatively little. I did publicity in Holland, and toward the end of one interview, the interviewer said that the book had made him angry because he'd believed most of it was true. He said, "Those diaries, for example. Those diaries! A standard nineteenth-century woman novelist's trick. And I fell for it!" What I'm saying is that part of the objection seems to be simply that the illusion works pretty well. Because it does, some people feel they have been seduced. And yet, isn't that what a novel is supposed to do—create an illusion of reality? ***Theory of War*** does say straightforwardly on the front that it *is* a novel; the factual material in it would fit into perhaps four pages. Most of Dickens is at least as factual; Frank Norris, Dreiser, Doctorow, Thomas Wolfe—all these are much more so.

I also read that there really isn't a lot of background history on selling children because it was illegal. Is that correct also?

The Emancipation Proclamation outlawed all slavery, but illegality was less important, I think, than the fact that these children were sold as individuals. There was no community around then—no slave community, so no communal memory. Also important is that there is always a strong element of shame in being a victim of any kind; most people and most families want only to forget.

Because my information on slavery was from the last century, I called the Anti-Slavery Society in London to find out if slavery existed in any important form today. I described what had happened to my grandfather, and the woman I talked to said, "This is very interesting because in 1956 the United Nations defined slavery in children. As nearly as I can remember the definition, it went like this: A slave child is 'any person under the age of 18, who is sold or given away for the purposes of the exploitation of his labor.' "

I asked how many children are in this state. She said that, setting aside children who work for a living—and in most countries of the world children work and work very hard for very long hours—and setting aside debt slavery and prostitution as well, she would put the figure at between one hundred and two hundred million. I was stunned.

Those figures surprise me. I would not have imagined such a practice to be so current and so extensive.

No, me either. I suppose again that the situation is so little known partly because the child is so often alone. The woman from the Anti-Slavery society pointed out that slave children today are very often transported across linguistic lines as well so that they don't even speak the language of the family into which they are sold. Such complete cutting off tends to enforce a great passivity. This doesn't do good things for the spirit. What is most remarkable about my grandfather is that he fought back. This is very rare.

Scott Silverman found your work "eloquent for its articulation of obsessive rage." Other reviewers have noted your skill in this area as well. How difficult was this to create within the story?

I got the story down in rough form, then tried to enter the mind of the character—my protagonist—who was living through the terrible life I'd laid out for him. I tried three different personalities for him before I hit on the enraged one. Playing out a character this way is somewhat theatrical, I suppose, but then my background to some degree explains such an approach. Besides, there is a wonderful freedom in letting yourself be furious without any bars.

What else can you describe about your writing process?

Once I've got a basic draft, I play out the part of the central characters, as I've said; then I take each of the other characters individually through the plot. I don't try to weave them together all at once. My approach does add up to many drafts. The first is just a crudely plotted sketch. Each character hammers out his or her part in a draft all to himself or herself, rather as a mechanic hammers out dents in a fender. The major characters usually get more than one draft. Then comes the knitting together, the catching of details that aren't consistent or fully worked out. When I can get through the manuscript in two days without having to stop long to fix things that trouble me, I know I'm nearing the end.

Initially **Theory of War** *was more successful abroad than in the United States. What do you feel accounts for this, especially when you consider its focus on American history and themes?*

I did get a grant for the book from National Endowment for the Arts; I did appear on the *Today* show; I did get some very good reviews and I did do a publicity tour, but the book still isn't doing well in the United States. I can't explain why. Nobody can. The *New York Times* didn't review it, even after I won the Whitbread, nor did the *Washington Post* or the *Boston Globe.* The Europeans, of course, feel that Americans turned away because they are ashamed of skeletons in the cupboard. They also figure Americans see the book as not politically correct.

The Europeans have been very generous to the book. So

far it has been translated into eight foreign languages. In England, as well as the Whitbread Novel of the Year and the Whitbread Book of the Year Awards, ***Theory of War*** narrowly missed the Booker list and was nominated for the Guardian Prize. It was very widely and very well reviewed here, and it hit number one on the best-seller list. In France it was the runner-up for the Prix Femina Etranger and is nominated for the Grand Prix des Lectrices de Elle 1995, to be decided in May.

Who are your primary literary influences?

My husband was the most important influence on me. Now that he's dead, I look mainly to film and television for new ways of working. I read almost not at all, but I'm sure writers I liked while I was still reading are important to what I do—writers such as Dostoyevsky, Kafka, Dickens.

What do you find most appealing about those authors?

In Dostoyevsky, the intensity; in Kafka, the element of fear; in Dickens, the vividness of the characters.

Could you expand on how your husband was an important influence?

I was married to Dexter Masters, a very fine American writer and one of the very finest of American editors. One day, before I'd written anything myself, I got an idea for a story for him to write. I tried and tried to explain this idea to him, and finally he said, "I can see a line or a phrase, but not a story. You're just going to have to write this one yourself." With his help, that's just what I did, and *Harper's Magazine* published the story, entitled **"A Variety of Religious Experience,"** in 1975. Dexter taught me to take exquisite pains over detail, to use resonance much as film uses music, to cut to the bone and to discard even a good idea if I couldn't manage to get it right.

You mentioned earlier that part of your background is theatrical. I know you had connections with ballet. Can you talk a little bit about that and how that relates to your writing?

I was a dancer with both the San Francisco Ballet and the New York City Ballet. It's an odd background for a writer, but not at all a wasted one—at least I don't think so. My feeling is that any technique is more like any other technique than no technique at all, and I borrow elements from ballet and from the theatrical trappings of ballet—ways of working—to use in writing. I wrote about my time as a dancer in a book that appeared in England in September to wonderful reviews. It came out first in the United States in 1982 under the title ***The Unmaking of a Dancer.*** Here it is called ***Prologue.***

What can you tell me about your new work?

I just delivered a manuscript—my third novel, to my agents. It goes to auction in London next week. It's medical in nature, heavily researched, largely based in the United States—a situation that started up in 1983, a very difficult and very scandalous medical situation. I wrote it first as nonfiction but couldn't sell it. One of my agents suggested I try it as a novel, which is what I've done. But it isn't by any means just a tract; it's a real novel with, I trust, some funny parts in it as well as a dark political message. Another agent is flying with it to America right this very day. It should be with an American publisher tomorrow. We will see what comes of it.

FURTHER READING

Criticism

Elson, John. "Boughten Boyhood." *Time* 141, No. 16 (19 April 1993): 69.

A positive assessment of *Theory of War.* Elson asserts that "at her best Brady writes with a poet's economy, evoking [the protagonist's] chaotic century in brief detonations of imagery."

Additional coverage of Brady's life and career is contained in the following source published by Gale Research: *Contemporary Authors,* Vol. 141.

Carolyn Forché
The Angel of History

Award: *Los Angeles Times* Book Award for Poetry

(Full name Carolyn Louise Forché) Born in 1950, Forché is an American poet, journalist, editor, and translator.

For further information on Forché's life and works, see *CLC,* Volumes 25 and 83.

INTRODUCTION

The Angel of History (1994) focuses on various atrocities of the twentieth century, including the Holocaust, the atomic bombing of Hiroshima, and the occupation of Paris by the Nazis. Divided into five sections, the volume employs a fragmented structure and is told in part by the Angel of History, a being which can record humanity's miseries but is unable to prevent them or the pain and suffering associated with them. Stressing the importance of remembrance and chance, Forché frequently assumes a multitude of voices as she relates her speakers' observations, fears, and haunted memories. In one poem, for example, she focuses on a group of Jewish children who, hiding from Nazis during World War II, are eventually discovered and marched to Auschwitz; in another poem, "The Garden Shukkei-en," a Japanese woman comments that she dislikes the color of a beautiful flower since it reminds her of "a woman's brain crushed under a roof"—a sight she witnessed during the atomic attack on Hiroshima. The latter poem, however, like other pieces in the collection, ends on a note of resigned hope. The speaker asserts: "We have not, after all these years, felt what you call happiness. / But at times, with good fortune, we experience something close. / As our life resembles life, and this garden the garden. / And in the silence surrounding what happened to us / / it is the bell to awaken God that we've heard ringing." *The Angel of History* also contains numerous allusions to quotes by French poet Paul Valéry, Austrian writer Georg Trakl, and Holocaust survivor Elie Wiesel. Noting Forché's desire to remember past events on personal and social levels—rather than as political abstractions, facts, or statistics—Susan Salter Reynolds observed: "[Forché] is not puzzling, not trying, first and foremost to figure out what to do with her own experience. She is, instead, speaking in the voices of the people whose stories are remembered. It is as though, beyond bearing witness and providing conscience, she has incorporated the history of others into her own genealogy."

PRINCIPAL WORKS

Gathering the Tribes (poetry) 1976
The Country between Us (poetry) 1982
Against Forgetting: Twentieth-Century Poetry of Witness [editor] (poetry) 1993
The Angel of History (poetry) 1994

CRITICISM

***Publishers Weekly* (review date 31 January 1994)**

SOURCE: A review of *The Angel of History,* in *Publishers Weekly,* Vol. 241, No. 5, January 31, 1994, pp. 77-8.

[*Here, the critic offers a favorable review of* The Angel of History.]

Though Forché's (***The Country Between Us***) previous books have been groundbreaking works of political and moral depth, this new volume may be the most remarkable. Ambitious and authentic, ***The Angel of History*** is an overarching book-length poem, composed in numbered sections, that invokes the horror of contemporary times in a mode reminiscent of Eliot's *The Waste Land.* Much as Eliot's poem refracted WW I, the vacuity of culture and the fragmentation of modern life, Forché considers the Holocaust, Hiroshima and genocide in Latin America—the dismal past that predicates the chaotic present. Her vehicle is the Angel of History, who confronts human cruelty and misery but can do no more than record them, as explained by Walter Benjamin in an epigraph: "The angel would like to stay, awaken the dead, and make whole what has been smashed. But . . . the storm irresistibly propels him into the future to which his back is turned, while the pile of debris before him grows skyward." Though the poetry is powerful, it is not always easily understandable; one must follow the Angel through serpentine lines, a disjointed and oblique nightmare whispered by an indeterminate narrator, and a splintered pastiche that borrows apocalyptic phrases from Elie Wiesel, Kafka, Canetti, Trakl, Char and Valery. But the journey ventured is well worth the occasional wrong turn: Forché has not only created poetry of consummate beauty, but has borne witness to the wounds of our collective history, fulfilling the conviction that "surely all art is the result of one's having been in danger, of having gone through an experience all the way to the end."

Kevin Walker (review date 22 May 1994)

SOURCE: "Inspired by War," in *Detroit Free Press,* Section G, May 22, 1994, p. 8.

[*In the following review, Walker favorably assesses* The Angel of History, *briefly comparing it to* The Country between Us *and noting Forché's focus on World War II, survival, and remembrance.*]

Carolyn Forche's second book, ***The Country Between Us,*** became one of the most talked-about books of poetry of the 1980s. The heart of it is a group of poems about the war in El Salvador. Forche wrote with haunting precision about the cruelty of that war and the questions of conscience it should have raised for all Americans.

In ***The Angel of History,*** Forche again bears witness to the shattering of lives. But her technique has evolved magnificently. In her 1981 work, she transformed suffering into the musical, unifying shape of the lyric poem. In ***The Angel of History,*** she has done something more challenging.

This book-length poem is as fragmented as a bombed-out house or a shattered mirror. But each puzzling fragment is exquisite, and the whole possesses a unity that defies easy understanding.

The Angel of History is a meditation on destruction, survival and memory. What the characters who float in and out of it like ghosts have in common is that their lives have been shaped irrevocably by the events of the World War II. Forche gives voice to survivors whose loved ones are all dead; to child victims who left behind only their names; to the countless human beings who were killed or ruined by events beyond their control and beyond their comprehension.

Like most of Forche's subject matter, this is grim territory. But ***The Angel of History*** is not a harrowing book, so much as an inspiring one. Forche has found a way of examining the unbearable that neither diminishes the terror nor drives the reader away.

The key to her success is the poem's unique blend of lucidity and elusiveness. Unwinding as it does in fragments of stories, wisps of personality, snapshots of landscapes, the poem resists the reader's desire to get a grip on it. It slips by like time itself. Left behind is the memory of wreckage, miraculously intertwined with the memory of beauty.

In *The Angel of History* Forché gives voice to survivors whose loved ones are all dead; to child victims who left behind only their names; to the countless human beings who were killed or ruined by events beyond their comprehension.

—Kevin Walker

In one passage, a survivor of Hiroshima stands in a restored ornamental garden in that city, considering her life and that of fellow survivors:

> We have not, all these years, felt what you call happiness,
> But at times, with good fortune, we experience something close,
> As our life resembles life, and this garden the garden.
> And in the silence surrounding what happened to us
> it is the bell to awaken God that we've heard ringing.

This entire book is as bright, as serene, and as tender as those lines. ***The Angel of History*** achieves what Forche hopes for when she writes,

> And so we revolt against silence with a bit of speaking.
> The page is a charred field where the dead would have written
> *We went on.*

Sue Russell (review date July 1994)

SOURCE: "The Workings of Chance and Memory," in *The Women's Review of Books,* Vol. XI, Nos. 10-11, July, 1994, p. 31.

[*In the following favorable review, Russell examines the themes and structure of* The Angel of History.]

With her latest collection, ***The Angel of History,*** Carolyn Forché proves once again that socially conscious poetry is not a contradiction in terms. When her first collection, ***Gathering the Tribes,*** won the coveted Yale Younger Poets prize in 1976, she was praised by Stanley Kunitz for the quality of her imagination, "at once passionate and tribal." Kunitz seems to be referring to Forché's empathic gift to see her way into other lives. Although these early poems document a connection to her own Slovak ancestry, they demonstrate as well a concern that moves beyond the boundaries of a particular family or cultural heritage toward a more global frame of reference. This global view is most clearly evident in ***The Angel of History,*** which takes as its subject nothing less than the devastations of war on every front in the latter part of the twentieth century.

It is illuminating to look back at the sources both within and outside her work which led Forché to this ambitious undertaking. With her second book, ***The Country Between Us,*** published in 1981, Forché's nascent political awareness was actualized by her experience with Amnesty International in El Salvador. Here she showed herself to be both poet and ethnographer, a participant observer whose reports from the field had the ring of truth. I bought the book at a B. Dalton store when it was in its third printing, which should say enough about its unique popularity among poetry collections. It was the rare occasion when a book that deserved to be read actually found its rightful audience.

In **"The Colonel,"** a prose poem from this earlier volume, the speaker conveys in simple, flat sentences an unforgettable story:

> I was asked how I enjoyed the country. There was a brief commercial in Spanish. His wife took everything away. There was some talk then of how difficult it had become to govern. The parrot said hello on the terrace. The colonel told it to shut up, and pushed himself from the table. My friend said to me with his eyes: say nothing. The colonel returned with a sack used to bring groceries home. He spilled many human ears on the table. They were like dried peach halves. There is no other way to say this . . .

The form of the poem will not allow for the shaping effect normally wrought by line breaks in free verse. By inference, such refinements would not be appropriate for the bald facts presented here. The prose poem can be seen as an appropriate vehicle for the poetry of witness. It enhances the implicit message: I have been there, I have seen these terrible things and now I must report them accurately. The tension between surface objectivity and underlying emotion comes to a head at the end of the poem, which breaks into another realm:

> He swept the ears to the floor with his arm and held the last of his wine in the air. Something for your poetry, no? he said. Some of the ears on the floor caught this scrap of his voice. Some of the ears on the floor were pressed to the ground.

In ***The Angel of History,*** that other realm is fully realized. Each of the book's five parts begins *in medias res* either within a historical moment or in the midst of a meditation on the nature of history itself. As readers, whether we enter through Vichy France, Hiroshima, or Terezinstadt, we find our own way through a complex weave of people, events and objects. In the first three sections, the narrator floats like an angel through the ruins of Europe, moving from a French sanitarium to the streets of occupied Paris and into the Czech republic that, according to a note, was the home of Forché's paternal ancestors. The trail leads inevitably to the death camps and cuts across time to a string of more recent events—most notably the Chernobyl nuclear disaster—in the same terrain.

In Part Four, three relatively short single poems examine the perspective of holocaust survivors, both from Hitler's camps (**"Elegy"**) and from Hiroshima (**"The Garden Shukkei-en"** and **"The Testimony of Light"**). The concluding section, "Book Codes," consists of three unpunctuated poems, partly fragments lifted from Wittgenstein, and partly commentary on the necessity of fragmentation. The familiar photographic image of the mushroom cloud hovers over the last several lines and reinvents itself as a generative image:

> smaller clouds spread out a golden
> screen
> given the task of painting wounds
> through the darkened town as though
> it had been light
> at the moment of the birth of this cloud

Perhaps the most striking element of the book is Forché's deep understanding of the workings of chance and memory. She explains in a note to ***The Angel of History*** that "The first-person, free-verse, lyric narrative poem of my earlier years has given way to a work which has desired its own bodying forth: polyphonic, broken, haunted, and in ruins, with no possibility of restoration." In the unnumbered sections of Part One, that "broken" or "haunted" narrative begins to define itself. The "I" of the poem is neither the poet nor a designated other but "a memory through which one hasn't lived."

Each of the five parts of *The Angel of History* begins *in medias res* either within a historical moment or in the midst of a meditation on the nature of history itself. As readers, whether we enter through Vichy France, Hiroshima, or Terezinstadt, we find our own way through a complex weave of people, events and objects.

—Sue Russell

I am a reader who has long admired those first-person lyric efforts that Forché has, for the moment, outgrown. I was therefore a bit sceptical in approaching this recent endeavor. Attempts at extended narrative, from Eliot and Pound to Suzanne Gardinier and Forché herself, seem to carry with them a heavy load of baggage that can be daunting even to the most generous of readers. I was afraid that the forceful clarity I have found in Forché's earlier work might be obscured by the complexities of the exercise. In other words, I was afraid that I would not be able to find vestiges of the poet in this new work.

What saves Forché from the postmodern trap, however, is the continuity between the persona of the current collection and that of her earlier work. Though the "I" may not be as close as it once was to the poet herself, both the thematic concerns and the precision of language remain constant.

This continuity is most evident through the presentation of specific details. In Part Three, "The Recording Angel," a singular image reminded me of that Salvadoran bag of ears:

Hundreds of small clay heads discovered while planting coffee
A telescope through which it was possible to watch a fly crawling the
  neighbors' roof tiles
The last-minute journey to the border
  for no reason, the secret house
  where sports trophies were kept
That weren't sports trophies
Someone is trying to kill me, he said . . .

While the narrator of **"The Colonel"** forced herself and, consequently, the reader, to stay with a single image, in these later lives the very concept of first-person narration is blurred through the use of sentence fragments and passive verbs.

These quick shifts in imagery are representative of the freedom of movement Forché has sought, which is in fact more cinematic than literary. Yet Forché is no omniscient "auteur" who controls the camera. Instead, I sense in these poems a suspension of authority, a willingness to channel other voices without losing the impact of a singular poetic intelligence.

Because of Forché's sharp, though changing, focus on individual details, the language is never distancing. Although the structure of the work as a whole is complex, and we may not always know who is speaking or who is being spoken to, the book is nonetheless fully inhabited by people and things. In Part Three, "The Recording Angel," for instance, we are made to see the "china cups" and hear the echo of "chiming tables" left in a house whose inhabitants abandon it and return after many years. One page later, we meet up with a Nazi sympathizer, "the woman with the shaved head seen twice in different arrondissements," whose spectral image more than hints at the depravity that encompasses the scene. And in Part Four, [in the poem] **"The Garden Shukkei-en,"** we encounter an elderly female survivor of Hiroshima who states matter-of-factly, "I don't like this particular red flower because / it reminds me of a woman's brain crushed under a roof."

The Angel of History may be difficult to describe, but it is also a difficult book to put down, or to forget. Images such as these have remained with me in the weeks during which I have lived with this book. Carolyn Forché has managed to write a poem that remains humble toward its sources without effacing her own distinctive voice. I hope that her rendering of twentieth-century events will also serve as a touchstone for the continuing discussion of how history is to be represented in a way that truly honors the lives that are lost.

Calvin Bedient (review date Summer 1994)

SOURCE: "Postlyrically yours," in *The Threepenny Review,* Vol. XV, No. 2, Summer, 1994, pp. 18-20.

[*In the excerpt below, Bedient offers a favorable assessment of* The Angel of History.]

Carolyn Forché's ***The Angel of History*** is instantly recognizable as a great book, the most humanitarian and aesthetically "inevitable" response to a half-century of atrocities that has yet been written in English. Each rereading becomes more hushed, more understanding, more painful, more rapt. A sort of bedrock of acquaintance with human misery, as of memory's capacity to witness it, emerges in lines that are each peculiarly forlorn: "The cry is cut from its stalk."

Forché creates—was given—a new tone, at once sensitive and bleak, a new rhythm, at once prose-like and exquisite, a new line and method of sequencing, at once fluid and fragmentary, frozen at the turn. Take the third unnumbered section of the title poem, which confronts the farmhouse in Izieu where forty-four Jewish children were "hidden April to April" during the war:

Within the house, the silence of God. Forty-
  four bedrolls, forty-four metal cups.
And *the silence of God is God.*

In Pithiviers and Beaune-la-Rolande, in Les
  Milles, Les Tourelles, Moussac and
  Aubagne,

the silence of God is God.

The children were taken to Poland.
The children were taken to Auschwitz in
  Poland

singing *Vous n'aurez pas l'Alsace*

et la Lorraine.
In a farmhouse still standing in Izieu, *le
  silence de Dieu est Dieu.*

Hypnotic, painfully ice-cold, the repetitions, the catalogue of place names (and they are beautiful: could God not have trusted speech in them?), the horridly mechanical primer's incremental creep from "to Poland" to "To Auschwitz in Poland," and Elie Wiesel's line on the inhuman purity of a silent God—these are part of an aesthetic which is unable to blame, explain, or console: a stunned aesthetic of bafflement, poised like an ear before *"le silence de Dieu."*

Forché is not concerned to connect up even related material closely and clearly; she is not mapping anything (except maybe silence). The gaps between her lines and sections count as much as the words, the artistry is half in the evocation of what cannot be retrieved from the ashes or forced from the silence. Exiled, displaced, ephemeral, cut off from the old dream of natural happiness, natural time, each line is an unfinished separation, an item in an infinite field of disappointment, forced into aimless drift, an untotalizable disaster implicit in it. The poet thus makes a small book huge. She earns her title.

Wallace Stevens's description of poetry, "particles of order, a single majesty," fits an earlier, a more naive kind of poetry than Forché's, whose "rage against chaos," in Stevens's words, is scarified into the angel of history's appalled witness of our times. Witness is not contemplation, it is far more passive; its goals are to see, tell, not forget, and withstand. Quick-pulsed, plangent activist in her famous book ***The Country Between Us,*** Forché is here encased in a giant block of ice, helpless, but no less compassionate for that. (The old voice starts up only once, in the most anonymous and jumbled of the long [sections], "The Recording Angel": "Each small act of defiance a force"). How do you *reach out* to "history"? To that which gives the lie to succession, to optimism? To that whose heart is extremity? The poet underwrites the pessimism of [Walter] Benjamin's sublime figure for history: "a storm is blowing in from Paradise; it has got caught in [the angel's] wings with such violence that [he] can no longer close them. The storm . . . propels him [backward] into the future . . . while the pile of debris before him grows skyward."

The Angel of History writes disaster. Maurice Blanchot's *The Writing of the Disaster* is the best single guide to its assumptions, to the stone-hard equanimity of

It isn't necessary to explain
The dead girl was thought to be with child
Until it was discovered that her belly had
  already been cut open
And a man's head placed where the child
  would have been

or to the tinge of horror in "Memory a wind passing through the blood trees within us," or to "the defenselessness for which there is no cure" (I quote from "The Recording Angel"), or to the conviction that "The worst is over. / The worst is yet to come," in words from **"The Testimony of Light."** The disaster, which is history's thumped-down trump card, cannot be thought; to think it, Blanchot says, "is to have no longer any future in which to think it." It can only be evoked, and with a "sort of disinterest, detached from the disaster"—disaster's chemical warfare having damaged the nerves. It is the affirmation and repetition of extremity, the fragmentariness of endemic disarray. At its threshold one is always turned back, yet there is no turning away. It makes of the anonymous continuity of humanity a rumor. To write the disaster is "to refuse to write—to write by way of this refusal"; to offer a text that is almost empty, and to which the reader has to jump to *failure's* intensity.

The poet's Czech grandmother ("They didn't want you to know the past. They were hoping in this way you could escape it") and other accidents of her history, including her travels with her photojournalist husband Harry Mattison to South Africa, Beirut, Paris, etc., have led her to this non-American acquaintance with extremity. But a blessed fatality of her nature, her liability to lose herself to others (and the effacement of the subject is anyway almost a precondition of writing poetry), explains it best. Like Simone Weil, Forché lacks whatever thickness it takes to refuse to see that history has been refusal for so many.

In the title poem, there is Ellie, once a refugee from the Nazis ("Winter took one of her sons and her own attempt to silence / him, the other")—the poet's ward mate in a Paris hospital, peeling skin from her arm like an opera glove: *"Le Dieu est un feu. A psychopath . . . I wish to leave life."* There is, also in Paris, a Salvadoran revenant ("And just now it was as if someone not alive were watching"), whose room, he says, was once ("filled with vultures . . . belching and vomiting flesh, / as you saw them at Puerto Diablo and El Playon . . . so fat with flesh they weren't able to fly"). Further, an identification with a Salvadoran woman whose eight-year-old letter Forché still carries ("It was years before my face would become hers . . . / As if it were possible to go on living for someone else"), who wrote, "Please, when you write, describe again how I looked in the white dress that improbable morning / when my random life was caught in a net of purpose." In the second long "The Notebook of Uprising," there is her grandmother, Anna ("Alenka: *You must not speak anymore. I am going to tell you"*), and Anna's niece, traced down in what is now the Czech Republic: "She stood on the landing in disbelief in Brno as if the war were translucent behind us, / the little ones in graves the size of pillows." And so on. The litany brings tears.

So much in ***The Angel of History*** is mysteriously beautiful, has the dully rich gleam of pewter, is so tinctured with the disaster ("The train rose along the bank above the tiled roofs, its windows blinded by mud and smoke"), and is so cumulative that it is misleading to single out passages, as if they were high points. The whole book must be picked up together, carefully, like the most fragile and most cutting of wonders.

But one of the three poems in Part IV, following the longer poems that make up the first three parts, will doubtless become an anthology piece (even though it deserves better). **"The Garden Shukkei-en"** finds the poet in Hiroshima. The poem ends with the Japanese woman guide saying in the restored garden:

I don't like this particular red flower because
it reminds me of a woman's brain crushed
  under a roof.

Perhaps my language is too precise, and
  therefore difficult to understand?

We have not, all these years, felt what you
  call happiness.
But at times, with good fortune, we experience something close.
As our life resembles life, and this garden
  the garden.
And in the silence surrounding what happened to us

it is the bell to awaken God that we've

heard ringing.

The pained eloquence is characteristic of the book. As for Eden in what "The Recording Angel" calls "the worst of centuries," it is but a simulacrum of a former paradise, painted in the red of disaster.

Don Bogen (review date 24 October 1994)

SOURCE: "Muses of History," in *The Nation*, New York, Vol. 259, No. 13, October 24, 1994, pp. 464-68.

[*In the excerpt below, Bogen extols Forché's ability to document historical atrocities, individual experience, and political vision in* The Angel of History, *noting that the book is a breakthrough from Forché's earlier works.*]

The history of our age is not the stuff of epic poetry. It has plenty of warfare, of course, but not much in the way of heroism; there is more bureaucratese than grandiloquence in the speeches of its leaders; and its chaotic pace would chew up any meter after a dithyramb or two. So what's a poet to do? Many tend their gardens. But a poetry that withdraws from the public concerns of its time for whatever reasons—aesthetic objections, information overload, lack of firsthand experience, indifference—impoverishes itself and its readers. We're left with the schizoid vision of the 6 o'clock news: a chaotic sense of the present—what was that country we're invading? —coupled with a handful of clichés that anesthetize the past. Poets of history like Neruda and Milosz take us beyond that split, revivifying the past as they uncover its links to the world today.

A poet of history inevitably offers some kind of political vision, and Carolyn Forché has long been aware of this dimension in her work. Her first book, ***Gathering the Tribes,*** which won the Yale Younger Poets Award in 1976, is grounded in a politics of identity: ethnic (with her Eastern European ancestors), spiritual (with Native Americans) and sexual. Her second collection, ***The Country Between Us*** (1981), moved toward a more overtly political stance, dramatizing her personal reaction to struggles in Europe, Vietnam and most notably El Salvador, where she worked as a human rights activist. This book derives much of its force from an insistence on the poet's witnessing of the events. Her well-known account of dinner with a Salvadoran colonel who collected the severed ears of his victims begins, "What you have heard is true. I was in his house."

For all its power, however, the limits of this approach have become clear to Forché in the thirteen years since her last book came out. But her new volume turns away from what she calls the "first-person, free-verse, lyric-narrative poem" of her earlier work. It reflects her increased awareness of the pitfalls of a reportorial approach to oppression: a naïve faith that verse will change the world, the unconscious egotism of the witness, traces of voyeurism in the portrayal of the oppressed. Her work compiling and editing the anthology ***Against Forgetting: Twentieth-Century Poetry of Witness*** has also been instrumental in moving her poetry beyond the politics of personal encounter. ***The Angel of History*** is rather an extended poetic meditation on the broader contexts—historical, aesthetic, philosophical—which include our century's atrocities. The collection represents a deeper and more complex engagement with her political concerns and a startling departure in style to achieve this. It's clearly a breakthrough.

Forché's new book is well aware of its situation at the end of the century. It takes its title from Walter Benjamin's "Theses on the Philosophy of History," in which history is seen as a growing pile of debris from what appears to the observing angel to be one single catastrophe; he looks back at it but can do nothing, as he is propelled continuously into an unknown future. His situation, of course, parallels that of the poet, and the fragmentary units with which Forché works have a rubblelike combination of specificity and disconnectedness. The core poetic material for ***The Angel of History*** is a body of shattered elegiac evocations, running from as little as a phrase to a few stanzas in length. Some of these arise from personal experience and memory, others from her reading, others from the words and experiences of real or imagined characters. To her credit, Forché has resisted the postmodern temptation to juggle with the ruins. Though aware of the slipperiness and essential relativity of language, she holds to the idea that history demands something more than an arbitrary order from those who would engage it.

At the heart of the book are the three long sequences with which it opens: "The Angel of History," "The Notebook of Uprising" and "The Recording Angel." As their titles suggest, these pieces are to some extent interwoven, sharing common concerns with the violence of our century and the challenge of getting it on paper. Within the one vast disaster that the angel sees, Forché singles out the Holocaust and Hiroshima as the two defining atrocities of our time, approaching them from different perspectives in the opening sequences (Parts I, II and III) and then defining her points more directly in the three short elegies of Part IV. The final section of the volume, "Book Codes" (Part V), sets the work in perspective by raising questions about the power of writing to deal with this material. Forché's goal in focusing on the two catastrophes is not so much to explain them—who could do that?—as to keep them from being forgotten or distorted as they recede in time and survivors die. If memory is, as she puts it in "The Notebook of Uprising," "a reliquary in a wall of silence," it's important to have scenes there that will continue to speak.

It's also important to make distinctions. As ***The Angel of History*** progresses, Forché's specific vision of the two atrocities becomes clear. The atomic bomb represents a single starting point for the age, "the moment of the birth of this cloud," as she puts it in **"Book Codes: III,"** while the death camps are the center of a web that binds us inextricably to the past. The obsessive, grinding, all-encompassing quality of the Holocaust—the way it intertwines the living and the dead, perpetrators, victims and those not yet born—comes out vividly in the poet's engagement with diverse sources, from the notes in a child's prayer book found at Theresienstadt—"V.K. 1940, hearts, a police doll wearing the star" ("The Notebook of Uprising")—to the deadened phrases of those who worked at the ovens (**"Elegy"**) and the fractured, multilingual testimony of the survivor Ellie in the title sequence. Everything about this topic is speaking, complex, demandingly human. Forché's treatment of Hiroshima, by contrast, captures the suddenness and horrible simplicity of the act:

> After the city vanished, they were car-
> ried on black mats from one place
> To another with no one to answer
> them
> Vultures watching from the white trees
> A portable safe found stuffed with
> charred paper
> An incense burner fused to its black
> prayer
> ("The Recording Angel")

The account is flat, end-stopped, largely unpunctuated, with everything in black and white, a list of seemingly disconnected facts inhabited by an anonymous dying "they." When a survivor speaks in **"The Garden Shukkei-en,"** her comments are hauntingly laconic, set off in brief stanzas of a line or two:

> Do you think for a moment we were
> human beings to them?
>
> We tried to dress our burns with vege-
> table oil.
>
> Perhaps my language is too precise,
> and therefore difficult to
> understand?

Forché uses these complementary formats—the polyglot and the muted, the intricate and the simple—to frame the brutality of our epoch. Each in its own way shows both the essentially unspeakable quality of the event and the necessity that the subject be engaged.

The differences between Forché's treatment of the Holocaust and that of Hiroshima suggest the wealth of possibilities her new style can bring to bear. Linked by themes and occasional repeated phrases as they are, the opening sequences represent distinct approaches to the horrors of our time. The first [sequence], "The Angel of History," works with fairly large units, scenes really—the story of Ellie, a hospital stay, the poet leaving Beirut, the birth of her son—which are presented early in the sequence and then broken, juxtaposed and repeated in variations of different lengths as the work progresses. Forché's mode here is not narrative but analytical, as if the encounter with Ellie were a jewel she holds up to the light and revolves, each facet presenting the scene in a different context. Viewed this way, the life of one survivor documents an era.

The second sequence, "The Notebook of Uprising," is, as the title suggests, more journal-like in approach, its twenty-eight numbered sections loosely following a trip to Eastern Europe where the poet finds the niece of her grandmother Anna in the Czech Republic. Instead of shifting angles here, Forché is digging through layers—Prague today, during the Warsaw Pact invasion, under the Nazis—to clarify what has lasted and what has been lost. Her lines have less of the documentary and more of the diary to them, with a focus on numinous moments and their ramifications, as in the second entry:

The core poetic material for *The Angel of History* is a body of shattered elegiac evocations, running from as little as a phrase to a few stanzas in length. Some of these arise from personal experience and memory, others from reading, others from the words and experiences of real or imagined characters.

—Don Bogen

> Anna stands in a ring of thawed snow,
> stirring a trash fire in an iron drum
> until her face
> flares, shriveled and intent, and
> sparks rise in the night along with
> pages of
> burning
> ash from the week's papers,
> one peeling away from the rest,
> an ashen page framed in brilliance.
>
> For a moment, the words are visible,
> even though fire has destroyed
> them, so
> transparent has the page
> become.
> The sparks from this fire hiss out
> among the stars and in thirty years
> appear
> as tracer rounds.
> *They didn't want you to know the past.*
> *They were hoping in this way you*
> *could escape it.*

The final sequence of ten large sections is the broadest in its focus and the most meditative. In big stanzas of long endstopped lines with minimal punctuation, "The Recording Angel" washes across passages of memory and description like a tide, gathering up references to the two previous sequences and quotations from René Char, Georg Trakl, Elias Canetti and others along with its own new material. The motifs underlying this sequence are broad, almost archetypes—a shipwreck, a child asking questions, a man walking and walking—and each section ends with a kind of residue of understanding, as the work's conclusions remain after the scenes have passed. The lyricism of the fourth is typical:

> On the water's map, little x's: a cross-
> stitched sampler of cries for help
> And yet every lost one has been seen,
> mornings in winter, and at night
> When the fishermen have cast their nets
> one too many times
> They surface, the lost, drawing great
> hillocks of breath
> We on the shore no longer vanish when
> the beacon strokes us
> The child's boat plies the water in imi-
> tation of boats
> Years they sought her, whose crew left
> on the water a sad Welsh hymn

Voices from a ketch lit by candles
Days pass and nothing occurs, nights
pass, nights, and life continues in its
passing
We must try then to send a message
ending with the word *night*

Forché's elegiac vision in "The Recording Angel" provides a moving conclusion to the three sequences. The poetic singing here is the most beautiful of Forché's modes in the book, but she has found an appropriately jagged music for the first sequence and an intimate density for the second. In each sequence she makes brilliant use of the possibilities her approach offers, controlling juxtapositions, variations on themes, repetition and sudden bursts of the new.

The "Book Codes" poems that conclude ***The Angel of History*** bring to the surface Forché's questions about the power and value of her craft. The last two—one carrying references to the Holocaust, the other to Hiroshima—are set in parallel forms of equal-length stanzas with closure on a haunting isolated line. The effect is striking aesthetically and emotionally:

an afternoon swallowing down whole
years its every hour
troops marching by in the snow until
they are transparent
from the woods through tall firs a wood
with no apparent end
cathedrals at the tip of our tongues with
countries not yet seen
whoever can cry should come here
("Book Codes: II")

The boldness of Forché's move at the end is typical of the volume as a whole. ***The Angel of History*** is challenging, ambitious poetry, and the book lives up to its claims.

Susan Salter Reynolds (essay date 13 November 1994)

SOURCE: "The Personal as Political," in *Los Angeles Times Book Review,* November 13, 1994, p. F.

[*Salter Reynolds is the assistant book editor for the* Los Angeles Times Book Review. *In the following essay, announcing that Forché is the recipient of the 1994* Los Angeles Times *Book Award for Poetry, she praises the fragmented structure and style of* The Angel of History *as well as its focus on the "social" realm.*]

When Carolyn Forché returned from El Salvador in 1980, where she had been working as a human rights activist, she wrote in her poem **"Return"**: "I go mad, for example, / in the Safeway, at the many heads / of lettuce, papaya and sugar, pineapples / and coffee, especially the coffee. / And when I speak with American men, / there is some absence of recognition."

It may not have been the first time that Forché was witness to the kind of cruelty El Salvador became known for at that time, but her response, recorded in ***The Country Between Us,*** became a sort of bible for puzzling over cruelty and the atrocities of war. The poems feel as though they were written when Forché came home, unable to reconcile daily life with what she had seen and heard. "Better / people than you were powerless" she wrote in **"Return."** "You have not returned to your country, / but to a life you never left."

These were Forché's poems of witness. If you were fortunate enough to read them in college, when history and the news and literature all left enormous black holes in your understanding; when debates in various seminars over the artificial/official separation of the personal and the political violated your still youthful instincts about how individuals should treat each other, when political science professors almost never let their students read poetry or novels, then you will never ever forget them, even if your well-worn copy was given away in a moment of generous weakness.

After we had lived with them for a while, digested her experiences, Forché's voice became part of our conscience. "To think of the writer as conscience of the world," Daniel Boorstin has written in a new collection of essays, "is only to recognize that the writer, as we have seen, is inevitably a divided self, condemned at the same time to express and to communicate, to speak for the writer and speak to others." Forché's next book, ***Against Forgetting: Twentieth Century Poetry of Witness*** collected more than 140 poets from five continents, poems in which the reader can hear "the trace of extremity . . . evidence of what occurred." These poems are written in this century, from the Armenian genocide to Tian An Men Square. The poets must have personally experienced what they write about, they must be considered important to their national literatures, and they must be "available in quality translation."

"What comes to us in the newspapers is not necessarily factual, nor is it necessarily cogent," Forché reminds. Seeing these poems together in one collection reinforces the fact that poetry is an active thing, a triumph of will over circumstance, as Forché paraphrases Walter Benjamin in her introduction: "a poem is itself an event." "The poetry of witness," she writes, "reclaims the social from the political and in so doing defends the individual against illegitimate forms of coercion."

With [***The Angel of History***] Forché gives her readers a place between the personal and the political, a realm she calls "the social," in which voices like that of the Hungarian poet Miklos Radnoti (1909-1944), whose widow found his last poems on his body in a mass grave of prisoners returned from Germany, are respected as historical evidence and testimony to the human spirit all at once: "I believe in miracles, forgot their days; / above me I see a bomber squadron cruise. I was just admiring, up there, your eyes' blue sheen" (from "Letter to My Wife," Larger Heidenau, above Zagubica in the mountains, August-September, 1944). All of these writers are victims, in one way or another, but their dignity is exquisite, and their experience must be trusted. One very fine form of revenge, a way of annihilating evil, a hopeful reader could conclude, is to make something beautiful.

The Angel of History, Forché's most recent collection of poems, are so very different from the poems in ***The Country Between Us***. She is not puzzling, not trying, first and foremost to figure out what to do with her own experience. She is, instead, speaking in the voices of the people whose stories are remembered. It is as though, beyond bearing witness and providing conscience, she has incorporated the history of others into her own genealogy. And there is some calm, some respite from what must be, by now, a terrible roaring inside her; respite in the form of children, pear trees, France and the French.

These poems don't have the neatness of the earlier poems, they are not distinct stories. They are a babble of fragments: "fragments together into a story before the shape of the whole / like a madman—time and again torn from my mouth / out of a nearby chimney each child's hand was taken / though this is not a fairy tale explained in advance" (from **"Book Codes: II"**). And, like the remains in El Playon or Puerto Diablo ("body dumps" in El Salvador), they cannot always be pieced back together to form whole bodies. They are, instead, as Forché wrote in **"The Testimony of Light,"** a poem about Hiroshima, "*Mugamu-chu:* without self, without center. Thrown up in the sky by a wind."

Additional coverage of Forché's life and career is contained in the following sources published by Gale Research: *Contemporary Authors,* Vols. 109, 117; *Contemporary Literary Criticism,* Vols. 25, 83; *Dictionary of Literary Biography,* Vol. 5; and *Poetry Criticism,* Vol. 10.

William Gaddis
A Frolic of His Own

Award: National Book Award for Fiction

Born in 1922, Gaddis is an American novelist.

For further information on his life and works, see *CLC,* Volumes 1, 3, 6, 8, 10, 19, and 43.

INTRODUCTION

Emphasizing litigiousness and greed as characteristics of contemporary American society, *A Frolic of His Own* (1994) focuses on Oliver Crease, his family, his friends, and the various lawsuits in which they are all enmeshed. Employing elements of humor and farce, Gaddis exhaustively details the absurdities of his characters' suits and subsequent countersuits. For example, Oliver is plaintiff in a plagiarism case he has brought against Constantine Kiester, a top Hollywood producer whose real name is Jonathan Livingston Siegal. Oliver is also, paradoxically, plaintiff and defendant in a suit concerning a hit-and-run accident in which he was hit by his own car—a Sosumi ("so sue me"). Taking its title from a British legal phrase used to describe an employee's actions which, though they resulted in on-the-job injuries, do not entitle the employee to compensation, *A Frolic of His Own* is largely noted for its satire of justice and law in contemporary American society and for its unusual narrative structure. Except for the inclusion of excerpts from Oliver's writings, legal documents, and trial transcripts, the novel is told primarily through dialogue that is unattributed and only lightly punctuated. Critics have praised Gaddis's realistic depiction of everyday speech—complete with pauses, interruptions, and unfinished thoughts—and stressed the difficulty such a narrative technique, reminiscent of stream-of-consciousness writing, places on readers. Steven Moore observed: "*A Frolic of His Own* is both cutting-edge, state-of-the-art fiction and a throwback to the great moral novels of Tolstoy and Dickens. That it can be both is just one of the many balancing acts it performs: It is bleak and pessimistic while howlingly funny; it is a deeply serious exploration of such lofty themes as justice and morality but is paced like a screwball comedy; it is avant-garde in its fictional techniques but traditional in conception and in the reading pleasures it offers; it is a damning indictment of the United States, Christianity and the legal system, but also a playful frolic of Gaddis's own."

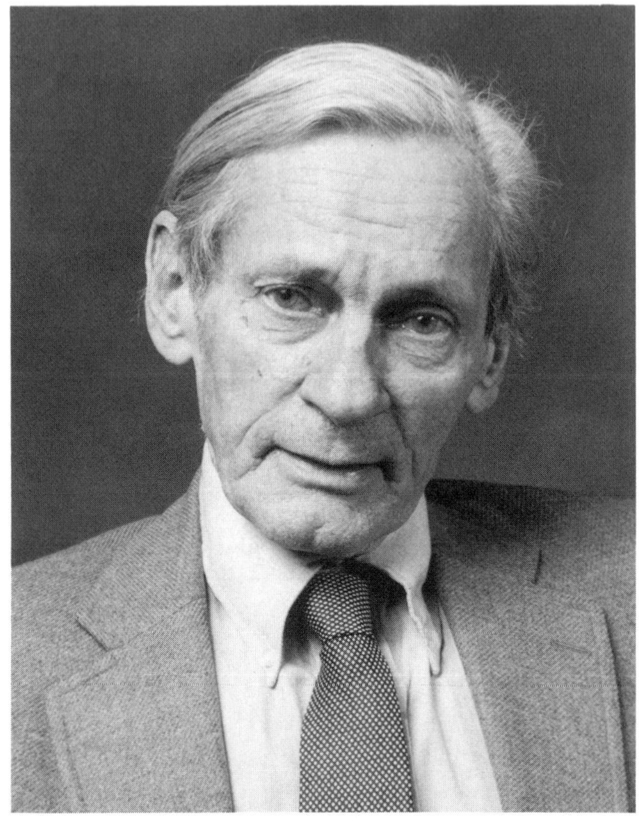

PRINCIPAL WORKS

**The Recognitions* (novel) 1955
**J R* (novel) 1975
Carpenter's Gothic (novel) 1985
A Frolic of His Own (novel) 1994

*The "corrected" versions of these works were both published in 1985.

CRITICISM

Michiko Kakutani (review date 4 January 1994)

SOURCE: "Plagiarism as the Metaphor for a Litigious Era," in *The New York Times,* January 4, 1994, p. C20.

[*In the mixed review below, Kakutani relates the plot, themes, and narrative structure of* A Frolic of His Own, *concluding that "Gaddis's provocative vision of modern society is purchased at a price, the price of hard work and frequent weariness on the part of the reader."*]

In ***The Recognitions,*** his monumental first novel published nearly 40 years ago, William Gaddis used the story of a would-be priest turned master forger to explore the loss of authenticity in the modern world, and the shifting relationships between life and art, art and faith. Those same themes—so pertinent in this post-modern era of recyclings and regurgitations—lie at the core of his long-winded, sometimes uproarious and often exhausting new novel ***A Frolic of His Own.*** This time, however, plagiarism, not counterfeiting, serves as the presiding metaphor; and the action takes place not in the world of art, but in the world of law.

Indeed, the idea behind ***A Frolic of His Own*** is idea theft, an increasingly common phenomenon in Hollywood that gained national attention in 1990, when Art Buchwald won a court victory against Paramount Pictures, contending that the idea for the 1988 Eddie Murphy film *Coming to America* had been stolen from a film treatment he had written in 1983. A similar lawsuit lies at the heart of ***A Frolic of His Own,*** a lawsuit that will snowball like the interminable lawsuit in *Bleak House,* into mayhem and madness for nearly everyone connected with the case, a lawsuit that will leave the reader with a darkly comic vision of a litigious society run perilously amok.

The instigator of Mr. Gaddis's fictional lawsuit is one Oscar Crease, a middle-aged college teacher, who has written an unproduced play called *Once at Antietam.* The play is ostensibly based on his grandfather's experiences in the Civil War, and also appears to draw heavily on the works of other writers, including Plato and Eugene O'Neill.

Oscar claims that he once submitted the play to a producer named Jonathan Livingston Siegal, who subsequently changed his name to Constantine Kiester and went on to be come a world-famous movie director. It is Oscar's contention that Kiester's latest blockbuster, a Civil War epic titled *The Blood in the Red, White and Blue,* is based on *Once at Antietam.* He is suing for compensatory and punitive damages.

Of course, things never proceed smoothly in Mr. Gaddis's novels, and Oscar's lawsuit is no exception. Even as Oscar's legal bills mount, his lawyer is imprisoned, and Oscar finds himself being sued by the O'Neill estate for plagiarizing *Mourning Becomes Electra.* At the same time, Oscar is also trying to recover damages in another lawsuit involving his own car, which ran over him while he was trying to jump-start it. Meanwhile, Oscar's father, a famous Federal Court judge, is trying to cope with the public outcry over his ruling in a case involving the accidental death of a dog named Spot, who became trapped in a piece of outdoor sculpture, a case that has spawned further lawsuits involving the creator of the sculpture, the town where the sculpture was erected and assorted entrepreneurs who want to cash in on Spot's untimely death. Oscar's brother-in-law, Harry; his girlfriend, Lily, and friends of his step-sister Christina are fielding lawsuits of their own.

Mr. Gaddis depicts all this litigation with the manic, slapstick energy of a Marx Brothers movie, a strategy that creates a counterpoint to his characters' spiritual lethargy while providing him with ample opportunities for satire. As in his second novel, ***JR,*** the American preoccupation with money and money-making is parodied, this time through the characters' relentless pursuit of so-called "damages" and "fairness." As in ***The Recognitions,*** the fragmented, fragmentary nature of contemporary society is repeatedly exposed: things fall apart in Mr. Gaddis's world; the center does not, cannot, hold.

Like storytelling, the law is supposed to serve as a tool, in Mr. Gaddis's words, for imposing or rescuing "order from the demeaning chaos in everyday life", but as his characters quickly discover, the law tends to be a poor substitute for justice. In ***A Frolic of His Own,*** the law links people together in purely adversarial relationships of mistrust, promoting a Kafkaesque sense of disintegration and crisis, rather than a sense of order.

Mr. Gaddis's own narrative method—refined through his last three novels and culminating in this volume—mirrors this philosophical outlook. There is almost no conventional narrative in ***A Frolic of His Own;*** most of the book consists of nothing but voices: characters creating themselves out of words, out of conversations, asides and ruminations. Heated conversations about death and money and sex are interrupted with murmurings about lunch and tea. Petty arguments about legal proceedings are sprinkled with allusions to Shakespeare and Plato. Long, tiresome extracts from Oscar's play are carefully laid out, as are jargon-filled legal briefs and opinions.

Despite Mr. Gaddis's antic humor, this can make for laborious reading. One has the sense that nothing has been edited out of Oscar's story; unlike conventional fictions, it does not feel sculptured or shaped. Instead, Mr. Gaddis seems to suggest, the reader is supposed to make order out of disorder, discern the patterns among the repetitions, ellipses and digressions. Even his characters tend to feel amorphous and poorly defined; they exist, after all, not as

Christopher Walker on the timeliness of *A Frolic of His Own:*

With *A Frolic of His Own,* Gaddis seems to have finally coincided with the *Zeitgeist.* American courtrooms are now televised theatres, and novels about the law are suddenly in vogue. However, unlike the legal thrillers of John Grisham and Scott Turow, which simply use the law as decoration, Gaddis's novel properly immerses itself in the intricacies of the law and explores the insanity of American legal practice.

Christopher Walker, in his "All in Order, Thanks," in The Observer, *27 February 1994.*

the completed creations of an omniscient novelist, but as modernist symbols of people in a continuous state of becoming.

As a result of this highly oblique approach, Mr. Gaddis's provocative vision of modern society is purchased at a price, the price of hard work and frequent weariness on the part of the reader.

Robert Towers (review date 9 January 1994)

SOURCE: "No Justice, Only the Law," in *The New York Times Book Review,* January 9, 1994, pp. 1, 22.

[*Towers is an American novelist and educator. In the following highly favorable review of* A Frolic of His Own, *he praises the novel's humor, satire, and focus on language and the law, suggesting that the reader not be discouraged by the difficulties of Gaddis's style.*]

William Gaddis is the formidably talented writer whose work—until ***A Frolic of His Own***—has been, I suspect, more likely to intimidate or repel his readers than to lure them into his fictional world. His first novel, ***The Recognitions*** (1955), is one of late modernism's sacred monsters, a 900-page display of polymathic erudition, which, though crowded with incident and allusion, shows minimal concern for narrative movement or the in-depth portrayal of any of its myriad characters. With ***JR*** (1975) Mr. Gaddis developed and ruthlessly exploited a technique of almost nonstop, scarcely punctuated dialogue, which he continued to employ in his next two novels. It is a technique that demands unflagging vigilance on the reader's part. I found the tone of both ***JR*** and ***Carpenter's Gothic*** (1985) so high-pitched, so unremittingly aggressive, as to blunt what might otherwise have been my pleasure in their satiric exuberance and mimetic brilliance. While there is still a good deal to be endured in his fourth novel, ***A Frolic of His Own,*** there is far more to be enjoyed than in any of his previous work.

Its opening sentence announces both the subject and the theme of the novel: "Justice?—You get justice in the next world, in this world you have the law." In ***A Frolic of His Own*** we do indeed have the law—and the language of litigation—in fantastic combinations and obsessive detail, materials from which Mr. Gaddis creates his harsh, misanthropic but often hilarious comedy. At the beginning, Oscar Crease, a major voice in this work composed of voices, is lying in a hospital, suffering from injuries (not very serious) inflicted by his own car, which ran over him while he was trying to hot-wire it. Oscar is thus both the owner of the car and its victim. There was no driver. What will his insurance company cover? Who can be sued? Can the maker of the car be sued for product liability since the car was in Park but slipped into Drive? Such are the issues that Oscar discusses—or rather rants about—with his stepsister, Christina, her lawyer husband, Harry Lutz, and the insurance adjuster who visits him in the hospital. Soon he is involved in a million-dollar suit for pain and disfigurement.

But this is only one of the legal matters with which the irascible Oscar is obsessed. A middle-aged community-college teacher with some inherited money and a conception of himself as "the last civilized man," Oscar has also written an unpublished play, *Once at Antietam,* derived from his grandfather's experiences in the Civil War. This high-minded play, he insists, has been plagiarized by a Hollywood producer-director (Constantine Kiester, a.k.a. Jonathan Livingston Siegal) who has turned it into a vulgar blockbuster movie (*The Blood in the Red White and Blue*) full of sex scenes and gory special effects. Obviously Oscar must sue for enormous damages, though he is warned that as a "little guy" he will face exorbitant expenses and little chance for victory.

Another—even funnier—legal carnival running through the novel involves Oscar and Christina's nonagenarian father, a distinguished Federal judge in whose awesome shadow Oscar has always lived. The case over which Judge Crease presides is worth a brief summary: A contentious sculptor called R. Szyrk has erected a towering, "site-specific" metal sculpture (*Cyclone Seven*) in a small Virginia village. A dog, Spot, belonging to a little boy, wanders into the intricate (and menacing) sculpture and is entrapped in its complex entrails. The village wants to rescue the dog, but the sculptor gets an injunction forbidding any tampering with his work of art. Judge Crease rules in favor of the sculptor, provoking a nationwide, televised campaign to "Save Spot." Here is Oscar talking (that is, ranting) to Christina on the subject:

> "America has taken Spot to its heart, did you see it last night? Every idiot in sight down there with something to sell, dog candy, hot dogs, Free Spot! buttons, Free Spot! T-shirts, Spot dolls with huge wet eyes and that whole hideous Cyclone Seven? peddling this take apart puzzle model and a game where you try to get the dog out with magnets shaped like a dog bone? Marching around for animal rights, artists' rights, black rights, right to life, abortion, gun control, Jesus loves and the flags, Stars and Stripes, Stars and Bars and then somebody. . . ."
>
> "Oscar, just. . . ."
>
> "Yes and then somebody throws a beer bottle and they. . . ."
>
> "And Father right in the midst of it, that's. . . ."
>
> "And why shouldn't he be! Why shouldn't he Christina he started it all didn't he? with that, that decision he wrote for this awful little dog? Schoolchildren sending in donations so this cheap sentimental vision of our great republic shall not perish from the earth."

These are only the major legal issues in ***A Frolic of His Own.*** Dozens of others—some very briefly touched upon, nearly all of them rich in absurdity—emerge from the matrix of the novel's nearly nonstop dialogue. For example, Trish, a rich friend of Christina's, who finds herself pregnant by a young man she picked up, engages one set of lawyers to sue a hospital for "foetal endangerment" and another set to defend her abortion against a suit brought by the father, demanding his paternal rights. In another case, one that has "soared beyond the $33 million mark" in legal costs, the Episcopal Church has sued Pepsico Inc. for trademark infringement and "libelous intent to disparage and make a mockery of plaintiff 's good name." (Reader: note the anagram in Pepsi-Cola.)

> ***A Frolic of His Own*** **is an exceptionally rich, even important novel.**
>
> ***—Robert Towers***

However, though his comic-satiric imagination seems endlessly fertile, Mr. Gaddis has other, more serious intentions in mind. Take the matter of language. When Christina complains that something is only a question of language, Harry cries out, "But, but damn it Christina that's what we're talking about! What do you think the law is, that's all it is, language." And when she complains that it's all a conspiracy, he replies, "Of course it is. . . . Every profession is a conspiracy against the public, every profession protects itself with a language of its own. . . . Language confronted by language turning language itself into theory till it's not about what it's about it's only about itself turned into a mere plaything." One suspects that the author's exasperation with the recent state of literary criticism is, among other things, reflected in this outburst. The novel's mockery of the legal profession, its minions and its dupes, is extended to include a wide spectrum of contemporary American culture—presented here, with corrosive Swiftian glee, as an unholy mess compounded of greed, ignorance, illiteracy, corruption and childish folly.

The major figures—Oscar, Christina and even Oscar's dopey girlfriend, Lily—reveal themselves (and are characterized by one another) with a vividness and immediacy that embrace pathos as well as comic futility. Oscar in particular is an arresting, even moving figure in the midst of farce. The big old house he lives in is in ruinous condition, the corridors full of boxes containing his "archives" (every piece of paper that's ever come his way, including illiterate student themes), and the chaos around him steadily mounts as the legal documents and outrageous bills pour in. As his fantasies of retribution and vindication soar, his condition deteriorates into a state of alcoholic childishness. Christina—herself a complex figure, at once imperious, worldly and needy—rails incessantly at her stepbrother but recognizes the quasi-tragic irony of his situation. [As she says to Harry]:

> "Oscar's done it again . . . setting himself up with these fantasies of producing his play when he wins this appeal and if he loses, this whole desperate pose as the gentleman poet, the last civilized man I mean he's just really so different from who he thinks he is and God only knows, when he loses. . . ."
>
> "Not when he loses, Christina. It's when this who he thinks he is loses, what the whole thing's all about isn't it? He goes off on a frolic of his own writes a play and expects the world to roll out the carpet for. . . ."
>
> "A frolic! Where in God's name did you get that, I mean have you ever seen anyone more deadly serious than. . . ."

And she concludes with a startling insight: that going off on a frolic of one's own is "really what the artist is finally all about."

One must not underestimate the obstacles that lie in the way of the appreciation, to say nothing of the enjoyment, of this remarkable novel. Some of these are inherent in the technique of nearly continuous, minimally punctuated speech (the author uses dashes to indicate dialogue). While the reader may marvel at Mr. Gaddis's powers of mimicry and his ability to evoke the distinct personalities of his characters through their spate of words, he is likely to feel bombarded, even assaulted, by the various voices clamoring for attention. The medium is exceptionally dense. The mere effort of sorting out the voices, of tracking them, can be exhausting.

Other obstacles seem gratuitous, even perverse. While old Judge Crease's legal opinions, quoted in their entirety, are perhaps witty enough to justify the stupefying legal jargon in which they are couched, there seems little excuse for subjecting the reader to 50 pages of verbatim, tiresomely repetitious testimony in one of Oscar's legal depositions. Or for quoting 40 or more pages of Oscar's high-minded, thematically significant but (in Christina's words) "long-winded" play. One could perhaps argue (perversely?) that the enduring of long stretches of tedium is a necessary part of the full esthetic experience that the book offers. In any case, I hope the reader will persevere. ***A Frolic of His Own*** is an exceptionally rich, even important novel. The payoff is more than worth the effort.

Malcolm Jones, Jr. (review date 17 January 1994)

SOURCE: "A Legal Lampoon Loses on Appeal," in *Newsweek,* Vol. CXXIII, No. 3, January 17, 1994, p. 52.

[*In the following review, Jones offers a negative appraisal of* A Frolic of His Own, *arguing that in this book Gaddis "hasn't met his own high standards" established with* The Recognitions, J R, *and* Carpenter's Gothic.]

Time has never been kind to the novelist William Gaddis. In the '50s his first novel, ***The Recognitions,*** helped inaugurate an era where so-called difficult writers were lionized. But while the Pynchons and Gasses and Coovers—writers with similarly dark visions who forsook traditional ways of telling a story—reaped the benefits of his labors, Gaddis toiled on in relative obscurity. Two decades later he published ***JR,*** and again he was ahead of the curve. That vicious satire of American business was the perfect '80s novel. Unfortunately, it appeared in 1975. Reviews were good, but sales were meager. In 1985, a similar fate befell ***Carpenter's Gothic,*** in which he savaged fundamentalist religion.

Now Gaddis has published ***A Frolic of His Own***, an extended satire on America's increasingly litigious ways.

Surely no theme could be more timely? Surely, too, we've grown accustomed to unusual narrative strategies. A novel written almost entirely in dialogue with no quotation marks—that's not too daunting these days. As for Gaddis's gloomy vision of American life, the greed, plagiarism and self-absorption that he describes would not look out of place on an episode of *Roseanne* or *The Simpsons.*

But there's the trouble. We've seen these literary somersaults and heard these jokes too often. And while Gaddis helped break such stylistic ground, the harsh truth is that here he hasn't met his own high standards. There's something too easy about this book. Its knee-jerk cynicism sounds unearned, its complications unwarranted. Intellectually and literarily, it's a lazy book.

The story of Oscar Crease, a dilettantish academic who fecklessly sues a movie company for pirating his Civil War play, the novel piles complication upon complication, lawsuit upon lawsuit. It is an orgy of chicanery that begins in frustration and ends in despair. In between, it is a tapestry of talk. Oscar, his lawyers, his family, his friends never stop yapping, rarely listen and refuse to learn. Periodically, Gaddis inserts legal briefs and excerpts from Oscar's lousy play, *Once at Antietam.*

Taken page by page, a lot of the writing is brilliant. Gaddis has a wonderful ear for the way people talk at each other, and he can mimic an insurance agent's spiel or a socialite's prattle with unsettling, hilarious accuracy. Near the end, he writes of an old judge's love for the law and the language: "because when you come down to it the law's only the language after all . . . and what better loves could a man have than those to get him through the night." That's one of the more heartfelt passages—it jumps out because passages like it are so rare. Most of the time Gaddis busies himself making litigants look like jerks or wearying the reader with jokey monikers like Jonathan Livingston Siegal.

At a writers' conference in 1985, Gaddis sought to distinguish himself from the likes of Danielle Steel by saying that she wrote books while he wrote "literature." Such arrogance would be easier to swallow if Gaddis gave his readers more for their trouble. But when you've slogged through 586 pages with a bore like Oscar Crease and learned little more than "people will do anything," you're apt to wonder if Ms. Steel's fans don't have the better part of the bargain.

Mark Kamine (review date 17-31 January 1994)

SOURCE: "Literary Trials and Tribulations," in *The New Leader,* Vol. LXXVII, No. 1, January 17-31, 1994, pp. 18-19.

[*Kamine is a short story writer and film consultant. In the review below, he offers praise for* A Frolic of His Own.]

William Gaddis stands alone. No other American novelist takes on the modernist challenge with comparable rigor or success. Few bother at all, beyond an easy self-reflexivity or the occasional insertion of Joycean interior monologue; most are content to explore 19th-century developments. The result is a conservative literary climate (albeit liberal politically) in which plot presides and innovation is adjunct to subject matter, not style. I don't mean to denigrate the importance of literature that breaches social barriers. I do, however, like to be reminded now and then of what drew me to literature in the first place. Gaddis, about once every 10 years (four novels since 1955), does this.

His latest work, ***A Frolic of His Own,*** challenges the reader from first page to last. Its dialogue is mostly unattributed, its descriptive passages are dense with events, allusions, everything but punctuation. Always difficult and occasionally exasperating, the novel is also immensely funny, moving and encyclopedic in its embrace of current concerns.

The central character, Oscar Crease, inhabits a dilapidated estate on Long Island. Housebound after running himself over while attempting to start his car, Oscar is nevertheless in the thick of events of national interest. The accident has made him the plaintiff in one lawsuit, and the release of a movie based on his grandfather's life has led him to file another, for plagiarism of his unpublished play. In the course of things Oscar's father, a Federal judge, hands down a couple of hilarious decisions—on a death by drowning during baptism and the fate of a dog trapped in a huge steel sculpture. And there are a dozen or so other suits, encompassing Oscar's girlfriend Lily's divorce and abortion, and his brother-in-law Harry's defense of Pepsi-Cola's right to its name.

Gaddis jams a deposition, Judge Crease's written decisions and numerous other legal documents into the text, along with excerpts from the play Oscar had written years before and charges was ripped off. The documents are priceless pastiches. The author takes obvious pleasure in couching some of his sharpest barbs in the formal strictures of legalese. When the sculptor seeks compensation for harm he alleges the dog has done to his creation, Gaddis sneaks in the perfect rejoinder:

> On the related charge of damages brought by plaintiff the standard for preliminary relief must first be addressed. . . . the court takes judicial notice in directing such claim to be made against the Village Board and the dog's master in tandem, since as in the question posed by the Merchant of Venice (I, iii, 122) "Hath a dog money?" the answer must be that it does not.

Reading the sculptor's further (unsuccessful) charge of character defamation, one can't help feeling Gaddis has past reviews of his own books in mind: ". . . yet to the court's knowledge none of this opprobrium however enviously and maliciously conceived and however stupid, careless, and ill informed in its publication has ever yet proved grounds for a successful action resulting in recovery. . . . In short, the artist is fair game and his cause is turmoil."

The book serves in some ways as a torts primer, touching on legal concepts such as proximate cause, product liability, wrongful death, and other incarnations of negligence. Even the title, explains one of the many lawyers we encounter, derives from a legal notion holding that an employee injured while working cannot recover damages if his injury results from an action inappropriate or unrelated to the task at hand.

As with the particular fields of endeavor that marked his earlier novels—art in ***The Recognitions,*** business in ***JR***—Gaddis turns the law here into a vehicle for comments about a broad range of issues. Thus we get keen observations on (and not-so-oblique references to) the contemporary state of literary criticism, multiculturalism, pop culture fetishism, violence in movies, religious fundamentalism, the hiring policies of corporate America, tabloid journalism, and activists of every stripe. Brother-in-law Harry might be speaking of Iran-contra:

> What you see in the headlines out of Washington every day, isn't it? caught redhanded destroying evidence, obstructing justice, committing perjury off on frolics of their own and when they get off on some technicality, everybody knows they're guilty but there's not enough there to prove it so they can proclaim they've been proved innocent, wrap themselves in the flag and they're heroes because now they believe it themselves.

An ongoing dialogue about art and its audience is particularly intriguing. Gaddis, after all, has spent much of his career maligned or ignored; although recently well-reviewed, I suspect he remains little read. His protagonist seems at times a buffoonish version of himself: Oscar's play is unread (except once, by the movie producer accused of plagiarism), he is unwilling to compromise, yet he thirsts for recognition and justice. Oscar's father, meanwhile, is excoriated by the local population for prohibiting the dog owner and the township from carving up a disliked avant-garde sculpture to save an animal. Gaddis milks this case for all it's worth—even bringing in a Southern Senator named Orney Bilk who says of high art: "Product of warped sick minds, sexual deviants, degenerates and foreigners. . . ." Sound familiar?

Not that the author comes down squarely on the side of exclusivist art. In fact, I can't help feeling he's reflecting his own goals when he has Oscar declare that Shakespeare "played to both the stalls and the pits."

That is not likely to be the happy fate of ***Frolic.*** It is tough going. Lack of punctuation ("He said he's not hungry for us to go ahead and eat. He's in there now watching some mystery with a peanut butter sandwich") is the least of its hurdles. Blink and you'll find yourself in mid-flashback, unaware of how you got there. Blink again ("And so she turned now to her guest over tea and coffee cups . . .") and you'll miss an indication—the "now"—that you've returned from the flashback to the novel's present. There are no chapter divisions and few page breaks to clue the reader in to shifts of time and place.

A Frolic of His Own **challenges the reader from first page to last. Its dialogue is mostly unattributed, its descriptive passages are dense with events, allusions, everything but punctuation. Always difficult and occasionally exasperating, the novel is also immensely funny, moving and encyclopedic in its embrace of current concerns.**

—Mark Kamine

The unattributed dialogue, jammed against the rapid-fire narration composed as often as not in long and frequently runon sentences, created in my mind an effect of incessant ranting. This verbal assault would be merely an annoyance were it not full of cutting humor ("Out in the country oh I know, it restores your faith in human nature not having to see anyone") and charged with manic energy ("All that, before a bottle of Chablis smoothed their way for the lobster, butter running down his thumb onto the white tablecloth, before the light and aerator were installed and the plants submerged in the [fish] tank, before another delivery brought more bills and anonymous personalized invitations and a script indecently titled from a playwright hopeful thirsting for production. . . ." Occasionally Gaddis even is willing to risk a dose of straightforward advice verging on wisdom, as when Oscar's brother-in-law attempts to assuage Oscar's guilt over his father's death: "Oscar can't you see! . . . What he tried to free you from while he was alive and now his death has finally done it, you're liberated! That's what this is all about, what a father's death is all about, any father, mine was a, when I was in law school he died. . . ."

Frolic is also rich in mundane detail—family spats, elaborate meals, off-color exchanges. Here is Gaddis' rendering of the climax and aftermath of a sexual encounter between Oscar's sister Christina and her husband Harry:

> . . . and his all panting earnest concentration on the burst that left his head buried on her shoulder, eyes closed, hers wide, as they slipped back in desultory concert to what remained of the day, of the lemon chicken and the shrimp in black bean sauce, the pointless flicker of dinner jackets and backless gowns on actors and actresses long dead and the papers, letters, briefs and memorandums—I mean do they have to be scattered all over the house, Harry? until at last the lights went out.

Such passages convey a sense of how time really passes, how one moment is replaced by another that gives rise to memory and complaint and on and on, unchecked and unstoppable. By novel's end I found myself thinking in the rhythms of Gaddis' prose. Although that sensation faded as well, I was glad to have experienced it. Anyone who invests the time that reading ***A Frolic of His Own*** demands will, I think, feel properly rewarded.

Michael Dirda (review date 23 January 1994)

SOURCE: "Caught in the Web of Words," in *Book World—The Washington Post*, January 23, 1994, pp. 1, 10.

[*In the following review, Dirda lauds the humorous aspects of* A Frolic of His Own, *calling the book "a superb comic novel."*]

How is it that the greatest fiction of our century has been so funny? Joyce and Proust, obviously; but think too of Evelyn Waugh, *Catch-22, Lolita,* much of *Invisible Man,* Pynchon, *The Master and Margarita,* Beckett, Borges. Nothing, it would seem, dates so quickly as the earnest. Really Serious Novels—by D. H. Lawrence, Hemingway, or Virginia Woolf—now sound tendentious, a bit histrionic, often downright embarrassing. Perhaps, to quote Lawrence himself, because ours is such a tragic age we instinctively refuse to take it tragically. There's simply no other way to keep on going when the world is so clearly a hell of fraud, phoniness and moral vacuity, a bloody arena of religious fanaticism, political bankruptcy, money-grubbing, and personal betrayal. We laugh to keep from weeping.

As a guide to this fallen world, our world, no one is better, or funnier, than William Gaddis. To his bitter, exhilarating task he brings the savage indignation of a Swift or Gogol, an insider's command of the lore and lingo of specialized groups (artists, financiers, lawyers), a drama-like approach to storytelling, and a high modernist's cunning use of leitmotifs and symbols. Oh yes, and an unwavering, rigorous artistry. Gaddis's books can be quite long, but if you shake them nothing will fall out: They are made to last.

Since his youthful masterpiece ***The Recognitions*** (1955)—a near-legendary account of inauthenticity, the spectre haunting so much post-romantic writing—Gaddis has produced only three other novels, and that number includes this latest, ***A Frolic of His Own.*** A modern Dunciad striking out at the abuses of what we are obliged to call the law, it is, I think, the most accessible of all his books, vivid with comic characters, especially among its supporting cast. Take the randy and conspicuously wealthy Trish. She blithely cheats her shoe repairman, breaks her mother's will (thus impoverishing an old family servant), never pays her bills, and, in a particularly dizzying moment, hires one set of lawyers to bring a suit "for foetal endangerment and another set to defend her abortion." During the novel's most hilarious scene, a kind of updated Mad Tea Party, this amoral socialite opens an expensive picnic hamper, only to begin chattering that "they've put in these horrid little plastic forks you'd think we were Kurds or something." She's just awful—and just perfect. I could listen to her forever.

In fact, nearly any page of ***A Frolic*** will elicit a laugh, or more often a rueful smile. A white-shoe law firm lives up to its name of Swyne & Dour. A sensitive newspaper story thoughtfully begins a sentence: "Speaking on condition that he not be identified, Village official J. Harriet Ruth . . ." A bill before Congress promises to "restore the arts to their pristine decorative function."

Certainly ***A Frolic of His Own*** deserves lots of readers here in Washington: It's all about civil suits, lawyers, greed, company loyalty, the proper and improper use of language, plagiarism, insurance scams, parental pressure, the thoughtless rich, venal evangelists, the relationship of the artist to society, the Civil War, the tensions between blacks and Jews, television, cornpone politicians, breast implants, and much, much more. Enriching the main narrative are judicial opinions, court decrees, depositions and two-thirds of a rather high-minded play called *Once in Antietam.* You get a lot for your money: But, then, that's what the law's all about, isn't it? "It's the money," as overworked lawyer Harry Lutz tells his wife Christina, "it's always the money. The rest is nothing but opera."

The novel's plot incorporates three main lawsuits, all of them touching the idealistic and innocent, pitiably ineffective, part-time American history professor Oscar Crease. In the most complicated case, Oscar is bringing suit because his car—a Japanese Sosumi—accidentally ran him over while he was hot-wiring its motor. This whole affair grows increasingly byzantine—at one point Oscar seems to be suing the owner of the vehicle, who is of course himself; ultimately he is told that "you might almost say that this is a suit between who you are and who you think you are."

The central lawsuit of ***A Frolic,*** however, revolves around Oscar's case against the blockbuster Civil War movie *The Blood in the Red, White and Blue,* which he maintains knowingly plagiarized his unproduced drama about his grandfather's life. In the course of this action he retains a black lawyer named Harold Basie (who turns out to be more than he seems), suffers cross-examination by a veddy high-tone Anglo-Indian attorney (who addresses people as "old sport"), and ultimately discovers the sorts of truths that Dickens made famous in the case of *Jarndyce* v. *Jarndyce* (in *Bleak House*). Against Oscar's two suits, Gaddis counterpoints an increasingly complex and farfetched case, presided over by Oscar's father, 97-year-old judge Thomas Crease, in which a small dog is trapped inside a modern sculpture and cannot be freed. The village of Tatamount wants to destroy the artwork to liberate Spot; the sculptor vehemently protests. The conflict leads to some splendid judicial humor and legal wordplay:

> The court finds sufficient urgency in the main action of this proceeding to reject defendants' assertions and cross motions for the reasons set forth below and grants summary judgment to plaintiff on the issue of his motion for a preliminary injunction to supersede the temporary restraining order now in place.

Who could argue with that?

In tone ***A Frolic of His Own*** ranges from Evelyn Waugh-like farce to deep outrage, from the accidental drowning of a born-again little boy undergoing baptism in the Pee Dee river at the hands of the unspeakable Reverend Ude to Oscar's frequent *cris du coeur.*

> All this crime, greed, corruption in the newspapers, you think they're just part of the times we're living in today? that our great Christian civilization is breaking down here right before

> our eyes? It's just the other way around . . . It's not the breakdown of our civilization that we're watching but its blossoming, greed and political corruption it's what America was built on in those years after the Civil War where it all got a start, so it's not whether corruption's a sign of decay but whether it's built into things right from the beginning.

Of course, high-tone Oscar himself succumbs to the lure of money; in fact, all the characters eventually fall prey to legal chicanery of one sort or another. "Justice?" as the novel says in its opening lines, "You get justice in the next world, in this world you have the law." Alas.

As in his previous novel, ***Carpenter's Gothic*** (1985), Gaddis contrives to set most of his drama in a single locale, here a run-down old family house on Long Island, where Oscar is recuperating from his injuries. In its windy rooms he shuffles about, guzzles Pinot Grigio, watches television—news programs about starving children, interrupted by inane commercials for laxatives, or specials about nature (symbolically red in tooth and claw)—and generally exasperates his sister Christina, his brother-in-law Harry, his ditzy and well-endowed girlfriend Lily, all the while fending off insurance adjusters, attorneys, scam-artists, realtors and other undesirables. The effect is a little like *Dead Souls* or the more humorous sections of *The Possessed,* where everyone seems half-crazy and no one ever plans to stop talking.

This dramatic quality is also reinforced by Gaddis's heavy reliance on dialogue (often unattributed and lightly punctuated), a technique first employed in his 1975 satiric masterpiece about America's obsession with money, ***JR,*** wherein an 11-year-old kid wheels and deals from telephone booths, and by so doing creates the world-wide JR Family of Companies. Such polyphony may seem initially confusing, but one quickly learns to recognize each character's distinctive speech patterns and verbal tics. By his "authorial absence," Gaddis once explained, "the characters create the situation," adding "it was the *flow* that I wanted, for the readers to read and be swept along, to participate. And enjoy it. And occasionally chuckle, laugh along the way."

This last remark makes clear that William Gaddis—now in his early seventies—wants to be read and enjoyed, not simply revered by a cult; he has never thought of himself as experimental, avant-garde or self-indulgently hermetic. Certainly ***A Frolic of His Own*** ought to earn him a wider audience, though impressed readers should go on, or rather back, to Gaddis's major works—***The Recognitions*** and ***JR***—which are just as enjoyable and even more ambitious in scope and accomplishment. There may be occasional longueurs to ***A Frolic***—Oscar's play, for instance—and the book's last 75 pages seem a little anticlimactic, but on the whole this remains a superb comic novel, one in which you begin by laughing at the characters and end by caring for them deeply. Through them Gaddis reminds us that perhaps only art and love can counter both the madness of the modern world ("it can't go on forever, can it?") and the sorrows delivered by what he has famously called "the unswerving punctuality of chance."

Sven Birkerts (review date 7 February 1994)

SOURCE: "Down by Law," in *The New Republic,* Vol. 210, No. 6, February 7, 1994, pp. 27-30.

[*Birkerts is an American critic and educator. In the following review, he discusses the plot and structure of* A Frolic of His Own, *noting the volume's relationship to Gaddis's previous works.*]

In recent years we hear William Gaddis spoken of in tones of breathless adoration—the outlaw late modernist, the father-figure to a generation of American novelists, the overcoat from which Pynchon, Gass and others emerged—or not at all. It is a difficult fate for the working novelist, who has not had the chance to be discussed and evaluated by readers alongside the critics. The reason is simple, and it somewhat indicts us as a culture: Gaddis is very difficult to read. In his second novel ***J. R.,*** which followed the more traditionally difficult ***The Recognitions*** (1955) by two decades, he announced a prose style that earned him much esteem and, I suspect, fewer real readers than even the pessimist might suppose.

Essentially, Gaddis mated the colloquial sprawl of the conversational novel à la Henry Green with some of the elliptical techniques of modernist cinema, including ceaseless movement of the camera (or narrative focus) and rapid-fire, breath-catching and confusing transitions that have the reader constantly scrambling for orientation. To make things harder, at least in that novel, Gaddis dispensed with all section breaks and chapters. The universe of J. R., its prodigious young protagonist, spun on and on in Mamet-meets-Milken conversational vortexes in which nothing ever stabilized. In the end the reader was left with the feeling of a high-speed skid on an icy surface and a vertigo of the moral sense.

J. R. did win the National Book Award in 1975, but the prize, while raising Gaddis's critical profile even higher, did little to promote sales or shelf recognition. Unread Gaddis remained unread. It was not until another decade passed that he made a bid for at least a small share of the market. ***Carpenter's Gothic*** was cut to normal dimensions—under 300 pages—was set in chapters and featured characters in relatively comprehensible situations. The novel was reviewed on the front page of *The New York Times Book Review.*

Readers more familiar with the reputation than the work now have reason to be grateful. For whatever reasons, Gaddis has, in ***A Frolic of His Own,*** produced his most accessible novel. Less dizzying in its transitions, more topical in presentation, easier on the eye because of its incorporation of diverse texts—legal opinions, long sections of a play—the novel may win Gaddis some of the audience that he deserves. At the same time, it must be said, when placed in the high-altitude ranks of his other work, his new book is not his very best. Top-heavy with legalistic obsession, it skimps on character and thereby undercuts its chances of making a strong moral connection to the material. Even so—and this nicely illustrates Gaddis's anomalous position—it is, in intelligence, wit and technical follow-through, leagues ahead of most so-called "serious" novels that are published these days.

A Frolic of His Own (the title is a legal locution referring to an employer's lack of culpability when an employee commits an indiscretion while not on company business) is pitched very close to the key of black humor. It tells the escalatingly preposterous story of Oscar Crease, a middle-aged history professor, and his descent into the maelstrom of litigation. We first encounter Crease in the hospital, where he is recovering from injuries incurred when his own car, which he was jump-starting, ran over him. Visiting, commiserating and setting the stage for the relentless hash and rehash of every new turn of events are Oscar's stepsister, Christina, and her lawyer husband, Harry. (They will later be joined by Oscar's loopy consort, Lily.) Though various bit players get their moments, much of the prose that follows and follows is familial conversation between these same characters, given in the customary Gaddis way, without quotation marks or helpful attribution.

Like all his books, this too is a strict school: let the attention slip for a second and you pay by having to work back to get it all straight. Here is a relatively easy bit between Oscar and Lily:

> —It's Bobbie! didn't I tell you it's always Bobbie?
>
> —God. What, look there are tissues right there by the lamp here, sit down and tell me all about it but, ow! my leg . . .
>
> —It's like a matte jersey only they have to let the skirt down with this real low-cut v-neck but I can pin it with that bunny rabbit pin you gave me that time when we went to that battlefield place where the motel had that bed with the magic fingers and you wanted me to, are you even listening to me?
>
> —Will you just tell me what happened?
>
> —Don't you remember? Where the bed kept jiggling and . . .
>
> —To Bobbie! What happened!
>
> —I told you didn't I? That he got this Porsche? I don't know what to do. Did you eat yet? All I had was some coffee. I'm starved, maybe it's something else feel right here, that lump? No inside, you can't feel through my clothes, did it get any bigger since last time? No, harder . . .

The legal action at the center of the plot, which Oscar initiates while still in the hospital, later acquiring a lawyer referred by Harry, involves the alleged theft by Constantine Kiester, a Hollywood producer, of the main idea of a play that Oscar had submitted to him years ago, when he worked as an agent by the name of Jonathan Livingston Siegal. The play itself, *Once at Antietam,* is loosely based on an experience of Crease's grandfather, who in later life became a jurist and a colleague on the bench of Oliver Wendell Holmes Jr. For complex reasons, the man had hired surrogates to fight for him in both the Union and Confederate armies, and both were, at least in the play, found dead on the battlefield, locked in one another's arms.

Kiester has used some of Crease's material in his hugely successful film, *The Blood in the Red White and Blue,* a film that owes a good part of its box-office appeal to its apparent repetition of controversial blood and guts footage from Kiester's previous vehicle, *Uruburu.* Crease's suit, which is woven through the novel, turns in part on Kiester's use of circumstances that Crease claims "belong" to him; but there is also a dispute over the playwright's own use of passages from Plato and Eugene O'Neill. Gaddis, via the nimble defense lawyer Madhar Pai (Kiester has, it turns out, retained Harry's firm, the Dickensianly named Swyne & Dour), lays open the issues involved in this increasingly volatile area of civil law. Here is Pai questioning Crease:

> Q: Again, you don't claim protection for that idea do you?
>
> A: I claim protection for the idea, too, yes, if the . . .
>
> Q: You do?
>
> A: . . . if the idea is copied in a vulgar, demeaning way.
>
> Q: The way it is expressed, is that what you mean? Can we separate the idea from its expression, sir? Do we understand each other?
>
> A: Yes, yes we understand each other. When the idea is used in the context of the expression, combined with the expression, then the idea becomes part of the abuse I'm referring to.
>
> Q: You don't claim any proprietary interest in the Civil War, do you?
>
> A: No, no no.
>
> Q: In the battle at Antietam, anymore than Shakespeare could lay a claim to the siege of Aleppo?
>
> A: No.

But Oscar's suit against Kiester is only part of the vast fabric of the novel. Linked to it in complex and resounding ways is another suit, *Szyrk* v. *the Village of Tatamount,* wherein Federal Judge Thomas Crease, Oscar's nonagenarian father, must sort out a dicey issue of liability. A dog, "Spot," has gotten trapped inside a large public sculpture, made by Szyrk. Community outrage rises against the artist's rights—and Gaddis gets to survey, and to mock, yet another arena of current controversy. Up on the fine points of jurisprudence and legal semantics, Gaddis is able to expose the vein of absurdity that runs through the American legal system, perhaps through law itself. He mocks the letter on behalf of the spirit, using what is finally only the most incremental exaggeration. Thus, we read in Judge Crease's opinion:

> We have, in other words, plaintiff claiming to act as an instrument of higher authority, namely "art," wherewith we may first cite its dictionary definition as "(1) Human effort to imitate, supplement, alter or counteract the work of nature." Notwithstanding that Cyclone Seven clearly answers this description, especially in its

> last emphasis, there remain certain fine distinctions posing some little difficulty for the average lay observer persuaded from habit and even education to regard sculptural art as beauty synonymous with truth in expressing harmony as visibly incarnate in the lineaments of Donatello's David, or as the very essence of the sublime manifest in the Milos Aphrodite, leaving him in the present instance quite unprepared to discriminate between sharp steel teeth as sharp steel teeth, and sharp steel teeth as artistic expressions of sharp steel teeth, obliging us for the purpose of this proceeding to confront the theory that in having become self-referential art is in itself theory without which it has no more substance than Sir Arthur Eddington's famous step "on a swarm of flies," here present in further exhibits by plaintiff drawn from prestigious art publications.

Quite early on in the book, still chair-ridden by his injuries, Oscar returns to his home—another of the vast and shambling pieces of New York real estate known to Gaddis readers. Ministered to by Christina and Lily, interrupted constantly by phone and mail and newspapers, Oscar settles in to wage his Quixotic battle. He schemes and rants, rising to righteousness and then lapsing into stale torpor. He is often described by the others in a near-coma, sitting in front of one of his red-in-tooth-and-claw nature programs (a not so subtle counterpart to the human activities) and swilling Pinot Grigio.

As entertainment, *A Frolic of His Own* is a tour de force. It is a profound entertainment. It is scalding and Swiftian, a darkly hilarious inquest into what we have come to now that we have turned from our trust in the sufficiency of the natural human bond, have surrendered accountability to surrogates and to systems we scarcely comprehend.

—Sven Birkerts

Once the basic premise is established, Gaddis's novel moves forward in the swirl of its interminable discussions, with interruptions simply initiating new discussion, the momentum only breaking when the author incorporates another chunk of Oscar's play or some portion of courtroom transcript or other legal business. The result is curiously surreal. Gaddis's absolute fidelity in rendering each conversational fidget, coupled with his refusal of any traditional subjective access, creates what feels like a self-contained universe of talk. Foregrounded thus, the speech displaces focus from the private to the public sphere. The reader feels trapped, every bit as much as if this were a stream of consciousness monologue. We realize how much we depend on our novelists to balance off inner and outer claims.

Frolic is claustrophobia-inducing. Not only is there no reprieve from talk, not only does the whole work unfold in the same few rooms, but the nature of the narrative itself is deeply, if not profoundly, cyclic. Same rooms, same people, different day, different day, different day, until the subliminal effect is realized and we grasp that however much things may change on the surface, the underlying law of human affairs is a recursive sameness, with day following day, season season and adaptative habit overriding all turmoils of loss and grief. A dark picture, but not the darkest possible; in Gaddis's world the wearying tow of sameness is mitigated, at least slightly, by the grumbling humor of his characters.

Unpacking the novel, we find it is wrapped in many skeins—countless encoded cross-references, myriad ironies and shimmers of sly wit. It pumps itself up with legal paradoxes and oddball twists and turns (Oscar urged to sue himself for his auto injury; Lily seeking damages for faulty breast implants; Harry arguing a case in which the anagrammatical connection between "Pepsi-Cola" and "Episcopal" is relevant; the preacher from ***Carpenter's Gothic*** being sued for drowning a child during a baptism . . .) and effectively turns America's legal fever into a trope for its overall spiritual and moral condition. There is outrage at the novel's heart, and Oscar is its principal conduit:

> I see all around us the criminal mind at large appropriating, literally stealing the fruits of the creative mind and the dedicated labors of others without even blinking, isn't that what's at the heart of this cancerous No Fault epidemic? This license for delinquency? Society created the criminal, society's responsible and so no one's responsible, isn't that the size of it, demolishing the pillar civilization rests upon, each individual's responsibility for the consequences of his own actions?

Gaddis is so effective at spinning his web of interlocking legalities that we begin to believe that there is no free place left, no crevice where one might stand and be unimplicated, unliable. The society has, to all appearances, grown together with the legal system. And as we see the system for what it is—a monster produced by the sleep of reason, or the wakefulness of it—we must deduce that madness has at last enveloped all.

Still, for all the power of this vision—its exacting specificity, its implied totality, its savage humor—the novel does not work on us as powerfully as it ought to. There are several reasons for this. The most injurious flaw of Gaddis's book is the relative inertness of its central characters. Oscar, Christina and Lily are all thin to the point of being types. They serve as voice-boxes, appliances for the generation of spoken material. Which, as it accumulates, tends less to reveal their depths than to overpower them. What they talk about discloses Gaddis's obsession with law, not their own characters.

This is aggravated, naturally, by the author's refusal to show the inward dimension. The reader must feel disappointment, for in previous works, such as ***J. R.*** and ***Carpenter's Gothic,*** where Gaddis also deployed speech almost exclusively, the verbal interplay does gradually create some understanding of the characters' pasts and of their motivations. Perhaps this is because in these novels the thematic focus is nowhere near so monomaniacal; the inclusion of extraneous narration allows us to assemble more convincingly complex identities for the players. Here, alas, we remain unpersuaded and, on a certain vital level, unengaged. Querulous Oscar rattles on, never more or less than himself, but never much more than the content of his grumpy rattling. Gaddis has made some effort, it is true, to draw in a theme relating to fathers; Oscar's play can be seen as an attempt to uncover a generational connection, but it lies flat on the storyboard. Free speech aplenty here, but we see it as an artistic strategy that has its limits.

Oscar's play poses more, and related, problems. Gaddis has let it be known that between the publication of ***The Recognitions*** and of ***J. R.*** he wrote a play about the Civil War and that parts of that play are now embedded in ***Frolic***. It is hard to say if the play constituted an advance intuition of this novel; perhaps Gaddis has simply sought to recycle previously written goods. But the question is finally moot. The portions of *Once at Antietam* included are strikingly without dramatic interest. If Oscar, Christina and Lily suffer from two-dimensionality, then the dramatis personae (identified as THOMAS, HIS MOTHER, THE MAJOR, etc.) perish of it. They speak with a kind of wooden hysteria (THOMAS: "A ram! But . . . by heaven! I'm being pressed for those profits now, the shareholders here . . . a ram! What the devil are they building a ram for!"). Their only possible reason for being is to give flesh to certain conceits that Gaddis means to echo and to play against his main narrative. Of these the most interesting are those surrogate soldiers who are found locked in a death embrace. Gaddis would seem to be giving us a figure for lawyers themselves, those proxy agents whom we hire to wage our own civil wars. The implications of self-murder (both soldiers *represent* Thomas) are given further, and absurd, resonance in the notion that Oscar might end up paying good money to sue himself for automotive self-injury.

Given Gaddis's extraordinary ear for dialogue, it is surprising that his dramaturgy is so weak. But maybe not. His brilliance is mimetic: he hears the dynamics of interchange at a threshold level. Drama, by contrast, requires an aptitude for symbolic condensation. Gaddis either cannot present his material this way, or he chooses not to—or maybe he wants us to judge Oscar as a second-rate talent. Looking at the whole trajectory of Gaddis's work, and recalling his own stated preoccupation with entropy as a universal and social condition (all his novels convey a sense of systems approaching the point of dissolution), I would guess that he finds drama aesthetically inadmissible, a kind of literary bad faith.

But this still does not explain the inclusion of long scenes from *Once at Antietam,* since they do almost nothing to further the needs of the work. If Oscar were developed as a character, if we could sound his subjective depths, then we might be able to read *through* the scenes, to calculate insights about the Creases from Oscar's treatment of family history. As things stand, however, we don't much care.

Finally, the whole edifice of American civil law, trenchantly as it is interrogated and mocked, is not fully exploited as a subject. We are constantly confirmed in our natural suspicions about the venality and the duplicity of it all; but we are never startled into reconsideration. Moreover, Gaddis has gotten himself stranded in paradox and irony. He is eager to point to the *danse macabre* of litigation, but has not, as it were, connected the superstructure to the base. The base, again, has to be the human, the personal. We see the dazzling, infuriating, insane-making whirl of litigation, but we grasp neither how it arises from, nor how it impinges upon, the individual. We have the pathology without the path.

Here the defense may object: since ***The Recognitions,*** Gaddis's whole fictional enterprise has been, after all, an exploration not only of the premise that God is dead, but also of the premise that the individual—the accountable individual of the social contract—is dead, too; and that only our fatally abstracted systems (financial in ***J. R.,*** legal in ***Frolic***) survive to orchestrate social behavior. In which case the critic must be wrong to call for more deeply coherent characters. To this I can only respond that in art, if nowhere else, the means and the ends must sometimes be separated. A novelist, no matter what his vision, has to know that the form is predicated, always has been, on the assumption of dynamic character; and that if one ceases to believe in character one had better be ready to do the honorable thing and find another expressive mode.

Still, as entertainment, ***A Frolic of His Own*** is a tour de force. It is a profound entertainment. It is scalding and Swiftian, a darkly hilarious inquest into what we have come to now that we have turned from our trust in the sufficiency of the natural human bond, have surrendered accountability to surrogates and to systems we scarcely comprehend. This is the wisdom of the novel, and of the devastating synopsis of its opening line: "Justice? —You get justice in the next world, in this world you have the law." Though of course we freed ourselves from the illusion of a next world long ago.

Jonathan Raban (review date 17 February 1994)

SOURCE: "At Home in Babel," in *The New York Review of Books,* Vol. XLI, No. 4, February 17, 1994, pp. 3-4, 6.

[*Raban is an English critic, educator, and editor. In the following review, he lauds Gaddis's characterizations, his focus on late twentieth-century life, and his use of dialogue, language, and farce in* A Frolic of His Own.]

Every William Gaddis novel tells its story in such a cryptic and allusive way that it can become a cerebral torture, like a crossword puzzle whose setter is named after a famous inquisitor—Torquemada, Ximenes. Reviewing ***JR*** in the *New Yorker* in 1975, George Steiner called it an "unreadable book"—a remark that got him into hot water with the professional Gaddisites, a solemn crew themselves given to sentences like "Read from this perspective, ***The Recognition*** demonstrates the essential alterity of the world, the meta-ethical virtue of agapistic ethics" [Gregory Comnes, in his 1994 *The Ethics of Indeterminacy in the Novels of William Gaddis*]. Certainly Gaddis tries one's readerly patience to breaking point, strewing the foreground of his fiction with obstacles designed to trip one up, slow one down, and generally bring one face to face with the (as it were) essential alterity of the novel as a willful tissue of words. Scaling ***The Recognitions*** and ***JR,*** one keeps coming on the remains of earlier readers who lost their footing and perished in the ascent.

Yet on most of the important counts, Gaddis is an engagingly oldfashioned writer. The Victorian spaciousness of his books is in keeping with their big Victorian subjects—forgery and authenticity, wills and legacies, the circulation of money, the workings of the law. His best characters, though never directly described, have a powerful fleshly presence on the page. The loutish pathos of J R, the boy capitalist, Liz and Paul Booth's burned-out marriage in ***Carpenter's Gothic,*** are examples of solidly credible realistic portraiture of the kind one feels that Trollope would have recognized and admired. More than any other writer I can think of, Gaddis really listens to the way we speak now. The talk in his novels is brilliantly rendered, with a wicked fidelity to its flimsy grammar, its elisions and hiatuses, its rush-and-stumble rhythms. When Gaddis's characters open their mouths, they're apt to give voice to sentences like car pileups in fog, with each new thought smashing into the rear of the one ahead and colliding with the oncoming traffic of another speaker's words.

If readers of Gaddis are often hard put to it to follow the novelist's drift, their difficulties are precisely mirrored by those of the characters inside the novel, as when Liz Booth sacks her Martinican cleaning woman in fractured Franglais:

> —Le mardi prochain Madame?
>
> —Next Tuesday yes will, well no. No I mean that's what I wanted to speak to you about, I mean qu'il ne serait pas nécessaire que, that it's maybe it's better to just wait and I call you again when I, que je vous téléphoner . . .
>
> —Vous ne voulez pas que je revienne.
>
> Yes well I mean but not next Tuesday, I mean I'll telephone you again I hope you understand Madame Socrate it's just that I, que votre travail est très bon everything looks lovely but . . .
>
> —J'comprends Madame . . . the door came open, —et la clef.
>
> —Oh the key yes, yes thank you merci I hope you, oh but wait, wait could you, est-ce que vous pouvez trouver le, les cartes. . . with a stabbing gesture at the mailbox, —là, dans le, des cartes . . . ?

Madame Socrate is not so named for nothing. Like a good reader, she understands that the static interference in which the message appears to be shrouded is in fact the message itself. As for the mysterious appearance of Descartes in the morning's mail, it is one of those suggestive coincidences with which Gaddis likes to tease, and sometimes torment, his readers.

He can be very funny, in a way that pointedly recalls the exasperated laughter of Evelyn Waugh, for whom Gaddis has often expressed his admiration in articles and interviews. Waugh's favorite cloak—that of the last surviving patrician in a fallen world of thugs and philistines—has been taken over by Gaddis and trimmed to a (slightly) more democratic American pattern. Like Waugh, Gaddis is funniest when he's gunning for the barbarians at the gate—for the culture of the game show, the shopping mall, the tabloid newspaper, the matchbook cover. Waugh saw the fall of Christendom in the rise of the commercial lower orders. Gaddis sees entropy: the world is not so much going to hell as suffering from the inevitable degradation of energy in a closed system, its language wearing out from overuse. So where Waugh invoked Ecclesiastes and the Book of Lamentations, Gaddis calls in Willard Gibbs and Norbert Wiener (which might in itself be seen as a kind of entropic diminishment). His eccentric personal version of thermodynamics chimes very closely with Waugh's eccentric personal theology, suggesting, perhaps, that gods, physicists, and novelists may share a common black humor as they contemplate the experiments in chaos over which they separately preside.

A Frolic of His Own, Gaddis's fourth novel in nearly forty years, is a country-house comedy, faster in pace and lighter in texture than anything he's done before. It reassembles themes, images, and a large number of characters from the earlier books. There's fresh news of Dr. Kissinger, the globe-trotting proctologist and cosmetic surgeon, of the Rev. Elton Ude, his son Bobby Joe, and of Wayne Fickert, the boy who was drowned by the Rev. Ude at a baptism in the Pee Dee River. The huge postmodernist sculpture, *Cyclone Seven,* last seen in ***JR,*** in the Long Island town where a child was trapped inside it, has here been moved to Tatamount, Virginia. Its steel jaws now imprison a dog named Spot. Oscar Crease, the gentleman-amateur playwright at the center of the story, is a reworked version of the character of Edward Bast in ***JR;*** his half-sister Christina and her friend Trish were schoolmates of Liz Booth and her friend Edie Grimes, the "Heiress Slain In Swank Suburb" of ***Carpenter's Gothic.*** Oscar Crease's play, *Once at Antietam,* had its first performance, in brief quotation, in ***JR,*** where it was the work of Thomas Eigen (and was dismissed by Jack Gibbs as "undigested Plato").

The Long Island house in which nearly all the action of the book takes place is (like the Bast family mansion in ***JR***) an incongruous genteel survivor from another age. Its roof leaks, its verandah sags, and—as a visiting realtor observes—it is in desperate need of the attentions of "old Mister Paintbrush to brighten things up." Its chief asset—worth several millions in "wetlands setbacks"—is a fine view from the drawing room of American literature's most famous pond, which has been trucked in from Massachusetts for the occasion of the book. Like Walden itself, the Crease place is ringed by suburbia: the chainsaws, whose "unanesthetized aerial surgery" began in ***JR,*** are within earshot of the house, and the driveway now leads straight to the debased language of Chic's Auto Body, Fred's Foto, and the R Dan Snively Memorial Parking Lot.

The hideous red-taloned woman who sells real estate (she envisions the house torn down and replaced by a new one, to be built by "this famous postmodern architect who's doing the place on the corner right down to the carpets and picture frames it will be quite a showplace") bears a strong resemblance to Mrs. Beaver and her plans for Hatton in *A Handful of Dust* (". . . supposing we covered the walls with white chromium plating and had natural sheepskin carpet . . . "). There may be another nod in Evelyn Waugh's direction in Gaddis's choice of the name of Crease. The only Crease I know of in the public domain is the Francis Crease who earned half a chapter to himself in Waugh's autobiography, *A Little Learning*—a neurotic calligrapher and dilettante of independent means who might be Oscar's twin.

Oscar Crease is the childish last scion of a distinguished legal family. His grandfather sat on the Supreme Court with Justice Holmes; his ninety-seven-year-old father is a judge in Virginia; in his fifty-odd years, Oscar has managed to write one unproduced play, based on what he believes to have been his grandfather's experience in the Civil-War. In a late and ill-advised bid for recognition, he sues the Hollywood producer of a Civil War epic called *The Blood in the Red White and Blue* for plagiarizing *Once at Antietam* and robbing him of his family history.

Broadly—very broadly—speaking, almost everyone in the novel is suing almost everyone else in sight for damages. Some are suing themselves—Oscar is both plaintiff and defendant in a personal injury suit involving his car, which ran over him when the ignition failed and he hot-wired it. People travel through these pages with their attorneys in tow much as people once used to travel with their maids. In the foreground are Oscar's chickenfeed pieces of litigation; in the background are the great cases of the day, like the $700 million suit, known in the tabloids as "Pop and Glow," brought by the Episcopal Church against Pepsi-Cola on the grounds that the church's good name has been stolen by means of an underhand anagram. For every suit there is a countersuit, for every judgment an appeal. Gaddis peoples the book with a throng of injured egos whose only means of asserting that they exist is to go to court. As Christina reasonably observes in the first page, "It's not simply the money . . . the money's just a yardstick isn't it. It's the only common reference people have for making other people take them as seriously as they take themselves."

Gaddis likes to set himself technical exercises. In ***JR*** he had to tell the story in dialogue; in ***Carpenter's Gothic*** he obeyed the classical unities of time, place, and action. ***A Frolic of His Own*** is in part an immensely skillful exercise in the mechanics of farce. It is a wonder that the ailing verandah of the house doesn't collapse under the weight of the stream of surprise exits and entrances of lawyers and litigants that it has to bear. Like all good farces, after the sound of laughter has subsided it turns out to have been in deadly earnest.

Gaddis is a mimic of genius and he runs the gamut of stylistic imitation from undetectable forgery to ribald satire. Oscar's play, for instance, of which the reader gets to see about seventy pages, is, unlike the usual text-within-a-text, a real play whose very unevenness convinces one of its authenticity. Brilliant passages, mostly in soliloquy, lead into long stilted debates, which themselves suddenly catch fire and come alive for a few minutes, then go dead again. Unlike the author of the novel, the playwright doesn't know how to move his characters on and off stage nearly fast enough. Yet the central confrontation, between Thomas, the southern heir to northern property, and Bagby, his agent, a commercial "new man" and an early example of the Barbarian genus, is engrossing enough to transcend the play's wonky stagecraft. *Once at Antietam*'s debts to Plato, first exposed in ***JR,*** are teased out here in detail by a smart Indian attorney, Madhar Pai, in a legal deposition taken during Crease's case against the Hollywood producer; but the play's more immediate debts are to the thoughtful, talkative middlebrow theater of the 1950s, to plays like Anouilh's *Antigone* and Bolt's *A Man for All Seasons* in which large moral questions were acted out by people in period costume, and it has a lot of their dusty charm.

The same goes for the legal documents that are interleaved throughout the book. The cases on which they touch may be farcical, but the attention paid to them by Gaddis's crew of lawyers and judges is of a quality for which one might reasonably pay Mr. Madhar Pai his fantastic hourly rate. This is not *Bleak House.* In ***A Frolic of His Own*** the language of the law is treated with affection and respect, and the lawyers themselves are honored as the last surviving instruments (even though some of them are very imperfect ones) of order in this disorderly world. The cleverest, most likable character in the novel is old Judge Crease, who appears in written opinions that combine a waspish common-sensicality with bouts of unexpected mental acrobatics. From Crease on *Szyrk* [the creator of the huge piece of sculpture *Cyclone Seven*] v. *Village of Tatamount et al.:*

> We have in other words plaintiff claiming to act as an instrument of higher authority, namely "art," wherewith we may first cite its dictionary definition as "(1) Human effort to imitate, supplement, alter or counteract the work of nature." Notwithstanding that Cyclone Seven clearly answers this description especially in its last emphasis, there remain certain fine distinctions posing some little difficulty for the average lay observer persuaded from habit and even education to regard sculptural art as beauty synonymous with truth in expressing harmony as visibly incarnate in the lineaments of Donatello's David, or as the very essence of the sublime manifest in the Milos Aphrodite, leaving him in the present instance quite unprepared to discriminate between sharp steel teeth as sharp steel teeth, and sharp steel teeth as artistic expressions of sharp steel teeth, obliging us for the purpose of this proceeding to confront the theory that in having become self referential art is in itself theory without which it has no more substance than Sir Arthur Eddington's famous step "on a swarm of flies," here present in further ex-

> hibits by plaintiff drawn from prestigious art publications and highly esteemed critics in the lay press, where they make their livings, recommending his sculptural creation in terms of slope, tangent, acceleration, force, energy and similar abstract extravagancies serving only a corresponding self referential confrontation of language with language and thereby, in reducing language itself to theory, rendering it a mere plaything, which exhibits the court finds frivolous.

This might be William Empson in a wig and gown. It is a fierce and well-grounded attack on trivial postmodernist pursuits and, in itself, a vindication of Gaddis's own way of writing novels.

True, all his books entail a "confrontation of language with language," but the confrontation is not "self-referential" and never reduces language to theory. In Gaddis's work, language is where we live and what we are. It's all we have. So the play *Once at Antietam* has its own power: it may not be a very good play, but it is, we are made to feel, the best play, the best reckoning with the paradox of his own history, that its author (call him Gaddis, or Eigen, or Oscar Crease) could make under the circumstances. So, too, Judge Crease's own legal opinion, laboring as it does to say something eloquent and true within the constricting conventional frame of the legal opinion, is the best that can be done under the circumstances, which in Gaddis are always adverse. ***A Frolic of His Own*** is not another novel about narratology: its sharp teeth are genuine sharp steel teeth.

In the most realistic way possible, Gaddis's characters have to struggle to stay afloat on the flux of late-century daily life. The Crease house is under permanent siege—its verandah stormed by callers, its phone ringing off the hook, newspapers piling up in the kitchen far faster than they can be read, and the television in the drawing room pouring out a continuous unlovely medley of bomb-blast pictures interspersed with *Jeopardy*-style questions ("Name three African countries beginning with C. . . . What breed of African antelope is named after an American car?") and commercials for laxatives and hemorrhoid creams. Oscar is addicted to nature programs, filmed to prove that animal life is as red in tooth and claw as the human variety. On the screen are exhibited pictures of such familiar domestic situations as: "two acorn woodpeckers sharing a nest where one laid an egg and the other ate it"; "the Australian red-back spider jumping into the female's jaws in the midst of mating which he continued undismayed as she chewed at his abdomen"; a "battle among the notorious burying beetles over the corpse of a mouse nicely scraped and embalmed by the victorious couple for their young to eat and then eating the young when they hatched to ensure the survivors of enough food for a stalwart new generation to start the whole thing over again." The TV set is kept switched on throughout the book: it is both a loud source of colored chaos and a faithful mirror of the Crease family in action. In the refrigerator, another chaos, a cole-slaw carton holds the "jelly implants" removed from the breasts of Oscar's infantile and dippy girlfriend, Lily.

In *A Frolic of His Own* Gaddis builds around the reader a magnificently ornate and intricate house of words. Every room is furnished in a different style, and one quickly loses count of the competing dialects and idiolects, archaic and modern, literary, legal, vernacular, that are represented here.

—Jonathan Raban

Gaddis is at his most Waugh-like in the formal grace with which he manages the wild disorder of the plot. The faster the whirlygig spins, the more one admires its ingenious workmanship. As in Waugh, the proprietor of the machine appears to be standing at some distance from it, his face perfectly impassive, while the riders scream.

Chaos is a state where the whole system of cause-and-effect appears to have given way, where everything happens by accident. In Gaddis's highly controlled version of chaos, the chance properties of the language itself, the puns, anagrams, and coincidental allusions, serve as vital connectors. So we get EPISCOPAL/PEPSICOLA—or the two brands of Japanese car that figure in this legal fiction, the Isuyu and the Sosumi—or the name, Jonathan Livingston Siegal, of the producer of *The Blood in the Red White and Blue*—or the way in which a negotiation over the forthcoming lunch break is recorded in a legal deposition as "Break, break, break on thy cold grey stones, O. . ." In a TV commercial for a diarrhea cure, a man is seen running for an airport bathroom; several hundred pages later in the novel, at an airport, an identical running figure is wrongfully accused of stealing a pocketbook belonging to Christina's friend Trish. In another chance collision, the infectious meter of Longfellow's *Hiawatha,* Oscar's favorite childhood poem, insidiously works its way into the later, hurrying scenes of the book, giving Longfellow the opportunity to write a description of Oscar's fishtank (where rapacious nature is again contained by glass):

> neither rose Ugudwash, the sunfish, nor the yellow perch the Sahwa like a sunbeam in the water banished here, with wind and wave, day and night and time itself from the domain of the discus by the daily halide lamp, silent pump and power filter, temperature and pH balance and the system of aeration, fed on silverside and flake food, vitamins and krill and beef heart in a patent spinach mixture to restore their pep and lustre spitting black worms from the feeder when a crew of new arrivals (live delivery guaranteed, air freight collect at thirty dollars) brought a Chinese algae eater, khuli loach and male beta, two black mollies and four neons and a pair of black skirt tetra cruising through the new laid fronds of the Madagascar lace plant.

The book is full of riffs and games like this, each one designed to forge some sort of punning link between one part of the battle and another. Taken together, they have the effect of falling into a pattern that grows more and more intricate the longer you look at it, like the sequence of enlargements in a Mandelbrot set.

Readers—and reviewers especially—ought to feel a disquieting pang of recognition as the climax of the book approaches and Oscar, armed with ice cream and Pinot Grigio, settles in front of the TV set to view the screening of *The Blood in the Red White and Blue,* the catchpenny epic, whose plot somewhat resembles that of his own play. The titles have barely started to roll before Oscar is off, reading into the images on the screen meanings that cannot possibly be there. By the time the Battle of Antietam starts, he has fallen into the language of a demented football commentator:

> —there! a man's shoulder blown off—look out! too late, the boy in butternut hit full in the open mouth, mere boys, mere boys in homespun and blue in a screaming frenzy of bayonets and shellfire—unbelievable, it's unbelievable look at that! Half the regiment wiped out at thirty feet we're taking the cornfield there's Meade, there's Meade in the midst of it there's Meade look at the flags, battle flags the Sixth Wisconsin, Pennsylvania regiments and three hundred of the Twelfth Massachusetts with two hundred casualties now! We're almost there, the Dunker church Georgia boys trying to get over the fence pffft! shot like laundry hung on a line listen! The Rebel yell listen to it, Hood's division counterattack makes your blood run cold they're coming through! Driving us back they're driving us back, A P Hill coming in from the East Wood I mean D H, D H Hill's division right into the, ooph! Battery B, six old brass cannon it's Battery B charging straight into it look at that! Double rounds of canister hitting them at fifty feet the whole Rebel column's blown to pieces blood everyplace, blood everyplace that's Mansfield, wild white beard's got to be General Mansfield Hooker sending him in with his XII Corps riding down the line waving his hat hear them cheering he's, yes he's hit, horse is down and Mansfield's hit in the stomach God, get him off the field!

No critic with a bee in his bonnet could be more capriciously inventive than Oscar as he deconstructs the blockbuster on the TV screen and reassembles it into a Super Bowl version of the Civil War. What Oscar sees here is neither the movie nor Antietam itself, but his and Gaddis's chief source of information on the battle, Bruce Catton's 1951 book, *Mr. Lincoln's Army.* Oscar's passionate explication of *The Blood in the Red White and Blue* turns out to be Gaddis's devastating parody of Catton's blow-by-blow, newspaperman's prose. (It's strange to turn to Catton's book after reading Gaddis: *Mr. Lincoln's Army* reads exactly like an overexcited football commentary . . .)

So it is with the silent pond beyond the window, whose prospect haunts the book. Again and again Christina (who is most nearly the reader's representative in the story) turns to it: while people fight in the drawing room, and animals dine off one another's carcasses on TV, and fish chase fish around the fishtank, life on the pond is orderly and serene. Things there happen in their seasons. The passage of time in the book, as autumn deepens into winter, is marked by the noiseless flight of wild duck, geese, and swans over the water. Each time the pond is sighted, it provokes a burst of beautiful, descriptive prose:

> And where they looked next morning the frozen pond was gone in an unblemished expanse of white under a leaden sky undisturbed by the flight of a single bird in the gelid stillness that had descended to seize every detail of reed and branch as though time itself were frozen out there threatening the clatter of teacups and silver and the siege of telephoning that had already begun with—well when, just tell me when I can talk to him, will you . . .

—beautiful, but anachronistic. To write like a contemporary of Thoreau (even a commaless contemporary of Thoreau) is something that can be managed only for a few clauses at a time, before the words are drowned out by the noisy desperation of the present moment. We're separated from the tranquility of the pond by a panel of glass and roughly 150 years.

Gaddis builds around the reader a magnificently ornate and intricate house of words. Every room is furnished in a different style, and one quickly loses count of the competing dialects and idiolects, archaic and modern, literary, legal, vernacular, that are represented here. Christina snaps at her husband: "I mean you talk about language how everything's language it seems that all language does is drive us apart" (which, of course, does exactly what it says). That Gaddis's tall building is Babel, where the Lord did confound the language of all the earth, hardly needs to be spelled out. What makes the novel so enjoyable is how very homely and familiar Babel is made to feel. There's a bed for us all in this oppressively realistic, beautifully designed Long Island madhouse.

Gary Amdahl (review date Spring 1994)

SOURCE: "Courting Lawyers and Whores," in *The Hungry Mind Review,* No. 29, Spring, 1994, pp. 34, 42-3.

[*In the excerpt below, Amdahl offers praise for* A Frolic of His Own.]

Adventure! How may one avail oneself of it in a culture gone mad with comfort and dreams of safety? I think there are two broad avenues radiating from the modern American self toward the perpetually fluorescent horizon of modern American adventure: one is *law* and the other is *medicine.* White-water rafting, mountaineering, alligator wrestling—certainly these activities are exciting and put one at risk, but they seem hobbylike compared to the harrowing, soul-chilling thrills of engaging in multiple lawsuits, or of contracting a fatal, high-profile disease and being at the mercy of the dark gods of insurance and technology. American adventures are adventures of money.

Two extraordinary novels, ***A Frolic of His Own,*** by William Gaddis, and *Butterfly Stories,* by William Vollmann, are dramatic cases in point, and constitute, in themselves, genuine (if literary) adventure. Resembling each other in almost no way (subject matter, structure, style, voice), the two novels share a great deal fundamentally. They are both *sui generis,* unmistakably and uncompromisingly original. They are technically innovative. They are dark, rich, solid, and occasionally sordid (especially the casually provocative *Butterfly,* but ***Frolic*** too, in a kind of helter-skelter subtext), comedies that make tragedies, even the best ones, seem lugubrious, lurid, and lead-footed, altogether the more pretentious and ineffective vehicles for transformation of human woe and catastrophe. And, most importantly, they are both, to quote one of Gaddis's characters, "trying to rescue the language."

A Frolic of His Own (the title is taken from English common law and refers to a deed committed by a servant that is not within the scope of his employment, that is not in the service of or at the behest of his master; e. g., an office worker shooting paper clips and putting out an eye, or, more broadly, *writing a novel*) is the story of one man and a handful of connected lawsuits. They range from personal injury and accidental death to divorce, plagiarism, and infringement. The lawsuits are initiated by a variety of plaintiffs: a small boy whose dog has been trapped in a horrific, menacing modern outdoor "public art" sculpture; the artist who created the sculpture and gets an injunction against its dismantling/destruction to save the dog; and the city, which wishes it to be removed permanently (these parties will reverse their positions 180 degrees before the novel is over). In another case, the Episcopal Church sues Pepsico, Inc., whom they claim is infringing on their trademark name with an anagram of it: Pepsi-Cola. The cases are conducted by a swarm of lawyers, from those who advertise on matchbook covers, to those on the run from the law themselves, to lawyers who are not really lawyers at all, to partners in prestigious "white shoe" firms and judges on the U.S. District Court.

The primary suits revolve around Oscar Crease, a playwriting professor of history at a community college on Long Island, whose father is a federal judge and whose grandfather sat on the Supreme Court. The first suit goes like this: Trying to hot-wire his car (a "Sosume"), Crease runs himself over. He then decides, since he is both the accident victim and the owner of the car, that the best course of action is to sue himself.

At first glance merely a bit of parody and slapstick, the ironic whine of the episode is amplified by the turn of nearly every page so that by the end of the novel it has become a howl of madness and despair. Crease wants "justice"; he wants his hospital bills paid, he wants a new car, he wants compensation for his injury and incapacity, he *wants wants wants* and believes that justice is *getting getting getting.* The irony, of course, depends on Crease's unwillingness to acknowledge his culpability. But this is precisely the acknowledgment that cannot be made in America. This is a no-fault world, a world of remote anonymous third-party reimbursement (someone else is paying, slice off a hunk, pad it, jack it up, put it on the tab), a world of money growing on trees and magician gardeners in those trees wearing suits and ties, hooting and rustling the leafy bills and keeping the branches just out of reach of frothing, leaping, wild-eyed victim/perpetrators. This is ***Frolic's*** central image and base melody (as I see and hear them).

The second suit has to do with Crease's play *Once at Antietam,* in which he tells the story of his famous grandfather, a Southerner who inherits a lucrative mine in the North and who ends up paying men to be his substitute in both the Union and Confederate armies (a common practice). The play, submitted years before to a TV producer in New York, turns up as a monster-budget Hollywood extravaganza, featuring state of the art sex acts and special-effects gore: *The Blood in the Red White and Blue.* Similar in many ways to his play, Crease charges its makers with a variety of crimes. *Once at Antietam* is a work of *art,* he insists over and over again; he wrote it because he is *a civilized man* who values philosophy and poetry, and all he wants is *justice,* as symbolized by *lots of money.*

A goodly portion of the play is reproduced in the novel (it may seem a little stately to readers used to Rabe, Shepard, Mamet, and Guare, but its counterpoint is both pleasing and necessary), and suffers close reading in one of the book's many *tour de force* legal parodies, a deposition of some fifty pages that raises a number of interesting questions about art, commerce, and ownership of intellectual property. Claiming that his work has been stolen and travestied, Crease, we soon realize, has himself borrowed from O'Neill's *Mourning Becomes Electra,* who in turn borrowed from Euripides, and owes a good deal to Plato, too, a lot of whose *Republic* pours (unattributed) from one of his character's mouths.

The complexity, depth, and range of ***Frolic*** are, I hope, clear enough. One of the marks of the great novel is its resistance to summary description, and ***Frolic*** (like all Gaddis's masterpieces) is overpowering in this regard. With its incredibly intricate weave of dramatic text, legal documents, and virtuoso dialogue, all connected with feverishly beautiful passages—or sinews of description—reading ***Frolic*** is something like listening to a life insurance salesman and biblical prophet—one who knows world literature forward and backward—interpret your wildest dreams.

Steven Moore (review date 25 April 1994)

SOURCE: "Reading the Riot Act," in *The Nation,* New York, Vol. 258, No. 16, April 25, 1994, pp. 569-71.

[*An American critic and educator, Moore is author and editor of several works on Gaddis. In the following highly laudatory review, he discusses the experience of reading* A Frolic of His Own *and questions the validity of critical assessments that denigrate the novel for its ostensible "difficulties."*]

The phrase "literary event" has been dulled by years of misuse by glib publicists; but no other phrase describes the appearance of a new novel by William Gaddis, one of this country's true literary giants. The review media's response to this literary event [the publication of ***A Frolic of His Own***] has been disheartening, however, as if nothing has changed in the forty years since Gaddis's first novel, ***The***

Recognitions, was panned. Then as now, the main charge is "difficulty," yet only in literature does this seem to be a sin. One rarely sees a music critic complain that Philip Glass expects too much of his listeners, or reads that Merce Cunningham expects too much from his audience. In diving competitions and magic acts the degree of difficulty is admired. But let a writer execute a difficult task with breath-taking technique, and mostly what's heard is heckling—whining and moaning about how much effort is involved in watching the artist work. What should be a privilege is treated like an affront.

In her review for the daily *New York Times,* the usually hardy Michiko Kakutani said the novel made for "laborious reading" and that "Mr. Gaddis's provocative vision of modern society is purchased at a price, the price of hard work and frequent weariness on the part of the reader." In the Sunday *New York Times Book Review,* Robert Towers also felt compelled to warn the unsuspecting reader that "One must not underestimate the obstacles that lie in the way of the appreciation, to say nothing of the enjoyment, of this remarkable novel," going on to call some of the obstacles "gratuitous, even perverse," (It's always the author's fault.) Sven Birkerts used the d-word as well in his *New Republic* review, though he was sharp enough to note that the neglect of Gaddis because of his alleged difficulty "somewhat indicts us as a culture." But he makes Gaddis sound like the strictest kind of taskmaster: "let the attention slip for a second and you pay by having to work back to get it all straight." Frank McConnell in the *Boston Globe* warned of "the holy arrogance of the demands it makes on the reader. The book dares you to struggle with it, and on every page taunts you that you may, after all, not be up to the fight." Toward the end of his review McConnell says, "This is a *very* hard book to read, but it works," though by that point most readers have probably been scared off. Running against the grain was a rather snotty squib in *Newsweek* by Malcolm Jones Jr., who took the opposite tack and complained that the book was too easy, too lazy, and chided Gaddis for not giving "his readers more for their trouble."

Is ***A Frolic of His Own*** that difficult, that exhausting? I devoured it in a weekend in a state of exhilaration and delight. Yes, you do have to keep your wits about you when reading Gaddis, but it's a rare privilege these days to be taken this seriously as a reader. Like Henry James, William Gaddis wants the kind of reader on whom nothing is lost. He doesn't talk down or assume you can't make connections. He expects that you've read a few books in your time, read the papers. This is literature, not a TV sitcom.

The point is not whether Gaddis is difficult or not but whether difficulty is such a bad thing in literature. Those who prefer easy listening may want easy reading, but others should find a novel bracing, challenging. In Gaddis's second novel, ***J R,*** Jack Gibbs is asked if his work in progress on technology and the arts is difficult, and he answers, "Difficult as I can make it." The difficulties Gibbs undergoes to get this book written, the breadth of his research and length of time he devotes to the task (after seventeen years he still isn't finished), show what sort of pact should exist between serious writers and serious readers.

Gaddis knows he's difficult (Gibbs is one of his personas in ***J R***), and consequently lightens the task somewhat by making his books very funny, filling them with all forms of humor, from limericks and low puns to learned wit and Olympian ironies. The absence of a comic element can make some difficult literary works a real grind—Pound's *Cantos,* say, or Broch's *Death of Virgil*—despite their other virtues. On the other hand, the comic element is what makes extremely difficult novels like Joyce's *Finnegans Wake* and Julián Rìos's *Larva* such a pleasure to wrestle with. And yet few reviewers convey the idea that Gaddis is essentially a comic novelist and that his books can be great fun—rather than an exercise in masochism—to read.

***A Frolic of His Own* is both cutting-edge, state-of-the-art fiction and a throwback to the great moral novels of Tolstoy and Dickens.**

—Steven Moore

The charges of difficulty have plagued Gaddis all his career. In *Fire the Bastards!* (1962), a scathing attack on the critical reception of Gaddis's first novel, Jack Green has a section called "The 'Difficult' Cliché" in which he quotes half a dozen reviewers voicing the same complaints about Gaddis as the current crop. (Green points out that a novel is difficult only if you read it like a textbook, in which each paragraph has to be mastered before moving on to the next. He also argues that a rich novel is always difficult, and asks "unless you hug impoverishment why worry?") Gaddis's ***J R,*** which is indeed his most difficult (though it is also *the* great American novel if ever there was one), seemed to prove most difficult for sophisticated mandarin reviewers like George Steiner in *The New Yorker;* those in the provinces, like Alicia Miller in the *Cleveland Plain Dealer,* had a wonderful time with it. Because of its shorter length, Gaddis's third novel, ***Carpenter's Gothic,*** got off comparatively easy, though there were those who complained of the close attention the novel demanded. The new book may be Gaddis's best mixture yet of complex and hilarious matters, of high art and good entertainment.

A Frolic of His Own is both cutting-edge, state-of-the-art fiction and a throwback to the great moral novels of Tolstoy and Dickens. That it can be both is just one of the many balancing acts it performs: It is bleak and pessimistic while howlingly funny; it is a deeply serious exploration of such lofty themes as justice and morality but is paced like a screwball comdey; it is avant-garde in its fictional techniques but traditional in conception and in the reading pleasures it offers; it is a damning indictment of the United States, Christianity and the legal system, but also a playful frolic of Gaddis's own.

The plot is too wonderfully complex to summarize here; suffice it to say, it concerns an interlocking set of lawsuits involving the Crease family: Oscar, a historian and playwright; Christina, his stepsister, married to a lawyer named Harry Lutz; and their father, Judge Thomas Crease, presiding over two cases in Virginia during the course of the novel. The story unfolds by way of Gaddis's trademark dialogue, so realistic it reads like unedited transcripts but which artfully conveys much information that normally would be consigned to expository narration. Here, for example, is how Oscar's flaky girlfriend, Lily, is introduced. Oscar asks her where she got the new BMW that Christina saw her driving, and she responds: "—It's just this person I borrowed it from Oscar. To come over and see you, I only wish she didn't dislike me so much. She just always makes me feel like a, she's so superior and smart and her clothes, she's just always so attractive for somebody her age and . . ." This occurs early in the novel, before Gaddis has described Christina, and now he doesn't need to: Lily has. ***J R*** was conveyed entirely in dialogue, but in ***A Frolic*** Gaddis includes passages from Oscar's play—necessary for the plot, but often tedious reading—and various legal opinions, brilliantly rendered in the majestic language of the law. One of them, first published a few years ago in *The New Yorker* as ***"Szyrk v. Village of Tatamount et al.,"*** is especially dazzling and contains one of the most eloquent defenses of venturesome art in our time. Noting that "risk of ridicule, of attracting defamatory attentions from his colleagues and even raucous demonstrations by an outraged public have ever been and remain the foreseeable lot of the serious artist," Judge Crease is another of Gaddis's personas, and it is this sense of artistic mission that makes Gaddis essential reading for our culture. He is the oldest of that generation of meganovelists that includes John Barth, Thomas Pynchon and Robert Coover, and while his artistry is as relentlessly inventive as theirs, he is more adept than they at cracking the whip of corrective satire, more concerned with rescuing American culture from itself by exposing its inherent contradictions and weaknesses. The next century's historians and sociologists will learn more from Gaddis than from any other American novelist of our time what went wrong with this century.

Despite its preoccupation with the law, ***A Frolic of His Own*** has nothing in common with the current crop of legal fictions. There are no courtroom scenes: Gaddis isn't interested in the histrionics of courtroom drama but rather in the role the law plays in attempting to impose order on disorderly conduct.

Justice, order, money and the law: Each of these nouns appears on the first page and together they form the compass points of the novel. The same concepts were at the heart of ***J R,*** but while there the emphasis was on money, here it is on the law. In the world according to Gaddis—made up of that devastating barrage of malice, madness and malfeasance reported nightly on the news—the law is less a system to insure order than a weapon that ridiculous, greedy people use to make "other people take them as seri-

An excerpt from *A Frolic of His Own*

—All right but, later yes listen, before they get here where are my glasses, listen. This might be useful in my complaint Mister Basie listen, it's a letter of Bernard Shaw talking about making movies from plays he says here 'set your analytical faculty, if you have any, to tabulate all the techniques involved in these extraordinary exhibitions . . .'

—Oscar, please . . .

—'Up to a certain point it pays. Most of the studios seem to live by it. But in such studios the dramatist can find no place. They know that they can do without him.'

—Oscar for God's sake what has this got to do with . . .

—'They don't even know, poor devils, that there is such a thing as a dramatic technique. Get drama and picture making separate in your mind, or you will make ruinous mistakes' and then he says . . .

—Might come in handy later on Oscar, see all we want right now is a few clearcut causes of action, opening guns you might say like this rejection, show they had their hands on it. You found that letter?

—I . . .

—Can't you simply say no Oscar? that you had that poor woman hauling a hundred heavy boxes down all those stairs and you don't really know whether it's in any of them? One letter, you expect to find one piece of paper in this whole mess, you've saved every letter anyone ever wrote you God only knows why they bothered, there are letters all over the place. What about that bundle you had me cart in to the hospital for no earthly reason but to cart them back out here, if you can't bear to simply throw them away you've a marvelous chance to get rid of them haven't you? this socalled historical society down there begging to add them to their distinguished collection?

—Why! For some doddering old women to paw through them wheezing over their sacred past, I've got my own archive haven't I? And this family correspondence they already claim to have should be in it too, it's mine isn't it? Ours?

—Why don't you ask your lawyer, he's sitting right here with the clock running.

—I don't have to ask anyone! It's our family correspondence, it's ours Mister Basie isn't it?

—Might have some trouble contesting who owns the actual letters but what they say, that still belongs to whoever said it, whoever wrote the letter, father, grandfather, grandmother, the rights pass right on down to the survivors. Might not be that bad an idea just to go ahead and register the copyright in your name, that way if some problem comes along you . . .

—Yes well do it then, you've got your yellow pad there write it down, can we do it?

William Gaddis, in his A Frolic of His Own, *Poseidon Press, 1994.*

ously as they take themselves" (also quoted from the first page; like an opera composer, Gaddis announces all his themes in the overture). Justice, order and the law are not synonymous terms, nor are they enough: The missing term (and thus absent from the first page but appearing later) is, simply, what is "right."

The novel is a stupendous achievement, filled with so much outrage, wit, wisdom and artistry that it makes other novels published in the past ten years look tepid and underachieved. (Despite his reservations, Sven Birkerts admitted that it is "leagues ahead of most so-called 'serious' novels that are published these days.") If you find it difficult you should be grateful, for you'll be engaged at the top of your abilities, discovering reading muscles you'd forgotten you ever had. And any exhaustion you feel afterward will be the good kind, as after sex or an invigorating workout. Go for the burn.

Michael Wood (review date 12 May 1994)

SOURCE: "So Sue Me," in *London Review of Books,* Vol. 16, No. 9, May 12, 1994, pp. 20-1.

[*Wood is an English-born critic, screenwriter, and educator. In the following review, he examines Gaddis's use of dialogue, wordplay, and humor in* A Frolic of His Own.]

It's hard to think of a writer who publishes a book every ten or twenty years as garrulous, or of a person who produces his fourth novel at the age of 72 as prolific; but we need some such terms if we are to begin to describe the extraordinary work of William Gaddis, born 1922, the author of ***The Recognitions*** (1955), ***JR*** (1975), ***Carpenter's Gothic*** (1985) and now ***A Frolic of His Own***.

Everyone talks in these novels, all the time and at length. They don't listen, or they barely listen; or they listen too late, so that what they finally hear confounds everything they have been saying. Their style, at least in the last three novels, is breathless and jumbled, often pronounless, dedicated to the present participle. From ***JR:***

> See life draining out of everything in sight call that beautiful? End of the day alone on that train, lights coming on in those little Connecticut towns stop and stare out at an empty street corner dry cheese sandwich charge you a dollar you wouldn't even put butter on it, finally pull into that desolate station scared to get off scared to stay on.

From ***Carpenter's Gothic:***

> Trying to get things together here look, getting things lined up everything's just about ready to fall in place so God damn many pressures, why I don't try to tell you everything I don't want to upset you. Try to give you the big picture you take one corner of it and run, jump like I said you jump to some conclusion the whole God damn thing falls to pieces like these flowers, I send these flowers you jump to some conclusion we end up arguing about flowers, see what I mean?

From ***A Frolic of His Own:***

> Like we just witnessed here right before our eyes how this Federal US judge just steps in there to suit his fancy and throws out a verdict reached after calm deliberation by a jury of you honest citizens black folk and white, right there in the Fourteenth Amendment in black and white, the jury that's the bulwark and cornerstone of American justice like you don't see in these dictator atheist countries.

And it's not just the characters who talk. The novels themselves are driven by a compulsion to discuss and argue, to let all these words out of the bag. Monologues merge into hectic narrative, often without warning; the narrators have purple passages, usually parodying some sort of fine writing, including Gaddis's own; texts are inserted into texts—handwritten homework and lists in ***JR,*** a play and sundry legal documents, with typescript to match, in ***A Frolic of His Own***. There is a need for words here, a sense of things to be said, of a world waiting for our wisdom, of ourselves needing to make an extended verbal mark on our habitat; and there is also—this is what makes these novels so brilliantly funny—a lucid and ironic awareness of how pointless and manic and self-centred this talk is. Talk is a kind of doomed buffoonery, wearing funny clothes and taking tumbles because it doesn't know how to get another job, or if there is another job, anywhere.

The books are crowded with voices and short on punctuation, but are they then unreadable? Some sort of late Modernist nightmare, experimental art at the end of its tether? This is what many hostile critics have said, and even a friendly critic, like William Gass (no relation, I think, except through the alphabet), introducing ***The Recognitions*** as a Penguin 20th-Century Classic, suggests we don't need or are not likely to finish reading the work. "Well, how many have actually arrived at the last page of Proust or completed *Finnegans Wake*? What does it mean to finish *Moby Dick,* anyway? Do not begin this book with any hope of that. This is a book you are meant to befriend.' The idea of befriending a book is attractive, but these are all the wrong comparisons, surely. Gaddis is not difficult or unapproachable, once we get the hang of his shifts from monologue to dialogue, and from dialogue to narrative. We pick up a habit, realise that the puns and misunderstandings and false starts that litter our reading are an unshakeable part of his and our world; that we are not missing things, just getting too much. If you say 'suit', to take an example from ***A Frolic of His Own,*** do you mean lawsuit or clothes? What if the point is the chance of slithering from one world to the other? If reference is always getting away from you; if it's not meaning that's the problem, but our not knowing where to hang it, or hanging it too soon in the wrong places?

There are lots of shifts of plot, always surprising, often hilarious; plenty of knockabout gags; endless amounts of shrewd observation of contemporary America, with its particular, self-consuming madnesses. The trouble with Gaddis is not his prose or the ambitions of his works. It's time. Our time, the time we haven't got. The books are wonderfully readable but you feel you need another life, or nothing else to do in this one, in order to read them. This feeling can be overcome.

The term 'a frolic of one's own', we learn in this new novel, is an ancient legal technicality. It describes the activities of an employee who is at work but engaged in private pursuits. The inference is that the employer is not liable for any damage that arises. It looks like a let-out, and Gaddis has a fine time applying it to God, as the always absent boss of people who say they are doing His work. American fundamentalism is one of Gaddis's favourite targets, and he develops here a black joke he started to sketch out in ***Carpenter's Gothic,*** where the Reverend Elton Ude inadvertently drowns a child he is trying to baptise. The case now comes to trial.

> There can be no question that, in bringing a new soul into the fold through the baptismal ceremony, he was engaged on his master's business much as, we may recall in Luke 2.49, this selfsame master at age 12 found lagging behind at the temple in Jerusalem by his anxious parents, rebuked them saying 'Wist ye not that I must be about my Father's business?' and not, in the word of a later English jurist, 'going on a frolic of his own'. In carrying out this solemn assignment, even were there reliable testimony that this omniscient master must have been aware of the risk and told his servant to act carefully, the law still holds him liable for a prevailing share in the consequences. In other words, the master may not delegate responsibility for the servant's acts to him, since under terms of their relationship he remains ultimately responsible for protecting his servant. This must hold all the more true where the instrument of imminent catastrophe is the master's to control, as must the crest and current of the Pee Dee River have been for one who had shown himself capable of stilling a great tempest to save a ship from foundering by merely rebuking the winds and the sea in Matthew 8.26, with which I am sure you are all familiar.

This is a piece of the judge's instructions to the jury, and it is full of sarcasm and mischief, fundamentalism turned against the fundamentalists. He is about to grant the unfortunate boy's father compensation in the amount of $19.76. But he (and Gaddis) are having fun with the idea of an act of God; and elsewhere Gaddis sets up the frolic of one's own as a definition of the artist. He or she is at work, and working, but not doing the job they are supposed to do; defecting even from their own projects. Does this make them deviant professionals, or just amateurs? Gaddis probably wants to say that it makes them unclassifiable. There is something sentimental and mystified about this claim, which implies an old romance of the ornery individualist, all rebellion and refusal. Still, Gaddis's world offers us plenty to refuse, and in context the frolic represents an escape not just from conformity but from the law itself, and from the idea that the law is ubiquitous and sufficient, 'all laws, and laws, and everything's laws', as a character says.

A Frolic of His Own is a book about language and desire; about how language misnames desire, perhaps must misname it; how a language like that of the law lives its own expensive life.

—Michael Wood

The chief frolickers in the novel are Oscar Crease, a (onetime) playwright and (casual) history instructor, described in the newspapers as 'a wealthy recluse living on Long Island'; and his 97-year-old father, the judge giving the instructions to the jury in Virginia. Oscar's girlfriend Lily thinks the papers have called him 'a wealthy excuse', which is perhaps more appropriate. He watches nature programmes on television, drinks a lot and broods over his various litigations. He is suing a car firm because his own car started while he was standing in front of it, and ran him over; and a movie company for plagiarising his play about the Civil War, a work which is in turn a rambling rip-off of O'Neill's *Mourning Becomes Electra* and *Desire Under the Elms,* with dashes of Plato and Rousseau and Camus thrown in. We have legal opinions, complaints, answers to complaints, depositions, more opinions, all done with admirable, patient attention to the detail and manner of the language of the law, touched with parodies and escapes, frolics of Gaddis's own, only in the lightest possible way. Oscar's case at first seems ludicrous, then plausible, then absolutely convincing: the movie took all of its essential plot and character features from him. It looks as if he's won, but then an appeal, accepting this indebtedness, gets a court to quantify. How large was Oscar's contribution to the financial success of the film, in comparison to that of the stars, the studio, the movie medium, salacious advertising, lots of nudity, bloody battles etc? You can hear Oscar's imagined money trickling away.

Meanwhile the judge has problems of his own, 'a lot on his plate', as the resentful, father-haunted Oscar keeps saying, with some satisfaction. Gaddis has really outdone himself in macabre humour here. A dog belonging to a black boy in the village of Tatamount, Va, runs into a large free-standing modern sculpture, called *Cyclone Seven,* and can't get out. The fire brigade is all set to release him with the aid of acetylene torches, when the artist, a fellow with a foreign name living in New York, gets an injunction to stop the village interfering with his masterpiece in any way. The judge, in another sarcastic opinion, upholds this injunction, the media arrive, and everyone wants a piece of this act, animal rights and artists' rights, local law and federal law, people making T-shirts, toys, the lot.

There is much malarkey along these lines, until the dog is killed by a bolt of lightning—an act of God or one of God's frolics—and the dispute now centres on the dog's remains, and the question of compensation for the bereaved boy. Most of the parties change sides several times, and at one point the village is anxious to keep the sculpture as it is because of the revenue it creates, while the artist wants to dismantle it and take it away. The judge is infuriating everyone, and there are calls for his impeachment.

The plot also involves Oscar's stepsister Christina and her husband Harry, a lawyer; a socialite friend of Christina's and her dog; a supposed lawyer who turns out to have forged his credentials; another lawyer with unbearable British manners and mannerisms. Oscar's father anonymously helps him out with his case, writing a brief that someone else presents; and dies. Oscar learns about this help, so there is a reconciliation, but only in two separate minds, and the judge did it for love of the law anyway. There are suits everywhere, bills mount up, careers are made and broken, but no one actually seems to win or lose. It's as if the Marx Brothers had rewritten *Bleak House.*

> —It's garaged at your, at the place of the accident I can't find the, what kind of car is it?
>
> —Sosumi.
>
> —I'm being quite serious, Mr Crease.
>
> —So am I! It's a Japanese car, a Sosumi.
>
> —Oh. Oh dear, yes I'm sorry, it's so hard to keep track of them all nowadays. We had a whole family killed last week in an Isuyu and I made a similar error.

Some of Gaddis's jokes are pretty broad—even broader than the above, like the name of the actor Robert Bredford, or the career of one Clint Westwood and his film *A Hatful of Sh*t*—and there is one long argument about the follies of organised religion that feels as if Gaddis, and not his characters, were indulging a bee in a bonnet. But the ingenuity and the intelligence of the comment on the law, and the speed with which people talk and things happen, take us into something beyond satire. In the following passage about a US Senator for North Carolina (the one we've already heard talking about dictator atheist countries), almost every clause has a fresh sting or gag:

> The latest disturbance centred about an outdoor pork barbecue rally for US Senator Orney Bilk, who is visiting the area on a campaign swing for the first time since he left his boyhood home in nearby Stinking Creek to enlist in the army following the end of hostilities in Southeast Asia. After graduating from army cooking school he was placed in charge of a field oven unit at Fort Bragg, NC.

The start of his senatorial career, no doubt. The language here is a trail of clues and disguises, and ***A Frolic of His Own*** is a book about language and desire; about how language misnames desire, perhaps must misname it; how a language like that of the law lives its own expensive life. 'I mean you talk about language how everything's language it seems that all language does is drive us apart.'

What people in this book think they want is money and fame and prestige, and they regard the law as the road to those things. But it's not even the road away from those things. It's what promotes those goals and consumes them, continues to dangle them ahead of every eager nose. A distinction is made several times between who Oscar is and who he thinks he is, and perhaps only the person he thinks he is can be made intelligible, to himself or others. Only the imagination can sue.

What people want, the novel strongly suggests, is *attention.* Harry the lawyer claims they want order, a form of fascism; but his wife Christina says they're just 'trying to be taken seriously'. That's what money is, she suggests: 'It's the only common reference people have for making other people take them as seriously as they take themselves, I mean that's all they're really asking for isn't it?' It's a generous estimate, and Christina, in her scatty, loquacious way, is a generous person. But it's also too much; more than anyone can expect in the world Gaddis elaborates for us.

Zachary Leader (review date 3 June 1994)

SOURCE: "Jarndyce USA," in *The Times Literary Supplement,* No. 4757, June 3, 1994, p. 22.

[*In the following, Leader favorably reviews* A Frolic of His Own.]

William Gaddis is now only obscure in one sense. At seventy-two, after long years of neglect, he has become a visible presence in American fiction, a modern—postmodern? modernist?—master. Gaddis has written four fiendishly clever and demanding novels: ***The Recognitions*** (1955), ***JR*** (1975), ***Carpenter's Gothic*** (1985), and now ***A Frolic of His Own,*** itself a comparative frolic at 586 pages. ***JR*** (726 pages) won the National Book Award in 1976, and last year, along with ***The Recognitions,*** was reissued as a Penguin Twentieth-Century Classic. Both volumes contain extravagantly admiring critical introductions and an impressive list of "suggestions for further reading". Gaddis himself, meanwhile, has won a MacArthur Fellowship, been elected to the American Academy of Arts and Letters, and was recently appointed official state author of New York, recognition that might well account for the new novel's relative accessibility.

Still, ***A Frolic of His Own*** is no day at the beach. As Gaddis himself puts it towards the end of ***JR,*** in words that apply to all his work: "Don't bring a God-damned thing to it can't take a God-damned thing from it", a message extracted from the following not-atypical passage of dialogue, part of a discussion of an unfinished novel "about random pattern and mechanization", entitled *"agapē" agape*":

> —Man I mean that's what I mean, like I mean if it says it why doesn't it say it? And I mean this is the name of the book agapē agape? that's the name of it?
>
> —Can't, look pē mark right over the God damned e pi eta pē agapē can't see God damn it? pi eta pē?
>
> —Man like who's supposed to know piéta I mean. . . .
>
> —Didn't Christ! didn't say pietà who God damned different Christ any God damned use

> look, book don't bring a God-damned thing to it can't take a God-damned thing from it don't know something look it up no God damned obligation encyclopaedia right here look it up ag, ag, glass golf wrong God damned volume . . .

This is not gibberish. It makes perfect sense, but you need patience to work it out, and time; once you've done so, you realize it's funny, or mildly funny, self-deprecating too, as at the end where looking things up isn't so easy. The new novel yields comparable rewards, but less grudgingly, being lighter, less clotted and clenched.

At the centre of ***A Frolic of His Own,*** lies Oscar Crease, all but prone in his defective motorized wheelchair, down but not out. Oscar's problem—it is only one of Oscar's problems—is that he's run himself over trying to hot-wire his Sosumi, another defective or "damage-feasant" motorized vehicle, close rival of the comparably priced Isuyu. So who do you sue? Usually in cases of defective vehicles, as in suits of all sorts, I sue you. Or you sue me. In Oscar's case, it is suggested, I sue I. Or, if you prefer, I sue me.

And why not, since Oscar's suing everyone else, often only seconds before everyone else countersues. Most importantly, Oscar is suing the film producer Constantine Kiester, née—or so he says—Jonathan Livingston, cannily customized for Hollywood to Jonathan Livingston Siegal. Siegal/Keister's blockbusting Civil War epic, *The Blood in the Red White and Blue,* a film with "the most widely discussed mass rape scene in screen history", lifts important ingredients, Oscar is convinced, from his unpublished play, *Once at Antietam,* based on what appear to have been his grandfather's Civil War experiences. This play is the only thing poor Oscar, a middle-aged college history teacher, failed offspring of a distinguished legal family, has managed to produce in a lifetime's amateurish dabbling (though, in fact, it never *has* been produced). The play is Oscar's last hope: for fame, fortune, fatherly favour or respect; it's a serious work, full of high-minded Socratic dialogue, much of it about justice, much of it lifted (in *hommage,* Oscar insists, a quite different matter) from Book One of *The Republic,* from *The Cratylus, The Crito,* from Rousseau, from Camus. We know this because Oscar is forever subjecting his lawyers to long and not always riveting readings from it (amounting to some seventy pages). Oscar wants justice, and he could do with the money.

Oscar's real problem, though, is everyone's problem, according to his perpetually exasperated step-sister, Christina: he wants recognition, attention, "to be taken seriously", principally by his father, a justice of another variety, though comparably absent, elusive, unstable. As Oscar keeps repeating, though, sometimes maliciously, sometimes pathetically, this father, ninety-seven-year-old Federal Court Justice Thomas Crease, has himself "a lot on his plate"—beginning with the inhibiting example of his own father, Supreme Court Justice Thomas Crease (this is a novel of entropy, of epic degeneration), Oliver Wendell Holmes Jr's great antagonist, a jurist "as obsessed with justice as Holmes was with the law", and no less absent, elusive, unstable, particularly at the bloody battle of Antietam. The grandfather's non-appearance, his shameful purchase of substitutes or surrogates in the battle, is the central action, or non-action, in Oscar's play.

More immediately, Oscar's father is busy—won't call, write, read his play—ruling on two mind-bogglingly complicated cases: the controversial *Cyclone Seven* trial, involving a massive free-standing civic sculpture, *Cyclone Seven,* located in the village of Tatamount, Virginia, and the no-less-convoluted and headline-grabbing trial of the Reverend Elton Ude of Mississippi, accused of negligence in the baptismal drowning of an infant named Wayne Frickert in the Pee Dee River. Ude, as it happens, is obliquely connected to the father of Oscar's dim-witted but well-endowed girlfriend, Lily, herself in litigation over defective breast implants. He also, as it happens, like a number of other characters, themes, incidents, and plot-points in the novel, appears elsewhere in Gaddis's work; in Ude's case, in ***Carpenter's Gothic***. It is not enough, in other words, to attend with unwavering concentration (and unless you do, you'll soon be lost) to the spiralling complexities of *this* plot; to do the novel's artfulness justice, you must know something of the plots of its notoriously inaccessible predecessors. This is a task that might daunt even Oscar's father, who rules on his cases impeccably, in long, carefully crafted and authentic-sounding judgments. These judgments, presented as typescripts or facsimiles, are full of acerbic good sense; they also provide the novel's only moments of stability, illusory flickers of presence, agency, closure, respite, justice even.

And then we're off again, appealing and countersuing, whittling down damages, running up costs, deposing, proceeding, filing, disclaiming. Christina's lawyer-husband, Harry, soon-to-be-senior-partner at the white shoe firm, Swyne and Dour, works himself to death on a trademark infringement case involving serious money, $700 million. Christina's socialite friend, Trish, also seriously rich (and the funniest character in the book, though her boyfriend, the fantastically clever and affected anglophile Jawaharlal "Jerry" Madhar Pie, Kiester's attorney, runs her a close second), hires one set of lawyers to bring damages "for foetal endangerment" and another "to defend her abortion", defrauds a devoted family retainer by breaking her mother's will ("I only wanted justice didn't I?"), ruins shopkeepers, never pays Swyne and Dour, then sues for its "abominable" behaviour over her bill.

Exaggerated? Fantastical? "If you permit the president of the United States to be sued and permit the case to go forward," warns President Clinton's lawyer, Richard S. Bennett (as reported in the *Washington Post* of May 6 1994), "there could be thousands of lawsuits. Your president would be tied down for 365 days a year being asked questions by lawyers." This sentence might almost have come from one of Oscar's lawyers. But lawyers alone aren't the problem; the novel's satire is only partly social or institutional. As Trish's example shows, lawyers too get used; or fired (if, say, they don't bill 2,000 hours); or driven into the ground with overwork, like poor Harry, whose entire estate is gobbled up by his employers, Swyne and Dour. The unscrupulousness of lawyers reflects a universal unscrupulousness, one the novel registers in tiny, casual details. "Speaking on condition that he not be identified,"

Oscar reads, "Village official J. Harret Ruth. . . ." So, too, with lawyerly heartlessness. "You'd think we were Kurds or something", wails Trish, outraged to discover "horrid little plastic forks" in her expensive picnic hamper. Oscar likes to spend hours in his darkened living-room drinking Pinot Grigio and watching nature programmes: insects devouring their mates, wild birds devouring their young. Who expects justice in such a world? We learn in the novel's opening sentence: "you get justice in the next world, in this world you have the law."

Which is doubly unfortunate, since just about the only sure thing in the novel is that there is no next world. This conclusion can be derived, with characteristic indirection, from the novel's title. "A frolic of his own", it turns out, is a legal phrase used in cases of imputed negligence: "the servant gets injured or injures somebody else on the job when he's not doing what he's hired for", explains Harry, "like an office worker puts out an eye shooting paperclips with a rubberband they say he's on a frolic of his own." When little Wayne Frickert drowns during baptism, according to Oscar's father, Reverend Elton Ude is "engaged on his master's business . . . and not, in the words of a later English jurist, 'going on a frolic of his own.' " The drowning, Justice Crease gloatingly instructs his redneck jury, is thus the "master's" (that is, God's) fault, especially since in this case "the instrument of imminent catastrophe is the master's to control, as must the crest and current of the Pee Dee river have been". God is indited in the novel for negligence—is absent, elusive, unstable.

Like "meaning" in general, and not just in the language of law. This is in part the message of Gaddis's neck-wrenching prose style, with its unattributed dialogue, absent or unstable punctuation, elusive syntax, hit-and-run transitions, as in the following near-miss: "Did you see that? his knuckles gone white on the wheel, —steps right in front of the car and holds up his hand, did you see that?" The chaotic style reflects a social condition, one marked by lack of control (as when Oscar suddenly veers into the rhythms of his favourite boyhood poem, *Hiawatha,* a wonderful effect), greed (being a sort of gabbling, like gorging), egomania and isolation (everybody talking, nobody listening); but it also reflects something deeper, a condition of language *per se.* "It all evaporates into language confronted by language turning language itself into theory till it's not what it's about it's only about itself." This is of a piece with the novel's wearying repetitions of scene and incident, its refusal to settle. What it suggests is a world of contingency, plurality, indeterminacy, a post-modern world.

Hence Gaddis's frequent association with Thomas Pynchon, whose novels are comparably cryptic, multivocal, centrifugal, entropic, and thus, it is argued, postmodern. But Gaddis also has strong modernist tendencies, in particular the modernist's nostalgia for lost value and unity. ***A Frolic of His Own*** is punctuated by brief, spare passages of natural description: time and again, Christina withdraws from the babble of Oscar's living-room, where most of the novel is set, to peer out of a window at the wintry landscape. This landscape, the chief selling point of the dilapidated Long Island estate Oscar has inherited, is dominated by what Jonathan Raban has wittily identified as "American literature's most famous frozen pond. . . trucked in from Massachusetts for the occasion of the book". Oscar's Long Island Walden functions in the novel as does, say, the remembered moment in the rose garden in Eliot's *Four Quartets,* every line of which Gaddis at one point considered incorporating into ***The Recognitions***. The wintry landscape, "as though time itself were frozen out there", recalls the cold afternoon light of Little Gidding; the country house milieu recalls Evelyn Waugh, an acknowledged influence, or the Shaw of *Heartbreak House.* What once was grand is falling to bits, doomed: the wind wraps Oscar's house "like shipwreck"; the veranda sags ominously, a lawsuit waiting to happen; predatory realtors loiter around the front drive; chainsaws whine from the adjoining development.

The barbarians, in other words, are at the gate, a modernist motif that connects to the novel's most prominent defect, its snobbishness. How else explain the slackness of "Clint Westwood", star of *A Hatful of Sh*t,* or his fellow star "Robert Bredford", or a senator named "Bilk", a southerner, from the town of "Stinking Creek". This is easy, unfunny, old-hat, quite unlike the legal satire, which derives its power in part from affection as well as knowledge. Gaddis makes fun of Oscar's delusions and pretentions, his uncool, antique organicism ("The whole thing builds towards the last act that's what any play is about isn't it?"), his disdain for massed America, for "the whole insignificant meaningless swarm", but at times Oscar's revulsion seems Gaddis's as well. This shared contempt recalls a shared background: Gaddis, too, grew up on Long Island in a small town swamped by development, suffered long years of neglect, wrote an unpublished play in the 1950s entitled *Once at Antietam.* Oscar, though, can't write, judging by his play (though it has its moments); could never, for instance, create a character like himself, one he then gleefully mocked. The happier resemblance is with Christina: funny, bitter, affectionate, up to her elbows in the world, yet also drawn, with blank solemnity, to the chilly beauty of the pond. In the end, it is Christina's spirit which dominates and redeems this bleak, brilliant, exhausting novel.

FURTHER READING

Criticism

Eder, Richard. "Literary Legalities." *Los Angeles Times Book Review* (9 January 1994): 3, 12.

Recounts Gaddis's comic portrait of legal issues in *A Frolic of His Own.*

Klawans, Stuart. "Further Frolics." *The Threepenny Review* XV, No. 2 (Summer 1994): 12-13.

Offers a comparative review of *A Frolic of His Own* and Catharine A. MacKinnon's *Only Words.*

McGonigle, Thomas. "Men in Suits." *Chicago Tribune—Books* (9 January 1994): 3.

Mixed assessment of *A Frolic of His Own.* Although describing *A Frolic of His Own* as "the wittiest novel to be published in many a year," McGonigle argues that the book's narrative structure and flawed characters may frustrate readers.

Additional coverage of Gaddis's life and career is contained in the following sources published by Gale Research: *Contemporary Authors,* Vols. 17-20, rev. ed.; *Contemporary Authors New Revision Series,* Vol. 21; *Contemporary Literary Criticism,* Vols. 1, 3, 6, 8, 10, 19, 43; *Dictionary of Literary Biography,* Vol. 2; and *Major 20th-Century Writers.*

Ernest J. Gaines
A Lesson before Dying

Award: National Book Critics Circle Award

(Full name Ernest James Gaines) Born in 1933, Gaines is an American novelist and short story writer.

For further information on Gaines's life and works, see *CLC,* Volumes 3, 11, and 18.

INTRODUCTION

A Lesson before Dying (1993) is Gaines's first major publication in ten years. Like all of his fiction, it is informed by his upbringing on a Louisiana plantation. Set in 1948 in rural Louisiana, *A Lesson before Dying* presents the story of Jefferson, a black man accused by a white community and sentenced to death for a murder and robbery he did not commit. His attorney's defense—that Jefferson would be incapable of planning and carrying out the crimes of which he is accused because he is merely a dumb animal incapable of independent thought—is unsuccessful. This reasoning, however, robs Jefferson of his self-respect and he withdraws into a nearly catatonic state. His godmother, Miss Emma, resolves that if he must die, "I want a man to go to that chair, on his own two feet." She enlists Grant Wiggins, a successful young black man, to be Jefferson's mentor and to help him find dignity while he awaits execution. Jonathan Yardley describes the book as "quintessential Gaines, a fine introduction to his world and his view of it for anyone unfamiliar with his work—and, for those who know that work, a welcome opportunity to return to familiar territory."

PRINCIPAL WORKS

Catherine Carmier (novel) 1964
Of Love and Dust (novel) 1967
Bloodline (short stories) 1968
The Autobiography of Miss Jane Pittman (novel) 1971
In My Father's House (novel) 1978
A Gathering of Old Men (novel) 1983
A Lesson before Dying (novel) 1993

CRITICISM

Jonathan Yardley (review date 28 March 1993)

SOURCE: "Nothing but a Man," in *Book World—The Washington Post,* March 28, 1993, p. 3.

[*Yardley is an American critic and educator who has written a weekly syndicated book review since 1974. In the following review, he favorably assesses* A Lesson before Dying.]

The year is 1948 [in ***A Lesson Before Dying***] and the place is rural Louisiana. "A white man had been killed during a robbery, and though two of the robbers had been killed on the spot, one had been captured, and he, too, would have to die." His name is Jefferson. He is a barely literate man-child, he was present at the killing purely by accident, and he almost certainly is innocent; but white justice in Bayonne, the seat of St. Raphael Parish, demands that he must die.

His lawyer does the best he can, considering the time and the circumstances. He portrays his client as a mere dumb animal incapable of coherent thought or action. "No, gentlemen," he tells the jury, "this skull here holds no plans. What you see here is a thing that acts on command. A thing to hold the handle of a plow, a thing to load your bales of cotton, a thing to dig your ditches, to chop your wood, to pull your corn. . . . What justice would there be to take this life? Justice, gentlemen? Why, I would just as soon put a hog in the electric chair as this."

To Miss Emma, Jefferson's ancient godmother, these last words have a terrible resonance. "I don't want them to kill no hog," she says. "I want a man to go to that chair, on his own two feet." She is speaking to Grant Wiggins, himself black and young, a teacher at a school for black children, whom she wants to take over the task of making Jefferson a "man." It is not an assignment he welcomes, as he tells his lover:

> "The public defender, trying to get him off, called him a dumb animal. He said it would be like tying a hog down in that chair and executing him—an animal that didn't know what any of it was all about. The jury, twelve white men good and true, still sentenced him to death. Now his godmother wants me to visit him and make him know—prove to these white men—that he's not a hog, that he's a man. I'm supposed to make him a man. Who am I? God? . . . What do I say to him? Do I know what a man is? Do I know how a man is supposed to die? I'm still trying to find out how a man should live. Am I supposed to tell someone how to die who has never lived?"

However reluctantly, Grant agrees to see what he can do. Miss Emma approaches her former employer to ask that he intercede with the sheriff so Grant can gain admission to Jefferson's cell. This in turn is followed by Grant's own interview with the sheriff—a humiliating encounter that is described with restraint and economy—after which he is permitted to proceed.

Thus the scene is set in ***A Lesson Before Dying,*** the eighth novel by Ernest J. Gaines, a writer who gained a measure of renown for ***The Autobiography of Miss Jane Pittman*** but has never really been given the recognition he deserves. Whether ***A Lesson Before Dying*** will change that is, as is usual in such matters, highly problematical, but in a just world it would. It is quintessential Gaines, a fine introduction to his world and his view of it for anyone unfamiliar with his work—and, for those who know that work, a welcome opportunity to return to familiar territory.

Gaines was born six decades ago on a Louisiana plantation. He was reared there, and it was there that his understanding of American life was shaped. He has traveled widely and lived in many places, but as he himself has readily acknowledged, rural Louisiana is where he feels most truly at home. It is there to which he returns, over and over again, in his fiction.

One of the many remarkable things about his work, and thus about Gaines himself, is the utter lack of overwrought emotion with which questions of race relations are treated. It is not that Gaines is incapable of anger. Quite to the contrary: "Twelve white men say a black man must die," he writes in this novel, "and another white man sets the date and time without consulting one black person. Justice?" Rather it is that he has the breadth and depth of mind to understand that generalizations are always suspect, that one must look at individual humans instead of stereotypes if there is to be any hope of understanding them.

Thus it is that one of the most sympathetic characters in ***A Lesson Before Dying*** is Paul, a white jailor who befriends Grant and quietly helps Jefferson. Thus it is that Jefferson is portrayed without sentimentality, as an ignorant man who must struggle against himself as well as against injustice. Thus it is that Grant is no cardboard hero but an immensely complex man who not merely is loath to take on a task he finds distasteful but also must resist the temptation to condescend to the uneducated man—so unlike himself except in being black—to whose cell he has so unhappily come.

He also admits, however grudgingly, his own complicity in the system of which Jefferson is a victim. Though whites regard him with disdain and a measure of apprehension—"You're smart," one of them tells him. "Maybe you're just a little too smart for your own good"—he knows that, like the black preacher who bows and scrapes, there is only so far that he can go. This is at the core of his appeal to Jefferson, the words that finally cut through the prisoner's hostility and resistance:

> "Do you know what a myth is, Jefferson? A myth is an old lie that people believe in. White people believe that they're better than anyone else on earth—and that's a myth. The last thing they ever want is to see a black man stand, and think, and show that common humanity that is in us all. It would destroy their myth. They would no longer have justification for having made us slaves and keeping us in the condition we are in. As long as none of us stand, they're safe. They're safe with me. They're safe with Reverend Ambrose. I don't want them to feel safe with you anymore."

The drama of the novel's final pages is psychological rather than actual; this is Louisiana in 1948, after all, and no one is going to ride to the rescue of a black man awaiting execution. Instead the questions involve how Jefferson will face his final hours and what the rest of the community, Grant most particularly, can learn from them—for the real lesson of the title is not learned by Jefferson but by others. Suffice it to say that the lesson is valuable and apt, presented in the modest but forceful terms that we have come to expect from Ernest J. Gaines.

Charles R. Larson (review date 9 May 1993)

SOURCE: "End as a Man," in *Chicago Tribune—Books,* May 9, 1993, p. 5.

[*Larson is an American novelist, editor, and critic. In the following positive review, he focuses on Gaines's treatment of human dignity and the "morality of connectedness" in* A Lesson before Dying.]

The incident that propels the narrative of Ernest J. Gaines' rich new novel is deceptively simple. Shortly after World War II, in a Cajun Louisiana town, a 21-year-old black man who is barely literate finds himself in the wrong place at the wrong time, an innocent bystander during the robbery of a liquor store. The white store owner is killed, as are the two black men who attempt to rob the store; Jefferson—who is just standing there—panics. He grabs a bottle of liquor and starts drinking it. Then he looks at the phone, knowing he should call someone, but he's never used a dial phone in his life. Flight seems the only option, but as he leaves the store, two white customers enter.

That event takes place at the beginning of ***A Lesson Before Dying,*** Gaines' most rewarding novel to date, and it's followed by a brief summary of Jefferson's trial. The 12 white jurors find him guilty, assuming he's an accomplice of the two other black men, and the judge sentences Jefferson to death by electrocution. Much of what follows in this often mesmerizing story focuses on Jefferson's slow rise to dignity and manhood.

The obstacle to be overcome is a derogatory remark made by the defense during the trial, supposedly to save Jefferson from the death sentence. The lawyer asks the jurors, "Do you see a man sitting here? Look at the shape of this skull, this face as flat as the palm of my hand. . . . Do you see a modicum of intelligence? Do you see anyone here who could plan a murder, a robbery . . . can plan anything? A cornered animal to strike quickly out of fear, a trait inherited from his ancestors in the deepest jungle of blackest Africa—yes, yes, that he can do—but to plan?. . . . No, gentlemen, this skull here holds no plans. What you see here is a thing that acts on command."

Finally, wrapping up his plea, the lawyer concludes, "What justice would there be to take his life? Justice, gentlemen. Why, I would just as soon put a hog in the electric chair as this."

***A Lesson before Dying* is a majestic, moving novel, an instant classic, a book that will be read, discussed and taught beyond the rest of our lives.**

—Charles R. Larson

The fallout from the lawyer's defense is devastating. In his cell, after receiving the death sentence, Jefferson is close to catatonic. As his aged godmother Emma and her friends try to make contact with him, he withdraws further into himself. In one wrenching scene when they bring him home-cooked food, he gets down on all fours and ruts around in the food without using his hands.

The complexity of this painful story is richly enhanced by Gaines's ironic narrator, Grant Wiggins. Only a few years older than Jefferson, Grant is college educated and a parish school teacher. Bitter in his own way and aloof from the community he has come to loathe, Grant is initially uninvolved, until his aunt (Miss Emma's friend) asks that he try to make Jefferson into a man. This quest for manhood becomes the emotional center of the story and a challenge for Grant himself to become reconnected to his people.

Assuming he will fail, Grant articulates his feelings to his mistress:

> "We black men have failed to protect our women since the time of slavery. We stay here in the South and are broken, or we run away and leave them alone to look after the children and themselves. So each time a male child is born, they hope he will be the one to change this vicious circle—which he never does. Because even though he wants to change it, and maybe even tries to change it, it is too heavy a burden because of all the others who have run away and left their burdens behind. So he, too, must run away if he is to hold on to his sanity and have a life of his own. . . . What she wants is for him, Jefferson, and me to change everything that has been going on for three hundred years."

Grant's task is further complicated by the local minister, who believes that saving Jefferson's soul is more important than making him into a man. The tensions between the teacher and the preacher add still another complex dimension to Gaines' formidable narrative.

Nowhere is the story more moving than in the scenes in which Grant and Jefferson are together in Jefferson's cell, agonizing over his horrific past—for Jefferson has been shaped not only by the animalistic designation thrust upon him in his 21st year but also by the deprivations of the previous 20.

When Grant can finally mention the unspeakable—the last day of Jefferson's life—Jefferson tells him, "I never got nothing I wanted in my whole life." When asked what he wants to eat that last day, Jefferson responds, "I want me a whole gallon of ice cream. . . . Ain't never had enough ice cream. Never had more than a nickel cone. Used to . . . hand the ice cream man my nickel, and he give me a little scoop on a cone. But now I'm go'n get me a whole gallon. That's what I want—a whole gallon. Eat it with a pot spoon."

More than any other novel about African American life in the United States, ***A Lesson Before Dying*** is about standing tall and being a man in the face of overwhelming adversity. And, equally important, Gaines' masterpiece is about what Ralph Ellison and William Faulkner would call the morality of connectedness, of each individual's responsibility to his community, to the brotherhood beyond his self. This majestic, moving novel is an instant classic, a book that will be read, discussed and taught beyond the rest of our lives.

Bob Summer (essay date 24 May 1993)

SOURCE: "Ernest J. Gaines," in *Publishers Weekly,* Vol. 240, No. 21, May 24, 1993, pp. 62, 64.

[*In the following excerpt, Summer examines the influence of Gaines's life on his novels.*]

Inspired by Turgenev's depictions of Russia's serfs, with whom he found parallels to the plantation slaves, [Gaines] began to write.

"I was 17 when I thought I could write a novel and send it to New York and get it published. But I didn't know a damn thing about doing it; I didn't even know how to type. I started in longhand, but my mother rented me a typewriter, which I typed on with one finger. I must have used the cheapest paper I could find, because we couldn't afford anything else. I cut the paper in half, the size of a book, and typed on both sides, single space. I thought it was pretty good. I wrapped in it brown paper, tied a string around it, and sent the thing off. It came back, of course."

After graduating from San Francisco State College (now the University of California-San Francisco) Gaines served in the army. He used $1000 he had saved, plus a small amount remaining from [his] $2500 Stegner Fellowship, to support himself while he tried to produce a saleable book. "After that ran out, I got a job in the Post Office," he says, adding, with a deep, rolling chuckle, "all artists get a job in the Post Office; even Faulkner did at one point."

The plot outline from his first amateurish effort—a young black man returns from California to his native South and falls in love with a woman in his old community—remained stubbornly alive, and Gaines determined to do it justice this time around. It took him five years. "I tried every point of view I could think of, but nothing worked. I knew I *had* to write a novel, but the truth is I didn't know how," he admits. Turgenev's *Fathers and Sons* provided the answer. "It's about a young man who goes back home to visit his people. He's changed since he left and plans a short stay. Then he falls in love with a beautiful woman. That's what I was writing about, so all the moves Turgenev made I followed. *Fathers and Sons* was my bible when I was writing ***Catherine Carmier.***"

The title of Gaines's first novel came from legendary editor Hiram Haydn at Atheneum, where the book was published in 1964. It met a cool response, however, and most of the 3500 first printing was remaindered. (Reprinted by North Point in the early '80s, it has just been reissued as a Vintage trade paperback.) Nevertheless, Gaines had found the place and voices that would continue to engage him as sources for his fiction.

His next three novels ***(Of Love and Dust; Bloodline; A Long Day in November),*** and a book for children, were published by Dial when E. L. Doctorow was editor-in-chief. Each is set in the region of his boyhood, a place of sugarcane and cotton fields where the people who work them say "mon" for mother, "gallery" (or "garry") for porch, and "fair" for a house party. While he did not base any of his characters directly on the people he knew in the quarter, he freely used the sounds of their voices and concentrated on capturing the rhythm of their speech.

His beloved Aunt Augusteen was the inspiration for the 110-year-old former slave who is the title character in ***The Autobiography of Miss Jane Pittman,*** which has sold over a million copies worldwide since its 1971 publication. Miss Jane, he points out, "was never my aunt physically. Miss Jane goes everywhere and does everything, and my aunt, who was crippled and could only crawl, could not. I never saw Aunt Augusteen in front of me when I was writing, but I felt her spirit." He dedicated the book to Augusteen, "who did not walk a day in her life but who taught me the importance of standing."

Miss Jane Pittman, which he researched in Baton Rouge libraries, took him two and a half years to write, but he feels that it had germinated for 38 years, his age when it was published. "Probably I couldn't have written it had I not come from Louisiana. I grew up listening to the old people in the quarter, and all that I heard, in some way, I buried in my subconsciousness. I just didn't begin putting it down on paper until I was 35. I wrote letters for those folks, too, as young Jimmy—my middle name is James—does in the novel. . . . I don't think I'm finished with those letters yet, although the people for whom I wrote them have been dead for 40 years or more. Maybe that's what I'm still trying to do as a writer."

Gaines says he has no particular audience in mind when he writes, just as he's certain that Turgenev, Joyce and Gertrude Stein—in whose *The Autobiography of Alice B. Toklas* he found the method he used to tell Miss Jane Pittman's life story—did not have him in mind either, although he's learned much from each.

"Wallace Stegner once asked me for whom I write, and I told him: no one. He said if he put a gun to me and forced an answer, what would I say. If he did that, I told him, I'd probably say I write for the black youth of the South, to make them aware of who they are. Who else, he asked. I said the white youth of the South to make them aware that unless they understand their black neighbors they cannot understand themselves. But, in fact, I have no intention of addressing any group over another. It's dangerous for writers to think of their audience. I try to write as well as I can, and that's tough enough."

In his last three novels from Knopf, where his editor is Ashbel Green, Gaines has focused on men, and in ***A Lesson Before Dying,*** as well as ***In My Father's House,*** he confronts the separation of black men from each other and their loss of mutual support. "My thesis is that black fathers and sons were separated in Africa in the 17th century and have not come back together since. They can eat across the table, but that is not the same as coming together."

In ***A Lesson Before Dying,*** a black schoolteacher and a young black fieldworker sentenced to be electrocuted for a crime at which he was a bystander are forced to do just that. "I've written a lot about men going to jail, and there are schoolteachers throughout my books—it was about the only thing an educated black in the South in the '40s, the time of the novel, could do for a living. I wanted to bring them together and see what a schoolteacher would say to someone in jail."

The novel is authenticated by what he learned from two lawyers in Louisiana who had defended young black men sentenced to death (one was mildly retarded and another went through the ordeal twice, because the electric chair malfunctioned the first time.) The seed for ***A Lesson Before Dying,*** however, was planted in the '60s in San Francisco, where Gaines's apartment is near Alcatraz. When he knew an execution was to take place there, he became so agitated that he had to go for a long walk. "Knowing when a man was going to the gas chamber made work impossible," he notes. Then he discovered that in Louisiana in the '40s, electrocutions were always held in the parish where the capital crime was committed, and always on Fridays between noon and 3 p.m. "Everything clicked for me then. Friday between 12 and 3, [the time of] Christ's crucifixion!" For a writer whose work attests to the endurance of the human spirit, the message was clear.

Michael Swindle (review date 30 May 1993)

SOURCE: "Louisiana Justice," in *Los Angeles Times Book Review,* May 30, 1993, p. 11.

[*In the following review of* A Lesson before Dying, *Swindle calls the story "enormously moving," but faults the novel's pace and dialogue.*]

One fall afternoon in rural south Louisiana in the late 1940s, a slow-witted young black man called Jefferson accepts a ride from two ne'er-do-wells, Brother and Bear. In the scene that serves as catalyst for Ernest Gaines' eighth novel, ***A Lesson Before Dying,*** Brother and Bear decide to detour by Alcee Grope's store to try to obtain a pint of wine on credit. When they are refused their request, guns are produced; two black men and the white grocer are left dead on the floor.

In a state of panic, Jefferson swills a half bottle of whiskey and pockets the money from the open cash drawer. Before he can flee, two white men enter the store. Jefferson is arrested, branded a co-conspirator in the robbery and put on trial for murder.

In his summation to the jury, Jefferson's defense attorney tells them that "this skull here holds no plans. What you see here is a thing that acts on command. A thing to hold the handle of a plow, a thing to load your bales of cotton, a thing to dig your ditches, to chop your wood, to pull your corn. That is what you see here, but you do not see anything capable of planning a robbery or a murder. He does not even know the size of his clothes or his shoes. . . . What justice would there be to take this life? Justice, gentlemen? Why, I would just as soon put a hog in the electric chair as this."

His words, demeaning as they are to poor Jefferson, fall on deaf ears. Given the time and place, the jury is comprised of 12 white men. With a black man standing accused of killing a white man, their verdict is a foregone conclusion: death by electrocution.

This verdict, and the reference to Jefferson being nothing more than a dumb animal, spurs the action of the novel, affecting the entire community, black and white, around the fictional town of Bayonne, the setting of all Gaines' works.

The story Gaines tells in *A Lesson Before Dying* is enormously moving. The author, a native of south Louisiana, unerringly evokes the place and time about which he writes. Some passages are redolent with the aura of a memoir.

—Michael Swindle

Most touched by the tragedy is Grant Wiggins, the book's narrator, who was raised by his aunt, Tante Lou, in "the quarter" adjacent to Henry Pichot's plantation, upon which all the residents are dependent for their livelihood. Educated at an out-of-state university, he has returned to the plantation to teach in the elementary school.

Because of his role in the black community, Grant is summoned by Miss Emma Glenn, Jefferson's "nannan" (godmother). She is grieved by the fate of the man-child she raised, but also deeply offended by the public defender's remarks. She wants Grant to visit Jefferson in jail and make him know, to prove to the white people, that he is a man and not an animal.

"I don't want them to kill no hog," she tells him. "I want a man to go to that chair, on his own two feet."

Grant's problem is that since returning to the quarter he has become tired of being committed. He hates teaching, feels he is running in place and needs "to go someplace where I can feel like I'm living."

He makes no effort to disguise his reluctance to take on this mission, telling Miss Emma that Jefferson is already dead. "The past 21 years," he says, "we've done all we could for Jefferson. He's dead now. And I can't raise the dead. All I can do is try to keep the others from ending up like this—but he's gone from us. There's nothing I can do anymore, nothing any of us can do anymore."

A strong position, but not strong enough to enable Grant to stand up under the moral pressure of his indomitable aunt and the immovable Miss Emma. They prevail and he endures—suffering humiliation from the white power structure that no longer has any use for him because he is "too educated," agonizing self-doubt and philosophical introspection over his religious belief, and stubborn resistance from his most important pupil. He is rewarded in the end with a success of sorts in the form of a semiliterate, but haunting, diary written by Jefferson during his last days.

The story Gaines tells in ***A Lesson Before Dying*** is enormously moving. The author, a native of south Louisiana, unerringly evokes the place and time about which he writes. Some passages are redolent with the aura of a memoir.

The pacing of the novel, however, is a bit too languorous, even for a Southern writer writing about Southern characters. Gaines' use of repetition wears thin over the course of the book. The reiterations accumulate without building on themselves to further the narrative. We are apprised of Jefferson's big brown eyes, with the whites too reddish, three times in less than half a page. On that same subject, the three white characters whose eyes are mentioned all have gray-blue eyes—though this may be a feature of white south Louisianans that I am unfamiliar with.

In a sub-plot involving Grant Wiggins and his love-interest, a fellow teacher, their exchanges are particularly stilted and clumsy, as evidenced by the following:

> "You want me here?" Vivian asked.
>
> I was not looking at her when she said it, and I could tell by her voice that she was not looking directly at me.
>
> "Yes," I said.
>
> She had been gazing down at the ground. Now she raised her eyes to me.
>
> "I love you Vivian," I said. "I want you to know that. I love you very much."
>
> "I hope you love me half as much as I love you."

Call this quibbling, if you will, but these flaws inflate a narrative that needs no such favor, hint that a writer did not get the editing he deserves, and tug the whole endeavor perilously close to the border of melodrama.

Bruce Bawer (review date 26 July 1993)

SOURCE: "Race, Justice and Integrity in the Old South," in *The Wall Street Journal,* July 26, 1993, p. A9.

[*Bawer is an American critic and editor. In the following largely positive review, he discusses the spiritual development of the characters in* A Lesson before Dying.]

Bayonne, the fictitious Louisiana river town in which Ernest J. Gaines has set all eight of his novels, is not far from the Mississippi lowlands immortalized by William Faulkner. Yet if Faulkner's lush, penetrating prose seems eminently suited to the region's sultry climate and racial tensions, Mr. Gaines's novels are written in a low-key, matter-of-fact prose that may surprise the first-time reader.

Consider, for example, Mr. Gaines's newest novel, ***A Lesson Before Dying,*** which takes place during the late 1940s. Jefferson, a guileless young black man, has been wrongly accused of complicity in the murder of a white liquor-store owner. His attorney tells the all-white jury that Jefferson is incapable of planning such a crime. For he is not a man, really, but "a thing to hold the handle of a plow, a thing to load your bales of cotton, a thing to dig your ditches, to chop your wood, to pull your corn."

The strategy doesn't work and Jefferson is sentenced to death. His ailing godmother has only one wish: that Jefferson—who has been as devastated by his lawyer's line of defense as by the verdict—will go to the electric chair with his head up, knowing himself to be not a "thing" but a man. To this end, she asks Grant Wiggins, the college-educated teacher at Bayonne's black school, to meet with Jefferson regularly. Wiggins (the narrator) is loath to get involved; he doesn't share the old lady's fervent religious faith and doesn't appreciate being put in a position where he has to toady to the ignorant white bigots who work at the jail house.

Wiggins is a Southern-black variation on that old Humphrey Bogart movie cliche, the cynical reluctant hero. He's constantly complaining about the pointlessness of his presence in Bayonne, where the only thing an educated black man can do is teach reading, writing and arithmetic to kids who will grow up to become field workers on some plantation. Yet as we learn from some contrived expository dialogue between Wiggins and his lover, Vivian (a one-dimensional character whose role never rises above the functional), he's already gone off to California once, only to return home. Deep down, he's committed to this place and feels needed here.

And indeed he is. By his conduct on the day of his execution, Jefferson will either inspire or demoralize his fellow blacks in Bayonne, and challenge or confirm his white executioners' image of blacks. Wiggins comes to realize that for Jefferson to see himself as a man is important not just to Jefferson but to the entire town.

So Wiggins perseveres. The breakthrough comes when Jefferson, who has been sad, surly and self-deprecating, turns to Wiggins and tells him to thank his students for sending him pecans. This line recalls the climactic scene in the celebrated 1974 TV movie ***The Autobiography of Miss Jane Pittman,*** based on Mr. Gaines's best-selling novel, in which the ancient Miss Jane strikes a blow for desegregation by drinking from a whites-only water fountain. Jefferson's thank you is a similar, seemingly trivial, everyday act that carries huge moral significance.

Mr. Gaines's fiction has continually attested to the psychological and symbolic importance of apparently minor gestures. Mr. Gaines reminds us movingly of many things: that the simplest of acts can be heroic, that it is important to set a moral example for others (especially the young), that struggles against inequity are carried on individual by individual and that everyone who participates in such struggles wages a battle not only in the world but within himself. By the book's end—which surprises with its power—it is clear not only what the lesson referred to in the title is, but also that Jefferson is not the only one who has learned it.

While this book's heart is most assuredly in the right place, it is, in a number of ways, rather disappointing. While Wiggins makes a credible enough protagonist, the transformation of Jefferson from self-disparaging "thing" to self-respecting man doesn't quite convince. Too often the book feels formulaic, written to outline. Its characters don't rise sufficiently off the page and its setting fails to burst into life with sights, smells and sounds.

Yet to complain about the lack of local color is to miss the point. Mr. Gaines's plain style ultimately proves appropriate because his book is less about the riverfront milieu than about the naked moral truths of these people's shared predicament. And Mr. Gaines knows that predicament inside out; he understands the workings of institutionalized prejudice and captures perfectly the complex tensions between black and white.

In the end, what is most surprising about this book is its tough, unsentimental spiritual power. Jefferson, whom we first encounter as a supposed subhuman, has by the final pages emerged (though Mr. Gaines doesn't lean too hard on the comparison) as a Christ figure, an exemplary victim, while Wiggins—whom his aunt condemns as an atheist—has grown from a secular into a spiritual teacher. Its deficiencies notwithstanding, ***A Lesson Before Dying*** is a very special book about prejudice, the value of individual integrity and the extraordinary resources of the human spirit.

Carl Senna (review date 8 August 1993)

SOURCE: "Dying like a Man: A Novel about Race and Dignity in the South," in *The New York Times Book Review,* August 8, 1993, p. 21.

[*In the following positive review of* A Lesson before Dying, *Senna emphasizes Gaines's ability to evoke the social climate of the South in the 1940s and its foreshadowing of the 1960s civil rights movement.*]

Near the end of Ernest J. Gaines's novel ***A Lesson Before Dying,*** set in the fictional town of Bayonne, La., in 1948, a white sheriff tells a condemned black man to write in his diary that he has been fairly treated. Although the prisoner assents, nothing could be farther from the truth in that squalid segregated jail, which is an extension of the oppressive Jim Crow world outside.

A black primary school teacher, Grant Wiggins, narrates the story of Jefferson, the prisoner, whose resignation to his execution lends credence to the lesson of Grant's own teacher, Matthew Antoine: the system of Jim Crow will break down educated men like Grant and prisoners like Jefferson to "the nigger you were born to be."

Grant struggles, at first without success, to restore a sense of human dignity to Jefferson, a semiliterate, cynical and bitter 21-year-old man, who accepts his own lawyer's depiction of him as "a hog" not worthy of the court's expense. The social distance between the college-educated Grant and Jefferson appears as great as that between the races, and class differences often frustrate their ability to communicate. It does not help that Grant has intervened only reluctantly, prompted by his aunt, a moralizing scold and a nag, and by Jefferson's godmother, Miss Emma.

Mr. Gaines, whose previous novels include ***A Gathering of Old Men*** and ***The Autobiography of Miss Jane Pittman,*** admirably manages to sustain the somber tone of the issues confronting the black citizens of Bayonne. What is at stake becomes clear. We find Grant vicariously sharing in the triumphs of Joe Louis and Jackie Robinson. The larger-than-life achievements of these black heroes make it intolerable to the black folks that Jefferson die ignobly. For that reason, Grant, who makes no secret of his disdain for Jefferson, reluctantly becomes their instrument in trying to save him from disgrace. Justice, or Jefferson's innocence, becomes secondary to the cause of racial image building—no trifling matter.

With the day of Jefferson's execution approaching, Grant begins to despair. Jefferson himself dismisses appeals from Grant and the blacks of Bayonne that he die with dignity—like a man, not like a hog.

Despite *A Lesson before Dying's* gallows humor and an atmosphere of pervasively harsh racism, the characters, black and white, are humanly complex.

—Carl Senna

To complicate the plot further, Grant must overcome another racial divide, crossing the color line to love a divorced Creole woman, Vivian Baptiste. She becomes yet another reason why Grant must save Jefferson's dignity, if not save him from execution. By rejecting Creole prejudice against blacks, Vivian must accept that she too has a stake in how Jefferson confronts the electric chair. She crosses the black-brown line, to the horror of other Creoles and the subtle animosity of Grant's black relatives.

It is a tribute to Mr. Gaines's skill that he makes the conflicts convincing. Jefferson, chained and securely behind bars, still has one freedom left, and that is the freedom to choose how he accepts death.

Despite the novel's gallows humor and an atmosphere of pervasively harsh racism, the characters, black and white, are humanly complex and have some redeeming quality. At the end, Jefferson's white jailer, in a moving epiphany, is so changed that he suggests the white-black alliance that will emerge a generation later to smash Jim Crow to bits.

The New England abolitionist preacher William Ellery Channing observed just before the Civil War that "there are seasons, in human affairs, of inward and outward revolution, when new depths seem to be broken up in the soul, when new wants are unfolded in multitudes, and a new and undefined good is thirsted for." ***A Lesson Before Dying,*** though it suffers an occasional stylistic lapse, powerfully evokes in its understated tone the "new wants" in the 1940's that created the revolution of the 1960's. Ernest J. Gaines has written a moving and truthful work of fiction.

Scott Jaschik (essay date 11 May 1994)

SOURCE: "A New Star in the Canon," in *The Chronicle of Higher Education,* Vol. XL, No. 36, May 11, 1994, pp. A23-4.

[*In the following essay, Jaschik discusses Gaines's views on his work as an author and educator, the extent of his influence as a Southern black writer, and his belief that an "appreciation of humanity" is the key to his success.*]

Ernest J. Gaines grins when he's told that more and more professors are now analyzing his novels in their classrooms. "They think they know more about me than I do myself," he says.

His amusement is easy to understand. He knows he is hard to categorize.

Mr. Gaines has joined the canon of African-American literature, yet he credits 19th-century Russian writers with inspiring his work. He is a male writer at a time when the stars of black literature are women. His fans applaud his empathetic portrayals of black men, yet Mr. Gaines's best-known creation is a woman, the title character of ***The Autobiography of Miss Jane Pittman.*** His novels unflinchingly portray the viciousness of white racism, yet faculty members say one reason they teach his works is that white students identify with the black characters.

Even classifying Mr. Gaines geographically is more difficult than it should be—considering that all of his fiction takes place in a county modeled on his birth-place of Pointe Coupée Parish in Louisiana. For although he spends each fall teaching at the nearby University of Southwestern Louisiana, he has written nearly every word of his eight books in San Francisco.

"I've been called a Southern writer who happened to live in the West, a California writer who writes about the South, a black writer, a Louisiana writer," Mr. Gaines says. "I don't know where I fit in and I don't give a damn."

Where Mr. Gaines fits in, increasingly, is in the nation's classrooms. Since its publication in 1971, ***Miss Jane Pittman*** has been widely taught in history and literature classes alike. Other Gaines works have also claimed students' and teachers' imaginations, especially ***A Gathering of Old Men*** and the short stories in ***Bloodline.***

Now, however, teaching Gaines may take off.

In the last year, his stock in academe shot up when he won one of the so-called genius awards given by the John D. and Catherine T. MacArthur Foundation.

He also won the National Book Critics Circle Award for his latest novel, ***A Lesson Before Dying.*** When Vintage brings out that book in paperback next month [June 1994], it is expected to start showing up on course reading lists as well. Selections from Mr. Gaines's work will be included in forthcoming anthologies of African-American literature from both McGraw-Hill and Norton, and he is already included in *The Heath Anthology of American Literature.*

Mr. Gaines's work is taught most often in literature classes, sometimes in survey courses and other times in specialized seminars on black or Southern writing. But other disciplines are also using his novels. John M. Grady, for example, teaches ***A Gathering of Old Men*** in a sociology class at Wheaton College (Mass.) to examine black-white relations.

Why has interest in teaching Mr. Gaines's work grown so rapidly?

"He is an extraordinary writer, and his compassion for both the victims and the victimizers in his books is outstanding," says Bernard W. Bell, a professor of English at Pennsylvania State University and author of the introduction to Mr. Gaines's writings in the McGraw-Hill anthology.

Mr. Bell says that Mr. Gaines's work is as important as his better-known contemporaries, such as Toni Morrison and Alice Walker. It could rise in public consciousness if more people—and professors—were willing to explore more than just a few black authors, he says.

At a time when racial tensions are simmering on many campuses, professors also say that his novels seem to inspire frank discussion among black and white students.

"My students are overwhelmingly middle-class whites, and sometimes I find that there are cultural reasons that prevent them from assimilating some work," says Cedric Gael Bryant, associate professor of English at Colby College. "But with Gaines there is an immediate identification, because he deals with timeless themes: love and hate and courage."

Lawrence Rodgers, a professor of English at Kansas State University, says the students in his African-American literature class—about half of whom are black and half are white—always respond well to ***A Gathering of Old Men.*** "I almost always teach that book last, but students who by that time in the semester are fairly grumpy about everything find that they just can't put it down."

He says the book affirms "the non-hierarchical traditions" in which black citizens worked together to help each other. The story tells how a group of old black men all claim responsibility for the killing of a cruel white man as a means of protecting the person who actually did it.

In the style of Faulkner, the story is told through the voices of those men and others—black and white, heroes and villains—who view the scene. "Gaines's ability to get inside white Southerners' heads is nothing short of phenomenal," Mr. Rodgers adds.

In largely black courses, too, faculty members report strong connections between their students and Mr. Gaines's characters. Willa G. Lowe is a professor of English at historically black Stillman College. She says her students focus on "the strong bonds among families, which are a great part of the African-American tradition."

Mr. Gaines's characters also inspire her students by the way they handle challenges, she says. "He writes about people who have been held back for so long, but have to make a positive statement about themselves before they leave this world."

Mr. Gaines's latest work, ***A Lesson Before Dying,*** deals with that issue explicitly. It is the story of Jefferson, a black man in late-1940's Louisiana who is about to be executed for a crime he didn't commit. Jefferson's lawyer—pleading unsuccessfully for his client's life before an all-white jury—argues that Jefferson is less than human. "I would just as soon put a hog in the electric chair as this," the lawyer says. That comment prompts Jefferson's godmother to recruit a young, cynical teacher, fresh out of a black college, to visit Jefferson in jail and teach him enough so that he can face death as a man.

What it means to be a man is at the heart of much of Mr. Gaines's work. In the short story **"The Sky Is Gray,"** a young boy describes the day his mother saves up enough money to take him to town to see a dentist for his toothache. Through the boy's eyes, the reader sees the mother imparting her values of responsibility and dignity.

The Autobiography of Miss Jane Pittman deals with similar themes as it tracks the treatment of blacks from the end of slavery to the start of the civil-rights movement.

Mr. Gaines says these themes come out of his earliest memories of growing up in Louisiana. Born in 1933, he was raised on a plantation with 11 younger siblings. "We didn't have running water, and my responsibility from the time I was 8 years old was to get the water. By the time I was 11 or 12 I was going out with my father to saw wood."

An aunt, Augusteen Jefferson, helped raise the large family, even though, for reasons nobody knew, she was unable to walk. "What I learned from her was a tremendous amount of discipline. She cooked for us and cleaned for us, even though she couldn't walk," he says. "We would bring her things and she would work at a little table and crawl around."

Mr. Gaines dedicated ***The Autobiography of Miss Jane Pittman*** to that aunt, who, he wrote, "did not walk a day in her life, but who taught me the importance of standing."

His aunt's disability also helped spur Mr. Gaines's writing. Since she couldn't move, friends would come to their small house and sit on the porch to talk. Hearing those stories, Mr. Gaines says, he picked up on the black oral tradition, which he mines for his novels.

Mr. Gaines picked up still more stories as a youth because he was known for being smart, and illiterate older people had him read and write letters for them.

At 15, he moved with his family to California, where he eventually enrolled at San Francisco State University and decided to become a writer. As he read American literature there in the mid-1950's, he found little that spoke to his experience. "I didn't read a single black author there. The only black character I knew was Othello, and he had been written by a white guy 300 years earlier."

Eventually, he was drawn to the 19th-century Russian writers, especially Dostoyevsky, Tolstoy, and Turgenev. The Russians attracted him because their portrayals of serfs were more realistic than anything he read by American writers about poor or black people.

Hemingway also made a lasting impact. Says Mr. Gaines: "I keep telling black students when I visit schools to read Hemingway to see how he writes about grace under pressure. No one has been under more pressure than blacks and not too many groups have come through as gracefully as we have."

Mr. Gaines says he realizes his views may not be popular with those who criticize the teaching of works by "dead white men." But he says that the push to add non-white writers to the curriculum, which he applauds, becomes foolish when it becomes a battle against everyone who was in the traditional canon.

"I think those dead white men should be read, but live black men and women should be read, too," he says. "I would tell any student to read Tolstoy, to read Twain, to read Hemingway, Shakespeare. I say, 'Read it. It can't hurt you.' "

All of his reading, combined with a writing fellowship in 1958 at Stanford University, started Mr. Gaines on his own career. His first novel, ***Catherine Carmier,*** was published in 1964 and he has steadily followed that with more work.

While Mr. Gaines always returned to Louisiana for visits, he made it his home base again in 1984, when he became a professor of English at the University of Southwestern Louisiana. The university approached him, he says, with the best deal possible: He teaches writing every fall and has the rest of the year for his novels. His students praise his patience. Some take his seminar many times.

Mr. Gaines says that teaching may slow down his writing, but he thinks that is a plus. He took seven years to write ***A Lesson Before Dying.*** "I probably would have written it much faster if I hadn't been teaching, but it probably wouldn't have had things that it has now."

Saying that he is "never in a hurry," Mr. Gaines writes his books out longhand and does extensive interviews to supplement his own experiences. For ***A Lesson Before Dying,*** he interviewed small-town sheriffs about their work and talked to death-row lawyers to learn about the impact of working with someone facing execution.

With the success of that book and his recent MacArthur grant, other universities have come courting, but Mr. Gaines says he is committed to Southwestern Louisiana and hopes to teach there for another 10 years before retiring. For now, he is battling carpal-tunnel syndrome through physical therapy so he can get to work on his next project: three novellas.

Two of the novellas will deal with an issue Mr. Gaines has touched on in previous work, the relationships between lighter- and darker-skinned black people. The third, tentatively titled *The Man Who Whipped Children,* will be about a black man on a plantation to whom parents went for help in disciplining their children.

The key to his success as a writer, he says, and what he hopes college students get from his work, is an appreciation of humanity. "I try to use characters whom people can identify with, and then put those characters in situations where people can think they might act the same way," he says.

"Of course the experience of my characters has been as a result of the color of their skin, but there is something deeper than that inside of us. They are black characters, but I aim at a humanity that makes them much more than the color of their skin."

Additional coverage of Gaines's life and career is contained in the following sources published by Gale Research: *Authors in the News,* Vol. 1; *Black Literature Criticism; Black Writers,* Vol. 2; *Concise Dictionary of American Literary Biography, 1968-1988; Contemporary Authors,* Vol. 9-12, rev. ed.; *Contemporary Authors New Revision Series,* Vols. 6, 24, and 42; *Contemporary Literary Criticism,* Vols. 3, 11, and 18; *Dictionary of Literary Biography,* Vols. 2 and 33; *Dictionary of Literary Biography Yearbook, 1980;* and *Major 20th-Century Writers.*

James Kelman
How Late It Was, How Late

Award: Booker Prize for Fiction

Born in 1946, Kelman is a Scottish novelist, short story writer, essayist, and dramatist.

For further information on Kelman's life and works, see *CLC,* Volume 58.

INTRODUCTION

How Late It Was, How Late (1994) concerns an unemployed, working-class Glaswegian named Sammy, an ex-convict who runs into trouble with the law while on a drunken binge. After being arrested and beaten by police, Sammy wakes up in a jail cell to discover that he is blind and unable to account for all the events that occurred between the onset of his binge and regaining consciousness. Described as both Kafkaesque and Joycean, the novel employs stream-of-consciousness and third-person narrative techniques, relating Sammy's passive attempts to deal with his blindness and his ruminations about his life and Scottish society. Although the work does not overtly concern itself with political themes, the relationship between the Scottish government and its working-class constituents as well as the relationship between Scotland and England are central to Sammy's observations. While praised for his psychological portrait of a working-class Scotsman and his focus on oppression, Kelman has been both lauded and castigated for his use of obscenity and dialogue in the novel. Noting that Kelman's excessive use of vulgarity and sexual references occasionally results in "a piling up of inarticulacies," Adam Mars-Jones has nevertheless asserted that "Glasgow speech and the attitudes it embodies are holy to this writer. To describe the local tongue as the language of resistance would be to understate [Kelman's] view of it; it is a language of truth in revelation."

PRINCIPAL WORKS

Not Not While the Giro, and Other Stories (short stories) 1983
The Busconductor Hines (novel) 1984
A Chancer (novel) 1985
Greyhound for Breakfast (short stories) 1987
A Disaffection (novel) 1989
The Burn (novel) 1992
Some Recent Attacks: Essays Cultural and Political (essays) 1992
How Late It Was, How Late (novel) 1994

CRITICISM

Brian Morton (review date 18 March 1994)

SOURCE: "Out of Sight," in *New Statesman & Society,* Vol. 7, No. 294, March 18, 1994, p. 56.

[*In the following, Morton offers a favorable review of* How Late It Was, How Late, *discussing Kelman's use of language and his focus on the dispossessed.*]

If fantasy is to be something other than mere wish-fulfilment, it requires a measure of resistance: either some collision with the boundaries of the actual, or else the resistance of language itself. Hubert Selby Junior's *The Room* offers an extreme example. A prisoner incarcerated in his own unconscious spins violent sexual fantasies in language that remains morbidly inchoate, without hope of redemption or escape.

James Kelman's new novel [***How Late It Was, How Late***] works fascinating variations on the same basic situation. The difference is that Sammy enjoys a measure of ambiguous freedom. He is sprung from custody in a cat-and-mouse exercise designed to get at something juicier than the mild duck-and-dive recidivism that has been Sammy's livelihood for years. The fundamental irony is that, while in the care of the "sodjers", Sammy has become blind.

One Sunday morning he wakes up, down a lane with a two-day hangover. Pulled in, he takes a routine kicking and a token spell in the lock-up before being released into a world that quite suddenly has been stripped of all familiar reference points: pubs, people, the sure connection of words and things. The flat is empty, his girlfriend gone with only the dim recollection of a row, and Sammy is unable to give a "satisfactory" account of his whereabouts on given days.

Unusually for Kelman, Sammy's CV is kept pretty thin. It is a recurring feature of his contacts with authority (both judicial and medical) that he is only "written up" in accordance with roles assigned to him by them. Kelman is unwilling to overplay the "Kafka" hand (a fashionable designation again), but there is a bleak comedy in Sammy's situation and sufficient vagueness in background events to suggest a grim futuristic scenario. Are the police only "soldiers" colloquially? Who are the "politicals" being sought?

Blindness offers a predicament in which language becomes more than usually sensitised. The tenor is much as usual for Kelman. Paragraphs drift away with a muttered "fucking" and an unpunctuated silence beyond. In the interrogation room, Sammy often fails to realise he is being addressed. The dialogue is peppered with silent ellipses. Questions are pursued in the brutally condescending third person ratified by police procedurals: "Mr Samuels doesn't seem to remember", "he", "him", "the customer". Even people who haven't been inside know the cops talk like this.

Dickens repented sharply of depriving his narrator of her sight. Kelman pushes it as far as it will go. His political agenda concerns social invisibility, the gaps in the netting through which people fall, the jeopardies of casual self-definition. There are brilliant cameos of form-filling, laden with jobsworth literalisms like "now what it says here" or "you've got to be one or the other".

Kelman is a passionately humane writer and a natural libertarian. The two don't always occur together. In all his fiction so far, and here centrally, he champions the dispossessed and the overlooked with unsentimental urgency. The novel's last words are "out of sight".

Ian Bell relating Kelman's belief in the political dangers of writing:

Write a book, [Kelman] says, on whatever subject you choose—South Africa, Aids, drugs, someone dying of asbestos disease—and you will be regarded as part of the establishment, as one of the perpetrators of the crimes. 'Their act of fellowship with the writer is a kind of appropriation, a method of extending domination over the subject, as if they also owned the experience of the novel. It's a kind of continuing disenfranchisement.'

Ian Bell, in his "Four Letter Truths," in The Observer, *March 27, 1994.*

Adam Mars-Jones (review date 1 April 1994)

SOURCE: "In Holy Boozers," in *The Times Literary Supplement,* No. 4748, April 1, 1994, p. 20.

[*Mars-Jones is an English critic, editor, and short story writer. In the mixed review below, he offers a thematic and stylistic discussion of* How Late It Was, How Late, *noting Kelman's political and linguistic focus.*]

When Julius Caesar taught himself to read without reading aloud—to safeguard military secrets—it was regarded as a troubling innovation. The general had taken language inside his head and made it private. Since then the scars of separation have long healed, but there persists at the back of some minds a fantasy of reunion: writing returning to the womb of speech.

In James Kelman's fiction, this fantasy of a defiant wholeness has a political agenda superimposed on it, which seems compatible but actually clashes: that of giving a voice to the voiceless, those whom society and literature ignore. Even this ambition is more alienated than it seems, since giving someone a voice implies the same power relation as taking a voice away, and restoring a voice to its throat is not a possibility but a dream of healing. Still, it's the way Kelman's two projects, the linguistic and the political, work against each other on the page that makes his writing so hard to enjoy—being brutally frank, so hard to read—and so much easier to praise instead.

It is no news that Kelman is an outstandingly negative writer, whose instinct is to fight deprivation with deprivation (a characteristic that colours even titles like ***Not not while the giro*** and ***A Disaffection***), but with ***How late it was, how late,*** the hefty new instalment of Strathclyde *arte povera,* he has set a new standard for himself.

His hero, Sammy, has no job and no home. He stays with his girlfriend Helen, but for the length of the book she is missing. This absence may be a judgment on Sammy or something more sinister (we never learn which). Sammy is missing something even more crucial to his welfare—his eyesight, lost perhaps for ever in the course of police interrogation. He was arrested after picking a fight on the street, while on the rebound from a drunken binge which cost him the memory of an entire day.

Missing Saturday, missing Helen, missing sight. This narrative of subtractions comes perilously close to being a subtraction of narrative. With sensory deprivation added to social, Sammy's unilluminated head, which is where we spend the whole book, is only fitfully a stimulating place to be. The most striking absentee, the most mourned by the reader, is ambient Glasgow, present only in shadowy memories, or muffled episodes of abrasive kindness.

Interior monologue is a highly artificial way of representing the mind's activity as speech, most effectively used as one element of a compound style. Served up raw and in quantity, unsustained by the world, it is highly indigestible. Kelman's dialogue positively skips along under the reader's eyes but there's not a great deal of it; Sammy's monologue is a long and weary trudge.

There is plenty of third-person in the book, but it brings with it no supplementary perspective and amounts to an alienated first. Cheating slightly, Kelman introduces the lyrics of country and western songs, laid out as poetry, for borrowed emotional resonance.

The few incidents of the novel could easily be accommodated in a short story; it can hardly be said that Kelman exploits the possibilities of the ampler genre. He establishes the seriousness of his project by brute duration, as if any invocation of the formal resources of the novel would sell Sammy into the slavery of writing.

For Kelman, authorial distance seems to be a form of literary imperialism. It is certainly an illusion, but so to be sure is the supersession of the author by his creature. In the first sentence of ***How late it was, how late,*** for instance, Kelman uses six semi-colons and a single colon, a near-exquisite piece of stopping that belongs to a different world from Sammy's. This other world is one which, among other things, would make political analysis possible. All Sammy can do is exemplify the sufferings of his region, his history and his class. The fact that his stoicism, a virtue on the personal level, is from a different point of view a guarantee that he will remain in his place, is an irony the book refuses to house.

Sammy drinks only a few pints in the course of the book, but whenever the characters refer to drinking establishments, their names (and nothing else in the book) are put into italics, like saints' names in a family Bible, or churches in Baedeker. It seems a curious form of bad faith for the author to vanish stridently from his text, while lingering slyly in nuances of punctuation, and in the respectful alcoholism of his italics.

For the first 200 pages of the book, before Sammy starts to re-enter the world around him, the reader has little to engage with beyond the authenticity of his language. Sometimes the effect is deliberately flat: "So all in all he had entered a new epoch on life's weary trail." Sometimes there is a dark flicker of wit: "Waiting rooms. Ye go into this room where ye wait. Hoping's the same. One of these days the cunts'll build entire fucking buildings just for that. Official hoping rooms, where ye just go in and hope for whatever the fuck ye feel like hoping for. One on every corner. Course they had them already: boozers."

Most often, though, the language is half-dead, half-alive, undeterred by the speaker's sudden sobriety (Sammy's blindness imposes a virtual house arrest) from bar-room philosophizing. Too much of the book is only kept by the prestige of dialect from sounding like banality or Beckett: "Ye just battered on, that was what ye did man ye battered on. What else can ye do? There's nothing else"; "Life, man, full of misunderstandings; nay cunt knows what ye're meaning"; "Ye blunder on and ye blunder on. That's what ye do"; "Life. Life could have been worse"; "Ye made wrong moves in life. It couldn't be denied"; "It was an effort. Life. That was how ye had to keep going."

On one singular occasion Kelman seeks to demonstrate that the acrid tang of Glasgow speech is not synonymous with benighted social attitudes. The subject is women:

> Ye wonder what they see in as well I mean being honest; men—christ almighty, a bunch of dirty bastards, literally, know what I'm talking about, sweaty socks and all that, smelly underpants. Course they've got nay choice, no unless maybe they're lesbian, then ye get tits bouncing against each other and it's all awkward and bumpy; same if it's guys, cocks and legs banging—that was what happened inside once, this guy that fancied Sammy trying to give him a kind of cuddle christ it was weird, fucking rough chins and these parts of yer body knocking the gether, yer knees as well man ye were aware of it, how ye didnay seem to merge right, maybe for the other thing but no cuddling, the guy actually said that to him he says, Sammy ye're holding me like a woman, I'm no a woman. Fine; fair enough, but how were ye supposed to do it, cause he hadnay wanted to hurt the guy, he liked him, know what I'm saying, he was a nice guy and aw that. Fucking hell man, life, difficult.

This passage of surrealistic liberalism from a narrator of considerable reflex belligerence can be put down to authorial wishful thinking, the strained neutrality of the word "merge" in this register its give-away.

In general, though, Glasgow speech and the attitudes it embodies are holy to this writer. To describe the local tongue as the language of resistance would be to understate his view of it; it is a language of truth in revelation. To most readers, admittedly, the words "bampot", "clatty" and "bammycain" will seem superior to the words "tosser", "dirty" and "nuthouse", either for reasons of regional loyalty or novelty. But are they really reliably superior, a million times better, enough to justify their constant incantatory repetition?

It is a paradoxical position, to feel that everything about people's lives can be corrupted or fouled except their speech, particularly when their speech is so freighted with *fucks,* adjectival *fucks,* adverbial *fucks* ("as *x* as fuck", "like fuck"), interpolated *fucks* ("enerfuckinggetic, enerfuckinggetised"), *fuck* cadenzas: "lonely, just fucking lonely, lonely lonely fucking lonely, lonely; that was his wife, lonely"; "That was the fucking story. Just as well she had went afore this, afore this fucking shit man this fucking blind shit, fucking blind blind blind fucking blind man blind a fucking blind bastard."

At moments like these, Kelman's aim as a writer—which might be imagined expressed as *no authority but in authenticity*—leads him into producing something curiously unaffecting, a piling up of inarticulacies. His prose becomes something to be consumed dutifully, not emetic or stimulant but good for you: cod liver oil. In his theology, the opposite of England/book/death is *Scotland, voice* and *life*. Yet a voice on the page is no longer a voice. Strange that he leaves it there stranded, and the reader stranded too.

Eric Jacobs (review date 2 April 1994)

SOURCE: "Eyeless and Legless in Glasgow," in *The Spectator,* Vol. 272, No. 8647, April 2, 1994, pp. 33-4.

[*In the review below, Jacobs provides an unfavorable assessment of* How Late It Was, How Late.]

[***How Late It was, How Late***] is not reader-friendly. Its 374 pages are not divided into parts or chapters. The only intervals in the text at which to take a much needed breather are infrequent double spaces between paragraphs, which mostly end with full stops, but sometimes don't.

Not that this joined up format is inappropriate, for we are in stream-of-consciousness country here. Sammy is a Glaswegian in his thirties with a long stretch in prison and some shorter stretches labouring on building sites behind him. He is currently living off social security, plus whatever else he can lay his hands on, including the flat of a girlfriend called Helen who is continuously expected but fails to show up throughout the length of the book. Wise woman.

Sammy goes on a two-day drinking binge, comes to in surprisingly good nick, picks a fight with some passing soldiers—'sodjers' to Sammy—and winds up in a police station, from which he somehow emerges blind. For the remaining 300-odd pages he struggles to cope with this unexpected disability.

The physical side of things Sammy, in fact, handles rather well. In no time at all he is rolling his own cigarettes, making himself cups of tea and opening tins in Helen's flat. It is life he can't handle. Sammy is a hopeless case, a loser for whom blindness seems not much of a handicap on top of all the others.

By rendering Sammy sightless, and therefore even more at the mercy of circumstance than he would ordinarily be, Mr Kelman surely invites us to apply the dread adjective 'Kafkaesque' to his situation. And by letting most of the action happen inside Sammy's head he just as surely invokes that other adjective to make one wary, 'Joycean'. One of these is enough for any novel to live with; two undoubtedly a surfeit.

There is a novel to be written about the Glasgow no-hoper: drunken, feckless, wandering, unable to hold on to a job or a woman, doomed to live off the meagre pickings of crime and the social services, and Mr Kelman is probably the person to write it. He understands his man. What he has actually written, however, is all too like an encounter in a Glasgow pub when you are sober and the man who buttonholes you is seriously drunk. He jabs you in the chest, blows smoke in your face, dribbles his drink all over and rambles incoherently on. F—is the most used word in his vocabulary, serving promiscuously as noun, adjective, verb and adverb. He laughs wheezily at his own jokes, which leave you cold when you can follow them. After not much of this, like Sammy, you want to run.

I see [literature] as a form of art and all that that entails. A lot of ritualistic behaviour that goes on in the literary establishment, it's charades, really. It's a form of colonisation, or a form of imperialism, and one of the effects of that is colonisation.

—James Kelman, in an interview with Ian Bell, in his "Four Letter Truths," in* The Observer, *March 27, 1994.

Andrew O'Hagan (review date 26 May 1994)

SOURCE: "The Paranoid Sublime," in *London Review of Books,* Vol. 16, No. 10, May 26, 1994, pp. 8-9.

[*In the following, O'Hagan offers a mixed assessment of* How Late It Was, How Late, *discussing the book's relationship to Kelman's other works and noting Kelman's preoccupation with politics, oppression, and the Scottish working class.*]

It was getting dark one sulphurous evening in Glasgow in the winter of 1990, when a pop-eyed cultural apparatchik—almost breathlessly ripe from a Chinese paper-lantern parade she'd just led through the naked streets of Carntyne—sat down beside me in a bar to the side of the City Chambers, to gab about the glories and horrors of Glasgow's reign as European City of Culture for that year. The city's better writers, it seemed, would have nothing to do with it. The £50 million jamboree, led by the municipal council, set its sights on ridding the city once and for ever of its razor-slashing, wife-battering, whisky-guzzling image; all to be blown away during a year-long bonanza; of painting and singing and exotic tumbling; with street-sweeping Bolivian choristers at the crack of dawn; with face-painting schools and afternoons of community theatre on Glasgow Green; and an evening of carry-on in the company of Pavarotti at 75 quid a throw. My bar companion flushed as she coasted through the vodkas, saying how pointless and infuriating it was that the better writers—whom we may as well call James Kelman, Alasdair Gray and Tom Leonard among others—wouldn't join in on the song. 'It's their loss,' she said. 'I mean, what do they want?'

A fairly good idea of what they wanted could be gleaned at that time from a visit to the Scotia Bar in Stockwell Street, where the dissidents met now and then to read their work and shout down the official festival. The group adopted the name Workers' City—which spelled out their opposition to that recently developed area around Blackfriars and Ingram Street known as Merchant City—and set about picketing some events and speaking and writing against them, convinced that most were a costly irrelevance and an insult to the real cultural and economic concerns of the majority of people living in the city. The producers of 'Glasgow's Glasgow', a hi-tech exhibition intended to celebrate Glasgow's social history, erected video displays in neon-lit cabinets, voice-responsive computers and the like, and installed them in a warren of renovated arches under a railway bridge by Central Station.

Workers' City reserved particular scorn for this place (which proved in the end to be a financial fiasco) and saw it only as an attempt by the Labour-run council to paint out Glasgow's less glossy history, the history, and actual situation, of most of its population. For their part, the festival organisers—like my tottering friend on the bar stool—came to believe the inhabitants of Workers' City were just unruly bores, spoil-sports and pains-in-the-arse; James Kelman later noted how he and his pals were described as 'misfits, dilettanti, well-heeled authors and critics; professional whingers, crypto-communists, self-proclaimed anarchists' and so on.

This animus is never unusual in Glasgow. In fact it's rather typical there—many of the worlds within Glasgow have spun, and continue to spin, on popular resentments to do with what kind of team you prefer or school you went to or street you live in or jumper you wear. And James Kelman, in his fiction, has concentrated on lives fully burdened with as many constantly disabling dislikes. But Glaswegian animus is not his subject; he would appear to have bigger fritters to fry.

Kelman's sense—his public position, if you like—is that his people, the particular underclass he writes about and has been part of, is a class of people whose internal differences melt away under the one Great Anglo-American Conglomerate of Establishment-and-Institutionally-Vested-Interests on Behalf of Imperialism, Racism and Associated Bad-Eggery. The message has been constantly, and often magically, clear: what the ex-working classes do to each other is one thing and bad enough—but nothing could ever match for badness what the big 'They' do to all of us together. Kafka's notion of the omnipotent state which could dispense with the nameless as a matter of whim, seems almost cosily camp next to Kelman's brutal Conspiracy of Universal Authorities bent on oppressing the Glasgow poor.

Sammy, the semi-wino whose person and consciousness lie at the centre of Kelman's new novel [***How late it was, how late***], wakes up in a police cell with a pounding head, a bruised one that carries no memory of how he got there and what the hell happened to his shoes. And he's stone blind. He sort of remembers a slippery scene, some altercation, out in the street, where he belted a copper ('a beautiful left cross man he fucking onered him one'); the coppers got a hold of him, and they most probably cuffed him and beat him, though he's not so sure of that. He knows he's lost a complete day, all day Saturday, since he went out on the razzle on Friday and was jailed Friday night. Once released, he starts groping his way down the road, slapping the walls with his palms to get some sense of where things are, though he has no clear idea of how to get home. He can hear, he thinks he can hear, people gibbering as they walk past:

> Mutter mutter. Somebody next to him. People going by. Fuck the people going by.
>
> Dear o dear he was stranded he was just bloody stranded. Bastards. Fucking bastards. Fucking joke. Fucking bastards. Sodjer fucking bastards. Sammy knew the fucking score. He knew the fucking score. He gulped; his mouth was dry, he coughed; catarrh; he bent his head and let it spill out his mouth to the pavement. He was still leaning against the window, now he pushed himself away. A groaning sound from the glass. He stepped sideways. He needed a fucking smoke, he needed a seat, a rest. This was crazy man it was fucking diabolical.

Once back in his flat, Sammy gets to grips with his new condition quicker than you might expect. (But then his demands are few: he maps out in his head the journeys he will have to make: 'the minimarket, the betting shop, the chemist. All the necessities. The local boozer stood by itself round the corner from there.') His girlfriend Helen is nowhere to be seen, and there's no sign of her even at the novel's end. He plays country tapes when feeling sorry for himself, makes a blind stick by cutting the head off a mop; still talking to himself in the old familiar way, he gasps for a fag, thinks of bumming one off his neighbour, hears music coming through the ceiling.

This stuff is close to perfect: Kelman identifies with characters like Sammy, he always has done, and he can slip first-person perceptions and psychological tics into a third-person narrative in an astonishing way. For someone who's made such a palaver about ways of talking, about speech I mean, he's actually not so very good at dialogue (not when you think of Peter McDougall or Roddy Doyle). It's the way people talk to themselves that he gets so brilliantly, so matchlessly. While the peripheral characters in his stories often exchange words in a pretty featureless manner, his central characters have always had a wonderful way with words, with parts of words and myriad inflections of the same word, as they form themselves inside their own heads.

The best bits of ***How late it was, how late*** contain a kind of mental vaudeville that brings Kelman's way with interior monologue to a point of precision beyond any he has reached before. Those who see what he does as a continuation of a European and existentialist tradition of fiction-writing will find the evidence for it here, among the talking mirrors embedded in those parts of the narrative most closely to do with Sammy's mind:

> He lay there all warm and comfy, the world gone, all the trials and tribulations, out the fucking window, just him existing in the middle of a massive big ocean, a wee toty island, just lying there, a whale drifting by, the mind getting set off by the music, it was some kind of christian thing for christ sake that was the fucking problem with country man it was like the sally army ye had to put up with god for a fucking half hour, ye heard good fiddles and banjos and it turned out to be a jesus-love-me effort
>
> never mind, never mind; ye let it go and ye stop fucking

> ye stop
>
> Aaahhh—the only problem being how ye're so vulnerable, just so relaxed, the ideal time for some cunt to reach ye—how easy it was, the ideal time, the ideal place, and he didnay have one weapon to hand; not one.

The narrator in Kelman's story **"By the Burn"**, a man on his way to an interview who stops on the bank of a stream and just stands staring, overcome by a cold tremor which brings to him the memory of his daughter, who died in a sandpit over by the other bank, is not unlike Sammy. Nor is Tammas, the signing-on gambler and lover and leaver in Kelman's second novel, ***A Chancer,*** or Patrick Doyle, the floundering schoolteacher in ***A Disaffection,*** who blows into a pair of industrial pipes he finds at the back of a club, captivated and comforted by their moaning. Like all these others, Sammy is the kind of man Kelman can commune with unreservedly—a very particular kind of Scottish man, of Kelman's age (48) or somewhere near it, who might steep his feet, then cut his toe-nails onto newspaper laid out on the living-room carpet; someone who will place a bet; who'll drink halves of whisky mixed with water, sometimes pints; one who'll be proud, who'll be on the dole or else hate the work they do; who'll loathe the police; who'll roll their own; who'll be good with money when they've got it, like Charles Donald in **"An Old Pub near the Angel"**, who gets some unexpected back-money from the broo and goes off smiling and waving to everyone, and buying them drink. It is the kind of man many of us grew up beside: one who's cantankerously knowing about what he knows, who's scornful of what he doesn't, and who never tires of telling people—especially people who also happen to be the wife—about the nature of other people's stupidity. Helen, who'd been giving Sammy the silent treatment before getting off her mark and leaving him, was, you might imagine, the kind of woman who has lived exclusively in step with her man's moods, habits and prejudices, one of those women whose lives are constituted by the paranoid behaviour of their men.

The Kelman man is a regular type, a person from Glasgow life, who comes to embody his author's political concerns. Both the type and the concerns are specific: they don't stand, as they're often called upon to do, for any contemporary group or new universality. Kelman has long been imagined, and has sometimes imagined himself, to represent and give voice to a whole class of the poor, located in Glasgow, who'd never effectively made it into fiction before. As far as such a thing suggests the kind of man I've been talking about, that is certainly true: Kelman has found a way into those heads in sometimes frighteningly original ways.

But Kelman-man is a working man from the days when the working classes could find work. Though his characters might also be out of work, and often hate what they do, the 'out of work' culture is clearly something quite different from what people leaving school now in Glasgow's housing schemes could recognise. Kelman brings to his writing priorities from another time, a time when working-class people worried about trade unions and overtime, demarcation and the futility of the work that they did. He mostly writes about a quite particular man of his own generation, someone who grows detached, gets disaffected, who might drink in the old way (who might even drink the old thing, like the infamous 'vino collapso' Lanny). He's a person who remembers the not-so-far-off days when hating your job and fucking off to Australia were the two biggest preoccupations you had.

Since 1980 (four years before the publication of Kelman's first novel, one year into Thatcher), drug-taking in housing schemes around Possilpark and Drumchapel—the very places you might find in Kelman's writing—has gone up by 700 per cent. Drugs are there to be seen, or got, in the playgrounds of some Glasgow schools. The growth of Aids in those places, the run of repossessions, the gangsterism, are all things that don't exist in the Glasgow of Kelman's underclass. The Glasgow housing schemes, and those which spread out around Glasgow, are not really the places of his writing, though they're generally thought to be. The experience of people who never expect to work again, of people, indeed, who leave school never having known what it's like to expect a job—these are people for whom Kelman's workerist lament might seem idealistic and alien even in the modes of its regret. Of course, no writer's to be blamed for their failure to write of things that don't concern or interest them. But Kelman in his paranoid essays, and his champions in their delirious reviews, too often deal in generalities when they speak of the denizens of working-class Glasgow: there is something spuriously lumpen about the groupings Kelman refers to, and something inattentive in his reckoning of their needs as far as he chooses to address them. It's not that he misrepresents the new non-workers or renders them in clichés as some writers do, it's simply that he doesn't *see* them in his fiction, though he chooses to speak on their behalf in his essays.

Some of the polemical dullness, at its most paranoid and ill-written in ***Some Recent Attacks: Essays Cultural and Political,*** unfortunately finds room in the novels. An indiscriminate loathing and distrust of officialdom, of inspectors and doctors, in ***The Bus Conductor Hines*** is very funny and very much part of the way the character Hines speaks in general, the way he describes himself and the world, especially when speaking to his son. But the DSS spooks, headmasters, pen-pushers and anyone-in-a-tie in his most recent fiction have been less and less funny, mere stooges, illustrations of an authorly idea. In ***How late it was, how late,*** Sammy—who comes loaded with nuance as one of Kelman's multi-dimensional traditional men—encounters a number of bureaucrats, all of whom are inordinately and absurdly irritating and unhelpful. He feels he's under surveillance since his mysterious doing-over by the police, someone might be keeping tabs on him, he may be bugged, the DSS bureaucrats note down everything he says—as does his doctor, a cardboard cut-out of a character whom Kelman figures as a kind of baby-eating monster from the CIA.

Sammy might have a claim for damages if he can prove he lost his sight in the police cells. He's pursued by a weirdo even more paranoid (again, with slightly less life) than himself, a guy with some typically vague way of obtaining private information, who aims to represent Sammy's claim against the dark knights of the state. The difference between Kafka's view of the state, or William Burroughs's or even George Orwell's, and that of James Kelman, is that Kelman believes his fiction offers a more or less literal depiction of how the state operates—it's not a surreal thing or a symbolic thing or a thing in the mind, for him it's an actuality. All the conspiratorial business in the new novel (the cover reproduces the sign you see on motorways to indicate that police cameras are in operation) takes us away time and again from Sammy's inner life and the way it alters and inflects the worlds around him.

Kelman wants to characterise the political antagonisms, the unknown powers, which oppress Sammy, but he can't come near to doing it convincingly, since Sammy's mysterious opponents are not people, not in the way he is; they are not from Glasgow or from anywhere else. They are deadening, posh-sounding caricatures, emanations from some malignant conglomeration of oppressive authorities. There is no energy or detail in the way they're represented—an absence the more remarkable in a novel where these things are so splendidly in evidence elsewhere. Kelman would appear to believe that his enemies, who are naturally the enemies of his central characters, are too inhumane to be rendered as regular humans committing inhumane acts.

James Kelman's most effective political act was, and is, his singular adaptation of the prose sentence to meet the demands of place and speech and, to a limited extent, economic reality on the west coast of Scotland. That's what he does best. At his worst, he indulges a series of paranoid fantasies—vague generalities which draw credibility from cases of negligence, fraud, mis-diagnosis, censorship and the like, all of which have firm bases in reality, but no relation to each other. He brings together any number of these institutional horror stories and fuck-ups, and banalises them to death. All this is done, we're to trust, on behalf of one or other of his favoured groupings, and done without much clear understanding of the evil institutions' specific natures or procedures or functions. You might be hard pushed to find anyone these days who didn't think the DSS and Scotland Yard and the BBC and the *Times* and the Department of Health, to name a few, are sometimes corrupt and irresponsible, but that's not the same as imagining them all to be in cahoots with each other, keen to oppress and flagellate and disenfranchise. This conspiracy guff—much like the habit of lumping a city's poor under one heading to be uniformly spoken for—comes about through a lazy philistinism and an illusion of subversion where the detail doesn't matter because it's all for the liberation of something good in the end. These broadsides, which Kelman drags out of his polemical essays and into his novels, contribute to a diminution of the complex lives actually being glanced off. This is from an essay titled **"English Literature and the Small Coterie"**, where Kelman writes of the failings of Salman Rushdie, in a way which might cause us to pause on his own technique:

> In a literary context one of the limited ways of using the stereotype technique creatively is to turn a prejudice on its head: the 'stereotyped' character is then revealed as an ordinary human being, with the specific qualities thereby demanded. Here the author of *The Satanic Verses* seems to me to fail too often for comfort and a case for 'insult' if not 'outrage' might conceivably be made by Afro-Caribbean black people, white working class people, people who have never received the benefits of higher education, people who 'do not speak properly' and people who look 'rat-faced' or 'piggy'. The work therefore contains a number of the stock characters and situations any politicised student of the English literary canon is well used to, and it places the novel in this mainstream. At schools and colleges and universities, in general, our students are taught *not to question* that such is the stuff of art. And if we genuinely demand free expression in our society then such stuff very often will be 'art'. It is within these terms that *The Satanic Verses* can be described as a good novel; perhaps ultimately, some would say, even a great one.
>
> . . . Apart from those who have described the novel as 'excellent', 'major', 'terrific', 'important', 'boring', 'bad', 'unreadable' etc, very little was heard from the literary establishment apart from spurious stuff to do with need to protect 'freedom of speech and expression'. This unwillingness or inability to examine the work in public is nothing short of pathetic. Yet it is quite understandable and not at all surprising. By implication such an undertaking would have been to examine not only the very ordinary human prejudice of the critics themselves, it would have been to expose the endemic racism, class bias and general élitism at the English end of the Anglo-American literary tradition.

At least when Hugh MacDiarmid published his late, late laments he could see the funny side, and had the good taste to call them things like 'England is our Enemy'.

The most interesting 'small coterie', incidentally, currently boiling its mighty stock in the literary hell-fires of London and Glasgow and Edinburgh, is the one which serves to promote Scottish writing. The much-hated 'literary establishment' could doubtless learn a thing or two about how to look after its own from the small crew of Scottish or Scots-loving novelists, poets, critics, publishers, journalists, booksellers and the rest, who enjoy nothing more than to pipe for their pals, with a wee blurb here and a dedication there (and don't be stuck if you need something drawn up for the cover, doll).

Kelman exists in close proximity to the people he sees himself writing about: he shares, as far as he can, in their struggles and speaks as they do. That's the kind of writer he is. So Kelman, you might think, is one who would recognise the folly in trying to shadow his people's sorry relationship with their non-elected government, in trying to shadow it, as he does, by claiming himself to be marginalised and excluded by a Literary and Cultural Government he neither knows nor sees, except when its derided representatives stand up to offer him prizes or praise. A writer who is compared, by all manner of people, to Beckett and Dostoevsky and Zola, who is nominated for literary prizes and published by mainstream publishers; who is on reading lists in universities all over the place; who'd be welcomed on many a cultural platform and be published by any good paper—such a writer, you might think, pays little respect to the reality of marginalised lives, to say nothing of censored artists, by so easily claiming for himself the status of underdog and enemy.

I recently took part in a television production devoted to Kelman's work. I arrived at the Glasgow production office when the film was more or less ready. There was a young woman there who was red-eyed and depleted from weeks of work on the programme; she'd clearly knocked her pan in trying to get it into some sort of decent shape, under the usual pressures. As I looked at her scurrying and typing and phoning and thinking, a guy told me of how they'd been fighting the executive, who'd only allow 17 'fucks' to be aired in the show. The tired woman and her colleagues had clearly fought for every one of them.

Then he told me of Mr Kelman, who gave the impression he was annoyed by the number of non-Scots working in the production office; so to save any trouble a Glaswegian boy was brought from downstairs, from another office, said my informer, just to sit and answer the phone in case He rang. Sometimes, when you ponder the power of the marginalised artist in this down-treading kingdom of ours, you have to laugh.

How Late It Was, How Late is a tour de force, both in its convincingly claustrophobic rendering of what it's like to be newly sightless and in its rhythmic prose, suggesting a Samuel Beckett nourished not on Proust and Joyce but on Waylon and Willie.

—David Gates, in his "Big Bummers from Britain," in* Newsweek, *January 23, 1995.

Sarah Lyall (essay date 29 November 1994)

SOURCE: "Booker Prize Winner Defends His Language," in *The New York Times,* November 29, 1994, pp. B1-B2.

[*In the essay below, Lyall comments on the controversy surrounding the Booker committee's decision to award Kelman the 1994 prize. She also discusses the impact of the prize on Kelman's life and relates his views on writing, literature, England, and the Scottish language.*]

No sooner had James Kelman's novel ***How Late It Was, How Late*** won this year's Booker Prize for fiction than a full scale furor erupted. One of the judges, Rabbi Julia Neuberger, declared that the book was unreadably bad and said that the awarding of the prize, Britain's most important, was a "disgrace." Simon Jenkins, a conservative columnist for *The Times* of London, called the award "literary vandalism." Several other critics sniped that the book should have been disqualified because of its heavy use of profanity.

Meanwhile, the British literary establishment huddled together defensively as Mr. Kelman appeared in a business suit at the black-tie Booker affair and, in his heavy Scottish accent, made a rousing case for the culture and language of "indigenous" people outside of London. "A fine line can exist between elitism and racism," he said. "On matters concerning language and culture, the distinction can sometimes cease to exist altogether."

Part stream of consciousness, part third-person narrative, sparsely punctuated, devoid of chapters and written entirely in the words and cadences of working-class Glasgow, ***How Late It Was, How Late*** does make for hard reading, which seems to explain some of the objections. But other critics have greeted the novel, the story of a down-and-out Glaswegian former convict who has a run-in with the police and wakes up to discover that he has suddenly gone blind, as a literary triumph.

Writing in *The Independent,* Janette Turner Hospital called Mr. Kelman a "poet and magician" and said the book was a "passionate, scintillating, brilliant song of a book."

It is nothing new for Mr. Kelman's work—which includes four other novels, a number of plays and about 100 short stories—to generate strong reactions, both for and against. He has been compared to James Joyce, to William Kennedy and to Samuel Beckett, but when the first Kelman short story was accepted by a magazine at York University in 1972, the printer refused to print it because of the profanity.

And in the mid-1970's, one publisher urged him to write more accessibly, saying, Mr. Kelman recalled in an interview in his home in a suburb of Glasgow, that "work written in Glaswegian dialect doesn't sell in America."

For the author, a slight man with haunting eyes and a grave manner that gives way easily to sardonic humor, the central issue is cultural imperialism through language. Recalling times when Glaswegian accents were banned from the radio, or when his two daughters were reprimanded in school for using the Scots "aye" instead of the English "yes," he said it was wrong to call the language of his work "vernacular" or "dialect."

"To me, those words are just another way of inferiorizing the language by indicating that there's a standard," he said. "The dictionary would use the term 'debased.' But it's the language! The living language, and it comes out of many different sources, including Scotland before the English arrived."

As angry as he might be about the criticisms, Mr. Kelman said that the Booker Prize had given him a useful opportunity to air his views about language and about the disenfranchised people who are his subjects. It has helped the book sell more than 20,000 copies in hard cover in Britain, and it certainly has raised the author's profile among pub-

Some people say my work has no value. They find a way of saying it's not literature, just oral tradition. Or perhaps that because you write from the point of view of people whose language is debased, then your language is debased, and therefore you're a debased writer, or really not a writer at all.

—James Kelman

lishers in the United States, where ***How Late It Was, How Late*** is to be published by W. W. Norton on Dec. 12.

The $30,000 prize has also had happy financial consequences for the often broke Mr. Kelman, who left school at the age of 15 and worked at a number of manual jobs even as he began writing some 20 years ago. Having spent his life in a series of apartments, he was able to move six months ago to a large house with its own garden. He has also invested in a new computer to replace his creaky grime-covered one, and his wife, a social worker for homeless people, has been able to reduce her working hours. What's more, Mr. Kelman said, the Booker brings a special kind of prestige to someone like him, one of a group of strong writers to emerge from Glasgow in recent years, including Jeff Torrington and Alasdair Gray.

"The meaning of the prize comes from other people," said Mr. Kelman, who chain-smokes cigarettes that he rolls himself. "I was aware of its importance from writers both from this community in Glasgow and the extended community in Scotland, and also other communities that you could say were in similar situations. Friends of mine who are Afro-Caribbean or from India or Pakistan, or Irish or American people, said they were amazed, astonished and delighted that this statement could have been made from the center of the city of London."

Particularly annoying to Mr. Kelman (although Mr. Kelman does his best not to look annoyed) has been the renewed criticism that his writing is shoddy and somehow subliterary. Referring to Mr. Kelman's protagonist and narrator, Sammy, Mr. Jenkins of *The Times,* for instance, said the book represented "the ramblings of a Glaswegian drunk." And another journalist took it upon himself to count how many times a particular obscenity appeared in ***How Late It Was,*** arriving at the impressive number of 4,000.

"Some people say my work has no value," Mr. Kelman said. "They find a way of saying it's not literature, just oral tradition. Or perhaps that because you write from the point of view of people whose language is debased, then your language is debased, and therefore you're a debased writer, or really not a writer at all."

"I've won a major prize before," he went on, referring to the James Tait Black Memorial Prize, which he won in 1989 for his novel ***A Disaffection,*** "and one of the people associated with it asked me if I ever revised my work."

Yes, Mr. Kelman said, he does revise, even more so because the language he uses is so singular. Well into his cigarette, perhaps his 10th in two hours, he launched into a fierce defense.

"In order to fight against the house style you have to justify every single comma," he said. "Every comma in my work is my comma. Every absence of a comma or full stop or semicolon or colon is my absence. You have to be much more precise and bloody pedantic. You have to revise and revise and proof at every bloody stage to insure that everything's spot on, especially because you're working in what other people regard as inconsistent ways, so you have to be really sure."

He stamped the cigarette out and began to roll another one. "You have to trust the fact that you're a writer."

Michiko Kakutani (review date 16 December 1994)

SOURCE: "Profane Wandering within the Idioms of Glasgow," in *The New York Times,* December 16, 1994, p. B8.

[*In the following, Kakutani offers a negative appraisal of* How Late It Was, How Late, *lamenting Kelman's reliance on profanity and portrait of a passive character.*]

How to describe James Kelman's new novel, ***How Late It Was, How Late?*** Think of one of Nathanael West's black comedies without the humor, combined with one of David Mamet's obscenity-laced plays without the poetry, combined with one of Samuel Beckett's novels without the philosophical subtext, and that should give you a pretty good idea of what this year's winner of the Booker Prize in Britain is like.

When the novel won that prestigious award this fall, there was an uproar in London, where detractors assailed the book's heavy use of profanity and its highly discursive narrative set down in Glaswegian slang.

As its critics claim, ***How Late It Was*** does indeed boast an amazing number of variations on a certain four-letter word: a word used, as many as 25 times a page, as all-purpose noun and adjective, adverb and verb. Take, for instance, the following expurgated passage:

> "[*Expletive deleted*] Charlie! Yedidnay [*expletive deleted*] need Charlie to tell ye may ye kidding! Get to [*expletive deleted*]. [*Expletive deleted*] bastards. Sammy had [*expletive deleted*] seen it, he had seen it. All he wanted was his due, that was all man his [*expletive deleted*] due. He had copped for it; copped for this and copped for that. [*Expletive deleted*] alright, O.K., O.K.; [*Expletive deleted*] yez!"

The novel's liberal use of such words and its willfully idiomatic narrative, however, have little to do with its more fundamental problems. As writers from James Joyce to Mr. Mamet to Patrick McCabe have demonstrated over the years, slang, vernacular and profanity can be turned, in the right hands, into a kind of poetry that delineates a world and a place as well as character and mood. Indeed the problems with Mr. Kelman's book have nothing to do with his raw materials; they have to do with his failure to use those materials to create a compelling voice, a sympathetic protagonist or a convincing story.

The narrative methods employed by Mr. Kelman in ***How Late It Was*** will be familiar to readers of his earlier books. As in ***A Disaffection*** (1989), a third-person interior monologue is used to depict a couple of days in a man's life, as he wanders aimlessly about the bars and streets of Glasgow. As in many of the stories in ***Greyhound for Breakfast*** (1987), the predominant mood is one of depression and vague anxiety, a sense of being trapped by circumstance and fate.

In fact the hero of ***How Late It Was*** often comes across as a parody of Mr. Kelman's earlier protagonists. Sammy, as he's called, isn't simply fond of drinking, as are so many Kelman characters; he has just spent a lost weekend that has left him lying in the gutter, with no memory of how he got there. Earlier Kelman people have been forced to cope with poverty, unemployment, lowered expectations; Sammy, an ex-con, has to cope with police arrest, a brutal police beating and a sudden case of blindness that may or may not be permanent. He responds, as most Kelman characters do, with a shrug: he is blasé about going to see a doctor, reluctant to press charges against the police, loath to seek any sort of compensation. "Look miss," he tells a woman inquiring about his condition, "what I'm saying is the polis didnay intend to make me lose my sight I mean if they went at me with a blade and then dug out my eyes then I'd be straight in for compensation, know what I mean, but they didnay, they gave me physical restraints, and I wound up with a dysfunction."

Sammy's first thought is that his estranged girlfriend, Helen, would find his predicament amusingly absurd; his second thought is that his blindness will prevent him from having to take most jobs offered by the unemployment commission.

In the course of ***How Late It Was*** a few things do happen. The police question Sammy about some of his ne'er-do-well acquaintances; they imply that Sammy knows more than he is telling; Sammy insists that he was drunk the previous weekend and can't remember a thing. When Sammy returns to the apartment he shares with Helen, he discovers that she has disappeared. Later, he spurns the efforts of a man who says he can help Sammy get compensation and help for his condition.

For most of the book, however, Sammy simply wanders around Glasgow, like many Kelman characters before him, stumbling from one bar to another, using a home-made walking stick to help him find his way. As he does so, his mind wanders from topic to topic. The reader learns a little about Sammy's childhood and his dabbling in petty crime; one learns considerably more about his difficulties in sleeping, his desire for cigarettes, his failure to bathe, all of which are mentioned time and time again. Sammy's bank of images and ideas feels depleted; so does Mr. Kelman's.

The reason it's impossible to sympathize with Sammy or his plight is that Mr. Kelman depicts him as an utterly passive creature devoid of any real inner life. The reader cannot comprehend his bizarrely nonchalant attitude toward his blindness, nor his lack of anger or confusion. One tires of his banal musings about men and women, his tiresome and repetitious observations about taking "it as it comes."

Perhaps Sammy's story is meant as some sort of metaphor for the existential predicament of modern man or the human condition in general, but as delineated by Mr. Kelman, it's little more than a tired tale about a foulmouthed blind man looking for a drink and trying to avoid getting run over by a bus.

FURTHER READING

Criticism

Bausch, Richard. "Auld Sammy After a Two-Day Binge." *The New York Times Book Review* (5 February 1995): 8.

Offers a positive review of *How Late It Was, How Late,* contending that the British controversy concerning its "salty" language is irrelevant since the prose precisely reflects the reality of a place and time.

Additional coverage of Kelman's life and career is contained in the following source published by Gale Research: *Contemporary Literary Criticism,* Vol. 58.

Yusef Komunyakaa
Neon Vernacular: New and Selected Poems

Award: Pulitzer Prize for Poetry and Kingsley Tufts Poetry Award

Born in 1947, Komunyakaa is an American poet and editor.

INTRODUCTION

Neon Vernacular (1993) includes work from several of Komunyakaa's previous volumes as well as various new poems. Like much of his verse, the collection is highly autobiographical and focuses on his identity as an African-American, his upbringing in the small community of Bogalusa, Louisiana, and his experiences as a soldier during the Vietnam War. Incorporating tales of anger, violence, death, racism, and poverty, his poems are often infused with rage and exhibit a pessimistic outlook on life. Critics note, however, that even when writing about emotionally wrenching events from his tour of duty in Vietnam or his relationship with his, at times, abusive father, Komunyakaa is frequently able to evoke feelings of tenderness and hope; in "We Never Know" he writes: "Our gun barrels / glowed white hot. / When I got to him, / a blue halo / of flies had already claimed him. / I pulled the crumpled photograph / from his fingers. / There's no other way / to say this: I fell in love. / The morning cleared again, / except for a distant mortar / & somewhere choppers taking off. / I slid the wallet into his pocket / & turned him over, so he wouldn't be / kissing the ground." Reviews of *Neon Vernacular* have additionally noted Komunyakaa's emphasis on music as well as the musicality of his writings. Robyn Selman asserted: "Like a brother less self-conscious than the poet, music as Komunyakaa hears it is not merely a celebration or even culmination of heritage and culture, but an alternate linguistic anatomy."

PRINCIPAL WORKS

Dedications and Other Darkhorses (poetry) 1977
Lost in the Bonewheel Factory (poetry) 1979
Copacetic (poetry) 1984
I Apologize for the Eyes in My Head (poetry) 1986
Toys in a Field (poetry) 1986
Dien cai dau (poetry) 1988
February in Sydney (poetry) 1989
The Jazz Poetry Anthology [editor, with Sascha Feinstein] (poetry) 1991
Magic City (poetry) 1992
Neon Vernacular: New and Selected Poems (poetry) 1993

CRITICISM

Lenard D. Moore (review date 15 March 1993)

SOURCE: A review of *Neon Vernacular: New and Selected Poems,* in *Library Journal,* Vol. 118, No. 5, March 15, 1993, p. 81.

[*Below, Moore favorably reviews* Neon Vernacular.]

[***Neon Vernacular: New and Selected Poems***] is comprised of poems from seven of Komunyakaa's previous collections. A master at interweaving memory and history to shape his experiences into narratives, Komunyakaa enriches his poems with details: "His fingernails are black / & torn from blows, / as if the hammer / declares its own angle of reference." Music has its special force with a rhythm that seems to enforce meaning: "Heartstring. Blessed wood / and every moment the thing's made of / ball of fatback / licked by fingers of fire." As an African American, Komunyakaa defines a culture with striking imagery that is often misunderstood by mainstream readers.

I never really approached [poetry] from the perspective of making a living. It was simply a need.

—Yusef Komunyakaa, in "Poetry Emotion" by Anna Quindlen, in* The New York Times, *16 April 1994.

R. S. Gwynn (review date Winter 1994)

SOURCE: "What the Center Holds," in *The Hudson Review,* Vol. XLVI, No. 4, Winter, 1994, pp. 741-50.

[*In the following excerpt, Gwynn discusses Komunyakaa's focus on jazz, Vietnam, family, and Louisiana in* Neon Vernacular.]

Yusef Komunyakaa is a poet whose work I have known mostly through anthology pieces, one of which, the beautiful **"Facing It,"** is the most poignant elegy that has been written about the Vietnam War. The "it," of course, is the Wall:

A white vet's image floats
closer to me, then his pale eyes
look through mine. I'm a window.
He's lost his right arm
inside the stone. In the black mirror
a woman's trying to erase names:
No, she's brushing a boy's hair.

It is a pleasure to have ***Neon Vernacular: New and Selected Poems*** in hand, a collection that gathers together poems from small press publications with those of three of Komunyakaa's books from Wesleyan (work from his most recent collection, ***Magic City,*** is not included). In all, it's a mixed bag, with the best work the newest. Komunyakaa has written about jazz and edited an anthology of poems on the subject, but too often his own jazz poems, like this passage from **"Elegy for Thelonious,"** consist of recitations of allusions that have little intrinsic interest:

Crepuscule with Nelly
plays inside the bowed head.
"Dig the Man Ray of piano!"
O Satisfaction
hot fingers blur
on those white rib keys.
Coming on the Hudson.
Monk's Dream.

When Komunyakaa is able to step back from the discographies and incorporate jazz-style riffs into his speech patterns, the effect is much more gratifying, as in **"Unnatural State of the Unicorn,"** where he asks a lover to set aside his academic, poetic, and assorted other credentials and simply "Introduce me first as a man." Here, his superb ear is much in evidence:

Before embossed limited editions,
before fat artichoke hearts marinated
in rich sauce & served with imported wines,
before antics & Agnus Dei,
before the stars in your eyes
mean birth sign or Impression,
I am a man.

Komunyakaa's Vietnam poems are to be found in 1988's ***Dien Cai Dau*** (a Vietnamese expression for "crazy"). He served as a correspondent during the conflict, and some of his descriptions of battle have an Ernie Pyle-like quality of compassion tinged with a journalist's unsparing eye for ironic detail:

He danced with tall grass
for a moment, like he was swaying
with a woman. Our gun barrels
glowed white-hot.
When I got to him,
a blue halo
of flies had already claimed him.

The most recent work in ***Neon Vernacular*** focuses on the poet's hometown of Bogalusa, Louisiana, a subject that he heretofore has not explored. Though Wesleyan's jacket copy is quick to note that Bogalusa was "once a center of Klan activity and later a focus of Civil Rights efforts," Komunyakaa's themes are rites of passage, friendship, and family. True, "The whole town smells / Like the world's oldest anger," but its source is the chemical plants and paper mills, "the cloudy / Commerce of wheels, of chemicals / That turn workers into pulp." I particularly like "Immigrants," a section of a long poem made up of scenes of growing up, for its unusual racial perspective, how blacks viewed "Guissipie, Misako, / & Goldberg" and other exotic imports to the South:

We showed them fishing holes
& guitar licks. Wax pompadours
Bristled like rooster combs,
But we couldn't stop loving them
Even after they sold us
Rotting fruit & meat,
With fingers pressed down
On the scales.

Probably the most impressive new poem is the last, a long elegy for the poet's father, a laborer who worked hard at everything, even making his children's Easter egg hunts a challenge, "hiding the eggs / In gopher holes & underneath roots." Some of Komunyakaa's memories are not easy, recalling his combative father's "Wanting me to believe / I shouldn't have been born / With hands & feet / If I didn't do / Your kind of work." Others capture delicate spots of time:

Sometimes you could be
That man on a red bicycle,

With me on the handlebars,
Just rolling along a country road
On the edge of July, honeysuckle
Lit with mosquito hawks.

At the end of a man's life, with his "name & features half / X-ed out," the old resentments have to be set aside. What is left is a son's lingering respect for the strength that "steered us through the flowering / Dogwood like a thread of blood."

Erik Ness (review date May 1994)

SOURCE: A review of *Neon Vernacular: New and Selected Poems,* in *The Progressive,* Vol. 58, No. 5, May, 1994, p. 50.

[*In the following excerpt, Ness remarks on the themes and subjects presented in* Neon Vernacular.]

For Yusef Komunyakaa, the experience that seared him into poetry was serving in Vietnam. In ***Neon Vernacular: New and Selected Poems,*** Vietnam stalks Komunyakaa. . . .

But for him, the atrocities [he witnessed] carry an extra burden. The first-person narrator cannot forget "how I helped ambush two Viet Cong / while plugged into the Grateful Dead," he writes in one of his previously published poems, **"Jungle Fever."** In some of the new poems, the same sentiment persists. **"Fever"** begins, "I took orders made my trail / Of blood, & you want me / To say it was right." He warns memorably: "You can hug flags into triangles, / But can't hide the blood / By tucking in the corners."

For shelter, Komunyakaa runs to women and to jazz, and many of his newer poems have a vibrant musicality about them. As he advises, "Don't try to make any sense / out of this; just let it take you / like Pres's tenor & keep you human."

Yet many of the poems are direct and readily comprehensible, especially those that wrestle with his father. The new poem, **"Songs for My Father,"** is as wrenching an Oedipal square-off as you'll find anywhere in contemporary letters.

Komunyakaa roots his poetry in his native Louisiana. He vividly describes the scenery and the people on the lower end of the economic scale whom he encounters every day—housekeepers, handymen, papermill workers, lawncutters. Growing up black in the South, he confronts the racism that is all around. In **"How I See Things,"** he asks: "Have we earned the right / to forget, forgive / ropes for holding / to moonstruck branches?"

There is a despairing vision that runs throughout, only partially leavened by the jazz and the sex. In one poem, he calls his body "a poorly rigged by-pass / along Desperado Ave." and in another, he says, "We were way stations / between sweatshops & heaven."

He provides some hope, however, in the new poem, **"Praising Dark Places."** He tells the story of lifting an old board and finding a scorpion, centipedes, and other life flourishing "in this cellular dirt / & calligraphy of excrement." That this society can persist beneath our view suggests the possibility of survival, and Komunyakaa says, "I am drawn again / To conception & birth."

Bruce Weber (essay date 2 May 1994)

SOURCE: "A Poet's Values: It's the Words over the Man," in *The New York Times,* May 2, 1994, pp. C11, C18.

[*In the article below, based on a conversation with Komunyakaa, Weber relates Komunyakaa's background and origins, various aspects of his writings, and his views on the writing process.*]

Yusef Komunyakaa, who won the Pulitzer Prize for poetry three weeks ago, is still receiving congratulations from acquaintances as he walks the hallways and quadrangles of the Indiana University campus here. People seem surprised to see him, as if he had been in hiding, calling out to him "Hey! Man of the hour!" and the like.

You would know he was a shy man just from the way he acknowledges his well-wishers, an embarrassed-seeming bow of the head, an abbreviated wave of the hand. And indeed, in the pantheon of poet stereotypes—the vitriolic, passionate drunkard is one; the wry, acerbic loner another—Mr. Komunyakaa, a professor of English, is more the dreamy intellectual, a Wordsworthian type whose worldly, philosophic mind might be stirred by something as homely and personal as a walk in a field of daffodils. Still, there's a way he gives off the sense of a cauldron, bubbling beneath the surface. He's not happy talking about himself.

"I'm happier talking about the process of writing, yes," he said. He's a dark-skinned man, with a broad nose and a dusting of salt-gray in his hair. His voice is a quiet country rumble, distinctly Southern, with a Cajunish tinge that betrays a childhood spent in Bogalusa, La. "Skeered," he'll say for scared; "paw-em" is how says the word poem.

"I'm even happier to have people read my work," he said. "I'm uncomfortable with the focus on the poet and not on the poem."

At 47, Mr. Komunyakaa (pronounced koh-mun-YAH-kuh) is something of a paradigm of the contemporary poet-academic. He is the author of eight books, including ***Neon Vernacular,*** the collection of new and selected poems for which he was awarded the Pulitzer, and he has been teaching a full load of graduate and undergraduate courses at Indiana since 1986. He taught at the University of New Orleans before that. He acknowledges poetry to be the most inaccessible of literary forms, requiring a commitment from readers that not many are willing to make. But he himself is committed to the relentless plumbing of ideas and the language needed to express them.

Poets need to be of eccentric and independent turn of mind, and Mr. Komunyakaa seems just that. He's pleased by ambiguity, complexity, resonance without clarity. His poems, many of which are built on fiercely autobiographical details—about his stint in Vietnam, about his childhood—deal with the stains that experience leaves on a life, and they are often achingly suggestive without resolution.

"I think of my poems as personal and public at the same time," he said. "You could say they serve as psychological overlays. One fits on top of the other, and hopefully there's an ongoing evolution of clarity."

In the language of his poems, too, is a sense of struggling to embrace complexity, images layered on images to create depth rather than simple revelation. He occasionally wishes he were a painter, he said, because the images in his poems often come from pictures that arise in his head and he has to work, experimenting, to approximate them.

"I like connecting the abstract to the concrete," he said. "There's a tension in that. I believe the reader or listener should be able to enter the poem as a participant. So I try to get past resolving poems."

Even in conversation he gravitates to anecdotes that are at once poignant and elliptical.

Take the story of his name. It is probably of West African derivation, the poet said, although he isn't sure. According to family legend, it was brought to this country by his grandfather.

"He slipped into this country from the West Indies, most likely Trinidad," Mr. Komunyakaa said. "He was a stowaway, I suppose. And the story was that he was wearing one boy's shoe and one girl's shoe."

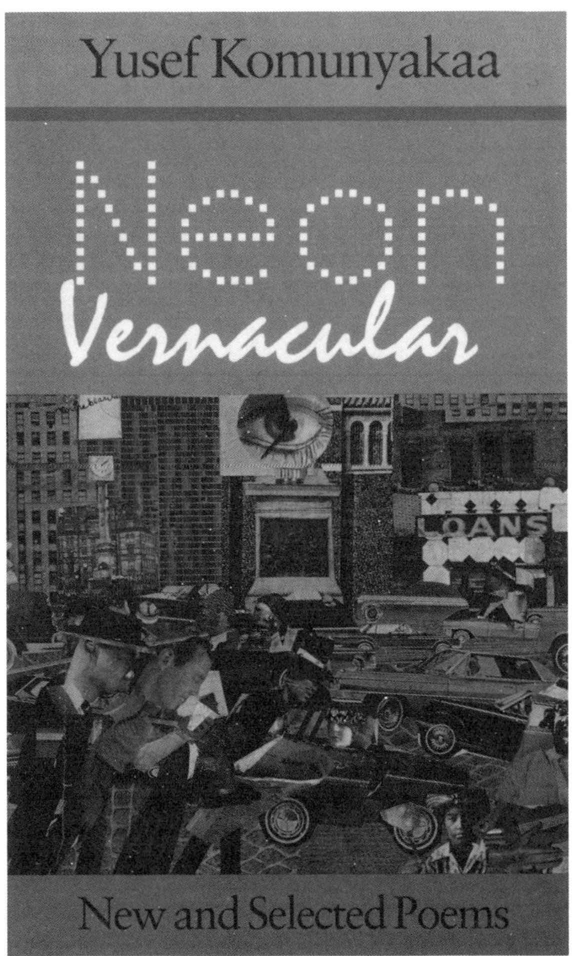

Cover of the prizewinning Neon Vernacular.

He is the oldest of five children "and the only one who reads poetry," Mr. Komunyakaa said. His father, who died in 1986, was a carpenter. Their relationship was clearly complicated.

"He taught me to learn the tools, that tools make a job easier, and I see that as paralleling the technique of poetry," Mr. Komunyakaa said. Relations between the two weren't smooth, however, and a poem in the new collection, **"Songs for My Father"** depicts the older man as both a hard worker and an angry, abusive philanderer. The poet's mother, when her marriage was over, moved to Phoenix, where she still lives.

Bogalusa, in the lowland toe of the Louisiana boot, north of Lake Ponchartrain on the Mississippi border, is a mill town. "Culturally it's desolate," Mr. Komunyakaa said. "It was a place where there was vegetation all over. In spring and summer, there was almost a psychological encroachment of it, as if everything was woven together. Growing up, I was always going into the woods and pulling things apart, the muscadine vines that had overtaken the oaks. There was a chemistry going on in the landscape, and I identified with it, so I kind of look for that wherever I go."

His first books were volumes of an encyclopedia his mother bought in a supermarket. He read the Bible through twice when he was a young teen-ager; then at 16, in a tiny church library, he came across James Baldwin's book of essays *Nobody Knows My Name,* which inspired him to write.

In 1969, Mr. Komunyakaa joined the Army and went to Vietnam. He served as an "information specialist," reporting from the front lines and editing for a military newspaper, *The Southern Call,* and winning a Bronze Star. When he returned home, he went to college, at the University of Colorado, then to graduate school at Colorado State University and the University of California at Irvine. In the peripatetic fashion of poets looking for a way to make a living, he pursued fellowships and teaching jobs in New England and, finally, New Orleans. It was there he met his wife, Mandy Sayer, an Australian novelist and short-story writer, whom he married in 1985. And it was there he embarked on the most fruitful period of his career.

"It took me 14 years to write poems about Vietnam," he said. "I had never thought about writing about it, and in a way I had been systematically writing around it."

While he was renovating a house in New Orleans in 1983, he said, he wrote his first Vietnam poem, periodically climbing down a ladder to write down lines in a notebook. "And it was as if I had uncapped some hidden place in me," he said. "Poem after poem came spilling out."

And indeed they still do. In the new collection, a poem called **"At the Screen Door"** describes the experience of a soldier returning home a changed man in ways he doesn't quite understand. He's watching a woman—his wife? his mother?—from outside the house; she doesn't see him yet. It ends this way:

Who is it
Waiting for me, a tall shadow
Unlit in the doorway, no more
Than an outline of the past?
I drop the duffle bag
& run before I know it.
Running toward her, the only one
I couldn't have surprised,
Who'd be here at daybreak
Watching a new day stumble
Through a whiplash of grass
Like a man drunk on the rage
Of being alive

Evidently, some demons lie not so dormant beneath Mr. Komunyakaa's serene exterior, and the impression was underscored when, apropos of nothing in particular, he began to speak about violence. It is endemic, of course, in American cities, like Phoenix, where his mother lives, he said. But it is even more deeply rooted in rural America.

"I grew up with guns around me," he said. "The rituals of violence. People hunting. Killing hogs, rabbits. Pragmatic violence. At the time it seemed pragmatic, but now I question it. In our culture we celebrate violence. All of our heroes have blood on their hands. I have a real problem with that."

In an interview that had otherwise been meandering and quiet, this was a moment of focus and fire. There's a poem in it, perhaps.

Additional coverage of Komunyakaa's life and career is contained in the following source published by Gale Research: *Dictionary of Literary Biography,* Vol. 120.

David Malouf
Remembering Babylon

Award: *Los Angeles Times* Book Award for Fiction

(Full name George Joseph David Malouf) Born in 1934, Malouf is an Australian novelist, poet, short fiction writer, playwright, librettist, and editor.

For further information on Malouf's life and works, see *CLC,* Volume 28.

INTRODUCTION

Updating the theme of the "noble savage," *Remembering Babylon* (1993) is set in nineteenth-century Australia and concerns Gemmy Fairley, an English citizen who was abandoned by shipmates as a child. After living with the aborigine people of Australia for a sixteen-year period, this "black white-feller" attempts to rejoin white Australian society, a community governed by European cultural norms and the English language. Variously regarded by some settlers as a curiosity, a potential ally against the aborigines, and an object of scientific wonder, Gemmy is also viewed with fear, loathing, and distrust. His reinitiation into white society, particularly after he is seen conversing with blacks in the aborigine dialect, culminates with several settlers attacking him. Eventually he abandons the "civilized" ways of the whites and rejoins Australia's indigenous community. Critics have lauded Malouf's focus on the relationship between politics, language, social stature, and personal and national identity in *Remembering Babylon,* praising the novel as a document of Australia's history, European settlement, and multifaceted population. Reviewers have additionally admired Malouf's use of Gemmy as a means of discussing the sublime in literature, the alienating and binding nature of language, and the paradox posed by the individual's need for acceptance and desire to distinguish between self and the "Other." In honoring Malouf with the *Los Angeles Times* Book Award for Fiction, judge Annette Smith stated: "Malouf's novel testifies all along to the confusion of languages. It demonstrates the demonic nature of words, both their destructive power and their creative force, as Gemmy's past and his new identity take form."

PRINCIPAL WORKS

**Bicycle, and Other Poems* (poetry) 1970
Neighbours in a Thicket (poetry) 1974
Johnno (novel) 1975
Poems, 1975-1976 (poetry) 1976
An Imaginary Life (novel) 1978
Wild Lemons (poetry) 1980
†Child's Play; The Bread of Time to Come (novellas) 1981
First Things Last (poetry) 1981
Selected Poems (poetry) 1981
Child's Play; Eustace; The Prowler (novella and short stories) 1982
Harland's Half Acre (novel) 1984
Antipodes (short stories) 1985
12 Edmondstone Street (memoir) 1985
Blood Relations (drama) 1988
The Great World (novel) 1990
Remembering Babylon (novel) 1993

*This work was published as *The Year of the Foxes, and Other Poems* in 1979.

†*The Bread of Time to Come* was published as *Fly Away Peter* in 1982.

CRITICISM

Peter Otto (essay date September 1993)

SOURCE: "Forgetting Colonialism," in *Meanjin*, Vol. 52, No. 3, September, 1993, pp. 545-58.

[*In the essay below, Otto analyzes Malouf's portrayal of male-female relationships, the sublime, the political, and the social in* Remembering Babylon, *noting Malouf's delineation of the evolution of Australia's colonial identity into a national identity.*]

> Whether this is Jerusalem or Babylon we know not.
>
> Blake, *The Four Zoas*

Remembering Babylon begins 'One day in the middle of the nineteenth century, when settlement in Queensland had advanced little more than halfway up the coast', at an imaginary line that purportedly divides colonial settlement from its Unknown. It may at first seem odd to associate this locale with Babylon but, as the first of the book's two epigraphs suggests, one of the title's allusions is to Blake's Babylon, a city formed by the dismemberment of Albion (England). The allusion suggests that colonial Australia is a dismembered Albion, formed by successive waves of transportation and migration. If the scattered pieces of Albion's body could be put back together again, then, according to Blake, Babylon would become Jerusalem once more and Albion would rise from the grave. Malouf attempts an analogous task in ***Remembering Babylon.*** The book re-members the divisions of colonial Australia, not to reconstruct an imperial Albion but to build a New Jerusalem of (Australian) national identity.

In the aftermath of the Mabo ruling and in the year of indigenous peoples, it hardly needs to be said that this project is fraught with difficulty. Phrases such as 'halfway up the coast' of Queensland and 'One day in the middle of the nineteenth century' will inevitably evoke two very different kinds of recollection. On the one hand, this locale might stand for the point from which a properly Australian identity springs. On the other hand, it is the site of violent dispossession. How is Malouf to re-member the different histories and cultures that collide at this point?

From the first pages of ***Remembering Babylon*** it is evident that the book sets out to re-member the former rather than the latter. It displaces the second set of recollections by translating the political into the psychological, and matters of history and politics into questions of creativity and aesthetics. The border between settlers and indigenous peoples is interpreted through a Romantic (or postmodern romantic) psychology and tropology which reads such encounters as thresholds or borders of consciousness. 'Halfway up the coast' of Queensland in the 'middle of the nineteenth century', one does not stumble across a site of dispossession or conflict between races; instead, one comes face to face with the Unknown. The book goes on to suggest that contact between European settlers and the Unknown occurs at a place just beyond the reach of imperial power where, thanks to the mysteries of the imagination, it becomes possible to build an authentic Australian identity.

The translation of the political into the aesthetic and psychological, and the accompanying metamorphosis of the colonial into the national, appears in different guises in other fictions by Malouf. One might describe ***Remembering Babylon*** as reformulating, in a more historically specific idiom, the mythology outlined in ***An Imaginary Life.*** It is instructive to trace some of the key moments in the erasure of the political in ***Remembering Babylon,*** and in particular the use of the sublime to orchestrate his re-membering of colonialism. I should underline that my concern is not with the views of Malouf as an individual, but with the implications of the discourse that structures this book. I take as given the literary virtuosity that makes Malouf one of Australia's most accomplished writers.

At the threshold between settler society and the Unknown, 'something extraordinary' occurs. Before the startled eyes of the McIvor children, Janet and Meg, and their cousin, Lachlan Beattie, something separates itself from the forbidden world on the other side of the line:

> a fragment of ti-tree swamp, some bit of the land over there that was forbidden to them, had detached itself from the band of grey that made up the far side of the swamp, and in a shape more like a watery, heat-struck mirage than a thing of substance, elongated and airily indistinct, was bowling, leaping, flying towards them.

The cousins' first thought is that they are being 'raided by blacks', but this conjecture turns out to be wrong:

> The stick-like legs, all knobbed at the joints, suggested a wounded water-bird, a brolga, or a human that . . . had been *changed* into a bird, but only halfway, and now, neither one thing nor the other, was hopping and flapping towards them out of a world over there, beyond the no-man's land of the swamp, that was the abode of everything savage and fearsome, and since it lay so far beyond experience, not just their own but their parents' too, of nightmare rumours, superstitions and all that belonged to Absolute Dark.

In the face of this threat from a being that eludes classification, the children's game of make-believe is disrupted, and they stand transfixed, almost as if turned to stone.

Even from this thumbnail sketch it is evident that Lachlan, Meg and Janet are actors in a drama belonging to the literature of the sublime. The opening pages of ***Remembering Babylon*** follow the first steps in the plot of the sublime: a state of harmony between subject and object (play or habitual activity) is disrupted by a superior power that brings 'irresistible might to bear' and then to a sense of blockage in which, as Edmund Burke described it [in *A Philosophical Enquiry into the Origin of Our Ideas of the Sublime and Beautiful*], all of the motions of the soul 'are suspended, with some degree of horror'. This moment of blockage is followed by a powerful sense of release, which for the male subject leads to a newly invigorated identity. This is achieved through a complex sequence of accommodations and transformations. First, the threatening force dissipates. Second, what was at first experienced as a disruptive, blocking force comes to be understood as a sign of a transcendental power that orders and stabilizes the world. The terms used to describe this power are quite diverse: God in the religious sublime, the self or the imagination in the Romantic sublime, language or desire in the postmodern sublime, and so on. Third, some of the might formerly attributed to the blocking agent is now transferred to the subject. As Burke explains,

> Now whatever . . . tends to raise a man in his own opinion, produces a sort of swelling and triumph that is extremely grateful to the human mind; and this swelling is never more perceived . . . than when without danger we are conversant with terrible objects, the mind always claiming to itself some part of the dignity and importance of the things which it contemplates.

In ***Remembering Babylon*** one can trace a very similar sequence of transformations and accommodations.

As if waking from a momentary trance, Lachlan steps 'resolutely' out in front of the girls in order to do 'what his manhood required him to do'. He raises his make-believe gun to his shoulder and confronts the phantom. This act of defiance has staggering results. First, the horrifying power turns out to be nothing more than Gemmy (or Jimmy) Fairley (or Farrelly). He is a white man, even though he has 'the mangy, half-starved look of a black'. Gemmy, it transpires, 'had been cast overboard from a passing ship' when he was thirteen and 'had been living since in the scrub country to the north with blacks'. As if in recognition that he stands at a border between worlds, Gemmy jumps onto the top rail of a fence and for a few moments balances between the world he has left and the one he is to enter. He is unable to remain at this point for long. Once he has confessed that he is 'a B-b-british object!' his descent into settler society is swift: Gemmy falls to the ground, crawls 'about with his nose in the dust', is advised to stop speaking in the Aboriginal language he has learnt, and is finally taken into custody by Lachlan and marched back to the white world.

Just as astonishingly, as the Unknown withers, Lachlan expands. It is as if some of the power that had once belonged to the Unknown has been transferred to him. As Lachlan prods the man he has taken prisoner, he hears 'sounds of such eager submissiveness' that his 'heart swelled'.

> He had a powerful sense of the springing of his torso from the roots of his belly. He had known nothing like this! He was bringing a prisoner in. Armed with nothing, too, but his own presumptuous daring and the power of make-believe.

The encounter with the Unknown transports Lachlan from the position of child to that of young adult, from the Imaginary to the Symbolic realm. As a young adult, the stick he wields has become 'what his gesture had claimed for it': the Phallus. He is now able to lay claim to the Law (he takes Gemmy into custody), language (he is the one able to translate Gemmy's attempts at communication) and masculine authority (he gives directions to his cousins, and they obey him).

Throughout the nineteenth and well into the twentieth century, the language of the sublime was frequently invoked by travellers, explorers and writers as a discourse appropriate for an encounter with an alien land or people. A representative instance of this usage can be seen in J. W. Gregory's *The Dead Heart of Australia* (1909), which offers an account of Gregory's journey around Lake Eyre in 1901-2. In the eleventh chapter of this book, Gregory describes an encounter that closely follows the scenario that I have been describing.

Gregory begins with an account of his boyhood 'yearning for the opportunity of travel', and his particular fascination with the desert, which promises a 'soothing solitude, and the exhilaration of its buoyant sense of freedom'. Unfortunately, when he enacts his dreams, reality stubbornly blocks his desires. The surface of the desert is 'black and rocky'; he gets sun blisters 'from the heat reflected from the ground'; 'a westerly gale' pelts him with 'coarse, black grit'; and the water he is carrying becomes 'warm and putrid, and almost poisonous'. As the narrative proceeds, the desert is personified as a fearsome adversary. What had been the source of a merely physical discomfort now produces an astounding catalogue of horrors:

> A vision rises before us of the desperate struggles of the lost explorer, and of the despair of his last mile's march. We begin to realise the agony of death by thirst, when the sun is burning like fire, and perhaps swarms of ants are stinging like a medieval 'jailer's daughter'. We then understand how Nature can rival the malignant tortures of the Inquisition.

Gregory responds to this adversary with a surprising degree of passion. He describes the desert as 'an enemy that *must* be fought' (my emphasis) and the sun 'in its fiery march' across the sky inspires feelings which 'sometimes approach to hatred'. Night, however, effects a miraculous deflation of the blocking power. The passive foe is softened, the active adversary is displaced by a faint light, and 'the demon dread of day' is exorcized: 'The air is cool and bracing; the low, brown hills that looked so near, but are so far, can no longer mock, or the mirage tantalise.' The desert's blocking force is displaced by a silence broken only by a 'barely perceptible humming' that 'one is tempted to believe' is the music of the spheres, 'such as that you dream'd about'. In touch with this transcendental order, Gregory is elevated and renewed.

Why should this elaborate scenario be used to describe an experience in the desert at the beginning of the twentieth century? Or, for that matter, why should Malouf use the sublime to describe an event that occurs in the 'middle of the nineteenth century', 'halfway up the coast' of Queensland? ***Remembering Babylon*** and *The Dead Heart of Australia* suggest at least three answers to these questions.

First, the sublime offers a powerful set of procedures for constructing a self in the face of an external threat. In effect it is a defence reaction that preserves the self against alterity. Second, the sublime consolidates this self by staging a drama that recapitulates a socially constructed division between the genders. In psychoanalytic terms, Lachlan's (and Gregory's) masculine identity is determined as much by his ability to separate himself from the feminine and the maternal (the pre-Oedipal world suggested by Gregory's dreams and Lachlan's make-believe) as by his willingness to take his father ('his manhood') as a model. The sublime offers an opportunity to effect this separation by dividing the world into two radically different groups: those who are overcome by 'power and irresistible might' and those who are able to assume this power as their own; the passive and the active; women and men.

In a colonial context, however, there is a third reason for the invocation of the sublime. The sublime offers a colonial (and post-colonial) society a drama in which the settler's encounter with an indigenous people and an alien land can be staged as an encounter with the Unknown. In so doing it re-inscribes the imaginary line that marks the furthest extent of settler expansion and Aboriginal dispossession as a limit of vision.

Pictured in this way, the politics of settlement is eclipsed by questions concerning the relation between centre and margin, Europe and Australia. In ***Remembering Babylon*** the boundary between white and black cultures becomes not so much a place of dispossession as the point where imperial power falters: it is a place 'only lightly connected to . . . the figure in an official uniform . . . and the Crown he represented, which held them all, a whole continent, in its grip'. A story of Oedipal rivalry deftly interprets and displaces the narrative of a conflict between races. This threshold turns out to be not merely a place where a masculine self can be consolidated, but a site where that self can expand, freed from the power of the centre.

***Remembering Babylon* suggests that contact between European settlers and the Unknown occurs at a place just beyond the reach of imperial power where, thanks to the mysteries of the imagination, it becomes possible to build an authentic Australian identity.**

—Peter Otto

Although the sublime may conclude with male swelling, this desired state is preceded by an experience of extreme subjection. The male subject is overcome, possessed, and moved by a power not his own. In the discourse of the sublime this experience is habitually described in the language of (a male vision of) sexual ecstasy. It is small cause for wonder that male writers are deeply ambivalent about this ravishing. In this brief moment they are the possessed rather than the possessor, the object rather than the subject.

Yet male writers, particularly in the twentieth century, are often fascinated by this experience of subjection. It suggests a state in which the social, civilized self is put aside in favour of an encounter with a more primitive, presocial and fundamental power. Writers such as Rilke, Lawrence, Yeats and Malouf figure the moment of sublime submission as a moment of inspiration in which the writer is in touch with the dark gods. The relation between the male self that emerges from the sublime and the 'female' state that is its immediate predecessor then becomes a question of the relation between the male writer and the (female) experience of inspiration and creativity. In ***Remembering Babylon,*** these questions are worked out in relation to Janet's experience of the sublime.

As is evident from Burke's notion of male 'swelling', the discourse of the sublime is far from gender-neutral. In the aesthetic discourse of the eighteenth and nineteenth centuries the sublime is masculine, while the beautiful is feminine; it would be unnatural for a woman to appropriate the power of the blocking agent. ***Remembering Babylon*** seems to share this view. Lachlan's mode of defence is not available to Janet or Meg. Instead, they remain passive, caught at the point of blockage, their minds filled by the object that confronts them. In this unenviable condition, their best defence is submission.

Before Gemmy's appearance, Janet and Meg are unwilling participants in Lachlan's game: 'They complained and dawdled and he had to exert all his gift for fantasy, his will too, which was stubborn, to keep them in the game.' Immediately after Gemmy has been taken prisoner, they silently accept the boy's 'new-found mastery' and 'let themselves be led'.

Remembering Babylon, however, claims more for the moment of subjection. It wants its readers to believe that Janet emerges with a premonition of a knowledge and power very different from that which is available to men. Her account of the sublime experience is at odds with the heroic narrative offered by Lachlan. Janet asserts that 'Me and Meg found [Gemmy], just as much as Lachlan' and that, if truth be told, the real agent of discovery is the dog. She proffers this deflationary narrative and waits expectantly for her parents to bring Lachlan down, because for her the experience is one in which her faculties were suspended, not one in which an active self was precipitated.

The different kinds of knowledge and power are first glimpsed through Gemmy's eyes. When Gemmy looks at Lachlan he never fails to see 'the power he had laid claim to with the pretence of arms'. Gemmy is therefore always ready 'to appease' the boy. Lachlan's power, the narrator observes, belongs 'to him because he was a boy; because, one day, the authority he had claimed . . . would be real'. By contrast, when Gemmy catches Janet looking at him he has the feeling 'that she was trying to see right into him, to catch his spirit'. Janet's knowledge arises from her ability to blur the boundaries between self and other, to allow others to 'enter her and reveal what they were'. As this knowledge is not predicated on the mastery of an object by a subject, Janet's power needs 'no witness' and is 'entirely her own'.

These radically different powers and knowledges reflect lives driven by different ambitions. Lachlan projects his desire out into the world. He is full of 'heroic visions in which the limitations of mere boyhood would at last be transcended'. By contrast, Janet is fascinated by a world beneath this one, by an identity more fundamental than the social.

> One day . . . picking idly at a scab on her knee, she was amazed, when the hard crust lifted, to discover a colour she had never seen before, and another skin, lustrous as pearl. A delicate pink, it might have belonged to some other creature altogether, and the thought came to her that if all the rough skin of her present self crusted and came off, what would be revealed, shining in sunlight, was this finer being that had somehow been covered up in her.

She feels as if she has been relieved of the weight of her own life, and 'the brighter being in her was very gently stirring and shifting its wings'.

This fantasy finds its most extreme form in the fifteenth chapter of the book. The primitive source of the sublime's 'power and irresistible might' here becomes a swarm of bees. Bees are a traditional symbol for primitive energy, either sexual or divine. ***Remembering Babylon*** allows both sets of associations to accrue. For Janet the bees suggest 'another life, quite independent of their human one', and evoke the fantasy that 'If she could escape . . . just for a moment, out of her personal mind into their communally single one, she would know at last what it was like to be an angel.' These intimations of violent possession and dispossession are given graphic form later in the chapter when the bees attack Janet:

> She just had time to see her hands covered with plushy, alive fur gloves before her whole body crusted over and she was blazingly gathered into the single sound they made, the single mind.

This barely disguised rape scene is figured by Malouf as a wedding. Janet's 'old mind' is put to one side and her 'new and separate mind' (provided by the bees) tells her that 'You are our bride'. This consummation provides her with a 'new' (spiritual) body and self; it is, however, also a conflagration which leaves her old body 'a charred stump, all crusted black and bubbling'.

In the sexual politics of this novel, male identity is defined in terms of the distance it has moved from the 'feminine'. Janet's metaphorical marriage through rape confirms the position she was allocated in the drama of the sublime: she is the defining other to male identity. But the masculine self is unable to divide itself once and for all from the feminine. In the Romantic discourse of ***Remembering Babylon,*** this is not simply because woman is the defining other to male identity, or that woman stands for all of the 'bodies' over which Lachlan's authority will be exerted. Janet's most crucial role at this point in the book is concerned with the status, in a colonial context, of the traditional identification of women and nature. Janet's possession by the bees confirms what was implicit in the drama of the sublime: woman can be possessed by the spirit of this new land. The sublime, therefore, is not merely the vehicle for the production of the Australian man; it also brings the truly Australian woman into being.

This second miracle performs a remarkable coup, a second displacement of the indigenous population. It is the white, female settler who now emerges as the authentic mouthpiece for Australia. She is the natural receptacle for the spirit of place: an Australian who stands, with her Platonic Adam, at the (expanding) edge of empire.

With the displacement of the conflict between settler and indigenous peoples, and the installation of Janet as authentic voice of the land, ***Remembering Babylon*** is set to begin its work of recollection. What it proceeds to remember is not the original inhabitants of the land, but a division itself produced by the sublime: a woman who speaks for the primitive voice of the land and a man who represents Australian political and social life. If achieved, this recollection would piece together an androgynous Australian identity. It would hold together the primitive and the civilized, the feminine and the masculine, those who submit and those who force others to submit. The focal point of this remembering is Gemmy.

Gemmy has a complex set of roles to play in this novel. He serves as a locus and catalyst for certain kinds of disorientation intrinsic to the colonial experience. First, as a white man who arrives in settler society from Aboriginal Australia rather than from Great Britain, he suggests a white civilization transposed to an alien context and so made strange. Second, he embodies the feared Unknown. Third, as a person who seems both black and white, he evokes fears of deracination and loss of racial purity. Gemmy also implies the possibility of a future identity and culture that is not simply black or white, Australian or European, but stands between these poles.

The anxiety Gemmy produces in the colonists is related both to their inability to categorize him and their desire not to recognize him. There is a bewildering proliferation of names and circumlocutions for him. Aside from the uncertainty as to whether he is Gemmy or Jimmy, Fairley or Farrelly, he is described as, or compared to, a 'blackfeller', 'plain savage, marionette' and moron, 'puppet', 'mongrel', 'pathetic, muddy-eyed, misshapen fellow', 'half-caste', 'run-a-way', 'straw-topped half-naked savage', 'black', 'nigger', parody of a white man, 'black white-feller' and 'white black man'.

Remembering Babylon provides what could be called an alphabet of possible responses to the unknowns that are given tangible form by Gemmy. Most of the settlers treat Gemmy in a way that is analogous to their treatment of the land, 'ringbarking and clearing and reducing it to what would make it, at last, just a bit like home'. These are the responses that produce the Babylon of the book's title by dividing white from black, the familiar from the unfamiliar, the known from the unknown, Australia from Europe and the present from both the past and the future.

Lachlan and Janet (along with a few of the other colonists) have a very different response to Gemmy. For them he is the focus of, and catalyst for, the remembering that is to heal colonial society. One might well ask what licenses Gemmy to play this role, for at first glance he appears to be a decidedly lacklustre hero. He is, at best, rather simple; and throughout the novel he acts in an oddly absent-minded, childlike way. Yet these disqualifications turn out to be his greatest assets.

The closest model for the character and role of Gemmy is the 'idiot boy' in Wordsworth's poem of the same name, whose simplicity is a sign that he has avoided socialization and is therefore still in touch with nature. This proximity to nature means that he is also close to the transcendental force that informs nature: the imagination. In this regard, the 'idiot boy' is like that staple of Romantic poetry (and second model for Gemmy), the Child. The Child, Wordsworth writes, is the 'best Philosopher', an 'Eye among the blind, / That, deaf and silent, read'st the eternal deep, / Haunted for ever by the eternal mind', because his imagination has not yet been tempered by the adult world of reality and social necessity. In Romanticism, 'idiot' and Child are often characterized as dwelling on the border between two worlds: they stand between, on the one hand, a paradisal world projected by the imagination and, on the other hand, a world determined by the artificial constraints of adult life. This is why for Lachlan and Janet what is most resonant about Gemmy is the transcendental power he implies as he stands balanced, on the top rail of the fence, between one world and the next. This power is the imagination, which for Romanticism is the active source of both human and physical nature and so represents the spring from which individual and national identity flows.

Once again, many of the key moments here can be found in narratives of colonization and exploration. In the final stages of Gregory's sublime encounter with the South Australian desert, he also discovers a vision of the future, of primitive nature, and of the imagination. As he lies under the stars, listening to the music of the spheres, he feels 'an irresistible attraction towards the better rest and fuller silence of the long, desert journey, that lies before us all'. This proleptic vision of a journey after death is coupled with the stirrings of primitive man:

> The simplicity of desert life, the uniformity of its conditions, the merciless severity of its forces, awaken in us the primitive man, lying beneath the carefully built-up fabric of social obligations. The unchanging face of Nature dimly stirs the beginnings of man. His pushing forward into the unknown is as the crown and completion of those beginnings.

Standing on the edge of the Unknown, pushing forward into the future and back into the past, produces an extraordinary sense of elation and inflation. For a moment, Gregory confides, 'a man sums up in himself the long experience of his race'.

This place between the past and the future, the primitive and the civilized, where a man can sum up the entire 'experience of his race' is, not surprisingly, one in which the imagination is free to act:

> To retain the knowledge and thought of the twentieth century while meeting the conditions of prehistoric man, to face the mystery of the unchanging desert, divested of the fetish-begotten fears that half paralysed the primitive races, gives that stimulus to the imagination, which is one of the highest joys given to man to feel.

In the last chapter of ***Remembering Babylon*** we see Lachlan Beattie, now a respectable politician in his late middle age, attempting to tie up 'one of the loose ends of his own life, which might otherwise have gone on bleeding for ever'. It is this that leads him back to Janet (now Sister Monica), Gemmy and the extraordinary event with which the book began. In these last pages we see the form that the remembering alluded to in the book's title will take:

> All that, fifty years ago. An age. They were living in another country. He could afford to admit now that it had not ended. Something Gemmy had touched off in them was what they were still living, both, in their different ways. It would end only when they were ended, and maybe not even then. They would come back, as they had now, from the far points they had moved away to, and stand side by side looking up at the figure outlined there against a streaming sky. Still balanced.

This passage effects a re-membering of child and adult, past and present, which recalls Wordsworth's economics of memory in the 'Immortality Ode'. Wordsworth's poem mourns the adult loss of the child's imagination through socialization, yet affirms that the child's imagination is still present to the adult through recollection and, moreover, that

> those first affections,
> Those shadowy recollections,
> Which, be they what they may,
> Are yet the fountain-light of all our day,
> Are yet a master-light of all our seeing.

The closing pages of ***Remembering Babylon*** also offer two answers to the question of what relation the now elderly Janet and Lachlan can have to their childhood and to Gemmy. Gemmy, like their youth, is no longer physically present. Lachlan discovers that he has been killed by white settlers (along with the Aboriginal people he has joined). Though Lachlan is not even sure where he was killed, he and Janet can still be with him in memory. Gemmy can still be the 'fountain-light' of their adult day.

Remembering their sublime encounter with Gemmy brings Janet and Lachlan back into relation with their childhood selves and experiences. In a Romantic psychology this is always therapeutic. It draws the fragmented identity of the adult back into relation with its source in the imagination of the child. At the same time, this recollection takes them back to a point where their very different trajectories have not yet diverged. Gemmy is a sign for the vanishing point in childhood (in the Imagination) where male and female, politician and nun, possessor and possessed, have not yet drawn apart.

The passage of fifty years that separates the temporal location of the book's final chapter from its beginning places this work of memory in a historical moment charged with significance: approximately ten years after federation and just before the First World War. In Australian mythology, both temporal markers imply a bringing together of disparate fragments into a new whole. As a result of the former, the colonies came together as a single nation. In the course of the latter, it is still sometimes asserted, a fledgling Australian nation forged a sense of collective identity. This is the vision that Malouf wants to be seen proleptically in Gemmy. If we return to the moment of contact between settlers and indigenous people, we will find, not Babylon, but the redemptive source of national identity in the imagination. The recollection of this beginning draws present-day Australia and colonial Australia into a whole; it opens the possibility of a nation built on the re-membering, the forging into one, of different peoples and states.

Perhaps the most startling thing about this redemptive narrative is the magnitude of what it has to forget in order to re-member, its transformation of a moment of violent dispossession into an anticipation of national unity. Something of the extent of this forgetting is oddly implied by the epigraphs with which Malouf begins this book. The first, included as epigraph to this essay, quotes words spoken by Ahania to her husband and king, Urizen, in Blake's *The Four Zoas.* Ahania claims not to know whether the fallen world she and Urizen inhabit is Jerusalem or Babylon. These words might at first seem apt, for ***Remembering Babylon*** is centred on the premise that the colonial experience harbours the still-living source of the Jerusalem of national identity. In *The Four Zoas,* however, Ahania equivocates about the nature of the reality she inhabits because she fears that Urizen will cast her out rather than hear the truth. Malouf does not quote the next line, in which Ahania details the full extent of the devastation which surrounds them: 'All is Confusion. All is tumult, & we alone are escaped.'

The book's second epigraph is even more ambivalent. It comes from an untitled poem by John Clare, which imagines an apocalyptic crisis of gigantic proportions:

> Strange shapes and void afflict the soul
> And shadow to the eye
> A world on fire while smoke seas roll
> And lightenings rend the sky
> The moon shall be as blood the sun
> Black as a thunder cloud
> The stars shall turn to blue and dun
> And heaven by darkness bowed
> Shall make suns dark and give no day
> When stars like skys shall be
> When heaven and earth shall pass away
> Wilt thou Remember me.

If one were to read these lines in the light of the last chapter of ***Remembering Babylon,*** the 'world on fire while smoke seas roll' might suggest the First World War. The final line would then allude to Janet's and Lachlan's therapeutic recollection of Gemmy. But if one were to take the first chapter of the book as the interpretative context for these lines, then 'A world on fire while smoke seas roll' could just as easily refer to the historical and political realities of colonization that ***Remembering Babylon*** displaces. The last line would then have a much more plangent tone. It would refer to the very things that ***Remembering Babylon*** works so hard to forget.

Michiko Kakutani (review date 19 October 1993)

SOURCE: "A 'Black White Man' in Colonial Australia," in *The New York Times,* October 19, 1993, p. C19.

[*In the following favorable review of* Remembering Babylon, *Kakutani praises Malouf's characterizations and his focus on Australian history.*]

The Babylon referred to in the title of David Malouf's new novel ***Remembering Babylon*** is Australia: a 19th-century frontier that many of its settlers regarded as Eden, a New World paradise where they might make a fresh start and begin new lives, tabula rasa. Yet as we learn in this astonishing novel, Australia was also a harsh, dangerous land, a place that brought out in its colonizers the dark passions of racism, brutality and hate.

Remembering Babylon, Mr. Malouf's seventh novel, takes place "one day in the middle of the 19th century" in a small British settlement in the desolate territory of Queensland on the eastern coast of Australia. Three young children, Janet and Meg McIvor and their cousin Lachlan, are playing at the edge of the family paddock, when they see something amazing: a creature that seems half animal, half child emerges from the wilderness (that "abode of everything savage and fearsome") and slowly makes its way towards them. A hopping and flapping bird, they think, or maybe a scarecrow "that had somehow caught the spark of life."

Lachlan takes a stick and aims it, like a gun, at the creature; and the creature, to the children's shock, issues a plea in their own language: "Do not shoot," it stutters. "I am a B-b-british object!"

> **There are passages of aching beauty in *Remembering Babylon* and passages of shocking degradation. Mr. Malouf has written a wonderfully wise and moving novel, a novel that turns the history and mythic past of Australia into a dazzling fable of human hope and imperfection.**
>
> ***—Michiko Kakutani***

The creature, it turns out, is a man named Gemmy Fairley, who grew up on the streets of London. Abused by a savage employer, he ended up going to sea, where he soon fell into the hands of equally savage sailors; at the age of 13, he was cast ashore on the coast of Australia and left to die in the bush. He has spent the last 16 years living in the wilderness with a group of aborigines.

Bewildered by Gemmy, the children bring him back to town—a gathering of buildings, really, a store and post office and a pub—where the other settlers are amazed and amused by the "black white man" they have found. There is much exclaiming and joshing about the attempts of this "marionette or imbecile" to ingratiate himself, and eventually the town minister attempts to quiz Gemmy about his past.

Much the way he was once taken in by the aborigines who found him close to death on the beach, Gemmy is taken in by Janet and Meg's parents, Jock and Ellen McIvor. He is to help out on the farm and assist with simple household tasks, jobs he is only too happy to perform.

As the weeks slowly pass, Gemmy becomes a part of the family and a friend and confidant of the children. A bond of "fearful protectiveness" develops among them: he is their playmate, companion and instructor in the ways of the bush.

Conflict between the settlers and the local aborigines accelerates, however, and the McIvors' neighbours come to view Gemmy with more and more suspicion. They begin questioning him about his former friends, trying, without much success, to get him to divulge information about aboriginal habits and intentions. After Gemmy is glimpsed speaking with two blacks, seeds of mistrust quickly sprout. Gemmy is no longer regarded as an entertaining simpleton; to many of the settlers, he has become a symbol of their starkest fears about the Other that lies beyond the flimsy fences of their settlement: their fears about the encroaching wilderness, their fears about "the Bogey, the Coal Man, Absolute Night."

Tension grows between the McIvors and the rest of the community, and one terrible night, it explodes: Gemmy is abducted, beaten and nearly killed. For Gemmy, that night is another awful replay of all the abuse he suffered as a child. For Jock McIvor, it is a night that shatters his trust in his neighbors and undermines his sense of purpose. For his children, it is a night that will initiate them into the brutalities of the grown-up world; for both Janet and Lachlan, it is a night that will determine the shape of the rest of their lives.

In relating the story of Gemmy and the McIvors, Mr. Malouf gives the reader an extraordinarily intimate sense of these inarticulate people's inner lives: their longing for connection in this vast, empty land, and their clumsy apprehension of both the kindnesses and cruelties others are capable of committing.

Through deft, quickly drawn cameos, Mr. Malouf also provides us with a sense of the community the McIvors inhabit. He introduces us to Mr. Frazer, the benevolent town minister, who's lost in his dreams of botany; the schoolmaster George Abbot, a young sourpuss of a man, embittered by his own inadequacies and failures; Mrs. Hutchence, the eccentric old woman who teaches Janet the mysteries of beekeeping, and Andy McKillop, an angry, half-witted farm hand, who yearns to stir up trouble.

As related by Mr. Malouf, the settlers' appalling mistreatment of Gemmy serves as a kind of frightening prelude to the far more violent "dispersals" and massacres that would be perpetrated on the aboriginal population in the years to come. Perhaps what makes his portrait of such acts so devastating is his understanding that they are a consequence of the settlers' own dreams: their dreams of creating a safe place in the wilderness for their families; their determination, in the face of illness and hardship and fear, to make a new life in a land free of memories and ghosts.

There are passages of aching beauty in ***Remembering Babylon*** and passages of shocking degradation. Mr. Malouf has written a wonderfully wise and moving novel, a novel that turns the history and mythic past of Australia into a dazzling fable of human hope and imperfection.

Richard Eder (review date 31 October 1993)

SOURCE: "Strangers in a Strange Land," in *Los Angeles Times Book Review,* October 31, 1993, pp. 3, 8.

[*An American critic and journalist, Eder received the Pulitzer Prize for Criticism in 1987. In the following review, he discusses Malouf's focus on alienation, colonialism, identity, and cultural conflict in* Remembering Babylon.]

There is no fully satisfactory word to oppose to *exile,* that forced removal and dismayed regret for a land that will always be home. Contemporary Australian writers need such a word; it would denote the forcible remover, and the dismay of occupying a land that will always be alien.

"Invader" doesn't quite do it. What such gifted authors as Rodney Hall, Janette Turner Hospital and Peter Carey conjure up is more like the notion of crime in Greek tragedy than in our present-day world: a transgression against the gods committed without knowledge or intention, but which must be paid for anyway. Explicitly or by remote implication, these authors evoke the land-spirits of the aboriginal culture as the deities who punish white settlers and their descendants by estrangement or even wreckage of the spirit.

David Malouf, too, makes settler estrangement the theme of his new novel ***Remembering Babylon.*** He uses it quite as powerfully as the others but in quite a different way. Where their writing is drastic and nightmarish, his is muted and elusive. They launch boulders over crags to demonstrate the force of gravity; he floats twigs and straw down a rivulet and demonstrates something similar. To use a film comparison, he is Ozu to their Kurosawa.

There is another difference. Running through Malouf's novel there is a note of reconciliation. Even the most penitential nightmare, he suggests, is a dream, which life undermines by its insistence on waking up. Malouf's story is a multiplicity of story fragments, in fact, and they persist in undermining each other. There is some disorientation in reading him from page to page, and a rich accumulating subtlety.

Remembering Babylon is placed at the settlement of Queensland, the steamy territory on the northeast coast. The settlers have a precarious footing in their enclaves, surrounded by swamp and gray endless wilderness. Shadows live in the wilderness, itinerant bands of aborigines who respect the shotgun-enforced boundaries by day, but at night wander through the farmers' lands and restless sleep.

One day a tattered, scarecrow-like figure lopes out of the horizon and approaches the little nephew and daughters of Jock and Ellen MacIvor, at play in the paddock. Lachlan, defending the Empire, raises a stick at him. "Do not shoot," the figure shouts. "I am a B-b-british object."

Gemmy Fairley was a London slum-child who became a ship's cabin boy. At 13 he was put ashore in the shallows off Queensland. We do not know why; Malouf's story is full of holes which, like lace, let through the blurred light of a larger reality. An aborigine band found him unconscious and gave him water. They took him for a sea-spirit and when he stood up, a sea-spirit turned to a child. For 16 years he wandered with them; they accepted him while patiently waiting for him to turn, as they saw it, fully human.

His arrival in the little settlement is an eruption that tests its inhabitants in different ways. There is intense curiosity. Mr. Frazer, the minister, patiently coaxes a story out of Gemmy's few English words and extravagant gestures. The young schoolteacher writes the story down, adding some details himself out of creative vanity. There are other distortions; Malouf writes a lovely spoof of how history is achieved. The saintly and solicitous Frazer supplies phrases out of sympathy for Gemmy's anguished stammering.

There is the settlers' fear of the Other, their antipathy for Gemmy's outlandish appearance, and their sense of duty toward what seems to be an unfortunate fellow white. "It was the mixture of monstrous strangeness and unwelcome likeness that made Gemmy Fairley so disturbing to them." Jock MacIvor, out of his wife's insistence and his own conscience, takes Gemmy in, but with nervous distaste. Others are more outspoken; eventually a gang abducts Gemmy at night, pushes him around and gives him a dunking.

Jock brings him back, then holds him in arms all night to calm him. Gemmy raises a double question for them all: Is he the Other or is he us; and who are we? The question turns Jock from a self-reliant settler to a man who begins to question himself, to look about him, to open up to his wife. In a tender night-scene, Ellen recalls the amiable crowding of lives in their native Scottish town. Once she saw a tightrope walker cross above the thronged street. She takes a few steps to show her husband. "Ah'd gie aenethin' t'hae seen it," he says. "You, Ah mean. T'hae seen you."

Less directly, Gemmy changes other lives. An epilogue shows Lachlan, the endearing young imperial boy, as an old politician whose rise is curtailed by an act of conscience. His cousin Janet, who burned with puzzled envy of his boy's freedom, will find a different identity in her mother's charity toward Gemmy, work with him and an old woman neighbor on her beehives and eventually, as a nun, become a renowned entomologist. Malouf is never insistent; far from stressing what happens to his characters, he lets them fall away or wander off. His touch can be as fugitive and suggestive as a trick of light.

Gemmy, awkward and misfitting, we feel intensely and never see entirely. He did not come to join the settlers, but to pull together a haunted memory. His stay is an act of exorcism. He never relinquishes what the aborigines instilled in him, and eventually he will quietly go back among them. Gathering plants with Frazer, he had sensed the hidden presence of a group of black watchers. He knew what they were seeing:

> He himself would have a clear light around him like the line that contained Mr. Frazer's drawings. It came from the energy set off where his spirit touched the spirits he was moving through. All they would see of Mr. Frazer was what the land itself saw: a shape, thin, featureless, that interposed itself a moment, like a mist or cloud, before the land blazed out in its full strength again and the shadow was gone, as if, in the long history of the place, it was too slight to endure, or had never been.

Malouf, however, does not condemn his whites to invisibility. They can open up to the country, he suggests. He speaks, above all, through the polymathic and inquisitive Rev. Frazer. Perhaps he will become more than a shadow. Botanizing with Gemmy, learning all the plant names and getting some wrong, he is the antithesis of the settler mentality that seeks to implant England in Australia. A vegetable idealist, he petitions the governor to alter the emphasis on growing lamb and wheat in favor of developing the continent's own native fruits and roots:

"This is what is intended by our coming here to make this place, too, part of the world's garden, but by changing ourselves rather than it, and adding thus to the richness and variety of things."

In its shrewd, lyrical evocation of time, place and the human condition, *Remembering Babylon* is a near masterpiece.

—Michael Upchurch, in his "Strangeness and Likeness," in* Chicago Tribune—Books, *November 28, 1993.

Alice Truax (review date 2 December 1993)

SOURCE: "The Wild Child," in *The New York Review of Books,* Vol. XL, No. 20, December 2, 1993, pp. 13-15.

[*In the review below, Truax offers a thematic discussion of* Remembering Babylon.]

The Australian writer David Malouf is fascinated with the power of words, an obsession he shares with the characters in his books. At the opening of his second novel, ***An Imaginary Life*** (1978), the poet Ovid has arrived at a desolate edge of the Roman Empire, where he has been banished for tweaking the emperor's nose once too often. His new home is a village of huts, pigs, and mud. No one reads Latin; no one can even understand what he is saying. He walks around ranting during the daytime, cut off from the essential working life of the village, and at night he writes letters, even when there is no one to read them:

> I speak to you, reader, as one who lives in another century, since this is the letter I will never send. . . .
>
> Have you heard my name? Ovid? Am I still known? Has some line of my writing escaped the banning of my books from all the libraries and their public burning, my expulsion from the Latin tongue? Has some secret admirer kept one of my poems and so preserved it, or committed it to memory? Do my lines still pass secretly somewhere from mouth to mouth? Has some phrase of mine slipped through as a quotation, unnoticed by the authorities, in another man's poem? Or in a letter? Or in a saying that has become part of common speech and cannot now be eradicated?
>
> Have I survived?

Malouf isn't particularly interested in the circumstances surrounding Ovid's censorship, nor does he seem to care very much about Ovid's enduring literary fame. But here Ovid is like the desperate man on a desert island who puts a message in a bottle and throws it into the sea. The desire to be recognized and remembered is always close to the heart of Malouf 's work—whether he is writing about a prisoner of war in southeast Asia or a lonely Roman poet. And for these yearning characters, language often defines the boundaries of their imagined worlds. Malouf rescues their "utterances," even when they are unspoken; he gives them room to grow, transplanted, in the reader's mind.

At the same time, Malouf is distrustful of words that are divorced from visceral experience: these can foster enchantment and delusion. Ovid's fortunes improve only after he abandons his sterile self-imprisonment in Latin and learns the language of the place where he now lives. A feral boy is then discovered in the woods, and the poet teaches him to speak; this linguistic challenge is what binds Ovid anew to the present. It therefore seems appropriate that Malouf 's own heady concerns, which pleasingly resurface in book after book, are increasingly fused with the immediate and the particular. In his new novel about nineteenth-century Australia, ***Remembering Babylon,*** almost every idea seems lovingly fleshed out, just as the most commonplace object or gesture—a teacup, the slicing of an apple—is alive with meaning.

Remembering Babylon begins in a remote Queensland community in the 1850s, and the farming families who live there—the transplanted McIvors and Corcorans and Sweetmans who've abandoned mine pits and blacksmithies to stake their claim—are unsure whether the new world will be their salvation or their downfall. There is no name yet for the dusty track that runs by the general store, no road attaching their settlement to the others along the coast. The newcomers have barely made a scratch on the vastness that surrounds them:

> It was disturbing, that: to have unknown country behind you as well as in front. When the hissing of the lamp died out the hut sank into silence. A child's murmuring out of sleep might keep it human for a moment, or a rustling of straw; but what you were left with when the last sleeper settled was the illimitable night, where it lay close over the land. You lay listening to the crash of animals through its underbrush, the crack, like a snapped bone, of a ring-barked tree out in a paddock, then its muffled fall; or some other, unidentifiable sound, louder, further off, that was an event in the land's history, no part of yours. The sense then of being submerged, of being hidden away in the depths of the country, but also lost, was very strong.

The massacres of the Australian aborigines are hinted at throughout ***Remembering Babylon,*** yet Malouf makes ready-made twentieth-century judgments about this historical catastrophe seem embarrassingly glib. Just as Pat Barker's recent novel *Regeneration* demands a strenuous moral reevaluation of the First World War by entangling the reader in Siegfried Sassoon's decision to resign from the army, Malouf forces you to experience not only the colonists' hatred, but also the fear that fosters it. The terrors engendered by this new land of upside-down seasons and wide skies seem almost equal to its opportunities. Cyclones. Floods. Natives who can come up on you without a sound, who refuse to recognize the authority of a fence. Jock McIvor dreams of snow, and his wife tells their children the stories of her own growing-up over and over. The faded dress with its pattern of larkspurs; the schoolmaster's slim French volumes, with their heroines named Ursule or Victorine: these are the settlers' talismans against the unknown, for Australia speaks a language that they do not understand.

It is out of this unfathomed, unfathomable territory that Gemmy Fairley emerges. On the blisteringly hot morning when the McIvor children first catch sight of him coming out of the swamp, they are already involved in a rather energetic game of make-believe—tracking wolves across the snowy forests of Russia—and at first they are mystified by what the creature bobbing awkwardly toward them *is:*

> The stick-like legs, all knobbed at the joints, suggested a wounded waterbird, a brolga, or a human that in the manner of the tales they told one another, all spells and curses, had been *changed* into a bird, but only halfway . . .

The children are frightened, but also utterly transfixed. Is he a scarecrow? Is he a black? By rights he *should* be a black, jumping out of the wilderness and running toward them in this eerie, incomprehensible way. But his hair is a shock of blond against his darkened skin. Lachlan, the boy, steps forward and gestures threateningly with his stick as though it were a gun. The creature squawks with alarm and leaps to the top rail of the fence. There, teetering, it stutters to justify its existence before being annihilated by the boy's imaginary weapon:

" 'Do not shoot,' it shouted. 'I am a B-b-british object!' "

After this astonishing statement. Gemmy falls off the fence and allows Lachlan to lead him back to the settlement, where he is considered quite a wondrous find.

Like Ovid, Gemmy is an outsider and an outcast, but of a far more ordinary sort: a white man, yes, but even so, a British object of little value—factory "maggot," rat-catcher's urchin—always defined by his usefulness to others. Sixteen years before, after a miserable stint as a much-abused ship's boy, Gemmy had been unceremoniously dumped overboard while he was sick with fever. Rescued by the aborigines, he has lived among them ever since.

Gemmy's years in Australia have not been unhappy ones, but he is haunted by a sense of his life before, a life that he can no longer remember. He lies by the aborigines' campfire at night and mysterious images come, unbidden, into his mind. Unsurprisingly, they are often contained in a word, like the seed locked in a fruit: " 'Boots' the darkness whispered—he caught only the breath of the word—and there they were: objects that made no sense here, that he saw propped up in front of a barred grate."

So when Gemmy learns that there are white-faced creatures living to the south, he goes to seek them out, knowing that he needs their language to coax out this other spirit that lives inside him and troubles his dreams. Soon he comes upon a man in a clearing, who is preparing to swing "a long-handled, bladed instrument." Gemmy watches from his hiding place:

> He was amazed. A kind of meaning clung to the image in the same way that the clothes he was wearing clung to the man, and when the blade flashed and jarred against wood, it struck home in him. *Axe.*
>
> The word flew into his head as fast and clear as the flash and whistle of its breath. *Axe. Axe.* Circles of meaning rippled away from the mark it blazed in the dark of his skull.

Gemmy is not escaping his present life, but attempting to reclaim his past, and as he circles the white community, observing, exploring, the language is as palpable to him as the chicken feed he shoves into his mouth and the clothes dancing on the line in the yard. The next day, when he runs toward the children, he wants to prove that "all that separated him from them was ground that could be covered."

Because the boy, Lachlan, feels that he discovered Gemmy, the McIvors agree to take him in. But, in a larger sense, the settlers can't seem to take him in; they find his presence among them strangely unnerving. What can it mean that, despite his lack of modesty, his goofy mannerisms, his humiliating desire to please, he is one of them?

> He had started out white. No question. When he fell in with the blacks—at thirteen, was it?—he had been like any other child, one of their own for instance. (That was hard to swallow.) But had he remained white? . . . Could you lose it? Not just language, but it. *It.*

The day following Gemmy's arrival, Mr. Frazer, the minister, brings Gemmy to the schoolhouse to examine him, instructing the schoolmaster, George Abbot, to take down his story. This dictation proves to be somewhat of a farce. Young Lachlan is Gemmy's best interpreter, but he is so rambunctious that he is finally banished from the schoolroom, leaving Gemmy in Mr. Frazer's well-meaning but far less capable hands. (Gemmy, anxious to be agreeable, eagerly accepts any interpretation Mr. Frazer offers, while Lachlan looks on, contemptuously, from the window.) Meanwhile Abbot, who is scornful of what he sees as the minister's gullibility, begins introducing fanciful elements of his own into the record. By the time Gemmy has finished, any sense that this is an accurate transcription of his experience—and whether, by implication, any such transcription is accurate—has been seriously compromised.

In *Remembering Babylon* Malouf forces you to experience not only the colonists' hatred, but also the fear that fosters it. The terrors engendered by this new land of upside-down seasons and wide skies seems almost equal to its opportunities.

—Alice Truax

The irony of this scene—which is at once comical, moving, and strangely upsetting—is less that Gemmy's life history, despite being elicited and recorded, is riddled with error than that for Gemmy the solemnity of the enterprise is completely authentic. "Magic, as Gemmy understood it, had been the essence of the occasion." He examines the ink-marked pages with reverence:

> He knew what writing was but had never himself learned the trick of it. As he handled the sheets and turned them this way and that, and caught the peculiar smell they gave off, his whole life was in his throat—tears, laughter too, a little—and he was filled with an immense gratitude. He had shown them what he was. He was known.

Like Ovid writing to his future readers, like Janet McIvor hunched over her needlework "as if her life was in every stitch," Gemmy possesses an intense desire to be pressed into the fabric of the world in some way that is both eternal and tangible. In one sense, Gemmy is distorted and diminished by this cobbled-together transcription, yet he is also exalted by the significance of its very existence. This contradiction is what prevents the scene from feeling narrowly moralistic. And is the illiterate Gemmy's assessment of the wonders of writing so different from the awe that all readers periodically experience throughout their lives?

> It did not surprise him—it was the nature of magic—that all that had happened to him, all his fortune good and bad, and so much sweat and pain, and miles travelled and bones picked and nights of freezing dew, and dreams, and dreams . . . should be reduced now to what a man could hold in his hand and slip into a pocket.

It is not only Gemmy who achieves a new self-consciousness: his very presence forces a new self-consciousness upon the colonists, and many of them find it an unwelcome one. The way he speaks English is especially galling:

> He was a parody of a white man. If you gave him a word for a thing, he could, after a good deal of huffing and blowing, repeat it, but the next time round you had to teach it to him all over again. He was imitation gone wrong, and the mere sight of it put you wrong too, made the whole business somehow foolish and open to doubt.

How do the McIvors put up with it? Slowly, inevitably, Gemmy's presence precipitates a reshuffling of loyalties. Old friendships are strained, new alliances spring up where none had previously existed. Malouf is particularly good at suggesting the profound disturbances and realignments that can occur within one person without being detected or remarked upon by others: the sudden terror of a despised farmhand; the fresh jealousy of a child. These assorted settlers, no less than Gemmy, have their own secret histories, and the brief glimpses Malouf offers us of their inner lives have the quality of revelation.

Although these harsh, hot landscapes of the Australian frontier are a hemisphere away from the Cornish coast and the florists of Bond Street, the loneliness of Malouf's characters is surprisingly reminiscent of Virginia Woolf; each one seems caught in an intricate prison of particularity. In ***Remembering Babylon,*** everyone important—Gemmy, Lachlan, Mr. Frazer, the schoolmaster, the various McIvors—is also very isolated, even when in the company of others. But their alienation is punctuated by brief moments of connectedness, like Mrs. Dalloway's sudden and clamorous happiness on a city street—"in the triumph and the jingle and the strange high singing of some aeroplane overhead was what she loved; life; London; this moment of June." Both writers celebrate that fragile and joyous sense of oneself in the world. In Woolf these moments are unearned. For Malouf's characters, though, they have a moral dimension; they are a form of blessing, and one must be ready to receive it.

In ***Remembering Babylon,*** Mr. Frazer is the only adult who sees that he can learn something from Gemmy, and they often go on field trips together—"to botanise," as Mr. Frazer calls it—in the surrounding countryside. Gemmy shows the minister the edible plants and vegetables, making him taste the scavenged tuber or berry, teaching him to sound out their strange names. Mr. Frazer jots them down phonetically in his notebook and then, to his companion's amazement, sketches the plant itself, bringing it to life again on the page. This is a quintessentially Maloufian exchange: it is almost as though—through Gemmy's language—the earth meets Mr. Frazer's enthusiastic curiosity with a corresponding eagerness to be known. Just as words in Malouf are always pressing against their limitations as mere words—he describes them as whistling, blazing, darkening a room—the natural world seems to respond to the human desire to perceive it, as though thrilling to a touch.

One suspects that it is the minister's lack of popularity in his profession that has brought him to this forsaken outpost, where he can't even supply his wife with a piano. But after spending time with Gemmy, Mr. Frazer's own ruminations on Australia take a visionary turn. At night, he takes out his notebooks and lets his imagination run wild with all he has learned. He marvels to think that early settlers starved to death in the midst of such abundance, unable, "*with their English eyes,*" to recognize it:

> *We must rub our eyes and look again, clear our minds of what we are looking for to see what is there. . . . Is there not a kind of refractory pride in it, an insistence that if the land will not present itself to us in terms that we know, we would rather die than take it as it is? For there is a truth here and it is this: that no continent lies outside God's bounty and his intention to provide for his children. He is a gardener and everything he makes is a garden.*

Just as Mr. Frazer helps Gemmy translate his life into English, Gemmy in turn helps translate the landscape of Australia into something comprehensible. Mr. Frazer learns, by defining the particular, to redefine the whole, and in so doing he finds himself transformed as well.

But while the minister fashions his paradise out of what he can see and feel and name, others in his flock are infusing more sinister mythologies with new life. Now, when Jock McIvor's neighbors regularly gather on the hillside at the day's end, they argue about the safety of allowing Gemmy to remain among them. And in the afternoons, the wives come to Ellen McIvor's to do their darning: What, their hostess wonders bitterly, did they talk about before Gemmy's arrival? Malouf captures perfectly the insidious, masturbatory tenor of their gossip:

> Didn't she find it hard sometimes to sit at the same table with him? Considering that he might be happier running about naked—goodness, remember that first day!—than in the shirts she washed for him. Oh and the trousers, of course! And eating grubs—imagine!—then potatoes and cold mutton. That is, if it wasn't something worse. Their own grandfathers, so they say. And wasn't she scared, just a little—well they knew *she* wasn't but they would be, it was a wonder really how calm she was—of the time he spent with the children. The little girls, for instance. . . . And did she really let him chop wood for her? Actually let him loose with an *axe?*

Here the whites wield the word "axe" as a sly justification for their own eventual violence; we've come a long way from Gemmy's moment of recognition in the clearing. When some blacks from Gemmy's tribe come to pay him a visit, they are sighted by a neighboring farmhand, and the news spreads through the settlement like contagion. Jock McIvor's neighbors are restless; soon he finds an obscenity smeared in human excrement on the side of his shed, seething with greenflies. The writing, so to speak, is on the wall.

Or is it? As the question of Gemmy's fate looms over the settlement, the reader waits for the event that will draw the principal characters together and test their moral mettle in some conclusive way. This inevitable climax never happens. Gemmy manages to tilt the story away from its predictable endings, and, finally, to give the reader the slip altogether, disappearing into the mysterious country that delivered him. He remains, for the time being, the subject of his own story, but we never hear the rest of it. Nor do we return to the settlement without him—the final section of the novel is about a reunion between Lachlan and Janet McIvor in another time and place altogether. Paradoxically, this narrative swerve makes Gemmy seem more real rather than less so. It is as though he has finally eluded even the manipulations of his creator.

This elusiveness is chronic in Malouf, and it may be one reason why he is not, after seven novels, better known in the United States. His endings often leave us hungry with questions, as if his world is merely an extension of our own—ragged, porous, burgeoning with unfinished stories. To hold onto this great world—to remember the names for all that will otherwise be lost, to find the words with which to grasp the present, to articulate one's visions of the future—is an unceasing challenge. Perhaps Malouf believes that to suggest otherwise, even in fiction, is a misguided deceit. Perhaps he refuses to fold Gemmy's story up with some final flourish because it isn't meant, finally, to be reduced to "what a man could hold in his hand and slip into a pocket." Once so dispensed with, it might be easier to forget.

In ***Remembering Babylon,*** Gemmy desperately wants to be known, both to himself and to others. Although Malouf won't answer the riddle of Gemmy's life, he does answer Gemmy's yearning for that life to be recognized. Malouf honors the desire for recognition in all of us. After all, the author does deliver Ovid's mournful letter safely into our hands. And in response to the lonely man's closing cry—"Have I survived?"—we can answer, "Yes. Yes."

Dwight Garner (review date Winter 1993-1994)

SOURCE: "Dark Terror," in *Hungry Mind Review,* No. 28, Winter, 1993-94, pp. 54-5.

[*In the review below, Garner favorably assesses* Remembering Babylon, *stating that this is "Malouf 's best book" to date.*]

The Australian writer David Malouf 's new novel is a compact import—at a lean two hundred pages, it's practically a novella—but it arrives with a mighty rumble behind it. In the U.K. ***Remembering Babylon*** is an odds-on bet to grab the Booker Prize, and elsewhere in Europe the book has been heralded as Malouf 's long-awaited breakthrough. The hype isn't mere woodsmoke: ***Remembering Babylon,*** a shrewd meditation on Australia's racial and cultural divides, has the intellectual heft and moral resonance of novels three times its length. It's Malouf 's best book, and it's a beauty.

Remembering Babylon's modest size wouldn't be worth remarking if Malouf 's last novel, ***The Great World*** (1990), hadn't spread itself across such a sprawling canvas. The book's World War II-era narrative followed an unlikely pair of misfits across several decades and continents, and it moved with the ruthless certainty of fate. As potent as ***The Great World*** was, though, ***Remembering Babylon*** focuses Malouf 's flame: his masterful sentences, which are artfully unmannered and oblique, have never marched forward to greater effect.

Remembering Babylon, Malouf 's seventh novel, is set in the "hostile and infelicitous" Australian north country of the 1840s, where a small band of European settlers has constructed a tenuous farming community. The existence they eke out is a mean, difficult one, and they're burdened with an uneasy sense "of being in a place that had not yet revealed all its influences on them." Worse, they live with a constant (if irrational) fear of Australia's aborigines—the "blackfellers." Malouf 's writing about dislocating terror in the face of an unknown enemy has a clear-eyed power that stops you short:

> It brought you slap up against a terror you thought you had learned, years back, to treat as childish: the Bogey, the Coal Man, Absolute Night. And now here it is, not two yards away, solid and breathing: a thing beside which all you have ever known of darkness, of *visible* darkness, seems but the merest shadow, and all you can summon up to the encounter, out of a lifetime lived on the other, the lighter side of things—shillings and pence, the Lord's Prayer, the half dozen tunes your fingers can pick out on the strings of a fiddle, the names and ages of your children, including the ones in the earth, your wife's touch on your naked belly, and the shy, soft affection you have for yourself—weakens and falls away before the apparition, out of nowhere, of a figure taller perhaps than you are and of a sooty blackness beyond black, utterly still, very close, yet so far off, even at a distance of five feet, that you cannot conceive how it can be here in the same space, the same moment with you.

Remembering Babylon is about what happens to these settlers when, quite by accident, a gaggle of children "capture" a strange apparition that's appeared at the edge of a swamp. Gemmy Fairley, a "straw-topped half-naked savage," is dragged into town, where the settlers learn his sorry history: At thirteen he'd been rudely tossed ashore by a merchant ship and taken in by aborigines. Sixteen years later this "in-between creature"—is he black, or is he white? the townspeople wonder—has emerged back into the world of the Europeans. (Gemmy hadn't actually intended to find the white world again; something in him merely wanted to "prove that all that separated him from them was ground that could be covered.")

The abiding theme in nearly all of Malouf 's work has been alienation—the terrible human divides wrought by race, class, and culture—and in Gemmy Fairley he has created a perfect lens through which to explore these concerns. Everyone in the community has a different reaction to Gemmy, and in their responses they speak far more about themselves than about him. For a while, most of the settlers treat Gemmy as a mere distraction. As the poor man "hummed and hooted and shot spittle out of his mouth" while trying to recall the few English words he once knew, the settlers revel in "the unaccustomed jollity of it, a noisy carnival." To them, Gemmy's a strange joke, "a parody of a white man."

The jollity turns to wariness, though, when Gemmy becomes a permanent fixture by moving in with one of the families. He unknowingly injects an element of poison into the community; he's a blank wall onto which they project their deepest fears about themselves and others. "Gemmy, just by being there, opened a gate on to things, things [a man] couldn't specify, even to himself, and did not want to ask about, that worried the soulcase out of him." Neighboring farmers begin to pressure the family to get rid of Gemmy; time-tested friendships are ripped apart during the debate about Gemmy's trustworthiness, a debate that ultimately turns crudely violent.

Malouf has dramatized this sort of difficult communion between "civilized" society and a seemingly part-human, part-animal presence before. In ***An Imaginary Life*** (1978), he imagines the Roman poet Ovid, while in a strange exile, becoming obsessed with a child who'd been living with wolves. But the earlier novel pales in comparison to Malouf 's performance here.

Part of Malouf 's achievement in ***Remembering Babylon*** is how much diverse life he packs into two hundred pages, without once cramping the narrative or losing the thread of this almost mythopoetic fable. For while Gemmy's tale provides the book's soul, Malouf skillfully interweaves numerous ancillary characters and dramas, each of which amplifies the issues surrounding Gemmy's alien status. Some of the book's best moments, in fact, emerge as the narrative skips back and forth in time, and the story is related from a multiplicity of perspectives.

Among the most potent and memorable scenes I've encountered in recent fiction, in fact, arrives when the daughter of the family that shelters Gemmy is set upon in a field by thousands upon thousands of bees. The girl sees "her hands covered with plushy, alive fur gloves before her whole body crusted over and she was blazingly gathered into the single sound they made, the single mind." But the bees don't bite, and as the girl surrenders her mind to their collective "unbodied" one, she has a quasi-religious experience—her life is irrevocably altered. (She ends up, actually, in a convent.)

In this scene and in so many others in ***Remembering Babylon,*** Malouf is writing not only of race—that is, our fear of that which is different. He's also underlining what social creatures we are—how we're ever so willing to surrender our individuality (i.e., our capacity for rational thought) in order to merge with a larger group. Our greatest urge is to fit in; we want to know *our* place, even if that means expelling those who don't fit. Our sociable selves are constantly at war with the rest of us.

For Malouf 's settlers, the need to feel grounded in a stable society is an undeniable yearning. Each of them feels rootless—as if they need to latch onto something quickly or they'll drift up into the dry air. It's so terrifyingly easy, as one lonely farm woman puts it, "to lose yourself in the immensities of the land, under a sky that opened too far in the direction of infinity." Life threatened to "sweep you right out of the door into a world where nothing, not a flat iron, not the names of your children on your lips, could hold you down against the vast upward expanse of your breath."

If the settlers worry about establishing firm roots lest they be swept out the door, Malouf 's sentences are a perfect mixture of earth and sky, of fact and feeling. He writes like a dream, never doing fandangos at his material's expense, never descending into glibness. His prose may, in fact, put some readers in mind of Cormac McCarthy's laconic but oddly expansive storytelling.

With ***Remembering Babylon*** Malouf has created an historical fiction that lives thrillingly in the present: the book's intellectual achievement (a subtle examination of race and its discontents) is never at odds with the book's onrushing narrative thrust. This is a novel that sorely tests what Malouf calls "the glow of the white man's authority."

The authority of Malouf 's art, however, is never once called into question.

An excerpt from *Remembering Babylon*

They were sly. They pretended to be pleased with him. He too was sly, but was less sure than he would have liked to be that he had told them nothing they might use. He leapt about, and with his heart very heavy in him, joked a little, and they narrowed their eyes, all smiles. 'Good boy, Gemmy,' Ned Corcoran said, as if he could have brained him.

But it was the other lot, those who were looking for the soft way, who gave him trouble. They could not understand why he was holding out on them. They were the peaceable ones, the ones who wanted to avoid bloodshed, couldn't he see that? Couldn't he tell the difference? Urgency made them desperate. They shouted at him, and then at one another.

And in fact a good deal of what they were after he could not have told, even if he had wanted to, for the simple reason that there were no words for it in their tongue; yet when, as sometimes happened, he fell back on the native word, the only one that could express it, their eyes went hard, as if the mere existence of a language they did not know was a provocation, a way of making them helpless. He did not intend it that way, but he too saw that it might be true. There was no way of existing in this land, or of making your way through it, unless you took into yourself, discovered on your breath, the sounds that linked up all the various parts of it and made them one. Without that you were blind, you were deaf, as he had been, at first, in their world. You blundered about seeing holes where in fact strong spirits were at work that had to be placated, and if you knew how to call them up, could be helpful. Half of what ought to have been bright and full of the breath of life to you was shrouded in mist.

David Malouf, in his Remembering Babylon, *Pantheon Books, 1993.*

Cynthia Blanche (review date January-February 1994)

SOURCE: "Artful," in *Quadrant,* Vol. XXXVIII, Nos. 1-2, January-February, 1994, pp. 115-17.

[*Blanche is a New South Wales novelist. In the excerpt below, she faults Malouf 's focus on characterization rather than theme in* Remembering Babylon.]

Remembering Babylon, David Malouf 's latest novel, is beautifully written, as indeed is everything that Malouf produces. It is a story about a small Queensland settlement in the mid-1800s and how the arrival of a man-creature from out of the bush affects it.

> . . . and its flamelike flickering, was not even, maybe, human. The stick-like legs, all knobbed at the joints, suggested a wounded waterbird, a brolga, or a human that in the manner of the tales they told one another, all spells and curses, had been *changed* into a bird, but only halfway, and now, neither one thing nor the other, was hopping and flapping towards them out of a world over there, beyond the no-man's-land of the swamp, that was the abode of everything savage and fearsome, and since it lay so far beyond experience, not just their own but their parents' too, of nightmare rumours, superstitions and all that belonged to Absolute Dark.

Gemmy, a white man, whose first appearance is thus described, has lived in the bush with the Aborigines for many years. No mother exists in his earliest memories, just himself as a sweeper in a timber mill. At the age of five or six, Gemmy became the ratcatcher Willett's assistant.

> When he plunges his arm into the musky dark and hauls the sewer-and ditch-rats out of the hot, drain-smelling interior, they squeal and tumble over one another's backs, and fight, using their teeth something horrible, and he gets many wounds that turn to open sores. He has scars all over his hands—one thumb is bitten through—and on his ears as well, since the rats, if they get the chance, will run up his body like squirrels up a tree trunk and fix their claws in his hair, till Willett untangles and tears them off. They get up the leg of his trousers too if they are not laced at the knees with string.

After escaping Willett at the age of twelve, Gemmy was press-ganged onto a sailing ship, then thrown overboard near Australia. He nearly drowned and Aborigines rescued him. When he at last emerges from the bush, sixteen years later, some of the members of the settlement take him into their hearts and hearths with kindness, while others hate and fear him and seek to destroy him. One day two blacks come out of the bush and sit with Gemmy.

> They spread the land out for him, gave him its waters to drink. As he took huge draughts of it, saw it light his flesh. Watched him, laughing, bathe in it, scooping great handfuls over his breast. In the little space of dust between them as they sat, they danced, beat up clouds, threw rainbows over their heads. Then they rose, exchanged the formalities of parting, and went. A day and a night it would take them to reach a place that was already humming all round him as he took up his hammer and sent the blows of it leaping with such clarity in the release of his spirit that they might be flying, he thought, thirty miles off, like stars his arms could fling over the furthest ridge to light their path.
>
> Then that bloke Andy appeared; came stumbling out of the scrub with his crooked jaw and restless, runaway eyes, and stood leaning on air, with the odd, empty look that anything, any madness might fill; hinting, demanding. The air around him was immediately infected, sucked into the emptiness he made just by stepping into it.

What a wonderful description of the effect a hostile, negative person can have on one!

There is much Gemmy has in common with Malouf 's Wild Boy of ***An Imaginary Life***. However, ***Remembering Babylon*** is not as successful. There is, for my taste, too much about too many characters that I don't find interesting, despite the fact that they all, in some way, feel alienated from their former lives. And new characters keep popping up even towards the end of the book. There is the promise of a good character in Mrs Hutchence, but she has a limited presence. Gemmy is the one really interesting character, and there is too little of him.

The theme is concerned with existing in a dimension of life at one remove from everyone else. But there is little story development and I'm afraid the whole thing, apart from some magic moments, is really rather dull.

Harvey Blume (review date February-March 1994)

SOURCE: A review of *Remembering Babylon,* in *Boston Review,* Vol. XIX, No. 1, February-March, 1994, pp. 32, 34.

[*Blume is an American novelist. In the following, he offers praise for* Remembering Babylon, *comparing the novel to Joseph Conrad's novella* Heart of Darkness *(1902).*]

There is an area forever associated with Joseph Conrad's *Heart of Darkness,* an area of meeting, crossover, mixture, transgression, an area inhabited—incarnated—by Kurtz. Kurtz is the renegade, the one who has abandoned western identity to assume unspeakable powers in an African forest hidden almost entirely from view of Belgium's river steamers. When Kurtz returns to, or is retrieved by, the West, it is only to rave eloquently and die. He never explains the mystery; he *is* the mystery. He can't articulate the taboo; he is the interdiction itself, the broken commandment, in his very being. The tablets of the law are shattered on the golden calf. Out of this collision comes a Kurtz.

David Malouf returns to this supercharged Conradian terrain and summons language strong enough to hold it open, to make it bearable, nearly, for the duration of his remarkable novel, ***Remembering Babylon***. Whereas Kurtz, invoked for most of *Heart of Darkness,* only materializes at the end, Malouf presents us with his creature of two worlds, his in-between, nearly at the beginning.

The first words Malouf gives him, though they may never, like Kurtz's "The horror! The horror!," course through our culture until uttered on screen by Marlon Brando, are memorable enough:

> " 'Do not shoot,' it shouted [to children who are not quite convinced that the creature they are looking at is human], 'I am a B-b-british object!' "

Indeed he was a "B-b-british object"—a young one, still a boy—until British seamen heaved him overboard near the coast of Australia sometime in the mid-19th century. Then he became an aboriginal object. For the aborigines, the boy's story begins when they find an incoherent crab-encrusted creature on the shore: the creature does something that approximates a dance and becomes, thereby, approximately human. The boy himself accepts this account of his origins except in dreams and in memories of a language he no longer speaks but has not entirely forgotten.

Malouf gives us access to the mind of Gemmy Fairly, as the boy is named by the whites—or at least as much access as Gemmy has to himself, for his mind is chambered, double, and at the same time incomplete. Gemmy struggles with familiar English words until whites avert their eyes, seeing in his search for simple sounds a sign of impairment or, worse, of treason—in any case, a mark of otherness that subverts their own identity. Gemmy compels them to ask themselves "the harder question. Could you lose it? Not just language but *it. It.*"

Gemmy has left the aborigines, among whom he has lived for years, to approach the settlement because whites offer him clues to his first memories of a tyrannical parent and the children among whom he once swarmed in an English sawmill, cleaning nuts and bolts and eating crusted machine oil as if it were candy. From the moment of his appearance among the whites—he is marched into town ahead of a boy brandishing the make-believe gun—we tremble for him.

His presence makes the hardest men among them harder still. His indistinctness—his being neither one thing nor the other, in age, culture, and appearance, his very jaw line reset by different consonants, different vowels—seems more than imbecilic to them; it seems monstrous. If his existence can be resolved at all in their minds it is that he must be a "blackfeller" disguised in white skin, a dangerous emissary of the outback. He worries "the soulcase" out of them: How long, we wonder, will they let him live?

Those few in the community who care for Gemmy despite fears of their own are gentled in the process. Like the others, they are immigrants from crowded places who have established tenancy on the land in blind terror of its expanse, its openness, and most of all its dark, nomadic inhabitants who seem to appear and disappear like shadows. Now they cross over, somehow, through Gemmy, to vision. They put down tools at odd times to marvel at themselves marveling at insects, flowers, birds pulling filaments out of running water. One man considers that previously he had been no more than "a sociable self, wrapped always in a communal warmth that protected it from dark matters and all the blinding light of things, but also from the knowledge that there was a place out there where the self might stand alone."

Occasionally—and always luminously—Malouf crosses all the way over through Gemmy to the world as seen by the aborigines. Once they seek Gemmy on the outskirts of town to telepathically transmit images of the land they used to travel together. Another time they stand squarely within the field of vision of the town's preacher who fails to see them because he cannot assimilate the raw shock of their presence. They, in turn, see him as no more than a "shape, thin, featureless, that interposed itself a moment, like a mist or cloud, before the land blazed out in its full strength again and the shadow was gone."

Gemmy sees from both sides; he is the fractured unity, the unobtainable translation. And though he is the crucial center of the book, other characters are drawn to a comparable depth. It is through two of them, children when they knew Gemmy and now middle-aged, that we look back on the denouement of the story. This break in the narrative, incidentally, is jarring. The leap from present to future, though it occurs near the end of the novel, remains the author's one questionable maneuver.

The writing, however, never falters. There are books we like so much we don't want to finish them. In this case the same applies to paragraphs and even sentences. And in keeping Kurtz-space open to us at maximum intensity, David Malouf has written a profound and poignant book.

Annette Smith (essay date 13 November 1994)

SOURCE: "The Tower of Babble," in *Los Angeles Times Book Review,* November 13, 1994, p. B.

[*An educator, Smith was one of the judges responsible for awarding Malouf the 1994* Los Angeles Times *Book Award for Fiction. In the essay below, she discusses Malouf's focus on language, boundaries, and the human condition in* Remembering Babylon.]

One day, in the middle of the last century, when white settlement was crawling, tentatively, up the coast of Queensland, three children were stopped in their games by the sight of a strange "thing" in the nearby swamps: perhaps "a human that in the manner of the tales they told one another . . . had been changed into a bird, but only halfway, and now, neither one thing nor the other, was hopping and flapping towards them out of a world . . . that was the abode of everything savage and fearsome . . . and of all that belonged to the Absolute Dark."

What they had taken for a lone aborigine raider turns out to be Gemmy Fairley, a "black white" with hair as blond as theirs. As the creature stands, scarecrow-like at the top of the boundary fence, facing a toy gun, he shouts "Do not shoot. . . . I am a B-b-british object!" One mark of a great novel, it might be said, is that its totality be already contained in its first few paragraphs, and such is certainly the case for ***Remembering Babylon,*** this year's winner of the *Los Angeles Times* Fiction Prize. In its first two pages alone, one understands that the book will be about boundaries, about encountering the Other, about metamorphosis and (through Gemmy Fairley's unwittingly accurate statement) about language.

David Malouf begins with this primal scene of the boundary fence—a fragile line between the white settlers and a continent so vast that the silence, when the hissing of the lamp dies out, engulfs them in the unknown. His simple plot covers the two years spent by Gemmy with the white Scottish community (following 16 spent with the aborigines), the various responses to him (from total acceptance to total rejection and nuances in between), the subtle changes in relationships precipitated by his presence, and finally his mysterious disappearance and a postscript reuniting two of the main protagonists, many years older and wiser. This plot, which resembles the story of Francois Truffaut's *Wild Child* and of Theodora Kroeber's Ishi in *Two Worlds,* is a recurrent one in Malouf 's work, testifying to his fascination with otherness and transformation. An Australian poet and novelist, he has previously published a fictionalized biography of Ovid, ***An Imaginary Life,*** in which Ovid befriends a wild child who, later during his exile in a decaying, rust-brown port town, will seem to him like a messenger, possibly a god.

Remembering Babylon **is elating, rather than depressing. Its final message is that men are capable of change and that even an imperfect change is better than none. Malouf wrote somewhere that "poems are acts of reconciliation." So, in a different way, is *Remembering Babylon.***

—Annette Smith

With Gemmy as a catalyst, many boundaries are redefined in ***Remembering Babylon,*** particularly those between races. The anti-colonial and racial themes are handled with a concern for historical and individual complexity. The ghostlike aborigines looming outside the limits of thc settlement constantly remind us that the whites are encroaching onto native territory. Nevertheless, Malouf legitimizes the settlers' claim to a land disputed foot by foot to the wilderness and empathizes with their need to cling to the only identity they know. If Gemmy, "this mixture of monstrous strangeness and unwelcome likeness," has changed his identity, not to mention skin color and (due to eroded teeth) face structure, "could you lose it? Not just language, but it. It." The very vagueness of the pronoun connotes the essential nature of that "it."

In any case, Malouf 's plea for tolerance goes beyond the racial context. While he finely satirizes empire builders in the person of Governor Lord Bowen and vividly evokes the hostility against Gemmy rampant in part of the community, he shows that Gemmy, as a rat-catcher's slave-boy in London, was indeed a "British object" long before his adoption by a native clan.

The Babylon in the title evokes therefore not only a parallel between the Israelites' captivity after the fall of Jerusalem and the colonists' nostalgia and isolation, but also the Tower of Babel, biblical site of the separation of languages and nations. Malouf 's novel testifies all along to the confusion of languages. It demonstrates the demonic nature of words, both their destructive power and their creative force, as Gemmy's past and his new identity take form, however spuriously, on records kept by a minister and schoolmaster.

Professors of literature and writers will, perhaps, read in this chapter not only an allegory of literature but also an allegory of the passage from oral to written culture, as Gemmy sniffs the sheets of paper on which his life has been inscribed. Finally, Malouf 's prose itself provides a subtle allegory on the separation of languages, for its ceremonial, slightly rugged unfolding seems to echo faintly some ancient biblical language that would have been lost forever with the Babel episode.

At the end of the tale, as suddenly as he has appeared, Gemmy walks away from the uncomfortable niche his goodwill and that of others had won him in the group and takes to the bush. We are not told exactly why. Nor shall we know for sure when and how he died, probably the victim of a minor colonial raid on Bushmen; nor which bones are the white ones amid the remains his friend Lachlan finds, several years later, in the forks of trees.

Yet the novel is elating, rather than depressing. Its final message is that men are capable of change and that even an imperfect change is better than none. Malouf wrote somewhere that "poems are acts of reconciliation." So, in a different way, is ***Remembering Babylon***. For we are linked to the Other in order to exist ourselves, and the gesture that gives is always the gesture that seeks.

FURTHER READING

Criticism

Sheppard, R. Z. "The Wild Man Within." *Time* 142, No. 17 (25 October 1993): 82, 85.

Favorable assessment of *Remembering Babylon.* Sheppard asserts that this is "a remarkably original book: a lyric history that is also a national contra-epic."

Additional coverage of Malouf 's life and career is contained in the following sources published by Gale Research: *Contemporary Authors,* Vol. 124; and *Contemporary Literary Criticism,* Vol. 28.

Kenzaburo Ōe
Nobel Prize in Literature

Born in 1935, Ōe is a Japanese novelist, short story writer, essayist, and critic.

For further information on Ōe's life and career, see *CLC,* Volumes 10 and 36.

INTRODUCTION

One of the foremost figures in contemporary Japanese literature, Ōe is highly regarded for intensely imagined and formally innovative novels examining the sense of alienation and anxiety among members of the post-World War II generation in Japan. Ōe's fiction is both profoundly intellectual and emotionally raw. Utilizing ideas from Jean-Paul Sartre's philosophy of existentialism, Ōe portrays the unique agonies and dilemmas of his characters with concrete precision in ways that point to the more universal significance of their suffering. Characterizing life as profoundly absurd, Ōe's works are deeply concerned with the implications of nuclear power, particularly in light of the atomic bombings of Hiroshima and Nagasaki.

Biographical Information

Born in a small village on the western Japanese island of Shikoku, Ōe was raised in a prominent Samurai family in accordance with traditional Japanese beliefs. Like most Japanese children of his generation, Ōe was taught to believe that the Emperor was a living god. When Emperor Hirohito personally announced in a radio broadcast Japan's surrender to the Allied military forces, Ōe and his schoolmates experienced a sense of devastation and disorientation which forever changed their perception of the world. Ōe described his emotions at this point in his life in his memoir *Genshuku na tsunawatari* (1974; *Solemnly Walking the Tightrope*): "the strange and disappointing fact was that the Emperor spoke in a human voice like any ordinary man." While Ōe lamented the sense of humiliation and guilt which Japan's defeat and occupation by American troops imposed on his generation, he also embraced the values of democracy which were instilled through the educational system of the occupation forces. While a student at Tokyo University, Ōe read widely in both traditional Japanese and modern Western literature. He was particularly influenced by such existentialist philosophers as Jean-Paul Sartre and Albert Camus, and by the American tradition of the "anti-hero," as represented in the works of such authors as Mark Twain, Herman Melville, William Faulkner, and Norman Mailer. Reflecting his ambitious and erudite reading habits, Ōe's early stories were awarded a number of prestigious literary prizes. In 1964 Ōe's first son was born with brain damage. While still concerned with the survival of heroic consciousness in an age of nuclear terror, Ōe subsequently incorporated the figure of his handicapped son into his fiction. According to the critic and translator John Nathan, Ōe began to write of heroes who "turn away from the lure of peril and adventure and seek instead, with the same urgency," a life of "certainty and consonance." A vocal anti-establishment, pro-democracy activist throughout his career, Ōe created a minor controversy in Japan when he rejected Japan's highest cultural honor—The Imperial Order of Culture, awarded days after he received the Nobel Prize—because he considered it a symbolic relic of the Imperial system and "would not recognize any authority, any value, higher than democracy."

Major Works

While still a university student, Ōe established his literary reputation with his first novella, *Shiiku* (1958; *The Catch*), which tells the story of a Japanese boy and a black American prisoner-of-war whose friendship is destroyed by the brutality of war. Ōe's first novel to gain international recognition, however, was *Kojinteki na taiken* (1964; *A Personal Matter*). The story of a twenty-seven-year-old man nicknamed "Bird" whose wife gives birth to a physically deformed and brain-damaged son, the novel ends on an apparently hopeful note with Bird's decision to keep his son alive. However, most critics emphasize that the style and overall thematic structure of *A Personal Matter* are more closely aligned with the pessimistic worldview of existentialism than with traditional narratives of tribulation and triumph. Ōe's concern with sickness and sexual perversion, as expressions of a deeper spiritual malaise, undercut the "happy" ending and signal Ōe's commitment to honestly portraying the darkest neuroses of contemporary humanity. Ōe's most universally acclaimed novel, *Man'en gannen no futtoboru* (1967; *The Silent Cry*), is a formally innovative and densely poetic portrayal of Takashi and Mitsusaburo, two brothers who clash over their differing interpretations of their tumultuous family history. Utilizing a method of temporal displacement and unity, Ōe constructs the narrative as the surreal juxtaposition of a political uprising in 1860 (the year Japan was forced to ratify a treaty opening up commerce with the United States) and the brothers' struggle a hundred years later. Violent to the point of psychosis, Takashi commits a brutal rape and murder, and betrays his elder brother in a secret land deal. To retaliate, Mitsusaburo conceals a crucial piece of knowledge about the Manengannen uprising, which has been Takashi's consuming obsession.

Takashi's eventual suicide bears an ironic correspondence to the story Mitsusaburo has concealed, and the novel ends with his guilty resignation to a life of passivity and regret. In addition to its complex narrative structure, *The Silent Cry* exhibits a preoccupation with violence and physical deformity which some critics have linked with the methods of "grotesque realism," a brand of exaggerated satire which was pioneered by the French Renaissance writer François Rabelais. In subsequent works, Ōe continued to employ complex methods of narrative displacement and juxtaposition, notably in *Dojidai gemu* (1979).

Critical Reception

Critical reaction to Ōe's works has been mostly adulatory. Despite the minor reservations of some critics with regard to its "happy" ending, *A Personal Matter* was internationally recognized as a masterpiece and a triumph of personal expression—a novel clearly autobiographical in content, but which transcends its literal narrative to symbolize the entire postwar spirit of malaise among Japanese intellectuals. *The Silent Cry* was lauded by the Nobel committee as "Ōe's major mature work," and its complex narrative framework has been compared with the "magic realism" of Colombian novelist and Nobel laureate Gabriel García Márquez. Many critics argue that Ōe's deliberate coalescence of modern Western and traditional Japanese forms has made him difficult to interpret and translate in either Japanese or English, and the fact that few of his works have been translated into English has limited the amount of criticism devoted to him outside of Japan. However, with the recognition attendant on his acceptance of the Nobel Prize, scholars foresee an influx of English translations and criticism in years to come.

PRINCIPAL WORKS

**Shiiku* [*The Catch*] (novella) 1958
Memushiri kouchi (novel) 1958
Warera no jidai (novel) 1959
Sakebigoe (novel) 1962
Hiroshimo nōto [*Hiroshima Notes*] (essays) 1963
Kojinteki na taiken [*A Personal Matter*] (novel) 1964
Man'en gannen no futtoboru [*The Silent Cry*] (novel) 1967
Nichijo seikatsu no boken (novel) 1971
Kozui wa waga tamashii ni oyobi (novel) 1973
Genshuku na tsunawatari [*Solemnly Walking the Tightrope*] (essays) 1974
Seinen no omei (novel) 1974
Pinchiranaa chosho [*The Pinchrunner Memorandum*] (novel) 1976
†Teach Us to Outgrow Our Madness (novellas) 1977
Dojidai gemu (novel) 1979
The Crazy Iris, and Other Stories of the Atomic Aftermath [editor] (short stories) 1984
Natsukashii toshi e no tegami (novel) 1987
Yureugoku (novel) 1994

*This novella was translated and published as *The Catch* in *The Shadow of Sunrise,* edited by Saeki Shoichi.

†This English-language collection contains the translated novellas *The Day He Himself Shall Wipe My Tears Away, Prize Stock, Teach Us to Outgrow Our Madness,* and *Aghwee the Sky Monster.*

OVERVIEWS

Michiko N. Wilson (essay date Winter 1981)

SOURCE: "Ōe's Obsessive Metaphor, Mori, the Idiot Son: Toward the Imagination of Satire, Regeneration, and Grotesque Realism," in *The Journal of Japanese Studies,* Vol. 7, No. 1, Winter, 1981, pp. 23-52.

[*Wilson is a critic and educator specializing in Japanese and comparative literature. In the following essay, she analyzes Ōe's variations on his most recurrent themes in five of his works and elucidates its relation to the genres of satire and "grotesque realism" as defined by structuralist theory.*]

Ōe Kenzaburo (1935-) is regarded in Japan and the United States as a leading postwar novelist. Deeply involved in contemporary issues, he makes a clean break from the literary traditions that nurtured such writers as the Nobel Prize winner Kawabata Yasunari (1899-1972), Shiga Naoya (1883-1972), and Mishima Yukio (1925-1970).

What is most innovative about Ōe's works is that he cultivates the techniques of Cervantes and Rabelais and follows in their footsteps. From 1964 on, by employing farce, travesty, satire, and "grotesque realism," which has debasement and laughter at its core, Ōe has challenged and turned upside down the notion of what Japanese literature should be. [In a footnote, Wilson notes that the term "grotesque realism" was coined by the Russian theorist Mikhail Bakhtin in his *Rabelais and His World,* 1968.] In contrast to Meiji-Taishō Realism, which is often characterized by a spirit of Confucian solemnity, Ōe tries to offer an alternative worldview by synthesizing in his artistic world the long-neglected elements of *gesaku*-like humor, the satiric, and especially the earthy qualities of folklore such as *Konjaku monogatari* (*Tales of Modern and Ancient Times*).

Ōe's originality also lies in the intensity of his message aimed at both the individual and the entire human race. Despite the extremely personal lyricism that runs through his works, his private universe, directed by what he calls "the Cosmic Will," offers immediacy and relevance to contemporary problems. Ōe believes that social, political, and environmental issues are as much "situations" created by man as man is the victim of his own "situations." For him "to outgrow" this insane world [Wilson is echoing and alluding here to the title of Ōe's collection, ***Teach Us to Outgrow Our Madness,*** 1977], grappling with the world's problems is the only way to survive. As much as the landing on the moon is a reality to contemporary man, the annihilation of mankind by nuclear war is a most immediate concern and reality to Ōe. [Wilson continues in a footnote: "In ***Hiroshima Nōto*** [***Hiroshima Notes***], Ōe talks about the journey he made to Hiroshima immediately after the birth of his first baby boy who was on the verge of dying in the incubator, and how he witnessed the enduring volition of the Hiroshima victims. 'I know very little about the Bible, but the gods who deluged the earth must have calculated on Noah's capability of restoring the human world before they sent the flood. Had Noah turned out to be a sluggard, a hysterical Jeremiah with no ability to restore the world, and had the postdeluvian world continued to be a wasteland, it would have certainly caused consternation among the gods in the heavens. . . . The atomic bomb that devastated Hiroshima was the worst deluge in the twentieth century. Amidst the great flood the people of Hiroshima immediately began to restore their world. By saving themselves, they also saved the souls of those who dropped the A-bomb. In the current deluge that we are faced with, the universal deluge frozen at this moment, yet ready to melt and engulf us at any time, the souls which the people of Hiroshima have saved include all the souls of humanity in the twentieth century seized with the cancer called "the possession of nuclear armaments." ' "]

Four Western literary figures—Auden, Sartre, Mailer, and Rabelais—stand out among those whose philosophy and literary techniques have had profound influences upon Ōe's consciousness. He reminisces in the notes to Part III in ***Solemn Tightrope Walking*** (1965), the first of three collections of essays: "My literary background was shaped like a triangle, the three points of which were Sartre, Norman Mailer, and postwar Japanese literature." Also, W. H. Auden often dominated Ōe's early discussions on literature in general:

> The things I learned from Auden are numerous, even though I had read Sartre before I came to know Auden. Auden especially taught me what a literary "image" is. I fantasized that, if I were to create an image as a novelist or a poet, I must grasp, as simply and accurately as possible, the nuance of a tiny wrinkle in the human heart, of the dark forest that conceals both a lion and a war. Also, the image must have a sense of shimmering specificity. I wanted to create an image in such a way that everything that exists in the world would go through a tunnel . . . penetrating straight into the human heart. [***Solemn Tightrope Walking***]

This statement contains three important points which Ōe has continuously insisted on: to promote social awareness, to demystify human behavior, and to liberate the human mind. With these issues in mind, Ōe struck upon another mentor whose intent and undaunting spirit of continuity (*jizokusei*) became his own.

He wrote in an essay called **"The Continuity of Norman Mailer,"** "one particular quality that grips the lifelong reader of Mailer is the sincerity of his continuity. . . . For example, in *Advertisement for Myself*, at the crossroads of his life, he edited his numerous essays and published them with his own comments. The consistent emotional impact his writings have upon the reader bespeaks not so much the superb journalistic talent inherent in Mailer as the continuity of purpose that is built into his individual works" [***Kujira no shimetsu suru hi*** (***The Day the Whales Shall be Annihilated***)].

Ōe shares Mailer's radical views on sex and politics. Politics interests Mailer so long as it is an integral part of man as a social being, that is to say, "politics as a part of everything else in life." While Ōe is encouraged by Sartre's statement that "one of the chief motives of artistic creation is certainly the need of feeling that we are essential in relationship to the world," he is also inspired by Mailer who believes that the purpose of art is "to intensify, even if necessary, to exacerbate, the moral consciousness of people." Mailer continues: "In particular, I think the novel is at its best the most moral of the art forms because it's the most immediate, the most overbearing, if you will. It is the most inescapable. One could argue much more easily about the meaning of a nonobjective painting or of music, or whatever. But in the novel, the meaning is there. It's much closer; one could argue about ambiguities, but, because one is using words, it's much closer to the sense of moral commandments, moral strictures" [*Advertisement For Myself*]. Parallel to this is the role of the artist, which, according to Mailer, is "to be as disturbing, as adventurous, as penetrating, as his energy and courage make possible."

One particular poem by Auden eventually came to represent the lifestyle of the prototype of Ōe's hero. It is entitled "Leap Before You Look"; its first stanza sums up the young hero's sentiments and action.

> The sense of danger must not disappear:
> The way is certainly both short and steep,
> However gradual it looks from here;
> Look if you like, but you will have to leap.

[In a footnote Wilson adds: "In 1958 Ōe wrote a short story with the same title about a 21-year-old college youth who is unable to 'leap' and gives in to the stagnant surroundings around him. His lifestyle and sentiments serve to represent the debilitation of Japanese people in general in postwar society. Later, Ōe borrowed a line, 'Teach Us to Outgrow Our Madness,' for the title of his story from Auden's long poem called 'Commentary' which appeared in *Journey to a War* (1939). . . ."]

For Ōe's hero, this sense of danger stimulates the need to act, the need to "intensify and exacerbate the moral consciousness of people." It is in this light that we are able to come to terms with the militant nature of Ōe's statement on the use of sex, which has often invited annoyance and dissatisfaction from Japanese critics. For example, he deplored the fact that his ambitious work, ***Warera no jidai*** (***Our Times,*** 1959), was dismissed as a novel of sexual perversion. "Almost every critic detested ***Our Times*** as if it were an ostracized slut" [***Solemn Tightrope Walking***]. In Ōe's narratives sexual terms and descriptions are meant to provoke the reader, to generate in his mind, as Ōe puts it, "an exaltation of an ideology"; by stimulating the mind and agitating the psyche, he hopes to dig "a vertical mine shaft" straight into the heart of the darkness of both the individual and of mankind. After all, sexuality is inseparably tied to what is at the root of human existence. What Ōe is aiming at is sobriety of mind with sex as a stimulant to one's consciousness, never sexual stupor.

Another Western literary mentor who has been a constant inspiration to Ōe is Rabelais. Paraphrasing the question an interviewer once put to Mailer, Ōe asks himself in one of his essays: "If I were to be exiled to a desert island and could take only a limited number of books with me, what would they be?" His immediate choice of *Gargantua and Pantagruel* by Rabelais foretells the direction he would take a decade later in creating ***The Pinchrunner Memorandum*** (1976), a novel of satire, laughter, and regeneration.

His admiration for Rabelais' work is restated in his 1976 article, **"Toward the Imagination of Buffoonery and Regeneration" ["Dōke to saisei e no sōzōryoku"]**, which supplies us with sufficient data to understand the intent and the range of the ambitious novel, ***The Pinchrunner Memorandum***. The novel is in many ways antithetical to post-Meiji realism and its succeeding literary traditions. It is in a way a violation of a taboo, in the sense that the combination of socio-political issues with Rabelaisian laughter, slapstick farce, satire, and "grotesque realism" has often been regarded as extraneous to the realm of "serious" literature, or *belles lettres*. Ōe also brings into the novel an element of the fantastic, which enjoyed considerable popularity among nineteenth-century Western writers. The result is that his work is remarkably free of cynicism, sentimentality, and pessimism.

In his early works written between 1957 and 1963, Ōe focuses on the degradation, humiliation, and chaos brought forth by the unconditional surrender of Japan in World War II. He relies heavily on explicit sexual terms in an attempt to portray the "adversities and the plight of the stagnant Japanese youth in the postwar society" [***Solemn Tightrope Walking***]. Unable to commit themselves to the making of history, these youth are in a state of "moratorium" (which later becomes Ōe's favorite word) in solitary confinement awaiting the moment of execution. Elsewhere, the humiliation of Occupied Japan is symbolized by an unemployed young man under the sway of a prostitute who caters only to foreigners. College youths and delinquent juveniles share the dream of an adventurous life which must exist somewhere outside Japan. Both groups are abandoned by adults, who are repulsed by their violence, obscene language, and aberrant sexual behavior. Out of these groups emerge the misfits who form a collective body to protect themselves from a hostile society, and a young intellectual who eventually settles down and brings up an idiot son.

With the appearance in 1964 of ***Aghwee the Sky Monster,*** Ōe's dominant theme shifts from an obsession with the lost war to the theme of madness. This second theme is deeply bound up with his personal experience: in June 1963 he became the father of a baby boy born with brain damage. In his five works written between 1964-1976, Ōe consistently employs the image of a corpulent father and his idiot son, and the theme of madness. These five works are ***Aghwee the Sky Monster*** (***Sora no kaibutsu Aguwee***), ***A Personal Matter*** (***Kojinteki na taiken,*** 1964), ***Teach Us to Outgrow Our Madness*** (***Warera no kyōki o ikinobiru michi o oshieyo,*** 1969), ***The Waters Are Come in unto My Soul*** (***Kōzui wa waga tamashii ni oyobi,*** 1973), and ***The Pinchrunner Memorandum*** (***Pinchirannaa chōsho,*** 1976). The presence of this "obsessive metaphor" of the father and the idiot son should not be dismissed merely as a repetition of an old theme, but rather we must consider the five works as one large narrative in progress. The repetition in Ōe's works is the key to the understanding of his literary universe and its structure, more essentially, of literature itself, and its tool, language. The pertinence of reciprocity of one work to another is well asserted by Todorov. "Just as the meaning of a part of the work is not exhausted in itself, but is revealed in its relation with other parts, a work in its entirety can never be read in a satisfactory and enlightening fashion if we do not put it in relation with other works, previous and contemporary" [*The Poetics of Prose*].

To apply Todorov's notion of reciprocity within the works of a single author, Ōe's five works under discussion can be categorized into what modern linguists refer to as a "syntagmatic" type, in which the second text reacts actively to the first, rather than a "paradigmatic" type which indicates the absence of the other text and does not function reciprocally. The first two works, ***Aghwee the Sky Monster*** and ***A Personal Matter,*** play off one another, creating the "syntagmatic" or "combinatory" relation between the two represented in the formula of the question/answer pair, or what Todorov calls, "a concealed polemic." The main polemic is: "Should I kill the monster baby or live with the monster?" The narrative movement in ***Aghwee*** is based on the following answer to the above question, "Yes, I should kill the baby (and I have murdered the baby)." ***A Personal Matter*** presents the other choice, "No, I should not kill the baby; I will live with the baby." By combining the first text with the second, the reader gains a clearer view of the conflict that the father must have experienced.

Once the resolution is made and the father carries out the decision, there emerges another question/answer: "Am I really the passive victim quietly enduring a bondage imposed by my idiot son who never rejects my words?" This polemic is the basis of the verbal structure of ***Teach Us to Outgrow Our Madness.***

Freedom from this artificially created bondage, the father's obsessive desire, means the establishment of a balanced relationship between the father and the son. It also means the exclusion of a mother or a wife, whose original role loses its impetus. In order to make their life a meaningful one, the pair must have contacts with the external world. Thus, in a way, ***The Waters Are Come in unto My Soul*** and ***The Pinchrunner Memorandum*** are adventure stories of the undaunted pair, the former story about the father who assumes the active role in the adventure, the latter about the idiot son who carries out the vision of the father and the son. Both stories end with a death: the father dies in ***The Waters,*** the son Mori in ***The Pinchrunner.*** The function of the pair is such that Ōe must end his story when the idiot son dies, because Ōe's works are ultimately about Mori the idiot son. In the following pages we shall closely examine the first four works about Mori, and their "syntagmatic," i.e., "combinatory," relations which unveil the intertextual figure of the father and the idiot son in a sequence.

A young father, the main character of ***Aghwee,*** kills his newborn baby by giving him only sugar water. When the autopsy reveals that the baby had a benign tumor, the father goes into self-confinement and becomes obsessed with the illusion (that is what the narrator and the reader are led to believe) of his baby flying down from the sky. The phantom baby, the size of a kangaroo in a white cotton nightgown, dwells in the sky. In other words, the murdered baby is transformed into a celestial being which is a part of the cosmic force. According to his ex-wife, however, the father's self-confinement is escapism.

The baby comes down from the sky to remind the father of his crime and taunt him. The illusion/reality is perhaps the father's insane desire to communicate and join with the baby whose only utterance in his brief life was "Aghwee!" In the end the baby fulfills the father's desire, or perhaps the baby tricks the father: "Suddenly D [the father] cried out and thrust both arms in front of him as if he were trying to rescue something; then he leaped in among those trucks and was struck to the ground." In other words, the father lets himself go for the first time in his life and *decides* to follow the baby. Already in this story are mythological elements or elements of the fantastic, which Ōe incorporates into ***The Pinchrunner Memorandum***. The kangaroo baby is not a passive victim eliminated by his own father, but a trickster-like character; he returns to haunt his murderer. The baby character does not exist in reality, but he does exist in the father's psyche. However, to the narrator who is hired to be the father's companion, the question persists to the end: Does it exist or not?

Seven months after [***Aghwee***] appeared, Ōe published ***A Personal Matter,*** which again centers around the father and his idiot son. Antithetical to the previous story, here the newborn baby escapes death by clinging stubbornly to life. Overwhelmed by the infant's physical and instinctive power to survive, the father resolves to live with his idiot son. This yet-to-be-named baby serves a double function: it is the father's personal tragedy as well as a symbol of the tragedy of mankind. For, prior to his decision to take care of the monster baby, in the midst of confusion, despair, and enervation, as he is about to carry out the murder of the baby, the father hears the news broadcast of the Soviet resumption of nuclear testing. At this moment the monster baby that governs his personal destiny seems to represent the fate of mankind in the face of nuclear war. "In a world shared by all those others, time was passing, a [sic] mankind's one and only time, and a destiny apprehended the world over as one and the same destiny was taking evil shape."

Bird, the baby's father, challenges the odds that are stacked up against him, that is to say, "the creation of misery for himself and the nurturing of a life that meant absolutely nothing to this world." Against these odds he repeats himself: "It's for my own good. It's so I can stop being a man who's always running away. . . . All I want is to stop being a man who continually runs away from responsibility." Here, Ōe's hero realizes the reversal of his relation to reality and to the world. The question, "Who am I?" is replaced by that of "What is my relation to the world?" or "What am I in relation to the world?" Ōe shares the Dostoevskian view that the most important thing is "not how the hero appears to the world, but . . . how the world appears to the hero and how the hero appears to himself" [Mikhail Bakhtin, *Problems of Dostoevsky's Poetics*].

Thus the baby is the beginning of the father's new life, a life of commitment to the world. We see in the following three stories, ***Teach Us [to Outgrow Our Madness]***, ***The Waters,*** and ***The Pinchrunner,*** how the odds are turned around, how the existence of an idiot son becomes part and parcel of the father's entire being. The identification of the father with the infant son gradually takes place at the end of ***A Personal Matter:*** "A week after the operation the baby had looked almost human; the following week it had begun to resemble Bird." Also, the final paragraph implies that the father is slowly emerging from an amorphous, suspended existence (*chūburarinko*), about to embark upon a risky adventure in the world where idiocy is an anomaly, digression from the norms set up by the intolerant society. The baby's presence will eventually liberate the father from the self-image he has indulged himself in. Ōe's works seek to explore "the sum total" of the hero's (later the pair's—the father and the idiot son) "consciousness and self-consciousness . . . the hero's final word about himself and about his world" [Bakhtin, *Dostoevsky's Poetics*].

In ***Teach Us*** Ōe strikes upon a name most appropriate for the idiot son who allegorically unites Ōe to the environment he himself grew up in, a valley in the deep forest of Shikoku Island (the background of ***The Catch,*** 1957). Mori, "forest" in Japanese and "death or idiocy" in Latin, becomes the axis upon which Ōe's literary universe spins and expands. At the same time Mori is also the destination to which Ōe returns. Throughout the story the reader is familiarized with the fat son, not by his real name Mori, but by his nickname Eeyore (which, according to the Japanese pronunciation, sounds like *"iiyō,"* meaning "It's O.K."!). Why so? We are told that the father initially meant to mock his son whose alternative was to die or be an idiot. "Could such existence be given a name?" "Every time he called the child by name [Mori] it seemed to him that he could hear, in the profound darkness in his head, his own lewd and repentent laughter mocking the entirety of his life." His cynicism turns against him, and he is the one to be mocked.

The corpulent father identifies with the moon-faced four-year-old son, and tries to live in his son's twilight world filled with pain, fear, and numbness. He believes or wants to believe that he is the only one who can function as a window to his son's murky mind, as "a pipeline of vision connecting his son's brain" with the outside world through the "conduit of their clasped hands." However, an incident occurs that forces the father to realize his son's adaptability: "My son can get along without me, as an idiot in an idiot's way. . . . The situation reverses: the fat man, believing that he has brought order, peace, and harmony to his son's fragile existence, must accept the truth.

It is the father who depends upon his idiot son for assurance, comfort, and equilibrium.

Thus, ***Teach Us*** tells of the initiation of a young father into the outside world filled with terror, pain, and numbness. It is also a story of a father yearning to go back to his childhood and to speak to his own father who continually ignored him. To the fat man, his own father's strange self-confinement in the darkness of the storehouse, his corpulence, silence, and sudden death is as much a mystery as the idiocy of his infant son. The desire to establish an intimacy, "the heavy bond of restraints," between himself and Mori betrays a chokingly painful question he dares not utter, "Why was my son born an idiot? Is this monster my creation?" In trying to answer this question, the fat man digs a mine in order to reach the core of the problem, of primeval existence, at the center of which stands Mori.

The father's quest must continue as he experiences Mori's growth. The Mori character is named Jin in ***The Waters Are Come in unto My Soul,*** a two-volume novel published in 1973. [In a footnote Wilson adds: "Watanabe Hiroshi speculates that the name Jin possibly comes from the German word, Sinn, meaning 'sense' and is probably used synonymously with the word, 'subconscious.' "] As if to make up for the poor eyesight the four-year-old Mori had to put up with, Jin, at the age of five, exhibits an extremely keen sense of sound. All day long, he listens to and identifies the songs of wild birds and whales recorded on tapes by his father. In flashbacks we learn about Jin's self-destructive impulses and the self-inflicted pain from which he was never free. Just as Mori's father began to feel the pains his son received from a scalding or an eye examination (which terrified Mori), Jin's father develops sudden fainting spells or experiences a scorching pain. Out of desperation, his wife agrees to let the pair of misfits start a new life on their own, a life of tranquillity in a refurbished nuclear bomb shelter, totally secluded from the humdrum of the external world.

I must comment briefly on the name, Ōki Isana, which the father took for himself upon venturing into a new life with Jin. Literally, the father's new name means Mr. Big-Tree Brave-Fish. Judging from this, what is evident is a sense of humor and the comical function assigned to the role of the father and the son as a pair. The father, claiming to be the agent for the souls of trees and whales, which he believes are the legitimate owners of the earth, exchanges telepathic communications with their spirits. When the entire human population is wiped out by nuclear war, he believes that he is to emerge out of the bomb shelter with Jin and return the earth to the trees and whales.

Jin seems to be a voiceless Jonah, a prophet, a representative of mankind about to be annihilated by nuclear war. Always calm and innocent, he repeats softly to himself the wild birds' names as he listens to the tapes. Here Ōe seems to be satirizing the sanctity of words and of human communication via words, i.e., the function of *parole* ("actual speech"). Incommunicability between the father and the idiot son, represented by the absence of speech, or of the reciprocity of words and ideas, transforms itself into comical Rabelaisian dialogues which dominate the narrative flow in both ***The Waters*** and ***The Pinchrunner.*** Divested of human deception, false seriousness, and manipulation, the father and his "parroting" son perform something beyond what verbal communication can achieve under normal circumstances.

In ***The Waters*** Ōe again takes up the image of misfits, which dominated his early works. It is significant that dropout characters calling themselves "Freedom Voyagers" form a comradeship with the father and Jin. The nonconformist groups consist of high school dropouts, ex-college students, a middle-aged Hiroshima survivor, "The Shrinking Man," and one female member, Inako, who in turn persuades a Self-Defense Corps member to join the crew. Ōe for the first time unites social outcasts, who heretofore struggled separately, to form a collective body to resist those who simply stigmatize them as "social cancer."

An ex-employee of a big corporation and son-in-law of a powerful conservative politician, Ōki Isana shares the lot of the non-revolutionary "Freedom Voyagers" and dies fighting for a vision, for the "goodness" of the earth, that is to say, the souls of trees and whales. What is amiss in the farcical repartee between the voyagers awaiting the final assault in the bomb shelter and a police riot squad surrounding the shelter, is the voice of Jin the idiot son, who has already been removed from the battle scene by the protective hands of Inako. What the reader and the father want to hear is Jin's soft-spoken voice intoning the words, "The end of the world is here," the Day of Judgment.

Ōe's fifth work under discussion, ***The Pinchrunner Memorandum,*** is symptomatic of everything he has so far written and insistently talked about in the past two decades. He has combined three dominant themes in the work: the embattlement of misfits, idiocy and averbalization, and the annihilation of the human race by nuclear war.

The Pinchrunner Memorandum is the story of a former nuclear engineer, a thirty-eight-year-old father who has an eight-year-old idiot son, Mori. This undaunted pair goes through a "miraculous transformation," with the father losing twenty years and Mori gaining twenty years. The grown-up Mori "speaks" in the voice of the Cosmic Will and transmits the message to the teenage father through the conduit of their clasped hands. Together they go out, aided by their faithful comrades and the Yamame Army, to eliminate the Patron ("The Big Shot A") of the underworld, who secretly plans to control Japan by financing the manufacturing of atomic bombs by two radical groups.

There are two central themes posited in the novel which need to be scrutinized carefully for us to grasp Ōe's semantic universe as a totality and a dynamic unity. The first is the theme of the "transformation" (*ten'kan*) or "metamorphosis," an essential element of fantastic literature. The second is concerned with the function of language and the speech art (verbalization) in relation to Mori, the idiot son.

The two themes are not as incompatible or incongruous as they seem. According to Todorov, the fantastic universe, being the exclusion of words "luck" or "chance," is based on a principle of a "pan-determinism." "It signifies that the limit between the physical and the mental, between matter and spirit, between word and thing, ceases to be impervious." In this sense, the notion of metamorphosis or transformation "constitutes a transgression of the separation between matter and mind as it is generally conceived" [Todorov, *The Fantastic: A Structural Approach to a Literary Genre,* 1975].

Identical with the fantastic universe is the world of drugs, the mystic, the psychotic, and, what is most relevant to our discussion, the primordial world of infancy. What characterizes the being of an infant is the effacement of the limit between subject and object, of the normal barrier between the self and the world (the other). To go a step further, his universe is a world without language. Such is the cosmic fusion which the transformed pair, Mori and his father, continuously approaches.

Like madness, Mori's idiocy is in effect a deviation from the norms set up by society or the "natural" world in which ordinary events occur; it is also a transgression of the laws of nature. Therefore, the only way Mori is allowed to exist is to become a part of the universe of the fantastic. The reader accepts Mori to the extent that he experiences a "hesitation" in the face of an apparently supernatural event, Mori's (the father's) miraculous transformation, which occurs in the context of natural, everyday life.

The central trait of the fantastic is ambiguity. "The fantastic confronts us with a dilemma: to believe or not to believe" [Todorov]. This element of ambiguity is maintained throughout ***The Pinchrunner Memorandum.*** First, the separation of the narrator (Mori's father) and his ghost writer (Hikaru's father), who receives the former's utterances through telephone calls, cassette tapes, and letters, and writes them down, is purposely weakened from the very beginning of the story. The concept of "double," the fusion of "I-Thou," is described in the first sentence of the novel:

> Words, beyond dispute, uttered by the other party: despite my clear memory of the circumstance under which the other party made the utterance, I feel the words gushed out of the recesses of my own soul.

Ōe also stresses the fact that these two fathers have a lot in common, and form a complementary relationship. Mori's father and Hikaru's father are both of the same generation and are both graduates of Tokyo University, the former with a science degree (nuclear physics) and the latter with a philosophy degree (literature). They both have idiot sons of the same age. Their initial encounter takes place on the school lawn where they wait absentmindedly for "their children" to finish their special class while watching the "brainy children different from theirs" noiselessly play baseball. Reminiscing about the sandlot baseball era he was brought up in, Mori's father mumbles to himself: "Nothing was as petrifying and intoxicating as being selected as a pinchrunner!" Immediately something inexplicable unites the two men. "At that instant, a cumbersome hot pipeline of the parent-child-like bond ran through us."

By the end of the first chapter we are prepared for the supernatural event to come, or, to be more exact, for the supernatural event that has already occurred but has not yet been reported. Then, the first narrator of the novel (Hikaru's father) is replaced by Mori's father (referred to as "the other party") who recounts the supernatural event that has overtaken him and his idiot son.

From the second chapter on, the relation between Mori's father and Hikaru's father becomes that of "the person who emits the text and the person who receives" [Todorov]. Ōe's narrative complicates this verbal structure even more by making the receiver of codes a ghost writer whose main job is to record the utterances or the speech act of Mori's father, not to decode them. We read at the beginning of the story the ghost writer's feeble claim that he is an independent entity and deserves to be treated as such: "Although my job originates in the words of the other party, the words must go through my flesh and consciousness before they can be put down on paper. I am expected to enter the mind of Mori's father, learn in detail his secret, and even temporarily must grasp the entirety of his being. However, I refuse to accept the reversal of this; I resent his constant habitation in my world."

What sustains the narrative construction of the supernatural event is the tripartite bond that unites the narrator (Mori's father) and the chronicler (Hikaru's father), with the reader sandwiched between the two. (Ōe also employs this structure in ***The Day He Himself Shall Wipe Our Tears Away.***) The narrator occasionally questions the ghost writer, "Do you doubt my words?" "I want you to write in such a way that your faltering voice would merge with my insistent voice of self-assertion and the two voices, one on top of the other, resonate together. The verbal account must be sustained by the tense opposition of my insistent words to your silent misgivings."

The adoption of a "ghost writer" intensifies the ambiguity of hesitation experienced by the reader and our "double" hero as the distinction between the narrator and the receiver of codes gradually ceases. The consciousness of the former begins to envelop the mental activities of the other. Also, as the word indicates, although a ghost writer physically exists, he has no claim to the work he is "writing." Conversely, since the real writer has nothing to do with the actual recording of his words, how can the reader really know that the utterance or the text is actually produced by the professed writer, and not by his ghost writer?

Mori's father gives the following reason why he is asking (actually imposing upon) Hikaru's father, whose profession is "writing," to become his scribe:

> I need someone to recognize my actions and thoughts, to record them in a "memorandum." I am about to embark upon a new adventure with Mori. Without the existence of a chronicler, I feel the adventure-to-come, and myself will be merely a mad illusion. A premonition tells me that our adventure will be a fantastic event; if the police ever got hold of my "memorandum," they would simply dismiss it as balderdash.

On the syntactic level, the novel is a "game" about the

narrator's gamble: on which side will the reader be? Will he believe the narrator's words or side with the faltering voice of the chronicler?

This hesitation, a dilemma whether to believe or not to believe, which is a verbal choice, is also directly linked with the father's fear and intense desire to be selected as a "pinchrunner." His main job is to steal a base and run: the crowd urges him to run. If he miscalculates in the situation, he loses and will be ordered back to sit on the bench. If he wins, he will become, even if temporarily, a hero. His choice is, "Should I stay or run?" The grown-up Mori says once via telepathy: "If the transformation means that we have to run, as a pinchrunner, for those who cannot run, or for those who do not know they must run, then we have to start running any minute now." The father/narrator must face this verbal choice, "Should I stay or run?" again and again. "I heard the voices of the spectator urging me to run, after an unexpected hit-and-run came about." In the end this verbal choice becomes the message of the story, the purpose of the adventure of the transformed pair, Mori and the father:

> I was resolved to assert my conviction that we are the chosen ones to run as a pinchrunner for mankind . . . We have already been selected and sent to the base with the instructions given to us by the coach of the Cosmic Will; we must concentrate our minds whether we should stand by cautiously or run. However, we must rely on our intuition in the end and must run on our own accord.

What the narrator anticipates eagerly from the fantastic event, i.e., the transformation, is to see his and Mori's consciousness expand and their flesh renewed and rejuvenated, which he believes is the fundamental hope cherished by the whole of humanity. In order to renew one's consciousness and flesh, old tissue and the entire past must die, because "renewal" must replace "death." The reversal of time is the key in fantastic literature. That is why the eight-year-old Mori, whose mental universe is that of an infant or a madman, sheds his old infant self, and becomes an "adult simulacrum of infancy" in a world without language. On the other hand, Mori's father steadily regresses and becomes "Mori's son," with the possibility of reverting back to infancy!

In recounting this supernatural event, Mori's father suffers from a terrible suspicion that gnaws at him. Isn't our transformation a terrible mistake? What is it that we are entrusted with by the Cosmic Will? Do we really have a mission to carry out? At one point, he begins to doubt the existence of the Cosmic Will, and instead begins to believe that the political domination of the Patron might be the very cause of their transformation. What pulls him out of this deep skepticism is Mori: at the age of twenty-eight, with his quiet smile, animated eyes and silence, he communicates with his teenage father. The narrator tells the chronicler: "This transformed Mori is the real Mori, the ultimate Mori, the beginning of Mori. So long as this Mori exists in reality, I will live through the life of 'transformation' with him, and carry out the job entrusted to us by the Cosmic Will."

The dreams and the imaginary/the illusory scattered throughout the verbal account indicate "the ambiguous vision" of the narrator that relies on the use of a stylistic device, modalization. Thus, the narrator talks of a possibility (and a hope) of one day decoding what must be stored in Mori's dark, murky brain:

> Like in a sealed cell, where dust *must* eventually accumulate over a long period of time, my words, the fine particles of dust, *might* one day form a heap and by natural ignition start into flame. At least Mori never rejects my words. Who knows, deep in the dim cell of Mori's twilight brain, the words transmitted to him through the eardrum *might* have been stored away like the sand in an hourglass.

At one point, the father imagines that Mori is a Socrates: "Listening quietly with genuine interest to whatever I tell him, Mori must be a man like Socrates who awakens you to your ignorance and raises you to a new level of knowledge." In the mind of the narrator, dream and reality, or the imaginary and the real, do not form separate and impermeable blocks. Time and again, Mori's father sees a dream of an extraordinary event that foretells their future: one such dream is about the Patron whom the pair helps gain total political power in Japan, power that extends to Korea, and the pageant they direct to celebrate his victory. However, the festival immediately turns itself into a celebration of the death of the Patron. The pair has rebelled against him and succeeds in the elimination of the evil force.

In the dream of the "Long March," Mori and the father are members of the Yamame Army which has in reality rescued the pair from the violent mob who refused to listen to Mori's message transmitted from the Cosmic Will. The pair is now a part of the collective body of "ideal people." The father recognizes among the Yamame soldiers those friends he encountered in his life. These are the people who have given him "a sense of fullness, stability, and finally the liberation of his soul." Passing right before him is a dear friend of his who strangled himself in Paris, accompanied by his lovely French wife. In reality he was the Yamame Army agent based in Europe. (This "friend" figure also appears in ***The Silent Cry.***) Gijin, the leader of the anti-nuclear movement from Shikoku, is also in the march "walking stiffly like a toy soldier with his hands clasped tight on his chest" as if he had been resurrected from death. The father's idol, Ōno Sakurao, walks right beside him. The sight of Hikaru and his father completes the list of comrades who join the Long March. The narrator tells the scribe: "After all, I have been telling a dream-like dream all along, ha ha!"

Dreams or the imaginary in the novel have a double-function. One is vaticinal in the sense that they are the harbingers of things to come; the other is to remove the boundaries between matter and spirit, the physical and the mental. What happens throughout the story is the materialization of the imaginary and the perceived. It also means that the entire verbal account, based on the sender of codes (narrator) and the receiver of codes (ghost writer), is turned upside down. The reader is uncertain whether the narrator and the ghost writer are really two separate people, or whether the entire verbal act originates in the real, rather than in the imaginary/the illusory, or "a dream-like dream."

This ambiguity or hesitation is not cleared away at the end of the novel. The narrator's "alternate plan" in case of his or Mori's death/arrest, is revealed to the ghost writer who is to substitute as the sender of codes to recount the end of their adventurous journey. We must assume that that is exactly what happens, and that the obstacle between the person who produces the text and the person who receives it collapses.

The aesthetic concept governing ***The Pinchrunner Memorandum*** comes from what Bakhtin defines as "grotesque realism" in his discussions of *Gargantua and Pantagruel.* In grotesque realism the bodily elements always have a deeply positive character given in an all-popular, festive, utopian setting. The cosmic, social, and bodily elements are parts of an indivisible whole, and presented not in a private, egotistic form or isolated from the other aspects of life, but as something universal, representing all the people. "The essential principle of grotesque realism is degradation, that is, the lowering of all that is high, spiritual, ideal, abstract; it is a transfer to the material level, to the sphere of earth and body in their indissoluble unity" [Bakhtin, *Rabelais*].

As we know, Rabelais challenged the authority of the still-medieval Church which inculcated fear and blind obedience in the minds of individuals. For this "battle," the great French satirist armed himself with a panoply of pots, frying pans, chopping knives, and with the urine and excrement of Gargantua and Pantagruel, which destroy yet fertilize the earth. Rabelais also knew that his criticism of the authority of Catholicism was a deadly one because he was an insider who was constantly exposed to the hypocrisy of clerical power. What he attempted to do was to turn the world and the conventional worldview upside down by demystifying "upward is heaven, downward is earth." According to Bakhtin, "Earth is an element that devours, swallows up (the grave, the womb) and at the same time an element of birth, or renascence (maternal breasts). Such is the meaning of 'upward' and 'downward' in their cosmic aspect, while in their purely bodily aspect, which is not clearly distinct from the cosmic, the upper part is the face or the head and the lower part is the genital organs, the belly, the buttocks."

Bakhtin's analysis sheds light on Ōe's constant reference to the lower part of the human body or bodily elements and copulation. The eight-year-old Mori, whose entire being exists in the need to eat, urinate, defecate, and sleep, is no longer an imbecile in the world of grotesque realism but becomes a positive being. He is acceptable in this world because he embodies the principle of degradation and debasement, which draws upon the excessive, the ludicrous, exaggeration, and earthiness. For example, at night Mori must still wear a diaper no longer big enough to cover his growing buttocks and erect penis. When we read the passage that describes Mori splashing urine all over the restroom, unable to properly aim his penis into the toilet, we do not find him pathetic, but laughable. Laughter degrades and yet materializes, writes Bakhtin. Degradation "has not only a destructive, negative aspect, but also a regenerating one." To degrade an object or a person implies hurling it or him down to "the zone in which conception of a new birth takes place" [Bakhtin].

Laughter in grotesque realism is shared by all people; it is a festive laughter which removes the barrier of human prejudice and deception, where "all men become conscious participants in that one world of laughter." It heals and regenerates. "Laughter must liberate the gay truth of the world from the veils of gloomy lies spun by the seriousness of fear, suffering, and violence."

Despite the fact that man is the only living creature endowed with laughter, when we think of laughter in the context of modern Japanese literature, we are struck by its poverty. It seems that laughter is "an ostracized slut" and has never been fully recognized as a proper ingredient for a novel. Watanabe Hiroshi offers one of the most satisfactory answers to the absence of laughter in modern Japanese literature. First, laughter is born out of the masses, the uneducated, common, ordinary people. It is the vulgar, simplistic, popular nature that is inherent in laughter. In other words, we can say that, by its very association with common folk, laughter has always occupied a "debased" position, and has been considered something frivolous and trivial. Secondly, Watanabe continues, it was extremely rare for laughter to become the source of inspiration and creativity in the days when Japanese intellectuals were busily engaged in "soul searching" or in carrying out their visionary mission.

In contrast to the vision pursued by the Meiji-Taishō intellectuals, Ōe's private quest and literary universe constantly draw upon the festiveness and universality of laughter. Farcical slapstick and travesty abound in ***The Pinchrunner Memorandum.*** Or, to put it another way, those incidents which we consider serious and earthshaking in the context of ordinary life, are debased and lowered down to the bodily elements of the earth. Nothing is vulgar in Ōe's universe: everything is told matter-of-factly in its utopian, all-popular organic whole.

For example, the novel describes a type of meeting (*hanseikai*) familiar to all Japanese. It is designed to "reflect upon" a past event in order to improve the situation, in the manner of a roundtable discussion. So the *hanseikai* is held to thank Mori's father for rescuing one of the children who gets caught in a malfunctioning automatic door of a supermarket where the whole "special class" has gone shopping. With the principal and the two embarrassed teachers in front of him, Mori's father goes into an eloquent tirade, trying to reevaluate and reform the entire system of the Special School and the function of the teachers who work under the system.

> The real help you can give to *our children* is to tell them what the world is really like out there and how to fend for themselves in society. Are you really teaching them what they need? All you are doing is teaching them how to control their limbs, barely enough to survive as imbeciles. . . . In the future society, who knows, they might teach *our children* how to control not only their limbs but how to dispose of the whole

Ōe in December 1994 being congratulated by King Carl Gustav of Sweden.

> body, ha ha, in other words, how to commit suicide? . . . In order to repel this authoritative power to weed out children like ours, we must teach them how to take up arms and defend themselves. As long as this world continues to be contaminated, the number of children like ours will increase rapidly. They will one day become scapegoats looked down upon as a loathsome minority.

The principal's reply to the radical alternative suggested by Mori's father takes the position that upholds the preservation of the status quo: "As a specialist in physical education, it has been my belief that education means to teach the unity of mind and spirit, and how to reconcile oneself with nature and society." This is a hackneyed statement repeated again and again to students in secondary education, and Mori's father is perfectly aware of the conventionality of the principal's response.

Mori's father immediately offers an alternative which is to teach their children music, that is, education through music. "Since *our children* have a keen sense of sound, we will make them specialists in music." He solemnly starts reading the memoirs on the record jacket written by a guru of Indian music. The reading session and meditation abruptly comes to an end when the prostitute mother of Saa-chan utters a loud protestation. The meeting deteriorates and turns into a shouting match between the mother and a woman teacher, the latter trying to restrain the verbal abuse the former directs against Mori's father:

> What the hell are you talking about? WHAT, WHAT, WHAT? *Our children* majoring in music? How about a kid who is hard of hearing like Saa-chan? Is she going to be discriminated against even in the special class? Don't you dare! . . . Why don't you pray for the well-being of your guru, guru, so that you won't goof off! You might as well grab the T.V. celebrity, Ōno Sakurao's fat butt! You, sexual pervert!

The meeting aborts itself, as the parents busily take care of their children who need to urinate, or get rid of the urine and feces of those children who could not wait. In the midst of this commotion sits Mori, quietly wetting himself.

What is at work in the comical, farcical descriptions that abound in ***The Pinchrunner Memorandum*** is travesty combined with cartoonization, or cartoonized travesty. Ōe is an inveterate cartoonist; as a cartoonist he is also very much aware of the power of satire, which responds "to the world with a mixture of laughter and indignation" [Matthew Hodgart, *Satire,* 1973]. In this sense, festive laughter that destroys the clerical authority during the "feast of fools" and the "feast of the ass" in the Middle Ages and the way of satire which turns the real world upside down, share a lot in common. Both grotesque realism and satire involve "a cathartic release of social tension." Bakhtin's analysis of Rabelaisian laughter and what Matthew Hodgart defines as satire complement each other in aiding us to unveil the constituents of Ōe's semantic world. "True satire demands," Hodgart writes, "a high degree both of commitment to and involvement with the painful problems of the world, and simultaneously a high degree of abstraction from the world. The criticism of the world is abstracted from its ordinary setting, say, political oratory and journalism, and transformed into a high form of 'play'; which gives us both the recognition of our responsibilities and irresponsible joy of make-believe."

In the above episode of "practical education" followed by the self- abortive *hanseikai,* Ōe treats an extremely serious and delicate subject, which directly concerns his personal life and the lives of those parents who have retarded children. However, the more serious the subject matter, the more he intentionally relaxes concern by exhibiting its process as ludicrous, because, as Elder Olson writes [in his 1975 *The Theory of Comedy*], "it [comedy] is most effectively comic when it treats of things which do arouse our concern." According to Ōe, to paraphrase Olson, there is always a serious element in buffoonery and cartoonization, and the ludicrous is seen only in comparison with the conventional.

The whole episode relies on the principle that the reader's only natural physical response is laughter and that this laughter is directed neither at the handicapped children nor at their defensive parents. What is being laughed at is the overall action, or the process that reveals the inadequate system of the Special School and its incompetent servants (the principal and the two teachers), who adamantly adhere to the status quo. The principal, a physical education major whose philosophy lies in the unification of mind and spirit, the reconciliation of society and nature, becomes the object of laughter. His comment has absolutely no value for the education of retarded children. Furthermore, he is just a paper pusher and has no interest in Special Education. In the end he takes advantage of the unexpected turn of events and slips out of the room "like a monkey," while the prostitute mother continues to bark up the wrong tree.

This incident contains, as in the case of all good satire, "an element of aggressive attack and a fantastic vision of the world transformed" [Hodgart]; however, what sets this episode off from conventional satire is the absence of contemptuous laughter or a bitter aftertaste. The overall spirit of satire is taken over by festive laughter which degrades and regenerates.

Another socio-political incident, nuclear hijacking, becomes the object of satire and Rabelaisian laughter in ***The Pinchrunner Memorandum.*** It all happens when the father (I call him the father here, even though the incident occurs prior to the birth of Mori, because the narrator has given him no other name besides *Mori-Chichi,* i.e., "Mori's father") is working as an engineer for a nuclear power plant. At one point in the story the father accompanies a driver and his assistant in broad daylight, completely unarmed and unguarded, hauling enough nuclear material to produce twenty A-bombs. A small, old-fashioned truck with a tarpaulin forces the power plant truck to a halt. Jumping out from under the tarpaulin are five or six men garbed like the "Tin Man" in *The Wizard of Oz,* each carrying a long cudgel (*sasumata*). When the father recognizes that the Tin Men's small truck is used to deliver school luncheons, his mind is seized with the fear and excitement he experienced as a pinchrunner in a sandlot baseball game when he was a boy. "How intoxicating and petrifying it was to be selected as a pinchrunner!" And he continues, "Once they load the truck with the plutonic acid and reuse the vehicle for delivering school luncheons in Tokyo, contamination will spread among the schoolchildren!" He makes up his mind to "run and steal the base," and jumps under the tarpaulin and squats down among barrels which contain the radiated green liquid. One of the barrels breaks open as the Tin Men prod the father with their cudgels, at which point, the father goes berserk and starts screaming wildly. "Everything is contaminated! Everything, the truck, the driveway, all of us! Alert! Alert!" He keeps on screaming until the Tin Men start fleeing from the scene, making terrible clink-clank noises in their cumbersome costumes.

In this episode the gravity of the situation—that is, the astronomical risk taken by handling plutonium and possessing nuclear power, and the possibility of radiation contamination—is debased to the level of comical combat between the hijackers and the hijacked. No Geiger counter, armed guards, or terrorism are involved. Things are turned around: the hijacked psychologically terrorizes the hijackers.

In another episode, the transformed pair, the teenage father and the grown-up Mori, attend an anti-nuclear meeting organized by Ōno Sakurao, a T.V. celebrity, and the Revolutionary Party. Above the stage set up by Ōno Sakurao is a banner "Nuclear Power in the Hands of Non-Authority," with Beethoven's string quartet "Serioso," Op. 95, playing in the background and intoxicating the whole audience. Mori's father, whose sexual prowess has been restored to that of an eighteen-year-old, is constantly aroused by the sight of his idol, Ōno Sakurao, on the stage. Attending the meeting with him and Mori are Mori's activist girl friend, Sayoko, the leader of the anti-nuclear forces in Shikoku Island, Gijin, and the Volunteer Mediator (*Shigan Chūsainin*) who constantly gets himself into trouble by trying to mediate the conflict between the two factions within the anti-nuclear forces, the Revolutionary Party and the Counter-Revolutionary Party.

The members of the Counter-Revolutionary Party who have infiltrated the audience start disrupting the meeting. The solemn political gathering, interrupted by a short-circuiting of the lighting system, degenerates into a commotion, and the commotion into a riot in which young activists of the Revolutionary Party start punching each other on the stage in the semi-darkness of disco-like flashing lights. The riot settles into a free-for-all, and the distinction between friend and foe is totally lost. Right below the stage Gijin bites the assailants back with his only weapon, his false teeth which have been knocked out of his mouth and which he uses as pincers. The Volunteer Mediator confronts the physical violence with his undaunted spirit, tenacity, and flexibility. On the stage, the mob, jostling, pushing, beating each other up, gleefully throws the T.V. celebrity into the air. What catches the eyes of the teenage father "in heat" is his beloved struggling helter-skelter, above the bobbing heads of the activists, trying to kick her way out. The valiant teenager rescues his "princess" and both retreat to a switchboard room backstage while the riot squad breaks into the meeting hall, "like tidal waves," and takes control. Mori's father assures Ōno Sakurao, "The riot squad won't dare come into this room with their metallic shields!" While he experiences "a fantastic orgasm" in making love to her, everything quiets down outside: the two take leave of the switchboard room with a flashlight which illuminates a big sign with a skull and crossbones, "KEEP OUT. HIGH VOLTAGE." Here we see the comical turn of events, copulation in the face of death, the anti-nuclear forces torn apart by factionalism.

All the various elements of grotesque realism are brought together in the eleventh chapter of ***The Pinchrunner Memorandum.*** The chapter, entitled, "The Arrival of the Buffoons," refers to the fifty people who come from the Patron's country to congregate outside the hospital to exorcise the evil spirits for their dying Patron. The country people throng around the building in pairs, disguised as *yakuza,* folk heroes, the Marx Brothers, Chaplin, A-bomb victims, Kamikaze pilots, etc.

The carnivalesque, all-popular, cosmic world is recreated in the gathering of these fifty buffoons. The father meditates upon sighting a pair of buffoons, a dwarf and his companion, an outlandishly corpulent woman: "Their very physical handicap satisfies the conditions of buffoonery, which is the degradation and debasement of the standard." Thus, for the first time, the idiot son Mori and the father have found a crowd in which they fit comfortably. The transformed pair joins the pressing throng in costumes which accentuate their transformation. Mori's father, in a rabbit-ear baby suit "as big as a kangaroo," moves steadily towards infancy, and Mori, in the costume of a Wizard, approaches senility.

The Patron, who is in reality a terrifying authority figure, becomes the clown to be mocked in this carnivalesque world: the buffoons are there to uncrown the dying "king," to let a new "king" reign. In other words, the only way the fifty country folk can overcome their fear of authority is to disguise themselves as buffoons, because only buffoonery, under the influence of a masquerade atmosphere, can summon the power of another world, a new world, a new ruler. We see here Ōe's attempt to indigenize buffoonery and the carnival, which have always existed as "little traditions" in the villages, but have been forgotten: "In an era in which the exterior of a city like Tokyo seems to have been buried under the debris of modernization, and where the idea of buffoonery seems virtually dead, subterranean society, like the world of the rain trout (iwana), can still offer us a place for the birth, growth, and death of buffoonery." [In a footnote Wilson explains: "*Iwana* (*Salvelinus pluvius*) belongs to the Charrs family, a kind of brook trout. Along with the fish called *yamame* (*Onchorhynchus masou*), this fish is used as a metaphor which embodies the ideal collectivity of the human race."]

As Ōe discusses in detail in **"Toward the Imagination of Buffoonery and Regeneration,"** the image of a buffoon is closely related to the mythological figure of the Winnebago Indians, the trickster ("The Foolish One"). Paul Radin calls the trickster "a breaker of the holy taboos, a destroyer of the most sacred objects," yet, to the Winnebago Indians, he is "a positive force, a builder." What takes place in the figure of the trickster is the gradual evolution "from an amorphous, instinctual unintegrated being into one with the lineaments of man and one foreshadowing man's psychical traits" [Paul Radin, *The Trickster,* 1975]. Radin sums up:

> Trickster is at one and the same time creator and destroyer, giver and negator, he who dupes others and who is always duped himself. He wills nothing consciously. At all times he is constrained to behave as he does from impulses over which he has no control. He knows neither good nor evil yet he is responsible for both. He possesses no values, moral or social, is at the mercy of his passions and appetites, yet through his actions all values come into being.

What we have in the trickster figure is an archetype of the jester and the buffoon, the ancestor of a Rabelaisian hero. One essential trait that characterizes the trickster, a creature still living in his unconscious, with the mentality of a child, is ambivalence. In this sense the idiot son Mori becomes Ōe's trickster. For example, as a small child, terrible misfortunes befall him. He falls into a hot bath, is bitten by a huge dog, and falls from a tree. Because of his self-destructive impulses, he beats himself up, and is beaten by his father, who accuses the son of abandoning him. Mori does not will anything and lives in the unconscious. Since he does not know the function of language, he is equated with desocialization, but, by his very presence and innocence, he regenerates those around him.

This notion of ambivalence, the simultaneous presence of the negative and the positive, is also the focal point of Bakhtin's discussions of grotesque realism. He notes that

> the grotesque image reflects a phenomenon in transformation, an as yet unfinished metamorphosis, of death and birth, growth and becoming. The relation to time is one determining trait of the grotesque image. The other indispensable trait is ambivalence. For in this image we find both poles of transformation, the old and the new, the dying and the procreating, the beginning and the end of the metamorphosis. [*Rabelais*]

Another element of ambivalence, i.e., the notion of a double, permeates many of the characters which appear in the novel. For example, there is the case of the driver and his assistant, who exchange *manzai*-like verbal repartee during the nuclear hijacking; also the pair of policemen, one "conciliatory," the other, "a threatening type," who keep the father's house under 24-hour surveillance. This antithetical pairing also extends to the two members of the Yamame Army whom the father nicknames Nōrifū (the Able Official) and Inutsura (Dog Face). Similarly the existence of the Revolutionary Party is not quite complete without the presence of the Counter-Revolutionary Party. Finally Ōno Sakurao, the woman counterpart of Gijin, represents along with the Yamame Army, an ideal collectivity of civilian power.

Throughout ***The Pinchrunner Memorandum,*** the transformed pair, Mori and the father, embodies this trait of ambivalence. The odd pair is portrayed as a double: "One a normal brother, the other a dwarf!" the father once tells the ghost writer. Their transformation reinforces the ambivalent nature of the grotesque imagery by each taking the other's place. In the gathering of fifty buffoons, the pair disguised as a kangaroo baby and a Wizard, becomes the very embodiment of ambivalence: both poles of transformation, the old and the new, the dying and procreating, the beginning and the end of the metamorphosis. Ōe's Gargantua and Pantagruel continue a spiral journey into the world of the fantastic and grotesque realism, exploring potentials and providing us at the same time with an entirely new outlook on the world.

Although the narratives of Ōe Kenzaburo . . . are deeply rooted in the indigenous culture of Japan, they are ultimately concerned with what is uniquely literary, not with what is uniquely Japanese. In this sense his narratives are "transcultural and transhistoric" to the core.

—Michiko N. Wilson, in his* The Marginal World of Ōe Kenzaburo: A Study in Themes and Techniques, *1986.

Emiko Sakurai (essay date Summer 1984)

SOURCE: "Kenzaburō Ōe: The Early Years," in *World Literature Today,* Vol. 58, No. 3, Summer, 1984, pp. 370-73.

[*In the following essay, Sakurai discusses the major influences on Ōe's early literary career, such as Japan's military defeat in 1945 and the works of such authors as Jean-Paul Sartre and traditional Haiku poets.*]

A highly regarded Japanese novelist, Shòhei Òoka, commented in 1977 that to discuss Kenzaburō Ōe would be to discuss one-quarter of a century of Japanese literature beginning in 1957. Few critics familiar with the development of that literature would disagree. Since becoming established as a writer in 1957 at age twenty-two, Ōe has produced an astonishing body of work that ranks at the forefront of contemporary Japanese fiction. He came on the literary scene a decade after a younger generation of writers referred to as *sengoha* (Postwar School) had launched a movement to discard outmoded traditions and achieve contemporaneity with world literature by exploring new ideas and techniques. Although the momentum created by the *sengoha* had already waned or changed direction by the time Ōe began to publish, he nonetheless succeeded in realizing the ideals of the movement and brought postwar literature to new heights.

Kenzaburō Ōe was born on 31 January 1935 in a village called Ōse on the island of Shikoku, the third son of a prominent samurai family. At the end of World War II he was a ten-year-old "village patriot" accustomed to being asked in school, "What would you do if the Emperor commanded you to die?" His knees trembling, he would reply: "I would die, Sir. I would cut open my belly and die." Because he had been taught that Emperor Hirohito was a living god, he was astounded on 15 August 1945 to hear the Emperor go on the radio and announce Japan's surrender. [As he wrote in ***Genshuku natsunawatari*** (***Solemnly Walking the Tightrope***)]:

> The strange and disappointing fact was that the Emperor spoke in a human voice like any ordinary man. Though we couldn't understand the speech, we heard his voice. One of my friends could even imitate it cleverly. We surrounded him, a boy in soiled shorts who spoke in the Emperor's voice, and laughed.
>
> Our laughter echoed in the summer morning stillness and disappeared into the clear, high sky. An instant later, anxiety tumbled out of the heavens and seized us impious children. We stared at one another in silence.

Ōe later wrote that the trauma left him squint-eyed for a time. Explaining twenty years later what turned him to fiction writing, Ōe said that the defeat, the feeling of being brought to his knees, "took seed" in August 1945 and grew into a lasting obsession in him and that only through literature could he cope with this obsession and manage to survive.

The defeat in World War II was a source of humiliation and guilt that the Japanese collectively suffered for a decade or more, a shame renewed daily by the presence of the Occupation forces, by the war trials, by the deprivation of daily necessities and by bombed-out city blocks. Powerful machinery was at work in General Douglas MacArthur's general headquarters [GHQ] to erase militarism from Japan forever, and the Japanese went through a long period of self-flagellation over the guilt of their militant past and of self-loathing for their new fifth-rate status. A boy of Ōe's sensitivity and precocity was bound to be deeply affected. The antiheroes of his early works—who resemble the author in many aspects—reflect the psychological ravages of that era. In one short story, **"Human Sheep"** (1958), Ōe describes a humiliating incident that a student of French like himself suffered on a bus at the hands of some American GI's.

Shortly after August 1945, a more encompassing censorship than the wartime publications code was clamped on the Japanese, and textbooks were probed with particular care for traces of militarism and emperor worship. The national education system was also revised, and when Ōe entered high school twenty months after the war, he was one of the first students to be educated under the new plan modeled after the American public school system.

The curriculum had been changed and he was no longer taught morality—a reading in anecdotes illustrative of traditional virtues such as filial piety and loyalty. The hour was devoted instead to the study of the new constitution speedily prepared by the order of the GHQ in the mold of the American constitution. Ōe's class, in addition, was given books on democracy and taught the subject by teachers recently returned from the war.

The details of Ōe's education have historical relevance. In a country never before vanquished, he is the only major writer ever to receive a secondary education under what was actually American occupation, following curricula devised by education specialists at the American GHQ and accumulating knowledge from books censored by them. The aim of that education was the rejection of traditional Japanese values in favor of the American value system. Receiving that education, Ōe became a strong proponent of democracy and a supporter of the new constitution, advocating them in writing and lectures. He became the spokesman for his generation in the new age and has been active in anti-establishment, human rights and humanitarian movements, demonstrating in the streets and staging hunger strikes.

By comparison, Yukio Mishima, born ten years before Ōe, received his secondary school education at the height of Japan's militarism. In the late fifties and sixties he glorified militarism and the emperor cult in such fictional works as the powerful short story "Patriotism" (1960). With revenues from his writing, he formed a private army of his own, outfitting the hundred members with stylish uniforms designed by a Parisian *haut couturier.* Mishima then demanded a revision of the constitution that outlawed war and called for a return to the imperial system. To achieve this end, he tried to incite an insurrection in 1970; on failing this, he committed ritual suicide. Subsequently Ōe parodied Mishima in a brilliant short novel, ***The Day He Himself Shall Wipe My Tears Away*** (1972). The protagonist is a seemingly deranged patient in a hospital who tries to relive an event that occurred on 15 August 1945, when his father led a band of army deserters on a suicide mission to rescue Japan from defeat and was shot down by the army. The father had been convinced of being consecrated in death because he was dying for the emperor, who is a living god, and the son spends the rest of his life reliving that glorious moment of consecration revealed to him by a colossal gold chrysanthemum in the sky.

In the village high school, Ōe's ambition had been to become a scientist, not a writer. But his teachers told him: "A scientist? You could *never* become a scientist." The basis for that opinion has never been discovered. Their student was clearly a genius. At the Scientific Invention Fair he submitted a "continous-type" mousetrap he invented that could conceivably catch, continuously, all the mice on the island of Shikoku. Ōe learned astronomy by reading on his own, and he also had a passion for geometry, solving geometric problems for pleasure. The teachers' cruel pronouncement threw him into a pit of despair, anger and shame and turned him into a lonely, morose, eccentric boy. He quit playing baseball and contracted intercostal neuralgia; unable to get along with others around him any longer, he turned to books for comfort.

Ōe's earliest reading was in tanka and haiku. He had been drawn since early childhood to Shiki Masaoka (1867-1902), a leading Meiji Era poet born in that same region (Ōe later attended the high school in Matsue City where Shiki had been educated). For years he also read Mokichi Saito (1882-1953), a tanka poet strongly influenced by Shiki. Because of his oldest brother's interest in haiku and tanka as a writer and collector, Ōe has admitted, he read most of the postwar publications in these genres. The poems he read should number close to 100,000, since Shiki's 1925 collection alone contained 12,700 haiku and Mokichi was also prolific.

After 1949, Ōe discovered the free-verse poets Tarō Tominaga (1901-25) and Chūya Nakahara (1907-37), to both of whom he acknowledges his indebtedness. The debt was partly owed to French poetry; Tominaga translated Baudelaire and, immensely affected by his poetry, wrote verse in the manner of the French symbolists. Nakahara started writing dadaist aphorisms at age fifteen, produced symbolist poems under the influence of Rimbaud and Verlaine and translated the collected poems of Rimbaud. During the same period, Ōe also became attracted to Poe, Eliot and Auden and later quoted them in his fiction. The titles for his short novels ***Teach Us to Outgrow Our Madness*** and ***Leap Before You Look*** come from Auden. "Although I have been periodically engrossed in French poetry, I keep coming back to Auden," Ōe says.

The poets of Ōe's boyhood were all men of extremely refined sensibility with added capacity to feel deeply because of their tragedies or illnesses. Shiki, for instance, suffered from tuberculosis all his adult life and wrote many of his poems while bedridden; Tominaga died of consumption at age twenty-four. They were lonely and melancholy men easily moved to tears. Their poems were subjective, self-absorbed and emotional, abounding in images from the natural world. Gifted in language and sensitive and withdrawn, especially after his father's sudden death when he was nine, Ōe shared several personal traits with these poets. After reading thousands of their poems annually and with great empathy during his formative years, Ōe naturally developed a literary personality like the personae in the poetry. Ōe's protagonists feel threatened by silence in the woods and sense the breathing of a small animal stirring in the dark. They are frequently fear-stricken, frustrated, humiliated, crushed, chagrined, mortified and ashamed, and are often on the verge of tears. When betrayed, cheated, humiliated, abused and cuckolded, they are too passive, too forgiving, devoid of the will and strength to fight back. Vengeance is unusual in Ōe's world. His characters tend to be self-destructive, sometimes out of a subconscious desire for self-punishment, which is a favorite theme of his in such works as ***Homo Sexualis*** (1963) and ***Man'en gannen no futtobōru*** (1967; ***The Silent Cry***).

Some critics view Ōe's unusual sensibilities as evidence of his essentially childlike nature. One critic even professes that he thinks of Ōe as an overgrown baby. There is undeniably a feeling of childlike innocence and purity about him; but Ōe's habit of overstatement and the influence of his favorite poets also have to be taken into account. In a 1905 tanka, for example, Mokichi described shedding tears while watching some wrestlers. When he was asked the reason for his tears, he explained that it moved him to see the wrestlers working so hard at their trade!

Poetry appears in abundance in Ōe's fiction. Critics called his early short story **"The Catch"** (1958) [which has also been published as a novella] a prose poem; in other stories some of his sentences resemble avant-garde verses. His writing is dense with natural images, particularly those of the birds and animals he grew up with in his mountain village, and no one can match Ōe's skill in the use of these images. The figures of speech that decorate his prose are occasionally too elaborate in fiction: "Hauling up my flabby, waterlogged body on the hook of consciousness much as one might reel in a dead sea toad, I clattered wildly down the staircase" [***The Silent Cry***].

In prose, Ōe's favorite book since childhood has been *The Adventures of Huckleberry Finn,* a copy of which was given to him during the war. Despite the emperor worship and wartime anti-Americanism, Huck Finn immediately became Ōe's hero. What won Ōe's lasting admiration was the agonizing decision Huck makes not to reveal the whereabouts of a runaway slave and to "go to Hell" instead. To a boy accustomed to being asked, "What would you do if the Emperor commanded you to die?" and not *totally* convinced of the sincerity of his answer, "I would cut open my belly and die, Sir," this was a supreme act of courage. In a 1966 article titled **"Huckleberry Finn and the Hero"** Ōe juxtaposed Charles Lindbergh, President John F. Kennedy and Huck Finn as heroes and praised Huck as the "representative American hero of all time." The admiration apparently inspired Ōe's teen-age adventure story ***Pluck the Flowers, Gun the Kids*** (1958).

In his fourteenth year Ōe was mesmerized by Dostoevsky's *Brothers Karamazov.* He was to write later that almost every year since that time he has spent one to several "holy weeks" reading only Dostoevsky.

—Emiko Sakurai

The writings of several postwar Japanese writers riveted Ōe's interest from about 1949. He read all the slick boy's adventure stories written by Jun Ishikawa (b. 1899) after the war, and he was entranced by Postwar School critic Kiyoteru Hanada's "Spirit of the Revival" (1947), an erudite book of literary theory based on Marxism. Deeply affected by Hanada's doctrines, Ōe later used Hanadian dialectics and heeded the critic's urging to writers not to neglect native traditions such as folklore in their pursuit of Western inspirations for their work. In his fiction he employed motifs from folklore such as festivals, sacrifices and burial rites and wrote two major novels based on the myths of his village and the history of his ancestors at a time when other writers were "foreignizing" characters and locales to make their work cosmopolitan. ***The Silent Cry*** and ***The Contemporaneity Game*** [***Dojidai Gemu,*** also published as ***A Game of Simultaneity,*** 1979] both won coveted prizes. When the eight-volume collection of literary and art criticism by the father of modern Japanese criticism, Hideo Kobayashi, started appearing in 1951, Ōe reverently read every page. He could not have had a better preparation for his writing career. When he began writing short stories four years later, they were masterfully plotted and proportioned.

In his fourteenth year Ōe was mesmerized by Dostoevsky's *Brothers Karamazov.* He was to write later that almost every year since that time he has spent one to several "holy weeks" reading only Dostoevsky.

> While reading Dostoevsky, I was free from anxiety, feeling myself stable, able to maintain an order, not committing suicide or becoming insane or starting an antisocial act. Even when I was unable to sleep, because I could curl up like a fetus and lie hidden in Dostoevsky's womb, I did not fear the shadows of night or death. [***Solemnly Walking the Tightrope***]

Sometime in late 1949 or early 1950, Ōe read a collection of short stories by Sartre in translation and found his description of the captives terrified of their approaching death in *Le mur* false. Ōe himself was being stricken nightly by fear of death, and he thought the portrayal could be more effectively handled. Dropping Sartre, he went on to Rimbaud, Baudelaire, Verlaine and Flaubert and did not return to Sartre until three years later, when he read *L'âge de raison.*

Admitted to Tokyo University in 1954, Ōe enrolled in the Literature Department and moved on two years later to the Department of French Literature. He was introduced to Rabelais by his principal professor, Kazuo Watanabe, an expert on Rabelaisian lore, but in 1956-57 Ōe was too absorbed in Sartre to become attracted to anyone else. Although he was studying classical French grammar and Balzac in the classroom, once he was back in his rooming house he would read absolutely nothing but Sartre. Particularly during vacations, he would devote all day to him—except for the last week, when he would try to write a one-act play or a short story for a prize offered on campus. Ōe's short story **"An Odd Job"** won the 1957 May Festival Prize and was published in the May issue of the university literary journal. The story attracted attention when Ken Hirano, a highly respected critic of the Postwar School and literary critic of the *Mainichi Shimbun,* praised it in the newspaper as a modernistic and artful work. Four more pieces by Ōe appeared in the following months in leading literary magazines and established his reputation as a student writer of extraordinary talent: **"Proud Are the Dead," "Other People's Legs," "The Plaster Mask"** and **"Time for Perjury."** In January 1958 Ōe won fame by narrowly losing the coveted Akutagawa

Prize for 1957 to writer Kōken Kai, his **"Proud Are the Dead"** vying against Kai's "Naked Emperor." So high was the critics' regard for Ōe's work that he received as many accolades as did Kai. Six months later he was awarded the 1958 prize for **"The Catch."**

"The Catch" was followed in February and March 1958 by **"Human Sheep," "Transportation"** and **"The Pigeon,"** and these and the previous five pieces—excepting **"Plaster Mask"** and **"Transportation"**—were collected in March 1958 under the title ***Proud Are the Dead.*** Regarding these efforts, Ōe, with his usual self-deprecation, credits Sartre:

> I thought I was singing with my own voice, but because of my daily habit of bogging down in the Sartrean mire, like a ventriloquist's grotesque, red-cheeked dummy, I was only miming Sartre's voice in a raw shriek. [***Solemnly Walking the Tightrope***]

Clearly there was no attempt at imitation; but there was much affinity and inspiration. Having survived war, defeat and occupation and being bewildered by the emptiness and enervation of a postwar wasteland similar to Sartre's, Ōe could easily identify with Sartre and his antiheroes. He saw himself and others of his generation as ensnared and incarcerated, devoid of real human solidarity and vitiated by incarceration, and he tried to depict that existence in a group of short stories that became ***Proud Are the Dead.*** In **"An Odd Job"** a student goes to work at a compound where dogs are tethered and beaten to death one by one. The student muses: "And who could say the same thing wouldn't happen to us? Helplessly leashed together, looking alike, hostility lost and individuality with it—us ambiguous Japanese students."

In **"Proud Are the Dead"** cadavers jostling one another in a tank in the cellar of a university hospital symbolize human existence within walls. The story recalls *Le mur,* in which the captives await their execution in a similar cellar. **"Other People's Legs"** describes the world of teenagers confined to wheelchairs for spinal tuberculosis in a sanatorium completely shut off from the outside world. In **"Time for Perjury"** a youth is tied to a chair and held under guard; in **"The Catch"** a downed black American airman is "raised" in the cellar by a ten-year-old boy in a wartime mountain village. Readers sensed in these works a certain foreignness; they were like translations from the writings of Camus, Sartre or Kafka. Ken Hirano lauded **"The Catch"** but commented that it did not describe an authentic Japanese village. With its rich images of animals, tribal chieftain and hunters, it is European in temper. The sanatorium in **"Other People's Legs,"** similarly, is nothing like those found in Japan. But Ōe was interested in philosophy, not authenticity. The critics, many of them specialists in some Western literature, were highly pleased with Ōe's "modernity"—by which they meant Western influence.

In June 1958 Ōe's first full-length novel, ***Pluck the Flowers, Gun the Kids,*** appeared to great acclaim. Also based on the theme of confinement, it treats the adventures of a group of teen-agers from a reformatory who occupy a deserted village. This was followed in October by ***Leap Before You Look,*** a collection of five novellas and short stories depicting the interrelations of foreigners and Japanese under occupation. In 1958 Ōe was also laboring on his thesis for graduation the following spring, a study of imagery in Sartre's fiction. (Incidentally, when Ōe met Sartre in Paris in 1961 and was asked which French author he read most in college, he was too shy to tell Sartre the truth. He finally whispered, "Racine.")

Ōe's early success as a writer has been the source of his enduring regret that he did not continue with his studies and accumulate experience first. He hears an inner voice that he should have heard in 1957: "What's the hurry, you're still young." Despite his enormous influence, he is not likely to get a sympathetic ear; because of that success, he has been invited abroad many times, starting in 1960 with a visit to China, where he met Mao, and he has become acquainted with several writers whom he admires: Norman Mailer, Saul Bellow and Gabriel García Márquez, for example, in addition to Sartre. He has gone on to publish eleven more bestselling novels, numerous critiques, reportages and essays, many of the latter on the art of writing. He must be the only author ever to write a bestseller titled ***The Technique of Fiction*** [***Shosetsu no Hoho,*** also published as ***Methods of the Novel,*** 1978], a book which only the initiated could comprehend. Clearly there is no need for apology. At age forty-nine, Kenzaburō Ōe has decades ahead of him in which to experiment and learn and present more masterpieces to his eager public.

Sanroku Yoshida (essay date Spring 1985)

SOURCE: "Kenzaburo Ōe: A New World of Imagination," in *Comparative Literature Studies,* Vol. 22, No. 1, Spring, 1985, pp. 80-95.

[*In the following essay, Yoshida argues for the universality of Ōe's fiction, citing its strong affinities with the "grotesque realism" of the French Renaissance writer François Rabelais.*]

In the modern history of Japan the most significant event was the defeat of Japan in the Second World War. It totally undermined the social and value system developed since the Meiji Restoration in 1868. The experience in Hiroshima and Nagasaki makes clear that one single bomb may mean instantaneous and simultaneous death for everybody on earth. And the real meaning of the nuclear age and its imminent danger is fully examined for the first time in the works of Kenzaburo Ōe. Even though the situations, characters, and incidents in his fiction are clearly Japanese, his unparalleled literary imagination makes his provocative and disturbing message universal. The problems he deals with are not only Japanese, but global. Ōe writes for the sake of the world's future.

While majoring in French literature at Tokyo University, Ōe avidly read Pascal, Camus, Sartre, Mailer, Faulkner, and Bellow. Like Shōyō Tsubouchi (1859-1935), who modernized Japanese literature, Ōe became familiar with contemporary trends of world literature, also influenced by wartime experiences and the postwar disorientation. With this background, Ōe has started to reform Japanese literature—to make it more committed and relevant to the human problems peculiar to the twentieth century. Ōe assigns a more active role to literature than that which Tsubouchi had given it nearly one hundred years ago—to "move the heart and stimulate the imagination." For Ōe, literature is not to "stimulate the imagination," but is a product of the imagination which should provide readers with a clear picture of the situation, physical or metaphysical, in which humans exist. Literature may also help the reader deal with the disillusionment that results from a realization of the meaninglessness of life. Furthermore, literature is to provide an individual or personal viewpoint, often antithetical to the ready-made and dominant one; thereby the novel functions as an antidote for such group psychology as exhibited in war.

According to Ōe's concept, therefore, political ideology has a legitimate place in literature; this again directly violates his predecessor's dictum. In his *Shosetsu Shinzui* (*Essence of the Novel,* 1885) Tsubouchi declared the independence of literature from what was called the "Political Novel," once fashionable in the pre- and early Meiji Period. The tradition of divorcing literature from political ideology has since been upheld in Japan. In other words, if literature is to remain serious it ought not deal with political issues. Ōe has violated that tradition by bringing into literature such political issues as disputes over nuclear energy, international treaties involving the use of nuclear weaponry, and the possible dangers of maintaining monarchy, even a symbolic monarchy.

Ōe's understanding of the world situation and its relationship to Japan makes him believe that political neutrality in literature is unacceptable, for the question involves human annihilation.

—Sanroku Yoshida

In one of his earlier novels, ***The Young Man Who Arrived Late*** (***Okurete Kita Seinen,*** 1962), Ōe deals with a young man who is helplessly disoriented after Japan's surrender by the Emperor's declaration of his change of status from divine to human, for the declaration cancels out the responsibilities for the war fought under his name. In a novella entitled ***The Day He Himself Shall Wipe My Tears Away*** (***Mizu kara Waga Mamida o Nugui Tamau Hi,*** 1971) [contained in Ōe's ***Teach Us To Outgrow Our Madness,*** 1977], Ōe symbolically presents the relationship between the Emperor and his Imperial Army on the eve of World War II and its result manifested in present-day Japan. His latest novel, ***A Game of Simultaneity*** (***Dōjidai Gēmu,*** 1979), explores the monarch's influence as a force in centralizing or controlling Japan's diversified folkloric culture.

Ōe's understanding of the world situation and its relationship to Japan makes him believe that political neutrality in literature is unacceptable, for the question involves human annihilation. Ōe's messages in ***The Flood unto my Soul*** (***Kozui wa Waga Tamashii ni Oyobi,*** 1973) and ***The Pinchrunner*** (***Pinchiran'na Chosho,*** 1976) are clearly antinuclear. [In ***Ōe Kenzaburo Dojidai Ronshu*** (***Essays on Contemporary Issues***), 1981] Ōe asks, "What can literature do when confronted with starving children?" His own answer to this question is that literature ought to be written from the viewpoint of starving people, because they are the majority of the world population. If literature is to be universal, it ought to be written from the perspective of the majority. And this is the only thing that literature can do for starving children. Ōe's message here is that literature should not exist for literature's sake, but should be actively involved in the issues vital to the existence of the majority, that is, the poor and the oppressed.

In an essay entitled **"Why Do Human Beings Create Literature?"** Ōe contends that the role of literature is as follows:

> Literature is a verbal endeavor made in order to recognize the meaning of one's being human at one's very root, with an overall understanding of one's relation to society, the world and the cosmos. Therefore, when a giant corporation, disrupting the natural cycle of life and death, exercises its large-scale violence over human beings—so large that it destroys the fundamental harmony between human beings and their society, the world and the cosmos—literature, standing on a human ground, will continue to protest against such violence.

It is true that the human problems of Tsubouchi's time were of a considerably different nature, but the philosophy of literature in the nineteenth century was to pursue truth in human life and to appreciate life. Basically life was precious and meaningful, and therefore death was tragic. However, toward the end of this century when, in the face of possible obliteration of humanity, death has lost its tragic quality, such political issues as nuclear weaponry and deterioration of the natural environment are not merely political but human issues. Ōe has departed far from the traditional literary tenets laid out by Tsubouchi; he allows wider latitude and gives new energy to literature, thus making it a vital activity of the human mind.

Sex is another element Ōe has been treating in a totally new fashion. In Japanese literary tradition, both before and after Tsubouchi, sex had never been so deeply and extensively explored. Ōe's predecessors always dealt with matters ancillary to human sexuality; therefore, sex was suggested more or less metaphorically or symbolically. This allusive and subtle treatment of sex is completely eliminated in Ōe, and sex is presented directly by depicting characters' sexual organs and acts with anatomical accuracy.

Ōe's treatment of sex seems to present images far removed from those of romantic literature, such as D. H. Lawrence's. In Ōe sex is brutal, repulsive, grossly distorted; therefore it presents a negative image. The sex described is often abnormal in form and in the relationships between the characters involved—abnormal also in the sense that it does not lead to healthy procreation.

The negative image of sex is presented in contrast to the

positive image of politics in Ōe's imaginative world. Political human beings are always alert to possible dangers, ready to fight, and therefore tend to differentiate themselves as individuals from the whole of society. Sexual human beings, by contrast, miss the danger signals in their sexual comfort, are satisfied in their stagnant state of mind, and tend to assimilate with society. Ōe, in other words, sees young people in modern Japan in such a stagnant state, and, in order to provoke them, repeatedly uses the motif of depraved sex and its negativity.

Ōe classifies sex in literature into two categories: one involves romantic and erotic treatment of sex; the other is a direct approach toward sex as the human core. Writers choosing the former try to identify themselves with the shadow of the past. The romantic-erotic treatment of sex may create a beautiful metaphorical world of emotion, but the more beautiful that world is, the farther removed it is from the actual state of being human. Ōe posits that literary examination of modern human beings can be done most effectively by the use of explicit sexual terminology:

> In the age of Stendhal, a clear mind [of the author] was efficient enough for analyzing the naked human being. In this century, with its two World Wars, a weapon called psychoanalysis was brought into literature. And today sexual terminology, sexual images are effective new weapons. In other words, in modern literature, only sexual images and terminology are shocking enough to break through [the outward protection of human beings]. [**"Modern Literature and Sex,"** in ***Essays on Contemporary Issues***]

Ōe's hyperbolic magnification of depravity in sex in his works seems to suggest a possible apocalypse. It recalls the visual presentation of the theme by Hieronymus Bosch, entitled the *Garden of Earthly Delights,* or *The Last Judgement.* The negativity of sex and pessimism concerning the future of mankind in Ōe's world are discussed in a later section of this essay.

Ōe emphasizes "imagination" time after time in his various essays. He certainly sets a higher value on "imagination" than on "realism" in its traditional sense. His incidents, situations, and characters are highly improbable, and yet they are often described with an air of matter-of-factness. Improbability is one of the major reasons why Japanese traditionalist critics review Ōe's works unfavorably. However, improbability in the light of everyday life, Ōe argues [in ***Methods of the Novel***], is an application of the technical theory called "defamiliarization." Victor Shklovsky, a Russian formalist critic, explains why and how a writer defamiliarizes familiar objects.

> Habitualization devours works, clothes, furniture, one's wife, and the fear of war. "If the whole complex lives of many people go on unconsciously, then such lives are as if they had never been." And art exists so that one may recover the sensation of life; it exists to make one feel things, to make the stone *stony.* The purpose of art is to impart the sensation of things as they are perceived and not as they are known. The technique of art is to make objects "unfamiliar," to make forms difficult, to increase the difficulty and length of perception because the process of perception is an aesthetic end in itself and must be prolonged. *Art is a way of experiencing the artfulness of an object; the object is not important.* [*Russian Formalist Criticism: Four Essays,* 1965]

Thus, increasingly, Ōe's imagination defamiliarizes and dehumanizes his characters: they do not have any ordinary names—ordinary names may induce "habitualization"—but often are referred to by an animal name or a general designation such as the "Righteous Man" or the "Man Who Would Not Come Down From Trees."

The major source of Ōe's literary technique is Rabelaisian grotesque realism, another form of defamiliarization. The images in grotesque realism are often of the human body, especially the lower part of it, and its natural material activities such as eating, drinking, defecation, and copulation. These bodily elements are definitely positive in the theory of the grotesque, since bodily activity is closely related to the soil, that is, nature. Nature, in turn, suggests rebirth and revitalization of life. Feces and urine function as intermediaries between human beings and soil; they embody the cycle of life. Ōe contends that in the nuclear age, with its everyday danger of annihilation and nuclear-related pollution, a deep understanding of the unity of human beings and nature in the context of a cosmic order is of vital importance and that the image system of grotesque realism is the most effective literary method to achieve the goal. Ōe concludes:

> Literature is a verbal structure that stops any movement directed toward one's inner self—movements that are separated from the material, bodily root of the entire world. Our literature should adopt the image system of grotesque realism as its integral part and, in so doing, should bring about a real regeneration of human life—in this way I intend to formulate the future of Japanese literature. [**"The Image System of Grotesque Realism,"** in ***Methods of the Novel***]

Ōe's literary technique of "defamiliarization" is, of course, directly in tune with Western modernism. This is only natural since he has been under heavy influence from Western literature. In addition, his mentor at the university was a scholar expert on *Gargantua and Pantagruel.* What is more important about Ōe's new world, however, is that he, as Shimei Futabatei (1864-1909) had a century earlier, has invented a new style—a style more efficient for his new motifs, images, and techniques. To the great dismay of traditionalists, he violates the natural flow of rhythm, natural syntax, elegance, suggestiveness, and sometimes even grammar of the language. Time will tell whether or not his style will influence Japanese culture in general, as was the case with Futabatei.

With all these revolutionary literary tenets, Ōe is an incredibly prolific and serious writer. He started his literary career at the age of twenty-three by winning the Akutagawa Prize for a short story, and since then [up to 1985] he has written eleven novels, about fifty short stories and novellas, and more than two hundred essays. His fiction deals with such human problems as estrangement, madness, and fear of nuclear annihilation; his essays are studies of other writers' works (East and West, present and past), analyses of literary theory, and of social and political criticism. He is popular among young readers but looked at askance by more traditional readers.

Until 1964, Ōe's works were based upon his experiences in, and observations of, society during the chaotic period immediately after Japan's defeat in World War II. (Ōe was ten years old when the war ended.) Specific incidents and episodes used in his fiction are probably pure products of his imagination, but the narrative situations are often identifiable with his own biographical data. His first novel, ***Plucking Buds and Shooting Lambs*** (***Me-mushiri Kouchi,*** 1958), is set in a mountain village, perhaps identifiable as his native village; ***Our Age*** (***Warera no Jidai,*** 1959), his second, is a story of a university student who, like Ōe himself, majors in French. ***The Young Man Who Arrived Late*** seems to reflect both his childhood experience and his university student life, especially the life of student political activists; street demonstrations and other activities by students in protest against the renewal of the U.S.-Japan Mutual Security Treaty became more and more violent during the first half of the sixties.

In 1964 Ōe's attention was directed to the possible danger of human annihilation by a nuclear holocaust when his newly born child had to undergo operations because of defective bone structure in the head. Ōe viewed the personal ordeal as overlapping the hardships of the atomic bomb survivors he met in Hiroshima. Between 1964 and 1976 Ōe wrote three major novels whose central motif is the main characters' mentally retarded son; ***A Personal Matter*** (***Kojinteki na Taiken,*** 1964), ***The Flood unto my Soul,*** and ***The Pinchrunner.*** The last two clearly present Ōe's pessimistic view of the likelihood of a nuclear apocalypse. Simultaneously Ōe explores his grim world view based on a notion of the ultimate cosmic confinement of human beings in ***The Silent Cry*** (***Manen Gan'nen no Futtoboru,*** 1967) and in ***A Game of Simultaneity.***

We shall discuss in the next two sections of this essay the obvious contradiction between theory and practice. The positive role of literature in society has been emphasized and the techniques of "defamiliarization" including grotesque realism were presented as the regenerating elements in literature and in life as well. The works of Ōe, however, do not convey such overtones, but rather present a pessimistic view of the future. This essay will first examine the relationship between sexual depravity and the nuclear apocalypse and then analyze Ōe's cosmic view and use of subterranean images as negative elements.

Ōe's world of sex is full of images apparently derived from the visual presentation of "the nightmarish humanity" of Hieronymus Bosch in such masterpieces as the *Garden of Earthly Delights* or *The Last Judgement.* In return, what Charles De Tolnay writes about Bosch seems to be readily applicable to Ōe:

> Whereas Hieronymus Bosch's contemporaries were content to solve formal problems within the frame work of the old religious themes, Bosch from the beginning set himself new tasks; to him art was a language which he used to express a view of the world, and his pictures are open books that address themselves to all the viewer's spiritual faculties. [*Hieronymus Bosch,* 1966]

Sex becomes a major concern for Ōe, as something deeply rooted in humanity, in his second novel, ***Our Age.*** Sex is never shown in a positive light, but always as something nightmarish and obsessive, as in Bosch's pictures. Because of the bold directness with which Ōe treats sex, it tends to create a repulsive effect and to suggest the apocalyptic end of mankind. The main character in ***Our Age*** is a decadent student who lives with a prostitute. He happens to find a chance to escape from his girl friend and to go to France in order to start a new life. Later, however, the hero becomes involved in underground revolutionary movements which deprive him of the chance to escape. In this novel, both politics and sex have negative images, and politics actually does ruin this young man's positive effort to get out of his stagnant life. This, of course, contradicts what Ōe formulates about politics and sex in his essays, and, in turn, it deepens the sense of confinement which leads only to despair and madness.

Sexual obsession remains the major motif in the novel ***Adventures in Everyday Life*** (***Nichijōseikatsu no Boken,*** 1964). The hero, Saikichi, leads an absurd life centering around various sexual adventures. The elements of absurdity and sex-related slapstick exist already in this novel in germinal form, which Ōe later develops fully in ***The Pinchrunner.*** The theme of nuclear apocalypse combined with sexual depravity gradually comes to the forefront of Ōe's imaginative world. Saikichi's suicide is triggered by the realization of his own inability to save the A-bomb victim from the pain of leukemia except by performing euthanasia. The motif of sex, as Ōe asserts, certainly creates negativity in ***Adventures in Everyday Life,*** but the negativity does not regenerate or revitalize human existence.

Bird, the protagonist in ***A Personal Matter,*** is confronted by a concrete problem—a problem threatening his future freedom in life—a deformed baby. Bird is devastated by a sense of shame since he has just fathered a monster baby and may now be trapped in a cage called "parental responsibilities." He takes shelter in the sexual world of his girl friend, Himiko, and in alcoholism as well, wishing death for the baby. Himiko resembles a nocturnal animal, a typical image of the classic grotesque—active only in the ominous atmosphere of night—and is presented as a sex expert who cures Bird's impotence by offering anal intercourse. The negative image of sex drives the dispirited Bird to a state of enervation. At this moment, Bird suddenly realizes that he cannot keep running away from his responsibilities forever, and decides to take care of the baby with his wife and parents-in-law.

If the perverted sexual acts with Himiko have brought this almost miraculous metamorphosis to Bird—an animal turns into a human being—then Bird's returning to his wife and baby ought to present a positive and vital image. The situation, however, is almost the same as before except that the baby's brain hernia has turned out to be a benign tumor, and the father now conforms to the social norm called "parental responsibilities." Furthermore, if Bird's return to his wife suggests a return to normalcy from the world of perverted sex, then the novel presents

In Ōe's world of imagination, deformity, possibly caused by nuclear contamination, is closely related to the obsession with perverted sex. In addition, these two elements combined seem to lead to the notion of an apocalyptic ending of the world.

—Sanroku Yoshida

a grim prophecy concerning the future of mankind, since that normalcy had produced a deformed child.

In Ōe's world of imagination, deformity, possibly caused by nuclear contamination, is closely related to the obsession with perverted sex. In addition, these two elements combined seem to lead to the notion of an apocalyptic ending of the world. The discovery of nuclear fission serves both as cause and effect. Therefore, deformity is a literary expression, as is the perverted sexual obsession, of the loss of faith in God in an age of crematoria and nuclear extermination; it epitomizes man's inability to reproduce himself. Thus, it becomes the major source of images for Ōe, who upholds the merits of the grotesque as literary expression. Friedrich Dürrenmatt, a Swiss author, who considers the grotesque as the only legitimate contemporary genre, contends that:

> . . . Our world led us inevitably to the grotesque as it did to the atom bomb, just as Hieronymus Bosch's apocalyptic paintings are grotesque in nature. The grotesque, however, is only a sensuous paradox, the shape of a shapelessness, the face of a faceless world; and just as our thinking seems unable to do without the concept of paradox, so is art, our world, which survives only because there is an atom bomb: in fear of it. [Quoted in Wolfgang Kayser, *The Grotesque in Art and Literature,* 1963]

The fear of nuclear holocaust is the main theme of the next novel in our discussion, ***The Flood unto my Soul.*** As the title suggests, it is a parody of the Biblical episode of Jonah, who is swallowed by a whale as the consequence of his disobedience to the word of God. The hero, Isana Ōki (Whale-Big Tree), lives in a nuclear shelter with his idiot son, Jin, but becomes involved with a group of social dropouts called the "Free Navigators." Their purpose is to prepare themselves for a seaborne escape, in the event of a nation-wide disaster, by stealing firearms, learning how to operate a schooner, and practicing combat drills. This escape plan is directly associated with another deluge. The novel concludes with Isana's death by drowning in the whale-like shelter in the midst of a shootout with the police.

The first grotesque motif of sex is presented in a character called the "Shrinking Man" and in his fate. The "Shrinking Man" is also a symbolic manifestation of the process of inevitable deformation in Ōe's **"Garden of Earthly Delights."** The shrinking starts on this man's thirty-second birthday; he feels as if a small metal ball is rolling up and down on his backbone, which makes him restless and leads him to the scales and the measuring tape.

> The sensation of shrinking in his body had been confirmed by his decreased measurements. It was a horrible confirmation, indeed. Seeing a picture of himself shrinking faster and faster, finally his inner organs crushed in a body as small as that of a monkey, and dying after a weak hiccup or two, he wept silently and hopelessly. He felt as if all of his emotional faculties had wilted. But at the same time, the shrinking dissolved immediately the sense of complication between body and consciousness, a knotty feeling which had been nagging him for several years. It was an extremely lonely but soothing sensation for him to be liberated from the hangup. [***The Flood unto my Soul***]

This sense of unity—or oneness—between flesh and consciousness is attained by diminishing all the mental faculties stored in his body except for sex; as his body shrinks, his phallus grows bigger in return. Actually he is gradually turning into one enormous phallus, and thereby becoming an entity whose body and consciousness are nothing but sex.

The ending of ***The Flood unto my Soul*** clearly suggests the fate of human beings who have violated the will of God. Furthermore, the fact that Isana is never saved, unlike Jonah, from the stomach of the whale, that is, the nuclear shelter, seems to indicate that the water in which Isana is drowned is actually a global deluge to annihilate mankind. Depraved sex has been a major reason for God's wrath in Biblical episodes, but now the invention of nuclear fission provides another reason since it disrupts the cosmic order; the punishment for this sin is obliteration of mankind by that same nuclear fission.

> Suppose in an hour the world's last war broke out, he [Isana] must walk back to his shelter with his son, Jin, before the heat and the shock waves of nuclear explosions hit this city, threading their way through the panicked crowd, with the aplomb and persistence of those who had lived only to prepare themselves for such a day. Until he could officially return the right to use the globe to the trees and the whales, he and his infant son must wait in the shelter calm and relaxed as if they themselves chose to be annihilated. The concrete wall of the shelter would glow with the intense heat and then the shock waves would reach the infant child's ears. Isana's wish, at that instant, would be to hear Jin whisper gently, "The end of the world, this is." [***The Flood unto my Soul***]

Isana's wish to wait for the last moment "calm and relaxed as if they themselves chose to be annihilated" is probably the manifestation of the Sartrean existential idea that man is doomed but not damned and should remain free to choose his fate. This may sound like nothing but a sophism, since on the eve of Doomsday it is the only option there is, but even so it is quintessential to be the master of one's existence.

The main character in ***The Pinchrunner,*** Mori (meaning

"forest" in Japanese and "death" in Latin), is the one who chooses his fate, activated and vitalized by the "Will of the Universe." By contrast, his father does not choose but is pushed around by the dominating power, called "Mr. A, the boss." The father, who is referred to only by the name "Mori/father," believes he was contaminated with plutonium when his wife became pregnant with Mori, and that, therefore, Mori is an idiot.

The novel is a fantasy-farce with full use of grotesque techniques and folkloric images. The central idea in the plot is transformation, a switch of identities between the father and son. This supernatural switch is made to take place by the "Will of the Universe." The thirty-eight-year-old father loses twenty years to his son, regaining the eighteen-year-old boy's sexual energy; his eight-year-old idiot son becomes a twenty-eight-year-old mature man and turns out to be a politically oriented assassin.

Ōe seems to be presenting a contrast between the sexually oriented and the politically oriented. The father, sexually oriented, used to work for Mr. A collecting information from foreign-language journals concerning the use of nuclear energy, which obviously helped Mr. A to establish nuclear generating plants. Mori/father later worked in one of these plants and was contaminated by highly toxic nuclear waste. As a result he was retired at full pay. Thus, Ōe creates a character whose situation is seemingly totally free from economic anxieties in the midst of physical dangers. Of course, this is also symbolic of Japan, economically booming, yet highly contaminated. The father is incapable of doing anything effective to save his son from idiocy or to secure his future well-being. Then, the switch takes place. Mori, the son, immediately attacks Mr. A, guided by the "Will of the Universe," while his father, now younger than the son, gets involved in the power struggle between factions of student activists over the issue of which student group should manufacture a nuclear bomb.

In spite of the author's conscious effort to create a ludicrous atmosphere, the characters' laughter, abundant and ringing literally all over the pages, sounds artificial and vacant. The vitality and regeneration expressed by folkloric images are overshadowed by deep pessimism about the possibility of a nuclear apocalypse, which seems even more pessimistic in a work filled with loud laughter.

The Silent Cry was published five years before ***The Flood unto my Soul,*** but it contains some strong thematic and technical similarities to the most recent Ōe novel, ***A Game of Simultaneity. The Silent Cry*** deals with the repeated experience of a historic incident by its posterity over several generations; in ***A Game of Simultaneity,*** the mythical and historical view of Japan in a cosmic context is presented. Increasingly Ōe is trying to grasp the meaningfulness or meaninglessness of human existence in his fatalistic view of life, using images from myth and history. The matter of sex, especially that of incest, is brought to the forefront for literary examination. And the notion that man is doomed and that the only destination for him is Hell, where he will be burned as a punishment for incest, seems to be pervasive. A picture entitled *Hell,* a family heirloom of the narrators in both novels, like Bosch's *Hell,* is a visual presentation of the fate of mankind.

The symbolic presentation of the space where human existence is rooted is indispensable for the development of the plot—the experiencing of incidents in the past by characters beyond the chronological sequence of time. Events, characters, narrative situations, all extremely symbolic and metaphorical, are oriented to space but not to temporal sequence. Thus, human experiences in various units of time and space can be analyzed and conceptualized in a systematic way as in a microcosmos, or as in myth, which synthesizes the cosmic picture in its totality.

The Nedokoro brothers (their name means "root-place") in ***The Silent Cry*** experience what their great-grandfather and his younger brother had experienced about a hundred years before. The great-granduncle, who escaped from the village in the legend, is the figure representing the antithesis of confinement for the Nedokoro brothers. The truth, however, confirms their fear; the great-granduncle had been kept secretly in the basement of the Nedokoro Mansion for the rest of his life. The confined view of life is also omnipresent in the incestuous relations between the brother and sister. Takashi, the younger brother, confesses:

> . . . I made up a tale about us [Takashi and his sister] being a couple of aristocrats whose family had come down in the world, and took an exaggerated pride in our descent from the great-grandfather and his brother. . . . I told her we were a special elite of two, and we wouldn't and mustn't get interested in anybody apart from each other. . . . [***The Silent Cry***]

This close tie between the brother and sister not only evolves into an obsession with incest, but also points to a primordial sexual unity, that is, hermaphroditism.

The narrator and his twin sister in ***A Game of Simultaneity*** present this sexual obsession in a more metaphorical and yet clearer way. They do not commit incest per se, but the brother cannot satisfy himself in sexual intercourse unless he imagines his sister's naked body. They are also a parody of the beginning part of the Japanese creation myth. The narrator of the novel, or the "one who records the myth and history of their village-nation-microcosmos," is named Tsuyuki: his sister, Tsuyumi. This slight difference in the last syllables in their names undoubtedly alludes to the incestuous brother and sister, Izanagi and Izanami, in the creation myth. Furthermore, the brother and sister in the novel are recorded as one person in the census bureau in order to cut down the heavy poll tax. The actual image of a hermaphrodite conceived by the narrator is a girl with a well-shaped penis and large testicles.

Another mythical aspect of the novel is the narrative situation. It suggests the process in which the *Kojiki* (*The Chronicles of Ancient Matters*) was compiled in the eighth century. The narrator's father, a Shinto priest, orders the son to keep a record of what he relates as the myth and history of the "village-nation-microcosmos." Unlike Hieda no Are, who told one authoritative version of the myth, the "Father/priest" provides many versions in plural points of view and the narrator tells them to his sister, not to the Emperor.

Events are told from plural viewpoints, and the chronological sequence of the events is intentionally rearranged, which makes it hard to pin down what actually happens in what order. It is safe, however, to assume that this much is clear: the village-nation-microcosmos was founded some time in the middle of the feudal period (around 1700) on the island of Shikoku by a number of expatriated samurai. These founding fathers live to be more than two hundred years old and become legendary giants. The leader of this group, named the "Destroyer," has been killed several times but always revives; his existence is ubiquitous, especially for the villagers. Ōe's nomenclature is always highly symbolic, but in this case, since the "Destroyer" is actually the "creator," it is paradoxical as well. This paradoxical nomenclature gives rise to several possible interpretations, which we shall discuss later. After the village-nation-microcosmos loses the "Fifty-Day War" against the Imperial Army, it is merged into a nation called Japan. The work is a satire of the modern world with its worship of sciencc-tcchnology, an attcmpt to cxamine human existence in relation to cosmology, and, above all, a dream-like, unreal story, lacking orientation to any everyday actuality, but told with stunning reality.

The fifty-day war is perhaps a caricature of the history of wars. It is basically jungle guerrilla warfare at the beginning, depending on the maze-like forest, bows and poison arrows (made out of bicycle spokes), knives, and a huge pond of human bodily waste. Then they start to use guns—guns converted from imported toy guns. The Imperial Army's field artillery shakes up the village, and it finally surrenders when the enemy threatens to burn down the forest.

The dehumanization and indiscriminate massacre of modern war, the cold bloodedness armed with insane logic reveals a grotesque picture; the villagers not recorded in the census paper are sentenced to death because they "do not exist."

Other aspects of history re-created in the novel are the agricultural land reform, disintegration of the multigeneration family and its replacement by the nuclear family, and liberation from sexual taboos—all of which took place in postwar Japan under the control of the American Occupation Army. The overwhelming power of Washington over Japan is presented as an inexplicable great noise, a supernatural phenomenon, filling the entire basin, afflicting everyone in the village. The quality and amount of the noise vary, depending on an individual as well as on the area in the basin, and, therefore, people start to leave their homes and property for a place where the damage to their eardrums and brains is minimal. This is a well-made parable; the sarcasm is the invention of earplugs—a character identifiable as the Emperor is the one who escapes all the postwar reforms by plugging up his ears.

The episode is not set in the postwar period, of course, in the history of the village-nation-microcosmos, which leaves ample room for ambiguity; and ambiguity in turn allows many other interpretations. One prime example of ambiguity is the "Destroyer." The "Destroyer" is an explosives expert and herbalist as well. Ironically he dies once while working at a dam construction site, by the accidental explosion of his own dynamite. But somehow he revives and returns. As an herbalist, he has a large herb garden and he is respected as a healer. Later, however, he is killed with the poison that his herb garden produced. In these episodes, the "Destroyer" seems to represent science-technology in which the ambivalence of construction-destruction, healer-killer, and life-death is an attribute.

The myth and history of the village-nation-microcosmos, told by the Father/priest to the narrator, is also listened to by the twin brothers, Apogii (apogee) and Perigii (perigee), specialists in celestial mechanics, as their names suggest. They try to find cosmological significance in the myth and history of the village and to locate its rightful unit of time and space in the universe. It is possible that the "Destroyer" is the embodiment of "entropy," the theory that the amount of disorder in the cosmos only increases as time passes. This is paradoxical in that one cannot keep creating without destroying what one has just created; in the final analysis, the figure of the "Destroyer" is a metaphorical composite both abstract and concrete, provoking a sense of ambiguity and ambivalence.

Ambiguity in the turn of events, as in the case of the "Destroyer," is often achieved by presenting more than one narrative, not exactly overlapping one another. This means Ōe consciously tries to minimize the effects of actuality in order to create a dream-like world with its own reality. The less actuality the novel attains, the more elusive and complex the structure of the novel becomes. The Father/priest begins his myth and history with the same repetitive phrase, "Some are not true stories, but you must listen as if they tell what actually happened. Understand?" This folkloric technique used extensively tends to resist the reader's effort to draw a clear picture of what is actually happening in the novel. Even though each incident is described clearly, the resulting picture is blurred since so many layers of images are superimposed.

Another ambiguity is the matter of time. There are six chapters in the novel, each being a letter from the narrator to his sister. The subject matter in each chapter has its own unity, with barely recognizable chronology. However, it is extremely difficult to establish the chronological relationship among the incidents in different chapters. Again, each incident is often presented with detailed realism, but if one tried to place the incident, judging from the metaphorically suggested meaning, in an actual historical period, one would find himself in a chronological maze with no outlet. Furthermore, in the last chapter, the narrator, wandering in the forest, with his naked body painted red, picks up pieces of the "Destroyer's" body, still unspoiled (even though they have been there for some years), in an attempt to reconstruct the "Destroyer." He also sees behind the trees the people who will be involved in the events yet to take place in the future.

What Ōe is experimenting with in this novel is condensing the passage of time to bring mythical and historical incidents hazy in the background to the foreground, and thereby to examine what human existence is, not only at this present moment but in a historical perspective. The novel must embrace the universe. It is a kind of universality that can go beyond one unit of time and space. For that purpose Ōe is trying to minimize life-like actuality and the obvious link between cause and effect. Thus, we have a huge picture of a dream-like, unreal world in which a multitude of incidents is displayed with vivid reality, like the works of Hieronymus Bosch. The picture is able to express even a millennium of human history. The narrator meditates on time in the cosmic framework as follows:

> . . . if one visits those planets in a spaceship, one will find each planet has its own time; in other words, there is another unit of time and space. If one can see an almost unlimited number of units of time and space on a huge expanse of spacescape, then one can see all the events in every branch of the global history of mankind taking place simultaneously. In that case, one can choose a single reality quite arbitrarily, as if playing a game, and rearrange the history of mankind as one wishes it to be. . . . [***A Game of Simultaneity***]

The timeless "Destroyer" in the timeless forest is the leitmotif of Ōe's cosmology, and the image system of grotesque realism ties his characters to the soil of the forest. However, the outcome of the novel still suggests a pessimistic view of life mainly plagued by depraved, incestuous sex. Politics destroys individuals; history buries people; and totalitarianism sends those who do not conform to the slaughterhouse.

The mythical element in this novel seems to suggest that human life is doomed in the endless cycle of incest, which invariably leads to insanity. If myth presents a clear picture of human existence in its totality in relationship to the world and the cosmos, we are becoming more and more insane as we continue to live generation after generation, since the poison is coming from the very act of reproduction. Like Mitsusaburo in ***The Silent Cry,*** one must accept the result of his insane brother's adultery; like Isana and his idiot son in ***The Flood unto my Soul,*** one must accept the result of nuclear science. There seems to be no opening in the womb-like or tomb-like village, and man in his claustrophobia is directed downward.

In the Western literary tradition that often inspired Ōe, the downward, subterranean human psyche, that is, the realm of grotesque realism, is associated with positive images, such as birth, revitalization, and regeneration. Mikhail Bakhtin argues in *Rabelais and His World:*

> . . . Degradation here means coming down to earth, the contact with earth as an element that swallows up and gives birth at the same time. To degrade is to bury, to sow, and to kill simultaneously, in order to bring forth something more and better. . . . [*Rabelais and His World*]

As we have discussed Ōe's works so far, however, it is hard to discover even an inkling of such positive connotation as to "bury, to sow, and to kill simultaneously, in order to bring forth something more and better." Ōe certainly presents pictures grim enough to alarm readers, but, instead of suggesting the advent of new hope, he perpetuates an ominous possibility that the outcome of rebirth and regeneration will be worse yet, for example, as in the form of insanity or of physical deformity. This unerasable pessimism probably derives from his observations that the natural flow of birth-death-rebirth is already extensively disrupted by the nuclear bombing in Japan and ever-spreading radioactive contamination all over the world. It is his uncompromising, penetrating insight that enables him to see the world and human existence in it with its in-

An excerpt from *The Silent Cry*

I stamped a hollow in the snow, thrust in the bundle of straw bent into a circle, and set fire to it. The fine down clinging to the skin of the pheasants burned first, giving off an oppressive odor. Almost at once, the bodies of the pheasants were crisscrossed with dark brown threads of melting animal matter, and the skin itself turned a dull color in the smoke, with beads of yellow fat rising here and there. It brought directly to mind something my dead friend had said about the photograph of the black who had been set fire to: "His body was so scorched and swollen that the details were blurred, like those of a crudely carved wooden doll."

Someone was standing behind me, peering with equal intensity at the same thing as myself. I turned and saw Takashi, his face so flushed with the heat of his fireside eloquence that I expected the falling snowflakes to melt on first contact. I felt sure that the pheasants with their scorched down had evoked much the same memories in him too.

"My friend who died told me you gave him a civil rights pamphlet when you met him in New York. He said it had a photo of a black who'd been burned alive."

"That right. A terrible picture, the sort of thing that tells you something about the essential nature of violence."

"Another thing he said was that you startled him by threatening to 'tell the truth.' He was worried because he got the impression you had some other 'truth' on your mind apart from what you actually talked about, but that you couldn't get it out. How about it—he never got his answer, but was the suspicion he died with at least well founded?"

Takashi went on peering at the pheasants, his eyes narrowed anxiously as though half blinded, not just by the light reflected by the snow onto his steadily paling cheeks, but also by something rising up within himself.

" 'Shall I tell you the truth?' —" he said. I felt sure he'd used the same voice in saying the same thing to my friend in New York. "It's a phrase from a young poet. I was forever quoting it at that period. I was thinking about the absolute truth which, if a man tells it, leaves him no alternative but to be killed by others, or kill himself, or go mad and turn into a monster. The kind of truth that once uttered leaves you clutching a bomb with the fuse irretrievably lit. What do you think, Mitsu—is the courage to tell others that kind of truth possible for ordinary flesh and blood?"

Kenzaburo Ōe, in his The Silent Cry, *Kodansha International, 1974.*

nate madness. This literary theme, deeply rooted in the conditions of Japan and the world as well, is treated in Western modernism, and thus, Ōe has created his own new world of imagination, universally relevant, in the age of nuclear anxiety.

AWARD ANNOUNCEMENTS

James Sterngold (essay date 14 October 1994)

SOURCE: "Kenzaburo Oe of Japan Wins Nobel in Literature," in *The New York Times,* October 14, 1994, pp. B1, B10.

[*In the following article, Sterngold reports on the Swedish Academy's decision to award Ōe the 1994 Nobel Prize in Literature.*]

The Swedish Academy announced today [October 14, 1994] in Stockholm that Kenzaburo Oe, a Japanese writer known for his powerful accounts of the atomic bombing of Hiroshima and his struggle to come to terms with a mentally handicapped son, had won the 1994 Nobel Prize in Literature.

Mr. Oe, 59, is just the second Japanese writer to capture the award. Yasunari Kawabata won it in 1968. But while Mr. Kawabata generally explored traditional Japanese themes with a delicate writing style, Mr. Oe has written politically charged tales filled with anger and a sense of betrayal, like the postwar generation he has come to represent.

Mr. Oe (pronounced OH-ay) came of age during the American occupation, after Japan's shattering defeat in World War II. He was recognized as a leading writer in the late 1950's when he was still a university student. While some authors found nothing but despair in those bleak years, Mr. Oe's left-wing political essays, short stories and lyrically written novels revolve around what critics generally describe as a core of hope and courage mixed with bitter humor. In perhaps his most famous novel, ***A Personal Matter*** first published in 1964, the protagonist plots the murder of his infant son, who has been born with severe brain damage, but finally realizes he must take responsibility for the child and embraces him.

Though he is one of Japan's most acclaimed authors, and had been mentioned in recent years as a potential Nobel winner, Ōe is relatively unknown in the United States and much of his writing has never been translated into English.

—James Sterngold

The influences on Mr. Oe's complex art range from Jean-Paul Sartre to the Mark Twain of *Huckleberry Finn.* The Swedish Academy noted the "poetic force" of Mr. Oe's beautifully rendered works, saying he "creates an imagined world where life and myth condense to form a disconcerting picture of the human predicament today." It also cited the impact of Japan's defeat on Mr. Oe's development as a writer. "The humiliation took a firm grip on him and has colored much of his work," the academy said. "He himself describes his writing as a way of exorcising demons."

In a telephone interview from his Tokyo home tonight, Mr. Oe, a voluble if somewhat solemn man, said the call from Stockholm, at a little before 9 P.M. local time, had come as a thunderbolt.

"It was a total surprise," he said. "Completely. Total."

While he has often spoken of his ambiguous feelings about Japan, he said he was proud the Swedish Academy recognized the strength of modern Japanese literature and hoped the prize would encourage others here.

"I believe I am a very Japanese writer," he said. "I have always wanted to write about our country, our society and feelings about the contemporary scene. But there is a big difference between us and classic Japanese literature."

He said that ultimately his writing was focused on a single concern. "I am writing about the dignity of human beings," he said, as a throng of reporters gathered in front of his home in a festive mood.

Mr. Oe is the 91st recipient of the Nobel Prize in Literature, which was won last year [1993] by Toni Morrison. The prize includes an award of $930,000.

Though he is one of Japan's most acclaimed authors, and had been mentioned in recent years as a potential Nobel winner, Mr. Oe is relatively unknown in the United States and much of his writing has never been translated into English. Several American publishers, including Kodansha America, Grove/Atlantic and M. E. Sharpe, have published his works in translation in the United States, and all said yesterday that they planned to make copies of the work more readily available.

Because the three previous winners—Derek Walcott, Nadine Gordimer and Ms. Morrison—write in English, speculation before today's announcement had centered on authors from Europe or Asia.

Among those considered in the running were the Belgian poet, playwright and novelist Hugo Claus, who writes in Flemish; the German novelist and playwright Peter Handke; the Dutch novelist Cees Nooteboom; the French writers Julien Gracq and Nathalie Sarraute; the Portuguese writers António Lobo Antunes and José Saramago, and the Swedish poet Tomas Transtromer. The Japanese novelist Shusaku Endo had also been considered a possible winner. The Irish poet Seamus Heaney was mentioned once again, and once again failed to take the prize.

The owlish, often detached-looking Mr. Oe grew up in a small village on the western island of Shikoku, a place steeped in Japan's rural traditions and wartime propaganda. The sense of wonder and security he seems to have felt in those innocent days, before the atomic bomb was dropped and an emperor he was taught to regard as divine announced that Japan had been defeated, appears again and again in his writing as a sort of Eden.

His early works, written while he was studying French literature at Tokyo University, are regarded as classics of the disillusionment his nation felt on seeing what Japan's leadership had done to the country. One of his first published stories, **"An Odd Job,"** describes a young man whose job is to bring dogs to a laboratory where they will be used in experiments. Looking at the huddled animals, he compares them to Japan's university students.

"That was the beginning of his literary odyssey," said John Nathan, a professor at the University of California at Santa Barbara, who translated several of Mr. Oe's early books into English. "He was the first Japanese writer taken thunderously as a serious writer while he was still a student."

Mr. Oe supported leftist causes, particularly opposition to the United States-Japan security treaty, which permits the maintenance of a string of American military bases across Japan. His popularity was near its peak during anti-treaty riots in 1960.

The birth of his son in 1963 altered his life and career. Mr. Oe's wife, Yukari, the daughter of a well-known author, Mansaku Itami, gave birth to a boy with serious brain damage. Just two months later, Mr. Oe visited Hiroshima and spoke with survivors of the atomic bombing.

Out of those experiences he produced ***A Personal Matter*** and ***Hiroshima Notes,*** an account of the courage of some of the survivors of the bombing in the face of the dehumanizing horror of the event.

He was the youngest of a generation of authors who responded to the war experience by depicting a world knocked off its center and surrounded by dark, irrational forces.

In the telephone interview he compared himself to Kobo Abe, the author of the surrealistic and disorienting novel *The Woman in the Dunes,* and Masuji Ibuse, best known for *Black Rain,* a novel about the victims of the atomic bombing.

"They created the way to the Nobel Prize," Mr. Oe said. "I am the youngest one of that group. I received the prize in their place."

Mr. Abe and Mr. Ibuse died in 1993.

Mr. Oe also acknowledged that the seriousness of his generation and its political agenda made it seem old-fashioned compared with young Japanese writers today, who have tended to be more introspective and concerned with materialism than with war.

"I am the last author who practices the old, very heavy, or sincere way of writing," Mr. Oe said.

While Mr. Oe has a reputation as a dour and at times overly earnest man, Mr. Nathan, who has known him for 30 years, said that the writer could be spontaneous and impish with friends.

"He does maintain a very solemn pose," Mr. Nathan said, "but the other side is that the guy can be a wild man." He described long evenings of drinking and wandering around Tokyo with Mr. Oe, who he described as given to pulling practical jokes on his friends.

Mr. Oe is a voracious reader, particularly of English-language and French authors. Mr. Nathan said an evening's conversation could take in everything from the tense used in a John Updike novel to W. H. Auden's poetry.

Another old friend of Mr. Oe's, Masao Miyoshi, a professor of literature at the University of California at San Diego, praised the author for the dazzling array of literary references that suffuse his writing.

"You have to think about someone like James Joyce living in the 1990's," Mr. Miyoshi said. He recalled his friend's reciting William Blake's epic poem "Jerusalem" in the original. "He remembers everything," Mr. Miyoshi said.

More recently, the theme of redemption has become more prevalent in Mr. Oe's work. This, too, may be related to his personal life. His son, Hikari (Japanese for light or light beam), has overcome his disability enough to become a composer.

In a documentary shown on Japanese television recently, Mr. Oe was shown completing the final pages of the last novel in a trilogy. He ended the book by declaring that with his son's new career launched, he would not write any further novels. He then penned in English a closing phrase, "Rejoyce."

James Sterngold (essay date 6 November 1994)

SOURCE: "Japan Asks Why a Prophet Bothers," in *The New York Times,* November 6, 1994, Section 4, p. 5.

[*In the following essay, Sterngold discusses Ōe's decision to reject Japan's Imperial Order of Culture—its highest cultural honor—and examines the Japanese public's reaction, which ranged from apathy to harsh opprobrium.*]

Except for a brief period during the 1960's, Kenzaburo Oe has been the sort of intellectual, left-leaning author who was well known among brooding Japanese undergraduates and scholars, but was not particularly widely read. Still, when he became the surprise choice for the Nobel Prize in Literature last month, most Japanese, even if they could not name any of his books, took pride in this affirmation of the richness of their culture. And they left the matter at that.

But Mr. Oe has not let them off so lightly. This owlish, fidgety man, who loves to talk in excited bursts, toss out French phrases and explicate *Moby Dick,* caused outrage by doing something dangerously unfashionable here: He took a stand on principle.

Just days after his Nobel Prize was announced, his name was hastily added to a list of eminences being given

Japan's highest cultural honor, the Imperial Order of Culture. When he received the call with that news, Mr. Oe said, he responded without hesitation—and rejected the award.

It was an almost unheard-of public affront in this polite country, particularly because the Emperor was involved. Worse, Mr. Oe did not bother with the elaborate ambiguities that accompany criticisms; he explained his thinking in plain terms. It seemed like the first shot in a potentially fiery public debate. In fact, it was not, and that may say more about Japan's current state of mind than Mr. Oe's politics.

For anyone familiar with his passionate, lyrical books—especially his morally charged analysis of the atomic bombing of Hiroshima—his reasoning could not have come as a surprise. At the peak of his popularity in the 1960's, he was a standard-bearer for an angry, disillusioned generation that welcomed the collapse of the authoritarian imperial system.

Mr. Oe says he regards the Emperor as an undemocratic relic and a reminder of the horrors of World War II, for which he holds the imperial system responsible.

"The reason I declined the cultural award was that I would not recognize any authority, any value, higher than democracy," Mr. Oe said in an interview, which was interrupted by the arrival of a police officer warning that rightists were planning a big demonstration in front of his house. "This is very simple, but very important."

He thought for a moment, and added, "I am in a very delicate situation."

Ōe says he regards the Emperor as an undemocratic relic and a reminder of the horrors of World War II, for which he holds the imperial system responsible.

—James Sterngold

That "situation" involves much more than the anger of the thuggish right-wing groups, which relish any opportunity to rev up their sound trucks and bellow tinny indignation. Mr. Oe's real problem is that he has found so little public sympathy for his stand, which seemed to leave most people angry or puzzled, but conspicuously unmoved. The thought that an ideal was worth fighting for struck people as quaint.

Indeed, the general reaction was like that of Kazuo Aichi, a former Defense Minister and a member of a reform movement in the parliament. "My own feeling was that he hadn't changed at all over the years," Mr. Aichi said in an interview. "I would have expected that he would have matured, so to speak, and accepted the award."

A man who had suddenly become the most famous author in the land had raised serious questions about the imperial system and Japan's odd, American-written constitution, and thus the more emotional issue of what it means to be Japanese. Japan is preparing for the 50th anniversary next summer of its surrender after World War II, a moment for reflection and debate. Also, with an odd coalition of Socialists and conservatives governing the country, Japan's basic political values are being questioned for the first time in four decades.

Still, Mr. Oe was greeted with what amounted to a scolding for pushing people to think so much. It was a revealing moment. Japan is admired for its competitive economy, the near absence of serious street crime and an unemployment rate of just 3 percent despite a severe recession. But what of its intellectual life?

"I think it's very interesting that the reaction in general to my tying my life to my principles was for people to say I'm old-fashioned," Mr. Oe said. "It says a lot about current attitudes in Japan."

Of course, the days when Washington bristled with impassioned protests about civil rights or Vietnam are long past, too—like the demonstrations and riots here opposing the American military presence.

But moral outrage lives on in the United States and elsewhere—just witness the debates over abortion or immigration. In Japan, rarely does any public debate stir such emotion. For example, there has been a long dispute over whether the military should participate in United Nations peacekeeping operations. But a contingent is now helping Rwandan refugees in Zaire, the third time the military has joined such an operation, and the public is quiescent.

Critics complain the lack of tension has taken a toll on the arts. The movie industry, which once turned out classics by artists like Akira Kurosawa, is now known for predictable formula dramas. The most popular movies come from Hollywood.

A number of experts look at literature as hollow and bloodless. "Oe's trying to do something no one else is trying to do: he's trying to do solid books," Donald Keene, a professor emeritus at Columbia University and the dean of Japanese literary experts in the West, said here. "If you go to a bookstore here, unless it is a very big bookstore, you won't find a real solid literary work. Authors today are writing for the passing tastes of a young audience. University students were the real market for serious books, but they don't really read them anymore. It's a very depressing period."

Mr. Keene added: "It is a statement on a prosperous country, a country that is very pleased with itself. People don't feel any sense of agitation."

That was evident this past summer, after the Socialists joined with their conservative foes, the Liberal Democrats, to form a government. During the cold war, the Socialists saw themselves as the nation's conscience, putting principle ahead of power as they fought for a pacifist foreign policy, a strong social welfare system and the closing of American bases here. The positions, however impractical, struck an emotional chord.

Last June, when the Socialists formed their awkward ruling coalition, they abandoned most of those principles. And the Socialist Prime Minister, Tomiichi Murayama, saw his ratings rise.

"Japan has lost the power to connect the principle or theory and reality," Mr. Oe said. "I think literature's value is in making those connections. That's the mission of literature. Morals are significant."

He admitted his disappointment at the generally tepid level of discussion of all the problems: "I was hoping that the 50th anniversary of the war's end would be a time to reflect, especially on Hiroshima and the use of nuclear bombs. But that kind of attitude does not exist in Japan. Not now."

INTERVIEWS

Kenzaburō Ōe with Sanroku Yoshida (interview date 7 June 1986)

SOURCE: An interview in *World Literature Today,* Vol. 62, No. 3, Summer, 1988, pp. 369-74.

[*In the following interview, which was conducted in 1986, Ōe discusses such topics as his literary and cultural influences and the style and techniques of his fiction.*]

[*Yoshida*]: *I met with Yōtarō Konaka yesterday. He said that recently Japanese society has created a peculiar mood in which it is rather difficult to discuss matters antinuclear, and that one may be considered childish or immature if one is antinuclear. The major theme of your* **Flood unto My Soul** *(1973),* **The Pinchrunner** *(1976), and other works is the deracination of mankind by nuclear holocaust. As the author of these novels, do you agree with such an assessment of the social climate?*

[Ōe]: I published a book called ***Hiroshima Notes*** (1965; Eng. 1981) twenty-three years ago. So it has been about a quarter of a century since I started to think about "Hiroshima." During that time, I have participated in the activities of a group called the Japan Confederation of A-Bomb and H-Bomb Sufferers Organizations; I have written and spoken in public in support of such movements as "Abolishment of Nuclear Weapons" and "Relief for Victims"; I have organized committees and councils for these movements as well; yet I do not think things are particularly difficult today. Twenty-four or twenty-five years ago, they were difficult—oh, well, not really difficult, but I was not supported by the majority of Japanese intellectuals. Many victims talked at those meetings, and they wrote about their ordeals. Nevertheless, Japanese scholars, whether they were scholars of English literature, sociologists, physicists, or well-known writers, seldom paid serious attention to such things—except for a handful of fine scholars such as Kazuo Watanabe, Masao Maruyama, and Professor Shūichi Katō. The situation now is about the same.

Four or five years ago, when American medium-range nuclear missiles put Europe in a very precarious position, an antinuclear movement spread from Europe to the United States. When there are such fervid antinuclear movements in Europe and the United States, Japanese intellectuals tend to follow their lead. Therefore, we had a large-scale antinuclear movement in Japan at that time. Now very little is going on. I have not been influenced by these ups and downs of the movements. I do what I have to do in writing my novels and critical essays.

I have been enchanted by existential philosophies, and naturally I am a very existential author. My main interest has been in examining man's existential situations.

—Kenzaburo Ōe

If Japanese critics say it is childish and naïve to oppose nuclear weapons, let me tell you the following: the American political scientist George Kennan, whose judgment I trust, argues in his book *The Nuclear Delusion* that political figures and nuclear weapons experts always ridicule antinuclear movements as manifestations of naïveté or childishness. However, it is the naïveté of the expert, in both diplomacy and nuclear weapons, that makes the existence of the world precarious. This is what George Kennan says, and I think this is also true in Japan. So there is no need to keep silent when you are called "childish." To be frank, I have to admit that there is perhaps something indeed quite childish about Japanese antinuclear movements. Nonetheless, one must try to embody one's ideals in one's works. If you don't do this, and you are called "childish," it is in part your own fault.

In your works, Mr. Ōe, there are many themes that had not been treated in Japanese literature before. When you started writing fiction, some readers were shocked because of your unique style, new themes, and new attitudes. I have been reading your works from the earliest ones to the most recent, and I know that your style is gradually changing. For example, in one of your earliest short stories, ***"Pigeon"*** *(1958), there is this sentence: "A sudden anger ravaged my chest." This is obviously written in the syntax of European languages. Did you create this new style because the traditional Japanese styles could not handle the kind of themes that you wished to treat in your fiction?*

First of all, the theme of nuclear deracination is not exactly new. Landing on the moon in a rocket is new. Of course, Edmond Rostand had his character talk about "The Journey to the Moon," and Wells wrote about the moon; but when man actually landed on the moon, that was completely new, and if you use that incident in literature, then you have an entirely new theme. The theme of nuclear deracination, however, is only partly new. The invention of nuclear fission made possible the atomic bomb, which killed many people, and nuclear weapons tend to intensify international tension. True, that is a new turn of events. But at the same time, as far as the notion of human annihilation is concerned, the theme is not new—it is partly in harmony with literary tradition (if I may use the word *tradition* as you used it). What I mean is that the notion of apocalypse in Christian tradition, for instance, or the Indian tradition of eschatology, or our tradition of Buddhist eschatology has been there for a long time. Therefore, I treat in my works the theme of the nuclear apocalypse as something partially rooted in a sort of global human tradition. It's not only me. The American author Bernard Malamud once wrote a novel, *God's Grace* (1982), in which he examines the problems of nuclear apocalypse in the context of the Judeo-Christian tradition.

In the period before I started writing, it was not in the tradition of Japanese literature to write novels in a way similar to that in which a philosopher or historian thinks. After the end of the war in 1945, for about ten years, postwar writers, under the influence of Dostoevsky, Hegel, Heidegger, or Sartre, wrote as the historian writes or the philosopher thinks or the social scientist analyzes. This was a new trend. I was influenced by these writers. I needed to think—think about Japanese society, the world, or about the human being—and when I started to write, I wrote in order to give novelistic expression to my thoughts. I was also reading French philosophers such as Sartre and Camus, so my writing was affected by them too, I suppose. I had an antipathy toward such people as Yasunari Kawabata or Jun'ichirō Tanizaki. I felt antagonistic toward established Japanese authors in general. First of all, they do not think logically. Their thoughts almost always become vague halfway. Furthermore, their thoughts are extremely simplistic. That's the way I thought about them when I was young; I do not necessarily think in the same way now.

I've been reading Kathleen Raine, a British literary critic and poet, who says the following about William Blake: "Blake's thoughts are full of ambiguities, but they are not vague." I thought Tanizaki, Kawabata, and other established writers were not ambiguous but vague. . . . Well, that's what I thought when I was young, anyway. As a rebellion, I tried to write as accurately as possible—for example, without using ellipsis. I tried not to omit any pronouns. As you know, the Japanese language is very effective when ellipsis is applied, but I was determined not to use it. Then my style became similar to that of a translation. By the way, most translations actually do not have any style. For example, Northrop Frye has been translated into Japanese, but the style is neither Frye's nor the translator's. You have to polish it up until it turns into a new style. I thought that kind of product—that is, something still in the process of translation—was interesting. A draft in which the two languages fight each other is provocative and full of resonance. So, my intention was to destroy the Japanese language by using a kind of syntax that cannot fit into Japanese. I was ambitious. I was writing novels with an extremely destructive intention.

In order to eliminate vagueness. . . .

Yes, in order to eliminate vagueness, I even defined certain words each time I used them in my works. But that was only in the early works. For the past ten years or so, I have been trying to create a new, exemplary Japanese style based on those earlier destructive activities of mine.

Especially in the more recent works, your style is in perfect accord with the rhythms of Japanese speech, isn't it?

That's because I used to compose Japanese *waka* poems.

Oh! That explains it. . . .

My brother is a *waka* poet. And I myself am more versed in classical Japanese literature than critics in general suspect. I am pretty good at haiku or *waka.* I composed quite a few *waka* between the ages of fifteen or sixteen and twenty, or thereabout. Still, I respect contemporary poets more than anybody else. I read a lot of modern Japanese poems. American poets like Auden and other foreign poets such as T. S. Eliot, Yeats, and Blake are very important to me. As you see, I am an avid reader of poetry, and I *am* interested in the rhythm of the Japanese language. I wrote ***Contemporary Games*** (1979) when I was forty-two or so. It is a kind of conclusion to all of my experimental novels. After that novel, for the past ten years, I've been trying to create yet another new style, a more comfortable one for Japanese; I don't mean to go back to the traditional style but to grope for a more acceptable one.

The role of Shōyō Tsubouchi (1859-1935), for example, was important in that he created a new style for new thoughts. . . .

Yes, but the ambitions of men of letters in regard to their style are always ambiguous. Take Shōyō's style, for instance. The capacity of Shōyō's style for conveying meaning or expressing thought was not as great as that of Enchō Sanyūtei (1839-1900), a popular storyteller and entertainer who was Shōyō's contemporary. Therefore, when Shimei Futabatei (1864-1909), Shōyō's disciple, tried to develop a new style for his *Drifting Clouds* (1889), he studied Enchō's style instead of his teacher's. A writer's thoughts about his style, as is obvious from Shōyō's case, are legitimate only half the time. No matter what the result may be, however, writers have to strive for new thoughts and new styles, especially at the start of a new age. Like Shōyō and Futabatei at the turning point of Japanese history after the Meiji Restoration (1868), I also tried to create a new style under the impact of Japan's surrender in the second world war.

Your use of Gothic or black letters first appeared, I believe, in **Our Age** *(1959). Later, in* **The Day He Himself Shall Wipe My Tears Away** *(1969; Eng. 1977),* **The Flood unto My Soul, The Pinchrunner,** *and* **Contemporary Games,** *you use that technique profusely. In recent stories, however, you put in Gothics only the dialogue of a character called Eeyore. What is your purpose in doing so? When I first encountered this, I wondered if there were any pictorial meaning on that particular page with the black letters.*

Well, any writer in any period or country is interested in typography. For example, Laurence Sterne, who wrote *A Sentimental Journey,* used dashes extensively in his novels. In Japan too, in the Meiji period when typography was introduced, writers tried out various interesting techniques. For example, the critic Chogyū Takayama (1871-

1902) put little circles, double circles, dots, and lines around his sentences in order to make these sentences stand out. The Russian critic Mikhail Bakhtin puts uneven spaces between letters by way of emphasis. This is a kind of defamiliarization in typography. I am very much interested in this sort of contrivance. It is possible to use various kinds of type at one time in order to make the pages more expressive. The Japanese language has three scripts: *katakana, hiragana* [two kinds of syllabaries], and *kanji* [Chinese characters], which we usually combine.

In **The Pinchrunner** *some parts are all in katakana.*

Yes, . . . and there is this interesting thing called *rubi* [the pronunciation key in one of the syllabaries of hard-to-read characters, usually given in small print beside the characters]. For example, if you write the kanji for "defamiliarization" and follow it with either the Russian or French equivalent in Japanese syllabic form as a *rubi,* then you can show in one space both the Japanese word and the foreign term from which the Japanese has originated. You can do the same thing using parentheses. You know, we have so many imported words in Japanese, and it is sometimes important to indicate the source. Thanks to the nature of the writing system, Japanese typography is very diversified. I consciously take advantage of this factor. . . .

In Inter Ice Age 4 *(1959; Eng. 1970) Kōbō Abe (b. 1924) filled several pages using only katakana. The translator of this work solved the problem by using capitals. If those works of yours are to be translated, some similar kind of device also has to be developed. How about Gothics or italics?*

Yes, I like italics. Those boldface types in my works can be considered as italics in English.

The Pinchrunner *is unique in that the style is interesting and different from that of other works. You must have invented this particular style to express the atmosphere of farce or slapstick. The major plot device in this work is the identity switch between father and son. How did you come up with such an interesting idea? Is there any particular work that you took as an example?*

There is no particular source. I live with my handicapped son. Sometimes our roles somehow get reversed in our conversations—jokingly, of course. The identity switch such as the one between sexes is in the tradition of European grotesque realism as a form of theater, like harlequinades. One example would be *Ferdydurke* by the Polish writer Witold Gombrowicz, in which an adult turns into a child. This is a novel that resembles mine, but it was not a source; I got the idea from my own life with my son. But, of course, I like this kind of novel.

I am also very much interested in slapstick. I like American slapstick movies. Among modern writers, Nathanael West, who wrote *The Day of the Locust,* is my favorite. Another example is *A Cool Million.* This is like an erotic gossip novel but is a slapstick. My interest in these works made me write ***The Pinchrunner.***

The most important focal point in ***The Pinchrunner,*** however, is its narration by a half-crazed, eccentric man. The problem of narration is certainly very important in the modern novel.

You mean "The plural viewpoint," in which one narrator narrates and another person writes it down?

Yes, that's right. That was a major experiment for me.

You use that technique in various pieces. The most complicated one is. . . .

The Day He Himself Shall Wipe My Tears Away.

And ***"The Trial of Plucking Buds and Shooting Lambs"*** *(1980). This one is very interesting and has an extremely intricate narrative structure.*

Critics completely ignored it.

They did? Completely?

Yes, absolutely.

Hmm. I wrote about it for an American journal.

Then that must be the only critical commentary on it in the entire world. (*Laughter*)

Anyway, the purpose of the plural viewpoint is to present reality with all its ambiguities and ambivalences.

Yes, you're right.

In **Contemporary Games** *a variety of viewpoints allow the author to present many different images of one reality, which overlap each other. The same episodes told many times by different characters, slightly different each time, create an image that is blurred, just like a picture out of focus. I think this blurred image is intentional and perhaps important. Could you elaborate on this point?*

I wrote a book entitled ***The Methods of the Novel*** (1978) in which I explained that the concept of ambiguity was very important for me. In the same sense of the word as in Kathleen Raine's comment about Blake, I wanted to present ambiguity in ***Contemporary Games***—that is to say, one reality conveying many meanings. Since regional folklore or regional myths contain this element of ambiguity, I clearly intended to delve into this matter in the regional myths. Now it's been ten years since I finished that book. I recently finished another novel on the same subject. The title is simply *M/T,* whose initials stand for "matriarch" and "trickster." This is another ***Contemporary Games*** told in a straightforward narrative by a reminiscing hero.

My intention was to destroy the Japanese language by using a kind of syntax that cannot fit into Japanese. I was ambitious. I was writing novels with an extremely destructive intention.

—Kenzaburo Ōe

These days literary critics talk abut "intertexts," which means the study of the relationship between two or more texts. I intend this recent novel of mine, *M/T,* to be read with such an intertextual connection between it and ***Contemporary Games***. If you read both of them, you will understand both very well, even if you don't make out each by itself.

Then, the relationship is similar to that between **Plucking Buds and Shooting Lambs** *(1958) and* ***"The Trial of Plucking Buds and Shooting Lambs,"*** *isn't it?*

Yes, except here it is the other way round.

Before **Hiroshima Notes** *and* **A Personal Matter** *(1964; Eng. 1968), I find in many of your works a motif of escape that reminds me of the biblical episode of Noah's ark. Did you have this in mind as the model when you were writing, for example,* ***"A Cry"*** *(1963) or* **The Flood unto My Soul?**

No, I didn't. Even though I read the Bible a lot, I have not thought of Noah's ark very much. I read the Bible through William Blake or Dante, and I don't think either of them has much interest in the Noah story.

But **The Flood unto My Soul** *has something to do with Jonah, doesn't it?*

Yes, I think Jonah is an interesting person. He is angry and prejudiced against God.

Because he is trapped. His situation is a metaphorical presentation of man's entrapment; man's struggle to get out of his confinement points to the leitmotiv of escape in your works.

I have been enchanted by existential philosophies, and naturally I am a very existential author. My main interest has been in examining man's existential situations. Recently, however, I have been more interested in preexistential philosophies—that is to say, my subject matter is not so directly related to existential philosophies any longer. More concrete elements in life, such as how to live with a handicapped child or how to think about the unclear age, are more important to me now. These days I choose motifs from actual life. I started out very existential, and I still am fundamentally, but to a lesser degree.

The image of Africa is recurrent in your works. To be exact, the heroes in **A Personal Matter,** ***"Adventures in Everyday Life"*** *(1964), and* **The Silent Cry** *(1967; Eng. 1974) all try to go to Africa.*

And in ***Our Age*** (1959) too.

In all these novels the image of Africa is ambiguous: sometimes it represents freedom, at other times danger or even death. Mr. Ōe, have you been to Africa?

Strangely enough, I haven't. Africa is a very romantic subject. Also, since I like Conrad, it is a Conradian image for me. A lot of difficulties, full of sufferings, and yet romantic—that is Africa for me. Another thing is that when I was a student, I was (and, still am) very much interested in the independence movements of the Third World. Africa has been, for me, a fantasized romantic haven from the real world rather than a place with ontological significance. To me Africa is what India or other Asian countries are to Western authors.

You have seriously treated the theme of sexuality in various novels. In one essay you divided all of humanity into two groups: sexual beings and political beings. Sexual beings live in the shadow of the past and are therefore romantic, whereas political beings are always alert to the changes of the world and look forward to the future. There seem to be two major assumptions about sex: first, humans are incessantly vulnerable to the entrapment of sex; second, the sexual depravity that you often treat is a means of defamiliarization.

Yes, I think you are right. I have used sexuality in my novels as a means of defamiliarization and have attempted to attach various meanings to it. I am different from D. H. Lawrence in that Lawrence at one time treated sex as the central theme of his novels; I have simply utilized sexual elements as the most concrete means to defamiliarize the mundane lives of human beings. I did this especially when I was in my twenties and thirties.

Speaking of defamiliarization, many characters in **The Flood unto My Soul,** *for example, are maimed: their hands are cut off, say. Some of them are very strangely shaped.*

Yes, . . . deformed.

They are like those human figures in Picasso's cubist paintings or like the grotesque people in Hieronymus Bosch's pictures. The prime example in **The Flood** *is the Shrinking Man, quite an astonishing invention.*

They may resemble Picasso or Bosch, but my interest was in dealing with the possibilities of living together with such strange objects as amputated parts of the human body or deformed persons. I am still writing about this, hoping to discover that it is comfortable to live with those bizarre creatures. At the beginning, I did not intentionally draw difficult and ugly elements into my world, but as I was groping for methods of defamiliarization, they were there. So, yes, you are right. They are a means to defamiliarize the familiar. The Shrinking Man, the example you mentioned, the model for him was Yukio Mishima. I based the character on Mishima. Every time I saw him, I thought of him as a shrinking man.

Could you elaborate on that?

If you realize that the Shrinking Man is a caricature of Mishima, then you will find some new ways to interpret that novel. For example, in things like homosexuality and the desire to punish himself. . . .

I see: you painted Yukio Mishima by using the technique of grotesque realism. In your essay titled ***"Why Do Human Beings Produce Literature?"*** *(1975) you argue that, if anybody disrupts the fundamental harmony between human beings and their society, the world and the cosmos, literature, based on a humanistic viewpoint, will continue to protest against such violence. When you say "the fundamental harmony," I don't think you mean simply being friendly to each other.*

In simple terms, literature should deal with the theme of the ostracized in family and in society. I have extended the theme of ostracism to include the cosmos. The question is how we can change the situation so that nobody is ostracized. That is to say, literature should create a model of the human being and his environment wherein nobody is discriminated against. This is the basis of my literature. The human being conceived by William Blake is not ostracized. The reason I read Blake and Dante is that I wish to see an image of the human being accepted in society and to enlarge my vision further so that I will be able to conceive the model human environment in a cosmic context. At this point the image of nuclear disaster comes in as an extremely disturbing element.

In the essay entitled ***"The Image System of Grotesque Realism"*** *in your book* **The Methods of the Novel** *you emphasize the importance of grotesque realism. You say, "Our literature should adopt the image system of grotesque realism as its integral part and, in so doing, should bring about a real regeneration of human life—in this way I intend to formulate the future of Japanese literature."*

Yes, that is my fundamental philosophy.

Yes, but in the cosmic context Japan is, of course, a part of the world. As a Japanese author, Mr. Ōe, do you ever write your novels for the sake of world readers?

When one of my pieces was translated into German, the German translator interviewed me. His last question was, "Is the German translation important to you?" I infuriated him by saying "No." I am not very enthusiastic either when a foreign publisher invites me to give a lecture on the occasion of a new publication of my translated work. The reason is that I am not optimistic that my books will find readers in foreign countries. Of course, I grew up under the influence of foreign literature. I have a profound sense of respect for the literatures of Germany, France, America, England, and Latin America as well. I am convinced, however, that literature should be written for people who live in the same country and in the same age as the author. Therefore, I never intentionally write for foreign readers. I strongly feel that I am writing for intellectuals living in this small country with me. If foreign readers happen to find the Japanese model of the human being and society presented in my works interesting, then I would simply be very happy.

With Yukio Mishima, it is a different story, I think. Even though he was very popular and was actually the king of the Japanese literati, Mishima could not trust Japanese criticism and turned to foreign readers. His death was a performance for the foreign audience, a very spectacular performance. The relationship between Mishima and the emperor system was rather dubious; the Japanese knew that. But from foreigners' point of view—say, an American reader's point of view—the Japanese emperor system is something inexplicable. Therefore, that final act by Mishima, tied in with the emperor system, appeared to be a kind of mystical thing. In actuality, he did it in order to entertain foreign readers.

I am always thinking of contemporary Japanese readers. That's why I sometimes get involved in antinuclear movements. If writers of the world became interested in the human models presented in my fiction, I would be very flattered. When I write, however, I only think of the Japanese audience. I am a local writer from the world's point of view. I read worldwide, though. I read Japanese novels, of course; but during the daytime, for about three hours every day, I read whatever I choose to study at the time: for example, Malcolm Lowry, Dante, Yeats, or Bakhtin. When I go to bed, since I quit drinking some time ago, I read Dickens by way of a nightcap. Reading foreign authors is the source of my nourishment. Nevertheless, insofar as I am writing in Japanese, I think I am writing for Japanese readers.

Kenzaburo Ōe with Kazuo Ishiguro (interview date 1991)

SOURCE: "Stronger Than Stereotype: A Conversation with Nobel Laureate Kenzaburo Oe," in *The Los Angeles Times Book Review,* October 30, 1994, p. 4.

[*A Japanese-born English novelist and critic, Ishiguro received widespread critical acclaim for* The Remains of the Day, *which was awarded the 1989 Booker Prize for Fiction. In the following excerpt from an interview originally published in 1991, Ōe discusses the Western view of Japanese culture and his role as an international figure.*]

[Ōe]: In my book ***The Silent Cry,*** I wrote about Shikoku. I was born and grew up in a mountain village on that island. When I was 18, I went to the University of Tokyo to study French literature. As a result, I found myself completely cut off from my village, both culturally and geographically. Around that time my grandmother died, and my mother was getting older. The legends and traditions and folklore of my village were being lost. Meanwhile, here I was in Tokyo, imagining and trying to remember those things. The act of trying to remember and the act of creating began to overlap. And that is the reason I began to write novels. I tried to write them using the methods of French literature that I had studied.

[*Ishiguro*]: *One of the reasons I think* **The Silent Cry** *is such a special work is that it's often difficult for a writer to get a certain distance from very personal events in his life that have touched and disturbed him. This book seems to stem from such an event, but at the same time you seem to have kept control, to have maintained an artistic discipline, so that it actually becomes a work of art that has meaning for everybody. It's not simply about Mr. Oe. It strikes me that one of the ways in which you manage that is a certain kind of humor, a unique tone. It's very different from the kind of humor found in most of Western literature, which is mainly based on jokes. In your books, everything has a peculiar sense of humor that is always on the verge of tragedy—a very dark humor. This is one of the ways in which you seem to have been able to keep under control events that must be very close to you. But do you think this sort of humor is something unique to your own writing, or have you gotten it from a larger Japanese tradition?*

I think that the problem of humor is a very important one. This is one of the points in which I differ from Yukio Mishima. Mishima was very strongly rooted in the traditions of Japanese literature, especially the traditions of the center—Tokyo or Kyoto—urban traditions. I come from a more peripheral tradition, that of a very provincial corner of the island of Shikoku. It's an extremely strange place, with a long history of maltreatment, out there beyond the reach of culture. I think my humor is the humor of the people who live in that place.

I would be quite interested to hear what you feel about Mishima. I'm often asked about Mishima in England—all the time, by journalists. They expect me to be an authority on Mishima because of my Japanese background. Mishima is very well known in England, and in the West generally, largely because of the way he died. But also I suspect that Mishima's image confirms certain stereotypical images of Japanese people for the West. Of course, committing seppuku [ritual suicide] is one of the clichés. He was politically very extreme. The problem is that the whole image of Mishima in the West hasn't helped people there form an intelligent approach to Japanese culture and Japanese people. It has perhaps helped people to remain locked in certain prejudices and very superficial, stereotypical images of what Japanese people are like. I wonder what you think about Mishima and the way he died, what that means for Japanese people, and what that means for a distinguished author such as yourself.

The observations you just made about the reception of Mishima in Europe are accurate. Mishima's entire life, certainly including his death by seppuku, was a kind of performance designed to present the image of an archetypal Japanese. Moreover, this image was not the kind that arises spontaneously from a Japanese mentality. It was the superficial image of a Japanese as seen from a European point of view a fantasy. Mishima acted out that image just as it was. He created himself exactly in accordance with it. That was the way he lived, and that was the way he died. Edward Said uses the word *orientalism* to refer to the impression held by Europeans of the Orient. He insists that orientalism is a view held by Europeans and has nothing to do with the people who actually live in the Orient. But Mishima thought the opposite. He said, in effect, "Your image of the Japanese is me." But what in fact happened is that Mishima presented a false image. As a result, the conception of Japanese people held by most Europeans has Mishima at one pole and people like Akio Morita, chairman of Sony, at the other pole. In my opinion, both poles are inaccurate.

I wonder, Mr. Oe, do you feel responsible for how Japanese people are perceived abroad? When you are writing your books, are you conscious of an international audience and of what the books will do to Western people's perceptions of Japan? Or do you not think about things like that?

I was interviewed once by a German television station. The interviewer had translated one of my books into German. He asked me whether it was very important to me to be translated into German. I said no, and a deathly silence fell over the studio. The reason I said no is simply that I write my books for Japanese readers rather than for foreigners. Moreover, the Japanese readers I have in mind are a limited group. The people I write for are people of my own generation, people who have had the same experiences as myself. So when I go abroad, or am translated abroad or criticized abroad, I feel rather indifferent about it. The responsibilities I feel are to Japanese readers, people who are living together with me in this environment.

I come from a peripheral tradition, that of a very provincial corner of the island of Shikoku. It's an extremely strange place, with a long history of maltreatment, out there beyond the reach of culture. I think my humor is the humor of the people who live in that place.

—Kenzaburo Ōe

Speaking as a reader, foreign literature is very important to me. William Blake is important to me. I've written one book based on Blake, and one based on Malcolm Lowry. Another book was about a Dante specialist who lives out in the country. So in that sense I have been much influenced by foreign literature. I read your books in English, for example. Naturally, I believe that a real novelist is international.

For some reason, Japanese writers tend to stay away from international writers' conferences. Up to now, at least, there have not been many authors who have gone abroad to speak out about Japan's place in the world, about the contradictions felt by Japanese writers in the midst of economic prosperity, about the things that trouble them deeply. So for my part I am trying to do that, little by little. Japan has many very capable businessmen and politicians, but as a novelist I want to speak out internationally about things that they never mention. And I think it is meaningful for writers from abroad, especially young writers like yourself, to come to Japan to look closely at this country and to meet Japanese intellectuals. I hope this will lead to a deeper understanding of things such as the difficult role played by Japanese intellectuals amid material prosperity, and to cultural encounters at a genuinely substantial level.

REVIEWS OF RECENT WORKS

Emiko Sakurai (review date Spring 1978)

SOURCE: A review of *Teach Us to Outgrow Our Madness,* in *World Literature Today,* Vol. 52, No. 2, Spring, 1978, pp. 345-46.

[*In the following review of the English publication of* Teach Us to Outgrow Our Madness, *Sakurai hails Ōe as a major international talent.*]

Teach Us to Outgrow Our Madness [translated by John Nathan] is the third publication in English of the extraordinary works of Kenzaburo Ōé, the most talented writer to emerge in Japan after World War II. Like his previous publications (***A Personal Matter,*** 1968, also translated by John Nathan, and ***The Silent Cry,*** 1975), this book is certain to surprise some Western readers who have come to expect delicate prose and exquisite imagery from a Japanese novelist. Having learned his craft from postwar American authors such as Norman Mailer and French existentialists such as Jean-Paul Sartre, rather than from *The Tale of Genji,* Ōé writes fiction that is more brutal and savage than exquisite or quaint. He was a twenty-two-year-old French major at Tokyo University when he won his first literary prize. Since then he has won virtually every literary award offered in Japan, including the coveted Akutagawa Prize in 1958 for ***Prize Stock,*** the earliest composition among the four short novels contained in the present book.

Prize Stock is a tightly knit tale of a black American flier's captivity in a mountain village during the War. Ōé referred to it as a "pastoral." But what a pastoral! Ōé superimposes a mythic, primeval society on the village and reveals the nature of man and conditions of human existence through a densely woven pattern of animal images. "Chilly, sweating stones" jut "like the swollen belly of a pupa," and "skin flush[es] hot as the innards of a freshly killed chicken." Symbolism is apparent as little boys in the opening scene "collect" well-shaped bones at a makeshift crematorium to use as medals and the black captive with a boar trap around his ankles is "reared" in the cellar. It is a powerful story that exploits all the elements of fiction.

The imagery of ***The Day He Himself Shall Wipe My Tears Away*** is just as striking. The narrator lies in a hospital wearing a pair of underwater goggles covered in dark cellophane and singing the song "Happy Days Are Here Again" in anticipation of death from liver cancer and return to an event in 1945 that ended his happy days. It is a technical as well as imagistic triumph. ***Aghwee the Sky Monster*** tells of a young composer haunted by the phantom of a kangaroo-sized baby in a white nightgown. ***Teach Us to Outgrow Our Madness*** is a tragicomic story of a fat man's obsession with his mentally defective son and the imagined madness of his own dead father. Both are original, well-plotted tales with vivid, if not likable characters and memorable scenes.

The four novellas vary in technique and style as well as subject matter but are alike in the theme of alienation (apparent in the images of the chained captive and the cancer patient waiting for liberation), in their absurdist, ironic, black-comic view of life and the use of anti-heroes. Artistic excellence characterizes all four. The translation is accurate and conveys the essence of the original, although some readers may prefer a more Anglicized, smooth-flowing rendition to Nathan's faithful-to-the-last-comma approach. ***Teach Us to Outgrow Our Madness*** is a book that should be read by everyone interested in contemporary fiction, for Ōé is as important a writer as Mailer or Updike.

Sanroku Yoshida (review date Summer 1988)

SOURCE: A review of *Natsukashii toshi e no tegami,* in *World Literature Today,* Vol. 62, No. 3, Summer, 1988, pp. 510-11.

[*In the following review, Yoshida hails* Natsukashii toshi e no tegami *as a technically daring "milestone in Ōe's career."*]

In the past Kenzaburō Ōe treated his concept of cosmos expansively in the novels ***Man'en gan'nen no futtobōru*** (1967; Eng. ***The Silent Cry,*** 1974) and ***Dojidai gemu*** (***Contemporary Games;*** 1979). In the former, folkloric elements are quintessential to the formation of his cosmos; in the latter, mythical allusions are also utilized. In his new novel [***Natsukashii toshi e no tegami,*** 1987] Ōe molds his microcosm on Dante's cosmology in *The Divine Comedy,* quoting from the work extensively.

The central theme of the novel is "the eternal dream time," an abstract structure in which the past, present, and future all overlap. The major organizing element in this time structure, however, is space, specifically the author's native village in the mountains of Shikoku, which was also the backdrop for the two novels mentioned above. In the title of the present volume, for example, *toshi* (year) is not used as a time indicator but rather to signify the combining of time and space into one concept. An English rendering of the title would be "Letters to the Time/Space of Fond Memories." This forms the novel's Dante-like cosmos.

Ōe borrows many characters, episodes, and images from his earlier works; in other words, he makes use of his own literary archetypes. Since, however, he presents them in a slightly different manner, this blurs the ontological meaning of the literary archetypes in the reader's mind and distills them into more abstract entities. Furthermore, the intertextual study of these distilled images between the present novel and its predecessors reveals a larger framework of Ōe's cosmology, in which the time/space concept is conceived.

Natsukashii toshi e no tegami is more autobiographical than anything that Ōe has ever written. In spite of its highly sophisticated theme, the narrative is easier to follow than that of ***Dojidai gemu.*** The overall tone is optimistic, which is not at all the case with ***Man'en gan'nen no futtobōru.*** The present novel is another milestone in Ōe's career and in Japanese literature as well.

Sanroku Yoshida (review date Spring 1991)

SOURCE: A review of *Chiryō-tō,* in *World Literature Today,* Vol. 65, No. 2, Spring, 1991, p. 368.

[*In the following review, Yoshida commends Ōe's* Chiryō-tō *as an imaginative and beautifully composed piece of science fiction.*]

In ***Chiryō-tō*** (***Towers of Healing***) the novelist Ōe Kenzaburō is concerned with the effect of a worldwide nuclear disaster, particularly its impact on the human race. He had previously developed this theme in ***Kōzui wa waga tamashii ni oyobi*** (***Flood onto My Soul;*** 1973), but here his earlier cataclysmic view has been replaced by a more optimistic outlook.

In the new novel, which was first serialized in *Hermes* (July 1989—March 1990), Ōe predicts a Persian Gulf crisis. The story is set at the beginning of the twenty-first century, and the use of nuclear weapons in the gulf has made the earth apparently uninhabitable. This has inspired an international project for immigration to a new earth, and at the beginning of the story the exodus of about a million people to that new earth in the spaceship *Star Ship* has already occurred. After ten years of scientific research and experiments on the new earth, the *Star Ship* returns to the old earth. This creates tension between the returnees and those who had been left behind.

The Star Ship Corporation, a government agency, serves as a secret police force over the people in what is now an Orwellian society. Intermarriage between the two groups is strongly discouraged, since the corporation is determined to protect the "pure blood" of the elite from possible AIDS contamination through contact with the other group. Passing a government-administered AIDS test has become a requirement in order for an old-earth person to marry a returnee. If the result of the test is positive, a thorough investigation is made to identify all persons with whom the applicant has had sexual contact. These persons are then ostracized.

***Chiryō-tō* is Ōe's first venture into science fiction, but it contains all the characteristics of his earlier works: the "great departure" from a difficult reality, the frequently existential impasse, the breakthrough, and the final advent of new hope.**

—*Sanroku Yoshida*

The novel focuses on an extended family of several generations, which includes both old-earth residents and returnees. One male is the head of the *Star Ship* project, and a brother is an underground activist who protests the project. Ōe's narrator, a young girl, belongs to the old-earth part of the family. She wants to marry a returnee but suspects she may have AIDS, having been repeatedly raped while held captive by a European terrorist group. Her family is thus a microcosm of the old-earth returnee society with all its problems and stigmas.

Eventually the narrator musters her courage and takes the AIDS test. The results are negative, and she is liberated from the spell of the disease. She learns from her future husband that the *Star Ship* crew discovered several tower-like buildings on the new earth. They were called "chiryō-tō" or "towers of healing," since whoever lies down in their coffinlike beds is irradiated and cured of all wounds and disease. The towers are also trees of life. As her future husband tells her this story, she becomes rejuvenated by the new life that is forming within her.

Chiryō-tō is Ōe's first venture into science fiction, but it contains all the characteristics of his earlier works: the "great departure" from a difficult reality, the frequently existential impasse, the breakthrough, and the final advent of new hope. As usual, Ōe is concerned with the social and political situation of the world, with the freedom and happiness of individuals, and with an ecologically healthy environment in which no one is ostracized. Instead of the intensity, urgency, shocking images, and difficult linguistic contrivances of his earlier works, however, here Ōe writes more in a vein of verisimilitude. In quiet colors he provides us with an example of how not to lose hope in our difficult days. More of Ōe's books should be translated into English so that a wider audience can listen to what this important writer from contemporary Japan has to say.

FURTHER READING

Criticism

"Reading Japan Through Its Writers: Abe Kobo and Oe Kenzaburo: The Problem of Selfhood in Contemporary Japan." *Book Forum* VII, No. 1 (1984): 30-1.

Comments on how contemporary Japanese culture is reflected in the works of Ōe and Abe Kōbō.

Enright, D. J. "Days of Marvelous Lays." *New York Review of Books* XI, No. 6 (10 October 1968): 35-7.

Negative review of *A Personal Matter* which considers the novel's ending to be contrived.

Gamerman, Amy. "Kenzaburo Oe Wins Nobel in Literature." *The Wall Street Journal* (14 October 1994): A9.

Reports on Ōe's selection as the Nobel Prize winner and offers a concise overview of his life and career.

Napier, Susan J. "Death and the Emperor: Mishima, Oe, and the Politics of Betrayal." *Journal of Asian Studies* 48, No. 1 (February 1989): 71-89.

Analyzes the "role of the Emperor" in the works of Ōe and Yukio Mishima. While Ōe is severely critical of the Emperor system, Mishima, who came of age during the 1930s, supported the Emperor for patriotic reasons.

———. *Escape from the Wasteland: Romanticism and Realism in the Fiction of Mishima Yukio and Oe Kenzaburo.* Cambridge: Harvard University Press, 1991, 258 p.

Critical study of selected works by Ōe and Yukio Mishima. Napier argues that Ōe and Mishima both "set up alternative fictional worlds of 'closed circles,' even of 'fairy tales,' which are 'outside the influence of time,' to contrast with the reality of modern Japan."

Nemoto, Reiko Tachibana. "Günter Grass's *The Tin Drum* and Oe Kenzaburo's *My Tears.*" *Contemporary Literature* 34, No. 4 (Winter 1993): 740-66.

Elucidates what Nemoto calls "a striking parallelism" between two novels by Ōe and Günter Grass. Nemoto argues that both "Grass and Oe insist that after Auschwitz and Hiroshima political neutrality in literature is unacceptable."

Remnick, David. "Reading Japan." *The New Yorker* LXX, No. 48 (6 February 1995): 38-44.

Discusses the facts of Ōe's personal life which account for his surprise announcement at the Nobel Prize ceremony that he would no longer write fiction.

Treat, John Whittier. "*Hiroshima Nōto* and Ōe Kenzaburō's Existentialist Other." *Harvard Journal of Asiatic Studies* 47, No. 1 (June 1987): 97-136.

Negative assessment of Ōe's *Hiroshima Notes* which is described as the ingenuous philosophizing of an author who is "a naive reader of history inversely attempting to comprehend a situation directly accessible only to its immediate victims."

Wilson, Michiko N. *The Marginal World of Oe Kenzaburo: A Study in Themes and Techniques.* New York: M. E. Sharpe, 1986, 160 p.

Discusses Ōe's fiction as a radical departure from traditional Japanese literature.

Additional coverage of Ōe's life and career is contained in the following sources published by Gale Research: *Contemporary Authors,* Vols. 97-100; *Contemporary Authors New Revision Series,* Vol. 36; *Contemporary Literary Criticism,* Vols. 10 and 36; and *Major 20th-Century Writers.*

Philip Roth
Operation Shylock: A Confession

Award: Faulkner Award for Fiction

(Full name Philip Milton Roth) Born in 1933, Roth is an American novelist, short story writer, autobiographer, essayist, and critic.

For further information on his life and works, see *CLC,* Volumes 1, 2, 3, 4, 6, 9, 15, 22, 31, 47, and 66.

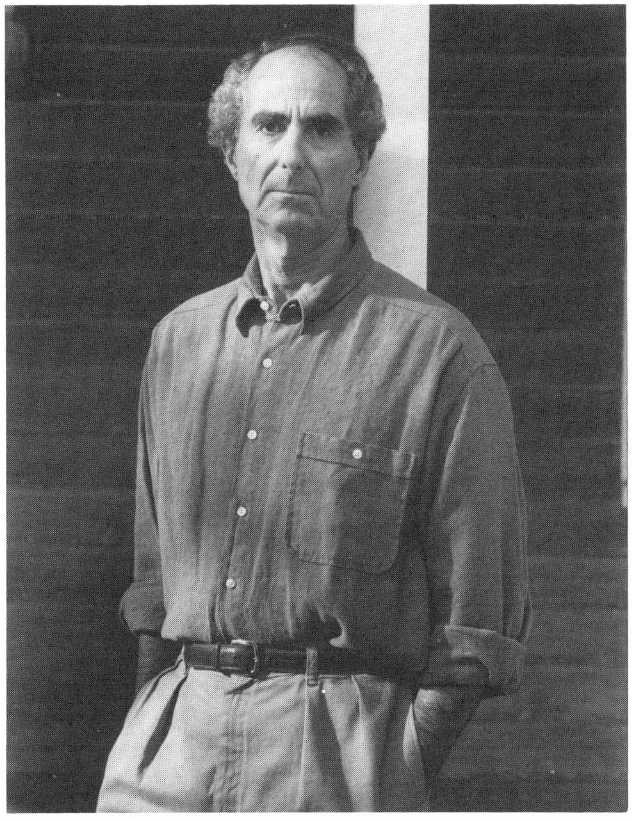

INTRODUCTION

Operation Shylock (1993) centers on a character named Philip Roth, who travels to Israel in 1988 after learning that a man claiming to be Philip Roth is in Jerusalem promoting a movement called "Diasporism." Roth eventually meets his impostor—a former private detective from Chicago who is dying of cancer—and gives him the nickname Moishe Pipik. Predicated on his belief that a future Muslim attack on Israel will prompt the Israelis to respond with nuclear weapons, Pipik contends that in order for Judaism to survive, all Ashkenazi Jews must return to Europe and relinquish Palestine to native Middle Easterners. The novel also concerns Roth's interaction with George Ziad, a Palestinian friend from Roth's college years who tries to recruit him to the Palestinian cause, and Louis B. Smilesburger, a Mossad spymaster who is trying to recruit Roth for "Operation Shylock," an Israeli intelligence scheme designed to uncover Jewish-American financial backers of the Palestine Liberation Organization (PLO). After many unsuccessful efforts, Smilesburger eventually convinces Roth to travel to Europe to spy on Ziad and his Jewish contacts. Although Israel's stance toward Palestinians, which Roth characterizes as combative and aggressive, is treated throughout *Operation Shylock* as damaging to the Diaspora, which is credited with producing many of Judaism's cultural achievements, Roth's final cooperation with Smilesburger suggests that there is a part of Roth that cannot turn away from Israel. Critical reaction to *Operation Shylock* has been mixed. While praising Roth's use of the doppelgänger and his elaborate development of themes concerning his Jewish identity, Judaism, the Diaspora, and the future of Israel, many commentators argue that the novel suffers from rhetorical excess and Roth's interest in self-presentation. Roth's incorporation of historical events and actual people in the work and his insistence that *Operation Shylock* is autobiographical and not a piece of fiction has also puzzled critics and generated controversy. Nevertheless, John Updike has contended that "this Dostoyevskian phantasmagoria is an impressive reassertion of artistic energy, and a brave expansion of Roth's 'densely overstocked little store of concerns' into the global marketplace. It should be read by anyone who cares about (1) Israel and its repercussions; (2) the development of the postmodern novel; (3) Philip Roth."

PRINCIPAL WORKS

Goodbye, Columbus, and Five Short Stories (novella and short stories) 1959
Letting Go (novel) 1962
When She Was Good (novel) 1967
Portnoy's Complaint (novel) 1969
Our Gang (novel) 1971
The Breast (novel) 1972
The Great American Novel (novel) 1973
My Life as a Man (novel) 1974
Reading Myself and Others (essays and criticism) 1975
The Professor of Desire (novel) 1977
**The Ghost Writer* (novel) 1979

**Zuckerman Unbound* (novel) 1981
**The Anatomy Lesson* (novel) 1983
The Counterlife (novel) 1986
The Facts: A Novelist's Autobiography (autobiography) 1988
Deception (novel) 1990
Patrimony: A True Story (memoir) 1990
Operation Shylock: A Confession (novel) 1993

*These works, along with the epilogue "The Prague Orgy," were published as *Zuckerman Bound: A Trilogy and Epilogue* in 1985.

CRITICISM

Richard Eder (review date 7 March 1993)

SOURCE: "Roth Contemplates His Pipik," in *Los Angeles Times Book Review,* March 7, 1993, pp. 3, 7.

[*Eder is an American critic who has won a citation for excellence in reviewing from the National Book Critics Circle as well as a Pulitzer Prize for Criticism. In the review below, he presents a mixed assessment of* Operation Shylock.]

"Mischief," Philip Roth writes partway through his new novel [***Operation Shylock: A Confession***], "is how some Jews get involved in living." He quotes his friend, the Israeli novelist Aharon Appelfeld, but it is hard not to think that Appelfeld was talking about Roth.

Almost more than the stories they tell, Roth's recent novels—particularly ***The Counterlife*** and ***Deception***—have been about the uncertain and illusory relationship he sets up between himself and his characters. Each book gives us a multiplicity of fictional Roths, directly or by means of alter egos, so that the teller and his tale keep changing places in a Pirandello-like contradance or pea-and-shell game.

It is disconcerting, and never more so than in ***Operation Shylock.*** It can be intrusive and self-absorbed. Look at me, not at my story, Roth seems to say, and he keeps butting in to switch places with it.

Yet this is only partly arbitrary. Method and story are joined. Always, Roth presents being Jewish as the most intense and extreme way of being human; and Jewish self-consciousness—morbid, comic, inspired—as a heightened form of human self-consciousness. But staring at things too hard causes double vision. Staring at yourself too hard fractures your sense of yourself.

Shylock gives us two fractured visions or, if you like, quadruple vision. Diaspora Jew confronts Israeli Jew, a theme introduced in ***Counterlife*** and now lavishly played out. At times, in fact, there are three double visions. An Arab voice is heard to complain with the scintillating lucidity that Roth is master of, but more faintly, as if even Roth could not quite handle sextuple.

A reader risks disappearing into his complexities. There is the author's suggestion—dangled, withdrawn, dangled, and very quietly canceled—that the story really took place and that its protagonist really does sign his royalty checks "Philip Roth." Occasionally, a genuine fact subverts the phantasmagoric account.

Shylock begins with a famous author named Philip who visits Israel in a state of Halcion-induced disorientation. There he meets a man named Philip Roth. The latter is urging Israelis of European descent to move back to a Europe that eagerly awaits them. ("Our Jews are back!" jubilant Polish crowds will cry out at the railroad station.) Unless they undertake this second Diaspora, he argues, there will be a second Holocaust, a mutually exterminating nuclear war with the Arabs.

Roth Two looks like Roth One. He wears the same tweed jacket with a button missing, fervently admires his books, and loyally detests his critics. Roth One naturally detests him and the confusing publicity he is creating. To distance himself, he gives his usurper the Yiddish sobriquet for an obstreperous child: Moishe Pipik.

Some distancing! Pipik means bellybutton, and that, of course, you can't cut off. Pipik is a fighter in the civil war that goes on inside Roth. Arguing that Jewish culture and ethics have been formed in the Diaspora, and that Israelis are coarse vulgarians, he flatters Roth's own Diaspora art. Pipik is a mad cartoon, of course, and the madness is reinforced by his ranting pleas to Roth not to disavow him. Pipik's warm and wholehearted Gentile lover, Jinx, adds to the rant by arguing that not only is Pipik an idealist, he is dying of cancer as well.

Guilt as thick as fuel oil powers Pipik's claim upon the narrator. A second claim is made by Ziad, a Palestinian-American schoolmate from Chicago who has settled on the West Bank to mourn his father's confiscated property and "to hate." Ziad's pleas mirror Pipik's; he, too, argues that the Jews in Israel have lost their soul and become oppressors. Taking Roth to be the author of the Second Diaspora plan, he attempts to recruit him for the Palestinian cause.

A third claim is addressed to the part of Roth that, despite his vulnerability to Pipik's and Ziad's arguments, cannot reject Israel. A Mr. Smilesburger first appears as a rich, doddering old Israeli who, seeming to take him for Pipik, gives him an enormous check to advance the cause. In fact, he is a high-ranking officer of Mossad, the Israeli equivalent of the CIA. He has Roth briefly kidnaped and then, appealing to his loyalty, assigns him to go to Athens to infiltrate a group of dovish Greek Jews with ties to the PLO.

Operation Shylock is less a novel than a dramatic monologue that alternately spurts above and sinks under its own voice.

—Richard Eder

These are, of course, the same people that Ziad wants him to meet. Everything in ***Shylock***—Mossad's name for the Athens project—has a double face. Smilesburger practices agentry upon Roth and so, much less efficiently, does Ziad. Yet each embodies an authentic moral and political position. Their respective monologues are passionate, moving and impaled upon paradox. They display the author at his most trenchant.

Smilesburger gives a searing defense of Israeli hawkishness. The Palestinians are essentially innocent, and the Israelis are guilty of their displacement, he affirms. He mocks Roth and other doves as hypocrites who want to have both Israel and their moral virtue. Hawks and doves will be hanged together if the Arabs win, he says. At the war-crimes trial, he will not argue the Holocaust or Biblical claims. He will say: "I did what I did to you because I did what I did to you."

It is *raison d'état* or, in the Hebrew phrase, *ein brera* (no other choice). Only Roth could make its advocate so stark and so human. As for Ziad's argument—that Israel has used the Holocaust to justify its suppression of the Palestinians—it comes across in a witty and original construction, but less vividly. Yet Ziad's present-day pain humanizes him, standing as it does against the inevitable abstraction of a far greater pain that is 40 years old.

Throughout the book, there are scenes from the trial of John Demjanjuk, the alleged Ivan the Terrible who killed thousands of Jews at Treblinka. Ziad contrasts the meticulousness and openness of the trial with the arbitrary and part-hidden violence used against the Palestinians. The Demjanjuk trial, he insists, is used to keep the Holocaust alive. The Roth character protests the incomparable difference in magnitude between the two cases.

The author is not after balances, though. ***Shylock*** is his characteristic headlong series of charges over the broken ground of unresolvable contradiction. When he is dealing with the contradictions between Israelis and Arabs, and between the Israeli Jews and those outside, the charges are exhilarating and as revealing in their rich paradox as anything he has done.

Bryan Cheyette on *Operation Shylock:*

In *Operation Shylock,* Roth wants to blur completely any distinction between reality and unreality or autobiography and fiction. He wishes, instead, to create an unauthored "plot" which dramatizes the "uncontrollability of real things". But this is not merely a writerly or solipsistic matter. What gives this work its considerable punch is that its fissured narrative—this is a novel that continually denies its own inventiveness—is situated in the Middle East which, in the late 1980s, was similarly split asunder.

Bryan Cheyette, in his "Me, Myself and I," in The Times Literary Supplement, *26 March 1993.*

There are long stretches, though, where Roth's self-absorption is so thick and extended as to screen out light, air and interest. The bright use of Pipik as a quixotic Diasporist and as one of Roth's alter egos dims in the long nighttime monologues where the *alter* drops off. Even weaker and more inert is Roth's treatment of Pipik's lover and defender, the Polish-American Jinx, who bills herself as a "recovering anti-semite," 12 steps and all. His paradox fails him; as their talk drags on and on, she becomes his sexy, long-winded, shiksa foil. ***Shylock*** is less a novel than a dramatic monologue that alternately spurts above and sinks under its own voice.

John Updike (review date 15 March 1993)

SOURCE: "Recruiting Raw Nerves," in *The New Yorker,* Vol. LXIX, No. 4, March 15, 1993, pp. 109-12.

[*A prizewinning novelist, short story writer, poet, dramatist, and critic, Updike is one of America's most distinguished men of letters. Best known for such novels as* Rabbit, Run *(1960),* Rabbit Redux *(1971), and* Rabbit Is Rich *(1981), he is a chronicler of life in Protestant, middle-class America. A contributor of literary reviews to various periodicals, he has frequently written the "Books" column in* The New Yorker *since 1955. In the following review, he remarks on theme and characterization in* Operation Shylock *and places the novel in the context of Roth's previous works.*]

Some readers may feel there has been too much Philip Roth in the writer's recent books—***The Facts,*** subtitled "A Novelist's Autobiography," with an eight-thousand-word afterword by the novelist's recurrent character Nathan Zuckerman (1988); ***Deception,*** an airy love tale, with wide margins, involving an American novelist called Philip living in London and conversing with a number of women in gusts of pure dialogue (1990); and ***Patrimony: A True Story,*** the gritty, moving account of Roth's father's slow death from a brain tumor and of his own coincidental open-heart surgery (1991). Such readers should be warned: there are *two* Philip Roths in his new novel, ***Operation Shylock: A Confession.*** The first one, an aging author minding his own business in New York and Connecticut, hears from friends in Israel that another Philip Roth has been in the news and is delivering a lecture in Jerusalem's King David Hotel on the topic "Diasporism: The Only Solution to the Jewish Problem." After a sleepless night, Philip I (let's call him) telephones the hotel and, upon inquiring if this is Philip Roth, is told, "It is, and who is this, please?"

The question is a profound one, and the concept of the double, in this novel, is never again as electrically spooky as in the long-distance phone call that is apparently answered by the caller. Later, in Jerusalem, Philip I meets Philip II, and at first finds the resemblance only approximate:

> I saw before me a face that I would not very likely have taken for my own had I found it looking back at me that morning from the mirror. . . . It was actually a conventionally better-looking face, a little less mismade than my own, with a more strongly defined chin and not so large a nose, one that, also, didn't flatten Jewishly like

> mine at the tip. It occurred to me that he looked like the after to my before in the plastic surgeon's advertisement.

We seem to have, at first blush, the figure of a nicer brother, like handsome, earnest Henry Zuckerman in ***The Counterlife*** (1987). At least since ***Portnoy's Complaint*** (1969), Roth's refractory central persona has been haunted by a moral shadow, the decent, civic-minded, asexual non-writer who is innocent of blame—blame from used and abandoned shiksas, and blame, in the exhaustively investigated case of Nathan Zuckerman, from outraged Jewish critics of the author's allegedly anti-Semitic fictions. But Philip II, "the Hollywooded version of my face so nebbishly pleading with me to try to calm down," is no mere shadow. The closer Philip I looks, the more exact the resemblance becomes, down to a "nub of tiny threadlets where the middle button had come off his jacket—I noticed because for some time now I'd been exhibiting a similar nub of threadlets where the middle button had yet again vanished from *my* jacket." The perfection of the duplication infuriates the original, whose charge of personality appropriation meets a wall of fawning verbosity. When Philip I demands, "Who are *you* and what are *you*? Answer me!," the answer comes back, "Your greatest admirer." Philip II supplies a cascade of grievances on the author's behalf (***"Portnoy's Complaint,*** not even nominated for a National Book Award!") and of fluent babble about Jung's mystical theory of "synchronicity" and his own theory of Diasporism, which would solve the dangerous problem of Israel by returning its million European Jews to Europe. In addition, he bursts into tears, twice, and reveals, without tears, that he (Philip II) is terminally ill of cancer.

If the repercussions and complications of this self-on-self grapple don't absolutely defy summary, they certainly don't invite it. The book is a species of international thriller: Philip I witnesses some of the trial of the alleged concentration-camp demon John Demjanjuk, ponders the purported diary of the Jewish martyr Leon Klinghoffer, and winds up, against his better judgment, performing as a spy in Athens and elsewhere for the Israeli intelligence service, the Mossad. ***Operation Shylock*** is, too, something of a medical thriller, and exhibits Roth's knowing way with pathology, no less masterly than Thomas Mann's. Philip I is slowly recovering from paralyzing mental distress induced by his taking Halcion in the aftermath of a botched knee operation, and the novel's Gentile femme fatale is a Chicago nurse called Jinx Possesski, whose descriptions of hospital life are authoritatively harrowing. Philip II, the lover who has saved her from the anti-Semitism contracted after prolonged exposure to Jewish doctors, wears a penile implant to compensate for the ill effects of cancer therapy, and the novel's father figure, a Mossad eminence bearing the genial name Louis B. Smilesburger, gets about on forearm crutches, has "that alarming boiled look of someone suffering from a skin disease," and shows a bald head "minutely furrowed and grooved like the shell of a hard-boiled egg whose dome has been fractured lightly by the back of a spoon." Roth's habitual polarities goy/Jew and hedonism/altruism have been augmented by sick/well and disintegration/integration. Jinx is trumpeted as "a voluptuously healthy-looking creature . . . somebody who was *well.*"

The novel is also a psychological thriller, centered on Philip I's frenzied and not unparanoid responses to the excessive stimuli of a few days in Israel—responses that are to be construed, we are told at the end, as steps in his recovery from the Halcion overdose and its sensations of disintegration. This particular infirmity, Roth readers will recall, figured in the last paragraph of ***The Facts,*** when Nathan Zuckerman assures the author, "I am distressed to hear that in the spring of 1987 what was to have been minor surgery turned into a prolonged physical ordeal that led to a depression that carried you to the edge of emotional and mental dissolution." Roth's œuvre presents an ever more intricately ramifying and transparent pseudo-autobiography: the first-person voice goes back to ***Goodbye Columbus*** (1959), the layered self-referentiality to ***My Life as a Man*** (1974), the serialized formalization of an alter ego to ***The Ghost Writer*** (1980). He should be commended for facing the fact that a fiction writer's life is his basic instrument of perception—that only the imagery we have personally gathered and unconsciously internalized possesses the color, warmth, intimate contour, and weight of authenticity the discriminating fiction reader demands. Rousseau's *Confessions* opened the door to the nineteenth-century novel, and Proust's autobiographical *Remembrance of Things Past* could be said to have closed it. In the post-Proust, postmodern, post-objective world of American fiction, Roth stands out as a working theorist of fictional reality, a marvellously precocious and accomplished realist who has tested the limits of realism: he has feverishly paced its boundaries and played games with its pretensions. The act of writing has become his fiction's central dramatic action. In this novel, which purports to be a confession, Philip II is a study in ongoing character creation. When he entertainingly and circumstantially describes his seamy career as a private detective in Chicago, his auditor, Philip I, feels doubts that echo the reader's own:

> I thought, He's got it all down pat from TV. If only I'd watched more *L.A. Law* and read less Dostoyevsky I'd know what's going on here, I'd know in two minutes what show it is exactly. Maybe motifs from fifteen shows, with a dozen detective movies thrown in. . . . Maybe it was the in-flight movie on El Al.

However, taking the trouble to invent a profession and to crib details from other, often equally fictional sources does, by drawing on the edges of the writer's imagination, make possible a wider personal truth—a dreamier level, as it were, of confession. Philip II, implausible and raddled as he is, is more of a character than Philip I, who seems, it must be allowed, slightly stiff. Like a Hemingway hero, Philip I has his dignity to protect, a certain rightness to uphold. Perhaps his neck is stiff from the effort of not letting his head be turned by all the compliments directed at him in the course of ***Operation Shylock.*** Along with his doppelgänger's slavish flattery, he hears himself described by an old Palestinian friend, George Ziad, as a model, non-Israeli Jew: "A Jew who has never been afraid to speak out about Jews. An independent Jew and he has suffered for it too." Ziad and Philip I were fellow graduate students at the University of Chicago in the fifties, and Ziad, now a professor in Israel, teaches ***Portnoy's Complaint*** to his students "to convince them that there are Jews in the world who are not in any way like these Jews we have here." The alluring Jinx Possesski reads Philip I's palm and, after assuring him that, according to his creases, his "sexual appetite is quite pure," tells him, "If I were reading the hands of a stranger and didn't know who you were, I would say it's sort of the hand of a . . . of a great leader." Clinchingly, Smilesburger, who by his final appearance has metamorphosed into the embodiment of enduring Jewish manhood ("The this-worldliness. The truthfulness. The intelligence. The malice. The comedy. The endurance. The acting. The injury. The impairment"), compliments Philip I on his spying assignment and his writing both: "First through our work together and then through your books, I have come to have considerable respect for you. . . . You are a fine man."

In the post-Proust, postmodern, post-objective world of American fiction, Roth stands out as a working theorist of fictional reality, a marvellously precocious and accomplished realist who has tested the limits of realism.

—John Updike

It's hard to wrap your mind around this paragon, whereas grotesque, sketchy Philip II has problems we can grasp: he is dying of cancer, he has been cursed with the name and appearance of a celebrity without being one, he must resort to a phallic prosthesis to satisfy his sexy girlfriend, he is enough tormented by the condition of post-Holocaust Jewry to have developed some crackpot schemes to remedy it. Through the plot's tangle and the steam of righteous indignation emitted by Philip I, this figment attracts our wonder and pity; his last days, and his incredible little afterlife as a dead sexual partner, commemorated in a letter from the faithful Jinx, stick in our minds, as images of the human condition having nothing to do with being a writer. "I AM THE YOU THAT IS NOT WORDS," Philip II tells Philip I, in capitals. For a writer, to be without words is to be without defenses, without immortality. Philip II is not the nice side of Philip I but his sick side, his mortal side, given phantasmal reality through the projective magic of fiction.

This magic is amply displayed in ***Operation Shylock,*** which, under the mysterious intensity of its inspiration, is as painstakingly written as it is elaborately developed. The passages introducing the characters, especially the female characters, are brilliantly, lushly evocative. Here is Jinx:

> Her whitish blond hair was worn casually pinned in a tousled bun at the back of her head, and she had a wide mouth, the warm interior of which she showed you, like a happy, panting dog, even when she wasn't speaking, as though she were taking your words in through her mouth, as though another's words were not received by the brain but processed—once past the small, even, splendidly white teeth and the pink, perfect gums—by the whole, radiant, happy-go-lucky thing.

George Ziad's wife, Anna, appears thus in their cavelike village home:

> Anna was a tiny, almost weightless woman whose anatomy's whole purpose seemed to be to furnish the housing for her astonishing eyes . . . intense and globular, eyes to see with in the dark, set like a lemur's in a triangular face not very much larger than a man's fist, and then there was the tent of the sweater enshrouding the anorexic rest of her and, peeping out at the bottom, two feet in baby's running shoes.

Yet, once they have been so vividly introduced, the characters turn out to be talking heads, faces attached to tirades. The novel is an orgy of argumentation; Roth, like Bernard Shaw, is as happy to shape an aria around a perverse or frivolous argument as around a heartfelt one. "That lubricious sensation that is fluency" seizes even our sensible Philip I as, too often mistaken for Philip II, he fervently expounds his double's theory of Diasporism, "calling for the de-Israelization of the Jews, on and on once again, obeying an intoxicating urge." One of the book's few taciturn characters, a Mossad strong-arm man, complains to him, "You speak too much. You speak speak speak." Though both Philips do much waxing wroth over a range of issues, the de-Israelization of the Jews—the claim that the embattled and therefore combative state of Israel has poisoned the Jewishness of the Diaspora—forms the dominant topic, argued from a pro-Jewish standpoint by Philip II and from a pro-Palestinian standpoint by George Ziad:

> "What *happens* when American Jews discover that they have been duped, that they have constructed an allegiance to Israel on the basis of irrational guilt, of vengeful fantasies, above all, *above all,* based on the most naive delusions about the moral identity of this state? *Because this state has no moral identity.* It has *forfeited* its moral identity, if ever it had any to begin with. By relentlessly institutionalizing the Holocaust it has even forfeited its claim to the Holocaust! The state of Israel has drawn the last of its moral credit out of the bank of the dead six million—this is what they have done by breaking the hands of Arab children on the orders of their illustrious minister of defense."

Though such views are put in the mouths of fictional characters, Roth's Zionist critics will not excuse him from their vigorous expression. "Name a raw nerve and you recruit it," Smilesburger tells Philip I after he has read this book. The ominous case of Salman Rushdie flickers into the author's mind: "Will the Mossad put a contract out on me the way the Ayatollah did with Rushdie?" If there were a Jewish Ayatollah, he might have issued his fatwa long ago, in the wake of those youthful short stories about goldbricking Jewish soldiers, bullying rabbis, Short Hills nouveaux riches, and little Jewish boys who can't understand why, if God could make the world in six days, He couldn't also impregnate a virgin.

Relentlessly honest, Roth recruits raw nerves, perhaps, because they make the fiercest soldiers in the battle of truth. Moral ambiguity, Semitic subdivision, has always been his chosen briar patch. His searching out of Jewishness is of a piece with the searching out of himself that has consumed so many pages and so many pleading, mocking, mocked alter egos. This, his most extended consideration of Jewishness, takes as its reference points not God's covenant with Abraham or the epic of Moses but affectionate memories of the Diaspora Jews of his boyhood's Newark. The myths of personal history have replaced those of a people's history. The only significant Old Testament reference is to Jacob's night-long wrestle with an unknown presence, which pairs nicely as an epigraph with Kierkegaard's assertion "The whole content of my being shrieks in contradiction against itself." Jacob's struggle with *another,* which gave Israel its name as "he who wrestles with God," has become, in echo of Christian self-abnegation, the self 's struggle with itself.

Never impressionistic in his style, Roth began with sensory facts, arranged and presented in a prose not quite colloquial but simple and clear. From ***Goodbye, Columbus:***

> I watched her move off. Her hands suddenly appeared behind her. She caught the bottom of her [bathing] suit between thumb and index finger and flicked what flesh had been showing back where it belonged. My blood jumped.
>
> That night, before dinner, I called her.

Under the stress of the intricate questions his later fiction poses, his sentences stretch and turn a bit stentorian: "However heroic the cause had seemed to Michael amid the patriotic graffiti decorating his bedroom walls in suburban Newton, he felt now as only an adolescent son can toward what he sees as an obstacle to his self-realization raised by an obtuse father mandating an outmoded way of life." A diagrammatic grayness creeps in as the complications thicken: "And what was *I* thinking? I was thinking, What are they thinking? I was thinking about Moishe Pipik and what *he* was thinking. . . . This is what I was thinking when I was not thinking the opposite and everything else." Not that Roth has quite forgotten the tricks of sensory actualization. Philip I sleeps with the delectable Jinx, and tells us nothing about the experience until, in the next chapter, while riding in a taxi, he remembers "that wordless vocal obbligato with which she'd flung herself upon the floodtide of her pleasure, the streaming throaty rising and falling, at once husky and murmurous, somewhere between the trilling of a tree toad and the purring of a cat." Later still, the experience washes back upon him less pleasantly: "I smelled her asleep in my trousers—she was that heavy, clinging, muttony stench and she was also that pleasingly unpleasing brackishness on the middle fingers of the hand that picked up the receiver of the ringing phone." But such sensory details are rare, and get rarer as the story goes on.

Somewhere after Philip I sleeps with Jinx, the novel stops pretending to coherence and becomes a dumping ground, it seems, for everything in Roth's copious file on Jewishness: a slangy American anti-Semitic monologue recorded by Philip II as a "work-out tape" for his Anti-Semites Anonymous program, the touchingly bland and banal journal of Leon Klinghoffer (fictional), searing testimony in the Demjanjuk trial (actual), and pages of uninterrupted discourse on the saintly nineteenth-century rabbi Chofetz Chaim and his desire that Jews abstain from *loshon hora*—evil speech, especially against other Jews. Perhaps the novel, whose events are centered on a few days in January of 1988, was too long in the working, and accumulated an awkward number of subsidiary inspirations. The headlines that haunt it—Demjanjuk, Klinghoffer, the case of Jonathan Pollard, the United States Navy officer who spied for Israel—also date it, as everything on the far side of the end of the Cold War is, for the time being, dated.

Operation Shylock, though it is as hot and strenuous as ***Deception*** was cool and diffident, shares with the previous novel an album quality, a sense of assembled monologues and interviews. Roth has taken to entrusting his message to the eloquence of his characters rather than to the movement of the plot. Plot be damned, he as good as says. Pausing midway to take stock on behalf of Philip I, he writes, "The story so far is frivolously plotted, overplotted, for his taste altogether too freakishly plotted, with outlandish events so wildly careening around every corner that there is nowhere for intelligence to establish a foothold and develop a perspective."

Well, theorists might argue, life isn't packaged in plots anymore, and why shouldn't a novel be a series of interviews, in this interview-mad age? Jinx Possesski's pilgrimage from working-class Catholic to fourteen-year-old hippie to born-again Protestant to anti-Semitic nurse to atheist consort of an anti-Zionist Jewish prophet is livelier than most tales you will read in *People* or hear on *Donahue.* But Roth, in his furious inventiveness and his passion for permutation, has become an exhausting author to be with. His characters seem to be on speed, up at all hours and talking until their mouths bleed. There are too many of them; they keep dropping out of sight, and when they reappear they don't talk the same. The plot is full of holes, and Roth, who becomes increasingly difficult to distinguish from Philip I, leaves out, for fully discussed security reasons, the crucial chapter in which he goes to Athens and spies for Israel and demonstrates, despite vicious rumors to the contrary, that he is a "loyal Jew" full of "Jewish patriotism."

This hard-pressed reviewer was reminded not only of Shaw but of *Hamlet,* which also has too many characters, numerous long speeches, and a vacillating, maddening hero who in the end shows the right stuff. Writing of *Hamlet,* T. S. Eliot coined, or gave fresh circulation to, the phrase "objective correlative," saying, "The supposed identity of Hamlet with his author is genuine to this point: that Hamlet's bafflement at the absence of objective equivalent to his feelings is a prolongation of the bafflement of his creator in the face of his artistic problem." Again, "In the character Hamlet is the buffoonery of an emotion which can find no outlet in action; in the dramatist it is the buffoonery of an emotion which he cannot express in art." All of Roth's work, and the history of mutual exacerbation between his work and his Jewish audience, lies behind the pained buffoonery of ***Operation Shylock.*** His narrowing, magnifying fascination with himself has penetrated to a quantum level of indeterminacy, where "what Jung calls 'the uncontrollability of real things' " takes over. The authorial ego's imaginative "self-subverting," which in the Zuckerman sequence conjured up counterlives of compelling solidity, in ***Operation Shylock*** slices things diaphanously thin. Still, this Dostoyevskian phantasmagoria is an impressive reassertion of artistic energy, and a brave expansion of Roth's "densely overstocked little store of concerns" into the global marketplace. It should be read by anyone who cares about (1) Israel and its repercussions; (2) the development of the postmodern novel; (3) Philip Roth.

An excerpt from *Operation Shylock: A Confession*

So eager was I to establish as fact that a dream had merely overflowed its banks that I got up to phone Aharon before it was even dawn. It was already an hour later in Jerusalem and he was a very early riser, but even if I had to risk waking him up, I felt I couldn't wait a minute longer to have him confirm that this business was all a mental aberration of mine and that no phone conversation had taken place between the two of us about another Philip Roth. Yet, once out of bed and on the way down to the kitchen to call him quietly from there, I recognized what a pipe dream it was to be telling myself that I had only been dreaming. I ought to be rushing to telephone not Aharon, I thought, but the Boston psychopharmacologist to ask if my uncertainty as to what was real meant that three months of being bombarded chemically by triazolam had left my brain cells permanently impaired. And the only reason to be phoning Aharon was to hear what new sightings he had to report. But why not bypass Aharon and inquire directly of the impostor himself what exactly he was out to achieve? By feigning "a reasonable perspective" I was only opening myself further to a dangerous renewal of delusion. If there was any place for me to be phoning at four fifty-five in the morning, it was suite 511 of the King David Hotel.

I thought very well of myself at breakfast for having made it back to bed at five without calling anyone; I felt settling over me that blissful sense of being in charge of one's life, a man who once again hubristically imagines himself at the helm of himself. Everything else might be a delusion, but the reasonable perspective was not.

Then the phone rang. "Philip? More good news. You are in the morning's paper." It was Aharon calling *me.*

"Wonderful. Which paper this time?"

"A Hebrew paper this time. An article about your visit to Lech Walesa. In Gdansk. This is where you were before you came to attend the Demjanjuk trial."

Had I been speaking to almost anyone else I might have been tempted to believe that I was being teased or toyed with. But however much pleasure Aharon may take in the ridiculous side of life, deliberately to perpetrate comic mischief, even of the most mildly addling variety, was simply incompatible with his ascetic, gravely gentle nature. He saw the joke, that was clear, but he wasn't in on it any more than I was.

Across from me Claire was drinking her coffee and looking through the *Guardian.* We were finishing breakfast. I hadn't been dreaming in New York and I wasn't dreaming now.

Philip Roth, in his Operation Shylock: A Confession, *Simon & Schuster, 1993.*

Robert Alter (review date 5 April 1993)

SOURCE: "The Spritzer," in *The New Republic,* Vol. 208, No. 14, April 5, 1993, pp. 31-4.

[*Alter is an American educator and critic. In the following review, he examines Roth's use of farce and the doppelgänger in* Operation Shylock.]

At least as far back as ***The Ghost Writer,*** which appeared in 1979, Philip Roth's fiction has exhibited an oddly correlated double development. The novels become more preoccupied with questions of Jewishness, the writer's relation to Israel, the Holocaust, anti-Semitism and the collectivity of Jews; and they become more self-reflexive, pondering the conundrums of their own fictionality or lack of it. These concerns were treated with the greatest imaginative richness in ***The Counterlife*** (1986), Roth's best book. His next novel, ***Deception*** (1990), was much thinner, cast entirely as a series of dialogues that record, among other things, a collision with genteel English anti-Semitism that impels the protagonist, as his mistress wryly notes, to "return to the bosom of the tribe." What he longs for, he has told her, is "Jews without shame. Complaining Jews who get under your skin. Brash Jews who eat with elbows on the table. Unaccommodating Jews, full of anger, insult, argument and impudence." This equation of Jewishness and rudeness has evidently been encouraged by Roth's personal trajectory from Newark to the realm of high culture, and its simplicity is disturbing; it has a peculiar congruence with the skewed argument of John Murray Cuddihy's once-controversial book *The Ordeal of Civility,* which abrasively bracketed Yid with id and portrayed the Jews as essentially a brusque, disruptive presence in the Christian world.

But the brash contentiousness that Roth has raised to an ideal suffuses the population, and the very mode of expression, of his new book [***Operation Shylock: A Confession***]. Written out of Roth's usual hyperconsciousness of the masterworks of European and American fiction, ***Operation Shylock*** provides a very late and very Jewish version of that pre-eminently nineteenth-century and early-modern figure, the doppelgänger. The first thing that catches the reader's eye after the table of contents is an epigraph in Hebrew cursive script, and its translation, "So Jacob was left alone, and a man wrestled with him until daybreak": the earliest literary double, Roth suggests, may have been that mysterious stranger who ambushed Jacob in Genesis 32. What follows is a "confession" by a fictional character named Philip Roth, who shares with the author of this novel a biography (born in Newark in 1933, and so on), a wife and a list of publications from ***Goodbye, Columbus*** to ***Patrimony.*** The experience of the protagonist in Jerusalem 1988, where most of the action takes place, is pure invention, though he also does a few things that the real Philip Roth did, such as interviewing his friend the Israeli writer Aharon Appelfeld and looking in at the trial of John Demjanjuk.

On his way to Jerusalem, Roth discovers that someone claiming to be Philip Roth has been running around Israel preaching a new doctrine that he calls "Diasporism." (The term, if not the doctrine, was invented by the British painter R.B. Kitaj, a friend of Roth's, in a small book called *The Diasporist Manifesto* that appeared a few years ago.) Proposing himself as a kind of Theodor Herzl in rapid reverse, he wants to lead all the Ashkenazi Jews out of Israel, where their physical existence is continually endangered by Arab hostility, and back to Europe, the cultural setting in which they flourished for centuries and which will now welcome them after the ghastly aberration of the Hitler years. (The Diasporist rather casually imagines he can safely leave the Sephardi Jews in Israel, because they are Middle Easterners like their putative brethren, the Arabs.)

When Philip Roth the narrator comes face to face with Philip Roth the doppelgänger, he discovers that the imposter is a dead ringer for himself, down to the khaki trousers, tieless Oxford shirt and frayed tweed jacket. The second Roth is a brilliant mimic or an authentic refraction of the first, but he is also a liar, a charlatan, a wild obsessive and an extravagant megalomaniac. Roth the narrator predictably responds to this bizarre duplication of himself with a mixture of rage, dismay, frustration, exasperation and fascination. Eternal A student of comparative literature, he is quick to identify the features of the double in nineteenth-century fiction, "fully materialized duplicates incarnating the hidden depravity of the respectable original."

Yet that literary precedent has only slight applicability to his own predicament. The literary figure of the double is indeed a dark fantasy, but in this book Roth makes its relation to fictional self-reflexivity more prominent than any grand psychological resonance of fantasy. He construes the double not as the embodiment of a hidden self, but rather as that other kind of doubling, much less threatening, which is the re-invention of the self for the purpose of a fiction. The narrator imagines the appearance of his double as a kind of retribution exacted from the novelist, who has repeatedly invented avatars of himself in his protagonists, straddling the borderline between fiction and autobiography: "It's Zuckerman, I thought whimsically, stupidly, escapistly, it's Kepesh, it's Tarnopol and Portnoy—it's all of them in one, broken free of print and mockingly reconstituted as a single satirical facsimile of me." Living a life by constantly reassembling himself in novelistic projections, he "ate of the fruit of the tree of fiction, and nothing, neither reality nor myself, has been the same since."

The second Philip Roth is also an ideological extrapolation, rather than a psychological excavation, of the first. That is, Roth the narrator (and the author) is a Jew deeply and sympathetically concerned with the culture and the society of Israel, but his ultimate allegiances are to the Diaspora that is his home, to the pungency and the vitality and the uninhibited freedom of the life that Jews have made for themselves there. Roth the double flamboyantly embodies these allegiances, though he does so with the high intensity of lunacy and with a political program (Diasporism, plus an organization for gentiles called Anti-Semites Anonymous) that is catastrophically quixotic.

Roth the ideological mountebank and a number of subsidiary characters—his luscious gentile mistress, an Israeli secret service operative, a Palestinian university chum of the narrator's who has returned to his native Ramallah and become a militant nationalist—are rendered with considerable verve. The question is whether they, together with the narrator's vivid and often acerbic reflections on the book's events, really add up to a novel. As usual, Roth has beaten his critics to this question. He repeatedly wonders whether the figures and the circumstances that have overtaken him bear any credible resemblance to reality. Of his double, he observes to Appelfeld, "He gives off none of the aura of a real person, none of the *coherence* of a real person. Or even the *in*coherence of a real person." Later he complains about the "general implausibility" of the plot in which he finds himself, "a total lack of gravity, reliance at too many key points on unlikely coincidence, an absence of inner coherence."

Such disclaimers built into the novel, together with its identification as a confession and its final note to the reader that "this confession is false," are stratagems to preempt criticism, and are familiar from earlier books by Roth. Compared with the flaunting of artifice and to the ambiguities between fiction and reality in a major self-reflexive novelist like Nabokov, they seem a little thin. They certainly do not sufficiently complicate the simple truth that Philip Roth is always writing about Philip Roth.

Perhaps it might be better to think of this book not as a novel but as a looser and less realistic fiction of the sort that Gide had in mind when he designated several of his longer narratives as *soties*—roughly, farces. In the farce, burlesque and exaggeration tend to displace realistic characterization, and plot may be willfully contrived for parodic ends or for the sheer play of elaborate artifice. There has been a tilt toward farce in many of Roth's novels, but with the exception of the negligible ***The Breast,*** it has never been so extreme as here. Roth seems to invite such a classification when he names the voluptuous shiksa Jinx Possesski and the undercover agent Smilesburger (with a wink to le Carré's Smiley), and has the narrator repeatedly refer to his double as Moishe Pipik (a mildly derogatory and weakly comic Yiddish epithet that means Moses Bellybutton). In a bedroom conversation with the aforesaid Jinx, the narrator actually spells out this sense of being caught not in a realistic novel, but in a farce: "it's *Hellza-*

poppin' with Possesski and Pipik, it's a gag a minute with you two madcap kids. . . . Diasporism is a plot for a Marx Brothers movie—Groucho selling Jews to Chancellor Kohl!"

Readers who make their way through ***Operation Shylock*** with the same expectations that they brought to ***The Professor of Desire*** or ***The Counterlife*** will be frustrated. What is called for, rather, is to let yourself go with the sheer farcical momentum of the narrative. But even such a forgiving attitude does not dispose of all the unresolved questions that the book raises: the tendency to rhetorical excess and melodramatic gesture on the part of its characters; the fact that everyone in the book, including Israelis with a presumably imperfect grasp of English, sounds exactly like Philip Roth; the sense of too many threads left dangling or abruptly torn off in the ending.

What survives such difficulties, however, is a great deal of talk, and that proves to be formidable enough. The book is really a series of encounters between performing selves, and the chief interest is in the verbal and emotional energy of the performances. This stand-up comedy is in part a reversion to ***Portnoy's Complaint,*** with the important difference that here the tenor of the talk is political and historical, not personal and psychological. The politics of Jewish existence after the Holocaust and the founding of Israel is the occasion for most of the displays. That existence, as Roth recognizes, is shot through with interesting and ironic conflict: Israeli versus Palestinian, Israeli culture versus Diaspora Jewish life, an untrammeled sense of Jewish self-affirmation versus a resurgence of anti-Semitism.

The effect of the performance is to play out the opposing lines of these conflicts, to allow the articulation of each position at the top of the decibel scale. As Roth conceives it, this habit of verbal extravagance is essentially Jewish, and probably also essentially neurotic. (There are some partial precedents in Dostoyevsky.) Even George Ziad, the militant Palestinian, proves to be in this respect thoroughly Jewish, though he waves a different flag: "The gush, the agitation, the volubility, the frenzy barely beneath the surface of every word he babbled, the nerve-racking sense he communicated of something aroused and decomposing all at the same time, of someone in a permanent state of imminent apoplexy." It is in vain that Smilesburger quotes to the narrator the injunction to silence—"Grant me that I should say nothing that is unnecessary"—of the early twentieth-century Polish rabbinical luminary Israel Ha-Cohen, who was known as the Chofetz Chaim and became a household name in the Orthodox Jewish world for his moralizing tracts against the abuses of speech. For everyone in this novel lives, irrepressibly, by outdoing through language.

Writing about Jewish theatrical traditions, the critic Benjamin Harshav has aptly characterized this distinctively Jewish mode of spectacular talkativeness:

> Such "Jewish discourse" [founded on Yiddish and the study of the Talmud but then manifested in all sorts of secular art-media] is talkative, argumentative, contrary, associative. Its typical traits include answering with examples, anecdotes, parables or questions, rather than with direct, logical replies; seeing the smallest detail as symbolic for universal issues; delving into meanings, connotations and associations of a single word, and leaping from a word or concrete item to abstract generalizations and theories.

When it is translated into fiction, this associative, exegetical, sometimes pugnacious mode of discourse produces neither linear plot development nor panoptic descriptive vision, but rather meandering verbal extravaganzas. Countless examples from Yiddish writers like Mendele and Sholom Aleichem (and from some older Hebrew writers) come to mind. Political positions in Roth's book are not analyzed or defined, they are played out as verbal vaudeville, as when Ziad complains of Israeli invocations of the Holocaust: "Marlboro has the Marlboro Man, Israel has its Holocaust Man . . . *for the smokescreen that hides everything, smoke holocaust.*" Or when the narrator's misgivings about his own futile Hebrew education as a child balloon into the airy fantasy of a wild set of comparisons:

> For one hour a day, three days a week, fresh from six-and-a-half hours of public school, we sat there and learned to write backwards, to write as though the sun rose in the west and the leaves fell in the spring, as though Canada lay to the south, Mexico to the north, and we put our shoes on before our socks.

These sundry performances are the kind of stand-up comedy—what Jewish comedians of the '50s used to call "spritz"—that seeks to engage urgent political ideas and issues of identity. The various characters express their extreme positions shrilly and uncompromisingly, if also sometimes amusingly. The narrator, a bundle of confusions and ambivalences, works back and forth dialectically between clashing perspectives. If, in the passage just quoted, he exposes the barrenness of after-school Jewish education in America, he proceeds, a couple of pages later, to an opposite perception. As he stares uncomprehendingly at the Hebrew script on a schoolroom blackboard in Jerusalem—it is the verse about Jacob and the angel—he reflects: "That cryptography whose signification I could no longer decode had marked me indelibly four decades ago; out of the inscrutable words written on this blackboard had evolved every English word I had ever written." Like all the unrestrained speakers of this book, Roth the narrator is no doubt exaggerating. But as with the other speakers, the exaggeration contains a kernel of insight.

There is something quite engaging about the way this Jewish affirmation is put, but again doubts linger. Hebrew, for a start, is reduced to mere display. For how, really, can the key to Roth's own work be an unintelligible language? How can a patently deadening Jewish education do anything more than deaden? As to the larger political questions raised by the novel, the splitting of selves and the clash of opposing performances do strike brilliant sparks; but one wonders whether the routines may not be in the end too easy a way to handle urgent and even excruciating dilemmas. The appeal of the Diaspora is articulated by a character who is a dazzling arguer, but crazy. The smoldering resentment of Palestinian nationalism is spelled out by a character who is a dazzling arguer, but even crazier. Where, in the end, are we supposed to stand?

At the beginning of Roth's career, the world of which that stifling Jewish schoolroom in Newark was an integral part figured either as an object of satirical representation or as a trap to break out of. Now, in a way that surely would have surprised his early critics in the Jewish community, Roth has created a fiction in which Jewishness, individually and collectively, is imagined as an ineluctable destiny with positive if troubling content, in which he can see himself as complement, antithesis and spiritual brother to Appelfeld, the Holocaust survivor who composes his fiction in that mysterious ancestral language that moves from right to left.

And even on the level of literary form, this aggressively loquacious narrative, warts and all, owes less to James and Conrad than to Sholom Aleichem and the Eastern European Jewish world. It is a world that Roth knows only through translation, and the remove somehow does not diminish the magnetism of the culture of origins; a filtered, second-generation American Jewish version of that culture has played a prominent role in Roth's work at least since ***Portnoy's Complaint.*** The centering of Israel and Jewish identity, and their treatment in a warm and positive light, is a relatively recent development in his work, and conspicuously evident in this new book. Roth has the skill to make these themes resonate, but their only sounding-box remains the limiting theater of self-presentation that remains the venue of all his novels.

Harold Bloom (review date 22 April 1993)

SOURCE: "Operation Roth," in *The New York Review of Books,* Vol. XL, No. 8, April 22, 1993, pp. 45-8.

[*Bloom is one of the most prominent contemporary American critics and literary theorists. Some of his best known works include* The Anxiety of Influence: A Theory of Poetry *(1973) and* Kabbalah and Criticism *(1974). In the review below, he discusses characterization and the theme of Jewishness in* Operation Shylock.]

When requested to choose an exemplary passage from his work for a New York Public Library *Commonplace Book,* Philip Roth came up with this, from ***Zuckerman Unbound*** (1981):

> Zuckerman was tall, but not as tall as Wilt Chamberlain. He was thin, but not as thin as Mahatma Gandhi. In his customary getup of tan corduroy coat, gray turtleneck sweater, and cotton khaki trousers he was neatly attired, but hardly Rubirosa. Nor was dark hair and a prominent nose the distinguishing mark in New York that it would have been in Reykjavik or Helsinki. But two, three, four times a week, they spotted him anyway. "It's Carnovsky!" "Hey, want to see my underwear, Gil?" In the beginning, when he heard someone call after him out on the street, he would wave hello to show what a good sport he was. It was the easiest thing to do, so he did it. Then the easiest thing was to pretend that he was hearing things, to realize that it was happening in a world that didn't exist. They had mistaken impersonation for confession and were calling out to a character who lived in a book. Zuckerman tried taking it as praise—he had made real people believe Carnovsky real too—but in the end he pretended he was only himself, and with his quick, small steps hurried on.

Twelve years later, in his new book ***Operation Shylock,*** Roth pretends he is only himself, and then doubles the pretense. We are given two fictional characters calling themselves Philip Roth, the as it were original Philip Roth and an impostor, who has arrived in Jerusalem usurping the novelist's identity in order to advance a counter-Zionist movement, a "new Diasporism" that urges Ashkenazi Israelis to return to their countries of origin, particularly in Europe. This idea, one of Roth's grand inventions, reminds me of Saki's short story "The Unrest-Cure," where an Unrest-cure could be defined as the equivalent of preaching Diasporism in Jerusalem:

> Well, you might stand as an Orange Candidate for Kilkenny, or do a course of district visiting in one of the Apache quarters of Paris, or give lectures in Berlin to prove that most of Wagner's music was written by Gambetta; and there's always the interior of Morocco to travel in. But, to be really effective, the Unrest-cure ought to be tried in the home.

Roth's career as a novelist has been one long Unrest-cure, in this sense, and has been tried in the home, if we take that home metaphorically as being the Jewish situation or condition. He has made himself the issue, the novelist as scapegoat, accused of Jewish self-hatred by Jews so defensive that they can't bear any criticism, however accurate or well-intentioned. It is rather late in the day for a Jewish writer to present himself as a moral prophet, but in his books Roth has dared to do so, making moral judgments on the relationship between parents and children, husbands and wives and lovers, and he has thus earned a lifetime of unrest. Indeed his new novel seems the apotheosis of a Jewish Unrest-cure.

Having endured so many unkind readings, Roth the novelist responded by making the entire Zuckerman saga his own ordeal, the saga of the novelist's travail at suffering his critics. This might have been intolerable had Roth forgotten or lost his comic gift, the uniquely painful laughter that he specializes in provoking. Poor Nathan Zuckerman going from scrape to disaster induces hilarity in us even as we wince at the humiliations that we endure with him, since his wounded dignity becomes our own.

Whether ***Operation Shylock*** marks the ultimate replacement of Zuckerman by "Philip Roth," his successor in the new novel is a much livelier fellow than the author of *Carnovsky.* Compared to the authentic "Philip Roth" (not the impostor) of ***Operation Shylock,*** the Zuckerman of ***The Counterlife, The Anatomy Lesson,*** etc., was more passive and conventional. Women thrust themselves on the hapless Zuckerman. He is besieged by nearly everyone he encounters, and responds ineffectually. But "Philip Roth," in ***Operation Shylock,*** is far more aggressive. Moreover, by narrowing the gap between author and protagonist (though the gap is certainly, as it has to be, still there), Roth the novelist has been able to create his most vivid character: fiercely comic, exuberant, stubbornly reasonable and unreasonably stubborn, lucid *in extremis,* above all immensely curious, about others as well as about himself.

It is irrelevant to accuse a comic genius of self-centeredness, whether the specialist in the aesthetics of outrage is W. C. Fields or Roth. The humorist, in portraying himself, gives us an exemplary figure, the person whose stance says: "We are here to be insulted." To that extent, ***Operation Shylock***'s "Philip Roth" is a descendant of the greatest of fictive humorists, Sir John Falstaff, who is there to be insulted and to return more, and more wittily than he receives. More than any other figure in literature, Falstaff is so intelligent a comedian that even his throwaway lines compel us to deep, prolonged meditation. So, too, Roth's new novel offers perspectives that are intensely serious.

Still, he has not written *Operation Falstaff,* but ***Operation Shylock,*** and the Jewish image, as always, remains his central concern. One of the throwaway phrases in ***The Counterlife*** is "Jews, who are to history what Eskimos are to snow." Roth's perspective has always been that of the endless blizzards of Jewish history. ***Portnoy's Complaint*** remains wonderfully funny on rereading, and is anything but a period piece. What is transparent is that book's willing and positive Jewishness; as much as ***Patrimony*** (1991), an account of his father's long dying, it is also a testament to the painful love for one's parents. The sorrows and absurdities of love—familial, personal, or for a people—have been Roth's true subject ever since. We do not expect a fierce satirist of Jewish life to be motivated by love for his targets, but that seems to me the innermost meaning of Roth's new novel.

In its first sentence ***Operation Shylock*** thrusts us into the midst of things, with a reference, dated January 1988, to the Jerusalem trial of John Demjanjuk, alleged by the Israeli prosecution to be the notorious Ivan the Terrible, the vicious guard of the Treblinka death camp. The pathos of the State of Israel, its salient feature to many Jews of the Diaspora, is certainly present in this novel, with its reminders of Holocaust horrors. But equally present are the harsh equivocations that seem to some necessary for the survival of the state, at least in its present boundaries. The hypocrisies and brutalities of Israeli policy toward the Palestinians emerge with frightening vividness in ***Operation Shylock,*** which nevertheless balances the hypocrisies and brutalities with a sense of the Israelis' desperation for survival. What emerges from Roth's novel is the terrible paradox that Israel is no escape from the burdens of the Diaspora.

Roth begins his "confession" (the book's subtitle) with the shock at being told of "the other Philip Roth" who is in Jerusalem to mount a crusade promoting "Diasporism: The Only Solution to the Jewish Problem." Rather than madden both myself and the readers of this review, I refer to the author of ***Operation Shylock*** as Roth, the central character in the novel as "Philip Roth," and the impostor as Moishe Pipik, the name assigned to him by "Philip Roth" in the book.

Moishe Pipik (Moses Bellybutton) is the eternal Yiddish little shot wishing to be a big shot. A rather shady private detective, Pipik longs for the worldly success of the author of ***Portnoy's Complaint*** and its successors. Unable to emulate his hero as a writer, the impostor chooses outrageous action. Pipik, in "Philip Roth's name, has secured an appointment with Lech Walesa, and has sold the Polish leader on his plan to persuade hordes of Jews voluntarily to return to Poland, traditional paradise for Jews! But even that is only a particle of Pipik's mad design. He is also the founder of Anti-Semites Anonymous, an organization which, like its model, urges its potential members to abstain from their addiction, while simultaneously recognizing that they are incurable.

Pipik is "Philip Roth" 's antithetical shadow: he looks like his original, dresses like him, has studied every mannerism, researched minutely the writer's childhood history. Uncanny as this is, it is persuasive, if only because "Philip Roth" frequently confides in us his worries that he is still in a state of Halcion-induced nervous breakdown. The theme of the double, which Poe handled without humor in "William Wilson," Roth treats both as Kafkan hallucination and as an American-Jewish comedy, set in Jerusalem during the hallucinatory trial of the supposed Ivan the Terrible of Treblinka.

What fascinates about ***Operation Shylock*** is the degree of the author's experimentation in shifting the boundaries between his life and his work. It may even be that Roth has succeeded in inventing a new kind of disciplined bewilderment for the reader, since it becomes difficult to hold in one's head at every moment all of the permutations of the Rothian persona.

One sees now that the crossing-point in Roth's career was ***The Counterlife,*** in which Zuckerman, the novelist, and his brother, who has fled his American family to settle in Israel, turn upon each other in a debate over whose life it was anyway, and who was stealing the other's identity. Whether or not Roth decides to bind his last four books together, they clearly are a tetralogy in which the novelist presents himself, along with his antithetical double or shadow self, as two opposing natures implacably set against each other. ***The Facts*** (1988), an ostensible autobiography centering upon Roth's education as a novelist, annoyed me when it first came out. It seemed to be what Roth's harshest critics consider his work to be: too clever, self-obsessed, a narcissistic reverie, but after ***Operation Shylock,*** I see that I misread it.

In its final section, ***The Facts*** explodes into a protest by Nathan Zuckerman against his author. Roth gets nearly five times the space for his narrative that Zuckerman gets for a reply, yet the fictional character's thirty-five pages are the most memorable in the book, since Zuckerman may not match Roth in intellect, but overdoes him as a rhetorician of outrage. This outrage is a direct expression of his fear that he may cease to exist if his portrayer turns to explicit autobiography. Urging against publication of ***The Facts,*** Zuckerman points to an apparent weakness in Roth's work that ***Operation Shylock*** has, I believe, transcended:

> As for characterization, you, Roth, are the least completely rendered of all your protagonists. Your gift is not to personalize your experience but to personify it, to embody it in the representation of a person who is *not* yourself. You are not an autobiographer, you're a personificator. . . . My guess is that you've written metamorphoses of yourself so many times, you no longer have any idea what *you* are or ever were. By now what you are is a walking text.

That last sentence spoken by character to author is nervy enough, but all of Zuckerman's letter seethes with the anxiety of a walking text that is about to be replaced; it is a fierce plea that cries out: Don't kill me!

The "Philip Roth" of ***Operation Shylock*** happily turns out to resemble Roth less than Zuckerman did. Indeed, "Philip Roth" is, I think, Roth's most vivid character, surpassing Portnoy, Tarnopol, the protagonist in ***My Life as a Man,*** Kepesh, who is the professor in ***The Professor of Desire,*** and the long-suffering and charmingly manic Zuckerman. I suspect that much of the reason for this is the presence of Moishe Pipik, the double, the not-so-secret sharer. With Pipik to fend off, "Philip Roth" is given a target, and thus the scope to become the fullest of Roth's characters in the variety of his sympathies. The initial pleasures a reader will take in this book will be its narrative exuberance, moral intelligence, and the high humor manifested throughout. But the most vivid impression, after several rereadings, is of the voice of "Philip Roth."

The theme of the double, which Poe handled without humor in "William Wilson," Roth treats in *Operation Shylock* both as Kafkan hallucination and as an American-Jewish comedy.

—Harold Bloom

Moishe Pipik, the double, has a remote ancestor in Alvin Pepler, the discredited TV quiz-kid who plagued the hero of ***Zuckerman Unbound*** by alternately praising and attacking him as the celebrated author of *Carnovsky.* In Pipik, Roth deliberately creates a more Dostoevskian double, at once in love with the idea of "Philip Roth," and helpless to cease his persecution of the writer. Pipik is a zealot, a terminal cancer patient in remission, and something of an idealistic thug. Both of his mad crusades, "Diasporism" and "Anti-Semites Anonymous," are animated by nightmare intimations of a ghastly double scenario: an all-out attack upon Israel by the entire Muslim world, and the inevitable reaction of the Israeli Doomsday Machine, its extensive nuclear arsenal.

Hovering behind Pipik is, of course, the shadow of Jonathan Pollard, the American Jew who spied for Israeli intelligence. But in the tangles of Roth's plot, it is not Pipik who is a Mossad agent, as might be suspected. It is "Philip Roth" who performs that role, in the Mossad's "Operation Shylock," whose purpose is to search out supposed secret American-Jewish financial backers of the Palestine Liberation Organization. Diasporism is Roth's pretext for the operation, and it spurs "Philip Roth" to manic impersonations of Pipik, which invariably improve upon the fantasies of the double who is being redoubled:

> No, I didn't stop for a very long time. On and on and on, obeying an impulse I did nothing to quash, ostentatiously free of uncertainty and without a trace of conscience to rein in my raving. I was telling them about the meeting of the World Diasporist Congress to take place in December, fittingly enough in Basel, the site of the first World Zionist Congress just ninety years ago. At that first Zionist Congress there had been only a couple of hundred delegates—*my* goal was to have twice that many, Jewish delegations from every European country where the Israeli Ashkenazis would soon resume the European Jewish life that Hitler had all but extinguished. Walesa, I told them, had already agreed to appear as keynote speaker or to send his wife in his behalf if he concluded that he could not safely leave Poland. I was talking about the Armenians, suddenly, about whom I knew nothing. "Did the Armenians suffer because they were in a Diaspora? No, because they were *at home* and the Turks moved in and massacred them *there.*" I heard myself next praising the greatest Diasporist of all, the father of the new Diasporist movement, Irving Berlin. "People ask where I got the idea. Well, I got it listening to the radio. The radio was playing 'Easter Parade' and I thought, But this is Jewish genius on a par with the Ten Commandments. God gave Moses the Ten Commandments and then He gave to Irving Berlin 'Easter Parade' and 'White Christmas.' The two holidays that celebrate the divinity of Christ—the divinity that's the very heart of the Jewish rejection of Christinity—and what does Irving Berlin brilliantly do? He de-Christs them both! Easter he turns into a fashion show and Christmas into a holiday about snow. Gone is the gore and the murder of Christ—down with the crucifix and up with the bonnet! *He turns their religion into schlock.* But nicely! Nicely! So nicely the goyim don't even know what hit 'em. They love it. *Everybody* loves it. The Jews especially. Jews loathe Jesus. People always tell me Jesus is Jewish. I never believe them. It's like when people used to tell me Cary Grant was Jewish. Bull*shit.* Jews don't want to *hear* about Jesus. And can you blame them? So—Bing Crosby replaces Jesus as the beloved Son of God, and the Jews, *the Jews,* go around whistling about Easter! And is that so disgraceful a means of defusing the enmity of centuries? Is anyone really dishonored by this? If schlockified Christianity is Christianity cleansed of Jew hatred, then three cheers for schlock. If supplanting Jesus Christ with snow can enable my people to cozy up to Christmas, then let it snow, let it snow, let it snow."

Here the voices of Roth and of "Philip Roth" fuse together. The irony cuts every which way, both celebrating and eviscerating the America of schlock, Gentile and Jewish.

When this mock-tirade reaches its apotheosis, there is something to offend nearly everyone, particularly Jews. "Better Irving Berlin than Ariel Sharon. Better Irving Berlin than the Wailing Wall. Better Irving Berlin than Holy Jerusalem! What does owning *Jerusalem,* of all places, have to do with being Jews in 1988?" This perhaps is "Philip Roth" disengaging from Roth, while surpassing Moishe Pipik in a Diasporism even more extreme than his.

Roth's comic art in ***Operation Shylock*** is an aesthetic leap beyond the complexities of ***The Counterlife*** in projecting alternate, shifting realities. What are the limits of Roth's assault on the imagination in ***Operation Shylock?*** One even begins to wonder whose photograph frowns at us on the dust jacket. Is it Roth or Moishe Pipik or "Philip Roth"? There is not an iota of difference in the quality of portraiture, in the novel, between Roth's friend, the Israeli novelist Aharon Appelfeld, and Appelfeld's foil or double, the Holocaust survivor, "Philip Roth" 's cousin Apter. Yet while Appelfeld is a real person and Apter is only a convincing fiction, Apter is in Roth's pages as strong a presence as Appelfeld. ***Operation Shylock*** ends with a "Note to the Reader" whose final sentence is: "this confession is false," but we are left uncertain just how false it is.

Both Moishe Pipik and "Philip Roth" are preoccupied with the still undecided case of Ivan the Terrible's true identity, itself a reflection of thematic doubling carried over into terrible reality. Roth in his mock preface speaks of "agreeing to undertake an intelligence-gathering operation for Israel's foreign intelligence service, the Mossad," clearly part of the fiction, but shifts abruptly to fact, to the case of John Demjanjuk who has been confused with Ivan Marchenko, the likely real Ivan the Terrible of the Treblinka death camp. Yet Roth adds the further detail: Demjanjuk continues to maintain his total innocence, even though German federal archives prove that he was in fact a guard at the Sobibor concentration camp. However the Marchenko/Demjanjuk case pending before the Israeli Supreme Court is decided, Roth here reinforces his theme of the ambivalence of guilt, even as he also selectively records the events of the Demjanjuk trial, and something of its impact upon Israel.

Moishe Pipik is a somewhat shadowy character, whose lifelong compulsion to become Philip Roth is not adequately explained. Doubles and secret-sharers vex all novelists and story-writers, if only because their quests necessarily involve either forsaking their own identities or an initial, perhaps preternatural, lack of any identity whatever. Pipik is something of the self-hating Jew or Jewish anti-Semite that Roth himself was accused of being in the bad old days. The other founding member of Pipik's Anti-Semites Anonymous is his girlfriend and nurse, a Polish-American enchantress named "Jinx" Possesski. As with Saul Bellow's female characters, Roth's tend not to be very convincing, and Jinx alas is no exception.

Indeed, the most successful characterizations in the novel, after that of the outraged and outrageous "Philip Roth," are not of his double and the double's girlfriend, but of the Palestinian and Israeli antagonists, emblematically presented as George Ziad, "Philip Roth" 's old friend from the University of Chicago Graduate School, and the Mossad officer Smilesburger. Ziad, who is evidently connected with the Palestine Liberation Organization, has an eloquence in his anti-Israeli harangues that rivals even as it satirizes much that I have read by champions of the Palestinian cause:

> These victorious Jews are terrible people. I don't just mean the Kahanes and the Sharons. I mean them *all,* the Yehoshuas and the Ozes included. The good ones who are against the occupation of the West Bank but not against the occupation of my father's house, the "beautiful Israelis" who want their Zionist thievery and their clean conscience too. They are no less superior than the rest of them—these beautiful Israelis are even *more* superior. . . . Who do they think they are, these provincial nobodies! Jailers! This is their great Jewish achievement—to make Jews into jailers and jetbomber pilots! And just suppose they were to succeed, suppose they were to win and have their way and every Arab in Nablus and every Arab in Hebron and every Arab in the Galilee and in Gaza, suppose every Arab in the world, were to disappear courtesy of the Jewish nuclear bomb, what would they have here fifty years from now? A noisy little state of no importance whatsoever. That's what the persecution and the destruction of the Palestinians will have been for—the creation of a Jewish Belgium, without even a Brussels to show for it.

Ziad, driven to the verge of breakdown by Israeli oppression, is without parallel in Roth's earlier work. For the first time, we are given a character who suffers outrageous treatment but who is not Roth's surrogate. Ziad's passion, his extraordinary command of irony, go beyond Portnoy's and Zuckerman's in their more domestic and self-deceived struggles for survival. Except for "Philip Roth," Ziad is ***Operation Shylock***'s most sympathetic character, more so than the ambiguous Smilesburger, who preaches against strife and slander between Jews, but is also a relentless representative of the Mossad. Smilesburger, although he is a humane and lucid critic of Jewish self-hatred, Jewish self-love, and Jewish feuding, and is keenly aware of Israeli injustice toward the Palestinians, is not in the least inhibited by the sufferings of his victims.

The contrast between Ziad and Smilesburger grants the Arab the pathos and the Israeli a subtle combination of pragmatic ruthlessness and wasted wisdom. Yet Roth is again exploiting the thematic ambivalence that governs his book, since the reader surmises that there is another doubling here. Ziad and Smilesburger, PLO and Mossad, are caught in the dialectic of becoming what each beholds in the other. Smilesburger becomes more passionately inclined to outflank the Palestinians, and Ziad is trapped in fantasies of violent revenge. Neither can attain an unambivalent understanding of the other's dilemma.

The epigraphs to ***Operation Shylock*** are from the Yahwist or J writer, the first authors in the Hebrew Bible, and from Kierkegaard, the two great ironic masters of primal ambivalence. "So Jacob was left alone, and a man wrestled with him until daybreak." I read that "man" as the Angel of Death, who represents the possible fate that Jacob fears to confront at the hands of his vengeful brother, Esau. Perhaps Pipik after all is an Esau, and precisely such a threat for Philip Roth. "The whole content of my being shrieks in contradiction against itself," writes Kierkegaard, who adds: "Existence is surely a debate." "Against itself" is Roth's reading of his own nature, of his art, and of life.

Shylock is introduced into the novel by David Supposnik, Tel Aviv rare book dealer and possible Shin Bet (Internal Security) agent. Supposnik, like Aharon Appelfeld a Holocaust survivor, associates "this modern trial of the Jew, this trial which never ends, . . . with the trial of Shylock." Roth employs Supposnik to cast aside Romantic and modern emphases on the supposed pathos of Shylock, and thus to return us to the stage Jew's "overwhelming Shakespearean reality, a terrifying Shakespearean aliveness." As Supposnik accurately says, because of Shylock: "the savage, repellent, and villainous Jew, deformed by hatred and revenge, entered as our doppelgänger into the consciousness of the enlightened West."

As the ultimate Jew, Shylock has caused immeasurable harm. It is refreshing to hear Supposnik's repudiation of nineteenth- and twentieth-century sentimentalizing of Shakespeare's farcical villain:

> The Victorian conception of Shylock, however—Shylock as a wronged Jew rightfully vengeful—the portrayal that descends through the Keans to Irving and into our century, is a vulgar sentimental offense not only against the genuine abhorrence of the Jew that animated Shakespeare and his era but to the long illustrious chronicle of European Jew-baiting. The hateful, hateable Jew whose artistic roots extend back to the Crucifixion pageants at York, whose endurance as the villain of history no less than of drama is unparalleled, the hook-nosed moneylender, the miserly, money-maddened, egotistical degenerate, the Jew who goes to *synagogue* to plan the murder of the virtuous Christian—*this* is Europe's Jew, the Jew expelled in 1290 by the English, the Jew banished in 1492 by the Spanish, the Jew terrorized by Poles, butchered by Russians, incinerated by Germans, spurned by the British and the Americans while the furnaces roared at Treblinka. The vile Victorian varnish that sought to humanize the Jew, to dignify the Jew, has never deceived the enlightened European mind about the three thousand ducats, never has and never will.

Is there a more memorable Jewish character in all of Western literature than Shylock? As a critic, not a novelist, I myself am unhappy at confessing that I do not know a stronger Jewish character than Shakespeare's anti-Semitic creation, who has an existence as convincing as Hamlet or Iago even though compared to Hamlet or Iago he speaks only very few lines. It is worth noting that when the virtuous Antonio, generous Christian, proves the authenticity of his piety by spitting and cursing at the Jew, and when he suggests that Shylock be compelled to convert to the true faith, or else face execution, this was Shakespeare's own quite gratuitous invention, and had no previous part in the pound-of-flesh tradition. The play, honestly interpreted and responsibly performed, as it was not in the recent Broadway production with Dustin Hoffman, would no longer be acceptable on a stage in New York City, for it is an anti-Semitic masterpiece, unmatched in its kind.

The strongest of all writers gave us a portrait never quite to be erased, however stage history and critical revisionism have labored to undo it during the last two centuries. Of all American-Jewish writers, Roth seems to know this best. Shylock, Roth intimates, is every Jew's dreaded double. Supposnik's shrewd and bitter tirade is the prelude to "Operation Shylock" proper, the mission upon which Philip Roth will embark on behalf of his Mossad handler who has taken the code-name of Smilesburger, and which brings the novel to its conclusion. The supposed Mossad operation, whose purpose is to unmask hidden Jewish supporters of the PLO, is clearly a fantastic invention, and Roth has "Philip Roth" refuse us any account of the procedure and details of the mission. The explicit justification given is that "Philip Roth" Mossad handlers have insisted on the omission "for security reasons," and the command is followed by the amateur agent.

But the fictive mission that "Philip Roth" undertakes, to Athens and to another, unnamed, city, is also a response to the potent myth of Shylock. For "Philip Roth" secret sharer is not the wretched Moishe Pipik (who is certainly an anti-Semite, and perhaps not Jewish); it is Shylock. "Philip Roth" says he cannot "name for himself what . . . was impinging on this decision." Was I, he asks, "succumbing . . . to a basic law of my existence, to the instinct for impersonations which I had so far enacted solely within the realm of fiction"? Yet by accepting Smilesburger's proposal, he leaves the reader free, I think, to decide that, for him, it may also be a mission against Jewish self-hatred, just as it is for Smilesburger.

At sixty, and with twenty books published, Roth in ***Operation Shylock*** confirms the gifts of comic invention and moral intelligence that he has brought to American prose fiction since 1959. A superb prose stylist, particularly skilled in dialogue, he now has developed the ability to absorb recalcitrant public materials into what earlier seemed personal obsessions. And though his context tends to remain stubbornly Jewish, he has developed fresh ways of opening out universal perspectives from Jewish dilemmas, whether they are American, Israeli, or European. The "Philip Roth" of ***Operation Shylock*** is very Jewish, and yet his misadventures could be those of any fictional character who has to battle for his identity against an impostor who has usurped it. That wrestling match, to win back one's own name, is a marvelous metaphor for Roth's struggle as a novelist, particularly in his later books, ***Zuckerman Bound***, ***The Counterlife***, and the quasi-tetralogy culminating in ***Operation Shylock***, which form a coherent succession of works difficult to match in recent American writing.

At the book's midpoint, "Philip Roth" says to Pipik, "You could have established a chapter of A-SA right in Vatican City. Meetings in the basement of St. Peter's Church. Full house every night. 'My name is Eugenio Pacelli. I'm a recovering anti-Semite.' Pipik, who sent you to me in my hour of need? Who made me this wonderful gift? Know what Heine liked to say? There is God, and his name is Aristophanes." That is Roth's comic Gospel, too. ***Operation Shylock*** answer to Shakespeare's Shylock is Aristophanes, whose mode of comedy—exuberant, outrageous, hallucinatory—has found in Roth a living master.

Along with being the first international contemporary Jewish novel, *Operation Shylock* is also a brilliant novel of ideas, a distinguished genre that is practiced in the United States today about as widely as the epic poem.

—Ted Solotaroff, in his "The Diasporist," in* The Nation, *7 June 1993.

Jenny Turner (review date 13 May 1993)

SOURCE: "Nicely! Nicely!" in *London Review of Books,* Vol. 15, No. 9, May 13, 1993, pp. 20-1.

[*In the following review, Turner speculates on Roth's motivation for writing* Operation Shylock *and other novels that feature a Philip Roth persona.*]

If you are anything like me, you will find yourself having to fight off a sort of sinking feeling as the new Philip Roth comes thudding into your life. What If A Lookalike Stranger Stole Your Name, Usurped Your Biography, And Went Around The World Pretending To Be You? the jacket flap blares: oh God help us, here we go again. You know there will be a lot of paranoid self-justification, in which the author revisits crimes against Jewry, against wives and against women in general committed in the novels he wrote ten, twenty, thirty years ago. There will be references, veiled or otherwise, to Roth's personal life, to an insurance salesman father and an English actress wife, to a huge heart bypass operation and a beautiful old clapboard hideaway in Connecticut. You know it will be up to some sort of interplay between real life and fiction, author and persona, history and His story. It is as if all that is left for the great American novel to do is to offer up narrative gizmology as a serious contender to portable computer games.

Unlike most of Philip Roth's recent novels, ***Operation Shylock*** does not feature Nathan Zuckerman, the celebrity-writer persona Roth adopted for his fiction from ***The Ghost Writer*** (1979) to ***The Counterlife*** (1987). Instead, ***Operation Shylock*** stars Philip Roth. Only there are two of them. One is Roth the famous and universally admired writer who gets bothered in the streets all the time, who lives in a clapboard hideaway in Connecticut and has an English actress wife called Claire. The other also appears to have the name Philip Roth on his passport, and looks enough like Roth I easily to be mistaken for him. Roth II is an American Jew from Chicago who worked as a private detective until becoming ill with cancer, one symptom of which is that he is prone to delusions—which may make him an even more proficient fictionaliser than is his counterpart the professional writer.

Lured to Israel by the apparition of Roth II, Roth I becomes embroiled in a plot which eventually involves him committing himself to work as an undercover agent for Mossad. Although it is not apparent what exactly his mission is, it has something to do with meeting Yasser Arafat and something to do with a conspiracy of rich Jews which, Mossad believes, funds the Palestinian liberation struggle out of guilt. According to various prefaces and afterwords, this is all completely true. And according to various journalists who have colluded with Roth's publicity in writing about this book before publication, Roth in the flesh and several of Roth's friends have verified it. Thus, as often happens with US fiction (remember the rumours that Thomas Pynchon was really J.D. Salinger under another name?), attention is deflected away from the substantive matter of the novel, and onto various gee-whizz discussions of supposedly Post-Modernist authorial behaviour—the adult version of the Phew-It-Was-Only-A-Dream-Or-Was-It metaphysic beloved of primary-school children.

For once you get into it, however, ***Operation Shylock*** is a much more interesting book than it appears. For when Roth I, the big-shot Jewish-American writer, comes face to face with Roth II, the minor-league Jewish-American shnorrer, it turns out that Roth II has a really big idea up his sleeve, an idea he calls Diasporism. According to Diasporism, the nation-state of Israel is at best a historically expedient construct which has long outgrown its usefulness, at worst a foolish misinterpretation of what it really means to be a Jew and living in the world. Thus all Israelis of Ashkenazi origin are forthwith to be encouraged to return to their ancestral homes in Europe, the better to fulfil their Diasporist destinies. In this way, a greatly reduced Jewish settlement will cease to be a belligerent presence in Palestine. As Roth II keeps pointing out, everybody thought Theodor Herzl was completely mad too, when he convened the first Zionist Congress in 1897.

Roth II has already visited Lech Walesa to discuss his plans, and fully understands that residual anti-semitism in the old Jewish heartlands of Poland, Lithuania, Germany may be a bit of a stumbling block to the peaceful execution of this exodus. Thus he has also set up an organisation called Anti-Semites Anonymous, complete with a 12-point programme aimed at nipping hate-dependency in the bud. He travels with his companion, Jinx Possesski, a Polish-American oncology nurse who used to be a raving anti-semite until she learned to give her life over to a power greater than herself. And he simply adores Roth I because he sees him as a prime example of modern Judaism's best hope, 'a Jew for whom authenticity as a Jew means living in the Diaspora, for whom the Diaspora is the normal condition and Zionism is the abnormality'.

As with the Israeli episodes of ***The Counterlife, Operation Shylock*** is structured as a series of monologues and set-pieces delivered by diversely deranged voices, tenuously linked by the author figure's movements around a crudely sketched-in Middle East. As in ***The Counterlife,*** Roth's imagined Israel is a cross between the *Purgatorio* and a psychotic filmset. But the version of Israel in ***Operation***

Shylock is a deeper and darker hellhole even than that of ***The Counterlife,*** for two main reasons. One, Roth's ostensible reason for being there is to watch Ivan Demjanjuk, a Ukrainian-American car-worker from Cleveland, being tried for war crimes he will have committed if he is proved to have been Ivan the Terrible, the notorious execution-chamber guard of Treblinka. And two, this is the Israel of 1988, the year of its 40th birthday celebrations, and of the brutal suppression of the Intifada.

Some of ***Shylock***'s satirical monologues are souped-up versions of themes Roth has often tackled before. There is Jinx Possesski telling of her past life as a born-again Christian, 'the fucked-up shiksa story, from the Scheherazade of fucked-up shiksas'. There is a phenomenally sly anti-semitic drone masking as a therapy tape from ASA:

> Look at Philip Roth, for God's sake. A real ugly buggy. A real asshole. . . . Now he's coming back into the Jewish fold again because he wants to win the Nobel Prize . . . Roth. Roth is just a fuckin' masturbator, a wanker, man, in the john, whackin' off.

There is a disquisition on Shylock himself. There is a long salt-cod-rabbinical ramble, as told by a Mossad agent, on why Jews must never commit *loshon hora*—viz. the telling of cruel stories against themselves.

Much of the material Roth has gathered into the ***Shylock*** bundle, however, is nothing short of stunning: fiction fulfilling one of its most honourable roles as a series of thought-experiments, giving voice to tangled, emotionally overdetermined ideas and theories that somebody somewhere is bound to be thinking anyway, and which are safer tried out in a novel than unleashed in their inchoate form on the world outside. There is Roth II on Diasporism, a piece of writing which has to be savoured carefully to be believed. There is an extraordinary tract on Jewish self-hatred as delivered by George Ziad, a wealthy Palestinian who has been driven to espouse the Diasporist cause after years spent watching his people being mowed down by Israeli batons and bullets: the unassuageable guilt of the American émigrés who inadvertently abandoned their poor old parents to Hitler; the utopian folly of the *aliyah* people who abandoned their ancestral Yiddish to found the modern Hebrew state. There is Roth himself on the greatest modern prophet of Diasporism, Irving Berlin: 'God gave Moses the Ten Commandments, and then He gave to Irving Berlin "Easter Parade" and "White Christmas". The two holidays that celebrate the divinity of Christ . . . *and he turns their religion into schlock!* But nicely! Nicely! So nicely the goyim don't even know what hit 'em!'

Whether or not these monologues eventually add up to more than the sum of their parts is debatable. For as usual they come embedded in page after page of stuff about writers and writing, tellers and tales, and other boring things like the customary hanky-panky with the fucked-up shiksa. It might be nice if Roth could try for once to do without all this Po-Mo business, but as it was his generation's discovery you can perhaps excuse him for having such an attachment to it. And the same goes for the Lego version of Bakhtinian polyphony by which he manages to write so much and so fiercely about burningly real political issues without ever taking an actual position on anything. Although of course it's Roth's prerogative as author of this novel to keep for himself a cosy little sinecure as the good guy, the fall guy, the one sane consciousness in a landscape littered with clapped-out crazies.

Is Philip Roth telling the truth when he claims already to have been co-opted as an undercover agent of the Zionist state? I would imagine not, and find myself cringing with sympathetic embarrassment at the thought of Roth, sixty-year-old two times winner of the US National Book Award, phoning up journalists, as it seems he really did to the *Independent*'s Mark Lawson, and speaking to them in funny voices. But then again, Roth would not be Roth if he were not clearly a man who knows the value of a gimmick when he sees one.

There are, however, several issues to be discussed around the theme of Roth and his mania for appearing to his audience in his various funny masks. But they are not the ones that people usually get excited about. According to one school of thought, as recently expounded by Mark Lawson, Roth is a gifted comic writer who has self-defeatingly limited the potential scope of his work by abandoning real life to write about celebrity-writer shenanigans, whether under cover of the Nathan Zuckerman persona or that of Roths I and II. Why, Lawson asked, could Roth not have followed John Updike in writing real novels like the *Rabbit* books, featuring a real fellow like Harry Angstrom? 'So if I'd made Zuckerman a Toyota dealer in Pennsylvania I'd've got away with it?' Roth replies. 'I think John is playing a what-if game. Suppose he had stayed in central Pennsylvania, what kind of life would he have had? So, in the Zuckerman books, I said, what if I were a writer. .. ?' Well, exactly, and nice of him to put it so politely.

Roth is not a writer who invents marvellously autonomous little fictional constructs which go on to interact with each other in a drama in which the author pretends to have no part. He is a writer who lets his personality sprawl openly across, through and around his every sentence: a rare gift, and one which, used wisely, can excuse many lapses into bravura and self-indulgence. This is not of course to say that Roth is necessarily any more 'honest' a writer than are those who choose to build tighter, more deliberately metaphorical fictions, only that he is working on a different plane of illusion. However, within even the world of recent Jewish-American letters, it is interesting to compare the impact of Roth's work with that of his polar opposite, Bernard Malamud. Nobody could accuse Malamud's tight and perfect fables of anything in the slightest bit crude or vulgar or self-advertising. Roth himself admitted as much in ***The Ghost Writer***, whose meta-hero, the saintly E. L. Lonoff, was read by most readers as a projection of Malamud-envy.

With hindsight and changing times, however, it becomes difficult to look at the cut-off self-enclosed worlds of Malamud's tales and see much going on other than a rather precious sort of Jewish-American kitsch. But Roth, even in his most slapdash and disappointing books, has the intimacy to reach a reader's heart, the force to bounce around and about the world outside the text. Roth, in other words, has *voice.* And Roth being Roth, he has defined this quality perfectly himself, as 'something that begins around the back of the knees and reaches well above the head'—the very words used by the noble Lonoff to encourage a neurotic young novelist in ***The Ghost Writer,*** the first of Philip Roth's famous Zuckerman books.

Everybody who reads Roth's work has something to say about the vexed Roth-Zuckerman relationship. But it isn't clear why everyone feels the need to make such a big deal of it. Pretty well all writers use personae of one sort or another; pretty well all fictional centres of consciousness represent their author's experience in some transformation or another. Imagine Kafka being invaded in Jewish Writers' Heaven by journalists wanting to know why he called his hero K in not one but two novels, and whether or not he had ever really turned into a giant insect! Writers use personae in order to access aspects of their minds unavailable to them except by underhand means. Whatever the subterfuge, it is used to outwit the policemen of the unconscious, and not to pull the wool over trusting readers' eyes.

There is no great mystery to Nathan Zuckerman. His usefulness and significance stare readers in the face. He is the device which has allowed Philip Roth, the self-hating Jewish-American assimilationist who can never take anything seriously, to dig deep into the ramifications of the Jewish experience yawning out in all directions beyond his Forties boyhood hometown of Newark, New Jersey. The first Zuckerman book, ***The Ghost Writer,*** allowed Roth to meet up with the archetypally irreproachable Jewish writer he in some ways seems to wish he was, the Malamud-Bashevis Singer cross that he called E. L. Lonoff. And ***The Ghost Writer*** also saw Roth first come face to face in fiction with the European Holocaust. It was the Zuckerman mask again that gave Roth the courage to take on contemporary Israel in ***The Counterlife,*** a novel which, like ***Operation Shylock,*** goes crashing around the country—an ideological bull in a china shop.

Under the fairly transparent cover of his various fictional masks. Philip Roth is doing one of the most ordinary things a person can ever do as he reaches maturity. He is digging deep into his ancestral fold. Moreover, he is doing it with the urgency of a man who, as he never ceases reminding us, has recently experienced two nasty brushes with his own mortality: when he underwent quintuple heart bypass surgery in 1989, as described in the memoir he wrote about his father, ***Patrimony*** (1991); and, as terrifyingly delineated in the opening chapter of ***Operation Shylock,*** in 1987, when a routine course of the now notorious soporific Halcion threw him headlong into a suicidal depression. Some readers seem to think it funny that Roth spends so much time telling them intimate things about his personal life. But really, the only joke is that a writer who spends most of his time showing himself to be just as attached as is the next guy to his parents, his brother Sandy, his English actress wife, his culture, his body, is treated like some sort of weirdo just because he likes to liven up his anecdotes with a bit of psychosexual hanky-panky and a few unexceptionally skilful authorial pranks.

Philip Roth is an artist whose imagination is inspired and structured by his sense of his own family history. He has never pretended to be anything other than a bright and ambitious lower-middle-class boy of Galician origin born in 1933 in Newark, New Jersey, and at bottom that is what he remains. The problem which motivates his fiction, however, is that it is not easy these days for liberal Diaspora Jews to figure out where exactly their ancestral fold belongs. Back in southern Poland, perhaps, in a nice little condo within easy reach of the Auschwitz railway junction. In a suburb of the new Jerusalem, seized from Egypt in 1967 and kept out of Arab hands only by force? In one of the Jewish retirement enclaves in Florida or someplace, where a sense of communal identity can be kept up only by clinging to an ill-remembered past? The urgency that is driving Roth to return in his writing to the Jewish past, and via Diasporism, to searching for a good sense of potential Jewish futures, is not only personal, but one of explosive political import.

Within a few decades, the Nazi Holocaust will have passed out of living memory. If the world were ever to have been able to wrest some sort of a positive from its experience and memory, there is ample evidence around that the opportunity has been missed. Headline-grabbing comparisons of Serbs to Nazis, or of Israel to the Final Solution, suggest only that some journalists will stop at nothing to make cheap thrills out of mass brutality while everybody else continues to do nothing. In the cultural sphere, writers of the post-war generation are starting to mess around with the image and memory of the Holocaust in a cavalier fashion that would have been unimaginable ten or twenty years ago: Martin Amis in *Time's Arrow,* D. M. Thomas in his recent *Pictures from an Exhibition,* the now banned British comic book, *Lord Horror.* In the States, businessmen are busily attempting to buy up bits of the Polish concentration camps in order to open Holocaust theme-parks.

Nobody, least of all Philip Roth himself, would pretend that Philip Roth, either I or II, has got to grips with the full dimension and scope even of the problems facing the Jewish people across the world towards the end of the 20th century, let alone any realistic solutions. Nobody, least of all Philip Roth himself, would ever expect him to: one of his most likeable qualities as a leading great American novelist across the years has been a calm and lucid refusal ever to make overblown claims as to what imaginative writing can be expected to do. Roth has never been particularly hot on practical politics, but in a way that is all to the good for his writing. It makes him stick with the stuff he really knows. However, as a quick glance through the essays and talks collected in ***Reading Myself and Others*** (1975, expanded 1985) will show, this is not to say that Roth is exactly an ivory-tower type mouthing off into hyperspace. For an anti-semitic self-hating rebel, jumped-up intellectual and shiksa-chaser, he appears to have been doing rather a lot of talks for Jewish community organisations, like the B'nai B'nth Anti-Defamation League, and he appears, moreover, to have been doing this sort of thing long before thoughts of heart attacks or the Nobel Prize could have sent him skittering back to the ancestral fold.

Philip Roth remains at bottom a deeply domestic novelist. He is uncomfortable in the savage arena that is Israel, and in great measure this explains the lapses and longeurs which bring ***Operation Shylock*** several times close to banality and boredom. That he has taken this risk suggests that he has taken on board the fact that to talk about a future, or even of a present, for the sort of comic Diaspora culture he most enjoys involves a confrontation with the fact of Israel. It is the fiction writer's prerogative that he can pretend to have discussed things which in real life remain almost entirely unaddressed.

FURTHER READING

Criticism

Brookhiser, Richard. "The Gripes of Roth." *National Review* XLV, No. 6 (29 March 1993): 68-9.

Unfavorable assessment of *Operation Shylock.*

Fein, Esther B. "Philip Roth Sees Double, And Maybe Triple, Too." *The New York Times* (9 March 1993): C13, C18.

Feature article based on an interview in which Roth discusses *Operation Shylock* and the Jewish-American novel.

Gray, Paul. "A Complaint: Double Vision." *Time* 141, No. 10 (8 March 1993): 68, 70.

Favorable assessment of *Operation Shylock* in which Gray contends that the "social and historical range of *Operation Shylock* is broader than anything the author has attempted before."

Halkin, Hillel. "How to Read Philip Roth." *Commentary* 97, No. 2 (February 1994): 43-8.

Presents an overview of Roth's works and suggests that the key to interpreting *Operation Shylock* is related to Roth's habitual blending of truth and fiction.

Kakutani, Michiko. "Of a Roth Within a Roth Within a Roth." *The New York Times* (4 March 1993): C17, C23.

Remarks that although much of the self-absorbed "talk" by the characters in *Operation Shylock* is "brilliantly rendered . . . it throws the book off balance, undermining its ingenious but fragile plot."

Koenig, Rhoda. "Torah de Force?" *New York* 26, No. 10 (8 March 1993): 83-4.

Provides a mixed review of *Operation Shylock.* Koenig faults Roth for taking liberties with the lives of real people in the novel but argues that "*Operation Shylock* is a good deal more vigorous and absorbing than anything Roth has written for a long time."

Louvish, Simon. "Rothology." *New Statesman and Society* 6, No. 247 (9 April 1993): 57.

Questions the validity of the events Roth describes in *Operation Shylock.*

Rubin, Merle. "Ironies within Ironies." *The Christian Science Monitor* (29 April 1993): 11.

Describes *Operation Shylock* as "an ongoing argument that its author is having with himself" and comments on the question of the novel's factuality.

Thomas, D. M. "Face to Face with His Double." *The New York Times Book Review* (7 March 1993): 1, 20-1.

Favorable review in which Thomas compares Roth's use of the double in *Operation Shylock* to that of Alexander Pushkin in his "Egyptian Nights."

Additional coverage of Roth's life and career is contained in the following sources published by Gale Research: *Bestsellers 1990,* No. 3; *Concise Dictionary of American Literary Biography, 1968-1988; Contemporary Authors,* Vols. 1-4, rev. ed.; *Contemporary Authors New Revision Series,* Vols. 1, 22, 36; *Contemporary Literary Criticism,* Vols. 1, 2, 3, 4, 6, 9, 15, 22, 31, 47, 66; *Dictionary of Literary Biography,* Vols. 2, 28; *Dictionary of Literary Biography Yearbook 1982; DISCovering Authors; Major 20th-Century Writers;* and *World Literature Criticism.*

Anna Deavere Smith
Twilight: Los Angeles, 1992

Award: OBIE Award for Best New American Play

Born in 1950, Smith is an American playwright and performer.

INTRODUCTION

Twilight (1993) is comprised of excerpts from interviews Smith conducted with numerous people following the April 1992 race riots in Los Angeles. The disturbance began after four white police officers who had been accused of severely beating a black man, Rodney King, were legally acquitted of any wrongdoing. The following uproar, which lasted for five days, resulted in widespread violence and looting throughout the city. In what is often referred to as her "one-woman show," Smith re-enacts many of the 175 interviews she conducted with various participants, protagonists, and bystanders. Smith performs the words of each character verbatim, assuming over twenty personas over the length of the play. Notable among these are former Los Angeles Police Department chief Daryl F. Gates, who was blamed for willfully ignoring the widespread violence; truck driver Reginald O. Denny, a white man who was severely beaten during the riots; and Maria, a member of the federal civil-rights jury which ultimately found the officers guilty. While *Twilight,* which is part of Smith's *On the Road: A Search for American Character* series, has sometimes been regarded more as a work of documentary than of theater, Smith has garnered much praise for her moving, thought-provoking, and realistic depiction of the social and psychological effects of the race riots on a diverse segment of Los Angeles's population. Critic Greg Evans has hailed Smith as a "profound talent" who "gives absolutely equitable and eloquent voice to the myriad communities touched by the riots and to individuals who otherwise would go uncounted."

PRINCIPAL WORKS*

On the Road, New York City (drama) 1982
Aunt Julia's Shoes (drama) 1983
Aye, Aye, Aye, I'm Integrated (drama) 1984
Charlayne Hunter Gault (drama) 1984
Building Bridges Not Walls (drama) 1985
On the Road: ACT (drama) 1986
Chlorophyll Post-Modernism and the Mother Goddess: A Convers/Ation (drama) 1988
Voices of Bay Area Women (drama) 1988
Gender Bending: On the Road Princeton University (drama) 1989
From the Outside Looking In (drama) 1990
Gender Bending: On the Road University of Pennsylvania (drama) 1990
On Black Identity and Black Theatre (drama) 1990
Fragments (drama) 1991
Identities Mirrors and Distortions I (drama) 1991
Identities Mirrors and Distortions II (drama) 1991
Identities Mirrors and Distortions III (drama) 1991
Identities Mirrors and Distortions IV (drama) 1991
Fires in the Mirror: Crown Heights, Brooklyn and Other Identities (drama) 1992
Twilight: Los Angeles, 1992 (drama) 1993

*All of the works listed here, except *Aye, Aye, Aye, I'm Integrated,* are part of Smith's *On the Road: A Search for American Character* series.

CRITICISM

Anna Deavere Smith with Steve Proffitt (interview date 11 July 1993)

SOURCE: An interview in *Los Angeles Times,* July 11, 1993, p. M3.

[*In the interview below, Smith discusses the effects of the 1992 race riots on Los Angeles and her reasons for writing* Twilight.]

One critic calls her the most exciting individual in current American theater. Another complains her work is emotionally unengaging and analytically shallow. She's been praised as a keen social observer of Los Angeles and condemned as an outsider who has exploited the city in tragedy. Whatever their opinions people are talking about Anna Deavere Smith and her one woman show, ***Twilight: Los Angeles, 1992.*** Her performance about the violence following the verdict in the Rodney G King-beating trial completes a five-week run at the Mark Taper next Sunday.

Smith, 42, sprang to prominence last year, with another one-woman show about a racial clash, ***Fires in the Mirror.*** Shortly after the verdict in the first King beating trial, the Taper's artistic director, Gordon Davidson saw her New York Public Theater production about the conflict between Orthodox Jews and African-Americans in the Crown Heights section of Brooklyn. He invited Smith to come to Los Angeles and mount a similar effort. ***Twilight*** is the result of some 175 interviews Smith conducted over a nine-month period with Angelenos whose lives were directly or indirectly touched by the riots.

Smith presents 26 characters—Koreans, African-Americans, Anglos and Latinos. She performs their words verbatim from transcripts of her taped interviews, portraying well-known figures like former LAPD Chief Daryl F. Gates, who complains about being the symbol of police brutality, and ordinary citizens like Elvira Evers, an expectant mother wounded by a gunshot during the violence following the Simi Valley verdict. Smith gives us a human glimpse of truck driver Reginald O. Denny, who describes his early days of recovery after being beaten at the intersection of Florence and Normandie. And she takes us inside the jury room of the federal civil-rights trial as Maria, one of the jurors, gives a humorous and profane accounting of the panel's deliberations.

Smith, born and raised in Baltimore, calls herself, "a repeater rather than a mimic." A 1977 graduate of San Francisco's American Conservatory Theatre, she got an odd lesson in the polities of race when casting agents said she was too light-skinned to play black characters. She soon started writing plays and teaching; in 1983, she began her series of interview-based performances—she calls this work ***On the Road: A Search for American Character.***

Smith currently teaches drama at Stanford, where she often has her students recreate TV talk shows in the verbatim style she uses in ***Twilight.*** She is tall and thin, a strict vegetarian whose face speaks of discipline. In conversation backstage at the Taper, Smith is alternately animated and guarded, at once quick to answer and then cautious, careful in crafting a reply.

. . . . .

[*Proffitt*]: *Do you remember what you were doing, and how you felt when you heard about the verdict in the original Rodney King-beating trial?*

[Smith]: I was in New York, and I was in rehearsal for the opening of ***Fires in the Mirror.*** That means that I was in the theater all the time, in a sort of black box. When I got home from rehearsal, there were all these messages on my machine, from friends, telling me what had happened in Los Angeles. My show was set to open, but we closed down—postponed it—just like everybody else. I was actually kind of glad. It made more sense to go to Times Square and see what was happening than to be performing, so that's exactly what I did.

It's hard to say what my emotional reactions were to the verdict. Just that I wasn't surprised. It was as if the steam had been let out of a high-pressure cooker. You know, I lived here in the late '80s, and taught at the University of Southern California, and I thought that it was such a peculiar environment. I think a lot of L.A. is something like USC—this incredible white culture living in the midst of color, and no obvious reaction to it at all. I mean, they have guards at the gate at USC—guards at the gate of a major university! And the guards chase young black boys away—I've seen it, chasing 8-year-old boys. And I don't think that is organic, or natural or good. So I suppose that the verdict did not surprise me.

When you were asked to come to L.A. and make a performance about the city exploding after the verdict, did you have any hesitation?

No, I didn't hesitate, because my other project had been about a similar situation. I was thinking a lot about race and the differences between people, and I wanted to come, to see the city, to know what happened here.

What did you expect to find here, and what surprised you?

I didn't expect anything. I go in without really knowing. I do what I call a search for discovery of character, which is the stuff you don't know. So I knew very little about the people I interviewed, and that is part of the relationship I developed with them.

I was, however, nervous about my own ethnocentricity, and I was concerned that I would bring to this process a structure of looking at race as only black and white, and I knew intellectually that I wanted to disrupt that. Because the issues in Los Angeles are really about very complicated interactions.

In putting this project together, what disturbed you the most?

What disturbed me and what made me happy at the same time was the degree with which people fall out of language when they try to tell me what happened here two Aprils ago. They don't have words. On the one hand, you say, what kind of education do these people have that they can't talk about race? On the other hand, I'm glad that there isn't a full articulation, because I am distrustful of that. Words can be, as Harold Pinter says, a strategy to cover nakedness. They can get in the way of a full understanding. But there is still something disturbing about otherwise fully educated people who can't talk about questions of race and the differences between people.

Was there anything that gave you reason for hope?

I think just about everyone who I interviewed for this show said something that gave me a glimmer of hope. And the other thing that gives me hope is that so many people want to come and see this show about race and pain—they could just say, "Who wants to bring that up again. Thank God, it was over in five days—why do we have to go through this again?" Because they do come makes me think that people want to know more—they want to revisit it, think about it and they want to change.

You know, Michael Jackson, the radio host, told me that everything in the world is here. If that's the case, then Los Angeles really is the racial frontier, and it can lead the way for the rest of the nation. It can turn pain into gold. It only takes opening hearts and relieving the mind of the work.

You held a number of discussions with audiences after your performances. What went on in those forums—what were people saying about where they want the city to go?

The discussions are important, because my goal is to bring people to the theater who normally wouldn't be in the same room together. It's using theater to create a kind of community. And in my show, people react differently. Sometimes, some people laugh, and others are offended by that laughter—so it's obvious that they are in an environment where people have differing points of view.

It's been lucky here that people don't really want to talk much about the performance—in New York, people always asked about how I learned lines, or dialects. Here in L.A., people get right down to talking about the city, and their lives—which is great. I see the play as a call, and the audience as part of the response to that call.

We had a very interesting post-play discussion a few weeks ago. There were a lot of younger people in the audience, high-school kids. And it was interesting that these young people tended to be much more hopeful than the older people. That's a great sign, because one way of looking at the younger generation is that they are kind of hopeless and in despair, but that doesn't seem to be across-the-board, by any means.

Some people have been critical of this performance, because there is no one in it who seems to have a unifying vision of Los Angeles. Do you think there is anyone in Los Angeles who has that vision?

Have you met anyone who has that vision? When people expect from me this one answer—some single, unifying thing—I feel so bad, because I just don't think that's fully intelligent right now.

You see, my work, at least at this moment, isn't about unifying. A unifying idea is not enough. It's why I don't really put my own point of view into the piece, because once you put forward a powerful voice, be it truth or not, it makes the other voices seem smaller. My work is about giving voice to the unheard, and reiterating the voice of the heard in such a way that you question, or re-examine, what is the truth. And we have to be able to tolerate more than one voice.

My main concern is theater, and theater does not reflect or mirror society. It has been stingy and selfish and it has to do better. And the way to make it better, and to make society better, is not to put out one voice that seems to bring us all together, because we are not all together: We are in fragments. Maybe what we can bring to the world is a society that achieves living together in peace in another way. Maybe this is a time to build bridges between multiple communities, rather than trying to come up with some sort of false unity. You know, interesting minds usually do hold more than one idea at a time.

An excerpt from *Twilight: Los Angeles, 1992*

Anonymous Male Juror "Your Heads in Shame"

As soon as we went
into the courtroom with the verdicts
there were
plainclothes policemen everywhere.
You know, I knew that
there would be people unhappy with the verdict,
but I didn't expect near
what happened,
If I had known
what was going to happen,
I mean, it's not,
It's not fair to say I would have voted a different
way.
I wouldn't have—
that's not our justice system—
but I would have written a note to the judge saying
I can't do this
because of what it put my family through.
We've been portrayed as white racists.
One of the most disturbing things, and a lot of the jurors
said that
the thing that bothered them that they received in the
mail
more
than anything else,
more than the threats, was a letter from the K.K.K.
saying.
We support you, and if you need our help, if you want
to join
our organization,
we'd welcome you into our fold.
And we all just were:
No, oh!
God!

Anna Deavere Smith, in her Twilight: Los Angeles, 1992, *from an excerpt in* The New York Times, *20 March 1994.*

But do you think there is someone—an L.A. messiah if you will—someone who can bring a sense of wholeness to this polyglot community?

I think there are small messiahs, and what we need to do is encourage these people to speak with one another and come out of that meeting with a big picture. We need to get Twilight [a proponent of gang truces] in the same room with [former *Los Angeles Times* publisher] Otis Chandler.

I wish there were a prophet who could touch the hearts of Angelenos in such a way that they would be less afraid of coming out and touching each other. Our institutions have not facilitated the growth of such a person—one who can speak for more than just himself. Nothing is encouraging the growth of that hybrid flower. And what that tells us is that we must prepare—now—so that in 20 years we do have that flower, an individual who can speak more than one language, for more than one type of person.

*The title of your performance—***Twilight***—resonates in a variety of ways. In your show, a character named Twilight talks about that time between the light and dark as being a sort of limbo. Do you see that as a metaphor for this city? Are we in Los Angeles caught between a past we reject and a future we can't quite grasp?*

That's what I'm gathering—that the city is in suspense and in suspension. What's gonna happen next? And not just in Los Angeles. I think American identity is in a kind of limbo right now.

To me, twilight also implies something about seeing and what we have to do to see. In twilight we have to look harder to see. The person named Twilight says that he doesn't think that night and dark are negative, he just thinks they are what comes first. I think that is a gorgeous and hopeful way to look at the dark period we are in now—that this is not negative, it's what comes first. And Twilight goes on to say that he sees the light as the knowledge and wisdom of the world. But almost implied in that is that knowledge alone is not enough.

If I have a single thing to say to the city of Los Angeles while I am here, it's what Twilight says—that to be a full human being, I cannot forever dwell in darkness. I cannot forever dwell in the idea of identifying only with those like me and understanding only my kind. That's the main thing I have to say.

One person at a time, one idea at a time, one temperament at a time, Smith builds up a rich, panoramic canvas of a national trauma.

—David Richards, in his "A One-Woman Riot Conjures Character Amid the Chaos," in* The New York Times, *24 March 1994.

Richard Hornby (review date Autumn 1993)

SOURCE: A review of *Twilight: Los Angeles, 1992,* in *The Hudson Review,* Vol. XLVI, No. 3, Autumn, 1993, pp. 534-35.

[*In the following excerpt, Hornby discusses Smith's performance in* Twilight: Los Angeles, 1992 *and praises the play as a representative example of American regional theater.*]

Twilight, like [***Fires in the Mirror***], deals with urban conflict, in this case the L.A. riots of April 1992. Smith interviewed hundreds of Los Angeleans involved in or affected by the riot (the latter group including almost everybody), and ended up performing 27 of them, including Reginald Denny, Police Chief Daryl F. Gates, and a wide range of others, rich and poor, black, white, Latino, and Asian. Rodney King apparently declined to be included, but his Aunt, Angela King, was interviewed and made the cut, as did an anonymous Simi Valley juror.

As Smith began her performance, I still felt dubious as to the point of it all. Why not simply edit the taped interviews to create a typically earnest PBS show, letting the people speak for themselves? But Smith's style of performance won me over. On the one hand, she does not, like a nightclub impressionist, transform herself totally into each character, but on the other hand, she does not, like a television reporter, just detachedly quote the characters' words. Her performances are fully energized, seeming to be driven from within. Using a simple bit of costume—a baseball cap, a tie, a floral skirt—as an emblem of each person, she reproduces the person's accent, rhythms, and body language, but always remains herself, a tall, striking, but not beautiful black woman. She becomes both herself *and* the character, a perfect example of the kind of "alienated" performance that Brecht called for, making the character distanced, strange, highlighted. The sincere but bland quality that occurs when someone is interviewed on TV was replaced by a heightened resonance; these all-too-familiar Los Angeleans became historic figures.

The historicism was heightened by the scrupulous neutrality that Smith maintained toward the characters, who represented the entire political spectrum. Whether depicting a gun store owner or a gunshot victim, she presented the person's words with complete sincerity, without any comment or non-verbal innuendo. Even her performance of Police Chief Gates, the most lampoonable figure in L.A. history, was simple and affecting. It remained for us, the audience, to ponder these figures and sort out our feelings toward them. The piece became a vehicle for the conception of our crazy city and its troubles, offering no solutions, but exposing all ideologies, confusions, and contradictions. Despite being performed by a single person, ***Twilight*** [is similar to] other historical, regional theatre plays . . . , with a large number of characters, historical scope, and an extroverted acting style. It is yet another example of how regional theatre in American has finally come of age.

Jan Stuart (review date 24 March 1994)

SOURCE: "*Twilight:* Group Therapy for a Nation," in *Newsday,* March 24, 1994.

[*In the following review, Stuart lauds Smith's deft handling of complex characters and situations in* Twilight.]

Toward the end of her heroic docu-theater event about the police beating of Rodney King and its violent aftermath, Anna Deavere Smith does something very, very clever.

Having impersonated dozens of participants in the 1992 Los Angeles maelstrom for some two hours, Smith steps into the shoes of Maria, a juror in the second Rodney King trial. We like Maria. She's theatrical, a spiky, pull-no-punches sort with a few choice words reserved for her fellow jurors. "Brain-dead," for starters.

One by one, Maria takes aim and caricatures each of her colleagues with their psychic pants down, constructing before our eyes a devastating archetype of group dynamics and the tortuous process by which strangers plow beyond their dissimilarities to get something done. Maria's impromptu performance is a panic—cathartically, bust-a-gut funny; as our laughter subsides, it may occur to us that the jury's breakthrough mirrors our own progress as we make our way through ***Twilight: Los Angeles, 1992.***

The Maria monologue, indeed, is a microcosm, a summing-up of the experience of watching this challenging "one-person" show. Following the model of ***Fires in the Mirror,*** Smith's journalistic kaleidoscope of the Crown Heights riots, ***Twilight: Los Angeles, 1992*** distills dozens of interviews she conducted with players in recent events. African- and Asian-American, white, rich, poor, women, men, brain-dead and alive, the contrasting perspectives pile up before us, each of them so steadfastly believing in the correctness of their positions. Well before it's over, we begin to wonder how anything as implicitly harmonious as a verdict is possible in a multicultural soup such as the United States.

The soup thickens as Smith moves away from Crown Heights and into the L.A. of ***Twilight,*** whose ethnic and class tensions reflect the broader spectrum of American culture directly affected by the King beating. The racial cauldron of ***Twilight*** spills over into the shooting of a 15-year-old African-American girl by a Korean-American shopkeeper, as well as the riot attack on white truck driver Reginald Denny that followed the trial of the four officers charged with beating King.

Sliding deftly between interviewees with the suggestive turn of a sweater, Smith lines up her characters in a boldly ironic juxtaposition that recalls the inspired oral histories of Studs Terkel and the political documentaries of Marcel Ophuls. The back-to-back proximity of her subjects provokes two responses: At first we notice the seemingly unbridgeable divide from one monologue to the next; then we are struck by the unexpected bonds. Reginald Denny, sweet-tempered, forgiving, a bit out of it, seems a world away from Paul Parker, the shrewd, rage-driven head of the defense committee for Denny's attackers. As we listen more, we begin to see the synchronicity in their notions of justice; the urgency with which each of them argues their cases is thrilling.

The heightened complexity of Smith's L.A. terrain is matched by a newfound subtlety in her performance (in contrast to George C. Wolfe's booming, projection-happy staging) and a more ambitious use of transcripts. Where ***Fires*** hugged to a formulaic procession of individual arias, ***Twilight*** often splices as many as three witnesses into a seamless rush of testimony, working up a fierce, cinematic intensity.

If Smith occasionally tosses us a few sacrificial lambs for those with the guilty need to feel superior (a braying, face-lifted real-estate agent who hides out at the Beverly Hills Hotel for the duration of the riots), she discourages the easy laugh and the foregone conclusion. Mostly, Smith gets us to listen. She validates, vigorously and humorously, the other side of the coin. She wants us to entertain the possibility of ambiguity.

By the time Maria launches into her tour-de-force vaudeville of a jury's A.A.-style confessional, we understand that we have already witnessed the same process. ***Twilight: Los Angeles, 1992*** is group therapy on a national scale based on the belief that we each have to dump our ugly personal baggage out on the table for all to see, before we can then get down to the difficult business of healing. Smith shows us how to do that with a breathtaking collage of real-life people who make us want to stand up and cheer, then sit back down and reflect.

Michael Feingold (review date 5 April 1994)

SOURCE: "Twilight's First Gleaming," in *The Village Voice,* Vol. XXXIX, No. 14, April 5, 1994, pp. 97, 100.

[*In the following review, Feingold praises Smith both as a performer and as a writer.*]

Roughly 10 minutes into ***Twilight: Los Angeles, 1992,*** Anna Deavere Smith disappears. I can't cite the exact moment; her material's so riveting that you only notice her absence after the fact. The artist, the selecting principle, has gone; what remains onstage is the life of L.A. before, during, and after the riots: men, women, and children, talking in a torrent of diverse languages, living out their anger, their pain, their injuries and resentments and joys and fears. Few stages have ever held such a huge, varied crowd; you meet, if my count is right, 46 people, from senators to gang members, opera stars to truck drivers.

And, aside from a minute flick of her distinguished chin as each new figure begins to speak, you never feel that Smith is manipulating or controlling your encounter with these people; she's mastered the art that conceals art, so that they seem to be talking to you from their hearts. Only the technology encircling her—audio, video, subtitles, shifting projection screens, set pieces that slide discreetly in and out—reminds you now and then that you're watching a show, not seeing an American city spill its guts. The technology stays in the background: With Smith only people matter.

This is, of course, her thesis as well as her aesthetic. Smith the interviewer may exercise an editor's selectivity, balancing points of view, arranging the story so that we see all sides; Smith the actress never tilts this balance, creating the slick excuses of head cop Daryl Gates with the same fullness as the mournful shrugs of Rodney King's aunt. To her, people's hesitations, repetitions, and desk-poundings are evidence, used not to prosecute the individual but to reveal the inner self.

Early on, there's what looks like a caricature of a shrill, silly white woman, the realtor Elaine Young; when a similarly shrill voice and extreme gestures are used later for Elaine Brown, once head of the Black Panther Party, you think, well, maybe these two women are more alike than either of them would suspect. Brown's shrillness doesn't hamper the good sense and compassion of her words; Young's are foolish, but harmless; you think, well, they could easily live in one community, who put so many barriers between them?

Smith carries this notion to the edge: One of the men who attacked Reginald Denny defends his act by bringing up Rodney King: "I wasn't raised to take ass whuppins like that and turn the other cheek." Later, a white female reporter, frenetically showing a tape of Denny's beating over and over, says, "I hate guns, but you know what? If my life is threatened, I'm not even going to hesitate, I'll pull that trigger." In anger as in compassion, the people come to resemble one another. Smith's most remarkable achievement is to make us see their underlying similarities by being so faithful to the differences. Inside the anger and hate, she finds sources of potential community.

Less a city than a centerless mass of urban sprawl, L.A.'s history and geography tell against it: the showbiz excesses of money and social dislocation; the insane disparity between rich and poor; the endless inpouring of people from Mexico, Asia, New York. City of dreams to others, L.A. has always been a secret horror to itself, rife with distrust and denial, snobbery and bigotry. The tales of police brutality go back for decades; even the lawyer for one of Rodney King's assailants has one to tell. Either a nightmare portent of our future, or a dying white elephant from our imperial past, the city sits there, imploding.

Telling the story of the riots from her 46 points of view, Smith in effect shows how to restructure the city: start over with the human factor. She begins as a Korean merchant (in Korean) and ends as a black gang leader discussing a truce. In between we see looters, victims, cops, bystanders, outsiders: A spokeswoman for the family of a black teenager shot by a storekeeper tells her, "Those Koreans all look alike." Rodney King's aunt says, "We were raised with all kinds of friends, Mexicans, Indians, blacks, whites, Chinese . . . Who'd have thought this would happen to us?"

A Latino artist recalls being beaten by cops in the zoot-suit riots of 1942; a white juror in the first trial moans like a stricken dog at having been praised for the verdict by the KKK. A Panamanian woman tells, imperturbably, how she was wounded by a stray bullet and, pregnant, made her way safely to the hospital. (Delivering her baby, doctors removed the bullet from its elbow.) Only moments later, Jessye Norman is there—yes, the svelte Smith, without artifice, plays Jessye Norman—to tell of having passed through L.A. the first day of the riots: "I think that if I were a teenager . . . and I felt I were being heard for the first time, it would not be singing as we know it. It would be a roar . . . it would come from the bottom of my feet."

Smith's triple ability—to evoke such statements, to recreate them so scrupulously, and to sculpt the assemblage so richly—is beyond anything else of its kind. Her inspiration may be the TV news bite; if so, she's a blazing reminder that the theater's not only faster and more vivid than the tube, but cuts deeper and reaches higher. She reaffirms, finally, that human beings are art's first concern, as they have to be a city's. ***Twilight*** is a gleam of hope for both theater and urban life; to watch it is like being present at the renegotiation of our shredded social contract.

Taken as a historical account of a seminal event, *Twilight* is valuable; as a symphony of voices echoing a maddeningly complex society at the end of this century, it is invaluable.

—Greg Evans, in a review of* Twilight: Los Angeles, 1992, *in* Variety, *28 March 1994.

Robert Brustein (review date 2 May 1994)

SOURCE: "P.C.—or Not P.C.," in *The New Republic,* Vol. 210, No. 18, May 2, 1994, pp. 29-31.

[*Brustein is a highly-regarded American drama critic. In the review of* Twilight *below, he comments on Smith's performance, her characterization, and her depiction of the multicultural issues surrounding the riots.*]

The most cogent commentators on our stormy times have unquestionably been not the columnists but the cartoonists, which is another way of noting that representational satire has more capacity than political commentary to relieve the pressures of a fractious age. On stage two inspired performers have recently been offering their own perspectives on the issues that divide us, and while the African American Anna Deavere Smith and the Jewish Jackie Mason seem worlds apart in tone, attitude, focus and ethnicity, they each provide more perspective on the nature of our discords than an army of op-ed pundits.

It is true that Smith might be more accurately described as a sociologist than as a satirist. Both in her previous ***Fires in the Mirror,*** which covered the Crown Heights affair, and in her current piece at the Joseph Papp Public Theater, ***Twilight: Los Angeles, 1992,*** which deals with the riots in South-Central L.A., she has drawn her material from interviews with the actual participants in those events. Still, Smith is not only an objective ear but a characterizing voice, and just as she shapes her text through editing and selection, so she achieves her emphasis through gesture and intonation. During the course of the evening the actress impersonates forty-six different people, capturing the essence of each character less through mimetic transformation, like an actor, than through the caricaturist's body English and vocal embellishments. Just look at her photographs: you'd never guess from any of those contorted head shots that she's an extremely handsome young woman.

Smith's subjects divide essentially into victims, victimizers and viewers, though it is sometimes difficult to determine which is which. If the former L.A. Police Chief Daryl Gates (defending himself against charges that he permitted the riots to rage while attending a fundraiser) and Sergeant Charles Duke (complaining that Officer Lawrence Powell was "weak and inefficient with the baton" because he wasn't allowed to use the "choke-hold") are clearly the patsies of the piece, the rioters, looters, gang members and assailants often appear more sinned against than sinning. A white juror in the first Rodney King trial—asked by a reporter, "Why are you hiding your heads in shame?"—is appalled to receive approving calls from the KKK. Keith Watson, one of those acquitted of beating Reginald Denny, justifies his rage and the burned-out vacant lots by saying "justice didn't work," while Paul Parker, chairperson of the Free the L.A. Four Defense Committee, charges "You kidnapped us, you raped our women . . . you expect us to feel something for the white boy?" One gringo-hating Latino, ranting against the "peckerwoods" and "rednecks" who have persecuted his family, expresses pleasure in the way Mexicans are able to terrify whites. Another Latino is encouraged by a policeman to "go for it, it's your neighborhood." A black woman "touring" in the white neighborhood loots I. Magnin because she finds it "very offensive" that rich stars should feel protected from rioting.

Then there are the other victims: the Asian shopkeepers who, in those tumultuous days, lost 90 percent of their stores and a number of their family members. At the same time that a spokesperson for a young black girl shot by a Korean shopkeeper (who was acquitted) is raging against Asians, Mrs. Young Soon Han, a former liquor store owner, speaks of her disenchantment with blacks. There were none in the Hollywood movies she saw in Korea; she thought this country was the best. Now "they" have destroyed the shops of innocent merchants simply because "we have a car and a house. . . . Where do I find justice? What about victims' rights?" Another store owner, inveighing against shoplifting and looting, remarks, "After that, I really hate this country, I really hate—we are not like customer and owner but more like *enemy.*"

"Enemy" and "hate" are the operative words of ***Twilight.*** With each ethnic group bristling at the other, one might think "cultural diversity" had become a euphemism for race war. A Mexican woman reporter, told her life is in danger, replies: "How could they think I was white?" The African American Parker boasts how "we burnt down the Koreans—they are like the Jews in this neighborhood." And this is countered not by appeals for tolerance but by counsels of caution, like those of Elaine Brown, former

Smith as Angela King, the aunt of Rodney King, in a 1993 production of Twilight.

Black Panther, reminding the gun-brandishing, swashbuckling looters about America's willingness to use its power: "Ask Saddam Hussein."

To judge by the interviews in ***Twilight,*** however, the Los Angeles riots caused a lot of soul-searching, and considerable guilt, among some white Americans. The experience certainly stimulated considerable generosity from Denny, who, pleading for recognition as a person rather than a color, expresses profound gratitude to the black people who risked their lives to save him. By contrast, others, such as a reporter named Judith Tur, wonder why South-Central blacks can't be more like Magic Johnson or Arthur Ashe, adding that "white people are getting so angry, they're going back fifty years." A suburban real estate agent named Elaine Young, who has had thirty-six silicone surgeries on her face, whines that "we don't have the freeway, we can't eat anywhere, everything's closed," meanwhile defending her decision to hole up in the Beverly Hills Hotel.

These are easy targets; and it is true that ***Twilight*** sometimes lacks the dialectical thickness, as well as the surprise and unpredictability, of ***Fires in the Mirror.*** Lasting over two hours, it seems too long *and* too short for its subject. The L.A. riots were a response to violence and injustice by means of violence and injustice, and the paradox still to be explored is how looting and burning Korean stores and destroying your own neighborhood, not to mention racial assaults on innocent people, could become acceptable means of protest against inequity and racism. With most of them still in shock, few of Smith's respondents are in a position to examine the irrationality of such acts unless, like Shelby Coffey, they cite "a vast, even Shakespearean range of motives."

Smith makes some effort to penetrate these motives by ending her piece with a poetic reflection by a gang member on the "limbo" twilight of crack addicts, but the metaphor somehow seems inadequate. Still, if she has not always gone beyond the events of this tragedy, she has powerfully dramatized a world of almost universal tension and hatred. George C. Wolfe's elaborate production, with its videos of King's beating and films of Los Angeles burning, is probably more appropriate for the coming Broadway move than for the stage of the Public. But it leaves us with a shocking sense of how America's hopes for racial harmony were left burning in the ashes of South-Central L.A.

Sean Mitchell (review date 12 June 1994)

SOURCE: "The Tangle over *Twilight,*" in *Los Angeles Times,* June 12, 1994, pp. 7, 48.

[*In the following excerpt, Mitchell discusses the controversy over whether* Twilight *should be characterized as journalism or art.*]

Anna Deavere Smith's one-woman play about the riots, ***Twilight: Los Angeles, 1992,*** now struggling to survive on Broadway after six weeks despite rapturous reviews and standing ovations, could gain additional longevity and respect if it wins either of the two major Tony Awards for which it is nominated tonight in New York.

Since its prominent premiere [in 1993] at the Mark Taper Forum, which commissioned it, ***Twilight*** has been both hailed as a sensational theatrical event and bedeviled by disagreement in the theater community and press as to how it should be measured—whether it is truly a work of the imagination and therefore pure dramatic art, or whether it is a form of journalism as performance art and therefore something less.

The argument was highlighted a few weeks ago when this year's Pulitzer Prize jury in drama disallowed ***Twilight*** for final consideration on the grounds that its language was not invented but gleaned from interviews. That it was even being discussed by the Pulitzer jury was an indication of how high the play had soared in the minds of some critics, while the decision to disqualify it for technical reasons might have been puzzling to anyone aware that the previous year's Pulitzer jury had judged Smith's earlier show ***Fires in the Mirror*** (similarly developed and performed, about ethnic battles in Brooklyn) a legitimate runner-up for the 1992 prize.

The Tony nominating committee evidently had no such qualms about ***Twilight,*** but to further confuse the general public, some will notice that while ***Twilight*** is one of the four Broadway plays up for best play (along with Tony Kushner's *Perestroika,* Robert Schenkkan's *The Kentucky Cycle* and Arthur Miller's *Broken Glass*), the play that won this year's Pulitzer, Edward Albee's *Three Tall Women,* is *not* represented tonight. That's because *Three Tall Women* is playing Off Broadway, and the Tonys stubbornly limit themselves (yes, still) to shows playing inside the geographical boundaries of the historic theater district in houses with at least 500 seats. . . .

[The] debate over ***Twilight's*** worthiness for these traditional honors is not so surprising given that it seems to be a wholly new form, dazzling but unfamiliar—and therefore a challenge and threat to established boundaries of official approbation.

Yet the debate is confounding all the same to those who believe that the first measure of any play or theater work—especially in today's beleaguered theater world—is whether it makes itself felt so strongly that people want to see it. And this certainly was true of ***Twilight*** in Los Angeles, where in its last weeks it broke box-office records for the Taper.

Smith, a San Francisco-based actress, assembled the two-hour piece from 200 tape-recorded interviews she conducted with all manner of people involved in or affected by the three days of violence and civil disturbance that began April 29, 1992. She described the intention of ***Twilight*** as "my search for the character of Los Angeles in the wake of the initial Rodney King verdict."

She revealed that character through her uncanny impersonations of roughly two dozen of the people she had interviewed, stretching her talent for mimicry from the voices of public figures like Reginald O. Denny, Daryl Gates and Stanley Sheinbaum to anonymous citizens white, black and brown. In a series of fast-moving monologues, she painted a swirling collage of a city at war with itself. And she did this, under the circumstances, with a considerable amount of humor and entertainment value.

The effect Smith achieved onstage was impressive, but what was she doing exactly? Or did it matter what we called it? It was not a play like *Our Town* or *Death of a Salesman,* nor was it a personal monologue of the kinds popularized by such writer-actors as Spalding Gray and Eric Bogosian.

It was nonfiction, but interpretive nonfiction, a theatrical relation perhaps to the literary forms of "nonfiction novelists" like Truman Capote, Norman Mailer and Joseph Wambaugh who combined reporting with novelistic narratives.

Searching for the roots of Smith's ***Twilight*** method in so-called "documentary theater," one looks all the way back to the fabled Living Newspaper of the Federal Theatre Project during the 1930s, the Group Theater's *Waiting for Lefty,* by Clifford Odets (that addressed the 1937 New York taxi strike) or to the earlier Taper shows *In the Matter of J. Robert Oppenheimer* (1968) and *The Trial of the Catonsville 9* (1971). There is, of course, the work of Emily Mann (*Still Life* and *Execution of Justice*), who directed ***Twilight*** at the Taper. Even so, there seems to be no clear precedent for what Smith has done at this professional level. She appears to have established a new genre, and at the moment she is a genre of one. This is a mixed blessing at awards time.

She has also been nominated for best featured actress in ***Twilight,*** but traditionalists in the theater may not be ready to grant her full status as a writer, as an established older American playwright confided to me recently, while requesting anonymity. "It's an eloquent performance all right, but there's a lot of concern among Tony voters that it's not a play," said the playwright.

Robert Schenkkan, author of *The Kentucky Cycle,* which won the 1992 Pulitzer and is nominated for a Tony tonight, holds a similar view. "From a dramaturgical point of view, it's not a work of the imagination," said Schenkkan. "This is not to take anything away from her performance, which is amazing. I think of it as performance art, not as a play."

Others feel differently.

"I think it's going to be an issue for some critics and some people in the theater," said Emily Mann, a leading proponent and practitioner of documentary theater. "But a lot of writing, if you will, goes into one of these pieces. There's an incredible amount of craft involved. You still have to make a play."

"I thought it was wonderful," said Wendy Wasserstein, the playwright who won the Pulitzer in 1989 for *The Heidi Chronicles* and one who speaks up in Smith's behalf. "I think of it as a work of art. There is an individual voice there, the eye of the observer. It's constructed in a theatrical way. It moves. It's documentary theater but it's different from 'docudrama' because she's dealing with character. It begins with character, which is what it has in common with a lot of other plays."

Tom Moore, who directed the Pulitzer-winning *'night Mother* on Broadway and the radio documentary play *Top Secret: The Battle for the Pentagon Papers* for L.A. Theatre Works, said about ***Twilight:*** "It's the way one shapes reality that makes theater. Not anyone could come up with a way of doing that. There's an argument to be made that she did write part of it since she asked the questions.

"Theater is becoming a form that no one thinks is relevant, and here is a piece that has shown relevance and vibrancy, that is important, clever, and well-done. So why in the world should it be excluded?"

"That connection that is madc bctwccn thc stagc and an audience and between the audience and the artist, that is what the theater is about," said Lloyd Richards, director of August Wilson's plays *Fences* (Pulitzer, 1987) and *The Piano Lesson* and for 30 years director [of] the National Playwrights Conference. Did he consider ***Twilight*** a play? "Categorizing it is something that's imposed on it. It's not what the art is about. One can say about something, what is the creative element in it? Sometimes assemblage is creative. I was moved or I was provoked or I was enraged or I was entertained by it. That's where it's at."

Oskar Eustis, a director at the Taper who worked with Smith as an adviser during the development of ***Twilight,*** made this observation: "Categories are invented before an art form is invented. When you have category confusion, the artists are usually ahead of the judges." . . .

There remains the question about ***Twilight:*** Will it last? Shouldn't the projected durability of a play or book or movie be a measure of its greatness or lack thereof? Probably, except that this is the most difficult of all standards to apply with any accuracy, given a glance at history. How many "classics" of just the last 25 years in the theater already qualify as answers to trivia questions?

Twilight seems a piece very much of the moment, an address to a city by a visitor who spent some time here and summed up her thoughts for the stage. But should this diminish its value? The Pulitzer jury concluded that Smith's work "is not reproducible by other performers because it relies for its authenticity on the performer's having done those interviews."

Smith herself disputes this conclusion and reasoning. But call it truth or call it fiction, it is hard to imagine an Anna Deavere Smith show without Anna Deavere Smith. Trying to read ***Twilight*** is only a little more fruitful than trying to read *A Chorus Line* or *Phantom of the Opera.* And in any case the published version differs significantly both from the staged version seen at the Taper and the one now on Broadway, which was altered again under a new director, George C. Wolfe, adding new characters (including a laughing Keith Watson, co-assailant of Reginald O. Denny). In a way, this continuous tinkering is just an additional problem for anyone trying to measure Smith for a formal gown of respectability. Because she is up to something else, asking audiences and the authorities to look at theater fundamentally as a work in progress, taking place one night at a time. This is possibly a radical idea.

FURTHER READING

Criticism

Barnes, Clive. "New Genre Dawns in *Twilight.*" *New York Post* (24 March 1994).

Lauds Smith for inventing a new theatrical genre that combines elements of documentary, journalism, and photography.

Feehr, Stephen. "Dousing Fires." *The Chicago Tribune,* No. 26 (26 December 1993): Section 6, p. 5.

Compares *Fires in the Mirror* and *Twilight.* Includes comments from Smith about her performances and her reasons for writing *Twilight.*

Kissel, Howard. "*Twilight* Offers a Riot of Detail, Slight Insight." *Daily News* (24 March 1994).

Faults Smith's characterization in *Twilight.*

Additional coverage of Smith's life and career is contained in the following source published by Gale Research: *Contemporary Authors,* Vol. 133.

In Memoriam

Cleanth Brooks

October 16, 1906—May 10, 1994

American critic and nonfiction writer.

For further information on Brooks's life and works, see *CLC,* Volume 24.

INTRODUCTION

One of the most influential of the World War II era "New Critics," Brooks championed a critical method characterized by a close reading of texts in which an individual work is evaluated solely on the basis of its internal components. Brooks was initially recognized as a critic of poetry, and his first major book, *Modern Poetry and the Tradition* (1939), presents his critical method through detailed analyses of several poems. In *The Well Wrought Urn,* originally published in 1947, he solidified his premises by arguing that poetry can be judged by the same criteria during any era. As John Paul Pritchard has noted, according to Brooks's theory, "[the] poet does not analyze actual experience like the historian; he synthesizes out of experience a simulacrum of reality that is in fact a new experience." This was a radical departure from the tenets of many literary historians and scholars who believed that the correct interpretation of a poem could only be obtained through an understanding of the social and political contexts of a poet's life. Likewise, biographers who considered the poet's intentions the most important factors in the analysis of poetry were equally reluctant to accept Brooks's ideas. In addition to studies on poetry, Brooks is highly regarded for his works on language and his books on William Faulkner. In such volumes as *The Relation of the Alabama-Georgia Dialect to the Provincial Dialects of Great Britain* (1935) and *The Language of the American South* (1985), he stressed that language and literature are inseparable fields of study and not reducible to linguistics, semiotics, and literature. In the area of Faulkner studies, Brooks's *William Faulkner: The Yoknapatawpha Country* (1963) is considered one of the most influential studies of the American novelist's settings and ideologies. However, numerous critics now question the merit of Brooks's work on Faulkner, arguing that Brooks's interest in validating conservative values of patriarchal and agrarian society unduly influenced his critical judgment. Highly controversial upon publication, Brooks's works continue to generate debate, with proponents lauding his penetrating exposition of literature and opponents charging that his emphasis on the text is too limiting.

PRINCIPAL WORKS

The Relation of the Alabama-Georgia Dialect to the Provincial Dialects of Great Britain (nonfiction) 1935
Understanding Poetry: An Anthology for College Students [editor with Robert Penn Warren] (criticism) 1938; enlarged and revised edition, 1950
Modern Poetry and the Tradition (criticism) 1939
**Understanding Fiction* [editor with Robert Penn Warren] (criticism) 1943
Understanding Drama [editor with Robert B. Heilman] (criticism) 1945; enlarged edition, 1948
The Well Wrought Urn: Studies in the Structure of Poetry (criticism) 1947; revised edition, 1968
Modern Rhetoric [with Robert Penn Warren] (nonfiction) 1949
Fundamentals of Good Writing: A Handbook of Modern Rhetoric [with Robert Penn Warren] (nonfiction) 1950

†*Literary Criticism: A Short History* [with William K. Wimsatt] (criticism) 1957
The Hidden God: Studies in Hemingway, Faulkner, Yeats, Eliot, and Warren (criticism) 1963
William Faulkner: The Yoknapatawpha Country (criticism) 1963
A Shaping Joy: Studies in the Writer's Craft (criticism) 1971
William Faulkner: Toward Yoknapatawpha and Beyond (criticism) 1978
William Faulkner: First Encounters (criticism) 1983
The Language of the American South (nonfiction) 1985
On the Prejudices, Predilections, and Firm Beliefs of William Faulkner (criticism) 1987
Historical Evidence and the Reading of Seventeenth-Century Poetry (criticism) 1991

*An abridged edition of this work was published as *The Scope of Fiction* in 1960.

†Part four of this work was published as *Modern Criticism: A Short History* in 1970.

OBITUARIES AND TRIBUTES

Herbert Mitgang (obituary date 12 May 1994)

SOURCE: An obituary in *The New York Times,* May 12, 1994, p. B14.

[*Mitgang is an American journalist, nonfiction writer, and critic. In the following obituary, he provides an overview of Brooks's life and career.*]

Cleanth Brooks, an educator, author and eminent Southern literary critic who helped spread the principles of the New Criticism movement throughout American universities, died on Tuesday at his home in New Haven. He was 87.

The cause was cancer of the esophagus, said the Beecher & Bennett funeral home in Hamden, Conn.

Mr. Brooks was the Gray Professor Emeritus of Rhetoric at Yale University, where he had been a member of the English faculty since 1947. He retired in 1975.

The New Critics advocated close reading of literary texts and detailed analysis, concentrating on semantics, meter, imagery, metaphor and symbol as well as references to history, biography and cultural background. In addition to Mr. Brooks, the main advocates of this approach were I. A. Richards, John Crowe Ransom, Allen Tate, R. P. Blackmur, Kenneth Burke and Robert Penn Warren.

Mr. Brooks's book ***Understanding Poetry*** (1938), written with Warren was considered a foundation stone of the New Criticism. The movement which had developed in the 1920's was continued in a 1941 book by Ransom called *The New Criticism.* In it, Ransom criticized other critics, including Richards, T. S. Eliot and Yvors Winters. The New Critics did not always agree with one another and by the 1960's, the movement lost its momentum.

Mr. Brooks, however, remained a "major influence," said David Marshall, the chairman of Yale's English department. "In the Yale English curriculum today, a basic course on major poets is still structured around a 'close' reading, which was the defining feature of the New Criticism," he said.

In the course of a distinguished writing and teaching career, Mr. Brooks also was a professor at Louisiana State University (1932-47) and, with Warren, edited *The Southern Review* from 1935-41. In addition, he taught at the University of Texas, the University of Michigan and the University of California at Los Angeles.

From 1964-66, he was cultural attaché at the United States Embassy in London. He was also affiliated with the Library of Congress as a Jefferson Lecturer and as a member of the library's council of scholars.

Mr. Brooks was the author of ***Modern Poetry and the Tradition*** (1939), ***The Well Wrought Urn*** (1947), ***The Hidden God*** (1963), ***The Language of the American South*** (1985) and several books on William Faulkner, including ***William Faulkner: The Yoknapatawpha Country*** (1963), ***William Faulkner: First Encounters*** (1983) and ***Firm Beliefs of William Faulkner*** (1987). With Warren, he also wrote ***Modern Rhetoric*** (1950).

Last year, he established the Cleanth Brooks graduate fellowships in the humanities at Yale. He said he was providing this financial support "because the humanities need all the help we can give them."

Mr. Brooks, who was born in Murray, Ky., was educated at Vanderbilt University, Tulane University and Oxford University, where he was a Rhodes Scholar. He was married in 1934 to Edith Amy Blanchard, who died in 1986. He is survived by his sister-in-law, Elinor Jacobs of Brenham, Tex.

The Times, London (obituary date 16 May 1994)

SOURCE: An obituary in *The Times,* London, May 16, 1994, p. 19.

[*Below, the critic surveys Brooks's career, characterizing his impact on literary studies as immense.*]

Cleanth Brooks was the most influential and widely-read exponent in his generation of what was known as "New Criticism"—a school of critical theory which came to dominate the teaching of literature on American campuses after the war. It was particularly in his own country, as a professor of rhetoric at Yale for nearly 30 years, that he made his impact, for in Britain F. R. Leavis had already completed much of the groundwork to the new critical approach during the 1930s.

Their theories on the importance of a literary work as a closed entity, the intrinsic worth of which could be measured through careful structural analysis rather than examination of its historical context, certainly had parallels. So, too, did the revolutionary impact each had on the teaching of literature at university level. But Brooks was the more concerned of the two to explore the links which might exist between creative writing and literary criticism, and in finding meaningful ways to discuss modern literature. He wrote poetry himself and published several of his best books with the poet and novelist Robert Penn Warren. Three of his works in particular—***Understanding Poetry*** (1938), ***Modern Poetry and the Tradition*** (1939), ***The Well Wrought Urn*** (1947)—became required reading for students for many years.

For his long tenure as Gray Professor of Rhetoric at Yale University, Brooks came to be seen as one of the grand old men of what was then the best English department in America. Until 1970, when such flag-bearers of post-structuralism as Paul de Man and J. Hillis Miller joined the faculty, New Criticism was the dominant version of literary theory in the country. Afterwards, the new French-influenced theorists came to see Brooks and his circle as reactionary, concerned only with the aesthetics of, and not with the politics behind, a poem. But Brooks always maintained that there was a real continuity between his own theories and the new ones. "Deconstruction is just the New Criticism with a bigger magnifying glass" he once said.

Cleanth Brooks was born in Murray, Kentucky, and educated at Vanderbilt and Tulane universities, and at Oxford as a Rhodes scholar. It was at Vanderbilt as a young man, that he had come under the influence of a literary group known as the Fugitives, of which the writer John Crowe Ransom was the guiding influence. Others in the group included its official leader Donald Davidson, Allen Tate, Merrill Moore and Robert Penn Warren. Their manifesto, *I'll Take My Stand* (1930), contained the blueprint for their anti-industrial "Southern Agrarian" programme.

Stimulated by their ideas, Brooks published his first work, a linguistic study entitled ***The Relation of the Alabama-Georgia Dialect to the Provincial Dialects of Great Britain*** in 1935. It offended some readers because it did not find a significant difference between the dialects of black and white or propose to discover for black dialects an origin in Africa.

To his students, Brooks appeared a gentle, quietly spoken man, with enormous authority. But, though he was a charming man in seminars, he remained essentially private outside the classroom, the quintessentially polite American Southern gentleman.

—The Times, *London*

Brooks moved to the faculty of Louisiana State University in 1932 and in 1947 became Gray Professor of Rhetoric at Yale University. Three years later his friend Robert Penn Warren joined him as Professor of English. Thus started the beginning of an extremely fruitful collaborative partnership, not only with joint authorship of books, but with the joint editorship of *The Southern Review,* which gave first publication to the work of many Southern writers. Brooks also contributed to *Poetry, The Kenyon Review, Virginia Quarterly Review, The New Republic* and *Saturday Review.*

As a teacher, Brooks encouraged his students to read modern works—*Jude the Obscure* was still considered by many in American universities to be a new novel—and, though he had started by concentrating on poetry, his interests moved increasingly towards fiction in later life. He was a lifelong champion of William Faulkner—then very much an unsung talent—producing two classic studies on his work.

In Britain his indirect influence for university teaching was immense, though not often recognised. He lived in London for two years from 1964 as cultural attaché to the American Embassy—the first time a professor had held the post. As such he was of enormous help to those trying to establish schools of American studies at English universities, in particular Malcolm Bradbury at the University of East Anglia.

To his students, Brooks appeared a gentle, quietly spoken man, with enormous authority. But, though he was a charming man in seminars, he remained essentially private outside the classroom, the quintessentially polite American Southern gentleman.

His wife Edith, whom he married in 1934, died in 1986. There were no children.

REVIEWS OF BROOKS'S RECENT WORKS

Monroe K. Spears (review date 7 May 1987)

SOURCE: " 'Kipper of de Vineyards,' " in *The New York Review of Books,* Vol. XXXIV, No. 8, May 7, 1987, pp. 38-41.

[*Spears is an American educator and critic. In the review below, he favorably assesses Brooks's* The Language of the American South, *noting his concern with the significance of language in the interpretation of literature.*]

That Cleanth Brooks, after a long and distinguished career as a literary critic, should now produce a book about language may surprise some readers. But it must be remembered that language was one of his strong early interests: among his first publications were ***The Relation of the Alabama-Georgia Dialect to the Provincial Dialects of Great Britain*** (1935) and **"The English Language of the South"** (1937, often reprinted). Besides, he is concerned here not with language for its own sake, but with its larger significances and particularly its relation to literature.

An innocent reader might easily take this short book for a pleasant but unimportant academic exercise. Yet, though never contentious, it takes firm positions on many controversial issues, and its affirmations, though tentatively and mildly made, are profound and wide reaching. The choice of subject itself might in some circles be regarded almost as a manifesto. For Mr. Brooks demonstrates that the study of language is highly relevant to the interpretation of literature, and although he says nothing whatever about matters of academic organization, this demonstration would seem to call into question the powerful trend in universities now to segregate language studies in separate departments of linguistics and semiotics, where the approach tends to be more "scientific" than humane.

Mr. Brooks begins by asserting, in opposition to the increasingly common view that such differences are superficial and trivial, the fundamental importance of the difference between northern and southern English. Citing the stubborn way the Welsh, the French Canadians, and the divided Belgians, for example, have held on to their native language "because they regarded it as a badge of their identity and because they felt that only through it could they express their inner beings, their attitudes and emotions, and even their own concepts of reality," he affirms that "the soul of a people is embodied in the language peculiar to them." He does not argue that southern English is really a separate language, of course, but rather that it is a distinct idiom and dialect. In his first lecture, **"Where It Came From,"** he describes its origin in terms so convincing that it takes an effort to recall how furiously they have been disputed. His first point is that all American English "obviously derives from the English that was spoken in Great Britain several centuries ago"; therefore "we Americans speak an old-fashioned English." It is English English that has changed, not American. For example, the broad *a* in such words as *path, last, laugh* was a nineteenth-century innovation in England, and the pronunciation of the final *g* in such words as *going, doing, thinking,* a still later one: the pronunciation of *g* was restored perhaps owing to the insistence of "the Victorian schoolmarm and her American counterpart" on pronouncing words as they were spelled. But if Americans in general are old-fashioned in pronunciation, southerners, especially in the coastal regions, are the most old-fashioned of all.

How account, then, for the differences between Southern pronunciation and that of Massachusetts Bay, for example, settled at roughly the same time? By considering place as well as time: that is, the part of England from which the early colonists of each region came. For example, in pronouncing *barn* the New Englander and southerner (unlike other Americans) agree in dropping the *r,* but use different vowel sounds, and Mr. Brooks suggests that the explanation is that their ancestors came from, respectively, East Anglia and southern England.

At this point, however, when to go further into the relations of American dialects to their English antecedents would require much definition and explanation, Mr. Brooks provides instead two striking illustrations of the resemblance between Coastal Southern and the dialect of southern England. Taking Joel Chandler Harris's Uncle Remus to illustrate Coastal Southern, he notes that his *gwine* is also characteristic of Hardy's Dorsetshire countrymen, and that his pronunciation of *pert* as *peart* and *muskmelon* as *mushmillion* is also recorded in Dorset. Even more strikingly, he quotes an 1860 rendering of a Sussex countryman speaking *The Song of Solomon.* It begins:

> "De song of songs, dat is Solomon's. . . . Cause of de smell of yer good intments, yer naüm is lik intment tipped out; derefore de maidens love ye. . . . Look not upan me, cause I be black, cause de sun has shoun upan me; my mother's childun was mad wud me; dey maüd me kipper of de vineyards; but my own vineyard I han't kipt. . . . My beloved spoke, an said to me: Git up, my love, my fair un, an come away. . . . Jest a liddle while âhter I passed by em, I foun him dat my soul loves. . . ."

How explain the startling resemblance? Since it is inconceivable that the Sussex countrymen could have learned their speech from American blacks, "the Englishmen who emigrated to the Southern states and from whom the black man necessarily had to learn his English—from whom else could he have learned it?—must have come predominantly from the counties of southern England." Mr. Brooks limits himself to a single feature, the pronunciation of *the, this,* and *that* as *de, dis,* and *dat.* Did southern white men ever use this pronunciation? Mr. Brooks shows that the forms are recorded in Sussex and Kent as early as the sixteenth century and as late as the 1960s, though they are now almost extinct. He then cites evidence that they survive among white southern Americans, though barely. Why did they become characteristic of blacks?

> The blacks, who were at first denied education and later on got only a rather poor and limited "book learning," held on to what their ancestors had learned by ear and which had been passed on to them through oral tradition. In short, they rather faithfully preserved what they had heard, were little influenced by spelling, and in general actually served as a conservative force.

Mr. Brooks notes that the blacks have influenced the language "through their intonation, through their own rhythms, through the development of striking metaphors, new word coinages, and fresh idioms." But he is at pains to deny that they perverted or corrupted it. Thus he rejects the common explanation that blacks in the nineteenth century and earlier were unable to pronounce *th:* "Uncle Remus apparently has no trouble with the voiceless *th:* he can say *thin, think,* and *thank* perfectly well. It is the voiced *th* that he regularly converts to a *d,* and this is exactly the distinction that the yeomen of Sussex and Kent were making back in the seventeenth century and continued to make for two centuries later." Summing up his "hypothesis," Mr. Brooks says that the "language of the South almost certainly came from the south of England." In addition to Kent and Sussex, Essex and London were, he says, probably important as sources of the early settlers' dialects.

Except for details (like initial voiced *th-* becoming *d-* in both Sussex and early Coastal Southern) and examples, Mr. Brooks's argument here is not new; it is basically the same one that he expounded in 1935, and generally in line with the views of dialect geographers such as Hans Kurath, Raven McDavid, and Frederic Cassidy (editor of the *Dictionary of American Regional English* [*DARE*], of which the first volume appeared this year). Though Mr. Brooks has never professed to be more than an amateur in these matters, his early work was enough to establish him in a curious role as archetypal dialect geographer—a kind of culture villain or bête noir to creolists and sociolinguists who hold fundamentally different views. (Dialect geographers believe geographical origin and distribution are the most important factors in the study of dialects; sociolinguists give primacy to sociological factors; and creolists to contact languages.) There is an intriguing parallel here to Mr. Brooks's equally curious role as archetypal New Critic, or bête noir to opponents of that equally mythical conspiracy. Why should a man who is personally so mild and inoffensive and who writes with such courtesy and moderation arouse such hostility? I don't understand it; I can only conjecture that the exceptional clarity and definiteness with which he states his positions make him an easy target.

J. L. Dillard, whose books *Black English* and *All-American English* I reviewed in [*The New York Review of Books*] some years ago ["You Makin' Sense" (November 16, 1972); "American, Black, Creole, Pidgin, and Spanish English" (July 17, 1975)], will serve as an example of the linguistic Young Turks. In his allegorical or mythical landscape, embattled creolists and sociolinguists are besieging the bastions of the Establishment, which are defended by dialect geographers. As a creolist, Mr. Dillard stresses the role of contact languages, pidgins, some of which became creoles. In the case of Black English, his thesis is that from Gullah (the Afro-English of the Sea Islands of South Carolina and Georgia, which everyone agrees was a genuine creole) developed a plantation creole which spread over the whole continent and eventually became black English.

Black English, or Black English Vernacular (BEV), as described by Mr. Dillard and his cohorts, is monolithic, the same in Detroit, New York, and Shreveport; it is a distinct and ethnic dialect, and where its peculiarities agree with those of white speech, it is because the whites were influenced by it. There are said to be structural differences between white and black English as well as differences in vocabulary, though Mr. Dillard has lately moderated his earlier views: in *Toward a Social History of American English* (1985), he says,

> Somewhere between the extremes of the one viewpoint that Black English differs only in "use" (discourse strategies, affective devices) from Standard English and the other that large numbers of Bantu or other African language words have survived must lie the truth about Black slang.

The most striking of these structural differentia are BEV invariant *be,* zero copula (*she a big woman*), and—Mr. Dillard's latest candidate for a unique characteristic—nonpassive preverbal *been* as anterior time marker, e.g., *I been had it a long time.* (He cites this form repeatedly both in his revision of Albert Marckwardt's *American English,* 1980, and his own 1985 book.)

Mr. Brooks says nothing of these controversies. He has always maintained (as have many professional linguists of all colors) that the blacks originally learned their English from the whites (and therefore learned the same regional English dialects), and that the only important difference is statistical: that is, because the blacks were more isolated and less educated, their language changed more slowly, and therefore more archaic or old-fashioned forms persisted. But in the present work he makes a point of acknowledging, as we have seen, that the blacks have influenced the language in important and valuable ways, not only through intonation and rhythm but through creating words and fresh and imaginative metaphors and idioms.

In his second and third lectures, Mr. Brooks engages in a kind of criticism that is so noncontroversial that, in other hands, it has a dreadful tendency toward banality. But Mr. Brooks makes it fascinating, partly because of his well-known perceptiveness and his brilliance in interpreting literature, and partly because of the skill with which he marshals the argument and makes clear its continuity with that of the first lecture in the book. The second lecture is called **"The Language of the Gentry and the Folk,"** and its point is not merely that the two are different, but that the close relation and interplay between them is the secret of southern writing, insofar as it has a secret. As Mr. Brooks puts it,

> The strength of even the more formal Southern writers stems from their knowledge of and rapport with the language spoken by the unlettered. . . . Our best writers have never held in contempt the speech of the folk or used it only for comic effects.

He begins with a quotation from Allen Tate's *The Fathers* (1938) in which the narrator describes his father's speech (in the antebellum South) as operating on four levels, ranging from Johnsonian formal to three kinds of conversational: first, with family and friends; second, with "plain people," abounding in many archaisms; and third, with Negroes, whose speech was "merely late seventeenth- or early eighteenth-century English ossified." "He would not have understood our conception of 'correct English.' Speech was like manners, an expression of sensibility and taste." Mr. Brooks remarks that this account "represents a giant's step beyond the received opinion of 1938 . . . and, I make bold to say, beyond even that commonly held today." After an example from Longstreet's *Georgia Scenes,* Mr. Brooks returns to Uncle Remus to consider another way in which the language of the folk can be used for literary effect. "Harris employs the dialect as it issues from the lips of Uncle Remus without ironic intent. He clearly admires its power to express the old man's wit and wisdom." There is no condescension toward either the medium or the character; to tell the stories without the dialect would deprive them of most of their charm. Mr. Brooks analyzes one of the stories to show its literary quality; its "comedy is firmly grounded in reality," and abounds in "sound insights into the human situation."

For examples of the language of the gentry in the antebellum South, Mr. Brooks quotes from another part of Tate's

The Fathers and the Cass Mastern section of Robert Penn Warren's *All the King's Men* that follows:

> So the Mantuan said, when Venus appeared and the true goddess was revealed by her gait. She came into the room and was the true goddess as revealed in her movement, and was, but for Divine Grace (if such be granted to a parcel of corruption such as I), my true damnation. She gave me her hand and spoke with a tingling huskiness which made me think of rubbing my hand upon a soft deep-piled cloth, like velvet, or upon a fur. It would not have been called a musical voice such as is generally admired. I know that, but I can only set down what effect it worked upon my own organs of hearing.

The latter quotation leads naturally to a contrasting quotation of one of Willie Stark's speeches from the same work:

> "Folks, there's going to be a leetle mite of trouble back in town. Between me and that Legislature-ful of hyena-headed, feist-faced, belly-dragging sons of slack-gutted she-wolves. If you know what I mean. Well, I been looking at them and their kind so long, I just figured I'd take me a little trip and see what human folks looked like in the face before I clean forgot. Well, you all look human. More or less. And sensible. In spite of what they're saying back in that Legislature and getting paid five dollars a day of your tax money for saying it."

From an earlier novel of Warren's, *At Heaven's Gate,* there is an example of Hill Southern dialect:

> [Marie] "would be done work and I would be waitin. Ax or layin to a crosscut all day, and I would see her comin out of that there kitchen and me waitin in the dark and the weariness was not nuthin. It was lak I was wakin up fresh and a sunbeam done smote you on the eyeball and roused you. . . .
>
> I never taken to likker lak I use to, and likker is a sin. But a man cannot be good out of plain human kindness. He cannot be good for it ain't in a pore man. He cannot be good unlest it is good in the light of Gods eye. Gods eye ain't on him and he just swaps one sin for another one, and it was worse maybe. I laid off likker but I swapped for another sin. I laid off likker for Marie but it was because of pore human love and not for Gods love."

Mr. Brooks then proceeds to another master of the various aspects of southern speech, Faulkner, whose "range extends across the whole spectrum of Coastal or Lowland Southern, literate and illiterate." He chooses as example one of my own favorites, "Pantaloon in Black," and notes that the dialect in which the young black man, Rider, speaks makes an important contribution to the effectiveness of the story: "Prettify it or formalize it, and the magical reality is lost." When Rider comes back to his cabin after the burial of his young wife Mannie, he finds her " 'standing in the kitchen door, looking at him.' "

> "Mannie," he said. "Hit's awright. Ah aint afraid." Then he took a step toward her, slow, not even raising his hand yet, and stopped. Then he took another step. But this time as soon as he moved she began to fade. He stopped at once, not breathing again, motionless, willing his eyes to see that she had stopped too. But she had not stopped. She was fading, going. "Wait," he said, talking as sweet as he had ever heard his voice speak to a woman: "Den lemme go wid you, honey." But she was going.

He deals briefly with two examples from *The Hamlet,* one showing the poetic speech of poor whites:

> They walked in a close clump, tramping their shadows into the road's mild dust, blotting the shadows of the burgeoning trees which soared, trunk branch and twig against the pale sky, delicate and finely thinned. They passed the dark store. Then the pear tree came in sight. It rose in mazed and silver immobility like exploding snow; the mockingbird still sang in it. "Look at that tree," Varner said. "It ought to make this year, sho."
>
> "Corn'll make this year too," one said.
>
> "A moon like this is good for every growing thing outen earth," Varner said. "I mind when we and Mrs. Varner was expecting Eula. Already had a mess of children and maybe we ought to quit them. But I wanted some more gals. Others had done married and moved away, and a passel of boys, soon as they get big enough to be worth anything, they aint got time to work. Got to set around store and talk. But a gal will stay home and work until she does get married. So there was a old woman told my mammy once that if a woman showed her belly to the full moon after she had done caught, it would be a gal. So Mrs. Varner taken and laid every night with the moon on her nekid belly, until it fulled and after. I could lay my ear to her belly and hear Eula kicking and scrouging like all get-out, feeling the moon."

The other renders satirically the speech of a Texas auctioneer:

> "Them ponies is gentle as a dove, boys. The man that buys them will get the best piece of horse-flesh he ever forked or druv for the money. Naturally they got spirit; I aint selling crowbait. Besides, who'd want Texas crowbait anyway, with Mississippi full of it?" His stare was still absent and unwinking; there was no mirth or humor in his voice and there was neither mirth nor humor in the single guffaw which came from the rear of the group. Two wagons were now drawing out of the road at the same time, up to the fence. The men got down from them and tied them to the fence and approached. "Come up, boys," the Texan said. "You're just in time to buy a good gentle horse cheap."

The final lecture in the book is called **"The Language in the Present Day."** Mr. Brooks here returns to the importance of rapport with the language of the folk in even the most formal southern writing, and convincingly illustrates this point by quoting passages from poems. In Warren's "Dragon Country" the narrator's use of words like *spectators* and *averted* marks him as a man of some education, with a knowledge of the great world outside. But we sense almost immediately that he grew up in the country, is thoroughly familiar with the local idiom, and can give an authentic report on the impact that this horror made on his neighbors. Thus he is doubly articulate and a convincing reporter on what occurred. He even uses the speech rhythms of the plain people.

But that was long back, in my youth,
  just the first of case after case.
The great hunts fizzled. You followed the track of disrepair,
Ruined fence, blood-smear, brush
  broken, but came in the end to a
  place
With weed unbent and leaf calm—
  and nothing, nothing, was there.
So what, in God's name, could men
  think when they couldn't bring to
  bay
That belly-dragging, earth-evil, but
  found that it took to air?
Thirty-thirty or buckshot might fail,
  but at least you could say
You had faced it—assuming, of
  course, that you had survived the
  affair.

John Crowe Ransom's lines are similarly local:

Autumn days in our section
Are the most used-up thing on earth
(Or in the waters under the earth)
Having no more color nor
  predilection
Than cornstalks too wet for the fire.

The colloquial element is strong even in Tate:

Man, dull criter of enormous head,
What would he look at in the coiling
  sky?

But for more obvious and extensive examples "of the literary artist's dependence upon the spoken language," he turns to prose fiction and discusses Eudora Welty's "The Petrified Man" and *The Ponder Heart.* Peter Taylor's "Miss Leonora When Last Seen" and "Guests" provide further examples of specifically southern kinds of speech and manners, and so does Flannery O'Connor's "The Enduring Chill"—again, one of my own particular favorites, a story at once devastatingly grim and increasingly hilarious. (Mr. Brooks quotes Robert Kiely's comparison of Joyce Carol Oates to Flannery O'Connor, ending, "If you take away the dialect, the laughter, and the redemption, that's right. She's just like Flannery O'Connor.") Finally, he discusses several passages from Walker Percy's novels. Every reader will want to add further examples—I think immediately of J. K. Toole, Padgett Powell, Ellen Gilchrist—but obviously there is no end to such additions.

In *The Language of the American South,* Brooks suggests that the close relation and interplay between the speech of folk and gentry, formal and colloquial, white and black, is the secret of the vitality of Southern language.

—Monroe K. Spears

At the end of the second lecture, Mr. Brooks raises the question whether it is the language that gives the southern writers their distinction or the material itself. Without going into this ultimate question of aesthetics, he suggests that it is not possible to make a sharp distinction between content and form: "When we try to describe one person to another . . . , what do we say? Not usually how or what that person ate, rarely what he wore, only occasionally how he managed his job—no, what we tell is *what he said* and, if we are good mimics, *how he said it.* We apparently consider a person's spoken words the true essence of his being."

The affirmation in [***The Language of the American South***] is, it seems to me, essentially the same one that is implicit or explicit in all Cleanth Brooks's more narrowly literary criticism. His vision is one of unity (and, though the phrase has grown unfashionable, one must add "organic," for the quality of aliveness is as important to Mr. Brooks as it was to Coleridge), of unity in diversity, of a fruitful tension between opposite and discordant qualities. Mr. Brooks has always maintained that attention to language is of fundamental importance in literary interpretation (or simply good reading), because we cannot separate the thing said from the words in which it is said, form from content, ideas or "messages" from metaphor, rhythm, and connotation, character from situation and narrative, and so on.

The work of art, as he sees it, exists in the interplay among all these elements, in the vision of the whole; to stress one element at the expense of the others is to distort it. In the present book he applies the same principle specifically to language, affirming its importance in literature and in life, and the value of diversity, of retaining the separate identities of Southern speech, as of other dialects and idioms, within the larger unity. As we have seen, he suggests that the close relation and interplay between folk and gentry, formal and colloquial, white and black, is the secret of the vitality of Southern language. He might be described as being against separatism: against segregating white from black English as, by implication, he is against separating the study of language from that of literature, and as he is certainly against taking any one element or aspect of the literary work for the whole. On the other hand, he is certainly opposed to the kind of total assimilation that would abolish or ignore all individual differences.

Mr. Brooks's writing, unobtrusive but highly effective in its patient logic and occasional eloquence, is very different from that of most people who deal with similar subjects. The older "establishment" linguists tend toward a dignified dullness (excepting some good and often entertaining writers such as James Sledd and the late Raven McDavid), while the "scientific" or hyphenated socio- and psycholinguists tend to ignore style and sometimes grammar, as if to demonstrate that they are not fussy about language. His conclusion is, however, one that I should think a linguist of any school would agree with enthusiastically. The most dangerous enemy of the Southern language, he says, is miseducation: "foolishly incorrect theories of what constitutes good English, an insistence on spelling pronunciations, and the propagation of bureaucratese, sociologese, and psychologese, which American business, politics, and academies seem to exude as a matter of course."

In many of his other books, Mr. Brooks has written eloquently about the relation between the debasement and corruption of our language by ruthless and manipulative people and our prevalent failure in commitment to any beliefs and in self-knowledge. To debauch the language is to debauch the minds of those who use it. He closes the present book with a comparison to Yeats's Ireland, which, like the South, had a vigorous oral literature and a brilliant written literature, mainly modern. Yeats's fear was that the mass of people would lose the virtues of the oral tradition without ever having achieved mastery of the written tradition; and Mr. Brooks fears that modern Southerners will have "lost the ability to tell a good yarn or appreciate it when told, and yet not be able to read with understanding and delight the great literature of the past and present. Such loss is not made up for by sitting bemused, watching a situation comedy or even the best programs of our public television networks for four or five hours a day." Genuine literature, he writes,

> is not a luxury commodity but neither is it an assembly-line product. It cannot be mass produced. It has to be hand made, fashioned by a genuine craftsman out of honest human emotions and experiences, in the making of which the indispensable material is our common language, in all its variety, complexity, and richness.

Eric Sundquist (review date 15 November 1987)

SOURCE: A review of *On the Prejudices, Predilections, and Firm Beliefs of William Faulkner,* in *The New York Times Book Review,* November 15, 1987, p. 27.

[*Sundquist is an American educator and critic. In the following review, he provides a mixed assessment of* On the Prejudices, Predilections, and Firm Beliefs of William Faulkner.]

His three previous books on Faulkner have established Cleanth Brooks as one of the novelist's leading critics in the last 30 years. Still, Mr. Brooks's interpretations of major works have not always been as influential as his insights into less studied aspects of the Faulkner canon. This most recent collection [***On the Prejudices, Predilections, and Firm Beliefs of William Faulkner***] of 12 essays, all but one of them first delivered as lectures dating as far back as 1971, is no exception. The essays that treat perennial Faulkner topics—the notion of community in his novels, his women characters or his values—are the least interesting of the group. More provocative are topical pieces arguing that the Fugitive poets praised Faulkner earlier than critics have claimed, or detailing the misconceptions of the South that have characterized most British reactions to Faulkner; or surprising literary observations, such as the wide-ranging and inventive essay on "motherless children" in Faulkner's novels. Likewise, Mr. Brooks's invocation of theories from other disciplines produces uneven results. Eric Voegelin's gnostic conception of history does not help us see Thomas Sutpen's flawed grand design in *Absalom, Absalom!* much more clearly; on the other hand, Christopher Lasch's notions about the managerial and professional invasion of the modern self turn out to be surprisingly consonant with Faulkner's view of the decay of individualism in his late and little-known essay, "On Privacy." Witty and gracefully written, Mr. Brooks's essays are perhaps too anecdotal, and the level of discussion often rather mundane. His focus on character and theme, at the expense of attention to Faulkner's style or recent research on Southern social history that more recent critics have examined, makes his perspective seem overly conventional. At the right moments, however, Mr. Brooks remains one of the most thoughtful and imaginative readers of Faulkner.

Frederick Crews (essay date 7 March 1991)

SOURCE: "The Strange Fate of William Faulkner," *The New York Review of Books,* Vol. XXXVIII, No. 5, March 7, 1991, pp. 47-52.

[*Crews is an American educator and critic. In the following excerpt from an essay that surveys several recent volumes of Faulkner criticism, he assails Brooks's recent and past interpretations of Faulkner's work as "Agrarian party line" and "indefensible."*]

By the postwar era the points of irreconcilable conflict between Agrarian/New Critics and ex-Marxist intellectuals had narrowed to an extraordinary degree. All were congregating in the academy, none were pressing activist causes, and for varying reasons they all could make their peace with both literary nationalism and international modernism as it was personified, however fastidiously, in "Mr. Eliot." Since there was much in Faulkner's work that could have caused unreconstructed Agrarians and Marxists alike to accuse him of political waywardness, this blurring of old antagonisms was crucial for the coming Faulkner boom. By the 1950s, moreover, a widespread revulsion against Soviet artistic regimentation had given Faulkner's stock still another lift, creating greater sympathy for his eccentric stylistic flights, his distrust of utopian agitators, and his individualistic probing of (formerly characterized as his morbid wallowing in) private regressions and fixations.

Vast in scope, morally engaged without being propagandistic, studded with complex image patterns, and intractable to ready explanation, Faulkner's newly republished writings beckoned as an inexhaustible-looking supply of raw material for what John Crowe Ransom, without derogatory intent, called Criticism, Inc. Thus Faulkner was destined to become the object of "an outpouring of critical attention," as one observer has noted, "such as no other writer, it may be, in the whole history of letters has received so near the time of his work, and such as only a few writers have received at any time" [Richard H. Brodhead, *Faulkner: New Perspectives,* 1983].

The main image of Faulkner to emerge from all that early attention, however, would necessarily reflect both the dominant critical style of the universities and the specific politics of the southern-born professors who largely shaped that style. For many years, and with surprisingly few exceptions, the academy contented itself with a formalist-Agrarian Faulkner—formalist, because his works were assumed to possess a unifying "moral vision," and Agrarian, because the alleged content of that vision flattered southern traditionalism without counting its cost in misery. The result was a body of criticism that occluded Faulkner's improvisation and interior debate, reduced his often daring characterizations to illustrated moral lessons, and subtly adulterated and softened his anguish over southern history.

The leading book in this vein also happens to have been, thus far, the most influential, as well as the most widely assailed, of all Faulkner studies: Cleanth Brooks's ***William Faulkner: The Yoknapatawpha Country*** (1963). Teachers still pull it from the shelf when they need to sort out Faulkner's bewildering social world, and even today one can discern its residual effect on critics who resent the main drift of contemporary criticism. To them, Brooks is not an ideologue but merely an affectionately objective critic who happens to know Faulkner's South at first hand. What Brooks actually gave us, however—and what became the leading strain of Faulkner criticism for a whole generation of teachers and students—was in effect the Agrarian party line.

For Brooks, Faulkner is primarily a spinner of instructive tales about the Old South and the New as they are typified in a single northern Mississippi county. In characteristic Agrarian style, the critic holds that the admittedly exploitative plantation system coexisted with a nobler, poorer South made up of independent white farmers whose values—courage, honor, perseverance, loyalty to family and village and religion—derived from a life of working the soil that their hardy forefathers had cleared from the wilderness. The chief offenses against those values, Brooks believes, can be found not in slavery, which was at least partially redeemed by its paternalism, but in secular northern materialism, especially as it corrupted the helpless South after 1865.

According to Brooks, Faulkner's novels relate the lingering consequences of that incursion while nevertheless showing how local solidarity has managed to survive as both a fact and a standard. "Community" thus becomes the central Faulknerian value in Brooks's hands, and "fanaticism" the error that inevitably brings about misfortune. In his view, for example, *Light in August* teaches us to beware the self-destructiveness of outsiders, like Joe Christmas and Joanna Burden, who lack a stable local identity and so cannot temper their extremism with mundane and humanizing involvements. And *Absalom, Absalom!* purportedly depicts a similar tragic flaw in Thomas Sutpen, whose fierce disregard of his neighbors leads to his eventual fall and, what seems almost worse, reveals him to be not a southerner at all but a generic American innocent driven by abstract (i.e., northern) notions.

As many recent critics have shown, these are highly dubious interpretations. The main reason for Brooks's dwindling appeal, however, lies not in this or that misreading but in the high price we must pay for assenting to his notion of community. Brooks would have us see an absolute opposition between Faulkner's criminals and zealots on one side and, on the other, the solidly rooted burghers and farmers of the town of Jefferson and its surrounding acres. But that provincial enclave as Faulkner depicts it looks like anything but a showcase of southern virtue. It is rather a bastion of segregation, chicanery, night-riding, lynching, and the routine oppression of women; and its antebellum record, in Faulkner's rendering, is no better, beginning with the theft of the land from gullible Indians and culminating in the incestuous union of Carothers McCaslin with his own half-white slave daughter and his racist spurning of the resultant child/grandchild. Brooks quite gratuitously assumes, and asks that we, too, assume, that all those crimes and vices are outweighed in Faulkner's scale of values by the bare fact of social cohesion among the conforming whites.

For a long while now, ***William Faulkner: The Yoknapatawpha Country*** has been an object of faint praise and increasingly fierce denunciation. Brooks, however, has continued to fill out his original picture of Faulkner, serenely addressing himself to various works and problems that had found no place in his first study. After ***William Faulkner: Toward Yoknapatawpha and Beyond*** (1978), came ***William Faulkner: First Encounters*** (1983), and then ***On the Prejudices, Predilections, and Firm Beliefs of William Faulkner*** (1987). Those books show an understandable decline of critical energy but no retreat from a position that now appears indefensible.

It would be pointless, then, to dwell on the shortcomings of Brooks's most recent collection of talks and essays. Suffice it to say that he remains determined to regard Faulkner's novels as the fictionalized illustration of holistic ideas, especially those that show off southern virtue to best advantage. "A great literary artist such as Faulkner," as he puts it, "helps the rest of the country and the rest of the world to understand us better." Some of the values thus paraded appear to unravel in the very act of being named—for example, "the feminine principle," which Faulkner is said to have treasured because male energies "require being checked and channeled into fruitful enterprises." Brooks's deeper liability, however, remains what it always was, the formalist's overeagerness to sift homilies from texts that could otherwise yield any number of disruptive implications.

Carol M. Andrews (essay date 1991)

SOURCE: "Cleanth Brooks on Faulkner: Yoknapatawpha and the Vanderbilt Tradition," in *The Vanderbilt Tradition: Essays in Honor of Thomas Daniel Young,* edited by Mark Royden Winchell, Louisiana State University Press, 1991, pp. 189-96.

[*An educator and critic, Andrews frequently writes about William Faulkner. In the essay below, she analyzes Brooks's studies of Faulkner.*]

Cleanth Brooks writes with an authority not easily matched in Faulkner criticism. His firsthand experience of southern culture, his comprehensive knowledge of literary tradition, and his clear sense of humanity enable him to cut through the absurdities and extravagances of much writing about Faulkner. Yet this very authority can pose a problem for the reader trying to understand the complexities of Faulkner's fiction; it can be difficult to separate Brooks's own critical precepts from the fictional world he makes so accessible to the reader. The New Criticism, which Brooks inherited from the Fugitives and developed into a revolutionary method for analyzing the verbal structures of a work of literature, carries with it the conservative values of a patriarchal, agrarian society. Focusing his study of Faulkner on the concept of community, one of the central concerns of the Vanderbilt group, Brooks sees in Yoknapatawpha an inherent order that may be a product of his own desire for order.

Although he dislikes the term "New Criticism," Brooks has long been considered one of the foremost practitioners of the approach. The New Critics—T. S. Eliot, I. A. Richards, and the Nashville group, particularly John Crowe Ransom, Allen Tate, and Robert Penn Warren—see the work of art as a self-contained entity, independent from biographical and historical considerations, that through its internal relationships imparts a unique vision of reality. Brooks states in ***Modern Poetry and the Tradition*** (1939) that

> Hobbes reduced the poet from the status of *maker* to that of *copyist* by making the imagination merely the file-clerk of the memory. He would have the poet take literally the phrase "to hold the mirror up to nature." A mirror can reflect the poetic object placed before it. But if we are to use the term mirror at all, it is rather a distortion mirror which the poet carries, or better still, a lens with which he gives a focus to experience. At all events, the emphasis must be placed on the poet's making.

As Frank Lentricchia points out [in "The Place of Cleanth Brooks," *Journal of Aesthetics and Art Criticism* XXXIX (Winter 1970)], the "lens" to which Brooks refers gives his theory a radical character when compared with the mirror of Aristotle and the lamp of Coleridge, for "his intention is no less than to elevate poetry to a unique position in human culture by giving the poem itself the autonomous capacity that will enable it to contribute to the very constitution of the total body of knowledge on which the culture stands."

The New Critics themselves apparently saw no conflict between their radical aesthetic philosophy and conservative social values. The Vanderbilt group felt the devastation of World War I as a loss of "a world order, a civilizational community," and therefore launched the Agrarian movement as a part of "the quest for a symbolism of community, for the restoration of a symbolism of order" [Lewis P. Simpson, introduction to *The Possibilities of Order: Cleanth Brooks and His Work,* edited by Simpson, 1976]. *I'll Take My Stand* (1930) fiercely decried the way that industrialism and progress had separated Americans from the humane values of Western civilization. Poetry, with its unique relationship to culture, could be one of the ways of linking the present with the past.

Brooks, who attended Vanderbilt as an undergraduate from 1924 to 1928, did not participate in the making of *I'll Take My Stand* but was deeply influenced by the "self-conscious, highly literate Vanderbilt clerisy." He applied their philosophy to literature in ***Modern Poetry and the Tradition,*** evaluating poetry according to its participation in the larger community of literary tradition. According to Brooks, the Victorians, as well as Americans such as Edgar Lee Masters and Carl Sandburg, wrote a "poetry of exclusion," limited and sentimental, that denied the poetic tradition preceding them. In contrast, John Donne, T. S. Eliot, and the Nashville group achieved a synthesis of past and present in a "poetry of inclusion," which Brooks sees as a more complex embodiment of reality. Ironically, then, the "New" Criticism is more a search for connections with an older tradition than it is a rejection of historicism. Like Eliot, Brooks values a poetic tradition that provides a community of voices.

Brooks also considers the text of a work to be a kind of community. In ***The Well-Wrought Urn*** (1947), his next full-length study, and ***A Shaping Joy: Studies in the Writer's Craft*** (1971), a much later collection of essays, he set himself the task of "discovering whether a poem is truly unified or chaotic, whether its parts are related or unrelated, whether it embodies order or is rent apart by disorder." Thus, as René Wellek points out [in "Cleanth Brooks, Critic of Critics," in Simpson], he was seeking in the structure of a poem the same connections and disjunctions he has found in literary tradition and civilization itself. But the "inclusiveness" of a poem is of a particular kind; "the principle is not one which involves the arrangement of the various elements into homogeneous groupings, pairing like with like. It unites the like with the unlike." The "total pattern" of a poem can "incorporate within itself items intrinsically beautiful or ugly, attractive or repulsive"; it makes use of irony, ambiguity, and paradox in order to produce a new ordering of reality.

Although this critical approach was developed for poetry, it seems admirably suited for Faulkner, who presents his readers with seemingly irreconcilable incongruities, contradictions, and paradoxes. When Brooks began to teach the Mississippi novelist's work at Yale in 1947, few critics had attempted to examine it for internal principles of order and coherence. George Marion O'Donnell (1939) and Malcolm Cowley (1946) had found organizing allegories or myths, Robert Penn Warren (1946) had written on recurrent themes and images, and Conrad Aiken (1939) and Warren Beck (1941) had analyzed style. But no one had attempted the synthesis of form and content that Brooks's approach to poetry would make possible.

Most of Brooks's work on Faulkner appears in four books: ***William Faulkner: The Yoknapatawpha Country*** (1963), ***William Faulkner: Toward Yoknapatawpha and Beyond*** (1978), ***William Faulkner: First Encounters*** (1983), and ***On the Prejudices, Predilections, and Firm Beliefs of William Faulkner*** (1987). ***The Hidden God,*** published in 1963 but originally delivered as lectures in 1955, contains a chapter entitled **"William Faulkner: Vision of Good and Evil,"** and several later essays published elsewhere are included in ***A Shaping Joy: Studies in the Writer's Craft*** (1971). The chapter from ***The Hidden God*** establishes some of the patterns Brooks sees as characteristic of Faulkner's world, but this essay merely sketches what ***The Yoknapatawpha Country*** develops in depth and detail.

In ***The Yoknapatawpha Country,*** Brooks set for himself what he called "the central critical task: to determine and evaluate the meaning of the work in the fullness of its depth and amplitude." The method of New Criticism, focusing on internal relations of the text itself, allowed him to avoid two dangers he saw in Faulkner criticism at the time he was writing: the sociological-historical approach that found Faulkner's subject matter trivial or distorted, and the "symbol-mongering" that lifted details out of context. Thus, to a great extent, his readings of the novels are corrective, but their strength is that they move beyond mere correction and present Faulkner's world as palpable, ordered, and profound.

In looking at Faulkner, Brooks focuses more on patterns of character and action than on the verbal patterns he examines so closely in his study of poetry. This shift can be seen in the themes he chooses to examine, which include "the role of the community, the theme of isolation and alienation, Puritanism under the hot Southern sun, the tension between the masculine and feminine principles, and the relation of the characters to the past." He examines the oppositions or polarities Faulkner so often presents in his novels—community and isolation, masculinity and femininity, present and past. Brooks resolves the tension of these oppositions by choosing one side by which to judge the other—community, masculine honor, the eternal feminine, the past—just as his teachers preferred the values of an earlier civilization to the dislocations of the present.

The chapter on *Light in August,* which in its focus on the community serves as a touchstone for Brooks's other readings, illustrates how he makes his judgments. Early in the chapter he describes the community as "the powerful though invisible force that quietly exerts itself in so much of Faulkner's work . . . the circumambient atmosphere, the essential ether of Faulkner's fiction." As an organizing principle, this sense of community might allow the mingling of contraries that is so crucial to Brooks's conception of literature: a community is defined by both its responsible citizens and its pariahs. Brooks pays careful attention to both sides of this contrast, considering the relation of all the outcasts to the community of Jefferson, but he finally comes down on the side of the community and its values: "The community is at once the field for man's action and the norm by which his action is judged and regulated." He distinguishes between Faulkner and other modern writers on the basis of community: "It sometimes seems that the sense of an organic community has all but disappeared from modern fiction, and the disappearance accounts for the terrifying self-consciousness and subjectivity of a great deal of modern writing. That Faulkner had some sense of an organic community still behind him was among his most important resources as a writer."

Brooks also makes a choice in terms of the novel's form; trying to decide between the possibilities of tragedy and comedy, he finds that the comic prevails: "Finally and generally, I believe, the mode is that of comedy. . . . Its function is to maintain sanity and human perspective in a scene of brutality and horror." Using one character by whom to evaluate the experience of the others, Brooks writes: "It is Lena and her instinct for nature, Lena and her rapport with the community, Lena as a link in the eternal progression from mother to daughter who provides the final norm for our judgment. In this connection Faulkner's abiding concern with man's endurance and his ability to suffer anything—compare the Nobel Prize speech—is worth remembering." Brooks does not allow for the radical questioning of the community's values implied in the life and death of Joe Christmas, a radicalism that cannot be contained by Lena's nonintellectual awareness. Faulkner, instead of placing a tragic story within a comic frame that contains it, uses the juxtaposition of the tragic and comic to reflect the complexity of experience.

When, in ***Toward Yoknapatawpha and Beyond,*** Brooks investigates the influence of romantic and decadent writers like Keats, Swinburne, Wilde, Gautier, Housman, and Eliot on the young Faulkner, he uses the traditional literary terms of romanticism and realism to define the poles of Faulkner's imagination. According to Brooks, Faulkner's invention of Yoknapatawpha County "provided him with a social context in which what was healthiest in his romanticism could live in fruitful tension with his realistic and detailed knowledge of the men and manners of his own land," while at the same time "the realistic, earthy life of Yoknapatawpha could be invested with the aura of the imagination, a mythic quality that could give vital import to what would otherwise have been drab and pedestrian."

In this second volume, Brooks also defines his understanding of Faulkner's modernism, again using the image of the lens to raise the question of localism versus universality: "The issues dealt with in his Yoknapatawpha novels ultimately concern universal human nature and they have reference to the world of the present. Faulkner uses Yoknapatawpha as a special lens that allows us to view with illuminating magnification and emphasis our own modernity." But Faulkner's modernism as seen by Brooks is not very modern. He continues to find in the novels "a coherent ethical and moral position that is traditional and conservative."

It is this last point, perhaps, that makes Brooks vulnerable to the charge of attempting to turn Faulkner into one of the Fugitives by claiming that Faulkner and they share the same values. Daniel Aaron, for example, says [in *The Unwritten War: American Writers and the Civil War,* 1973] that "the exegesis of Warren and especially of Cleanth

Brooks influenced Faulkner scholarship so profoundly, in fact, that the differences between him and the Nashville group have been obscured." This accusation is hardly fair or accurate, as no criticism that I know of has confused the two. In his reply **"Faulkner and the Fugitive-Agrarians,"** Brooks denies that his and Warren's work was designed to make it appear that Faulkner shared their views: "In any case, Faulkner was too big to be attracted into anybody else's orbit. Warren and I would have been fools to think so."

Aaron argues, essentially, that Faulkner viewed the South with a certain detachment, whereas the Fugitives wrote southern propaganda. Brooks points out what he sees as Aaron's oversimplification by appealing to the texts, demonstrating that the Fugitives shared with Faulkner the need for southern self-criticism and that Faulkner shared with them the idea that there were certain southern virtues "worth defending and preserving." Ironically, Brooks thus does consciously what Aaron has accused him of doing unconsciously (finding a common ground for Faulkner and the Fugitives), but as he does so his close exegetical approach maintains the integrity of the texts at hand.

A more serious problem is raised by John Duvall in his essay "Faulkner's Critics and Women: The Voice of the Community" [in Doreen Fowler and Ann J. Abadie, eds., *Faulkner and Women: Faulkner and Yoknapatawpha, 1985,* 1986]. He uses Brooks as an example of "how Faulkner critics often appropriate the voices of the Southern community (as represented in Faulkner's novels and short stories) for their own writing practices." His criticism shows how such a point of view remains partial:

> Brooks, the outside interpreter, consistently (if indirectly) identifies Faulkner with the utterances of certain male characters who exhibit benevolent paternalism. Such interpretive moments are a strategy of containment, and rhetorical violence adheres in the deductive leap to formations beginning "For Faulkner . . ." since they are always an appeal to the authority of the author, part of critics' attempts to legitimate their readings.

So many of Faulkner's novels find their subject matter in the multiple ways in which characters make meaning for themselves that it is impossible to reduce his view to one conservative, patriarchal version of southern history.

One side of Faulkner, the public figure given to pronouncements about what he called "the eternal verities"—qualities like pride and sacrifice and pity—does seem to reinforce Brooks's interpretation. Yet many characteristics of the novels themselves call this side of Faulkner into question. In constructing a "cosmos of his own," Faulkner seemed to need to distance the actual world from the artistic construct. He wrote many of his novels about absent characters who become the objects of narrative obsessions, with the symbolizing imaginations of the narrators replacing any real dealings with another person. He often gave up one narrative stance to adopt multiple narrative voices that, in their isolation, preclude the sharing of values necessary to a true community. His radical experiments with form, which cause no two novels to be alike, reflect an alien world, not a familiar one, with the dislocations of modernism part of their purpose. Faulkner does seem to share Brooks's idea of the work of art as an autotelic entity, as in the image of the vase "like that which the old Roman kept at his bedside" in Faulkner's posthumously published introduction to *The Sound and the Fury,* yet the interconnections among the novels complicate the issue, making the whole of Faulkner's work one intricate world.

On the one hand, New Criticism separates the work of art from politics, social issues, and even the historical context in which it was produced; on the other hand, the conservative values of its practitioners project or create a historical context that may distort the work. Brooks solves this conflict to his own satisfaction by seeing his traditional values as universal, inhering in human experience itself and therefore quite rightly represented in a work of art that separates itself from historical flux. The idea of a community of shared values in a self-contained work of art thus seems to him to be a natural, even necessary correlation. His conservatism, however, may not allow him to see the radicalism of Faulkner's experiments in fiction.

Michael L. Hall (review date Spring 1992)

SOURCE: "Well Wrought Facts," in *The Sewanee Review,* Vol. C, No. 2, Spring, 1992, pp. xxxviii-xli.

[*Below, Hall favorably reviews* Historical Evidence and the Reading of Seventeenth-Century Poetry *and compares it to Brooks's earlier work* The Well Wrought Urn.]

Historical Evidence and the Reading of Seventeenth-Century Poetry will be especially rewarding, as the title suggests, for readers interested in the good minor poetry of the seventeenth century. Some familiarity with the poets collected by H. J. C. Grierson and Geoffrey Bullough in their once standard *Oxford Book of Seventeenth-Century Verse* (1934), a book earlier generations of English doctoral students studied in preparation for oral qualifying examinations, would be helpful, but is not essential. The more general sort of educated readers will be happy to learn, however, that with ***Historical Evidence*** Cleanth Brooks also continues his lifelong project of teaching us how to read, understand, and appreciate literature.

Most obviously ***Historical Evidence*** may be approached as the demonstration Brooks claims it is of a method of reading old poems. In his introduction he remarks that his choice of seventeenth-century poetry was somewhat arbitrary, that he might just as well have performed his demonstrations with poems of a different period. He says he was "seriously tempted to choose poems printed between 1840 and 1890." He intends primarily to demonstrate that history is a valuable component of literary criticism: "Sometimes the biographer, the literary historian, and the lexicographer hold the keys necessary for unlocking a poem's full meaning, especially if the poem dates from an earlier time." Those startled to discover that Brooks still believes poems have meaning, full or otherwise, should be forewarned that he also speaks throughout this book of "literary value."

Brooks makes no effort, though, to join in recent critical debates. Nor is ***Historical Evidence*** a belated attempt, after more than forty years, to provide a corrective for the New Critical practices of ***The Well Wrought Urn*** (1947). In a brief epilogue Brooks notes connections between the two books and draws some obvious conclusions, but he makes no apologies. There remains, nevertheless, a complicated relationship between ***Historical Evidence*** and ***The Well Wrought Urn*** that should not be passed over lightly. Both books are, after all, demonstrations of interpretive practices that are usually applied to short lyric poems. Both begin with basic critical or theoretical assumptions but move quickly to specific examples. Both reprint the texts of the poems and rely heavily on close readings.

In other respects the two books offer contrasting mirror images. ***The Well Wrought Urn*** performs readings of some of the best-known poets of the canon: Donne, Shakespeare, Milton, Herrick, Pope, Gray, Wordsworth, Keats, Tennyson, and Yeats. In many ways Brooks intended his earlier book to show that New Critical methods would work in all periods and on all poets. With ***Historical Evidence*** he turns to minor poets of a single period and to poems nearly forgotten by everyone, save an older generation of literary scholars and a few specialists in the seventeenth century—poems by Henry King, Richard Corbett, James Shirley, Aurelian Townshend, Sir Richard Fanshawe, Lord Herbert of Cherbury, Sir Richard Lovelace, and Andrew Marvell. With the exception of Marvell's "To His Coy Mistress," "The Garden," and "Horatian Ode upon Cromwell's Return from Ireland," and perhaps not even excepting the last, these poems and poets will not be well known.

The Well Wrought Urn relies on familiarity and takes history and biography for granted, although not entirely. From time to time Brooks may remind us that "legend" "in Donne's time meant 'the life of a saint,' " or recall that Herrick was an Anglican parson to complicate the irony of "Corrina's Going A-Maying," or allude to the allegoric figures "which clutter a great abbey church such as that at Bath or at Westminster" to explain references in Gray's "Elegy." But in ***Historical Evidence*** he expects unfamiliarity and performs virtuoso readings by means of detailed historical and biographical references, as well as frequent recourse to the OED and other sources for contemporary seventeenth-century meanings of a poem's words. His learned and sensible account of Marvell's use of the word *glew* in "To His Coy Mistress" should finally dispatch any lingering notion that the poet thought his young lady was coated in "youthful glue."

Despite these contrasts, however, the two books are finally much more alike than they are different. Both exhibit a range of address now almost absent from literary criticism. Both concentrate attention on literary qualities now more often ignored than illuminated. Both insist on the necessity to let the poem "speak for itself" even after the historical evidence is presented, even against this evidence. After a particularly effective reading of Henry King's "An Exequy To his Matchlesse never to be forgotten Friend," Brooks reminds us that the Anglican Bishop who so lamented the loss of his wife Anne, and who in the final stanzas of his most successful poem looks forward to his reunion with her in death, "I shall at last sitt downe by Thee," not only may have married again but certainly was not reunited with Anne in a common grave, since as bishop of Chichester he was buried in his cathedral. Then Brooks challenges us with a familiar question: "Let us suppose that some scholar should come upon documentary evidence that Bishop King had remarried. Ought we in that case to think less of 'The Exequy'?" His answer comes as no surprise to readers of ***The Well Wrought Urn.*** After demonstrating that we cannot fully understand the meaning of King's "Exequy" without recourse to history and biography, Brooks reminds us that "this magnificent poem stands above and apart from all the vicissitudes of King's personal life" and "now enjoys a life of its own, not to be affected by what subsequently happened to its author or what he caused to happen."

Brooks's impressive range of address in ***Historical Evidence*** results in part from his allusions, often to poems that appeared in ***The Well Wrought Urn,*** but also to other poems both of the seventeenth century and afterward. The discussions of Hardy's poetry are a particular bonus, especially the comparison of "The Country Wedding" and John Hall's "On a Gentleman and His Wife," in which Brooks shows us why we may prefer Hardy to Hall, and why this is a poetic judgment on the relative success of the two poems as poems. Similarly his reading of James Shirley's "The glories of our blood and state" compares Shirley's poem to Gray's "Elegy," and then more briefly Gray's to Milton's "Il Penseroso," and finally concludes with a reading of Hardy's "In Time of 'The Breaking of Nations.' " None of these allusions is incidental. Each helps to demonstrate connections between the specific historical context a poem may have grown out of and its ability to make contact with larger human universals.

Not that Brooks ignores differences. Noting contrasts is an important part of his method of reading, but his point is that the specific historical reading must give into a larger context that includes our knowledge of other periods and other styles of poetry. Brooks intends to demonstrate, finally, that his method of historical reading is not antiquarian but serves a larger purpose, and part of that purpose is to remind us why we would want to read these old poems, or any other works of literature, in the first place: "No one has ever doubted that poems (and novels and plays) are products of the culture out of which they came, and consequently at some level they must reflect that culture. But that fact does not prevent our assessing these literary documents on other levels, including what they can tell us about ourselves and about the universal human condition."

Additional coverage of Brooks's life and career is contained in the following sources published by Gale Research: *Contemporary Authors,* Vols. 17-20 (rev. ed.), 145; *Contemporary Authors New Revision Series,* Vols. 33, 35; *Contemporary Literary Criticism,* Vol. 24; *Dictionary of Literary Biography,* Vol. 63; and *Major 20th-Century Writers.*

Elias Canetti

July 25, 1905—August 14, 1994

Bulgarian-born novelist, essayist, playwright, nonfiction writer, autobiographer, and translator.

For further information on Canetti's life and works, see *CLC,* Volumes 3, 14, 25, and 75.

INTRODUCTION

The recipient of the 1981 Nobel Prize in Literature, Canetti is best known for his only novel, *Die Blendung* (1935-36; *Auto-da-Fé* and *The Tower of Babel*), and his treatise on mass behavior, *Masse und Macht* (1960; *Crowds and Power*). Born in Rutschuk (now Ruse), Bulgaria, Canetti lived in various countries throughout Europe, and his national identity is, subsequently, often a matter of dispute: he has been identified as Turkish, Bulgarian, German, British, Austrian, and Swiss. His early years were spent in London, Vienna, and several European German-speaking countries, and in the 1920s he immersed himself in the cultural life of Berlin and Vienna, associating with famed novelists and artists of the day. In the 1930s Canetti fled to England after the annexation of Austria by Germany and the anti-Semitic violence of Kristallnacht, events which, many critics claim, confirmed his desire to make the study of individual psychology, mass psychology, and crowd phenomena his life work. Canetti's well-known *Auto-da-Fé,* a study of obsessed individuals, details the ruin of Peter Kien, a world-renowned sinologist completely engrossed with his 25,000-volume library. The other major characters in the novel also exhibit obsessions that dominate their lives: Kien's housekeeper, Therese Krumbholz, is preoccupied with satisfying her appetites for money and sex; Benedikt Pfaff, the manager of Kien's apartment house, with seizing money and power; and a dwarf, Fischerle, with becoming a wealthy and famous chess champion. *Auto-da-Fé* satirizes the greed, cruelty, and intolerance of each of these individuals, all of whom, though victims themselves, readily join in the persecution of one another. Observing that Canetti's portrait of a world populated by cruel, obsessive personalities accurately reflects European society in the 1920s and 1930s, critics note that his complex narrative technique provides a penetrating understanding of his characters' psychopathy. *Crowds and Power,* the product of thirty years of labor, draws on literature, anthropology, and science in an attempt to explain the origins, behavior, and significance of crowds as forces in society. Organized as a large volume of brief, aphoristic essays explaining various aspects and examples of mass psychology, the book scrutinizes crowds and crowd-like phenomena found in nature, mythology, and history. Canetti created his own terminology for discussing mass phenomena in *Crowds and Power,* disregarded modern scientific studies of crowds, and ignored important contemporary examples of crowd behavior and crowd manipulators, most notably Adolf Hitler, the volume is considered highly original in its approach as well as easily accessible to the average reader. Thomas H. Falk observed: "Further studies [will] surely confirm the Nobel Prize tribute: In his versatile writings the cosmopolitan Canetti attacks the sicknesses of our age and serves the cause of humanity with intellectual passion and moral responsibility." Additionally known for his plays and autobiographies, Canetti was also the recipient of numerous other awards, including the Georg Büchner Prize, the Franz Kafka Prize, and the Great Service Cross of the Federal Republic of Germany.

PRINCIPAL WORKS

Die Blendung [*Auto-da-Fé* and *The Tower of Babel*] (novel) 1935-36
Fritz Wotruba [*Fritz Wotruba*] (criticism) 1955
**Die Befristeten* [*Life-Terms* and *The Numbered*] (drama) 1956
Masse und Macht [*Crowds and Power*] (nonfiction) 1960
***Dramen* (dramas) 1964
Aufzeichnungen 1942-1948 (aphorisms) 1965
†*Hochzeit* [*The Wedding*] (drama) 1965
‡*Die Komödie der Eitelkeit* [*Comedy of Vanity*] (drama) 1965
Die Stimmen von Marrakesch: Aufzeichnungen nach einer Reise [*The Voices of Marrakesh: A Record of a Visit*] (travelogue) 1967
Der andere Prozeß: Kafkas Briefe an Felice [*Kafka's Other Trial: The Letters to Felice*] (criticism) 1969
Alle vergeudete Verebrung: Aufzeichnungen 1949-1960 (aphorisms) 1970
Die gespaltene Zukunft: Aufsätze und Gespräche (essays) 1972
Macht und Überleben: Drei Essays (essays) 1972
Die Provinz des Menschen: Aufzeichnungen 1942-1972 [*The Human Province*] (aphorisms) 1973
Der Ohrenzeuge: Fünfzig Charaktere [*Earwitness: Fifty Characters*] (sketches) 1974
Das Gewissen der Worte [*The Conscience of Words*] (essays) 1975
Der Beruf des Dichters (essay) 1976
Die gerettete Zunge: Geschichte einer Jugend [*The Tongue Set Free: Remembrance of a European Childhood*] (autobiography) 1977
Die Fackel im Ohr: Lebensgeschichte 1921-1931 [*The Torch in My Ear*] (autobiography) 1980
Das Augenspiel: Lebensgeschichte 1931-1937 [*The Play of the Eyes*] (autobiography) 1985
Das Geheimherz der Uhr: Aufzeichnungen 1973-1985 [*The Secret Heart of the Clock: Notes, Aphorisms, Fragments 1973-1985*] (aphorisms) 1987
Die Fliegenpein [*The Agony of Flies*] (sketches, notes, aphorisms) 1992

*This work was first published in 1964 in *Dramen.*

**This work contains *Hochzeit, Die Komödie der Eitelkeit,* and *Die Befristeten.*

†This work was written in 1931-32 and first published in 1964 in *Dramen,* but never performed until 1965.

‡This work, written in 1933-34, was first published in 1950, but never performed until 1965.

TRIBUTES AND OBITUARIES

Sidney Rosenfeld (essay date Winter 1982)

SOURCE: "1981 Nobel Laureate Elias Canetti: A Writer Apart," in *World Literature Today,* Vol. 56, No. 1, Winter, 1982, pp. 5-9.

[*In the following essay, which was written after Canetti was awarded the Nobel Prize for Literature in 1981, Rosenfeld provides an overview of Canetti's life, career, and major works, focusing on his critical reception and the problematic nature of his national identity.*]

At first glance, if it was at the *New York Times,* the news that the 1981 Nobel Prize in Literature was awarded to Elias Canetti would seem to belie Ivar Ivask's observation [in *World Literature Today* 55, No. 2] that, in vying for recognition, "major writers from major languages have more support than major authors from minor literatures." The *Times*'s front-page article bore the heading "Bulgarian Wins the Nobel Prize for Literature," and the continuation was captioned "Bulgarian Writer Wins Nobel Prize." The content of the article made evident, however, that Canetti belongs not in the second but in the first category. He is a major German-language writer and, one must insist, no more a Bulgarian writer than I. B. Singer, the 1978 laureate, is a Polish writer, or Czesław Miłosz, last year's prize recipient, a Lithuanian writer—however great the debt of these authors to their birthlands may be.

To be sure, Elias Canetti was born in Bulgaria (in 1905), but he did not acquire its language as his mother tongue. Rather, his first language was Ladino, the Old Spanish of the Sephardic Jews, and whatever Bulgarian he had learned he soon lost when he was taken to England as a child of six. Moreover, while his mother stemmed from one of the country's oldest Sephardic families, his paternal grandparents had moved to Bulgaria from Adrianople, and like many of the Sephardim, they retained Turkish citizenship. Canetti too was a Turkish subject. Nevertheless, the problem of where he belongs as a writer can be resolved simply if it is conceded that someone who writes in German is a German author. Yet the question of this author's personal identity, of his "nationality," which is not German, cannot be dismissed. It touches upon the heart of his work and the fascination he has exercised on an international audience that has grown ever larger through the years. This identity is inseparably linked with a life history that, if it is to be properly understood, must be traced back almost five centuries to Inquisitional Spain.

The surname Canetti is, of course, neither Slavic nor Germanic. It is an Italianized form of the place-name Canete and derives from the city of the family's origins between Cuenca and Valencia. Before the mass emigration of Bulgarian Jews to Israel after World War II—to its lasting honor, Bulgaria had saved them from annihilation—such names as Canetti, Arditti (the maiden name of the laureate's mother), Morenzi or Almosino were hardly uncommon in the larger towns of the Kingdom. They could, in fact, be encountered throughout the Balkans and still farther reaches of the Turkish domain to which thousands of Spanish Jews had fled from the terror of the Inquisition, among them the writer's own forebears. But Canetti was fated to become a *German* writer, and in the German-speaking countries, where he spent his most formative years, such names are rare. They catch both the eye and the ear and mark their owner as an outsider, all the more when they are identified, as the name Canetti is today, with an art so profoundly expressive of a nation's history and character as its literature.

The conjecture may be warranted that the rarity of the name itself and exotic appeal such rarity creates inspired the fairly consistent cover and dust-jacket designs of Canetti's books. Particularly the American editions, but also the German originals, forcefully display the author's surname, alone, in imposingly bold type across the front and back, so that it greatly overshadows the title. But despite its prominence, the name does not jump out to greet the viewer. It stands commandingly on its threshold, as it were, declaring the presence of a writer who challenges more than he invites the reader to venture acquaintance with him. Whoever takes up this challenge discovers an author who has secured for himself an elevated and very distinct place in German letters on terms of his own. He requires of the reader a high degree of concentration; he demands too the readiness to relinquish what is familiar and assuring and to follow him, the writer, on paths that may lead into realms of absurdity and madness. The reader must be willing to persist with him in his unconventional pursuit of themes and interests that resist traditional modes of portrayal: the hateful tyranny of death over human existence, the dynamics and interplay of crowds and power, the world of myth and magic, the essence and authority of literary genius.

In citing Canetti's "original and most vigorously profiled personality," the Swedish Academy confirmed what has become a universally accepted view. Also, the interviews that have appeared during the past two decades attest to these same qualities, consistently revealing an artist-thinker of striking originality and commanding presence. Even so individual and formidable a discussion partner as Theodor Adorno pales and seems disadvantaged in conversation with him. Indeed, there appears to exist no discrepancy between the man and the writer; Canetti's personal presence and the presence projected in his books are equally intense and absorbing. The acquaintance with the oeuvre would genuinely seem to represent a full and authentic acquaintance with the author's personality itself. Thus the evident displeasure with which the laureate declined to grant interviews after the award was publicized—"Whoever wants to know something should read my books"—reflected a readily experienced truth and can find justification on grounds that lie beyond the sheer desire for privacy.

Canetti's fascination as an artist-intellectual is starkly revealed in the two major works that established his literary eminence—which until today remains the eminence of the solitary outsider; they are the novel ***Die Blendung*** (translated as ***Auto-da-Fé***), first published in 1935, and the encyclopedic study ***Masse und Macht*** (***Crowds and Power***), on which he labored for twenty years before it finally appeared in 1960. The extraordinary claim he made for the latter work, namely that in it he had "succeeded in grabbing this century by the throat," can be applied to the novel also—if ***Auto-da-Fé*** is viewed as an artistic-symbolic portrayal of the unspoken but clearly underlying thesis of ***Crowds and Power:*** that the two great calamities of the twentieth century, Hitlerism and Stalinism, arose from the dialectical interaction of human masses, which tyrants can create and exploit, and the problem of power and paranoia. The accomplishment of the novel lies in Canetti's narrative transformation of this thesis, which he was to elaborate in ***Crowds and Power*** only years later. In the story of the private scholar Peter Kien he portrayed an intellectual so estranged from reality—the "Head Without a World"—and so hostile to it that he could end only in self-destruction. The flames that engulf the "greatest Sinologist of his time" amid the gigantic mass of his books—the novel teems with symbolic masses—forebode the ruin that was soon to descend on Canetti's Europe.

Auto-da-Fé has gained its author a respected place within the cosmopolitan Central European narrative tradition that is represented by the Austrian novelists Kafka, Musil and Broch, with whom he is most often associated. It has been recognized also as a precursor of trends that were to culminate only twenty years later in the literature of the absurd. It has been described as an "experimental novel without stylistic experiments," and as such it demonstrates Canetti's originality in the most telling way. He discussed the book's narrative strategy in the following manner [in his ***The Conscience of Words***]:

> One day, the thought came to me that the world should not be depicted as in earlier novels, from one writer's standpoint, as it were; the world had *crumbled,* and only if one had the courage to show it in its crumbled state could one possibly offer an authentic conception of it. However, this did not mean that one had to tackle a chaotic book, in which nothing was comprehensible anymore; on the contrary, a writer had to invent extreme individuals with the most rigorous consistency, like the individuals the world consisted of, and he had to place these extreme individuals next to one another in their separateness.

The total elimination of "one writer's standpoint" contributes more than any other narrative device to the novel's stunning effect. Canetti succeeded fully in neutralizing his narrator: he has been given no authoritative and distinguishing voice, but rather he becomes the ever-changing echo of the sundry voices that inhabit the story; he accompanies its "extreme individuals" on a compulsive course through their microcosmic world as though they, and their world, were whole and not "crumbled." For the narrator, unlike the author, Kien and his tormentors are seemingly unexceptional; his tone betrays no judgment, and he offers no guidance. The reader is directly faced with the madness of this world—which is conjured up, moreover, in a language that is wholly lucid and concrete—and left to fend for himself in its threatening midst. Such abandonment is unaccustomed and very probably helps to account for the frequently heard criticisms that the novel is "too difficult" (or even incomprehensible), that reading it is disturbing or eerie. ***Auto-da-Fé*** surely is difficult, but its essential difficulties are not formal and stylistic ones. Rather, they are difficulties that arise from the novel's inherent demand that the reader consciously confront as real, and reject, the madness it portrays and for which it offers no antidote.

The 1947 American edition of ***Auto-da-Fé*** was significantly titled ***The Tower of Babel,*** thus reflecting the narrative's chaotic world of extreme individuals in the unbridgeable separateness that Canetti embodied in the peculiarities of their speech. Still other titles, these of his own choosing, underscore the prime function in his writing of individualized speech, of what he has termed the "acoustic citation." A collection of grotesque satirical character sketches is called ***Der Ohrenzeuge*** (1974; translated as ***Earwitness,*** 1979); in the portrait devoted to the title character, the "Earwitness" himself, the reader learns that "his ear is better and more faithful than any gadget, nothing is erased, nothing is blocked, . . . he accurately registers even things he does not understand and delivers them unaltered if people wish him to do so." The first volume of Canetti's autobiography is entitled ***Die gerettete Zunge*** (1977; ***The Tongue Set Free,*** 1979), and the second ***Die Fackel im Ohr*** (1980), literally ***The Torch in the Ear***. This latter title—which the planned American translation will reportedly not bear—refers to the journal *Die Fackel* (*The Torch*), which the Viennese satirist and polemicist Karl Kraus edited and wrote from 1899 until his death in 1936. For some five years, in Vienna, Kraus exercised a spiritual and intellectual dictatorship over Canetti, who found himself merged into the "hunting pack" that he perceived in the enthralled audiences at Kraus's celebrated readings. In order to regain the freedom of his own judgments, Canetti was compelled to liberate himself from this powerful hold; but he confessed lasting gratitude to Kraus for the gift of *hearing* that he had received from him: "Since hearing him, it has not been possible for me not to do my own hearing."

The start of work on ***Auto-da-Fé*** coincided with Canetti's self-liberation from the oppressive sway of Karl Kraus and suggests that Kraus's inspiration had been internally set free and could now become productive. The kinship of Canetti's novel with Kraus's gigantic drama of World War I, *Die letzten Tage der Menschheit* (*The Last Days of Mankind;* 1919), is evident. It is not a kinship that arises from imitation but rather a kinship of artistic and ethical persuasion. In countless variants of human speech, captured in their subtlest pitches and shadings, Kraus had brought to life and condemned the same "crumbled" world that Canetti now undertook to evoke in ***Auto-da-Fé***—by means of what he called the "acoustic mask." For Canetti, it is through speech that people assume shape and form, are clearly delineated from every angle, are differentiated one from another. "A person's speech-shape," he explained, "the stable character of his speech, this language that arose with him, that he alone possesses, that will pass with him, is what I call his acoustic mask." Canetti has left no doubt that his sensitivity for this phenomenon was honed by Karl Kraus. But he must have been uncommonly receptive to the nuances of individual speech from his earliest years on.

Not only was his mother tongue, Ladino, not the language of his birthplace, it was also not the sole language of his home. To each other his parents spoke German, which he was unable to comprehend. What is better suited to stir curiosity and awaken the desire for initiation and possession than the secrets parents withhold from their children! Indeed, Canetti's resentment toward his mother for such exclusion vanished only when she began teaching him German in his ninth year. From his grandfather, moreover, he heard songs in Turkish, and from the peasant girls who lived in his home as serving women he heard fairy tales in Bulgarian (which he later mysteriously retained only in German). And to complicate these circumstances further, there were the Hebrew prayers, readings and songs on holidays, in which the boy participated with a feeling of importance though without understanding the ancient language. Upon this multilingual beginning followed two years in England, from 1911 to 1913, when the young Canetti started school and read his first books, in English. From 1913 until he completed the gymnasium eleven years later, he changed countries three times and lived successively in Vienna, Zürich and Frankfurt—each city with its own peculiarities of German idiom. Against this background it is no wonder that Canetti became an "earwitness," a master of the "acoustic citation," and that, in addition, he acquired the cosmopolitan sensitivities that enabled the encompassing vision not only of ***Auto-da-Fé*** but also of his second major work, ***Crowds and Power.***

The title of this massive study—which is as strikingly original as ***Auto-da-Fé*** and likewise reveals Canetti as a writer apart—announces its theme with self-assured succinctness. But its method and scope cannot be characterized without the help of an ungainly procession of academically-robed adjectives such as: anthropological, ethnological, sociological, philosophical, psychological. In a spectacular feat of intellectual synthesis Canetti joined the disciplines to which they apply and produced an absolutely novel inquiry into the interdynamics of masses and power. Not only did he accomplish this in a language that is clear and concrete to the same degree that the subjects of his investigation are dark and elusive, but he did it also in declared independence of the scientific-theoretical schools that have shaped our contemporary view of these subjects. To both the praise, if not to say amazement, and the skepticism of Canetti's commentators, ***Crowds and Power*** refers nowhere to either Sigmund Freud or Karl Marx, nor does it show any debt to them. Canetti consciously excluded them from his reflections, in part because of critical doubts and a goodly measure of personal rejection, but more significantly because he was determined to start anew, as it were, to go at his task, as he stressed, in a "completely naïve" way, to develop his own terminology and to attain his own results. The richness and complexity of his study frustrate the attempt to define these results within a common conceptual framework or to distill some single theory from them.

Praise for ***Crowds and Power,*** which has been acclaimed as a revolutionary work, has usually centered on the author's intellectual breadth, imagination and originality rather than on the practical or theoretical value of his findings. He had set out to seize his century by the throat, but the century, as a historical and political reality, is absent from his book. Its undeniable hermetic quality has elicited the criticism that ***Crowds and Power*** is "lost," "unscientific," "idiosyncratic." Such criticism, which has sometimes amounted to rejection, must be seen as a consequence of the book's most-cited characteristic, its originality. Whether this work will ultimately be regarded as a grand curiosity or accepted as a valid contribution to the analysis of mass behavior and the politics of tyranny, and thus to human survival, will be decided by the kinds of thought and ideas it proves itself able to stimulate. Will Canetti's insights be incorporated into the systems of knowledge that help to determine social and political planning? Can they be employed to help reconcile the destructive global rivalries between West and East and, increasingly, North and South? Canetti himself demonstrated in his essay **"Hitler, According to Speer"** that such questions need not be academic, that they possess genuine content, and that ***Crowds and Power,*** for all its seeming exoticism, may bear directly on the most crucial problems of contemporary existence.

The awarding of the Nobel Prize to Canetti produced news reports that showed considerable uncertainty or, in some instances, plain helplessness. Inherent in much of the commentary was the not unfamiliar question on this annual occasion: Who *is* he? Or perhaps, Who's *he!* Yet Canetti is not new to the American literary scene. In fact, he had achieved recognition in America—and even more in England—before he gained prominence in Germany. Both ***Auto-da-Fé*** and ***Crowds and Power*** were acknowledged early as remarkable works by an unusually gifted author. There were three successive printings of ***Auto-da-Fé*** in England in 1946-47 and four more between 1962 and 1973; during the years 1947-79 there were four printings in America. ***Crowds and Power*** first appeared in both countries in 1962, and in America it has been issued three times since. Starting in 1978, Seabury Press in New York has published another five of Canetti's works in translation. Nonetheless, it is fair to say that since the early 1960s his repute has grown most steadily and his stature has been acknowledged most firmly in Germany—although he did not reach a popular audience there until ***Die gerettete Zunge*** appeared in 1977.

Canetti himself will probably not be impressed by his new prominence; fame has never been his goal. But now that it has come, the intriguing question arises of what country, or countries, will want to share it with him; and along with this question there arises once again that of his identity. The answer given at the outset still holds: As a writer in German, Canetti is—like Kafka, the German-speaking Jew from Czech Prague whom he esteems—a German writer. But again like Kafka, he is one who evades neat categorization. The term "writer in exile" has often been applied to him, but its validity is not apparent. From what homeland was Canetti exiled? Given his personal history, the answer that he had found his sole homeland in the German language is more than just metaphorical. Although he was forced to flee from Austria—where he had lived from 1924 to 1938—when it was joined to the Greater Germany of the Third Reich, he did not permit himself to be banished from the realm of the German language. Perhaps the most moving statement he has made in this context is the following from the year 1944 [in his ***The Human Province***]:

> The language of my intellect will remain German—because I am Jewish. Whatever remains of the land which has been laid waste in every way—I wish to preserve it in me as a Jew. *Their* destiny too is mine; but I bring along a universal human legacy. I want to give back to their language what I owe it. I want to contribute to their having something that others can be grateful for.

This is not the declaration of a writer in exile, but of one for whom language and vocation together have created an identity that lies beyond any geographical or national-political boundaries. Yet even within the cultural sphere of the German language and its literature, it is the identity of a writer who comprehends himself as an outsider. Both in defiance and gratitude he wishes to return to *their* language what he owes it.

Even when Canetti himself speaks of "the two great expulsions" in his past, that of his forebears from Spain and that of the Jews from Nazi Germany, the one appears to be as close to him and as vivid as the other; he is not evoking an exile that can be translated into the terms of literary history and national identities. Rather, he is placing himself within a tradition that permits identifications of mythical dimension. At the end of an insightful discussion with the novelist Horst Bienek, Canetti said:

> Sometimes I think myself to be a Spanish poet in the German language. When I read the old Spaniards, for example *Celestina* or Quevedo's *Sueños,* I believe that I myself am speaking in them. No one knows who he really is. It gives me strength to know at least this much. [**"Gespräch mit Horst Bienek,"** in ***Die geteilte Zukunft***]

The persuasion that no one has full knowledge of his identity does not imply a diminution but rather an enrichment of the self—which for Canetti is the product of millennia of human experience. He intends it quite literally when he claims affinity with the old Spanish poets. He, the German writer, is the offspring of untold ancestors who emerged from the obscurity of history in medieval Spain and who remain present in his personality five centuries later. Their becoming and being are an inseparable part of his own; their cultural experience is alive in him.

Fundamental to this belief and indeed to Canetti's entire thought is the concept of transformation, a phenomenon in which he sees the origins of mankind as well as the essence of human existence. Nowhere does the boldness of this concept, as he has interpreted it, become so apparent as in his assertions [in **"Gespräch mit Horst Bienek"**] that "man is the sum of all the animals into which he transformed himself in the course of his history." But less drastically, Canetti has applied it also to his view of work and profession in the life of each individual, stating his conviction [in **"Gespräch mit Joachim Schickel"** in ***Die geteilte Zukunft***] that "the individual, and really every individual, possesses a totality of natural bents and that in the last analysis many of these bents derive from the rich store of old transformations. No one is really a unity and should live as a unity." It is this belief in the multiple character of the self that underlies Canetti's often-cited opposition to the "division of labor" and helps to explain one of the most salient characteristics of his writing: its unusual range and diversity.

At seventy-six, Canetti has hardly concluded his oeuvre. A sequel to ***Crowds and Power***—whose tentative appearance he has announced more than once—has been awaiting its definitive form for at least a decade. During the same period he has been cautiously withholding from publication several works of fiction. They are said to include two more novels and some plays, all in advanced stages of completion. The two volumes of his autobiography, which appeared within three years of each other, in 1977 and 1980, extend only to 1931; thus a third volume would seem likely, perhaps in the near future. With a writer so thoroughly distinctive as Canetti, all predictions are precarious but for one: that from his solitary place, outside the traditional literary categories, he will continue to fascinate a steadily growing readership with works of high originality and challenging symbolic vision.

Roger Kimball on Canetti's life and memoirs:

[In attempting to place] Canetti's memoirs within his *oeuvre,* it is difficult not to conclude that his real masterpiece was not his life's work but his life, not the story of Professor Kien or the nature of crowds but his own story, the story of becoming Elias Canetti. It is for the account they give us of this absorbing story that they will be read long After *Auto-da-Fé* and *Crowds and Power* become historical curiosities.

Roger Kimball in his "Becoming Elias Canetti," in The New Criterion, *September, 1986.*

Edward Rothstein (review date 8-15 January 1990)

SOURCE: "Dreams of Disappearance," in *The New Republic,* Vol. 202, Nos. 2-3, January 8-15, 1990, pp. 33-6, 38-9.

[*Rothstein is an American critic. In the following review of several of Canetti's memoirs, he discusses various aspects of Canetti's life and works.*]

On a trip to Morocco, Elias Canetti was attracted again and again to the great square in the middle of Marrakesh. It was not the bustle of haggling merchants or the sights of starving camels that drew his attention, but a small brown bundle huddling on the ground—a bundle "consisting not even of a voice but of a single sound." The bundle produced a drawn out buzzing "e-e-e-e-e-e-e-e" that just went on and on, audible beneath all the cries of the square.

Canetti saw neither the mouth that produced this sound, nor any part of the face, nor the body, just a hooded cloak and a shapeless mass. He did not know whether the creature was tall or short, whether it was carried to its begging place in the square or walked there on its own, whether it had arms with which to pick up the coins tossed on the ground. Canetti felt helpless before it, not because of imagined horrors of deformity, but because he felt there was something sacred about the bundle, which he called the "unseen"; he could not unveil or approach it. He imagined that the unremitting vowel sound was Allah's name called out by a tongueless mouth. And what he felt, most peculiarly, was pride: "I was proud of the bundle because it was alive." It persisted, reappeared, never silent, producing its diligent mournful cry.

Canetti is a peculiar writer, not least because it is possible to imagine him seeking that bundle not just in Marrakesh but wherever his wanderings took him. He is the traveler determinedly selecting the "unseen" and the "tongueless" from the voices surrounding him in the marketplace, picking out the crippled call from the badgering, begging voices. This gives him a peculiar perspective, a view of the world that elevates the eccentric and denigrates the familiar, that despises those who would make their way through the world on ordinary terms and honors those who are hobbled by it but pursue within themselves an unseen, unheard quest.

Canetti peoples his books with such figures: an aging Sinologist who disdains humanity and lives only for the sake of his 25,000-book library, a paraplegic philosopher who reads by turning pages with his tongue, a disturbed widow who in a nightly ritual solemnly licks the back of photos of her late husband, a five-year-old boy who chases his young cousin with an ax intending to kill her because she won't show him her school notebooks. Only the first of these is a fictional creation. The others are characters in his memoirs. The last was Canetti himself.

It is hard to know what to make of him, in fact, so exotic are his visions, so eccentric is his vision. In 1981 he was awarded the Nobel Prize for literature, but anyone coming upon ***The Secret Heart of the Clock,*** his most recent book in English, would have a difficult time imagining why. It is the sort of book that is meant to bring the reader closer to the writer—a collection of notes and aphorisms and fragments confided to notebooks between 1973 and 1985. They range from images that must have just come to mind ("the sieve of his self-confidence" is the entire text of one) to hypothetical imaginings of lands and worlds in which our natural order is overturned and strange events become the rule ("a country where the language is changed every ten years," or "the land without brothers: no one has more than one child," or "a land where people burst with a little pop"). In these jottings, merely the evocation of these strangely premised universes is supposed to suffice for illumination.

Yet there are also more revealing hints of something more personal. "My melancholy is never free of anger," he writes. "Among writers I am one who rages." Or, "Only in fear am I completely myself." And in 1980, at the age of 75, "The very last thing in my life that still makes an impression on me: animals." Rage, fear, resentment, and misanthropic sentiments seem to accompany a sort of abstract "adoration of humanity." "One who reveres the worst—man—believes in its transformation," Canetti asserts; and we begin to wonder what this worst is, and what are the grounds for the adoration and the transformation that Canetti lays out in the writings of his career.

The life and the career are relatively uncomplicated, except for their restless movement. Canetti was born in 1905 in Ruschuk, Bulgaria, to a family of Sephardic Jewish merchants. He spoke Ladino, German, Bulgarian, and English before he was seven. (He was writing Latin poetry by the time he was 14.) His family moved to Manchester when he was eight, where his father died suddenly. Canetti's education was a sampling of Europe's best: schools in England, Vienna, and Zurich, including a doctorate in chemistry from the University of Vienna in 1929. Six years later, his novel, ***Auto-da-Fé,*** was published in German (as ***Die Blendung***). By then he had set out on what he called his "life work," which took nearly three decades, and was published in English in 1962 as ***Crowds and Power***. There were also plays, essays, the account of the visit to Marrakesh; and in 1977 Canetti began publishing his memoirs, three volumes of which have appeared in English so far.

But this life of adopted countries and languages and ambitions yielded sentiments that were anything but simple. As Susan Sontag has written, Canetti's life was "rich in displacements"; and so he cultivated a manner of displacement and detachment. He admired such 20th century German writers as Musil and Kafka, and he seemed to imitate the allusive baroque quality of the first and the psychological paralysis of the second. But the youthful ***Auto-da-Fé*** also resists such comparisons. Canetti saw it as one of a series of books about modern types, about perverse figures who reacted to the world's horrors with obsessive peculiarity. He envisioned a Religious Fanatic, a Collector, an Actor, an Enemy of Death.

He got only as far as this novel, about a Book Man. Its main character, Kien, knows little about the world other than what is described by his scholarly texts. His universe is gradually taken over by a thuggish, illiterate cleaning woman with a starched skirt, who knows as little about her charge as he does about her. He is abused, imprisoned, and even tortured by her, all the while spinning absurd interpretations about the world created around him: a modern Don Quixote, beaten by the windmill. It is impossible to read this novel without horror, but no sympathy is permitted. Kien is actually something less than human, a bundle of bones and muscle whose delusions about the powers of language and learning have turned him into a pathetic organism who can live only in a cage bounded by his books; his final act is to set fire to his prized library, and to himself. The grotesques and brutes and cripples of this novel could hardly be imagined mourning at this pyre of Western civilization; they practically inspire its flames.

After years of rejections, the novel was published in 1935, sponsored by the philistine owner of a newspaper in Strasbourg who refused to read it. The patron thought, correctly, that he would have found it repellent; he sponsored it, incorrectly, because he imagined the book's horrors would serve as a cautionary warning against the dangers of our century. But Canetti does not exactly caution against the bleak universe of his novel. He is immersed in it, he is a believer in its apocalyptic tone, in its universal scorn; he calls its brutal account "graffiti on the walls of a new Pompei." *Kant Catches Fire* was Canetti's original title. Kant, who was devoted to the universal characteristics of thought, is destroyed: nothing is shared, everything said is misunderstood, there are no a prioris, no categorical imperatives.

Canetti may have viewed this sort of creaturely nihilism as the only authentic response to a crazed universe. But this recurrent (and by now tiresome) trope of our century haunts Canetti's other major book as well. ***Crowds and Power*** has the same insistence on a single theme that gives ***Auto-da-Fé*** its exhausting grip, though here the theme is unlimited by time or circumstance. All of human enterprise is seen as a manifestation of the drive to form crowds. The book ranges over the customs of primitive cultures, the metaphorical significance of rain and sand, the nature of tyranny. It is obsessed with the acts of primitive man—cannibalism, massacres, savagery—but it is clear that the obsession derives from the contemporary world: "It is not for a European of the 20th century to regard himself as above savagery." The formation of crowds becomes the primary fact of history; the imperial urge to increase one's numbers is the prime mover of peoples, the fundamental cause of battles, a biological need that is both an intoxication and a refuge. The book is as exhausting and distressing as the novel. With it, Canetti thought he was "grabbing this century by the throat."

Judging from some of the notebook entries in ***The Secret Heart of the Clock,*** Canetti is anxious, several decades later, to reinterpret his ideas, to give their peculiarity a better ground. That is one reason for his memoirs: "I ought to embed my ideas in their place of origin, to make them appear more natural. It is possible that by doing that, I would give them a different accent. I don't want to correct anything, but I want to retrieve the life that is part of the ideas, bring it in close and let it flow back into them." He wants to present what he calls "the tradition of a life," thus connecting the grand abstractions of ***Crowds and Power*** and the relentless obsessions of ***Auto-da-Fé*** with his own experience.

This attempt, it turns out, is extraordinarily revealing. Canetti would like to see himself as he sees that bundle—as a prideful, persistent, diligent presence, attempting to reach some discontented accommodation with the wayward world. He would also like to find some way of negotiating what he calls "the fluid boundary between individuals and types," between the ways in which concrete persons relate to the abstract and representative figures he so habitually imagines. The three volumes of memoirs published so far in English—***The Tongue Set Free, The Torch in My Ear,*** and ***The Play of the Eyes***—are accounts of the growth of the artist as a young man, learning to speak and hear and see. These tales, which barely bring the author to the age of 30, prepare the way for the production of his own more abstract cries in his novel, plays, criticism, and sociological analysis. They are an extraordinary literary achievement, more supple and suggestive than any of the works that gave Canetti the reputation he is recollecting.

The narratives of the earlier volumes are the most novelistic. They recall a youth speckled with relatives of gargantuan talent and elephantine pride, and a mother at once brilliant and hysterical, determining Canetti's displacements from country after country, drilling him in the German "mother" tongue in which he still writes. She reads him Strindberg nightly before he is in his teens, and promises him that she will never remarry; ridicules any hint of sentimentality that appears in her son, and leaves in him a dark, consuming hatred mixed with debt and worship.

But though the first volume is the most extraordinary in its shape and achievement, it is the third volume that is the most suggestive about Canetti's intellectual project. In ***The Play of the Eyes,*** Canetti begins to move within the marketplace of writers, artists, and ideas of the early 1930s in Vienna, finding in the midst of an age he has called "swift, menacing, and rich," the extreme, the exaggerated, the grotesque. Even if, at the time of many of these memories, ***Auto-da-Fé*** was still unpublished, and his plays—***The Wedding*** and ***Comedy of Vanities***—were still unstaged, Canetti was gaining a reputation for dramatic readings of these works at the homes of patrons, where, in the close-knit intellectual society of Vienna, he soon enough met the major literary figures of the time and the place. The performer recounts what he faced as he read: the great German novelist Hermann Broch flirting with Alma Mahler's beautiful daughter Anna instead of paying attention, Franz Werfel rudely interrupting his reading with scathing insults, James Joyce cryptically tossing a "wretched comment" at the expectant author. Canetti finds the universal rejection bracing, strengthening him for his life work: "It is defeats of such catastrophic proportions that keep a writer alive."

These memoirs are also an act of possession, a settling of old scores. There is, for example, a portrait of Heinrich Scherchen, the conductor who championed contemporary music during the early decades of the century. Canetti notes Scherchen's recurrent approach to building power: finding novelty, courting fashion, seducing key figures into his circle. He flatters Canetti with praise, then asks him conspiratorially to deliver a letter to Anna Mahler. But Canetti—strong-willed and strong-headed—soon becomes a rival for Anna's affections, and enmity with Scherchen follows. The very account becomes Canetti's delayed revenge. Canetti writes of the conductor: "At last I had before my eyes a perfect specimen of something I was determined to understand and portray: a dictator." Then he tells of the dictator at work. At a banquet Scherchen proclaims he will read everybody's palm. The 28-year-old author listens to the conductor's manipulative predictions for each of the guests; but a particularly cruel verdict is passed on Canetti's own hand. The 81-year-old memoirist writes, with a wry sense of vengeance against his nemesis: "I alone was doomed to die before my thirtieth birthday."

The memoirist seems to stalk through his own recollections, with a kind of animal determination, like a lion following its prey. Nearly everything is recounted with a primitive, simple clarity. And no slight is left unslighted. ***The Play of the Eyes*** seems to be about the play of power in the human animal. Every person in this memoir in some sense engages in a contest with the author, dominating him or being dominated by him. Canetti did indeed take an ax and attempt to murder his cousin for not showing him her notebooks. His literary assaults are more calculated, worked out with the care of a caricaturist, early self and late self in expert collusion.

The caricature comes in the exaggeration of a single feature of a person, the focus on a part of the physiognomy or personality. Thus Werfel, who slighted Canetti with both his literary judgment and his manners, becomes a rancid physical elaboration of his paunch. He "overflowed with sentiment, his fat belly gurgled with love and feeling, one expected to find little puddles on the floor around him and was almost disappointed to find it dry." The aging Alma Mahler is desiccated, grotesque, a mere appendage to the "trophies" of love and triumph she had collected about her and displayed to Canetti's horror. Hermann Broch is embodied in his "breath"—the respiration that Canetti finds in the man's posture and presence as well as in the movements of his prose and atmospheric style. The technique of caricature is present even in the titles of each volume of these memoirs that name parts of the sensing body. It is, I think, the way Canetti sees: individuals turn into representatives of types, their particularities becoming, as in the shrieking bundle or the churning crowd, exhausted by a single peculiarity.

The eyes of this third volume are themselves caricatures, revealing, commanding, demanding. They belong first to Anna, Alma Mahler's daughter with whom Canetti falls in love only to be suddenly and unpredictably cut off. Anna's "play of the eyes" is dangerous, seductive and enchanting; her eyes fix him, glittering, like a deep lake or pool. So powerful are they that her blunt and sudden rejection of Canetti has something "sublime" about it, as if such behavior were the natural right of a beautiful animal. "A woman endowed with such eyes," Canetti is told at one point by a friend, "couldn't help herself, she was a slave to the needs of her eyes, not as victim but as huntress."

The play of the eyes is also something that is far from private. It is a visible play that is meant to get the response of another. It is the play of the public life, the play of reputation and interaction and power. When Canetti is in the midst of a reading and sees Broch and Anna engaged in the "play of the eyes," or when he himself stares down Werfel and his "jutting right eye" at a concert, these are life and death games being played with these agents of power.

So potent are they that blindness becomes at once a great fear and a great relief. In ***Auto-da-Fé*** Kien feigns blindness to escape the power of his starched-skirted temptress and keeper Therese. And the original German title of the novel—***The Blinding***—is one that suggests Kien's escape, his punishment, and his revenge, all at once, in a world in which sight is delusion. The blinding in ***The Play of the Eyes*** occurs figuratively, with the death of Canetti's mother, with whom he struggled so bitterly in earlier volumes. "She lay there, emaciated," Canetti writes, "reduced to pale skin, with deep black holes instead of eyes." But it is also clear, during the ineffably moving pages of this recollection, that the author himself cannot escape the vision of his mother's eyes: "Her breathing grew weaker, but the power of her eyes grew stronger." They are the eyes that taught him about power. In their power to seduce, to intoxicate, to capture, to expand, they display an individualized version of the power of crowds: they are the crowd-organs of the human face.

Canetti's "tradition of a life" soon enough connects with the ideas of his work. The memoirs display the workings of power in the individual. ***Crowds and Power,*** a book more often praised than read, explores it in large groups. It is easy to imagine such a preoccupation developing on the eve of the Second World War, which was to have, as Canetti writes in ***The Play of the Eyes,*** the "proud and gluttonous appetite of a biblical Assyrian war." Clearly the crowds of Hitler are the ones that haunt Canetti's excavations into the primitive past.

Canetti was not, of course, alone in his choice of subject. Freud's ghost hovers over this text, his study of group psychology gnawed to pieces without ever being mentioned; and the study of massification was the preoccupation also of Ortega y Gasset and the Frankfurt School. But Canetti's approach was eclectic, stubbornly idiosyncratic. He expends his most brilliant energies establishing a sort of typological catalog of crowds: closed crowds and open crowds, slow crowds and fast crowds, feast crowds and flight crowds. There are crowds that have a quickly attainable goal, crowds created by a threat, crowds created in a closed space. But the primary urge of all crowds is to expand, to dissolve the individual in its mass. "The crowd always wants to grow."

Each type of crowd goes about its project in a different way, generating phenomena ranging from religious movements (a slow-moving crowd, closed to the uninitiated, heading toward its ever distant goal) to war (involving double and opposing crowds dependent on each other for their goals and existence). Under Canetti's gaze, the crowd becomes an organism, a beast that crouches under the phenomena of world history. The result is a sort of mystical primitivism. Everything has its roots not only in a primal crowd instinct, but in the life of primitive man. The voices and the passions of primitive man come to be the dominant voices and passions of all culture's life.

Unlike, say, Max Weber, who catalogued types of religious and social behavior with a complicated understanding of, and respect for, rational life and the material world, Canetti's universe is strangely shrunken, like some cannibal's trophy head. The primitive becomes the measure of all phenomena; and our heritage in animal life becomes the explanation of all power and evil. Canetti weaves haunting images, but he means them to be explanations. The eating and the chewing of food become the model for power's workings, the grid of man's teeth the model for the prison, and so on. Even the diagnoses of modern psychology are "explained" as if they were episodes in the life of a hunter-gatherer: "hysteria" is described as a preparation for flight, "mania" as a desire to capture one's prey. Crowds, he writes, are so much more nakedly visible today because they are freed from the bounds of traditional religion and displayed in their "biological state." It is a state of unquenchable appetite and insurmountable waste. "How should there be value," Canetti asks, "in a life that resembles an intestinal tract?"

It is no wonder that Canetti has had so little influence with his theories, or that ***Crowds and Power*** loses its impact (and its organization) after its themes are stated. There is no place to take them. Canetti's findings are more evocative than instructive: one isn't clear by the end how totalitarianism developed, or how crowd instincts can be modified, or how civilization develops, or why positing an instinct for crowds is any more revealing than positing (with Freud) an instinct for death. By the time Canetti concludes his book with a discussion of the paranoid personality of Schreber (a case made famous by Freud), the implied equivalence between Schreber and Hitler is banal and unrevealing.

For all its acknowledgement of the ugly sides of human life, Canetti's analysis is oddly naive. The impulse for crowds is so universal that it is trivial. Canetti even finds the powers of the crowd in swarms of microscopic spermatozoa: "200 million of these animalcules set out together on their way," he solemnly proclaims. "They all have the same goal and, except for one, they all perish on the way." And when Canetti does turn practical in his analysis—as in his survey of the political scene at the end of the 1950s—he again reduces historical complexities to typology. He comments, for example, that the "modern frenzy for increase" in economic production is eliminating the old notion of war between double crowds. As a result, he suggests, sport can replace war as a "crowd phenomenon" on a "worldwide scale." But until the Olympics pacify man's animal nature, social life becomes almost completely a matter of nature's law. Canetti is a primitive determinist.

But the memoirs also show another side, a sort of aesthetic faith that is as pervasive as nature's evil workings, and is peculiarly unmoving. That faith is in the role of the writer as a fighter against power. In Canetti's vision, power detests the possibilities of imagination, for power "is sufficient unto itself and wills only itself." Imagination's ability to create other worlds, other situations, other beings, is a freedom that is a threat. Canetti calls this writerly power "transformation" or "metamorphosis"—against which "a ruler wages continuous warfare." The writer's calling is to be "the keeper of metamorphosis," who can undo, through voice and word, the grip of power and the crowd by first eluding it, and then transforming it. "Of all man's gifts transformation is the best . . . after all the crimes he has committed it is his justification and crowning glory."

This displays a rather Romantic faith in the power of the imagination. Indeed, there are indications that Canetti attaches a magical power to transformation itself; it is in some sense redemptive, an alternative to a Nature (and a Society) red in tooth and claw. He sees metamorphosis as a literal transformation of a world, a force that has nearly physical impact. The eyes play with power, but redemption comes with the setting free of the tongue, the writer's tool.

This theme is never argued, it is only asserted with the calmness of unquestioned faith. It is also why at the heart of ***The Play of the Eyes,*** with its tales of domination and submission, there is also a dissenting quest, a search for a truly good man who neither courts power nor submits to it, an articulate version of that helpless bundle in Marrakesh. Here Canetti's idealism reaches full bloom. He claims to find such a man in a person named Dr. Sonne. Sonne looks like Karl Kraus, the Viennese writer to whom Canetti was almost religiously devoted for a time. But unlike Kraus, his tool is not satire or citation or scorn, but a refined, kind intellect. The effusive Canetti tells us nothing about the man's life or his past; there are no details, not even Sonne's true name. He simply asserts that Sonne possessed encyclopedic knowledge and wisdom. It is enough that Canetti calls him the "angel Gabriel," a "supreme authority" whose name—the Sun—is the "source and . . . end of all life."

But if Canetti tells us nothing about him, it is because ideal goodness for Canetti is a sort of nothingness, an abstention from all power play, even from the attempt to survive. When Canetti discovers that Sonne actually once wrote some Hebrew poetry, it is a mark against him. Only in non-activity, in withdrawal, could Sonne, the writer who doesn't write, attain sainthood. Canetti intimately understands Kafka and his urge for withdrawal from the world; Sonne is Canetti's Samsa. The writer is at his best when he has practiced metamorphosis, and turned himself into an insect or cripple, like the paralyzed philosopher in ***The Torch in the Ear*** who can only read his books by using his tongue to turn the pages. The cripple, the isolate, the solitary dreamer: there is Canetti's answer to a life he compares to passage through an intestinal tract. Would that wailing bundle in Marrakesh ever sully itself with power?

This leaves Canetti with very few choices. For, as these memoirs show again and again, the very act of living involves an incessant play with power. What is the writer to do, then, in his withdrawal from the world? The only choice is to reject life as it really is, ordinary life, with all its struggles and its preoccupations, to say no to it, again and again. This rejection can mean arguing that life is indeed little more than an intestinal tract, a realm of biological waste and stifled impulse, treating the figures who move through it as caricatures, as exaggerated and distorted versions of what was once called "human." This Canetti often does, mixing his disdain with a cold propriety. One does not read Canetti for his empathy for the inner life of others; he is too preoccupied with caricature and type, too busy schematically outlining the person's relationship to himself and to the "play of the eyes." One of his books, ***Earwitness,*** is nothing more than a collection of 50 caricatures.

But the rejection of life can also mean idealizing humanity in the abstract while despairing of it in the particular, disdaining all that is specific for the sake of something indefinite and ideal. This is Canetti's other impulse. Educated as a Sephardic Jew, he declares, for example, that though he was an avid learner of languages, a collector of myths, a student of ancient religions, he deliberately avoided getting acquainted with the Hebrew Bible. "It would have narrowed me down to learn more about things that were so close to my origins, though I had preserved a keen interest in every other religion."

So Canetti declares himself a sort of universalist. He must keep the world out of focus long enough to escape his own will to power. Compassion exists only globally and generally: "I care about the life of every human being," he boasts in ***The Torch in My Ear,*** "and not just that of my neighbor." But he loves the idea of man too much not to despise the particular. There is an oddly inhuman quality to Canetti's humanism. His compassion even extends to the inanimate. He speaks of the great pity he has for drops of water: they are irrevocably separated from the ocean, their home.

According to such a view of life, living itself is a sign of something like sin, not Original but Intrinsic. The very act of living is a sign that one has succumbed to temptation. "Survival," Canetti has said, "is at the core of everything that we . . . call power." For Canetti, the survivor survives because he stands over other corpses. Canetti's survivor is not the figure that any student of World War II, of Canetti's war, might imagine: a man or woman who managed, by chance or character or strength or faith, to avoid being plowed under by murderous machinery let loose. He is, rather, the manager of such machinery, his survival a sign of complicity. "Few readers," Canetti writes, "can have finished the chapters on the survivor without some feeling of disgust. But it was my intention to hunt him out in all his hiding-places and show him for what he is and always has been. He has been glorified as a hero and obeyed as a ruler, but fundamentally he is always the same. . . . The survivor is mankind's worst evil, its curse and perhaps its doom." The survivor commands, he rules, he kills.

Here Canetti's humanism becomes really frightening, his primitivism, his idealism, his disgust at the particular seem to echo precisely the sentiments of his enemies during the last war. His description is, again, caricature. Is survival simply the key fact? Are there not different kinds of survivors? Are all who survived the war really guilty? Was there no value in resistance? Would their death have been philosophically preferable? And what happened to Canetti's own Bulgarian family during the war? Such distinctions would distract Canetti from his attempts at caricature and condemnation.

And if survival itself becomes a curse, what is left? "Hitherto the only answer to man's passionate desire for survival has been a creative solitude which earns immortality for itself; and this, by definition, can be the solution only for a few." This is his own alibi: immortality through writing and withdrawal. But this is hardly a solution to the problems Canetti has constructed for himself. The memoirs prove it. They are written in the fray, uneasy and unforgiving. Indeed, in ***The Secret Heart of the Clock,*** Canetti begins to recognize that he is the survivor he has so forthrightly condemned. He notes "the *guilt* of surviving, which you have always felt." It is the guilt of life and particularity, the guilt that suffuses his memoirs and gives them their crisp brilliance. Expunging that guilt is nothing less than suicide. "It would be beautiful to disappear," Canetti says in another aphorism, "nowhere to be found." There should be no mark left, not even of absence: "It would be beautiful to be the only one to know that you have disappeared."

So Canetti's writings are torn by paradox. His own recollections are tales of domination and submission, of power and play. And yet he dreams again and again of escape, of disappearance, of the elimination of all particularity, of absorption into universality, of an oblivion that grants him a peculiar immortality. But is not this dream of dissolution also a yearning for a crowd? A crowd of words, not a crowd of men; but still Canetti wishes to submerge himself.

"Why should it be important what you thought?" Canetti asks himself in ***The Secret Heart of the Clock.*** It is a rare moment in Canetti's work, when the author is not a guilty survivor, a universal visionary, a grand theoretician, a seeker of revenge, when he is, simply, a man. "Since you have not achieved anything, anything at all, it can just as well disappear." This is an uncharacteristic retreat, the writer submitting to death because he believes, at least for a moment, that his work will not survive. The despair passes quickly, but there is another entry, more provocative and more revelatory, in the journals for 1985, the year in which Canetti turned 80:

> The whole enormous apparatus you have erected serves no purpose. It doesn't save anyone. It gives a false appearance of strength, no more than a boast, and is from beginning to end as helpless as any other scheme.
>
> The truth is that you have not yet found out what would be the right and valid and humanly useful attitude. You haven't gone beyond saying no.

Elias Canetti is, without a doubt, one of the great creative artists and seminal thinkers of the twentieth century. Much superb scholarship has been devoted to his work in the years since his writings have increased in number and circulation, but much more remains to be done.

—Thomas H. Falk, in his* Elias Canetti, *Twayne Publishers, 1993.

William Grimes (obituary date 19 August 1994)

SOURCE: An obituary in *The New York Times,* August 19, 1994, p. A25.

[*In the following, Grimes briefly traces Canetti's life and career.*]

Elias Canetti, a novelist, playwright and cultural historian who won the Nobel Prize in Literature in 1981, died on Saturday in Zurich. He was 89 and had homes in London and Zurich.

On Wednesday, he was buried next to James Joyce.

Mr. Canetti, a Bulgarian who wrote in German, spent much of his creative life analyzing the individual and the social and political forces that weighed against him in the 20th century. He first wrote on the subject in ***Crowds and Power,*** published in 1935, just two years after Hitler came to power. Mr. Canetti returned to the theme in his old age in a multi-volume autobiography that traces his, and 20th-century Europe's, artistic and intellectual development.

Mr. Canetti was born to a family of Sephardic Jews in the port city of Ruschuk in what is now Bulgaria. When he was 6, the family moved to Manchester, England, and a year later, after Mr. Canetti's father had died, the family moved to Vienna, and later to Zurich and Frankfurt. Mr. Canetti grew up speaking German, English, French and Bulgarian.

To please his mother, he earned a doctorate in chemistry from the University of Vienna, but he had set his sights on becoming a writer. He made an auspicious beginning with the novel ***Auto-da-Fé,*** the story of a reclusive scholar whose loutish wife forces him out of his apartment into the real world, where he undergoes degradation and torment before setting fire to himself and his books. The novel was perceived as an attack on fascism and was banned in Germany.

Mr. Canetti wrote two plays, ***The Wedding*** and ***The Comedy of Vanity,*** before fleeing first to Paris and eventually to London ahead of the Nazis. While taking part in a violent demonstration in Vienna in 1927, he had become fascinated by the nature of crowds, and in London he began researching ***Crowds and Power,*** drawing on folklore, myth and anthropology to explain mass psychology and the allure of dictators. The book, which Mr. Canetti called "my life's work," was not completed until 1960. While writing it, he kept note-books and journals that were later published as ***The Human Province*** (1972).

In addition to several plays, his other works included the books ***Voices of Marrakesh*** (1967), ***The Conscience of Words*** (1979), ***Earwitness: Fifty Characters*** (1982) and ***Kafka's Other Trial*** (1988) ***The Secret Heart of the Clock*** (1989) and ***The Agony of Flies*** (1994).

The literary project that consumed his later years was an autobiography that recounted his spiritual and intellectual coming of age, and his encounters with such seminal artists as Bertolt, Brecht, Karl Kraus, Isaac Babel and Georg Grosz. The first three volumes were ***The Tongue Set Free*** (1979), ***The Torch in My Ear*** (1982) and ***The Play of the Eyes*** (1986). He completed a fourth volume of memoirs, as yet untitled, that will be published by Farrar, Straus & Giroux.

He is survived by his daughter, Johanna.

***The Times,* London (obituary date 19 August 1994)**

SOURCE: An obituary in *The Times,* London, August 19, 1994, p. 19.

[*In the obituary below, the critic provides a broad survey of Canetti's life and career.*]

Elias Canetti was the first British citizen to win the Nobel

In truth [Canetti's] was the great poetic voice of this century which knew better than any other how to discredit death.

—Claudio Magris, in "Claudio Magris on Canetti," in Salmagundi, *Fall, 1994-Winter, 1995.*

Prize for Literature after Winston Churchill in 1953. He had lived in London from 1938 until the 1970s when he moved to Zurich, but few outside an informed minority in this country had heard of him when the Nobel Committee made its decision in 1981. The citation made mention of "his broad outlook, a wealth of ideas and artistic powers", but the remarkable thing was how frustratingly little of what was, in any case, a slim body of work had been translated from the German.

However, several of his books have achieved classic status. The first was a novel, ***Die Blendung*** (1935), translated into English in 1946. The second was a massive anthropological study on the psychology, history and political implications of the crowd, ***Masse und Macht*** (1960), translated as ***Crowds and Power*** two years later. More recently, three volumes of memoirs published between 1977 and 1985—***The Tongue set Free, The Torch in my Ear*** and ***The Play of the Eyes***—have provided an unrivalled portrait of the vanished world of prewar European Jewry, and have won him many new readers.

Canetti was by nature an intensely reclusive man, and his response to sudden fame was to retreat even further from public view. It was not until 1985 that he lifted a ten-year boycott that restricted half of his books from being published in Britain—a protest apparently at his prolonged neglect by British publishers and critics, though he never fully explained his motives.

His reputation within the Continental intellectual community had been secured long before this, however, and his work favourably compared to Karl Kraus, Franz Kafka and Robert Musil—the writer Canetti placed highest among the moderns. Canetti's own work was marked by an intense awareness of the latent violence of language. George Steiner wrote of him: "He knows, as did the Greek tragedians, that words uttered in fury or despair will literally destroy those at whom they are flung; that political justice and injustice are woven into the words of the law." To certain themes he returned obsessively: the psychology of crowds; the nature of power; and the precarious relationship between the individual and the state.

He was born in Ruschuk, Bulgaria, a child of the Spanish-Jewish Diaspora. His father, Jacques Canetti, was a businessman, his mother Mathilde Arditi a possessive and gifted woman. His first language was the Sephardic tongue Ladino (a combination of medieval Spanish, Hebrew, Turkish and other elements).

After his parents settled in Manchester when he was six, he picked up English. Two years later his father died; Canetti and his mother moved to Vienna, where German became his main language and the one in which he was to write his books. His education was multinational—schools in England, Zurich, Frankfurt, were followed by the University of Vienna, where he obtained a doctorate in chemistry in 1929.

In 1934, while working on ***Die Blendung*** he escaped his mother's influence by marrying Venetia Taubner-Calderón, the woman who, as "Veza", dominates his memoirs. His father-substitute was the great journalist Karl Kraus, whose stand against the modern vulgarisation of culture Canetti made his own.

Canetti's obsession with crowds and mass violence had begun at the age of nine, when he and his mother were attacked by a mob in Berlin. He had first seen large demonstrations in Zurich at the time of the runaway inflation in the 1920s, and on July 15, 1927, he witnessed the marching of a crowd of protesting workers on the Palace of Justice in Vienna. The Palace was set alight and some 90 unarmed demonstrators were killed. Canetti, though terrified, walked over afterwards and examined the corpses. This horrific scene marked a turning-point for him.

Increasingly confirmed in his bleak view of the world by a visit to Berlin in 1929, Canetti planned a series of eight novels intended to be a "*comédie humaine* of madness". He later described what he had in mind: "It seemed no longer possible to me to get to grips with the world by means of conventional realistic fiction" (Canetti had been particularly influenced, up to that point, by Balzac). "The world had fallen too much apart, as it were, in all directions."

In the event, only one book was ever written, ***Die Blendung*** (***The Blinding,*** 1935), translated into English under the supervision of Canetti by the historian C.V. Wedgwood 11 years later as ***Auto da Fé*** and in America as ***Tower of Babel.*** It was published in Germany in an extended version in 1965.

The book was originally intended to be entitled *Kant Catches Fire,* though Canetti found the pain of this working title too hard to endure. He was reluctant, however to separate from the idea of fire completely. Kant became instead a brilliant and obsessed Sinologist, Peter Kien (the German for resinous pinewood), a man blinded to reality by scholarship. Kien marries a rapacious housekeeper who conspires with the caretaker to oust her husband from his beloved library and apartment. Cut off from his work, rudderless and adrift in the grotesque underworld of Vienna, Kien begins to believe that he is literally carrying his library around in his head. He sinks into despair, finally returns to his library and sets the books and Chinese scrolls alight, thus burning himself alive in the process in one vast symbolic conflagration.

The narrative voice remains ironic throughout, enabling Canetti to treat ponderous themes—the proximity of abstract thought to madness; the psychology of Fascism; the role of language in society; the decline of liberal humanism—as black comedy. It was a work of extraordinary intellectual maturity and formal strength, which the 30-year-old Canetti would never again achieve in fiction.

But it also presented, by virtue of its terrible pessimism and its fragmentary narrative form, a strenuous challenge to readers. Reviewers complained of its dreadful morbidity, its insane humour, its rigid symbolism. *The Times* dismissed it as "ponderous and trivial". Only a few immediately appreciated its quality, among them Thomas Mann. Kate O'Brien thought it a "mad, magnificent work which we are not able to endure . . . but of which we dare not deny the genius or the justification."

Gradually the book's underground reputation grew. After the *Anschluss* the Canettis had emigrated and settled in Hampstead, where the presence of so many other German-speaking Jews was reassuring. Canetti had given up work on the other seven novels, feeling that, as far as fiction went, he had said everything he could in ***Die Blendung.*** But he was still possessed with certain ideas, as he recalled in his autobiography: "The problem of masses had occupied me since 1925 and that of power had become associated with it only a little later. But until shortly before the war they were not my only concern."

At this point Canetti resolved to devote himself to the problem rigorously and scientifically. The result, and the major work of his London years, was that massive hybrid of a book, ***Masse und Macht*** (1960), translated as ***Crowds and Power*** in 1962. It was an extraordinarily courageous and lengthy project ("the very slight prospect that [this endeavour] might succeed makes every kind of effort worthwhile" he recalled) and was not without faults. But, for all that, it remains a stimulating book, revealing Canetti as a genuine polymath—as Salman Rushdie remarked, "a sort of prestructuralist Levi-Strauss crossed with James Frazer of *The Golden Bough*". Bushmen, Shia Muslims, Byzantine emperors, even orchestral conductors—all were raided as examples of the component elements of power.

Canetti's other work, with the exception of a brilliant short essay on Franz Kafka, ***The Other Trial*** (1969), was not so widely read, not least because so little of it was available in translation. His plays, which he had been writing since the 1930s, were intimately connected with his studies, and have so far been regarded as more interesting on the printed page than in performance. Written in Viennese dialogue, they were also almost impossible to render in English: ***Hochzeit*** (***The Wedding,*** 1932), ***Die Komödie der Eitelkeit*** (***Comedy of Vanity,*** 1934), ***Die Befristeten,*** performed in England in 1956 as ***The Numbered.*** They were collected as ***Dramen*** in 1964.

Meanwhile ***Die Blendung,*** after its third edition appeared in Germany in 1965, was beginning to achieve proper recognition. In 1966 Canetti received the Literature Prize of the City of Vienna and in the 1972 the much-coveted George Büchner Prize. Then in 1981, nearly half a century after his masterpiece and to the surprise of almost everybody, he was awarded the Nobel Prize for Literature. This was in part due to what the committee felt (rightly or wrongly) was the tarnished political record of the Argentinian Jorge Luis Borges. And there were other more obvious candidates. But in choosing Canetti, the committee were affirming the importance of ***Die Blendung,*** which was by then being compared to the greatest novels of the century, in the tradition of Hermann Broch and Robert Musil.

Canetti remained scrupulously economical with his publications in later life, though these included travel writings—particularly the charming ***The Voices of Marakesh*** (1978)—and his three much acclaimed volumes of autobiography. He maintained two homes, in London and Zurich, in the latter of which he died.

His first wife died in 1963 and there were no children. His second wife, Hera, died in 1988. He leaves a daughter from his second marriage.

Additional coverage of Canetti's life and career is contained in the following sources published by Gale Research: *Contemporary Authors,* Vols. 21-24 (rev. ed.), 146; *Contemporary Authors New Revision Series,* Vol. 23; *Contemporary Literary Criticism,* Vols. 3, 14, 25, 75; *Dictionary of Literary Biography,* Vols. 85, 124; and *Major 20th-Century Writers.*

Alice Childress

October 12, 1920—August 14, 1994

American dramatist, screenwriter, novelist, editor, and author of children's books.

For further information on Childress's life and works, see *CLC,* Volumes 12 and 15.

INTRODUCTION

Childress is primarily known for her young adult novel *A Hero Ain't Nothin' but a Sandwich* (1973). A highly controversial work that was part of a censorship case brought before the United States Supreme Court, the novel is set in Harlem and details a teenager's growing addiction to heroin. Each chapter of the book, which was a finalist for the National Book Award for Fiction in 1974 and which earned Childress a Lewis Carroll Shelf Award in 1975, is told from the perspective of various individuals with whom the protagonist interacts, including his drug pusher, peers, teachers, and family members. Childress is additionally known for her work as a playwright. Although often characterized as a critically neglected dramatist, Childress was instrumental in the genesis of black theater in America in the twentieth century: with *Gold through the Trees* (1952) she became the first black woman to have a play professionally produced on the American stage, and with *Trouble in Mind* (1955) she became the first woman to win an OBIE Award. In her dramas, which include *Florence* (1949), *Wedding Band* (1966), *Wine in the Wilderness* (1969), *Sea Island Song* (1977), and *Moms* (1987), Childress frequently focused on such topics as African-American history, racism, miscegenation, drug abuse, and black-white relations. Many of these works, like *A Hero Ain't Nothin' but a Sandwich,* have been the subject of controversy. Childress, however, never sought notoriety and maintained that she drew her inspiration from everyday life and people. In a 1984 essay entitled "A Candle in a Gale Wind," she stated: "[I] write about those who come in second, or not at all . . . and the intricate and magnificent patterns of a loser's life. No matter how many celebrities we may accrue, they cannot substitute for the masses of human beings. My writing attempts to interpret the 'ordinary' because they are not ordinary. Each human is uniquely different. Like snowflakes, the human pattern is never cast twice. We are uncommonly and marvelously intricate in thought and action, our problems are most complex and, too often, silently borne."

PRINCIPAL WORKS

Florence (drama) 1949
Just a Little Simple [adaptor; from the short story collection *Simple Speaks His Mind* by Langston Hughes] (drama) 1950
Gold through the Trees (drama) 1952
Trouble in Mind (drama) 1955
Like One of the Family: Conversations from a Domestic's Life (prose) 1956
Wedding Band: A Love/Hate Story in Black and White (drama) 1966
The Freedom Drum (drama) 1969; also performed as *Young Martin Luther King,* 1969
String [adaptor; from the short story "A Piece of String" by Guy de Maupassant] (drama) 1969
Wine in the Wilderness: A Comedy-Drama (drama) 1969
Wine in the Wilderness (screenplay) 1969
Mojo: A Black Love Story (drama) 1970

A Hero Ain't Nothin' but a Sandwich (novel) 1973
Wedding Band (screenplay) 1973
When the Rattlesnake Sounds (drama) [first publication] 1975
Let's Hear It for the Queen (drama) [first publication] 1976
**Sea Island Song* (drama) 1977
A Hero Ain't Nothin' but a Sandwich (screenplay) 1978
A Short Walk (novel) 1979
String (screenplay) 1979
Rainbow Jordan (novel) 1981
Moms: A Praise Play for a Black Comedienne (drama) 1987
Those Other People (novel) 1989

*This work has also been produced as *Gullah.*

INTERVIEW

Alice Childress with Kathleen Betsko and Rachel Koenig (interview date 1987)

SOURCE: An interview in *Interviews with Contemporary Women Playwrights,* edited by Kathleen Betsko and Rachel Koenig, Beech Tree Books, 1987, pp. 62-74.

[*In the following excerpt, Childress discusses her works and writing process.*]

[Childress]: I wrote my play ***Wedding Band*** as a remembrance of the intellectual poor. The poor, genteel and sensitive people who are seamstresses, coal carriers, candymakers, sharecroppers, bakers, baby caretakers, housewives, foot soldiers, penny-candy sellers, vegetable peelers, who are somehow able to sustain within themselves the poet's heart, sensitivity and appreciation of pure emotion, the ability to freely spend tears and laughter without saving them up for a rainy day. I was raised by and among such people living on the poorest blocks in Harlem and have met many more on the boundary lines of the segregated life—the places where black, white, brown, yellow and red sometimes meet—in bus stations, train and plane waiting rooms, on lines where we pay gas, light and telephone bills.

Wedding Band kept coming at me from hidden, unexpected places, the characters called on my mind while I was trying to write something else, demanding attention, getting together, coming into being. It was a play I did not want to write, about people few others wanted to hear from . . . I thought. It somehow seemed to be answering back all the stage and screen stories about rich, white landowners and their "octoroon" mistresses.

Such stories meant nothing in my life. I am a black woman of light complexion, have no white relatives except on the other side of slavery, and have experienced the sweetness, joy and bitterness of living almost entirely within the Harlem community. I really did not wish to beat the drum for an interracial couple and yet there they were in front of me, not giving a damn about public opinion of this or that past day. It was like being possessed by rebel spirits, ideas clinging, taking over and starting my day for me. Instead of a joyous experience, writing the play became a trial, a rough journey through reams of paper. Characters know; they won't be fooled, not even by their medium, the writer. They *allow* you to write them, pushing you along until they're satisfied that they've done their thing to the utmost of your ability.

I was born in Charleston, South Carolina, and raised on 118th Street between Lenox and Fifth avenues in Harlem, New York City. My grandmother and her friends were not ashamed of living: "Got it to do!" they said. When people were ill, neighbors rallied and brought various home remedies to the bedside, seldom a doctor. Those days are almost gone, thank God. Who wants to live with one foot in hell just for the sake of nostalgia? Our time is forever now! Today our youngsters can freely discuss sex. Soon they will even be able to openly discuss one of the results of sex—life. I also remember death, funerals, just before it went out of style to have the last service within the home instead of at the undertaking parlor. In one corner of the kitchen, a big truckdriver of a man wept tears into a large handkerchief, his shoulders shaking with grief: "Why did she leave us? Only last week I was talking to her and answered real short: 'Shut up.' I said that to her . . . and now she's gone." And those there gathered answered him with healing words of comfort: "Well, God knows you loved her, don't take it so hard, you did your best." They brought him through that day. Other men, richer and smarter, had to go through three years of therapy to find the reasons why and why and why . . . and to know there's always another way. On our block there was prostitution, but we were so damned blind until even the prostitutes were called "Miss" Margaret or "Miss" Beatrice or whatever. And they did not beckon to men until our backs were turned, most of the time. Heroin was not yet King of the Ghetto and a boy would not dream of killing his grandmother or hurting his mama or her friends in order to pour cooked opium dust through a hole in his arm. But they weren't "the good old days." The only good days are ahead. The characters kept chasing me down. Men in love with "nothing to offer." Women who couldn't or wouldn't hold back their emotions "for the sake of the race." They tap at the brain and move a pen to action in the middle of the night. They are alive, they really are, pushing and shoving interfering creators out of the way. Now, in this slot of time, they return singing old songs about inner discovery. Other characters keep knocking at our doors, pushing, pulling, tearing at seams of life. Poets, novelists, painters, playwrights stand around shifting from foot to foot, trying to keep score. Ordinary people know more about how to live with love and hate than given credit for . . . even though they're never seen on talk shows.

[*Interviewer*]: *There was a difference between the white criticism of* **Wedding Band** [*a play whose central characters are an interracial couple; it premiered in 1966*] *and what the black critics had to say, wasn't there?*

The white criticism was that the interracial couple needn't have stayed [in a Jim Crow state], that they could have gone away; they felt the male character, the white baker, should have turned his back on his mother and sister and escaped. Now, that's a very hard thing for poor people to do. It's easier for wealthy people. They can leave *and* send money home to their dependents. This baker *is* his family's livelihood. His mother contributed all of her money to his small bakery shop. For him to walk away from family and debts is almost unheard of in poor communities.

The black critics' objections were: Why talk about this interracial issue at all? Why couldn't I just write about a black couple? It may have sounded as though I were praising interracial love but, in fact, this was not my objective. In almost everything I write there are black couples, and there is also one in ***Wedding Band***. But this was a true story my grandmother had told me, about a black woman named Miss Julia, who lived across the street from her in South Carolina and who "kept company" with a white butcher. I made him a baker in the play because I thought it would be more palatable for the audience than butchering. Black critics felt that the character I based on Miss Julia should not have wanted to marry a white man, no matter that this situation often occurs in real life. The black audience would have been more comfortable if Julia had rejected her white lover. That was true even of the last production of the play at Joe Papp's theater. [The New York Shakespeare Festival, Public Theatre, 1972]. It had been done earlier at the University of Michigan at Ann Arbor [1966] and in Chicago, where we had our greatest success. Black audiences in Chicago really liked the play. They sold out the whole six weeks, standing room only; you couldn't get tickets.

Did you find less resistance to your artistic vision in the publishing world?

Yes I did. I didn't have to fight and struggle as in the theater because, almost by accident, an editor [at Coward McCann] came to me who knew of my playwriting—the late Ferdinand Monjo, who was also a noted children's author. He said, "Alice, you've said so much about drugs in your writing, why don't you really put some time into it and do a book?" That's how I came to write ***A Hero Ain't Nothin' but a Sandwich***. He told me it had to be a young adult book because he was a young adult book editor, and young adults needed such a book.

In **A Hero . . .** *each chapter represents a different character's point of view: the boy on drugs, the boy's mother, the boy's teacher, and so on. Is this an instance of your playwright's training overlapping into your fiction?*

Yes—theater and film. I was very impressed by the film *Rashomon* [by Japanese director Akira Kurosawa]. A woman was raped; she tells her story and the other characters tell their stories. Each one's version of the event is reenacted within the film. But all were *lying* except one, who was observing from a distance. And when he tells what happened, you understand why all the others lied. But I do an opposite thing. In my writing, all the stories differ, but I see that you can get ten *different* stories out of people *all telling the truth*. We don't all view things the same way, each perspective is different. Many-leveled narration is something I do well. It's true to theater. When I'm writing a character that I see as a villain, I try to take the villain's side and believe in the righteousness of the villainous act. In ***A Hero . . .*** we pondered long about cutting out the drug pusher's side of the story.

Because it was a book for young people?

Yes. The drug pusher is so convincing about the rightness of the acts and the reader feels for him. Monjo was very helpful. After a great deal of talk about it, we decided to leave the character in.

A Hero *went as far as the Supreme Court in a book-banning case, along with books by eight other authors. Will you discuss censorship?*

Nine books got to the Supreme Court, and mine was one of them. I don't know if I'm the first or only woman whose book got to the Supreme Court on a banning. They also banned Hawthorne's *The Scarlet Letter* because it was sympathetic to an unmarried pregnant woman. In one school, the authorities banned *Romeo and Juliet,* saying the Nurse was a poor role model because Juliet's parents had hired her to take care of their daughter, and there she was passing notes and arranging liaisons, covering up that Romeo and Juliet were seeing each other. Another school banned all of Shakespeare's plays *except Romeo and Juliet.*

Some people say, "I like this book, such a beautiful book shouldn't be banned." But they don't mind it when a book they *don't* like is banned. I feel we must be against banning regardless of whether we like a book. We do not have to accept its content and quality, we do not have to read or accept a book at all—but to ban it is wrong.

Do you have any particular criteria you use to judge what is bad and what is helpful in criticism?

Yes. I weigh it and think about it. If ten people read or see a play at different times and they all zero in on the same trouble spot, the problem might not be *exactly* what they are expressing, but the playwright knows that there is *something* there that needs to be cleared up. I have an instinctive feeling when someone is giving me "wrong" criticism. I'm wary when I've labored over something for five years and someone comes over and tells me in five minutes, "Do this, do that, change this . . ." Well, you can't just trust and do what you are told. But at the same time, you must be open to "good" criticism. You have to get off by yourself and find out if it's merely your ego that is suffering. The viewer of a film or play doesn't have to spend all the years you've spent to know the ending is upsetting to them.

Do you care if your endings are upsetting to the audience?

No, I don't, but I do care if the audience feels something is unbelievable or a lie. All fiction is tampering with the truth, but it bothers me if something seems like it's been thrown in just to make the script "work." I can't make a character do or say something that I don't think this character would do or say just because the audience would prefer it. But I do have to listen to a director or producer on whether a scene is too long, whether the progression of the play is being held up because of it. It's not only what the play has to say, but how it flows. If it's too long, it's too long. I don't care for lengthy plays—four, six, eight hours long. I don't want to go back the next night to see how it ends. I want to sit in one session, and see and hear a play all the way through, I want it all to fit, there and then. Some people criticize the "well-made" play, but it is not to be knocked. If you buy a suit you want it to be well made. You don't want the tailor to experiment; we want something dependable; well, *I* do. . . .

You've published several novels. Have they influenced your playwriting? Have you mastered something in your fiction that helps you to create the "well-made" play?

It's the other way around. The theater influences my novel writing. I feel each chapter is a scene. But when writing novels, I find description difficult. With plays, after we've described the set, we're free of that. We don't *have to* describe the sun rising or the sound of rain. Someone else brings lighting, set, costumes and sound to life for us. Playwrights are specialists in dialogue, situation and conflict; and they must make it all happen within a limited time and space. The novel is more permissive. When I'm writing a book, I visualize it all on a stage. I'm very pleased when critics say my novels feel like plays. I've learned to lean on theater instead of breaking with it. I came to theater first, acted for eleven years with the American Negro Theater and started writing out of that experience. When writing a novel or a play I act out all the parts. I've actually gotten up, walked around and played out a scene when I've run into difficulty with the writing . . . moved through all the entrances and exits. Making theater is more than how you feel and speak, it's how you move. You have to work it out, act it out, think it out, as if on a stage. I also think that way about a book.

You were an actress first . . .

Oh, yes. I was in the original cast of *Anna Lucasta* [1944] on Broadway. I've also worked a little in television and movies. But racial prejudice was such that I was considered "too light" to play my real self and they would not cast light-skinned blacks in white roles. I realized I had to have some other way of creating. I love acting, the art of acting, but not the business of acting and auditioning. Most of the time, I didn't like the parts they wanted me to play. Unless one is lucky enough to get a lot of stage work, creativity is cut off or underexercised. I decided I'd rather create from the start, create good roles I'd like to play by writing them. I found, however, I wasn't interested in writing parts for myself. I've never written anything for me—though I've been tempted. When my work is presented, I feel I belong out front. I want to be the beholder, the audience.

What exactly bothered you about the roles you played as an actress?

They were stereotypes, "packaged" situations. I don't necessarily mean derogatory stereotypes, but too predictable. "The black" would do one thing, "the white" another thing, and, of course, by the end they would all come together and resolve their differences—packaged solutions.

It's all very well to just take any old play and cast it from different races with no further comment—a nice exercise in democracy, a social service to one another—but I think there is something very particular about different races and religious backgrounds in America that has yet to be fully explored.

Do you mean that in the effort to be "universal," we are losing something about the parochial?

Yes. Some of the greatest plays have come from Sean O'Casey, *Irish* playwright, who wrote *about* the poor Irish, *for* the Irish. Look at the works of Sholem Aleichem and [Isaac] Peretz—out of the blood and bones of Jewish tradition. The black poet, Paul Laurence Dunbar, works the same sort of magic about particular people.

Rosemary Curb on Childress's literary aims and critical acceptance:

Despite her impressive array of published books and produced plays, Alice Childress has asserted that she harbored no ambition to become recognized as a great writer when she began her playwriting career in the late 1940s. She wrote her first play because she loved theatre, and black theatre needed good material. Her work has achieved prominence in the literary and academic world, won awards, and reaped financial gain in the publishing and theatrical marketplaces—but these were not her prime motivations for writing. She sought to promote social justice. However, a cursory study of some of her best serious plays—*Wedding Band, Wine in the Wilderness, Trouble in Mind,* and *Mojo*—reveals that racial and sexual prejudice as well as academic and political discrimination have kept her work from reaching large audiences and from being given the recognition it deserves.

Rosemary Curb, in her "Alice Childress," in Dictionary of Literary Biography: Twentieth-Century American Dramatists, *Volume 7, Bruccoli Clark, 1981.*

You're working on a novel about Dunbar now. Did you research extensively?

Yes. Writing about New York City in 1895, I have to find out what it was like here at that time, what products were being used, what clothing was in style. You try to get the underlying feel of the times. . . . My writing stops when I don't know what my characters would have done in certain situations . . . what they did in houses without bathrooms. . . . This often entails reading articles and books that have nothing to do with your story but which reveal the ambience of the period. I'm writing about African-Americans, but in my research have fallen headlong into the Jewish life of the late eighteen hundreds, immigrants coming from Europe, the teeming streets of the Lower East Side. All of these details help a story to bloom. Also, I try not to write in the past tense.

Another feature of your theater training perhaps?

It's more theatrical to write in the present tense, and more interesting. I have Paul Laurence Dunbar and his sweetheart walking across the Brooklyn Bridge when it was two years old, when people were afraid to cross it. I have them talking about the newness of it.

How did your interest in Dunbar evolve?

I'm writing about Paul and his wife, Alice—their personal relationship. I read many published papers and correspondence they exchanged. I went down South and visited with their niece, and saw hundreds of original letters in faded ink. I decided to write about the four years they were married. Their union was turbulent. . . . Frightening. They were obviously in love but also tried to destroy one another. I liked the drama of it all . . . and the historical aspect. . . .

If someone had offered you a stage for the Dunbar story, as Coward McCann offered to publish a book [**A Hero . . .**], *would you have written it as a play?*

That would have been delightful . . . but a play would have been more difficult. A book is more lenient than the stage, which has such space and time limitations I'd have to throw out half of my story.

Why did you put your piece **Gullah** *on the stage instead of into a novel?*

It would have been simpler to write it as a novel, I felt moved to write a play. I started once on it—a big long thing—but it didn't hang together well. Then I tried again and that didn't work either. Sometime later, the South Carolina Commission on the Arts wanted a play specific to South Carolina. They only wanted a hour-long piece so that it could tour schools all over the state. Well, I said I'd boil down what I had, and make a short version. My husband, Nathan Woodard, composed music for it. We were quite pleased with the result and stopped worrying about it being full-length.

Gullah is a name for a language, isn't it? A very musical language specific to certain islands off the coast of South Carolina. How did this language evolve?

It's a poetry of the people, and embodies their poetic expression and poetic feeling. During the time of slavery, Africans were often sold in mixed lots of different nationalities and languages, because their owners didn't want them to communicate with one another. You see, there were about seven hundred fifty different tongues spoken throughout Africa. So the slave traders hit upon the idea of forming groups, "parcels," by selecting one slave from each nationality. The various groups were sold for labor on different islands off the South Carolinian coast, and a language evolved from the many African languages mixed with English and even a little German. Some people think the word *Gullah* came from people trying to say *Angola*. They became known as Gola or Gullah people. Island isolation helped preserve the Africanisms that blacks on the mainland soon lost through assimilation. My stepfather was born on one of those islands. After he died (on Edisto Island), some of his people came to visit us in New York. I could hardly understand a word. Now, of course, there are bridges, businesses have opened, property has been bought for homes and resorts. The South Carolina Commission on the Arts didn't want us to use the title ***Gullah***. The word is sometimes spoken in a prejudicial way to mock country people and the way they talk. The play was called ***Sea Island Song*** down there but it sounded too Hawaiian, misleading, I thought. When we came back North I went back to the original ***Gullah***.

What's happening to the people and their culture?

They are being scattered and shattered. That's partly what ***Gullah*** is about. Their way of life is ebbing away. Their African baskets take weeks to weave. We live in an age of plastic and metal. They can't make a livelihood working with their hands. That's the problem.

Is that true of all the arts these days, do you think?

It feels that way. The longer you take to make something, the less you are paid. If a publisher pays you an advance and it takes you six months to write something, that's what you make for six months' work. If it takes three years to write it, you still make the same amount of money. So some writers do tend to think about what they can whip together fairly fast. It's not satisfying; sometimes you have to let the work go with regret. I don't think I've ever really "finished" anything to my satisfaction . . . no matter how long I've worked on the material.

You've said the less a writer understands the faster he or she can write . . .

Yes. And you're forgiven for what you don't know. But when you understand your material, you can't shove it along at great speed. When you "know," there is a pleasure in taking time, in stopping yourself, in choosing another direction. As my present editor, Refna Wilkins, once said to me, "Alice, you always pick the hard way." I ask myself if it's healthy, choosing the more difficult road. I guess the bottom line about writing is that it's a torturous process, but the beautiful part is there's a deep, indescribable, inexplicable *satisfaction* in having written. A feeling of elevation and joy afterward that is greater than the despair of sitting there and doing it. I don't enjoy the writing process. I like writing when I have completed it.

OBITUARIES

Sheila Rule (obituary date 19 August 1994)

SOURCE: An obituary in *The New York Times,* August 19, 1994, p. A24.

[*In the following, Rule provides a brief overview of Childress's career.*]

Alice Childress, an actress and a writer of plays and novels, including ***A Hero Ain't Nothin' but a Sandwich,*** died on Sunday at Astoria General Hospital in Queens. She was 77 and lived in Manhattan.

The cause was cancer, said her husband, Nathan Woodard.

In 1973, in a review of ***A Hero Ain't Nothin' but a Sand-***

wich in *The New York Times,* the playwright Ed Bullins wrote: "There are too few books that convince us that reading is one of the supreme gifts of being human. Alice Childress, in her short, brilliant study of a 13-year-old black heroin user, achieves this feat in a masterly way."

In the mid-1970's, the book was at the center of a controversy when a Long Island school district banned it and works by Kurt Vonnegut Jr., Langston Hughes and others on the grounds that they contained obscenities and other material considered offensive. Ms. Childress adapted her novel for a 1978 film that starred Cicely Tyson and Paul Winfield.

Among her other books were ***Rainbow Jordan, Those Other People, When the Rattlesnake Sounds, Let's Hear It for the Queen, Like One of the Family*** and ***A Short Walk.***

One of her plays was ***Wedding Band,*** an interracial love story set in Charleston, S.C., at the time of World War I. Ms. Childress wrote the play in 1965 but was unable to find a New York producer until the New York Shakespeare Festival presented it in 1972. In a review of a 1979 production of the play, Richard Eder wrote in *The Times* that the ideas in ***Wedding Band*** were "like wildflowers growing in their own ground; not, as in works of less art, like cut flowers sorted and offered by the dozen at a florist shop." ABC later produced the play for television, but eight of the network's affiliates declined to carry the show because of its theme and earthy dialogue.

Her other plays included ***Florence, Gold Through the Trees, Just a Little Simple, Trouble in Mind, String*** and ***Mojo.*** With Mr. Woodard, she wrote musicals including ***Young Martin Luther King, Sea Island Song, Gullah*** and ***Moms (A Praise Play for a Black Comedienne),*** about Jackie (Moms) Mabley.

Ms. Childress was born in Charleston . . . . Before she turned to writing, she was an actress with the American Negro Theater, and acted in the original company of *Anna Lucasta.* At the time of her death, she was working on a novel for young adults about her African great-grandmother, a slave until the age of 12, and her Scotch-Irish great-grandmother.

In addition to her husband, she is survived by a granddaughter, Marilyn Alice Lee of Brooklyn.

OVERVIEWS

Jeanne-Marie A. Miller (essay date June 1977)

SOURCE: "Images of Black Women in Plays by Black Playwrights," in *CLA Journal,* Vol. XX, No. 4, June, 1977, pp. 494-507.

[*In the following excerpt, Miller discusses Childress's depiction of black women in her best-known plays.*]

In 1933, in an essay entitled "Negro Character as Seen by White Authors," the brilliant scholar-critic Sterling A. Brown wrote that Blacks had met with as great injustice in the literature of America as they had in the life of their country. In American literature, then, including the drama, Blacks had been depicted most often as negative stereotypes: the contented slave, the wretched freeman, the comic Negro, the brute Negro, the tragic mulatto, the local color Negro, and the exotic primitive. Black female characters have been scarce in only one of these categories—the brute Negro. They have been most plentiful as the faithful servant. In American drama, where, seemingly, many more roles have been written for men than women, Black or white, it is the Black female character who has faced double discrimination—that of sex and race.

As early as the nineteenth century Black women have been written about by playwrights of their own race. Melinda, in William Wells Brown's *The Escape,* for example, is a mulatto who is not tragic, and Rachel, in Angelina Grimke's early twentieth-century play of the same name, is a young, educated, middle-class Black woman who protests against the indignities suffered by her race. Though there were many plays written by Blacks after the dawn of the twentieth century, the Civil Rights Movement of the 1950's and the Black Consciousness Movement of the 1960's produced many new Black playwrights who brought to the stage their intimate inside visions of Black life and the role that Black women play in it.

Alice Childress, a veteran actress, director, and playwright, in several published plays, has placed a Black woman at the center. Childress noted early [in her **"A Woman Playwright Speaks Her Mind,"** in *Anthology of the American Negro,* edited by Lindsay Patterson, 1969] that the Black woman had been absent as an important subject in popular American drama except as an "empty and decharacterized faithful servant."

Childress' ***Florence,*** a short one-act play, is set in a railroad station waiting room in a very small town in the South. The time of the play is the recent past. Emphasized is the misunderstanding by whites of Blacks, brought on by prejudice and laws that keep the two races apart. The rail separating the two races in the station is symbolic.

In the station a Black woman of little means, with a cardboard suitcase and her lunch in a shoebox, has a chance meeting with a white woman also bound for New York. In the conversation that takes place between them, the prejudices of the whites and their myths about Blacks are exposed, such as that of the tragic mulatto. Revealed also is the determination to keep Blacks in the places set aside for them by whites. Marge, the Black woman's daughter living at home, has accepted her place; Florence, the daughter seeking an acting career in New York, has not. Because of the revelations of the white woman, Florence's mother, enroute originally to bring her daughter home and end her fumbling New York career, changes her mind and instead mails the travel money to Florence so that she can remain where she is. Thus, a docile-appearing Black woman, who stays in her place in the South, acts to help her child transcend the barriers placed there by those trying to circumscribe her existence.

Childress' two-act comedy ***Trouble in Mind,*** while concentrating on discrimination in the American theatre, also brings into focus the troublesome racial conditions in the United States of the 1950's. The framework of ***Trouble in Mind*** is the rehearsal of the play *Chaos in Belleville,* a melodrama with an anti-lynching theme, in reality a white writer's distorted view of Blacks. The principal character, Wiletta Mayer, a middle-aged Black actress, a veteran of "colored" musicals, appears at first to have found a way to survive in the prejudiced world of the theatre. Coerced by the white director, however, she explodes and reveals her long pent-up frustrations. Specifically, Wiletta disagrees with the action of the character she is playing—a Black mother who sends her son out to be lynched by a mob seething with hatred because the Black man had tried to vote. Wiletta, alone among the play's interracial cast, demands script changes that will portray Black life realistically. Though she loses her job in the attempt, she in no way seems to regret the stand she has taken after a lifetime of acceptance.

In ***Wine in the Wilderness,*** Tommy Marie, a young Black woman from the ghetto, teaches real pride to her newly acquired middle-class acquaintances. This play is set during the Black revolutionary period of the 1960's. It is one of those Harlem summers popularly described as long and hot. A riot is taking place outside the apartment of Bill, a Black artist currently engaged in painting a triptych entitled *Wine in the Wilderness*—three images of Black womanhood. Two canvases have been completed: one depicting innocent Black girlhood and the other, perfect Black womanhood, an African queen, this artist's statement on what a Black woman should be. The third canvas is empty because Bill has not found a suitable model for the lost Black woman, the leavings of society. Unknown to Tommy, she has been picked out by two of Bill's friends to serve as the model for that hopeless creature. At first sight Tommy is unpolished and untutored but is essentially a warm, likeable human being. Once a live-in domestic and now a factory worker, at the present time she has been burned out and then locked out of her apartment as a result of the riot.

Later, dressed in an African throw cloth and with her cheap wig removed, Tommy undergoes a transformation as she overhears Bill, to whom she is attracted, describe his painting of the African queen. Believing that he is referring to her, she assumes the qualities he praises: "Regal . . . grand . . . magnificent, fantastic. . . ." For the first time she feels loved and admired. While Bill is trying to get into the mood to paint her, she recites the history of the Black Elks and the A. M. E. Zion Church, all part of her background. With her new look and the new knowledge he has gained about her, Bill cannot now paint Tommy as he had intended, for she no longer fits the image he sought.

The next day Oldtimer, a hanger-on, unthinkingly tells Tommy about the three-part painting and the unflattering role she was to play in it. She, in anger, teaches Bill and his middle-class friends about themselves—the hatred they have for "flesh and blood Blacks"—the masses, as if they, the others, have no problems. To the white racist, they are all "niggers" she tells them. But she has learned—she is "Wine in the Wilderness," "a woman that's a real one and a good one," not one on canvas that cannot talk back. The real thing is *inside,* she states.

Bill changes the thrust of his painting. Oldtimer—"the guy who was here before there were scholarships and grants and stuff like that, the guy they kept outta the schools, the man the factories wouldn't hire, the union wouldn't let him join . . ."—becomes one part of the painting; Bill's two friends—"Young Man and Woman workin' together to do our thing"—become another. Tommy, the model for the center canvas, is "Wine in the Wilderness," who has come "through the biggest riot of all, . . . 'Slavery' " and is still moving on against obstacles placed there by both whites and her own people. Bill's painting takes on flesh. Tommy has been the catalyst for change.

Unlike Childress' other plays, ***Wedding Band*** is set in an earlier period—South Carolina in 1918. The central character, Julia Augustine, the Black woman around whom the story revolves, is an attractive woman in her thirties. A talented seamstress, she has only an eighth-grade education. The play opens on the tenth anniversary of her ill-fated love affair with Herman, a white baker who has a small shop. This illegal love affair is the theme of the play. In direct violation of South Carolina's laws against miscegenation, the pair has been meeting and loving clandestinely for years. On this day, in celebration of their anniversary, Herman gives Julia a wedding band on a thin chain to be worn around her neck. This day, too, is the first that Julia has spent in this impoverished neighborhood. She has moved often because her forbidden love affair has caused her to be ostracized by both Blacks and whites.

A series of encounters clearly delineates the kind of woman Julia really is. Though she is lonely between Herman's visits and sometimes allows wine to fill in the void, she is a woman of strength. She endures the criticism of her affair. She is unselfish, warm, and forgiving. With compassion she reads a letter to a new neighbor who cannot read. Unknown to her lover's mother, Julia sews and shops for her. When confronted by this woman who hates her and whose rigid racism drives her to exclaim that she would rather be dead than disgraced, Julia rises to her full strength and spews out the hatred that momentarily engulfs her. And even in her sorrow she is able to give a Black soldier a fitting sendoff to the war and the promise that the world will be better for all Blacks after the war's termination. In the end, Julia forgives her weak, timid lover who is dying from influenza. He could never leave South Carolina for a region more suitable for their love and marriage, he explains, because he had to repay his mother the money she gave him for the bakery. In reality, history stands between Julia and Herman. South Carolina belongs to both of them, but together they could never openly share the state. The promised escape to the North and marriage never materialize. Julia stands at the end of a long line of Childress' strong Black women characters. In this backyard community setting of ***Wedding Band*** are other images of Black womanhood—the self-appointed representative of her race, the mother protecting her son from the dangers awaiting him in the white South, and the woman, abused by a previous husband, waiting loyally for the return of her thoughtful and kind merchant marine lover.

Childress on "breaking ground":

I never was interested in being the first woman to do anything. I always felt that I should be the 50th or 100th. Women were kept out of everything. It almost made it sound like women were not quite right enough or accomplished enough, especially when I hear "the first Black woman." When people are shut out of something for so long, it seems ironic when there's so much going on about "the first."

Alice Childress, in an interview with Elizabeth Brown-Guillory, in Sage, *Spring, 1987.*

John O. Killens (essay date 1984)

SOURCE: "The Literary Genius of Alice Childress," in *Black Women Writers (1950-1980): A Critical Evaluation,* edited by Mari Evans, Anchor Press/Doubleday, 1984, pp. 129-33.

[*In the following essay, Killens discusses various aspects of Childress's career, lauding her numerous accomplishments.*]

There were the Childress plays up at the Club Baron in Harlem in the late forties and early fifties, including ***Florence, Just a Little Simple, Gold Through the Trees*** (a play about Harriet Tubman), every one of them an exuberant celebration of the Black experience with emphasis always on the heroic aspect of that experience in the constant struggle against racist oppression. One left the theater after an evening with Alice Childress imbued with pride and with the spirit to struggle. It was as if whenever Alice Childress sat before the typewriter she heard the voice of Frederick Douglass speaking to her down through the ages of a universal truth that is never outmoded, a truth that time can never render obsolete: *"If there is no struggle there is no progress. . . . Find out just what any people will quietly submit to and you have found out the exact measure of injustice and wrong which will be imposed upon them, and these will continue till they are resisted with either words or blows or with both."* (Emphasis mine.)

Then there was the experience in the Village in 1955 at the Greenwich Mews with her play *Trouble in Mind.* What I had felt uptown about her artistic potential, her power as a great humorist, came into full bloom. If my memory serves me, it was a comedic drama about a group of Black actors trying to make a go of it in a play conceived and directed by a "well-meaning" white man. In this play Childress demonstrated a talent and ability to write humor that had social impact. Even though one laughed throughout the entire presentation, there was, inescapably, the understanding that although one was having an undeniably emotional and a profoundly intellectual experience, it was also political. One of Childress's great gifts: to have you laughing, not at the characters but with them. It is a rare gift that does not come easily. Humor is of serious import, not a thing to take for granted. One gets the feeling that the writer loves the people she writes about. Love of life and people, accent on struggle, humor as a cultural weapon. *Love, struggle, humor.* These are the hallmarks of her craft, of her artistry; these, like a trademark or a fingerprint.

In the volume entitled ***Like One of the Family,*** the writer uses satire and humor as a cutting edge against prejudice and hypocrisy. ***Like One of the Family*** utilizes a series of conversations between Mildred, a Black domestic, and her friend Marge. Segments of these chapters were first published in a Black weekly newspaper. From the first page to the last, ***Family*** is ethnic, it is idiomatic, it is in the great tradition of signifying; notwithstanding, it is universal. For example, here is a quotation from the very first chapter.

> Hi Marge! I had me one hectic day . . . Well, I had to take out my crystal ball and give Mrs. C . . . a thorough reading . . . When she has company, for example, she'll holler out to me from the living room to the kitchen. "Mildred dear! Be sure and eat both of those lamb chops for your lunch!" Now you know she wasn't doing a thing but trying to prove to company how "good and kind" she was to the servant, she had told me already to eat those chops. Today she had a girlfriend of hers over to lunch . . . and she called me over to introduce me to the woman. Oh no, Marge! I didn't object to that at all. I greeted the lady and then went back to my work . . . And then it started! I could hear her talkin' just as loud . . . and she says to her friend, "We just love her! She's like one of the family and she just adores our little Carol! We don't know what we would do without her! We don't think of her as a servant!"
>
> . . . When the guest leaves I go in the living room and says, "Mrs. C . . . I want to have a talk with you."
>
> "By all means," she says.
>
> I drew up a chair and read her thusly: "Mrs. C . . . , you are a pretty nice person to work for, but I wish you would please stop talking about me like I was a cocker spaniel or a poll parrot or a kitten . . . Now you just sit there and hear me out.
>
> In the first place, you do not love me; you may be fond of me, but that is all. In the second place, I am not just like one of the family at all! The family eats in the dining room and I eat in the kitchen. Your mama borrows your lace tablecloth for her company and your son entertains his friends in your parlor, your daughter takes her afternoon nap on the living room couch and the puppy sleeps on your satin spread . . . and whenever your husband gets tired of something you are talkin' about he says, 'Oh, for Pete's sake, forget it . . .' So you can see I am not just like one of the family.

> Now for another thing, I do not just adore your little Carol. I think she is a likeable child, but she is also fresh and sassy. I know you call it 'uninhibited' and that is the way you want your child to be, but luckily my mother taught me some inhibitions or else I would smack little Carol once in a while when she's talkin' to you like you're a dog, but I just laugh it off the way you do because she is your child and I am not like one of the family.
>
> Now when you say, 'We don't know what we'd do without her' this is a polite lie . . . because I know that if I dropped dead or had a stroke, you would get somebody to replace me.
>
> You think it is a compliment when you say, 'We don't think of her as a servant . . . ,' but after I have worked myself into a sweat cleaning the bathroom and the kitchen . . . making the beds . . . cooking the lunch . . . washing the dishes and ironing Carol's pinafores . . . I do not feel like no weekend guest. I feel like a servant, and in the face of that I have been meaning to ask you for a slight raise which will make me feel much better toward everyone here and make me know my work's appreciated.
>
> Now I hope you will stop talkin' about me in my presence and that we will get along like a good employer and employee should."
>
> Marge! She was almost speechless but she apologized and said she'd talk to her husband about a raise . . . I knew things were progressing because Carol came in the kitchen and she did not say, "I want some bread and jam!" but she did say, "Please, Mildred, will you fix me a slice of bread and jam!"
>
> I'm going upstairs, Marge. Just look . . . You done messed up that buttonhole.

The work brings to mind Langston Hughes' man of the people, Jesse B. Semple. Childress's humor is in the profoundest tradition, i.e., humor with a political vengeance. What Mildred is really talking about is the face of oppression in the domestic arena: the tacky ways of the white folk she works for, how they work the hell out of her, but how, when it serves their own egotistical purposes, showing off, they suddenly refer to her as one of the family. "Why, she's just like one of the family!"—*the one that's never invited to sit at the dinner table,* not that sitting at the table would be a big deal for Mildred.

Childress's drama ***Wedding Band,*** a play about an ailing white man and a Black woman living together in a Carolina town, details the Black woman's struggle against the racist attitudes of the town and against the members of the white man's middle-class family who are outraged by the relationship. Childress's other writings had seemed to have a total and timely relevance to the Black experience in the U.S. of A.; ***Wedding Band*** was a deviation. Perhaps the critic's own mood or bias was at fault. For one who was involved artistically, creatively, intellectually, and actively in the human rights struggle unfolding at the time, it is difficult, even in retrospect, to empathize or identify with the heroine's struggle for her relationship with the white man, symbolically the enemy incarnate of Black hopes and aspirations. Nevertheless, again, at the heart of ***Wedding Band*** was the element of Black struggle, albeit a struggle difficult to relate to. As usual, the art and craftsmanship were fine; the message, however, appeared out of sync with the times.

Her novel ***A Hero Ain't Nothin' But a Sandwich*** was adapted for a film production. It is the story of Benjie, a thirteen-year-old drug addict. There are some awesomely beautiful and powerful moments in this novel. One that comes immediately and vividly to mind is the poignant scene in which Butler Craig, the "stepfather," saves spaced-out Benjie from falling from a Harlem rooftop, even as the boy begs his stepfather to let him go. " 'Let go, Butler . . . let me die. Drop me, man!' He's flailing his legs, trying to work loose my hold, hollerin and fighting to die. 'Let me be dead!' "

There are times in the book, however, when the characters, the victims, in this novel are their worst enemies. They appear unable to get out of their own way. Perhaps life is a treadmill, but the enemy of the people, the hand of the oppressor, is not clearly delineated in this one. Mari Evans says: "To identify the enemy is to free the people." Which just goes to prove that no one is perfect. Even an expert marksperson like Alice Childress does not hit the bull's-eye every time she picks up the rifle.

Alice Childress's latest and most rewarding novel is ***A Short Walk.*** "Life is just a short walk from the cradle to the grave—and it sure behooves us to be kind to one another along the way." This is the saga of Cora James from just before her fifth birthday in a racist Charleston, South Carolina.

Alice Childress brings the history of the times alive, as we, along with Cora James, join the Garvey movement, the U.N.I.A. (Universal Negro Improvement Association), the fabulous pomp, the militant pageantry, the grand and colorful parades through Harlem, the African Orthodox Church. It's all here, along with the struggle for race pride and identification with Africa. "Back to Africa!"—"Africa for the Africans! At home and abroad!" You've seen it written about many times before, but never has it come alive like this. It is history relived. We go with the Movement's ship, the Black Star Line's S.S. *Frederick Douglass* (Yarmouth) on its maiden voyage to Cuba. The writer's genius, her artistry, is her ability to totally involve you in the happenings, as you, the reader, happen along with them. You emerge from the spell of her writing with the feeling of a lived experience.

Alice Childress is a tremendously gifted artist who has consistently used her genius to effect change in the world: to change the image we have of ourselves as human beings, Black and white. Her primary and special concern has been the African image. She knew that Black was beautiful when so many of us thought that Black Beauty was the name of a storybook horse, a figment of a writer's fantasy. Her gift has been used as an instrument against oppression; notwithstanding, she is always the consummate artist, telling her story powerfully and artistically. Her writing is always realistic, avoiding somehow the indulgence

An excerpt from *A Hero Ain't Nothin' but a Sandwich*

I tole Benjie, "No matter how much skag a guy gets, he will still feel low when he comes down, cause he knows that everybody is kickin on his ass and gettin themselves a case of the weirdo jollies outta seein him sweat for his next fix." Fact is, I seen a pusher make a junkie *beg* for his dose, before he would even sell it to him. You ready for that? Not me. All that talk bout bein a chicken, if you don't let somebody use your veins for a horse racin track, goes on past my head and I'm feelin no pain, dig?

I don't be preachin a sermon on the subject cause everybody don't dig bein told how dumb-ass they actin. To a cat that digs bein stoned, I say, "Right on, *kill* yourself, man." He be thinkin that sound good and will give you a full grin, like you his main boon. But I hate to hit down too hard on some these little junk men, cause many are good cats. Didn't junk knock Benjie down?

One time a guy name Carwell sold me some joints. I looked up Benjie, so we could try us a pot high. We went up the steps leadin to the roof in a house on the next block a beat-up, fallin-down place where we know ain't no super give a damn. We on the steps smokin, suckin in the smoke like we been seein and hearin bout. I'm little bit older than they are, makes me cooler than them. Carwell and Benjie takin off and goin on, "Uuuuuuu-weee, um high, man. Groovin, this is it, man." I'm feelin kinda simple-ass cause all that ain't happenin for me. I feel sorta so-what—but no big thing. The roof door is open, and I could see blue sky and a white cloud straight up over my head, so it's there, dig? Remind me of the time I went in on a sixty-five-cent pinta wine—muscatel, it give me a headache hangover. Pot high, for me, is a dumb kinda don't-give-a-damn, but I know it's a high, and I'm sorta quietly lookin it over and tryin to figure it out. I got what you call a inquisitive mind. Benjie and Carwell, they makin talk.

"This it!"

"Live or die, make me no difference."

I'm layin back studyin sky and their voices . . . . just waitin for the high to pass. Nothin left of me but one dumb, sad feelin. I don't dig bein lost, I'm better off found. Carwell say, "I know a stud who buys grass by the bag!" I don't like Carwell, his eyes ugly, hard brown buttons. You got to *stay* stoned to stand Carwell a-tall, I'm still not likin him even with the high on. Losin yourself is for some, but it ain't for others. It ain't for me.

Benjie had a long stringa spit hangin offa his bottom lip. I'm lookin at spit, seein sky through a roof door, and turnin my bread over to the button-eyed Carwell. It ain't for me, dig? I really don't need no knockin out. I'm sorry how Benjie is now gettin caught up and expandin on the program.

Alice Childress, in her A Hero Ain't Nothin' but a Sandwich, *Coward, McCann & Geoghegan, 1973, reprinted by Avon Flare Books, 1982.*

of wallowing in quagmires of despair and pessimism. After all, life *is* a short walk. There is so little time and so much living to achieve. Perhaps her greatest gift, along with her satiric bent and the thematic accent on struggle, is the leitmotif of love for people, particularly her own people. I have come away from most of her writing feeling mighty damn proud of the human race, especially the African aspect of it. Portraying it with great fidelity in all of its meanness, its pettiness, its prejudices, its superstitions, Childress captures most of all its capacity to overcome, to be better than it is, or ever could be, its monumental capacity for change.

At a writers' conference sponsored in 1974 at Howard University by Dr. Stephen Henderson and the Institute for the Arts and Humanities, writer Toni Cade Bambara said: "The responsibility of an artist representing an oppressed people is to make revolution irresistible." At the same time, when so many Black writers have decided that the thing to do is to "get over" with the great white racist publishing establishment, despite the price one may be forced to pay in terms of self-esteem, human dignity, and artistic integrity, Childress has made a deliberate choice of weapons; she has chosen the weapon of creative struggle. Black blessings on you, Alice Childress.

Elizabeth Brown-Guillory (essay date 1988)

SOURCE: "Alice Childress, Lorraine Hansberry, Ntozake Shange: Carving a Place for Themselves on the American Stage," in *Their Place on the Stage: Black Women Playwrights in America,* Greenwood Press, 1988, pp. 25-49.

[*An American educator and playwright, Brown-Guillory is the author of several works on contemporary drama. In the following excerpt, she offers an overview of Childress's principal plays, acknowledging her contributions to African-American drama.*]

Alice Childress is the only black woman playwright in America whose plays have been written, produced, and published over a period of four decades. Like a giant in a straitjacket, Childress has remained faithful to the American theater even when it has looked upon her with blind eyes and turned to her with deaf ears. Having had plays produced in New York City, across the United States, and in Europe, Childress' legacy to the American theater is monumental. In her thirty-eight years of writing for the American stage, Childress admits that she has never compromised her vision. Her sagacity and total commitment became apparent when she, almost in a whisper commented [in an interview conducted in 1987], "I will not keep quiet, and I will not stop telling the truth." Though she writes mainly about the genteel poor, a diverse audience looks to her for the truth that she gives to them in numerous small doses and without adulteration.

Alice Childress has written plays that incorporate the liturgy of the black church, traditional music, African mythology, folklore, and fantasy. She has experimented by writing sociopolitical, romantic, biographical, historical, and feminist plays. Striving to find new and dynamic ways of expressing old themes in an historically conservative theater, Childress has opened the door for other black playwrights, particularly Hansberry and Shange, to make dramaturgical advances. Her litany of "firsts" invariably paved the way for a line of black women playwrights to insist upon craft and integrity over commercialism. Doris Abramson [in her *Negro Playwrights in the American Theatre, 1925-1959*] writes, "Alice Childress has been, from the beginning, a crusader and a writer who refuses to compromise. . . . She refuses productions of her plays if the producer wants to change them in any way that distorts her intentions."

Alice Childress writes about poor women for whom the act of living is sheer heroism. In fact, Childress' own background resembles that of the heroines in her plays. In a recent essay, **"Knowing the Human Condition"** [in *Black American Literature and Humanism,* edited by R. Baxter Miller, 1981], Childress acknowledges that her grandmother was a slave. Claiming that she is neither proud nor ashamed of her past, Childress has observed:

> I was raised in Harlem by very poor people. My grandmother who went to fifth grade in the Jim Crow school system of South Carolina inspired me to observe what was around me and write about it without false pride or shame.

Indeed, her poor, dejected heroines are depicted as morally strong, sometimes vulnerable, but resilient. She portrays these women honestly as they fight daily battles not just to survive but to survive whole.

Childress' contributions to the American theater have been varied and consistent. In the early 1940s, Childress helped to found the American Negro Theater (ANT), a phenomenal organization that served as a beacon of hope for countless black playwrights, actors, and producers, such as Sidney Poitier, Ossie Davis, Ruby Dee, Frank Silvera, and others. ANT, like the African Grove Theatre that was founded in 1821-1822 and marks the beginning of "alternative theatre" for blacks, has been instrumental in institutionalizing black theater. Another major achievement of Childress, a long time Broadway and off-Broadway actress, and a member of the Author's League of the Dramatists' Guild, is that she was instrumental in the early 1950s in initiating advanced, guaranteed pay for union off-Broadway contracts in New York City.

Childress became one of the beneficiaries of her efforts to establish equity standards for off-Broadway productions. Her first two plays, ***Just a Little Simple*** (1950) and ***Gold Through the Trees*** (1952), were the first plays by a black woman to be professionally produced, i.e., performed by unionized actors. Three years later, Childress became the first black woman to win the Obie Award for the best original, off-Broadway play of the year with her production of ***Trouble in Mind*** (1955), which was subsequently produced by the BBC in London. Ten years later, Childress' ***Wedding Band*** (1966) was broadcast nationally on ABC television. ***Wine in the Wilderness*** (1969) was presented on National Educational Television (NET). With all of the kudos of a seasoned playwright, the author basked in the glory of the officially designated Alice Childress Week in Columbia and Charleston during the production of ***Sea Island Song*** (1979), commissioned by the South Carolina Arts Commission to capture the flavor of the Gullah-speaking people of the area.

As a result of Childress' innovative achievements and commitment to quality theater, she has been the recipient of a host of awards and honors, including writer-in-residence at the MacDowell Colony; featured author on a BBC panel discussion on "The Negro in the American Theater;" winner of a Rockefeller grant administered through The New Dramatists and a John Golden Fund for Playwrights; and a Harvard appointment to the Radcliffe Institute for Independent Study (now Mary Ingraham Bunting Institute), from which she received a graduate medal for work completed during her tenure.

Serving as spokesperson for the masses of poor, Childress continues to write about "the complexity of relationships between blacks and whites and the various ways blacks survive in contemporary society" [Dedria Bryfonski, ed., *Contemporary Literary Criticism,* Vol. 12, 1980]. Sharply observant and unsentimental, she is one of the most influential theater pioneers whose works serve as a precursor to the black naturalistic plays of the 1960s, and whose efforts substantially shaped the ethnic theater of black experience of the 1970s and 1980s.

Alice Childress, born on October 12, 1920, in Charleston South Carolina, is an actress, playwright, novelist, essayist, columnist, lecturer, and theater consultant. At the age of five, Childress boarded a train for New York where she grew up in Harlem. Childress attended Public School 81, The Julia Ward Howe Junior High School and, for three years, Wadleigh High School, at which time she had to drop out because both her grandmother and mother had died, leaving her to fend for herself. Forced to assume the responsibility of teaching herself, Childress discovered the public library and attempted to read two books a day.

Beginning in the early 1940s, Childress began establishing herself as an actress and writer, during which time she worked to support herself and her only child, Jean, in a number of odd jobs, including assistant machinist, photo retoucher, domestic worker, salesperson, and insurance agent. [Trudier] Harris believes that "the variety of experiences and the constant contact with working-class people undoubtedly influenced Childress' approach to the development of characters and her overall writing philosophy. Her characters in fiction and drama included domestic workers, washerwomen, seamstresses, and the unemployed, as well as dancers, artists, and teachers. . . ."

Childress' first play, ***Florence,*** produced by the American Negro Theatre in 1949, levels an indictment against presumptuous whites who think they know more about blacks than blacks know about themselves. It is also a play about a need for blacks to reject stereotyped roles. On another level, ***Florence*** pays tribute to black parents who encourage their children to reach their fullest potential at all cost. It reveals Childress' superb skill at characterization, dialogue, and conflict.

Florence is set in a Jim Crow railway station where Mama discovers that Mrs. Carter, a white liberal, is irrepressibly racist. Mama, awaiting a train bound for Harlem, confides in Mrs. Carter that her daughter has been able to secure only minor and infrequent theater roles. Vehemently trying to persuade Mama to make Florence give up her dreams of becoming an actress before she becomes completely disillusioned, Mrs. Carter explains that Florence's efforts are futile, especially since she, a white woman, is an actress who cannot find work. Mama becomes outraged when, after asking her to help her daughter, Mrs. Carter speaks of getting Florence a job as a maid. Resolving not to go to New York, Mama sends her last money to Florence with a note attached saying "keep trying."

The theme of rejecting stereotypes and of not compromising one's integrity is further explored in Childress' ***Trouble in Mind,*** which was produced at the Greenwich Mews Theatre in New York in 1955. Running for ninety-one performances, ***Trouble in Mind*** won for Childress the Obie Award for the best original off-Broadway play of the 1955-1956 season and was subsequently produced twice in 1964 by the BBC in London. When offered a Broadway option, Childress refused because the producer wanted her to make radical script changes. Alice Childress says of her rejection of the Broadway offer, "Most of our problems have not seen the light of day in our works, and much has been pruned from our manuscripts before the public has been allowed a glimpse of a finished work. It is ironical that those who oppose us are in a position to dictate the quality of our contributions" [Abramson].

Childress' ***Trouble in Mind*** needed "pruning" because it is a satiric drama about white writers, producers, and directors who, because they are ignorant of blacks, support or defend inaccurate portraits. Childress insists in this drama that blacks must maintain their integrity and identity in the theater, refusing to accept roles that characterize them as exotic or half-human creatures, regardless of the monetary losses.

Making use of the play-within-a-play, ***Trouble in Mind*** is set on a Broadway stage where the characters rehearse *Chaos in Belleville,* a play written by a white about blacks. Wiletta Mayer, a veteran black actress, offends the sensibilities of the white director when she asserts that no black mother, as in *Chaos in Belleville,* would tell her son to give himself up to be lynched, regardless of his innocence or guilt. Appalled by other untruths, Wiletta announces that she will not perform unless some changes are made in the script. Because of her frankness, she is summarily dropped from the cast.

Trouble in Mind, Childress' first professionally produced play outside of Harlem, received glowing reviews. Loften Mitchell, in *Black Drama* [1967], commented, "Now the professional theatre saw her outside of her native Harlem, writing with swift stabs of humor, her perception and her consummate dramatic gifts." Equally laudatory is the assessment made by Arthur Gelb of the *New York Times* [5 November 1955], who says that Childress has "some witty and penetrating things to say about the dearth of roles for Negro actors in contemporary theatre, the cut-throat competition for these parts and the fact that Negro actors often find themselves playing stereotyped roles in which they cannot bring themselves to believe."

GREENWICH MEWS THEATRE

141 West 13th Street

FIRE NOTICE: The exit indicated by a red light and sign nearest to the seat you occupy is the shortest route to the street. In the event of fire please do not run — WALK TO THAT EXIT.
EDWARD CAVANAGH, FIRE COMMISSIONER.

THE GREENWICH MEWS THEATRE

presents

TROUBLE IN MIND

by ALICE CHILDRESS

Directed by CLARICE TAYLOR and ALICE CHILDRESS

Setting and Lighting by Vincent Sorrentino

A community project sponsored by the Village Presbyterian Church and Brotherhood Synagogue

THE CAST

(In order of appearance)

Hoodan .... JOHNNY BARRACUDA
Pop .... LIAM LENIHAN
Wiletta Mayer .... CLARICE TAYLOR
John Neville .... CHARLES BETTIS
Millie Davis .... HILDA HAYNES
Sheldon Forrester .... HOWARD AUGUSTA
Judith Sears .... STEPHANIE ELLIOT
Al Manners .... JAMES McMAHON
Eddie Fenton .... HAL ENGLAND

ACT ONE: The Brick Box Theatre in New York City. 10 a.m. Monday morning.

ACT TWO: Ten Minutes later.

There will be a ten minute intermission between the acts.

PRODUCTION STAFF

Artistic Director .... LILY TURNER
Administrative Coordinator .... STELLA HOLT
Stage Manager .... HOWARD AUGUSTA
Production Assistants .... DOROTHY BARRY, MAURICE BUGEAUD, ANITA HONIS, BILL KELLOGG, LINDA STEINBERG

Playbill for Trouble in Mind.

Like ***Trouble in Mind, Wedding Band*** (1966) was deemed controversial and missed Broadway because of Childress' refusal to make script changes that would alter her intent. Produced at the University of Michigan in 1969, and at the Public Theatre in New York during the 1972-1973 season, ***Wedding Band*** became the first play by Childress to be televised nationally on ABC in 1974. ***Wedding Band*** centers around an interracial love affair that is destroyed by white and black bigotry. The theme that emerges is that blacks and whites must learn to judge each other on individual merit, instead of blaming an entire race each time a white-black relationship, intimate or casual, terminates.

Set in a small town in South Carolina in 1918, the plot revolves around Julia and Herman, who have been secretly meeting for ten years because of state laws forbidding interracial marriage. Giving Julia a wedding band on a chain that she can wear only around her neck until they leave the South, Herman encourages her to go to New York to prepare for his coming within a year, at which time he hopes to have settled a debt owed his mother. Calamity strikes when Herman falls sick with influenza at Julia's house in the heart of the black community, an occurrence that outrages both whites and blacks. The promised escape to the North never materializes, and Herman dies in Julia's arms.

Wedding Band, subtitled *A Love/Hate Story in Black and White,* received mixed reviews. Clive Barnes of the *New York Times* wrote [27 October 1972], "Indeed its strength lies very much in the poignancy of its star-cross'd lovers, but whereas Shakespeare's lovers had a fighting chance, there is no way that Julia and Herman are going to beat the system. Niggers and crackers are more irreconcilable than any Montagues and Capulets." In quite a different vein, Loften Mitchell [in *The Crisis* (April 1965)] commented, "Miss Childress writes with a sharp, satiric touch. . . . Characterizations are piercing, her observations devastating. . . . The play reaches a rousing climax when the Negro woman defines for a white woman exactly what the Negro has meant in terms of Southern lives."

Following ***Wedding Band,*** Childress wrote ***Wine in the Wilderness,*** which was aired on National Educational Television (NET) in 1969. Set in Harlem in 1960 during a race riot, this play pokes fun at bourgeois affectation and is one of the first plays about middle-class Negro life by a black woman playwright. Childress levels an attack at blacks who scream blackness, brotherhood, and togetherness but who have no love or empathy for poor, uneducated, and unrefined blacks. Tomorrow Marie, the dynamic heroine, is dragged in from the violence of the riots only to experience the emotional violence inherent in the discovery that her new associates think that she is the dregs of society, a poor black woman who is crass. Serving as a catalyst for the growth of Bill Jameson, Cynthia, and Sonny-Man, Tomorrow Marie calls them phoney niggers and teaches them the ugliness of their own superciliousness.

Wine in the Wilderness is Childress at her best. Hatch and Shine [in *Black Theater USA: Forty-Five Plays by Black Americans, 1847-1974,* 1974] note that, "The beauty of ***Wine in the Wilderness*** is in part due to the author's sensitive treatment of Tommy. . . . Alice Childress has created a powerful, new black heroine who emerges from the depths of the black community, offering a sharp contrast to the typically strong 'Mama' figure that dominates such plays as *Raisin in the Sun.*"

Another play by Childress in which the heroine serves as a catalyst for growth is ***Mojo: A Black Love Story,*** produced at the New Harlem Theatre in 1970. ***Mojo*** is a domestic drama dealing with the misfortunes and misunderstandings of a poverty-stricken black couple who, though they love each other, have spent the bulk of their lives apart and hurting. Teddy's ex-wife, Irene, returns unexpectedly for emotional support as she readies herself for cancer surgery. Each recalls the mistakes of earlier days and comes to realize the strength fostered by uncovering past anger, wounds, and fears. Childress' perceptions are devastatingly accurate in this complex drama where people are pressured into causing each other pain because of financial exigency. The author skillfully, but without condoning or relieving the black couple of their past indiscretions, depicts two people who have survived rats, garbage, and minimum wages earned for cleaning toilets.

Unlike Childress' other plays, her historical dramas have not met with a great deal of success. Barbara Molette argues [in *Black World* (April 1976)], "It's not that black playwrights have not written historical plays; it's that we have a difficult time getting them produced." Like the early black women playwrights of the Harlem Renaissance, such as May Miller and Georgia Douglas Johnson, Alice Childress' historical heroines have remained silent. One case in point is Childress' ***When the Rattlesnake Sounds*** (1975), which has no record of a professional production. This children's play illustrates Harriet Tubman's commitment, strength, and fear during the days of the Underground Railroad. Childress' talent in this play has not gone unrecognized as critic Zena Sutherland comments [in *Bulletin of the Center for Children's Books* (May 1976)], "the play is moving because of its subject and impressive because of the deftness with which Childress develops characters and background in so brief and static a setting."

Alice Childress writes because she is compelled to tell the truth about black life in America. According to C. W. E. Bigsby, in *A Critical Introduction to Twentieth-Century American Drama* [1985], "Childress' humanism is evident, and her resistance to ruling political and cultural orthodoxies apparent." She is a writer of great discipline, power, substance, wit, and integrity. A pioneer in the theater, Childress' steadfast efforts of forty years have substantially shaped black playwriting in America.

Additional coverage of Childress's life and career is contained in the following sources published by Gale Research: *Authors and Artists for Young Adults,* Vol. 8; *Black Literature Criticism; Black Writers,* Vol. 2; *Children's Literature Review,* Vol. 14; *Contemporary Authors,* Vols. 45-48, 146; *Contemporary Authors New Revision Series,* Vols. 3, 27; *Contemporary Literary Criticism,* Vols. 12, 15; *Drama Criticism,* Vol. 4; *Dictionary of Literary Biography,* Vols. 7, 38; *Junior DISCovering Authors; Major Authors and Illustrators for Children and Young Adults; Major 20th-Century Writers;* and *Something about the Author,* Vols. 7, 48.

Ralph Ellison

March 1, 1914—April 16, 1994

(Full name Ralph Waldo Ellison) American novelist, essayist, short story writer, critic, and editor.

For further information on Ellison's life and works, see *CLC,* Volumes 1, 3, 11, and 54.

INTRODUCTION

One of the most influential and accomplished American authors of the twentieth century, Ellison is best known for his highly acclaimed novel *Invisible Man* (1952). Honored with a National Book Award for Fiction, *Invisible Man* is regarded as a masterpiece for its complex treatment of individuality, self-awareness, and the repression and betrayal associated with race relations in America. Employing naturalistic, expressionistic, and surrealistic elements, Ellison combined concerns of European and African-American literature in *Invisible Man* to chronicle an unnamed black youth's quest for self-identity in a hostile world. Narrating his story from an underground cell, the anonymous protagonist describes his experiences as a student in the South, his travels in Harlem following his undeserved expulsion from college, his work with a political organization named the Brotherhood, and his participation in the Harlem race riots of the 1940s; he explains in the prologue that he is involuntarily invisible—and has thus gone underground—because society sees him only in terms of racial stereotypes. Although some critics have faulted Ellison's style in this work as occasionally excessive, *Invisible Man* has consistently been praised for its poetic, ambiguous form, its sustained blend of tragedy and comedy, and its complex symbolism and characterizations. A meticulous craftsman, Ellison was working on his long-awaited second novel at the time of his death. Additionally known as an essayist and nonfiction writer, Ellison collected twenty-two years of reviews, criticism, and interviews concerning such subjects as art, music, literature, and the influence of the black experience on American culture in *Shadow and Act* (1964). This volume is often considered autobiographical in intent and is noted for its lucidity and the insights it provides into *Invisible Man. Going to the Territory* (1986), which contains speeches, reviews, and interviews written since 1957, echoes many of the concerns of *Shadow and Act.* Making use of ironic humor in the manner of *Invisible Man,* Ellison here reflected on and paid tribute to such personal influences and creative mentors as Richard Wright and Duke Ellington. Although Ellison has historically been recognized as a seminal figure in contemporary literature, critical reception of his work has been largely influenced by the changing political milieu of American society in the latter half of the twentieth century. Nevertheless, commentators have continued to stress the universal themes and sophisticated nature of his oeuvre. Richard Corliss observed: "Ellison's writing was too refined, elaborate, to be spray painted on a tenement wall. He was a celebrator as much as a denouncer of the nation that bred him. In his multicolored vision, America was not just a violent jungle but a vibrant jumble of many cultures and temperaments; it mingled melody, harmony, dissonance and ad-lib genius, like the jazz that Ellison played, wrote about and loved."

PRINCIPAL WORKS

*"Flying Home" (short story) 1944; published in journal *Cross Section*

*"King of the Bingo Game" (short story) 1944; published in journal *Tomorrow*

Invisible Man (novel) 1952
"Out of the Hospital and under the Bar" (short story) 1963; published in *Soon, One Morning: New Writing by American Negroes, 1940-1962*
Shadow and Act (essays and interviews) 1964
Going to the Territory (essays, lectures, and interviews) 1986

*These works were also published in *Dark Symphony: Negro Literature in America* in 1968.

OBITUARIES AND TRIBUTES

David Remnick (essay date 14 March 1994)

SOURCE: "Visible Man," in *The New Yorker,* Vol. LXX, No. 14, March 14, 1994, pp. 34-8.

[In the essay below, written on the occasion of Ellison's eightieth birthday, Remnick provides an overview of Ellison's career, discussing the writer's unfinished second novel, his critical reputation, his contributions to American society, and the value of Invisible Man.*]*

In a modest apartment overlooking the Hudson, at the weld of northern Harlem and southern Washington Heights, Ralph Ellison confronts his "work in progress." He has been at this for nearly forty years, and rare is the day that he does not doubt his progress. He wakes early, goes out to buy a paper on Broadway, returns, and, when he has exhausted the possibilities of the *Times* and the *Today* show, when the coffee and the toast are gone, he flicks on the computer in his study and reads the passage he finished the day before. "The hardest part of the morning is that first hour, just getting the rhythm," Ellison says. "So much depends on continuity. I'll go back to get a sense of its rhythm and see what it will suggest, and go on from there. But very often I'll start in the morning by looking back at the work from the day before and it ain't worth a damn." When that happens, as it does more frequently than he would like, Ellison will turn away and stare out the window, watching the river flow.

Ralph Ellison turned eighty on March 1st, and his peculiarly modern burden, the burden of a second act, grows heavier with age. The man is far too composed, too regal, to betray the weight of it, but the soul must weary of its persistence. So great was the celebration in 1952 for his first (and only) novel, ***Invisible Man***, that the sound of critical applause, rattling medals, and whispered expectations took years to fade. Few novels have ever entered the canon so quickly. Ellison won the National Book Award, the Presidential Medal of Freedom, the Chevalier de l'Ordre des Artes et Lettres, a place in the American Academy of Arts and Letters, and a position at New York University as Albert Schweitzer Professor of Humanities. Here and there, critics' and readers' polls would declare ***Invisible Man*** the greatest American novel of the postwar period or of the century. Ellison's rite-of-passage novel absorbed everything from black folklore to Dostoyevski's *Notes from Underground*, creating something entirely new, lasting, and American. It was translated into seventeen languages, and the Modern Library produced an edition. But at the end of all this lingered the nervous, American question: What's next?

Ellison did not intend to distinguish his career with such an austerity of publication. By 1955, he had begun a novel set mainly in the South and in Washington, D.C. At the center of the story—as far as we know it from a few published extracts—are the community and the language of the black church and the relationship between a black preacher and a friend who eventually becomes a senator and a notorious racist. After a few years of writing, Ellison was not shy about showing excerpts to friends like Saul Bellow and the novelist and cultural historian Albert Murray. He was not reluctant to publish a piece here and there in literary quarterlies.

For a while, expectations for the book soared. "I shared a house with Ralph in the late fifties in Tivoli, New York, along the Hudson in Dutchess County," Bellow says. "At that time, he was hard at work on the book, and he let me read a considerable portion of it—a couple of hundred pages, at least, as I remember. We were running a magazine at the time called *The Noble Savage*, and we published an excerpt of Ralph's manuscript called **'Cadillac Flambé.'** But all of it was marvellous stuff, easily on a level with ***Invisible Man***."

A couple of weeks before his birthday, I called on Ellison at his home. The apartment is lined and stacked with books. Here and there are African sculptures and piles of papers, mostly correspondence. As he and his wife, Fanny, showed me around, a small cloud of cigar smoke still hovered over his computer in the study. Slender and graceful, with the courtly elegance of his friend Duke Ellington, Ellison looks fifteen years younger than he is; a man of old-fashioned Southern grace, he is polite in the high style, careful in conversation almost to the point of deliberate, if ironic, dullness. I said that his friends have often remarked on the gap in style between the turbulence of ***Invisible Man*** and the reserve of its author.

"Well, one inherits a style from the people one grows up with," Ellison said, referring to his childhood in Oklahoma, which was segregated at the time but had never been a slave state. He studied composition at Booker T. Washington's Tuskegee Institute, in Macon County, Alabama—and was the intellectual star of his class—before coming to New York, in 1937. "I am rather passionate about some of the inequities that are part of the country," he went on. "But why should a writer be different? No one asks a surgeon to be different. He has to be a surgeon first. He has to know the techniques and traditions of surgery. That's how I approach writing. I would do the same thing if I were an opera singer. Black opera singers have to master the tradition. We all have at least double identities."

For a while, Ellison skated amiably, and elliptically, around various questions of the day, but when the subject turned to his work in progress, the book that Bellow had remembered so vividly, the one that Albert Murray used to hear Ellison read aloud from, he seemed, at first, a little startled. Then, as he described a fire two decades ago at his old summer house, in Plainfield, Massachusetts, he slumped back in his chair, resigned, his voice lowering into a growly whisper. "There was, of course, a traumatic event involved with the book," he began. "We lost a summer house and, with it, a good part of the novel. It wasn't the entire manuscript, but it was over three hundred and sixty pages. There was no copy. We had stayed up in the country into November, in the Berkshires. We went to do some shopping and came back and the house was burning. An electrical failure. And, being in the country with a little volunteer fire department—well, they were off fighting another fire and didn't make it. They never got it put out. It all burned down. They came and tried, but in the country it's difficult to get water, especially there."

Ellison's friends say that it was years before he went back to work on the novel; some say three or four, others five or six. Albert Murray, who lives across town, off Lenox Avenue, and has known Ellison since they were students together at Tuskegee, had told me, "Ralph was just devastated. He just closed in on himself for a long time. He didn't see anyone or go anywhere. At a certain point, you knew not to say much about it. A wall, Ralph's reserve, went up all around him." Ellison was reduced to trying to summon up his novel from memory or from the memories of those who had read it or heard him read it.

When I asked Ellison how much time he lost, he was quiet for a while, and then he said, in a tone that suggested we were talking about someone else and the question was merely *interesting,* "You know, I'm not sure. It's kind of blurred for me. But the novel has got my attention now. I work every day, so there will be something very soon. After the fire, I had certain notes here in the city and a pretty good idea of where I wanted to go. Snatches of it had been published. And I did a lot of teaching after that. Let's say I was disoriented, but I worked on it. I don't know how long the interruption was. Maybe four or five years. It wasn't as if I weren't working. I was trying to reimagine the situation. The characters are the same and the mixture of language is the same. But nuances are different. After all, when I write I am discovering things. One development suggests another, a phrase will reveal things. You just try to get through it.

"Letting go of the book is difficult, because I'm so uncertain. I want it to be of quality. With ***Invisible Man,*** I wasn't all that certain, but I had friends like Stanley Edgar Hyman, who worked on *The New Yorker,* and who was invaluable to me. There's a photograph of Stanley reading ***Invisible Man*** in Francis Steegmuller's office. I'll always remember: he looked up at me and said, 'Say, this thing is funny!' When you are younger, you are so eager to be published. I am eager to publish this book. That's why I stay here, and not in the country. I'm eager to finish it and see how it turns out."

Ellison's readers can be greedy and hope for more novels and essays—come to think of it, a memoir would be nice, too—but what's done is done and, in a sense, is more than enough. On the occasion of his eightieth birthday, it becomes clearer than ever that ***Invisible Man*** and his two collections of essays, ***Shadow and Act*** (1964) and ***Going to the Territory*** (1986), are the urtexts for a loose coalition of black American intellectuals who represent an integrationist vision of the country's history and culture. Ellison's books are a foundation for talents as various as the novelists Charles Johnson, John Edgar Wideman, Leon Forrest, and James Alan McPherson; the critics Shelby Steele, Henry Louis Gates, Jr., and Stanley Crouch; the poet Michael S. Harper. When Johnson, for instance, received the National Book Award, in 1990, for his novel *Middle Passage,* he devoted his entire acceptance speech to a celebration of Ellison. Johnson said he hoped that the nineteen-nineties would see the emergence of a "black American fiction" that takes Ellison as its inspiration, "one that enables us as a people—as a culture—to move from narrow complaint to broad celebration."

The publication of ***Invisible Man*** predates the civil-rights movement of the nineteen-sixties, the drama of Malcolm X, and the rise of Afrocentrism, and yet it anticipates, or answers, all of these. The demagogic figure of Ras the Destroyer in the novel is based, no doubt, on Marcus Garvey, but it turns out to be a prescient depiction of the Farrakhans to come. The lancing portrait of the Brotherhood was modelled on the Communist Party of the nineteen-thirties, but it stands for all the doctrinaire utopianism and fakery to come. The metaphor of the paint factory and the mixing of black paint into white anticipates a sane multiculturalism, a vision of American culture as an inextricable blend. Unlike so much fiction labelled somehow as ethnic, ***Invisible Man*** is a universal novel. From the first lines to the very last ("Who knows but that, on the lower frequencies, I speak for you?"), it insists on the widest possible audience.

In Ellison's view, America is not made up of separate, free-floating cultures but, rather, of a constant interplay and exchange. In the essays, he describes slaves on a Southern plantation watching white people dance and then transforming those European steps into something that is American; he speaks of what Ella Fitzgerald has done with the songs of Rodgers and Hart, what white rock bands did with the blues; he watches the black kids in Harlem in their baggy hip-hop gear walking down Broadway, and on the same day he sees white suburban kids on television affecting the same style. What Ellison has called the "interchange, appropriation, and integration" of American culture is evident in the music we hear, the games we play, the books we read, the clothes we wear, the food we eat. For him, integration is not merely an aspiration but a given, a fact of cultural and political life. Without pity or excessive pride, Ellison also sketches the facts of his own life—especially his self-discovery, first through music, then literature—to describe the American phenomenon. ***Invisible Man*** itself looks not only to the experience of Ralph Ellison at Tuskegee Institute or in Harlem but to Ralph Ellison in the library, the young reader that Albert Murray remembers as "always looking to the top shelf." When Ellison finally came to New York, Richard Wright and Langston Hughes became literary mentors and friends, but their influence was secondary, following a youthful tear through Eliot, Pound, Faulkner, Hemingway, Stein, and Dostoyevski. Out of many, one.

Ellison's vision of American life and culture has not always sat well with critics, black or white. For the Black Arts Movement of the nineteen-sixties and seventies, ***Invisible Man*** and its author lacked the necessary rage. Amiri Baraka (LeRoi Jones) and other nationalists denounced Ellison from platform after platform. And that had its wounding effect, especially in the academy.

In 1969, Charles Johnson dropped by the library at Southern Illinois University's new black-studies program. "Where can I find a copy of ***Invisible Man?***" he asked the librarian.

"We don't carry it," came the answer.

"Really? Why not?"

"Because Ralph Ellison is not a black writer," the librarian said.

An extreme example, no doubt, but it suggests the climate of the time. "When Ellison got an award in 1965 for the best novel since the Second World War, people were still under the sway of the vision that came from Martin Luther King," Stanley Crouch, the author of *Notes of a Hanging Judge,* told me. "Once the black-power separatist agenda came along, and once white people showed that they preferred some kind of sadomasochistic rhetorical ritual to anything serious, Ellison's position began to lose ground. That's been the central problem in Afro-American affairs since the black-power-cum-Marxist vision took over the discussion. We have had to deal with one or another intellectual fast-food version of that these last twenty-five years or so. What it comes down to is that Ellison perceives Afro-American history in terms of the grand sweep of American life, not in terms of sheer victimhood. And that has been very difficult in the wake of the whole Malcolm X, 'You didn't land at Plymouth Rock, Plymouth Rock landed on you' thing."

"Let's face it," Henry Louis Gates, Jr., the chairman of the Afro-American studies program at Harvard, said. "Ellison was shut out, and Richard Wright was elected godfather of the Black Arts Movement of the nineteen-sixties, because, Wright's hero in *Native Son,* Bigger Thomas, cuts off a white girl's head and stuffs her in a furnace. For Ellison, the revolutionary political act was not separation; it was the staking of a claim for the Negro in the construction of an honestly public American culture. Wright's real message was not that different, but no one wanted to see that."

The resistance to Ellison's vision was by no means limited to black critics. In "Black Boys and Native Sons," an essay published in *Dissent,* Irving Howe adopted a strangely patronizing tone to celebrate Richard Wright's authenticity and to reprimand James Baldwin and Ellison for failing to possess a similar sense of rage. Howe declared himself astonished by "the apparent freedom [***Invisible Man***] displays from the ideological and emotional penalties suffered by Negroes in this country."

Ellison's passionate reply, **"The World and the Jug,"** was published in *The New Leader,* and can be read as a manifesto, a defense of his vision and art, and of the life that created them:

> Evidently Howe feels that unrelieved suffering is the only "real" Negro experience, and that the true Negro writer must be ferocious. But there is also an American Negro tradition which teaches one to deflect racial provocation and to master and contain pain. It is a tradition which abhors as obscene any trading on one's own anguish for gain and sympathy; which springs not from a desire to deny the harshness of existence but from a will to deal with it as men at their best have always done. . . . It would seem to me, therefore, that the question of how the "sociology of his existence" presses upon a Negro writer's work depends upon how much of his life the individual writer is able to transform into art. What moves a writer to eloquence is less meaningful than what he makes of it. . . . One unfamiliar with what Howe stands for would get the impression that when he looks at a Negro he sees not a human being but an abstract embodiment of living hell. He seems never to have considered that American Negro life (and here he is encouraged by certain Negro "spokesmen") is, for the Negro who must live it, not only a burden (and not always that) but also a discipline.

Ellison's answer to Howe was, in a sense, an elaboration of the first paragraph of ***Invisible Man,*** with the hero's demand to be seen as himself, as "flesh and bone, fiber and liquids—and I might even be said to possess a mind." The mind of Ellison has been deeply influential. Even if Leonard Jeffries and Molefi Kete Asante have been successful

went back to Tatlock and others that I had had disagreements long before college. I had always seemed to arouse the anger of some of the fellows, though without intention at first, then later by design . It was an antagonism that arose simply from my interest in other things, from my ambition to put aside the things around me and take up other ways... I'd been too clever for them though and all that was away and past. I could not reawaken the old anger against them now although it would have been a relief from the bewilderment of having no one to turn against in my confusion. Suddenly as the bus came to a stop I realized that I had been humming the tune which the man ahead of me had been whistling, the words now sounding in my head:

O well they picked poor Robin clean
O well they picked poor Robin clean
Well they tied poor Robin to a stump,
Lawd, they picked all the feathers round from
Robin's rump.

O well they picked poor Robin
Poor old Robin
They picked poor Robin
Clean.

I yanked down upon the cord and hurried from the bus at the next stop, looking into the man's innocent face as I went past. His thin, whistle like the sound of tissue paper blown against the teeh of a comb followed me out through the roar of the motor. I stood watching the bus move off, half expecting the man to leap from the door and follow me wherever I went, whistling his old forgotten jingle about bare rumped robin. I had to reassure myself that the man knew nothing about me, had never seen me before and that his whistling of that particular tune had been accidental, but I wasn't quiet sure. Nothing that happened to me seemed accidental, only unexaplainable, for now I was growing more andmore certain that all that had happened to me was part of a plan. It had to be; there had to be some order about

Typescript page of Invisible Man.

in imposing dubious Afrocentric programs on the City College of New York and Temple University, even if such ideas have trickled into school systems as far-flung as Portland's and Atlanta's, Ellison's godchildren have been at least as influential in stating their case. His integrationist position has shaped black-studies programs at Harvard, Princeton, Yale, Stanford, and many other leading universities.

"Ellison grants blacks their uniqueness without separating us from the larger culture," Shelby Steele, the author of *The Content of Our Character,* said. "After reading Ellison, you realize that talk of a 'white culture' or 'black culture' is simplification. In the academy, identity politics is often the thing, and people would prefer to deal with finite categories: 'black culture,' 'white culture,' 'Hispanic culture,' and so on. Nationalist politics gets more attention, because it's more flamboyant, more glamorous, more controversial. It's better press. But the vast majority of black people in this country are not nationalist. My sense of the problem has to do with the nature of black politics, an oppression-based politics since the nineteen-sixties. People like me, who believe that there are some difficulties of black life that are not the result of oppression, are just branded conservatives, no matter what the range of opinion."

Stanley Crouch sees the ambivalence toward Ellison as a symptom of the separatist drift represented by Ras the Destroyer. "Ellison knew a long time ago what the dangers were," Crouch said. "All the dangers are in ***Invisible Man.*** The dangers of demagoguery. The dangers of trying to hold up a rational position in a country that can become hysterical about race, from either side. You see, the race hysteria that was dominated by white people for the bulk of time Afro-Americans have been in America was overtaken by the black-power-, Malcolm X-derived, pro-Louis Farrakhan, anti-American, romantic Third World stuff that came up in the sixties. You had thugs, like Huey Newton, who were celebrated as great revolutionaries. You had West Indians, like Stokely Carmichael, who were calling for the violent overthrow of the country. You had LeRoi Jones ranting anti-Semitism from one coast to the other, and black students on campus cheering and howling. And that's going on now. If people had paid more attention to what Ellison had to say in 1952, we might have got beyond some of the stuff we're in."

Leon Forrest, a black novelist Ellison took time to praise in our meeting, told me, "Ralph goes back to a fundamental tradition in African-American life. He's what we used to call a race man. Areas that seem conservative, supporting businesses in the community, respecting the workingman, the family—that's part of it. A race man means you're in a barbershop conversation, and there might be a nationalist, an N.A.A.C.P. man, whatever, but they're all concerned with getting African-Americans ahead in the community. I know Ralph had a lot of respect for many of the things Adam Clayton Powell stood for at first, the way Powell broke the back of Tammany Hall, though not the shrill things he said at the end of his life. Ralph is for a robust onslaught against racism but, at the same time, for building within the race. What's happened is that there hasn't been enough building within the race: our families, our businesses, the inner strength of the people.

"What disappoints him today is that not enough black Americans are learning from the possibilities of the book. We don't read enough. His own literature is informed by a vast library, and yet we are cutting ourselves off from that. You've got a problem in Afro-American society these days: if a woman has a niece and a nephew, she'll give the niece a copy of a Toni Morrison book and take the nephew to the Bulls game. We don't do nearly enough to enrich our kids in the middle class in our body of literature—the body that fashioned Ralph Ellison's imagination and scholarship."

An excerpt from *Invisible Man*

I leaned against a stone wall along the park, thinking of Jack and Hambro and of the day's events and shook with rage. It was all a swindle, an obscene swindle! They had set themselves up to describe the world. What did they know of us, except that we numbered so many, worked on certain jobs, offered so many votes, and provided so many marchers for some protest parade of theirs? I leaned there, aching to humiliate them, to refute them. And now all past humiliations became precious parts of my experience, and for the first time, leaning against that stone wall in the sweltering night, I began to accept my past and, as I accepted it, I felt memories welling up within me. It was as though I'd learned suddenly to look around corners; images of past humiliations flickered through my head and I saw that they were more than separate experiences. They were me; they defined me. I was my experiences and my experiences were me, and no blind men, no matter how powerful they became, even if they conquered the world, could take that, or change one single itch, taunt, laugh, cry, scar, ache, rage or pain of it. They were blind, bat blind, moving only by the echoed sounds of their own voices. And because they were blind they would destroy themselves and I'd help them. I laughed. Here I had thought they accepted me because they felt that color made no difference, when in reality it made no difference because they didn't see either color or men . . . For all they were concerned, we were so many names scribbled on fake ballots, to be used at their convenience and when not needed to be filed away. It was a joke, an absurd joke. And now I looked around a corner of my mind and saw Jack and Norton and Emerson merge into one single white figure. They were very much the same, each attempting to force his picture of reality upon me and neither giving a hoot in hell for how things looked to me. I was simply a material, a natural resource to be used. I had switched from the arrogant absurdity of Norton and Emerson to that of Jack and the Brotherhood, and it all came out the same—except I now recognized my invisibility.

Ralph Ellison, in his Invisible Man, *Random House, 1952.*

Sixteen friends and associates gathered on March 1st at Le Périgord, on the East Side, to celebrate Ralph Waldo Ellison's birth. Once the food and not a little wine had been consumed, Albert Murray, by way of toasting his friend, recalled his youthful admiration for Ellison as the smartest, and smartest-dressed, upperclassman at Tuskegee. It was, of course, impressive to Murray that Ellison always seemed to check out the best books in the library, but it was at least as daunting for him to set eyes on the nascent elegance of Ellison, a slender concertmaster in his two-tone shoes, bow tie, contrasting slacks, and whatever else the best haberdasher in Oklahoma had to offer. "I even remember the poetry Ralph wrote," Murray said. " 'Death is nothing, / Life is nothing, / How beautiful these two nothings!' "

"Thanks for remembering so much," Ellison said, smiling and rising to his feet. All evening long, he had been reminiscing at the table, about his friends in jazz, his ill-advised attempt to play the trumpet not long ago in the presence of Wynton Marsalis, his pleasure in everything from the poems of Robinson Jeffers to the liturgy of the black Episcopal church. And then, turning to Murray, he said, "Isn't it interesting and worth a bit of thought that from Booker T. Washington's school, which was supposed to instruct youngsters in a vocation, two reasonably literate writers emerged? Isn't that just part of the unexpectedness of the American experience? It behooves us to keep a close eye on this process of Americanness. My grandparents were slaves. See how short a time it's been? I grew up reading Twain and then, after all those Aunt Jemima roles, those Stepin Fetchit roles, roles with their own subtleties, here comes this voice from Mississippi, William Faulkner. It just goes to show that you can't be Southern without being black, and you can't be a black Southerner without being white. Think of L.B.J. Think of Hugo Black. There are a lot of subtleties based on race that we *will* ourselves not to perceive, but at our peril. The truth is that the quality of Americanness, that thing the kids invariably give voice to, will always come out." And to that everyone raised a glass.

Burt A. Folkart (obituary date 17 April 1994)

SOURCE: An obituary in *Los Angeles Times,* April 17, 1994, pp. A1, A22.

[*In the following, Folkart offers praise for* Invisible Man *and provides an overview of Ellison's life.*]

Ralph Ellison, whose only novel, ***Invisible Man,*** became not only a dramatic cry for racial understanding but a work cherished over four decades for its complex yet poignant literary style, died Saturday [April 16, 1994].

He was 80.

Ellison, whose essays and novel propelled him into the front ranks of 20th-Century American fiction, died of pancreatic cancer at his home in Harlem, said Joe Fox, his editor at Random House, Ellison's publisher.

Fox said Ellison had been ill for only a short time. Random House had a party for him on March 1 to celebrate his 80th birthday and "he was perfectly fine," Fox said.

When ***Invisible Man*** was published in 1952, its author was a virtually unknown history and music student whose influences ranged from Langston Hughes to Mark Twain.

After 16 weeks on the bestseller lists and a National Book Award, Ralph Waldo Ellison (he was named after the philosopher-essayist) had become a household name among readers, regardless of color. His lone published novel—he had worked on a second but most of the manuscript perished in a fire—has not been out of print since.

Critics, scholars and readers see it as a convoluted study of a young black man who is struggling to affirm and make meaningful his race. He makes war on the twin standards of segregation that had forced him out of the mainstream and made him feel that he was less than a man.

Ellison himself was not only a sensitive youth in some conflict with his color, but an English scholar fascinated with the literature of his time.

His contention that American blacks were invisible because they were seen only as stereotypes, was couched in the classic, stylistic tumult of T. S. Eliot and the psychological myth of James Joyce.

Ellison found the impetus and strength to respond to the stereotype in the popular music of his day, saying years later that blues singer Jimmy Rushing "represented, gave voice to, something which was very affirming of Negro life, feelings which you couldn't really put into words."

But it was a Fats Waller lyric that he credited with driving him to focus the painful introspection of autobiography that was evidenced in ***Invisible Man.***

"What did I do," asked the plaintive refrain, "to be so black and blue?"

The first lines of ***Invisible Man*** have become among the best known in American literature:

> I am an invisible man. No, I am not a spook like those who haunted Edgar Allan Poe; nor am I one of your Hollywood-movie ectoplasms. I am a man of substance, of flesh and bone, fiber and liquids—and I might even be said to possess a mind. I am invisible, understand, simply because people refuse to see me.

The book tells of a young man from the South who journeys to Harlem.

The nameless narrator finds a symbol of oppression there that Ellison dubbed the "Monopolated Light and Power Company." The central character moves from sight to blindness, from shadow to sun, as he battles the monolith in a plot difficult to summarize because of its personal and literary allusions.

The Negro (Ellison generally preferred that word to black) protagonist even incurs the enmity of his own people while managing to somehow drain power (control) from his arch-foe.

The mysterious journey takes place above ground except for Prologue and Epilogue, which occur in the narrator's Underground Chamber near Harlem.

"Who knows," the narrator wonders at the end, "but that on the lower frequencies, I speak for you?"

Invisible Man has been called a near-perfect example of the German *Bildungsroman* or a psychological and educational work that both informs and entertains.

Invisible Man has been translated into Czech, Danish, Dutch, Finnish, French, German, Hebrew, Swedish and Japanese.

Ellison later published two collections of essays and was working on restoring his second novel at the time of his death.

Unlike his narrator, Ellison was not a true son of the South. He was born in Oklahoma City to a construction worker father who died when he was 3 and raised by his mother who did domestic work to support them. But he said he still found in that frontier land vestiges of racial prejudice despite the more fluid relationships between whites and blacks.

In interviews with such newspapers as the *Chicago Tribune,* he loved to talk of how the city had set up a separate library for blacks but a black minister continued to insist on using the main, segregated branch.

City officials became disgusted and threw great piles of books into an abandoned pool hall. As a result, young Ellison found himself with free access to the world's greatest minds.

He spent three years studying classical composition at Alabama's Tuskegee Institute and then headed to New York, where, like his protagonist in the novel, he became a writer. He came under the guidance of Richard Wright, the most prominent black writer of the time. Wright introduced him to *Native Son,* Wright's early, definitive work of the black experience, while poet Hughes introduced Ellison to Andre Malraux, the French essayist and Marxist.

Ellison said he took the best from both while also falling under the influence of Dostoevsky, Conrad, Eliot and Joyce.

Wright was the first to publish Ellison's writings in a magazine he was then editing.

During World War II, Ellison served in the Merchant Marine and returned ready to write a novel about a black American soldier captured by the Germans.

What happened instead, he said, was that he was obsessed with his existence that he saw only as "invisible." The book that came from that dark thought took seven years to write.

Ellison did not live long enough to completely reconstruct his second novel, which he said featured the childhood reminiscences of Cleothus, at 300 pounds the biggest kid in the first grade. He did publish the two collections of essays, ***Shadow and Act*** in 1964 and ***Going to the Territory*** in 1986.

Ellison taught and lectured at Yale, Rutgers, New York University, the University of Chicago and Bard College in New York.

His awards included the nation's highest civilian honor—the Medal of Freedom—and membership in its most prestigious literary organization, the American Academy Institute of Arts and Letters.

In his late years Ellison said he had sought to create works of literary merit built on scaffolds of social causes.

What he perceived as current pessimism among blacks concerned him.

"I don't think the country can afford (it)," Ellison said. "By some strange quirk of American fate it is the Afro-American who has sustained the nation's optimism. If we can be optimistic down at the bottom of the social pyramid, then everyone else can afford to look and say, 'If they still believe, what the hell are we complaining about.' "

Ellison is survived by his wife, Fanny, and a brother.

Richard D. Lyons (obituary date 17 April 1994)

SOURCE: An obituary in *The New York Times,* April 17, 1994, p. 38.

[*Lyons is an American journalist. In the excerpt below, he provides an overview of Ellison's life.*]

Ralph Ellison, whose widely read novel ***Invisible Man*** was a stark account of racial alienation that foreshadowed the attention Americans eventually paid to divisions in their midst, died yesterday [16 April 1994] in his apartment on Riverside Drive. He was 80.

The cause was pancreatic cancer, said his editor, Joe Fox.

Mr. Ellison's seminal novel, ***Invisible Man,*** which was written over a seven-year period and published by Random House in 1952, is a chronicle of a young black man's awakening to racial discrimination and his battle against the refusal of Americans to see him apart from his ethnic background, which in turn leads to humiliation and disillusionment.

Invisible Man has been viewed as one of the most important works of fiction in the 20th century, has been read by millions, influenced dozens of younger writers and established Mr. Ellison as one of the major American writers of the 20th century.

Mr. Ellison's short stories, essays, reviews and criticisms also have been widely published over the years; one collection was printed by Random House in 1964 under the title ***Shadow and Act.*** The second and last collection ***Going to the Territory,*** came out in 1986.

Yet Mr. Ellison's long-awaited second novel proved to be a struggle and has yet to emerge.

Mr. Fox said yesterday that the second novel "does exist. It is very long, I don't know the name, but it is not a sequel to ***Invisible Man.***" The book was started in the late 1950's. The initial work on the book was destroyed in a fire in his home upstate, and that was so devastating that he did not resume work on it for several years.

"Just recently Ralph told me that I would be getting the book soon, and I know that he had been working on it every day, but that he was having trouble with what he termed 'transitions.' "

Mr. Fox said he was unsure whether the reference was to transitions in periods described in the work, or transitions between the time periods in which they were written, which have spanned 30 years.

Invisible Man, was almost instantly acclaimed as the work of a major new author. It remained on the best seller lists for 16 weeks and millions of copies have been printed since its first publication. ***Invisible Man*** had been reprinted many times and is a standard work of American fiction in the nation's schools and colleges.

The book is the story of an unnamed, idealistic young black man growing up in a segregated community in the South, attending a Negro college and moving to New York to become involved in civil rights issues only to retreat, amid confusion and violence, into invisibility.

Hundreds of thousands of readers have felt themselves tingle to the flatly stated passion of the book's opening lines:

"I am an invisible man. No, I am not a spook like those who haunted Edgar Allan Poe; nor am I one of your Hollywood-movie ectoplasms. I am a man of substance, of flesh and bone, fiber and liquids—and I might even be said to possess a mind. I am invisible, understand, simply because people refuse to see me . . ."

And 572 pages later the unnamed narrator was to evolve into the spokesman for all races when he asks in the book's last line: "Who knows but that, on the lower frequencies, I speak for you?"

The author of these now epic lines was born in Oklahoma City. His full name was Ralph Waldo Ellison, for the essayist Ralph Waldo Emerson. Mr. Ellison was the son of Lewis Ellison, a vendor of ice and coal who died accidentally when the boy was only 3 years old. He was raised by his mother, Ida, who worked as a domestic. ***Invisible Man*** is dedicated to her and Mr. Ellison attributed his activist streak to a mother who had recruited black votes for the Socialist Party.

Mr. Ellison began playing the trumpet at age 8, played in his high school band and knew blues singer Jimmy Rushing and trumpeter Hot Lips Page. Also drawn to writing, Mr. Ellison was to say later that his early exposure to the works of Ernest Hemingway and T.S. Eliot impressed him deeply and that he began to connect such writing with his experiences "within the Negro communities in which I grew up."

However, his environment was not segregated. Mr. Ellison was to recall years later that, in the Oklahoma City society of that time, his parents "had many white friends who came to the house when I was quite small, so that any feelings of distrust I was to develop toward whites later on were modified by those with whom I had warm relations."

He studied classical composition at Tuskegee Institute in Alabama, which he reached by riding freight trains. He stayed at Tuskegee from 1933 to 1936, before moving to New York where he worked with the Federal Writers Project.

During a stay in Harlem during his junior year in college, Mr. Ellison met the poet Langston Hughes and the novelist Richard Wright, who several years later published *Native Son.*

Mr. Wright, 6 years older than Mr. Ellison, became a friend. Mr. Wright encouraged him to persevere with writing and short stories followed, including, in 1944, **"King of the Bingo Game"** and **"Flying Home."**

During World War II, Mr. Ellison served in the Merchant Marine as a cook, and became ill from his ship's contaminated water supply. At the end of hostilities, he visited a friend in Vermont and one day typed "I am an invisible man" and the novel started. He recalled later, however, he didn't know what those words represented at the start, and had no idea what had inspired the idea.

Yet the words and the ideas were to strike a resonant chord among the public, but also among American intellectuals. Over the years such authors as Kurt Vonnegut and Joseph Heller have credited Mr. Ellison with having influenced them.

Saul Bellow hailed "what a great thing it is when a brilliant individual victory occurs, like Mr. Ellison's, proving that a truly heroic quality can exist among our contemporaries . . . (the tone) is tragicomic, poetic, the tone of the very strongest sort of creative intelligence."

Mr. Ellison was to teach creative writing at New York University, while also serving as a visiting scholar at many other institutions such as the University of Chicago, Rutgers University and Yale University.

Mr. Ellison is survived by his wife of 48 years, Fanny, and a brother, Herbert of Los Angeles.

Charles Johnson (essay date 18 April 1994)

SOURCE: "The Singular Vision of Ralph Ellison," in *The Washington Post,* April 18, 1994, pp. C1, C4.

[*An American novelist, essayist, short story writer, and scriptwriter, Johnson is best known for his novel* Middle Passage *(1990), which earned him a National Book Award. In the essay below, he offers high praise for Ellison and his writings.*]

"What on earth was hiding behind the face of things?" the Everyman narrator of ***Invisible Man*** asks himself in Ralph Ellison's perennial masterpiece. His unique dilemma, and ours, is the formidable task of freeing himself from the blinding social illusions that render races and individuals invisible to each other. Only after a harrowing, roller coaster ride of betrayals and revelations above and below America's 20th century intellectual landscape does he achieve the liberating discovery that, for all the ideologies we impose upon experience, we cannot escape the chaos, the mysterious, untamed life that churns beneath official history, the "seen," and ensures the triumph of the imagination.

By any measure, ***Invisible Man***—the one great work of Ellison, who died Saturday [16 April 1994] at age 80—is the most complex, multilayered and challenging novel about race and being and the preservation of democratic ideals in American literature. Fellow writers read Ellison with awe and gratitude. Some, of course, read him with jealousy, because everything one could want in a novel is here: humor, suspense, black history (that is, American history) from which Ellison's inexhaustible imagination teases forth truth from beneath mere facts, fuguelike prose, meditations on the nature of perception, and a rogues' gallery of characters so essentially drawn that in their naked humanity we can recognize their spirits in our contemporaries 42 years after the book's publication.

Added to that, and perhaps most impressive of all, Ellison's expansive rite-of-passage is the very idea of artistic generosity. Its exuberant, Hegelian movements gracefully blend diverse literary genres and traditions, from Mark Twain to William Faulkner, from the slave narrative to the surrealistic Kafkaesque parable, from black folklore to Freud, forever forcing us to see in the novel's technique the spirit of democracy. Spanning South and North, it traces the comic progress of a nameless black student from a state college aswim in the contradictions of Booker T. Washington's reliance on white philanthropy, to New York, where Marxists and black nationalists are engaged in a Harlem turf war.

And, as if this were not enough, Ellison gave our age a new metaphor for social alienation. His definition of "invisibility" is so common now, so much a part of the culture and language—like a coin handled by billions—that it is automatically invoked when we talk about the situation of American blacks, and for any social group we willingly refuse to see.

In the late 1960s when I was a college student and came of age in an anti-intellectual climate thick with separatist arguments for the necessity of a "black aesthetic," when both Ellison and poet Robert Hayden were snubbed by those under the spell of black cultural nationalism, and when so many black critics denied the idea of "universality" in literature and life, I stumbled upon ***Invisible Man*** and spent three memorable nights not so much reading as dreaming, absorbing and being altered by his remarkable adventure of ideas and artistic possibility, though I knew—at age 20—I was missing far more than I grasped.

But each time I returned to Ellison's book, teaching the novel many times over 25 years, I found new imaginative and intellectual portals to enter, more layers of meaning to peel away. Of the thousands of American novels I have read, his has been the most reliable guide for giving a young writer full access to his ethnicity and his Yankeeness. The social and spiritual dangers depicted in ***Invisible Man,*** the various forms of self-inflicted "blindness" and the intricacies of racial collision are so exhaustively treated in this single, metamorphic machine of a book that every 10 years or so we are obliged to check our cultural progress and failures against its admonitions.

Despite his groundbreaking achievements, the awards with which he was showered when ***Invisible Man*** was published, and the direction his work gave to a generation of black writers who came of age in the 1960s, Ellison's novel has often presented too severe an intellectual and moral challenge for readers reluctant to abandon simplistic formulas about race in America.

Indeed, his book once inspired rage. In his 1952 review, writer John Oliver Killens said, "The Negro people need Ralph Ellison's ***Invisible Man*** like we need a hole in the head or a stab in the back. . . . It is a vicious distortion of Negro life." Equally critical was Amiri Baraka, who dismissed Ellison as a middle-class Negro for his insistence that mastery of literary craft must take priority over politics in a writer's apprenticeship. For Ellison that apprenticeship included T. S. Eliot as well as Langston Hughes, Pound and Hemingway, alongside Richard Wright, Gertrude Stein and Dostoevsky together with the blues.

Fortunately, ***Invisible Man*** also can be enjoyed on the level of rousing entertainment, as a thrilling odyssey that follows a naive but ambitious young man through an entire universe of unforgettable characters and events. There is Mr. Norton, one of the white founders of a black college—"a trustee of consciousness"—who believes Negroes are his "fate" and discovers his deepest fears and desires mirrored back at him by Jim Trueblood, a black sharecropper who has committed incest.

No less startling is Dr. Bledsoe, the minister administrator of a school that features a "bronze statue of the college Founder, the cold Father symbol, his hands outstretched in the breathtaking gesture of lifting a veil that flutters in hand, metallic folds above the face of a kneeling slave; and I stand puzzled," says Ellison's protagonist, "unable to decide whether the veil is really being lifted, or lowered more firmly in place; whether I am witnessing a revelation or a more efficient blinding."

On and on they come; mythic characters spun from the social paradoxes of the uniquely American belief in (and failure to achieve) equality—Lucius Brockay, the black laborer installed in the bowels of Liberty Paints, the "machine within the machine"; Brother Jack, leader of an organization dedicated to "working for a better world for all people," but racist to its core and eager to eliminate people "like dead limbs that must be pruned away" if they fail to serve the group's purpose; and Ras the Exhorter, a Harlem demagogue encapsulating in one powerful figure Afrocentric thought from Marcus Garvey to Malcolm X to, even today, Leonard Jeffries ("You think I'm crazy, it is c'ase I speak bahd English? Hell, it ain't my mama tongue, mahn. I'm African")—all of them blind, Ellison says, to his protagonist's humanity, his individuality, and the synthetic, creolizing process long at work in this country, making each and every one of us, whether we like it or not, a cultural mongrel.

That underlying experience, which so many in the universe of ***Invisible Man*** fail to see, is delivered by Ellison in several astonishing scenes most novelists would give their first-born children to have created. One is the cryptic paint factory episode, where "Optic White" is mixed with 10 drops of black "dope," which is expected to disappear into the "purest white that can be found," but instead reveals a "gray tinge"—a blending of the two into one that changes the identity of both.

Another is the Harlem eviction scene in which the possessions of an old black couple thrown onto the street become a doorway for experiencing black history from the Civil War forward. A third, the most striking episode of all, is the Rinehart section, at once hilarious and profound as it dramatizes the polymorphous character of human seeing, the fluidity of the self, and portrays "history" as a mental construct beyond which lies "a world . . . without boundaries."

As might be expected, appreciating the achievement of Ellison's fiction inevitably means taking seriously both the singular aesthetic position that makes it possible and his notion of the Negro's crucial role in this country's evolution—an understanding shared by most of our elders born early in the century.

Read his 1981 introduction to ***Invisible Man.*** There, Ellison confronts, then triumphantly solves a problem that had long haunted the fiction of a young nation known for the strong, anti-intellectual strains in its culture. It is "the question of why most protagonists of Afro-American fiction (not to mention the black characters in fiction by whites) were without intellectual depth. Too often they were figures caught up in the most intense forms of social struggle, subject to the most extreme forms of the human predicament but yet seldom able to articulate the issues which tortured them. . . ."

However, his happy (for us) discovery, one that everyone concerned about "multi-culturalism" would do well to memorize, was that, "by a trick of fate (and our racial problems notwithstanding), *the human imagination is integrative—and the same is true of the centrifugal force that inspirits the democratic process.*" (Italics mine.)

Such an insight enabled him to envision and execute the visionary work that had been part of our literary canon for 40 years. In theorizing about it, he said, "I would have to provide him [Invisible Man] with something of a worldview, give him a consciousness in which serious philosophical questions could be raised, provide him with a range of diction that could play upon the richness of our readily shared vernacular speech and of American types as they operated on various levels of society."

Hoping to create "a fiction which, leaving sociology to the scientists, arrived at the truth about the human condition, here and now, with all the bright magic of a fairy tale," Ellison devoted five years to the novel's execution. His theory led him into lasting insights, edging him toward a way to sing the unseen so often in the novel that even his casual asides cannot be ignored, as when Invisible Man thinks of his literature class, where he studied James Joyce, and his teacher observes:

> Stephen's problem, like ours, was not actually one of creating the uncreated conscience of his race, but of creating the *uncreated features of his face.* Our task is that of making ourselves individuals. The conscience of a race is the gift of its individuals who see, evaluate, record. . . . We create the race by creating ourselves and then to our great astonishment we will have created something far more important: We will have created a culture. Why waste time creating a conscience for something that doesn't exist? For, you see, blood and skin do not think!

Because no author could hope for more than to work in this wonderful, Ellisonesque spirit of inclusion, I dedicated my acceptance speech for the National Book Award in fiction to Ralph Ellison when my third novel, *Middle Passage,* won this prize in 1990. It seemed to me the very least I could do in the presence of an elder who forged a place in American culture for the possibility of the fiction I dreamed of writing. For a man who, when the global list of the most valuable authors of the 20th century is finally composed, will be among those at the pinnacle.

In his magnificent novel *Invisible Man,* Ellison, as artist, helped to save the life of the mind and spirit by giving his nation something to live for and to live by, even as he challenged his readers to think profoundly and analytically about the disease of racism and the contradictions between our democratic ideals and the capricious attitudes that characterize our rigged value system.

—Leon Forrest, in his "Ralph Ellison Remembered," in* Chicago Tribune— Books, *24 April 1994.

Stanley Crouch (essay date 9 May 1994)

SOURCE: "The Oklahoma Kid," in *The New Republic,* Vol. 210, No. 19, May 9, 1994, pp. 23-5.

[*Crouch is an American poet, essayist, playwright, educator, editor, and critic. In the following overview of Ellison's life, he relates Ellison's personality, critical reception, and literary aims.*]

When Ralph Ellison saddled up the pony of death and took that long, lonesome ride into eternity on Saturday morning, April 16, the quality of American civilization was markedly diminished. He had always traveled on a ridge above the most petty definitions of race and had given us a much richer image of ourselves as Americans, no matter how we arrived here, what we looked like or how we were made. Alone of the internationally famous Negro writers of the last half-century, Ellison had maintained his position as a citizen of this nation. His deservedly celebrated 1952 novel, ***Invisible Man,*** his two collections of essays—***Shadow and Act*** and ***Going to the Territory***—the public addresses he gave and what he read and published from the most-awaited second novel in this country's literary history spoke always of the styles, the intrigues, the ideas, the lamentations and the desires that bewitchingly reached across race, religion, class and sex to make us all Americans. This champion of democratic narrative wasn't taken in by any of the professional distortions of identity that have now produced not the astonishing orchestra of individuals our country always promises, but a new Babel of opportunism and naïveté, one we will inevitably defeat with a vital, home-made counterpoint.

Ellison had been trained as a musician, intending to become a concert composer. But the books got him and he boldly took on the job of ordering the dissonance and the consonance of our culture into the orchestrated onomatopoeia that is the possibility of the novel at its highest level of success. At every point, he was definitely the Oklahoma Kid—part Negro, part white, part Indian and full of the international lore a man of his ambition had to know. I sometimes thought of him as riding tall into the expanses of the American experience, able to drink the tart water of the cactus, smooth his way through the Indian nations, gamble all night long, lie before the fire with a book, distinguish the calls of the birds and the animals from the signals of the enemy, gallop wild and woolly into the big city with a new swing the way the Count Basie band had, then bring order to the pages of his work with an electrified magic pen that was both a warrior's lance and a conductor's wand.

In our time, there is a burden to straight shooting, and Ellison accepted it. Those troubles snake all the way back to the '30s, when the Marxist influence began to reduce the intricacies of American problems to a set of stock accusations and dull but romantic ideas about dictatorial paradises rising from the will of the workers. Because Ellison had come through all of that and, like Richard Wright, had rejected it, he was prepared for the political bedlam of the '60s. He refused to forgo his vision of democracy as an expression of high-minded but realistic courage, one that demanded faith and vigilant engagement. His tutoring by blues musicians and the world of blues music had given him a philosophical ease in face of the perpetual dilemmas of human existence. What he wrote of Afro-Americans at their best expressed his own sensibility as surely as the tar of that deceptively silent baby stuck to Br'er Rabbit:

> There is no point in complaining over the past or apologizing for one's fate. But for blacks, there are no hiding places down here, neither in country or city. They are an American people who are geared to what is and who yet are driven by a sense of what it *is* possible for human life to be in this society. The nation could not survive being deprived of their presence because, by the irony implicit in the dynamics of American democracy, they symbolize both its most stringent testing and the possibility of its greatest human freedom.

The most stringent testing that Ellison himself had to face was the rejection of his stance and his work by the intellectual zip coons of black nationalism. The Oklahoma Kid took every emotional and psychological blow thrown at him; he didn't submit to the barbarian gate-rattlers who intimidated so many into accepting a new segregation as a form of self-expression and ethnic authenticity. He knew that segregation was never less than an instrument of cowardice and rejected it. Those sufficiently misled tried to drum Ellison all the way out of the Afro-American experience and were not beyond calling him names to his face. They didn't know they were messing with the wrong man. The writer had the same kind of leathery hide possessed by those dusky Western demons who broke horses, drove cattle and wore the scars left by arrowheads and desperado bullets. Fanny Ellison, his wife of forty-eight years, recalled a luncheon where the embattled novelist sat next to one of the black power literary stooges so anxious to bring him down. Ellison said to him, "I'm a street boy; I'm mean, and I have a dirty mouth." It was an announcement of his essence and a declaration of war.

Ellison wasn't a street boy like the ones who sell pornographic novelties under the banner of rap, their nihilism made superficially complex by the editing and overlaying processes of the recording studio. He was from the same spiritual corner as Louis Armstrong, who knew of cutting and shooting but had danced in the gutter while doggedly staring at the stars. He was also of Duke Ellington's persuasion, an artist bent on the democratic eloquence that speaks most indelibly through the tragicomic resolution of the primitive and the sophisticated. Citing the peerless bandleading composer and the great trumpeter in **"Homage to Duke Ellington on His Birthday,"** Ellison clarified once more his aesthetic vision of how artistic quality both added to the social promise of the nation and helped protect it against vernacular demons:

> Even though few recognized it, such artists as Ellington and Louis Armstrong were the stewards of our vaunted American optimism and guardians against the creeping irrationality which ever plagues our form of society. They created great entertainment, but for them (ironically) and for us (unconsciously) their music was a rejection of that chaos and license which characterized the so-called jazz age associated with F. Scott Fitzgerald, and which has returned once more to haunt the nation. Place Ellington with Hemingway, they are both larger than life, both masters of that which is most enduring in the human enterprise: the power of man to define himself against the ravages of time through artistic style.

Sneering at the tedious political pulp that would shrink Negro experience to no more than a social soap opera, the Oklahoma Kid, cigar in his teeth and fingers at his keyboard, strove to make his knowledge of race in conflict and confluence a wildly orchestrated metaphor for all of human life. He sought combinations of the concrete and the mythic, the excitement of intricate ideas and the boisterous flare-ups of fantasy. Ellison was too sophisticated to stumble into the dungeon of "magic realism," feeding on surreal hardtack and water. Like the Alejo Carpentier of *Reasons of State,* Ellison knew that the fusions and frissons of race and culture in the Western Hemisphere supply all that is needed for an unforced way out of convention. The miscegenated multiplications of human meaning and effort allow shocking syncopations of fictional narrative and endless variations on hilarity, horror and inspiration.

The Oklahoma Kid told one writer that craft was an aspect of morality and that is perhaps why his unfinished novel took so long, even given the incineration of a manuscript near completion in the middle '60s. His ambition might have gotten the best of him. Ellison refused to say when he thought he would finish the book. This led some to assert that he was some sort of a coward who couldn't face the possibility that the novel might not be up to snuff, that critics with sharpened teeth might gnaw at it like wild dogs, that a second novel might prove the first no more than a fluke. Those who heard him read from the manuscript during the early and middle '80s doubted the skeptics. What Saul Bellow wrote of ***Invisible Man*** in 1952 was still quite true:

> I was keenly aware, as I read this book, of a very significant kind of independence in writing. For there is a "way" for Negro novelists to go at their problems, just as there are Jewish or Italian "ways." Mr. Ellison has not adopted a minority tone. If he had done so, he would have failed to establish a true middle-of-consciousness for everyone.

At Baruch College in 1983 he delivered a lecture titled **"On Becoming a Writer,"** stressing the freedom from the limitations of segregation that reading granted. Around 1924 books from the downtown library were jammed into a pool hall in the Negro section of Oklahoma City. As older men told tales, laughed and gambled, the young Ellison investigated the unalphabetized books, which meant that a volume of fairy tales might be right next to a volume of Freud. While the books took him into worlds much broader than those he then knew, they also made it possible for him to better appreciate the contrasting humanity of a state in which a large number of whites and Negroes had facial features and skin tones affected to greater or lesser degrees by Indian blood. Ellison's Oklahoma City was informed as much by those formally educated as by jazz musicians like Lester Young and Charlie Christian, who took innovative positions in the band battles and jam sessions of the era. Local aspirations were extended by the precedents of college-educated Negroes from the Eastern Seaboard who took on the missionary goal of traveling and educating their less fortunate brethren after the smoke of the Civil War cleared and the spiritual lion of freedom was roaring at the social limitations imposed by racism. The message of the lecture was that the shaping of language and the comprehension of it amplified that roar in the soul of the young Oklahoma Kid, allowing him to do battle with the riddles of human life and affirm the victories evident in the verve of Negro culture.

In later readings given at the Library of Congress, The New School and the Sixty-Third Street YMCA in Manhattan, Ellison made it clear who he was. Whether or not the

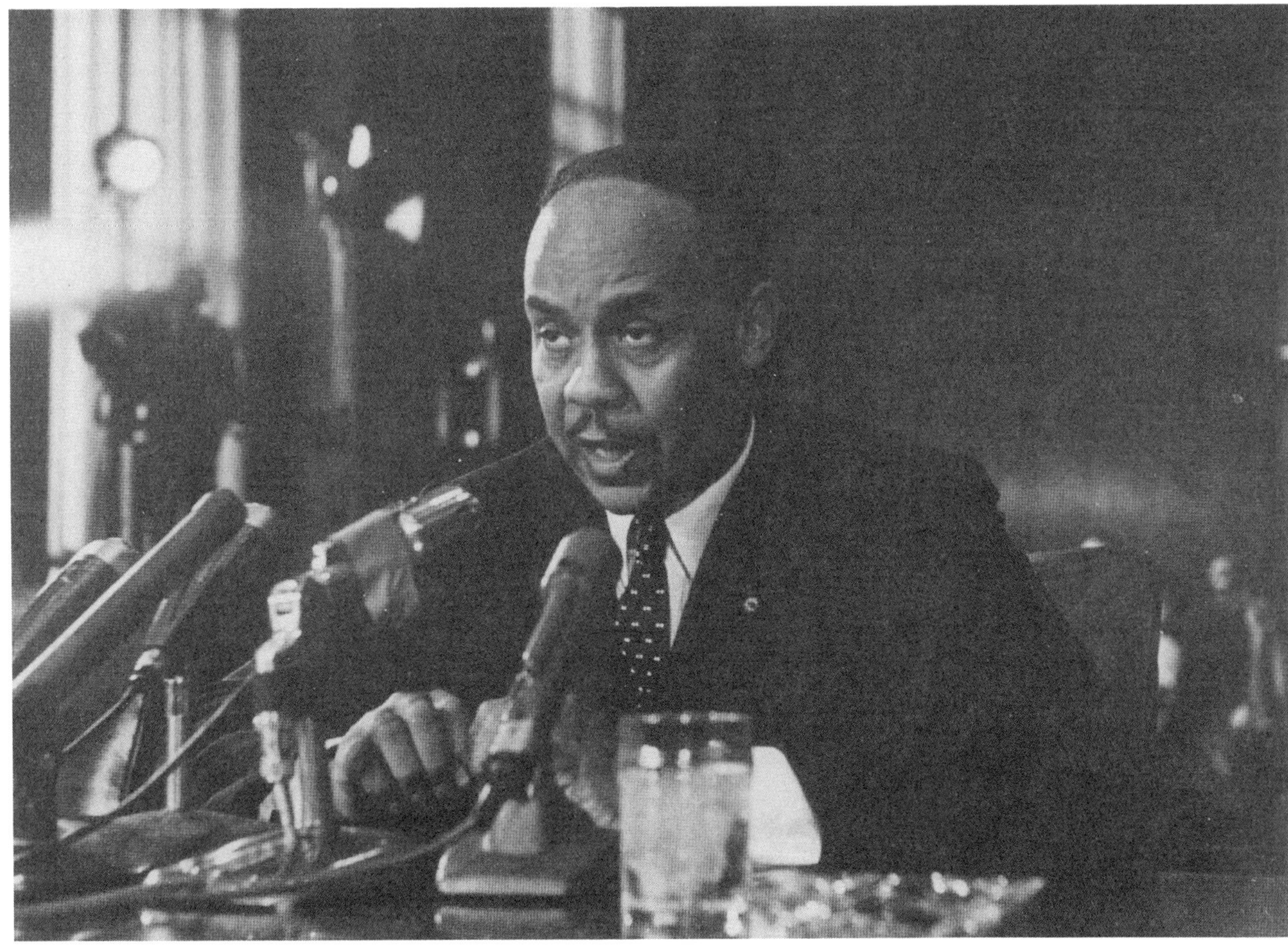

Ellison in 1966 appearing before a Senate subcommittee hearing on the problems of big cities.

novel ever reached publication, each time he gave public voice to his words, those writers in attendance had an opportunity to witness just how big a lariat the old master was twirling. With ***Invisible Man,*** he brought the resonance of genius to his variations on the Southern themes of racial misunderstandings and the disillusionment with Northern radicalism found in the full text of Richard Wright's *American Hunger.* The later work made it clear that he had advanced upon his initial ambitions and raised what was already a richly ironic style to a level of Melvillian complexity.

Taken by his readings, this writer looked up everything Ellison had published from the work-in-progress, some of it dating back to 1960. One of the themes was corruption and its charisma. A prominent character was a Southern senator named Sunraider. His tale was perfectly Ellisonian. A very light-skinned Negro or a white child who somehow found himself part of a traveling revival unit of Negroes, Sunraider, then known as Bliss, was "brought back from the dead" before various tent congregations. Leaving his background and misusing the lessons of his mentor, the Negro preacher Hickman, Bliss went into politics, changed his name and became famous for the public speaking he had learned at the knees of black people.

In **"Hickman Arrives,"** the wounded Sunraider lies in the hospital after an assassination attempt, dreaming about his past, recalling himself nervously sucking air through a rubber tube inside a coffin as Hickman whipped up the congregation in the tent. But caught by the spirit, Hickman goes on longer than usual. Bliss is awestruck by the spontaneous eloquence as he trembles inside the wooden cigar. Chaos takes over the counterfeit Lazarus routine when a white woman claiming to be Bliss's mother bursts into the act. The hypnotic corruption at the center of the revival meeting, the fooling people for their own good and to prove the greatness of God, is a tool Bliss uses quite differently when he becomes a pro-segregation senator. Nothing is ever simple in Ellison, nor is his vision naive. In essence, Ellison was saying that Negroes, because of their charismatic relationship to American culture, have the moral responsibility to use their gifts with as much integrity as possible. Otherwise, they might unintentionally contribute to the disorder that always pushes at our culture's borders.

If the novel ever appears, good; if it doesn't, Ellison's contribution to the higher possibilities of our society won't be diminished. He outlasted two generations of attackers, the white and black writers and critics who hated ***Invisible Man*** and those from the black power era who found him too "white," too "European," too "middle-class." With each passing year his already published rendition of American life grew stronger and his work spoke ever more accurately of what came to pass—the fluid shifts of social position, the tragedies of corruption, the unpredictable turns that pivot on our technology and on how we interpret our heritage as improvising Americans, people whose roots stretch into Africa, Europe, Asia and both directions in this hemisphere; people who remake sometimes perfectly and sometimes too swiftly; people who will never realize their potential unless we take on the challenge of democratic recognition, of understanding that both good and evil, folly and corruption, excellence and mediocrity can come from any place in the society. Ralph Ellison, the Oklahoma Kid, knew that we can never count on closed theories, on limiting explanations of our history—or any history. The only thing we can count on is the chaos that ever threatens our humanity and the willingness the best of us have to stand up to it. When we get lucky, as we Americans have so often, people like Ralph Ellison rear the hooves of their horses up toward the sky, then charge, taking every risk necessary to sustain the vitality of our civilization.

Additional coverage of Ellison's life and career is contained in the following sources published by Gale Research: *Black Literature Criticism; Black Writers,* Vol. 1; *Concise Dictionary of American Literary Biography, 1941-1968; Contemporary Authors,* Vols. 9-12 (rev. ed.), 145; *Contemporary Authors New Revision Series,* Vol. 24; *Contemporary Literary Criticism,* Vols. 1, 3, 11, 54; *Dictionary of Literary Biography,* Vols. 2, 76; *DISCovering Authors; Major 20th-Century Writers;* and *World Literature Criticism.*

Eugène Ionesco

November 26, 1909—March 28, 1994

Romanian-born French playwright, essayist, novelist, autobiographer, and critic.

For further information on Ionesco's life and works, see *CLC,* Volumes 1, 4, 6, 9, 11, 15, and 41.

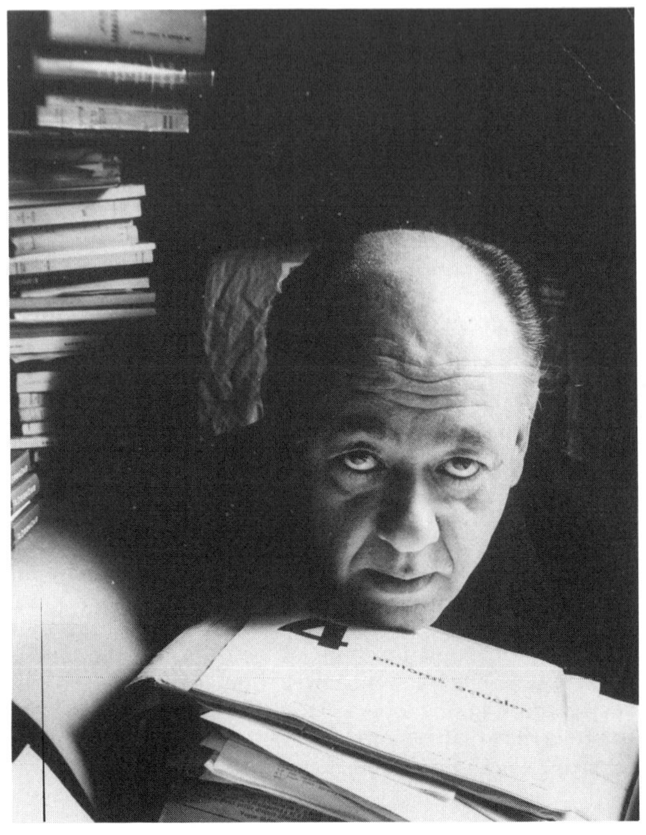

INTRODUCTION

A key innovator along with Samuel Beckett and Jean Genêt in creating the "Theater of the Absurd," Ionesco produced darkly comic portraits of the human condition by exploring such themes as alienation, the impossibility of communication between human beings, and the destructive forces of modern society. Born in Romania, he spent his first thirteen years in France, then lived in Romania for fourteen years before settling in Paris. Ionesco wrote primarily in French, and such critics as John Lahr contend that "[Ionesco's] estrangement from his native tongue gave him a feeling for the confusion created by language and its inadequacy to make sense of reality." The problematic nature of language and communication is a dominant theme in Ionesco's early works. In *La cantatrice chauve* (1950; *The Bald Soprano*), for instance, the dialogue among the characters disintegrates from clichés to meaningless sounds. To address the absurdity of life, alienation, and the loss of identity experienced by people in the twentieth century, Ionesco often employed the metaphor of multiplying objects; for example, in *Les chaises* (1952; *The Chairs*) an old man's desperate belief in reason and rationality is mocked by the play's setting—a room that becomes increasingly filled with empty chairs. Beginning in the late 1950s, he wrote four plays centering on Bérenger, a modern-day Everyman. In *Rhinocéros* (1959; *Rhinoceros*), in which everyone except Bérenger becomes a rhinoceros, Ionesco attacked mindless conformity and mob mentality. Death also became an overriding concern in many of Ionesco's later works. His last play, *Voyages chez les morts* (1980; *Journeys among the Dead*), for example, features protagonists that engage in conversations with the deceased. Ionesco quit writing plays in 1980 and subsequently devoted his time to painting and autobiography. Commenting on Ionesco's significance to contemporary theater and his innovative techniques, Edward Albee has argued that "we would diminish Ionesco. . . were we to suggest he was little more than a bag of tricks. His concerns with individual freedom, identity and rationalism place him higher than that. He was a major force in shaping nontraditional drama in the second half of the 20th century."

PRINCIPAL WORKS

Non [*Non*] (criticism) 1934
La cantatrice chauve [*The Bald Soprano*] (drama) 1950
La leçon [*The Lesson*] (drama) 1951
Les chaises [*The Chairs*] (drama) 1952
Victimes du devoir [*Victims of Duty*] (drama) 1953
Amédée; ou, comment s'en débarrasser [*Amédée; or, How to Get Rid of It*] (drama) 1954
Jacques; ou, la soumission [*Jack; or, The Submission*] (drama) 1955
Le nouveau locataire [*The New Tenant*] (drama) 1957
Tueur sans gages [*The Killer*] (drama) 1958
Rhinocéros [*Rhinoceros*] (drama) 1959
Notes et contre-notes [*Notes and Counter-notes*] (essays, addresses, and lectures) 1962
Le piéton de l'air [*A Stroll in the Air*] (drama) 1962

Le roi se meurt [*Exit the King*] (drama) 1962
La soif et la faim [*Hunger and Thirst*] (drama) 1964
Présent passé, passé présent [*Present Past, Past Present*] (autobiography) 1968
Jeux de massacre [*The Killing Game*] (drama) 1970
Le solitaire [*The Hermit*] (novel) 1972
L'homme aux valises [*Man with Bags*] (drama) 1975
Voyages chex les morts: Thèmes et variations [*Journeys among the Dead*] (drama) 1980
La quête intermittente (autobiography) 1988
Théâtre complet (dramas) 1992

OBITUARIES AND TRIBUTES

Mel Gussow (obituary date 29 March 1994)

SOURCE: An obituary in *The New York Times,* March 29, 1994, pp. A1, D21.

[*Gussow is an American editor, educator, biographer, and critic. In the following obituary, he provides an overview of Ionesco's life and works.*]

Eugène Ionesco, whose wildly innovative plays, among them ***Rhinoceros, The Bald Soprano*** and ***The Chairs,*** overturned conventions of contemporary theater and had a profound effect on a new generation of playwrights, died yesterday in Paris, where he lived. He was 84.

His death was announced by the French Cultural Ministry. The cause was not reported.

Mr. Ionesco's "anti-plays" satirized modern society while discovering new uses of language and theatrical techniques. Inspired by silent film clowns and vaudeville, he was a playful playwright, clownish in his own personality as well as in his work onstage. With outrageous comedy, he attacked the most serious subjects: blind conformity and totalitarianism, despair and death. Repeatedly he challenged—and accosted—the audience and his critics. As he said, "The human drama is as absurd as it is painful."

Along with Samuel Beckett and Jean Genet, he was one of a trinity of pioneering experimental playwrights who lived and worked in Paris. Although there were thematic bridges among the three, Mr. Ionesco's distinction was in his fanciful surrealism and sense of Dada. Among the playwrights he influenced were Tom Stoppard, Fernando Arrabal, Edward Albee, Tina Howe and Christopher Durang. Mr. Ionesco was among the playwrights often grouped as practitioners of the Theater of the Absurd. He objected to the label, preferring, he said, the Theater of Derision.

In his work, he turned drawing-room comedy on its head (***The Bald Soprano***), had a stage filled with empty chairs (***The Chairs***) and transformed man into beast (***Rhinoceros***). Although his playwriting career did not begin until he was 40, he wrote 28 plays as well as several books of memoirs. The plays have been performed around the world in various languages, although in recent years his work has been neglected in the United States. Throughout his career, he was an imaginative iconoclast who could create the most bizarre imagery.

Rhinoceros, in its 1961 Broadway production, proved to be his breakthrough play, enriched by Zero Mostel's virtuosic performance, in which he transmogrified himself from man to rhinoceros without altering his makeup or costume. Roaring, bellowing, hilarious Mostel put the playwright on the international theatrical map, and ***Rhinoceros*** ran for 241 performances. But the play was only one of many that insured Mr. Ionesco's stature.

Despite his reputation for controversy, he saw himself as a preserver of theater, a classicist and "a supreme realist." He insisted that he wrote archetypes, not stereotypes. As he said in 1958, "I believe that the aim of the avant-garde should be to rediscover—not invent—in their purest state, the permanent forms and forgotten ideals of the theater." He added: "I make no claim to have succeeded in this. But others will succeed, and show that all truth and reality is classical and eternal."

He was "the Molière of the 20th century," said Rosette C. Lamont, the author of *Ionesco's Imperatives: The Politics of Culture* and an acknowledged authority on Ionesco's work. "Like Molière in his late plays," she continued, "In Ionesco's plays, there is a seamless amalgam of the comic and tragic." In her eyes, he was a master of the "metaphysical farce," an oxymoron that the playwright accepted as accurate.

I believe that the aim of the avant-garde should be to rediscover—not invent—in their purest state, the permanent forms and forgotten ideals of the theater.

—Eugène Ionesco

Eugène Ionesco was born in Slatina, Romania, on Nov. 26, 1909, although he took three years off his age and claimed 1912 as his birth year, presumably because he wanted to have made his name before the age of 40. His father was Romanian, his mother French.

As a child, he lived in Paris. In an article titled **"Experience in the Theater,"** he remembered his introduction to a world that would preoccupy him for a lifetime. The Punch and Judy show in the Luxembourg Gardens fascinated him as the puppets "talked, moved, clubbed each other." It was, he said, "the spectacle of the world itself . . . presented itself to me in an infinitely simplified and caricatured form, as if to underline its grotesque and brutal truth."

In 1922, he returned to Romania, where he went to high school and later studied at Bucharest University. At first he wrote poetry, not plays (except for a historical drama he wrote at 13). He married Rodica Burileanu in 1936;

eight years later, their daughter, Marie-France, was born. Both his wife and daughter survive.

In 1939, Mr. Ionesco moved back to France and worked for a publisher. He became a French citizen and remained there for the rest of his life. During World War II, he and his wife were in hiding in the south of France.

The Bald Soprano (***La Cantatrice Chauve***) was inspired by his own attempts to learn English by using an English-French conversational manual. Copying out phrases, he realized he was relearning obvious truths, that there are seven days in a week and that the ceiling is above, the floor below. Carrying that premise to ridiculous, word-spinning heights, he wrote his first play—and no bald soprano appeared onstage. An actor improvised those words, and Mr. Ionesco seized upon them and changed the play's title from "English Made Easy."

The play was intended, he said, as "a parody of human behavior and therefore a parody of theater, too." Presented in 1950 at the tiny Théâtre des Noctambules in Paris, it received some initially hostile reviews but became the catapult for his career. More than 40 years later, the play is still running in another theater in Paris.

The Bald Soprano was quickly followed by ***The Lesson*** (1951), ***Jack or the Submission*** and ***The Chairs*** (1952) and ***Victims of Duty*** (1953), all of which certified his avant-garde credentials. In ***Amédée, or How to Get Rid of It*** (1954), a corpse grows larger and larger until it takes over the stage, and in ***The New Tenant*** (1956), a man rents a new apartment and the furniture takes over the stage. These and other works are filled with sight gags and silent comedy as well as intricate plays on words.

Rhinoceros brought him his widest public. Jean-Louis Barrault starred in the play in Paris and Laurence Olivier in London. But it was the Broadway production, directed by Joseph Anthony and starring Zero Mostel and Eli Wallach, that brought him his greatest celebrity. Mostel later starred in an unsuccessful film version of the play, directed by Tom O'Horgan. ***Rhinoceros*** and other plays charted the progress of Mr. Ionesco's Everyman, a character named Berenger.

In 1960, ***The Killer,*** a comedy about a serial killer in "the radiant city," had a brief run Off Broadway, and in 1968 Ellis Raab directed ***Exit the King*** on Broadway. From then on, Mr. Ionesco was often absent from the New York theater. Some of his plays were presented in regional theater, with the United States premiere of ***Macbett*** at the Yale Repertory Theater in 1973. Taking off from Shakespeare, he regarded *Macbeth* as a grotesque joke. How else could he explain mass murder, a favorite subject for his dark comic contemplation?

Throughout his life, he said he was apolitical, a fact he often disproved in his plays, especially those in his later period, like ***A Stroll in the Air,*** (a cosmic walk with reference to World War II and the Holocaust) and ***Man With Bags,*** a play about exile, in which a traveler is adrift in a world without place names. (Is there life without geography?) His last play, ***Journeys Among the Dead*** was scheduled to be performed at the Guggenheim Museum in 1980 but never opened. In his own life, the playwright often took strong stands on public issues, speaking out about the rights of dissidents.

Mr. Ionesco also wrote a novel (***The Hermit***) and short stories, dramatic theory (***Notes and Counter Notes***), memoirs (***Fragments of a Journal, Present Past Past Present*** and ***The Intermittent Quest***) and fairy tales for children. He also painted and made lithographs; in the 1980's he stopped writing plays, and devoted much of his time to painting and exhibiting his artwork.

In 1970, he was elected a member of the French Academy. In his address to the Academy, he spoke of his faith in illogicality, the confusion of rules and the impotence of intelligence.

On a number of occasions, he visited the United States, in 1988 for the first New York International Festival of the Arts. He delivered a lecture titled **"Who Needs Theater Anymore?"** His pithy answer: "Tout le monde." Looking back at ***The Bald Soprano,*** he said that at the time "it was a pleasure to destroy language." Now, he said, he found "the disintegration of language tragic."

In his early 20's, he wrote about his reasons for wanting to be a writer: "To allow others to share in the astonishment of being, the dazzlement of existence, and to shout to God and other human beings our anguish, letting it be known that we were there."

Edward Albee (essay date 10 April 1994)

SOURCE: "Edward Albee Salutes a Great Vaudevillian," in *The New York Times,* April 10, 1994, p. 12.

[*A three-time winner of the Pulitzer Prize, Albee is an American playwright, scriptwriter, poet, and short story writer. In the following tribute, he remarks on how Ionesco influenced his approach to drama.*]

While I wasn't exactly born in a trunk—well, I may have been, for I never knew my natural parents, their habits—my adopting family was involved with vaudeville. They were not jugglers or comedians—more's the pity—but owner-management, the Keith Albee Vaudeville Circuit.

The house I tried to grow up in was frequented by performers, and the likes of Ed Wynn and Victor Moore dandled me when I was a tot. My family had me go to the theater when I was a little boy, and my first theatrical memory is of *Jumbo* at the old Hippodrome—Jimmy Durante and an elephant, great Rodgers and Hart songs, and a toy they hawked in the auditorium to kids like me, a Krazy Kat-like flexible figure on a hand-held board, manipulated from beneath by rings on strings. Doubtless I enjoyed the songs, the elephant and Durante; I know I loved the toy.

Time passed. I moved through my bewildered adolescence and into my chaotic 20's, accumulating theater experiences on the way. (I was lucky: I lived in New York.)

When I was 14—and subjected to military school for my sins—I found Shakespeare, and reasoned that the problem was the language; maybe a rewriting, a simplification, would allow us to follow the plots better. I abandoned this theory when I left military school. Later, I experienced Chekhov, Pirandello, Ibsen—feeling no need to rewrite them.

Chance and good fortune took me to the premieres of *The Iceman Cometh* and *The Skin of Our Teeth* and *The Glass Menagerie.* I was still writing not very good poetry then but had given up on the novel as too much work. I had not yet realized that with the short story—at least in my case—practice does not make perfect, and, in drama, the three-act sex farce I had composed at 13 had not led me to further attempts at writing plays.

But what an exciting time we all had in New York City in the late 40's and 50's—those of us who lived in and with the arts: the concerts of avant-garde music at McMillan Theater at Columbia University, the exhibits of Constructivist and Abstract Expressionist paintings at the galleries, the explosion of foreign authors in translation—Sartre, Camus, the Nouvelle Vague, the Italian Realists Berto, Verga, Moravia, and on and on.

And in the theater in the 1950's there occurred a series of events that changed the rules of playwriting—the premieres in America of plays by that great vaudeville act, Beckett, Ionesco and Genet.

So profound was the effect of these playwrights that the term Theater of the Absurd was invented to encompass (and isolate, alas) their accomplishment, although Ionesco was the only one of the three for whom the term was valid.

The reactionaries were applied, the audience for conventional plays was bewildered, and an entire generation of us suddenly decided to be playwrights, liberated by these three. The exuberance, the during, the sleight-of-hand, the deepest laughter in the deepest dark broke all the rules for us and showed us that the familiar, the safe, the predictable was the true Theater of the Absurd.

If we can tie Beckett to the Existentialists and Genet to a kind of solitary confinement of the spirit, then we must relate Ionesco to Dadaism and Surrealism—movements not a part of mainstream American culture. Ionesco's preoccupation with the collapse of language, as well as such matters as major characters who never appear, furniture (and corpses) growing as the drama proceeds, and people becoming rhinoceroses before our (very) eyes, influenced a lot of us.

As Pinter's debt to Beckett can be found in much of his work, my own stylistic sources for *The American Dream* and *The Sandbox* are clearly to be found in Ionesco. (Indeed, the first several pages of *The American Dream* were so obviously an intended homage to the Romanian-French master that I was startled when some critics insisted it was imitation—an Ionesco-like situation?)

We would diminish Ionesco, however, were we to suggest he was little more than a bag of tricks. His concerns with individual freedom, identity and rationalism place him higher than that. He was a major force in shaping nontraditional drama in the second half of the 20th century.

Beckett has gone on to be an acknowledged master, albeit almost buried by the scholars; Genet is still sniffed suspiciously by the wary, who are profoundly frightened by the primal violence of his vision, and Ionesco—the most playful of the three, the most purely "experimental," though every bit as reality grounded and tough as the others—has been neglected.

There's no point in dwelling on this. A hundred years down the line—unless the viruses have taken over—we'll see it all sort itself out.

And now Ionesco can write no longer; he has joined the others. As a character I like says, in a play I admire, "That particular vaudeville act is playing the cloud circuit now."

What an act it was, and what a hard act to follow!

John Lahr (essay date 11 April 1994)

SOURCE: "Eugène Ionesco," in *The New Yorker,* Vol. LXX, No. 8, April 11, 1994, p. 94.

[*Lahr is an American critic, nonfiction writer, playwright, and novelist. In the following tribute, he surveys the themes and techniques of Ionesco's works.*]

Eugène Ionesco, who died last week, was an entrepreneur of his own uncertainties. "There are no alternatives," he said about his first, short play, ***The Bald Soprano*** (1950). "If man is not tragic, he is ridiculous and painful, 'comic' in fact, and by revealing his absurdity one can achieve a sort of tragedy." Giddy with a sense of absence and of abdication, Ionesco's plays sounded a new note of frivolity at the beginning of the fifties which tweaked both the committed ideologues of the left and the boulevardiers of the right, and pushed theatre beyond the boundaries of logic and sociology. His plays often spoke in hilarious non sequiturs (***The Bald Soprano; The Lesson,*** 1951; ***The Chairs,*** 1952), in the crazy symmetry of dreams (***Victims of Duty,*** 1953), and in fantastical transformations (***Amédée, or How to Get Rid of It,*** 1954; ***Rhinoceros,*** 1960)—and they all announced a refusal to suffer while acting out the dislocation and the strange emptiness he found in the world.

Born in Romania in [1909], Ionesco spent most of his first thirteen years in France, dreaming alternately of being a saint and a warrior. Between the ages of thirteen and twenty-seven, he lived in Romania, and then he returned to Paris to live and write in his second language. His estrangement from his native tongue gave him a feeling for the confusion created by language and its inadequacy to make sense of reality, and also left him with an exile's rootlessness, which comes across in the floating world of his plays. His first experience of theatre, he wrote in 1958, was in Paris: growing up near the Luxembourg Gardens, he frequently watched puppet shows there. "I could stay there, entranced for whole days . . . spellbound by the sight of these puppets that talked, moved and clubbed each other. It was the spectacle of the world itself." Ionesco's plays, with their surrealist narratives and acid thoughts, almost immediately embroiled him with the literary establishment. "I think that writers like Sartre, Osborne, Miller, Brecht, etc., are simply the new *auteurs du boulevard,* representatives of a left-wing conformism which is just as lamentable as the right-wing sort," Ionesco, an anarchist in the face of all orthodoxies, wrote.

Ionesco wrote clown plays that disguised their intellect and insolence in the high jinks of visual surprise.

—John Lahr

Ionesco was a pint-size renegade. He had a clown's face—a rutted forehead and a bald pate that gave him a memorably comical double-dome appearance. It seemed apt that he wrote clown plays that disguised their intellect and insolence in the high jinks of visual surprise. "The theatre is the appearance of the unexpected," he said. His best jokes were sight gags whose impact was multiplied by a comic exaggeration and conveyed, in lucid metaphors, an almost childlike appreciation of life's weirdness. In ***The Chairs,*** the stage is inundated with a whirlwind of seats for an invisible audience, which never comes to hear an orator who turns out to be mute; in ***Amédée,*** Ionesco's first full-length play, a couple share their apartment with a corpse (a symbol of their dead love), which gets bigger and bigger; in ***Rhinoceros,*** an allegory of totalitarian conformity, the world proliferates with rhinos. Ionesco's theatrical world was one of danger, disconnection, and daring. "Personally, I regard existence as a misfortune," he said. Ionesco was a kind of Zanni of remorse. As he lets a character in ***Jack, or the Submission*** (1955) sing, "There's no one else like me on earth / I'm full of light and gloom and mirth."

REVIEWS OF IONESCO'S RECENT WORKS

Virgil Nemoianu (review date 6 February 1987)

SOURCE: "Intuitions and Subversions," in *The Times Literary Supplement,* No. 4375, February 6, 1987, p. 141.

[*Nemoianu is a Romanian-born American educator and critic. In the review below, he comments on Ionesco's concerns and literary method in* Non.]

Those who have marvelled at Ionesco's radical experimentalism may not realize that his mature work was actually a toning-down of the much more ferocious radicalism of his youth. At twenty-two he was still in Bucharest. He had read widely, but unsystematically. His intuitions and emotions were surprisingly deep, varied and precise for such a young man, and he had an incredible self-confidence and capacity for challenging whatever was accepted. His first book was called simply ***No*** [***Non***] and more than half of it is a calm and relentless demolition of some of Romania's greatest living writers. These (Arghezi, Barbu, Camil Petrescu) were not venerable traditionalists, but the shining lights of the Modernist wave, often resented for their novelty. Yet in 1934 Ionesco saw in their works the outlines of an emergent canon, and immediately set about subverting it. In the book he is paradoxical, violent and unjust, but also brilliant and amusing, and above all right on the broader issues, even when he is being prejudiced on specific ones.

To repair some of these local injustices the present French translation [of ***Non***] is accompanied by two critical essays (by Eugen Simion and Ileana Gregori), by the translator's notes and by a generous introductory disclaimer from Ionesco himself. Here he makes the melancholy observation that the fifty years that have elapsed have turned a text that was intended as a critique of the (normal) vicissitudes of any literary commonwealth into a celebration of a society brimming with freedom, variety, and creative ferment. This is only to some extent an effect of nostalgia, and much more a result of the dreary and stupefying dictatorship that has kept hold of Romania over the past four decades.

The interest of the book is not primarily historical, however, but to be found in its tragi-comical musings about literature and life. Ionesco first reveals himself as a critical relativist. Even as he is lambasting the poetry of Arghezi, he remarks that he might well decide one day to argue the opposite case. Whenever I engage in a polemic, he suggests, an inner voice tells me that the other side is right. He illustrates this ambivalence very spiritedly by taking the first novel of his friend, the future historian of religion, Mircea Eliade, and writing two directly opposite reviews of it, one highly laudatory, the other remorselessly panning. Ultimately aesthetic value itself is cast into doubt—a shocking heresy in a culture like that of Romania, in which the beautiful had traditionally been thought of as higher than either the true or the good. That God must go the same way is inevitable. Ionesco writes: "If God exists, why write literature? And if He doesn't, why write literature?" He perhaps means to say, even more paradoxically, that if literature has no value, then it matters little whether God exists or not. What certainly did matter to this bright and sassy young man was the existence of death: the most moving and hilarious pages in the book are his "intermezzi" on human identity and its cessation. Aptly enough the crowning essay argues for the relativity of death itself, but this, like whistling in a graveyard, seems to offer only a contrived optimism.

In *Non* Ionesco is paradoxical, violent and unjust, but also brilliant and amusing, and above all right on the broader issues, even when he is being prejudiced on specific ones.

—Virgil Nemoianu

Along the way there are many delightful things in ***Non:*** portraits of literati and instructions to the ambitious literary beginner, in the ironic vein of an eighteenth-century essay; and many amusing displays of arrogance, as when Ionesco proclaims his competence at provoking scandals, or when he favourably compares his own talent, rhythm and verve as a writer to a rival's lack of coherence and plodding style. (Marie-France Ionesco's translation here catches very well the scapegrace charm and self-deprecatory posturing of sensibility and intelligence that had not yet found their vehicle.)

Not that ***Non*** is always self-indulgent and whimsical. Ionesco intimates more than once that he should be seen as a follower of the nineteenth-century *junimist* movement, which advocated continual self-criticism if Romania was to develop towards civilization, and which itself gained some political power in its day. His negative attitude towards established Romanian writers is usually based on references to the literary values of Proust or Valéry. Similarly, his approach to literature only seems anarchical: in fact it displays an intuitive and effective use of what we would now call deconstruction or reception theory.

Finally, there are scattered but often memorable comments here on metaphysical alienation and on loneliness, on the impossibility of authentic self-expression in language, or the limits of morality, and in particular on the way in which the poetic, the absurd, and the imaginative coincide. "We emerge from nothingness not with a discourse, but with a scream or an astonished glance", the twenty-one-year-old Ionesco admonishes his readers. These are the views and perceptions that were to become the mainstay of his *oeuvre* and can be much better understood after reading ***Non.***

Marguerite Dorian (review date Spring 1987)

SOURCE: A review of *Non,* in *World Literature Today,* Vol. 61, No. 2, Spring, 1987, pp. 272-73.

[*Dorian is a Romanian-born novelist, poet, and short story writer who now lives in the United States. In the following review, she remarks favorably on* Non.]

Surfacing in Marie-France Ionesco's excellent translation half a century after the scandal it caused upon its original publication in Bucharest in 1934, the mélange of literary criticism, texts on Romanian literature and culture, and philosophic and existential notes titled ***Non*** is, more than anything else, a contribution to an inquiry into creativity, as we observe the metamorphoses that a writer's themes and motifs undergo with time and in relation to the circumstances of his life. Among writers in exile, displaced and alienated, with their struggle to adjust or resist adjustment and their performance in a foreign language from within a foreign culture, Eugène Ionesco is yet another extraordinary case: perfectly bilingual, taking his French from his mother and his Romanian from his father, Ionesco spent his childhood in France and his adolescence and youth in Romania, in the midst of Romanian literary life. He returned to France as a mature man and an obscure Romanian writer to become the playwright who has altered contemporary theatre. ***Non*** is a book from Ionesco's first literary career in Romania, an episode practically unknown to his Western readers.

Without much concern for structure, the kaleidoscopic material of the book is divided into two parts: a series of critical essays intended to demolish the glory of three literary lions of the time, the poets Tudor Arghezi and Ion Barbu and the novelist Camil Petrescu; and a collection of texts on Romanian culture and literature attempting a methodology of literary criticism. The work's unity resides in the aggressive and contemptuous tone of the young author, who does not hesitate to provoke and insult his readers while making his point, and in the young Ionesco's theory of "the identity of opposites," which he develops and applies throughout. The theory demonstrates gleefully—and brilliantly at times—the vanity of attempting to take a position in literary criticism, as Ionesco writes parallel reviews on the same subject and demolishes in one what he has just praised in the other.

The theatre seems absent from the preoccupations in ***Non,*** yet one can sense the future dramatist in the language always at high tide and in the way Ionesco stages his argumentations. It is this verbal energy, undiscovered at the time, which often thrusts the book out of its intended literary genre and into the realm of drama.

Written in the early thirties, the essays on Romanian culture should be read in the context of that time. In the disenchanted aftermath of World War I the generation of Romanian intellectuals concerned with the cultural crisis of their country are faced with two choices: cultural isolation brought on by an emphasis on Romanian traditional values as a source of creativity or an adaptation of Western values to Romanian cultural life, resulting in "cultural colonization." Ionesco offers the second alternative as a remedial program to what he believes to be a second-rate culture. His attitude is dictated not only by his bilingual and bicultural makeup, but also by a reaction to the tragic and complex circumstances of the thirties, when the ideologues of the rising Romanian fascism began to adapt some of the ideas of this generation, particularly the ones which exalt Romanian traditional values.

If the demolition of Romanian literary idols and the literary gossip of the thirties are less interesting to Ionesco's readers today, the personal notes scattered throughout ***Non*** complete the author's Romanian diaries, published partially in his ***Présent passé, passé présent*** and in ***Journal en miettes*** and invite a rereading of the interviews in *Entre la vie et le rêve.* Disengaged from the catcalls and the grimaces of the enfant terrible, they disclose the terrors and epiphanies of the writer and offer the fragile and vibrant poetry of Ionesco's future prose, a poetry which does not surface in his theatre. His feud with the terror of dying and the betrayal of language, two of the themes of his future plays, are also sketched here.

Non is a book against literature, a paradox sustained by the verbal energy of its author. "It was written by an angry adolescent," Ionesco warns in his 1986 preface, but "aside from some clumsiness and incoherences, what was said then, I continue to say and write, in the deepest and most spiritual sense, throughout my life." Indeed, one of the more recent interviews with Ionesco contains almost word for word a leitmotiv from ***Non:*** "The basic problem is that if God exists, what is the point of literature? And if He doesn't exist, what is the point of literature? Either way," adds the present-day Ionesco, "my writing, the only thing I have succeeded in doing, is invalidated."

Two helpful essays, "Portrait of an Epoch" by E. Simionescu and "The Irony in *Non*" by I. Gregori, provide the necessary background information and a knowledgeable commentary.

Victor Brombert (review date 15 February 1988)

SOURCE: "Le misérable," in *The New Republic,* Vol. 198, No. 7, February 15, 1988, pp. 39-41.

[*Brombert is an American educator and critic who specializes in nineteenth-century French literature. In the following review, he offers a mixed assessment of Ionesco's attack on Victor Hugo in* Hugoliad.]

When young Eugène Ionesco wrote his outrageous attack on Victor Hugo, ridiculing among other things Hugo's institutionalized glory as an Académicien, little did he know (he, the rebel who claimed to cherish failure) that he himself would one day be solemnly installed as an "immortal" member of the Académie Française. Such are the ironies of literary fate; and Ionesco's ***Hugoliad,*** a "demolition" of the great French poet, and an attack on all literary ambition, is ironic in more sense than one.

Hugoliad: or The Grotesque and Tragic Life of Victor Hugo, first published in a Romanian journal of the 1930s, is a preposterous text. On second thought, however, the unlikely encounter between the future dramatist of the absurd and Hugo seems almost unavoidable. Ionesco, the 26-year-old demystifier, was bothered, as were so many writers of his generation, by what was regarded as Hugo's grandiloquence, theatrical postures, pretenses at spiritual elevation, flabbiness, and hopelessly naive faith in human progress. Ionesco's debunking of Hugo is an anti-biography as much as it is an anti-hagiography.

The picture of Hugo presented in this ferocious deflation is that of a literary parvenu with limited intelligence but a monstrous capacity for work, a manipulator of extravagant metaphors totally lacking in lucidity, a master of self-praise endowed with nothing more than a resonant "tenor's voice" that hardly qualified him to pose as philosopher, statesman, reformer, and prophet. According to Ionesco, Hugo was completely perverted by vanity, he never lived authentically, and his body of writing amounts to nothing but a big "void."

Hugoliad is a book of laughter and excess. Caricature alternates with pastiche and nasty paraphrase of Hugo's most sentimental verses, which are taken out of context. Ionesco relentlessly fictionalizes ludicrous, intimate scenes in which Hugo insists on reading his own lines to his wife and to his mistress. Even while making love he cannot stop versifying. In fact, everything around Hugo seems to be contaminated with logorrhea; the flowers themselves produce Hugolian rhymes.

The mockery is occasionally amusing and inventive, but it is heavy-handed, and ultimately tedious. Only the aphoristic verve keeps the text going. Right or wrong, Ionesco will score with amateurs of wit-at-any-cost when he asserts that Hugo "spoke of silence with noise," that he is a master of "platitudes in color," that the only reason his work survived is that it is unreadable. When Ionesco speaks of Hugo's congenital bad taste and unscrupulousness, however, and accuses him of being simultaneously a hypocrite and a prodigy of mediocrity, even admirers of epigrammatic raillery might wonder, Why such a loathing, such acerbity, such wild overstatements?

The answers may well be more interesting than the animosity (real or feigned) toward the man and the writer named Hugo. For ***Hugoliad*** goes beyond an individual case, no matter how notorious. In its sarcastic and violently unjust way, it is a meditation on literary success, on the nature of genius, on literature as an institution. This "exercise in mischief" (Ionesco's own term), written in large part for the pleasure of scandalizing, has broader implications. As Gelu Ionescu puts it in a postcript, Hugo was "the prototype of the author/authority" for Ionesco. He embodied the monstrosity of genius seen as a spiritually deficient being, as the exact opposite of the saint.

The young rebel's venomous satire reveals, then, a deeper need for protest. Ionesco's first book, a collection of criticism characteristically titled ***No,*** questioned the status of literature ("If God exists, why write literature? And if He doesn't, why write literature?") in terms that betray not only a distrust of literature and of men of letters, but also a latent idealism. The indictment of the Man of Letters who lays claim to sacerdotal powers, and thereby becomes guilty of "a rape of the soul of things," corresponds to a notion of poetry that, for all its explicitly modernist negativity, hides a hopeless quest for purity. Poetry is thus opposed to literature. For poetry, in this perspective, can never be rhetoric; it is not discourse, but an outcry, a moan free from all logic and immanent in its "transcendental primitiveness." Better still, it is silence.

These yearnings for authenticity and sincerity in (and against) literature, this desire to master literary craft in order to unlearn it and to gain emancipation from eloquence, were features of the anti-Hugo feelings that set in after 1885, the year of his death; it was a reaction that lasted for several generations. Ionesco's stance is thus not at all atypical in a period that produced Gide's famous answer, when asked who was the greatest French poet: "Victor Hugo, alas." Ionesco himself speaks of a "psychology of the historical moment." The young rebel, who may have shocked pious readers in Romania, appears in fact far from original in the context of France, where anti-Hugo virulence was fashionable at the time he wrote ***Hugoliad.*** It is revealing that in his anti-Hugolian fervor, Ionesco goes so far as to second the disparaging statements of the notorious reactionary and anti-Semite Charles Maurras.

It is indeed remarkable how conventional an enfant terrible Ionesco was. All the smug commonplaces of the anti-Hugo set are here. But that is precisely why ***Hugoliad*** is such an interesting document, why it deserved to be exhumed from an old Romanian review, translated from Romanian into French, and then from French into English. As a verbose epigram, it helps give Cocteau's witty quip its full value (for Cocteau's words imply admiration too): "Victor Hugo was a madman who thought he was Victor Hugo."

Genuine wit tolerates no redundancy. One might leave it at that, were it not that ***Hugoliad*** also contains a great deal of vituperative nonsense. To describe Hugo as enrolled in "the school of vanity and insensitivity," to dismiss his writings as "only a spilt bucket, straw and dirty water," is bad enough. But it is downright silly to claim that the notoriously limited Adèle Hugo had a much greater poetic sensibility than her husband, that the poet could have learned the meaning of poetry and authenticity from her. And it is absurd, to say the least, to assert that the author of *Les Contemplations* was "too busy to be able to think of either his life or his death." Even more deplorable is young Ionesco's bad taste, as he makes crude fun of Hugo's grief on hearing of his daughter's death by drowning (Ionesco describes Hugo in the process of downing his beer, chewing sausage, and gulping an "insufficiently masticated crumb of bread"), accusing him moreover of converting his grief into literature, and of being in the habit of defiling his dead.

Ionesco knows no bounds in his zest to revile the posthumous glory of Hugo. He accuses him (the ultimate absurdity) of political cowardice and betrayal, of having been a fellow traveler joining each political party as it came into power. The truth is exactly the opposite, as was demonstrated by (among many other less momentous episodes) Hugo's early endorsement of Louis Bonaparte in the brief days of the Second Republic, and by his fierce opposition to him after the dictatorial coup d'état of 1851, which transformed the president into an emperor and drove Hugo into almost 20 years of uncompromising exile.

To set the record straight after so many patent falsehoods would be pedantic. Only two points need be made. First, belittling Hugo's poetry in the name of modernity, which according to Ionesco "demolished" his poetic edifice, does not take into account the very apostles of modernity—Baudelaire, Flaubert, Rimbaud in particular—who stood in awe of the enormity of Hugo's genius, and of the splendor of his verse and vision. Mallarmé would not allow anyone to speak ill of Hugo in his presence. Second, belittling Hugo the man and public figure makes hardly any sense at all in view of his life-long struggle against the death penalty, against cruelty and oppression of every kind, and his ceaseless defense of the disinherited and the exploited—which was not merely verbal or literary. Among other acts of courage, Hugo offered his hospitality to the hunted members of the defeated Commune, at considerable risk to his own safety.

Ionesco's distortions are surprising. But even more surprising is the insensitivity to what is radical, and radically modern, in Hugo's work: his sense of the grotesque, his subversion of the tragic code, his fictions about the revolutionary laughter of the slave rebelling against the laughing master. It is ironic that Ionesco, whose sense of the grotesque informs so much of his work, should have been so unaware of the significance of the poem "Le Satyre" or the novel *L'Homme qui rit* (*The Man Who Laughs*).

Ionesco's notion of the grotesque is evidently of a lesser nature. It tends to reduce the human figure to the ridiculous and the deformed ("hairs, bulges on top of and underneath other bulges. . . ," as he puts it in ***Hugoliad***). Hugo integrated his sense of the ludicrous and the absurd into a broader, more generous vision. By contrast, Ionesco's skepticism about any rhetoric of ideals may well be a form of frustrated idealism, but such intolerance of the language of ennoblement has its limitations. Hugo may have known that our human sorrows are, as Ionesco puts it, "earthworm sorrows"; but he also believed that human beings can and should rise above them.

Iordan Chimet on Ionesco:

Ever since his earliest writings, Ionesco has condemned, in vicious metaphors, modern man's spiritual agony. . . . A prophet, a Cassandra reborn in an agonizing age, Ionesco will predict disaster in each of his works—not the disasters of an unforeseeable future, but those of the present time. 'Apocalypse according to Ionesco' does not depict a possible Inferno, but the real everyday inferno which is part of the human being. . . . Death is the only truth, the only certainty. Life continues to be man's only chance of reaching Paradise, but life deprived of spirit becomes more and more a part of Hell. I, for one, do not think that this is Ionesco's final answer. In fact, it is not the answer that counts, but the debate, the dialogue, the question in itself. I have always believed that the End can turn into a New Beginning. Someday, tomorrow maybe, Ionesco—or one of his spectators—will be able to build up Hope again from the various suggestions of pain, to turn the curse into an incantation, to dissipate the present nightmare, to raise the siege around the Radiant City. I am looking forward to the moment when Ionesco will give contemporary Sodom a chance.

Iordan Chimet as quoted by William Riggan, in his "Jurors and Candidates for the 1986 Neustadt International Prize for Literature: Critical Perspectives," in World Literature Today, *Winter, 1986.*

John Weightman (review date 15-21 April 1988)

SOURCE: "A Pair of Despairers," in *The Times Literary Supplement,* No. 4437, April 15-21, 1988, p. 416.

[*Weightman is an English educator and critic. In the following excerpt, he presents a mixed assessment of* La quête intermittente.]

On reading this latest, and bleakest, instalment of Ionesco's diary, ***La Quête intermittente,*** I am reminded of the well-worn anecdote I first came across in the old Gaspey-Otto-Sauer German-Language Manual. An anonymous patient comes to consult a nerve specialist about his depression. The doctor listens to his complaints, prescribes a placebo and concludes with the suggestion: "Go and see a performance by the clown, Grock. He's sure to cheer you up." "Alas!" replies the patient, "I am Grock."

Ionesco, who has made millions laugh, at least with his early plays, is, from his own account, the unhappiest of mortals, and now, in his late seventies, his depression is so acute that it no longer transmutes itself into art, but goes straight down on to paper in a sort of ritual of self-purging lamentation. As he says, the function of a writer is to write, so, in the absence of creative ideas, he just describes the anguish of everyday living as he endures it, along with Madame Ionesco, in a country rest-home belonging to the French Society of Authors. The only sign of art in the book is that he loads every rift with gloom, until the blackness is sometimes on the point of toppling over into humour in spite of itself.

His title would seem to indicate that the root of his misery is metaphysical, and indeed he can be considered an archetypal case of the lapsed, or would-be, believer trying in vain to establish communion with the transcendent. He repeats the religious polarity of the light and the dark which, for many years now, has been running through his plays. At some very rare moments in the past, he enjoyed experiences of ineffable illumination, and he longs, without success, to return to the state in which they were possible. Meanwhile, existence is an excruciating martyrdom: his health is a constant concern, he worries about his wife and daughter, his celebrity seems to be on the wane (he now has to spell out his name to ignorant telephone operators), people are even forgetting that it was he who invented the Theatre of the Absurd, how unfair that the Nobel Prize should have been given to Beckett rather than to him, and so on.

Any average depressive, who relishes learning about the miseries of the rich and famous, will get great satisfaction from this book. But it raises the question: how far is Ionesco's wretchedness the dark night of the soul in the absence of God, and how far a pathological affliction, a clinical depression, that is, an unfortunate consequence of his body chemistry? He himself doesn't try to distinguish between the two mental states, either because it doesn't occur to him to do so, or perhaps because he senses that critical self-analysis might destroy the unity of his Jeremiah or Job-like tone. However, it is precisely in this connection that a welcome gleam of apparently unintended comedy creeps back into the text.

This is clearest in a passage about the sanitary arrangements in the rest-home. The provision of lavatories is inadequate, so that Ionesco's erratic bowel-functions cannot be catered for in peace, but involve him in a distressing game of hide-and-seek with the other guests. Now, it is an obvious proof of our Fallen Nature that we have bowels—the Angels are free of such encumbrances—but, on the everyday level, the problem is not metaphysical but practical. Ionesco, who owns more than one private residence and is presumably not short of cash, could depart immediately for any number of comfort stations. If he chooses to stay, it must be because he needs the discomfort to feed his neurosis which, in this case at least, is not a metaphysical worry or quest but an unexplained pathological syndrome looking for justifications. Had he seen things fully in this light, his diary, instead of being an honest but one-dimensional document, might have become a partly comic work, with himself as the central character—a sort of Don Quixote of the Misdirected Complaint.

Rosette C. Lamont (review date Summer 1988)

SOURCE: A review of *La quête intermittente,* in *World Literature Today,* Vol. 62, No. 3, Summer, 1988, pp. 435-36.

[*A French-born American educator and critic, Lamont is the author of* Ionesco *(1973) and* The Two Faces of Ionesco *(1977). Below, she favorably assesses* La quête intermittente.]

Dedicated to his wife and daughter Rodica and Marie-France, Ionesco's latest intimate journal [***La quete intermittente***], possibly the ultimate volume of his pensées, is a moving love letter to the guardians of his life, the two women without whose watchful love he feels he would not remain alive. Again and again, Ionesco speaks of his hope that he will not outlive his frail, tiny wife, who took upon her narrow shoulders the full weight of a sacred trust:

> Elle vit dans le dévouement. Elle va m'accompagner jusqu'au bout. . . . Elle ne mourra pas avant moi . . . elle a reçu de façon mystique cette mission de ma mère, à laquelle elle n'a pas failli. . . . Cela va au-delà du mariage, au-delà de l'amour le plus fort, c'est un engagement mystérieux, spirituel et religieux qu'elle a tenu, qu'elle tient.

The book begins with a description of the 12 July 1986 celebration of the Ionescos' golden wedding anniversary. It is being held in the Swiss village of Saint Gall, where the publisher of art books, Francesco Larese, has given the writer the possibility of developing his talent as a painter and lithographer. Ionesco writes: "La couleur, ô ma vie, couleurs, mes paroles dernières, couleurs . . . accompagnez-moi, aidez-moi, vivez pour que je sois, couleurs, vous, figures vivantes, signes de la vie, parures." Many friends have gathered for this important occasion, but Ionesco also names the dead friends and relatives who have remained part of his conscious and subconscious life. Wars and revolutions have tossed this typical European family all over the world: "On ne compte que quelques survivants de cet immense naufrage."

One of the moving aspects of Ionesco's confessional memoirs is his mea culpa vis-à-vis his wife: "Ô, ma Rodi, ma femme, la jolie demoiselle Burileanu que j'ai épousée, et que je na'i pas su rendre heureuse. Je lui ai fait du mal, je l'ai trompée, je l'ai insultée parfois, . . . j'ai honte devant ma fille, devant moi-même, devant Dieu." The writer also worries about their daughter, a spinster who chose to devote her life to the care of her aged parents. Although Marie-France teaches dramatic literature at the school of "la rue Blanche," her father is haunted by the unrealistic fear that the two women may remain destitute after his death. When this happens, will Marie-France still keep her identity, the only self-definition she has: "Sera-t-elle encore la fille d'Eugène Ionesco? Saura-t-on, ne saura-t-on pas qui ètais-je. Pour savoir ce qu'elle est, qu'elle est."

The title of the book betrays Ionesco's religious doubts

punctuated by the need to believe that God exists. He prays: "God, make me believe in You!" The overwhelming emphasis on doubt, however, brings him close to Montaigne, without the latter's enlightened serenity. Like the ailing creator of the essay, Ionesco does not hesitate to describe in detail the body's failings: rare, difficult bowel movements coaxed by a suppository every second day, the race for the facilities in the château's long hallways, a deficient circulation which reminds the writer of the icy end of life, a pronounced limp. Can one become reconciled to such a paltry existence? And yet it is still life: looking at an abundant, joyous French street market, he exclaims, "Le marché au dessus, et en dessous les égouts à merde."

Alas, the mind is no purer than the body, and Ionesco lets some of his literary envy surface. Above all, he reveals his rage at the esteem enjoyed by Samuel Beckett. People ought not to say that Beckett invented the absurd, he claims: "Les journalistes et les historiens littéraires amateurs commettent une désinformation dont je suis victime, et qui est calculée." He was the first, he almost shouts, with ***La cantatrice chauve*** in 1950. He even claims to have written his first absurdist text in Romania, in 1943: "Je peux facilement en fournir des preuves." This indignation is demeaning. The rest of the book, however, reveals once again a complex, sensitive man, one who has never grown into adulthood. Perhaps an artist must remain a child.

Patricia Rigg on Ionesco's Berenger plays:

The fragmented structure of this four-part series of plays [*The Killer, Rhinoceros, A Stroll in the Air,* and *Exit the King*] gives the impression that time is ironically timeless, fluid and relative, rather than static and absolute, but it also draws attention to the related central irony of all literature, which is that it pretends to freeze time by imposing order on chaos. "Organized chaos" undermines all suggestions that drama, or any other art form, can be truly representations in any way other than representative of the ambiguity of the human condition. The incredible abundance of the human imagination is glorious, but the glory is undermined by recognition that one cannot depend on a finite faculty to be a means of transcendence of the limitations of humanity. . . . [When] the four Berenger plays are understood to be a development of contradicting impulses which work simultaneously—the awareness of both the ontological becoming which specifies essence and the limitations of human knowledge which define existence—then I think perhaps we are better able to understand Ionesco's dilemma in trying to "get used" to an existence which is moment by moment in a state of transition. Berenger is able to see the beauty that arises out of a chaotic universe only when the veils intended to make of it something static are removed, and this is a beauty of change for the sake of change and of vitality and unpredictability. But with this beauty comes skepticism that such a process can ever be understood in the flashes of insight to which we are limited, and, if it is understood, that it can ever be represented. These simultaneous impulses elicit fear, but as a Romantic Ironist, Ionesco's fear is a positive force because it compels not complacency and Existential paralysis, but the creative impulses which maintain the process.

Patricia Rigg, in her "Ionesco's Berenger: Existential Philosopher or Philosophical Ironist?" in Modern Drama, *December, 1992.*

Michael Sheringham (review date 25 September 1992)

SOURCE: "Honours for a Mad Baby," in *The Times Literary Supplement,* No. 4669, September 25, 1992, p. 15.

[*In the following review of* Théâtre complet, *an edition of Ionesco's plays edited by Emmanuel Jacquart, Sheringham surveys the themes of Ionesco's works.*]

It is good to know that a rainy afternoon in Paris can still be enlivened by exposure to the world of Ionesco at the pocket-sized Théâtre de la Huchette. ***La Cantatrice chauve*** has been running there uninterruptedly since 1957, clocking up those eminently forgettable statistics, familiar from *The Mousetrap*—this many changes of cast, this many thousand performances, this many costumes, vases, antimacassars. . . . Still crazy after all these years, the Smiths chunter on in their amiably sinister way, the Martins play out theatre's sexiest recognition scene, the fire-chief, hit by recession, hustles door to door for even the teeny-weeniest conflagration, while the maid, who has clearly foresuffered all, keeps a forensic eye on the proceedings, knowing it will probably end as usual with all parties barking of birth, copulation and death. As one staggers out in the quest of liquid refreshment, it is odd to recall that the man responsible for these avant-garde shenanigans has become a pillar of the establishment, who proudly sports a French Academician's sword and regalia, has his plays performed at the Comédie Française, and has now been consecrated by incorporation in the Pléiade collection alongside Molière and Claudel.

Although tempting, it would be misleading to plot Ionesco's career as a course from young turk to old buffer. A quadragenarian in the decade where he contributed, less absent-mindedly than Samuel Beckett, to one of the greatest upheavals in theatre history, the author of ***La Cantatrice chauve,*** first performed in 1950, was by then a survivor with a complex personal history already imprinted in the lugubrious eyes, the way with a bottle and the somewhat frantic temperament which, for the fellow dramatist and *névrosé* Arthur Adamov, gave him the air of a "bébé fou". Born in Bucharest in 1909, transplanted to France at the age of two, Ionesco was brought up speaking French while his overbearing Romanian father beavered away at his law exams, paying scant attention to the impoverished family. Surprisingly, in circumstances that remain mysterious despite Emmanuel Jacquart's probings, Ionesco returned at the age of thirteen to Romania, whither his father had decamped some time earlier, divorcing his French wife on a trumped-up pretext and marrying a woman who, it seems, could scarcely bear to be in the same room as him and was in turn duly loathed by her stepson.

Between 1922 and 1938, Ionesco learnt to be a Romanian, playing the part so well that by the age of twenty-nine he was a prominent figure on the literary scene, well known for his poems and iconoclastic critical essays. But as the sound of jackboots grew uncomfortably loud, he found it expedient to sign up for a Sorbonne doctorate (quickly abandoned) on "Sin and Death in French Poetry since Baudelaire", and by the outbreak of war he was in Paris with his young wife, learning once more to be an alien.

The universe of Ionesco's early one-act plays and sketches is at once domestic and linguistic. It is in the couple's drawing-room, the family home, the scholar's den, the old folk's abode, the bachelor pad that talk ceases to be merely the currency of human exchange or the barometer of psychological truth and, shoving aside identity, communication and motive, becomes a perilous and disquieting zone. But language here is double. Allowed to proliferate at the expense of sense, words replace thought, scouring out the inner life and leaving their victims prey to the merely atavistic, or else, as in ***La Leçon,*** subject to a lethal coercion the more frightening for being clearly beyond the control of those ostensibly in charge.

Yet for Ionesco, words can also be the harbingers of wonder. Freed of its craven subordination to logic, language can become a playground; ride the surf of words, Ionesco suggests, and you may experience the euphoric release which attends the fundamental experience (recollected from childhood at La Chapelle-Anthenaise) he calls *évanescence.* While the old man in ***Les Chaises*** clings doggedly to the idea that he has a message for humanity, he is beset only by the void, manifested unforgettably by the rows of empty chairs. More sagacious, his wife Sémiramis urges him to make up his own world in his head, to make himself a nest in words relieved of their impossible mission to anchor down a stable reality. The doubleness of language is especially patent in ***Jacques ou la soumission,*** where it is the mind-numbing idiolect of the family group which exacts Jacques's submission to bourgeois conventions, but where, equally, it is a ludic and childlike manipulation of words (notably the word *chat*), a revelling in the free play of the signifier, which provides him and Roberte with their escape route into a private world of freedom and fantasy.

Ionesco's early plays work best when waves of psychic disquiet with which they are imbued (and whose autobiographical basis is progressively disclosed in works such as ***Journal en miettes,*** 1967), are transmitted not simply by mean of oneiric atmosphere but via concrete stage images. Where Beckett's is a world of progressive deprivation, Ionesco is the poet of proliferation: more and more chairs, more cups and saucers, more briefcases, more rhinoceroses. In ***Le nouveau locataire,*** the tenant, deaf to the landlady's prattle, fusses over the exact disposition of his furniture, but is only satisfied when, as more and more desks and chairs and sideboards are piled insanely on top of each other, he cocoons himself in the last empty corner and politely asks for the light to be extinguished. Apart from the visual image, the key here is the build-up, the sure sense of theatrical rhythm, the feeling for ritual (the same performance every night) and an idiom which, however paroxysmic, remains rooted in comedy, a mode Ionesco finds harsher, less forgiving than tragedy.

Stung by the accusation (levelled by Kenneth Tynan among others) that his plays were irrelevant, Ionesco eschewed Beckettian silence and lambasted his critics for their ideological blindness—the age's great malady, as he has never stopped insisting. But he also changed his act. The more elaborate plays of his middle period, centred on the Everyman figure of Bérenger, have as their main theme the opposition between various forms of false consciousness and the acute sense of the human condition available only to the solitary individual. If Bérenger alone (in ***Tueur sans gages***) tries to fight the killer who lurks in the radiant city, it is not because he is better or smarter than others but because his lack of social standing immunizes him against the terrible indifference of the crowd. Similarly, in ***Rhinocéros*** (1960), it is not the power to resist which prevents Bérenger from joining the stampede to become a rhinoceros but a radical naiveté, a lack of "side", which simply won't allow him to ditch his humanity even when he wants to.

Rhinocéros, graced by Barrault and Olivier in the part of Berenger, was an international success, and so, after the inane ***Le Piéton de l'air,*** was the last play of the cycle, ***Le Roi se meurt*** (1962), where King Bérenger gives moving testimony to what was by now emerging as his creator's central obsession, the absurdist's absurdity, the fact of death itself. These more substantial and accessible plays made Ionesco acceptable to a wider theatre-going public, but it took all the craft of skilled directors to bring off what the playwright called "la projection sur scène du monde de dedans", to make something manageable out of a "matière théâtrale" dredged up from "mes rêves, mes angoisses, mes désirs obscurs, mes contradictions intérieures . . .". If part of Ionesco's charm continued to lie in the brightly lit, weightless French (closer to Tintin and Astérix than to Racine or Giraudoux) in which his characters conversed, he was all too ready to provide it in vast quantities, encrusting his dramatic structures with a cladding his cannier directors found it necessary to thin out.

It is a pity in this regard that Jacquart's generally scrupulous and comprehensive edition [***Théâtre complet***] provides only the final performed version of the texts even when earlier ones are extant. In its original version (still the one most generally available), ***Tueur sans gages*** comprised vast tracts of material which held up the action disastrously but cast interesting light on Ionesco's strengths and limitations, and it would be interesting to view this alongside the "version pour la scène". Jacquart, it must be said, makes ample amends by including very interesting production notes commissioned from some of Ionesco's most distinguished directors—Barrault, Lavelli, Serrault, Mauclair, Planchon—and by providing stage photographs, many of them featuring Ionesco regulars (such as Tsilla Chelton, latterly a hit as the outrageous old lady in the film *Tatie Danielle*), about whom much useful information is given.

La Soif et la faim, staged by Jean-Marie Serrault at the Comédie Française in 1966, marked a second major turning-point. From then on, Ionesco does not so much write plays as supply compliant producers with the latest fragmentary bulletins from the inner theatre of his memories, dreams and fantasies, often already recorded in his diaries (***Passé présent, présent passé,*** 1968). Spiritual autobiography becomes the predominant mode of his theatre, the quest its principal motif, and the discontinuous series of *tableaux* its staple device (Ionesco in this last respect falls in with the dominant dramaturgical trends of the period). At its least successful, as in ***Ce formidable bordel!*** (1973) or ***L'Homme aux valises*** (1975), the results can be fairly dire—on both page and stage. Unlike his friend and compatriot Mircea Eliade, Ionesco has little flair for comparative religion, and the eclectic myths and symbols in which he clads his personal search for tranquillity often have a woefully superannuated air. Things liven up when he resumes the struggle with his doughtiest antagonist—death. ***Jeux de massacre*** (1970), and to a lesser extent ***Macbett*** (1972), Ionesco's *grand guignol* version of Shakespeare, convey something of the old mayhem. Gross and frenetic, the *tableaux* of ***Jeux de Massacre*** involve a wide range of settings—prison, hospital, town hall—and characters of all ages and types who have one thing in common: by the end of the scene in which they appear, they will have been mown down by the plague which stalks the town in the shape of a hooded monk.

Just as deathly but twice as weird is ***Voyages chez les morts*** (1981), adapted by Roger Planchon at Villeurbanne in 1983 under the title *Spectacle Ionesco.* The denizens of Death City turn out to be mostly long-gone members of the Ionesco family circle, including his mother, father and stepfather, and the author seemingly wants us to witness his attempts to square things with them once and for all. If it looks as if this was destined to be his last play, it is good to see from Jacquart's chronology that the playwright has kept busy in the past decade, travelling, painting and searching for peace. He deserves it: warts and all, Ionesco is to be cherished, not least because the "bébé fou" still lurks beneath the academician's uniform.

Additional coverage of Ionesco's life and career is contained in the following sources published by Gale Research: *Contemporary Authors,* Vols. 9-12 (rev. ed.), 144; *Contemporary Literary Criticism,* Vols. 1, 4, 6, 9, 11, 15, 41; *DISCovering Authors; Major 20th-Century Writers; Something About the Author,* Vol. 7; and *World Literature Criticism.*

Dennis Potter

May 17, 1935—June 7, 1994

(Born Dennis Christopher George Potter) English playwright, screenwriter, novelist, nonfiction writer, and director.

For further information on his life and works, see *CLC*, Volume 58.

INTRODUCTION

Widely acclaimed for his television plays *Pennies from Heaven* (1978) and *The Singing Detective* (1986), Potter is regarded as one of the best writers in England and as a great innovator in the medium of television. Black humor and a devout belief in the redemptive power of the imagination are prominent characteristics of Potter's writing, which he once described as "non-naturalism," or a blend of fantasy and realism that allowed him to explore characters' inner worlds and varying psychological states. Potter was born and raised in the Forest of Dean in western England, a coal mining community where many of his works are set and about which he wrote in *The Changing Forest* (1962). As a student at Oxford, he developed his interest in politics, and in his senior year wrote his first book, *The Glittering Coffin* (1960), a stinging indictment of Oxford, the class system, and English social institutions. His political ideals led him to an unsuccessful run for public office in 1964. Around this time he suffered the onset of a debilitating form of arthritis known as psoriatic arthropathy, an extremely painful disease that causes the skin to blister and the joints to swell. Disillusioned and depressed, Potter turned to writing plays. His early works, *Vote, Vote, Vote for Nigel Barton* (1965) and *Stand Up, Nigel Barton* (1965), deal with his political experiences and established his reputation for highly creative, yet highly controversial work; the BBC deemed *Vote, Vote, Vote* offensive to England's Labour Party and changed the ending. Potter's subsequent works continued to challenge the public's sensibilities and, in Vincent Canby's words, make "writing for television respectable." In 1978 the BBC aired Potter's six-part miniseries *Pennies from Heaven*. Extremely popular with British television viewers, this work tells the story of a libidinous 1930s sheet music salesman whose quest for a life as happy as those described in the popular songs he sells leads him eventually to hang for a murder he did not commit. *Pennies from Heaven* inaugurated a favorite technique of Potter's in which characters lip-synch the words to songs on the soundtrack. This was used to great sentimental and ironic effect in *The Singing Detective,* considered by many critics to be Potter's greatest work. Here, a writer of detective fiction named Philip Marlow, suffering from psoriatic arthropathy and hospital-bound, retreats into dreams and reveries—in which he becomes the hero of his own fiction—in order to overcome his pain. In February of 1994 Potter was diagnosed with pancreatic cancer. He worked aggressively in his remaining months—aided by the controlled use of morphine—to finish two more television plays, *Cold Lazarus* (1994) and *Karaoke* (1994).

PRINCIPAL WORKS

The Glittering Coffin (nonfiction) 1960
The Changing Forest: Life in the Forest of Dean Today (nonfiction) 1962
The Confidence Course (television play) 1965
Stand Up, Nigel Barton (television play) 1965
Vote, Vote, Vote for Nigel Barton (television play) 1965
Almost Cinderella (television play) 1966

Son of Man (television play) 1969
Lay Down Your Arms (television play) 1970
Traitor (television play) 1971
Follow the Yellow Brick Road (television play) 1972
Hide and Seek (novel) 1973
Only Make Believe (television play) 1973
Joe's Ark (television play) 1974
**Schmoedipus* [adaptor; from a novel by Angus Wilson] (television play) 1974
†*Brimstone and Treacle* (drama) 1976
Double Dare (television play) 1976
Where Adam Stood [adaptor; from the autobiography of Edmund Gosse] (television play) 1976
‡*Pennies from Heaven* (television play) 1978
Blue Remembered Hills (television play) 1979
Blade on a Feather (television play) 1980
Cream in My Coffee (television play) 1980
Rain on the Roof (television play) 1980
Gorky Park [adaptor; from the novel by Martin Cruz Smith] (screenplay) 1983
Dreamchild (screenplay) 1985
The Singing Detective (television play) 1986
Ticket to Ride (novel) 1986
§*Blackeyes* (novel) 1987
Christabel [adaptor; from a memoir by Christabel Bielenberg] (television play) 1988
Track 29 (screenplay) 1988
Secret Friends (film) 1992
Lipstick on Your Collar (television play) 1993
Cold Lazarus (television play) 1994
Karaoke (television play) 1994

*Potter based his screenplay for Nicolas Roeg's 1988 film *Track 29* on this work.

†Potter also wrote the screenplay for the 1982 film version of this work directed by Richard Loncraine.

‡Potter also wrote the screenplay for the 1981 film version of this work directed by Herbert Ross. He also expanded the television play into novel form in 1982.

§Potter adapted this work for television in 1989.

INTERVIEW

Dennis Potter with Melvyn Bragg (interview date March 1994)

SOURCE: An interview in *The New York Times,* June 12, 1994, p. H30.

[*Bragg is an English writer and TV personality. In the following excerpt from an interview first broadcast in England in early 1994, Potter discusses how the knowledge of his imminent death and its attendant physical pain have affected his outlook and his work.*]

Given his commitment not to novels or to plays but to what he considered the inherently democratic and implicitly subversive medium of television, it made perfect sense for [Dennis Potter] to make his farewell in a televised interview.

In March, Melvyn Bragg, an English author and television personality, and Michael Grade, the chief executive officer of Channel 4, invited Potter for a televised conversation with Mr. Bragg. The tape was edited by Mr. Bragg and broadcast in Britain on April 5, after which Potter withdrew from public life to concentrate on his last two plays.

The telecast attracted enormous attention in Britain, partly for its almost gruesome intimacy, with Potter twisting nervously in his seat as he let loose with a stream of political polemics, personal justifications and near-religious epiphanies. Particularly discomforting were his occasional swigs of liquid morphine to dull his pain. Potter explored the eerie and insidious effects of morphine in his final work, a short story written last month for *The Daily Telegraph* of London.

The following is an edited transcript of the Potter-Bragg conversation, which has not been shown in the United States. A footnote: A few days ago, acceding to Potter's plea, Channel 4 and the BBC announced plans to cooperate in the joint presentation, tentatively set for next year, of his final two, now lamentably posthumous, plays, ***Karaoke*** and ***Cold Lazarus***.

. . . . .

[*Bragg*]: *How long have you been working on this new thing?*

[Potter]: Since I knew what was happening. I hope I've got enough days to finish it. I'm keeping to a very hard schedule, I'm driving myself. Even when I walk up and down—with the pain you sometimes have to keep moving—I still have the pen in my hand to make sure I can put a sentence down when it eases.

It's like that. It keeps me going. There'd be no point in remaining if I didn't, because there's no treatment possible; it's just blanking out pain with morphine. So it's finding a balance—if you blank it out totally, you can't work. It's one of those ratios that you have to work out daily.

How and when did you find out that you'd got this cancer?

Well I knew for sure on St. Valentine's Day—like a little gift, a little kiss from somebody.

I've been working since then flat out at strange hours, because I'm done in the evenings, mostly because of the morphine. Also the pain is very energy-sapping. But I do find that I can be at my desk at 5 in the morning, and I'm keeping to a schedule of pages, and I will and do meet that schedule every day.

Obviously, I had to attend to my affairs as well. I remember reading that phrase when I was a kid: "He had time to tend to his affairs."

But what it's given me also. . . . As a child, I know for a fact that I was a coward, a physical coward. And I'm really a cripplingly shy person. I hate new situations, new people, with almost a dread.

Now those two consequences in your adult life can really create seriously wrong impressions of yourself, to yourself and to other people, because you try and compensate. That can lead to aggression and the reverse of shy—arrogance, if you like—because you wear it like a cloak. But to let that drop and find out that in fact, at the last, thank God, you're not actually a coward—I haven't shed a tear since I knew. I grieve for my family, and friends who know me closest, obviously, and they're going through it in a sense more than I am.

I've discovered also what you always know to be true, but you never know it till you know it, if you follow. I remember Martin Amis saying something about how when you reach your 40's, middle age, nobody has ever told you what it's like.

Well, it's the same with knowing about death. We're the one animal that knows that we're going to die, and yet we carry on paying our mortgages, doing our jobs, moving about, behaving as though there's eternity in a sense, and we tend to forget that life can only be defined in the present tense.

It is, and it is now only. As much as we would like to call back yesterday and indeed ache to sometimes, we can't. It's in us, but it's not there in front of us. And however predictable tomorrow is, no matter how predictable it is, there's the element on the unpredictable.

. . . . .

That nowness becomes so vivid to me now, that in a perverse sort of way, I'm almost serene, I can celebrate life. Below my window, for example, the blossom is out in full. It's a plum tree. It looks like apple blossom, but it's white. And instead of saying, "Oh, that's nice blossom," looking at it through the window when I'm writing, it is whitest, frothiest, blossomiest blossom that there ever could be.

Things are both more trivial than they ever were, and the difference between the trivial and the important doesn't seem to matter—but the *nowness* of everything is absolutely wondrous.

And if people could see that—there's no way of telling you, you have to experience it—the glory of it, if you like, the comfort of it, the reassurance. . . . Not that I'm interested in reassuring people, you know. The fact is that if you see the present tense, boy, do you see it, and boy, can you celebrate it!

You said earlier that it wasn't to do with believing that life was eternal, but have you any feeling from the position you're in, that it might be? You've said that you've never quite thrown off the idea of believing in God, and it features in a lot of your work.

Well, I don't know. God's a rumor, if you like. Christianity or indeed any other religion that is a religion because of fear of death or hope that there is something beyond death does not interest me. What kind of cruel old bugger is God if it's terror that is the ruling edifice, the structure of religion? And too often, for too many people, it is. Now that to me isn't religion.

Religion has always been—I've said it before, but it doesn't matter, I won't get many more chances to repeat myself—thank God, religion to me has always been the wound, not the bandage. I don't see the point of not acknowledging the pain and the misery and the grief of the world, and if you say, "Ah, but God understands" or through that you come to a greater appreciation, I then think, "That's not God, that's not my God, that's not how I see God."

I see God in us or with us, if I see God at all, as shreds and particles and rumors, some knowledge that we have, some feeling why we sing and dance and act, why we paint, why we love, why make art.

All the things that separate us from the purely animal in us are palpably there, and you can call them what you like, and you can theologize about them, and you can build great structures of belief about them. The fact is they are there and I have no means of knowing whether that thereness in some sense doesn't cling to what I call me.

When I go flat out, I go flat out and write with a passion I've never felt. I feel I can write anything at the moment. I feel I can fly with it. I feel I can really communicate what I'm about, and what I feel.

—Dennis Potter

When you knew you had cancer, one of the things you decided to do was write. What are you writing? We're about a month on from when you were told, on Feb. 14..

Yeah, I've done a lot. First of all I was on the point of delivering something that had been commissioned quite a long time ago, called ***Karaoke,*** for the BBC.

Although there's a little bit set in the karaoke clubs, obviously karaoke is a metaphor: there's the music, and you have your little line, you can sing it, and everything is written for you, and that is the way life feels to a lot of people. For some, you haven't got much space, and even the space you've got, although you use your own voice, the words are written for you.

I was on the point of delivering it, then as soon as I knew I was going to die, I thought: I can't deliver this, whatever I'm doing now is my last work, and I want to be proud. I want it to be fitting, a memorial, I want to continue to speak.

And at the same time I had this, to me, very exciting idea—I would say that, but I do feel the excitement of it—I'm doing with Channel 4, which I'm calling ***Cold Lazarus,*** and you'll see why. I'm trying to join two things together that are currently in the air.

One is virtual reality, where you put on goggles and gloves, and you can land a plane, simulated, or—they hope, and this is the commercial money behind it—you can almost feel that you're having sex with Marilyn Monroe or somebody. Virtual reality will invade the entertainment business but also your own sense of reality.

The other is cryogenics—that is, deep-freeze—technology at absolute zero temperatures. In California they are actually freezing bodies of people, very rich people—and there are some corporations making quite a lot of nice money out of this—for eventual regeneration, when they can cure whatever it is they died of. They've honed that down now, I discover. They only need to freeze the head. They've managed apparently to regenerate some frozen rat brain cells.

I have this series, where there's the head in its case, and all the electrodes are attached to it, and as they gradually allow and stimulate the billions upon billions of brain cells, they discover that one's alive and there is memory there everywhere, real memory.

We're talking about 400 years from now, and that real memory is of the 1930's, 1940's, 1950's, 1960's, in other words, my memories or what I choose to make my memories. And to stimulate those memories, they have to use virtual-reality memories as well.

Now what I want to do, and I'm floating this now publicly, so I'm going to compromise some people. ***Karaoke*** is BBC. ***Cold Lazarus*** is Channel 4. I want the man whose head is in the box, spilling out memories of the real world that I know, to be the man who is the central character of ***Karaoke***.

All I hope is that I've got enough days to finish it, and I'm working all the hours I can. I've got a doctor, Paul Downey, whose name should be celebrated if I do finish this, who has so gently and carefully led me to a balance between pain control and mental control, where I can work. He's given me the liberty, and he's had the intelligence to see that I can create a space to do 10 pages a day, flat out.

When I go flat out, I go flat out and with a passion I've never felt. I feel I can write anything at the moment. I feel I can fly with it. I feel I can really communicate what I'm about, and what I feel.

My only regret would be to die four pages too soon. If I can finish, then I'm quite happy to go. I don't mind. I am quite serene. I haven't had a single moment of terror since they told me. I know I'm going to die, whether it's in four weeks' time, five, six. It might be longer—I might make eight, nine, ten, who knows?

The histology of it suggests that I should already be dead, but I know what's keeping me going. . . . I've written so much of it I know, and I've got the same feeling that I had with ***Singing Detective*** and ***Pennies From Heaven*** and ***Blue Remembered Hills,*** only more so. I would go out with—I can now be arrogant and boastful—I could go out with a fitting memorial.

That'll have to do. I'm done.

OBITUARIES AND TRIBUTES

William Grimes (obituary date 8 June 1994)

SOURCE: An obituary in *The New York Times,* June 8, 1994, p. 11.

[*In the following obituary, Grimes recounts the highlights of Potter's life and career.*]

Dennis Potter, the caustic and controversial writer of the innovative British television dramas ***The Singing Detective*** and ***Pennies from Heaven,*** died yesterday at his home near Ross-on-Wye, England, about 100 miles west of London. He was 59.

The cause was cancer. In an interview earlier this year, for a segment of the British television program *Without Walls* that was broadcast on April 5, Mr. Potter revealed that on Valentine's Day he had been told he was suffering from cancer of the pancreas, and that it had spread to his liver.

Mr. Potter wrote novels and screenplays, but it was in television, which he referred to as "the greatest of all media" because of its accessibility, that he preferred to work. He took audacious liberties with television drama, infusing it with new life by turning its conventions upside down.

He was best known for ***The Singing Detective,*** about a writer of crime novels who, while lying in a hospital bed and being treated for a skin disease, sees his life, his fictional characters and the contents of his unconscious parade before him. The spectacle is a kind of surreal musical, sprinkled with popular songs from the 1930's and 40's. Michael Gambon played the central character, Philip Marlowe. Most critics took Marlowe to represent Mr. Potter, who struggled for the last 30 years of his life with psoriatic arthropathy, a debilitating skin disease.

The Singing Detective, which ran more than six hours, was first shown in Britain in 1986 and in the United States in 1988.

"For me, writing is partly a cry of the soul," Mr. Potter told an interviewer in 1989. "But at the same time I'm bringing back the results of a journey that many people don't get the chance to make, to whatever hinterland it is where all those dark figures fibber and jeer and fly at you."

Mr. Potter was born in Joyford Hill, Gloucestershire, the son of a coal miner. When Dennis was 14, the family moved to London, where he excelled in school, eventually winning a scholarship to New College, Oxford. At Oxford, he was active in the Labor Club, appeared in student productions, edited a student magazine and wrote ***The Glittering Coffin,*** an indictment of England's social ills.

After receiving a degree with honors in 1959, he wrote and produced documentaries at the British Broadcasting Corporation as member of the current-affairs staff. He also contributed articles on politics to *The New Statesman.* From 1961-64, he worked for the *The Daily Herald* of London, now defunct, first as a feature writer and later as its television critic. In the 1964 general election, he ran unsuccessfully as the Labor candidate for East Hertfordshire.

Shortly before the campaign, Mr. Potter suffered his first attack of psoriatic arthropathy. After his electoral defeat, he went into seclusion and began writing television plays. He first made his mark in 1965 with ***Vote Vote Vote for Nigel Barton,*** a tragicomedy about a young Labor candidate's campaign for Parliament. It was followed by ***Stand Up, Nigel Barton***. The two works were later combined in a successful stage play.

Mr. Potter repeatedly found himself at the center of controversy. The Nigel Barton plays were broadcast by the BBC only after changes were made to avoid offending the Labor Party's leadership. ***Son of Man*** was attacked for its presentation of Jesus as a man tormented by doubts about his own divinity. In 1966, the BBC asked him to rewrite ***Almost Cinderella,*** an updated fairy tale in which Prince Charming strangles Cinderella at midnight. ***Brimstone and Treacle,*** about a brain-damaged teen-age girl who is cured after being raped by the Devil, was made in 1976 but not broadcast until 1987.

"They get hopping mad sometimes," Mr. Potter said of the public reaction to his work. "But so be it. That's what television is for, too."

In all, he wrote more than 30 television plays. He often expressed his confidence in television and in the notion of a popular culture. In the "Without Walls" interview, the last interview he granted, Mr. Potter told Melvyn Bragg he had never tried to be daring. "I never felt the need to," he said. "It came out of the need to do what I was doing."

In ***Blue Remembered Hills,*** for example, he cast adults as children, he said, because only adult actors could deliver the lengthy speeches in the script, and they made the use of flashbacks more efficient.

Mr. Potter first began to make a reputation in the United States in the late 1970's, when ***Pennies from Heaven*** was televised. The series, about a Depression-era sheet-music salesman (played by Bob Hoskins), was shown on public television. As in ***The Singing Detective,*** the characters sang popular songs from the period in lip sync. The series was later made into a film, with Steve Martin in the lead role. Mr. Potter wrote the screenplay.

"I wanted to write about the way that cheap songs are inheritors of something else," Mr. Potter said. The popular music he used, he said, stirred profound associations and memories for the average person. "Cheap songs have something of the Psalms of David about them," he said. "They do illuminate."

In 1984, his ***Blade on the Feather,*** an indictment of the upper classes was broadcast on public television in the United States. John J. O'Connor, writing in a review in *The New York Times,* said the series "takes on the proportions of a John le Carre thriller as arranged by Harold Pinter."

Christabel, televised in America in 1989, told the true story of Christabel Bielenberg, an Anglo-Irish woman in Germany who rescued her husband from the Gestapo after he was arrested for plotting to assassinate Hitler.

Although Mr. Potter did his best-known work for television, he ventured into fiction and film as well. He wrote the screenplays for ***Gorky Park*** (1983), ***Dreamchild*** (1985) and ***Track 29*** (1989). He was both screenwriter and director of ***Secret Friends*** (1992), which was loosely based on his 1986 novel, ***Ticket to Ride***.

His other novels are ***Hide and Seek*** (1973), ***Pennies from Heaven*** (1982) and ***Blackeyes*** (1987). He also wrote a book of nonfiction, ***The Changing Forest: Life in the Forest of Dean Today*** (1962).

Mr. Potter's most recent work to be broadcast in America was ***Cream in My Coffee*** (1990), the story of an old couple at a seaside resort and the evolution of their unhappy marriage, told through flashbacks and songs.

This year, he was at work on two television projects. In ***Karaoke,*** he explored the pastime of singing in karaoke clubs as a metaphor for the social constraints that force most people into assuming roles, and leading lives, which have been written for them. ***Cold Lazarus*** presents a character preserved through cryogenic freezing; after he is revived four centuries after his death, his memories are used to feed a giant entertainment industry.

"I feel I can write anything at the moment," Mr. Potter said in his last interview. "I can fly. My only regret is if I die four pages too soon. If I can finish, I'm quite happy to go."

He finished both projects before dying.

Last week, Mr. Potter's wife, Margaret, whom he described as "my rock, my center," for having nursed him through of many periods of illness, died of breast cancer. He is survived by a son, Robert, and two daughters, Sarah and Jane.

John J. O'Connor (essay date 9 June 1994)

SOURCE: "The Potter Legacy: Faith in Quality TV," in *The New York Times,* June 9, 1994, pp. C15, C18.

[*In the following excerpt, O'Connor lauds the stylistic and thematic depth of Potter's work in television, praising him for believing in the intelligence of the viewer and for resisting the commercializing tendencies of the medium.*]

Dennis Potter died this week. And so did a powerful voice cantankerously insisting that television, which he always praised as the most democratic medium, could be far more than a tireless purveyor of fluffy diversions. Mr. Potter, who was 59, wrote novels, plays and screenplays, but his talents flourished most splendidly, and often controversially, in television drama. If the medium can lay claim to masterpieces, two would have to be the Potter mini-series: ***Pennies From Heaven*** and ***The Singing Detective***.

Probing themes of reality and illusion, sex and death, public and personal betrayal, Mr. Potter had boundless contempt for timid industry accountants or feel-good critics who refused to acknowledge that television could be as serious and significant as literature or films at their best. His credo: "A confidence in common culture, an assumption that people are very much brighter than the market men say they are, that something in them is capable of responding to things that are very complex."

Suffering since his mid-20's from psoriatic arthropathy, a severely painful and frequently debilitating combination of psoriasis and arthritis, Mr. Potter was hardly the most genial of men. An executive at the BBC, where the writer did the bulk of his work, once delicately described the organization's relationship with Mr. Potter as "stormy," emphasizing that this was hardly out of line with a person embodying "scathing irreverence, wit and a highly charged vision of the world."

At a 1992 lunch arranged by the Museum of Television and Radio to open an extensive retrospective on "The Television of Dennis Potter," the bristling writer offered horrifyingly vivid descriptions of his skin problems and then for good measure, fixing his gleefully diabolical eyes on a television critic with an Irish surname, spoke of sensing "the smell of the bog." The response of a smile seemed to disappoint him momentarily.

Mr. Potter's own roots were in England in the Forest of Dean, close to the border of Wales. There is in much of his work the unmistakable touch of the outsider, once removed from the mainstream by either geography or, as so graphically portrayed in ***The Singing Detective,*** some dreadful physical ailment. Past and present, fact and fiction, love and hate can melt into each other effortlessly, part Freud, part Proust. In ***Blade on the Feather,*** produced for the BBC in the early 1980's, Mr. Potter pondered the phenomenon of treason among England's privileged classes and had a character conclude, "The upper class loves only what it owns, and it doesn't quite own enough of England anymore."

On religion, he could be seemingly blasphemous, describing God as "a code word for all kinds of humbug and hypocrisy and institutionalized pap." Yet he told one interviewer that as far as he and the Almighty were concerned, "There's a relationship." Mr. Potter's only question: "God, are you there? And if not, why not?"

All of which is obviously far removed from the concerns of standard television. In a world that is being Disneyfied into theme parks and an amorphous something called family entertainment, Mr. Potter insisted on being aggressively adult. That included occasionally blunt language, sexual candor and even a bit of nudity. Nothing was prurient, but the mix was unusual enough to strike fear into the hearts of notoriously cautious broadcasters.

When ***The Singing Detective*** was first shown on public television in this country, it was denied a cushy *Masterpiece Theater* showcase and scheduled instead late at night, outside of prime time. One of Mr. Potter's last works, the deliciously impudent mini-series ***Lipstick on Your Collar,*** produced in Britain for Channel 4, has so far been unable to find an American outlet.

In a medium devoted to tidy solutions, Mr. Potter insisted on playing the renegade. A character summed up the Potter vision of life this way: "All clues, No solutions. That's the way things are." It is not a concept amenable to formulaic pop culture Mr. Potter saw television as a tool "its very generality drawing the specific out of you." His use of popular songs, suddenly popping out of lip-synching mouths, became a marvelous device for tapping into worlds of complicated memory.

The question now: How many Dennis Potters, if any, will be allowed to survive in television's future? He was scornful of American commercial television, arguing that "that's what happens when you hand over a powerful machine to the hucksters." And these are hucksters reluctant to support even the solidly rated *N.Y.P.D. Blue* because of organized protests over rather innocuous content.

Probing themes of reality and illusion, sex and death, public and personal betrayal, Mr. Potter had boundless contempt for timid industry accountants or feel-good critics who refused to acknowledge that television could be as serious and significant as literature or films at their best.

—John J. O'Connor

Mr. Potter was nearly as gloomy about British television, noting that as technology enables the medium to become universal, international co-productions, assembled by committees, assume greater importance while the voices of individual writers grow more distant. The inevitable upshot, Mr. Potter said, is that "more doors shut down."

Troubled and sometimes troublesome, Mr. Potter will long remain a seminal and major figure in the initial phase of the newfangled contraption called television. He was among the far too precious few who did not believe that television entertainment had to pass quickly into oblivion, that the medium was more important than assorted bottom-line anxieties. That's a notion that just won't go away. I certainly hope not.

John Naughton (essay date 12 June 1994)

SOURCE: "Potent Cliches and Painful Truths," in *The Observer,* June 12, 1994, p. 5.

[*In the following essay, Naughton eulogizes Potter's life and career, describing him as a "great artist" and "the first—and so far the only—television dramatist to produce works which approach the complexity and power of great novelists."*]

It was his handwriting I noticed first: gossamer-thin strokes of a felt-tip pen, like the trail of a literary spider. I was working on the *New Stateman* at the time (the early Seventies), and he was our television critic. Someone (probably his wife, Margaret, who died of cancer two weeks ago) used to bring in his copy on Wednesdays. In my ignorance, I asked why it wasn't typed like everyone else's, and someone had to explain to me that his arthritis made it impossible for him to use a typewriter, or even a conventional ball-point or fountain pen. The wispy script that he turned in every week had probably caused him more pain in two hours than I had experienced in 20 years. It was my first inkling of the forcefulness and courage which characterised Dennis Potter in life—and in dying.

'What is his legacy?' a radio interviewer asked me on Tuesday. At one level, the answer is obvious: a body of dramatic work of astonishing vigour and originality, including three masterpieces—***Pennies from Heaven*** (1978), ***Blue Remembered Hills*** (1979) and ***The Singing Detective*** (1986)—which will live for as long as people gather in the dark to watch television screens. He has even left us two posthumous gifts—***Karaoke*** and ***Cold Lazarus***—which he slaved to complete before succumbing to cancer, together with typically elaborate demands as to how they should be realised and broadcast.

But at another level he left us a worked example of how a writer should engage with his society. He had passionate beliefs about social justice, a hatred of snobbery and prejudice, a fantastic nose for cant, and a withering contempt for what Margaret Thatcher, John Major and Rupert Murdoch have done to the country he loved. He felt they were turning a fundamentally decent society into an indecent one, and 'common decency' was a value he prized very greatly. In that sense, Potter had a fierce integrity reminiscent of George Orwell. Like Orwell, he was also exceedingly prolific—stupendously so when you consider his medical history, for he was struck down by severe psoriatic arthropathy in his twenties. In 29 years he turned out 42 screenplays, of which many were striking and some were unforgettable. From the beginning he displayed an extraordinary ability for getting up people's noses. The closing sequence of ***Vote, Vote, Vote for Nigel Barton*** (1965), his play about the disillusioning effect of political campaigning, for example, originally closed with a two-fingered salute to the electoral process that was edited out by a terrified BBC.

Potter's plays address the great transcendental issues which have always bedevilled humankind: life, death, love, betrayal, good, evil, God and the devil and, most of all, the relationship between childhood and what comes after. And they addressed these subjects in ways which were entirely alien to television.

—John Naughton

The extent to which he terrified broadcasting executives is one measure of Potter's integrity. When ***Brimstone and Treacle*** was completed in 1976, the then Director-General, Alasdair Milne, refused to screen it saying that it was 'nauseating' and 'diabolical'. Potter replied that it was meant to be both of these things. The play was a variation on the pious 'visitation' story in which a family with a brain-damaged daughter is visited by a mysterious stranger who effects a miraculous transformation. What frightened the horses—and the D-G—was the fact that the stranger was the devil incarnate, and that rape was the instrument of liberation. The tape was held in the BBC archives for more than a decade and eventually to be shown in 1987.

The years from 1976 to 1986 were the most creative of Potter's career. They were the years of ***Pennies from Heaven, Blue Remembered Hills*** and ***The Singing Detective***—all products of an author who had really hit his stride. Some people have linked this creative sunburst with a change in the medication which Potter took to try and alleviate the crippling effects of his illness. This seems over-deterministic, especially to anyone familiar with Methotrexate, the drug to which he switched. The truth is that ***Pennies from Heaven*** revealed a writer who had finally attained total control of his medium. What made Potter special was that whereas other dramatists wrote for television, he *wrote television*. Unlike many of his counterparts, he put no camera directions into his scripts. But it was always obvious to the reader what kind of visual treatment he had in mind. 'When a close-up is necessary', said Jon Amiel, director of ***The Singing Detective,*** 'he will describe an event in such detail that the only conceivable way to match the intensity of that description is with a close-up. What Dennis's writing does, rather than insist on or direct you to do something, is to inspire you to do something with the same passion and the same specificity.'

Nobody before or since has understood the grammar of television as well as Potter, or used it to such powerful effect. He understood its ability to shock and to haunt. He knew the power of images, especially subliminal ones, and the potency of cliches. One sees this especially in his use of popular music from ***Pennies from Heaven*** onwards. At first, people thought this was a gimmick or an affectation, and it is true that sometimes Potter used music to 'distract, tickle, upset' the viewer. At other times he used it to provide a poignant or ironic counterpoint to the visual images. The hospital scene in ***The Singing Detective*** opens with shots of Philip Marlow crucified by psoriasis while on the soundtrack someone sings 'I've Got You Under My Skin'. And the cathartic climax of the series—the scene where Philip as a young boy comes upon his mother copulating with her lover in the wood—is overlaid with 'The Teddy Bears' Picnic': 'If you go down to the woods today, you'd better not go alone. / It's lovely out in the woods today, but better to stay at home . . .' Potter's use of music was no gimmick, but a way of getting to parts of one's psyche that other media simply cannot reach. Singing in the pain, you might say.

He was a great artist because he was the first—and so far the only—television dramatist to produce works which approach the complexity and power of great novelists. His plays address the great transcendental issues which have always bedevilled humankind: life, death, love, betrayal, good, evil, God and the devil and, most of all, the relationship between childhood and what comes after. And they addressed these subjects in ways which were entirely alien to television. People sometimes complained that they found his works hard to follow, and indeed in one sense they were because he believed in making the viewer work. Potter fought all his life against what he called 'the tyranny of narrative' and the received wisdom that televised drama essentially consisted of a chronological sequence of causes and effects, varied only by flashback. His aim was to disorient the viewer, often by shock tactics, to force him or her away from the powerful naturalism of television. No one ever slept at the back when Dennis Potter was on.

Sometimes he achieved this with simple devices—like using adults to play children in ***Blue Remembered Hills,*** the greatest play ever written about the cruelty of childhood and our inability to leave it. But more often he did it by placing impediments in the flow that puzzled or enraged viewers—until they had worked at it hard enough to understand the purpose of such obstacles. ***The Singing Detective,*** for example, is structured like a psychoanalytical exploration, with all its diversions, confusions and dead ends—and the assumption that the keys to adult neuroses are to be found in the dark recesses of childhood. It is littered with clues and motifs which linger in the mind long after the credits have rolled. Few televised works repay a second viewing; but you could watch ***The Singing Detective*** 50 times over and still feel enriched by the experience.

In lamenting his loss, therefore, we should also celebrate his wonderful talent, and feel grateful that we lived at a time when there was a television service equal to his needs. In his final interview with Melvyn Bragg, Potter talked about his childhood and going to chapel and the words of hymn number 787. 'Will there be any stars in my crown when the evening sun goes down? / When I wake with the blessed in the mansion of rest.' Yes, Dennis, there will, there will. And thanks for the memories.

REVIEWS OF POTTER'S RECENT WORKS

Paul Delany (review date Winter 1988-89)

SOURCE: "Potterland," in *The Dalhousie Review,* Vol. 68, No. 4, Winter, 1988-89, pp. 511-21.

[*In the following essay, Delany reviews several of Potter's works, including* Pennies from Heaven, The Singing Detective, Christabel, *and the two novels* Ticket to Ride *and* Blackeyes.]

> I was born into a coalminer's cottage in a stony village in what was then a relatively isolated Forest of Dean that heaves up in half-hidden layers of grey and green between two rivers on the assertively English side of the border with Wales. Brass bands, rugby football, nonconformist chapels with names like Zion and Salem, the sound of silicotic old men from the now closed mines spitting the dust out of their rattling chests. Secret places. Unknown caves. A mother who was a Londoner, bringing occasional uncles with outlandish Fulham or Hammersmith tongue, who did not say 'thee' and 'thou.' And when the teacher at the junior school left the room, which had windows too high for a child to look out of, she would say, 'Come out to the front, Dennis, and tell a story.' That was meant as a reward, or a compliment: it was, of course, a punishment. [***Waiting For the Boat: Dennis Potter on Television***]

The village was Joyford Hill, Gloucestershire; the two rivers enclosing the Forest are the Severn and the Wye; the schoolboy was Dennis Potter. Fifty years earlier, D. H. Lawrence had moved up and out from his mining village, and raged at the cost of uprooting himself. But whereas Lawrence became a compulsive wanderer, Potter has returned to live only a few miles from his birthplace, probing obsessively at questions deeply rooted in his childhood: innocence, betrayal, sexuality, the nature of evil itself. Like one of those little pellets that expands into a flower when put in water, Potter's buried childhood in the Forest of Dean has blossomed into a career of more than thirty television plays, many screenplays, three novels, and perhaps the biggest audience, in Britain, of any serious writer in this century.

When John Berger examined the fate of a country doctor in the Forest, in *A Fortunate Man* (1967), he saw in the foresters' lives a desperate narrowness and deprivation. Potter's transformation of his childhood into art calls that judgment into question; though he was not, of course, a typical forest child. His mother was an outsider; his exceptional intelligence set him apart from his schoolmates; and he suffered an unnamed psychic wound, "something foul and terrible that happened to me when I was ten years old, caught by an adult's appetite and abused out of innocence" [***Waiting For the Boat***]. All these things worked to expel him from the "tight, warm mesh" of working-class life. When he was fourteen his family moved to Hammersmith, known for its ornate suspension bridge over the Thames (the setting for some crucial scenes in his plays). Unhappy in London, Potter's father returned to the Forest after two years. Dennis stayed in Hammersmith, already launched on a path that would steadily distance him from his father's world: first St. Clement Dane's Grammar School; then National Service as a Russian-language clerk in the War Office; then a scholarship to New College, Oxford where he edited the literary magazine *Isis,* and wrote a book—***The Glittering Coffin***—attacking the system that was hurrying him on to success.

From Oxford Potter went to the BBC where he helped produce a documentary on the Forest of Dean, "Between Two Rivers" (1960). Before long he quarrelled with his superiors and signed on with the *Daily Herald,* the only serious newspaper that supported Labour. On the side he wrote sketches for *That Was The Week That Was,* a TV series that made fun of everything typically English and was, typically, rewarded with enormous popularity. In 1964 Potter stood as a Labour candidate for a safe Tory seat, and duly lost; disillusioned with practical politics he wrote two TV plays about the experience, ***Vote, Vote, Vote for Nigel Barton*** and ***Stand Up For Nigel Barton.***

The first of these was produced by the BBC and then cancelled on the day it was due to be shown, on the grounds that it treated parliamentary democracy with contempt and "shat on the Queen." This was the beginning of Potter's running battle with the people who decide what is shown on TV. Eventually he re-wrote the last ten minutes of ***Vote, Vote, Vote*** and persuaded the BBC to show it, along with its companion piece. His plays have been seen on British TV virtually every year since. "Television," he said in 1970, "is the only medium that really counts for me. . . . [It] is the biggest platform and you should kick and fight and bite your way into it. It's true that television is endemically a trivialising medium, but it doesn't follow that it *has* to be. Television is the true national theatre."

Television drama has been an important cultural genre in Britain since TV service began in 1936. At first, directors just made a few minor adjustments to stage plays before sending them out in the new medium. This mode survives in the costumed nostalgia of *Masterpiece Theatre,* the main representative of the British genre on North American television. The tremendous popularity of such dramas—15 million people watched *The Forsyte Saga* in Britain—rests on their conventional narrative form and faithful reconstruction of period settings. But there is also another tradition, critical rather than nostalgic, and using a complex narrative vocabulary derived from modernist literature and film. Potter's achievement has been to push that complexity to the limit, yet bring a mass audience along with him.

[Jan Bussell's *The Art of Television,* an] early guide for television playwrights gave the following advice:

> Scenes between twos and threes are what television wants: quiet, intimate stuff which the camera can get right into. Five people on the set for any length of time is a producer's headache, meaning constant regrouping and cutting from shot to shot in order to show viewers what the characters look like in close-up.

Potter has favored this "natural" scale for television, which also has the advantage, for him, of foregrounding the writer's words rather than the sound and spectacle of large-screen movies. He has observed, also, that the compact scenes of studio productions find a counterpart on the *receiving* end: the media's massive audience is the sum of millions of miniature audiences, each watching the dramatic action in the family setting where they also live out their own reality. In ***The Singing Detective,*** Potter brilliantly uses cutting to show the close-range emotional interplay between characters. In a scene at a workingmen's club, for example, Philip's father sings the Inkspots' "Do I Worry" in harmony with his wife's lover, while the wife plays the piano and nine-year-old Philip watches, entranced. A series of closeups show how all are connected yet all have different interests and understandings; in the background, a leering audience sees all.

Masterpiece Theatre series like *Upstairs, Downstairs* presented an integral national past. Although masters and servants lived in different parts of the house, they were really one big family (with, of course, the inevitable squabbles); and the nation was simply a bigger family yet. The classic setting for such fables was the Edwardian era, the most convenient one to appropriate because it was just beyond the reach of the general living memory. Potter has challenged this formula for representing the British past. His own use of history only goes back as far as the thirties: the decade of his birth (in 1935, the year in which ***Pennies From Heaven*** is set) and thus, for him, the origin of a *continuous* personal and collective popular culture. He has lovingly re-created that culture in his plays, but not as any comfortably nostalgic living museum. Rather, he has cobbled together his private experiences and obsessions into a mythic "Potterland"—which has nonetheless become as definitive a popular image of the period from 1935 to 1950 as Dickens's version of the Victorian age. Potterland is shaped like a dumb-bell, with the Forest of Dean at one end, London at the other, and the railway connecting them. London really means Hammersmith, for boyhood memories, and Paddington, where trains from the West Country arrive to a neighborhood of whores, transients and [as he puts it in ***Ticket to Ride***] "Arabs facing away from Mecca." Trains and whores are Potter obsessions; some of the others are dance music before the rock-and-roll era, Russian spies, cowboys (and America, generally, as a mythic opposite of Britain), the bombing of German cities by the RAF, cigarettes, betrayals, art deco interiors, neurotic schoolteachers, the Oedipus complex, and everybody's childhood.

But these elements are only the backdrop to Potter's dramatic world; what really matters is the action that takes place there. Each Potter play contributes a new perspective to a lifetime imaginative project, the constant reworking of unresolvable contradictions between child and adult, past and present, belief and scepticism, fantasy and reality. Underlying them all is Potter's fervent but totally unorthodox Christianity. "There is, in the end, no such thing as a *simple* faith," he has observed [in his introduction to ***Bristone and Treacle***], "and we cannot even begin to define 'good' and 'evil' without being aware of the interaction between the two."

Potter's Forest of Dean is still haunted by Wordsworth, who walked there with Dorothy in 1798, composing "Tintern Abbey" as he went. But *the* Wordsworth poem, for Potter, is the "Immortality Ode." If "the child is father to the man," Potter is only too well aware of how the abused child gives birth to the crippled adult. In ***Pennies From Heaven,*** the loving schoolteacher Eileen asks her headmaster why he beats his pupils; he answers that he is making sure that when they grow up they will be able to hold down a job in the mines. His belief in punishment combines with religious and nationalist fanaticism: society must be ruled by teachers, police, judges and an angry God at the top of it all. Eileen, and even more her lover Arthur, are overgrown children who try to escape the beating reserved for them. "Nobody ever, ever stops yearning" says Eileen, when she is fired by her head for getting pregnant; his reply is that "they jolly well better had." (In a characteristic Potter turn of the screw, the head cherishes an unrequited yearning for Eileen, and gives her a generous gift to help her on her way).

Evicted from her forest idyll, Eileen takes the train to Paddington; when her money runs out she goes on the streets and changes her name to "Lulu," after the whore in Pabst's film of Wedekind's *Pandora's Box.* Soon she is cheating and even killing with such gusto that the viewer has to wonder if "she always had it in her." This is certainly the message of ***Blue Remembered Hills*** (1979), where the continuity between children and grown-ups is made literal by having the children played by adult actors. Across the English Channel, the Second World War is raging; in the Forest of Dean, a gang of children are acting it out in their play. War needs victims and they have one to torment, a gentle half-witted hanger-on; at the end, they lock him in a barn where he is burned alive. But are they just imitating what is offered them, or is the real war an example of how an earlier generation are now able to enact their childish desires on a bigger scale? Why do children follow the worst of their own kind, and persecute the good; and why can't the adults—who are never seen in the play—impose morality on their children? Having the children played by adults suggests that there *is* no real older generation to control the play, just as there is, perhaps, no God to set limits to the malice of man.

Blue Remembered Hills suggests that we must live inside the iron cage of morality and necessity, for fear of the worse horrors outside it. Potter's heroes and heroines are people who know this, but still dream of escape. The key to those dreams is often the popular music of the thirties and forties—which, Potter has said, "not only invokes in many of us the characteristically bitter-sweet (and totally useless) emotions of nostalgia, but also carries within its bright and easy bounce, or silkily blue ribbons of sobbing 'regret,' the faint and haunting outlines of 'thoughts that lie too deep for tears.' " The hero of ***Pennies From Heaven*** is a travelling salesman for this music, an ordinary sensual man who insists that something in his songs *must* be real. In his semidetached suburban house he lives a life of chronic frustration with his frigid, snobbish wife. At home there is a constant battle between lower-middle class gentility and his own feckless hedonism; but outside, he can let his fantasies bloom, driving towards the Forest of Dean to the strains of "Roll Along, Prairie Moon."

Eileen, buried in her little country schoolhouse, is just as eager to escape from her own cage. But by the time she and Arthur decide to cut loose together, both have been fatally compromised: Eileen has become a whore, and Arthur has taken his wife's inheritance to set up a record shop. By sheer mischance, Arthur has become a suspect in the rape and murder of a blind girl near Gloucester. Bitter in her abandonment, his wife tells a detective of how Arthur had talked her into putting lipstick on her nipples and doing the housework without any knickers on. In his stiflingly genteel accent, the detective observes that "a man like that is capable of anything"; and the final nail in Arthur's coffin is that the murdered girl's knickers were also missing. Arthur goes on the run, clinging to his old dream of escaping to America, "a world where songs come true." What he gets instead is the gallows—not because he committed any crime, but because he always preferred a lie to the truth. In the end, Potter seems to be saying that one can live in two worlds at once—one of the songs, one of reality—but to try and combine them is fatal.

In ***The Singing Detective,*** Potter makes his most ambitious and moving attempt at unity of vision. We begin with a view of one Philip Marlow sitting in a hospital bed like Job on his dunghill, his face looking like meat that has been boiled and left out to rot, his hands gnarled into stumps. Like Potter himself he is a child of the Forest, a writer, and a victim for many years of psoriatic arthropathy. When Potter was first attacked by this awful disease, in his mid-twenties, he felt it as a self-punishment for betraying the working-class community in which he had grown up. Now, he is more inclined to see it as just a stroke of genetic bad luck. But in ***The Singing Detective*** it is the visible sign of Marlow's unwholesome moral state: his guilty childhood, his present self-enclosure, and the paranoid world of his recurrent fevers.

Marlow's purulent face repeatedly fills the screen, with an expression either of sullen withdrawal or of wide-eyed terror when his hallucinations start to take over. The viewer must get used to being flipped between four distinct worlds and levels of reality. One is Marlow's present crucifixion, among the motley inhabitants of the cardiac and skin ward of a London hospital. Second is his memory of the events that have put him there, in the spring of 1945 when he was nine years old. Third is a favorite diversion, to imagine himself as P. Marlow, detective—the hero of a thriller he has written, *The Singing Detective* [in an endnote, Delany adds: "The difference between 'Marlow' and Raymond Chandler's 'Marlowe' is part of a recurrent theme: 'One letter's all there is between trick and prick,' as Marlow's wife puts it"]. Fourth is the morbid delusion that his wife and his literary agent are sleeping together while conspiring to sell an old screenplay of *The Singing Detective* to Hollywood and pocket the proceeds.

The inner world of ***The Singing Detective*** is unabashedly Freudian. Freud speaks of fantasy as essentially wish-fulfilment, "which carries about it traces of its origin from the occasion which provoked it and from the memory. Thus past, present and future are strung together, as it were, on the thread of the wish that runs through them." Marlow suffers from an Orestes complex, adoring his father and unable to cope with the horror of seeing his mother "shagged" by her lover in the Forest. The parents separate, with Mr. Marlow remaining at his job in the mine and Mrs. Marlow going with Philip to her parents in Hammersmith. When Philip confronts her with his knowledge of her adultery, she drowns herself in the Thames. Philip goes back to his father, and spends hours up a tree brooding on the "sticky betrayals" of sex; metaphorically he is still there as an adult, cut off from love by his obsession that every woman is a hateful trinity of mother, wife and whore.

But Marlow is more than just a self-righteous male puritan. He is haunted by guilt for "killing" his mother, but also for the gratuitous crime of having previously sneaked back to his schoolroom and deposited a turd on his teacher's desk. The teacher, a grotesque moral terrorist, suspects Philip of the crime; but in a moment of inspiration he accuses the class half-wit, who had earlier made a face at him. The witch hunt is on as the other children rush to corroborate Philip's story; he will go free, while Mark Binney will get "the Big Stick . . . across your behind, and in front of the whole school." Soon afterwards a strange mark appears on Philip's forearm—the mark of Cain, a first sign of his life-long psoriasis. Binney ends up in a mental hospital, turned into a "complete nutter" by the unjust punishment; Philip's adult confinement in the hospital ward is the only way he can find to atone for the events of 1945, until his psychiatrist sets him free.

The Singing Detective uses the popular music of the forties, but much less insistently and winningly than ***Pennies From Heaven.*** Its backbone is the superb evocation of Philip's childhood, touchingly re-created by Alison Steadman as Mrs. Marlow, Jim Carter as her husband, and Lyndon Davies as Philip. The parallel plots are a more mixed bag; but the series is driven along by Potter's emotional intensity and by his amazing inventiveness in shuffling together his four levels of meaning. There is no natural continuity of narrative, only a rapid flight from one mental association to another. One can imagine the story being told equally well through many different sequences of narrative elements. Nonetheless, ***The Singing Detective*** never declines into an exercise in post-modern smoke and mirrors, because its central theme is such a painfully direct exorcism of guilt, betrayal and sexual disability. Indeed, if there is a criticism to be made it is that the series ends up as a commercial for psychoanalysis, releasing its hero into a sunwashed landscape of health and marital love that is scarcely credible after the dark journey that had led up to it.

Television is the only medium that really counts for me. It is the biggest platform and you should kick and fight and bite your way into it. It's true that television is endemically a trivialising medium, but it doesn't follow that it *has* to be. Television is the true national theatre.

—Dennis Potter

The two novels Potter has written since ***The Singing Detective, Ticket To Ride*** (1986) and ***Blackeyes*** (1987), also deal with the construction of identity from spare parts of real or imagined experience. In ***Ticket To Ride*** the hero is a commercial artist who retires to the country with his wife to paint what he really loves, British wildflowers; but a nervous breakdown strips him of his memory and leaves him looking for his identity among the whores of Paddington. As he puzzles out his past, it seems that his wife may have been a call girl before he met her, and that he may even have killed her before finding himself on a train to London with no identifying papers on him. ***Blackeyes,*** even more of a puzzle, uses ***The Singing Detective***'s device of presenting parallel texts that are as confusedly intertwined as snakes in a basket. The anti-hero of the book is Maurice Kingsley, a has-been novelist; like Sir John Betjeman in real life, he is still fixated on his childhood teddy-bear. Just when everyone has written him off he triumphs with a novel, *Sugar Bush,* that he wrote by picking the brains of his niece Jessica, a former model. At the end, the unnamed author of ***Blackeyes*** stuffs Kingsley and Jessica back into the text and kills them off—while the model "Blackeyes" escapes from the story into a happy life in the "real" world.

Both novels leave an impression of being work for the left hand, despite the skill with which Potter juggles his *trompe l'oeil* plots. His moral target here is contemporary Thatcherite London, where the old genteel classes rub shoulders with the new opportunists. For all Potter's loathing of this milieu, his barbs often glance off its hard and shiny surface. The British class system is a constant preoccupation in his work; but his roots and loyalties are best seen at the first line of conflict, where the working class encounters the repressive respectability of the lower middle class. ***Ticket to Ride*** and ***Blackeyes*** also lack the taproot into the past that reveals the deep continuity between child and man. Finally, one must recognize that in the collaborative art of television Potter's scripts have profited from Britain's tremendous wealth of talent in acting and production. A final judgment on ***Blackeyes,*** at least, should be reserved for Potter's forthcoming adaptation of it for TV.

Meanwhile Potter has also written ***Christabel,*** a 1988 series for the BBC. Here the problem is not any slightness of theme, but rather the problem of how to represent, on the small screen, an overwhelming historical reality. In 1978 Potter wrote a savage review of the American mini-series *Holocaust,* in which he argued that commercial television is intrinsically disqualified from showing past horrors with decency. ***Christabel*** tries to strip Nazism of the *kitsch* that has adhered to it over the decades. Here, we see it simply as a political movement that tested the conscience of the average German in many small matters of daily life. There are no apocalyptic scenes of battle or atrocity, except as they are conveyed by the stories of people who were there, or as they are seen in fragments: a bombed street, an encounter with a SS man in a railway carriage, a village lad being taken round the corner to be shot. Potter seems to have throttled down his imagination to follow as closely as possible the memoirs of the actual Christabel Bielenberg, an upper-class Englishwoman who married a German in the thirties. But ***Christabel*** lacks the cumulative detail and cultural authority achieved by the West German series *Heimat* in covering similar ground. Representing the Black Forest (where Christabel took refuge in 1943-45) as a middle-European Forest of Dean, populated by peasants with rustic English accents, only confuses the question of national guilt. There is a universal concern, it is true, with what Christabel calls "that silver thread [of conscience] which must run through people's lives, ruling how far they should go and no further." But conscience in Nazi Germany was exercised within specific terms imposed by history. German guilt over the extermination of Jews, gypsies and homosexuals cannot be crudely equated with, say, British guilt over the saturation bombing of civilians (though the latter also needs to be brought to account—which Christabel is more ready to do in her book than Potter in his script).

Christabel still has its powerful moments, when it matches Bielenberg's aim in her very impressive book: to look out, with decency and precision, at the myriad small-scale moral decisions that steered Germany through its national crisis. But too much of the series reverses that point of view, looking in *at* Christabel instead of looking out *with* her. Continual lingering views of the highlighted face of Elizabeth Hurley—appealing as she may be in her nubile ingenuousness—are so many diversions from the true centre of the story: the question of how these events came to happen. The problem of evil is treated most directly by Potter in ***Joe's Ark*** (1974), where a devout Welsh nonconformist must watch his eighteen-year-old daughter die of cancer. Potter can be bitterly contemptuous of "the dishonesty or special pleading which is, alas, so characteristic of demoralised Christians." Yet he has also testified to his journey, in the seventies, from "an in-turned spiritual nihilism and on towards a new and (for me) starting but exhilarating trust in the order of things." Dramatizing the ultimate horrors of our century, ***Christabel*** simply places moral contradictions face to face, without any presumption by the author that *he* is able to resolve them. In one scene added by Potter to Bielenberg's narrative, a rabbi advances on an SS officer like a figure of judgment, crying at him: "God sees what you do!" The rabbi is promptly shot and dumped into a mass grave with his fellow victims. In another scene, a children's choir singing "Silent Night" is crosscut with the piano-wire hanging of those who conspired against Hitler in 1944, as if the children's seraphic gazes are turned on *that.* Does God see the same things that man sees, or does he turn his face away from them? There is a mystery worth dwelling on in ***Christabel***—the same mystery, finally, as the one pondered by that nine-year-old boy in his tree, in the Forest of Dean, in 1945: "When I grow up, everything ool be *all right.* Won't it, God? . . . When I grow up, I be going to be—*a detective.* . . . I'll find out. I'll find out who did it!"

Julie Salamon (review date 13 February 1992)

SOURCE: "A Painter's Descent into Sick Fantasy," in *The Wall Street Journal,* February 13, 1992, p. A17.

[*In the following review, Salamon praises* Secret Friends *as a beautiful "twisted joke."*]

Secret Friends is the perfect movie for people who hate Valentine's Day. In this unnerving portrait of sick love Alan Bates plays a middle-aged man who can no longer distinguish between his fantasy life and the real thing—mainly because he's spent such a long time propping up reality with make-believe.

But this is no dense psychological study in any conventional sense. This is the film directing debut of Dennis Potter, whose unique, darkly comic sensibility has been developed mainly in British television shows like ***Pennies From Heaven*** and ***The Singing Detective***. Mr. Potter has written novels as well, and several film scripts, including the American film version of ***Pennies From Heaven*** and ***Dreamchild.***

Mr. Potter's work has always revealed a fascination with glossy American pop culture of the 1930s. He understands the power of that breezily sentimental music that gave people a way to express feelings that seemed impossibly romantic given the troubles the real world had to offer. He's also terribly cynical about the possibilities of non-fantasy relationships.

In this first feature, which he also wrote, Mr. Potter tells the story of a man named John whose idea of romance is a very special one. He's convinced his very young wife that they need to pretend that she was a prostitute when they met. He has become dependent on this notion, and so has she. She consents to make believe that sex between them is a financial transaction. Their "foreplay" consists of her pretending they've agreed on a price, then saying, "Whatever else you may care to give me is a personal transaction between you and me."

But she's grown tired of the game, afraid of it. She and her husband have begun to hate themselves and one another for basing their lust and affection on a nasty fiction. In fact, they'd like to kill one another—or someone. Also, he's become impossible to live with in more prosaic ways. He gets furious at her for playing music too loudly.

This may be the stuff of a psychological thriller, but Mr. Potter plays it as a twisted joke—a very stylish one at that. The movie is very pretty and bright, punctuated by images of a nightclub combo playing music that sounds very much like '30s jazz (but which was cleverly composed for the picture by Nicholas Russell-Pavier). The camera work is spirited and wonderfully composed, the work of Sue Gibson, whose first film was recently released, *Hear My Song.*

Mr. Potter pops in and out of John's head, filling the screen with his real life and memories as well as his fake ones, and you're never sure which is which. The story is literally a journey into John's psyche. He's traveling on a train—a very nice train, in a first-class dining car. He can't remember who he is, but starts to figure it out in flashes.

We learn that John is a painter of wildflowers and that he paints in the airy, handsome attic studio of his lovely home. He looks like what he is, the well-heeled country squire.

But the creator of these pretty, pristine drawings dreams of killing his wife, and is consumed by self-loathing. He is actually very repulsive, a man filled with bitterness, especially toward women. With his fleshy face and fake dark hair, Mr. Bates immediately gets across John's creepiness. The miracle of his performance is that he makes John bearable and frequently morbidly funny.

His fantasies are wide-ranging. They go back to his childhood as the son of a country minister with a mean spirit. He taught his son about wildflowers but as subjects of cruel quizzing. In John's dreams, his mother simply sat and watched, knitting. His refuge was his "secret friend," the inner voice that allowed him to rebel.

You start to understand why John views all physical pleasure as gross. People eating beautifully arranged food look piggish. John stares down at his dining-car lunch in shock and wonders why he's sitting there with a dead fish in front of him. When he unwraps a chocolate in a hotel room he eats it with a sickening, violent frenzy. When he touches his wife, dressed in prim, comfortable clothes, he must imagine her with long red fingernails and an electric blue dress slit all the way up her thigh.

Gina Bellman has the right looks for Helen, his wife—sexy and neurotic. She's quite believable as the confused object of John's fantasy life, but has a tendency toward overdoing it. Her eyes bulge a bit too anxiously.

As John drifts in and out of his inner ruminations, he notices that the two businessmen sitting across from him in the train's diner are watching him. When he notices them noticing him, he incorporates them into his fantasy life; they become characters in his mental flashes. These two are hilarious, obviously appalled at the rudeness of this man daring to have a nervous breakdown while they're trying to have lunch.

Additional coverage of Potter's life and career is contained in the following sources published by Gale Research: *Contemporary Authors,* Vols. 107, 145; *Contemporary Authors New Revision Series,* Vol. 33; *Contemporary Literary Criticism,* Vol. 58; and *Major 20th-Century Writers.*

Obituaries

In addition to the authors represented in the In Memoriam section of the *Yearbook*, the following notable writers died during 1994:

Lindsay Gordon Anderson
April 17, 1923—August 30, 1994
Indian-born British film and stage director

The director of such films as *This Sporting Life* (1963), *If...* (1969), and *O Lucky Man!* (1973), Anderson was a proponent of the British "Free Cinema" movement which emphasized the artist's responsibility toward society and the individual. In his manifesto article "Stand Up! Stand Up!" (1956) Anderson lashed out at critics and filmmakers, urging them to develop a greater social consciousness and focus on "the significance of the everyday" in their work. For example, in *This Sporting Life* Anderson attacked the emotionally repressive structures of British society, while in *If...* he condemned the British public school system for stifling the creative development of students. Also a documentary filmmaker, Anderson won an Academy award for *Thursday Children* (1953), which concerns a school for deaf children. More recently Anderson directed *The Whales of August* (1987), which starred Lillian Gish and Bette Davis. [For further information on Anderson's life and career, see *CLC,* Volume 20.]

Robert Albert Bloch
April 5, 1917—September 23, 1994
American novelist, short story writer, and screenwriter

Best known as the author of *Psycho* (1959), the novel which served as the basis for the film by Alfred Hitchcock, Bloch wrote over twenty novels, hundreds of short stories, and numerous film and television scripts in a variety of genres, including mystery, horror, science fiction, fantasy, and humor. Bloch, who sold his first short story to the pulp fiction magazine *Weird Tales* when he was seventeen, was inspired and encouraged to write in his early teens by master horror writer H. P. Lovecraft, with whom he corresponded and developed a lifelong friendship. Bloch earned his living for many years contributing stories to pulp magazines and writing scripts for various horror films and for such television series as *Alfred Hitchcock Presents* and *Star Trek*. Described by writer Harlan Ellison as "the kindest, gentlest human being who ever lived," Bloch befriended and encouraged many young writers in addition to Ellison who have since become famous, notably Stephen King and Ray Bradbury. Arguing that Bloch was attracted to dark, sinister themes and characters because they "were so utterly alien to him," Ellison concluded that Bloch "was surely on a level with Poe." [For further information on Bloch's life and career, see *CLC,* Volume 33.]

Charles Bukowski
August 16, 1920—March 9, 1994
German-born American poet, short story writer, novelist, and screenwriter

A prolific and seminal figure in underground literature, Bukowski is best known for writings in which he caustically indicted bourgeois American society while celebrating the lives of alcoholics, prostitutes, decadent writers, and other desperate characters in and around Los Angeles. In his early poems, for example those collected in *Longshot Pomes for Broke Players* (1962), Bukowski introduced his characteristic protagonist: the unstudied, self-exiled poet who rejects the public and the literary world in order to maintain his freedom and uniqueness as a writer; such subsequent collections as *Poems Written before Jumping out of an 8-story Window* (1968) and *Fire Station* (1970) deal in concrete, realistic terms with acts of rape, sodomy, deceit, and violence, focusing in particular on male-female relationships characterized by physical and emotional abuse. Like his poetry, Bukowski's fiction is considered largely autobiographical and has been both praised and vilified by critics. For example, while some commentators find his short story collections *Notes of a Dirty Old Man* (1969) and *Erections, Ejaculations, Exhibitions, and General Tales of Ordinary Madness* (1972) misogynistic and formulaic, others laud them as pointed analyses of the short-sightedness, pettiness, and spiritual bankruptcy of American society. Bukowski is also known for the novels *Post Office* (1971), *Factotum* (1975), *Ham on Rye* (1982), and *Barfly* (1984), all of which concern Henry Chinaski, a hardened alcoholic. Bukowski wrote the screenplay for the 1987 film version of *Barfly,* which featured Faye Dunaway and Mickey Rourke, and was directed by Barbet Schroeder. [For further information on Bukowski's life and career, see *CLC,* Volumes 2, 5, 9, 41, and 82.]

Amy Clampitt
June 15, 1920—September 10, 1994
American poet, essayist, and editor

Clampitt is known as a poetic stylist whose verse is characterized by vivid, baroque vocabulary, intricate syntax, attention to detail, and revealing metaphors. In her first full-length book, *Kingfisher* (1983), published when she was sixty-three, Clampitt combined a focus on nature with musings on life, death, and love. *What the Light Was Like* (1985), her critically acclaimed second collection of poetry, focuses on images of light and dark, and has been compared to the work of John Keats. Her other works include *Multitudes, Multitudes* (1974) and *Archaic Figure* (1987). [For further information on Clampitt's life and work, see *CLC*, Volume 32.]

James Edmund Du Maresq Clavell
October 10, 1925—September 6, 1994
English-born American novelist, screenwriter, film director,
and author of children's books

Clavell is known primarily for his best-selling novel *Shōgun* (1975) and his other fictional works that focus on East Asian customs, history, and economic and political power struggles. Clavell worked as a screenwriter in the 1950s and 1960s; his most notable work included writing *The Fly* (1958) and writing, directing, and producing *To Sir with Love* (1967). Although it was immensely popular with general readers, *Shōgun* received mixed reviews from specialists. For example, Asian historian Henry Smith lauded the novel for "[conveying] more information about Japan to more people than all the combined writings of scholars, journalists and novelists since the Pacific War." Other scholars and critics, however, questioned the authenticity of Clavell's portrait of feudal Japan and accused him of willfully distorting reality and sensationalizing history. In response, Clavell stated that he has "played with history—the where and how and who and why and when of it—to suit my own reality and, perhaps, to tell the real history of what came to pass." [For further information on Clavell's life and career, see *CLC,* Volumes 6, 25, and 87.]

Erik Homburger Erikson
June 15, 1902—May 12, 1994
German-born American psychoanalyst, writer, and biographer

Erikson was one of the most influential psychoanalysts of the twentieth century. Although he studied under Sigmund and Anna Freud, he developed his own theory of human psychological development and was one of the first to explain how societal and cultural influences might contribute to an individual's emotional life. Retaining the Freudian concept of the ego, Erikson theorized that human development follows a series of eight predetermined stages. He believed that each stage is characterized by a particular crisis and that the resolution of each crisis substantially contributes to the individual's personality. These ideas are explored in such works as *Childhood and Society* (1950), *Identity and the Life Cycle* (1967), and *The Life Cycle Completed: A Review* (1982). Erikson is also known for his books *Gandhi's Truth: On the Origins of Militant Non-violence* (1969), which won both a National Book Award and the Pulitzer Prize, and *Young Man Luther: A Study in Psychoanalysis and History* (1958), his renowned and controversial "psychobiography" of Martin Luther. His own belief in nonviolent political activism, as well as his views on the nature of personal and professional crises, was tested when he chose to resign from the University of California in 1950 rather than sign a statement of loyalty during a period of intense anti-Communist sentiment. In 1987 the Erik Erikson Center was founded at the medical center of Harvard University, from which Erikson retired as professor emeritus in 1970.

Albert Goldman
April 15, 1927—March 28, 1994
American biographer, critic, educator, and editor

Goldman was best known for his controversial biographies of pop music icons Elvis Presley and John Lennon. Published in 1981, *Elvis* portrayed the rock legend as selfish, lazy, greedy, and addicted to drugs and food. Responding to charges of self-indulgence and character assassination, Goldman insisted that his portrait of Presley maintained a scrupulous fidelity to the facts of his subject's life; critic Roy Blount, Jr. described *Elvis* as a "morbidly fascinating biography." Goldman's book on ex-Beatle John Lennon, *The Lives of John Lennon* (1988), met with similar censure for its negative and judgmental portrayal of Lennon's later years. A one-time English professor who shifted his attention to contemporary popular culture, Goldman's other writings include *Ladies and Gentlemen, Lenny Bruce!* (1974), *Carnival at Rio* (1978), *Grass Roots: Marijuana in America Today* (1979), *Disco* (1979), *Sound Bites* (1992), and an unfinished biography of rock singer Jim Morrison.

Clement Greenberg
January 16, 1909—May 7, 1994
American critic and editor

One of the most widely-known and respected American art critics of this century, Greenberg came to prominence in the 1950s as an impassioned advocate for the works of Jackson Pollock and other members of the Abstract Expressionist movement. He began his career art in criticism in the 1930s as a regular contributor to the famous left-wing periodical *Partisan Review,* the forum for what would later be known as the "New York Intellectuals" school. Greenberg championed the work of Pollock—whose unique "drip" method of applying paint to monumental canvases was originally met with skepticism and confusion—at a time when the artist was earning little money on the Works Progress Administration Federal Arts Project. Greenberg's influence on the American art scene extended beyond his writings—he was a personal friend of numerous artists and frequently visited their studios to comment on work in progress. Although he published little after the early 1960s, Greenberg remained a venerable figure in the art world until his death.

Lewis M. Grizzard, Jr.
October 20, 1946—March 20, 1994
American journalist and nonfiction writer

A nationally syndicated columnist who spent most of his journalistic career at *The Atlanta Journal-Constitution*, Grizzard was the author of twenty books, most of them humorous observations of his own life that bore such striking titles as *Elvis Is Dead, and I Don't Feel So Good Myself* (1984), *Don't Bend Over in the Garden, Granny, You Know Them Taters Got Eyes* (1988), and *Chili Dawgs Always Bark at Night* (1989). Grizzard began his career as the sports editor of a local paper while he was attending the University of Georgia. Hired by *The Atlanta Journal* soon after he graduated, he became the executive sports editor when he was twenty-three. Plagued by a congenital defect of the aorta, Grizzard underwent several heart surgeries. *They Tore Out My Heart and Stomped That Sucker Flat* (1982), about his first operation, was his best-selling book.

Joan Mary Harrison
June 20, 1909—August 14, 1994
English screenwriter and film producer

Harrison began her career in film as secretary to Alfred Hitchcock and soon collaborated with him on many of his best screenplays, including *Rebecca* (1940), *Foreign Correspondent* (1940), *Suspicion* (1941), and *Saboteur* (1942). One of the few female producers in Hollywood, Harrison produced films by such noted directors as Robert Siodmak (*Phantom Lady*, 1944) and Jacques Tourneur (*Circle of Danger*, 1950). Film scholar Jeanine Basinger has noted that "all of Harrison's films have these qualities in common: excellent women characters, who are frequently intrepid in their response to danger and death; a low-key, subtle suggestion of violence rather than overt blood and gore; and excellent production values, with handsome sets and modish costumes." Harrison produced the acclaimed television series *Alfred Hitchcock Presents* from 1953 to 1964. She was married to spy novelist Eric Ambler.

Ely Jacques Kahn, Jr.
December 4, 1916—May 28, 1994
American journalist, nonfiction writer, biographer, and autobiographer

A staff writer for *The New Yorker* since 1937, Kahn wrote twenty-seven books and is credited with inventing the biographical profile article. Beginning with *The New Yorker* while he was still a senior at Harvard University, Kahn became the magazine's war correspondent during World War II and the Korean War. His military experiences resulted in three books, *The Army Life* (1942), *The Peculiar War* (1952), and *The Stragglers* (1962); in this last work, Kahn related stories of Japanese soldiers who continued to live in jungles and "fight" for many years after the Korean War ended. Kahn was an inveterate traveler and wrote many articles and books on places in Asia and Africa. His most famous writings, however, were his *New Yorker* profiles of such unique individuals as the King of Morocco, Frank Sinatra, David Rockefeller, and Joe Pepitone. Kahn made these articles one of the most prominent and popular features of *The New Yorker*.

Robert Edwin Lee
October 15, 1918—July 8, 1994
American dramatist, scriptwriter, and screenwriter

Lee is best known for *Inherit the Wind* (1955). Written in collaboration with Lee's longtime partner, Jerome Lawrence, *Inherit the Wind* is a fictionalized account of the famous "Scopes monkey trial," which focused on the teaching of Darwinian evolution and Biblical creationism in American schools. Lee and Lawrence were also responsible for the drama *The Night Thoreau Spent in Jail* (1970), another reconstruction of American historical events. Other popular plays, movies, and musicals that Lee produced include *Look Ma, I'm Dancin'* (1948), *Auntie Mame* (1956), and *First Monday in October* (1975). Prior to his death, Lee finished a novel about General Robert E. Lee, to whom he was not related.

Leonid Maximovich Leonov
June 1, 1899—August 8, 1994
Russian novelist and playwright

A writer of considerable fame and importance in Soviet Russia, Leonov's novels and plays are notable for their pro-Soviet Socialist stance. Although his earliest works, including *Konets melkogo cheloveka* (1922; *The End of Insignificant Man*) and *Barsuki* (1924; *The Badgers*), reflect the influences of Honoré de Balzac and Fyodor Dostoevsky and garnered international acclaim, Leonov's later works have been faulted for slavishly reflecting the official Soviet demand for "socialist realism" in all art works. Nevertheless, some critics point to *Sot* (1930; *Soviet River*), *Skutarevsky* (1932), and *Russkiy les* (1953; *The Russian Forest*), an allegory some view as an attack on Stalin's purges, as examples of how Leonov used the conventions of "socialist realism" to disguise his true objections to Soviet policies. Leonov received many prestigious Soviet awards and honors, including the Lenin Prize on four separate occasions. He also remained an active and influential member of the Soviet Academies of Science and Writers, and was a deputy of the U.S.S.R. Supreme Soviet from 1946 to 1970.

Richard Milhous Nixon
January 9, 1913—April 22, 1994
American politician, memoirist, and nonfiction writer

Nixon was one of the United States's most controversial presidents—the only one forced to resign under threat of impeachment. Originally a lawyer, he entered Congress in the 1940s, serving as senator from California and later as vice president to Dwight D. Eisenhower. In 1968 Nixon was elected president. His administration was praised for several achievements in foreign affairs: notably opening relations with Communist China and establishing détente with the Soviet Union; eventually ending U.S. involvement in the Vietnam War; and for brokering an Arab-Israeli peace accord. However, Nixon's accomplishments are invariably discussed in relation to the "Watergate" scandal that brought his administration down: the arrest of Republican-sponsored burglars who attempted to steal documents from and plant listening devices in the Democratic National Committee headquarters in the Watergate building during his second term. The hearings that followed exposed the corruption of high-ranking White House officials and implicated the president in illegal activities. In retirement, Nixon wrote his autobiography, *RN: The Memoirs of Richard Nixon* (1978), and a number of books on foreign and domestic affairs, including *The Real War* (1980), *Real Peace* (1983), *No More Vietnams* (1985) and *In the Arena: A Memoir of Victory, Defeat and Renewal* (1990). His later years were characterized by increasing public visibility and the attempt to refurbish his persona and his place in history. Public opinion toward him began to thaw, and at his death his contributions to world peace were emphasized.

Michael O'Donoghue
January 5, 1940—November 9, 1994
American television writer, screenwriter, and humorist

Best known for his work as a writer and occasional performer on the television series *Saturday Night Live* during the mid-1970s, O'Donoghue perfected a mordant and sometimes shocking brand of humor that has since proved highly influential. Starting out as a freelance writer for underground avant-garde magazines in the 1960s, he later wrote for *National Lampoon* magazine as well as the "National Lampoon Radio Hour," where he first worked with Gilda Radner, Chevy Chase, and John Belushi. O'Donoghue was one of the original writers and performers on *Saturday Night Live*, writing many of the show's most famous sketches and appearing as the infinitely cynical character Mr. Mike, whose "Least Loved Bedtime Stories" were gruesome and disillusioning tales for children. His screenwriting credits include *Mr. Mike's Mondo Video* (1979), *Gilda Live* (1980), and *Scrooged* (1988).

Juan Carlos Onetti
July 1, 1909—May 30, 1994
Uruguayan-born Spanish novelist, short story writer, poet, and editor

One of Latin America's most distinguished writers, Onetti is known for works in which he explored such themes as despair, alienation, and the realities of urban life. While not generally known outside Latin America, Onetti has been praised for his lyricism, imaginative use of language and narration, and blending of fantasy and realism. Onetti's creation of the imaginary setting of Santa Maria, which recurs in several of his novels and is said to be modeled after the Uruguayan capital of Montevideo, has also led many critics to compare him to William Faulkner, creator of fictional Yoknapatawpha County. While Onetti wrote over thirty works, only two of his novels have been translated into English, *La vida breve* (1950; *A Brief Life*) and *El astillero* (1961; *The Shipyard*). After many years of neglect, Onetti began to receive critical acclaim and attention during the 1960s. He was awarded the National Literature Prize of Uruguay in 1963 and the Jose Enrique Rodo Prize, his country's most distinguished literary award, in 1991. Onetti also won the Cervantes Prize for his contribution to literature in Spanish in 1980. After being jailed in 1974 for antagonizing Uruguay's military regime with his writings, Onetti left for Madrid in 1976. He became a Spanish citizen in 1985. [For further information on Onetti's life and work, see *CLC,* Volumes 7 and 10.]

John James Osborne
December 12, 1929—December 24, 1994
English playwright, screenwriter, and autobiographer

Famous for his first major play, *Look Back in Anger* (1956), Osborne was one of a group of playwrights known as the "Angry Young Men"—which included John Wain, Kingsley Amis, and John Braine—who initiated a new era in English theater characterized by aggressive social criticism, authentic portrayals of working-class life, and antiheroic characters. Osborne, whose father died in 1940 and whose mother was the object of his passionate, lifelong hatred, left home in his late teens to become an actor and began writing plays when he was nineteen. In addition to *Look Back in Anger*, his most famous works include *The Entertainer* (1957), written at the request of Laurence Olivier who starred as a second-rate music hall comedian; *Luther* (1961), in which Albert Finney played Martin Luther; and the Academy Award-winning screenplay for the film *Tom Jones* (1964). Notorious for his heavydrinking and irascible personality, Osborne was married five times and fathered a daughter with screenwriter and film critic Penelope Gilliat. [For further information on Osborne's life and career, see *CLC*, Volumes 1, 2, 5, 11, and 45.]

Sir Karl Raimund Popper
July 28, 1902—September 17, 1994
Austrian-born English philosopher

Known for his ideas on history, Marxism, and science, Popper is credited with providing much of the intellectual framework for the British Conservative Party under Margaret Thatcher during the 1980s. Two of his most influential works—*The Open Society and Its Enemies* (1945) and *The Poverty of Historicism* (1957)—attack Marxism and postulate that human history is not controlled by laws but rather by the unpredictable growth of knowledge. In *Logik der Forschung: Zur Erkenntnistheorie der modernen Naturwissenschaft* (1935; *The Logic of Scientific Discovery*) and *Conjectures and Refutations: The Growth of Scientific Knowledge* (1962), Popper presented his views on science, arguing that scientific theory advances not through the methodical accumulation of data but rather by an alternating process of adventurous guessing followed by rigorous testing to falsify new concepts. Born in Austria to Jewish parents, he left for New Zealand in 1937 and later moved to London, England, where he held the position of professor of Logic and Scientific Method at the London School of Economics from 1949 to 1969. He was knighted in 1965.

John Preston
December 11, 1945—April 27, 1994
American novelist, short story writer, nonfiction writer, and editor

Founder of the Gay House Inc. and Gay Community Services of Minneapolis, Preston was editor of the national gay and lesbian newspaper *The Advocate* from 1975 to 1976 before deciding to write full time. Among his best known fictional works are the 1983 novel about an aging homosexual entitled *Franny, the Queen of Provincetown* (1983); the short story collection *I Once Had a Master, and Other Tales of Erotic Love* (1984); and numerous mass-market paperback novels published under various pseudonyms. His nonfiction includes *Safe Sex: The Ultimate Erotic Guide* (1987), which he authored with Glenn Swann, and *Personal Dispatches: Writers Confront AIDS* (1989), which he edited.

Richard McClure Scarry
June 5, 1919—April 30, 1994
American author and illustrator of children's books

An extraordinarily prolific and popular children's author, Scarry wrote over 200 books that have sold more than 100 million copies and been translated into thirty languages. After studying drawing at the Boston Museum School and serving in the army during World War II, Scarry began illustrating books for other authors. His first major success as both author and illustrator was with *Richard Scarry's Best Word Book Ever* (1963), which defines and depicts over 1400 words and objects. His wife Patricia has explained that he "considered himself an educator more than anything."

Randy Shilts
August 8, 1951—February 17, 1994
American journalist and nonfiction writer

Known as the first openly gay journalist at a major American newspaper, Shilts is credited with focusing national attention on Acquired Immunodeficiency Syndrome (AIDS) and other more strictly gay-related issues through his writing in *The San Francisco Chronicle* and his book-length study, *And the Band Played On* (1987), a history of America's response to the AIDS epidemic. Both this study and Shilts's *Conduct Unbecoming* (1993) are considered highly influential documents in the movement to promote equal rights for gays and lesbians. Cleve Jones, founder of the Names Project that produced the AIDS quilt, asserted that Shilts's writings are "without question the most important works of literature affecting gay people." [For further information on Shilts's life and career, see *CLC*, Volume 85.]

John Innes Mackintosh Stewart
September 30, 1906—November 12, 1994
British novelist, short story writer, critic, and educator

A prolific and popular author of sophisticated mystery novels, J. I. M. Stewart was also respected for his chronicles of the erudite social milieu of Oxford University, where he was a English professor for many years. Among his most notable works are his "A Staircase in Surrey" quintet, which presents an endearing autobiographical portrait of his eccentric and creative associates at Oxford, and a series of mysteries featuring the resourceful and learned Inspector Sir John Appleby. In addition to his highly popular autobiographical and mystery novels, Stewart was a respected scholar whose critical studies of Rudyard Kipling, Joseph Conrad, and Thomas Hardy received praise from numerous reviewers. In addition, his *Eight Modern Writers* (1963), the fifteenth volume in the "Oxford History of English Literature" series, was widely praised for its balanced and authoritative expository analysis of early twentieth-century English literature. [For further information on Stewart's life and career, see *CLC*, Volumes 7, 14, and 32.]

Julian Gustave Symons
May 30, 1912—November 19, 1994
English novelist, short story writer, poet, editor, historian, critic, biographer, and radio and television writer

Well regarded as a poet, critic, and biographer, Symons is best known as the author of several highly praised crime novels, including *The Color of Murder* (1957), *The Progress of a Crime* (1960), and *The Man Who Killed Himself* (1967). Born to Russian-Jewish immigrant parents in London, Symons wrote romantic, Trotskyite poetry before World War II. After serving in the British army, he worked in advertising and then reviewed books for the *Manchester Evening News*. The publication of his first crime novel, *The Immaterial Murder Case* (1945), marked the beginning of his long and prolific literary career, which included many esteemed nonfiction works, notably *Bloody Murder* (1972), a study of the crime genre, and *The Tell-Tale Heart: The Life and Works of Edgar Allan Poe* (1978). In 1976 Symons succeeded Agatha Christie as president of the Detection Club. [For further information on Symons's life and career, see *CLC*, Volumes 2, 14, and 32.]

Mary TallMountain
1918—September 2, 1994
American poet, essayist, and short story writer

A Native American writer of Russian and Athabascan descent, TallMountain is best known for her poetry collection *There Is No Word for Goodbye* (1981), winner of a 1982-83 Pushcart Prize, and her *The Light on the Tent Wall: A Bridging* (1990), a volume of essays, poems, and short stories. Her works incorporate her interest in Christian and Native spirituality, imagery and symbols drawn from her Athabascan heritage and childhood in rural Alaska, and her belief in humanity's need to remember the past and commune with the natural world. She is also the author of the verse collection *A Quick Brush of Wings* (1991).

Mai Elisabeth Zetterling
May 24, 1925—March 15, 1994
Swedish actress, film director, screenwriter, novelist, autobiographer, short story writer, and author of children's literature

Internationally acclaimed for her acting in such films as Alf Sjoberg's *Hets* (1947; *Torment*) and, most recently, Nicholas Roeg's *The Witches* (1990), Zetterling was also a highly accomplished filmmaker and author. Beginning in the 1960s, she made several documentaries dealing with northern European political and social issues. Her first fiction film, the fifteen-minute antiwar movie *The War Game* (1963), won the Gold Lion award at the Venice Film Festival. As a director of feature films, which include *Alskande par* (1964; *Loving Couples*), *Nattlek* (1966; *Night Games*), *Scrubbers* (1983), and *Amorosa* (1986), she explored loneliness, obsession, feminine sexuality, and the role of women in society. As an author, Zetterling received much acclaim for the autobiographical volume *All Those Tomorrows* (1985), her short stories, and her children's books, in particular, *The Rain's Hat* (1978), which she adapted and directed for television. When she died, Zetterling was directing a film based on her screenplay *The Woman Who Cleaned the World.*

Topics in Literature: 1994

Electronic "Books": Hypertext and Hyperfiction

INTRODUCTION

With the development of CD-Rom technology and the transfer of such reference works as encyclopedias and dictionaries to compact disc, much recent debate among publishers and software producers has centered on the future of books as bound volumes of text printed on paper and their possible eclipse by CD-Rom and other electronic formats. Contending that books are outdated and cumbersome, proponents of CD-Rom stress that the physical space to information ratio is much higher for CD-Roms and that CD-Roms offer sound, moving pictures, and instantaneous cross-referencing capabilities unmatched by books. Proponents of books, however, note that the traditional book is much more durable and easy to transport than CD-Roms, which require a computer; that many of the searching capabilities available with electronic texts are not very useful; and that sales of CD-Roms, despite their hype, have rarely met expectations. Defenders of the traditional book see few advantages to reading literature on a computer screen versus paper.

A small but growing number of writers are developing a new genre of fictional works—known as hyperfictions—that exploit the hypertextual capabilities of computers and can only be read in an electronic format. Hypertext, briefly defined, is a system of electronically linked blocks of text that are not designed to be read in any particular sequential order. For instance, Stuart Moulthrop's hyperfictive novel about the Gulf War, *Victory Garden* (1993), features nearly one thousand blocks of text with approximately two thousand eight hundred different links between them. The reader of hyperfiction decides in what order the text will be read by selecting from a set of options attached to each block of text. Critics of hyperfiction note that the new genre challenges the traditional view of reading as a linear process, promotes multiple readings of works, and encourages associative thinking. In addition to creating new works, some scholars have identified ways in which hypertext can be used in the reading and study of traditional works of literature. For instance, hypertext might aid a student reading John Milton's *Paradise Lost* (1667) by providing quick and easily accessible explanations of allusions and references in the text. Commenting on the impact of hypertext capabilities on canonized works, Jay David Bolter has stated: "Rather than eliminating works of the past or making them irrelevant, the electronic writing space gives them a new 'typography.' For hypertext is the typography of the electronic medium."

REPRESENTATIVE WORKS OF HYPERFICTION DISCUSSED BELOW

Gibson, William, and Ashbaugh, Dennis
Agrippa (A Book of the Dead) 1993
Guyer, Carolyn
"Izme Pass" [with Martha Petry] 1991
Quibbling 1993
Humphrey, Clark
The Perfect Couple 1993
Joyce, Michael
Afternoon, a Story 1987
"WOE" 1991
Larsen, Deena
Marble Springs 1993
Malloy, Judy
Its Name Was Penelope 1993
McDaid, John
Uncle Buddy's Phantom Funhouse 1993
Moran, Monica
Ambulance: An Electronic Novel 1993
Moulthrop, Stuart
Victory Garden 1993
Roach, Greg, and Crossley, David
The Madness of Roland 1993
Swigart, Rob
Portal 1986

BOOKS VERSUS CD-ROMS

Sarah Lyall (essay date 14 August 1994)

SOURCE: "Are These Books, or What? CD-ROM and the Literary Industry," in *The New York Times Book Review,* August 14, 1994, pp. 3, 20-1.

[*In the following essay, Lyall discusses the future of books and CD-Roms.*]

This spring William H. Gates, the plugged-in chairman of the Microsoft Corporation and a man who lives for his computer, announced that he wanted to publish a definitive 300-page discussion of his views on the information revolution—where it had been and where it was going. But when it came time to choose a format, Mr. Gates rejected the familiar tools of his trade: on-line services, floppy disks, CD-ROM's, all the hardware and all the software. He turned to a technology that has been around since the mid-15th century. He decided to sell his book as a book.

You can't get more conventional. Books are cunning and resilient creatures. They have survived world wars and revolutions and totalitarian regimes and the waxing and waning of other media, including magazines, newspapers, radio, movies, videos, records, tapes, compact disks and television. Whenever their end was predicted, books managed to defy their own death sentences and spring back to life. Books have persevered so effectively, in fact, that in 1993 more of them were sold in the United States than in any year before, $18 billion worth.

But at no time since 1450, when Johann Gutenberg introduced books to the masses by fashioning the first printing press using movable type, has the book business been at such a confusing and potentially treacherous juncture. Publishers are still competing for a share of an increasingly distracted public's attention. But now they are also struggling over control of their own industry, and over the definition of what a book is. The competition is coming not from other forms of entertainment, but from computer and software companies that are experimenting with new formats: books on CD-ROM, books on floppy disk, books that can be read on a portable personal computer using a little card and some batteries, books that incorporate voices, music and movies, books that fly wholly or in parts through on-line services and arrive directly on screen.

For publishing executives from the old school, this translates into a heady time of trying to decide how much to embrace the new technology, or even (for some) whether to embrace it at all. They are scared, and they should be, considering the type of advice they're hearing from non-publishers like Gregory Rawlins, a computer science professor at Indiana University. "If you're not part of the steam-roller," he told a group of university press publishers recently, "you're part of the road."

Predictions of the imminent death of serious publishing are old news. But they've gained more urgency in recent years, as more and more once-autonomous publishers find themselves tiny specks on the balance sheet of some huge entertainment conglomerate that also owns record companies, television stations, movie studios and sports teams. People are getting hired and fired; divisions are being bought, sold and folded; publishers are starting "new media" departments that combine books with other forms of media, and serious books seem to be selling fewer copies than ever, supplanted by one-shot celebrity biographies and sure-fire genre books. And into this volatile environment have entered companies that seek to question publishers' raisons d'être and the very notion of what defines a book. Is a book, they ask, a collection of words fashioned into a poem or a narrative or a play printed on paper, bound with a cover, opened and closed at will and stored on a shelf with others of its kind, as has been done for 500 years? Or is a book the ideas contained within, regardless of their format? Can you stack them up and put them in a CD rack? Can you put them on a tiny little credit card, insert the card in a portable computer and read them on a screen? Can you add music and video? "We only invest in the creation of one product here, the book," said Jack Romanos, the president of the consumer group at Simon & Schuster. "But the book's gone in five different directions."

What matters is content, Mr. Romanos said, something publishers have in spades. The question is how to put it to use. "In the past, you said, 'What sort of book, how many pages, what's the trim size, what's the market?' " said Nancy Dickinson, the director of advanced media at HarperCollins. "Now you say, 'How would this idea work if I could see video or hear sound? How would this make it more accessible and a richer experience for the customer?' "

For traditional publishers, so steeped in old habits that many editors still regularly edit manuscripts on paper (even when the author turns in a version on disk), evolving into something different looks to be a bumpy and confusing proposition. Though Ms. Dickinson's department has counterparts at every big book publisher in New York, new media divisions tend to consist of a small band of computer literates preaching to the company's uninitiated, resistant masses. Publishers are stubbornly holding on to electronic rights in case their books go electronic, and most large companies have already produced half a dozen or so general interest multimedia titles on CD-ROM or floppy disk. But they're not sure what the future will require.

One thing that does seem clear is that in the lucrative academic and reference markets, new media are quickly overtaking traditional books, and for good reason. Consider the Encyclopaedia Britannica. The complete set costs more than $1,500, weighs 118 pounds and takes up more than four feet of shelf space. A commensurate encyclopedia on CD-ROM—Microsoft's Encarta, for instance—costs $99.99, holds up to 650 megabytes of data, weighs under an ounce, and could fit in your purse. And it's rich with extras. Look up Beethoven, for instance, and the text of the regular entry appears on your screen. Click your mouse and you can listen to a 30-second snippet from the Ninth Symphony. Click again and you can learn how Wagner was influenced by Beethoven, and hear the results. Look up Edvard Munch, click your mouse and see a high-resolution version of *The Scream* appear on your screen.

It's the same with dictionaries. Looking up a word in, say, the Oxford English Dictionary requires hauling an unwieldy volume down from a shelf and then hauling another volume down, too, if the first definition piqued your interest in a new word somewhere else. For the condensed version of the dictionary, the only one most people can afford, you need a magnifying glass to read the type. But all the volumes can fit on a single CD-ROM, which can store up to 300,000 pages of text and do cross-referencing in a flash.

Donald Norman, who founded the department of cognitive science at the University of California, San Diego, and who now holds Apple Computer's highest research position, said: "Within 10 years, dictionaries will essentially all be electronic. They will win because they offer ease of access and readability."

Books on floppy disk are useful for quick cross-referencing. And with its video and audio components, the CD-ROM also lends itself naturally to other reference works, books that teach you, for instance, how to adjust the brakes on your Trans Am, install a shelf in the basement, learn American Sign Language, plant a rosebush, truss a chicken, or search through thousands of choices to find a film to rent on Sunday night. Companies like Byron Preiss Multimedia, which began as a conventional book packager, are beginning to take traditional titles and make them reference works. A forthcoming CD-ROM based on John Steinbeck's *Grapes of Wrath* allows readers to see photographs that inspired Steinbeck, a map of the Joad family's route through Oklahoma and video interviews with people in Steinbeck's life. Somewhere in there lurks the novel's text, which seems almost beside the point next to the souped-up new features. But Byron Preiss himself insists that *The Grapes of Wrath* on CD-ROM will never supplant *The Grapes of Wrath,* the book. "It doesn't replace the experience of sitting in bed reading," he said. "It coexists, and it amplifies the book."

Electronic publishing is making a serious impact in children's books. "What is clear is that children are much more comfortable with technology," said Randi Benton, who recently set up Random House's new media division. The company recently embarked on a joint venture with Broderbund Software, an interactive children's software company, to start Living Books, which provide lively sounds, elaborate graphics and hundreds of things to play with in such stories as Aesop's fable "The Tortoise and the Hare" and Mercer Mayer's *Just Grandma and Me.* Such books—which have sold tens of thousands of copies already—are somewhere between computer games and hypertext fiction, a new computer-based format that turns traditional beginning-to-end narrative on its head by affording the reader the thoroughly post-modern opportunity to skip from place to place in the text, creating his own story and arriving at his own ending.

"I think the idea that this next generation is going to start at page 1 and go to page 284 and then close the book is wrong," said the president of Warner Books, Laurence J. Kirshbaum, who recently discovered the joys of an on-line world when he got himself hooked up to the Internet. "This is a generation that has been raised on MTV and a multitude of stimuli. They don't think linearly; they think mosaically. And they're much more used to getting their information from talking and listening than from reading books."

It's easy to be seduced by the new products, but part of the trick for publishers these days is to avoid investing too much in technology that might burn out as completely as LP records. Richard Sarnoff, who heads the new media group of Bantam Doubleday Dell, said, "We have to decide what is likely to augment, and what is likely to cannibalize, our business." Big publishers have several ways to go. They can buy their own software companies. They can form copublishing partnerships, as Putnam did when it made a deal with Sony to publish H. R. Haldeman's diaries, Putnam in hard cover and Sony on CD-ROM. They can embark on joint ventures or buy stakes in multimedia companies.

But mixing multimedia publishers with traditional book publishers seems counterintuitive, like mixing milk with grapefruit juice. They speak different languages. They look at their products, and at the world, in different ways. Even the word "product," applied to books, would seem anathema to editors of the old school. This spring Jason Epstein, the editorial director of Random House's adult trade group, ventured into the offices of Voyager, a Manhattan software company, one morning to talk to his former assistant, 26-year-old Maryam Mohit. Ms. Mohit, one of a flotilla of young editors who have left traditional publishing houses to join new media companies, showed him one of her latest works, the CD-ROM version of Marvin Minsky's *Society of Mind.* Mr. Epstein looked at the video of a tiny Marvin Minsky gesticulating at a lectern, listened to Mr. Minsky's speech on the speakers, and then spotted a turgid sentence on the screen, where the text was printed out. That's what he focused on. "I would have edited that," he said.

"The mentality of a CD-ROM publisher is different from that of a book publisher," said Michael Lynton, until recently the senior vice president for publishing at the Walt Disney Company, whose publishing arm, Hyperion Books, is investing in new media projects. "People go into book publishing and bookselling because they want to be involved with words and books. They don't want to make money. If they do, they've made a serious mistake. The CD-ROM people, and the gaming community—those people are in love with games, in love with computers and in love with making money. They have no problem talking about units."

Many publishing houses suffer from a generational divide in which their staffs can be split in two: the ones who grew up with computers and the ones who didn't. Traditional editors read *The New York Review of Books,* not *Wired* magazine; many even still use their old manual typewriters, edit by pencil, and feel unnerved by, even afraid of, computers.

At Penguin U.S.A., many editors are being gingerly exposed to new media by a 28-year-old vice president, Julie Hansen, who administers a lab where employees can drop in and play with a CD-ROM unit for the first time.

Voyager, which recently abandoned its headquarters in southern California for an enormous converted loft in Soho, has the atmosphere of a computer company: large open spaces broken up by partitions, chicly casual workers without official titles, a buzz of new ideas. In an interview about the future of books, the president, Bob Stein, was wearing a pair of baggy trousers and a T-shirt reading "Free All Political Prisoners." "Will books exist? I think that's the wrong question," Mr. Stein said. "Humans have tremendous capacity to find imaginative uses for old media, and books will be with us for generations. But the locus of important intellectual communication is going to shift away from books. The complexity of palate that authors have with these new media is going to draw them in."

Mr. Stein envisions a creative brain drain that will pull authors toward the new media. "One hundred years ago, if you were going to write stories the only choice would be plays or novels," he said. "Now, you're already thinking about the movies. And with CD-ROM's, you can create the intimate experience of a novel and the experience of video, audio and film."

Art Spiegelman is one author who has now worked in both media. Voyager recently put out the CD-ROM version of *Maus*, his critically acclaimed comic-book depiction of the Holocaust. It includes audio interviews with his father, who figured prominently in *Maus;* aerial photographs of concentration camps, and dozens of early sketches Mr. Spiegelman made when he put *Maus* together. "The least interesting thing about the ROM is the book itself, because it was conceived as a book," Mr. Spiegelman said. "But I don't see it as competitive with a book, any more than going to the theater is competitive or watching television is competitive. On some vague level it's a plea for attention, but the experience is a different one."

The new formats are likely to have a great effect on the production and distribution of books. For one thing, making a CD-ROM costs about 68 cents and can be done virtually instantaneously, while making a book costs between $2 and $3.50. For another, CD-ROM's are sold mostly in software stores, not traditional bookstores. They come in big, clunky boxes shrouded in glossy packaging, and they're arranged according to which machines they're compatible with—not according to subject. They're impossible to browse through, in the manner of a book, unless the store sets up a computer demonstration area. "The traditional bookstore is an extraordinary resource for the publisher because you get people on the staff who have a lot of product knowledge and can be incredibly helpful to the customer," Dan McNamee, a partner in a business called the Publishing and Media Group, said. "But they tend to be very uncomfortable with electronic products. On the other hand, software distributors are not used to providing support for highly varied product lines. And they can talk about technology, but they're not used to talking about content."

But some people envision a time when bookstores themselves might be obsolete. Why would you need to walk into a store, they say, when books come on little disks for your personal computer, or when they're made more widely available through places like the On-Line Bookstore, which is based in Massachusetts and sells books through the Internet? Although bookstore executives like Steve Riggio, the executive vice president of Barnes & Noble, say they envision their stores metamorphosing into information superstores, it's unclear how this will happen.

Despite the obvious advantages of electronic books, visions of a future world confined indoors—working, playing, communicating, reading and shopping via computer—have so far vastly outpaced the realities, particularly when it comes to books. Tens of millions of people have the capacity to read books on floppy disk, but they don't. And at this point, according to industry figures, only about 5 million households have CD-ROM attachments on their computers. The number is expected to increase to more than 10 million by the end of the year; new models of old computers are sold almost exclusively now with CD-ROM attachments. But it will take a long time before everyone has the equipment.

We've come up with a beautifully browsable invention that needs no electricity and exists in a readable form no matter what happens. If the end of civilization comes and we lose electricity, we can hold a CD-ROM up to the light and it has totemic value, but we have no past.

—Nicholson Baker

Meanwhile, computer companies are scrambling to come up with a technology that mimics a book completely, that can put text on a screen as effectively as on paper, but none have succeeded yet. Devices like the Powerbook and the Sony Bookman still don't come close to matching the experience of reading a paper-and-print book while curled up in a chair, in bed, on the train, under a tree, in an airplane. "The machines have to be a lot better," said Jack Hoeft, the chief executive of Bantam Doubleday Dell. "As the technology improves, I expect that they will be, and then people who want to read a book on a computer reader can do it that way."

But probably they won't want to. Olafur Olafsson, the 32-year-old president of Sony Electronic Publishing, who also happens to be the best-selling novelist of all time in his native Iceland, says, "Novels on a computer screen don't do the job." Sitting in his upper-floor office with a picture-window view of Central Park, he plucked the Alfred A. Knopf translation of his latest novel, *Absolution*, from his desk. Under no circumstances, he said, would he want to read it on a computer screen. "Maybe if you had something of this dimension and this weight and as easy to hold as this book," he said. "The screen would have to be easy to read, it wouldn't be able to suffer from heat and glare, and you could easily go back and forth from page to page. But I don't see that technology arriving any time soon." And after all, the modern book is the result of centuries of trial and error during which people wrote on bark, on parchment, on vellum, on clay, on scrolls, on stone, chiseling characters into surfaces or copying them out by hand.

"The book has been with us for about 500 years," said Donald Norman of Apple Computer, who recently published a book, *Things That Make Us Smart*, which argues that technology sometimes runs away with itself, dazzling and tyrannizing people instead of serving them by making life simpler. "People think it's unsophisticated technologically, but the book has evolved into an extremely convenient and sophisticated artifact. It uses modern paper, with good contrast and good quality print. The typefaces themselves have evolved over many years, the design and layout have evolved in esthetic quality and utility. And in many ways, the book is a good random access device that's extremely easy to scan through."

The novelist Nicholson Baker said: "We've come up with a beautifully browsable invention that needs no electricity and exists in a readable form no matter what happens. If the end of civilization comes and we lose electricity, we can hold a CD-ROM up to the light and it has totemic value, but we have no past."

There's more to it than that. In an instant culture, books represent our more ruminative, deliberate and thoughtful side. Earlier this year Bill Henderson, the editor of the Pushcart Press in Wainscott, L.I., founded a group called the Lead Pencil Club. The idea came to him when he was reading Doris Grumbach's memoir *Extra Innings,* which describes her grumpy ill will toward all her electronic gadgets. The club is devoted to the superiority of non-technology. Its motto is "Not So Fast," and the book is one of its favorite devices.

"America's the only country that doesn't have a past," Mr. Henderson said. "We've become speed freaks, and things like faxes and E-mail contribute to our national amnesia. Books don't allow that to happen. You go to the library and you see the past out there and you can browse at leisure. And a book is personal—you can hold it in your hand, turn down its pages, write in the margins, carry it to the beach. It's a cliché, but you can. I don't think we're going to put up with the demise of the book."

And if Mr. Gates at Microsoft likes computers so much, you might ask, why did he decide to publish his forthcoming book the regular way? "The medium is appropriate," said Jonathan Lazarus, the vice president of systems strategy at Microsoft, who negotiated Mr. Gates's book project—for $2.5 million—with Penguin U.S.A. "There's a certain test of one's credibility and ideas when you have to put them in 300 pages of prose. We've grown up in a society where we learn a lot from books and where books are a well-understood way to get information. If I said to you, 'I'd like you to learn all about fly fishing,' you wouldn't be surprised if I said, 'Here's a book about fly fishing to read.' "

As Mr. Norman, whose book about the tyrannies of technology is about to come out in a new CD-ROM version, said, "If you really want to read my book, I'd recommend the paper version."

D. T. Max (essay date September 1994)

SOURCE: "The End of the Book?" in *The Atlantic Monthly,* Vol. 274, No. 3, September, 1994, pp. 61-2, 64, 67-8, 70-1.

[In the essay below, Max compares books with CD-Roms and speculates on the future of both.]

An office-party atmosphere pervaded the headquarters of *Wired* magazine, the newly created oracle of the computer-literate generation. *Wired* is housed on the third floor of a flat, low brick building with plain-pine interiors in an industrial section of San Francisco south of Market Street. The area is known as Multimedia Gulch, for the scores of small companies working in the neighborhood which mix sound, video, and text into experimental interactive multimedia computer products that they hope will one day sell millions of copies. *Wired* is not an ordinary computer magazine: it promises the faithful reader not mere computing power—something available from a grown-up computer magazine like *Macworld,* which happens to be across the street—but, more important, hipness, the same sense of being ahead of the curve that once attached to a new Bob Dylan album or Richard Brautigan book.

The weekday afternoon I was there, hero sandwiches lay on the table, the magazine's pet gray parrot was hanging outside its cage, and young men and women with sophisticated eyewear sat rapt before their computer screens. The reference folders and lay-out paraphernalia common to magazine editorial departments were scattered around. The ringing of the phones was constant. When I had first called *Wired*'s co-founder, Louis Rossetto, in the summer of 1993, I got through to him immediately, and he had, if anything, too much time to speculate about the shape of things to come. Several months later I had to go through a secretary and a publicist for my interview, and once I arrived, I was made to wait while more-urgent calls were put through. What happened in the interim is that the information highway became a hot subject. Rossetto was now every media journalist's and Hollywood agent's first call.

What I wanted from Louis Rossetto was his opinion on whether the rise of the computer culture that his magazine covered would end with the elimination by CD-ROMS and networked computer databases of the hardcover, the paperback, and the world of libraries and literate culture that had grown up alongside them. Was print on its way out? And if it was, what would happen to the publishers who had for generations put out books, and to the writers who had written them? Or was there something special about the book that would ensure that no technical innovation could ever supplant it? Would the book resist the CD-ROM and the Internet just as it has resisted radio, television, and the movies?

Finally I was taken into the sunlit confines of his office. Bookshelves ran along one wall. A forty-five-year-old career journalist with shoulder-grazing gray hair, Rossetto is a late convert to computers. He spent much of the 1980s in Europe, and gives off a mild sense of disengagement—there is a touch of the sixties about him, as there is about much else in the Gulch. Now he set out his vision of a fast-changing computerized, paperless, nearly book-free society, and did so with a certainty that would frighten even someone whose sense of equilibrium, unlike mine, did not involve visits to bookstores or the belief that last year's laptop is basically good enough. "The changes going on in the world now are literally a revolution in progress, a revolution that makes political revolution seem like a game," Rossetto, who recently sold a minority interest in his magazine to Condé Nast, said.

> It will revolutionize how people work, how they communicate, and how they entertain themselves, and it is the biggest engine for change in our world today. We're looking at the end of a twenty- or thirty- or forty-year process, from the invention of tubes to transistors to fiber-optic and cable to the development of cable networks, until we've reached critical mass today.

I asked if there was no downside, no tradeoff for all that information in the world that was to come. "It doesn't keep me up at night, I admit," he said.

> Written information is a relatively new phenomenon. Depositing it and being able to reference it centuries later is not common human experience. In some ways what is happening with on-line is a return to our earlier oral tradition. In other ways, it is utterly new, a direct connection of minds. Humans have always been isolated, and now we're starting to see electronic connections generating an intellectual organism of their own, literally a quantum leap beyond our experience with consciousness.

This is classic 1990s cybervisionarism, repeated up and down the halls of *Wired* and echoed throughout the Bay area, and it derives directly from the teenage-male personalities of the hackers who created the computer industry: cyberspace will be like a better kind of school.

There are three principal articles of faith behind this vision. 1) The classroom will be huge: the linking of information worldwide will cause a democratic explosion in the accessibility of knowledge. 2) The classroom will be messy: the sense of information as an orderly and retrievable quantity will decline, and you won't necessarily be able to find what you're looking for in cyberspace at any given time. 3) There will be no teachers: the "controllers of information"—censors, editors, and studio executives—will disappear, and the gates of public discourse will swing open before everyone who can get on-line. Anyone can publish; anyone can read what is published; anyone can comment on what he or she has read. Rossetto had been delineating his vision for twenty minutes, but suddenly it was time to go. An assistant popped in to pull him into an editorial meeting. "I have a pretty cynical view of most of the American media," Rossetto said before leaving (read: "You'll get this wrong. You'll be hostile"). "Their jobs are at stake, because their businesses are threatened. Take *Time* magazine. What function would it have in the modern world?"

One look at *Wired* suggests a gap between message and messenger. *Wired* looks more radical than it is. It cheerleads and debunks its subjects using editorial formulas that came in with the nineteenth-century magazine—a fictional takeoff on Microsoft, written by Douglas Coupland, the author of *Generation X;* a classic star cover on Laurie Anderson, "America's multimediatrix"—rather than harnessing any global back-and-forth among literate minds. Although *Wired* communicates extensively by E-mail with its readers, conducts forums, and makes back issues available on-line, its much-repeated goal of creating a magazine—currently called *HotWired*—that is especially designed to exist electronically remains fuzzy. For the moment this is no open democracy, and *Wired* is no computer screen—its bright graphics would make a fashion magazine envious. *Wired* celebrates what doesn't yet exist by exploiting a format that does: it's as if a scribe copied out a manuscript extolling the beauty that would one day be print.

Overhyped or not, interactive multimedia do hold vast potential for the companies that in the next decades back the right products in the right formats. Multimedia are not new—a child's pop-up book is one example, and an illustrated pre-Gutenberg Bible is another. But interactive multimedia as envisioned by the computer industry (especially if television cables or telephone wires are reconfigured to accommodate two-way high-quality video digital transmissions—technologies that may be in place on a national scale sometime around the millennium) have great potential, because they would persuade consumers to bring software into their homes as they brought it into their offices in the 1980s. Who wouldn't want a screen that accessed all currently existing forms of information, from mail to movies, and did so with great convenience and flexibility?

Even if this vision is only partly realized, the book, the newspaper, and the video will be hard-pressed to maintain their place in our culture. Look at the book without sentiment and its limitations are evident: books can excite the imagination, but they can't literally make you see and hear. "What is the use of a book without pictures or conversations?" Lewis Carroll's Alice grouses, before tumbling down the rabbit hole into the more absorbing precincts of Wonderland, in one of the favorite texts of hackers. Interactive-multimedia designers, with their brew of sights, sounds, and words, believe that they could keep Alice (her age puts her very much in their target group) above-ground and interested. Or a multimedia designer could expand the book's plot line, giving the reader the choice of whether Alice goes down the hole or decides to stick around and read alongside her sister on the riverbank. The reader could hear Alice's voice, or ask her questions about herself, the answers to which are only implicit in the book.

When something intrigues the readers of a printed book, they have to wrestle with an index and then, perhaps, go to a library to find out more about the subject; they can't just hit a search button to log on to a database attached to the book and read something else on the same subject, as they can on a computer. "I decided books were obsolete thirty-four years ago," says Ted Nelson, an early computer hacker who coined the word "hypertext" in the early sixties to describe how knowledge would be accessed if all information were available simultaneously. "I have thousands of books and I love them. It's only intertwining I want more of."

But such intertwining—a vast linkage of electronic text across databases worldwide—would inevitably push the printed word to the margins and replace it with sleeker, more efficient text conveyers. It is not the viability of text itself that is in question. On the contrary, whether paper gives way to the computer screen or not, there is little question that words as the cornerstone of communication are safe. *"Littera scripta manet,"* an anonymous Roman wrote; "The written word endures." This is a comforting quotation—typically if erroneously attributed to the poet Horace—that writers about multimedia are fond of using. In fact, words are multiplying wildly. In the world of computers they are a bargain compared with images: cheap to transport and easy to store. Probably more words are put out in a week by the 20 million people who use the loosely strung computer networks that constitute the Internet than are published by all major American publishing companies in a year. There's a "Poetry Corner" and bulletin boards where new novels get posted constantly. In a recent announcement a nonprofit organization called Project Gutenberg, run out of a university in Illinois, presented as its mysteriously precise goal "To Give Away One Trillion E[lectronic] Text Files [of classic books] by December 21, 2001." When I mentioned the scope of fiction on the Internet to the novelist John Updike, he said lightly, "I imagine most of that stuff on the information highway is roadkill anyway." And of course he is right. But his is a minority opinion outside the circles of tastemakers.

Text and books are not, however, joined at the hip—words don't need print. "Books on paper are a medium unto themselves," Louis Rossetto says, "and my sense is that anything that is stand-alone is a dead end." But even to Rossetto a world completely without books seems unlikely. One view is that the book will become the equivalent of the horse after the invention of the automobile or the phonograph record after the arrival of the compact disc—a thing for eccentrics, hobbyists, and historians. It will not disappear, but it will become obsolete. Multimedia programmers themselves disagree sharply on whether this will come to pass in five years, ten years, or never. One question is whether there is money to be made in the production of multimedia. Another is how good multimedia products will ever be, for by industry admission they are not very good now. The great majority of the 3,000 multimedia products launched last year were little more than rudimentary efforts. "I think that there are fewer than thirty titles with good, solid, deep information out there," Rick Fischer, the director of product development at Sony Electronic Publishing, says. "The majority of titles are kind of pseudo-multimedia. People are still learning how to do this." Besides, computer companies are not as excited by books as they are by games, which represent an ever-increasing share of the market. Sony, for example, has backed an interactive game version of its movie *Bram Stoker's Dracula*—Harker races against rats, wolves, and flaming torches to slay the Prince of Darkness—rather than the book *Dracula,* 300 pages of print that could be augmented with perhaps a moving illustration or two.

Publishers are terrified. They have read a thousand times that one day we will play games, shop, watch movies, read books, and do research all on our computer or television screens. Computer companies are skillful at bluffing one another, forever claiming that they are nearly ready to release a hot new product, which is in truth barely in prototype. This kind of nonproduct has the nickname "vaporware" within the industry. But publishers, unfamiliar with computer culture, believe the hype. In the past year *Publishers Weekly* ran six major stories on how CD-ROM and the Internet will remake publishing. The comments of Laurence Kirshbaum, the president of Warner Books, a subsidiary of Time Warner, were not untypical: "I don't know if there's the smell of crisis in the air, but there should be. Publishers should be sleeping badly these days. They have to be prepared to compete with software giants like [Microsoft's chairman] Bill Gates." Publishers are most of all afraid of doing nothing—as hardback publishers did when they ignored the paperback explosion of the 1960s and 1970s. So they are rushing to form electronic-publishing divisions and to find partners in the software business. "Eighteen months ago no one was talking about multimedia and CD-ROMS seriously, and now everyone is deeply involved and deeply conscious of them," says Alberto Vitale, the chairman of the normally cautious Random House, Inc., which has signed a co-venture deal with Broderbund, a leading children's software developer in Novato, California, to create children's interactive multimedia. Putting Dr. Seuss on CD-ROM is one of their first efforts. The Palo Alto "media kitchen" owned by Viacom, where the company's film, television, and book divisions cooperate—at least theoretically—on interactive-multimedia research, is designing new travel guides: why actually go to San Francisco when by 1995 you will be able to take a virtual walking tour on a Frommer CD-ROM? Interest has even percolated into the last redoubt of traditional publishing, the firm of Alfred A. Knopf. Since its inception Knopf has placed great emphasis on the book as handsome object. But Knopf's president attended the first International Illustrated Book and New Media Publishing Market fair, held earlier this year, which was designated to introduce multimedia's various content providers to one another. (The fact that the fair was in Cannes probably did not hurt attendance.)

Behind the stampede into electronic publishing is doubtless a widespread feeling among those in conventional publishing that the industry is in dire, if ill-defined, trouble. A decade-long trend among major publishers toward publishing fewer trade books recently had an impact on four imprints in just two months, most notably a near-total cutback of Harcourt, Bracc's tradc dcpartment (the publishers of T.S. Eliot, Virginia Woolf, and Alice Walker) and the closing of Ticknor & Fields adult books, a Houghton Mifflin imprint (which included William Gass and Robert Stone among its authors). Aggressive marketing has allowed publishers to sell more copies of their top titles, creating the illusion of pink-cheeked health in some years. But after decades of competition from radio, television, movies, videos, and Americans' increasingly long workdays, it is hard to imagine how the publishers of mainstream fiction and nonfiction in book form will ever again publish as many titles as they did in the past; after all, popular fiction magazines never recovered from the advent of radio serials. Giants like Doubleday and Putnam publish perhaps a third as many hardcover books as they did ten years ago, and McGraw-Hill, once the publisher of Vladimir Nabokov and hundreds of other authors, is out of the new-trade-book business altogether. Recently Random House sent a glass-is-half-full letter to book-review editors, letting them know that the company would be making their jobs easier by publishing fewer books. According to a 1993 survey by Dataquest, a San Jose information-technology market-research firm, most employees in the multimedia-content industry come from traditional print backgrounds. And the extremely rudimentary employment statistics that exist for the publishing industry show a decline since the late 1980s in New York-based publishing jobs, though it is hardly enough of one to confirm a sea change in publishing's fortunes, or to suggest that Armageddon is around the corner. Last year nearly 50,000 new titles destined for bookstores were published, and total consumer-reference CD-ROM software sales amounted to only about three percent of trade-book sales.

Besides, the computer industry acknowledges that what most readers think of as books—that is, novels and nonfiction text—gain nothing from being on screen; the appeal of the product depends on the quality of the prose and the research, neither of which is enhanced by current screens. Whether you scroll down a screen or turn a page to read *The Bridges of Madison County* makes a great deal of difference in the quality of the reading experience. "I just don't personally believe in reading novels on a computer screen," says Olaf Olafsson, the president of Sony Electronic Publishing and the author of *Absolution,* a novel published in March by Pantheon Books. He says that he would never want to see his own work on a computer: "There's a lot of content that's now being delivered on paper that's fine on paper." The book has great advantages over the computer: it's light and it's cheap. That it has changed little in 400 years suggests an uncommonly apt design. John Updike says,

> It seems to me the book has not just aesthetic values—the charming little clothy box of the thing, the smell of the glue, even the print, which has its own beauty. But there's something about the sensation of ink on paper that is in some sense a thing, a phenomenon rather than an epiphenomenon. I can't break the association of electric trash with the computer screen. Words on the screen give the sense of being just another passing electronic wriggle.

You can drop a book in the bathtub, dry it out on the radiator, and still read it. You can put it in the attic, pull it out 200 years later, and probably decipher the words. You can curl up in bed with it or get suntan lotion on it. These are definitely not possibilities suggested by the computer. A well-thumbed paperback copy of John Grisham blowing in a beach breeze represents a technological stronghold the computer may never invade.

Lovers of literature (and schlock) may not see much change, then, but that doesn't mean publishers are in for an easy ride. Novels, nonfiction, and belles lettres are a prestige sideshow for publishers—they amount to only a few billion dollars in a roughly $18 billion book industry. Take dictionaries and encyclopedias, which are in effect databases in book form. The hand cannot match a computer chip in accessing given references, which constitutes the primary function of such works. Last year the 1989 edition of the *Oxford English Dictionary,* the flagship publication of the 400-year-old university press, sold four times as many copies in a new CD-ROM version as in its traditional twenty-volume book form. The company has said that the next print edition, due in a decade, may well be the last. At an October, 1993, celebration at the New York Public Library in honor of the publication of the fifth edition of the *Columbia Encyclopedia* in both book form and (a year hence) on CD-ROM, one guest speaker commented that the next edition, whenever it was ready, might well not have a paper counterpart. There was barely an objection from the audience.

Publishers are divided over the fate of so-called "soft reference titles"—cookbooks and how-to books—and children's books. These are huge markets, and the question is whether electronic books will capture them or expand on them. "My generation may be the last . . . to have a strong visceral affection for books," Janet Wikler, a former director of advanced media at Harper Collins, told *Publishers Weekly* last year.

What publishers have not stopped to consider is whether consumers like CD-ROMS in the first place—or how comfortable they will ever be with networked, digitalized, downloaded books when they become available. It may be a question of technical proficiency: how many families possess the sophistication to use Microsoft's new CD-ROM Musical Instruments—a charming visual and audio tour of the instruments of the world which is perfect for six-year-olds? The product requires either a multimedia computer or "a Multimedia PC upgrade kit, which includes CD-ROM drive (with CD-DA outputs, sustained 150K/second transfer rate and a maximum seek time of 1 second while using no more than 40% of the CPU's processing power)." Electronic encyclopedias have all but driven print encyclopedias out of the market in large part because they are "bundled"—sold at a deep discount to computer-hardware manufacturers to be included free when the consumer buys a CD-ROM drive. This is roughly like giving the consumer a book if he will only buy a lamp. "Traditional publishers may be a Luddite elite, but software publishers are arrogant sheep," says Michael Mellin, a multimedia executive who until last year was the publisher of Random House's electronic-publishing division. "One thing publishers don't realize is that there hasn't been a comparable kick in sales of CD-ROM multimedia titles given the rise in the number of CD-ROM drives installed." In other words, books on CD-ROM don't sell—at least not yet. A study of the industry last year found that of those people who had bought a CD-ROM drive, fewer than half had returned to the computer store to buy new discs. Compare this with the way the compact-disc player caught on in the mid-1980s. Interactive multimedia may turn out to be the biggest bust since the paperless office. One former industry executive describes multimedia as "a solution in search of a problem, doing what other things do already, only slightly less well."

Publishers derive their impressions of the awesome potential of multimedia from products like Microsoft's much publicized Encarta CD-ROM, a magnificent encyclopedia with text drawn from Funk & Wagnall's twenty-nine-volume encyclopedia and augmented by hundreds of video and audio clips. Alice would have fun with this: she could listen to bird calls and African drums, or experiment with changing the moon's orbit. (She could also click on Bill Gates's name and hear his nasal assurance that Microsoft "has never wavered from the vision" of a personal computer "on every desk and in every home." This was not part of Funk & Wagnall's original text.) But having been five years in development, employing a hundred people at its peak, and reportedly costing Microsoft well upward of $5 million, Encarta may be something of a Potemkin Village, meant for credulous competitors to marvel at. The company has dropped the price from $395 to $139 to try to get consumers to buy it.

The question may not be whether, given enough time, CD-ROMS and the Internet can replace books, but whether they should.

—D. T. Max

Paper has limitations, but the computer may have more. As a physical object, it is hardly comforting. "Who'd want to go to bed with a Powerbook?" John Baker, a vice-president at Broderbund, asks. And even if the laptop goes on shrinking, its screen, whose components represent nearly all the machine's cost, remains at best a chore to read. At the Xerox Palo Alto Research Center (where the receptionist's cubicle still houses an IBM Selective typewriter) is a display room with half a dozen prototype six-million-pixel AMLCD screens. The quiet hum of the room, the bright white lighting, the clean, flat antiseptic surfaces, give the impression of an aspirin commercial. "It was clear to us that no reader was going to read a book off any of the current screens for more than ten minutes," says Malcolm Thompson, the chief technologist. "We hoped to change that." A large annotated poster on the wall illustrates point for point the screen's superiority to paper, as in an old-fashioned magazine ad. This flat panel display is indeed better than commercial screens, but it is neither as flexible nor as mobile as a book, and it still depends on fickle battery power. A twentysomething software marketer who began as an editorial assistant in book publishing points out, "A book requires one good eye, one good light source, and one good finger."

In the heart of official Washington, D.C., down the street from the Capitol and at the same intersection as the Supreme Court and the Library of Congress, stands an incongruous statue of Puck, whom the *Oxford Companion to English Literature,* soon to be issued on CD-ROM, defines as "a goblin," and whom Microsoft Encarta passes over in favor of "puck," which it defines solely as a mouse-like device with crosshairs printed on it, used in engineering applications. The 1930s building next to the statue is the Folger Shakespeare Library. Two flights below the reading room, designed in the style of a Tudor banquet hall, next to which librarians and scholars click quietly on laptops and log on to the Internet's Shaksper reference group for the latest scholarly chatter, is a locked bank gate. Behind it is what librarians call a "short-title catalogue vault"—in other words, a very-rare-book room. This main room—there is another—is rectangular, carpeted in red, and kept permanently at 68 degrees. Sprinkler valves are interspersed among eight evenly spaced shelves of books dating from 1475 to 1640 and lit by harsh institutional light. Of these books 180 are the only copies of their titles left in the world: you can spot them by the small blue slips reading "Unique" which modestly poke out from their tops. At the end of the room is a long shelf on which stacks of oversize volumes rest on their sides: these are nearly a third of the surviving First Folio editions of the plays of Williams Shakespeare. When the First Folios were printed, in the 1620s, printing was still an inexact art. Each page had to be checked by hand, and the volumes are full of mistakes: backward type, ill-cut pages, and variant lines. Several copies lack the 1602 tragedy *Troilus and Cressida,* owing to a copyright dispute. And yet, 370 years after they came off the printing press, you can still pull down these books and read them. The pages are often lightly cockled and foxed, because the folio was printed on mid-priced rag paper, but the type is still bright and the volume falls open easily. You can balance it on your lap and run your finger along the page to feel the paper grain in that sensuous gesture known to centuries of book readers: here is knowledge.

In 1620 Francis Bacon ranked printing, along with gunpowder and the compass, as one of the three inventions that had "changed the appearance and state of the whole world." Indeed, the existence of multiple identical copies of texts that are nearly indelibly recorded, permanently retrievable, and widely decipherable has determined so much of modern history that what the world would be like without printing can only be guessed at. More books likely came into existence in the fifty years after the Gutenberg Bible than in the millennium that preceded it. "Printing was a huge change for Western culture," says Paul Saffo, who studies the effect of technology on society at the Institute for the Future, in Menlo Park (where the receptionist also uses an IBM Selectric). "The dominant intellectual skill before the age of print was the art of memory." And now we may be going back.

For the question may not be whether, given enough time, CD-ROMS and the Internet can replace books, but whether they should. Ours is a culture that has made a fetish of impermanence. Paperbacks disintegrate, Polaroids fade, video images wear out. Perhaps the first novel ever written specifically to be read on a computer and to take advantage of the concept of hypertext—the structuring of written passages to allow the reader to take different paths through the story—was Rob Swigart's *Portal,* published in 1986 and designed for the Apple Macintosh, among other computers of its day. The Apple Macintosh was superseded months later by the more sophisticated Macintosh SE, which, according to Swigart, could not run his hypertext novel. Over time people threw out their old computers (fewer and fewer new programs could be run on them), and so *Portal* became for the most part unreadable. A similar fate will befall literary works of the future if they are committed not to paper but to transitional technology like diskettes, CD-ROMS, and Unix tapes—candidates, with eight-track tapes, Betamax, and the Apple Macintosh, for rapid obscurity. "It's not clear, with fifty incompatible standards around, what will survive," says Ted Nelson, the computer pioneer, who has grown disenchanted with the forces commercializing the Internet. "The so-called information age is really the age of information lost." Software companies don't care—early moviemakers didn't worry that they were filming on volatile stock. In a graphic dramatization of this mad dash to obsolescence, in 1992 the author William Gibson, who coined the term "cyberspace," created an autobiographical story on computer disc called "Agrippa." "Agrippa" is encoded to erase itself entirely as the purchaser plays the story. Only thirty-five copies were printed, and those who bought it left it intact. One copy was somehow pirated and sent out onto the Internet, where anyone could copy it. Many users did, but who and where is not consistently indexed, nor are the copies permanent—the Internet is anarchic. "The original disc is already almost obsolete on Macintoshes," says Kevin Begos, the publisher of "Agrippa." "Within four or five years it will get very hard to find a machine that will run it." Collectors will soon find Gibson's story gone before they can destroy it themselves.

HYPERTEXT AND HYPERFICTION

George P. Landow (essay date 1990)

SOURCE: "Changing Texts, Changing Readers: Hypertext in Literary Education, Criticism, and Scholarship," in *Reorientations: Critical Theories and Pedagogies,* edited by Bruce Henricksen and Thaïs E. Morgan, University of Illinois Press, 1990, pp. 133-61.

[*Landow is an American educator and critic whose works include* Hypermedia and Literary Studies *(1991),* Hypertext: The Convergence of Contemporary Critical Theory and Technology *(1992), and* The Digital Word: Text-Based Computing in the Humanities *(1993). In the excerpt below, based on his experiences at Brown University where literature courses have used hypertext in the classroom, he defines the distinguishing characteristics of hypertext and remarks on its potential impact on the reading and study of literature.*]

It is eight P.M., and after having helped put the children to bed, Professor Jones settles into her favorite chair and reaches for her copy of Milton's *Paradise Lost* to prepare for tomorrow's class. A scholar who specializes in the poetry of Milton's time, she returns to the poem as one returns to meet an old friend. Reading the poem's opening pages, she once again encounters allusions to the Old Testament, and because she knows how seventeenth-century Christians commonly read these passages, she perceives connections both to a passage in Genesis and to its radical Christian transformations. Furthermore, her previous acquaintance with Milton allows her to recall other passages later in *Paradise Lost* that refer to this and related parts of the Bible. At the same time, she recognizes that the poem's opening lines pay homage to Homer, Virgil, Dante, and Spenser and simultaneously issue them a challenge.

Meanwhile, John H. Smith, one of the most conscientious students in Professor Jones's survey of English literature, begins to prepare for class. What kind of poem, what kind of text, does he encounter? Whereas Professor Jones experiences the great seventeenth-century epic situated within a field of relations and connections, her student encounters a far barer, less connected, reduced poem, most of whose allusions go unrecognized and almost all of whose challenges pass by unperceived. An unusually mature student, he pauses in his reading to check the footnotes for the meaning of unfamiliar words and allusions, a few of which he finds explained. Suppose one could find a way to allow Smith to experience some of the connections obvious to Professor Jones. Suppose he could touch the opening lines of *Paradise Lost,* for instance, and the relevant passages from Homer, Virgil, and the Bible would appear, or that he could touch another line and immediately receive a choice of other mentions of the same idea or image later in the poem or elsewhere in Milton's other writings—or, for that matter, interpretations and critical judgments made since the poem's first publication.

Hypertext, or electronically linked text, enables students to do all these things. Unlike books, which contain physically isolated texts, hypertext emphasizes connections and relations, and in doing so changes the ways texts exist and the ways we read them. It also changes the roles of author and reader, teacher and student.

Because hypertext has the power to change the way we understand and experience texts, it offers radical promises and challenges to students, teachers, and theorists of literature. *Hypertext,* a term coined by Theodor H. Nelson in the 1960s, refers to nonsequentially read (and written) texts: "Both an author's tool and a reader's medium, a hypertext document system allows authors or groups of authors to *link* information together, create *paths* through a corpus of related material, *annotate* existing texts, and create notes that point readers to either bibliographic data or the body of the referenced text. . . . Readers can browse through linked, cross-referenced, annotated texts in an orderly but nonsequential manner" [Nicole Yankelovich, Norman Meyrowitz, and Andries van Dam, "Reading and Writing the Electronic Book," *IEEE Computer* 18 (1985)]. Writers on hypertext trace the notion to a 1945 article by Vannevar Bush in *Atlantic Monthly* that called for mechanically linked information retrieval machines in the midst of what was already becoming an explosion of information. In the 1960s Douglas C. Englebart and Nelson began to design computer systems that could implement some of these notions of linked texts, and today *hypertext* refers almost exclusively to electronic hypertext systems that rely on computing equipment and software.

Originally the idea of hypertext did not depend upon computers. In fact, the standard scholarly article in the humanities or physical sciences perfectly embodies the underlying notions of hypertext as nonsequentially read text. For example, in reading a critical article on James Joyce's

Ulysses, one reads through the main text, encounters a number or symbol that indicates the presence of a foot- or endnote, and leaves the main text to read it. The note might contain a citation of passages in *Ulysses* that support the argument in question as well as information about the author's indebtedness to other scholars, disagreement with them, and so on. The note might also summon up information about sources, influences, and parallels in other literary texts. In each case, the reader can follow the link to another text indicated by the note, thus moving entirely outside the text of the article itself. Having completed reading the note or having decided that it does not warrant a careful reading at the moment, one returns to the main text and continues reading until one encounters another note, at which point one again leaves the main text. This combination of excursionary reading outside the main text and returning to it constitutes the basic experience of hypertext.

Suppose now that one could simply touch the page where the symbol of a note or reference appeared and instantly bring into view the material contained in a note or even the entire other text—here all of *Ulysses*—to which that note refers. Scholarly articles situate themselves within a field of such relations, but the print medium keeps most of these intertexts out of sight and relatively difficult to follow because the referenced (or linked) materials lie spatially distant from the corresponding note. In contrast, electronic hypertext makes individual references easy to follow and the entire field of textual interconnections easy to navigate. Changing the rapidity and ease with which one can orient oneself within such a context of information radically changes both the experience of reading and ultimately the nature of what is read. For example, if we had a hypertext system in which our putative Joyce article existed linked to all the materials it cited, it would appear to the reader as part of a much larger system whose totality might count more than the individual document. The article would now be woven much more tightly into its context than would its traditional print technology counterpart. The ease with which readers traverse such a system has additional consequences for as they move through this web of texts, they continually shift its center—and hence the focus or organizing principle of their investigation and experience. Hypertext, in other words, provides an infinitely recenterable system whose provisional point of focus depends upon the reader, who becomes truly a user of knowledge.

Hypertext offers enormous possibilities to the student and teacher of literature, all of which derive from its fundamental connectivity, a quality that greatly speeds up certain processes involved in skilled reading and critical thinking, while also making them far easier to carry out. The greater speed of making connections in hypertext permits and encourages sophisticated forms of analysis. . . .

Hypertext has the capacity to emphasize intertextuality in a way that page-bound text in books cannot. Scholarly articles, as we have seen, offer an obvious example of explicit hypertextuality in nonelectronic form. Conversely, any work of literature—which for the sake of argument and economy I shall here confine in a most arbitrary way to mean canonical literature of the sort we read and teach in universities—offers an instance of implicit hypertext in nonelectronic form. Take Joyce's *Ulysses,* for example. If one looks, say, at the "Nausicaa" section in which Bloom watches Gerty McDowell on the beach, one notes that Joyce's text here "alludes" or "refers" (the terms we usually employ) to many other texts or phenomena that one can treat as texts, including the Nausicaa section of *The Odyssey,* the advertisements and articles in the women's magazines that suffuse and inform Gerty's thoughts, facts about contemporary Dublin and the Catholic Church, and other passages within the novel. Again, one can envisage a hypertext presentation of the novel that would link this section not only to the kinds of materials mentioned, but also to other works in Joyce's career, critical commentary, and textual variants. Hypertext here permits one to make explicit, though not necessarily intrusive, the linked materials that an educated reader perceives surrounding the novel.

[In "Is There an Intertext in This Text?: Literary and Interdisciplinary Approaches to Intertextuality," *American Journal of Semiotics* 3 (1985)] Thaïs Morgan suggests that intertextuality, "as a structural analysis of texts in relation to the larger system of signifying practices or uses of signs in culture," shifts attention from the triad constituted by author/work/tradition to another constituted by text/discourse/culture. In so doing, "intertextuality replaces the evolutionary model of literary history with a structural or synchronic model of literature as a sign system. The most salient effect of this strategic change is to free the literary text from psychological, sociological, and historical determinisms, opening it up to an apparently infinite play of relationships." Morgan describes well a major implication of hypertext (and hypermedia) intertextuality: one gains an opening up, a freedom to create and perceive interconnections occurs. Nonetheless, although hypertext intertextuality would seem to devalue any historic or other reductionism, it in no way prevents those interested in reading by means of author and tradition from doing so. Our experiments [with students at Brown University using *Context32,* a series of linked documents,] thus far suggest that hypertext does not necessarily turn one's attention away from such traditional critical approaches. What is perhaps most interesting about hypertext, though, lies not in whether it fulfills certain claims of structuralist and poststructuralist criticism, but that it provides a rich means of testing them.

Intermedia does not work in the manner of most first-generation computer-assisted instruction. Most such programs and materials, which follow the model of printed workbooks, take the user through a pre-arranged sequence of exercises and experiences. Such systems constrain the users by forcing them to follow a single sequence or relatively few possible sequences. Intermedia, in contrast, reflects the fundamental characteristic of hypertext and hypermedia systems: they are bodies of linked texts that have no primary axis of organization. In other words, Intermedia has no center. Although this absence of a center can create problems for the teacher and researcher, it also means that anyone who uses Intermedia makes his or her own interests the de facto organizing principle (or center) for the investigation at the moment. One experiences Intermedia as an infinitely decenterable and recenterable system.

Hypertext then is related to the ideas of Jacques Derrida and Louis Althusser, both of whom emphasize the need to shift vantage points by decentering discussion. As Derrida points out in "Structure, Sign, and Play in the Discourse of the Human Sciences," the process or procedure he calls decentering has played an essential role in intellectual change. For example, "Ethnology could have been born as a science only at the moment when a de-centering had come about: at the moment when European culture—and, in consequence, the history of metaphysics and of its concepts—had been *dislocated,* driven from its locus, and forced to stop considering itself as the culture of reference." Derrida makes no claim that an intellectual or ideological center is in any way "bad," for as he explains in response to a query from Serge Doubrovsky, "I didn't say that there was no center, that we could get along without a center. I believe that the center is a function, not a being—a reality, but a function. And this function is absolutely indispensable" [Richard Macksey and Eugenio Donato, *The Structuralist Controversy: The Languages of Criticism and the Sciences of Man,* 1972].

Intermedia, like all hypertext systems, permits the individual user to choose his or her own center of investigation and experience. What this principle means in practice is that *Context32* does not lock the student into any kind of organization or hierarchy. For the person who chooses to organize a session on the system by making use of author overview files, moving from [the Keats overview or OV] to Tennyson OV, the system would represent an old-fashioned, traditional, and author-centered survey course. On the other hand, nothing constrains the student to work in this manner, and any students who wish to investigate the validity of period generalizations could organize their sessions in terms of such periods by using the Victorian and Romantic OV files as starting or midpoints, while others could begin with ideological or critical notions, such as overviews of Feminism or the Victorian Novel. In practice, however, students employ *Context32* as a text-centered system, since they tend to focus upon individual works with the result that even if they begin sessions by entering the system at an individual author overview file, they tend to spend most time with files devoted to individual works, moving between poem and poem (Swinburne's "Laus Veneris" and Keats's "La Belle Dame sans Merci") and between poem and informational texts ("Laus Veneris" and files on chivalry, medieval revival, courtly love, Wagner, and so on).

As the capacity of hypertext systems to be infinitely recenterable suggests, they have the corollary characteristics of being antihierarchical and democratic in several different ways. First, as the authors of "Reading and Writing the Electronic Book" point out, in such systems "Ideally, authors and readers should have the same set of integrated tools that allow them to browse through other material during the document preparation process and to add annotations and original links as they progress through an information web. In effect, the boundary between author and reader should largely disappear." One sign of the disappearance of boundaries between author and reader is the fact that the reader, not the author, largely determines how the reader moves through the system, for the reader can determine the order and principle of investigation. Intermedia has the potential, thus far only partially realized, to be a democratic or multicentered system in yet another way: as students who use the system contribute their comments and individual documents, the sharp division between author and reader that characterizes page-bound text begins to blur with several interesting implications: first, by contributing to the system, student users accept some responsibility for materials anyone can read; second, students thus establish a community of learning, demonstrating to themselves that a large part of any investigation rests on the work of others.

Hypertext offers enormous possibilities to the student and teacher of literature, all of which derive from its fundamental connectivity, a quality that greatly speeds up certain processes involved in skilled reading and critical thinking, while also making them far easier to carry out.

—George P. Landow

Although students, particularly beginning students, do not have sufficient knowledge of either primary materials or their contexts to create adequate treatments of more complex issues, they often produce excellent brief discussions of relatively limited, specific topics, such as aspects of technique in specific texts or ways in which one text relates to others. Although students in the survey contributed relatively little original material to *Context32,* those in English 61, the Victorian poetry seminar, contributed much more. Members of this and subsequent classes have created a wide range of materials including brief comparative essays, annotated bibliographies, analyses of particular passages, annotations to maps or other graphical materials illuminating individual works, and their own versions of concept maps and literary relation files. . . .

Intermedia's emphasis upon connections and relations encourages students to integrate materials from a single course with everything else they know.

There is another form of democratization or absence of hierarchy: in hypertext systems, links inside and outside a text—intertextual and intratextual connections between points of text (including images)—become equivalent, thus bringing texts closer together and blurring the boundaries among them. Consider what happens to the distinction between intra- and intertextual links in Milton in a hypertext system like Intermedia. Examples of hypertext intratextual links could be created by Milton's various descriptions of himself as prophet or inspired poet in *Paradise Lost* or by linking his citations to Gen. 3:15 within the poem. Intertextual links, in contrast, are exemplified by links between a particular passage in *Paradise Lost* that mentions prophecy and his other writings in prose or poetry that make similar points as well as those between this passage in the poem and biblical texts, scriptural commentaries throughout the ages, comparable or contrasting poetic statements by others, and scholarly comment by students of literature. Similarly, Miltonic citations of the biblical text about the heel of man crushing the serpent's head and being in turn bruised by the serpent link to the biblical passage and its traditional interpretations as well as to other literary allusions and scholarly comment upon all these subjects. Hypertext linking simply allows one to speed up the usual process of making connections while providing a means of graphing such transactions—if one can apply the word *simply* to such a radically transformative procedure. The speed with which one can move between passages and points in sets of texts promises to change the way we read and write, just as high-speed number-crunching computing changed various scientific fields by making possible investigations that before had required too much time or risk. We do not know all the ways hypertext will affect reading (and production) of texts, but one effect is already clear: the distinction between intratextuality and intertextuality will become harder to maintain than it is with book technology, and this crucial change comes from the fact that electronic linking permits the reader to move with equal facility between points inside a text and those outside of it. Once one can move with equal facility between the opening section of *Paradise Lost* and a passage in book 12 thousands of lines "away," or between that opening section and a particular anterior French text or modern scholarly comment, then, in an important sense, the discreteness of texts, which print culture creates, has radically changed and possibly disappeared.

These observations about hypertext suggest that computers bring us much closer to a culture whose qualities have more in common with those of preliterate humans than even Walter J. Ong has been willing to admit. In *Orality and Literacy* he argues that computers have brought us into what he terms an age of "secondary orality" that "has striking resemblances to the old [oral, preliterate culture] in its participatory mystique, its fostering of a communal sense, its concentration on the present moment, and even its use of formulas." Nonetheless, although Ong finds interesting parallels between a computer culture and a purely oral one, he still insists, "The sequential processing and spatializing of the word, initiated by writing and raised to a new order of intensity by print, is further intensified by the computer, which maximizes commitment of the word to space and to (electronic) local motion and optimizes analytic sequentiality by making it virtually instantaneous." In fact, hypertext systems, which insert every text into a web of relations, produce a very different effect, for they allow nonsequential reading and thinking.

Such nonsequential reading weakens the boundaries of the text, either correcting the artificial isolation of the text from its contexts or violating one of the chief qualities of the book, depending on one's point of view. Another possible result of hypertext may also be disconcerting. As Ong points out, books, unlike their authors, cannot really be challenged: "The author might be challenged if only he or she could be reached, but the author cannot be reached in any book. There is no way to refute a text. After absolutely total and devastating refutation, it says exactly the same thing as before. This is one reason why 'the book says' is popularly tantamount to 'it is true.' It is also one reason why books have been burnt. A text stating what the whole world knows is false will state falsehood forever, so long as the text exists." The question arises, however, if hypertext situates texts in a field of other texts, can any individual work that has been addressed by another still speak so forcefully? One can imagine hypertext presentations of books (or the equivalent) in which the reader can call up all the reviews and comments on that book, which would then inevitably exist as part of a complex dialogue rather than as the embodiment of one voice or thought that speaks unceasingly and authoritatively.

As one might expect at this relatively early stage in the history of hypertext systems, those involved in developing them have devoted most attention to the simple fact of linking and to the effects upon discourse of such electronically linked text. Now we need to develop a rhetoric and stylistics of hypertext. To begin with, we must recognize that although hypertext redefines some of the basic characteristics of page-bound, printed discourse, such as the rigidly hierarchical distinction in scholarly works between a main text and its annotation, it still depends upon many of the same organizing principles that make page-bound discourse coherent and even pleasurable to read.

Jay David Bolter on hypertext and the history of typography:

Rather than eliminating works of the past or making them irrelevant, the electronic writing space gives them a new "typography." For hypertext is the typography of the electronic medium. A text always undergoes typographical changes as it moves from one writing space to another. The Greek classics, for example, have moved from the papyrus roll, to codex, and finally the printed book. When we read a paperback edition in English of Plato's dialogues or Sophocles' tragedy, we are aware of the translation from ancient Greek to a modern language. But we should also remember that the original text had no book or scene divisions, no paragraphing, no indices, no punctuation, and even no word division. All these conventions of modern printing make significant organizational intrusions into the original work. They make reading Sophocles easier, but they change the Sophocles that we read. We would find it very difficult to read an English manuscript of the fourteenth century, or even an early printed book, because of the visual conventions. Electronic versions of old texts will not violate their sanctity for the first time: these texts have always been subject to typographic change; they have already been violated.

Jay David Bolter, in "Topographic Writing: Hypertext and the Electronic Writing Space," in Hypermedia and Literary Studies, *edited by Paul Delany and George P. Landow, The MIT Press, 1991.*

Designers of hypertext and hypermedia materials confront two related problems, the first of which is how to indicate the destination of links, and the second, how to welcome the user on arrival at that destination. Drawing upon the analogy of travel, one can say that the first problem concerns *exit* or *departure* information and the second *arrival* or *entrance* information. In both cases the designer must decide what users need to know at each end of a hypertext link to make use of what they find there. The general issue here is one of interpretation—namely, how much interpretation in the form of encoding or markup must the designer-author attach to the points at which one both leaves and enters a text?

John Slatin (essay date 1991)

SOURCE: "Reading Hypertext: Order and Coherence in a New Medium," in *Hypermedia and Literary Studies,* edited by Paul Delany and George P. Landow, The MIT Press, 1991, pp. 153-69.

[*An American educator and critic, Slatin has written several essays on hypertext. In the following essay, he remarks on the continuities and differences between hypertext and conventional text.*]

The basic point I have to make is almost embarrassingly simple: hypertext is very different from more traditional forms of text. The differences are a function of technology, and are so various, at once so minute and so vast, as to make hypertext a new medium for thought and expression—the first verbal medium, after programming languages, to emerge from the computer revolution. (The computer has spawned new media in the visual arts and music as well.) As a new medium, hypertext is also very different from both word processing and desktop publishing, two other computer technologies which have had an enormous impact on the production of texts. Both word processing and desktop publishing have as their goal the production of conventional printed documents, whereas hypertext exists and can exist only online, only in the computer. A new medium involves both a new practice and a new rhetoric, a new body of theory. I hope this paper will serve as a step in that direction.

The first requirement for a rhetoric of hypertext is that it must take the computer actively into account as a medium for composition and thought—not just as a presentational device and not simply as an extension of the typewriter. This means different things, depending on the level of abstraction at which one stands. At some levels, for example, one has to deal not only with knowledge as constructed by humans for humans, but also with data structures, with the representation—or, more accurately, the reconstruction—of knowledge (if the term still applies) in hardware and software. It means, also, that the rhetoric itself must be abstract, like Wallace Stevens's Supreme Fiction, in order to permit movement up and down the ladder of abstraction and to permit the articulation of principles that will enable practice. By the same token, the rhetoric of hypertext will have to be capable of change: for it is tied to a still immature (perhaps perpetually immature) technology which is itself changing at an exponential rate.

On the assumption, then, that description is the first step toward theory, I will contrast hypertext with more traditional text. I will focus on the assumptions each makes about what readers do and the ways in which those assumptions about reading affect the author's understanding of composition. For the purposes of this discussion, taking the computer into account means that we have to find ways of talking about "documents" that have multiple points of entry, multiple exit points, and multiple pathways between points of entry and exit points. Moreover, we must find ways to talk about the still more exciting kinds of activity fostered by this proliferation of possibilities: I mean interactive reading and its more or less inevitable concomitant, interactive writing, or co-authorship.

Widespread literacy is a comparatively recent phenomenon—that is to say that in Western societies such as those of Europe, and North America, general literacy is at best a couple of hundred years old. But Western culture was a print culture long before the coming of general literacy, and the text environment we are all familiar with is the product of fully mature, highly stable manuscript and print technologies which have been in place for many centuries. Our principles and strategies for effective written communication are therefore based on long-established assumptions about readers and reading. It will be helpful to consider these assumptions briefly before going on to discuss the different assumptions embedded in the design of hypertext and hypermedia systems.

The assumption that reading is a sequential and continuous process is the foundation on which everything else rests. The reader is expected to begin at a clearly marked point whose appropriateness has been determined by the author—usually with considerable effort: one of the hardest moments in any writing project is to figure out where to start—and to proceed from that beginning to an ending which is just as clearly marked and which has also been determined by the author in accordance with his or her understanding of the subject matter and the reader. The reader's progress from the beginning to the end of the text follows a route which has been carefully laid out for the sole purpose of ensuring that the reader does indeed get from the beginning to the end in the way writer wants him or her to get there.

All but the most naive and inexperienced writers recognize that all but the most naive and inexperienced readers inevitably and rightly make inferences about what's going to happen next, on the basis of what they have already read—not only in the current text, but in other texts resembling it. The reader's perception of the predictability of a given text is an important factor in his or her qualitative evaluation of the text.

Prediction operates on a number of different levels and is determined by different things at different levels of abstraction. The predictability of a given text is a function of the relationships among phenomena at microscopic, macroscopic, and metatextual levels of abstraction. At the microscopic levels, the reader's ability to predict the course of the text from moment to moment is a function of such factors as paragraphing, sentence length, complexity of phrasing, vocabulary, and so on—that is, the factors that are evaluated in producing a so-called "readability index." Indeed, one might descend even further down the ladder of abstraction and argue that prediction takes place at the graphemic or phonemic levels as well. At the macroscopic levels, the reader is aware of such things as general subject matter, topics and subtopics and the structural devices organizing the text as a whole—sections, chapters, and subchapters, and so forth. At this level the reader is also at least subliminally aware of such things as how much more material there is to read. On what we might call the metatextual level, the reader makes inferences about the text as a whole, based on his or her understanding of the larger context to which s/he regards the text as belonging. These inferences are often implicit, or else they may take the form of mental or marginal annotations; in any case, they are outside the text and separate from it. But, as I shall explain later on, they are *integral* to hypertext.

The end product of the writing process is a text written or printed on paper, and then, often, sewn or glued or otherwise bound between covers. This is obvious, I know, and yet it needs to be said. Every writer has had the awful experience of opening a book or article hot off the press, only to stare in horror at a glaring error in a crucial passage that somehow escaped the most agonizing scrutiny. The fixity of the printed text as an object in physical space makes the text as an object in mental space seem equally stable and fixed. Or at least that's how we tend to want it. As Richard Lanham has said, "It was establishing the original text that the Renaissance scholars thought their main task, and generations of textual editors since have renewed their labors. The aim of all this was to fix the text forever" ["Convergent Pressures: Social, Technological, Theoretical," *Conference on the Future of Doctoral Studies in English,* Wayzata, Minnesota, April 1987]. The continuing controversy over Hans-Walter Gabler's edition of Joyce's *Ulysses* makes abundantly clear just how intense the desire "to fix the text forever" can be. Gabler's reconception of the editing process may have occurred "independently of his decision to use the computer," but the controversy over his "synoptic" version of *Ulysses* offers a clear illustration of the way computers will revolutionize our understanding of text. Every word in Gabler's synoptic text was written by Joyce himself—and yet the final "reading text" is a text no one ever wrote—it had never existed prior to its publication. (In this sense, Gabler's *Ulysses* resembles Benoit Mandelbrot's fractals, in which recursive mathematical formulae are graphically plotted to produce visual structures that, while in some cases resembling phenomena in the day-to-day world, have no counterpart in that world.) Gabler's is a simulated *Ulysses,* like the *Don Quixote* that would be produced by Borges' Pierre Menard if Menard were real and if he had a computer. This is what becomes of the work of art in an age of electronic reproduction. Text is always mutable, always subject to inadvertent error and deliberate change, and it has to be coerced into standing still—that's why publishers charge you money if you make too many changes in a text after it's been typeset.

For all these reasons—because a text looks like a permanent thing, because readers expect to begin at the beginning and end at the end and to know which is which (that's why students so often begin the last paragraph with *In conclusion*), because readers expect to get from beginning to end *via* a clearly-marked route—sequence is of paramount concern to a writer. Much of his or her effort goes into figuring out the correct sequence for the material that's going to be presented. The writer's job in this context is to contrive a sequence that will not only determine the reader's experience and understanding of the material but will also seem to the reader to have been the only possible sequence for that material; you want it to seem to have been somehow inevitable.

Of course this inevitability has a good deal to do with the issue of predictability I raised earlier. Readers have to be able to predict what will come next, at least up to a point, or they start to feel lost, which makes them start to feel nervous, which makes them want to put down what they're reading and go watch a football game or something—at which point the writer has failed miserably. But the flip side is just as bad, and the end result is going to be the same.

Writing that's too predictable is governed by a presupposition succinctly expressed by a certain hotel chain's ad campaigns. The presupposition that there should be "no surprises" may be fine for hotels. But it becomes a fundamental conceptual error where writing is concerned.

The informational value of a given document is not simply a function of the quantity of data it presents or the facts it contains. At one level of abstraction, what we call information may indeed consist in numbers, dates, and other data, other facts. But as Gregory Bateson says [in his *Mind and Nature: A Necessary Unity,* 1980], "All receipt of information is necessarily receipt of the news of *difference.*" At a somewhat higher level of abstraction, therefore, none of these data can be considered information until they have been contextualized, arranged in such a way that both the significant differences and the significant relationships among them may become apparent to the intended reader. In Christopher Dede's terms, this is when information becomes knowledge. In other words, as literary artists and their readers have always known, there can be no information without surprise.

Rhetoric typically has little to say about the physical processes by which a text is brought into being. Or I could put it even more strongly and say that rhetoric has traditionally been indifferent to the technology of communication. One reason for this indifference is that the technology is so mature that it's simply taken for granted, so that it is essentially invisible *as* technology. There was a point in history, of course, when writing itself was a radically innovative technology and was regarded as such, as Eric A. Havelock, Father Walter J. Ong, and Richard Lanham have shown us. The computerization of writing has similarly made the technology itself highly visible, especially in the cases of desktop publishing and hypertext/hypermedia. By contrast with traditional text, hypertext and hypermedia depend upon an emergent technology which is still immature and still subject to radical transformation; indeed, all indications are that accelerating change is an inherent characteristic of this technology. It may *never* stabilize. Thus rhetoric for hypertext cannot afford to disregard the technological substrate upon which composition and reading depend.

There are many continuities between conventional text and hypertext. Anyone involved in creating a hyperdocument will still have to worry about the problems I've outlined so far. But hypertext is a very different kind of beast than a conventional text, and creating a hyperdocument poses some very different problems as well. The remainder of this paper will concentrate on those differences and their implications.

First of all, the hyperdocument may well contain material from several different media such as text, graphics, video, and sound. While this is an important factor, I don't think it's decisive. After all, printed books often contain text, line drawings, tables of data, reproductions of visual images, and so forth—though of course they cannot manage full motion video or sound. Besides containing different types of materials than those to be found in printed text, the hyperdocument is likely to contain considerably more material than a printed book. Again, this is not a decisive difference in itself: encyclopedias also contain an enormous quantity of material. The quantity of material in a hyperdocument does pose problems, and it does make for complexity. But the greatest difference between text and hypertext is not in the relative quantity of material each form handles: it's in the technology that handles the material.

What makes all the difference in the world is the fact that hypertext exists and can exist only in an online environment. This is crucial, not just because it substitutes monitors, keyboards, and mice for the customary physical apparatus associated with text—paper, books, pencils, and so forth. The fact that hypertext exists only in the online environment is crucial because, as Douglas Hofstadter says [in his *Metamagical Themas: Questing for the Essence of Mind and Pattern,* 1986], "It is the organization of memory that defines what concepts are." Hypertext uses machine memory in a way that has no analogue in the traditional text environment, where composition relies on the organization of human memory. It is the organization of memory in the computer and in the mind that defines hypertext and makes it fundamentally different from conventional text.

In such an environment, the problem is not simply to develop effective strategies for implementing well known and long established principles of effective communication. On the contrary, one of the chief functions of rhetoric in the hypertext environment is to discover the principles of effective communication and then develop ways of implementing those principles through the available technology.

The rapidly evolving technological environment makes hypertext possible by permitting the embodiment of a very different set of assumptions about readers and reading—and about thinking. These assumptions in turn form the basis for decisions made in the process of creating a hyperdocument.

Reading, in hypertext, is understood as a discontinuous or non-linear process which, like thinking, is associative in nature, as opposed to the sequential process envisioned by conventional text. Associative thinking is more difficult to follow than linear thinking. Linear thinking specifies the steps it has taken; associative thinking is discontinuous—a series of jumps like the movement of electrons or the movements of the mind in creating metaphor. This discontinuity is not fortuitous; rather, as Stewart Brand points out [in his *The Media Lab: Inventing the Future at MIT,* 1987], it is a basic aspect of the digital encoding of information. Brand offers the illuminating contrast between the surface of a traditional phonograph album, with its continuous grooves, and the surface of a compact disc, with its distinct, discontinuous pits.

Reading in this sense has little to do with traditional notions of beginning at the beginning and going through to the end. Instead, the reader begins at a point of his or her own choosing—a point chosen from a potentially very large number of possible starting points. The reader proceeds from there by following a series of links connecting documents to one another, exiting not at a point defined by the author as "The End" but rather when s/he has had enough. Accordingly, the most common metaphors in discussions of hypertext equate reading with the navigation or traversal of large, open (and usually poorly-charted) spaces. As Jeff Conklin has pointed out [in his *A Survey of Hypertext,* 1986], because the hyperdocument contains so much material, and because relations between the components of the hyperdocument are not always spelled out, there is a significant danger that the reader will get lost or become badly disoriented.

The difficulty is compounded because hypertext systems tend to envision three different types of readers: the reader as browser, as user, or as co-author. The relationship between these three classes can be fuzzy and therefore difficult to manage. One function a rhetoric for hypertext will have to serve will be to provide ways of negotiating it.

The browser is someone who wanders rather aimlessly (but not carelessly) through an area, picking things up and putting them down as curiosity or momentary interest dictates. In this respect the browser is someone who reads for pleasure, with this important difference: there is no expectation that the browser will go through all of the available material; often the expectation is just the reverse. It is difficult to predict the browser's pathway through the material—and in fact it is less important to predict the pathway the browser will take than it is to provide a backtracking mechanism, what Mark Bernstein calls [in "The Bookmark and the Compass: Orientation Tools for Hypertext Users," in *ACM SIGOIS Bulletin* (October 1988)] a Hansel-&-Gretel trail of breadcrumbs to allow the browser to re-trace his or her steps at will. (Of course this same mechanism is essential for readers in the two remaining categories as well.)

By contrast with the browser, the user is a reader with a clear—and often clearly limited—purpose. He or she enters the hyperdocument in search, usually, of specific information and leaves it again after locating that information. The user's path is relatively predictable, provided those who have created the hyperdocument have a sufficient understanding of the task domain. In these respects, then, the user resembles a typical student doing the assigned reading for a course. But there is also an important difference between the user and the student, which is most clearly recognized from the vantage-point of the author rather than the reader. The author(s) of a hypertext documentation system (for, e.g., a software product like Microsoft QuickBASIC 4.5) will have met their goal when the user finds the information s/he needs and returns to the work in progress. The instructor designing a set of hypertext course materials may well not be satisfied with such an outcome, however: the instructor aims at a dynamic process, in which the student moves among three different states: from a user the student becomes a browser (and may then become a user once again). Ultimately, the student becomes fully involved as *co-author.* Thus what looks like a hierarchy of readers collapses.

One of the most important differences between conventional text and hypertext is that most hypertext systems, though not all, allow readers to interact with the system to such an extent that some readers may become actively involved in the creation of an evolving hyperdocument.

—John Slatin

One of the most important differences between conventional text and hypertext is that most hypertext systems, though not all, allow readers to interact with the system to such an extent that some readers may become actively involved in the creation of an evolving hyperdocument. Co-authorship may take a number of different forms—from relatively simple, brief annotations of or comments on existing material, to the creation of new links connecting material not previously linked, to the modification of existing material or the creation of new materials, or both. Both literary theorists (e.g., Wolfgang Iser, Paul Ricoeur, Stanley Fish) and cognitive scientists like Jerome Bruner have talked for years about the reader's involvement in the construction of textual meaning. But hypertext's capacity for literally interactive reading and co-authorship represents a radical departure from traditional relationships between readers and texts. The implications of this departure from traditional relationships between readers and texts are enormous, both for the creative arts and for education: as many theorists now agree, understanding comes about when the mind acts upon the material. Marshall McLuhan's distinction between hot and cool media is relevant here—a cool medium being one that invites active participation, a hot one being one before which one sits passively. McLuhan was thinking, of course, about the difference between print and television, but one might argue that hypertext combines the heat and visual excitement of film, video, and television with text's cool invitation to participate.

"Writing," in the hypertext environment, becomes the more comprehensive activity called "authoring." Authoring may involve not only the composition of text, but also screen layout and other things that fall under the general rubric of interface design; it may also involve a certain amount of programming (as in Apple's HyperCard, where complex navigational and other processes are scripted by the stack's author). Perhaps most importantly, authoring involves the creation and management of links between nodes.

Ted Nelson, who coined the term "hypertext," defines hypertext [in his *Literary Machines,* 1987] as "nonsequential writing." This means writing in which the logical connections between elements are primarily associative rather than syllogistic, as in conventional text. One implication of this is that the hyperdocument "grows" by a process of accretion, whereas the conventional document tends to have been winnowed out of a larger mass of material. That is, in preparing to write a conventional document, you almost inevitably assemble more material than you can possibly use; the closer you come to final copy, the more you find yourself excluding material that "doesn't fit" the subject as you've finally defined it. Hypertext, by contrast, is an inclusive medium. Thanks to the capability of creating nodes and links, material not linearly related to the point being discussed at the moment but still associated with that point may be placed in a node of its own and linked to other nodes as appropriate; the material need not be thrown away. In much the same way, no individual point of view need be excluded.

This inclusiveness makes it unlikely that any one individual will see all the elements making up the system. It also means that the hyperdocument is in fact a collection of possible documents, any one of which may be actualized by readers pursuing or creating links between elements of the system.

The end product of the authoring process, the hyperdocument, is not a closed system, like a book; it is rather an open and dynamic system. The hyperdocument is an online system or network whose constituents are of two basic types: nodes and links. Nodes may consist of documents, images, or other materials electronically connected—linked—to one or more other documents or images. Very likely, the different nodes will represent the work of quite a few individuals, who may have been working at different times and in different locations. Indeed, one impetus for the development of hypertext systems has been in the need to address exactly this issue among members of development teams. The development of protocols and procedures for co-authorship thus becomes an important issue. So does the development of procedures for moving through the system.

The reader's progress through a conventional text is governed by the arrangement of the material; the burden of prediction falls more heavily upon the reader than on the writer. This situation becomes considerably more complicated in hypertext. Given a system of discrete and interconnected nodes, the reader/user must decide which links to follow; in order to make that decision intelligently, s/he must be able to make reliable predictions about the consequences of particular choices. But the freedom of movement and action available to the reader—a freedom including the possibility of co-authorship—means that the hypertext author has to make predictions as well: for the author, the difficulty at any given moment is to provide freedom of movement and interaction, while at the same time remaining able to predict where the reader/user will go next. The most effective solution here, I think, will be to treat each node as if it were certain to be the reader's next destination. This is time-consuming in the short run, but in the long run probably saves time by creating a more readily usable system.

This brings us to the issue of linkage, the mechanism that creates the hyperdocument and allows the reader to move through it. Douglas Hofstadter has suggested that the perception of relatedness is a defining characteristic—perhaps *the* defining characteristic—of intelligent behavior. Hypertext embodies this idea, for everything in hypertext depends upon linkage, upon connectivity between and among the various elements in the system. Linkage, in hypertext, plays a role corresponding to that of sequence in conventional text. A hypertext link is the electronic representation of a perceived relationship between two pieces of material, which become nodes once the relationship has been instantiated electronically. That is, the link *simulates* the connections in the mind of the author or reader; and it is precisely because the electronic link is only a simulation that problems will arise.

The interdependency of links and nodes is such that it is impossible to talk about one without talking about the other. Thus the question of how to define a node (*block* is an alternative term in the literature on hypertext) leads to additional questions about linkage. These lead in turn to questions about structure and coherence, and so back again to the issue of prediction.

A node is any object which is linked to another object. It may be as large as an entire book or as small as a single character (theoretically, it could be as small as a single pixel [picture element] on a display), though such extremes seem hardly practical; it may consist of a document or a block of text within a larger document; it may be a drawing, a digitized photograph, a (digitized) detail of a painting, a sound recording, a motion picture, or a scene—even a frame—from a motion picture.

There is no set answer to the question, how big should a node be? just as there is no set answer to the question, how long is a paragraph? Like the paragraph, the hypertext node is a way of structuring attention, and its boundaries, like those of the paragraph, are somewhat arbitrary. A node may contain a single paragraph; it may contain many; it may contain something else entirely. Jeff Conklin offers criteria for guidance in determining node size. To what extent, he asks, is the information in question so tightly bound together that (a) you always want to view it together; (b) you never want to take it apart; and (c) you rarely even want to reference parts of it outside of the context of the rest. In other words, a node is an integrated and self-sufficient unit; its size will be a function of the complexity of the integration. This in turn is contingent upon the author's perception of the nature of the material it contains and the relation of that material to other things in the hyperdocument.

The individual node, then, behaves in certain respects like a more conventional text. But the node is not just a self-contained unit. A node cannot, by definition, be entirely free of links—a node is a knot, is always embedded in a system—and that connectedness in turn gives the node its definition. "A node is something through which other things pass, and which is created by their passage" [John M. Slatin, "Hypertext and the Teaching of Writing," in Edward Barrett's *Text, Context, and Hypertext,* 1988].

A text becomes a node when it is electronically placed in relation to other materials (documentary or otherwise), which may (or may not) already contain links to other elements within the system. The difficulty here, of course, is that what are to me self-evident associations may not be even faintly apparent to you, and vice versa. This imposes an obligation on the author(s) of a hyperdocument which has no exact parallel for the writer of conventional text: the nodes must seem complete in themselves, yet at the same time their relations to other nodes must be intelligible. The problem of relationality here is analogous to the problems of intertextuality confronting readers of, say 20th-century poetry. This problem becomes increasingly challenging as the hyperdocument expands. Links exist for many different reasons—that is, to represent many different kinds of relationships between objects; the more links there are between the current node and other elements of the hyperdocument, then, the greater the necessity of identifying the attached material clearly—especially when the reader is allowed considerable freedom in choosing among the available links.

These identifiers carry an enormous burden. Indeed they are often asked to do the kind of explanatory work that ordinarily takes several sentences or paragraphs. Not surprisingly, there are several different methods of identifying link or node types. Some hypertext systems, such as MCC's gIBIS, use "typed nodes," while others—Xerox PARC's NoteCards, for example—employ "link types." These systems allow the co-author creating a new node to choose from a list of predefined relationship categories, whose names then become part of the node or link.

HyperTIES, developed by Ben Shneiderman at the University of Maryland and distributed by Cognetics Corporation, offers a variation on this approach, by encouraging the author to compose a brief (two-line) description of the linked node. In HyperTIES, where reading is defined primarily as browsing and where browsing is completely separate from authoring, activating a link is a two-step process. The first step, clicking on a highlighted word or phrase, brings up the description of the attached node; the second step either brings up the attached node or returns the browser to the current screen.

The developers of Intermedia at Brown University have chosen a third alternative. Links belong to "webs" rather than to documents; webs are displayed onscreen as visual maps. An Intermedia document is first displayed as if it were freestanding; then, when the user opens a web, the links belonging to that web are displayed. This approach allows an individual node to be placed within multiple frames of reference, or "webs," while avoiding both the screen clutter and the mental clutter that can accrue so easily when multiple links radiate to and from a node. Which links the user sees will depend upon which web s/he has elected to open.

As the Intermedia approach suggests, one way to address the question of how many links a node should have is by turning it into the question of how many links should be displayed at any moment. Research on memory suggests that we can hang on to between five and seven "chunks" of information at a time, and that creating links between these chunks is a way to increase the effective size of the chunk. However, the number of chunks that can be retained decreases in inverse proportion to their size.

Probably no single method of identifying nodes and their relationships to other nodes is adequate to all needs; some combination will be needed. Choosing from a list of predefined relationships has certain advantages, since there is a strong likelihood that a newly created node will fall within an existing classification. However, the list must offer real choices without becoming so big as to make choice impossible. And co-authors will still want to be able to define and use new categories. Co-authors may also wish to give a fuller description of the attached node than the list approach permits; something like the HyperTIES strategy becomes appropriate here. And when a given node has multiple links to and from other nodes, it may be advisable to use an Intermedia-style mapping strategy.

The approach you choose to the problem of identifying links and nodes will depend on several factors: your understanding of the ways in which the material is related; your sense of who your readers are (are they primarily browsers? users? co-authors?). Your sense of what you want those readers to do is especially important.

You don't have to worry about interactive readers when you write a conventional text—the only thing you want the reader to do is to go on to the next sentence. But in hypertext, where there are a number of possible "next sentences" or nodes for the reader to go on to, you do have to make some decisions about what ought to happen next. That is, do you care whether the reader (a) opens a specific node or sequence of nodes; (b) chooses more or less randomly from the available links; (c) creates a new node, linking it not only to the current node but also to such other nodes as the reader—now a co-author—deems appropriate?

If you want the reader to open a specific node or sequence of nodes, you can either try to influence the reader's course of action, for example by highlighting a "preferred pathway" through the material, or you can simply pre-empt the reader's choice by automating the sequence or hiding links you don't want the reader to pursue. (Though if you take that route you give up many of the advantages of hypertext, it seems to me.) Or if you don't have a preference about the sequence the reader follows, you may opt not to give directions, leaving the choice of which links to activate—or whether to activate any link at all—entirely up to the reader. If you want to encourage response—that is if you want the reader actually to get involved as a co-author—you should say so somewhere on the screen and make it as easy as possible for the reader to change roles. In HyperCard, for instance, you can script a button to open up a text field with a date/time stamp and the name of the new co-author; you can even let the co-author enter keywords to make later searches faster.

I've already said that the author of a hyperdocument has a hard time trying to predict where the reader will go from any given point. The reader who activates a link often has a hard time, too, because it can be so difficult to predict what the result will be. The more cryptic the link or node identifiers are, the harder it is for the reader to predict the results of activating a particular link. The harder it is to make such predictions, the greater the likelihood that the reader will simply opt out of the process in frustration. And even if the reader does go ahead there is no guarantee that s/he will know the place when s/he gets there.

The reader has to make several different kinds of predictions. First, s/he has to predict the kind of material s/he will encounter upon activating a link. It would be quite distressing, for example, to activate a link in the expectation of moving to a narrative explanation of some issue, if in fact the associated node contains only raw data in tabular form. Second, s/he makes some predictions about the content of the node: at the most general level, the reader makes some kind of assumption about the closeness of the relationship between the current node and the material linked to it.

The questions of link and node labeling which are obviously of such central importance here impinge on the issue of predictability at what I have been calling the macroscopic level. At the microscopic level, predictability revolves around such things as screen-design: typography, visual effects, layout of information on the screen, and so forth, all have an impact on the reader's ability to organize the material in his or her own mind, and thus on his or her ability to operate effectively within the hypertext environment.

Typographical conventions are such that the reader of a conventional text has a pretty good idea what kind of object will appear next. The period at the end of a sentence leads one to expect a capital letter and the beginning of a new object belonging to the same class—a new sentence; the blank space at the end of a paragraph signals the beginning of a new paragraph; and so on. The signals in hypertext systems aren't nearly so clear.

Because the technology isn't mature enough yet to support a single set of conventions, each hypertext system has to develop its own conventions. For that reason, it is probably necessary to incorporate procedural discussions about these conventions into the hyperdocument itself; thus one element of the hyperdocument will be an ongoing critique of its own procedures. Participants might consider, for example, whether to assign specific fonts to individual co-authors so that their contributions can be readily identified; text styles might be assigned to specific node or link types; a question might always be italicized, for instance, while an explanation might be underlined; and so on. Color can be used for similar purposes in systems where color is available. So can visual effects such as wipes, dissolves, and zooms, which are available in HyperCard. These and other special effects can easily become distracting or even annoying, but if particular devices are consistently and intelligently used in association with particular node types, they can also function as more or less subliminal aids to prediction, helping the reader to perceive the hyperdocument as coherent.

We regard a conventional text as coherent to the extent that all the material it contains strikes us being (a) related in an appropriately direct way to the subject and to the author's thesis; and (b) arranged in the appropriate sequence. The perception of coherence in hypertext seems to me much more problematic, however, though I don't have time to do more than suggest what might be involved. Nor do I know enough to do more than that.

I think of hypertext coherence as appearing at the metatextual level—that is, at the level where the reader perceives what Gregory Bateson calls "the pattern which connects." The "pattern which connects" is the organizing notion around which all the disparate elements of the hyperdocument revolve. (An author's feel for "the pattern which connects" plays a significant part in decisions about node size and linkage as well.) This can be a relatively straightforward thing—a given hyperdocument might contain all the materials generated during a particular design project, for instance. This metatextual level is perhaps best represented by a visual map of some kind, whose nodes would open up to map subordinate patterns. This map ought to be readily accessible from any point in the hyperdocument, which suggests that it might be "iconized" and placed at a consistent screen location. This sounds simple enough, perhaps; but it becomes problematic again when we remember that we're dealing with a fluid system and multiple participants, and we start to ask whose understanding such maps represent. Maybe there needs to be a facility to allow any user to create such a map, whether for private consideration only or for public use might be up to the reader/co-author.

Conceptually, hypertext has a place, I think, in any environment where it's necessary or desirable to bring together large, complex, highly diversified bodies of information in such a way as to emphasize their interconnectedness—especially if physical space is at a premium, as of course it is on board a space station or an orbital device, or in a control room—or, for that matter, in a classroom.

Perhaps the greatest value of hypertext is in its ability to link enormous quantities of material that, in a conventional text environment, would be kept separate, perhaps even in different buildings, so that things which someone perceives as being related do in fact become related. Hypertext is weakest when it comes to spelling out what these relationships entail; it is important to say this, because the techniques for explanation are quite highly developed within traditional rhetoric, and it would be a mistake to abandon them as outmoded.

Hypertext places different demands on both readers and authors than those facing readers and authors of conventional text. The principal reason for this, in my view, is that hypertext is truly a new medium. Employing the full resources of technology to represent and correlate information, hypertext grants both readers and authors an unprecedented degree of freedom to arrange materials as they deem best, and it permits interaction between readers and authors to an unprecedented degree. In so transforming the methods of organization which have served traditional text for millennia, hypertext requires authors and system designers to find new methods of indicating relationships, representing and constructing knowledge, and achieving coherence.

Robert Coover on hypertext and reading:

With hypertext we focus, both as writers and as readers, on structure as much as on prose, for we are made aware suddenly of the shapes of narratives that are often hidden in print stories. The most radical new element that comes to the fore in hypertext is the system of multidirectional and often labyrinthine linkages we are invited or obliged to create. Indeed the creative imagination often becomes more preoccupied with linkage, routing and mapping than with statement or style, or with what we would call character or plot (two traditional narrative elements that are decidedly in jeopardy). We are always astonished to discover how much of the reading and writing experience occurs in the interstices and trajectories *between* text fragments. That is to say, the text fragments are like stepping stones, there for our safety, but the real *current* of the narratives runs between them.

Robert Coover, in his "The End of Books," in The New York Times Book Review, *21 June 1992.*

Jay David Bolter (essay date 1991)

SOURCE: "Interactive Fiction," in *Writing Space: The Computer, Hypertext, and the History of Writing,* Lawrence Erlbaum Associates, 1991, pp. 121-46.

[*In the following excerpt, in which he discusses Michael Joyce's interactive text "Afternoon" (1987) at length, Bolter places interactive fiction within the context of Modernism and suggests possibilities that the genre offers to authors and readers.*]

Bibliographic databases and technical documents have long been regarded as legitimate texts for the computer: novels, short stories, and poems have not. It is true that many novelists now use word processors to prepare manuscripts for publication as printed books. But very few have attempted to write fiction to be read in the electronic space—that is, nonlinear fiction, which invites the reader to conduct a dialogue with the text. Yet fiction belongs just as naturally in this new technology as all the more pragmatic forms of writing. Fiction, at least modern fiction, is by nature open to experiment, and being open and open-ended is precisely the quality that the computer lends to all writing. The flexibility of electronic text makes for a new form of imaginative writing that has already been named "interactive fiction."

We are just emerging from the nickelodeon era of interactive fiction, and the computer's equivalent of the nickelodeon is the adventure game (which costs rather more than a nickel). In an adventure game the player has a mythical world to explore—a dungeon or an enchanted forest or valley. The computer describes the scene, and the player issues simple commands such as "go ahead," "enter the room," "pick up the dagger," "get gold," and the like. The goal is to amass treasure and dispatch monsters, although sometimes the game is more sophisticated, casting the player in the role of a detective who must solve a murder or other mystery. Even the simplest of these games is a kind of fiction. The computer presents the player with a text, and the player's job is to understand and respond to that text. Depending upon the response, the computer presents more text and awaits a further response. The player, then, is a reader, but an unusually powerful reader, for his or her decisions determine what text will next appear. Admittedly the text of most of the current games is simple-minded, but the method of presentation is not. While a printed novel presents its episodes in one order, the electronic writing space removes that restriction for fiction as it does for the essay. Instead of a single string of paragraphs, the author lays out a textual space within which his or her fiction operates. The reader joins in actively constructing the text by selecting a particular order of episodes at the time of reading. Within each episode, the reader is still compelled to read what the author has written. But the movement between episodes is determined by the responses of the reader, his or her interactions with or intrusions into the text, and the reader's experience of the fiction depends upon these interactions.

In its simplest form, interactive fiction requires only [two elements]: episodes (topics) and decision points (links) between episodes. The episodes may be paragraphs of prose or poetry, they may include bit-mapped graphics as well, and they may be of any length. Their length will establish the rhythm of the story—how long the reader remains a conventional reader before he or she is called on to participate in the selection of the next episode. At the end of each episode, the author inserts a set of links to other episodes together with a procedure for choosing which link to follow. Each link may require a different response from the reader or a different condition in the computer system. The reader may answer a question posed in the text; there will be one link for each possible reader response. The computer can also keep track of the previous episodes readers have visited, so that they may be barred from visiting one episode before they visit another. Many other tests are possible, but even with the simple matching technique and the tracking of previously visited episodes, the author can create a fictional space of great flexibility. Readers may be allowed to examine a story in chronological order, in reverse chronology, or in a complicated sequence of flashbacks and returns. They may follow one character through the story, and then return to follow another. A reader might play the role of the detective trying to solve a murder, a role familiar from the computerized adventure games. A reader might be asked to influence events in a novel by choosing episodes that promise to bring two characters together or to punish an evil character for his or her deeds: each choice would define a new course for the story. Such multiple plots, however, are only one possibility for interactive fiction. The electronic writing space can accommodate many other literary strategies. It could offer the reader several different perspectives on a fixed set of events. In this case the reader would not be able to affect the course of the story, but the reader could switch back and forth among narrators, each with his or her own point of view. An electronic text could also establish relationships among episodes that are not narrative at all: a poet could define multiple reading orders for an anthology of his or her poems—according to theme, image, time of the year, or other criteria under the poet's or the reader's control.

It is important to realize that electronic fiction in this sense is not automatic fiction. The computer does not create the verbal text: it presents that text to the reader according to the author's preconditions. The locus of creativity remains with the author and the reader, although the balance between the two has shifted. Nor is electronic fiction necessarily random. The author may put any number of restrictions on the reading order. The extent of the reader's choices and therefore the reader's freedom in examining the literary space depends upon the links that the author creates between episodes. The reader may have to choose from among a few alternatives or may range widely through the work. Each author can relinquish as much or as little control as he or she chooses; the author has a new literary dimension with which to work.

What the author and reader can do with this literary dimension is shown in "Afternoon" by Michael Joyce (1987), one of the first examples of this new genre of interactive fiction. "Afternoon" combines the literary sophistication of a printed work with the immediacy of a computerized adventure game. "Afternoon" is a fiction and a game at the same time, and yet its visual structure is very simple. The reader confronts a window on the computer screen: episodes of "Afternoon," containing from one to a few hundred words, will appear successively in the window. At the bottom of the screen is a small bar, where the reader types replies in order to move to the next episode; the reader may also initiate movement by selecting a word from the current episode in the window. All the text of the episodes was written by Michael Joyce, but the particular order in which the episodes are visited is determined at the time of reading.

"Afternoon" begins:

> I try to recall winter. 'As if it were yesterday?' she says, but I do not signify one way or another.
>
> By five the sun sets and the afternoon melt freezes again across the black top into crystal octopi and palms of ice—rivers and continents beset by fear, and we walk out to the car, the

> snow moaning beneath our boots and the oaks exploding in series along the fenceline on the horizon, the shrapnel settling like relics, the echoing thundering off far ice.
>
> This was the essence of wood, these fragments say. And this darkness is air. 'Poetry' she says, without emotion, one way or another.
>
> Do you want to hear about it?

If the reader types yes, then a link will flash another episode on the screen, whose first sentences are:

> She had been a client of Wert's wife for some time. Nothing serious, nothing awful, merely general unhappiness and the need of a woman so strong to have friends. . . .

If the reader types no, another episode will appear beginning:

> I understand how you feel. Nothing is more empty than heat. Seen so starkly the world holds wonder only in the expanses of clover where the bees work. . . .

"Afternoon" does not accept no as the reader's last word: instead, it moves the reader along a different path. But the reader has other choices as well: he or she can select a particular word directly from the text (such as "poetry," "winter," or "yesterday" in the first episode). Certain words in each window will "yield" and branch to another episode. If the reader defaults by hitting the Return key, then yet another link will be followed. Many different responses will cause the text to move, but until the reader responds with some action of the keyboard or the mouse, the text of an episode remains on the screen, conventional prose (occasionally poetry) to be read in the conventional way.

One voice in a later episode in "Afternoon" describes the reading experience this way:

> In my mind the story, as it has formed, takes on margins. Each margin will yield to the impatient, or wary, reader. You can answer yes at the beginning and page through on a wave of Returns, or page through directly—again using Returns—without that first interaction.
> These are not versions, but the story itself in long lines. Otherwise, however, the center is all—Thoreau or Brer Rabbit, each preferred the bramble. I've discovered more there too, and the real interaction, if that is possible, is in pursuit of texture. . . .

This is the great difference between "Afternoon" and a fiction written on and for paper. There is no single story of which each reading is a version, because each reading determines the story as it goes. We could say that there is no story at all; there are only readings. Or if we say that the story of "Afternoon" is the sum of all its readings, then we must understand the story as a structure that can embrace contradictory outcomes. Each reading is a different turning within a universe of paths set up by the author. Reading "Afternoon" several times is like exploring a vast house or castle. The reader proceeds often down the same corridors and through familiar rooms. But often too the reader comes upon a new hallway not previously explored or finds a previously locked door suddenly giving way to the touch. Gradually, the reader pushes back the margins of this electronics space—as in a computer game in which the descent down a stairway reveals a whole new level of the dungeon. "Afternoon" is constructed so as to remind the reader of the origins of electronic fiction in the computerized adventure games.

"Afternoon" is metaphorically related to computer video games as well. It is like a video game in which the player pilots a spaceship around planetary obstacles that each exert a gravitational force. Readers of "Afternoon" move along paths with their own inertia, while at the same time experiencing the attraction of various parts of the fiction as they move by. It is easy to fall into an orbit around one set of episodes, one focus of the story. Readers find themselves returning to the same episodes again and again, trying to break free by giving different answers and therefore choosing different paths. When it succeeds, this strategy may then push the reader into another orbit.

The planets in "Afternoon" 's solar system are characters and key events. The characters include a poet named Peter who is working as a technical writer for a software company; his employer Wert, Wert's wife Lolly, and another employee in the company with the unlikely classical name of Nausicaa. Peter's is the narrative voice through most of the episodes, but the reader may follow paths in which each of the two women also narrate. Various paths concern the history of these characters, and the reader can find himself or herself parked in an orbit around one of them. The events in "Afternoon" may be significant in the traditional narrative sense: one is an automobile accident which may have killed Peter's former wife and his son. But one of the most gravitationally powerful events is commonplace: Peter has lunch with his employer. What makes the event important is that it is a structural crossroad: the intersection of many narrative paths. Peter's lunch may be the occasion for him to think about Wert's wife, or about his own affair with Nausicaa, or about the crazy computer project on which he is engaged. The significance of the lunch episode depends upon where the reader has been before and where the reader goes next. In some readings "Afternoon" is a picaresque novel in which the characters seem to stay put while the reader wanders.

Sometimes there is only one path leading from a given episode; sometimes there are several. The author's control of the narrative is inversely proportional to the number of paths and the kinds of responses expected of the reader. A single path gives the author the same degree of control as a printed book—in fact, even more control, because the reader cannot flip pages or turn to the back of the book; the reader must simply hit return and go on. An episode with many paths offers the reader the opportunity to head in any of several directions, although the reader may only be aware of this freedom after he or she has returned to the episode many times. And even after visiting all the episodes, the reader has still not exhausted the writing space. The significance of the episodes changes depending upon the order of reading. At one point several characters are invited to tell about themselves. If they do this early in the reading, then their subsequent words and deeds will be measured against this history. Nausicaa, for example, who seems a benign presence, turns out to have been a drug addict and prostitute. If the reader comes upon the self-revelatory episodes late in the reading, then these episodes must be read as explanation and justification of what went before. In either case, we find ourselves invoking familiar literary structures in the effort to make sense of this electronic fiction. The difference is that both (contradictory) structures coexist in the same electronic space, and, at least after several readings, the reader becomes aware of this double presence, so that he or she must reflect on the difference between the two possible readings.

The presence or absence of paths changes the feel of a particular part of the fiction. Wherever the choices narrow to a single path, "Afternoon" becomes a conventional story: it imitates the narrow space of the printed book before broadening again into its "natural" electronic space. The capacity to imitate the printed book is one important way in which "Afternoon" makes its comment on the nature of reading. Each of its paths seems to be a mixture of the accidental and the inexorable. Paths can have narrative force, as when Peter tries to find out whether his wife and son have been in an automobile accident. Following this trajectory makes the story quite linear. Peter fights his way through various telephone calls, in an effort to get information, at the same time reticent to make the most direct calls, that is, to take the most direct path to the information he anticipates. As readers we must do the same: we must be careful about our answers at the end of each episode in order to stay with this narrative strand. A wrong answer will shunt us to another path from which it may be difficult to return to Peter's frantic calls. This is a perfect example of the way in which electronic fiction can take into itself the experience of reading. The need of the reader to struggle with the story mirrors the struggle that the character goes through. "Afternoon" becomes an allegory of the act of reading. The struggle for meaning is enacted by the characters in "Afternoon," which is by now a conventional theme of 20th-century literature. What is new is that the allegory is played out by the reader as he or she reads. "Afternoon" becomes the reader's story in this remarkable way. Readers experience the story as they read: their actions in calling forth the story, their desire to make the story happen and to make sense of what happens, are inevitably reflected in the story itself.

"Afternoon" is about the problem of its own reading. This will certainly be the problem that confronts us with all interactive fiction, at least in the early days of this new form. As an example of topographic writing, "Afternoon" asks us to consider how we are to appreciate the multiplicity of such writing. The writing space of "Afternoon" can be represented by a diagram with squares for the episodes and arrows for the links between episodes. The whole diagram is vast, since "Afternoon" has over 500 episodes and over 900 connections. . . .

The reader never sees this diagrammed structure: the reader's experience of "Afternoon" is one-dimensional, as he or she follows paths from one episode to another. Instead, the reader must gain an intuition of the spatial structure as he or she proceeds in time. This task is rather like that of a mathematician who attempts to envision a four-dimensional object by looking at several projections in three dimensions. Each projection is a snapshot, and the snapshots must be synthesized to win a sense of the whole. For the reader of "Afternoon," each reading is one projection of the geometry of the whole; the whole is the sum of all the possible ways in which "Afternoon" may be read.

The geometry of electronic fiction need not be defined solely in terms of the plot. In "Afternoon," the important events seldom vary on different readings. Instead, it is the characters' reactions and interactions that vary. The electronic writer can exploit other organizing principles of modern printed fiction, such as the stream of consciousness of one character or the points of view of several characters. Linked rings of episodes would be particularly effective for presenting multiple points of view. "Afternoon" has what we might call a subspace in which Lolly and Nausicaa tell their stories, each in several episodes and each ending more or less where she began. There is also the possibility of narrating the same events from different points of view, a technique familiar from Faulkner's *The Sound and the Fury* and Durrell's *Alexandria Quartet.* In the electronic medium the reader can be given more degrees of freedom than is possible in print; he or she may be allowed to flip back and forth among episodes, comparing one narrator's version against the others'.

The author might choose to build a narrative hierarchy by presenting the same events, for example, from three points of view, where the first point of view is in some sense superior to the second and the second to the third. The author might think of these as the divine, the heroic, and the satiric perspectives. From the satiric perspective, events are a confusion, as we normally experience them, making only a provisional sense that dissolves again into chaos. Imagine the dramatic story of Oedipus, told from the perspective of the shepherd who failed to obey the order to kill baby Oedipus and instead gave him away. After many years, this well-meaning shepherd is brought before Oedipus the king, threatened, and made to reveal what he did with the baby. He is then released and left to ponder the horror of Oedipus' crime and his own revelation. From the heroic perspective, events take on greater clarity and urgency, as Oedipus himself would tell the story. The third, divine perspective is omniscient and also detached, for the heroic sense of engagement is lost. It is the story of Oedipus as narrated by Apollo. . . .

Each of the levels contains six episodes from one perspective, corresponding to the scenes of the play. The reader begins on the lower (the satiric) level, and the task is to break into a higher realm of understanding. . . . Thus, as the reader is visiting one episode on the satiric plane, he or she may succeed in jumping to the heroic plane and instantly see the same event in a new light. The divine level should clearly be harder to reach than the heroic, and yet its presentation of events might be so cold and crystalline that the reader may wonder whether attaining this level was in fact worth the effort. This geometry omits the choral odes which divide the scenes of Sophocles' play. We could include these and have them serve as foci where the change of point of view might occur. The odes, like operatic arias, often take place in a time that is outside the conventional time of the dramatic action, pulling the reader or listener away from the plot to reflect upon the significance of past and possible future action. They provide a perfect moment for a shift in point of view.

In this Sophoclean structure, each level is in the same narrative mode: each tells a story in the first person. We can also imagine a structure in which each level contains a different mode of discourse—prose, drama, narrative poetry, lyric poetry, and so on. There is no need to limit the modes to fiction: the same experience could also be treated in historical prose and in scientific prose with mathematics. Each level would then be presenting a different aspect of written reality. The fictive level describes a man seated at a mahogany desk writing a letter; the poetic describes the scratch of the quill pen upon paper and the sound of the sand used to blot the ink; the historical discusses literacy in Victorian England; and the scientific explains how ink disperses into the pores of the paper. In the electronic organization the author can refract reality into a series of such perspectives without destroying the rhythm or comprehensibility of the text. Readers do not have to contend with all facets of the event at once; instead, the order in which they examine the various facets determines their experience of the text.

The preceding geometries are suggestions; many others are possible. They simply show how we might envision the spatial expression of a multiplicity of temporal experiences provided by any one electronic text. Electronic literature is not static, nor is it "timeless": it exists in "real time," as computer specialists call it, the time that the user passes in front of his or her terminal. The fiction realizes itself on the computer screen and then rolls or blinks out of sight and is gone. The reader might produce the same sequence of screens on the next day, but for any large structure of episodes, exact repetition is unlikely. As readers develop an aesthetic sense for this new medium, they may no longer care about perfect repetition or long preservation.

On the other hand, repetition and return take on new significance in interactive fiction, because in its own way the computer is capable of endless repetition. If the writer is clever, he or she can arrange it so that the reader seldom duplicates a previous fiction, but can always have something like it again. We may judge the success of a work by its ability to adapt to new readings and yet preserve its essence. It may be with readings as with dreams: important ones may not return, but they are never entirely lost either. Conversely we may judge works by their ability to defy categories—to have no essence and so to be different for each reading. In no case can the author in the electronic medium claim to have erected a monument more lasting than bronze; the author must instead delight in writing, like Archimedes, in sand (or silicon).

Playfulness is a defining quality of this new medium. Electronic literature will remain a game, just as all computer programming is a game. We have seen that such literature grows out of the computer games that are popular today. In video games, the kind depicting spacecraft and deadly robots, the player competes against the programmer, who has defined goals and put obstacles in the player's path. The emphasis is on the player, not the programmer, who is an anonymous employee of some software firm. Even in the simplest form of electronic fiction described above, the author/programmer is as important as the reader/player, and the relationship between author and reader may take a variety of forms: they may work cooperatively or competitively. No matter how competitive, the experience of reading in the electronic medium remains a game, rather than a combat, in the sense that it has no finality. The reader may win one day and lose the next. The computer erases the program and offers the reader a fresh start—all wounds healed. Anyone who has written a program knows that the computer has a genius for getting completely and hilariously off track. Fortunately, it is possible to drop everything and start over. This quality will carry over into electronic literature. Every reading of "Afternoon" can be a new afternoon, or the reader can choose to pick up the fiction where he or she left it in the last session. The impermanence of electronic literature cuts both ways: as there is no lasting success, there is also no failure that needs to last. By contrast, there is a solemnity at the center of printed literature—even comedy, romance, and satire—because of the immutability of the printed page.

Interactive fiction is both innovative and traditional. It is certainly new to automate the presentation of text. However, in disrupting the stability of the text, interactive fiction belongs in a tradition of experimental literature that has marked the 20th century.

—Jay David Bolter

Interactive fiction is both innovative and traditional. It is certainly new to automate the presentation of text, so that the reader's decisions are automatically registered and cause other words to appear. However, in disrupting the stability of the text, interactive fiction belongs in a tradition of experimental literature (if we may use this oxymoron) that has marked the 20th century—the era of modernism, futurism, Dada, surrealism, letterism, the nouveau roman, concrete poetry, and other movements of greater or lesser influence. The experiments of Dada, for example, were aimed at breaking down all structures of established art and literature, and in that breakdown the Dadaists worked in the same spirit as writers now work in the electronic medium. Jean Arp wrote that in his poems: "I tore apart sentences, words, syllables. I tried to break down the language into atoms, in order to approach the creative." Tristan Tzara proposed a poetics of destruction, when he gave this recipe for creating a Dada poem: "To make a dadaist poem. Take a newspaper. Take a pair of scissors. Choose an article as long as you are planning to make your poem. Cut out the article. Then cut out each of the words that make up this article and put them in a bag. Shake it gently. Then take out the scraps one after the other in the order in which they left the bag. Copy conscientiously. The poem will be like you. . . ."

Dada was an early and influential example of the modern will to experiment. The modern attack was often aimed at the conventions of the realistic novel that told its story with a clear and cogent rhythm of events. In the course of their attack, modern authors found themselves straining at the limitations of the printed page. Because the linear-hierarchical presentation of the printed book was so well suited to the conventions of plot and characters of the realistic novel, to attack the form of the novel was also to attack the technology of print. The French led the way with the nouveau roman and Philip Sollers and the Tel Quel group. From France and elsewhere, we have had programmed novels and aleatory novels. All these were instances of subversion: they worked from within, attempting to undercut the conventions of printed literature while themselves remaining printed books.

Most of the important literature of the 20th century has been accused of subversion. The avant-garde movements like Dada were never so radical as they claimed to be; they were instead extending or perhaps caricaturing the mainstream. Joyce, Virginia Woolf, Pound, T.S. Eliot, and others all participated in the breakdown of traditions of narrative prose and poetry; breaking with such traditions was the definition of being modern. Pound and Eliot set about to replace the narrative element in poetry with fragmented anecdotes or mythical paradigms. Joyce and Woolf devised new ways of structuring their works based on stream of consciousness or on multiple layers of topical and mythical organization. All of these writers were trying to set up new relationships between the moment-by-moment experience of reading a text and our perception of the organizing and controlling structures of the text. The surprising fact is that topographic writing in the space provided by the computer is a natural extension of their work. Topographic writing redefines the tradition of modernism for a new medium. To put it another way, modern authors have already been writing topographically, but they have been using the medium of print, which is not well suited to that mode of writing.

The experimentation with and fragmentation of the form of the novel is certainly older than modernism: it dates back at least to the 18th century. The whole tradition of experimentation needs now to be reconsidered in the light of the electronic medium, since each previous experiment in print suggests ways in which writing may now break free of the influence of print. In another sense all novels embody a struggle between the linear flow of the narrative and the associative trains of thought touched off by the narrative, and the electronic medium provides a new perspective on that struggle. The history of the novel itself will need to be rewritten, so that we understand works by authors from Laurence Sterne to Jorge Luis Borges not only as explorations of the limits of the printed page but also as models for electronic writing. It is as if these authors had been waiting for the computer to free them from print. And in fact, many of their works could be transferred to the electronic writing space and playfully reconstructed there. From this perspective, interactive fiction is the inevitable next step, like the take-off of an airplane that has been gaining speed on the runway. As with the speeding airplane, the moment of take-off for interactive fiction is a matter of definition. . . .

There are so many experimental novels and novelists today that any choice among them is arbitrary. The will to experiment even extends to children's fiction: books in the series entitled "Choose Your Own Adventure" or "Find Your Fate" offer young readers something like the computerized adventure game. Each book contains a garden of forking paths, from among which the reader must choose. At the bottom of page 18, one may read: "If you choose to risk the curse, turn to page 29. If you press on down the tunnel, turn to page 42." Thus, the book sacrifices the linear order of pages to allow for multiple reading. There are many of these programmed novels, some for adult readers. The novel *Rayuela* by the Latin American writer Cortázar offers two possible reading orders: one a linear narrative and the other a satirical comment on that narrative. Other writers who have experimented with fragmented narrative include Raymond Queneau, Italo Calvino, and Michel Butor.

One experiment seems to have achieved an anonymous notoriety: everyone seems to have heard of this work, although very few know its title or author. Marc Saporta's *Composition No. 1* was published in France in 1962, and the English translation, a work consisting of about 150 unnumbered pages, appeared in the following year. This fiction consists of loose sheets of paper, each containing one or a few paragraphs printed on one side. The sheets (at least in the English version) are somewhat larger than octavo, larger than a deck of playing cards, to which the author compares them. In the introduction, which is printed on the box and also appears as one of the pages, the author explains:

> The reader is requested to shuffle these pages like a deck of cards, to cut, if he likes, with his left hand, as at a fortuneteller's. The order the pages then assume will orient X's fate. For time and the order of events control a man's life more than the nature of such events. . . . A life is composed of many elements. But the number of possible compositions is infinite.

Composition No. 1 consists of passages in the story of X, a character we learn about only through his reflection in the events and other characters of the narrative. X, an unsavory figure, is married to Marianne, has a mistress named Dagmar, and also rapes a girl named Helga. He apparently steals to support the compulsions of his neurotic wife, and he possibly dies in an automobile accident. By way of redemption, he seems to have played some role in the French resistance, although this strand in the story is the most obscure.

It is Saporta's tour de force that the reader is able to figure out this much from the experience of reading the pages one at a time. Each page is necessarily only a vignette. Even for a contemporary reader, accustomed to fragmentation and suspension, the natural impulse is to turn the page in order to find out what happens next. But the next page bears no immediate relation to the previous action. This fiction is not static: on most pages there is action or at least dialogue that promises to advance our knowledge of the characters. We get the impression that we are reading pages torn from a conventional novel. We find ourselves searching for their "proper" order—that is, for an order that makes chronological and causal sense. We become literary detectives, since the pieces in this puzzle are topical elements in a written text. Connecting these topics reminds us of papyrology or other scholarly detective work with the fragmentary remains of ancient writings. It is always the papyrologist's hope that newly found fragments will turn out to be part of a known or, better still, unknown, but identifiable ancient work—that both the text and its context will be revealed. We feel that hope as we read Saporta. Indeed, to call the work "fragmented" is to assume that it was originally whole, that the fragments belong in one order.

As 20th-century readers, we are prepared for the focus to shift from one page of a fiction to another. But we want to find a reason for such shifts. Each time we shuffle the pages, some intriguing juxtapositions happen by chance. It is a characteristic of our literary imagination that we can so often provide an interpretation for these juxtapositions. Whatever order falls out is a lesson in the nature of reading. We become active readers, fashioning texts as we shuffle pages. Saporta's trick makes us uniquely aware of the effect of narrative order upon the reading experience, as we see in practice what we are always told in theory. There is not one possible order for the episodes but a broad class of acceptable orders, each producing its own literary effect. Some orders are better than a simple chronological story, and many are worse. The number of reading orders for Saporta's composition is not infinite, as the author claims. If there are 150 pages in the set, then the number of possible presentations is 150! —a number with 263 digits, but still finite. *Composition No. 1* has necessary limits: as Sharon Spencer points out [in her *Space, Time, and Structure in the Modern Novel,* 1971], in every possible rearrangement of its pages we will still have a portrait of X, the silent, second character in each fragmentary scene.

Composition No. 1 is an exercise in choice within a large but still limited fictional universe. . . . Saporta's universe is one of French existential romanticism, fascinated by the interplay of chance and fate. Moreover, Saporta seems to be working in a different direction from the one we have been considering for topographic writing in the computer. The author of *Composition No. 1* apparently disavows responsibility for the structure of his work. In seeming to deny form, he displaces the formal responsibility onto his reader. In fact, *Composition No. 1* has form; otherwise, it could not remain recognizable as a work of fiction. There are loose formal relations that exist among the pages when read in any order—relations established, for example, by the comparison of two female characters. Moreover, each paragraph or page is itself a conventional formal structure. Saporta's style is characterized by precise images and rhetorical effects: on each page, not a single word seems out of place. The precision on the page is in marked contrast to the disorder that prevails between pages and requires a different strategy of interpretation. On the page we may assume that the author is in complete control, and we may examine every mark of punctuation for nuances of meaning. Moving between two pages, we can only ask ourselves more general questions: how, for example, did the author arrange the beginning and ending of each page to make them fit together smoothly in any order?

Saporta's experiment in chance fiction seems to be an inevitable step in the exhaustion of printed literature. When all the other methods of fragmenting the novel have been tried, what remains but to tear the pages out of the book one by one and hand them to the reader? From the ideal of perfect structural control, Saporta brings us to the abdication of control. But we can also see in Saporta's experiment, and in others like it, not only the end of printed fiction, but also a bridge to the literature of the electronic medium.

Composition No. 1 brings us back to "Afternoon," for Saporta's work is an "Afternoon" under the limitations that print imposes. Each page of *Composition No. 1* is a topographic unit, like an episode of "Afternoon" as it appears on the screen. In both fictions, the burden of constructing the text is thrown back upon the reader. And in both cases the reader struggles to make narrative sense of the episodes as they present themselves: to construct from these disordered episodes a story in which characters act with reasonable and explicit motives. In *Composition No. 1* we may resort to stacking the pages in piles. In "Afternoon" the medium itself resists that solution, since we cannot get at the episodes except by typing responses, and even then the episodes appear only one at a time.

If we put *Composition No. 1* and "Afternoon" side by side, we see all the more clearly how our desire for a story has been fostered by thousands of years of reading in manuscript and print. When we read and write in these older technologies, we are compelled to narrow the possibilities into a single narrative. We have not yet learned to read and write "multiply," as Stuart Moulthrop has described it [in his "Text, Authority, and the Fiction of Forking Paths," unpublished manuscript], in part because our technologies of literacy have suggested just the opposite: that we must read and write linearly. To read multiply is to resist the temptation to close off possible courses of action; it is to keep open multiple explanations for the same event or character. It is an almost impossible task for the reader to remain open in a medium as perfected as that of print. Saporta must tear his novel apart in order to resist the perfection of print, and still our first impulse is to try to put the novel back together.

"Afternoon," on the other hand, does openly and with ease what experimental writers in print could do only with great difficulty. It offers a narrative that encompasses contradictory possibilities. In "Afternoon" an automobile accident both does and does not occur; the narrator does and does not lose his son; he does and does not have a love affair. The story itself does and does not end:

> Closure is, as in any fiction, a suspect quality, although here it is made manifest. When the story no longer progresses, or when it cycles, or when

> you tire of the paths, the experience of reading it ends. Even so, there are likely to be more opportunities than you think there are at first. A word which doesn't yield the first time you read a section may take you elsewhere if you choose it when you encounter the section again; and sometimes what seems a loop, like memory, heads off again in another direction.
>
> There is no simple way to say this.

There is no simple way to say this in the linear writing of print. But "Afternoon" embodies the idea of openness with utter simplicity. What is unnatural in print becomes natural in the electronic medium and will soon no longer need saying at all, because it can be shown.

All our topographic writers in print . . . are "difficult" writers, and the difficulty is that they challenge the reader to read multiply. They call to the reader's attention the painful contrast between the temporal flow of narrated events and the interruptions and reversals that the act of writing imposes upon those events. All their experimental works are self-consciously concerned with the problem of writing. That concern is shown by the difficult relationship between the narrator and text, between the text and its reader, or both. The difficulty in writing (and therefore in reading) appears with Tristram Shandy, who is always getting further behind experience as he writes, and again and again in the 20th century. Saporta and Cortázar must give special instructions to their readers. *Finnegans Wake* may well be the most demanding book that has ever been published and critically received. In each case, the printed fiction must work against its medium in order to be topographic. There is a conflict between the printed volume as a frame and the text that is enframed. The frame is not adequate to contain and delimit the text, which is constantly threatening to spill out of its container.

By contrast, the computer provides a frame that gives way as the text strains against it; the stubbornness of the printed book suddenly disappears. In "Afternoon" the margins "yield" to the reader. The elements of the text are no longer fragments of a prior whole, but instead form a space of shifting possibilities. In this shifting electronic space, writers will need a new concept of structure. In place of a closed and unitary structure, they must learn to conceive of their text as a structure of possible structures. The writer must practice a kind of second-order writing, creating coherent lines for the reader to discover without closing off the possibilities prematurely or arbitrarily. This writing of the second order will be the special contribution of the electronic medium to the history of literature.

The computer gives the reader the opportunity to touch the text itself, an opportunity never available in print, where the text lies on a plane inaccessible to the reader. Readers of a printed book can write over or deface the text, but they cannot write in it. In the electronic medium readers cannot avoid writing the text itself, since every choice they make is an act of writing. The author of "Afternoon" wrote the prose and poetry for each episode, and he fashioned electronic structures of expectation and fulfillment on analogy with the static structures of printed fiction. But in giving the reader a role in realizing those structures, he has also ceded some of his traditional responsibility as author. This sharing of responsibility points the way in which electronic writing will continue to develop: we can envision an electronic fiction in which the reader is invited to alter existing episodes and links and add new ones. In this way the reader becomes a second author, who can then hand the changed text over to other readers for the same treatment. Electronic fiction can operate anywhere along the spectrum from rigid control by the author to full collaboration between author and reader. The promise of this new medium is to explore all the ways in which the reader can participate in the making of the text. Stuart Moulthrop suggests that the reader should be ". . . invited not just to enter a garden of forking paths, but to expand and revise the ground plan at will. This would cause a substantial shift in the balance of authority, one with enormous implications for the idea of literature itself; but it would nonetheless be a logical development of writing in the electronic medium."

The reader's intervention may come at any level of the electronic text. We have been considering fixed episodes and their connections, but the reader could also intervene to change the text itself. Such intervention could begin with simple letter substitution and typographic changes, perhaps under constraints programmed by the author. Letter substitutions can change words into other words or into nonsense that may suggest several words at once. Typography can be altered to make the text visually more exciting. Such changes too have been prefigured by writers in print. Mallarmé with his spatial poems such as "Coup de dès" and Apollinaire with his *calligrammes* were followed by the Dadaists, by LeMaître, and more recently by the writers of "concrete" poetry, who deployed letters and words in defiance of the conventions of lines and strophes. Concrete poetry too was an expression of the growing dissatisfaction with the medium of print in the 20th century. Concrete poetry too belongs in the computer; indeed, the computer makes possible truly kinetic poetry, a poetry in which letters and words can dance across the screen before the reader's eyes.

The poet William Dickey has already begun to create interactive poems. In "Heresy: A Hyperpoem," words, images, and icons compete on the screen for the reader's attention. The poem is a network of many screens, and the reader moves from one screen to others by activating one of the snowflake-shaped icons. Each screen is a different arrangement of verbal text and image; each vigorously asserts its visual identity. The typography of this hypertext encourages the reader to examine and savor each screen before activating an icon to move on. Sometimes the verbal text penetrates the graphic image. . . . Sometimes the spatial arrangement of text against the white background reminds us of the experiments of Mallarmé or LeMaître.

In "Heresy," as in "Afternoon," each textual unit is static; the reader sets the hypertext in motion by moving between fixed units. In future kinetic poems, however, the reader might also intervene to control the speed and direction or the way in which words coalesce and divide. He or she may participate in the reordering of the ultimate constituents of writing—letters, words, and graphic symbols. The reordering of such symbols *is* writing: it is all that any writer can ever do. This insight, which has been laboriously demonstrated and violently contested in the printed literature of the 20th century, becomes a simple and unavoidable fact in the electronic medium. Multiple reading passes inevitably into multiple writing.

Electronic fiction is technologically complicated in that it requires a computer and the sophisticated arrangement of text and graphics on a videoscreen. But it is conceptually simple—simpler than writing for print, where the writer must always force his or her text into a single line of argument or narrative. The computer frees the writer from the now tired artifice of linear writing, but the price of this new freedom for the writer is that the writer must allow the reader to intervene in the writing space.

Harry Goldstein (review date March-April 1994)

SOURCE: "The Changing Shape of Fiction," in *Utne Reader,* No. 62, March-April, 1994, pp. 131-32.

[*Below, Goldstein comments on the new field of hyperfiction and reviews several works in the genre.*]

Despite its dramatic name, hyperfiction—the latest craze in hightech literature—is basically software: You load it onto your computer and use certain tools to navigate through it. And what a ride it is.

In hyperfiction, you don't just read, you make choices. It's the classic existentialist dilemma manifested in the reading process. You're at least partially responsible for creating (by choice or actual writing) what you read, so you can never just snuggle up with your laptop and get lost in the story. Rather, you *can* get lost in the story, but it's your responsibility to find the way out, if indeed you want to get out, which is all up to you. There's no comfort in watching the pages between you and the end of the book evaporate in the sure knowledge that the end is in sight. And there's no such thing as reading ahead to the last page to find out who killed whom. There is no closure to a work of hyperfiction. When you stop reading, that's the end—of that particular reading of the fiction.

Some works, such as *Quibbling* or *Hypertext Quarterly,* give you a reading map of the hypertext—a sort of topographical representation of the blocks of text, or lexias. By clicking on links—highlighted words or phrases—you can zoom into another set of lexias (and characters and storylines). Other hyperfictions allow you to type in a word, which may lead you anywhere. And almost all hyperfictions allow you to point the mouse, click on any word that might strike your fancy, and see where *that* takes you. Several hyperfictions indicate, by means of underlining, boxes, or boldface, certain words or phrases that have a link to another part of the hypertext.

Most readers, conditioned by novels and short stories, have traditional expectations when they first encounter hyperfiction: They want to know who did what, and why. Hyperfiction plays with these expectations, especially with the need to perceive an established order. You still read for plot, for characters and their motivations, and for the key to the mystery, but hyperfiction demands a spatial rather than a linear reading. Each lexia consists of several surfaces that interact differently with other text blocks and links, resulting in an almost boundless web of interconnections. Not only is there room for a vast range of interpretations, but hyperfiction actively encourages multiplex reactions and interactions.

Hyperfiction constitutes a radically new genre, quite distinct from the so-called expanded novels (published by Voyager)—novels adapted for computers and souped up with hypertext components, but which you read more or less as you would a book between covers. Hyperfiction empowers readers and overturns traditional notions of author and reader. Stuart Moulthrop, hypertext critic and author of *Victory Garden,* distinguishes between two kinds of hyperfiction—exploratory and constructive—in his essay "Polymers, Paranoia, and the Rhetoric of Hypertext" in the spring 1991 issue of *Writing on the Edge.* According to Moulthrop, an exploratory hyperfiction—which includes most commercially available hypertexts—allows the reader to " 'transform' the textual body by following alternative paths or linkways" while the hyperfiction "retains its fundamental identity under all transformations. . . . The maze may have many permutations, the circuit many switchings, but in all of them the user still circulates through the same mechanized volume." Constructive hyperfiction, which arrived in the commercial sphere with the November 1993 publication of Deena Larsen's *Marble Springs,* allows you to add your own words to the hypertext and send your additions back to the publisher to be included in subsequent editions. *Marble Springs* points to the future of constructive hyperfiction, which lies in the proliferation of computer networks where many reader/writers will collaborate on projects made open-ended by virtue of their virtual existence as malleable data in cyberspace.

Most readers, conditioned by novels and short stories, have traditional expectations when they first encounter hyperfiction: They want to know who did what, and why. Hyperfiction plays with these expectations, especially with the need to perceive an established order.

—Harry Goldstein

Hyperfiction addresses a fundamental issue that faces all writers: In a society where people are more willing to consume images than read, hypertext seems like a wordsmith's dream. Finally, here's a vehicle for writing that is as fast as the microprocessor that paints the words on the screens, the words taking on a visual quality that can compete with pictures. Ultimately, however, hyperfictions must still succeed first as writing: Are the characters worth following through the labyrinth of a hyperfiction? Is the narrative structure engaging, its complexity challenging or its simplicity aesthetically pleasing? Is the language fresh? Most importantly, does the writer have something new to say in addition to having a new way to say it?

The hyperfictions reviewed here run on an Apple Macintosh Plus and more powerful models and are available for IBM compatibles in Windows format except where noted. Although they will run on 1 MB of RAM, they run slowly, so 2 MB is suggested, and required where indicated.

"Afternoon, a story" by Michael Joyce. One of the very first hypertext fictions and still one of the most fascinating, "Afternoon, a story" doesn't have any mapping graphics that allow you to see where you are in the whole scheme of things, but is so engrossing that you can get lost in it and not care. The lyrical intensity of the language lures you through a structure that is simultaneously compelling and perplexing.

"Afternoon" affords a remarkable amount of freedom. If you find yourself pursuing a link that doesn't interest you and remember seeing one a few screens back that looked more promising, you can backtrack to find it. A cascade of returns can be very entertaining, the words dancing on the screen, revealing the hyperfiction not as printed matter but as something more ephemeral. And when you turn off the computer, you might find that the voices of "Afternoon" linger in your ear, speaking of the intrigue that you sensed rippling just beneath the surface, waiting to be uncovered the next time you venture into the fiction.

Ambulance: An Electronic Novel by Monica Moran. Produced by the prolific Jaime Levy, *Ambulance* is the latest in a series of cyberzines published by Levy's New York-based Electronic Hollywood. Monica Moran's very linear narrative tells the story of a group of twentysomethings who crash their car somewhere in the Hollywood hills. A serial killer spies the accident from his house and decides to collect our band of hapless travelers and take them back to his house, where grim mayhem ensues. *Ambulance* combines Levy's cinematic sensibility with hypertextual flashbacks and some engaging multimedia effects, including bass samples by alternative rocker Mike Watt and illustrations by Jaime Hernandez (of the *Love and Rockets* comic book series). By turns amusing and grisly, *Ambulance* requires less work on the part of the reader than hyperfictions more consciously concerned with putting into practice the theories of Derrida and Barthes and the fictional visions of Borges and Pynchon.

The Madness of Roland by Greg Roach, with animation by David Crossley. The most striking things about *Roland* are its animation, videos, sound, look—in short, everything but the text of this multimedia extravaganza whose list of credits resembles that of a movie production. As hyperfiction becomes more geared toward a primarily image-literate audience, collaborative hypermedia efforts of this sort will undoubtedly increase. Unfortunately, *Roland* points to one of the pitfalls: Mediocre writing will never be able to compete with wow-'em special effects. Requires CD-ROM player for Macintosh or MPC machine and Video for Windows for IBM compatibles.

Marble Springs by Deena Larsen. The first to invite the reader to collaborate on subsequent editions by writing characters and creating links, this hyperfiction is very much an *Our Town* brought to hypertext. You enter the work via the Marble Springs cemetery to discover a ghost town where women have woven the fabric of the town's history. In addition to the usual assortment of text-based links, the map of Marble Springs provides one way of getting into the fiction; you choose certain geographical locations and discover—or write—the lives of the inhabitants. This is easily the most demanding hypertext on the market in the range of choices the reader is given, from perusing actual bibliographies detailing the research that went into reconstructing an Old West town to collaborating with Deena Larsen and other readers. Requires HyperCard 2.0 and 2 MB of RAM; available for Macintosh only.

Victory Garden by Stuart Moulthrop. *Victory Garden* is hyperfiction about the Gulf War by noted Thomas Pynchon critic Stuart Moulthrop. One of the most complex hypertexts now available, with an astonishing number of lexias and links, *Victory Garden* explores reactions to the war in letters and scenes from Saudi Arabia featuring college student and reservist Emily Runbird, media coverage of the war, military technobabble, and protests at the college Emily attended before she was shipped off. Moulthrop has taken a historical event and given it back to us through almost 1,000 blocks of text and 2,800 links; careful characterizations; numerous storylines, plots, and subplots; and an incisive critique of news media, the war, and the war's media audience. The Gulf War was presented to the public in fragments. Moulthrop has used hyperfiction to link real and imagined fragments, allowing the reader to do what the media and the government made impossible: to explore the story of the war, and of ourselves, for ourselves.

IMPLICATIONS FOR PUBLISHING, LIBRARIES, AND THE PUBLIC

Eldred Smith (essay date 1 February 1992)

SOURCE: "The Print Prison," in *Library Journal,* Vol. 117, No. 2, February 1, 1992, pp. 48-51.

[*In the following essay, Smith remarks on the weaknesses of the print medium, particularly as it relates to scholarly publishing, and suggests ways in which the academic community could benefit from electronic information technology.*]

It is no exaggeration that the invention of printing liberated the spread and advancement of knowledge. No field or discipline remained untouched, and most were transformed by printing's ability to disseminate and preserve information inexpensively and with an ease and reliability never previously imagined. The ensuing rapid rise of print publication also exerted a liberating influence on the growth and development of libraries.

It is, however, becoming increasingly clear that the book

and other print products have also had a limiting effect on knowledge's spread and advancement. Print imprisons knowledge by the very means through which it promotes its availability: access to the contents of a book can only be achieved if one physically possesses a copy of that book.

The need to invest their efforts and resources in managing book collections has effectively imprisoned librarians and libraries as well. Research librarians, in particular, have little capacity left over to assist their clientele with quick and effective access to the information that they seek, a substantial and increasingly important need as scholarship and its written record continue to expand and proliferate. Rather, research librarians have generally had to leave scholars and students to their own devices in coping with enormous collections and a very complex bibliographic apparatus.

The new electronic information technology has begun to demonstrate print's limitations more clearly than any other development over the past 500 years, precisely because it provides the means to overcome these limitations. Indeed, as the electronic age progresses, it is gradually freeing recorded knowledge from its print confinement. This development, in turn, has the capacity to free librarians and libraries from their imprisonment by the book, providing that librarians seize the opportunity to transform their libraries from print repositories to electronic information centers.

As Elizabeth A. Eisenstein has demonstrated at length in her indispensable study *The Printing Press as an Agent of Change* (1980), printing literally transformed every significant field of human activity. Science, art, law, exploration and discovery, politics, education—none was the same after the printed book replaced the manuscript as the primary means of recording and preserving information. Although a number of printing's characteristics were important in exerting this influence, its ability to produce a large number of identical copies of a work, quickly and cheaply, was particularly significant.

Not only did this allow for an ease and breadth of information distribution that was unheard of previously, it also guaranteed that the text in each individual copy of a work was precisely the same as that in every other copy. During the manuscript era, no such guarantee could be made or accepted. Indeed, no matter the care with which scribes pursued their task, mistakes were inevitable and, in many cases, substantial. As a consequence, it was impossible to establish a body of generally accepted detailed knowledge in any field. It is certainly no accident that encyclopedias and other codifications knowledge began to appear only after printing became well established and widely used. Scholarship as we know it today, which builds incrementally on the documented and accepted work of others, was literally made possible by the creation and distribution of printed records.

Libraries existed for centuries, even millennia, before the introduction of print; however, the modern library, as it has evolved since the 15th century, is a creature of the printed book. The standardized features of the book, which every reader takes for granted, are also a product of print culture. Cataloging and classification, which organize and control multimillion-volume collections, derive directly from information provided by standardized title pages, tables of contents, and indexes, through the use of systems that have all been developed and established during the print era.

Although printing liberated the growth and spread of information, this liberation was far from complete. In order to disseminate information through print, it is necessary to package this information in the form of a book, newspaper, journal, or other product, which must then be dispersed in multiple copies. Because printed information is spread through the distribution of books and other print products, anyone seeking information must acquire copies of these products in order to have access to the information that they contain.

Organization and preservation of printed information requires the organization and preservation of the books, journals, and other carriers of such information. The basic paradox of print publication, therefore, is that information is restricted by the very vehicle that was designed to promote its availability—the book or other print product.

This paradox has affected the progress and spread of scholarship. Despite its enormously liberating impact on the growth of knowledge, print publication has also limited and constrained that growth. These limitations have been of two kinds: first, limits on quick and effective dissemination; second, limits on convenient and efficient access.

Limits on dissemination have been most evident in the difficulties that scholars encounter in having their works published expeditiously. Delays of months are expected, and delays of years are not uncommon. Librarians, struggling to keep pace with a constantly increasing number of monographs and journals, may perceive that too much is being published. In truth, as scholarship continues to expand, a growing amount of material deemed worthy of distribution remains unpublished because the resources do not exist to print and distribute everything of value.

Furthermore, even published works receive only limited circulation. Dependent upon sales to cover ever-expanding printing and distribution costs, scholarly book publishing has witnessed a long and gradual decline in purchase by both individuals and libraries. As a consequence, these publications are reaching a diminishing portion of their constituency, and they are reaching that constituency much more slowly because both individuals and libraries are increasingly dependent upon sharing copies.

Limits on access are, in many respects, even more severe. It has been impossible, throughout the print era, to gather a complete collection of the world's scholarly publications or to create a comprehensive and convenient bibliographic apparatus to control this publication. In fact, collections are becoming less complete and more scattered, and the bibliographic apparatus is growing increasingly complex and difficult to use effectively. Scholars must either invest larger and larger amounts of their time and energy in gathering the information that they need, or they must rely more heavily upon informal and selective information-seeking practices, such as consultation with colleagues and citation searching.

The paradox of information's entrapment in the very mechanism that distributes it has resulted in librarians and libraries being bound by this same mechanism. Librarians invest most of their energies in acquiring, cataloging, and managing collections of books and other print products. Far too little of their time is left over for the substantive assistance with the use of these collections that their clientele require.

This is particularly true for research librarians, who have the special responsibility of preserving and maintaining the record of world scholarship. In their constant struggle to accomplish this with limited resources, research librarians find themselves hard pressed to provide effective information service.

With the rise of the new electronic information technology, print's shortcomings are becoming more evident and more bothersome.

—Eldred Smith

The limitations of print have gone generally unrecognized until recently. The book has long been celebrated as a remarkably cheap, convenient, and effective means of information transfer, and this is still generally the case. With the rise of the new electronic information technology, however, print's shortcomings are becoming more evident and more bothersome. This is occurring in many areas of human activity, including the informal, prepublication stages of scholarship. Not only are scholars in a growing number of disciplines making greater and greater use of computers to store and manipulate data, they are using electronic mail to communicate worldwide with colleagues in the pursuit of common or collaborative research objectives.

The attraction of E-mail is that it offers the advantages of print with few of print's shortcomings. Like print, E-mail can communicate identical text to a number of different parties across considerable distances. Unlike print, E-mail can communicate almost instantly. It also allow the receiving parties to preserve the information they receive either in print or in electronic form, and it also enables them to manipulate the text they receive in a variety of ways. This capability adds appreciably to scholars' convenience in sharing information and ideas through the research process.

Similarly, electronic technology can also free scholarly publication, the more formal process of scholarly communication, from the limitations imposed by print. Delays resulting from queueing for an opening in a journal issue or scheduling a print run for a monograph, coupled with the time required to produce and distribute print products, are unnecessary in an electronic communication system that does not require print packaging. Once a work has been reviewed, accepted, and edited, it can be made available electronically. Similarly, electronic publication need impose no limit on volume of publication. Everything that has passed muster with reviewers and editors can be distributed in potentially unlimited number.

Such distribution cannot, however, be accomplished through the well-established print channels that have developed over the past 500 years. It is increasingly evident that this elaborate system of journals and monographs will be neither effective nor necessary for electronic dissemination. What will replace it? This is the problem that now perplexes scholars, publishers, and librarians as they look ahead toward passage from the print to the electronic information environment.

The answer to this question is inextricably tied to solution of the print era's information access problems: the scattered, incomplete, highly redundant collections and complex, incomplete bibliographic apparatus that have been characteristic of this period. Research libraries, which properly aspire to be comprehensive in their collections, inevitably fail due to the enormous difficulty and expense of acquiring and maintaining such a large number of print products. Because of the incompleteness and dispersal of print collections, the bibliographic apparatus that has been developed to control them has been largely uncoordinated, and it is rife with both duplication and omission.

Correction of these problems requires the gathering of a single comprehensive collection, including all extant current, past, and future scholarly publication. Such a collection is possible in the electronic era. Furthermore, just as scattered and incomplete collections have frustrated the creation of a single complete, consistent, and comprehensive bibliographic apparatus, it is precisely such an apparatus that can and must be established to maintain and control a single unified collection.

Of course, both the collection and the apparatus would be electronic. They would be accessible anywhere, using the worldwide communications structure that presently exists. Desired portions could be retrieved on computer screens, transferred to local data stores, and even printed out on printers. Although much work would certainly be required to plan and implement such a collection and apparatus, no substantial technical problem lies in the way of its accomplishment.

What is necessary is a new electronic mode of distributing scholarly publication that is both coordinated and consistent. This can be achieved by establishing a database of scholarship to which electronic copies are contributed. Electronic copy is now produced for the vast majority of publications, as a prelude to print. Rather than relying on the limitations, costs, and imperfections of the print distribution system, as in the past, publication of a work of scholarship would be accomplished by its deposit in a generally accessible electronic database, where its index would be integrated with the indexes of all other publications, and it would be properly cataloged.

This mode of publication would be advantageous to the

nonprofit societies and universities that comprise the vast majority of scholarly publishers, particularly in North America. It would relieve them of the enormous financial and other burdens of printing and marketing. Without damaging their editorial role in any way, it would allow them to publish each work as soon as it had passed review and been edited. All limitations on volume of publication would be removed.

Scholars would benefit through prompt publication, the removal of external limitations on publishability, and improved access. The single, complete archive of scholarship, controlled by a comprehensive, consistent index, and available on their office, laboratory, or home personal computers, would provide scholars with a convenience and reliability heretofore unknown. If this were coupled with genuine information service provided by local campus libraries, scholars' information access would improve manyfold.

The librarian would benefit as well. Relieved of the increasingly frustrating burden of managing larger and larger collections that contain a steadily dwindling portion of world scholarly publication, research librarians could concentrate on providing substantive information service, drawing upon the electronic database of scholarship as well as the other electronic databases that are being and will continue to be established. Campus libraries would be transformed into information centers by providing a range of programs from current awareness services, to alert scholars to new publications of interest as soon as they were deposited in the scholarly database, to searches of that database and of other information stores.

Presumed barriers, such as copyright and technological compatibility, would effectively be removed by the shift in publication mode on the part of nonprofit publishers (for which copyright is more of an authentication protection than an economic benefit) and the establishment of a single database of scholarship. Commercial publishers that are presently distributing works of scholarship—a far more extensive practice in Western Europe than in the United States, but certainly a problem for all research libraries—would probably resist the establishment of an electronic scholarly database, particularly if no user fees were levied, as they would not have to be for nonprofit publications. Such resistance could, however, be addressed in a number of ways. Fees could be implemented for access to commercial publications only. Conversely, copyrighted publications could be barred from the database until their copyrights expired.

In practice, it is doubtful that such measures would have to be applied for very long. If electronic publication through a scholarly database could assure scholars of prompt availability and widespread distribution of their works, it is highly unlikely that they would continue to use the slower and less accessible print vehicle. Quickly, electronic publication by means of the scholarly database would become the standard.

Today's publishers offer electronic journals, modeled on the print journal. CD-ROMs distribute electronic information in multiple copies, depriving it of the convenience and flexibility that are the new technology's most outstanding features. Librarians find themselves struggling through a transition period, still caught up in practices of the past as they attempt to redefine these practices in line with the capabilities of the future.

Nevertheless, the genie is emerging from the bottle. The most constraining features of the print era are gradually yielding to the greater capabilities of the new technology. Scholars, scholarly publishers, research librarians—all are being liberated from the book's limitations.

This does not mean that the book will not be with us, at least through the foreseeable future. What it does mean is that the new technology will replace print in performing an increasing number of functions, wherever its performance proves superior. One of those functions, clearly, is distribution and use of scholarly information.

This argument suggests a certain inevitability, as though all one had to do was sit back and await the transformation. Perhaps it may happen that way, in the long run. If, however, one seeks the best result in a reasonable period of time, it is well not to rely on destiny.

Librarians are in a critical position to direct this transition. Indeed, no one but research librarians, working with scholars, scholarly publishers, and academic leaders, can design and implement such a change. In the final analysis, then, research librarians must assume responsibility to free themselves from the boundaries of the book, as they move forward into the next millennium.

Carol Robinson (essay date 6 September 1993)

SOURCE: "Publishing's Electronic Future," in *Publishers Weekly,* Vol. 240, No. 36, September 6, 1993, pp. 46-8, 50, 52.

[*In the essay below, which is based on interviews with numerous people in the publishing industry, Robinson addresses questions regarding the future of publishing, including distribution, genres, media, copyright law, and marketing.*]

The industrial world is in the throes of a technological revolution in which the rate of change has never been as fast or the boundaries that normally separate one industry from another as blurred. Communications, computing, entertainment and publishing industries are beginning to converge, creating new kinds of alliances. What does it all mean for publishing? Who are the visionaries in publishing today, and how will they take advantage of the opportunities that come with technological change?

To answer some of these questions, and to try to find out what the tradebook publishing industry thinks about the prospects for the millennium 2000, a diverse but representative group of 32 people, including publishers, directors of new media, literary agents, new media packagers, marketing consultants and copyright experts were interviewed.

. . . . .

Everyone agrees that, in a scant seven years, publishing as

we know it will be different, but there is little shared vision of the future. In fact, there was some general discomfort about how things might look by the year 2000. Some smaller publishers even said they were "out in left field" or simply "not prepared to answer." One straightforward publisher of a large company admitted that the changes in technology make him nervous. Perhaps the discomfort is due to previous experiences some of the larger publishers have had in trying to pioneer when neither the technology nor the market were ready.

Four major issues emerged in response to this question. The first involved the fate of the book itself.

Rather expectedly, most people interviewed do not believe the book will ever disappear, although they can imagine some fairly dramatic changes by the year 2000. What they call the "revolution" will happen first in the reference world. "I think that business and reference publishers will lead the way for the new technology—providing all of us with raw data of what works and doesn't," says Larry Kirshbaum, CEO of Warner Books. The talk right now is that encyclopedias will continue to sell as hardcover books even though consumers can now buy the same information for less money with the added benefit of the search capacity of an interactive CD-ROM. Kenzi Sugihara, v-p and publisher of Random House Reference and Electronic Publishing, points out, however, that "electronic publishing is expanding faster than many of us expected. The installed base of CD-ROM drives is now expected to double every year." He predicts that by the year 2000, "telecommunications will take off as the next major distribution medium for publishers." Jack Romanos, president of the Consumer Group of Paramount Publishing, agrees that the industry will be revolutionized for nonfiction books. "We will slowly convert popular reference titles as the electronic installed base starts to grow. It is not essential to be the first to develop electronic books; many courageous people will get hammered in the beginning," he cautions.

If publishers are unwilling to admit that certain books may not make good business sense to continue to publish in hardcover, they are adamant about the staying power of the book format. Kirshbaum cautions anyone who has "the idea of a book, especially in fiction, going away. Let's not bury Mr. Gutenberg yet."

Peter Kindersley, president of Dorling Kindersley, does not agree. "We've almost exhausted the linear textbook as a way of getting information," he says. "An innovative blend of pictures and words creates more of a wraparound experience." He thinks that "interactive media meets the human need for freedom of exploration, where we can search for patterns out of our existing world."

Literary agent Richard Curtis, whose science fiction authors have already catapulted him into the 21st century, predicts that changes in publishing will be technology-driven rather than market-driven. "We are now in the twilight of the printed word," he declares, though careful to add that "twilights can take a long time."

Janet Wikler, group v-p and director of advanced media of HarperCollins, takes Curtis's warning about the future of books in an interesting direction. She believes that "interactive media form the basis of entirely new businesses that are not simply byproducts of our traditional businesses." She adds that "my generation may be the last to be predominantly verbal, to have a strong visceral affection for books—the smell of paper, the look of type. The book publishing industry depends on verbal literacy, while new media depend on comfort with technology. Most of the children in school right now have that kind of comfort, while their parents often don't."

Currently, publishers still expect to offer consumers options for nonfiction titles. And indeed some of the early offerings have been produced simultaneously in hardcover and CD-ROM formats. *Clinton, Portrait of Victory,* produced by Epicenter Communications and published by Warner Books, is an example of such a dual production. Matthew Naythans, its producer, thinks "most buyers for the CD-ROM option bought it in addition to the book."

One major stumbling block for book publishers who may wish to develop electronic properties is the lack of a standard platform, and this turned out to be the second major topic of discussion.

Charles Hayward, Little, Brown CEO, articulated a concern about making the right platform decision when a lot of money is at stake. He predicts that "there will be either a hard disk for television or an interactive service—the platform isn't clear yet. People do tend to get worried as a result."

Most publishers are taking a wait-and-see attitude. Both inside and outside the industry, there are examples of companies that chose the wrong technology or who enthusiastically produced something using a new technology before a sufficient base was there. (Betamax, anyone?) Peter Mayer, CEO of the Penguin Group, is concerned that "neither the hardware nor the software that could drive the publishing industry is agreed upon. Besides, we have not yet heard the consumer speak." Della Van Heyst, director of the Stanford Publishing Course, predicts that "online publishing will have a greater impact on traditional publishing than CD-ROM."

Michael Mellin, consulting editor at large for Random House, says he is not nervous about the platform issue. "What is needed is editorial judgment," Mellin says. "We have made some strategic partnerships with technology companies that also have a lot to gain from digitizing information and entertainment, and we will continue to do this."

Wikler agrees that the platform issue should not be the central concern. "We need to work with some platforms now that have a large enough installed base. But later we can adapt to other platforms as well. The important thing is to establish the vision of a company. There will never again be an era of certainty. We need to learn to live with change and variety."

There may not be agreement about the platform issue, but there does seem to be consensus on the third major issue—consumer acceptance. Quality content at good value, all agreed, will be crucial to building markets for the new media. Wikler thinks "with interactive media there needs to be a new way of thinking about content, and it will have to be more revolutionary than the process of adapting books for movies. With interactive media, the user decides where to start and what to do. The product needs to be created in such a way that it can enhance the power of the user."

As to coexistence with existing books, John Papanek, editor-in-chief of Time Life Inc., is one of several publishing executives who see "new media as incremental revenue, which will broaden audiences for books in general." Jack Romanos is in the same camp. opting for acquiring a property once and producing it in several formats. However, he is quick to point out that "electronic books need to have multimedia value-added."

Publishing contracts that existed before electronic rights were ever discussed often do not protect the current publishers of an author's work, leaving conversion to an electronic format entirely in the hands of the author of his/her estate. Already there has been some house-jumping around electronic rights, and outside companies like Microsoft, Voyager, Sony and Paramount Communications are beginning to grab rights to properties that have not been nailed down.

How best to staff and organize for new media development was the fourth major issue considered, and Peter Mayer is one of a few executives to predict a need to develop his organization to be more flexible. "It's unclear," he says, "whether the same staffs that exist in publishing companies today will be appropriate to the creation, marketing and selling of new products in the world of interactive media. It may be that new media, at least over time, will have to be staffed by people who think in terms of new media itself, as opposed to those who think of a simplistic transference of product from one media format to another."

Who will be the leaders in this new world? Michael Mellin predicts that "the existing leaders in tradebook publishing will be the same further down the line, because no one else knows how to create titles people want to exchange money for. They will harvest the fruits of technology created by other industries."

Michael Wolff, a digital publisher and multimedia consultant, does not agree. He thinks "the new technology will change the definition of who publishers are and what publishers do."

Janet Wikler feels that "whoever goes after market share aggressively will be the future leaders." She sees three choices for tradebook publishers: "They can make a commitment to invest in the future, expand their market share and experience renewed growth; they can dabble, by licensing content to outside companies, in which case they give away the biggest rewards; or they can do nothing at all, in which case their businesses will grow smaller."

Size should be a question of strategy, not a negative outcome from wishing the marketplace would stay the same when it is, in fact, undergoing rapid change. If a publisher wishes to be small by design, then small can be positive. Ironically, it is a large publisher who envisions some opportunities for small publishers. Peter Mayer speaks eloquently about "the high creativity at the production and design end in the world of desktop publishing."

Scott Walker, publisher of Graywolf Press, one of the oldest of the independent literary publishers, is somewhat in sync with Mayer's view of market opportunities for independent, creative publishers. "Since we can operate on all cylinders and afford to change more quickly," he says, "we will produce tasty little CD-ROMs while the big publishers will go in for larger entertainments such as Anne Rice Smellavision."

Charlie Winton, president of Publishers Group West, predicts that "the number of small publishers doing desktop publishing will continue to expand geometrically." The challenge for small publishers is to distinguish themselves from the crowd by establishing a memorable new media imprint. One such company, Broderbund Software, is already gaining a reputation for creative multimedia for children, especially for the Grandma titles and the Carmen Sandiego series.

Most publishers either have found or are currently looking for software partners to whom they may license their content on a short-term basis. Both Random House and Penguin are finding partners. Mayer's strategy for Penguin is to continue to make some strategic acquisitions and/or joint ventures. "We will also license other vendors to adapt products for us in some cases."

Dorling Kindersley has gone as far as forming a limited partnership with Microsoft, and already some of their earliest CD-ROMs have exceeded sales expectations. Paramount Publishing, for its part, has access to a "media kitchen" for electronic research and development through its parent company, and Time-Life plans for new media creation seem to be coming from in-house resources as well. Graywolf plans to develop CD-ROM titles at some point in the future through a limited partnership, while Warner Books took advantage of an opportunity to buy an existing CD-ROM as part of a package from a developer. Most publishers anticipate a new breed of book packager with CD-ROM capability entering the industry in droves.

Putnam's CEO Phyllis Grann says, "Putnam has gone into the children's market with interactive media in a coventure with Bertelsmann. In 1993-94, seven CD-ROM titles will be developed for both the Macintosh and Windows-based computers." Disney will also be a big player in the children's market, utilizing its vast resources of animated content and special-effects technology.

Competition inside and outside the industry for market share should be fierce. One way for publishers to protect themselves from outside competition—both from foreign competitors and computer and communications companies who are busy buying up electronic rights for intellectual content—could be to get together to decide on industry standards.

One such consortium, the Atrium Group, is concerned exclusively with new media, and funds the National Demonstration Laboratory at the Library of Congress. Atrium currently has 19 members (among them, Microsoft, IBM, Paramount Publishing, Bell Atlantic and Philips Interactive of America) who meet with Jacqueline Hess, director of the National Demonstration Laboratory. The group discusses such common issues as intellectual rights, the developing information highway and international information flow.

There was a surprising amount of unanimity in answer to the question of genres. The list consisted of genres that can easily be converted into new media—travel, cookbooks, gardening, how-to, reference, biography, diet, financial, science fiction, children's literature and adult games (where there is some learning involved). This will happen in different ways. Some books will be adapted, like David Macaulay's bestselling *The Way Things Work,* a natural for the electronic format with its bits of information that can be expanded and linked. Other disks will pull together information from several books, while some will be created from scratch.

The Voyager Company, a nine-year-old publisher, is one of several pioneers in interactive media, bringing together for the first time a literary sensibility, technological know-how and business skills. Voyager now offers 30 CD-ROM titles, including some for children, and "Expanded Books," floppy disks designed for students and scholars.

New media consultant and producer Dr. Dana Ardi suggests that "after reference and how-to, publishers need to plan for the next wave of entertainment/enlightenment." Who knows, maybe even poetry will take off. Although Larry Kirshbaum says "electronic poetry is an oxymoron," Voyager's CD-ROM *Poetry in Motion* has given niche publishers something to think about.

Book agent Jack Scovil, formerly of the Scott Meredith Agency and now of Scovil, Chichak & Galen, thinks that history books lend themselves to new media. He imagines that "Ken Burns's miniseries of the Civil War, possibly including some virtual reality techniques to place you on the battlefield, might work well on CD-ROM."

Most people in the industry do not think fiction lends itself to new media, though Peter Kindersley doesn't agree. He foresees that "even the novel will become interactive, and therefore more experimental." Scott Walker also predicts that interactive fiction, or hyperfiction, and multimedia narrative will become a new genre.

The pioneer of interactive fiction is Robert Coover, who teaches a Hypertext Fiction Workshop at Brown University. Hyperfiction is also taught at multimedia studies programs in many other universities. However, it is only now that authoring devices are becoming more affordable, although they may still be hard to learn. The Voyager Company's co-director of marketing, Todd Wade, says "the industry is waiting for authoring tools to become fluent and rich enough to support the production of titles that are simple enough to operate and compelling to navigate."

It's not surprising that most people interviewed see the kids of today as the new readers of tomorrow. What is new is how they picture them. Janet Wikler describes this new generation as "more right-brain than left—more visual, more intuitive, more instinctive." Phyllis Grann believes this generation of kids will grow up reading from hand-held computers, although she sees that day as a long way off. "Still," Grann warns, "to prepare for it, we need to become technically astute now." Jack Romanos agrees. He thinks that "the job of the publisher is to stay ahead of the market in terms of taste, so we are looking at the next generation of readers now."

Papanek, Mellin and W. W. Norton president Donald Lamm all think that college campuses are where new media will take off first. This age group is the most computer literate and has the need to learn. All the books currently available to scholars could lend themselves to new media—from economic treatises to literary classics—and many publishers feel that by the end of the decade they will be sending the contents of their textbooks across this network, possibly to be printed on demand in campus bookstores.

Several publishers and agents agree that the consumers who now buy CD-ROM titles are probably the same people who were the first to buy VCRs. Since CD-ROMs are mainly sold in computer stores, it makes sense that the buyers are technologically sophisticated or gadget-oriented. Peter Ginsberg, president of Curtis Brown Ltd., says: "They are the ones who we feel will help shape the future of CD-ROMs and how books are developed in that format."

Phyllis Grann says, "We always respond to quality and readability in our selection of book titles. The same will be true for new media." However, Jacqueline Hess does not think quality content is enough to determine success. "New media require new standards of evaluative criteria," she says, adding that multimedia producers must pay attention to suggested pathways for user navigation because so much rich information can be overwhelming for a user.

John Papanek predicts that "publishers will take more risks in making selections for new media because their profit margins are better than those in book publishing, despite the higher up-front costs."

Making selections for new media brings us to the question of who will write the text. Richard Curtis thinks that "with technological changes in the industry, the role of the author must without question become subordinated to that of the producer." He refers to such individuals as *auteurs,* the term used for artistic filmmakers.

Jack Scovil anticipates that "the multimedia writer most likely will be just one person on a team."

New media gurus agree on the need to reconsider the whole issue of sales channels for the product. Although superstores have more space and carry more titles, there is some question whether a bookstore is the best or only environment for display and demonstration of CD-ROMs.

Right now CD-ROMs are mainly sold in computer and software stores. Michael Mellin thinks "store chains that are already selling books and other media could become multimedia stores selling many titles in many formats.

Bookstores can deal with complexity of titles better than software stores." Todd Wade believes bookstores are open to distributing CD-ROMs. "They are afraid of missing out on an opportunity, as they did with video distribution," he says. And, in fact, Apple and Voyager are planning to test-market bookstore sales of their products at a demonstration kiosk.

Richard Curits predicts, "The major bookstore chains will be bought up by large electronic companies." But Donald Lamm cautions us "not to forget the fudge brownie factor," suggesting that "the need for human contact may become even more important in a cold, technological world. Bookstores, especially bookstores that offer a warm, engaging, responsive environment, may become even more popular as places to go."

Len Riggio, CEO of Barnes & Noble, has made a point of creating the warm sense of place espoused by Lamm and others—a place to sit and leaf through a book. Furthermore, Riggio strongly believes that in the year 2000, books will still make great gifts: "No one's going to give someone a dot."

Munro Magruder, of BMR Associates, a West Coast management consulting firm to the media business, believes the distinctions between entertainment products retailers will become increasingly blurred. "Some of the large superstores, including chains like Tower and Borders and independents like The Tattered Cover, are already embracing an 'entertainment boutique' concept, carrying a range of product offerings that includes books, audio, video and recorded music. When you add electronic delivery into the retailing equation, physical inventory limitations become less of a consideration."

Future electronic delivery of books remains a controversial issue, inspiring the following disparate opinions.

Nion McEvoy, editor-in-chief of Chronicle Books, predicts that "by the year 2000 universal texts will be downloaded to a retailer and the customers will be able to compose their own anthologies at the booksite." Riggio thinks such a service would be "too time-consuming and not economically feasible." However, Mellin believes that it could work, particularly for college bookstores. "There is no question that the price of an already published book would be lower if it is printed digitally on site," says Mellin.

McEvoy agrees with Magruder that "as a result of electronic distribution, there will be less need for physical inventory of information books in a store."

But Stephen M. Lewers, president of paperback publishing at Houghton Mifflin, points out an irony about on-demand printing. "There is no question that for certain kinds of titles, especially out-of-print ones, it is far more efficient. But the end result is a paperback book," he says, suggesting that "on-demand printing for out-of-print books could take place on the publishing house floor if the technology is there."

Glenn Hausman of BiblioBytes sells and distributes books, some of which have gone out of print, through the Internet. Users download a file and read a book on a screen or print pages, in their own chosen typeface. Hausman says, "Traditional publishers are not yet prepared to enter into this market. They don't have the technical know-how and they don't want to alienate existing distribution channels." Yet Barnes & Noble already has an electronic mail-order catalogue on Compuserve, and Waldenbooks is also online. "Perhaps," Scott Walker predicts, "there could be new kinds of bookstores, such as community bookstores or TV subscription book clubs as a result of on-demand printing."

Electronic distribution does not have to be viewed as a threat. There are some advantages, perhaps for everyone. Mellin says that "once we're all networked together, it will also revolutionize the way sales are handled. Orders will be fulfilled instantaneously, and through network connections we can download in-store promotional brochures. We will become better collaborators with bookstores on getting our books to the public."

The future possibilities of customer-designed product is what visionaries like to think about. On-demand ordering takes away the guessing game of how many copies to publish and how many to buy. Janet Wikler believes that "we are now entering the world of mass customization."

Jack Romanos says that "traditional rights packages will get smaller because the reprint issue will become less important. And there will be more coordination in English-language publishing on a worldwide basis. Foreign-language rights will continue to be licensed for the foreseeable future."

John Taylor Williams, copyright law expert and literary agent of Boston's Palmer & Dodge, says, "The grant to a publisher in a standard contract has traditionally included general wording which encompassed 'all new media formats.' Once audio rights became hot properties, authors, agents and publishers began to pay more attention to the bounds of that grant. Now much more negotiating takes place over the specific rights the author will grant. But I already see a tension, since some publishers' new stragetic partners—such as Apple, Microsoft and Voyager—are anxious to create multimedia versions of publishers' backlists."

He sums up: "Electronic access is a boon for authors and publishers alike; but respect for copyright ownership shouldn't get lost in the melee."

The question of copyright in an electronic world is a tough one. John Taylor Williams says that "online infringement of copyright occurs when one copy of a work in electronic form is bought and then downloaded, that is, copied by the end user. Further infringement occurs when the downloaded copy is made accessible to multiple users via a network." He sees "enforcing electronic rights as a matter of control by license or by a built-in mechanism that monitors usage by the end-user. There will be a need for an electronic tag, some equivalent of a bar code, so that usage will be passed on to a copyright center."

Scott Walker thinks an organization like Compuserve could keep track of downloading from the Internet or any network. To get online a user needs to enter a password, which would be easy to track. Others suggest that publishers need to work right now with the Library of Congress to find a way to monitor usage for copyright. However, Carol Risher, v-p for copyright and new technology of the AAP, does not think "any government agency would have the marketplace experience needed for assessing copyright fees. There is a lot of potential revenue at stake here. The Copyright Clearance Center has, in fact, captured $28 million in copyright fees that might otherwise have been lost to the industry from copy centers."

According to Dana Ardi, "Companies need to change the way they are organized and form team efforts across all business units to come up with successful new media products." She also believes they need to change their thinking about platforms. "Why does there have to be one standard?" she asks. "Why can't this be a multi-platform opportunity?" She says "there are three areas of concern that the industry needs to get together to address. They are: 1) sorting out how the 'guilds' [segments of the industry] will interact; 2) the problem of copyright; and 3) the challenge of finding new and emerging channels of distribution for new media." And in an enthusiastic outburst that best sums up the hopes of more forward-looking publishers about the future of publishing, she adds, "We must begin to publish, taking full advantage of the new tools that the technology will provide."

FURTHER READING

Criticism

Bolter, Jay David. "The Computer, Hypertext, and Classical Studies." *American Journal of Philology* 112, No. 4 (Winter 1991): 541-45.

Suggests future uses of hypertext in classical studies.

Birkerts, Sven. *The Gutenberg Elegies: The Fate of Reading in an Electronic Age.* Boston: Faber & Faber, 1994, 231 p.

Collection of essays concerning the shift from print to electronic media. Birkerts argues that "the complexity and distinctiveness of spoken and written expression are deeply bound to traditions of print literacy."

Christopher, L. Carol. "Closing the Gap." *The Quill* 82, No. 1 (January 1994): 27-9.

Comments on the implications of electronic publishing and the information highway for newspapers, readers, and journalists.

Coover, Robert. "Hyperfiction: Novels for the Computer." *The New York Times Book Review* (29 August 1993): 1, 8-10.

Reviews Stuart Moulthrop's hyperfictive novel *Victory Garden* and comments on the genre of hyperfiction and its effects on the reading experience.

———."And Hypertext Is Only the Beginning. Watch Out!" *The New York Times Book Review* (29 August 1993): 8-9.

Discusses hypertext, hypermedia, and the state of hypertext fiction. Coover notes: "Hypertext, in effect, introduces 'purpose' or 'design' into the scatter of electronic writing, and its principal tool for doing this is its linking mechanism: in place of print's linear, page-turning route, it offers a network of alternate paths through a set of text spaces by way of designated links."

———. "And Now, Boot Up the Reviews." *The New York Times Book Review* (29 August 1993): 10-12.

Reviews eleven hyperfictions, including Michael Joyce's *Afternoon, A Story,* Judy Malloy's *Its Name Was Penelope,* and Stuart Moulthrop's *Victory Garden.*

Delany, Paul, and Landow, George P., eds. *Hypermedia and Literary Studies.* Cambridge, Mass.: The MIT Press, 352 p.

Collection of essays covering various aspects of the theory and application of hypertext to the creation and study of literature.

Elmer-Dewitt, Philip. "Bards of the Internet." *Time* 144, No. 1 (4 July 1994): 66-7.

Remarks on the quality of writing found on the Internet.

Jonas, Gerald. "The Disappearing $2,000 Book." *The New York Times Book Review* (29 August 1993): 12-13.

Comments on William Gibson and Dennis Ashbaugh's *Agrippa (A Book of the Dead),* which contains artwork by Ashbaugh and a short story by Gibson. Noting that a computer virus destroys the text of the short story as it is read, Jonas draws parallels between the nature of *Agrippa* and the future of traditional books.

Kenner, Hugh. "Electronic Books." *Byte* 18, No. 12 (November 1993): 404.

Argues that much of the software available with electronic books is not very useful.

Korn, Eric. "Miracles of Miniaturization." *The Times Literary Supplement,* No. 4476 (13-19 January 1989): 34.

Mixed review of the CD-ROM version of the *Oxford English Dictionary.*

Lewis, Peter H. "Library of Congress Offering to Feed Data Superhighway." *The New York Times* (12 September 1994): B1, B4.

Discusses plans of the Library of Congress to convert parts of its holdings to electronic form.

Princenthal, Nancy. "The Technology of Poetry." *American Book Review* 15, No. 1 (April-May 1993): 7.

Favorably reviews Judy Malloy's hyperfiction *Its Name Was Penelope.*

Reynolds, Louis R., and Derose, Steven J. "Electronic Books." *Byte* 17, No. 6 (June 1992): 263-68.

Surveys the history and development of electronic books and hypertext.

Schmidt, Stanley. "A Powerful New Tool for Writers: Hypertext." *Writer's Digest* 70, No. 2 (February 1990): 35-7.

Suggests how a writer might use hypertext software packages to organize notes for a novel.

Steiner, Clyde. "The Future of Electronic Publishing: Two Views." *Publishers Weekly* 240, No. 1 (4 January 1993): 38.

Summarizes the views of two publishing industry executives on the roles printers and publishers will play in the future of electronic book publishing.

Trudeau, Garry. "Great Leaping Illustrations! It Works!" *The New York Times Book Review* (13 November 1994): 56.

Favorably reviews the CD-ROM version of David Macaulay's book *The Way Things Work* (1988).

Welsch, Erwin K. "Hypertext, Hypermedia, and the Humanities." *Library Trends* 40, No. 4 (Spring 1992): 614-46.

Relates the history and origins of hypertext and hypermedia and examines the past, present, and future uses of these technologies by librarians and humanist scholars.

Zimmer, Carl. "Floppy Fiction." *Discover* 10, No. 11 (November 1989): 34, 36.

Briefly describes hyperfiction and the different types of software used to create it.

Graphic Narratives

INTRODUCTION

Aimed primarily at adults, graphic narratives present fiction and nonfiction featuring complex plots and serious themes in a comic-book format. One of the first adaptations of literature to a graphic narrative format occurred in 1941 when Albert Kanter launched the *Classics Comics* series, later renamed *Classics Illustrated.* With graphic versions of such diverse classics as Sir Walter Scott's *Ivanhoe* (1820), Lewis Carroll's *Alice's Adventures in Wonderland* (1865), William Shakespeare's *Hamlet* (1600-01), Fyodor Dostoyevsky's *Crime and Punishment* (1866), and Homer's *The Iliad,* the series flourished in the United States from 1941 through 1971—when the publisher stopped reprinting old titles. In 1990 Berkley, First Publishing, and Classics Media Group revived *Classics Illustrated;* other publishers and writers have produced similar types of works. Paul Karasik and David Mazzucchelli, for instance, adapted Paul Auster's *City of Glass* (1985), and Robert Crumb and David Zane Mairowitz have collaborated on graphic versions of numerous works by Franz Kafka. Proponents of graphic narrative adaptations argue that such material will promote cultural literacy by introducing adolescents to works they might not otherwise read. Detractors contend that graphic versions oversimplify the original's content and discourage people from reading.

Writers and illustrators have also developed original fiction and nonfiction works in the graphic narrative format. Distinct from traditional comic books in their subject matter and level of thematic complexity, graphic novels—which appear as serials, collections, or in single volumes—usually feature numerous, highly-developed characters interacting in a complex plot within a naturalistic setting. For instance, the series *Love and Rockets,* drawn and written by Gilbert Hernandez and Jaime Hernandez, emphasizes rural Central Americans dealing with conflicts between capitalist and communist forces. The series also deals with the personal trials of Hispanic Americans living in barrios. Other works in the genre, such as Alan Moore and Dave Gibbons's *Watchmen* (1987), feature superheroes but depict them in a realistic setting and treat them in a sophisticated, revisionist manner. As Russell Schechter has argued, *Watchmen* "through its reflexive, comic-within-a-comic structure, . . . deconstructs—verbally and visually—50 years of comic book conventions." Nonfiction graphic narratives include Larry Gonick's *The Cartoon History of the Universe* (1990) and *The Cartoon History of the Universe II* (1994), which treat world history from the Big Bang through the decline of the Roman Empire; Joyce Brabner and Tom Yeates's *Flashpoint* (1989), a journalistic account of the Central Intelligence Agency's attempt to assassinate Eden Pastora, a Nicaraguan *contra;* Harvey Pekar, Joyce Brabner, and Frank Stack's *Our Cancer Year* (1994), a memoir of Pekar's struggle with cancer; and Joe Sacco's *Palestine* (1994), an account of his visit to the West Bank in the early 1990s. Commenting on *Maus: A Survivor's Tale II* (1991), Art Spiegelman's Pulitzer Prize-winning graphic narrative about the Holocaust, James Colbert wrote: "It is, indeed, unusual to think of authentic novels as having pictures. The notion is so new that, although comics are an indigenous, truly American art form, we haven't even figured out what to call such works. *Comic book* seems diminutive, even pejorative. A *graphic novel* seems like something Madonna would write. But lest we forget, the *other* definition of novel is 'new and not resembling something formerly known or used; original or striking, especially in conception or style.' "

REPRESENTATIVE WORKS DISCUSSED BELOW

Acocella, Marisa
Just Who the Hell Is SHE, Anyway? (novel) 1994

Bergin, John
Bone Saw [editor, with James O'Barr] (anthology) 1993
From Inside (novel) 1994

Brabner, Joyce, and Yeates, Tom
Flashpoint: The La Penca Bombing (nonfiction) 1989; published in *Brought to Light*

Chaykin, Howard
Time² (novel) 1986
The Shadow: Blood and Judgment (novel) 1987
Time²: The Satisfaction of Black Mariah (novel) 1987

Crumb, Robert, and Mairowitz, David Zane
Kafka for Beginners [*Introducing Kafka*] (fiction and nonfiction) 1993

DeMatteis, J. M.
Greenberg the Vampire [with Mark Badger] (novel) 1986
Moonshadow [with Jon J. Muth, Kevin Nowlan, and Kent Williams] (novel) 1989

Gaiman, Neil
Brief Lives [with Jill Thompson and Vince Locke] (novel) 1994

Gonick, Larry
The Cartoon History of the Universe: Volumes 1-7, From the Big Bang to Alexander the Great (history) 1990
The Cartoon History of the Universe II: Volumes 8-13, From the Springtime of China to the Fall of Rome (history) 1994
Helfer, Andrew, and Baker, Kyle
Justice, Inc. (novel) 1989
Hernandez, Gilbert
Love and Rockets [with Jaime Hernandez] (series) 1984-
Heartbreak Soup (novel) 1988
Poison River (novel) 1994
Karasik, Paul, and Mazzucchelli, David
City of Glass [adaptors; from the novel by Paul Auster] (novel) 1994
Koike, Kazuo, and Kojima, Goseki
Lone Wolf & Cub (novel) 1988
Mack, Stan
Stan Mack's Real Life American Revolution (history) 1994
Messner-Loebs, William
The Journey Saga, Volume 1: Tall Tales (novel) 1987
The Journey Saga, Volume 2: Bad Weather (novel) 1991
Miller, Frank
Batman: The Dark Knight Returns [with Klaus Janson and Lynn Varley] (novel) 1986
Electra: Assassin [with Bill Sienkiewicz] (novel) 1987
Moore, Alan
Watchmen [with Dave Gibbons] (novel) 1987
Batman: The Killing Joke [with Brian Bolland] (novel) 1988
Shadowplay: The Secret Team [with Bill Sienkiewicz] (nonfiction) 1989; published in *Brought to Light*
V for Vendetta [with David Lloyd] (novel) 1991
Munoz, Jose, and Sampayo, Carlos
Joe's Bar (novel) 1988
Nocenti, Ann, and Bolton, John
Someplace Strange (novel) 1988
Otomo, Katsuhiro
Akira (novel) 1984
Pekar, Harvey
American Splendor (novel) 1986
Our Cancer Year [with Joyce Brabner and Frank Stack] (nonfiction) 1994
Prado, Miguelanxo
Streak of Chalk (novel) 1994
Robinson, James, and Elliot, Phil
Illegal Alien (science fiction) 1994
Sacco, Joe
Palestine (nonfiction) 1994
Sim, Dave, and Gerhard
Cerebus (novel) 1987
High Society (novel) 1987
Church and State. 2 vols. (novel) 1989
Jaka's Story (novel) 1990
Spiegelman, Art
Maus: A Survivor's Tale: My Father Bleeds History (novel) 1986
Maus: A Survivor's Tale II: And Here My Troubles Began (novel) 1991
Vance, James, and Burr, Dan
Kings in Disguise (novel) 1990
Zarate, Oscar, and Sayle, Alexei
Geoffrey the Tube Train and the Fat Comedian (novel) 1987
Zelenetz, Alan, and Vess, Charles
The Raven Banner (novel) 1985

HISTORY AND OVERVIEWS

Russell Schechter (essay date August 1989)

SOURCE: "Kat and Maus," in *Communication Research,* Vol. 16, No. 4, August, 1989, pp. 552-62.

[*In the excerpt below, Schechter contends that Alan Moore and Dave Gibbons's graphic novel* Watchmen *and Art Spiegelman's* Maus *are postmodern works that validate the comic form.*]

Criticism of the postmodernist enterprise as ultimately empty might well be a tendential parochialism. If one is going to live by the argument that modern works have an aura that is extant but different from that of traditional works, one must accept the possibility of a distinctive postmodern aura resulting from recombinant pastiche and possibly different from both traditional and modern forms. *Watchmen,* the recent postmodern comic book by Alan Moore and Dave Gibbons (1987), provides ample evidence for the argument. Although comic books began as compilations of newspaper strips, the two forms quickly developed in their own—though closely related—directions. *Watchmen,* designed for a late-teen and adult readership, reflects an origin in postmodernity: Its impact depends on the reader's acceptance of the distance of the "meta" position.

The subject of this comic is the comics. It lays bare the abundant absurdities of what has been a mostly juvenile, underachieving form in an extremely sophisticated and adult manner. In part through its reflexive, comic-within-a-comic structure, *Watchmen* deconstructs—verbally and visually—50 years of comic book conventions, making visible what has always remained latent: the psychopathology of heroes, the fascistic trajectory of adolescent power fantasies, and rampant misogyny, among many other elements central to the form's thematics.

Watchmen explodes the fantasy world of the comics at the same time that it spins a compelling yet inescapably archetypal comic book yarn. In spite of its elegant, labyrinthine structure and delightfully detailed panel design, however, the book ultimately (and purposefully?) succumbs to many of the same themes and techniques it intends to deconstruct. One revels in *Watchmen*'s cleverly engineered contradictions even as one is suckered into the narrative's grand operatic flow.

The problem with *Watchmen* is that, like Daffy Duck's famous self-immolation act, it can be done only once. Even though I am willing to be convinced that art was involved when "performance artist" Joe Coleman first went on stage to bite off the head of a mouse, by the time he chewed off his fiftieth rodent noggin it was merely embarrassing. Like so much (post-) avant-gardist work, the point is made the first time and, though perhaps worth repeating until everyone gets it, all repetitions after that become less than redundant. So, too, with *Watchmen.*

Although both *Watchmen* and [Jay Cantor's novel *Krazy Kat* (1987)] are energetic and innovative in their own ways, and there remains more than two thousand years of art to deconstruct and reassemble, the prospect of a long walk down a short *bricolage* pier is less than appealing. This is not to imply any fundamental limitations of the postmodernist agenda, nor that the job of deconstructing the past is to be taken lightly, but the seemingly endless recycling and reappropriation of cultural icons does seem to be emblematic of postmodern production—production highly rationalized in that all art becomes standardized in the process of meaning removal. If the past serves the present well, it is only because the past has been *preprocessed:* It is instantly recognizable at the surface, a dereferentialized surface now stripped of meaning and structure and thus aura. The routinization of authentic cultural items in postmodern production may prove every bit as savage as that enacted on traditional work by mechanically reproduced simulacra. If so, the question of whether the postmodern can be regarded as a truly autonomous epoch remains open to debate.

If there is an overwhelming bleakness to the notion of a rationalized postmodern aesthetic, there remain works that, while not necessarily revolutionary in a paradigm-breaking sense, are at least transcendent within the constraints of the dominant aesthetic. One such work that glows with an irrefutable authenticity, a beacon powerful enough to penetrate even the dense gloom of the postmodern malaise, is *Maus,* Art Spiegelman's (1986) masterful and moving biography of his father's experiences in Nazi Germany.

Although "Holocaust comic" is a perversely exquisite oxymoron, *Maus* represents not only validation of the comic form but fulfillment of the best possibilities inherent in the postmodern validation of the "baser" media. Originally appearing in the pages of *Raw,* an irregularly published magazine of innovative comic and graphic art, the first six chapters of the as-yet-unfinished story of *Maus* have been assembled in a single volume by Pantheon Books. Drawn in appropriately stark black-and-white and subtitled "A Survivor's Tale," *Maus* tells two stories: the frustrating present-day relationship of Spiegelman and his widowed father and the mad nightmare of his parents' survival in Auschwitz.

All of the characters in *Maus,* in a classic tradition of the comic form, are depicted as animals: The Jews are mice, the Nazis cats, the Poles pigs. These choices of species may be obvious, but are effective nonetheless. Every character is as real, every emotion as true, and every episode as harrowing as anything from Elie Weisel or Primo Levi or A. Anatolii.

Spiegelman has a remarkable ear not only for how people say things, but for what their words do and do not mean. The balloons his words appear in are not the overblown casings of hyperreal hyperbole, but delicate shells containing pearls of stripped-down truth. Without ever resorting to the crude phoneticisms of a Tom Wolfe, Spiegelman creates believable dialogue and convincing inflections for Polish collaborators and Borscht Belt bungalow dwellers alike. His deliberately pared-down drawing style, which renders the faces of various characters virtually identical, is sparse in detail but dense with feeling: Characters become knowable for themselves as complicated and fully developed personalities. The darkness of Spiegelman's vision reproduces the atmosphere of the time, with an impact as shattering and—perhaps most surprising—as immediate as a masterwork like the Alain Resnais film *Night and Fog.*

There are, no doubt, those who will ask, in the spirit of Dwight Macdonald, why such a story need be told as a comic. Given the author's remarkable talent and irrefutable authenticity, why not tell the tale in a conventional literary or biographical form? That is the wrong question, one which assumes that there is necessity and value in maintaining rigid hierarchies between high culture and low, midcult and mass. The more progressive impulses of postmodernism bring us to the comic form with a more appropriate question: Why not?

Maus refutes all objections to the comic as a complex and meaningful medium. Although some of *Maus*'s impact may result from the novelty of experiencing such a story in so different a form, it demonstrates the possibility of countering rationalization—and not only by toying with those forces à la *Watchmen.* Other works that work against the rationalized grain include *Stray Toasters,* Bill Sienkiewicz's astonishing transgenre comic book, and Lynda Barry's weekly strip *Ernie Pook's Comeek,* which plays with nostalgia without succumbing to it.

Postmodernism leads us to consider that the limitations of a medium may be minor relative to the artist's breadth of vision and depth of devotion. Whether this idea surfaces—or is itself reduced to mere surface—will determine the position that postmodernism finally occupies in the judgment of history.

Keith R. A. DeCandido (essay date 15 March 1990)

SOURCE: "Picture This: Graphic Novels in Libraries," in *Library Journal,* Vol. 115, No. 5, March 15, 1990, pp. 50-5.

[*DeCandido is a librarian and a reviewer for* The Comics Journal. *In the following excerpt, he presents a general description of the graphic novel genre, suggests where to acquire graphic novels, and surveys some of the available works.*]

Not many libraries have discovered graphic novels yet. The *American Heritage Dictionary* has not discovered them yet either; it does not define the term. A graphic novel is a self-contained story that uses a combination of text and art to articulate the plot. It is equivalent in content to a long short story or a short novel (or novella, or novellini, as the old *New Yorker* cartoon has it) and is in some ways a larger version of a comic book. It differs from the *fotonovela* in that the art is generally drawn in a graphic novel; photographs are used in the *fotonovela.*

The comic book as we know it has its origins in the Depression era. William M. Gaines, one of the masterminds behind the EC Horror Comics of the 1950s and *Mad* magazine, claims that his father originated the comic book in the mid-1930s by placing Sunday funnies into a booklike format. The idea caught on, and comics were not only used to collect funnies, but were created independently. In the 1940s, patriotic superheroes and soldiers were used to propagandize the war effort; in the 1950s, superheroes gave way to romance and horror.

Like everything else, comics came under fire by McCarthy-era paranoia, and the Comics Code Authority, a glorified censorship squad, was formed to keep comics in line. (It should be noted that the code is next to useless these days—it comes from the same mindset as the movie ratings system, and is even less relevant.) The superhero was revitalized in the early 1960s with Marvel's line of quasi-realistic heroes. In the late 1960s and 1970s, the underground comix creators began publishing graphic novels that moved away from the Comics Code and clichéd superheroes. In the 1980s, The Big Two, Marvel and DC, started expanding into graphic novels. The form is more flexible in size and shape, and allows greater creative freedom. Today, graphic novels are plentiful, from all publishers, in all shapes and sizes.

Generally graphic novels are either the size of a magazine (more like the late lamented *Ms.* or *LJ* than *Rolling Stone* or *Mirabella*), and usually printed on glossy paper for crisper artwork. Others are as large as regular, newsprint comics. Some are original, self-contained stories, others are collections of serialized chapters (à la 19th-century novels by Dickens and others).

The term "graphic novel" is a misnomer; while "graphic" is certainly accurate, "novel" is not; they are shorter than a standard novel. Maybe we could call them "graphic novellinis"? Comics critics have debated the question in the pages of such magazines as *The Comics Journal (CJ), Comics Buyer's Guide, Amazing Heroes,* and *Comics Interview,* with little result. Some have tried "graphic album" (used by *CBG* in their annual fan poll), but that sounds too much like an LP decorated with a cartoon. Carter Scholz, in *CJ* once proposed "graphic installment." Finally, the critics sigh, scratch their heads, and put "graphic novel" in quotes. . . .

One of the current problems that libraries may have in attempting to collect graphic novels is that the system of distribution is different from what libraries generally use. The librarian who selects graphic novels for the New York Public Library (Research) is forced to buy at Forbidden Planet (a N.Y. store specializing in sf, fantasy, and graphic literature). Queries to major publishers and distributors about dealings with libraries were met with confused or negative responses, though many expressed a desire (or at least a willingness) to deal with libraries. First Publishing (the largest of the non-Marvel-or-DC publishers) representatives regularly speak to librarians at the American Booksellers Association convention, however, even they have no special arrangement with libraries.

The principal reason for this is the rigidity of the distribution system of graphic literature. Publishers send books directly to distributors, who send books directly to newsstands and comic specialty shops. Of the two largest distributors, Diamond has no arrangements with any libraries, and Capital City sends material only to two or three.

Some libraries have begun to collect graphic literature, but very few have anything beyond a few titles. Boston Public Library only carries Art Spiegelman's *Maus.* Baltimore County Public Library only carries Batman-oriented material due to recent demand. (According to Mary Paulus of BCPL, they base their purchases on materials information cards submitted by readers, and graphic literature apparently is not requested much.)

Sam Bennett at Kansas City Public Library, Mo., says they buy a few, mainly based on reviews in *Publishers Weekly,* and he does look out for interesting things. The Kansas City Art Institute Library, Mo., the New Orleans Public Library, and Salem Public Library, Mass. (among others) order very little, if any; indeed, many librarians we contacted for this article needed a detailed explanation of what a graphic novel is. We were able to identify one place with a large graphic collection, the Bowling Green State University Popular Culture Library, Ohio. In fact, it was the only one polled that unhesitatingly gave a long list of titles it carried.

Bookdealers were just as disappointing. Mike Nicita of Golden-Lee said that they do carry graphic novels, but libraries don't order in any magnitude "worth mentioning in your article," a sentiment echoed by Sandy Rose of Brodart. Ingram's Larry Price could not determine if they carried graphic literature or not—it is not classified as a separate genre, and is therefore untraceable. Jean Srnecz of Baker & Taylor said much the same thing, adding that graphic novels have not "emerged as a major publishing category." B&T does carry graphic literature, but it is not publicized separately. . . .

The traditional age group for comic book purchasers is in the upper teens (based on the respondents to *CBG*'s annual poll). Graphic novels capture a higher age group, mid-20s, due to their generally greater sophistication. Few of the best of graphic novels come from Marvel or DC, nor do they involve superheroes overmuch. Although people in tights and capes are the backbone of the industry, they are in the minority in the literary art form.

The themes are no different from any other literature: some form of conflict, usually between "good" and "evil," or dealing with the intricacies of interpersonal relationships. That about covers every plot from Shakespeare to Danielle Steel. Graphic literature is unique in that it combines representation with words. It is not simply art conveying a story, nor just words, but the combination that sets the medium apart (this is why many of the best works are written and drawn by the same person).

If one must categorize it, it should have its own denomination, rather than being lumped in with art books, or sf/fantasy, or "pop," or (as some bookstores do for whatever arcane reason) humor. Since the form has only recently gained anything resembling mainstream acceptance, it is still feeling its way around, so one cannot blame those who don't know how to treat it. . . .

Any library contemplating a graphic collection should definitely consider the following as musts, in order of merit. This list is by no means complete, but would make an excellent start.

Maus by Art Spiegelman is collected from the pages of *RAW,* an anthology comic put out by Spiegelman and his wife, Françoise Mouly. It is a biographical tale of Spiegelman's father, Vladek, detailing his trials as a Jew in Europe during World War II. Besides the sheer power of the story, Spiegelman twists the "talking animal" convention used often in comics (and also by George Orwell in *Animal Farm*). Jews are mice, Germans, cats, Poles, pigs, and Americans, dogs. A second volume, *Mauschwitz,* is being serialized in *RAW.* Libraries that collect Holocaust literature should consider this.

Cerebus, High Society, and *Church and State* (2 vols.) by Dave Sim, with Gerhard, is Sim's monthly comic, planned as a massive 300-issue story in separate installments (Sim feels 300 comic books will have enough content to qualify as a novel). Each installment has been collected into one (or two) massive volumes. The first, *Cerebus,* collects issues prior to Sim's decision to make this one big story, and is marred by crude stories and cruder art, but should be included for completeness. Although ostensibly the story of a walking, talking, obnoxious aardvark in a medieval land of humans, Sim does an excellent job of detailing the nuances and peculiarities of political power (*High Society*), religious authority (the two-volume *Church and State*) and personal relationships (*Jaka's Story,* still in progress in the monthly book). The art, with tones and background inking by Gerhard, is magnificent.

Watchmen by Alan Moore and Dave Gibbons got notice in the mainstream press, as it takes the superhero convention and grounds it in reality. Moore and Gibbons do not just present a world with superheroes, but *this* world, with the addition of a "superhero" fad around the late 1930s, early 1940s. Grown men and women acted as vigilantes in funny suits. This concept itself alters little, but when a true superman (called "Dr. Manhattan") arrives, everything changes. The balance of power shifts, the United States wins the Vietnam War, Nixon remains president for a third, fourth, and fifth term, and numerous other significant changes, all because the government has a superman working for it. ("God exists," one perceptive scientist remarks, "and he's American.") Moore and Gibbons take the superhero to its ultimate, to a level mainstream comics couldn't possibly attain. The attention to detail is superb, and by the time you finish (probably, despite its length, in one sitting), you are stunned.

Moonshadow by J.M. DeMatteis and Jon J. Muth, with Kevin Nowlan and Kent Williams could easily be subtitled "Candide in Space." Moonshadow's mother is a hippie who was plucked from the Earth in the early 1970s by the G'l Doses, an enigmatic race of beings that look like balls of light with beatific smiles, who flit about the galaxy operating on pure whim, plucking beings from all manner of worlds. One of those G'l Doses is Moon's father, and it is that father that boots Moon & Co. (his mother; his cat, Frodo; his unwilling companion, the lecherous Ira) into space. Throughout his travels—referred to by the older Moonshadow, narrating in flashback, as his search for enlightenment—he encounters all manner of beings, learns of love and hate, war and peace. DeMatteis writes with joy of life, of love, and of literature (each chapter opens with a relevant quote, from Blake to Beckett to Tolkien to Carroll). Moon's quest is in many ways the Romantic quest of so many early-19th-century poets, and Muth's watercolor art with Nowlan's calligraphic letters only augment the feeling of wonder and delight in exploration and discovery.

American Splendor by Harvey Pekar and others. Any random sampling of issues in this series would do nicely, or one could purchase the collection. Pekar does "slice-of-life" work (with a multitude of artists, including the infamous and weird R. Crumb), specifically from his own life. Pekar gives pieces of his experiences, delightful in their mundanity, comfortable in their familiarity, and made enjoyable by his remarkable skill with dialect.

Love and Rockets by Jaime and Gilbert Hernandez is available in the monthly magazines, and many collections in varying formats. These brothers work separately to different ends, but both have remarkable storytelling abilities. Gilbert's main focus is rural Central Americans living in the middle of (or perhaps in spite of) conflicting capitalist and communist forces. Jaime's characters live in urban barrios, also on the low end of the economic spectrum, and he chronicles their crazed personal crises. Gilbert has also done more abstract work recently, including "Frida" in *Love and Rockets* #28, a magnificent portrait of Frida Kahlo, artist and wife of artist Diego Rivera.

The Journey Saga. Vol. 1: *Tall Tales* by William Messner-Loebs is the first collection of the "Journey" series, the story of Josh "Wolverine" MacAllistaire, a trapper in early 1800s Michigan, a frontier rife with story possibilities. Messner-Loebs has a charmingly laid-back narrative style ("Black bears in the wild, as a rule, stood three-foot at the shoulder and measured six foot from flank to snout. They weighed close on three hundred pound . . . 'Course, some were bigger . . ."), and a mishmash of French, German, and American (both native and colonial) people, not to mention wildlife, who fall in and out of Josh's life. Josh counters his daily tumult with a simple commonsense approach that belies a terrible ferocity. Brilliant storytelling, with good attention to historical detail. Can be considered historical fiction.

Batman: The Dark Knight Returns by Frank Miller, with Klaus Janson and Lynn Varley is a high-quality superhero comic, but still a superhero comic. There are numerous inconsistencies that Miller (and his editors Denny O'Neil and Dick Giordano) glossed over, but this is perhaps the ultimate Batman story, with superb, larger-than-life art, and is primarily responsible for the present Bat-mania of which the *Batman* movie is the climax.

The following titles are not musts, but worth-looking-ats. . . .

AARGH stands for Artists Against Rampant Government Homophobia, and was published as a backlash against Proposition 28. That British law effectively enables the government to censor the very concept of homosexuality from British cultural life. It contains contributions from various artists (see also *StripAIDS USA*).

Any Similarity to Persons Living or Dead Is Purely Coincidental by Drew and Josh Alan Friedman takes loony pokes at popular culture.

Batman: The Killing Joke by Alan Moore and Brian Bolland focuses on the relationship between Batman and the Joker far more devilishly and horrifically than the *Batman* movie.

Brought to Light by Alan Moore, Joyce Brabner, Tom Yeates, Bill Sienkiewicz, and Paul Mavrides was supposed to be jointly published by Eclipse and DC, but DC's parent corporation, Warner Bros., pulled out, fearing possible reprisals. This "graphic docudrama" features two stories severely critical of our government, involving the "secret wars" conducted by the CIA and National Security Council in Central America. It was done in conjunction with the Christic Institute's legal suit against the U.S. government. Moore and Sienkiewicz's story is the better of the two, but both will shatter any illusions one might have about covert activities perpetrated by the United States. . . .

The Cowboy Wally Show by Kyle Baker is a satiric treatment of television politics.

Elektra: Assassin by Frank Miller and Bill Sienkiewicz is an overwhelmingly surreal look at government—sort of. Very strange and very good.

The Greatest Batman Stories Ever Told and *The Greatest Joker Stories Ever Told* present companion pieces to present Bat mania, and include some very interesting stories from the late 1930s to the early 1980s.

Greenberg the Vampire by J.M. DeMatteis and Mark Badger is the hilarious story of a neurotic, Jewish, horror-fiction-writing vampire.

Joe's Bar by Jose Munoz and Carlos Sampayo is the story of a local Manhattan bar told with surprising realism considering the two Argentine creators have never been to New York. Gritty and dark.

Justice, Inc. by Andrew Helfer and Kyle Baker takes the Avenger, the old radio hero who could alter his facial features, and uses it to critique the CIA's practice of overthrowing legitimate (and socialistic) governments and replacing them with dictatorships. Very skilled.

Lone Wolf & Cub by Kazuo Koike and Goseki Kojima tells the story of a ronin (a samurai without a lord), formerly the shogun's executioner, who travels the road of the assassin, hoping someday to avenge his family's murder. He travels with his very young child. Very Japanese in style and narrative.

Neat Stuff by Peter C. Bagge. If you picture Roger Rabbit's eyes bulging, that's Bagge's people, only they are like that all the time. His portrayals of scuzzy characters are hysterical.

The Raven Banner by Alan Zelenetz and Charles Vess is a charming tale of Norse mythology with beautiful painted art by Vess.

The Shadow: Blood and Judgment by Howard Chaykin portrays the 1980s-ization of the radio hero. Convoluted and violent, but interesting.

Someplace Strange by Ann Nocenti and John Bolton tells the story of two kids and a punk who travel to an alternate universe. Excellent character study, and weird art.

Starstruck by Elaine Lee and Michael Wm. Kaluta is sf as a cross between William Gibson's cyberpunk books and Douglas Adams's *Hitchhiker's Guide to the Galaxy* series. Gorgeous art.

Stray Toasters by Bill Sienkiewicz. Congratulations if you can follow the plot. Abstract, surreal, peculiar, and warped.

StripAIDS USA is like *AARGH*, an AIDS benefit. This is primarily by American artists, reacting against misconceptions about both the disease, and those who get it.

Time² and *Time²: The Satisfaction of Black Mariah* by Howard Chaykin has jazz music, gangland warfare, adultery, violence, and more convoluted plot twists than previously believed possible. Larger-than-life art in the vein of Miller's *Dark Knight*.

V for Vendetta by Alan Moore and David Lloyd is a frightening treatment of totalitarian, post-World War III Britain, and a statement on where Britain is now heading.

X-Men: God Loves, Man Kills by Chris Claremont and Brent Eric Anderson is a fascinating study in racial prejudice and the influence of tunnel-minded televangelists, especially in light of the Swaggart and Jim and Tammy imbroglios that have occurred since its publication.

Pagan Kennedy (essay date 19 March 1990)

SOURCE: "P. C. Comics," in *The Nation*, New York, Vol. 250, No. 11, March 19, 1990, pp. 386-89.

[In the essay below, Kennedy comments on the history of comic book publishing in the United States and discusses the distinctive qualities and appeal of several graphic novels.]

By 1969, *Zap Comix* had become so much a totem of the underground San Francisco scene that its editor, ninety-pound weakling Robert Crumb, was finally able to get laid. As he relates in a recent cartoon story, "I made up for all those years of deprivation by lunging maniacally at women I was attracted to . . . squeezing faces and humping legs. . . . I usually got away with it . . . famous eccentric artist, you know." His *Zap* included everything from instructions for smoking a joint to the adventures of Wonder Wart-Hog, in which the main character, unable to get it up, uses his snout instead. Underground comix, distributed through head shops along with bongs and roach clips, were ancillary to (male) hippie culture: They were kinky and they were druggy, and if they were too loud, then you were too old.

I discovered comic books that same year. I was 7 and I bought mine at Dart Drug while Dad browsed through the lawn-care aisle. Like most girls my age, my tastes ran toward *Casper, the Friendly Ghost, Wendy the White Witch* and *Richie Rich, the Poor Little Rich Boy.* Their titles were tellingly oxymoronic—in their candy-colored world, even ghosts, witches and capitalists were cute. And they, unlike the superhero stories the boys read, taught that goodness meant goody-two-shoeism: Rather than a strong left hook, girls' heroes got by on politeness, obedience and proper grooming. If Casper inadvertently scared human beings with his spooky looks, he, the spirit world's answer to Uncle Tom, would win them back with his courteousness. And Richie, that prig in the Little Lord Fauntleroy suit, always minded his millionaire dad.

Why was there such a tremendous gap between the fluff that companies like Marvel, DC Comics and Harvey Comics dished out to us kids and the acid humor of the undergrounds? One reason may have been a 1954 book by Frederic Wertham called *Seduction of the Innocent.* Wertham accused comic books of causing everything from juvenile delinquency to bad grammar. The book prompted a televised Senate hearing, and the subdued publishers formed the Comics Code Authority of America, which drew up guidelines that put the quirkier titles, notably those of Entertaining Comics (EC), out of business. *Mad,* which became enormously influential for 1960s underground cartoonists, was the only EC survivor—albeit as the tamer *Mad Magazine.*

Moreover, DC, Marvel and other biggies turned the creation of comic books into an assembly line. One artist drew according to a writer's script; another inked in the drawing; another put in color; another, the lettering. Of course, artists and writers seldom received royalties on their work or owned the characters they developed, a policy that insured that they would churn out copy.

Many of those who formed the underground had been kids when EC—which specialized in torn-off limbs, eyeballs popping out of skulls and Twilight Zone plot twists—was put on trial. Faced with a system in which comics that didn't meet the code couldn't get shelf space, publishers such as Last Gasp Eco-Funnies and The Rip Off Press printed up their own books and distributed them directly or through porno and head shops.

Not only did these presses seek to encourage free expression, they also tried to overturn the exploitative behavior of the mainstream companies. As Jack Jaxon, one of the founders of Rip Off, wrote in 1971, "Publishers of comix work with the artists in what virtually amounts to a partnership arrangement. . . . We [artists] also retain the copyright to our published work." Jaxon's manifesto, reprinted in 1989 by *Blab!,* included an epilogue in which he admitted, "Perhaps I was hasty in predicting the eventual collapse of the mainstream industry."

Indeed, as the 1970s wore on, head shops fell afoul of the law, and the underground—tied to a waning hippie subculture—began to wither away.

But with the 1980s, two alternative titles, *RAW* and *Weirdo,* arrived to resuscitate the scene. On the face of it, they had a lot in common: Both were edited by veterans of the 1960s underground, and both showcased the work of old and new talents in the potpourri style of literary magazines. But in sensibility, they couldn't have been farther apart. Art Spiegelman's edgy, European *RAW* was printed on pages at least as large as *Interview*'s and would have looked equally at home on a Soho coffee table. The large format and high-quality paper showed off each panel as a work of art, not merely a device to further the story at hand. Even when *RAW* artists drew in primitive and scratchy styles, you knew it was because they were more tortured and sensitive than you'd ever be.

R. Crumb's *Weirdo* also embraced primitive art styles, but in the American snot-dripping-out-of-the-nose tradition of Big Daddy Roth, renowned for his monsters driving hot rods. The inclusion of Crumb's own work in *Weirdo* tended to overshadow that of other artists, fine as many of them were. With his witty confessional style (tales of high-school foot fetishism, fr'instance) and drawings reminiscent of 1920s cartoons, Crumb was more a guru than a peer to other weirdos.

However, it was Spiegelman who most affected the way comic books are marketed. His masterpiece *Maus—A Survivor's Tale* recounts his father's experiences in a concentration camp, showing Jews as mice and Germans as cats. This "graphic novel" trailblazed comics' migration from the ghetto of special-interest markets to the (relatively) big bucks of book publishing. At first serialized in *RAW, Maus* was picked up by Pantheon and sold through bookstores—at a rate of 1,000 copies a week at one point. *RAW* itself is now put out by Penguin, alas in book format rather than as a coffee-table magazine.

But even after America's introduction to the graphic novel, relatively few comic books have made it into B. Daltons or Waldenbooks. For the rest, the "direct market" store—those comic book boutiques that stock both collector's items and the latest titles—has taken the place of the head shop, accounting for two-thirds of all comic books sold in the country. Such stores provide a venue for experimental works that otherwise might not get distributed. In addition, the specialty shops serve as hangouts where comics cognoscenti can meet to discuss the death of Robin or pick up more than the latest issue of *X-Men.*

What's perhaps most interesting about these stores, when you consider the antipathy between the mainstream and undergrounds in the 1960s, is that *Zap* (still going) now sits side by side with *Spiderman* on the shelves. The differences between the mainstream and the alternatives are falling away.

The big guys, eyeing an audience that now ranges in age from 13 to 29 (but which is still almost completely male), are scrambling to be arty and adult. In 1986, the same year *Maus* came out, megalith DC Comics published its own graphic novel, a Batman story called *The Dark Knight Returns.* The book marked several departures for DC. First, rather than having been churned out entirely in assembly-line fashion, it bears the distinctive stamp of one person, writer and penciler Frank Miller. Second, its themes aim unwaveringly at an older audience: Batman copes with the aging of his body, a soul as dark as his enemies' and, last but not least, nuclear war. In addition, *The Dark Knight,* first put out as a serialized comic, was published as a perfect-bound book on slick paper rather than on newsprint. At $12.95, few kids would be able to afford this comic book—indeed, it might put a strain on some adults' allowances.

But don't let its gussied-up looks fool you: *The Dark Knight* is just more of the same schlock. Miller adopts an easy nihilism to justify Batman's make-'em-die-screaming philosophy. The book has been hailed for reviving the vampirish 1930s Batman, but one would hope it is only fanboys weaned on costumed-hero books who are insisting that *The Dark Knight* qualifies as literature.

Watchmen, also serialized and later published in book form by DC, tackles the same hero-gone-wrong theme: The title is taken from the epigraph to the Tower Commission report, "Who watches the watchmen?" While you wouldn't want to call this book literature either, it's a lot more sophisticated than *The Dark Night.* Scriptwriter Alan Moore portrays costumed heroes as both bungling do-gooders and Lieutenant Calley-style sleazebags. In short, they're just like the folks we see on the news except they have a thing for leotards and masks. *Watchmen* may be a bit simple-minded, but it deserves recognition for the innovations it brings to the graphic novel form. Certain images appear and reappear with cinematic subtlety—for instance, a bloody "happy face" graces the first and last panels of the book. In addition, Moore and artist Dave Gibbons weave ersatz book excerpts, newspaper articles and even an EC-style comic book into the story line.

Recently, DC has been trying to grab an even artier market with an imprint called Piranha Press. For those not hip to the situation, these comic books may look like they're produced by an alternative press: Nowhere, except in the fine print on the inside cover, is it apparent that the comic books are put out by DC. With the exception of *The Drowned Girl,* every one of Piranha's titles wants to be bleak but is instead banal. The worst, because it tries the hardest to look punk and pained, is *Beautiful Stories for Ugly Children,* which pairs scratchy, angry drawings with poorly written, angry narratives. It's as if some executive had puzzled over Gary Panter's *Invasion of the Elvis Zombies*—a book with a surreal text and apocalyptic illustrations that was lavishly published by *RAW* but is now out of print—and thought, "Hell, what's the big deal? We can do this."

While DC tries to serve up its comics raw, or at least medium-rare, the "ground-level" companies (as they're called now that they've come up from underground) are mimicking the marketing techniques of the big guys. Unlike 1960s comix publishers, which tended to put out one title that included the work of many artists, today's ground-levels often sell each artist's work under a different title. These appear in standard, or better-quality, comic book form and are serialized, just like the lowly superhero book.

The foremost of these alternative publishers is Fantagraphics Books, which serializes Jaime and Gilbert Hernandez's work in *Love and Rockets.* Jaime draws and writes about a group of Latino punks in California; brother Gilbert, about the Central American anytown of Palomar. *Love and Rockets,* which has drawn a cult following, was the comic book that got me hooked again; except for the odd *RAW* (too pricey), I'd stopped reading comics after I grew out of *Betty and Veronica.*

It was Jaime Hernandez's "Locas" story (1986's No. 15 was the first issue I came across) that plunged me into a comics ecstasy I hadn't known since I was 10. Hernandez brings to life a group of neurotic, odd and headstrong women. In issue No. 15, for instance, Maggie, a pretty and plump *pocha,* fixes a truck for some Mexican brothers she has nicknamed Los Tres Estoogies, but is humiliated when they offer her money. Maggie sleeps in the same bed with Hopey, but it's not clear whether they're lovers. Hopey, a skinny, combat-booted Chicana, is in one of those punk bands that can never quite get off the ground: The singer's on drugs, the bassist takes herself too seriously and no one can agree whether the band should be called "Greg Brady Image" or "Our Wives Look Best to Us." Best of all, Hernandez draws in a style copped from Archie comics. He exaggerates facial expressions—for instance, drops of sweat fly from anxious characters—and displays a superb command of body language.

The drawings in boys' comic books are meant to convey movement, to help the reader feel what it's like to kick someone in the face or jump across a rooftop. To this end, artists play with perspective—they foreshorten bodies, let huge fists pop out of the panel. Girls' comic books, on the other hand, employ close-ups of faces, subtle expressions and body movements to supplement the dialogue. Hernandez's use of the visual idioms of girls' comic books—as much as his convincing and independent women characters—made *Love and Rockets,* for this girl raised on a Richie Rich diet, instantly familiar and readable.

However, Jaime Hernandez did not originally use the visual language of girls' comics, nor was he always a feminist. Maggie, for instance, started out as a curvy sci-fi babe, a mechanic who fixed hovercrafts and robots. Over the years, Hernandez pruned the fantastic elements from his world to concentrate on the characters. Recently, when he had Maggie gain weight, letters of protest poured in, attesting that a mostly male audience still may not be ready for realism, especially when that means real women.

Brother Gilbert Hernandez has an equal respect for strong women. His mythical Central American town is patrolled by a woman sheriff. In Palomar, where "men are men and women need a sense of humor," females lay down the law. And his *Heartbreak Soup* series brings to comics the feeling of Latin literature with its weave of plots and subplots and its Marquezian touches—ghosts appear casually among the living, and people dine on giant slugs. In an interview with *The Comics Journal,* he explained the origins of his new work (like Jaime, he started out with sci-fi babes): "There were always great stories that we'd heard from our uncles and aunts and our grandmother . . . about when they were living in Mexico. . . . And we thought, 'If we could just tell those stories somehow . . .' But we figured that nobody white could understand this. We were naïve." Appropriately, Gilbert's drawing style shows the influences of painter Frida Kahlo and Mexican folk artists.

In *Love and Rockets,* Fantagraphics debuted Dan Clowes's cool camp detective story, and soon after he had his own serial called *Lloyd Llewellyn.* Clowes looks through X-ray specs at a world of late-nite cocktail lounges, *Mad Magazine* beatniks and killer sex kittens, amid which bumbles private dick Llewellyn. Several months ago Clowes embarked on a new title, *Eightball,* which allows him to mock more than just B movies. Issue No. 1 mercilessly makes fun of commercial comicdom in a story about a publishing czar who convinces his artists to work without pay by sermonizing, "These are our six flagship titles: The Army-Bots, Infinity Hombre, Musclemaster, The 10-Year Robot War, New Age Krystyll and Marionette Squad! . . . They will one day be read in classrooms and quoted by scholars!"

Another Fantagraphics artist, Carol Lay, also gets her

An excerpt from From Hell *by Alan Moore and Eddie Campbell.*

point across by camping it up. Her *Good Girls* series parodies true-confession comics of the 1950s and 1960s—imitating their drawing style while undercutting their message of conformity. Lay's heroine Irene has, well, an unusual love problem. Raised in an African tribe, Irene has had her face molded and ritually scarred (it looks something like a telephone). When her blind boyfriend asks to feel her features, this leads to—Sob! —heartbreak. Even so, Irene refuses plastic surgery. She knows she's beautiful even if the world doesn't.

Other titles gaining followings and garnering praise are *Jim* (Fantagraphics), a psychedelic romp through the author's dream life; *Yummy Fur* (Vortex Comics), which links story lines about aliens, a sewer underworld and a portal to another dimension through a dead man's anus; and *Unsupervised Existence* (Fantagraphics), whose characters are the type of P.C. marginals you might meet at your food co-op.

The diversity of new titles suggests that publishers are still feeling out the possibilities of the comic book form. One role might be educational—as much as that might make some parents shudder. For instance, Will Eisner (creator of *The Spirit*) noted in a recent *New York Times Book Review* essay that the comic book manuals he worked on for the military persistently outperformed its traditional training methods.

Meanwhile, a 1987 comic book published by the Central Committee for Conscientious Objectors, *Real War Stories,* may have helped teach kids not to step into the recruiting office at all. It adapted real interviews to detail the horrors of war and the military's sexism and racism. Particularly moving was the final story, about El Salvador. A boy hears gunshots at night and in the morning finds soldiers hosing down the streets. The next panel shows a close-up of the water disappearing down the gutter: It's red. The comic won the critical acclaim of the war machine itself, in a fashion. Military officials have alleged that *Real War Stories* threatens national security.

I have my own hopes for the form. To survive today as an artist, one must identify oneself as a specialist—writer, draftsperson, painter. It's not so different from the division of labor enforced by the big comics companies, where pencilers seldom are allowed to write their own scripts.

Thus, if the comic book can be liberated from the assembly line, it may come to represent one of the few venues for those whose talents don't fall into any one category. Fantagraphics, for example, will this year publish a collection of the stories, comics, illustrations and paintings of Kenneth Smith.

Like film, comic books are far more sensual than pure language, and therefore have the potential to appeal to a large popular audience, as they do in Europe and Japan. Unlike film, comic books can be produced by one person with little more investment than some boards, brushes and pens. No wonder the form has so often been on the wrong side of the law, associated with longhairs and lefties: As visceral as film, as silent as a book, and as easy to produce as finding an idle photocopier, the comic book is inherently subversive.

Mikal Gilmore (essay date 17 May 1990)

SOURCE: "Hot Comic Books," in *Rolling Stone,* Issue 578, May 17, 1990, pp. 57, 60, 62, 64, 65.

[*In the following essay, Gilmore remarks on the early development of the graphic novel genre and surveys the work of several writers.*]

"Batman doesn't exist," British comic writer Alan Moore is saying. "There *aren't* any characters like that in the real world, and the real world is what we should be writing about."

It is late on a blustery winter evening, and Moore is seated in the living room of his row house in the small town of Northampton, England, showing some of the finished pages from *Big Numbers*—his new twelve-part opus about small-town community, millennial convulsion and fractal mathematics. Tall, gracious and voluble, Moore is probably the most respected and visionary talent in comics today.

A fervent believer that comics can prove as sophisticated as any narrative medium around, Moore is convinced that for the art form to mature and gain acceptance, it must cast aside its overworked superhero mythologies and begin to look toward the real world as a source of ideas and inspiration. "It's not very useful to know that Batman is a psychopath," Moore says. "It *is* useful to know why your corner grocer might be one, or why Margaret Thatcher or George Bush are possibly psychopaths. But not Batman, because you are never going to meet him."

Welcome to the increasingly high-reaching (and contentious) world of the modern-day comic book—or, if you prefer, the graphic narrative—one of the most adventurous storytelling mediums of the day. If that seems like a reckless or surprising claim—if comics seem like a disreputable pop form, catering largely to adolescent fantasies of sex and violence—well, look again. In recent years, American and British writers and artists have taken the conventions of the comic book, with its formulaic monsters and superheroes, and fashioned ingenious narratives about characters trying to wrest hope and peace from lives riddled with pain and horror. Now some of the best of these authors, like Moore, are casting out fantastic elements altogether and shaping stories in which characters live, love, hope, lose, have sex, kill, abide and die for familiar human purposes. In the process, comics are winning new, hip cachet and a new literary credibility. In fact, to a devoted and growing coterie of fans, the comics medium is now undergoing the sort of exciting creative explosion that film and pop music enjoyed in the 1960s.

The roots of this rite of passage go back to the early 1980s, when a lanky author-artist named Frank Miller took over a flagging Marvel title called *Daredevil.* By bringing a film noir-inspired style to the comic's art and plots and by placing the central character in a more lifelike, sordid reality, Miller single-handedly invented the superhero revisionist movement that still rages today. Through the 1980s, authors like Miller, Jaime and Gilbert Hernandez (*Love and Rockets*), Art Spiegelman (*RAW* and *Maus*) and Alan Moore (who turned DC's failing *Swamp Thing* into a brainy horror series) were producing works that were revitalizing a long-devalued art form. In particular, Miller's *Batman: The Dark Knight Returns*—a brutal fantasy about comics' oldest superhero-detective waging his last fateful campaign against a backdrop of political apocalypse—became the biggest-selling work in the medium's history and brought a new, decidedly more adult readership into the marketplace. But it was with Moore's 1986 masterwork *Watchmen* that comics came fully into their own. A twelve-part story about a group of hard-bitten heroes who fight to save an America that few of them believe in any longer, *Watchmen* was not only savvy commentary on the dangers and appeals of the superhero archetype, it was also astute political analysis and a peerless thriller. To read it was to understand the power and depth that this renascent art form could wield.

At the same time, books like *Watchmen* and *Dark Knight* were also receiving scrutiny from critics who still regarded comics as primarily an agency for children and were alarmed by the medium's new, darker themes. "[Comics] have forsaken campy repartee and outlandishly Byzantine plots for a steady diet of remorseless violence," wrote Joe Queenan in the *New York Times Magazine.* "[Their] vindictive, sadistic tone . . . is best exemplified by Alan Moore, author of *Watchmen.*" Apparently nervous about this sort of criticism, DC Comics—the publisher of *Dark Knight, Watchmen* and all Batman and Superman titles—proposed a ratings system for its books, similar to the label guidelines that the Parents' Music Resource Center had devised for pop albums. Moore and Miller balked at having their work rated or censored and found they could no longer work in good conscience with the comics industry they had helped rejuvenate.

In the wake of Moore and Miller's departure, the comics mainstream idled. Major publishers like DC and Marvel simply saw the unprecedented sales of revisionist superhero tales as affirmation of the genre's renewed viability and flooded the market with them. "At the moment," says Moore, "there are a lot of self-consciously hip comics around, showing grim psychological portraits of established comic characters. It may be making lots of money, but in the long run, it isn't doing comics any good."

What *is* doing comics good, though, is the work currently being produced on the medium's fringe. Books like Chester Brown's *Yummy Fur,* Dave Sim's *Cerebus,* the Hernandez Brothers' *Love and Rockets,* Jamie Delano's *Hellblazer* and Neil Gaiman's *Sandman* are telling smart and compelling tales. And now, Alan Moore and Frank Miller—who are pretty much the Beatles and Rolling Stones of the comics world—are getting ready to join that fringe. In the months ahead, both authors will be presenting ambitious new multipart projects for independent comics companies. If an intricate, form-shattering work like *Big Numbers* can sell in significant numbers, it might effectively challenge the superhero stranglehold of the major publishers.

These same projects also represent how varied comics are becoming. In recent years, Miller and Moore have grown apart artistically, so that now their work represents opposing sides of a debate over both the form and the content that comics should pursue. Moore, of course, no longer has patience with tales of heroes and supernaturalism. "I can walk out my front door," he says, "go down to the corner shop, and the first person I would meet—whoever they might be—would be infinitely more complex and interesting than the Man of Steel or the Caped Crusader."

Miller, meantime, still finds great resonance in tales about heroics. "Heroic melodrama is a very clear and compelling form," he says. "Like Hitchcock said, melodrama *is* reality, with all the boring parts taken out."

There is merit to both perspectives. Superhero tours de force like *Watchmen* and *The Dark Knight Returns* are exciting ways of telling big stories about big issues. Meanwhile, finely detailed real-life dramas like *Big Numbers* or Gilbert Hernandez's *Blood of Palomar* eloquently address all those "smaller" concerns that preoccupy most of us in our day-to-day lives. Either approach amounts to an honorable attempt to tell important truths, and the best work of the new breed will endure as much as any art of our time.

Superhero tours de force are exciting ways of telling big stories about big issues. Meanwhile, finely detailed real-life dramas eloquently address all those "smaller" concerns that preoccupy most of us in our day-to-day lives. Either approach amounts to an honorable attempt to tell important truths, and the best work of the new breed will endure as much as any art of our time.

—Mikal Gilmore

Here's a list of the most laudable work that comic books presently have to offer. If you like, look at it as a consumer guide to powerfully inventive alternative entertainment.

But be advised: Like the best film, literature or music, the new comics are telling stories about the world around us. Sometimes those stories, like that world, are sweet or hilarious; sometimes they're horrific, though ultimately humane. You can decide for yourself which—if any—you want to spend some time with.

Big Numbers, by Alan Moore and Bill Sienkiewicz (Mad Love); *From Hell,* by Moore and Eddie Campbell (Spider-Baby); *Lost Girls,* by Moore and Melinda Gebbie (Spider-Baby). If comics have a Renaissance man, it is Alan Moore, who is launching three new projects. The work Moore seems to be staking both his reputation and livelihood on is *Big Numbers,* a twelve-part, bimonthly square-shaped book that is being drawn and painted in a naturalistic style by *Stray Toasters*' Bill Sienkiewicz. Five hundred pages of knotty construction, *Big Numbers* will chronicle the lives of roughly forty characters in the small English town of Hampton (based on Moore's hometown, Northampton), where a community is being transformed and displaced by the impact of a sprawling new shopping mall. "What I want to look at," says Moore, "is the sort of political, economic, climatic and emotional turbulence that most Western communities are going through. I want to suggest a new way of seeing it, using the new science of fractal mathematics—the science of chaos that finds order in seemingly random events—as a metaphor to illuminate our times. This all may sound very high-flown, and it may fall far short, but you have to aim high in these things."

From Hell—which is being serialized as sixteen chapters in the quarterly horror anthology *Taboo*—may prove even more impressive. Illustrated in a dread-steeped black-and-white style by British artist Eddie Campbell, *From Hell* is, as Moore describes it, "an investigation into the web of fact and fiction and meaning and mythology that surrounds the Whitechapel murders—more famously known as the Jack the Ripper case. I've tried to approach it as a holistic detective would: A murder is a very complex human event with a complex anatomy, and you would not only have to solve the crime but also the entire social structure in which it occurred. *From Hell* isn't a horror story; it's an attempt to use comics to examine history."

Though Moore reveals Jack the Ripper's identity early in the narrative, he also notes that Jack's guilt was hardly singular. "To many of the men in Victorian England—and in the world since—Jack was a potent symbol, a hero," he says. "Now England has a prime minister who promises a return to Victorian values. One of the questions *From Hell* will necessarily raise is, do we *really* want to go back to those values?"

Also coming up in *Taboo* will be *Lost Girls,* a thirty-part, 240-page novel, illustrated by American artist Melinda Gebbie, that begins as a tale of erotica and ends up examining the sexual subconscious of the twentieth century.

Give Me Liberty, by Frank Miller and Dave Gibbons (Dark Horse); *Hard Boiled,* by Miller and Geof Darrow (Dark Horse); *Elektra Lives Again,* by Miller and Lynn Varley (Epic). "Most of the heroes I'm drawn to are angry and empowered by inner demons," says Frank Miller, who with his groundbreaking *Dark Knight Returns* aimed to reveal the almost psychotic obsessions at the heart of Batman's vigilante quest. "I love the idea of this character taking all the evil inside him and managing to wield it like a weapon in a direction that serves some sort of good. In fact, my heroes are often defined by their ability *not* to become villains themselves."

Now, after a lengthy hiatus (brought on in part by writing the screenplay for *Robo Cop 2*), Miller is returning to comics with several ventures that examine the meaning and cost of heroism. The first, *Give Me Liberty* (drawn by British artist Dave Gibbons, who collaborated with Moore on *Watchmen*) is a four-part series about a young black woman, Martha Washington, who searches for her American birthright against the landscape of a futuristic America that is under martial law in the face of an upcoming civil war. "At the beginning," Miller says, "Martha is simply a survivor. Her chief motivation is freedom, even though she can't define it at first. The story is loaded with political aspects, but it isn't an effort to put forth a utopian ideal. My adventure stuff is made more enjoyable by a certain amount of political parody, but mostly it *is* parody. I don't think a comic is the first place to look for political solutions."

Appearing concurrently with *Liberty* will be *Hard Boiled.* A mystery about a pitiless cyborg in search of his memory and his purpose, *Hard Boiled* features the vividly violent and sexual imagery of Geof Darrow, a remarkable illustrator whose flair for detail, combined with his gift for depicting movement, results in art that is intricate, kinetic and thoroughly outrageous. *Hard Boiled* is going to incense many of the people who see it—and may even reignite the debate about censorship in comic books.

Later this year, Miller returns to what remains his most popular creation: Elektra, a female ninja assassin whom he introduced a decade ago in the pages of Marvel's *Daredevil,* with a brutal story line that left Elektra dead and left Matt Murdock, the blind lawyer who is Daredevil, a helpless hero. Now, in *Elektra Lives Again,* Miller resolves Murdock and Elektra's broken romance. Written and drawn by Miller and colored by Lynn Varley, *Elektra Lives Again* is stunningly beautiful and also deeply unsettling. "In many ways, it is a horror story," says Miller. "A man's dead lover is coming back to life—and he finds he has a raving sexual passion for this total embodiment of death, though what he can't see is that she's a male creation. I don't mean to sound too pretentious about it, because it also has lots of sword fights and chase scenes."

Is Miller at all concerned about the controversy that books like *Hard Boiled* and *Elektra Lives Again*—with their fixations on violence and aberrant sexuality—might provoke? "Actually, I think this is the kind of thing we're going to see a bit more in comics," he says. "There's an explosion of freedom coming, and some writers and artists are going to want to find out what happens when you do this more extreme stuff—what it does to your story, and to your reading experience. I know *I'd* like to know more about that. I've been in the field for twelve years, and this is the first time I've had this kind of freedom."

Love and Rockets, by Jaime and Gilbert Hernandez; *The Death of Speedy,* by Jaime Hernandez; *Blood of Palomar,* by Gilbert Hernandez (all Fantagraphics). For nearly a decade, *Love and Rockets* has been American fiction's best-kept secret. Written and drawn by two Los Angeles-area brothers, Jaime and Gilbert Hernandez, the quarterly comic chronicles the development of two different Hispanic communities of friends, families, lovers, rivals and interlopers, enlivening them with acutely observed characterizations that are often hilarious, sometimes tragic and never forgettable. Jaime's stories, set in a modern-day East L.A. barrio, follow the exploits of Maggie and Hopey, two punk-bred young women, as they fight, kiss, make up, play rock & roll, fall in love and endure heartaching losses on the road to adulthood. But it is Gilbert's stories—about the everyday lives of people who dream and die in the south-of-the-border village of Palomar—that have the greater impact and depth. In particular, his *Blood of Palomar* is among the most powerful American novels of recent years. A killer is stalking Palomar, lovers are trading partners and betraying each other's hopes, children are spurning negligent parents and leaving home—in short, known values and connections are falling apart. The story progresses to an obvious end, then Gilbert blindsides you: One of *Love and Rockets'* loveliest creations sets out to redeem the precious ideal of human fraternity and moves toward a shocking choice that leaves Palomar changed forever. If you read only one graphic novel, make this the one.

Yummy Fur and *Ed the Happy Clown,* by Chester Brown (Vortex). *Yummy Fur* is as delightful as comics get. That is, if *delightful* is the right word for a book that, for a time, featured an ongoing tale about a star-crossed clown named Ed, who somehow got the head of an other-dimensional Ronald Reagan transplanted to the head of his (Ed's) penis. With the aid of Josie—a sexy, nude vampire—Ed spent several issues more or less in pursuit of his rightful penis head (he never got the original one back, but he *did* get a bigger one, if that's any consolation).

These days, the Ed saga has gone the way of writer-artist Chester Brown's attention span (though, thankfully, it's been collected in an *Ed the Happy Clown* book). Brown is now writing autobiographical stories that are as funny and uncomfortably familiar as any from our private lives.

A consensus of the writers, artists, editors and publishers interviewed for this article named *Yummy Fur* as the best comic series being published today—though its childlike art, uncompromising mix of sexual and religious themes (the companion feature, "Mark," is a straightforward, unsentimental adaptation of the gospel according to Saint Mark), and Brown's passion for bodily functions (which outstrips even David Lynch's obsessions) are hardly for everybody's taste.

"I love the beautiful way Chester Brown cartoons," says Frank Miller. "I love the twisted corridors he takes you down, and the utter abandon with which he lets you see all his demons. It's a completely personal statement, without any attempt to be either a polemic or a crowd pleaser."

Hellblazer, by Jamie Delano, with various artists (DC Comics). John Constantine, a hard-boiled occultist and Sting look-alike, was invented by Alan Moore as a punky, impudent foil for the most solemn vegetable the world has known, Swamp Thing. In the last two years, in the hands of Moore's lifelong friend Jamie Delano, Constantine has evolved into the best character in comics: a haunted man whose meddling in the darkest secrets of the universe often ends up costing his friends their lives. "John Constantine is Philip Marlowe without compassion, Sam Spade without integrity," writes novelist Shaun Hutson. Delano puts it more pointedly: "You wouldn't want him to move next door to you, that's for sure.

"I want the book to reflect reality," says Delano, "the idea that there *is* horror in the real world, in the political history of the world, and it isn't necessarily good for us to be distracted from it. One of the really valid functions of horror is subversion—and I'm into it."

Hellblazer's current story line—"The Family Man,"

about a serial killer who murders Constantine's father and then stalks the hero himself (and whose misanthropy implies a certain kinship with Constantine)—is Delano's best to date.

The Sandman, by Neil Gaiman, with Mike Dringenberg and Malcolm Jones III (DC Comics). Along with *Hellblazer,* DC Comics' *Sandman* is one of the more radical books presented by a major publisher. Written by Neil Gaiman, the most prolific and poetic writer that British comics have produced since Alan Moore, *Sandman* is the story of the god of dreams' attempt to bring order to the realm of the nocturnal. By entering the dark places where gods, demons, succubi and frail humans dream, Sandman must also wrestle with their most secret hurts and hopes.

"I'd like the stories to be as varied and unpredictable as dreams themselves," says Gaiman, "which means that the Sandman should be willing to follow the human subconscious wherever it may go, even into the darker realm of internal mythologies."

Gaiman says he plans to remain on *Sandman* until about issue 40. "I've always known where this book is going, what its last panel will be," he says. "I'd like to turn out a good book once a month. I mean, why *shouldn't* there be good mainstream comics?"

DC is presently releasing a trade-paperback edition of *Sandman,* issues 8 through 16, which collects Gaiman's recent story line "The Doll's House."

Cerebus, by Dave Sim, with Gerhard (Aardvark/Vanaheim). Dave Sim's *Cerebus* is the most voluminous, intricate novel-style work in comics. Sim began the book in 1977 as a self-published parody of *Conan the Barbarian.* It made for a rollicking read, sold respectably and proved that by refusing to compromise one's ambitions, a comic's creator could not only make money but assert more control over the destiny and integrity of his creation. Sim has handled his central character, a misanthropic aardvark, with remarkable depth, imagination and maturing talent and intelligence. In recent years, *Cerebus* has become a sophisticated means for exploring critical questions about politics, history, economy and theocracy. Mostly, Sim is writing about the high costs of emotional isolation, and he does so with grace and heart, though also with a certain keen, mean humor. The comic's current tale, "Jaka's Story," is about the fragility of human (and aardvark) love.

In the last year or two, Sim has collected the *Cerebus* tales into four bound volumes—*Cerebus, High Society* and *Church & State,* volumes 1 and 2. Collectively, they function as a riveting, continuous 2200-page novel. "With silly little Cerebus the Aardvark," says artist and publisher Stephen Bissette, "Dave Sim is doing comics on the level of Henry Miller." And then some.

Animal Man, by Grant Morrison, with Chas Truog and Doug Hazlewood (DC Comics). The only superhero-revisionist book on this list, but what a prize. Written by an up-and coming Scottish superstar (author of the overwrought, overpriced *Arkham Asylum*), *Animal Man* is the chronicle of a sometimes zealous, sometimes uncertain animal-rights activist.

In the series' most inspired single issue, "The Coyote Gospel," a broken man journeys into the desert to slay a humanlike wolf-devil whom he blames for his terrible misfortune. What the man doesn't know is, the wolf isn't a wolf at all: He is a Wile E. Coyote lookalike, and he is the bravest and saddest creature in the world. In fact, he's . . . well, he's the savior of the modern world, and he is prepared to die endless horrible deaths for the sins of the violent world around him. The man and the coyote meet in the desert. They kill each other—and then, in a brilliant moment of revelation that invokes Chuck Jones's classic "Duck Amuck" cartoon, Morrison makes plain who is really behind all the killing and who really benefits from it.

Plastic Forks, by Ted McKeever (Epic). Like Chester Brown, Ted McKeever is producing some of the most idiosyncratic, antic work around. With books like *Transit* and *Eddy Current* (the latter an outlandish satire on both superheroes and the PMRC), McKeever developed a magnificently crude chiaroscuro style that seemed playful on the surface but was an effective vehicle for telling unpredictable stories. *Plastic Forks* has even more elaborate ambitions: It is a beautifully colored, five-part science-fiction mystery about an attempt to cure sexual disease by developing a shocking form of asexual reproduction. But maybe the strangest thing about *Plastic Forks* is that, as unorthodox as McKeever's work may be, it is being published by a major mainstream publisher—an accomplishment that may bode well for the industry's maturation.

"Like a lot of comic artists today," says McKeever, "I *hate* superheroes, and I'd love to see the marketplace become more diversified. We have a long ways to go, but with books like *Love and Rockets* and *Yummy Fur* on the market, there's more and more hope. Comics are one of the best places in the world right now for young writers and artists to be working—not because they're a stepping-stone to something bigger, like film, but because, in and of themselves, they're simply one of the most creative mediums going. In the end, the point isn't whether you work for the majors or for the independents. The point is to do this work as intelligently as it deserves to be done."

Frank McConnell (essay date 28 February 1992)

SOURCE: "Comic Relief: From 'Gilgamesh' to 'Spider-man,' " in *Commonweal,* Vol. CXIX, No. 4, February 28, 1992, pp. 21-2.

[*In the essay below, McConnell remarks on the development of comics and their relationship to society and traditional literature.*]

The first time I assigned a comic book—Frank Miller's grimly revisionist Batman saga, *The Dark Knight Returns*—for my course in "The Art of Narrative," the consensus of my colleagues (I heard it through the grapevine) was "God—what's he trying to do *now?*"

Well, maybe just be honest. The fact is—though you're not going to hear it from many of the tenured priesthood of what Ezra Pound contemptuously called "Kulchur"—that some of the best and most human fiction in America, not to mention the rest of the world, is appearing not as "novels" but as that more-than-faintly-contemptible form, the comic book.

Of course, the publishers refer to them as "graphic novels" these days. That's the same sort of uneasy semantic bourgeoisification that got people to stop talking about "movies" and start talking about "film" or even—bleah!—"cinema." What the hell: like all high churchisms, it's a bother, but a harmless one. You want we should call the chopped liver, already, a *pâté? Sei gesund.*

In fact, like the movies, and like jazz, and for interesting reasons *not* like TV, the comic book is a true mass-cult art form that grows up against the sanctions of the cultural establishment, aka the good-taste fascists, and elaborates its special genius and energy in a fierce and defiant faith in itself. Jazz and the movies had a head start. They both began somewhere around the beginning of the century, so by now they've convinced all but the most dunderheaded that they are among the central imaginative glories of the age. The comic book really began about forty years later. And right now, just on time, it's approaching the kind of shimmering zenith jazz and the movies both hit in the midthirties to the midforties.

The American comic book as a serious visionary enterprise was born around 1938 when two dreamy, shy Jewish kids from Cleveland named Jerry Siegel and Joe Shuster took their handdrawn concept to a New York publisher who had been publishing "animal funnies" and gangster comics for some years.

What kind of story would a skinny, pushed-around kid from *Cleveland,* for crying out loud, invent? A story, maybe, about a skinny, pushed-around, four-eyed reporter for a great metropolitan newspaper who was *really* a strange visitor from another planet with powers and abilities far beyond those of mortal men? Bingo. And if I have to tell you who I'm talking about, then *you* must be a strange visitor, etc.

Just a sad adolescent fantasy, right? Right: like *Sister Carrie, The Great Gatsby,* and virtually every other novel written here since 1900. And Superman's popularity was so immense and unshakable that it made the publisher—D.C. Comics—the first and still the all-but-unbeatable giant in the industry. And two years later a seventeen-year-old kid named Bob Kane, who loved the dark, brooding world of German Expressionist films, invented Superman's inevitable complement: a wealthy, powerful, attractive guy who was *really,* because of a deep and unhealable psychic wound, a compulsively vengeful, nocturnal guerrilla? Batman: natch.

All the immense later elaboration of the "superhero" comic in the forties and fifties comes out of the yin/yang tension between these two myths. And myths they are: it's been said that no Indian ever reads the *Mahabharata* for the first time, and likewise no American—unless you were raised by, say, a sect of vegetarian neo-Babylonians—ever needs to be *told* who Superman and Batman are. They are two crucial ways of finding a "real" identity, a self you can call your own and hold onto against the encroachments and impingements of the "real" world, the everyday life of the city which, as all us adolescents know, is in some subtle way out to get us.

As Paul Tillich argues, the religious quest, the quest for an authentic self, is always caught between the irreconcilables of transcendence and immanence. It's why Supes and Bats are less interesting for what they do than what they are (how many times can you save the world or clean up Gotham City?): Superman's problem is that he's really God and Batman's is that he really isn't.

Now around the sixties, the time of our *public* national coming-apart, the comics began "outing" this always-latent tension. Suddenly, the difficulties of being *Clark Kent* or *Bruce Wayne* became as important as those of their alter egos. And a new line of heroes, from Stan Lee's Marvel Comics, were developed just *for* their neuroses and hangups (e.g., Spiderman, Daredevil, and most poignantly Captain America, a WW II character resurrected during Vietnam and now agonized by the lost certainties of his patriotism). It was about this time, by the way, that I realized nobody *does* grow up, exorcised my expensively acquired snobbism, and began reading the damn things again. Could it be, asked the aesthetic Yalie, tremblingly reading *Fantastic Four* #167, that this stuff is as good as the Holy Cross fifth-grader had thought it was?

Yup. And it was going to get better.

From the late seventies, at least, and through the eighties, the art has matured and—just as Ellington and Basie did for Jelly Roll Morton—reaffirmed and validated the genius of its earlier manifestations. Frank Miller's four-part series, *The Dark Knight Returns,* is a stunning reexamination of the Superman/Batman mythos in terms of Reaganamerica's internal decay: and a major source not only for Tim Burton's *Batman* film, but for a lot of what I've been saying here. Bruce Wayne, now fiftyish, retired and heavy-drinking, decides to become Batman again because he is outraged at the urban sprawl. His opponent—now an agent of the Fed—is, of course, Superman. And the final confrontation is as apocalyptic as the Reagan/Bush world deserves.

Even more intricately, Alan Moore has produced a series of self-contained narratives—*V for Vendetta, Miracleman,* and *Watchman*—which with increasing genius (there is no other word) explores the idea of the comic book altogether as a psychic mechanism for dealing with the killing dubieties of our end of the century. I can't begin to describe the brilliance of, say, *Watchman.* But read it and then tell *me* that it's less admirable than Coover or Pynchon or Mailer or DeLillo.

And then there's *The Sandman.* It's a comic written by Neil Gaiman (like Moore, one of those transatlantic Brits), and for the life of me I can't think of a more fascinating enterprise in contemporary fiction. Listen:

Gaiman has invented, out of whole cloth, a mythology not just of the comics but of storytelling itself: storytelling, which I take to be the quintessentially human activity, from *Gilgamesh* to *American Psycho.* The world of *The*

Sandman is *our* world, populated by ordinary, variously screwed-up folks, and it contains no superheroes. It is, however, haunted by gods. Well, not gods, exactly, but a family of seven characters who are called "The Endless," who are anthropomorphic projections of the essential human fears and aspirations, who are projections of our own condition and therefore are the *origins* of all gods and mythologies: and who *know* that that is all they are. Their names are Destiny, Death, Dream, Desire, Delirium, and Despair, and the seventh sibling, who has mysteriously departed, is unnamed. And the central character, Dream, who is profoundly uncertain of his ultimate involvement with human life, is not just "Dream" but the "Shaper of Form," that is, the narrative urge incarnate. *Sandman,* in other words, is evolving into a web, nearly Joycean, of interrelated tales, invoking all the world's major myths, whose ultimate assertion is the heroic hopelessness of a man as the storytelling animal.

"Postmodern" is a phrase lit. crit. types like to apply to contemporary writing that celebrates the equivalence of all truths and the breakdown of all certainties, even the certainty of the nobility of the human adventure itself. And "the death of literature" is a phrase lovingly applied by critics of the postmodern for what they see as the betrayal of the humanistic tradition.

Well, hey: I'm here to tell you that the one phrase is pointless and the other one is silly. If you think literature is dead, or if you think that authentic mythmaking is somehow impossible in the computer age, you probably can't read and you've sure been shopping in the wrong bookstores. Check out Miller, Moore, or Gaiman.

Gordon Nore (essay date November 1992)

SOURCE: "Beyond Superman," in *The Progressive,* Vol. 56, No. 11, November, 1992, p. 12.

[*In the following essay, Nore discusses the thematic concerns that distinguish graphic novels from other comics.*]

For generations of young readers in North America, comic books have been the ultimate reserve of escapism: Saturday mornings, a trip to the corner store, a soda, and a furtive dawdle with *The Flash* or *Superman.*

The superhero comics for kids are still around, of course, but so is a growing subculture of alternative comics aimed primarily at adults. Their sales barely register a blip against the mammoth DC and Marvel Comics, but they are carving a new niche in the comic culture.

Instead of superheroes, the grown-up consumers of comics—at least some of them—prefer narratives by real people. Instead of guileless showdowns between good and evil, they elect for the murky reality of unresolved conflict.

One icon consigned to the comic scrap heap is the "great man" theory of history. Tome Press, a division of Caliber Press, in Plymouth, Michigan, has published some fifty comics based on historical themes. One of these, *Suppressed! History and Violence in America,* is a disturbing look at the American past. It begins, predictably, with Christopher Columbus, but soon exhumes a cache of odious cruelties and deceptions. Among them: the Zoot Suit Riots, in which armed forces marched through the streets and beat on anyone—especially Mexican- and African-Americans—who wore the baggy apparel; William Randolph Hearst's 1930s anti-marijuana campaign, contrived to discredit hemp products in favor of the less efficient but more profitable wood-pulp paper.

In other comics, the writers and illustrators *are* the story. There's Seth. The first installment of his autobiographical series, *Palooka-ville,* published by Drawn & Quarterly Press in Montreal, begins with the creator introducing a young counterculture version of himself. Seth dyes his eyebrows, goatee, and shoulder-length hair "C-9, Shwartzkoff Igora Royale/silver platinum blond" so he looks like an albino. While riding on the Toronto subway to meet his girlfriend, he is brutalized by queer-bashers who think he is gay.

"The appeal for the reader is an opportunity to see a story well told," says Seth (the artist, not the comic-book character), "a peek into someone else's life that you don't get in the general media, somewhere you can deal with any kind of subject."

Ottawa comic book expert Jon Bell agrees: "It's a sign of a new maturity in the comic milieu—they [publishers, artists, and readers] have come to realize that we are looking at a new medium. It is, in fact, a graphic narrative, and it can be used in a variety of ways."

One way comics are being used—just as parents and teachers have always feared—is to get across subversive messages to kids. *Real War Stories* is a comic book published by Citizen Soldier, a nonprofit organization of soldiers and veterans whose aim is to get teenagers to think before they enlist. Topics in one recent issue include treatment of gays and lesbians in the military, misleading recruiting practices, violent training techniques, and a brief history of racism and sexism in the service.

World War 3, an overtly political comic produced by a collective of artists, includes stark, sophisticated graphics, and unexpected, sometimes existential storylines.

"The movement to a narrative format is a natural progression," observes Drawn & Quarterly's Chris Oliveros. "Historically, a lot of comic books are based on one-page gags; the format wouldn't go beyond that. What's interesting about this stuff is that you're not limited by the medium. Hopefully, it will go much further."

Peter Plagens and Yahlin Chang (essay date 5 September 1994)

SOURCE: "Drawing on the Dark Side," in *Newsweek,* Vol. CXXIV, No. 10, September 5, 1994, p. 70.

[*In the essay below, Plagens and Chang focus on Neon Lit's efforts to transform classic literary texts into graphic novels.*]

Comic books have gotten a lot less comic over the years. Today's typical readers—skateboard adolescents and some Gen-Xers—are interested in mesomorphic su-

[Graphic novels] have little in common with the traditional comic of cardboard super-heroes and rudimentary plot. The new books are long, beautifully and painstakingly illustrated, with a large number of characters and complex narrative.

—An article entitled "The Comic Novel," in* The Economist, *October 24, 1987.

perheroes and fur-clad warlocks. Now comic books are taking a more serious step away from funny-ha-ha toward funny-peculiar. Neon Lit, an imprint of Avon Books founded by poet Bob Callahan, has just come out with a comic-book version of Paul Auster's sinisterly minimalist novel *City of Glass.* Comic books—or "graphic novels," as they're called when aimed at readers who aren't kids—have taken on literary fiction before. But those were the pictorial Cliffs Notes called Classics Illustrated. This is the first time the form has tried to interpret serious contemporary literature.

Auster's Bret-Easton-Ellis-with-brains darkness and stripped-down narrative lend themselves superbly to graphic interpretation. Under art director Art Spiegelman (Pulitzer Prize-winning author/artist of the graphic novel *Maus*), artist David Mazzucchelli (illustrator of *Batman: Year One*) and writer Paul Karasik have given Auster's metaphysical detective story a spare, almost crude adaptation. The drawing is brushy and blunt, the verbatim selections from the text are flinty and the layout is a metaphor for the progressive collapse of the protagonist's mind. It works—though perhaps not as elegantly as the original novel. Which is to say you're just about as depressed and mystified as when you finish the all-text version.

Neon Lit has other books underway in the series: Barry Gifford's *Perdita Durango* (a sequel to *Wild at Heart*) and William Lindsay Gresham's *Nightmare Alley.* The imprint also wants to tackle such authors as Albert Camus, Italo Calvino and Umberto Eco. Can these remain as faithful to their sources as *City* is to Auster's book? Avon Editor in Chief Bob Mecoy enthuses about the graphic-novel form: "It's like hearing Ella Fitzgerald take on a Cole Porter tune. This is the jazz version."

Nonsense, says critic Sven Birkerts, who's written about Auster's fiction. He describes Neon Lit's project as "absurd." "If you took a particular movement of Mozart and got the basic melody and did it as Muzak, you could argue that the melody was all there . . . But it's still Muzak." Or, as some suggest, "MTV literature" and "paper movies." But Auster, who received about $4,000 as an advance and had the right of approval, is no snob. He says Neon Lit's *City of Glass* goes beyond a "cinematic approach [into] something that can only be done through drawing." With just a hunch about Yuppie tastes, and no market research, Neon Lit is hoping that particular something has commercial potential. The first printing is 16,000 copies—more than for many literary novels. Meanwhile, DC Comics (home of Superman) is planning its own graphic novels: a Paradox Press original mystery line with such well-known crime writers as John Wagner and Jerome Charyn, and some original serious fiction. One book is about a young gay man growing up in the South during the civil-rights movement.

Neon Lit's project may offend some critics, but it's an almost inevitable development. Our democratic culture keeps itself vital neither through the erecting of impenetrable walls between high art and low art, nor the willy-nilly erasing of standards and boundaries. It triumphs with inventive hybrids like jazz, movies and modern dance. The serious graphic novel may become one of them. Did somebody say *Spiderman's Remembrances of Things Past*?

Calvin Reid (essay date 19 September 1994)

SOURCE: "Graphics Go Literary," in *Publishers Weekly,* Vol. 241, No. 38, September 19, 1994, pp. 20, 22.

[In the essay below, Reid comments on publishers' interest in and efforts to promote the graphic novel genre.]

Even if you've never read or wanted to read a comic book, you've probably found yourself reading an article *about* comics. And not just in "alternative" papers, but in mainstream bastions like *Forbes,* the *New York Times* and *U.S. News & World Report.* Superhero and action comics form the biggest part of the $1.3 billion U.S. comics market and have captured media attention with their obsessive and free-spending readership and huge commercial potential for movie and merchandising tie-ins.

However, while chain bookstores and comics specialty stores have enthusiastically accepted trade paperback compilations of superhero fantasies, if you happen to publish comics that don't feature bodybuilding specimens and apocalyptic battles, you can feel a little bit out of it. But comics publishing does have its literary niche—trade paperback and occasionally even hardcover books that are as thoughtfully wrought as a prose work from a literary imprint. (Comics publishers mostly distribute trade paper to the general bookstore market and hardcover editions to comics specialty stores.)

This fall is distinguished by an unusual number of titles that aim to impress artistically as much as the superheroes do by dint of market size. Although the readership for these is small in comparison to mega-selling series, it is nevertheless growing incrementally and sustaining a wide range of work.

A very good example is the Neon Lit series from Avon Books. Editor Bob Mecoy has put together a team to produce a series of book-length adaptations of mystery novels. Just released is the debut volume, Paul Auster's critically acclaimed *City of Glass* adapted by writer Paul Karasik and artist David Mazzucchelli. "We believe in the genre," asserts Mecoy, pointing to a 25,000-copy first printing. Called "stunning" and "masterful" by *PW*'s reviewer, this is the first in a series that will be edited by Bob

Callahan and designed by Art Spiegelman, Pulitzer Prize winner for *Maus.*

Mecoy describes Neon Lit as an effort "to open the mystery genre and speak to the contemporary graphics scene with books of literary and classic noir, aimed at mystery readers, graphic novel readers, people who are interested in 'cutting edge' cultural phenomena and Generation X readers who see comics as just another book." The Neon Lit series may eventually number 20 titles, with William Gresham's 1946 *Nightmare Alley* and Barry Gifford's *Perdita Durango* scheduled for next year.

In addition, Avon also plans to publish a nonfiction title, *Stan Mack's Real Life American Revolution* by the eponymous *Village Voice* cartoonist, a pictorial account of the "chaos, kings, lunatics and loudmouths" that launched this great nation.

Spiegelman—whose illustrations are featured in the November reissue of the book-length poem *The Wild Party* by Joseph Moncure March—emphasizes that to find its audience, Neon Lit "must be nursed" by the Avon sales and marketing departments. "Neon Lit is another attempt to storm the citadel with a peashooter," says Spiegelman, reminding us that *Maus* was turned down by about 15 publishers before Pantheon took a chance.

"*Maus* was published against all odds and has much in common with what we're doing here," maintains Spiegelman. He adds that on the sales front, "display boxes would help, and publishers and booksellers need to give careful attention to reviewers and book buyers who have expressed an interest in comics."

Gary Groth, publisher of Fantagraphic Books, a Seattle-based comics house specializing in "alternative" works (i.e., no superheroes) worries that too much media hype will result in trade publishers losing interest when the comics they produce register only modest sales. But he also reckons that "there is much better material being published now than ever before. Unfortunately, you can't always find it in the stores." While Fantagraphics' better selling titles are published in print runs of around 10,000, Groth is publishing more trade paperbacks than ever before (from 12 five years ago to 24 today), and steady sales keep them all in print.

This fall Fantagraphics is publishing *Poison River* by the critically acclaimed Mexican-American artist Gilbert Hernandez, as well as Joe Sacco's nonfiction work, *Palestine. Poison River* is a Latin-American epic that tells the story of Luba, one of the women featured in Hernandez's ongoing stories about the fictional Central American village of Palomar. *Palestine* is a kind of funky *From Beirut to Jerusalem,* chronicling Sacco's visit to the West Bank and Gaza Strip to document the Palestinian resistance.

Terry Nantier of the New York City-based NBM Publishing is more optimistic about the market for serious comics, asserting that "book readers will cross over to the kind of material we publish once people realize just where comics are heading and how interesting they are." This month, NBM is releasing *Streak of Chalk* by Spanish artist Miguelanxo Prado, an enigmatic love story and the first title to be released from NBM's new graphic fiction imprint, ComicsLit.

Citing 20%-50% growth in revenues over the last three years, NBM—which publishes comics in trade paper and hardcover only—has gone from about 15 titles per year to about 25 now, with growth as well in more sales per title. Nantier points out that certain large stores, like "Borders and big independents like Tattered Cover and Powell's do a good job at selling our books." But he also laments that, in general, independents have "stepped back a bit, which is a shame. They are losing a chance to distinguish themselves from the chains."

NBM is known for publishing European comics artists in translation, among whom are Hugo Pratt, Jacques Tardi and Milo Minara; Americans include Rick Geary, P. Craig Russell and Peter Kuper.

Even DC Comics, one of the big two in superheroes, along with Marvel, has made a commitment to presenting a broader variety of comics through its Vertigo and Paradox Press imprints. These imprints, says Andrew Helfer, editor of Paradox, are aimed as much at the general book trade as at specialty stores. According to Helfer, "the chains are very interested."

In November, Vertigo will publish the trade paperback edition of *Brief Lives* the eighth book in the Sandman series (all still in print). Paradox Press will begin releasing a series of tongue-in-cheek nonfiction titles, including *Urban Legends,* a 224-page, large-format anthology that recounts stories about life in the big city. Next spring look for the debut of Paradox Press's mystery and fiction series pairing such writers as Jerome Charyn and Joel Rose with several different visual artists in a series whose format (5½" X 8" trade paper) and price (under $12) are designed to appeal to a wide readership.

There's more. Larry Gonick's *Cartoon History of the Universe II* is arriving in October, alongside the post-feminist feminist satire *Just Who the Hell Is SHE, Anyway?* by Marisa Acocella. And celebrating its 25th anniversary, Kitchen Sink Press is publishing *From Inside* by John Bergin, a dark tale of a dreamlike journey through a world of misery and terror; and *Illegal Alien* by James Robinson and Phil Elliot, a weird and witty science fiction work set in 1963 that combines space aliens, the mob, ray guns and—what else—mohair suits.

THE *CLASSICS ILLUSTRATED* SERIES

Beth Levine (essay date 24 November 1989)

SOURCE: "Berkley, First and CMG Join to Revive Classics Illustrated," in *Publishers Weekly,* Vol. 236, No. 20, November 24, 1989, p. 48.

[*In the following essay, Levine remarks on the revival of the* Classics Illustrated *series.*]

"Classics Illustrated". . . . For millions, the name conjures up the midnight hours they spent reading by flashlight under the bedcovers. For others, the comic book versions of such titles as *Moby Dick* and *David Copperfield* symbolize the only way they survived English lit. In February, Berkley, First Publishing and Classics Media Group will revive the once-popular series with all-new full-color art and text in a perfect-bound graphic novel format, priced at $3.75 per book.

In this unusual joint venture, Berkley will distribute the titles to the bookstores and deal with publicity, promotion and advertising. First Publishing will handle editing, production and distribution to specialist comic book outlets, while Classics Media Group manages audio, video, TV and film rights. Classics Illustrated was previously published from 1941 to 1972; in its heyday, the series sold 25 million copies a week. (Berkley et al. plan more modest, though yet unannounced, first printings.) Why revive a format that lost steam 17 years ago?

"There's a disturbing degree of illiteracy in America today . . . and we think that Classics Illustrated is a very smart way to get people reading again," says First publisher Rick Obadiah.

In order to ensure that the series reflects the original novels, writers and publishers are working with various literacy organizations, two of which—the Chicago chapter of Volunteers for Literacy and Associated Reading Services—have given the project their stamp of approval. To critics who say that the series will discourage people from reading the originals, Obadiah counters, "These are in no way meant as substitutes for the novels themselves; we hope they'll be used as introductions, and encourage readers to seek out the originals."

Obadiah feels that the range of potential readers is greater than it was during the series' previous incarnation. "The average comic book readers are not 10 years old anymore; they're in their high teens. And we estimate the readers of our comics and graphic novels are even older, probably in their mid-20s. In Europe and Japan, many adults read comics. We feel we'll appeal to a very wide spectrum."

Two years ago, the three companies bought the Classics Illustrated property from Frawley Enterprises. But it was First that initially became aware of the potential for graphic novels back in 1984 when it published the Beowulf legend in that format. Obadiah talked a very hesitant Waldenbooks into taking the title and it subsequently went on the chain's bestseller list. Soon after that, the publisher released graphic novels based on L. Frank Baum's *Wizard of Oz,* which were also successful. Berkley took on bookstore distribution of the company's graphic novels three years ago, and is now experimenting with distribution of First comic books as well.

Classics Illustrated will be launched in February with *Great Expectations, Through the Looking Glass, Moby Dick* and *The Raven. Hamlet* and *The Scarlet Letter* will be released in March, and *The Count of Monte Cristo* and *Dr. Jekyll and Mr. Hyde* in April. One new title a month will follow thereafter. If these prove successful, titles from the Classics Junior line may also be issued.

The writers and artists who are working on the series have varied backgrounds, bringing experience from children's books, advertising, adult and juvenile comics, etc., to Classics Illustrated. Writers include Charles Dixon, Steven Grant and Stefan Petrucha; among the participating artists are Gerald Forton, Tristan Schane and Dan Spiegle. Rick Geary, Bill Sienkiewicz and Gahan Wilson will be both writing and illustrating.

Berkley plans to promote the books with a publicity campaign aimed at both the educational buyer and the regular consumer. Publicity director Donna Gould says that the company hopes to get mainstream review attention: "We're going to let the media know that Classics Illustrated is back in a very big way."

REVIEWS OF RECENT WORKS

Roz Kaveney (review date 18-25 December 1987-1 January 1988)

SOURCE: "Eaten by a Lion or Something," in *New Statesman,* Vol. 114, Nos. 2960-2962, December 12-25, 1987-January 1, 1988, pp. 41-2.

[*Below, Kaveney reviews several graphic novels including* Outrageous Tales from the Old Testament *from Knockabout Publishers and Jose Munoz and Carlos Sampayo's collaboration entitled* Joe's Bar.]

When we were all very young, the reverend Marcus Morris attempted to channel our taste for comics into that brand of liberal Christian imperialism so skillfully preached in *Eagle* and *Girl.* In between Belle of the Ballet and Dan Dare, we had to sit more often than we cared to through famous stories from the Bible, all of them done in excruciating, stilted good taste.

And some of us grew up to be the artists and writers who have contributed to Knockabout's *Outrageous Tales from the Old Testament,* which goes to show that blasphemy is a matter of having a complex relationship with your past and your roots.

Outrageous Tales has already been greeted with tabloid and rent-a-quote MP outrange—and, of course, with vague threats of prosecution from Mary Whitehouse. In some measure, it would have failed in its purpose had it not been.

Knockabout has been prosecuted and persecuted for a variety of underground comics published or imported and there is a certain amount of anticipated *schadenfreude* in their production of a volume which, for the most part, takes stories from the Bible and handles them straightforwardly. It avoids, in other words, the mealy-mouthed toning-down that most Christians prefer when dealing with the Old Testament. Here these are stories of brutal murder, human sacrifice, rape, mutilation and massacre, and in this they are utterly faithful to their original. Dame Jill Knight MP may well be correct in her concern that all this mayhem will inspire imitation; what, at its best, the Knockabout collection does is boobytrap the Christian Right into the position of having logically (not that logic applies) to disown the original as well as the Knockabout versions.

Having said which, it must also be said that some of the sections misfire, either through being merely dull—the Creation myth section for example—or by miscalculations like the gratuitous and stereotyped homophobia of some of the Journey to Bethlehem (Judges) section. There is nothing subversive about clichéd subscription to a dominant and oppressive discourse.

At its best, *Outrageous Tales* is not only a potential *cause célèbre* but a handy sampler of some of the most interesting talents working in comics in Britain. It also shows a useful fusing of the underground and mainstream traditions. Notable are Hunter Emerson and Alan Moore's collaboration on the murderous implications of the sexual prohibitions of Leviticus, the gleeful rendition of Jael and Sisera by Julie Hollings, the OTT superheroics of Samson and a particularly muscular Delilah as drawn by Graham Higgins. There is also a beautiful and sombre minor extract from Kings, written by Neil Gaiman and drawn by Dave McKean: "The moral of this story is . . . Never listen to anyone who says God told him what you ought to be doing, not even a prophet, or you'll be eaten by a lion on your way home or something."

The rising of a new wave of comics talent in the UK has not gone unnoticed by the US moguls of DC and Marvel, of course, and the quest for "the New Alan Moore" proceeds apace, with generous contracts being waved around whenever said moguls hit London. Gaiman and McKean are compromising with the superhero comic ethos in what promises to be a stunningly beautiful and terrifying reevaluation of the minor superheroine, Black Orchid, while we are already seeing the results of another headhunt in the writing of Jamie Delano on *Hellblazer.* Delano has taken over John Constantine, the low-rent exorcist from Moore's *Swamp Thing,* and is putting him through various excursions into the demotic demonic. *Hellblazer 3* has a McKean cover of Constantine standing by a vampire-toothed Thatcher poster and brings him into contact with "Demon Yuppies, Soul-Brokers from Hell" who foreclose on their earthly counterparts while jogging, handing round a handy toot or listening to CDs of *Tears of Atlantis Re-Awaken the Dessicated souls of Hiroshima.* No one could ever accuse Delano of subtlety, but he has found the right Chandler-cum-Sting voice for his character and has a nice line in *film noir* dialogue and class hatred.

Not that native American talent is failing to do some moderately interesting things all of its own. Howard Chaykin clinched his reputation with the split-screen-revolutionary and perversely sexual antics of the early issues of his *American Flagg,* but seemed to be going more than a little adrift with the uncritical and undiluted vigilantism of his episodes of *The Shadow* and the inventive, but frequently grossly stereotypical, world of zombie musicians and demon hookers that he is creating in *Times Squared.*

His resurrection of the WWII *Blackhawk* is another matter entirely, with its plump fighter ace compromised by premature anti-fascism while wise-cracking his way around the fleshpots of the East with a similarly pudgy-sexy woman Soviet agent. When Chaykin is dealing with the '80s, or with a future that satirises them, tendencies to the prurient and aesthetically authoritarian set the teeth on edge. In this nostalgic '40s hommage, played for sardonicism and for keeps, they somehow do no worse than confirm one's doubts about a supposedly more innocent age. Chaykin is a mad-dog talent, but his uncomfortable aspects go with a real vigour and a commitment to non-linear narrative and innovative use of the comic's grid that compels respect.

A minor aspect of the effect of the junta on Argentine life has been the exile of talents like those of Oscar Zarate, Jose Munoz and Carlos Sampayo. Zarate's version of Marlowe's Faust had stunning moments but failed through its overdone attempts to make the play's themes directly relevant to the 20th-century through the crudest of iconographic borrowings and levellings of parallels. His work with Alexei Sayle on *Geoffrey the Tube Train and the Fat Comedian* turns what might have been a rather crass combination of anthropomorphic whimsy and self-indulgent monologue into something with edge and bite. Zarate's visions of reptilian admen, glazed commuters and demon fish make the book tremble, far more than his Faust ever did, on the brink of hell.

Munoz and Sampayo have produced, in the four sections of *Joe's Bar,* a vision of New York as the jungle of those cities informed by exiles' combination of dread, homesickness and constant surprise. This is the America of cheap coffee and roach-filled rooms we've seen often before, but never from quite this vantage point. Munoz has a line in dark, distorted interiors and angrily mad faces which brings something new to the field, something with a different kind of passion. The field of the comic and the graphic novel is a shaker into which ever more exotic ingredients are being poured, with results that few can yet foresee.

Mark Sinker (review date 29 July 1988)

SOURCE: "Barrio Culture," in *New Statesman & Society,* Vol. 1, No. 7, July 29, 1988, pp. 48-9.

[*In the review below, Sinker remarks on the work of Gilbert and Jaime Hernandez, noting their focus on strong women characters and Hispanic themes in their graphic novels and comics.*]

The way to make money on adult comic books in the late eighties is to put the monthly issues together into glossy compilations and sell them as "graphic novels". The new market can avoid the wait and has its literary ego stroked a little, too.

But comics aren't novels and novels aren't comics. So it's appropriate that a character in Gilbert "Beto" Hernandez's strip *Heartbreak Soup*—from the comic *Love & Rockets,* written and drawn by Gilbert and his brother Jaime—is seen discussing *One Hundred Years Of Solitude* in a faintly pretentious way only a short while before his wife throws him and the book out of their house.

Heartbreak Soup is in fact one of the few extended strips where the comparison with the novel (in particular the magic realist novel) really makes much sense. But the brothers' heightened punk sensibility is important in its own right, a spearhead of a new wave of comic books.

Heartbreak Soup is set in a mythical (Mexican?) village called Palomar and spans a 30-year period in the life of the community, an ironic weave of sex and death and other mysteries, the affairs, feuds and obsessions of the villagers. *Love & Rockets,* its companion strip, is set in the *barrio* district of an unnamed Californian(?) city and focuses on a small group of hispanic punk girl teenagers, their blurred gender identification and doomed communal idealism.

Thanks to an overlong love affair with detectives, caped crusaders and other lawless lawbringers, comics will always be associated with explicit violence and sublimated sex. What makes *Love & Rockets* so remarkable is the casual way in which this has been reversed, almost feminised. Men aren't central to either strip. In *Heartbreak Soup,* they're dominated (even terrorised) by a community of tough, smart, highly sexual women. In *Love & Rockets,* Maggie Chascarrillo (a romantic with a weight problem) and Hopey Glass (a barely reformed delinquent) are occasional lovers, in classically punky fashion: more or less disinterested, except when they're not.

On one hand, there's the cross-border contrast between a dislocated and poverty-stricken modern third world community and a marginal refusenik subculture in a deteriorating capitalist society. On the other, there's a fascinating tension being worked up between a stereotypical hispanic worldview—think of the origins of the word 'macho'—and the brothers' charged and complex vision of changing sexual norms. The US punk underground continues to be fairly healthily radical in its attitudes to sexual equality—it's the hispanic spin the picture's given here that makes it so compelling, a distinctly un-WASP social coding.

The hispanic community in the United States will soon be the largest ethnic minority. It's surely no accident that the most innovative and perceptive of the new American comics comes from the heart of a rising culture. And—compared to the novels of Marquez, for example—it's unlikely to be absorbed and neutralised by any elitist literary establishment.

Publishers Weekly (review date 17 February 1989)

SOURCE: A review of *Brought to Light,* in *Publishers Weekly,* Vol. 235, No. 7, February 17, 1989, p. 73.

[In the following review, the critic comments on the political focus of the omnibus volume containing the graphic novels Flashpoint *and* Shadowplay.]

In this long-awaited documentary comic book [*Brought to Light,* which collects two works], [Joyce] Brabner, co-author of the comic book *Real War Stories,* and political illustrator Tom Yeates have produced a straightforward and competently illustrated journalistic account [*Flashpoint: The La Penca Bombing*] of the CIA's pivotal attempt to assassinate independent Nicaraguan *contra* leader Eden Pastora in a bombing at La Penca. The second story, *Shadowplay,* by celebrated comics writer [Alan] Moore, and the acclaimed illustrator/author [Bill] Sienkiewicz, is a masterly satiric expose of "The Secret Team" that came to direct the Reagan administration's covert war in Nicaragua. Moore, in combination with Sienkiewicz's viciously parodic drawings, has produced a scathing black comedy documenting the CIA's long history as a criminal shadow government. The wretched choice of format—the two stories are bound back to back, upside down—defeats easy reference between the two related works, all the more galling since *Shadowplay* provides a broader context for understanding the La Penca bombing.

Publishers Weekly (review date 27 July 1990)

SOURCE: A review of *The Cartoon History of the Universe: Volumes 1-7, From the Big Bang to Alexander the Great,* in *Publishers Weekly,* Vol. 237, No. 30, July 27, 1990, p. 227.

[Below, the critic comments on the subjects covered in Larry Gonick's The Cartoon History of the Universe, *praising the volume's humor and attempts at revisionism.]*

Gonick's hilariously informative history of the planet [*The Cartoon History of the Universe*] is a great addition to the growing field of comics trade books. Starting with the Big Bang theory and moving on to the "evolution of everything," he manages to cover three billion years—from the origins of cellular life to the fossil and dinosaur periods that followed, right up to the first appearance of hominids—all with casual erudition, silly humor and delightfully cartoony black-and-white drawings. But Gonick doesn't stop there. He reinstates the record of women (their theoretical role in the development of agriculture and the matrilineal clans of the neolithic era) as well as accurately restoring black racial characteristics to the Egyptian dynasties. He also surveys other highly evolved ancient civilizations: the Sumerians, the Hittites, the Assyrians and the Israelites. Gonick cheerfully conjures rulers, warriors and slaves alike, many stumbling around in the desert, as they form the foundations for Western civilization. This is Gonick's first book.

Publishers Weekly (review date 27 July 1990)

SOURCE: A review of *Kings in Disguise,* in *Publishers Weekly,* Vol. 237, No. 30, July 27, 1990, p. 227.

[In the following review, the critic favorably comments on Kings in Disguise.]

It's 1932, the height of the Depression, in Marian, Calif. The Bloch family is teetering on the brink of dissolution. Mr. Bloch, widowed and alcoholic, can't or won't find work. Teenage son Albert has lost respect for him and 12-year-old Freddie, mesmerized by Hollywood movies, is too young to comprehend the social forces that are rending the fabric of his life. After the father disappears and Albert is injured trying to steal money for food, Freddie, suddenly alone, heads for his father's last known address in Detroit. He's befriended by Sammy (who calls himself "the King of Spain"), a troubled and sickly vagabond who teaches him how to survive as a hobo, coping with hunger and the danger of riding the freight trains. The two develop a deeply felt attachment as they travel together, braving labor riots and anti-Semitism. Advancing classic themes, [*Kings in Disguise,* James] Vance's Harvey Award-winning story of a young man forced to become an adult is touching. [Dan] Burr's black-and-white drawings are crisply rendered and abound in historical details. This collaboration by two newcomers is an outstanding example of mature comic book storytelling.

Tom Easton (review date January 1991)

SOURCE: A review of *V for Vendetta,* in *Analog Science Fiction/Science Fact,* Vol. CXI, Nos. 1 & 2, January, 1991, pp. 308-09.

[*Below, Easton favorably reviews* V for Vendetta.]

And now! Once more! It's comics time! Warner Books keeps bringing out the "graphic novels," and some of them are pretty good. The latest to arrive on my desk is *V for Vendetta,* by Alan Moore and David Lloyd. It first appeared in England, beginning in the early '80s, and now you have a chance to enjoy it too.

The authors avoided comics formalisms such as thought balloons and captions, telling their tale quite successfully with little more than pictures and dialog. That tale deals with a fascist England arisen from the rigors of a mild nuclear war. Wogs, queers, and liberals have all disappeared in concentration camps. The survivors, even the party higher-ups, are routinely brutalized. Cameras and microphones are everywhere. The news is managed. Freedom, justice, and independent thought are forgotten.

But here is V! Masked, cone-hatted, caped, a Guy Fawkes figure blowing up Parliament, the Old Bailey, and more. Attacking the fascist tyranny, forcing it to stumble and fall, stimulating the people to grasp their freedom once more. A classic theme, but well told. I enjoyed the book.

James Colbert (review date 8 November 1992)

SOURCE: "On *Maus II,*" in *Los Angeles Times Book Review,* November 8, 1992, pp. 2, 11.

[*Colbert is an American novelist and critic. In the review below, he remarks on the themes and innovative style of Spiegelman's* Maus *and* Maus II.]

There is no question that the story of the Holocaust needs to be told and retold; but a very real danger is that too much retelling creates resentment, more than a barrier to remembering and understanding, a persistent ill will. "Many [younger Germans] have had it up to *here* with Holocaust stories," Art Spiegelman writes. "These things happened before they were even born. Why should *they* feel guilty?" Why should any of us feel guilt who, apparently, had nothing to do with the atrocities committed in Hitler's Germany?

But Mr. Spiegelman provides the answer to those questions: "I feel so inadequate trying to reconstruct a reality that was worse than my darkest dreams." A reality that was, in fact, so terrifying that the worst possible consequence results: Many choose not to address it at all. Of its many extraordinary achievements, perhaps most significant is that by relating a story of hideous inhumanity in non-human terms, *Maus* and *Maus II* allow us as readers to go outside ourselves and to look objectively at ourselves and at otherwise unspeakable events. And while the presentation is enormously effective (and while the events Mr. Spiegelman relates are factually accurate, in most ways a memoir), the fact is, too, that these events did not take place among mice, cats and dogs. That is fiction—and it is fiction of the very first order.

Maus II is the continuing story of one survivor's tale of Auschwitz and Dachau and of boxcars filled with people and left for weeks. It is the story of a son's search for understanding of events that, inevitably, shaped his life as well. In this story, Jews are drawn as mice, Nazis as cats, Americans as dogs. The pages are divided into captioned, illustrated frames.

It is, indeed, unusual to think of authentic novels as having pictures. The notion is so new that, although comics are an indigenous, truly American art form, we haven't even figured out what to call such works. *Comic book* seems diminutive, even pejorative. A *graphic novel* seems like something Madonna would write. But lest we forget, the *other* definition of novel is "new and not resembling something formerly known or used; original or striking, especially in conception or style." In this regard, there is no doubt that *Maus II* richly deserves this year's prize for *fiction,* a prize that is reserved for the novel—with or without pictures.

Had Spiegelman truly known beforehand the scope of the work he was undertaking, no one could have blamed him if he had simply called it off. The idea of relating a narrative as complex as a son's attempt to unravel his parents' history, to place within that history the son's relationship with his father and to meld the whole into a compelling narrative begets a multilayered task, a tapestry of present and past. Yet in telling his parents' (Vladek's and Anja's) story, Spiegelman is able to convey not only the horrors the survivors endured but also the terrors foisted on the generation that followed.

"I had nightmares," the fictional Artie reveals to his wife, "about S.S. men coming into my class and dragging all us Jewish kids away. . . . Sometimes I'd fantasize Zyklon B coming out of our shower instead of water."

And later, Artie's wife asks him, "What's that noise?"

"Oh, nothing—just Vladek," he replies. "He's moaning in his sleep again. When I was a kid I thought that was the noise *all* grown-ups made while they slept."

In this way, *Maus II* makes the experience resonate and come back to haunt us all. Add to such vignettes a subtle use of language, authentic rhythms and patterns of speech achieved by oddly placed prepositional phrases and modifiers, a keen eye for detail, an astonishing graphic style, and you begin to understand the brilliantly innovative fabric of *Maus II,* as deceptively simple as a canon—and no less complex. *Maus II* is an extraordinary accomplishment, a new way of looking at experience. But it comes, too, with knowledge of its own limitations, an ominous warning.

"Look at how many books have already been written about the Holocaust," Artie's therapist, Dr. Pavel, notes. "What's the point? People haven't changed. . . . Maybe they need a newer, bigger Holocaust."

For the very last frame of *Maus II,* Spiegelman has drawn his parents' tombstone. In one way it is a sad ending, illustrating the inevitability of death no matter the quality of the life or the courage shown; but in another way, for this story it is the only ending possible, for it gives certain proof that the lessons learned *can* survive from one generation to the next. The story will continue to be told. And retold. Each in our own way, we are all survivors of that horror—something we forget at our peril.

Marty Cohen (review date February-March 1993)

SOURCE: "Honey I Nuked the Kids," in *The American Book Review,* Vol. 14, No. 6, February-March, 1993, p. 5.

[*Cohen is a nonfiction writer, poet, and critic. In the following review of* Bone Saw *and* Akira, *he remarks on their tone and subject matter, arguing that although both works violate cultural tabus, both fail to shock or "move" the reader.*]

The heart of the graphic novel beats with the violation of tabu. Starting from the postliterate premise that pictures, rather than words, can be the primary carrier of meaning, artists of the graphic novel movement take something from the Sunday funnies, something from the 1960s underground comics, something from surrealist montage, and plenty from Saturday matinee serials, Warner Brothers cartoons, and *The Terminator,* to wallow in the rag and bone shop of art and culture, asserting themselves with fury and sardonic detachment.

There are violations, and then there are violations. The difference between *Akira,* written and illustrated by Katsuhiro Otomo, and *Bone Saw* No. 1, edited by John Bergin and James O'Barr, is readily defined. When you study the pages of *Akira* on a crowded commuter train, the passenger next to you gets up and leaves with disdain. When you read *Bone Saw,* the passenger gets up with revulsion and seats himself or herself as far away as possible.

Subject matter(s). *Bone Saw,* although nominally a magazine or anthology, is unified in theme—unlike, say, *Raw,* the leading periodical of the graphic novel movement, whose editors, Art Spiegelman and Françoise Mouly, display a taste for a range of visual styles, subject matters, and tones. Bergin and O'Barr's central concern is announced in their title, iconicized in the running logo of a rotary saw blade. Human dismemberment is featured in twelve of nineteen items; child abuse in nine; medical experimentation (is this Burroughs's Dr. Benway being homaged, or Harold Ramis's Unnecessary Surgeon? —both, with further respects paid to Drs. Moreau, Mengele, and Mabuse) in seven. Images from warfare, cyberpunkdom, and contemporary urban violence are other recurring themes. There is only the slightest nod to the realistic tradition of the Sunday paper's "Apartment 3G" or Harvey Pekar's Cleveland (the setting for *American Splendor*), no plain vanilla sex or relationships. Instead we see amputations, drugs, maggots eating monkey brains, babies discarded in garbage pails, coprophilia, pedophilia, sodomy, incest, bondage, and scatology.

By comparison, the world of *Akira,* a tale of anomie and doggedness set in Neo-Tokyo thirty-eight years after World War III, is innocent and familiar. *Akira* is an ongoing series of graphic novels (Books 4-6, reviewed here, appeared in Japan in 1984) and relatively tame compared to other Japanese comic books that appeal to a class of youth sometimes characterized as "radically bored." A film adaptation of *Akira* that adds a 100-decibel soundtrack to the graphic elements has played to enthusiastic festival audiences in the United States.

What propels the plotless *Akira* is the aimless curiosity of its youthful protagonists. Delinquents, mutants, rebels without families or focus, they form alliances based on convenience and jealousy. The adults are better defined, if only because they are recognizable types: a muscled colonel; a toad-like opposition party leader; the mushroom-pale-and-squat (she is also a mutant) leader of a religious cult. Akira, who looks like a sleepy six-year-old, passes from faction to faction in a cryogenic stupor; warming up at last in Book 6, he lets out a scream and levels a major portion of Neo-Tokyo with psychic energy. Instantly he is adored as Master Akira, the figurehead leader of a provisional government based on terror, forced drug use, xenophobia, and resentment—as if the recent catastrophe had been caused by someone else.

The images are in the standard glossy palette of graphic novels. Details of city life are delineated in modest detail, moderately well drawn, although it is impossible to tell the difference between green tea and green bile; between broken glass and leaded glass, or, for that matter, between one character and another, most of whom are drawn with an interchangeable insipidity and androgyny. Mutant or not, the players can withstand major mayhem, including laser beams, cannon wounds, falls from skyscrapers, and so forth, without sitting out more than a few panels; then again, a few people have their heads explode in psychic duels, which slows them down permanently. In Books 4-6 there is little sex (one interrupted kiss, one aborted gang rape, one small if fatal orgy) and little reason to care whether or not Neo-Tokyo will survive Akira's next migraine headache. *New Yorker* cartoonist Jack Ziegler, in "Hole: the Complete Soundtrack" captured the plot of *Akira* in eight panels (small hole appears, hole expands, planet disappears) with as much conviction, and without the fuss.

A few of the pieces in *Bone Saw* stand out amid the obsessions and pathologies. "Tomorrow Never Knows," a little time-travel parable about the JFK assassination by Lawrence Watt-Evans (accompanied by a black and white drawing that would not have looked out of place in *Galaxy* thirty years ago) could serve as a tonic for those who in an Oliver-Stoned haze have forgotten that JFK played more than a minor role in the escalation of the war in Viet-

An excerpt from Church and State Volume I *by Dave Sim and Gerhard.*

nam. The other piece that makes *Bone Saw* pleasurable is a parody—we are alerted to this by the drawing of a coyote holding a signboard that reads, "Parody"—of roadrunner cartoons. "Slave Cylinder," by coeditor O'Barr, based on a story by Jeff Holland, features a punk drug fiend named Henry, a talking car, a backseat full of rats (more intelligent and more vicious than Henry), and a gang of Coyote Boys who ride on ingenious motorcycles whose seats are set into the middle of their rear wheels. Self-reverential and over the edge, with visual references to Chuck Jones, Buster Keaton, *Mad Max, A Clockwork Orange,* and other contemporary high and low vulgarities, "Slave Cylinder" is framed by an "Official Disclaimer" and by Holland's ur-text, "LSD Test Animal," of which one of the rats says, "Yo kiddes!! Lissen up, here's jeff 's original story so's you all can see how o'barr butchered it [*sic*]." O'Barr has translated the written concept to graphic form with eyeball-popping verve.

Two purely visual entries, Rene J. Cigler's "Child with Head Wounds" and cover artist Jared Pankin's "The Railroad Man" seem to be multimedia constructions, photographed to no particular advantage. Confronting them in three dimensions might be moving. The more purely graphic undertakings, except for Michael Manning's proleptic visions of nuclear war and punk rock, are crude and amateurish, and seem to suffer from over-inking.

Will *Bone Saw* develop a stable (wrong word, perhaps) of artists capable of depicting more than voluntary amputations, infanticide, and mayhem? During the height of the Vietnam War, Clayton Eshleman printed in an early issue of the seminal little magazine *Caterpillar* a pair of horrifying photographs of napalm-burned children. In a later issue Eshleman wrote that he was "ceasing to validate the present war . . . at this point in my life I want to validate what I want to exist. That generation be swallowed up in regeneration." What do Bergin and O'Barr—or Otomo—wish to validate?

The confrontation with tabu does not succeed very well either in *Bone Saw* or *Akira,* because there is no conviction that the tabus matter. With s & m garb on the couturier runway, not just in sex clubs, with the possibility of nuclear accidents in everyday's paper, how are the artists to shock? There must be some community of values before values can be violated.

The inmates of *Arkham Asylum: A Serious House on Seri-*

ous Earth, a graphic novel featuring Batman written by Grant Morrison and illustrated by Dave McKean, commit the same violations that *Bone Saw* favors—medical torture, child rape, dismemberment, scatology—but with more impact. It is not just because Morrison is graphically more resourceful than Otomo or Bergin and O'Barr's artists. (And slicker, with clearer allegiances to the comic book tradition than the *Bone Saw* crew, while taking more risks with its conventions than Otomo.) It is also that we care about (one might say, *valorize*) Batman, in a way that we do not care about the worlds of *Akira* or *Bone Saw.* The creatures of Otomo, Bergin, and O'Barr do not respect any limits: religion, science, politics, ethics, family count for nothing. Disintegration is the norm, not reconciliation or healing. What remains is a bitter sense of adolescent nay-saying, the notion that a silent child is worth more than a functioning adult. Akira—a Little Boy Bomb drawn with an impassive face—levels his own city merely by breaking his silence; this may show attitude, but it cannot be construed as morally superior to dropping a bomb in wartime. Akira and the Bone Sawyers are driven by fury, egocentrism, and self-pity. In the end they fail to move us because—unlike the denizens of the more pretentious and febrile Arkham Asylum—they involve nothing serious or sacred in their Grand Guignol violations.

Bill Jones (review date February-March 1993)

SOURCE: "Boundless Schizophrenic World," in *The American Book Review,* Vol. 14, No. 6, February-March, 1993, pp. 6-7.

[*Jones is an artist and writer. In the review below, he focuses on the graphic and visual aspects of Spiegelman's* Maus, *calling it "a true work of art."*]

Art Spiegelman's wrenching visual narrative *Maus* portrays in verbatim, often tape-recorded dialogue and comics-formatted drawings Vladek Spiegelman's intricately detailed Holocaust survival story. Art Spiegelman, founder of *Raw* comics, where *Maus* was first published, relates the complex story by disguising each ethnic group as a particular animal; Jews are mice, Germans cats, and Poles pigs. The simple substitution sets up the adversarial relationships between the groups graphically in a way that only pictures can. The Germans terrorize Jews in a way that can be described only as a cat-and-mouse game. Yet the conceit never reads as a cliché. But what makes Art Spiegelman's comics rendering of his father's story unique is the younger Spiegelman's uncanny ability to place himself in this survivor's tale. Art is there not only as author and artist, not just as recipient and recorder—as is often the case with children of Holocaust survivors—but as inheritor of a brutal and painful legacy. And in the way that only the schizophrenic, time-boundless world of underground comics offers, Spiegelman moves forward and back, in and out of time, telling the story of the story's telling, wrapped within the father's compelling narrative. In this way the account of the making of this work of art, emotional and physical, over a two-year span, is revealed as a kind of demystified subtext.

Vladek Spiegelman, who died August 18, 1982, was by his son's vivid account a difficult and irascible man. He is gruff and cruel to his second wife Mala. Anja, Vladek's first love and soul mate at Auschwitz, and Art Spiegelman's mother, committed suicide in 1968. As the confused and beleaguered Mala says in one frame, "He's more attached to things than to people."

Experiencing Vladek's story in this visual onslaught, the reader could easily enough forgive him his miserly ways which compel him to count and recount everything from pills to crackers—it was such constant miserliness that saved Vladek and his beloved Anja from the death grip of the Nazis. But Art Spiegelman cannot forgive, locked as he is into the hell of a survivor's legacy. The son can only come to empathize with his father through the story and its retelling. And it is telling, the way Spiegelman's phantasmagoric drawing style is held in check by the constant need to cover every detail in text and in image.

Near the center of the first volume—*Maus* in its book form comes in two volumes—Vladek, quite by accident, finds a copy of an obscure underground comic from years before in which Art tells the story of his mother's suicide. "In 1968 when I was twenty my mother killed herself . . . she left no note," Spiegelman, dressed in prison uniform, looking like a camp survivor, tells us in the first frame. The distorted comics portrayal, which reminds one stylistically of German expressionist woodcuts, forms the dark-hearted secret at the center of both Vladek's and Art's stories. The stylistic shift in drawing from this earlier document, *Prisoner on the Hell Planet,* to that of *Maus* is critical to the emotional tone of the survivor's tale. Gone is the hallucinatory distortion, replaced by the conceit of the mouse, cat, and pig personae that represent the various ethnicities of the protagonists. But more than this it is the consistency, the regularity of the drawings that shows Spiegelman's dogged commitment to his project. The effect—people as mice, cats, and pigs aside—is one of stark realism. There is a simplicity of line that makes possible this complex and revealing undertaking.

Being a purveyor of abstraction in art, I missed *Maus* in its *Raw* comics incarnation. I could not imagine how a comics rendering could get at the heart of a survivor's story without demeaning the memory of those who perished in the Holocaust. But it is the maximal effect of the endless exposition traditional to the comics genre that makes *Maus* so intriguing and allows Spiegelman to do more than record another tale of horror. *Maus* is a true work of art, an honest and direct expression of the generational effects of the tragedy that befell the millions who perished and those who survived. Near the end of the second volume, a photograph appears set in among the black and white drawings. As Vladek tells his son, "I passed once a photo place what had a camp uniform—a new and clean one—to make souvenir photos," we see a still proud, unbroken Vladek, healthy and well fed, shortly after the war has ended. He had the photo taken to send to Anja, to prove he was still alive. The photo—dropped in as it were—stands in stark contrast to the drawn comics. It does something the drawings can't by showing how Vladek appeared; his attitude shows in his stance and facial expression. But seeing the photo also tells us something about what only the drawings can say, in their docudramatic way, linked as they are to the hand of one of the story's protagonists, about the experience of being there, in prewar Poland, in the ghetto, in the camps, and on *Hell Planet* with Artie, sharing his father's anguish.

There are two photos hidden away in the pages of *Maus.* The first comes from the inset of *Prisoner on the Hell Planet,* and shows a ten-year-old Artie and his mother a decade before her suicide. She does not look proud and upright like Vladek's picture just after the war. Anja in 1958 still bears the full weight of the aftermath of the Holocaust. It is a rare work that can, in such a short passage, with simple elegance of line through direct and honest emotion, encompass the whole of the Holocaust and its continuing legacy.

Publishers Weekly (review date 18 July 1994)

SOURCE: A review of *City of Glass,* in *Publishers Weekly,* Vol. 241, No. 29, July 18, 1994, p. 241.

[In the review below, the critic favorably assesses the graphic adaptation of Paul Auster's novel City of Glass.]

[Paul] Auster's acclaimed novel *City of Glass,* a dreamlike meditation on language and fiction in the form of a detective novel, has been translated into comics form to stunning effect. And while [Paul] Karasik's faithful adaptation of Auster's crisp prose partially obscures its author's sly allusions to the act of writing itself, [David] Mazzuchelli's black-and-white illustrations capture and expand on Auster's precise documentation of place, psychological development and pedagogical improvisation with unusual style, simplicity and graphic facility. This combination story, lecture and literary deconstruction begins when New York City detective novelist Daniel Quinn answers a wrong number. Donning the personas of both the detective he created and his own creator, Auster himself, Quinn attempts to protect a young man, who as a child was kept without light or language for nine years as his lunatic academic father tried to discover "God's Language." In Quinn, the roles of fictional detective and creator/novelist are interchangeable; and the processes by which these two carry out their investigative work—the fanatical collection of random detail, obsessive observation and recording, and an almost monastic introspection—serve as sublime indications of the serendipitous mix of chance, language and invention at root of the art of fiction. This is a masterful addition to the growing library of serious comics works.

Publishers Weekly (review date 8 August 1994)

SOURCE: A review of *Our Cancer Year,* in *Publishers Weekly,* Vol. 241, No. 32, August 8, 1994, p. 420.

[Below, the critic offers a positive assessment of Our Cancer Year.]

[Joined by his wife and collaborator Joyce Brabner and illustrator Frank Stack, Harvey Pekar's] first book-length comics narrative [*Our Cancer Year*] is by turns amusing, frightening, moving and quietly entertaining. As always, Pekar's work records his apparently ordinary life as a hospital clerk in Cleveland while simultaneously capturing the epiphanic combination of mundanity and awkward, sporadic nobility of everyday life. In 1990, Pekar was diagnosed with lymphoma and needed chemotherapy. By the time the disease was discovered, the couple was in the midst of buying a house (a tremendous worry to Pekar, who fretted about both the money and corruptions of bourgeois creature comforts). Brabner, a self-described "comic book journalist," had to oversee both the new house and a sick and very difficult husband. Pekar's cancer treatment and suffering will take your breath away, but there's a happy ending; and the book (and their marriage) is distinguished by Brabner's great tenderness and determination in the middle of Pekar's medical nightmare. Stack's brisk and elegantly gestural black-and-white drawings wonderfully delineate this captivating story of love, community, recuperation and international friendship.

Publishers Weekly (review date 8 August 1994)

SOURCE: A review of *Streak of Chalk,* in *Publishers Weekly,* Vol. 241, No. 32, August 8, 1994, p. 420.

[In the following review, the critic comments favorably on Miguelanxo Prado's Streak of Chalk, *praising Prado's skill in evoking mood with his choice of setting and use of color.]*

Nick Bantock's *Griffin and Sabine* meets John Fowles's *The Magus* in [*Streak of Chalk,* Miguelanxo Prado's] graphic novel about curious characters on a spit of uncharted island in the middle of nowhere. The island, with its deserted lighthouse, general store/bar/inn, and two sullen inhabitants easily seems mysterious. Add to that a few guarded, secretive visitors and this isolated atmosphere needs little imagination—on the part of reader or characters—to make ordinary circumstances seem sinister, perhaps murderous. Although the story is sparse, there's intrigue, sex and, more importantly, Spanish artist Prado's sumptuous illustrations and exquisite use of colors, to keep the reader's attention. Starting with vividly clear greens and blues, the colors change with the mood of the narrative, with lavender-streaked shadows moving in as the mystery grows, while deeper blues and reddish browns signal violence and loss. A fine first title from NBM's just launched ComicsLit imprint of graphic novels from around the world.

Publishers Weekly (review date 22 August 1994)

SOURCE: A review of *Poison River,* in *Publishers Weekly,* Vol. 241, No. 34, August 22, 1994, p. 52.

[Below, the critic lauds Gilbert Hernandez's complex plot, striking characters, and vivid dialogue in Poison River.]

Along with his brother Jaime, Gilbert Hernandez (*Love and Rockets X*) has produced some of the best comics work of the last 10 years. *Poison River* is the story of one his most engaging characters, Luba—self-possessed, intelligent and iconoclastically sexy—in the years before she arrived in Palomar, Hernandez's mythological Central American village. We meet Maria, Luba's mother, beautiful, pampered and recklessly promiscuous. Maria's husband discovers that Luba is the result of a tool-shed tryst with Eduardo, a poor Indian worker and kicks mother, child and lover out into poverty. Glamorous Maria abandons the other two in turn, and much later a teenage Luba meets her future husband Peter Rios, conga player and small-time (soon to be big-time) gangster who takes her away to a life of privilege. But their meeting is not by chance and Rios's peculiar sexual obsessions (women's navels and well-hung chorus "girls") are driven by carnal memories of the exquisite Maria. Indeed Luba's new life (and the men in it) is much like her mother's—lavishly sheltered by violent anticommunist gangsters, who murder and terrorize the local "leftists" in the name of "business" and right-wing patriotism. Hernandez has written an epic Latin American melodrama of lost identity, political violence and polymorphous sexuality. And while his complex plotting is occasionally confusing, his characterizations, dialogue and relationships are vividly, emotionally engaging. A brilliant draftsman, Hernandez presents a wide range of facial and physical types, all rendered with an expressive facility and a deft comic flourish.

Publishers Weekly (review date 29 August 1994)

SOURCE: A review of *Palestine,* in *Publishers Weekly,* Vol. 241, No. 35, August 29, 1994, p. 71.

[*Here, the critic offers a highly laudatory assessment of Joe Sacco's nonfiction book* Palestine.]

Sacco spent two months during the winter of 1991-92 living in Jerusalem and visiting the West Bank and the Gaza Strip to see for himself what life was like for Palestinians under the Israeli occupation. He has produced [*Palestine*] a fascinating you-are-there-with-me comics account as impressive for its idiosyncratic personal tone as for its scrupulous documentation of human-rights abuses and lively accounts of ordinary Palestinians (in East Jerusalem, the West Bank towns and the decrepit refugee camps). In this volume (the sequel will focus on the Gaza Strip and more recent events), he details his encounters, discussions and interviews with a wide range of West Bank personalities: Arab shopkeepers, refugees from 1948, rock-throwing Palestinian teenagers, teachers, intellectuals, former prisoners, Israeli soldiers, members of the peace movement, American Jews and some terrorists as well. Like other rights investigators, he documents some of the better known abuses—arbitrary beatings by the IDF, administrative detention (arrest without charges), house demolitions and appalling prison conditions—especially at the notorious Ansar III prison. His final section is a wry but typically informative section on the position of Palestinian women in a society in which wife battering is "part of Arab culture." His drawings are simply wonderful, combining great facility and compositional invention with a fluid line and a gift for the economical use of intensive linear detail. There is nothing else quite like this in alternative comics.

Publishers Weekly (review date 19 September 1994)

SOURCE: A review of *The Cartoon History of the Universe II,* in *Publishers Weekly,* Vol. 241, No. 38, September 19, 1994, p. 64.

[*The following is a positive appraisal of* The Cartoon History of the Universe II.]

[In *The Cartoon History of the Universe II* Larry] Gonick has done it again with a diffuse but deep excavation into early civilizations from ancient China to the Germanic tribes. In some ways, Gonick asks a lot of American readership's occidental training by detailing every dynastic hotshot from the Orient. This also being a fertile time for the development of religious cults, Gonick spends much time on Christ (whom he insists on calling "Jeshua ben Joseph"), Confucius, (not, one might note, Lao Tsu or K'ung futsze), Buddha and the like. Gonick's main focus is not to outline the contributions that allowed their teachings to survive the centuries, but rather to humanize them, and some come across as fanatical seekers simply looking for a following, a good meal, a wicked battle, a girlfriend or a shower. The artist's style is versatile and engaging, and his asides, puns and parenthetical references do much to keep the reader's attention throughout this tome, but that cannot entirely make up for the fact that some of this history is just plain dry. However, aficionados of cartoon blood, backstabbing, sex and history will love this volume, and might find a place for it near their encyclopedias.

Publishers Weekly (review date 19 September 1994)

SOURCE: A review of *Just Who the Hell Is She, Anyway?* in *Publishers Weekly,* Vol. 241, No. 38, September 19, 1994, p. 64.

[*In the following review, the critic offers a mixed assessment of* Just Who the Hell Is She, Anyway?, *a graphic novel by Marisa Acocella.*]

The original *She* was launched as a regular comics feature of *Mirabella* in 1993 and quickly became a reader favorite. [In *Just Who the Hell Is She, Anyway?,* Marisa] Acocella continues her efforts to create a character that embodies the cultural history of a generation of upper-middle class white women. A post-feminist everywoman, *She* is impatient with the status quo even in the womb. A child of suburbia stuck with gender-based expectations, *She* manages to both laugh at and deconstruct these conventions, wryly acknowledging the role they play in shaping her life ("Barbie did introduce the concept of 'man as accessory' "). *She* wants to play *with* the boys in every sense of the word, and, after leaving home (and her "(s)mother"), she gets her chance by joining the corporate media world. But for all her revolutionary rants, Acocella's heroine is just a neo-material girl with a rebel attitude *cum* pose. Which shallow trend shall I *choose* to be now, she seems to say—the sad result of viewing life as a succession of pop phenomena. She's pissed (like other "power babes" in her circle) that boys have all the fun but that's about it. *She* is fun, but ultimately is more about social climbing than social change. Acocella's drawing is barely adequate, but her page layouts are lively and carry the story well.

Karal Ann Marling (review date 9 October 1994)

SOURCE: "An Angst Even Shopping Cannot Cure," in *The New York Times Book Review,* October 9, 1994, p. 11.

[*In the following review, Marling compares* Just Who the Hell Is She, Anyway? *to Japanese graphic novels and comments on its feminist themes.*]

SHE is the daughter of (S)mother and Dad, the latter lost in a perpetual twilight zone in which visions of split-level houses, stacks of cash and female legs in fishnet stockings dance like sugarplums before his eyes. SHE, the product of a tract-house suburb and an indecisive skirmish with the liberal arts, is now single and in her 30's, a vice president at a Madison Avenue advertising agency, with a corner office and a galloping premature midlife crisis that even shopping cannot cure. You know you're in trouble when life is so burdensome that you conjure up angst-ridden fashion fantasies about Chanel doing cut-rate black rubber suits. And SHE does. The cartoonist (and Young & Rubicam vice president) Marisa Acocella first began to chronicle her almost-too-hip-to-bear SHE-ness in a comic strip in *Mirabella* magazine last year. *Just Who the Hell Is SHE, Anyway?* is her full-blown biography, and a dandy novel in pictures.

In Japan, the comic-format novel—the *manga*—is the reading of choice on public transit. Thick and meaty, about the size of a John Grisham hardback, each Japanese comic is pitched at a specific segment of the audience: samurai stories for macho guys, sedate "salaryman" adventures for corporate drones, inventive erotica for sexual athletes and even works tailored for players of mah-jongg and pachinko. Many readers slip their purchases into fabric covers, so nobody can tell that the officious salaryman on the seat opposite is actually reading a so-called ladies' comic, with a title—almost always in English—like *Be Love.* The *Be Love* school of comic art features idealized romance, agonizing career choices, great clothes, beautiful men and women with Western features, and passionate girl-girl friendships.

Just Who the Hell Is SHE, Anyway? is a first-rate ladies' comic in the Japanese mode. All the key elements are there. SHE has sweet pre-teen dreams of riding around in a limo with Paul McCartney; moments of corporate rebellion (a nocturnal raid with a bottle of white-out changes the self-important "Startle Me" motto on her boss's door to "Start Me"); girlfriends (she hangs out with "Power Babes," who have names like Sandra the Command-a and Lo-Lisa); boys *du jour* of little consequence; and fabulous clothes, including the junior half of a mother-and-daughter Pucci set acquired after a family fight. (When Dad misbehaves, (S)mother says to the 6-year-old SHE, "IT'LL REALLY COST HIM!")

The graphic format does wonders for the story. Big emotions get big letters. Identity choices are represented as paper dolls who borrow glamour duds from Audrey Hepburn or perky cutout hairdos from Mary Tyler Moore to define the current version of SHE. When pregnant, (S)mother wears wild Pucci patterns that swell around her fecund figure. When lost in thought, SHE appears in close-up, her Maybelline eyes cast heavenward, her caterpillar lips parted, her one perfect never-to-be-bitten nail poised invitingly before a pearly incisor. The style gives the title character a pseudo-ironic sensibility, as if Roy Lichtenstein had taken entirely too seriously the current Marvel Comics style sheet for drawing mega-babes.

Ms. Acocella is a tart critic of pop culture, taking deadly aim at a variety of icons and anti-icons, from feminine deodorant commericials on television to Barbie dolls (Ken is a wuss) and Oreos. But Ms. Acocella is at her best when SHE, playing the American Everywoman, details the plight of the second-generation feminist for whom Betty Friedan is summed up in an ancient slogan ("We wore girdles on our bodies and girdles on our minds") and Gloria Steinem is "the patron saint of miniskirts," complete with halo. Like the rest of us, SHE hasn't quite sorted it all out yet: the biological clock, the boy-toys, the corporate rat race, the remote chance that Chanel will introduce a line of black rubber suits at bargain prices.

***Publishers Weekly* (review date 24 October 1994)**

SOURCE: A review of *Brief Lives,* in *Publishers Weekly,* Vol. 241, No. 43, October 24, 1994, pp. 57-8.

[*Below, the critic offers a mixed assessment of* Brief Lives.]

[Neil] Gaiman's very popular Sandman series (this is the eighth book in the series) continues with [*Brief Lives*] another tale of the Endless, the family of mythic cosmic beings that govern the psychic and physical realms of Dream, Desire, Despair, Destiny, Delirium, Destruction and Death. Morpheus, Lord of Dreams and the central figure in the series, is asked by his sister, the unstable and touchingly demented Delirium, to help locate their brother Destruction. Destruction abandoned his duties 300 years ago (about the time of the Enlightenment), dropping out of sight after a prescient and despairing glimpse of the rise of human reason and its own destructive proclivities. The grimly ironic Morpheus and his whimsically erratic sister travel among the mortals of earth in search of their brother and ultimately learn something of Destruction's reasons for abdicating. Gaiman's works often follow the plots of classical and mythical narratives and *Brief Lives,* like his other works, can often look and sound as ponderous as a bad period costume movie. But his works are also driven by sharply drawn characters and his knack for capturing the patterns of intimacy, even in an otherworldly setting, can be affecting. [Jill] Thompson and [Neil] Locke contribute subtle and vividly colored drawings, rendered in an awkward but agile line.

***Publishers Weekly* (review date 24 October 1994)**

SOURCE: A review of *Stan Mack's Real Life American Revolution,* in *Publishers Weekly,* Vol. 241, No. 43, October 24, 1994, p. 58.

[*In the positive review below, the critic remarks on the subjects covered in Stan Mack's historical book* Stan Mack's Real Life American Revolution.]

Longtime *Village Voice* cartoonist [Stan] Mack has taken his talent for rendering the frenzied variety of life in New

York City and produced a cheerful and informative history of the American Revolution [entitled *Stan Mack's Real Life American Revolution*]. Delightfully illustrated in his distinctive minimalist cartoon style, Mack's first original book-length effort puts the "real life" back into our revolutionary roots, providing capsule portraits of the prominent activists of the time, along with their many idiosyncracies, comic flaws and strategic bungling. He provides amusing sketches of early anti-British activists like James Otis and Sam Adams, notes the nature of the Enlightenment and New England Puritanism and outlines the many hated tax laws that preceded the Boston Tea Party and the Revolutionary War. Just as important, he depicts the ongoing clashes between the colonial aristocracy, new merchant classes, urban laborers and farmers over the country's developing economy. He also profiles the important but restricted roles of African slaves and freemen and women in the war, as well as the formidable presence of Native American nations. Ending with the ratification of the Constitution, Mack celebrates the document while pointing to its flaws—the continuance of slavery, destruction of native cultures and lack of rights for women and whites without property.

Publishers Weekly (review date 24 October 1994)

SOURCE: A review of *From Inside,* in *Publishers Weekly,* Vol. 241, No. 43, October 24, 1994, p. 58.

[*Below, the critic offers a mixed review of John Bergin's nuclear-winter novel,* From Inside.]

In this strange, post-apocalyptic birth story [titled *From Inside*], a pregnant woman sees her husband fry during the nuclear flash before she manages to escape on a train with other survivors. The group travels through the wreckage of a bleak world looking for food, shelter and a suitable place to stop the train. Along the way, the passengers overcome a host of chilling obstacles, the least of which is the woman's complicated childbirth. Understandably depressed, the woman is ambivalent about her baby, unable to reconcile the new life of her child with the fast approaching death of the world. Any symbolic connection between the train traveling through the refuse of a planet and a child leaving the womb is lost in too many scenes of fire, destruction and mounting series of wicked dreams. [John] Bergin's dark artwork aptly illustrates the desperation at the end of the world, with appropriately apocalyptic red and brown overtones evoking blood and fire. With a suggested soundtrack for readers, this rarely breaks out of it's pretentious vision, but it is a valiant try.

FURTHER READING

Criticism

Berman, Avis. "Art Spiegelman: The Maus that Roared." *Artnews* 92, No. 5 (May 1993): 63-4.

Examines the making of *Maus* and its use of a comic-book format.

DeCandido, Keith R. A. "Comic 'Books.' " *Library Journal* 116, No. 10 (1 June 1991): 134.

Provides brief reviews of several graphic novels, including Dave Sim and Gerhard's *Jaka's Story.*

Kaveney, Roz. "Strip Shows." *New Statesman* 113, No. 2926 (24 April 1987): 26-7.

Remarks on several contemporary graphic novels, including Gilbert Hernandez's *Heartbreak Soup.*

Larson, Kay. "Of Mice and Men." *New York* 25, No. 2 (13 January 1992): 65-6.

Discusses Art Spiegelman's two-volume *Maus: A Survivor's Tale,* arguing that "the comic-book format, merging historical nightmare and ordinary reality, allowed Spiegelman to conflate those two extremes and point toward their enormity."

Nicholls, Richard E. "Detective Comics." *The New York Times Book Review* (2 October 1994): 32.

Briefly reviews *City of Glass.*

Prescott, Peter S., and Sawhill, Ray. "The Comic Book (Gulp!) Grows Up." *Newsweek* CXI, No. 3 (18 January 1988): 70-1.

Discusses the changing focus of comic books from escapism to naturalistic stories of adult anxieties.

Review of *Death: The High Cost of Living,* by Neil Gaiman, Chris Bachalo, Mark Buckingham, and Dave McKean. *Publishers Weekly* 241, No. 8 (21 February 1994): 248.

Mixed review of *Death.* The critic notes that "while Gaiman brings a gritty urban contemporaneity to the fantasy genre, the story . . . suffers from a TV script-like sensibility."

Smoler, Fredric Paul. "Teen Arts." *The Nation* 245, No. 11 (10 October 1987): 386-87.

Reviews *Watchmen* by Alan Moore and Dave Gibbons, noting the work's appeal and political themes.

Spence, Jonathan. "Then Came the Fall of Rome (Splat!)." *The New York Times Book Review* (18 December 1994): 15-16.

Favorably reviews Larry Gonick's *The Cartoon History of the Universe* and *The Cartoon History of the Universe II,* but laments that the multimedia CD-Rom version of the first book is "basically a filmed copy of the original text."

Sylvia Plath and the Nature of Biography

INTRODUCTION

With the advance publication of *The Silent Woman* (1994) in the *New Yorker* in August 1993, Janet Malcolm reopened debate about the life of poet Sylvia Plath and raised some larger issues about the nature of biography itself. Suggesting that the motives of biographers are less than altruistic, if not intrusive, Malcolm's book concentrates on her lengthy research process, particularly dealing with Olwyn Hughes, the executor of Plath's literary estate, and interviewing other Plath biographers to discuss how writing their biographies affected them personally. Among the issues Malcolm addresses is the right to privacy of living persons who were associated with the biographer's subject and how those rights interfere with the biographer's attempt to produce an accurate portrait. Indeed, Malcolm questions the efficacy of the biographer's project—capturing a person's life—and wonders if the biographer is, in fact, more of a burglar than a benefactor. Several other writers have also pondered this predicament. B. L. Reid, for instance, argues in *Necessary Lives* (1990) that "biography ought to be as well written as a novel; but it should not try to be, or to feel like, a novel. Biography becomes a fine art when it performs superbly within the right limits of its own nature. . . . One must be wary of the tempting 'high *Priori* road,' as Pope calls it: of fitting data into preconceived designs, the temptation to neaten and intensify and thereby to falsify the often disorderly order of time. Biography's strength and its integrity are ones of subject matter, of honorable and tasteful treatment of an interesting subject."

What makes biographies of Plath so controversial is that her widower, the English poet Ted Hughes, is still an active writer who insists, through his sister Olwyn Hughes, on maintaining a high degree of privacy concerning his years with Plath. This has made research difficult for Plath's biographers, who have been denied access to many of Plath's journals and letters, key sources that biographers of other individuals often take for granted. Once considered a noble genre, whose standard was James Boswell's *Life of Samuel Johnson* (1791), biography in recent years has become increasingly dependent on the lurid details of its subject's life, becoming a psychology of an artist's pathology instead of an exploration of the guiding principles and philosophies that underscored a person's life. This penchant for deviant details—a trait Malcolm readily recognizes in her own biographical pursuits—prompts her to compare the biographer to "the professional burglar, breaking into a house, rifling through certain drawers that he has good reason to think contain the jewelry and money, and triumphantly bearing his loot away . . ." and to characterize biography as "the medium through which the remaining secrets of the famous dead are taken from them and dumped out in full view of the world." Thus, she defends Hughes's noncooperation with Plath's biographers as his attempt to guard his privacy and honor his wife's memory.

REPRESENTATIVE WORKS DISCUSSED BELOW

Hamilton, Ian
Keepers of the Flame: Literary Estates and the Rise of Biography (criticism) 1992

Malcolm, Janet
The Journalist and the Murderer (nonfiction) 1990
The Silent Woman (biography) 1994

Plath, Sylvia
Letters Home: Correspondence 1950-1963 [edited by Aurelia Schober Plath] (letters) 1975
The Journals of Sylvia Plath [edited by Ted Hughes and Frances McCullough] (journals) 1982

Reid, B. L.
Necessary Lives: Biographical Reflections (criticism) 1990

Stevenson, Anne
Bitter Fame: A Life of Sylvia Plath (biography) 1989

Wagner-Martin, Linda
Telling Women's Lives: The New Biography (criticism) 1994

THE NATURE OF BIOGRAPHY

Dee Horne (essay date 1992)

SOURCE: "Biography in Disguise: Sylvia Plath's Journals," in *Wascana Review,* Vol. 27, No. 1, 1992, pp. 90-104.

[*In the following essay, Horne details how Plath's published journals were manipulated by Hughes and his editor, thus providing a skewed rendering of Plath's life. Horne concludes that there is always room for interpretation in biography, even when analyzing works written by the subject.*]

> It's hopeless to "get life" if you don't keep notebooks.
>
> Now to do what I must, then to do what I want: this book too becomes a litany of dreams, of directives and imperatives. [*The Journals of Sylvia Plath,* 1982]

Many critics have erroneously labelled Plath a confessional writer. As Judith Kroll accurately observes in *Chapters in a Mythology,* Plath is not a confessional writer because her writing has distinctive characteristics which do not conform to those of confessional writers such as Robert Lowell and Anne Sexton:

> In a great deal of the work of Robert Lowell and Anne Sexton, often considered the paradigm 'confessional' poets, the voice—intensely personal and almost journalistic—is the direct voice of the author in an everyday role. In Plath the personal concerns and everyday role are transmuted into something impersonal, by being absorbed into a timeless mythic system. The poetry of Lowell and Sexton relates their narratives; in Plath—although many narrative details of her mythic system are drawn from her life—the emphasis is more on expressing the structure of her state of being. 'Confessional' poetry usually comprises a plurality of concerns—politics, the writing of poetry, marriage, aging, fame, and so on—that remain relatively independent. But in Plath's poetry, there is one overriding concern: the problem of rebirth or transcendence; and nearly everything in her poetry contributes either to the statement or to the envisioned resolution of this problem.

Kroll's analysis of the characteristics of the confessional writer might also be applied to Plath's journal. She is not a confessional poet, nor does she use her journal as a confessor. The journals play an important role in the creative evolution of her writing.

Plath started keeping a journal when she was a child and remained an avid journal writer up to her death. Though most have been preserved, we are unable to read the journals kept just prior to her death because Ted Hughes took the term 'literary executor' quite literally:

> The journals exist in an assortment of notebooks and bunches of loose sheets. This selection contains perhaps a third of the whole bulk, which is now in The Neilson Library at Smith College. Two more notebooks survived for a while, maroon-backed ledgers like the '57-'59 volume, and continued the record from late '59 to within three days of her death. The last of these contained entries for several months, and I destroyed it because I did not want her children to have to read it (in those days I regarded forgetfulness as an essential part of survival). The other disappeared.

By destroying this late journal, Hughes has done a disservice to Plath and to scholars and other interested readers. In all probability both of these missing journals would have shed light on Plath and the "Ariel" poems which constitute her crowning achievement.

The editors of Plath's journals, Frances McCullough and Ted Hughes, have altered the surviving journals significantly. In the published American edition of *The Journals of Sylvia Plath,* the writing often appears fragmented as Plath shifts from one topic to another. A comparison of the published Smith Journal (1950-1953) to the original manuscript, however, reveals that the published edition edits, and often deletes, much of Plath's creativity and sensuality as well as her pain and anger. The discrepancy between the Smith Journal (1950-1953) in this published edition and the original manuscript is a demonstration of the misleading effects of the editorial omissions. Clearly the reader's critical interpretation of Plath's Smith Journal (1950-1953) and understanding of her as an individual and a writer, too, is revised.

McCullough and Hughes also alter the text by making additions, inserting material chronologically from other fragments and notebooks, "ordering" her journals on false grounds. For example, they insert Plath's notes about her attack of sinusitis (October 17 [-19], 1951)—which is not in the bound volume of the original manuscript, but is a six page manuscript. Later on, they insert Plath's poem "Infirmary Blues," thereby establishing a link between the journal and a finished poem which was not included in the original Smith Journal (1950-1953). Near the end of the published edition, the editors include an entry dated May 14 which corresponds to page 414 of the original Smith Journal (1950-1953) in which they omit the last six pages. More importantly, they neglect to state specifically that the subsequent entries in their edition are not part of the original Smith Journal (1950-1953). Plath's reflections, for example, on the executions of Ethel and Julius Rosenberg, which she later uses in the beginning of *The Bell Jar,* are found in a one page typescript (June 19, 1953) which Plath typed on the reverse side of Street & Smith Publications interoffice memorandum paper, and not in the Smith Journal at all. Similarly, her "Letter to an Over-grown Over-protected, Scared Spoiled Baby" is found in a three page typescript.

As is the case of the Smith Journal (1950-1953), the subsequent section entitled "Cambridge 1955-57" in the published edition is misleading because the editors do not state that they are culling material from a variety of journals. Plath did, in fact, keep a journal entitled "Cambridge Diary" (January 3-March 11, 1957), but this is only a ten page typescript. In addition, the editors add editorial commentary, changes in punctuation for the sake of conformity, and make omissions in both content and style. While all three of these editorial decisions are noteworthy, the fact that they are made 'silently' is disturbing.

The central question the editor of journals must consider is whether or not to print the manuscript in its entirety. In *From Writer to Reader: Studies in Editorial Method,* Philip Gaskell states:

> Although they were not written for publication, the literary quality of diaries, collections of letters, etc., may be great, and they may be edited for publication. Here it is the original document itself that is the finished product, and there is every reason to make the manuscript as copy-text and to reproduce it without normalization.

> The only difficulty is likely to be that of representing the author's manuscript conventions readably and economically by means of typographical symbols.

McCullough and Hughes, however, intervene by making omissions and additions from other journals and by normalizing punctuation for the sake of condensation and readability. The underlying implication is that these measures will eliminate redundancy and tedium, making the journals more interesting and accessible to the general public; but the major problem with this approach is that the reader does not see the author's version of her life, but rather that of the editors. McCullough and Hughes provide a selective portrait of Plath because they eliminate much of her early writing, writing that included, interestingly, much eroticism.

In the editor's note, McCullough states the basic editorial principles for omissions, which I quote at length:

> We have tried, in the cutting of the work, to stick to a few basic principles: to include what seem to us the most important elements relating to her work, her inner life, and her valiant struggle to find herself and her voice. This leaves a great deal of material by the road: countless numbers of sketches, prospective poems and stories, lists of characters' names, detailed descriptions of rooms, places, people, and other elements related to her work. *Obviously there are also lots of missing pages of ordinary commentary that seemed not particularly relevant to any of the basic concerns of the book.* Because it is very early—in terms of the ages of Plath's survivors—to release such a document, there has been special concern for those who must live out their lives as characters in this drama. There are quite a few nasty bits missing—Plath had a very sharp tongue and tended to use it on nearly everybody, even people of whom she was inordinately fond (Paul and Clarissa Roche, for instance, who take some tartness in this book and yet were very close to Plath right up until the end). So, some of the more devastating comments are missing—these are marked '(omission)' to distinguish them from ordinary cuts—*of intimacies—that have the effect of diminishing Plath's eroticism, which was quite strong.* In the later Smith College section and the Devon section a few names have been changed. (emphasis mine)

The editors do not define what is "relevant," but leave the reader wondering what could possibly be *ir*relevant. Plath presumably found the material of sufficient relevant to her "inner life" and "struggle to find herself" to record it on paper.

McCullough and Hughes omit approximately one quarter of the original Smith Journal (1950-1953). One page of the original manuscript is roughly the same as one typed page in the published edition because Plath wrote in such a large book. She wrote 420 pages while the published edition only devotes eighty-eight pages to the section entitled "Smith College." The practical exigencies of shaping a book-length manuscript were undoubtedly a strong editorial consideration, but the omissions are so extensive and alter our perception of Plath *and* her journal significantly. While it is not possible to prove that the editors made cuts due to personal reasons in the Smith Journal (1950-1953), there is evidence in later unpublished journals which suggests that personal concerns played a substantial part in the cutting and deleting process. In a typescript dated (August 28, 1957-October 14, 1958), for example, there are excerpts from an autograph manuscript of 186 pages (sealed). These were written while Plath was teaching at Smith College and while she lived in Boston. These excerpts correspond to pages 174-263 in the published American edition of Plath's journals. The editors typed these parts of Plath's journals and cuts were made, although it is impossible to ascertain how much material was omitted.

On the typescript copy supplied by the Plath Estate there are cuts made with a thick black marker. These deletions fall into three categories: references to men Plath knew; gossip; and references to Ted Hughes. The references to men are often scathing portraits of people who were probably still alive; thus, there are frequent name changes, presumably to protect both the editors and the living. The editing, however, is *selective,* and not consistent. While the sections in which Plath gossips about friends, faculty members at Smith and contemporary poets are often acerbic, they are none the less important. Of the three categories of deleted materials, the references to Ted Hughes are the most noticeable. In one section where Plath is writing about Ted and friends, a section is cut out with scissors. In addition, the editors delete references to Ted in which he criticizes Plath's poetry and suggests that she change some of the words—deletions that change Ted's own image favourably. There are also numerous references to Ted in the supplied typescript where Plath expresses her bitterness and anger toward him and observes the ways in which he has negatively changed her. She also expresses her feelings of inferiority of living in his shadow. At one point, she records the adultery of some Smith professors, her premonitions about Ted's unfaithfulness, and later, her believed confirmation of it when she sees him returning from Paradise Pond with another woman.

Plath's self-professed powerlessness in life, ironically, persists in death as well. Certain cuts to Plath's journals suggest that the editors allowed personal reasons to influence their editorial decisions.

—Dee Horne

These deletions are important because the editors have censored Plath's anger and altered the public's perception of her personality. In addition, Plath's loss of trust and fears of betrayal and abandonment are relevant to our appreciation of her poetry in which she transforms these personal feelings into central themes. Thus the deletion of Plath's bitterness and anger toward Ted alters the way that we perceive Plath and read her journals; the deletion serves not only to dismiss, but also to invalidate her anger and her right to *express* it, even posthumously. In reality, anger often motivated her. In the published journal, for instance, she writes, "Fury jams the gullet and spreads poison, but, as soon as I start to write, dissipates, flows out into the figure of the letters: writing as therapy?" Moreover, as the "Ariel" poems illustrate, Plath needed to express her anger in order to write without inhibition and to liberate her own voice. Plath's self-professed powerlessness in life, ironically, persists in death as well. The cuts in this autograph suggest that the editors allowed personal reasons to influence their editorial decision here, and it is likely that personal reasons also influenced their editing of the Smith Journal (1950-1953) manuscript.

Oddly, the working typescript of the next journal (December 12, 1958-November 15, 1959) contains proposed omissions which are often ignored and reproduced in the published edition. Upon first inspection of the suggested omissions, it appears that one of the editors suggests the cuts in order to protect people: there are name changes, suggested deletions of references to prominent writers and to Plath's mother and her spouse. Plath expressed her hatred of her mother and jealousy of—and competition with—her brother. She also discusses her feeling of being unloved by her mother and her anguish over the loss of her father. In addition, she discusses how these feelings, not her rejection from Frank O'Connor's writing course (as her mother suggests), were the underlying factors behind her suicide attempt.

By and large, these suggested omissions are ignored and faithfully reproduced in a section which covers Plath's psychoanalysis and work with her therapist, Dr. Ruth Beuscher, in the "Boston 1958-1959" section of the published text. Here Plath acknowledges her fears of being barren and considers how, if this is true, this will affect Ted. There is also a suggested (but ignored) cut in which Plath discusses one of Ted's stories. She reveals her admiration of the story and offers critical suggestions about how he might edit it. The fact that the proposed cuts were largely ignored suggests that there was a conflict between editors regarding editorial principles and that the person who wished to make the cuts was allowing personal feelings to influence editorial decisions.

In a 1962 typescript, there are twenty-nine pages in which Plath keeps "Notes on Neighbours" in North Devon (including her description of Rose and Percy B and Charlie Pollard). But the editors omit Plath's moving and unusually frank description of her labour and delivery of her son, Nicholas. This omission is important because it shows that the editors have reconstructed Plath to suit their own image of her and, in so doing, that they have deprived her of the right to express her feelings. They have also prevented the reader from seeing that Plath did strip away her masks and reveal her true feelings in her journals alone (these masks remain in *Letters Home*).

In this entry, Plath describes her sense of loss of control while in labour. She feels as though she is being controlled and possessed by a "black force" (the baby) and records her initial feeling of alienation after the delivery: "I felt no surge of love." In *Letters Home,* Plath constructs a completely different picture of her labour and delivery for her mother:

> Then at 5 minutes to 12, as the doctor was on his way over, this great bluish, glistening boy shot out into the bed in a tidal wave of water that drenched all four of us to the skin, howling lustily. It was an amazing sight. I *immediately sat up and felt wonderful—no tears, nothing.* (emphasis mine)

From the reading of Plath's journal account, one can see that Plath revised her own feelings in letters to others, yet expressed them in the journals.

Plath used her feelings and experiences during her labour and delivery as recorded in the journals for her radio poem, "*Three Women:* A Poem for Three Voices." In this poem, Plath describes three women and their ambivalent feelings about their about-to-be-born child. She portrays their feelings of loss of control and alienation. One woman has a son, one miscarries, and the one has a daughter whom she chooses to abandon. The third woman perceives the birth of the child as a form of self-annihilation: "I should have murdered this, that murders me," while the second woman perceives herself as "a heroine of the peripheral." Even the first woman has moments of apprehension in which she fears the vulnerability of love and the parental responsibility: "It is a terrible thing / To be so open: it is as if my heart / Put on a face and walked into the world."

As Wendy Owen suggests [in her dissertation " 'A Riddle in Nine Syllables': Female Creativity in the Poetry of Sylvia Plath," Yale University, 1985], Plath's portrait of the pregnant woman is another area in which she explores her own conflicts about her role in the creative process:

> Like most women coming of age in the 1950's, Plath must have felt tremendous pressure to bear a child. To be pregnant would be to prove visibly that she had fulfilled one of femininity's most important requirements. On the other hand, Plath expresses fear that having a child, even being pregnant, will take from her the time, energy and concentration she needs for her writing. Plath seemed to know that her writing, however painful and unsatisfying at times, was essential to her well-being. And so she continually struggled with her identity as Earth Mother and her identity as a poet. (. . .) The pregnant woman is yet another arena in which Plath plays out her contradictory sense of self as a creator.

Plath's divergent accounts of her labour and delivery reveal her conflict between her need to write honestly and her desire to please and protect her mother, a conflict that is nullified by the editors of her journal.

The most blatant distortion in the published journals is that created by the omission of intimacies which "have the effect of diminishing Plath's eroticism." The majority of the omissions in the Smith Journal (1950-1953) are in this area. Almost all of Plath's entries about men are deleted except those about Ted Hughes, the Norton brothers, and select references to some of the dates she had at Smith. Yet even these are condensed so much that the reader of the published journals does not see Plath's pervasive sensuality and eroticism. The original manuscript also leaves the reader with a much stronger sense of the social pressures she experienced as a young woman at an all-women's college in the fifties. For Plath, the entries in which she expresses her sensuality are, like the rest of her journal, significant because she saw these experiences as raw material for her writing. In an entry which is omitted from the published journal, Plath writes, "Perhaps someday I'll crawl back home, beaten, defeated. But not as long as I can make stories out of my heartbreak, beauty out of my sorrow." These entries are also important because they show that she struggles not only to define herself within her romantic relationships but also, paradoxically, to assert her independence and individuality with her writing.

Throughout her journals, Plath struggles between societal and cultural expectations of women as nurturers who place the needs of others first and her personal ambitions to write—to assert her own needs and individuality. Her greatest fear is that her own goals will become subordinate to, and hence dissolved in, those of her prospective spouse. In an early entry which is omitted in the published journal, Plath analyzes her fear of intimacy and unwittingly foreshadows her later separation and divorce from Ted Hughes: "I can only end up with one, and I must leave many lonely by the wayside. So that is all for now. Perhaps someday someone will leave me by the wayside. And that will be poetic justice.—"

In the foreword to the published journals, Hughes stresses the value that Plath's journals have as an autobiography which records her internal struggles:

> This is where her journals demonstrate their difference in kind from all her other writings. Here she set down her day to day struggle with her warring selves, *for herself only.* This is her autobiography, far from complete, but complex and accurate, where *she strove to see herself honestly and fought her way through the unmaking and remaking of herself.* And the Sylvia Plath we can divine here is the closest we can now get to the real person in her daily life. (emphasis mine) [In an endnote, the critic states: "I do not believe that Plath, or any journal writer, wrote for herself only. Even if she did not consciously consider the eventuality of a reader, the very act of expressing her ideas on paper meant that there was the possibility that, as Gaskell argues, someone at some point in time would read them. By deleting and editing much of Plath's anger and sensuality, the editors prevent the reader from seeing Plath's authentic voice and self."]

Herein lies another contradiction in the application of editorial principles, because if the editors present Plath's manuscript as autobiography—that is, as a record of her vision of herself—then editorial omissions will misrepresent and distort Plath's testimony by providing the reader with only a partial, incomplete portrait. [In an endnote, the critic adds: "Autobiography, I contend, is distinct from the journal because it is a more selective and self-conscious form. The author is more conscious of the reader and selectively crafts the picture of herself that she wants the reader to see. The less structured and defined journal form, on the other hand, enables the writer to explore different aspects of herself and different modes of expression. Moreover, a journal has the illusion of privacy which enables the writer to dismiss the idea of a reader from her conscious thought when actively writing."]

The omissions in the Smith Journal (1950-1953) adversely affect our reading of Plath's journals by altering the physical structure as well as the content of her manuscript. In reading the published edition, the reader lacks any sense of the physical format of the original Smith manuscript. Plath wrote in a black hard-bound volume, labelled "LAW NOTES" on the spine, which has lined and numbered pages with a vertical line a third of the way across from the left side. The physical format of a journal often affects the way an author writes. In Plath's case, the hard-bound pages might be seen to suggest permanence. Unlike a loose leaf notebook, bound pages are not meant to be removed. Plath did not rip out any pages and only occasionally crossed out what she wrote. This physical format, then lends itself to a structured, well-thought-out style of writing. However, the physical size and weight of the book would have proved cumbersome and the numerous fragments of writing on memorandum paper and scrap paper housed in the Smith collection suggest that Plath did not always carry this book with her. Hence, this book was more conducive to reflective, premeditated writing than to spontaneous, fleeting impressions.

Unlike many journal writers, Plath rarely dates her entries, but instead numbers each one in the upper left-hand side. Moreover, she does not restrict herself to the pre-set pagination. At times, there are several entries on a page while at other times an entry may be as long as ten or fifteen pages. This method indicates some attempt to organize her thoughts into structurally and thematically unified entries. Each entry often has a theme and a unified beginning, middle, and end. Plath presents a theme, expands on it, and returns to her theme in the closure—much like the structure of a formal essay. Frequently, the following entry expands to a point made in the preceding entry and this linkage continues until she has explored as many different aspects of the theme as possible. The editors, by omitting the numbers of the entries, prevent the reader from seeing the evolution of Plath's ideas. By deleting the beginning paragraph of the entry and making subsequent cuts throughout, the editors make Plath's writing appear fragmented and disjointed.

In the editorial commentary prior to the section they entitle "Northampton," the editors acknowledge that the omissions alter the narrative:

> In September of 1950 Plath entered her freshman year at Smith College with several scholarships. Entries from this period in the journal are not dated, and in any *case so many cuts have been made in the text that the reader should not be encouraged to attempt to read these excerpts in a close narrative way, but rather thematically.* While Plath was under extreme pressure to perform scholastically, in order to keep her scholarships and to maintain her own high academic standards, she felt an equal pressure to be ac-

> cepted socially, especially with men, and *a great passion for her own creative work—poems and stories.* (emphasis mine)

A more accurate title of their published edition would be *Extracts of the Journals of Sylvia Plath.*

The original Smith Journal (1950-1953) and subsequent journals show the extent to which Plath was committed to her writing. While the Smith Journal (1950-1953) is not a writer's notebook in the same way that some of her later journals are, it is important insofar as Plath kept numbered entries in which she formally structured her ideas. By omitting these numbered entries and altering the structure of her entries, the published journals prevent the reader from seeing this important function of Plath's Smith Journal (1950-1953). Plath uses her journals as a preparation for her real writing. It is a place in which she practises her writing and retrieves her authentic self.

At times, the journals convey Plath's immaturity and naïveté, but this, too, is relevant because it reminds the reader that Plath wrote this journal when she was a young woman. Further, it serves to highlight those other parts of her journal in which she often expresses a wisdom and perceptiveness far beyond her years. For a woman in the 1950's to express her sensuality so openly, even in the relative privacy of a journal, is in itself remarkable. What also emerges in this journal is Plath's perpetual conflict between her desire to express her sensuality and passion openly, and her need to conform with a society in which such expression was taboo. The primacy of Plath's sensuality proves the extent to which the *published* journals have influenced Plath scholarship. This may account for why so few critics have examined this aspect of her poetry.

The published journals, then, are not Plath's own. The predominant impression that the published journals give is that Plath is a self-preoccupied, driven woman and writer. Although there is some truth in this assessment, it is only a partial truth. What the published journals do not show is the extent to which passion—both in terms of her sexuality and her creativity—and anger fuel her writing. The omissions distort the original manuscripts and typescripts because they give no indication of the frequency of which, or the context in which, she expresses her creativity and feelings, and thereby minimize the central roles that these aspects of her personality play in her life and her writing.

The omissions in the published edition of the journals thus produce a biased picture of Plath's professional and personal development. This is not to say that a reader must know Plath's personal history in order to appreciate and understand her poetry, although such knowledge is certainly useful. But the voicing of both personal and creative passions is essential to an autobiography of a writer, which is what the editors purport to present. And if an autobiography is to be valid, then it must be the writer's, not the editors', version of her life. Once it becomes the editors', it ceases to be autobiography and becomes biography. And indeed, McCullough and Hughes cross this generic boundary, without acknowledging that they do so. Ironically, the poet's self-revelation in her journals has been transformed into yet another disguise, providing the public with yet another mask of Sylvia Plath.

Ian Hamilton (essay date 1992)

SOURCE: "Provisional Posterities: Sylvia Plath and Philip Larkin," in *Keepers of the Flame: Literary Estates and the Rise of Biography,* Hutchinson, 1992, pp. 291-310.

[*Hamilton is an English poet, biographer, critic, and editor. His biographies include* Robert Lowell: A Biography *(1982) and* In Search of J. D. Salinger *(1988). In the following excerpt, he traces the history of Plath's biographies from her death in 1963 to the present and examines how Hughes's role developed as Plath's reputation grew and changed.*]

For literary keepers of the flame, the Copyright Act of 1911 represented a significant upgrading, an access of power. Under the new law, an author's legatee had fifty years' control of published work, together with perpetual ownership of any writings which remained unpublished at the author's death. Keepers could look forward to a lifetime's reign, a lifetime's proceeds. With fifty years in view, their sense of having a double duty—to respect the dead and to maximise the takings—was bound to seem both more delicate and weightier than under the old rules. Obedience to what the lost loved one 'would have wished' might not always turn out to be good for business.

But then, as we have seen, that obedience had always been elastic. Most readily lauded among keepers of the flame is Max Brod, who defied Franz Kafka's instruction that 'Everything I leave behind me . . . is to be burned unread even to the last page.' Most often vilified is Spencer Curtis Brown, who scorned Somerset Maugham's not dissimilar decree: 'I direct that there shall be no biography or publication of my letters and that my literary executor and trustees are to refuse permission for such publication and any assistance to any person who wishes or attempts such publication.' Max Brod, of course, saved Kafka's now-celebrated novels from the fire; Curtis Brown merely sanctioned a biography: 'Many people may think I have acted wrongly,' he said. 'Only one man could have given me a clear decision, and he was the man who had sufficient confidence in me to place his reputation in my hands.'

Brod's defence, which no one pressed him for, was that when Kafka made his 'will'—actually a note addressed to Brod—he was in one of his depressions (his 'self-critical tendencies had reached their peak') and in any case he had been warned that his instructions would be disobeyed: 'Franz knew that my refusal was in earnest, and at the end, if he had still intended these wishes to be carried out, he would have appointed another executor.' Curtis Brown's defence, which few seem to have quite swallowed, was that 'when Maugham made this stipulation and when I accepted it, neither of us could foresee how many books would be written about him. Some were written with great responsibility, some with apparent lack of it. But even the most conscientious have been unable, for lack of access to the material, to give a true picture of his final tragic years.' Curtis Brown's own 'true picture' of those final years was that the author of *Cakes and Ale* had turned into a fairly poisonous old toad. The sanctioned biography, by Ted Morgan, was strongly supportive of this view.

George Orwell was another who said he wanted no biography, and there are now two 'authorised' versions of his Life, the second of these none too admiring of the dead widow who had authorised and then disowned the first. W. H. Auden asked his executor Edward Mendelson to assist in 'making a biography impossible'. 'Biographies are always superfluous and usually in bad taste,' he used to say, and when he died the estate published his request that friends should destroy any letters they had had from him: how many of them did we'll never know, but in any case by that date—1973—most of Auden's correspondence had found its way into the libraries. Auden did not, however, formally veto a biography. After some head-scratching, Mendelson decided that his instructions were 'flexible enough to be bent backwards'. As with Maugham, the executor contended that his hand was forced by a flood of unofficial memoirs. And Auden, the compulsive aphorist, came to his aid: 'What every author hopes to receive from posterity—a hope usually disappointed—is justice.'

T. S. Eliot added a memorandum to his will: 'I do not wish my executors to facilitate or countenance the writing of a biography of me.' His widow Valerie has done what she was told, or asked: she has not sanctioned a biography and her gradual and meticulous unveiling of the poet's letters has made it difficult for unauthorised enquirers to make headway. And yet it is not at all certain that her husband would have approved her publication of his *Waste Land* drafts. And what about the song 'Memory' in *Cats?* 'Memory', says the sleevenote of the *Cats* LP, 'includes lines from and suggested by "Rhapsody on a Windy Night" ' together with 'additional material by Trevor Nunn'. Eliot loved the music-hall, we know, and he hungered for theatrical success, but a taste for Marie Lloyd does not necessarily betoken a taste for Andrew Lloyd Webber. Scholars who have had trouble with the Eliot estate on the matter of permissions might well go a bit sulky when they hear Grizabella mew about those 'burnt out ends of smoky days, the stale cold smell of morning / A street lamp dies, another night is over, another day is dawning.'

The Eliot estate is still a so-called 'live' estate, and will remain so until 2015. Until that date, if Mrs Eliot holds to the no-biography ruling, critics will have trouble reading the Eliot life into the Eliot work, and vice versa. When Peter Ackroyd wrote his unsanctioned biography of Eliot in 1984, he was refused permission to quote from the poet's published work, 'except for purposes of fair comment in a critical context'—which is what the law allows. If he had wished to trace in detail the imprint on Eliot's verse of, say, his terrible first marriage, he would have been obliged to tread with feline stealth: a line here, a couple of lines there, with lashings of critical fair comment. As it was, he made no effort to get round the ruling; he merely put up a few signposts, as in: 'The image of a man who believes himself to have committed a crime, and the notion of a secret which leads to guilt and feelings of worthlessness, are significant aspects of [Eliot's] later drama.' Of course, with Eliot, the biographer was fairly certain that his signposts could be followed, that readers knew the work or had it readily to hand. Ackroyd in truth was not much inhibited by the quotation ban: he claimed that it helped him to tell his tale more crisply. It might have been different if the subject had been a fiction writer of large output and small fame.

It might have been different too if Eliot had been like Sylvia Plath and had 'deliberately used the details of [his] everyday life as raw material for art'. Of Plath's case, A. Alvarez has observed:

> A casual visitor or unexpected telephone call, a cut, a bruise, a kitchen bowl, a candlestick, everything became usable, charged with meaning, transformed. Her poems are full of references and images which seem impenetrable at this distance but which could mostly be explained by a scholar with full access to the details of her life.

Arguments about what is or should be meant by 'full access' to the details of Sylvia Plath's life have been on the go for the past twenty-five years, and are raging even now. When she committed suicide in 1963, not much was known about her life *or* work. She had published one book of poems, *The Colossus,* a pseudonymous novel, *The Bell Jar,* and she was married to Ted Hughes, a well-known poet from whom she seemed to have learned plenty. The poems that would shortly make her name were written during the last two years of her life; some of them, the most spectacular, during the last weeks. On the Sunday after Plath's death, Alvarez printed an obituary notice in *The Observer,* together with four poems. The impact was immediate, and eerie. In one poem, 'Edge', a woman imag-

Sylvia Plath.

ines her own suicide: 'The woman is perfected / Her dead / Body wears the smile of accomplishment.' In another, 'The Fearful':

> This woman on the telephone
> Says she is a man, not a woman.
>
> The mask increases, eats the worm,
> Stripes for mouth and eyes and nose,
>
> The voice of the woman hollows—
> More and more like a dead one,
>
> Worms in the glottal stops.

Read alongside a terse announcement of Plath's death, at the age of thirty-one, the lines seemed to insist on an inquisitive response: 'How?', 'Why?' and 'Who?'

It was not until the late 1960s that these questions were brought up in public. The appearance of *Ariel* in 1965 made it possible, indeed necessary, to make mention of the suicide. Most critics settled for respectful talk about the price Sylvia Plath had had to pay, the 'sacrifice' she had made in order to achieve this last 'blood jet' of brilliantly angry and despairing verse. There was also much emphasis on the so-called 'public' dimension of the poems. Plath's rather modishly dragged-in references to Nazi concentration camps were grasped at as evidence of imaginative courage: 'Sylvia Plath *became* a woman being transported to Auschwitz on the death-trains,' wrote George Steiner. When 'Daddy' was discussed, there was no problem about explaining why Plath imagined her dead father as a Nazi, but there were other bits of the poem which at this stage had to be ignored:

> I made a model of you,
> A man in black with a Meinkampf look
>
> And a love of the rack and the screw,
> And I said I do, I do.

Sylvia Plath died intestate, and Ted Hughes inherited her copyrights. The couple had separated a few months before she died, and not amicably, but they had not divorced. There were two young children of the marriage. Hughes's inheritance was scarcely to be envied. There was a great mass of unpublished writing, principally journals and poems, and not all of it, in his view, deserved to be kept. One of the journals, covering the last weeks of her life, he at once elected to destroy: 'because I did not want the children to see it.' And he may well have felt tempted to deal similarly with certain of the poems. During her last months, much of his wife's creative fury had been aimed at *him.* As executor, he was now required to publicise insults and accusations to which he could make no dignified riposte: how do you *reply* to a good poem—by pointing out that it exaggerates, tells lies?

When Hughes came to assemble the manuscript of *Ariel,* he decided to present the late work 'cautiously'; he 'omitted some of the more personally aggressive poems from 1962, and might have omitted one or two more if she had not already published them in magazines'. (The omitted poems appeared in 1971, in *Winter Trees.*) His policy, it seemed, would be one of gradual disclosure. At the time no one complained. In 1969, he appointed a biographer, Lois Ames, and 'undertook to help her exclusively in the usual way (to give her his own records and recollections, make available Sylvia's diaries, notebooks, correspondence, manuscripts, etc. and to request family and friends to give their full cooperation)'. Contracts were drawn up with publishers in the UK and US, stipulating delivery by 1975. Ames's agreement with Hughes granted her 'exclusive help until December 1977'.

How Lois Ames might have performed we can but guess, for she did not deliver. Over the years her research 'slowed to a standstill'. In the meantime, though, the exclusivity clause could be used to deter other would-be investigators. By the end of the 1960s, there was a burgeoning Plath cult and Hughes began to look to his defences, to exhibit a certain touchiness on the matter of how to 'interpret' his wife's death. He did not seem to mind the event being glorified by the likes of Anne Sexton: 'We talked death with burned-up intensity, both of us drawn to it like moths to an electric light bulb. Sucking on it!' But when the Leavisite critic David Holbrook contended, in 1968, that some of the *Ariel* poems might set a bad example to the young, the estate refused him permission to make quotations from her work. The objection was to Holbrook's use of the terms 'schizoid' and 'insane'. Olwyn Hughes, Ted's sister and by now acting as literary agent to the Plath estate, explained that Holbrook's theories 'seriously misrepresented' the dead poet 'as an individual and as an artist'. Holbrook manfully struck back:

> It may be that in public debate my readers will decide that I am as poor a literary critic as Miss Hughes says I am. But she is still trying to suppress the debate altogether, which is my point. Her implication that an author's agent has the right to decide whether or not a work is good enough as *criticism* to allow copyright permission for it to be published is, I suggest, quite unacceptable to the world of scholarship and letters.

Because Holbrook was constantly writing letters to the newspapers about this or that sickness in the culture, nobody rallied to his aid. But even his worst enemies could see that he did have a point.

Three years later, the estate was at it again, and this time the offender was none other than Alvarez, Plath's first, most influential champion. Of Holbrook, Olwyn Hughes complained that he 'never knew Sylvia Plath in her lifetime'. Alvarez's offence, it soon transpired, was that he did. In 1971, he published a study of suicide, *The Savage God,* in which he gave an account of his relationship with Plath. During her last months, she had from time to time visited him at his London flat, often bearing new poems, which she read aloud to him. A critic's nightmare, one might think, but in this case Alvarez was bewitched. Plath's poems seemed to him an extraordinary vindication of his own critical position. He had lately ridiculed the 'gentility principle' that vitiated most current English verse and had called for a new poetry of psychic risk: the risk was that by voyaging in search of their 'unquiet buried selves' artists might indeed go mad, or die, or both. As he saw it, Plath's was an accidental death; she gambled, and she lost. 'She had always been a bit of a gambler, used to taking risks. The authority of her poetry was in part due to her brave persistence in following the thread of her inspiration right down to the Minotaur's lair.'

In terms of biography, of circumstantial reportage, the memoir was highly reticent: Hughes was a friend. Alvarez knew that the marriage had ended because of Hughes's involvement with another woman, but he said nothing of this; there had, he implied, been merely a collision of two giant talents. It was a surprise, therefore, when—on the appearance in *The Observer* of an extract from *The Savage God* (the first of two, it was announced)—there was an outcry from the Plath estate. Ted Hughes wanted the serialisation stopped, he said, because the memoir had been 'written and published without my having been consulted in any way'. He objected to Alvarez's 'misremembering' of private conversations they had had:

> Mr Alvarez's main *trouvé* is that Sylvia Plath 'gambled' with her death and he uses this to drag her in as an example in close-up, an unusual type of suicide who happened to be his friend (and only incidentally as the now very public poet) to fill the longest and most sensational chapter in his general history of suicide. This particular fantasy of her gamble was, in fact, a notion of mine, which haunted me at the time, and which I aired to him, even though it went against the findings of the coroner, and against other details which I imparted to no one.
>
> His facts are material for fiction, second-hand scraps, glimpses and half-experiences, resurfacing after seven years, imaginatively reshaped and acceptably explained to the author. They have nothing to do with the truth of an event far more important to Sylvia Plath's family than to Mr Alvarez or any of his readers.

It was in order to protect Plath's family, the adult members now and 'her children throughout their future' that he wanted the memoir withdrawn 'from any wider circulation'. *The Observer* cancelled the second extract. Replying to Hughes, Alvarez sounded genuinely hurt and baffled. He could understand Hughes's instinct to defend 'his privacy and that of his children', and he was also aware that the 'authorised version of Sylvia's last months will appear in the official biography' but 'I see no reason why this should stand in the way of an account by another person who was also involved—though, God knows, not very willingly—in the affair.' And as to not having checked it out with Hughes: 'I was not writing a memoir of him: I was writing about Sylvia Plath.'

Alvarez had reason to be puzzled: what *was* it that had got up Hughes's nose? The 'risk' theory might be wrong, but it was just a theory. Robert Lowell, six years before, had written: 'These poems are playing Russian roulette with six cartridges in the cylinder, a game of "Chicken", the wheels of both cars locked and unable to swerve.' This was the preface to the American edition of *Ariel,* which Hughes himself had ushered into print. But Lowell was Lowell, and he had been careful to say 'these poems' and not 'she'. And his only personal recollection of Plath was of her attending one of his Boston University poetry classes in the 1950s, when—he had to admit—she had made more impression than the poems, which somehow never 'sank very deep into my awareness'. He also said nothing about Hughes. Alvarez, on the other hand, had in his memoir attempted to distinguish the Hughes style of self-exploration from that of his wife. The rustic Hughes, it was suggested, lived more familiarly with his dark gods than she could. 'Her intensity was of the nerves, something urban.' Hughes, although as worldly as the next man when he wished to be, was genuinely *primitivo;* he 'had never properly been civilised or had, at least, never properly believed in his civilisation'. But could the author of the blood-drenched *Crow* (1970) seriously object to being thought of as possessing 'a quality of threat beneath his shrewd, laconic manner', 'some dark side of the self which had nothing to do with the young literary man'?

Alvarez's memoir was probably Hughes's first experience of what was to become for him a lifetime's horror. From now on, he was able to perceive, the Plath biography would need to appropriate at least one chapter from the biography of Hughes. Anybody who took an interest in her life could claim the right to poke about in his. Hughes, by all accounts, was a taciturn personality, pre-Plath. There is no evidence that he had any taste for the confessional. His poetry, for all its love of violence, tended to be void of personality. Oddly enough, the best way of getting any near-intimate sense of what he might be like was to consult the verses and stories that he wrote for children.

It was not until the early 1970s that Sylvia Plath became a celebrity in the commercial book world. A rough check of her bibliography shows that about four-fifths of all recorded writings on her—aside from book reviews—was done in that decade. In 1970, *The Bell Jar* was published in the United States and it launched her into stardom. Plath herself once described her first novel as a 'potboiler' and it was turned down in the 1960s by Harper and Row, its 1970 publisher. But with *Ariel* and the suicide behind it, so to speak, this thin study of late-adolescent breakdown was an immediate bestseller, a campus cult, a movie, and so on. And as the women's movement got into its stride, Plath was assimilated to the ideology. Articles with titles like 'Reading Women's Poetry: the Meaning and our Lives' or 'Male Authority and Female Identity in Sylvia Plath' began appearing in the journals. Post-graduate theses were embarked on: 'The Woman as Hero', 'The Quest for Self', 'Power and Vulnerability in the Poetry of Sylvia Plath'. The girl who won the *Mademoiselle* fiction prize in 1951 was in 1972 up for 'reconsideration' in the inaugural issue of *Ms.* magazine. And as Plath was reconsidered, so was Hughes. Under feminist scrutiny, he was found to epitomise 'the enemy, the monster who had all but murdered her'.

Post-1970, then, Hughes's relationship with the 'audience' was forced to undergo a change. Because of his wife's death, the manner of it, and because of her posthumous literary fame, he now had to justify his privateness. For the poet Hughes there could be not much subtlety of interaction between artist and inquisitor. If he were to burn his own diaries in a fit of privacy, he would surely be accused of interfering with Plath Studies. And the situation was for him further complicated by his knowledge that Plath was an eloquent distortionist; she was very good at making her enemies look bad. Her friends too: she used to describe Ted Hughes adoringly as a 'colossus', 'a large hulking healthy Adam . . . with a voice like the thunder of God', 'a huge Goliath'—praise for which he would later have to pay. She made things up, played roles and put on masks:

> Some were camouflage cliché façades, defensive mechanisms, involuntary. And some were deliberate poses, attempts to find the key to one style or another. They were the visible faces of her lesser selves, her false or provisional selves, the minor roles of her inner drama. Though I spent every day with her for six years, and was rarely separated from her for more than two or three hours at a time, I never saw her show her real self to anybody—except, perhaps, in the last three months of her life.

Hughes believed that he knew Plath, or knew the several Plaths—lesser, provisional and real—better than anyone else could. Her death, and the anger that went into it, the death-poems, ought to be understood as a drama of 're-birth', a destroying of fabricated selves and a breaking through into the 'real'.

Hughes would no doubt have preferred to keep Plath Studies at this level of abstraction. The hate-objects in *Ariel* and *Winter Trees* were often male, admittedly, but they were male-*figures,* archetypes, not individual chaps. For Plath to become 'real' in those last months, she had to conquer and destroy the psychic tyranny of those male-gods who had controlled her lesser lives. Did it matter who, in actuality, they were? A father, a lover, a merging or confusing of the two: this was the radical configuration. When it came to studying the verse, the important evidence was already on display, and if the evidence was justly scrutinised, Plath's fear and hatred of other women could scarcely be ignored. This is perhaps to travesty Hughes's thinking, but he did seem to believe something of the sort. For instance, Judith Kroll's *Chapters in a Mythology* is one of the few books about Plath that Hughes is known to have admired; Kroll's approach is anti-biographical, heavy with archetypes, and expounds a 'false-selves' thesis that roughly corresponds with his.

Perhaps the early Seventies would have been the right time for Hughes to have applied the brakes. He could have brought out a *Collected Poems* and embargoed all other material for fifty years. With only the poems to go on, his accusers would have been thrown back on speculation and hearsay. But then speculation and hearsay could hurt too, as Hughes was soon to learn. In 1976 a deeply unauthorised biography by Edward Butscher appeared in the United States. Butscher in 1972 had solicited the estate's cooperation and had been rebuffed: the Ames arrangement was invoked. He had persisted, though, and his book leaned heavily on the 'living witness' method of research. The witnesses prepared to speak were, of course, no friends of Hughes. During her last chaotic months, Plath had done a lot of talking: more than one neighbour or acquaintance could boast of having been her special confidante. In an attempt to block the book, the estate refused Butscher permission to quote from Plath's writings, but he and his US publisher ignored the ban, reckoning—correctly—that Hughes would not pursue a transatlantic lawsuit. (Many years later, Hughes had cause to regret not suing Butscher. When a film was made of *The Bell Jar,* a Dr Jane Anderson complained that a lesbian character in it had been based on her: she used Butscher's text as evidence. Hughes was arraigned for having 'failed to control what Mr Butscher wrote about the plaintiff' and the whole affair, he said, 'consumed five years and cost several people—but not Butscher—many hundreds of thousands of dollars'.)

As Sylvia Plath's executor, Hughes had a duty, he believed, 'to permit publication of whatever contributes to a fuller appreciation of the author'. Despite all the peculiar circumstances, the overlaps, the general prejudice, his own loathing of biography ought not to be imposed on her. *Ariel,* he had to acknowledge:

> supplies little of the incidental circumstances or the crucial inner drama that produced it. Maybe it is this very bareness of circumstantial detail that has excited the wilder fantasies projected by others in Sylvia Plath's name. We respond to the speech, that fascinating substance, which is everywhere fully itself, nowhere diluted and ordinary—but we can only discuss it, or communicate our feelings about it, in terms of those externals, the drama of her psychological makeup, the accidents of her life.

There was a money angle too. By the mid-1970s Hughes did not need his sister to tell him that the Plath industry, now at its peak and not guaranteed to last, could provide security for the two children.

Whatever the reasoning, the estate in the end opted for a policy of staged and monitored publication, releasing a bit here, a bit there. First, in 1976, came *Letters Home,* a collection of Sylvia's letters to Aurelia, her mother. Hughes had given Aurelia the copyright of these on condition that he could retain some measure of control. Thus, when reviewers discovered that there were a number of excisions, they rumbled sternly about censorship. It turned out that, although Hughes *had* asked for certain cuts, not all of these were self-defensive. He removed 'some wicked comments about people she knew' and a few of the more 'syrupy' descriptions of himself. The book's editor, Frances McCollough, was 'amazed to see how much he allowed through'. She herself had had the task of cutting the original manuscript by half. The real problem with *Letters Home* was that the letters themselves were almost unreadably affected. They displayed one of the least endearing of Plath's provisional or unreal selves: the chirpy, high-achieving self she kept on tap for mother. Faced with accusations of a Hughes paint-job, McCollough was obliged to spell out what ought to have been obvious: 'Anyone who remembers his own letters home will recognise at once that if there is a censor's hand at work here, it is the daughter's, not the mother's.'

The estate itself was less level-toned in its response to the reviews of *Letters Home,* possibly because the book's publication coincided with the 'illegal' Butscher Life: the two volumes were being noticed side by side. When Karl Miller, in the *New York Review of Books,* expressed what might to most readers have seemed a decent sympathy for Hughes's plight, Olwyn Hughes accused him of writing 'in guise of indignation on my brother's behalf'. Miller's crime was that he had given more space to Butscher's 'patently rubbishy hotch-potch' than to the near-official *Letters Home.* A belligerence was in the air and Olwyn was beginning to make a name for herself. As Hughes retreated into a volcanic silence, his sister could be found outfront, mixing it with the 'libbers' and the ghouls, 'who treat Sylvia Plath's family as though they are characters in some work of fiction, or a hundred years dead, and proper subjects for speculation and academic dissection'.

Since the mid-1970s, there have been further, but not dissimilar outbreaks of controversy. The estate has been criticised for censoring Plath's *Journals,* for delaying the *Collected Poems,* for harassing the feminist biographer Linda Wagner-Martin and for leaning on their own appointee, Anne Stevenson, whose 1989 Life of Plath confessed to being 'almost a work of dual authorship—the co-author being, of course, Olwyn.

The Stevenson biography was a curious affair. As the estate's answer to two decades of misrepresentation, it was always likely to sound somewhat irritably partisan, pro-Hughes, and perhaps if Hughes himself had chosen this opportunity to have his say, the book might have had a more cordial reception. As it was, he distanced himself from the whole enterprise ('Hughes asked me to address all questions relating to his personal life to Olwyn,' Stevenson recalls), and his sister seized the reins. So eager was Olwyn to ensure that Ted should at last be treated fairly that she strong-armed a large part of the biography into an appearance of ill-natured bias, and in the process made Stevenson seem got at and confused—one minute thanking Olwyn for her help, the next complaining that her own input had been 'olwynized', and all in all coming to regret the whole assignment: 'It was clear to me at a very early stage that Olwyn Hughes badly needed to tell her side of Sylvia's story. It was a side no one as yet had heard, chiefly because no one would listen.'

The message of Anne Stevenson's *Bitter Fame* could not in truth have been delivered in person by Ted Hughes: the narrative suggests that only a man of the most saintly temperament could have lived with the devil-woman Plath for twenty-four hours, let alone six years. In the end, after many a wearying explosion, even the ever-patient Hughes had had to get some air. To force such a reading into shape, Plath of course had to be represented at her worst: jealous, success-hungry, manipulative, and—since the childhood loss of her over-adored father—suicidally inclined. She was a victim, to be sure, but not of Hughes, nor of any other dominating male. Her own disordered psyche was to blame. And yet, apart from the poems, there was nothing very heroic about the ways in which she tried to cope with her affliction. Most of the time, she had come over as petty, mean-minded, self-absorbed, a rather shrill and nasty bore. The book reeked of exasperation, and thus rather played into the hands of hostile Plathologists, those commentators who had now and then felt the rough edge of Olwyn's tongue and had retaliated by building small careers out of policing the estate.

In the year of Stevenson's biography, Ted Hughes was obliged to emerge from his burrow to answer charges that really could not be ignored: (a) that his first wife's grave lay derelict and unmarked in a remote Yorkshire churchyard and (b) that on the night of her funeral he had attended a 'highspirited and boisterous party with bongo drums'. In the latter case, Hughes had recourse to the law, and was thus branded as a bully-litigant: the bongo-party anecdote had been dredged from the faulty memory of a near-penniless 82-year-old. On the matter of the grave, he wrote letters to the press, explaining that the headstone, having been regularly vandalised by feminists who objected to the inscription 'Sylvia Plath Hughes', was in the repair shop of a local mason: 'I asked him to give it another go. If he has not yet done so, I'm sure I agree with him that there is no hurry.'

Hughes's account of his trial-by-gravestone was restrained enough, and rather touching. He had originally wanted to put the legal name Sylvia Hughes on the memorial but had then added the Plath because 'I knew well enough in 1963 what she had brought off in that name, and I wished to honour it. That was the beginning and end of my thoughts about the name.' Then came the desecrations: riveted lead letters were levered off the stone, restored, and then removed again—three times. Even the shells and beach pebbles he had placed about the plot were carried off. Small wonder that he now 'simply wished to preserve for a while longer something of the private remnant valued by her living family'. To judge from these letters, Hughes was tired of the whole carry-on, but there was also an anger to be felt, an anger that had been building up over the twenty-five years in which he served as keeper of the Plath inheritance; an inheritance which had come to him but was not really his:

> In the years soon after her death, when scholars approached me, I tried to take their apparently serious concern for the truth about Sylvia Plath seriously. But I learned my lesson early. The honourable few who have justified my trust have been few indeed. With others, if I tried too hard to tell them exactly how something happened, in the hope of correcting some fantasy, I was quite likely to be accused of trying to suppress Free Speech. In general, my refusal to have anything to do with the Plath Fantasia has been regarded as an attempt to suppress Free Speech. Where my correction was accepted, it rarely displaced a fantasy. More often, it was added to the repertoire, as a variant hypothesis. It would then become itself a source of new speculations which sooner or later, somewhere or other, would be preferred to it. The truth simply tends to produce more lies. . . .
>
> A rational observer might conclude (correctly in my opinion) that the Fantasia about Sylvia Plath is more needed than the facts. Where that leaves respect for the truth of her life (and mine) or for her memory, or for literary tradition, I do not know.

James Atlas (essay date 12 December 1993)

SOURCE: "The Biographer and the Murderer," in *The New York Times Magazine,* December 12, 1993, pp. 74-5.

[*Atlas is an American poet, biographer, and critic. At the time this article was published, he was at work on a biography of Saul Bellow. In the following essay, he discusses the changing nature of biography, contending that current books, including* The Silent Woman, *tend to revel more in scandalous details than serious scholarship.*]

Biography is getting bad press these days. A "lowly trade," Martin Amis pronounced it, reviewing Andrew Motion's biography of Philip Larkin. "Something horrid has recently befallen the craft of biography," lamented Arthur M. Schlesinger Jr. in *The New Republic,* deploring the glut of gossipy new lives on the market. Joyce Carol Oates even coined a word to describe the genre: *pathography*—biographies that revel in "dysfunction and disaster, illnesses and pratfalls, failed marriages and failed careers, alcoholism and breakdowns and outrageous conduct."

Now biographers themselves have joined the chorus. "Biography as a form has become the revenge of little people on big people," noted Edmund White, the biographer of Jean Genet, in *The New York Times Book Review* a few weeks ago.

How mild even these objurgations seem in the wake of *The Silent Woman,* Janet Malcolm's book-length anatomy of Sylvia Plath and her biographers in *The New Yorker*—the first salvo in what has become a virtual assault against the whole enterprise. Malcolm is not one to tiptoe around her subject; *The Journalist and the Murderer,* her previous book, led off with the now famous declaration that "every journalist who is not too stupid or too full of himself to notice what is going on knows that what he does is morally indefensible." That was just a warm-up; compared with the charges lodged against biographers in her latest diatribe, stupidity and arrogance are venial crimes. Biography is a spurious art, claims Malcolm: the orderly narrative it creates is illusory; the "facts" aren't facts at all, but literary inventions. Worse—and here Malcolm goes in for the kill—the pretense of biographical objectivity conceals a darker purpose. The biographer's real intent is to enact revenge: "The writer, like the murderer, needs a motive."

A biographer's heart sinks. To be linked, even metaphorically, with murder is of a different magnitude of culpability than being accused of moral turpitude.

Of course, one could lay the blame for this depressing indictment on a few bad apples—guys like Joe McGinniss, whose character Malcolm so memorably eviscerated in *The Journalist and the Murderer,* depicting him as a weaselly betrayer of his subjects. Certainly *The Last Brother,* McGinniss's "biography" (it was Michael Kelly, writing in *GQ,* who put quotes around the word) of Ted Kennedy, hasn't done the profession any good. Encrusted with allegations of plagiarism, with a craven author's note that admits thoughts and dialogue were "created" by the author, *The Last Brother* is, even by the standards of celebrity journalism, a sordid spectacle. Joe Klein, reviewing McGinniss's opus in *The New Republic* last month, went Oates one better, calling it an "odiography."

It could be that all this sniping is partly the fault of us biographers. At a recent Harvard conference on biography, three of the conferees quoted the passage from Malcolm's *New Yorker* article in which she compared the biographer to a thief. "It had become a crux," said Phyllis Rose, the author of *Parallel Lives* and one of the quoters. "I was trying to express my sense of my own transgressions as a biographer." There *is* a seedy aspect to the business—Malcolm calls it "busybodyism"—that must trouble the sleep of all but the most thick-skinned biographer. Who among us hasn't looked up from the avid perusal of our subject's private mail and recalled with embarrassment the "publishing scoundrel" in Henry James's *The Aspern Papers,* pawing through the desk of a dead poet's lover in search of their correspondence? We all have a touch of Jeffrey Aspern in us. (Or people think we do: A cartoon in *The New Yorker* shows a man and a woman talking in bed while a rumpled scholar rifles their desk. "Ignore him," the man counsels his mate. "He's the guy who's writing that unauthorized biography of me.")

Janet Malcolm, to her credit, tried to monitor this tendency within herself. Time and again, she confesses to her own complicity in the very process she condemns. "My narrative of Rose has an edge," she writes of her interview with a literary critic, Jacqueline Rose. "My silver-plated scissors are ever at the ready to take snips at her." The writer's treachery is Malcolm's great theme.

The one person she lets off is Ted Hughes, an "electrically attractive man" whose letters are "so deeply, mysteriously moving" as to fill the normally unsentimental Malcolm with feelings of "intense sympathy and affection." Why does she idealize this man she doesn't know? Because Malcolm identifies with him. "I, too, had been attacked in the press," she writes, acknowledging (as she failed to do in *The Journalist and the Murderer*) Jeffrey Masson's headline-making libel suit. "I had been there—on the helpless side of the journalist-subject equation." The connection is hard to miss: Just as Ted Hughes has been mercilessly scrutinized, his private life examined in the court of public opinion, so Janet Malcolm, the defendant in one of the most widely covered trials of our time, now stands exposed to the world. Like Hughes, Malcolm has been—literally—on trial.

All art is a form of autobiography. That Malcolm's work parallels her life doesn't bother me. Indeed, its subjectivity is what makes it such an absorbing read. For all her malevolence, Malcolm is an exciting writer, a mesmerizing stylist whose own voice and sensibility leap off the page. The most interesting character in her narrative is herself. Yet of all the characters in *The Silent Woman,* this is the one who eludes her. She never quite grasps the depth of her own destructive impulses.

For Malcolm, the biographer is a voyeur, a "burglar"—in a word, *bad.* But isn't it possible to be motivated by other, more benign impulses? For instance, the wish to commemorate? Richard Ellmann, in his biography of James Joyce, achieved a considerable feat of imaginative empathy. His Joyce stands before us in all his human qualities, both exalted and base—in all his *goodness* as well as his badness. Ellmann (he was my tutor at Oxford) had a profound affinity with his subject's dual nature. He was as fascinated by Joyce's sympathy for ordinary people, his lack of pretension, as by his taste for pornography. Ellmann's *Joyce* doesn't idealize; neither does it desecrate.

Saul Bellow has often said that a novelist is a reader moved to emulation. So is a biographer. When I undertook to write the biography of Delmore Schwartz, it wasn't to unearth his dirty secrets. No one cared about them, anyway; he was a nearly forgotten figure. I had admired his early poems, so incandescent with promise, and his classic story "In Dreams Begin Responsibilities," published in *Partisan Review* to great acclaim when he was only 24. Three decades later, he died alone in a midtown Manhattan fleabag. What happened in the interval? The work made me curious about the life. "Affection for one leads to interest in the other, the two sentiments tend to join, and the results of affection and interest often illuminate both the fiery clay and the wrought jar"—that was Richard Ellmann's credo.

All biographical narrative, claims Janet Malcolm, is "stale, hashed over, told and retold, dubious, unauthentic, suspect." Memory is "monstrously unreliable," vitiated by "epistemological insecurity." Why is she so adamant on this point? Because if authorial objectivity is a myth—if Malcolm had been tried by a jury of deconstructionists instead of 12 ordinary citizens—she would have been acquitted. But there *are* facts. That Saul Bellow, two weeks after his 21st birthday, officially changed his first name from Solomon provides a clue to the name changes of his characters. Charles Citrine, the hero of *Humboldt's Gift,* was originally Tsitrine; Tommy Wilhelm in *Seize the Day* was born Wilhelm Adler; Dr. Shawmut, the narrator of Bellow's story "Him With His Foot in His Mouth," came from a family named Shamus, "or, even more degrading, Untershamus." Surely this persistent literary theme is clarified by the biographical fact. Why did Solomon become Saul? And why did his two older brothers choose to be called Bellows, adding an s? Was Bellow asserting his independence? Defying his father? The biographer can only speculate. But that speculation is informed by a knowledge of the subject's character—by intuition and research; by *facts.*

Janet Malcolm depicts the biographer as a nosy, intrusive figure, invading his subject's private papers. But isn't there usually some collusion? Samuel Johnson gave more than tacit cooperation to his biographer; he made himself available night after night in the coffee-houses of London, furnished Boswell with correspondence, even read his biographer's notes—in effect sat for his portrait. T. S. Eliot, famous for his reticence, accepted posterity's interest in his life; he wrote a "private paper" about his troubled marriage to Vivienne Haigh-Wood and assumed that his voluminous correspondence with Emily Hale, a schoolteacher with whom he had a long flirtation, would eventually be read. (It's sequestered at Princeton until 2020—but at least it's there.) Even Ted Hughes, whom Malcolm apotheosizes as a saintly poet beset by biographical jackals, is no recluse; over the years, as she herself discloses, he has tirelessly advanced his case in various literary forums. "Why, if he is so keen to own the facts of his life, has he distributed them so freely to the reading public?" Why, indeed?

A piety surrounds this issue. "My father turned down the vast majority of magazines and talk shows that came calling," wrote Janna Malamud Smith, the daughter of Bernard Malamud, in "Where Does a Writer's Family Draw the Line?," an essay in *The New York Times Book Review.* It's true: Bernard Malamud was an intensely private man. "He wanted people to read his books, not about him." Yet one of his most appealing novels, *Dubin's Lives,* is about a biographer—a highly sympathetic figure, one might add. "He loved biographies," the novelist's daughter admits, "read them throughout his life, always underlining, carefully, word by word, the parts that grabbed him." Too bad. There won't be a biography of Malamud—not if his daughter can help it. "If an audience for his fiction persists, my grandchildren might wish to make public Bernard Malamud's private letters and journals," Smith concludes. "I doubt I will." That's her prerogative—which doesn't necessarily mean it was the writer's wish. One day when I was visiting with Malamud in his study, he pulled open a file cabinet and pointed to the papers and letters within, neatly arranged in manila folders. "Someday a person could make something interesting out of this," he said.

B. L. Reid on the nature of biography:

When a biography sets out to produce the shapes and excitements of prose fiction it begins to falsify its own nature and it fails to fulfill its basic function of truthful chronicle, of the ordering of fact within the discipline of time. Certainly biography ought to be well written. I am reminded of Ezra Pound's early fiat: "Poetry ought to be at least as well written as prose." Biography ought to be as well written as a novel; but it should not try to be, or to feel like, a novel. Biography becomes a fine art when it performs superbly within the right limits of its own nature.

Biography should be decently selective rather than drudgingly inclusive: it should spare us the truly trivial. But it should not fear to find certain small things significant: "This Flemish picture," Boswell called his book, accurately and with proper fondness. The biographer should let his material form its own shapes: lives do form patterns, but patterns accumulate one piece at a time. One must be wary of the tempting "high *Priori* road," as Pope calls it: of fitting data into preconceived designs, the temptation to neaten and intensify and thereby to falsify the often disorderly order of time. Biography's strength and its integrity are ones of subject matter, of honorable and tasteful treatment of an interesting subject.

B. L. Reid, in his Necessary Lives: Biographical Reflections, *University of Missouri Press, 1990.*

Richard Holmes, the biographer of Coleridge and Shelley, describes the moment when, having gone to Paris to try his hand at a novel, he came across a photograph of Baudelaire by the 19th-century photographer Nadar: "The old sensations of being drawn into another life began to assail me almost with a sense of fatality." Every biographer has known this moment—the serendipitous discovery of a bundle of letters or a forgotten manuscript that kindles all at once the hope of insight. To recover and bring forth, to preserve against oblivion the documents that give texture to a life, those "fossils of feeling" that Janet Malcolm holds up as the one verifiable artifact of truth—is that such a scurrilous vocation?

Victoria Glendinning (review date 23 October 1994)

SOURCE: "Whose Life Is It Anyway?: Why One Prefers a Biographer of One's Own," in *Los Angeles Times Book Review,* October 23, 1994, pp. 2, 8.

[*Glendinning is an English biographer and novelist whose biographies include* Elizabeth Bowen: Portrait of a Writer *(1977) and* Edith Sitwell: A Unicorn Among Lions *(1981). In the following review of Ian Hamilton's* Keepers of the Flame: Literary Estates and the Rise of Biography *(1992), she recounts how biography has changed through the years as those close to an author have sought to control what is said about that person. She also raises questions about the appropriateness of certain details in biographies and illustrates cases in literary history where opportunism on the part of the living ran rampant.*]

What is posterity? Nothing but "an unending jostle of vanities, appetites and fears," concludes Ian Hamilton at the end of [*Keepers of the Flame,*] a book that is quite surprisingly entertaining and suggestive. One might not suppose that a work subtitled "Literary Estates and the Rise of Biography" would give one cause to laugh aloud, but it does. Hamilton is a British poet, an editor and himself the biographer of Robert Lowell and, notoriously, of J.D. Salinger (well, he tried). For all his scholarship, he writes here with the immediacy, economy and ease of a witty man talking over a bottle of wine.

The "keepers of the flame" are the friends, relations, devotees, literary executors and biographers, in whose hands lies what Hamilton calls the "after-fame" of great writers. We live in an era of copious, candid and some would say intrusive, biography. The questions Hamilton addresses about the history and ethics of the genre were never more topical. "How much should a biographer tell? How much should an executor suppress? And what would the biographee have wanted—do we know?"

He proceeds chronologically, by means of case histories, each marking some change or development in the perceived function of the custodians of greatness. This leads us into the history of publishing and of the law on copyright, into the company of some egregious crooks and creeps, and into some stimulatingly unprovable statements from Hamilton. The poet and priest John Donne (d. 1631), for example, was "the first" important writer to leave a substantial collection of letters, and his no-good son was "the first" to see that there was money to be made from a literary parent's leavings. Edmund Curll, the 18th-Century publisher, was "the first" to cash in on scurrilous instant biographies. Robert Burns was "the first" to have his frailties exposed by a biographer (he drank himself to death). Just occasionally, Hamilton is wrong. He writes that Thackeray's daughter "vetoed all thoughts of a biography," thus fueling speculation about skeletons in cupboards; in fact, she commissioned Trollope to write a book about her father, which he did. Admittedly, she gave him very little material to work on.

The book is full of tasty details about cabinets and laundry baskets of letters and manuscripts falling into greedy hands or being used as wrapping paper for groceries. Keepers of the flame tended to be self-appointed. The poet Andrew Marvell's landlady posed as his wife in order to get money owed to his estate. Sir William Davenant liked it to be thought that he was Shakespeare's illegitimate son. Thomas Hardy had the bright idea of controlling his after-fame by ghosting his own biography, ostensibly authored by his second wife.

The book is free from academic pedantry. Hamilton remarks that Johnson's life of Dryden contains "the funniest and cruelest" of the "many wildly improbable" accounts of Dryden's funeral, quoting none of them, and thus whetting the reader's desire to find out more. Likewise, he writes of William Warburton, the adviser and editor of Alexander Pope, that Pope guided him to a rich wife "and then (via her very rich uncle) to a bishopric and a palatial estate." Most scholars would have ruined their narrative flow by dutifully identifying, if only in a footnote, the "very rich uncle."

Not Ian Hamilton. His pace and semi-satirical tone extract the maximum entertainment value from pompous literary mayhem. He writes with informed malice about the frequent rivalry between a dead author's self-aggrandizing "best friends" as to who is the true keeper of the flame. Disciples are often catty about co-disciples. One reviewer of *The Life of Dickens* by his friend and champion John Forster complained that it "should not be called *The Life of Dickens* but *The History of Dickens' Relations to Mr. Forster.*" Yet Forster was cavalier about his hero's materials. He chopped extracts out of Dickens' letters (discarding the tattered remains) and pasted them into his manuscript, which was thrown away afterward by the printers. Boswell was the most successful flame-keeper of all time, making the relationship between subject and biographer the central pillar of his *Life of Dr. Johnson,* to the extent that Boswell is now a more lively commercial proposition than Johnson himself.

They believed in "definitive" biography in the past, and possessive jealousy such as John Forster's found destruction preferable to the gaze of alien eyes. John Cam Hobhouse, neurotically possessive about the late Lord Byron, engineered the burning of his idol's autobiography, unread, because it had been shown to Tom Moore and not to him. Hobhouse was uneasy lest there be something uncomplimentary about himself in it.

When Henry James was given a private view of Byron's

scandalous private papers he was so appalled that he went home and destroyed 40 years accumulation of his own correspondence, manuscripts and notebooks, expressing an "utter and absolute abhorrence" of any biography of himself. And what was the upshot? Leon Edel's five-volume *Life of Henry James,* and four volumes of letters.

Henry James did not have much to hide, or else it remains hidden. He is an exception. Readers are sometimes shocked when they discover that authors whose books they admire were less than admirable in private life. Hamilton poses the most difficult question that biographers and critics must address: "Does poetic genius excuse or mitigate bad conduct; does/should knowing about the life have a bearing on how we read the work?"

In the 19th Century, most spouses and devotees thought it their duty to suppress all evidence of "bad conduct." Biographers worked "to the sound of snipping scissors and paper crackling in the grate. . . . After the funeral would come the slamming of doors, the scrubbing of marble and then, within two years or so, the emergence of what Gladstone called 'a reticence in three volumes.' " George Eliot's reputation for unrelenting high seriousness was largely established by her widower's cutting all jokes and familiar turns of speech out of her published letters and journals.

The problems remain much the same today. The biographer of a modern subject is caught between wanting to tell "the truth" and the need to maintain good relations with informants and access to the archive. The eternal dispute, as identified by Henry James, between "the public and the private, between curiosity and delicacy" may have been resolved to Kitty Kelley's satisfaction, but it still exercises most biographers.

Coming to our own time, Hamilton is sharp about the costiveness of T.S. Eliot's window in publishing his letters and declining to authorize a biography, while she allows Eliot's words to be mixed with Trevor Nunn's in the song "Memory" in the lucrative show *Cats;* Hamilton pays tribute to Peter Ackroyd's subtly "widow-proof" account of Eliot's life. Yet he shows sympathy with Ted Hughes who, as he writes, cannot even destroy any of his own private papers without being accused of interfering with "Plath Studies."

This book was first published in Britain two years ago—before the very pertinent furor caused by the publication of the biography of Philip Larkin by Andrew Motion and of Larkin's Letters, before the contentious overview of the saga of the Plath biographies by Janet Malcolm in the *New Yorker,* before the proposal for a new and Draconian "Privacy Bill" in Britain, and before it was decided that the 50-year copyright period should be increased in Britain to 70 years, in the interests of harmonization within the European Union. It would have been helpful, in the American edition, to have had an afterword on these matters.

Hamilton's own position is that writers must, in the first instance, be their own keepers of the flame: In other words, having read this review, you should at once burn all your diaries and love letters. Or not; as Izaak Walton wrote in the 17th Century, a wish for self-perpetuation is "rooted in the very nature of man." But you should never, Hamilton thinks, burn anyone else's private papers. Larkin in his last illness requested that his diaries be destroyed. His friend Monica Jones shredded the 25 volumes within hours of his death. She did not have to. However vehement the wishes of the deceased in this regard, you are not in (British) law obliged to fulfill them.

There are evidently still moral imperatives stronger than the tug of literary history or the law of the land. But there's little any author can do about eliminating indiscreet letters written to other people; they are probably already in the Humanities Research Center at the University of Texas at Austin anyway, nicely filed and catalogued. Only the law of copyright, and a stalwart keeper of the flame, can protect you. On the evidence of this book, writers should choose the keepers of their flame very carefully indeed. As Dryden wrote to his young protege, the playwright Congreve:

> Be kind to my Remains; and oh defend
> Against Your Judgement Your departed Friend!

Carol Muske (review date 6 November 1994)

SOURCE: "Oppressed by Narrative," in *The New York Times Book Review,* November 6, 1994, p. 18.

[*Muske is an American educator, poet, novelist, and critic. In the following review of Linda Wagner-Martin's book* Telling Women's Lives *(1994), she rejects the author's thesis that women's lives, because of their non-linear nature, do not lend themselves to traditional biography.*]

With *Telling Women's Lives,* Linda Wagner-Martin erects a shaky platform from which to leap headlong into the swirling waters of controversy engulfing the genre of biography. Here's a sample quotation from her introduction:

"The lives of real people have always been more interesting than stories about fictional characters; we may temporarily believe in the exploits of imaginary human beings, but biography wears better."

That will come as news to those of us permanently obsessed with Anna Karenina, Sula or Holden Caulfield. In light of this quick dispatch of imaginative writing, it is particularly ironic that Ms. Wagner-Martin's overall premise is deeply indebted to fiction, its structures and strategies. These she borrows at will to document the routine "fictionalization" process that occurs in biography; thus she comes up with the rather familiar conclusion that biographies are inventions, as are (to the extent that the impulse to render character is innately speculative) the subjects of biography.

This thinking would seem to reduce biography to the level of second-class creative writing, and contradict her own initial division of the two genres. But Ms. Wagner-Martin, a professor of English and comparative literature at the University of North Carolina who is herself a biographer—and one who, in 1987, after publication of her *Sylvia Plath: A Biography,* was caught in the inevitable commotion surrounding Plath—has bigger conflicts in mind. Ms. Wagner-Martin soon moves away from analysis of biography as fiction and begins to psychoanalyze the genre itself. It is about "conceptualization," she says, it is the "enactment of cultural performance," and just as the self in everyday life constructs the appearance of a consistent identity, so the biographer must represent that manufactured self whole.

The biographer, Ms. Wagner-Martin says, must decide if the performance self that the real self projects is credible. The biographer then constructs a narrative, either supporting or refuting this performance self. The traditional biographer has a difficult time with life stories of women because, she says, "few women—even women like Eleanor Roosevelt—live public lives" or possess well-developed performance selves. And further:

"Harder to discover, private events may be ones purposely kept secret by the subject (such as sexual abuse, dislike for parents, dislike by parents or other unfortunate childhood or adolescent happenings)."

The neglect of women and their stories is tragic and irrefutable; what is questionable is Ms. Wagner-Martin's certainty that there is a particular kind of life story unique to women. Narrative itself is her enemy. She does not believe that women's experience fits neatly into a linear arrangement. And, she says, critics are only looking for the performance narrative to praise:

"When the biographer fails to meet the most traditional of biography's rules—to provide a structure of external event as a setting for the subject's life story—critics are disgruntled."

She includes among the disgruntled William H. Pritchard, whose review in *The New York Times Book Review* of Ann Hulbert's *Interior Castle* (a 1992 biography of Jean Stafford) reveals his attempt, she says, to "put biography back into a more traditional mode." In the passage she quotes, Mr. Pritchard warns that probing a "subject's childhood, sexual and domestic conflicts, obsessions and compulsions" should not be mistaken for better understanding: "In fact, the more fully we become acquainted with people—in real life or in biography—the more ultimately mysterious and unfathomable they may become."

This passage could not make clearer the argument between Ms. Wagner-Martin and what she calls traditional critics. Mr. Pritchard is not, in her view, raising questions about how we interpret human experience; rather, he is attempting to repress and restrict real-self stories of women's lives. It becomes clear that for her, the revelation of repressed detail qualifies as the unprejudiced examination of interior life. She is unlike Janet Malcolm, who in *The Silent Woman,* her new book on Sylvia Plath, Ted Hughes and their biographers, finds the task of determining individual motive largely elusive, and moves farther *inward,* into questions of how the biographer is both seduced and repelled by her subject, eventually wondering what purpose biography finally serves. Ms. Wagner-Martin moves outward into cultural analysis.

She has no serious questions about the impossibility of one human being rendering another's life story whole and accessible within language. Rather, she has answers for readers and writers alike, providing, oddly, her own performance narrative. Here it is: The reason there are not many, or many effective, biographies of women is the failure of the genre itself, as conceived and executed by men—and by women who attempt to tell women's life stories in "traditional" form—and as bolstered by critics. These restrictions have made the correct recounting of women's lives unlikely.

But Ms. Wagner-Martin sees hope in "new ways," which include structures "dependent less on chronology than on 'moments of being.' " She does not, however, provide many examples from biography, drawing instead on the use of "recognizable voice" in fiction, memoir and autobiography by women.

Presumably, once these "new ways" are firmly in place, all women will live happily ever after, at least within the confines of Reconstituted Biography. At least, that's the way the story is supposed to go. *Middlemarch,* anyone?

Janet Malcolm (essay date 1994)

SOURCE: *The Silent Woman: Sylvia Plath and Ted Hughes,* Alfred A. Knopf, 1994, 213 p.

[*A nonfiction writer and biographer, Malcolm is well-known for her contributions to* The New Yorker. *In the following excerpt, first published in* The New Yorker *in slightly different form in August 1993, she explains the "transgressive nature of biography" and how she became interested in the controversy surrounding the Plath biographies.*]

Life, as we all know, does not reliably offer—as art does—a second (and a third and a thirtieth) chance to tinker with a problem, but Ted Hughes's history seems to be uncommonly bare of the moments of mercy that allow one to undo or redo one's actions and thus feel that life isn't entirely tragic. Whatever Hughes might have undone or redone in his relationship to Sylvia Plath, the opportunity was taken from him when she committed suicide, in February of 1963, by putting her head in a gas oven as her two small children slept in a bedroom nearby, which she had sealed against gas fumes, and where she had placed mugs of milk and a plate of bread for them to find when they awoke. Plath and Hughes were not living together at the time of her death. They had been married for six years—she was thirty and he was thirty-two when she died—and had separated the previous fall in a turbulent way. There was another woman. It is a situation that many young married couples find themselves in—one that perhaps more couples find themselves in than don't—but it is a situation that ordinarily doesn't last: the couple either reconnects or dissolves. Life goes on. The pain and bitterness and exciting awfulness of sexual jealousy and sexual guilt recede and disappear. People grow older. They forgive themselves and each other, and may even come to realize that what they are forgiving themselves and each other for is youth.

But a person who dies at thirty in the middle of a messy separation remains forever fixed in the mess. To the readers of her poetry and her biography, Sylvia Plath will always be young and in a rage over Hughes's unfaithfulness. She will never reach the age when the tumults of young adulthood can be looked back upon with rueful sympathy and without anger and vengefulness. Ted Hughes has reached this age—he reached it some time ago—but he has been cheated of the peace that age brings by the posthumous fame of Plath and by the public's fascination with the story of her life. Since he was part of that life—the most interesting figure in it during its final six years—he, too, remains fixed in the chaos and confusion of its final period. Like Prometheus, whose ravaged liver was daily reconstituted so it could be daily reravaged, Hughes has had to watch his young self being picked over by biographers, scholars, critics, article writers, and newspaper journalists. Strangers who Hughes feels know nothing about his marriage to Plath write about it with proprietary authority. "I hope each of us owns the facts of her or his own life," Hughes wrote in a letter to the *Independent* in April, 1989, when he had been goaded by a particularly intrusive article. But, of course, as everyone knows who has ever heard a piece of gossip, we do not "own" the facts of our lives at all. This ownership passes out of our hands at birth, at the moment we are first observed. The organs of publicity that have proliferated in our time are only an extension and a magnification of society's fundamental and incorrigible nosiness. Our business is everybody's business, should anybody wish to make it so. The concept of privacy is a sort of screen to hide the fact that almost none is possible in a social universe. In any struggle between the public's inviolable right to be diverted and an individual's wish to be left alone, the public almost always prevails. After we are dead, the pretense that we may somehow be protected against the world's careless malice is abandoned. The branch of the law that putatively protects our good name against libel and slander withdraws from us indifferently. The dead cannot be libelled or slandered. They are without legal recourse.

Biography is the medium through which the remaining secrets of the famous dead are taken from them and dumped out in full view of the world. The biographer at work, indeed, is like the professional burglar, breaking into a house, rifling through certain drawers that he has good reason to think contain the jewelry and money, and triumphantly bearing his loot away. The voyeurism and busybodyism that impel writers and readers of biography alike are obscured by an apparatus of scholarship designed to give the enterprise an appearance of banklike blandness and solidity. The biographer is portrayed almost as a kind of benefactor. He is seen as sacrificing years of his life to his task, tirelessly sitting in archives and libraries and patiently conducting interviews with witnesses. There is no length he will not go to, and the more his book reflects his industry the more the reader believes that he is having an elevating literary experience, rather than simply listening to backstairs gossip and reading other people's mail. The transgressive nature of biography is rarely acknowledged, but it is the only explanation for biography's status as a popular genre. The reader's amazing tolerance (which he would extend to no novel written half as badly as most biographies) makes sense only when seen as a kind of collusion between him and the biographer in an excitingly forbidden undertaking: tiptoeing down the corridor together, to stand in front of the bedroom door and try to peep through the keyhole.

Biography is the medium through which the remaining secrets of the famous dead are taken from them and dumped out in full view of the world.

—Janet Malcolm

Every now and then, a biography comes along that strangely displeases the public. Something causes the reader to back away from the writer and refuse to accompany him down the corridor. What the reader has usually heard in the text—what has alerted him to danger—is the sound of doubt, the sound of a crack opening in the wall of the biographer's self-assurance. As a burglar should not pause to discuss with his accomplice the rights and wrongs of burglary while he is jimmying a lock, so a biographer ought not to introduce doubts about the legitimacy of the biographical enterprise. The biography-loving public does not want to hear that biography is a flawed genre. It prefers to believe that certain biographers are bad guys.

This is what happened to Anne Stevenson, the author of a biography of Sylvia Plath called *Bitter Fame,* which is by far the most intelligent and the only aesthetically satisfying of the five biographies of Plath written to date. The other four are: *Sylvia Plath: Method and Madness* (1976), by Edward Butscher; *Sylvia Plath: A Biography* (1987), by Linda Wagner-Martin; *The Death and Life of Sylvia Plath* (1991), by Ronald Hayman; and *Rough Magic: A Biography of Sylvia Plath* (1991), by Paul Alexander. In Stevenson's book, which was published in 1989, the cracking of the wall was all too audible. *Bitter Fame* was brutally attacked, and Anne Stevenson herself was pilloried; the book became known and continues to be known in the Plath world as a "bad" book. The misdeed for which Stevenson could not be forgiven was to hesitate before the keyhole. "Any biography of Sylvia Plath written during the lifetimes of her family and friends must take their vulnerability into consideration, even if completeness suffers from it," she wrote in her preface. This is a most remarkable—in fact, a thoroughly subversive—statement for a biographer to make. To take vulnerability into consideration! To show compunction! To spare feelings! To not push as far as one can! What is the woman thinking of? The biographer's business, like the journalist's, is to satisfy the reader's curiosity, not to place limits on it. He is supposed to go out and bring back the goods—the malevolent secrets that have been quietly burning in archives and libraries and in the minds of contemporaries who have been biding their time, waiting for the biographer's knock on their doors. Some of the secrets are difficult to bring away, and some, jealously guarded by relatives, are even impossible. Relatives are the biographer's natural enemies; they are like the hostile tribes an explorer encounters and must ruthlessly subdue to claim his territory. If the relatives behave like friendly tribes, as they occasionally do—if they propose to cooperate with the biographer, even to the point of making him "official" or "authorized"—he still has to assert his authority and strut about to show that he is the big white man and they are just the naked savages. Thus, for example, when Bernard Crick agreed to be George Orwell's authorized biographer he first had to ritually bring Orwell's widow to her knees. "She agreed to my firm condition that as well as complete access to the papers, I should have an absolute and prior waiver of copyright so that I could quote what I liked and write what I liked. These were hard terms, even if the only terms on which, I think, a scholar should and can take on a contemporary biography," Crick writes with weary pride in an essay entitled "On the Difficulties of Writing Biography in General and of Orwell's in Particular." When Sonia Orwell read excerpts from Crick's manuscript and realized the worthlessness of the trinkets she had traded her territory for (her fantasy that Crick saw Orwell exactly as she saw him, and viewed her marriage to Orwell exactly as she viewed it), she tried to rescind the agreement. She could not do so, of course. Crick's statement is a model of biographical rectitude. His "hard terms" are the reader's guarantee of quality, like the standards set by the Food and Drug Administration. They assure the reader that he is getting something pure and wholesome, not something that has been tampered with.

When Anne Stevenson's biography arrived, it looked like damaged goods. The wrapping was coming undone, the label looked funny, there was no nice piece of cotton at the top of the bottle. Along with the odd statement about the book's intentional incompleteness, there was a most suspicious-looking Author's Note on the opening page. "In writing this biography, I have received a great deal of help from Olwyn Hughes," Stevenson said. (Olwyn Hughes is Ted Hughes's older sister and the former literary agent to the Plath estate.) "Ms. Hughes's contributions to the text have made it almost a work of dual authorship. I am particularly grateful for the work she did on the last four chapters and on the *Ariel* poems of the autumn of 1962." The note ended with an asterisk that led to a footnote citing exactly which poems Olwyn Hughes had done work on. As if all this weren't peculiar enough, the Author's Note in the published book differed from the Author's Note in the galleys sent to reviewers, which read, "This biography of Sylvia Plath is the result of a three-year dialogue between the author and Olwyn Hughes, agent to the Plath Estate. Ms. Hughes has contributed so liberally to the text that this is in effect a work of joint authorship."

Anne Stevenson apparently had not subdued the natives but had been captured by them and subjected to God knows what tortures. The book she had finally staggered back to civilization with was repudiated as a piece of worthless native propaganda, rather than the "truthful" and "objective" work it should have been. She was seen as having been used by Ted and Olwyn Hughes to put forward their version of Ted Hughes's relations with Plath. Hughes has been extremely reticent about his life with Plath; he has written no memoir, he gives no interviews, his writings about her work (in a number of introductions to volumes of her poetry and prose) are always about the work, and touch on biography only when it relates to the work. It evidently occurred to no one that if Hughes was indeed speaking about his marriage to Plath through Stevenson this might add to the biography's value, not decrease it.

When I first read *Bitter Fame,* in the late summer of 1989, I knew nothing of the charged situation surrounding it, nor was I impelled by any great interest in Sylvia Plath. The book had been sent to me by its publisher, and what aroused my interest was the name Anne Stevenson. Anne had been a fellow student of mine at the University of Michigan in the 1950s. She was in the class ahead of me, and I did not know her, but I knew of her, as the daughter of an eminent and popular professor of philosophy and as a girl who was arty—who wrote poetry that appeared in *Generation,* the university's literary magazine, and who had won the Hopwood award, a serious literary prize. She had once been pointed out to me on the street: thin and pretty, with an atmosphere of awkward intensity and passion about her, gesticulating, surrounded by interesting-looking boys. In those days, I greatly admired artiness, and Anne Stevenson was one of the figures who glowed with a special incandescence in my imagination. She seemed to embody and to have come by naturally all the romantic qualities that I and my fellow fainthearted rebels against the dreariness of the Eisenhower years yearned toward, as we stumblingly, and largely unsuccessfully, attempted to live out our fantasies of nonconformity. Over the years, I watched Anne achieve the literary success she had been headed toward at Michigan. I had begun to write, too, but I did not envy or feel competitive with her: she was in a different sphere, a higher, almost sacred place—the stratosphere of poetry. Moreover, she had married an Englishman and moved to England—the England of E. M. Forster, G. B. Shaw, Max Beerbohm, Virginia Woolf, Lytton Strachey, Henry James, T. S. Eliot, D. H. Lawrence—and that only fixed her the more firmly in my imagination as a figure of literary romance. When, in the mid-seventies, I read Anne's book-length poem *Correspondences,* a kind of novel in letters, a chronicle of quiet (and sometimes not so quiet) domestic despair over several generations, my vague admiration found a sturdy object. The book showed Anne to be not only a poet of arresting technical accomplishment but a woman who had lived, and could speak about her encounters with the real in a tough, modern woman's voice. (She could also modulate it into the softer tones of nineteenth-century moral thought.)

The years passed, and one day a poem by Anne Stevenson appeared in the *Times Literary Supplement* entitled "A Legacy: On My Fiftieth Birthday." Anne was now a grand literary lady. Her poem was full of poets and editors and critics and friends and children and dogs, and its tone of intimate allusiveness evoked a society of remarkable people meeting in each other's burnished houses and talking about literature and ideas in their quiet, kind English voices. I briefly considered writing Anne a note of congratulation and identifying myself as an old Michigan schoolmate—and didn't. Her society seemed too closed, sufficient unto itself.

More years went by when I didn't hear or think about Anne Stevenson; then *Bitter Fame* brought her into my imaginative life again. I read the early chapters about Plath's childhood and adolescence and college years with pangs of rueful recognition—the three of us were almost the same age—and with a certain surprise at the accuracy and authority of Anne's evocation of what it had been like to be a young person living in America in 1950s. How did Anne know about it? I had placed her far above and beyond the shames and humiliations and hypocrisies in which the rest of us were helplessly implicated. Evidently, she knew about them all too well. "Middle-class teenage Americans in the 1950s subscribed to an amazing code of sexual frustration," she writes, and continues:

> Everything was permissible to girls in the way of intimacy except the one thing such intimacies were intended to bring about. Both partners in the ritual of experimental sex conceded that "dating" went something like this: preliminary talking and polite mutual inspection led to dancing, which often shifted into "necking," which—assuming continuous progress—concluded in the quasi-masturbation of "petting" on the family sofa, or, in more affluent circumstances, in the back seat of a car. Very occasionally intercourse might, inadvertently, take place; but as a rule, if the partners went to the same school or considered themselves subject to the same moral pressures, they stopped just short of it.

When writing of how Plath, in her senior year at Smith, daringly matriculated from petting to sleeping with her boyfriends, and deceived her mother about her activities, Anne is moved to observe: "Many women who, like myself, were students in America in the 1950s will remember duplicities of this kind. Sylvia's double standard was quite usual, as was the acceptable face she assumed in letters to her mother. My own letters home of the time were not dissimilar."

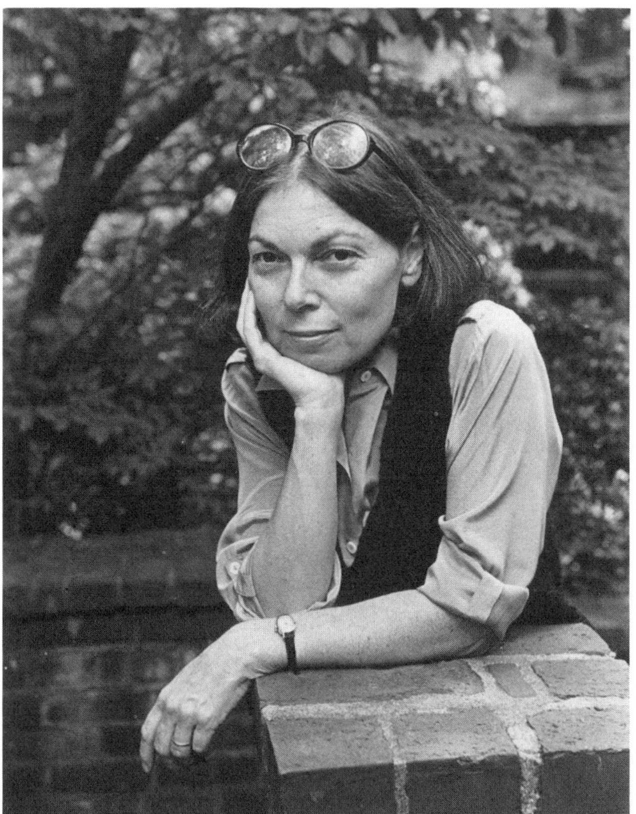

Janet Malcolm.

The early chapters of *Bitter Fame* pulled me back into a period that I still find troubling to recall, precisely because duplicity was so closely woven into its fabric. We lied to our parents and we lied to each other and we lied to ourselves, so addicted to deception had we become. We were an uneasy, shifty-eyed generation. Only a few of us could see how it was with us. When Ted Hughes writes about the struggle of Plath's "true self" to emerge from her false one, he is surely writing about a historical as well as a personal crisis. The nineteenth century came to an end in America only in the 1960s; the desperate pretense that the two World Wars had left the world as unchanged as the Boer War had left it was finally stripped away by the sexual revolution, the women's movement, the civil rights movement, the environmental movement, the Vietnam War protests. Sylvia Plath and Anne Stevenson and I came of age in the period when the need to keep up the pretense was especially strong: no one was prepared—least of all the shaken returning G.I.'s—to face the post-Hiroshima and post-Auschwitz world. At the end of her life, Plath looked, with unnerving steadiness, at the Gorgon; her late poems name and invoke the bomb and the death camps. She was able—she had been elected—to confront what most of the rest of us fearfully shrank from. "For goodness sake, stop being so *frightened* of everything, Mother!" she wrote to Aurelia Plath in October, 1962. "Almost every other word in your letter is 'frightened.' " In the same letter she said:

> Now stop trying to get me to write about "decent courageous people"—read the *Ladies' Home Journal* for those! It's too bad my poems frighten you—but you've always been afraid of reading or seeing the world's hardest things—like Hiroshima, the Inquisition or Belsen.

But Plath's engagement with "the world's hardest things" came only just before she killed herself. (Robert Lowell wrote in his introduction to *Ariel,* "This poetry and life are not a career; they tell that life, even when disciplined, is simply not worth it.") The history of her life—as it has now been told in the five biographies and in innumerable essays and critical studies—is a signature story of the fearful, double-faced fifties. Plath embodies in a vivid, almost emblematic way the schizoid character of the period. She is the divided self par excellence. The taut surrealism of the late poems and the slack, girls'-book realism of her life (as rendered by Plath's biographers and by her own autobiographical writings) are grotesquely incongruous. The photographs of Plath as a vacuous girl of the fifties, with dark lipstick and blond hair, add to one's sense of the jarring disparity between the life and the work. In *Bitter Fame,* writing with the affectionate asperity of a sibling, Anne Stevenson draws a portrait of Plath as a highly self-involved and confused, unstable, driven, perfectionistic, rather humorless young woman, whose suicide remains a mystery, as does the source of her art, and who doesn't add up.

As I read the book, certain vague, dissatisfied thoughts I had had while reading other biographies began to come into sharper focus. It was only later, when the bad report of the book had spread and I had learned about some of the circumstances of its writing, that I understood why it gave the sense of being as much about the problems of biographical writing as about Sylvia Plath. At the time, I thought that it was Sylvia Plath herself who was mischievously subverting the biographer's project. The many voices in which the dead girl spoke—the voices of the journals, of her letters, of *The Bell Jar,* of the short stories, of the early poems, of the *Ariel* poems—mocked the whole idea of biographical narrative. The more Anne Stevenson fleshed out Plath's biography with quotations from her writings, the thinner, paradoxically, did her own narrative seem. The voices began to take over the book and to speak to the reader over the biographer's head. They whispered, "Listen to me, not to her. I am authentic. I speak with authority. Go to the full texts of the journals, the letters home, and the rest. They will tell you what you want to know." These voices were joined by another chorus—that of people who had actually known Plath. These, too, said, "Don't listen to Anne Stevenson. She didn't know Sylvia. I knew Sylvia. Let me tell you about her. Read my correspondence with her. Read my memoir." Three of these voices were particularly loud—those of Lucas Myers, Dido Merwin, and Richard Murphy, who had written memoirs of Plath and Hughes that appeared as appendixes in *Bitter Fame.* One of them, Merwin's, entitled "Vessel of Wrath," rose to the pitch of a shriek. The memoir caused a sensation: it was deplored because of its intemperateness.

Dido Merwin couldn't stand Plath, and had waited thirty years to tell the world what she thought of her former "friend," depicting her as the unbearable wife of a long-suffering martyr. According to Merwin, the wonder was not that Hughes left Plath but that he "stuck it out as long as he did." After the separation, Merwin writes, she asked Hughes "what had been hardest to take during the time he and Sylvia were together," and he revealed that Plath, in a fit of jealous rage, had torn into small pieces all his work in progress of the winter of 1961, as well as his copy of Shakespeare. Merwin also recalls as if it had happened yesterday a disastrous visit that Plath and Hughes paid her and her then husband, the poet W. S. Merwin, at their farmhouse, in the Dordogne. Plath "used up all the hot water, repeatedly helped herself from the fridge (breakfasting on what one had planned to serve for lunch, etc.), and rearranged the furniture in their bedroom." She cast such a pall with her sulking (though her appetite never diminished, Merwin notes, as she tells of balefully watching Plath attack a fine foie gras "for all the world as though it were 'Aunt Dot's meat loaf' ") that Hughes had to cut the visit short. Anne Stevenson was heavily criticized for giving an "unbalanced" idea of Plath by including this venomous portrait in her biography.

In fact, where Anne Stevenson made her mistake of balance was not in including such a negative view of Plath but in including such a subversively lively piece of writing. The limitations of biographical writing are never more evident than when one turns from it to writing in another genre; and when, led by a footnote, I turned from the text of *Bitter Fame* to Dido Merwin's memoir I felt as if I had been freed from prison. The hushed cautiousness, the solemn weighing of "evidence," the humble "she must have felt"s and "he probably thought"s of biographical writing had given way to a high-spirited subjectivity. Writing in her own voice as her own person, fettered by no rules of epistemological deportment, Dido could let rip. She knew exactly how she felt and what she thought. The contrast between the omniscient narrator of *Bitter Fame,* whose mantle of pallid judiciousness Anne Stevenson was obliged to wear, and the robustly intemperate "I" of the Merwin memoir is striking. Merwin's portrait of Plath is a self-portrait of Merwin, of course. It is she, rather than Plath, who emerges, larger than life, from "Vessel of Wrath," and whose obliterating vividness led readers into their error of questioning Anne Stevenson's motives.

REVIEWS OF *THE SILENT WOMAN*

Phoebe Pettingell (review date 14-28 March 1994)

SOURCE: "Plath and the Perils of Biography," in *The New Leader,* Vol. LXXVII, No. 3, March 14-28, 1994, pp. 14-15.

[*In the following review of* The Silent Woman, *Pettingell praises Malcolm's journalistic and self-conscious approach to biography.*]

Janet Malcolm has created a literary niche for herself as a chronicler of quarrels. Ten years ago, *In the Freud Archives* gave us a blow-by-blow account of orthodox Freudians duking it out with their master's detractors. In 1990, *The Journalist and the Murderer* depicted the feud between an Army doctor convicted of killing his family and a friendly writer with whom he cooperated in hopes of exoneration, but whose book ultimately concurred with the court. Not one to pull her own punches, Malcolm lets us see how people talk to a reporter, how in seeking to control a story they usually reveal the very information they later regret having mentioned. Her tales are gripping precisely because she zeroes in on the essence of a personality. Without being disengaged—her own opinions do emerge, and tend to be strong—she fashions portraits that, favorable or not, retain the feel of authenticity.

Now, in *The Silent Woman: Sylvia Plath and Ted Hughes,* Malcolm explores the conflicts inherent in accurately describing the life of a dead contemporary author. For her model she has chosen one of the most fierce and public battles ever fought between a literary estate and aspiring biographers. Since Malcolm's style depends on startling metaphors, it comes as no surprise that she sees those biographers as players in a gothic poker game, taking place "in a room so dark and gloomy that one has a hard time seeing one's hand; one is apt to make mistakes." In the next room lies "an open coffin surrounded by candles. A small old woman sits in a straight-backed chair reading a manual of stenography." A tall, graying man, all in black, enters where the players are gathered, followed by a tall woman who glares malevolently at them. Will these rather menacing characters help or hinder the game? Nothing becomes clear until the bidding starts.

The main figures in this allegory are Plath's survivors. The old woman is her mother, Aurelia, with whom Sylvia had a close but difficult relationship. Ted Hughes, now England's Poet Laureate, is the tall man, the husband whose desertion inspired Plath's most powerful and angry verse. Because she left no will when she killed herself in 1963, her writings and other properties automatically passed to him. The tall woman is his sister, Olwyn Hughes, a literary agent who administered the estate until her retirement in 1991. Her overriding concern was, and remains, to defend her brother from the "libbers" she imagines to be Sylvia's champions and his adversaries. Many Plath scholars, identifying strongly with the rage and hurt their heroine expressed against her husband during her last months, cannot forgive him—even 30 years later—for censoring parts of her *Journals* or for controlling their freedom to quote from her in print. Malcolm shows how the situation is both oppressive and tantalizing for Plath's would-be biographers: Each hopes to be the one to illuminate what actually happened and voice the feelings of the "silent woman" in the casket, whose poetry still speaks so loudly.

Plath is considered a "confessional" poet. Thus it is commonly assumed that by studying her personality and the events of her life, readers can better understand the desperation of what Emily Dickinson would have called her "letter to the world." Yet of the five biographies to date (*Silent Woman* does not properly belong to the genre), Anne Stevenson's *Bitter Fame* alone confronts the enigma at the heart of Plath's work. Her writings, public and private, indicate that she deliberately discarded the image of "a nice person" in favor of a grittier truth. She was obviously driven by private demons we cannot fully fathom. Malcolm rightly points out that "The taut surrealism of the late poems and the slack, girl's book realism of her life (as recorded by biographers and by her own biographical writings) are grotesquely incongruous." In short, "she doesn't add up." But how does one go about filling in the lacunae in one's knowledge of a dead person? Witnesses prove contradictory, so one ends up trying to collate the paper trail of a lifetime. Family keepers of that material, however, will frequently turn hostile if their vision of the deceased is not accepted.

From the time of his wife's death, Ted Hughes has been what Malcolm terms "Plath's greatest critic, elucidator, and (you could almost say) impresario." His enemies, recalling her best-known poem, "Daddy," crudely mark him as the "man in black with a Meinkampf look / And a love of the rack and the screw," persecuting her defenders to hide his own moral complicity in her death. This view does not jibe with reality. If Hughes had wanted to escape blame, he might better have suppressed the furious poems of the *Ariel* manuscript altogether. Had he done so, Plath probably would never have come to public notice. He has instead faithfully kept her flame burning bright before literary audiences. Nevertheless, he insists on his right to preserve an undistorted portrait of Plath for their two children—infants at the time she died—whom he and Olwyn raised. With good reason, if unrealistically, he also resents having his own life hashed over. When Hughes bitterly protests the way "writers move onto the living because they can no longer feel the difference between [them] and the dead," and charges that they ransack their subjects' "psyches and reinvent them however they please," readers of recent biographies know exactly what he is talking about.

Malcolm's research uncovered clumsy errors in the handling of Plath's estate, but no self-serving omissions by Hughes. In fact, she clarifies how a serious tactical misstep he made set in motion a chain of events that had quite the opposite effect. In 1970 Hughes wanted money to buy a new house, so he decided to reprint Plath's autobiographical novel *The Bell Jar.* Aurelia Plath was understandably upset, for the book contained highly unflattering portraits of her family and friends, as well as an account of Sylvia's first suicide attempt while in college. Previously it had been published under a pseudonym and only in England, to avoid inflicting pain on its American subjects. Hughes was within his legal rights. The friction the novel's appearance caused, though, soon escalated into a war between husband and mother over the poet's image. Both sides started releasing private letters and journals to support their contrasting impressions of "the real Sylvia." Malcolm notes that the eventual result was something neither anticipated nor wanted: Public attention began to focus on the details of Plath's life more than on her poetry.

In one of her most memorable passages Malcolm writes: "The voyeurism and busybodyism that impel writers and readers of biography alike are obscured by an apparatus of scholarship designed to give the enterprise an appearance of banklike blandness and solidity. The biographer is portrayed almost as a benefactor . . . sacrificing years of his life to his task . . . and the more his book reflects his industry the more the reader believes that he is having an elevating literary experience, rather than simply listening to backstairs gossip and reading other people's mail." A number of individual lives have been reshaped—usually for the worse—by getting caught up in the thicket surrounding Plath. Malcolm, observing that there have been countless similar exploitations of the survivors of a biographer's dead subject, cites the case of George Orwell's widow, Sonia, and his authorized biographer, Bernard Crick.

After two accounts of Plath's life were published—both fairly innocuous to an outsider's eye, yet hurtful to those who figured in her history—the estate made another unfortunate move. Hughes decided to "cooperate," through his sister, with Anne Stevenson in order to correct what he and Olwyn agreed were the failings of the earlier books. An American poet about Plath's age, Stevenson too had moved to England. Her approach seems sensible and balanced to an impartial reader. All the same, it drew fire from every side. Reviewers accused her of "selling out" to the estate and assuming an advocate's role for the

Hugheses. The notoriously difficult Olwyn, meanwhile, felt Stevenson had not listened to the family enough and never forgave her for it. In Malcolm's view, *Bitter Fame* is "the most intelligent and only esthetically satisfying" life of Plath thus far. She takes up cudgels against those who, reacting to its connection with the estate, have written it off as an attack on a heroine unable to respond. Mostly, she suggests, these are the people eager "to wrest from Hughes the power over [Plath's] literary remains which he acquired when she died." They insist that no one may criticize the deceased, although living members of the family are fair game.

Malcolm confesses to appreciating Anne Stevenson's predicament because she herself has "written an unpopular book . . . and been attacked in the press." The allusion is to *In the Freud Archives.* Malcolm had claimed that one of its subjects, a Freudian apostate, used his position in that august institution to hunt for documents that might discredit the founder of psychoanalysis. He sued her for defamation and she was widely presumed to have intruded her own Freudian bias into her tale. At her trial she countered (with little success) that such a charge distorts both the offending portrait and her purpose. On one level, *The Silent Woman* is a continuation of her defense.

All writers wear "the blinders of narrative," she argues, since any attempt to tell a coherent story necessitates editing the material. Inevitably, some issues get left out and others are magnified. As she did the interviews for this work, Malcolm tells us, she paid particular attention to the way each person molded "the Plath legend." Some made it a melodrama between the good girl and the bad guy. A postmodernist critic who had done a study that saw everything Plath wrote as dreamlike, allowing infinite speculation, confided that an outraged letter from Hughes over her reading of one poem as a bisexual fantasy caused her to feel physically threatened. In Malcolm's own complicated interpretation, Hughes emerges a compelling and sympathetic figure. Doubtless many will charge her again with being grossly biased. But that would miss her fundamental point. Her thoughtful book proclaims that too many contemporary biographies do violence to reality by treating it merely as a form of literature, complete with black-or-white characters, a tidy plot and a Hollywood moral.

Caryn James (review date 27 March 1994)

SOURCE: "The Importance of Being Biased," in *The New York Times Book Review,* March 27, 1994, pp. 1, 18-20.

[*In the following review, James describes how Malcolm's investigation into Plath's life was fueled by her sympathy for Ted Hughes and how* The Silent Woman *presents a revisionist view of Hughes's influence on Plath and her biographers.*]

In small cemetery in Yorkshire is a gravestone that reads "Sylvia Plath Hughes, 1932-1963." Or at least that's what it usually reads. For a while in the late 1980's, vandals kept creeping into the cemetery and scraping away the word "Hughes." The poet's husband, Ted Hughes, had his family name restored, only to find it scraped off again, at least three times. No one ever discovered the vandals' identities, but it was assumed that they were enraged Plath devotees who had bought into a popular, simple-minded myth. She was St. Sylvia, the genius housewife driven to despair and suicide because of her adulterous husband. He was a poet too, but also a garden-variety 1950's-style oppressor, who metaphorically held open the oven door.

Who owns Sylvia? The tug-of-war began soon after Plath's final, best poems were gathered in *Ariel,* in 1965. (To anyone under 50, that slim volume now carries the unmistakable whiff of sophomore year in college.) And the debate gained a new flurry of interest last August, when *The Silent Woman,* by Janet Malcolm, appeared in *The New Yorker.* Now published as a book subtitled "Sylvia Plath & Ted Hughes," it details the angry wrangling between Plath's biographers and the Hughes family for control of Plath's image.

On one side are the hagiographers, armed with a now-glorified tale: the young American alone with two small children, rising at dawn in a brutal English winter to write her fierce, blackhearted poems about death. On the other is Ted Hughes, then her estranged husband. Arguably as great a poet as Plath and now England's poet laureate, he has nonetheless been best known over the years as the man who let Sylvia down. It seems odd that Ms. Malcolm doesn't mention Plath's defaced headstone in *The Silent Woman,* for this book is her passionate attempt to restore the Hughes name to a position of honor.

She takes Mr. Hughes's side against 30 years' worth of disgruntled critics and biographers. As executor of his wife's estate, Mr. Hughes can grant or deny permission to quote from the cache of Plath's poetry, letters, journals and manuscripts. His sister, Olwyn, was the estate's agent until three years ago. It was Olwyn Hughes who dealt directly with the writers, bearing messages from her elusive brother as if from the oracle. Together, the Hugheses were famous for the hard time they gave to anyone who disagreed with them about Plath.

Few essays in recent years have caused anything like the buzz *The Silent Woman* did when it first appeared, but Sylvia Plath was the least of it. While the English fuss about poets' graves, Americans gossip about litigation and celebrity journalists. The word was that *The Silent Woman* was all about Janet Malcolm.

—Caryn James

Ms. Malcolm's approach is rich and theatrical. *The Silent Woman* is to literary skulduggery what *All the President's Men* was to Watergate, with Ms. Malcolm casting herself in the Woodward-Bernstein role. As she races around England, a reporter going from one genteel teatime interview to the next, she artfully turns the story of Ted, Olwyn and the shaping of the dead poet's legend into a high human drama about a tragic, maligned widower and his devoted sister. Few essays in recent years have caused anything like the buzz *The Silent Woman* did when it first appeared, but Sylvia Plath was the least of it. While the English fuss about poets' graves, Americans gossip about litigation and celebrity journalists. The word was that *The Silent Woman* was all about Janet Malcolm.

Well, it's certainly not about Plath, who emerges as an enigma, a shadowy set of contradictory anecdotes. Some say she was mad, others maddening; she may well have been both. In *The Silent Woman,* she is usually the bone and the hank of hair over which two camps are feuding. Though Ms. Malcolm positions herself in the Hughes camp, the great strength of the book is that Plath becomes the excuse for page after page of deep and provocative questions. Her broader subject, Ms. Malcolm writes, is biography itself, "a flawed genre" in which "the pose of fair-mindedness, the charade of evenhandedness, the striking of an attitude of detachment can never be more than rhetorical ruses."

These are explosive words from someone with Janet Malcolm's notoriety. Just two months before the *New Yorker* essay appeared, Ms. Malcolm lost a famous libel suit, which has dragged on for 10 years and isn't over yet. The psychoanalyst Jeffrey Masson sued her and *The New Yorker* over a 1983 article that later became a book, *In the Freud Archives.* Last June, a jury found that Ms. Malcolm had fabricated five quotations, two of them libelous. But the jury could not agree on damages, and a retrial was ordered. (*The New Yorker* was declared not legally responsible, and the magazine was detached from the suit.)

Ms. Malcolm's legal troubles cast a tiny shadow over *The Silent Woman,* not because her quotations seem suspect but because she is so coy. She cannot angrily accuse one Plath biographer of skirting "the limits of libel law" without making a reader wonder why she chose such loaded words. But the woman who is set to go back to court is different from the Janet Malcolm who appears as a character, on stage, in her book. The offstage Janet Malcolm is the one who at her trial could not produce tape recordings of all her challenged quotations and who strung together remarks from two different interviews as if they were one. Most reporters would think it's safer to rob a bank. Still, the journalistic lessons of her legal case are crashingly banal—always tape everything and don't monkey with the quotes—and irrelevant to *The Silent Woman.*

The Janet Malcolm in the book is an idealized version of her journalistic self. She lucidly unravels the Plath controversy. She makes a vehement, though finally unconvincing, case for Mr. Hughes as a man helplessly "imprisoned in the Plath legend." Most important, she raises indispensable, uncomfortable issues that journalists and biographers should be brave enough to face. In an age of rampant celebrity journalism, it would be foolish to dismiss her claim that biography's appeal is based on "voyeurism and busybodyism," however high-minded the subject. And what reporter can disagree when she peers beneath the ritual dance of the interview, with its "outward resemblance to an ordinary friendly meeting," and finds two people trying to use and outwit each other? These are the existential questions of journalism: profoundly important and totally paralyzing if you think about them for too long. It may be the ultimate paradox that they are framed by someone whose own methods are in dispute.

The Silent Woman gives dazzling shape to Ms. Malcolm's theories. True to her sense that a biographer must have a bias to be any good, she sets out to persuade her readers that Ted Hughes has been unfairly treated, as if he too were already dead and fair game for history's cruelty and voyeurism. Metaphors become one of her most effective weapons. The "flood of information" about Sylvia Plath, she writes, "could be likened to an oil spill in the devastation it wreaked among Plath's survivors, who to this day are like birds covered with black ooze." She realizes that some of the survivors helped create the oil spill. In 1975, Plath's mother published *Letters Home,* a volume of her daughter's good-girl correspondence. Mr. Hughes published Plath's journals in 1982. But those facts don't erase the image of the Hugheses covered in slime.

Ms. Malcolm praises Anne Stevenson, whose 1989 book, *Bitter Fame: A Life of Sylvia Plath,* presents the poet as a difficult, selfish, abrasive personality. The biographer's cooperation with Olwyn Hughes was fraught with the kind of journalistic danger that was bound to intrigue Ms. Malcolm. The situation echoes a case Ms. Malcolm wrote about in *The Journalist and the Murderer,* the 1990 book on journalism to which *The Silent Woman* becomes a companion piece. In the earlier work, Ms. Malcolm examined a literary lawsuit and turned it into an essay on journalistic ethics. Jeffrey MacDonald, a convicted murderer, sued Joe McGinniss for fraud and breach of contract. Mr. McGinniss made a deal to write the MacDonald story, acted like a friend, then published *Fatal Vision,* which made Dr. MacDonald look guilty.

Ms. Stevenson made no deal with the Plath estate. But for years Olwyn Hughes fed her facts, sources and ideas. In exchange, she expected—and almost got—control over the book's content. Olwyn Hughes's encouragement was a "spider's invitation," Ms. Malcolm says, and cheers the biographer for breaking free. Still, she assumes the generous attitude that when Olwyn Hughes interfered with writers, it was done for the sake of protecting her beleaguered brother.

It is in the portrait of Ted Hughes that Ms. Malcolm loses control, romanticizing him almost as much as the young, infatuated Sylvia Plath did. He is compared to Prometheus and to Chekhov. He suffers "punishment by biography." Even his letters to other people make Ms. Malcolm react with "intense sympathy and affection," as if she were in the throes of a schoolgirl crush.

Mr. Hughes's heroic status owes much to the fact that Ms. Malcolm never meets him. She wrote to him at the start of her project, in care of his sister (the recommended way to reach him), requesting an interview. Olwyn Hughes answered the letter and met with the author. If Ms. Malcolm ever met Ted Hughes—or even tried again to reach him—

Sylvia Plath and her husband, Ted Hughes, in 1958.

she doesn't mention it here. She snoops outside his house once, and is deeply ashamed of herself for doing so. Another reporter might have carried away some delicious detail. She sees "a fully stocked bird feeder," which prompts "a return of my feeling of tenderness toward Hughes."

She even turns around Plath's best-known poem, "Daddy," citing the lines "Daddy, you can lie back now. / There's a stake in your fat black heart." In Ms. Malcolm's metaphor, "Hughes has never been able to drive the stake through Plath's heart and free himself from her hold." He is tormented by biographers and curiosity seekers, "stand-ins for the Undead woman herself."

Ms. Malcolm is more convincing in those rare moments when she achieves a conscious "hardening of the heart against Ted Hughes." He allowed Plath's autobiographical novel, *The Bell Jar,* to be published posthumously in the United States because he needed money to buy a house (his third). "He had evidently exchanged his right to privacy for a piece of real estate," she writes. One of the disillusioning truths offered in *The Silent Woman* is that all biographical subjects eventually become pieces of property, with writers feuding over the corpus left behind.

Ms. Malcolm finally had her own skirmish about permission to quote from Plath and from Ted Hughes's letters. She refused to let Mr. Hughes read her manuscript before making his decision, as he had asked through his publisher. She compromised and let him see the paragraphs on either side of the quotations. If she had stood on principle, Mr. Hughes would not have seen any of her writing. But then he might have refused to let her quote what she needed; the book would have been damaged or even destroyed. Ms. Malcolm's idealized journalistic self has vanished from this incident, replaced by a pragmatic one.

Her version of Woodward and Bernstein turns out to be the reporter as antihero. That is what makes *The Silent Woman* such an astute journalistic chronicle, disturbingly in touch with its times.

Michiko Kakutani (review date 5 April 1994)

SOURCE: "Taking Sides in Polemics Over Plath," in *The New York Times,* April 5, 1994, pp. C13, C17.

[*In the following review of* The Silent Woman, *Kakutani outlines the longstanding libel case against Malcolm for her previous book,* The Journalist and the Murderer *(1990), and its relevance to Malcolm's biography of Plath.*]

Before we get to Janet Malcolm's vexing new book, *The Silent Woman: Sylvia Plath and Ted Hughes,* which originally appeared in different form as a single voluminous article in *The New Yorker* last year, a little history is in order.

To begin with, the volume stands as a kind of bookend to Ms. Malcolm's earlier book *The Journalist and the Murderer* (1990), a heated attack on the author Joe McGinniss for betraying the trust of the convicted murderer Dr. Jeffrey MacDonald. For Ms. Malcolm, Mr. McGinniss's act—befriending Dr. MacDonald and subsequently writing a defamatory book about him—was a paradigm for the relationship between journalists and their subjects. Indeed, she went on to make a damning generalization about journalists as a group.

"Every journalist who is not too stupid or too full of himself to notice what is going on knows that what he does is morally indefensible," she wrote in *The Journalist and the Murderer.* "He is a kind of confidence man, preying on people's vanity, ignorance or loneliness, gaining their trust and betraying them without remorse."

Curiously enough, the vague accusations Ms. Malcolm was hurling at fellow journalists were also being hurled—very specifically—at her by Jeffrey M. Masson, a principal subject of a 1983 article she wrote for *The New Yorker.* Last June, a Federal jury concluded that Ms. Malcolm had indeed defamed Mr. Masson with five fabricated quotations, but deadlocked over damages. A retrial is scheduled.

All of which brings us to Ms. Malcolm's latest book, *The Silent Woman,* a book that's meant to do for biographers what *The Journalist and the Murderer* tried to do for journalists. The volume draws analogies between the biographer at work and "the professional burglar," who breaks into a house, rifles "through certain drawers" and triumphantly bears his loot away. Ms. Malcolm says in passing that the book was shaped by her own experience (during the Masson trial) of being "attacked in the press."

"I had been there—on the helpless side of the journalist-subject equation," she writes. "Now my journalist's 'objectivity' was impaired."

Given the evidence presented at the Masson trial, one must certainly question what sort of "objectivity" Ms. Malcolm ever possessed, and *The Silent Woman* serves only to ratify this perception.

On the surface, the volume gives us some interesting insights into the continuing literary feuds being fought over the memory of the poet Sylvia Plath, who committed suicide in 1963. On one side are Plath's former husband, the poet Ted Hughes, and his sister Olwyn Hughes, who have controlled access to Plath's papers. On the other side are those Plath friends, critics and biographers who suggest that the Hugheses have been obstructive in their handling of the estate. To some Plath admirers who have tried to portray Mr. Hughes as an overbearing husband who dominated his wife in life and death, Mr. Hughes has responded that critics and biographers have willfully tried to reinvent the image of his wife and their marriage, while cruelly ransacking his own psyche.

Ms. Malcolm comes down firmly on the side of Ted Hughes, whom she depicts as a kind of archetypal victim of the predatory biographer: "Like Prometheus, whose ravaged liver was daily reconstituted so it could be daily reravaged, Hughes has had to watch his young self being picked over by biographers, scholars, critics, article writers and newspaper journalists."

Ms. Malcolm also hails Mr. Hughes's literary gifts ("he writes with brilliant, exasperated intelligence and a kind of Chekovian largeheartedness and melancholy"), his physical attractiveness and his "helpless honesty." She writes of the "tenderness" she feels for the man, and even of the "identification" she feels with his typing style.

In fact, Ms. Malcolm's belief in Mr. Hughes is so ardent that it makes her want to find ways to dismiss the work of critics whom Mr. Hughes has opposed, including Jacqueline Rose's critically acclaimed book *The Haunting of Sylvia Plath.*

"In another context—if, that is, I had read *The Haunting of Sylvia Plath* as a book on a subject in which I had no investment—I would have felt nothing but admiration for it," Ms. Malcolm writes, "since I tend to support the new literary theorists in their debate with the traditionalists. But in the Plath-Hughes debate my sympathies are with the Hugheses, and thus, like a lawyer defending a case he knows to be weak and yet obscurely feels is just, I steel myself against the attractions of the opposition's most powerful and plausible witness." In other words: don't bother me with evidence; my mind's already made up.

From time to time, Ms. Malcolm seems to realize just how superficial and blindered her polemical approach to the Plath-Hughes debate really is. But instead of working harder—interviewing people in greater depth, talking to additional sources, collecting further facts—she tries to extrapolate her own limitations to the genre of biography-writing in general.

After a brief afternoon chat with one of Plath's former friends and her husband, Ms. Malcolm sighs: "What did I know about them? How inadequate and off the mark my account must be! The biographer commits the same offense when he proposes to solve the mystery that is a life with 'data' no less meager (when you consider the monstrous mass that accrues from the moment-by-moment events of a life) and interpretations no less crass (when you consider what a fine-tuned, custom-made instrument human motivation is)."

The thing is, there is a serious problem with Ms. Malcolm's reasoning here. Yes, there has been a deplorable rise in recent years of biographical smear jobs, and yes, all biography and history are to some degree fragmentary and provisional. This does not mean, however, that all efforts to discern the truth are futile or that all efforts to do so are equal or equally suspect.

Fortunately for the reader, the sloppy journalistic ethics evinced by Ms. Malcolm (in her reporting on Jeffrey Masson) and Joe McGinniss (in *Fatal Vision* and *The Last Brother*) aren't shared by all reporters. And for Ms. Malcolm to suggest that her own shortcomings are in any way representative of the vocations of journalism or biography writing in general seems not only solipsistic, but profoundly disingenuous.

Mary Cantwell (review date 17 April 1994)

SOURCE: "Plath, Hughes and Malcolm: A Metaphysical Ménage à Trois," in *The New York Times,* April 17, 1994, p. E16.

[*In this brief review of* The Silent Woman, *Cantwell stresses the elusive nature of biography and the futility of its quest to summarize a person's life.*]

On Feb. 11, 1963, a young American named Sylvia Plath stuck her head in the gas oven of her London home. It was not the first time she had attempted suicide. This time she succeeded. Ms. Plath was survived by her husband, two children, her mother, her brother, some short fiction, a brief autobiographical novel and many poems. The last of them, collected in a book called *Ariel,* were written with a passion that insures their permanence—as their author was the first to realize. "I am writing the best poems of my life," she wrote her mother a few months before her death. "They will make my name."

Since February 1963 Sylvia Plath has captured the attention of several biographers, countless English professors and a legion of women who saw in her work, and in her life and death, some curious reflection of themselves. Her husband, to whom she once gave the kind of encomium Emily Brontë might have given Heathcliff, also fascinates.

"I met the strongest man in the world," she wrote on the coming together of Sylvia Plath and Ted Hughes, ". . . with a voice like the thunder of God—a singer, storyteller, lion and world-wanderer, a vagabond who will never stop." When she died, they were divorcing. His eye had moved elsewhere.

Thirty-one years later the vagabond is England's poet laureate, *Ariel* still flies from bookstores and the Plath legend has attracted yet another recorder, Janet Malcolm. Only what Ms. Malcolm is recording, in *The Silent Woman,* is less the legend itself than the difficulties faced by those who *would* record it. "The strongest man in the world" is their greatest difficulty: he controls Plath's estate, maintains an almost palpable silence about their marriage and admits to having misplaced, perhaps for all time, one of her journals and to destroying another. Even so Ms. Malcolm, who has previously concentrated much of her formidable intelligence on the sins of journalists, has not the heart to damn him.

Not only is she on his side, she even sounds a bit like the young, besotted Plath when she describes the trials he has endured as a suicide's relict. "Like Prometheus, whose ravaged liver was daily reconstituted so it could be daily reravaged, Hughes has had to watch his young self being picked over by biographers, scholars, critics, article writers and newspaper journalists."

The picking over will presumably continue long after Mr. Hughes is as absent from this earth as his first wife. By then the misplaced journal may have surfaced, along with ream after ream of new material about this talented woman and this talented man.

Chances are, however, that neither of them—and Ms. Plath in particular—will ever be truly pinned down to paper. The reason, though, will have little to do either with material too fragile to build upon or with material so copious it hides the telling details. Rather it has to do with the sheer, but endlessly alluring, impossibility of the biographer's craft.

Richard Holmes, who has written books about Shelley and Coleridge, parsed the problem perfectly in his magical *Footsteps of a Romantic Biographer.* Mr. Holmes had tried, and failed, to "find" Robert Louis Stevenson by duplicating the journey Stevenson described in *Travels With a Donkey.* In doing so, however, he found his métier.

" 'Biography,' " he wrote, "meant a book about someone's life. Only, for me, it was to become a kind of pursuit, a tracking of the physical trail of someone's path through the past, a following of footsteps. You would never catch them, no, you would never quite catch them. But, maybe, if you were lucky, you might write about the pursuit of that flying figure in such a way as to bring it alive in the present. . . . You cannot freeze them, you cannot pinpoint them, at any particular turn in the road, bend of the river, view from the window. They are always in motion, carrying their past lives over into the future."

Anna Fels (review date 16 May 1994)

SOURCE: "The Flash of the Knife," in *The Nation,* New York, Vol. 258, No. 19, May 16, 1994, pp. 670-73.

[*In the following review of* The Silent Woman, *Fels praises the intensity of Malcolm's writing and maintains that it is Ted Hughes, Plath's husband, who is the silent one.*]

Janet Malcolm's new book, *The Silent Woman: Sylvia Plath and Ted Hughes,* is a brilliant literary tour de force that reads like a thriller. On one level Malcolm's subject is biography, the psychological complexity and potential destructiveness of this genre. She explores the legacy of the poet Sylvia Plath and its impact on those who knew her—or tried to write about her. But on another level it is about the crimes that people commit against one another. Malcolm's awareness of these crimes gives the book a kind of lurid intensity. Murder, burglary, brutal attacks, women brought to their knees—the metaphors she chooses have a striking violence. Nor is it only the metaphors. In this and in her other books real crimes have occurred. There are bodies. The question of whodunit has a real as well as a psychological dimension.

But this is no Agatha Christie tale in which a large group of suspects is rounded up and alibis checked. Malcolm's subject has always been dyads, two-person relationships and the distortions and violations to which they inevitably give rise. The two members can be husband and wife, mother and child, psychiatrist and patient, biographer and subject, journalist and interviewee. Often several of these dyads are linked, forming chains of culpability and victimization. In *The Silent Woman* Malcolm writes about Anne Stevenson, a much-criticized biographer of Plath, Stevenson's relationship to Ted Hughes (and his sister Olwyn Hughes, who has long served as his stalking horse) and finally Hughes's relationship with Plath.

In her earlier books Malcolm was a relatively inconspicuous observer of such relationships. But several years ago she found herself embroiled in a lawsuit brought by one of her subjects. Perhaps because of this development, Malcolm has now included herself prominently in the series of relationships she explores here—she, too, is a link in the chain. Her self-examination in the biographer's role is the thread that holds the book together.

But it is a sharply conflicted role. Malcolm bitterly attacks biographers as exploitative and self-serving, brutalizing their subjects for their own gain. At the same time, she is engaged in her own obsessive pursuit of a subject who is opposing her project: Ted Hughes denied her any interviews. This contradiction in her stance gives the book a strangely gripping, almost poignant quality. Malcolm herself is trapped within the matrix she describes, showing us her own struggles with voyeurism, manipulation and covert agendas even as she enacts these dramas with Plath's family and friends. Malcolm tries to convince us that she is supremely aware of what she is doing, letting us in on her writerly crime even as she commits it. But at times the reader is left wondering if this self-observation is not serving as the most disarming of cover-ups. Nor is it clear that Malcolm is always aware of what she is up to. In this Dostoyevskian tale of biographical "soul murder," Malcolm is at once Raskolnikov and the police inspector.

Throughout the book we see Malcolm traveling around a raw, wintry England interviewing the aging friends and acquaintances of Plath. They themselves are a chilling sight—fragile with their swollen, arthritic limbs, but undiminished in their passionate, deeply partisan views on Plath. Malcolm captures these encounters in her breathtakingly lucid, observant style, rendering the smell and feel and look of their rooms and their lives. The clarity and wit of her portraits make for reading that feels like a clandestine pleasure. Jacqueline Rose, a poststructuralist who has written an acclaimed book on Plath, is described as "a small, attractive woman in her early forties, wearing a short and close-fitting skirt and a sweater, whose face was framed by a great deal of artfully unruly blond hair, and whose whole person was surrounded by a kind of nimbus of self-possession." The hapless spouse of an interviewee who wanders into Malcolm's view is immortalized in a thumbnail sketch: "William brought a pot of tea and a plate of cookies made from blameless natural ingredients. He then retired to his office, a room filled with computer equipment and a photocopier." The characters that emerge from the gloomy British landscape range from the heroically portrayed Hughes to the low comedy figure of Plath's downstairs neighbor, Trevor Thomas, who sourly recites his litany about Plath's last days. The complexity, contradictions and self-interest of their differing views are deftly set forth.

But beneath this carapace of observations about how people experience one another and the uses to which they put their knowledge, Malcolm, like all the other characters in the book, has chosen a specific tale to tell about Plath—and she has her own reasons for telling it. In Malcolm's inimitable words, "The writer, like the murderer, needs a motive." In her forthright way Malcolm states that "I, too, have taken a side—that of the Hugheses and Anne Stevenson—and I, too, draw on my sympathies and antipathies and experiences to support it. . . . In the Plath-Hughes debate my sympathies are with the Hugheses . . . like a lawyer defending a case he knows to be weak yet obscurely feels is just. . . ."

Given the stylistic brilliance and intellectual sophistication of this book, the story Malcolm chooses to tell has an oddly girlish quality. It's a story about three women—Janet Malcolm, Anne Stevenson and Sylvia Plath—all of whom came of age in the United States in the 1950s, all of whom became renowned writers, and two of whom moved to England and married Englishmen. Malcolm knew of Stevenson in college, and Stevenson was to Malcolm what Plath would later become to a generation of women: "She was in a different sphere, a higher, almost sacred place—the stratosphere of poetry. Moreover, she had married an Englishman." Importantly, Stevenson, like Plath, had a daring sexuality, "with an atmosphere of awkward intensity and passion about her, gesticulating, surrounded by interesting-looking boys."

The subplot of this book is Malcolm's rendering of the relationships of each of these women to Ted Hughes—Plath's stormy and ultimately destructive relationship, Stevenson's well-meaning but bungled attempt to collaborate with Hughes and finally Malcolm's own (literary) rescue of him. In her depictions of these two other women, you feel Malcolm's willed effort to be fair, but their portraits, like the one of Rose, have little warmth or generosity. Praise given on one page is often undercut on the next. Stevenson, whom Malcolm purports to champion, in fact is characterized as a rather bedraggled figure; talented, striving to do the right thing, but insecure and inept, an ex-alcoholic with a confused, chaotic life.

Only once does Malcolm appear to have a glimmer of the dynamic underlying her description of these women. Meditating on a subtle awkwardness, a "charged 'moment,' " that occurred in a conversation with Rose, she briefly has the conviction that "something unexpected and complicated had occurred. I remember feeling that she and I were struggling over something—were having a fight about some central, unacceptable thing. . . ." She then goes on to simultaneously identify and deny the "unacceptable thing": "Jacqueline Rose and I were fighting over Ted Hughes." No sooner is this said than she hastens to repudiate it. The observation is embedded in a description of the unreliability of such conclusions and of biographical information in general.

That Malcolm decided to wade in to rescue such a "weak case" as Hughes should not come as a surprise to anyone who has read her recent books. One could argue that in each of the last three books she comes to the defense of a beleaguered man accused of a crime. And that in each case Malcolm takes elaborate pains to discredit the accusers. She indirectly "saves" Freud from Masson's allegation that Freud willfully ignored the sexual abuse of women patients. She pillories the author Joe McGinniss and raises the possibility that his subject, Jeffrey MacDonald, may not have murdered his wife (and children). And now Malcolm has chosen Hughes, a man who has had two wives commit suicide and who has been widely vilified for his treatment of Plath.

Perhaps because of the impulse that Malcolm feels to defend Hughes, as she moves from her wonderful, tough descriptions of the more peripheral characters toward her two central characters—Plath and Hughes—her portraits become less convincing. Her admiration for Hughes, despite (or perhaps because of) never having met him, is surprisingly starry-eyed. He is for her, as for Plath, the "overgrown Adonis/Aryan superman." He is described as having a "Chekhovian largeheartedness" and is compared to Prometheus; women are said to become literally weak in the knees at the sight of him. "When he writes about Plath he renders all other writings about her crude and trivial."

Malcolm's prose at times has an almost swooning quality. She writes that, reading a letter of Hughes to Stevenson, "I felt my identification with its typing swell into a feeling of intense sympathy and affection for the writer. . . . Critics will wrestle with the question of what gives [the letters] their peculiar power, why they are so deeply, mysteriously moving." In one amazing scene, she makes a pilgrimage to look at Hughes's house and has a *frisson* of pleasure as she realizes from a recently filled bird feeder that "the Hugheses were not away, that my intrusion might not be going unmarked. . . . I felt a return of my feeling of tenderness towards Hughes."

But although Malcolm succeeds in demonstrating that Hughes's life has been deformed by Plath's death, she never addresses the many contradictions in Hughes's chosen role as victim. Malcolm has the writerly integrity to supply us with enough facts to make the inconsistencies evident, but we are left without an explanation that is consonant with Malcolm's characterization. Hughes bitterly denounces the invasion of his privacy and the opportunistic use of Plath's writings by scholars. Yet he sold *The Bell Jar* to buy a second country house—despite the pain this move caused Plath's mother. The sale of the book then provoked further disclosures by Plath's mother in an effort to exonerate herself. Hughes destroyed at least one and possibly two of Plath's notebooks, pleading that he did it to protect their children. But obviously these could have been preserved in a library and made unavailable for the next century if he had wished: Hughes was protecting himself. Hughes's infidelities are also dismissed. It's a situation, Malcolm writes, that "perhaps more couples find themselves in than don't. . . ." Surely two wives who committed suicide and the murder of one of his children by his second wife go beyond the normal course of youthful mistakes and marital woes. This unsettling theme is neither examined nor explained.

Malcolm's uncritical portrait of Hughes has as its counterpart the largely unflattering portrait of the Silent Woman—Sylvia Plath. Amazingly, Plath, at first glance the victim of the piece, is revealed to be the murderer—a sleight of hand Agatha Christie would be proud of. Her death itself, her "silence," turns out to be the murder weapon: "It is Plath's (Medusan) speechlessness that is the deadly, punishing weapon." Her silence is described as threatening, unnerving—aggression. Malcolm's admiration of Plath's poetry is grudging. The *Ariel* poems are described as the "waste products" of her madness. During the last months of her life, when Plath was suffering from a severe clinical depression in the setting of her recent separation, she is described as "running actual fevers as well as figurative ones of jealous rage and bathetic self-pity."

It is of course Hughes who has been silent and has refused to speak to anyone writing on Plath. Destroying Plath's writing is certainly the imposition of an irrevocable silence.

—Anna Fels

Malcolm's depiction of Plath as the Silent Woman is perhaps the strangest distortion of the entire book. Plath is, after all, the only person mentioned in this book who will undoubtedly continue to be heard from for a long time to come. Each time her poems are quoted in the book this fact is underlined. It was even more striking when the book was published as an essay in *The New Yorker* with the full texts of many of Plath's most powerful poems alongside it. In letters, fiction, journals and poems, Plath is very far from silent. The book includes a wonderful quote from Elizabeth Hardwick, who heard Plath in a BBC recording: "These bitter poems . . . were 'beautifully' read, projected in full-throated, plump, diction-perfect, Englishy, mesmerizing cadences, all round and rapid, and paced and spaced. Poor recessive Massachusetts had been erased. 'I have done it again!' " It is hard to think of Plath as silent. Paradoxically, it is of course Hughes who has been silent and has refused to speak to anyone writing on Plath. Destroying Plath's writing is certainly the imposition of an irrevocable silence.

But if Malcolm's motives at times appear to overwhelm the material, at many others she's wonderfully clear-eyed. And when she does intrude, Malcolm tries to warn us about the writer's animus, her calculations. The distortions are there, but they are a price worth paying for the depth and insight and sheer pleasure in Malcolm's narrative. Despite her cautions we become transfixed by a story that has all the elements of a great mystery: sex, murder, betrayals, suicide. But in this tale the crimes are as hidden as the evidence. It is only as we follow Malcolm into her deep psychological investigation that we begin to see the lineaments of true criminality. Like the guileless interviewees described by Malcolm, who always agree to talk to the writer, her readers cannot help being drawn into her endeavor. As Malcolm put it in the last line of her prior book: "And still they say yes when a journalist calls, and still they are astonished when they see the flash of the knife."

FURTHER READING

Biography

Alexander, Paul. *Rough Magic: A Biography of Sylvia Plath.* New York: Viking, 1991, 402 p.

Largely implicates Hughes in Plath's death. Alexander forgoes literary analysis of Plath's work in favor of tracing the lives of those affected by Plath's death and her rising popularity since 1962.

Butscher, Edward. *Sylvia Plath: Method and Madness.* New York: Seabury Press, 1976, 388 p.

Presents a psychological portrait of Plath and her various personae, discusses how she integrated these identities into her life and art, and analyzes the formation of the Plath legend.

Hayman, Ronald. *The Death and Life of Sylvia Plath.* New York: Birch Lane Press, 1991, 235 p.

Writes of Plath's life, her college boyfriends, and the circumstances leading to her death. Hayman also relates the details of Plath's psychological history and Hughes's infidelity.

Wagner-Martin, Linda. *Sylvia Plath: A Biography.* New York: Simon & Schuster, 1987, 282 p.

Focuses on Plath's desire to become the perfect wife and mother. Wagner-Martin, who was denied permission to quote from Plath's works, argues that Plath's quest led her to defer her development as a writer.

Criticism

Alexander, Paul, ed. *Ariel Ascending: Writings about Sylvia Plath.* New York: Harper & Row, 1985, 218 p.

Collects essays on Plath by such critics as Joyce Carol Oates and Elizabeth Hardwick as well as observations written by Anne Sexton, Ted Hughes, and Aurelia Plath.

Bredsdorff, Thomas. "The Biographical Pursuit: Biography as a Tool of Literary Criticism." *Orbis Litterarum: International Review of Literary Studies* 44, No. 2 (1989): 181-90.

Maintains that biography is a useful tool in critically assessing "less than perfect" literary works, such as Plath's poetry.

Butscher, Edward, ed. *Sylvia Plath: The Woman and the Work.* New York: Dodd, Mead, 1977, 242 p.

Includes memoirs written especially for this volume by seven people who knew Plath, as well as other previously published criticism.

Christiansen, Rupert. "Hanging Out the Washing." *The Spectator* 269, No. 8578 (5 December 1992): 45-6.

Negative review of Ian Hamilton's *Keepers of the Flame.* Christiansen argues that the book is "unfocused" and does not deeply explore the history of biography or sufficiently ponder philosophical and moral issues.

Frank, Elizabeth. "A Long Romance with Death." *The New York Times Book Review* (6 October 1991): 14-16.

Reviews *The Death and Life of Sylvia Plath* and *Rough Magic.* Frank applauds Hughes's silence regarding Plath but states that "no adequate biography can possibly be written as long as the Plath estate continues to exact editorial compliance as the price of full quotation."

Friendly, Fred W. "Was Trust Betrayed?" *The New York Times Book Review* (25 February 1990): 1, 41-2.

Discusses Janet Malcolm's claim that biography and journalism are voyeuristic as he reviews Malcolm's *The Journalist and the Murderer,* in which Malcolm asserted that Joe McGinniss, the author of *Fatal Vision,* misrepresented himself in order to gain access to the murder defendant Jeffrey MacDonald.

Pinsky, Robert. "Playing the Tragedy Queen." *The New York Times Book Review* (27 August 1991): 11.

Concedes that Anne Stevenson's suggestion in *Bitter Fame* that "Plath suffered the airless egocentrism of one in love with an ideal self" is plausible but notes that Olwyn Hughes's role in writing the book may leave many readers uncomfortable with the unsympathetic way in which the biography unfolds.

Rose, Jacqueline. *The Haunting of Sylvia Plath.* Cambridge, Mass.: Harvard University Press, 1992, 288 p.

Contends that various interpretations of Plath have arisen over the years because of the disturbing and troubling nature of her life and work.

Showalter, Elaine. "Risky Business." *The London Review of Books* 16, No. 8 (22 September 1994): 19.

Ambivalent review of Linda Wagner-Martin's *Telling Women's Lives.* Showalter traces the rise of the women's biography genre and takes issue with Wagner-Martin's belief that only women are qualified to write biographies of women.

Treglown, Jeremy. "Beware the Biographer." *The Times Literary Supplement,* No. 4674 (30 October 1992): 9.

Calls *Keepers of the Flame* "absorbing and drily funny." Treglown appreciates Hamilton's treatment of Henry James and Philip Larkin, but laments the author's failure to explore at length the ramifications of copyright legislation and the ethics of consent involved in biographical writing.

Additional coverage of Plath's life and career is contained in the following sources published by Gale Research: *Concise Dictionary of American Literary Biography, 1941-1968; Contemporary Authors,* Vols. 19-20; *Contemporary Authors New Revision Series,* Vol. 34; *Contemporary Authors Permanent Series,* Vol. 2; *Contemporary Literary Criticism,* Vols. 1, 2, 3, 5, 9, 11, 14, 17, 50, 51, 62; *Dictionary of Literary Biography,* Vols. 5, 6; *DISCovering Authors; Major 20th-Century Writers; Poetry Criticism,* Vol. 1; and *World Literature Criticism.*

□ Contemporary Literary Criticism

Indexes

Literary Criticism Series
Cumulative Author Index
Cumulative Topic Index
Cumulative Nationality Index
Title Index, Volume 86

How to Use This Index

The main references

Calvino, Italo
1923-1985.....CLC 5, 8, 11, 22, 33, 39, 73; SSC 3

list all author entries in the following Gale Literary Criticism series:

BLC = *Black Literature Criticism*
CLC = *Contemporary Literary Criticism*
CLR = *Children's Literature Review*
CMLC = *Classical and Medieval Literature Criticism*
DA = *DISCovering Authors*
DC = *Drama Criticism*
HLC = *Hispanic Literature Criticism*
LC = *Literature Criticism from 1400 to 1800*
NCLC = *Nineteenth-Century Literature Criticism*
PC = *Poetry Criticism*
SSC = *Short Story Criticism*
TCLC = *Twentieth-Century Literary Criticism*
WLC = *World Literature Criticism, 1500 to the Present*

The cross-references

See also CANR 23; CA 85-88;
obituary CA 116

list all author entries in the following Gale biographical and literary sources:

AAYA = *Authors & Artists for Young Adults*
AITN = *Authors in the News*
BEST = *Bestsellers*
BW = *Black Writers*
CA = *Contemporary Authors*
CAAS = *Contemporary Authors Autobiography Series*
CABS = *Contemporary Authors Bibliographical Series*
CANR = *Contemporary Authors New Revision Series*
CAP = *Contemporary Authors Permanent Series*
CDALB = *Concise Dictionary of American Literary Biography*
CDBLB = *Concise Dictionary of British Literary Biography*
DLB = *Dictionary of Literary Biography*
DLBD = *Dictionary of Literary Biography Documentary Series*
DLBY = *Dictionary of Literary Biography Yearbook*
HW = *Hispanic Writers*
JRDA = *Junior DISCovering Authors*
MAICYA = *Major Authors and Illustrators for Children and Young Adults*
MTCW = *Major 20th-Century Writers*
NNAL = *Native North American Literature*
SAAS = *Something about the Author Autobiography Series*
SATA = *Something about the Author*
YABC = *Yesterday's Authors of Books for Children*

Literary Criticism Series Cumulative Author Index

Aldiss, Brian W(ilson) 1925- . . . . **CLC 5, 14, 40**
See also CA 5-8R; CAAS 2; CANR 5, 28; DLB 14; MTCW; SATA 34

Alegria, Claribel 1924- . . . . **CLC 75**
See also CA 131; CAAS 15; DLB 145; HW

Alegria, Fernando 1918- . . . . **CLC 57**
See also CA 9-12R; CANR 5, 32; HW

Aleichem, Sholom . . . . **TCLC 1, 35**
See also Rabinovitch, Sholem

Aleixandre, Vicente 1898-1984 . . . **CLC 9, 36**
See also CA 85-88; 114; CANR 26; DLB 108; HW; MTCW

Alepoudelis, Odysseus
See Elytis, Odysseus

Aleshkovsky, Joseph 1929-
See Aleshkovsky, Yuz
See also CA 121; 128

Aleshkovsky, Yuz . . . . **CLC 44**
See also Aleshkovsky, Joseph

Alexander, Lloyd (Chudley) 1924- . . **CLC 35**
See also AAYA 1; CA 1-4R; CANR 1, 24, 38; CLR 1, 5; DLB 52; JRDA; MAICYA; MTCW; SAAS 19; SATA 3, 49, 81

Alfau, Felipe 1902- . . . . **CLC 66**
See also CA 137

Alger, Horatio, Jr. 1832-1899 . . . . . **NCLC 8**
See also DLB 42; SATA 16

Algren, Nelson 1909-1981 . . . . **CLC 4, 10, 33**
See also CA 13-16R; 103; CANR 20; CDALB 1941-1968; DLB 9; DLBY 81, 82; MTCW

Ali, Ahmed 1910- . . . . **CLC 69**
See also CA 25-28R; CANR 15, 34

Alighieri, Dante 1265-1321 . . . . **CMLC 3**

Allan, John B.
See Westlake, Donald E(dwin)

Allen, Edward 1948- . . . . **CLC 59**

Allen, Paula Gunn 1939- . . . . **CLC 84**
See also CA 112; 143; NNAL

Allen, Roland
See Ayckbourn, Alan

Allen, Sarah A.
See Hopkins, Pauline Elizabeth

Allen, Woody 1935- . . . . **CLC 16, 52**
See also AAYA 10; CA 33-36R; CANR 27, 38; DLB 44; MTCW

Allende, Isabel 1942- . . . . **CLC 39, 57; HLC**
See also CA 125; 130; DLB 145; HW; MTCW

Alleyn, Ellen
See Rossetti, Christina (Georgina)

Allingham, Margery (Louise) 1904-1966 . . . . **CLC 19**
See also CA 5-8R; 25-28R; CANR 4; DLB 77; MTCW

Allingham, William 1824-1889 . . . **NCLC 25**
See also DLB 35

Allison, Dorothy E. 1949- . . . . **CLC 78**
See also CA 140

Allston, Washington 1779-1843 . . . . **NCLC 2**
See also DLB 1

Almedingen, E. M. . . . . **CLC 12**
See also Almedingen, Martha Edith von
See also SATA 3

Almedingen, Martha Edith von 1898-1971
See Almedingen, E. M.
See also CA 1-4R; CANR 1

Almqvist, Carl Jonas Love 1793-1866 . . . . **NCLC 42**

Alonso, Damaso 1898-1990 . . . . **CLC 14**
See also CA 110; 131; 130; DLB 108; HW

Alov
See Gogol, Nikolai (Vasilyevich)

Alta 1942- . . . . **CLC 19**
See also CA 57-60

Alter, Robert B(ernard) 1935- . . . . . . **CLC 34**
See also CA 49-52; CANR 1, 47

Alther, Lisa 1944- . . . . **CLC 7, 41**
See also CA 65-68; CANR 12, 30; MTCW

Altman, Robert 1925- . . . . **CLC 16**
See also CA 73-76; CANR 43

Alvarez, A(lfred) 1929- . . . . **CLC 5, 13**
See also CA 1-4R; CANR 3, 33; DLB 14, 40

Alvarez, Alejandro Rodriguez 1903-1965
See Casona, Alejandro
See also CA 131; 93-96; HW

Amado, Jorge 1912- . . . . . **CLC 13, 40; HLC**
See also CA 77-80; CANR 35; DLB 113; MTCW

Ambler, Eric 1909- . . . . **CLC 4, 6, 9**
See also CA 9-12R; CANR 7, 38; DLB 77; MTCW

Amichai, Yehuda 1924- . . . . . . **CLC 9, 22, 57**
See also CA 85-88; CANR 46; MTCW

Amiel, Henri Frederic 1821-1881 . . **NCLC 4**

Amis, Kingsley (William) 1922- . . **CLC 1, 2, 3, 5, 8, 13, 40, 44; DA**
See also AITN 2; CA 9-12R; CANR 8, 28; CDBLB 1945-1960; DLB 15, 27, 100, 139; MTCW

Amis, Martin (Louis) 1949- . . . . **CLC 4, 9, 38, 62**
See also BEST 90:3; CA 65-68; CANR 8, 27; DLB 14

Ammons, A(rchie) R(andolph) 1926- . . . . **CLC 2, 3, 5, 8, 9, 25, 57**
See also AITN 1; CA 9-12R; CANR 6, 36; DLB 5; MTCW

Amo, Tauraatua i
See Adams, Henry (Brooks)

Anand, Mulk Raj 1905- . . . . **CLC 23**
See also CA 65-68; CANR 32; MTCW

Anatol
See Schnitzler, Arthur

Anaya, Rudolfo A(lfonso) 1937- . . . . **CLC 23; HLC**
See also CA 45-48; CAAS 4; CANR 1, 32; DLB 82; HW 1; MTCW

Andersen, Hans Christian 1805-1875 . . **NCLC 7; DA; SSC 6; WLC**
See also CLR 6; MAICYA; YABC 1

Anderson, C. Farley
See Mencken, H(enry) L(ouis); Nathan, George Jean

Anderson, Jessica (Margaret) Queale . . . . **CLC 37**
See also CA 9-12R; CANR 4

Anderson, Jon (Victor) 1940- . . . . **CLC 9**
See also CA 25-28R; CANR 20

Anderson, Lindsay (Gordon) 1923-1994 . . . . **CLC 20**
See also CA 125; 128; 146

Anderson, Maxwell 1888-1959 . . . . . **TCLC 2**
See also CA 105; DLB 7

Anderson, Poul (William) 1926- . . . . **CLC 15**
See also AAYA 5; CA 1-4R; CAAS 2; CANR 2, 15, 34; DLB 8; MTCW; SATA 39

Anderson, Robert (Woodruff) 1917- . . . . **CLC 23**
See also AITN 1; CA 21-24R; CANR 32; DLB 7

Anderson, Sherwood 1876-1941 . . . . **TCLC 1, 10, 24; DA; SSC 1; WLC**
See also CA 104; 121; CDALB 1917-1929; DLB 4, 9, 86; DLBD 1; MTCW

Andouard
See Giraudoux, (Hippolyte) Jean

Andrade, Carlos Drummond de . . . . . . **CLC 18**
See also Drummond de Andrade, Carlos

Andrade, Mario de 1893-1945 . . . . . **TCLC 43**

Andreas-Salome, Lou 1861-1937 . . . **TCLC 56**
See also DLB 66

Andrewes, Lancelot 1555-1626 . . . . **LC 5**

Andrews, Cicily Fairfield
See West, Rebecca

Andrews, Elton V.
See Pohl, Frederik

Andreyev, Leonid (Nikolaevich) 1871-1919 . . . . **TCLC 3**
See also CA 104

Andric, Ivo 1892-1975 . . . . **CLC 8**
See also CA 81-84; 57-60; CANR 43; DLB 147; MTCW

Angelique, Pierre
See Bataille, Georges

Angell, Roger 1920- . . . . **CLC 26**
See also CA 57-60; CANR 13, 44

Angelou, Maya 1928- . . . . **CLC 12, 35, 64, 77; BLC; DA**
See also AAYA 7; BW 2; CA 65-68; CANR 19, 42; DLB 38; MTCW; SATA 49

Annensky, Innokenty Fyodorovich 1856-1909 . . . . **TCLC 14**
See also CA 110

Anon, Charles Robert
See Pessoa, Fernando (Antonio Nogueira)

Anouilh, Jean (Marie Lucien Pierre) 1910-1987 . . . . . . **CLC 1, 3, 8, 13, 40, 50**
See also CA 17-20R; 123; CANR 32; MTCW

Anthony, Florence
See Ai

Anthony, John
See Ciardi, John (Anthony)

Anthony, Peter
See Shaffer, Anthony (Joshua); Shaffer, Peter (Levin)

Anthony, Piers 1934- . . . . **CLC 35**
See also AAYA 11; CA 21-24R; CANR 28; DLB 8; MTCW

Antoine, Marc
See Proust, (Valentin-Louis-George-Eugene-) Marcel

Antoninus, Brother
See Everson, William (Oliver)

Antonioni, Michelangelo 1912- . . . . . **CLC 20**
See also CA 73-76; CANR 45

Antschel, Paul 1920-1970
See Celan, Paul
See also CA 85-88; CANR 33; MTCW

Anwar, Chairil 1922-1949 . . . . **TCLC 22**
See also CA 121

Apollinaire, Guillaume . . **TCLC 3, 8, 51; PC 7**
See also Kostrowitzki, Wilhelm Apollinaris de

Appelfeld, Aharon 1932- . . . . **CLC 23, 47**
See also CA 112; 133

Apple, Max (Isaac) 1941- . . . . **CLC 9, 33**
See also CA 81-84; CANR 19; DLB 130

Appleman, Philip (Dean) 1926- . . . . . **CLC 51**
See also CA 13-16R; CAAS 18; CANR 6, 29

Appleton, Lawrence
See Lovecraft, H(oward) P(hillips)

Apteryx
See Eliot, T(homas) S(tearns)

Apuleius, (Lucius Madaurensis)
125(?)-175(?) . . . . **CMLC 1**

Aquin, Hubert 1929-1977. . . . . **CLC 15**
See also CA 105; DLB 53

Aragon, Louis 1897-1982 . . . . **CLC 3, 22**
See also CA 69-72; 108; CANR 28; DLB 72; MTCW

Arany, Janos 1817-1882. . . . . **NCLC 34**

Arbuthnot, John 1667-1735 . . . . **LC 1**
See also DLB 101

Archer, Herbert Winslow
See Mencken, H(enry) L(ouis)

Archer, Jeffrey (Howard) 1940- . . . . **CLC 28**
See also BEST 89:3; CA 77-80; CANR 22

Archer, Jules 1915- . . . . **CLC 12**
See also CA 9-12R; CANR 6; SAAS 5; SATA 4

Archer, Lee
See Ellison, Harlan (Jay)

Arden, John 1930- . . . . **CLC 6, 13, 15**
See also CA 13-16R; CAAS 4; CANR 31; DLB 13; MTCW

Arenas, Reinaldo
1943-1990 . . . . **CLC 41; HLC**
See also CA 124; 128; 133; DLB 145; HW

Arendt, Hannah 1906-1975 . . . . **CLC 66**
See also CA 17-20R; 61-64; CANR 26; MTCW

Aretino, Pietro 1492-1556 . . . . **LC 12**

Arghezi, Tudor. **CLC 80**
See also Theodorescu, Ion N.

Arguedas, Jose Maria
1911-1969 . . . . **CLC 10, 18**
See also CA 89-92; DLB 113; HW

Argueta, Manlio 1936- . . . . **CLC 31**
See also CA 131; DLB 145; HW

Ariosto, Ludovico 1474-1533 . . . . **LC 6**

Aristides
See Epstein, Joseph

Aristophanes
450B.C.-385B.C. . . . **CMLC 4; DA; DC 2**

Arlt, Roberto (Godofredo Christophersen)
1900-1942 . . . . **TCLC 29; HLC**
See also CA 123; 131; HW

Armah, Ayi Kwei 1939- . . . . **CLC 5, 33; BLC**
See also BW 1; CA 61-64; CANR 21; DLB 117; MTCW

Armatrading, Joan 1950- . . . . **CLC 17**
See also CA 114

Arnette, Robert
See Silverberg, Robert

Arnim, Achim von (Ludwig Joachim von Arnim) 1781-1831 . . . . **NCLC 5**
See also DLB 90

Arnim, Bettina von 1785-1859 . . . . **NCLC 38**
See also DLB 90

Arnold, Matthew
1822-1888 . . . . . **NCLC 6, 29; DA; PC 5; WLC**
See also CDBLB 1832-1890; DLB 32, 57

Arnold, Thomas 1795-1842 . . . . . . **NCLC 18**
See also DLB 55

Arnow, Harriette (Louisa) Simpson
1908-1986 . . . . **CLC 2, 7, 18**
See also CA 9-12R; 118; CANR 14; DLB 6; MTCW; SATA 42; SATA-Obit 47

Arp, Hans
See Arp, Jean

Arp, Jean 1887-1966. . . . . **CLC 5**
See also CA 81-84; 25-28R; CANR 42

Arrabal
See Arrabal, Fernando

Arrabal, Fernando 1932- . . . **CLC 2, 9, 18, 58**
See also CA 9-12R; CANR 15

Arrick, Fran. . . . . **CLC 30**

Artaud, Antonin 1896-1948 . . . . . **TCLC 3, 36**
See also CA 104

Arthur, Ruth M(abel) 1905-1979. . . . **CLC 12**
See also CA 9-12R; 85-88; CANR 4; SATA 7, 26

Artsybashev, Mikhail (Petrovich)
1878-1927 . . . . **TCLC 31**

Arundel, Honor (Morfydd)
1919-1973 . . . . **CLC 17**
See also CA 21-22; 41-44R; CAP 2; CLR 35; SATA 4; SATA-Obit 24

Asch, Sholem 1880-1957 . . . . **TCLC 3**
See also CA 105

Ash, Shalom
See Asch, Sholem

Ashbery, John (Lawrence)
1927- . . . . . . **CLC 2, 3, 4, 6, 9, 13, 15, 25, 41, 77**
See also CA 5-8R; CANR 9, 37; DLB 5; DLBY 81; MTCW

Ashdown, Clifford
See Freeman, R(ichard) Austin

Ashe, Gordon
See Creasey, John

Ashton-Warner, Sylvia (Constance)
1908-1984 . . . . **CLC 19**
See also CA 69-72; 112; CANR 29; MTCW

Asimov, Isaac
1920-1992 . . . . . . **CLC 1, 3, 9, 19, 26, 76**
See also AAYA 13; BEST 90:2; CA 1-4R; 137; CANR 2, 19, 36; CLR 12; DLB 8; DLBY 92; JRDA; MAICYA; MTCW; SATA 1, 26, 74

Astley, Thea (Beatrice May)
1925- . . . . **CLC 41**
See also CA 65-68; CANR 11, 43

Aston, James
See White, T(erence) H(anbury)

Asturias, Miguel Angel
1899-1974 . . . . **CLC 3, 8, 13; HLC**
See also CA 25-28; 49-52; CANR 32; CAP 2; DLB 113; HW; MTCW

Atares, Carlos Saura
See Saura (Atares), Carlos

Atheling, William
See Pound, Ezra (Weston Loomis)

Atheling, William, Jr.
See Blish, James (Benjamin)

Atherton, Gertrude (Franklin Horn)
1857-1948 . . . . **TCLC 2**
See also CA 104; DLB 9, 78

Atherton, Lucius
See Masters, Edgar Lee

Atkins, Jack
See Harris, Mark

Atticus
See Fleming, Ian (Lancaster)

Atwood, Margaret (Eleanor)
1939- . . . . . **CLC 2, 3, 4, 8, 13, 15, 25, 44, 84; DA; PC 8; SSC 2; WLC**
See also AAYA 12; BEST 89:2; CA 49-52; CANR 3, 24, 33; DLB 53; MTCW; SATA 50

Aubigny, Pierre d'
See Mencken, H(enry) L(ouis)

Aubin, Penelope 1685-1731(?) . . . . **LC 9**
See also DLB 39

Auchincloss, Louis (Stanton)
1917- . . . . **CLC 4, 6, 9, 18, 45**
See also CA 1-4R; CANR 6, 29; DLB 2; DLBY 80; MTCW

Auden, W(ystan) H(ugh)
1907-1973 . . . . . . **CLC 1, 2, 3, 4, 6, 9, 11, 14, 43; DA; PC 1; WLC**
See also CA 9-12R; 45-48; CANR 5; CDBLB 1914-1945; DLB 10, 20; MTCW

Audiberti, Jacques 1900-1965 . . . . . . **CLC 38**
See also CA 25-28R

Audubon, John James
1785-1851 . . . . **NCLC 47**

Auel, Jean M(arie) 1936- . . . . **CLC 31**
See also AAYA 7; BEST 90:4; CA 103; CANR 21

Auerbach, Erich 1892-1957 . . . . **TCLC 43**
See also CA 118

Brathwaite, Edward Kamau 1930-... **CLC 11**
See also BW 2; CA 25-28R; CANR 11, 26, 47; DLB 125

Brautigan, Richard (Gary) 1935-1984 .... **CLC 1, 3, 5, 9, 12, 34, 42**
See also CA 53-56; 113; CANR 34; DLB 2, 5; DLBY 80, 84; MTCW; SATA 56

Braverman, Kate 1950- .... **CLC 67**
See also CA 89-92

Brecht, Bertolt 1898-1956 ...... **TCLC 1, 6, 13, 35; DA; DC 3; WLC**
See also CA 104; 133; DLB 56, 124; MTCW

Brecht, Eugen Berthold Friedrich
See Brecht, Bertolt

Bremer, Fredrika 1801-1865 ..... **NCLC 11**

Brennan, Christopher John 1870-1932 .... **TCLC 17**
See also CA 117

Brennan, Maeve 1917-............. **CLC 5**
See also CA 81-84

Brentano, Clemens (Maria) 1778-1842 .... **NCLC 1**
See also DLB 90

Brent of Bin Bin
See Franklin, (Stella Maraia Sarah) Miles

Brenton, Howard 1942- .... **CLC 31**
See also CA 69-72; CANR 33; DLB 13; MTCW

Breslin, James 1930-
See Breslin, Jimmy
See also CA 73-76; CANR 31; MTCW

Breslin, Jimmy .... **CLC 4, 43**
See also Breslin, James
See also AITN 1

Bresson, Robert 1907- .... **CLC 16**
See also CA 110

Breton, Andre 1896-1966... **CLC 2, 9, 15, 54**
See also CA 19-20; 25-28R; CANR 40; CAP 2; DLB 65; MTCW

Breytenbach, Breyten 1939(?)- .. **CLC 23, 37**
See also CA 113; 129

Bridgers, Sue Ellen 1942- .... **CLC 26**
See also AAYA 8; CA 65-68; CANR 11, 36; CLR 18; DLB 52; JRDA; MAICYA; SAAS 1; SATA 22

Bridges, Robert (Seymour) 1844-1930 .... **TCLC 1**
See also CA 104; CDBLB 1890-1914; DLB 19, 98

Bridie, James..................... **TCLC 3**
See also Mavor, Osborne Henry
See also DLB 10

Brin, David 1950-................ **CLC 34**
See also CA 102; CANR 24; SATA 65

Brink, Andre (Philippus) 1935- .... **CLC 18, 36**
See also CA 104; CANR 39; MTCW

Brinsmead, H(esba) F(ay) 1922- .... **CLC 21**
See also CA 21-24R; CANR 10; MAICYA; SAAS 5; SATA 18, 78

Brittain, Vera (Mary) 1893(?)-1970 .... **CLC 23**
See also CA 13-16; 25-28R; CAP 1; MTCW

Broch, Hermann 1886-1951....... **TCLC 20**
See also CA 117; DLB 85, 124

Brock, Rose
See Hansen, Joseph

Brodkey, Harold 1930-............ **CLC 56**
See also CA 111; DLB 130

Brodsky, Iosif Alexandrovich 1940-
See Brodsky, Joseph
See also AITN 1; CA 41-44R; CANR 37; MTCW

Brodsky, Joseph .. **CLC 4, 6, 13, 36, 50; PC 9**
See also Brodsky, Iosif Alexandrovich

Brodsky, Michael Mark 1948- ..... **CLC 19**
See also CA 102; CANR 18, 41

Bromell, Henry 1947-............. **CLC 5**
See also CA 53-56; CANR 9

Bromfield, Louis (Brucker) 1896-1956 .... **TCLC 11**
See also CA 107; DLB 4, 9, 86

Broner, E(sther) M(asserman) 1930- .... **CLC 19**
See also CA 17-20R; CANR 8, 25; DLB 28

Bronk, William 1918-............. **CLC 10**
See also CA 89-92; CANR 23

Bronstein, Lev Davidovich
See Trotsky, Leon

Bronte, Anne 1820-1849.......... **NCLC 4**
See also DLB 21

Bronte, Charlotte 1816-1855 ... **NCLC 3, 8, 33; DA; WLC**
See also CDBLB 1832-1890; DLB 21

Bronte, (Jane) Emily 1818-1848 .... **NCLC 16, 35; DA; PC 8; WLC**
See also CDBLB 1832-1890; DLB 21, 32

Brooke, Frances 1724-1789 .... **LC 6**
See also DLB 39, 99

Brooke, Henry 1703(?)-1783 .... **LC 1**
See also DLB 39

Brooke, Rupert (Chawner) 1887-1915 .... **TCLC 2, 7; DA; WLC**
See also CA 104; 132; CDBLB 1914-1945; DLB 19; MTCW

Brooke-Haven, P.
See Wodehouse, P(elham) G(renville)

Brooke-Rose, Christine 1926- ...... **CLC 40**
See also CA 13-16R; DLB 14

Brookner, Anita 1928- ...... **CLC 32, 34, 51**
See also CA 114; 120; CANR 37; DLBY 87; MTCW

Brooks, Cleanth 1906-1994 ..... **CLC 24, 86**
See also CA 17-20R; 145; CANR 33, 35; DLB 63; MTCW

Brooks, George
See Baum, L(yman) Frank

Brooks, Gwendolyn 1917- ...... **CLC 1, 2, 4, 5, 15, 49; BLC; DA; PC 7; WLC**
See also AITN 1; BW 2; CA 1-4R; CANR 1, 27; CDALB 1941-1968; CLR 27; DLB 5, 76; MTCW; SATA 6

Brooks, Mel...................... **CLC 12**
See also Kaminsky, Melvin
See also AAYA 13; DLB 26

Brooks, Peter 1938- .... **CLC 34**
See also CA 45-48; CANR 1

Brooks, Van Wyck 1886-1963...... **CLC 29**
See also CA 1-4R; CANR 6; DLB 45, 63, 103

Brophy, Brigid (Antonia) 1929- .... **CLC 6, 11, 29**
See also CA 5-8R; CAAS 4; CANR 25; DLB 14; MTCW

Brosman, Catharine Savage 1934-.... **CLC 9**
See also CA 61-64; CANR 21, 46

Brother Antoninus
See Everson, William (Oliver)

Broughton, T(homas) Alan 1936- ... **CLC 19**
See also CA 45-48; CANR 2, 23

Broumas, Olga 1949- .... **CLC 10, 73**
See also CA 85-88; CANR 20

Brown, Charles Brockden 1771-1810 .... **NCLC 22**
See also CDALB 1640-1865; DLB 37, 59, 73

Brown, Christy 1932-1981 .... **CLC 63**
See also CA 105; 104; DLB 14

Brown, Claude 1937- .... **CLC 30; BLC**
See also AAYA 7; BW 1; CA 73-76

Brown, Dee (Alexander) 1908- .. **CLC 18, 47**
See also CA 13-16R; CAAS 6; CANR 11, 45; DLBY 80; MTCW; SATA 5

Brown, George
See Wertmueller, Lina

Brown, George Douglas 1869-1902 .... **TCLC 28**

Brown, George Mackay 1921-.... **CLC 5, 48**
See also CA 21-24R; CAAS 6; CANR 12, 37; DLB 14, 27, 139; MTCW; SATA 35

Brown, (William) Larry 1951-...... **CLC 73**
See also CA 130; 134

Brown, Moses
See Barrett, William (Christopher)

Brown, Rita Mae 1944- ..... **CLC 18, 43, 79**
See also CA 45-48; CANR 2, 11, 35; MTCW

Brown, Roderick (Langmere) Haig-
See Haig-Brown, Roderick (Langmere)

Brown, Rosellen 1939- .... **CLC 32**
See also CA 77-80; CAAS 10; CANR 14, 44

Brown, Sterling Allen 1901-1989 .... **CLC 1, 23, 59; BLC**
See also BW 1; CA 85-88; 127; CANR 26; DLB 48, 51, 63; MTCW

Brown, Will
See Ainsworth, William Harrison

Brown, William Wells 1813-1884 .... **NCLC 2; BLC; DC 1**
See also DLB 3, 50

Browne, (Clyde) Jackson 1948(?)-... **CLC 21**
See also CA 120

Browning, Elizabeth Barrett 1806-1861 ..... **NCLC 1, 16; DA; PC 6; WLC**
See also CDBLB 1832-1890; DLB 32

Cary, (Arthur) Joyce (Lunel) 1888-1957 . . . . **TCLC 1, 29**
See also CA 104; CDBLB 1914-1945; DLB 15, 100

Casanova de Seingalt, Giovanni Jacopo 1725-1798 . . . . **LC 13**

Casares, Adolfo Bioy
See Bioy Casares, Adolfo

Casely-Hayford, J(oseph) E(phraim) 1866-1930 . . . . **TCLC 24; BLC**
See also BW 2; CA 123

Casey, John (Dudley) 1939- . . . . **CLC 59**
See also BEST 90:2; CA 69-72; CANR 23

Casey, Michael 1947- . . . . **CLC 2**
See also CA 65-68; DLB 5

Casey, Patrick
See Thurman, Wallace (Henry)

Casey, Warren (Peter) 1935-1988 . . . **CLC 12**
See also CA 101; 127

Casona, Alejandro . . . . **CLC 49**
See also Alvarez, Alejandro Rodriguez

Cassavetes, John 1929-1989 . . . . **CLC 20**
See also CA 85-88; 127

Cassill, R(onald) V(erlin) 1919- . . . **CLC 4, 23**
See also CA 9-12R; CAAS 1; CANR 7, 45; DLB 6

Cassity, (Allen) Turner 1929- . . . . **CLC 6, 42**
See also CA 17-20R; CAAS 8; CANR 11; DLB 105

Castaneda, Carlos 1931(?)- . . . . **CLC 12**
See also CA 25-28R; CANR 32; HW; MTCW

Castedo, Elena 1937- . . . . **CLC 65**
See also CA 132

Castedo-Ellerman, Elena
See Castedo, Elena

Castellanos, Rosario 1925-1974 . . . . **CLC 66; HLC**
See also CA 131; 53-56; DLB 113; HW

Castelvetro, Lodovico 1505-1571 . . . . . **LC 12**

Castiglione, Baldassare 1478-1529 . . . **LC 12**

Castle, Robert
See Hamilton, Edmond

Castro, Guillen de 1569-1631 . . . . **LC 19**

Castro, Rosalia de 1837-1885 . . . . . **NCLC 3**

Cather, Willa
See Cather, Willa Sibert

Cather, Willa Sibert 1873-1947 . . . . **TCLC 1, 11, 31; DA; SSC 2; WLC**
See also CA 104; 128; CDALB 1865-1917; DLB 9, 54, 78; DLBD 1; MTCW; SATA 30

Catton, (Charles) Bruce 1899-1978 . . . . **CLC 35**
See also AITN 1; CA 5-8R; 81-84; CANR 7; DLB 17; SATA 2; SATA-Obit 24

Cauldwell, Frank
See King, Francis (Henry)

Caunitz, William J. 1933- . . . . **CLC 34**
See also BEST 89:3; CA 125; 130

Causley, Charles (Stanley) 1917- . . . . . **CLC 7**
See also CA 9-12R; CANR 5, 35; CLR 30; DLB 27; MTCW; SATA 3, 66

Caute, David 1936- . . . . **CLC 29**
See also CA 1-4R; CAAS 4; CANR 1, 33; DLB 14

Cavafy, C(onstantine) P(eter) . . . . . . **TCLC 2, 7**
See also Kavafis, Konstantinos Petrou

Cavallo, Evelyn
See Spark, Muriel (Sarah)

Cavanna, Betty . . . . **CLC 12**
See also Harrison, Elizabeth Cavanna
See also JRDA; MAICYA; SAAS 4; SATA 1, 30

Caxton, William 1421(?)-1491(?) . . . . . **LC 17**

Cayrol, Jean 1911- . . . . **CLC 11**
See also CA 89-92; DLB 83

Cela, Camilo Jose 1916- . . . . **CLC 4, 13, 59; HLC**
See also BEST 90:2; CA 21-24R; CAAS 10; CANR 21, 32; DLBY 89; HW; MTCW

Celan, Paul . . . . . . **CLC 10, 19, 53, 82; PC 10**
See also Antschel, Paul
See also DLB 69

Celine, Louis-Ferdinand . . . . **CLC 1, 3, 4, 7, 9, 15, 47**
See also Destouches, Louis-Ferdinand
See also DLB 72

Cellini, Benvenuto 1500-1571 . . . . **LC 7**

Cendrars, Blaise
See Sauser-Hall, Frederic

Cernuda (y Bidon), Luis 1902-1963 . . . . **CLC 54**
See also CA 131; 89-92; DLB 134; HW

Cervantes (Saavedra), Miguel de 1547-1616 . . . . . . **LC 6, 23; DA; SSC 12; WLC**

Cesaire, Aime (Fernand) 1913- . . . . **CLC 19, 32; BLC**
See also BW 2; CA 65-68; CANR 24, 43; MTCW

Chabon, Michael 1965(?)- . . . . **CLC 55**
See also CA 139

Chabrol, Claude 1930- . . . . **CLC 16**
See also CA 110

Challans, Mary 1905-1983
See Renault, Mary
See also CA 81-84; 111; SATA 23; SATA-Obit 36

Challis, George
See Faust, Frederick (Schiller)

Chambers, Aidan 1934- . . . . **CLC 35**
See also CA 25-28R; CANR 12, 31; JRDA; MAICYA; SAAS 12; SATA 1, 69

Chambers, James 1948-
See Cliff, Jimmy
See also CA 124

Chambers, Jessie
See Lawrence, D(avid) H(erbert Richards)

Chambers, Robert W. 1865-1933 . . . **TCLC 41**

Chandler, Raymond (Thornton) 1888-1959 . . . . **TCLC 1, 7**
See also CA 104; 129; CDALB 1929-1941; DLBD 6; MTCW

Chang, Jung 1952- . . . . **CLC 71**
See also CA 142

Channing, William Ellery 1780-1842 . . . . **NCLC 17**
See also DLB 1, 59

Chaplin, Charles Spencer 1889-1977 . . . . **CLC 16**
See also Chaplin, Charlie
See also CA 81-84; 73-76

Chaplin, Charlie
See Chaplin, Charles Spencer
See also DLB 44

Chapman, George 1559(?)-1634 . . . . . . **LC 22**
See also DLB 62, 121

Chapman, Graham 1941-1989 . . . . . . **CLC 21**
See also Monty Python
See also CA 116; 129; CANR 35

Chapman, John Jay 1862-1933 . . . . . **TCLC 7**
See also CA 104

Chapman, Walker
See Silverberg, Robert

Chappell, Fred (Davis) 1936- . . . . **CLC 40, 78**
See also CA 5-8R; CAAS 4; CANR 8, 33; DLB 6, 105

Char, Rene(-Emile) 1907-1988 . . . . **CLC 9, 11, 14, 55**
See also CA 13-16R; 124; CANR 32; MTCW

Charby, Jay
See Ellison, Harlan (Jay)

Chardin, Pierre Teilhard de
See Teilhard de Chardin, (Marie Joseph) Pierre

Charles I 1600-1649 . . . . **LC 13**

Charyn, Jerome 1937- . . . . **CLC 5, 8, 18**
See also CA 5-8R; CAAS 1; CANR 7; DLBY 83; MTCW

Chase, Mary (Coyle) 1907-1981 . . . . . . **DC 1**
See also CA 77-80; 105; SATA 17; SATA-Obit 29

Chase, Mary Ellen 1887-1973 . . . . **CLC 2**
See also CA 13-16; 41-44R; CAP 1; SATA 10

Chase, Nicholas
See Hyde, Anthony

Chateaubriand, Francois Rene de 1768-1848 . . . . **NCLC 3**
See also DLB 119

Chatterje, Sarat Chandra 1876-1936(?)
See Chatterji, Saratchandra
See also CA 109

Chatterji, Bankim Chandra 1838-1894 . . . . **NCLC 19**

Chatterji, Saratchandra . . . . **TCLC 13**
See also Chatterje, Sarat Chandra

Chatterton, Thomas 1752-1770 . . . . **LC 3**
See also DLB 109

Chatwin, (Charles) Bruce 1940-1989 . . . . **CLC 28, 57, 59**
See also AAYA 4; BEST 90:1; CA 85-88; 127

Chaucer, Daniel
See Ford, Ford Madox

Copeland, Stewart (Armstrong) 1952- .... **CLC 26**

Coppard, A(lfred) E(dgar) 1878-1957 .... **TCLC 5**
See also CA 114; YABC 1

Coppee, Francois 1842-1908 ...... **TCLC 25**

Coppola, Francis Ford 1939- .... **CLC 16**
See also CA 77-80; CANR 40; DLB 44

Corbiere, Tristan 1845-1875 ..... **NCLC 43**

Corcoran, Barbara 1911- .... **CLC 17**
See also AAYA 14; CA 21-24R; CAAS 2; CANR 11, 28; DLB 52; JRDA; SATA 3, 77

Cordelier, Maurice
See Giraudoux, (Hippolyte) Jean

Corelli, Marie 1855-1924 .... **TCLC 51**
See also Mackay, Mary
See also DLB 34

Corman, Cid .... **CLC 9**
See also Corman, Sidney
See also CAAS 2; DLB 5

Corman, Sidney 1924-
See Corman, Cid
See also CA 85-88; CANR 44

Cormier, Robert (Edmund) 1925- .... **CLC 12, 30; DA**
See also AAYA 3; CA 1-4R; CANR 5, 23; CDALB 1968-1988; CLR 12; DLB 52; JRDA; MAICYA; MTCW; SATA 10, 45

Corn, Alfred (DeWitt III) 1943- .... **CLC 33**
See also CA 104; CANR 44; DLB 120; DLBY 80

Cornwell, David (John Moore) 1931- .... **CLC 9, 15**
See also le Carre, John
See also CA 5-8R; CANR 13, 33; MTCW

Corso, (Nunzio) Gregory 1930- ... **CLC 1, 11**
See also CA 5-8R; CANR 41; DLB 5, 16; MTCW

Cortazar, Julio 1914-1984 ...... **CLC 2, 3, 5, 10, 13, 15, 33, 34; HLC; SSC 7**
See also CA 21-24R; CANR 12, 32; DLB 113; HW; MTCW

Corwin, Cecil
See Kornbluth, C(yril) M.

Cosic, Dobrica 1921- .... **CLC 14**
See also CA 122; 138

Costain, Thomas B(ertram) 1885-1965 .... **CLC 30**
See also CA 5-8R; 25-28R; DLB 9

Costantini, Humberto 1924(?)-1987 .... **CLC 49**
See also CA 131; 122; HW

Costello, Elvis 1955- .... **CLC 21**

Cotter, Joseph Seamon Sr. 1861-1949 .... **TCLC 28; BLC**
See also BW 1; CA 124; DLB 50

Couch, Arthur Thomas Quiller
See Quiller-Couch, Arthur Thomas

Coulton, James
See Hansen, Joseph

Couperus, Louis (Marie Anne) 1863-1923 .... **TCLC 15**
See also CA 115

Coupland, Douglas 1961- .... **CLC 85**
See also CA 142

Court, Wesli
See Turco, Lewis (Putnam)

Courtenay, Bryce 1933- .... **CLC 59**
See also CA 138

Courtney, Robert
See Ellison, Harlan (Jay)

Cousteau, Jacques-Yves 1910- ...... **CLC 30**
See also CA 65-68; CANR 15; MTCW; SATA 38

Coward, Noel (Peirce) 1899-1973 .... **CLC 1, 9, 29, 51**
See also AITN 1; CA 17-18; 41-44R; CANR 35; CAP 2; CDBLB 1914-1945; DLB 10; MTCW

Cowley, Malcolm 1898-1989 .... **CLC 39**
See also CA 5-8R; 128; CANR 3; DLB 4, 48; DLBY 81, 89; MTCW

Cowper, William 1731-1800 .... **NCLC 8**
See also DLB 104, 109

Cox, William Trevor 1928- ... **CLC 9, 14, 71**
See also Trevor, William
See also CA 9-12R; CANR 4, 37; DLB 14; MTCW

Coyne, P. J.
See Masters, Hilary

Cozzens, James Gould 1903-1978 .... **CLC 1, 4, 11**
See also CA 9-12R; 81-84; CANR 19; CDALB 1941-1968; DLB 9; DLBD 2; DLBY 84; MTCW

Crabbe, George 1754-1832 .... **NCLC 26**
See also DLB 93

Craig, A. A.
See Anderson, Poul (William)

Craik, Dinah Maria (Mulock) 1826-1887 .... **NCLC 38**
See also DLB 35; MAICYA; SATA 34

Cram, Ralph Adams 1863-1942 .... **TCLC 45**

Crane, (Harold) Hart 1899-1932 .... **TCLC 2, 5; DA; PC 3; WLC**
See also CA 104; 127; CDALB 1917-1929; DLB 4, 48; MTCW

Crane, R(onald) S(almon) 1886-1967 .... **CLC 27**
See also CA 85-88; DLB 63

Crane, Stephen (Townley) 1871-1900 .... **TCLC 11, 17, 32; DA; SSC 7; WLC**
See also CA 109; 140; CDALB 1865-1917; DLB 12, 54, 78; YABC 2

Crase, Douglas 1944- .... **CLC 58**
See also CA 106

Crashaw, Richard 1612(?)-1649 ...... **LC 24**
See also DLB 126

Craven, Margaret 1901-1980 .... **CLC 17**
See also CA 103

Crawford, F(rancis) Marion 1854-1909 .... **TCLC 10**
See also CA 107; DLB 71

Crawford, Isabella Valancy 1850-1887 .... **NCLC 12**
See also DLB 92

Crayon, Geoffrey
See Irving, Washington

Creasey, John 1908-1973 .... **CLC 11**
See also CA 5-8R; 41-44R; CANR 8; DLB 77; MTCW

Crebillon, Claude Prosper Jolyot de (fils) 1707-1777 .... **LC 1**

Credo
See Creasey, John

Creeley, Robert (White) 1926- ..... **CLC 1, 2, 4, 8, 11, 15, 36, 78**
See also CA 1-4R; CAAS 10; CANR 23, 43; DLB 5, 16; MTCW

Crews, Harry (Eugene) 1935- .... **CLC 6, 23, 49**
See also AITN 1; CA 25-28R; CANR 20; DLB 6, 143; MTCW

Crichton, (John) Michael 1942- .... **CLC 2, 6, 54**
See also AAYA 10; AITN 2; CA 25-28R; CANR 13, 40; DLBY 81; JRDA; MTCW; SATA 9

Crispin, Edmund .... **CLC 22**
See also Montgomery, (Robert) Bruce
See also DLB 87

Cristofer, Michael 1945(?)- .... **CLC 28**
See also CA 110; DLB 7

Croce, Benedetto 1866-1952 ...... **TCLC 37**
See also CA 120

Crockett, David 1786-1836 .... **NCLC 8**
See also DLB 3, 11

Crockett, Davy
See Crockett, David

Crofts, Freeman Wills 1879-1957 .... **TCLC 55**
See also CA 115; DLB 77

Croker, John Wilson 1780-1857 .. **NCLC 10**
See also DLB 110

Crommelynck, Fernand 1885-1970 .. **CLC 75**
See also CA 89-92

Cronin, A(rchibald) J(oseph) 1896-1981 .... **CLC 32**
See also CA 1-4R; 102; CANR 5; SATA 47; SATA-Obit 25

Cross, Amanda
See Heilbrun, Carolyn G(old)

Crothers, Rachel 1878(?)-1958 ..... **TCLC 19**
See also CA 113; DLB 7

Croves, Hal
See Traven, B.

Crowfield, Christopher
See Stowe, Harriet (Elizabeth) Beecher

Crowley, Aleister .... **TCLC 7**
See also Crowley, Edward Alexander

Crowley, Edward Alexander 1875-1947
See Crowley, Aleister
See also CA 104

Crowley, John 1942- .... **CLC 57**
See also CA 61-64; CANR 43; DLBY 82; SATA 65

Crud
See Crumb, R(obert)

Crumarums
See Crumb, R(obert)

Doyle, Arthur Conan 1859-1930 .... **TCLC 7; DA; SSC 12; WLC**
See also AAYA 14; CA 104; 122; CDBLB 1890-1914; DLB 18, 70; MTCW; SATA 24

Doyle, Conan
See Doyle, Arthur Conan

Doyle, John
See Graves, Robert (von Ranke)

Doyle, Roddy 1958(?)- .... **CLC 81**
See also AAYA 14; CA 143

Doyle, Sir A. Conan
See Doyle, Arthur Conan

Doyle, Sir Arthur Conan
See Doyle, Arthur Conan

Dr. A
See Asimov, Isaac; Silverstein, Alvin

Drabble, Margaret 1939- .... **CLC 2, 3, 5, 8, 10, 22, 53**
See also CA 13-16R; CANR 18, 35; CDBLB 1960 to Present; DLB 14; MTCW; SATA 48

Drapier, M. B.
See Swift, Jonathan

Drayham, James
See Mencken, H(enry) L(ouis)

Drayton, Michael 1563-1631......... **LC 8**

Dreadstone, Carl
See Campbell, (John) Ramsey

Dreiser, Theodore (Herman Albert) 1871-1945 .... **TCLC 10, 18, 35; DA; WLC**
See also CA 106; 132; CDALB 1865-1917; DLB 9, 12, 102, 137; DLBD 1; MTCW

Drexler, Rosalyn 1926- .... **CLC 2, 6**
See also CA 81-84

Dreyer, Carl Theodor 1889-1968.... **CLC 16**
See also CA 116

Drieu la Rochelle, Pierre(-Eugene) 1893-1945 .... **TCLC 21**
See also CA 117; DLB 72

Drinkwater, John 1882-1937...... **TCLC 57**
See also CA 109; DLB 10, 19

Drop Shot
See Cable, George Washington

Droste-Hulshoff, Annette Freiin von 1797-1848 .... **NCLC 3**
See also DLB 133

Drummond, Walter
See Silverberg, Robert

Drummond, William Henry 1854-1907 .... **TCLC 25**
See also DLB 92

Drummond de Andrade, Carlos 1902-1987 .... **CLC 18**
See also Andrade, Carlos Drummond de
See also CA 132; 123

Drury, Allen (Stuart) 1918-........ **CLC 37**
See also CA 57-60; CANR 18

Dryden, John 1631-1700 ... **LC 3, 21; DA; DC 3; WLC**
See also CDBLB 1660-1789; DLB 80, 101, 131

Duberman, Martin 1930-........... **CLC 8**
See also CA 1-4R; CANR 2

Dubie, Norman (Evans) 1945-...... **CLC 36**
See also CA 69-72; CANR 12; DLB 120

Du Bois, W(illiam) E(dward) B(urghardt) 1868-1963 ...... **CLC 1, 2, 13, 64; BLC; DA; WLC**
See also BW 1; CA 85-88; CANR 34; CDALB 1865-1917; DLB 47, 50, 91; MTCW; SATA 42

Dubus, Andre 1936-... **CLC 13, 36; SSC 15**
See also CA 21-24R; CANR 17; DLB 130

Duca Minimo
See D'Annunzio, Gabriele

Ducharme, Rejean 1941- .... **CLC 74**
See also DLB 60

Duclos, Charles Pinot 1704-1772 ..... **LC 1**

Dudek, Louis 1918- .... **CLC 11, 19**
See also CA 45-48; CAAS 14; CANR 1; DLB 88

Duerrenmatt, Friedrich 1921-1990 ...... **CLC 1, 4, 8, 11, 15, 43**
See also CA 17-20R; CANR 33; DLB 69, 124; MTCW

Duffy, Bruce (?)-................. **CLC 50**

Duffy, Maureen 1933- .... **CLC 37**
See also CA 25-28R; CANR 33; DLB 14; MTCW

Dugan, Alan 1923- .... **CLC 2, 6**
See also CA 81-84; DLB 5

du Gard, Roger Martin
See Martin du Gard, Roger

Duhamel, Georges 1884-1966 .... **CLC 8**
See also CA 81-84; 25-28R; CANR 35; DLB 65; MTCW

Dujardin, Edouard (Emile Louis) 1861-1949 .... **TCLC 13**
See also CA 109; DLB 123

Dumas, Alexandre (Davy de la Pailleterie) 1802-1870 .... **NCLC 11; DA; WLC**
See also DLB 119; SATA 18

Dumas, Alexandre 1824-1895 .... **NCLC 9; DC 1**

Dumas, Claudine
See Malzberg, Barry N(athaniel)

Dumas, Henry L. 1934-1968 ..... **CLC 6, 62**
See also BW 1; CA 85-88; DLB 41

du Maurier, Daphne 1907-1989 .... **CLC 6, 11, 59**
See also CA 5-8R; 128; CANR 6; MTCW; SATA 27; SATA-Obit 60

Dunbar, Paul Laurence 1872-1906 ...... **TCLC 2, 12; BLC; DA; PC 5; SSC 8; WLC**
See also BW 1; CA 104; 124; CDALB 1865-1917; DLB 50, 54, 78; SATA 34

Dunbar, William 1460(?)-1530(?) .... **LC 20**
See also DLB 132, 146

Duncan, Lois 1934-............... **CLC 26**
See also AAYA 4; CA 1-4R; CANR 2, 23, 36; CLR 29; JRDA; MAICYA; SAAS 2; SATA 1, 36, 75

Duncan, Robert (Edward) 1919-1988 .... **CLC 1, 2, 4, 7, 15, 41, 55; PC 2**
See also CA 9-12R; 124; CANR 28; DLB 5, 16; MTCW

Dunlap, William 1766-1839....... **NCLC 2**
See also DLB 30, 37, 59

Dunn, Douglas (Eaglesham) 1942- .... **CLC 6, 40**
See also CA 45-48; CANR 2, 33; DLB 40; MTCW

Dunn, Katherine (Karen) 1945-..... **CLC 71**
See also CA 33-36R

Dunn, Stephen 1939- .... **CLC 36**
See also CA 33-36R; CANR 12; DLB 105

Dunne, Finley Peter 1867-1936.... **TCLC 28**
See also CA 108; DLB 11, 23

Dunne, John Gregory 1932-........ **CLC 28**
See also CA 25-28R; CANR 14; DLBY 80

Dunsany, Edward John Moreton Drax Plunkett 1878-1957
See Dunsany, Lord
See also CA 104; DLB 10

Dunsany, Lord.................... **TCLC 2**
See also Dunsany, Edward John Moreton Drax Plunkett
See also DLB 77

du Perry, Jean
See Simenon, Georges (Jacques Christian)

Durang, Christopher (Ferdinand) 1949- .... **CLC 27, 38**
See also CA 105

Duras, Marguerite 1914- ...... **CLC 3, 6, 11, 20, 34, 40, 68**
See also CA 25-28R; DLB 83; MTCW

Durban, (Rosa) Pam 1947-......... **CLC 39**
See also CA 123

Durcan, Paul 1944-............ **CLC 43, 70**
See also CA 134

Durkheim, Emile 1858-1917 ...... **TCLC 55**

Durrell, Lawrence (George) 1912-1990 .... **CLC 1, 4, 6, 8, 13, 27, 41**
See also CA 9-12R; 132; CANR 40; CDBLB 1945-1960; DLB 15, 27; DLBY 90; MTCW

Durrenmatt, Friedrich
See Duerrenmatt, Friedrich

Dutt, Toru 1856-1877........... **NCLC 29**

Dwight, Timothy 1752-1817...... **NCLC 13**
See also DLB 37

Dworkin, Andrea 1946- .... **CLC 43**
See also CA 77-80; CANR 16, 39; MTCW

Dwyer, Deanna
See Koontz, Dean R(ay)

Dwyer, K. R.
See Koontz, Dean R(ay)

Dylan, Bob 1941- ...... **CLC 3, 4, 6, 12, 77**
See also CA 41-44R; DLB 16

Eagleton, Terence (Francis) 1943-
See Eagleton, Terry
See also CA 57-60; CANR 7, 23; MTCW

Eagleton, Terry .... **CLC 63**
See also Eagleton, Terence (Francis)

Early, Jack
See Scoppettone, Sandra

East, Michael
See West, Morris L(anglo)

Eastaway, Edward
See Thomas, (Philip) Edward

Eastlake, William (Derry) 1917- ..... **CLC 8**
See also CA 5-8R; CAAS 1; CANR 5; DLB 6

Eastman, Charles A(lexander) 1858-1939 .... **TCLC 55**
See also NNAL; YABC 1

Eberhart, Richard (Ghormley) 1904- .... **CLC 3, 11, 19, 56**
See also CA 1-4R; CANR 2; CDALB 1941-1968; DLB 48; MTCW

Eberstadt, Fernanda 1960- .... **CLC 39**
See also CA 136

Echegaray (y Eizaguirre), Jose (Maria Waldo) 1832-1916 .... **TCLC 4**
See also CA 104; CANR 32; HW; MTCW

Echeverria, (Jose) Esteban (Antonino) 1805-1851 .... **NCLC 18**

Echo
See Proust, (Valentin-Louis-George-Eugene-) Marcel

Eckert, Allan W. 1931- .... **CLC 17**
See also CA 13-16R; CANR 14, 45; SATA 27, 29

Eckhart, Meister 1260(?)-1328(?) .. **CMLC 9**
See also DLB 115

Eckmar, F. R.
See de Hartog, Jan

Eco, Umberto 1932- .... **CLC 28, 60**
See also BEST 90:1; CA 77-80; CANR 12, 33; MTCW

Eddison, E(ric) R(ucker) 1882-1945 .... **TCLC 15**
See also CA 109

Edel, (Joseph) Leon 1907- ...... **CLC 29, 34**
See also CA 1-4R; CANR 1, 22; DLB 103

Eden, Emily 1797-1869 .... **NCLC 10**

Edgar, David 1948- .... **CLC 42**
See also CA 57-60; CANR 12; DLB 13; MTCW

Edgerton, Clyde (Carlyle) 1944- .... **CLC 39**
See also CA 118; 134

Edgeworth, Maria 1767-1849 ...... **NCLC 1**
See also DLB 116; SATA 21

Edmonds, Paul
See Kuttner, Henry

Edmonds, Walter D(umaux) 1903- .. **CLC 35**
See also CA 5-8R; CANR 2; DLB 9; MAICYA; SAAS 4; SATA 1, 27

Edmondson, Wallace
See Ellison, Harlan (Jay)

Edson, Russell .... **CLC 13**
See also CA 33-36R

Edwards, Bronwen Elizabeth
See Rose, Wendy

Edwards, G(erald) B(asil) 1899-1976 .... **CLC 25**
See also CA 110

Edwards, Gus 1939- .... **CLC 43**
See also CA 108

Edwards, Jonathan 1703-1758 .... **LC 7; DA**
See also DLB 24

Efron, Marina Ivanovna Tsvetaeva
See Tsvetaeva (Efron), Marina (Ivanovna)

Ehle, John (Marsden, Jr.) 1925- .... **CLC 27**
See also CA 9-12R

Ehrenbourg, Ilya (Grigoryevich)
See Ehrenburg, Ilya (Grigoryevich)

Ehrenburg, Ilya (Grigoryevich) 1891-1967 .... **CLC 18, 34, 62**
See also CA 102; 25-28R

Ehrenburg, Ilyo (Grigoryevich)
See Ehrenburg, Ilya (Grigoryevich)

Eich, Guenter 1907-1972 .... **CLC 15**
See also CA 111; 93-96; DLB 69, 124

Eichendorff, Joseph Freiherr von 1788-1857 .... **NCLC 8**
See also DLB 90

Eigner, Larry .... **CLC 9**
See also Eigner, Laurence (Joel)
See also DLB 5

Eigner, Laurence (Joel) 1927-
See Eigner, Larry
See also CA 9-12R; CANR 6

Eiseley, Loren Corey 1907-1977 ..... **CLC 7**
See also AAYA 5; CA 1-4R; 73-76; CANR 6

Eisenstadt, Jill 1963- .... **CLC 50**
See also CA 140

Eisenstein, Sergei (Mikhailovich) 1898-1948 .... **TCLC 57**
See also CA 114

Eisner, Simon
See Kornbluth, C(yril) M.

Ekeloef, (Bengt) Gunnar 1907-1968 .... **CLC 27**
See also CA 123; 25-28R

Ekelof, (Bengt) Gunnar
See Ekeloef, (Bengt) Gunnar

Ekwensi, C. O. D.
See Ekwensi, Cyprian (Odiatu Duaka)

Ekwensi, Cyprian (Odiatu Duaka) 1921- .... **CLC 4; BLC**
See also BW 2; CA 29-32R; CANR 18, 42; DLB 117; MTCW; SATA 66

Elaine .... **TCLC 18**
See also Leverson, Ada

El Crummo
See Crumb, R(obert)

Elia
See Lamb, Charles

Eliade, Mircea 1907-1986 .... **CLC 19**
See also CA 65-68; 119; CANR 30; MTCW

Eliot, A. D.
See Jewett, (Theodora) Sarah Orne

Eliot, Alice
See Jewett, (Theodora) Sarah Orne

Eliot, Dan
See Silverberg, Robert

Eliot, George 1819-1880 .... **NCLC 4, 13, 23, 41; DA; WLC**
See also CDBLB 1832-1890; DLB 21, 35, 55

Eliot, John 1604-1690 .... **LC 5**
See also DLB 24

Eliot, T(homas) S(tearns) 1888-1965 ..... **CLC 1, 2, 3, 6, 9, 10, 13, 15, 24, 34, 41, 55, 57; DA; PC 5; WLC 2**
See also CA 5-8R; 25-28R; CANR 41; CDALB 1929-1941; DLB 7, 10, 45, 63; DLBY 88; MTCW

Elizabeth 1866-1941 .... **TCLC 41**

Elkin, Stanley L(awrence) 1930- ... **CLC 4, 6, 9, 14, 27, 51; SSC 12**
See also CA 9-12R; CANR 8, 46; DLB 2, 28; DLBY 80; MTCW

Elledge, Scott .... **CLC 34**

Elliott, Don
See Silverberg, Robert

Elliott, George P(aul) 1918-1980 ..... **CLC 2**
See also CA 1-4R; 97-100; CANR 2

Elliott, Janice 1931- .... **CLC 47**
See also CA 13-16R; CANR 8, 29; DLB 14

Elliott, Sumner Locke 1917-1991 ... **CLC 38**
See also CA 5-8R; 134; CANR 2, 21

Elliott, William
See Bradbury, Ray (Douglas)

Ellis, A. E. .... **CLC 7**

Ellis, Alice Thomas .... **CLC 40**
See also Haycraft, Anna

Ellis, Bret Easton 1964- .... **CLC 39, 71**
See also AAYA 2; CA 118; 123

Ellis, (Henry) Havelock 1859-1939 .... **TCLC 14**
See also CA 109

Ellis, Landon
See Ellison, Harlan (Jay)

Ellis, Trey 1962- .... **CLC 55**

Ellison, Harlan (Jay) 1934- .... **CLC 1, 13, 42; SSC 14**
See also CA 5-8R; CANR 5, 46; DLB 8; MTCW

Ellison, Ralph (Waldo) 1914-1994 .... **CLC 1, 3, 11, 54, 86; BLC; DA; WLC**
See also BW 1; CA 9-12R; 145; CANR 24; CDALB 1941-1968; DLB 2, 76; MTCW

Ellmann, Lucy (Elizabeth) 1956- .... **CLC 61**
See also CA 128

Ellmann, Richard (David) 1918-1987 .... **CLC 50**
See also BEST 89:2; CA 1-4R; 122; CANR 2, 28; DLB 103; DLBY 87; MTCW

Elman, Richard 1934- .... **CLC 19**
See also CA 17-20R; CAAS 3; CANR 47

Elron
See Hubbard, L(afayette) Ron(ald)

Eluard, Paul .... **TCLC 7, 41**
See also Grindel, Eugene

Elyot, Sir Thomas 1490(?)-1546 ..... **LC 11**

Elytis, Odysseus 1911- .... **CLC 15, 49**
See also CA 102; MTCW

Emecheta, (Florence Onye) Buchi 1944- .... **CLC 14, 48; BLC**
See also BW 2; CA 81-84; CANR 27; DLB 117; MTCW; SATA 66

Emerson, Ralph Waldo 1803-1882 ...... **NCLC 1, 38; DA; WLC**
See also CDALB 1640-1865; DLB 1, 59, 73

Eminescu, Mihail 1850-1889 ..... **NCLC 33**

Empson, William 1906-1984 .... **CLC 3, 8, 19, 33, 34**
See also CA 17-20R; 112; CANR 31; DLB 20; MTCW

Enchi Fumiko (Ueda) 1905-1986.... **CLC 31**
See also CA 129; 121

Ende, Michael (Andreas Helmuth) 1929- .... **CLC 31**
See also CA 118; 124; CANR 36; CLR 14; DLB 75; MAICYA; SATA 42, 61

Endo, Shusaku 1923- ..... **CLC 7, 14, 19, 54**
See also CA 29-32R; CANR 21; MTCW

Engel, Marian 1933-1985.......... **CLC 36**
See also CA 25-28R; CANR 12; DLB 53

Engelhardt, Frederick
See Hubbard, L(afayette) Ron(ald)

Enright, D(ennis) J(oseph) 1920- .... **CLC 4, 8, 31**
See also CA 1-4R; CANR 1, 42; DLB 27; SATA 25

Enzensberger, Hans Magnus 1929- .... **CLC 43**
See also CA 116; 119

Ephron, Nora 1941- .... **CLC 17, 31**
See also AITN 2; CA 65-68; CANR 12, 39

Epsilon
See Betjeman, John

Epstein, Daniel Mark 1948- .... **CLC 7**
See also CA 49-52; CANR 2

Epstein, Jacob 1956- .... **CLC 19**
See also CA 114

Epstein, Joseph 1937-............. **CLC 39**
See also CA 112; 119

Epstein, Leslie 1938- .... **CLC 27**
See also CA 73-76; CAAS 12; CANR 23

Equiano, Olaudah 1745(?)-1797 .... **LC 16; BLC**
See also DLB 37, 50

Erasmus, Desiderius 1469(?)-1536.... **LC 16**

Erdman, Paul E(mil) 1932- .... **CLC 25**
See also AITN 1; CA 61-64; CANR 13, 43

Erdrich, Louise 1954-.......... **CLC 39, 54**
See also AAYA 10; BEST 89:1; CA 114; CANR 41; MTCW; NNAL

Erenburg, Ilya (Grigoryevich)
See Ehrenburg, Ilya (Grigoryevich)

Erickson, Stephen Michael 1950-
See Erickson, Steve
See also CA 129

Erickson, Steve .... **CLC 64**
See also Erickson, Stephen Michael

Ericson, Walter
See Fast, Howard (Melvin)

Eriksson, Buntel
See Bergman, (Ernst) Ingmar

Eschenbach, Wolfram von
See Wolfram von Eschenbach

Eseki, Bruno
See Mphahlele, Ezekiel

Esenin, Sergei (Alexandrovich) 1895-1925 .... **TCLC 4**
See also CA 104

Eshleman, Clayton 1935-........... **CLC 7**
See also CA 33-36R; CAAS 6; DLB 5

Espriella, Don Manuel Alvarez
See Southey, Robert

Espriu, Salvador 1913-1985......... **CLC 9**
See also CA 115; DLB 134

Espronceda, Jose de 1808-1842... **NCLC 39**

Esse, James
See Stephens, James

Esterbrook, Tom
See Hubbard, L(afayette) Ron(ald)

Estleman, Loren D. 1952- .... **CLC 48**
See also CA 85-88; CANR 27; MTCW

Eugenides, Jeffrey 1960(?)- .... **CLC 81**
See also CA 144

Euripides c. 485B.C.-406B.C. .... **DC 4**
See also DA

Evan, Evin
See Faust, Frederick (Schiller)

Evans, Evan
See Faust, Frederick (Schiller)

Evans, Marian
See Eliot, George

Evans, Mary Ann
See Eliot, George

Evarts, Esther
See Benson, Sally

Everett, Percival L. 1956- .... **CLC 57**
See also BW 2; CA 129

Everson, R(onald) G(ilmour) 1903- .... **CLC 27**
See also CA 17-20R; DLB 88

Everson, William (Oliver) 1912-1994 .... **CLC 1, 5, 14**
See also CA 9-12R; 145; CANR 20; DLB 5, 16; MTCW

Evtushenko, Evgenii Aleksandrovich
See Yevtushenko, Yevgeny (Alexandrovich)

Ewart, Gavin (Buchanan) 1916- .... **CLC 13, 46**
See also CA 89-92; CANR 17, 46; DLB 40; MTCW

Ewers, Hanns Heinz 1871-1943 ... **TCLC 12**
See also CA 109

Ewing, Frederick R.
See Sturgeon, Theodore (Hamilton)

Exley, Frederick (Earl) 1929-1992 .... **CLC 6, 11**
See also AITN 2; CA 81-84; 138; DLB 143; DLBY 81

Eynhardt, Guillermo
See Quiroga, Horacio (Sylvestre)

Ezekiel, Nissim 1924-............ **CLC 61**
See also CA 61-64

Ezekiel, Tish O'Dowd 1943- .... **CLC 34**
See also CA 129

Fadeyev, A.
See Bulgya, Alexander Alexandrovich

Fadeyev, Alexander............... **TCLC 53**
See also Bulgya, Alexander Alexandrovich

Fagen, Donald 1948-.............. **CLC 26**

Fainzilberg, Ilya Arnoldovich 1897-1937
See Ilf, Ilya
See also CA 120

Fair, Ronald L. 1932-............. **CLC 18**
See also BW 1; CA 69-72; CANR 25; DLB 33

Fairbairns, Zoe (Ann) 1948- .... **CLC 32**
See also CA 103; CANR 21

Falco, Gian
See Papini, Giovanni

Falconer, James
See Kirkup, James

Falconer, Kenneth
See Kornbluth, C(yril) M.

Falkland, Samuel
See Heijermans, Herman

Fallaci, Oriana 1930- .... **CLC 11**
See also CA 77-80; CANR 15; MTCW

Faludy, George 1913-............. **CLC 42**
See also CA 21-24R

Faludy, Gyoergy
See Faludy, George

Fanon, Frantz 1925-1961..... **CLC 74; BLC**
See also BW 1; CA 116; 89-92

Fanshawe, Ann 1625-1680.......... **LC 11**

Fante, John (Thomas) 1911-1983 ... **CLC 60**
See also CA 69-72; 109; CANR 23; DLB 130; DLBY 83

Farah, Nuruddin 1945-....... **CLC 53; BLC**
See also BW 2; CA 106; DLB 125

Fargue, Leon-Paul 1876(?)-1947... **TCLC 11**
See also CA 109

Farigoule, Louis
See Romains, Jules

Farina, Richard 1936(?)-1966 .... **CLC 9**
See also CA 81-84; 25-28R

Farley, Walter (Lorimer) 1915-1989 .... **CLC 17**
See also CA 17-20R; CANR 8, 29; DLB 22; JRDA; MAICYA; SATA 2, 43

Farmer, Philip Jose 1918-....... **CLC 1, 19**
See also CA 1-4R; CANR 4, 35; DLB 8; MTCW

Farquhar, George 1677-1707........ **LC 21**
See also DLB 84

Farrell, J(ames) G(ordon) 1935-1979 .... **CLC 6**
See also CA 73-76; 89-92; CANR 36; DLB 14; MTCW

Farrell, James T(homas) 1904-1979 .... **CLC 1, 4, 8, 11, 66**
See also CA 5-8R; 89-92; CANR 9; DLB 4, 9, 86; DLBD 2; MTCW

Farren, Richard J.
See Betjeman, John

Farren, Richard M.
See Betjeman, John

Fassbinder, Rainer Werner 1946-1982 .... **CLC 20**
See also CA 93-96; 106; CANR 31

Fast, Howard (Melvin) 1914- ...... **CLC 23**
See also CA 1-4R; CAAS 18; CANR 1, 33; DLB 9; SATA 7

Faulcon, Robert
See Holdstock, Robert P.

Faulkner, William (Cuthbert) 1897-1962 ..... **CLC 1, 3, 6, 8, 9, 11, 14, 18, 28, 52, 68; DA; SSC 1; WLC**
See also AAYA 7; CA 81-84; CANR 33; CDALB 1929-1941; DLB 9, 11, 44, 102; DLBD 2; DLBY 86; MTCW

Fauset, Jessie Redmon 1884(?)-1961 .... **CLC 19, 54; BLC**
See also BW 1; CA 109; DLB 51

Faust, Frederick (Schiller) 1892-1944(?) .... **TCLC 49**
See also CA 108

Faust, Irvin 1924-................. **CLC 8**
See also CA 33-36R; CANR 28; DLB 2, 28; DLBY 80

Fawkes, Guy
See Benchley, Robert (Charles)

Fearing, Kenneth (Flexner) 1902-1961 .... **CLC 51**
See also CA 93-96; DLB 9

Fecamps, Elise
See Creasey, John

Federman, Raymond 1928- ...... **CLC 6, 47**
See also CA 17-20R; CAAS 8; CANR 10, 43; DLBY 80

Federspiel, J(uerg) F. 1931-........ **CLC 42**

Feiffer, Jules (Ralph) 1929-.... **CLC 2, 8, 64**
See also AAYA 3; CA 17-20R; CANR 30; DLB 7, 44; MTCW; SATA 8, 61

Feige, Hermann Albert Otto Maximilian
See Traven, B.

Feinberg, David B. 1956-.......... **CLC 59**
See also CA 135

Feinstein, Elaine 1930-............ **CLC 36**
See also CA 69-72; CAAS 1; CANR 31; DLB 14, 40; MTCW

Feldman, Irving (Mordecai) 1928-.... **CLC 7**
See also CA 1-4R; CANR 1

Fellini, Federico 1920-1993 ..... **CLC 16, 85**
See also CA 65-68; 143; CANR 33

Felsen, Henry Gregor 1916- .... **CLC 17**
See also CA 1-4R; CANR 1; SAAS 2; SATA 1

Fenton, James Martin 1949-....... **CLC 32**
See also CA 102; DLB 40

Ferber, Edna 1887-1968........... **CLC 18**
See also AITN 1; CA 5-8R; 25-28R; DLB 9, 28, 86; MTCW; SATA 7

Ferguson, Helen
See Kavan, Anna

Ferguson, Samuel 1810-1886..... **NCLC 33**
See also DLB 32

Ferling, Lawrence
See Ferlinghetti, Lawrence (Monsanto)

Ferlinghetti, Lawrence (Monsanto) 1919(?)- .... **CLC 2, 6, 10, 27; PC 1**
See also CA 5-8R; CANR 3, 41; CDALB 1941-1968; DLB 5, 16; MTCW

Fernandez, Vicente Garcia Huidobro
See Huidobro Fernandez, Vicente Garcia

Ferrer, Gabriel (Francisco Victor) Miro
See Miro (Ferrer), Gabriel (Francisco Victor)

Ferrier, Susan (Edmonstone) 1782-1854 .... **NCLC 8**
See also DLB 116

Ferrigno, Robert 1948(?)-.......... **CLC 65**
See also CA 140

Feuchtwanger, Lion 1884-1958 ..... **TCLC 3**
See also CA 104; DLB 66

Feuillet, Octave 1821-1890 ...... **NCLC 45**

Feydeau, Georges (Leon Jules Marie) 1862-1921 .... **TCLC 22**
See also CA 113

Ficino, Marsilio 1433-1499 .... **LC 12**

Fiedeler, Hans
See Doeblin, Alfred

Fiedler, Leslie A(aron) 1917- .... **CLC 4, 13, 24**
See also CA 9-12R; CANR 7; DLB 28, 67; MTCW

Field, Andrew 1938-.............. **CLC 44**
See also CA 97-100; CANR 25

Field, Eugene 1850-1895 .... **NCLC 3**
See also DLB 23, 42, 140; MAICYA; SATA 16

Field, Gans T.
See Wellman, Manly Wade

Field, Michael .... **TCLC 43**

Field, Peter
See Hobson, Laura Z(ametkin)

Fielding, Henry 1707-1754 .... **LC 1; DA; WLC**
See also CDBLB 1660-1789; DLB 39, 84, 101

Fielding, Sarah 1710-1768........... **LC 1**
See also DLB 39

Fierstein, Harvey (Forbes) 1954- ... **CLC 33**
See also CA 123; 129

Figes, Eva 1932-................. **CLC 31**
See also CA 53-56; CANR 4, 44; DLB 14

Finch, Robert (Duer Claydon) 1900- .... **CLC 18**
See also CA 57-60; CANR 9, 24; DLB 88

Findley, Timothy 1930- .... **CLC 27**
See also CA 25-28R; CANR 12, 42; DLB 53

Fink, William
See Mencken, H(enry) L(ouis)

Firbank, Louis 1942-
See Reed, Lou
See also CA 117

Firbank, (Arthur Annesley) Ronald 1886-1926 .... **TCLC 1**
See also CA 104; DLB 36

Fisher, M(ary) F(rances) K(ennedy) 1908-1992 .... **CLC 76**
See also CA 77-80; 138; CANR 44

Fisher, Roy 1930-................ **CLC 25**
See also CA 81-84; CAAS 10; CANR 16; DLB 40

Fisher, Rudolph 1897-1934 .... **TCLC 11; BLC**
See also BW 1; CA 107; 124; DLB 51, 102

Fisher, Vardis (Alvero) 1895-1968.... **CLC 7**
See also CA 5-8R; 25-28R; DLB 9

Fiske, Tarleton
See Bloch, Robert (Albert)

Fitch, Clarke
See Sinclair, Upton (Beall)

Fitch, John IV
See Cormier, Robert (Edmund)

Fitzgerald, Captain Hugh
See Baum, L(yman) Frank

FitzGerald, Edward 1809-1883 .... **NCLC 9**
See also DLB 32

Fitzgerald, F(rancis) Scott (Key) 1896-1940 .... **TCLC 1, 6, 14, 28, 55; DA; SSC 6; WLC**
See also AITN 1; CA 110; 123; CDALB 1917-1929; DLB 4, 9, 86; DLBD 1; DLBY 81; MTCW

Fitzgerald, Penelope 1916-... **CLC 19, 51, 61**
See also CA 85-88; CAAS 10; DLB 14

Fitzgerald, Robert (Stuart) 1910-1985 .... **CLC 39**
See also CA 1-4R; 114; CANR 1; DLBY 80

FitzGerald, Robert D(avid) 1902-1987 .... **CLC 19**
See also CA 17-20R

Fitzgerald, Zelda (Sayre) 1900-1948 .... **TCLC 52**
See also CA 117; 126; DLBY 84

Flanagan, Thomas (James Bonner) 1923- .... **CLC 25, 52**
See also CA 108; DLBY 80; MTCW

Flaubert, Gustave 1821-1880 .... **NCLC 2, 10, 19; DA; SSC 11; WLC**
See also DLB 119

Flecker, (Herman) James Elroy 1884-1915 .... **TCLC 43**
See also CA 109; DLB 10, 19

Fleming, Ian (Lancaster) 1908-1964 .... **CLC 3, 30**
See also CA 5-8R; CDBLB 1945-1960; DLB 87; MTCW; SATA 9

Fleming, Thomas (James) 1927- .... **CLC 37**
See also CA 5-8R; CANR 10; SATA 8

Fletcher, John Gould 1886-1950... **TCLC 35**
See also CA 107; DLB 4, 45

Fleur, Paul
See Pohl, Frederik

Flooglebuckle, Al
See Spiegelman, Art

Flying Officer X
See Bates, H(erbert) E(rnest)

Fo, Dario 1926-.................. **CLC 32**
See also CA 116; 128; MTCW

Fogarty, Jonathan Titulescu Esq.
See Farrell, James T(homas)

Gates, Henry Louis, Jr. 1950- . . . . . . **CLC 65**
See also BW 2; CA 109; CANR 25; DLB 67

Gautier, Theophile 1811-1872 . . . . . **NCLC 1**
See also DLB 119

Gawsworth, John
See Bates, H(erbert) E(rnest)

Gaye, Marvin (Penze) 1939-1984 . . . **CLC 26**
See also CA 112

Gebler, Carlo (Ernest) 1954- . . . . **CLC 39**
See also CA 119; 133

Gee, Maggie (Mary) 1948- . . . . **CLC 57**
See also CA 130

Gee, Maurice (Gough) 1931- . . . . **CLC 29**
See also CA 97-100; SATA 46

Gelbart, Larry (Simon) 1923- . . . **CLC 21, 61**
See also CA 73-76; CANR 45

Gelber, Jack 1932- . . . . **CLC 1, 6, 14, 79**
See also CA 1-4R; CANR 2; DLB 7

Gellhorn, Martha (Ellis) 1908- . . **CLC 14, 60**
See also CA 77-80; CANR 44; DLBY 82

Genet, Jean
1910-1986 . . . **CLC 1, 2, 5, 10, 14, 44, 46**
See also CA 13-16R; CANR 18; DLB 72; DLBY 86; MTCW

Gent, Peter 1942- . . . . **CLC 29**
See also AITN 1; CA 89-92; DLBY 82

Gentlewoman in New England, A
See Bradstreet, Anne

Gentlewoman in Those Parts, A
See Bradstreet, Anne

George, Jean Craighead 1919- . . . . . . **CLC 35**
See also AAYA 8; CA 5-8R; CANR 25; CLR 1; DLB 52; JRDA; MAICYA; SATA 2, 68

George, Stefan (Anton)
1868-1933 . . . . **TCLC 2, 14**
See also CA 104

Georges, Georges Martin
See Simenon, Georges (Jacques Christian)

Gerhardi, William Alexander
See Gerhardie, William Alexander

Gerhardie, William Alexander
1895-1977 . . . . **CLC 5**
See also CA 25-28R; 73-76; CANR 18; DLB 36

Gerstler, Amy 1956- . . . . **CLC 70**

Gertler, T. . . . . **CLC 34**
See also CA 116; 121

Ghalib 1797-1869 . . . . **NCLC 39**

Ghelderode, Michel de
1898-1962 . . . . **CLC 6, 11**
See also CA 85-88; CANR 40

Ghiselin, Brewster 1903- . . . . **CLC 23**
See also CA 13-16R; CAAS 10; CANR 13

Ghose, Zulfikar 1935- . . . . **CLC 42**
See also CA 65-68

Ghosh, Amitav 1956- . . . . **CLC 44**

Giacosa, Giuseppe 1847-1906 . . . . . . **TCLC 7**
See also CA 104

Gibb, Lee
See Waterhouse, Keith (Spencer)

Gibbon, Lewis Grassic . . . . **TCLC 4**
See also Mitchell, James Leslie

Gibbons, Kaye 1960- . . . . **CLC 50**

Gibran, Kahlil
1883-1931 . . . . **TCLC 1, 9; PC 9**
See also CA 104

Gibson, William 1914- . . . . **CLC 23; DA**
See also CA 9-12R; CANR 9, 42; DLB 7; SATA 66

Gibson, William (Ford) 1948- . . . **CLC 39, 63**
See also AAYA 12; CA 126; 133

Gide, Andre (Paul Guillaume)
1869-1951 . . . . **TCLC 5, 12, 36; DA; SSC 13; WLC**
See also CA 104; 124; DLB 65; MTCW

Gifford, Barry (Colby) 1946- . . . . **CLC 34**
See also CA 65-68; CANR 9, 30, 40

Gilbert, W(illiam) S(chwenck)
1836-1911 . . . . **TCLC 3**
See also CA 104; SATA 36

Gilbreth, Frank B., Jr. 1911- . . . . **CLC 17**
See also CA 9-12R; SATA 2

Gilchrist, Ellen 1935- . . **CLC 34, 48; SSC 14**
See also CA 113; 116; CANR 41; DLB 130; MTCW

Giles, Molly 1942- . . . . **CLC 39**
See also CA 126

Gill, Patrick
See Creasey, John

Gilliam, Terry (Vance) 1940- . . . . **CLC 21**
See also Monty Python
See also CA 108; 113; CANR 35

Gillian, Jerry
See Gilliam, Terry (Vance)

Gilliatt, Penelope (Ann Douglass)
1932-1993 . . . . **CLC 2, 10, 13, 53**
See also AITN 2; CA 13-16R; 141; DLB 14

Gilman, Charlotte (Anna) Perkins (Stetson)
1860-1935 . . . . **TCLC 9, 37; SSC 13**
See also CA 106

Gilmour, David 1949- . . . . **CLC 35**
See also CA 138

Gilpin, William 1724-1804 . . . . **NCLC 30**

Gilray, J. D.
See Mencken, H(enry) L(ouis)

Gilroy, Frank D(aniel) 1925- . . . . **CLC 2**
See also CA 81-84; CANR 32; DLB 7

Ginsberg, Allen
1926- . . . . . . **CLC 1, 2, 3, 4, 6, 13, 36, 69; DA; PC 4; WLC 3**
See also AITN 1; CA 1-4R; CANR 2, 41; CDALB 1941-1968; DLB 5, 16; MTCW

Ginzburg, Natalia
1916-1991 . . . . **CLC 5, 11, 54, 70**
See also CA 85-88; 135; CANR 33; MTCW

Giono, Jean 1895-1970 . . . . **CLC 4, 11**
See also CA 45-48; 29-32R; CANR 2, 35; DLB 72; MTCW

Giovanni, Nikki
1943- . . . . . . **CLC 2, 4, 19, 64; BLC; DA**
See also AITN 1; BW 2; CA 29-32R; CAAS 6; CANR 18, 41; CLR 6; DLB 5, 41; MAICYA; MTCW; SATA 24

Giovene, Andrea 1904- . . . . **CLC 7**
See also CA 85-88

Gippius, Zinaida (Nikolayevna) 1869-1945
See Hippius, Zinaida
See also CA 106

Giraudoux, (Hippolyte) Jean
1882-1944 . . . . **TCLC 2, 7**
See also CA 104; DLB 65

Gironella, Jose Maria 1917- . . . . **CLC 11**
See also CA 101

Gissing, George (Robert)
1857-1903 . . . . **TCLC 3, 24, 47**
See also CA 105; DLB 18, 135

Giurlani, Aldo
See Palazzeschi, Aldo

Gladkov, Fyodor (Vasilyevich)
1883-1958 . . . . **TCLC 27**

Glanville, Brian (Lester) 1931- . . . . . . **CLC 6**
See also CA 5-8R; CAAS 9; CANR 3; DLB 15, 139; SATA 42

Glasgow, Ellen (Anderson Gholson)
1873(?)-1945 . . . . **TCLC 2, 7**
See also CA 104; DLB 9, 12

Glaspell, Susan (Keating)
1882(?)-1948 . . . . **TCLC 55**
See also CA 110; DLB 7, 9, 78; YABC 2

Glassco, John 1909-1981 . . . . **CLC 9**
See also CA 13-16R; 102; CANR 15; DLB 68

Glasscock, Amnesia
See Steinbeck, John (Ernst)

Glasser, Ronald J. 1940(?)- . . . . **CLC 37**

Glassman, Joyce
See Johnson, Joyce

Glendinning, Victoria 1937- . . . . **CLC 50**
See also CA 120; 127

Glissant, Edouard 1928- . . . . **CLC 10, 68**

Gloag, Julian 1930- . . . . **CLC 40**
See also AITN 1; CA 65-68; CANR 10

Glowacki, Aleksander
See Prus, Boleslaw

Glueck, Louise (Elisabeth)
1943- . . . . **CLC 7, 22, 44, 81**
See also CA 33-36R; CANR 40; DLB 5

Gobineau, Joseph Arthur (Comte) de
1816-1882 . . . . **NCLC 17**
See also DLB 123

Godard, Jean-Luc 1930- . . . . **CLC 20**
See also CA 93-96

Godden, (Margaret) Rumer 1907- . . . **CLC 53**
See also AAYA 6; CA 5-8R; CANR 4, 27, 36; CLR 20; MAICYA; SAAS 12; SATA 3, 36

Godoy Alcayaga, Lucila 1889-1957
See Mistral, Gabriela
See also BW 2; CA 104; 131; HW; MTCW

Godwin, Gail (Kathleen)
1937- . . . . **CLC 5, 8, 22, 31, 69**
See also CA 29-32R; CANR 15, 43; DLB 6; MTCW

Godwin, William 1756-1836 . . . . . . **NCLC 14**
See also CDBLB 1789-1832; DLB 39, 104, 142

Gray, Spalding 1941- .... **CLC 49**
See also CA 128

Gray, Thomas
1716-1771 ...... **LC 4; DA; PC 2; WLC**
See also CDBLB 1660-1789; DLB 109

Grayson, David
See Baker, Ray Stannard

Grayson, Richard (A.) 1951- .... **CLC 38**
See also CA 85-88; CANR 14, 31

Greeley, Andrew M(oran) 1928- .... **CLC 28**
See also CA 5-8R; CAAS 7; CANR 7, 43; MTCW

Green, Brian
See Card, Orson Scott

Green, Hannah
See Greenberg, Joanne (Goldenberg)

Green, Hannah .... **CLC 3**
See also CA 73-76

Green, Henry .... **CLC 2, 13**
See also Yorke, Henry Vincent
See also DLB 15

Green, Julian (Hartridge) 1900-
See Green, Julien
See also CA 21-24R; CANR 33; DLB 4, 72; MTCW

Green, Julien .... **CLC 3, 11, 77**
See also Green, Julian (Hartridge)

Green, Paul (Eliot) 1894-1981 ...... **CLC 25**
See also AITN 1; CA 5-8R; 103; CANR 3; DLB 7, 9; DLBY 81

Greenberg, Ivan 1908-1973
See Rahv, Philip
See also CA 85-88

Greenberg, Joanne (Goldenberg)
1932- .... **CLC 7, 30**
See also AAYA 12; CA 5-8R; CANR 14, 32; SATA 25

Greenberg, Richard 1959(?)- .... **CLC 57**
See also CA 138

Greene, Bette 1934- .... **CLC 30**
See also AAYA 7; CA 53-56; CANR 4; CLR 2; JRDA; MAICYA; SAAS 16; SATA 8

Greene, Gael .... **CLC 8**
See also CA 13-16R; CANR 10

Greene, Graham
1904-1991 .... **CLC 1, 3, 6, 9, 14, 18, 27, 37, 70, 72; DA; WLC**
See also AITN 2; CA 13-16R; 133; CANR 35; CDBLB 1945-1960; DLB 13, 15, 77, 100; DLBY 91; MTCW; SATA 20

Greer, Richard
See Silverberg, Robert

Greer, Richard
See Silverberg, Robert

Gregor, Arthur 1923- .... **CLC 9**
See also CA 25-28R; CAAS 10; CANR 11; SATA 36

Gregor, Lee
See Pohl, Frederik

Gregory, Isabella Augusta (Persse)
1852-1932 .... **TCLC 1**
See also CA 104; DLB 10

Gregory, J. Dennis
See Williams, John A(lfred)

Grendon, Stephen
See Derleth, August (William)

Grenville, Kate 1950- .... **CLC 61**
See also CA 118

Grenville, Pelham
See Wodehouse, P(elham) G(renville)

Greve, Felix Paul (Berthold Friedrich)
1879-1948
See Grove, Frederick Philip
See also CA 104; 141

Grey, Zane 1872-1939 .... **TCLC 6**
See also CA 104; 132; DLB 9; MTCW

Grieg, (Johan) Nordahl (Brun)
1902-1943 .... **TCLC 10**
See also CA 107

Grieve, C(hristopher) M(urray)
1892-1978 .... **CLC 11, 19**
See also MacDiarmid, Hugh
See also CA 5-8R; 85-88; CANR 33; MTCW

Griffin, Gerald 1803-1840 .... **NCLC 7**

Griffin, John Howard 1920-1980 .... **CLC 68**
See also AITN 1; CA 1-4R; 101; CANR 2

Griffin, Peter 1942- .... **CLC 39**
See also CA 136

Griffiths, Trevor 1935- .... **CLC 13, 52**
See also CA 97-100; CANR 45; DLB 13

Grigson, Geoffrey (Edward Harvey)
1905-1985 .... **CLC 7, 39**
See also CA 25-28R; 118; CANR 20, 33; DLB 27; MTCW

Grillparzer, Franz 1791-1872 ...... **NCLC 1**
See also DLB 133

Grimble, Reverend Charles James
See Eliot, T(homas) S(tearns)

Grimke, Charlotte L(ottie) Forten
1837(?)-1914
See Forten, Charlotte L.
See also BW 1; CA 117; 124

Grimm, Jacob Ludwig Karl
1785-1863 .... **NCLC 3**
See also DLB 90; MAICYA; SATA 22

Grimm, Wilhelm Karl 1786-1859 .. **NCLC 3**
See also DLB 90; MAICYA; SATA 22

Grimmelshausen, Johann Jakob Christoffel von 1621-1676 .... **LC 6**

Grindel, Eugene 1895-1952
See Eluard, Paul
See also CA 104

Grisham, John 1955- .... **CLC 84**
See also AAYA 14; CA 138; CANR 47

Grossman, David 1954- .... **CLC 67**
See also CA 138

Grossman, Vasily (Semenovich)
1905-1964 .... **CLC 41**
See also CA 124; 130; MTCW

Grove, Frederick Philip .... **TCLC 4**
See also Greve, Felix Paul (Berthold Friedrich)
See also DLB 92

Grubb
See Crumb, R(obert)

Grumbach, Doris (Isaac)
1918- .... **CLC 13, 22, 64**
See also CA 5-8R; CAAS 2; CANR 9, 42

Grundtvig, Nicolai Frederik Severin
1783-1872 .... **NCLC 1**

Grunge
See Crumb, R(obert)

Grunwald, Lisa 1959- .... **CLC 44**
See also CA 120

Guare, John 1938- .... **CLC 8, 14, 29, 67**
See also CA 73-76; CANR 21; DLB 7; MTCW

Gudjonsson, Halldor Kiljan 1902-
See Laxness, Halldor
See also CA 103

Guenter, Erich
See Eich, Guenter

Guest, Barbara 1920- .... **CLC 34**
See also CA 25-28R; CANR 11, 44; DLB 5

Guest, Judith (Ann) 1936- .... **CLC 8, 30**
See also AAYA 7; CA 77-80; CANR 15; MTCW

Guild, Nicholas M. 1944- .... **CLC 33**
See also CA 93-96

Guillemin, Jacques
See Sartre, Jean-Paul

Guillen, Jorge 1893-1984 .... **CLC 11**
See also CA 89-92; 112; DLB 108; HW

Guillen (y Batista), Nicolas (Cristobal)
1902-1989 ..... **CLC 48, 79; BLC; HLC**
See also BW 2; CA 116; 125; 129; HW

Guillevic, (Eugene) 1907- .... **CLC 33**
See also CA 93-96

Guillois
See Desnos, Robert

Guiney, Louise Imogen
1861-1920 .... **TCLC 41**
See also DLB 54

Guiraldes, Ricardo (Guillermo)
1886-1927 .... **TCLC 39**
See also CA 131; HW; MTCW

Gunn, Bill .... **CLC 5**
See also Gunn, William Harrison
See also DLB 38

Gunn, Thom(son William)
1929- .... **CLC 3, 6, 18, 32, 81**
See also CA 17-20R; CANR 9, 33; CDBLB 1960 to Present; DLB 27; MTCW

Gunn, William Harrison 1934(?)-1989
See Gunn, Bill
See also AITN 1; BW 1; CA 13-16R; 128; CANR 12, 25

Gunnars, Kristjana 1948- .... **CLC 69**
See also CA 113; DLB 60

Gurganus, Allan 1947- .... **CLC 70**
See also BEST 90:1; CA 135

Gurney, A(lbert) R(amsdell), Jr.
1930- .... **CLC 32, 50, 54**
See also CA 77-80; CANR 32

Gurney, Ivor (Bertie) 1890-1937 ... **TCLC 33**

Gurney, Peter
See Gurney, A(lbert) R(amsdell), Jr.

Guro, Elena 1877-1913 .... **TCLC 56**

Harris, George Washington 1814-1869 .... **NCLC 23**
See also DLB 3, 11

Harris, Joel Chandler 1848-1908 ... **TCLC 2**
See also CA 104; 137; DLB 11, 23, 42, 78, 91; MAICYA; YABC 1

Harris, John (Wyndham Parkes Lucas) Beynon 1903-1969
See Wyndham, John
See also CA 102; 89-92

Harris, MacDonald .... **CLC 9**
See also Heiney, Donald (William)

Harris, Mark 1922- .... **CLC 19**
See also CA 5-8R; CAAS 3; CANR 2; DLB 2; DLBY 80

Harris, (Theodore) Wilson 1921-.... **CLC 25**
See also BW 2; CA 65-68; CAAS 16; CANR 11, 27; DLB 117; MTCW

Harrison, Elizabeth Cavanna 1909-
See Cavanna, Betty
See also CA 9-12R; CANR 6, 27

Harrison, Harry (Max) 1925-...... **CLC 42**
See also CA 1-4R; CANR 5, 21; DLB 8; SATA 4

Harrison, James (Thomas) 1937- .... **CLC 6, 14, 33, 66**
See also CA 13-16R; CANR 8; DLBY 82

Harrison, Jim
See Harrison, James (Thomas)

Harrison, Kathryn 1961- .... **CLC 70**
See also CA 144

Harrison, Tony 1937-............. **CLC 43**
See also CA 65-68; CANR 44; DLB 40; MTCW

Harriss, Will(ard Irvin) 1922-...... **CLC 34**
See also CA 111

Harson, Sley
See Ellison, Harlan (Jay)

Hart, Ellis
See Ellison, Harlan (Jay)

Hart, Josephine 1942(?)- .... **CLC 70**
See also CA 138

Hart, Moss 1904-1961 .... **CLC 66**
See also CA 109; 89-92; DLB 7

Harte, (Francis) Bret(t) 1836(?)-1902 .... **TCLC 1, 25; DA; SSC 8; WLC**
See also CA 104; 140; CDALB 1865-1917; DLB 12, 64, 74, 79; SATA 26

Hartley, L(eslie) P(oles) 1895-1972 .... **CLC 2, 22**
See also CA 45-48; 37-40R; CANR 33; DLB 15, 139; MTCW

Hartman, Geoffrey H. 1929-....... **CLC 27**
See also CA 117; 125; DLB 67

Haruf, Kent 19(?)- .... **CLC 34**

Harwood, Ronald 1934-........... **CLC 32**
See also CA 1-4R; CANR 4; DLB 13

Hasek, Jaroslav (Matej Frantisek) 1883-1923 .... **TCLC 4**
See also CA 104; 129; MTCW

Hass, Robert 1941-............ **CLC 18, 39**
See also CA 111; CANR 30; DLB 105

Hastings, Hudson
See Kuttner, Henry

Hastings, Selina .... **CLC 44**

Hatteras, Amelia
See Mencken, H(enry) L(ouis)

Hatteras, Owen .... **TCLC 18**
See also Mencken, H(enry) L(ouis); Nathan, George Jean

Hauptmann, Gerhart (Johann Robert) 1862-1946 .... **TCLC 4**
See also CA 104; DLB 66, 118

Havel, Vaclav 1936-........ **CLC 25, 58, 65**
See also CA 104; CANR 36; MTCW

Haviaras, Stratis .... **CLC 33**
See also Chaviaras, Strates

Hawes, Stephen 1475(?)-1523(?) ..... **LC 17**

Hawkes, John (Clendennin Burne, Jr.) 1925- ...... **CLC 1, 2, 3, 4, 7, 9, 14, 15, 27, 49**
See also CA 1-4R; CANR 2, 47; DLB 2, 7; DLBY 80; MTCW

Hawking, S. W.
See Hawking, Stephen W(illiam)

Hawking, Stephen W(illiam) 1942- .... **CLC 63**
See also AAYA 13; BEST 89:1; CA 126; 129

Hawthorne, Julian 1846-1934 ..... **TCLC 25**

Hawthorne, Nathaniel 1804-1864 ...... **NCLC 39; DA; SSC 3; WLC**
See also CDALB 1640-1865; DLB 1, 74; YABC 2

Haxton, Josephine Ayres 1921-
See Douglas, Ellen
See also CA 115; CANR 41

Hayaseca y Eizaguirre, Jorge
See Echegaray (y Eizaguirre), Jose (Maria Waldo)

Hayashi Fumiko 1904-1951....... **TCLC 27**

Haycraft, Anna
See Ellis, Alice Thomas
See also CA 122

Hayden, Robert E(arl) 1913-1980 ...... **CLC 5, 9, 14, 37; BLC; DA; PC 6**
See also BW 1; CA 69-72; 97-100; CABS 2; CANR 24; CDALB 1941-1968; DLB 5, 76; MTCW; SATA 19; SATA-Obit 26

Hayford, J(oseph) E(phraim) Casely
See Casely-Hayford, J(oseph) E(phraim)

Hayman, Ronald 1932-........... **CLC 44**
See also CA 25-28R; CANR 18

Haywood, Eliza (Fowler) 1693(?)-1756 .... **LC 1**

Hazlitt, William 1778-1830...... **NCLC 29**
See also DLB 110

Hazzard, Shirley 1931- .... **CLC 18**
See also CA 9-12R; CANR 4; DLBY 82; MTCW

Head, Bessie 1937-1986... **CLC 25, 67; BLC**
See also BW 2; CA 29-32R; 119; CANR 25; DLB 117; MTCW

Headon, (Nicky) Topper 1956(?)- ... **CLC 30**

Heaney, Seamus (Justin) 1939- .... **CLC 5, 7, 14, 25, 37, 74**
See also CA 85-88; CANR 25; CDBLB 1960 to Present; DLB 40; MTCW

Hearn, (Patricio) Lafcadio (Tessima Carlos) 1850-1904 .... **TCLC 9**
See also CA 105; DLB 12, 78

Hearne, Vicki 1946-.............. **CLC 56**
See also CA 139

Hearon, Shelby 1931-............. **CLC 63**
See also AITN 2; CA 25-28R; CANR 18

Heat-Moon, William Least .... **CLC 29**
See also Trogdon, William (Lewis)
See also AAYA 9

Hebbel, Friedrich 1813-1863 ..... **NCLC 43**
See also DLB 129

Hebert, Anne 1916- .... **CLC 4, 13, 29**
See also CA 85-88; DLB 68; MTCW

Hecht, Anthony (Evan) 1923- .... **CLC 8, 13, 19**
See also CA 9-12R; CANR 6; DLB 5

Hecht, Ben 1894-1964 .... **CLC 8**
See also CA 85-88; DLB 7, 9, 25, 26, 28, 86

Hedayat, Sadeq 1903-1951........ **TCLC 21**
See also CA 120

Hegel, Georg Wilhelm Friedrich 1770-1831 .... **NCLC 46**
See also DLB 90

Heidegger, Martin 1889-1976 ...... **CLC 24**
See also CA 81-84; 65-68; CANR 34; MTCW

Heidenstam, (Carl Gustaf) Verner von 1859-1940 .... **TCLC 5**
See also CA 104

Heifner, Jack 1946-.............. **CLC 11**
See also CA 105; CANR 47

Heijermans, Herman 1864-1924 ... **TCLC 24**
See also CA 123

Heilbrun, Carolyn G(old) 1926-..... **CLC 25**
See also CA 45-48; CANR 1, 28

Heine, Heinrich 1797-1856 .... **NCLC 4**
See also DLB 90

Heinemann, Larry (Curtiss) 1944- .. **CLC 50**
See also CA 110; CANR 31; DLBD 9

Heiney, Donald (William) 1921-1993
See Harris, MacDonald
See also CA 1-4R; 142; CANR 3

Heinlein, Robert A(nson) 1907-1988 ...... **CLC 1, 3, 8, 14, 26, 55**
See also CA 1-4R; 125; CANR 1, 20; DLB 8; JRDA; MAICYA; MTCW; SATA 9, 69; SATA-Obit 56

Helforth, John
See Doolittle, Hilda

Hellenhofferu, Vojtech Kapristian z
See Hasek, Jaroslav (Matej Frantisek)

Heller, Joseph 1923- .... **CLC 1, 3, 5, 8, 11, 36, 63; DA; WLC**
See also AITN 1; CA 5-8R; CABS 1; CANR 8, 42; DLB 2, 28; DLBY 80; MTCW

Hellman, Lillian (Florence) 1906-1984 ...... **CLC 2, 4, 8, 14, 18, 34, 44, 52; DC 1**
See also AITN 1, 2; CA 13-16R; 112; CANR 33; DLB 7; DLBY 84; MTCW

Helprin, Mark 1947- ..... **CLC 7, 10, 22, 32**
See also CA 81-84; CANR 47; DLBY 85; MTCW

Helvetius, Claude-Adrien 1715-1771 .... **LC 26**

Helyar, Jane Penelope Josephine 1933-
See Poole, Josephine
See also CA 21-24R; CANR 10, 26

Hemans, Felicia 1793-1835 ...... **NCLC 29**
See also DLB 96

Hemingway, Ernest (Miller) 1899-1961 .... **CLC 1, 3, 6, 8, 10, 13, 19, 30, 34, 39, 41, 44, 50, 61, 80; DA; SSC 1; WLC**
See also CA 77-80; CANR 34; CDALB 1917-1929; DLB 4, 9, 102; DLBD 1; DLBY 81, 87; MTCW

Hempel, Amy 1951- .... **CLC 39**
See also CA 118; 137

Henderson, F. C.
See Mencken, H(enry) L(ouis)

Henderson, Sylvia
See Ashton-Warner, Sylvia (Constance)

Henley, Beth .... **CLC 23**
See also Henley, Elizabeth Becker
See also CABS 3; DLBY 86

Henley, Elizabeth Becker 1952-
See Henley, Beth
See also CA 107; CANR 32; MTCW

Henley, William Ernest 1849-1903 .... **TCLC 8**
See also CA 105; DLB 19

Hennissart, Martha
See Lathen, Emma
See also CA 85-88

Henry, O. .... **TCLC 1, 19; SSC 5; WLC**
See also Porter, William Sydney

Henry, Patrick 1736- .... **LC 25**
See also CA 145

Henryson, Robert 1430(?)-1506(?).... **LC 20**
See also DLB 146

Henry VIII 1491-1547............. **LC 10**

Henschke, Alfred
See Klabund

Hentoff, Nat(han Irving) 1925- ..... **CLC 26**
See also AAYA 4; CA 1-4R; CAAS 6; CANR 5, 25; CLR 1; JRDA; MAICYA; SATA 27, 42, 69

Heppenstall, (John) Rayner 1911-1981 .... **CLC 10**
See also CA 1-4R; 103; CANR 29

Herbert, Frank (Patrick) 1920-1986 ...... **CLC 12, 23, 35, 44, 85**
See also CA 53-56; 118; CANR 5, 43; DLB 8; MTCW; SATA 9, 37; SATA-Obit 47

Herbert, George 1593-1633 .... **LC 24; PC 4**
See also CDBLB Before 1660; DLB 126

Herbert, Zbigniew 1924- .... **CLC 9, 43**
See also CA 89-92; CANR 36; MTCW

Herbst, Josephine (Frey) 1897-1969 .... **CLC 34**
See also CA 5-8R; 25-28R; DLB 9

Hergesheimer, Joseph 1880-1954 .... **TCLC 11**
See also CA 109; DLB 102, 9

Herlihy, James Leo 1927-1993 ...... **CLC 6**
See also CA 1-4R; 143; CANR 2

Hermogenes fl. c. 175- .... **CMLC 6**

Hernandez, Jose 1834-1886...... **NCLC 17**

Herrick, Robert 1591-1674 .... **LC 13; DA; PC 9**
See also DLB 126

Herring, Guilles
See Somerville, Edith

Herriot, James 1916- .... **CLC 12**
See also Wight, James Alfred
See also AAYA 1; CANR 40

Herrmann, Dorothy 1941- .... **CLC 44**
See also CA 107

Herrmann, Taffy
See Herrmann, Dorothy

Hersey, John (Richard) 1914-1993 .... **CLC 1, 2, 7, 9, 40, 81**
See also CA 17-20R; 140; CANR 33; DLB 6; MTCW; SATA 25; SATA-Obit 76

Herzen, Aleksandr Ivanovich 1812-1870 .... **NCLC 10**

Herzl, Theodor 1860-1904........ **TCLC 36**

Herzog, Werner 1942- .... **CLC 16**
See also CA 89-92

Hesiod c. 8th cent. B.C.- .... **CMLC 5**

Hesse, Hermann 1877-1962 .... **CLC 1, 2, 3, 6, 11, 17, 25, 69; DA; SSC 9; WLC**
See also CA 17-18; CAP 2; DLB 66; MTCW; SATA 50

Hewes, Cady
See De Voto, Bernard (Augustine)

Heyen, William 1940- .... **CLC 13, 18**
See also CA 33-36R; CAAS 9; DLB 5

Heyerdahl, Thor 1914- .... **CLC 26**
See also CA 5-8R; CANR 5, 22; MTCW; SATA 2, 52

Heym, Georg (Theodor Franz Arthur) 1887-1912 .... **TCLC 9**
See also CA 106

Heym, Stefan 1913- .... **CLC 41**
See also CA 9-12R; CANR 4; DLB 69

Heyse, Paul (Johann Ludwig von) 1830-1914 .... **TCLC 8**
See also CA 104; DLB 129

Hibbert, Eleanor Alice Burford 1906-1993 .... **CLC 7**
See also BEST 90:4; CA 17-20R; 140; CANR 9, 28; SATA 2; SATA-Obit 74

Higgins, George V(incent) 1939- .... **CLC 4, 7, 10, 18**
See also CA 77-80; CAAS 5; CANR 17; DLB 2; DLBY 81; MTCW

Higginson, Thomas Wentworth 1823-1911 .... **TCLC 36**
See also DLB 1, 64

Highet, Helen
See MacInnes, Helen (Clark)

Highsmith, (Mary) Patricia 1921- .... **CLC 2, 4, 14, 42**
See also CA 1-4R; CANR 1, 20; MTCW

Highwater, Jamake (Mamake) 1942(?)- .... **CLC 12**
See also AAYA 7; CA 65-68; CAAS 7; CANR 10, 34; CLR 17; DLB 52; DLBY 85; JRDA; MAICYA; SATA 30, 32, 69

Hijuelos, Oscar 1951- ...... **CLC 65; HLC**
See also BEST 90:1; CA 123; DLB 145; HW

Hikmet, Nazim 1902(?)-1963....... **CLC 40**
See also CA 141; 93-96

Hildesheimer, Wolfgang 1916-1991 .... **CLC 49**
See also CA 101; 135; DLB 69, 124

Hill, Geoffrey (William) 1932- .... **CLC 5, 8, 18, 45**
See also CA 81-84; CANR 21; CDBLB 1960 to Present; DLB 40; MTCW

Hill, George Roy 1921- .... **CLC 26**
See also CA 110; 122

Hill, John
See Koontz, Dean R(ay)

Hill, Susan (Elizabeth) 1942- .... **CLC 4**
See also CA 33-36R; CANR 29; DLB 14, 139; MTCW

Hillerman, Tony 1925- .... **CLC 62**
See also AAYA 6; BEST 89:1; CA 29-32R; CANR 21, 42; SATA 6

Hillesum, Etty 1914-1943 .... **TCLC 49**
See also CA 137

Hilliard, Noel (Harvey) 1929- ...... **CLC 15**
See also CA 9-12R; CANR 7

Hillis, Rick 1956- .... **CLC 66**
See also CA 134

Hilton, James 1900-1954......... **TCLC 21**
See also CA 108; DLB 34, 77; SATA 34

Himes, Chester (Bomar) 1909-1984 .... **CLC 2, 4, 7, 18, 58; BLC**
See also BW 2; CA 25-28R; 114; CANR 22; DLB 2, 76, 143; MTCW

Hinde, Thomas .... **CLC 6, 11**
See also Chitty, Thomas Willes

Hindin, Nathan
See Bloch, Robert (Albert)

Hine, (William) Daryl 1936- .... **CLC 15**
See also CA 1-4R; CAAS 15; CANR 1, 20; DLB 60

Hinkson, Katharine Tynan
See Tynan, Katharine

Hinton, S(usan) E(loise) 1950- .... **CLC 30; DA**
See also AAYA 2; CA 81-84; CANR 32; CLR 3, 23; JRDA; MAICYA; MTCW; SATA 19, 58

Hippius, Zinaida .... **TCLC 9**
See also Gippius, Zinaida (Nikolayevna)

Hiraoka, Kimitake 1925-1970
See Mishima, Yukio
See also CA 97-100; 29-32R; MTCW

Hirsch, E(ric) D(onald), Jr. 1928- . . . **CLC 79**
See also CA 25-28R; CANR 27; DLB 67; MTCW

Hirsch, Edward 1950- . . . . **CLC 31, 50**
See also CA 104; CANR 20, 42; DLB 120

Hitchcock, Alfred (Joseph) 1899-1980 . . . . **CLC 16**
See also CA 97-100; SATA 27; SATA-Obit 24

Hitler, Adolf 1889-1945 . . . . **TCLC 53**
See also CA 117

Hoagland, Edward 1932- . . . . **CLC 28**
See also CA 1-4R; CANR 2, 31; DLB 6; SATA 51

Hoban, Russell (Conwell) 1925- . . **CLC 7, 25**
See also CA 5-8R; CANR 23, 37; CLR 3; DLB 52; MAICYA; MTCW; SATA 1, 40, 78

Hobbs, Perry
See Blackmur, R(ichard) P(almer)

Hobson, Laura Z(ametkin) 1900-1986 . . . . **CLC 7, 25**
See also CA 17-20R; 118; DLB 28; SATA 52

Hochhuth, Rolf 1931- . . . . **CLC 4, 11, 18**
See also CA 5-8R; CANR 33; DLB 124; MTCW

Hochman, Sandra 1936- . . . . **CLC 3, 8**
See also CA 5-8R; DLB 5

Hochwaelder, Fritz 1911-1986 . . . . . . **CLC 36**
See also CA 29-32R; 120; CANR 42; MTCW

Hochwalder, Fritz
See Hochwaelder, Fritz

Hocking, Mary (Eunice) 1921- . . . . . **CLC 13**
See also CA 101; CANR 18, 40

Hodgins, Jack 1938- . . . . **CLC 23**
See also CA 93-96; DLB 60

Hodgson, William Hope 1877(?)-1918 . . . . **TCLC 13**
See also CA 111; DLB 70

Hoffman, Alice 1952- . . . . **CLC 51**
See also CA 77-80; CANR 34; MTCW

Hoffman, Daniel (Gerard) 1923- . . . . **CLC 6, 13, 23**
See also CA 1-4R; CANR 4; DLB 5

Hoffman, Stanley 1944- . . . . **CLC 5**
See also CA 77-80

Hoffman, William M(oses) 1939- . . . **CLC 40**
See also CA 57-60; CANR 11

Hoffmann, E(rnst) T(heodor) A(madeus) 1776-1822 . . . . **NCLC 2; SSC 13**
See also DLB 90; SATA 27

Hofmann, Gert 1931- . . . . **CLC 54**
See also CA 128

Hofmannsthal, Hugo von 1874-1929 . . . . **TCLC 11; DC 4**
See also CA 106; DLB 81, 118

Hogan, Linda 1947- . . . . **CLC 73**
See also CA 120; CANR 45; NNAL

Hogarth, Charles
See Creasey, John

Hogg, James 1770-1835 . . . . **NCLC 4**
See also DLB 93, 116

Holbach, Paul Henri Thiry Baron 1723-1789 . . . . **LC 14**

Holberg, Ludvig 1684-1754 . . . . **LC 6**

Holden, Ursula 1921- . . . . **CLC 18**
See also CA 101; CAAS 8; CANR 22

Holderlin, (Johann Christian) Friedrich 1770-1843 . . . . **NCLC 16; PC 4**

Holdstock, Robert
See Holdstock, Robert P.

Holdstock, Robert P. 1948- . . . . **CLC 39**
See also CA 131

Holland, Isabelle 1920- . . . . **CLC 21**
See also AAYA 11; CA 21-24R; CANR 10, 25, 47; JRDA; MAICYA; SATA 8, 70

Holland, Marcus
See Caldwell, (Janet Miriam) Taylor (Holland)

Hollander, John 1929- . . . . . . **CLC 2, 5, 8, 14**
See also CA 1-4R; CANR 1; DLB 5; SATA 13

Hollander, Paul
See Silverberg, Robert

Holleran, Andrew 1943(?)- . . . . **CLC 38**
See also CA 144

Hollinghurst, Alan 1954- . . . . **CLC 55**
See also CA 114

Hollis, Jim
See Summers, Hollis (Spurgeon, Jr.)

Holmes, John
See Souster, (Holmes) Raymond

Holmes, John Clellon 1926-1988 . . . . **CLC 56**
See also CA 9-12R; 125; CANR 4; DLB 16

Holmes, Oliver Wendell 1809-1894 . . . . **NCLC 14**
See also CDALB 1640-1865; DLB 1; SATA 34

Holmes, Raymond
See Souster, (Holmes) Raymond

Holt, Victoria
See Hibbert, Eleanor Alice Burford

Holub, Miroslav 1923- . . . . **CLC 4**
See also CA 21-24R; CANR 10

Homer c. 8th cent. B.C.- . . . . . **CMLC 1; DA**

Honig, Edwin 1919- . . . . **CLC 33**
See also CA 5-8R; CAAS 8; CANR 4, 45; DLB 5

Hood, Hugh (John Blagdon) 1928- . . . . **CLC 15, 28**
See also CA 49-52; CAAS 17; CANR 1, 33; DLB 53

Hood, Thomas 1799-1845 . . . . **NCLC 16**
See also DLB 96

Hooker, (Peter) Jeremy 1941- . . . . . . **CLC 43**
See also CA 77-80; CANR 22; DLB 40

Hope, A(lec) D(erwent) 1907- . . . . **CLC 3, 51**
See also CA 21-24R; CANR 33; MTCW

Hope, Brian
See Creasey, John

Hope, Christopher (David Tully) 1944- . . . . **CLC 52**
See also CA 106; CANR 47; SATA 62

Hopkins, Gerard Manley 1844-1889 . . . . **NCLC 17; DA; WLC**
See also CDBLB 1890-1914; DLB 35, 57

Hopkins, John (Richard) 1931- . . . . . . **CLC 4**
See also CA 85-88

Hopkins, Pauline Elizabeth 1859-1930 . . . . **TCLC 28; BLC**
See also BW 2; CA 141; DLB 50

Hopkinson, Francis 1737-1791 . . . . . . **LC 25**
See also DLB 31

Hopley-Woolrich, Cornell George 1903-1968
See Woolrich, Cornell
See also CA 13-14; CAP 1

Horatio
See Proust, (Valentin-Louis-George-Eugene-) Marcel

Horgan, Paul 1903- . . . . **CLC 9, 53**
See also CA 13-16R; CANR 9, 35; DLB 102; DLBY 85; MTCW; SATA 13

Horn, Peter
See Kuttner, Henry

Hornem, Horace Esq.
See Byron, George Gordon (Noel)

Horovitz, Israel (Arthur) 1939- . . . . . **CLC 56**
See also CA 33-36R; CANR 46; DLB 7

Horvath, Odon von
See Horvath, Oedoen von
See also DLB 85, 124

Horvath, Oedoen von 1901-1938 . . . **TCLC 45**
See also Horvath, Odon von
See also CA 118

Horwitz, Julius 1920-1986 . . . . **CLC 14**
See also CA 9-12R; 119; CANR 12

Hospital, Janette Turner 1942- . . . . . **CLC 42**
See also CA 108

Hostos, E. M. de
See Hostos (y Bonilla), Eugenio Maria de

Hostos, Eugenio M. de
See Hostos (y Bonilla), Eugenio Maria de

Hostos, Eugenio Maria
See Hostos (y Bonilla), Eugenio Maria de

Hostos (y Bonilla), Eugenio Maria de 1839-1903 . . . . **TCLC 24**
See also CA 123; 131; HW

Houdini
See Lovecraft, H(oward) P(hillips)

Hougan, Carolyn 1943- . . . . **CLC 34**
See also CA 139

Household, Geoffrey (Edward West) 1900-1988 . . . . **CLC 11**
See also CA 77-80; 126; DLB 87; SATA 14; SATA-Obit 59

Housman, A(lfred) E(dward) 1859-1936 . . . . . . **TCLC 1, 10; DA; PC 2**
See also CA 104; 125; DLB 19; MTCW

Housman, Laurence 1865-1959 . . . . . **TCLC 7**
See also CA 106; DLB 10; SATA 25

Howard, Elizabeth Jane 1923- . . . **CLC 7, 29**
See also CA 5-8R; CANR 8

Howard, Maureen 1930- . . . . . **CLC 5, 14, 46**
See also CA 53-56; CANR 31; DLBY 83; MTCW

Ingalls, Rachel (Holmes) 1940- . . . . . **CLC 42**
See also CA 123; 127

Ingamells, Rex 1913-1955 . . . . **TCLC 35**

Inge, William Motter
1913-1973 . . . . **CLC 1, 8, 19**
See also CA 9-12R; CDALB 1941-1968; DLB 7; MTCW

Ingelow, Jean 1820-1897 . . . . **NCLC 39**
See also DLB 35; SATA 33

Ingram, Willis J.
See Harris, Mark

Innaurato, Albert (F.) 1948(?)- . . **CLC 21, 60**
See also CA 115; 122

Innes, Michael
See Stewart, J(ohn) I(nnes) M(ackintosh)

Ionesco, Eugene
1909-1994 . . . . **CLC 1, 4, 6, 9, 11, 15, 41, 86; DA; WLC**
See also CA 9-12R; 144; MTCW; SATA 7; SATA-Obit 79

Iqbal, Muhammad 1873-1938 . . . . . **TCLC 28**

Ireland, Patrick
See O'Doherty, Brian

Iron, Ralph
See Schreiner, Olive (Emilie Albertina)

Irving, John (Winslow)
1942- . . . . **CLC 13, 23, 38**
See also AAYA 8; BEST 89:3; CA 25-28R; CANR 28; DLB 6; DLBY 82; MTCW

Irving, Washington
1783-1859 . . . . **NCLC 2, 19; DA; SSC 2; WLC**
See also CDALB 1640-1865; DLB 3, 11, 30, 59, 73, 74; YABC 2

Irwin, P. K.
See Page, P(atricia) K(athleen)

Isaacs, Susan 1943- . . . . **CLC 32**
See also BEST 89:1; CA 89-92; CANR 20, 41; MTCW

Isherwood, Christopher (William Bradshaw)
1904-1986 . . . . **CLC 1, 9, 11, 14, 44**
See also CA 13-16R; 117; CANR 35; DLB 15; DLBY 86; MTCW

Ishiguro, Kazuo 1954- . . . . . . **CLC 27, 56, 59**
See also BEST 90:2; CA 120; MTCW

Ishikawa Takuboku
1886(?)-1912 . . . . **TCLC 15; PC 10**
See also CA 113

Iskander, Fazil 1929- . . . . **CLC 47**
See also CA 102

Ivan IV 1530-1584 . . . . **LC 17**

Ivanov, Vyacheslav Ivanovich
1866-1949 . . . . **TCLC 33**
See also CA 122

Ivask, Ivar Vidrik 1927-1992 . . . . **CLC 14**
See also CA 37-40R; 139; CANR 24

Jackson, Daniel
See Wingrove, David (John)

Jackson, Jesse 1908-1983 . . . . **CLC 12**
See also BW 1; CA 25-28R; 109; CANR 27; CLR 28; MAICYA; SATA 2, 29; SATA-Obit 48

Jackson, Laura (Riding) 1901-1991
See Riding, Laura
See also CA 65-68; 135; CANR 28; DLB 48

Jackson, Sam
See Trumbo, Dalton

Jackson, Sara
See Wingrove, David (John)

Jackson, Shirley
1919-1965 . . . . . **CLC 11, 60; DA; SSC 9; WLC**
See also AAYA 9; CA 1-4R; 25-28R; CANR 4; CDALB 1941-1968; DLB 6; SATA 2

Jacob, (Cyprien-)Max 1876-1944 . . . **TCLC 6**
See also CA 104

Jacobs, Jim 1942- . . . . **CLC 12**
See also CA 97-100

Jacobs, W(illiam) W(ymark)
1863-1943 . . . . **TCLC 22**
See also CA 121; DLB 135

Jacobsen, Jens Peter 1847-1885 . . **NCLC 34**

Jacobsen, Josephine 1908- . . . . **CLC 48**
See also CA 33-36R; CAAS 18; CANR 23

Jacobson, Dan 1929- . . . . **CLC 4, 14**
See also CA 1-4R; CANR 2, 25; DLB 14; MTCW

Jacqueline
See Carpentier (y Valmont), Alejo

Jagger, Mick 1944- . . . . **CLC 17**

Jakes, John (William) 1932- . . . . **CLC 29**
See also BEST 89:4; CA 57-60; CANR 10, 43; DLBY 83; MTCW; SATA 62

James, Andrew
See Kirkup, James

James, C(yril) L(ionel) R(obert)
1901-1989 . . . . **CLC 33**
See also BW 2; CA 117; 125; 128; DLB 125; MTCW

James, Daniel (Lewis) 1911-1988
See Santiago, Danny
See also CA 125

James, Dynely
See Mayne, William (James Carter)

James, Henry
1843-1916 . . . . . . **TCLC 2, 11, 24, 40, 47; DA; SSC 8; WLC**
See also CA 104; 132; CDALB 1865-1917; DLB 12, 71, 74; MTCW

James, M. R.
See James, Montague (Rhodes)

James, Montague (Rhodes)
1862-1936 . . . . **TCLC 6; SSC 16**
See also CA 104

James, P. D. . . . . **CLC 18, 46**
See also White, Phyllis Dorothy James
See also BEST 90:2; CDBLB 1960 to Present; DLB 87

James, Philip
See Moorcock, Michael (John)

James, William 1842-1910 . . . . . **TCLC 15, 32**
See also CA 109

James I 1394-1437 . . . . **LC 20**

Jameson, Anna 1794-1860 . . . . **NCLC 43**
See also DLB 99

Jami, Nur al-Din 'Abd al-Rahman
1414-1492 . . . . **LC 9**

Jandl, Ernst 1925- . . . . **CLC 34**

Janowitz, Tama 1957- . . . . **CLC 43**
See also CA 106

Jarrell, Randall
1914-1965 . . . . **CLC 1, 2, 6, 9, 13, 49**
See also CA 5-8R; 25-28R; CABS 2; CANR 6, 34; CDALB 1941-1968; CLR 6; DLB 48, 52; MAICYA; MTCW; SATA 7

Jarry, Alfred 1873-1907 . . . . **TCLC 2, 14**
See also CA 104

Jarvis, E. K.
See Bloch, Robert (Albert); Ellison, Harlan (Jay); Silverberg, Robert

Jeake, Samuel, Jr.
See Aiken, Conrad (Potter)

Jean Paul 1763-1825 . . . . **NCLC 7**

Jefferies, (John) Richard
1848-1887 . . . . **NCLC 47**
See also DLB 98, 141; SATA 16

Jeffers, (John) Robinson
1887-1962 . . . . **CLC 2, 3, 11, 15, 54; DA; WLC**
See also CA 85-88; CANR 35; CDALB 1917-1929; DLB 45; MTCW

Jefferson, Janet
See Mencken, H(enry) L(ouis)

Jefferson, Thomas 1743-1826 . . . . **NCLC 11**
See also CDALB 1640-1865; DLB 31

Jeffrey, Francis 1773-1850 . . . . **NCLC 33**
See also DLB 107

Jelakowitch, Ivan
See Heijermans, Herman

Jellicoe, (Patricia) Ann 1927- . . . . . . **CLC 27**
See also CA 85-88; DLB 13

Jen, Gish . . . . **CLC 70**
See also Jen, Lillian

Jen, Lillian 1956(?)-
See Jen, Gish
See also CA 135

Jenkins, (John) Robin 1912- . . . . **CLC 52**
See also CA 1-4R; CANR 1; DLB 14

Jennings, Elizabeth (Joan)
1926- . . . . **CLC 5, 14**
See also CA 61-64; CAAS 5; CANR 8, 39; DLB 27; MTCW; SATA 66

Jennings, Waylon 1937- . . . . **CLC 21**

Jensen, Johannes V. 1873-1950 . . . . **TCLC 41**

Jensen, Laura (Linnea) 1948- . . . . . . **CLC 37**
See also CA 103

Jerome, Jerome K(lapka)
1859-1927 . . . . **TCLC 23**
See also CA 119; DLB 10, 34, 135

Jerrold, Douglas William
1803-1857 . . . . **NCLC 2**

Jewett, (Theodora) Sarah Orne
1849-1909 . . . . **TCLC 1, 22; SSC 6**
See also CA 108; 127; DLB 12, 74; SATA 15

Jewsbury, Geraldine (Endsor)
1812-1880 . . . . **NCLC 22**
See also DLB 21

Kallman, Chester (Simon) 1921-1975 .... **CLC 2**
See also CA 45-48; 53-56; CANR 3

Kaminsky, Melvin 1926-
See Brooks, Mel
See also CA 65-68; CANR 16

Kaminsky, Stuart M(elvin) 1934- ... **CLC 59**
See also CA 73-76; CANR 29

Kane, Paul
See Simon, Paul

Kane, Wilson
See Bloch, Robert (Albert)

Kanin, Garson 1912-.............. **CLC 22**
See also AITN 1; CA 5-8R; CANR 7; DLB 7

Kaniuk, Yoram 1930-............. **CLC 19**
See also CA 134

Kant, Immanuel 1724-1804 ...... **NCLC 27**
See also DLB 94

Kantor, MacKinlay 1904-1977 ...... **CLC 7**
See also CA 61-64; 73-76; DLB 9, 102

Kaplan, David Michael 1946- ...... **CLC 50**

Kaplan, James 1951- .... **CLC 59**
See also CA 135

Karageorge, Michael
See Anderson, Poul (William)

Karamzin, Nikolai Mikhailovich 1766-1826 .... **NCLC 3**

Karapanou, Margarita 1946-....... **CLC 13**
See also CA 101

Karinthy, Frigyes 1887-1938...... **TCLC 47**

Karl, Frederick R(obert) 1927-..... **CLC 34**
See also CA 5-8R; CANR 3, 44

Kastel, Warren
See Silverberg, Robert

Kataev, Evgeny Petrovich 1903-1942
See Petrov, Evgeny
See also CA 120

Kataphusin
See Ruskin, John

Katz, Steve 1935-................ **CLC 47**
See also CA 25-28R; CAAS 14; CANR 12; DLBY 83

Kauffman, Janet 1945-............ **CLC 42**
See also CA 117; CANR 43; DLBY 86

Kaufman, Bob (Garnell) 1925-1986 .... **CLC 49**
See also BW 1; CA 41-44R; 118; CANR 22; DLB 16, 41

Kaufman, George S. 1889-1961..... **CLC 38**
See also CA 108; 93-96; DLB 7

Kaufman, Sue .... **CLC 3, 8**
See also Barondess, Sue K(aufman)

Kavafis, Konstantinos Petrou 1863-1933
See Cavafy, C(onstantine) P(eter)
See also CA 104

Kavan, Anna 1901-1968...... **CLC 5, 13, 82**
See also CA 5-8R; CANR 6; MTCW

Kavanagh, Dan
See Barnes, Julian

Kavanagh, Patrick (Joseph) 1904-1967 .... **CLC 22**
See also CA 123; 25-28R; DLB 15, 20; MTCW

Kawabata, Yasunari 1899-1972 ..... **CLC 2, 5, 9, 18; SSC 17**
See also CA 93-96; 33-36R

Kaye, M(ary) M(argaret) 1909-..... **CLC 28**
See also CA 89-92; CANR 24; MTCW; SATA 62

Kaye, Mollie
See Kaye, M(ary) M(argaret)

Kaye-Smith, Sheila 1887-1956..... **TCLC 20**
See also CA 118; DLB 36

Kaymor, Patrice Maguilene
See Senghor, Leopold Sedar

Kazan, Elia 1909-........... **CLC 6, 16, 63**
See also CA 21-24R; CANR 32

Kazantzakis, Nikos 1883(?)-1957 .... **TCLC 2, 5, 33**
See also CA 105; 132; MTCW

Kazin, Alfred 1915- .... **CLC 34, 38**
See also CA 1-4R; CAAS 7; CANR 1, 45; DLB 67

Keane, Mary Nesta (Skrine) 1904-
See Keane, Molly
See also CA 108; 114

Keane, Molly..................... **CLC 31**
See also Keane, Mary Nesta (Skrine)

Keates, Jonathan 19(?)- .... **CLC 34**

Keaton, Buster 1895-1966 .... **CLC 20**

Keats, John 1795-1821 ... **NCLC 8; DA; PC 1; WLC**
See also CDBLB 1789-1832; DLB 96, 110

Keene, Donald 1922- .... **CLC 34**
See also CA 1-4R; CANR 5

Keillor, Garrison.................. **CLC 40**
See also Keillor, Gary (Edward)
See also AAYA 2; BEST 89:3; DLBY 87; SATA 58

Keillor, Gary (Edward) 1942-
See Keillor, Garrison
See also CA 111; 117; CANR 36; MTCW

Keith, Michael
See Hubbard, L(afayette) Ron(ald)

Keller, Gottfried 1819-1890....... **NCLC 2**
See also DLB 129

Kellerman, Jonathan 1949- .... **CLC 44**
See also BEST 90:1; CA 106; CANR 29

Kelley, William Melvin 1937-...... **CLC 22**
See also BW 1; CA 77-80; CANR 27; DLB 33

Kellogg, Marjorie 1922-............ **CLC 2**
See also CA 81-84

Kellow, Kathleen
See Hibbert, Eleanor Alice Burford

Kelly, M(ilton) T(erry) 1947-....... **CLC 55**
See also CA 97-100; CANR 19, 43

Kelman, James 1946-.......... **CLC 58, 86**

Kemal, Yashar 1923- .... **CLC 14, 29**
See also CA 89-92; CANR 44

Kemble, Fanny 1809-1893 .... **NCLC 18**
See also DLB 32

Kemelman, Harry 1908-............ **CLC 2**
See also AITN 1; CA 9-12R; CANR 6; DLB 28

Kempe, Margery 1373(?)-1440(?) ..... **LC 6**
See also DLB 146

Kempis, Thomas a 1380-1471 .... **LC 11**

Kendall, Henry 1839-1882....... **NCLC 12**

Keneally, Thomas (Michael) 1935- ...... **CLC 5, 8, 10, 14, 19, 27, 43**
See also CA 85-88; CANR 10; MTCW

Kennedy, Adrienne (Lita) 1931- .... **CLC 66; BLC; DC 5**
See also BW 2; CA 103; CAAS 20; CABS 3; CANR 26; DLB 38

Kennedy, John Pendleton 1795-1870 .... **NCLC 2**
See also DLB 3

Kennedy, Joseph Charles 1929-
See Kennedy, X. J.
See also CA 1-4R; CANR 4, 30, 40; SATA 14

Kennedy, William 1928-... **CLC 6, 28, 34, 53**
See also AAYA 1; CA 85-88; CANR 14, 31; DLB 143; DLBY 85; MTCW; SATA 57

Kennedy, X. J................... **CLC 8, 42**
See also Kennedy, Joseph Charles
See also CAAS 9; CLR 27; DLB 5

Kent, Kelvin
See Kuttner, Henry

Kenton, Maxwell
See Southern, Terry

Kenyon, Robert O.
See Kuttner, Henry

Kerouac, Jack ..... **CLC 1, 2, 3, 5, 14, 29, 61**
See also Kerouac, Jean-Louis Lebris de
See also CDALB 1941-1968; DLB 2, 16; DLBD 3

Kerouac, Jean-Louis Lebris de 1922-1969
See Kerouac, Jack
See also AITN 1; CA 5-8R; 25-28R; CANR 26; DA; MTCW; WLC

Kerr, Jean 1923-................. **CLC 22**
See also CA 5-8R; CANR 7

Kerr, M. E..................... **CLC 12, 35**
See also Meaker, Marijane (Agnes)
See also AAYA 2; CLR 29; SAAS 1

Kerr, Robert .... **CLC 55**

Kerrigan, (Thomas) Anthony 1918- .... **CLC 4, 6**
See also CA 49-52; CAAS 11; CANR 4

Kerry, Lois
See Duncan, Lois

Kesey, Ken (Elton) 1935- ...... **CLC 1, 3, 6, 11, 46, 64; DA; WLC**
See also CA 1-4R; CANR 22, 38; CDALB 1968-1988; DLB 2, 16; MTCW; SATA 66

Kesselring, Joseph (Otto) 1902-1967 .... **CLC 45**

Kessler, Jascha (Frederick) 1929-.... **CLC 4**
See also CA 17-20R; CANR 8

Landon, Letitia Elizabeth 1802-1838 . . . . **NCLC 15**
See also DLB 96

Landor, Walter Savage 1775-1864 . . . . **NCLC 14**
See also DLB 93, 107

Landwirth, Heinz 1927-
See Lind, Jakov
See also CA 9-12R; CANR 7

Lane, Patrick 1939- . . . . **CLC 25**
See also CA 97-100; DLB 53

Lang, Andrew 1844-1912 . . . . **TCLC 16**
See also CA 114; 137; DLB 98, 141; MAICYA; SATA 16

Lang, Fritz 1890-1976 . . . . **CLC 20**
See also CA 77-80; 69-72; CANR 30

Lange, John
See Crichton, (John) Michael

Langer, Elinor 1939- . . . . **CLC 34**
See also CA 121

Langland, William 1330(?)-1400(?) . . . . **LC 19; DA**
See also DLB 146

Langstaff, Launcelot
See Irving, Washington

Lanier, Sidney 1842-1881 . . . . **NCLC 6**
See also DLB 64; MAICYA; SATA 18

Lanyer, Aemilia 1569-1645 . . . . **LC 10**

Lao Tzu . . . . **CMLC 7**

Lapine, James (Elliot) 1949- . . . . **CLC 39**
See also CA 123; 130

Larbaud, Valery (Nicolas) 1881-1957 . . . . **TCLC 9**
See also CA 106

Lardner, Ring
See Lardner, Ring(gold) W(ilmer)

Lardner, Ring W., Jr.
See Lardner, Ring(gold) W(ilmer)

Lardner, Ring(gold) W(ilmer) 1885-1933 . . . . **TCLC 2, 14**
See also CA 104; 131; CDALB 1917-1929; DLB 11, 25, 86; MTCW

Laredo, Betty
See Codrescu, Andrei

Larkin, Maia
See Wojciechowska, Maia (Teresa)

Larkin, Philip (Arthur) 1922-1985 . . . . **CLC 3, 5, 8, 9, 13, 18, 33, 39, 64**
See also CA 5-8R; 117; CANR 24; CDBLB 1960 to Present; DLB 27; MTCW

Larra (y Sanchez de Castro), Mariano Jose de 1809-1837 . . . . **NCLC 17**

Larsen, Eric 1941- . . . . **CLC 55**
See also CA 132

Larsen, Nella 1891-1964 . . . . . **CLC 37; BLC**
See also BW 1; CA 125; DLB 51

Larson, Charles R(aymond) 1938- . . . **CLC 31**
See also CA 53-56; CANR 4

Lasker-Schueler, Else 1869-1945 . . **TCLC 57**
See also DLB 66, 124

Latham, Jean Lee 1902- . . . . **CLC 12**
See also AITN 1; CA 5-8R; CANR 7; MAICYA; SATA 2, 68

Latham, Mavis
See Clark, Mavis Thorpe

Lathen, Emma . . . . **CLC 2**
See also Hennissart, Martha; Latsis, Mary J(ane)

Lathrop, Francis
See Leiber, Fritz (Reuter, Jr.)

Latsis, Mary J(ane)
See Lathen, Emma
See also CA 85-88

Lattimore, Richmond (Alexander) 1906-1984 . . . . **CLC 3**
See also CA 1-4R; 112; CANR 1

Laughlin, James 1914- . . . . **CLC 49**
See also CA 21-24R; CANR 9, 45; DLB 48

Laurence, (Jean) Margaret (Wemyss) 1926-1987 . . **CLC 3, 6, 13, 50, 62; SSC 7**
See also CA 5-8R; 121; CANR 33; DLB 53; MTCW; SATA-Obit 50

Laurent, Antoine 1952- . . . . **CLC 50**

Lauscher, Hermann
See Hesse, Hermann

Lautreamont, Comte de 1846-1870 . . . . **NCLC 12; SSC 14**

Laverty, Donald
See Blish, James (Benjamin)

Lavin, Mary 1912- . . . . . . **CLC 4, 18; SSC 4**
See also CA 9-12R; CANR 33; DLB 15; MTCW

Lavond, Paul Dennis
See Kornbluth, C(yril) M.; Pohl, Frederik

Lawler, Raymond Evenor 1922- . . . . **CLC 58**
See also CA 103

Lawrence, D(avid) H(erbert Richards) 1885-1930 . . . . **TCLC 2, 9, 16, 33, 48; DA; SSC 4; WLC**
See also CA 104; 121; CDBLB 1914-1945; DLB 10, 19, 36, 98; MTCW

Lawrence, T(homas) E(dward) 1888-1935 . . . . **TCLC 18**
See also Dale, Colin
See also CA 115

Lawrence of Arabia
See Lawrence, T(homas) E(dward)

Lawson, Henry (Archibald Hertzberg) 1867-1922 . . . . **TCLC 27**
See also CA 120

Lawton, Dennis
See Faust, Frederick (Schiller)

Laxness, Halldor . . . . **CLC 25**
See also Gudjonsson, Halldor Kiljan

Layamon fl. c. 1200- . . . . **CMLC 10**
See also DLB 146

Laye, Camara 1928-1980 . . . **CLC 4, 38; BLC**
See also BW 1; CA 85-88; 97-100; CANR 25; MTCW

Layton, Irving (Peter) 1912- . . . . . **CLC 2, 15**
See also CA 1-4R; CANR 2, 33, 43; DLB 88; MTCW

Lazarus, Emma 1849-1887 . . . . **NCLC 8**

Lazarus, Felix
See Cable, George Washington

Lazarus, Henry
See Slavitt, David R(ytman)

Lea, Joan
See Neufeld, John (Arthur)

Leacock, Stephen (Butler) 1869-1944 . . . . **TCLC 2**
See also CA 104; 141; DLB 92

Lear, Edward 1812-1888 . . . . **NCLC 3**
See also CLR 1; DLB 32; MAICYA; SATA 18

Lear, Norman (Milton) 1922- . . . . . . **CLC 12**
See also CA 73-76

Leavis, F(rank) R(aymond) 1895-1978 . . . . **CLC 24**
See also CA 21-24R; 77-80; CANR 44; MTCW

Leavitt, David 1961- . . . . **CLC 34**
See also CA 116; 122; DLB 130

Leblanc, Maurice (Marie Emile) 1864-1941 . . . . **TCLC 49**
See also CA 110

Lebowitz, Fran(ces Ann) 1951(?)- . . . . **CLC 11, 36**
See also CA 81-84; CANR 14; MTCW

Lebrecht, Peter
See Tieck, (Johann) Ludwig

le Carre, John . . . . **CLC 3, 5, 9, 15, 28**
See also Cornwell, David (John Moore)
See also BEST 89:4; CDBLB 1960 to Present; DLB 87

Le Clezio, J(ean) M(arie) G(ustave) 1940- . . . . **CLC 31**
See also CA 116; 128; DLB 83

Leconte de Lisle, Charles-Marie-Rene 1818-1894 . . . . **NCLC 29**

Le Coq, Monsieur
See Simenon, Georges (Jacques Christian)

Leduc, Violette 1907-1972 . . . . **CLC 22**
See also CA 13-14; 33-36R; CAP 1

Ledwidge, Francis 1887(?)-1917 . . . **TCLC 23**
See also CA 123; DLB 20

Lee, Andrea 1953- . . . . **CLC 36; BLC**
See also BW 1; CA 125

Lee, Andrew
See Auchincloss, Louis (Stanton)

Lee, Don L. . . . . **CLC 2**
See also Madhubuti, Haki R.

Lee, George W(ashington) 1894-1976 . . . . **CLC 52; BLC**
See also BW 1; CA 125; DLB 51

Lee, (Nelle) Harper 1926- . . . . **CLC 12, 60; DA; WLC**
See also AAYA 13; CA 13-16R; CDALB 1941-1968; DLB 6; MTCW; SATA 11

Lee, Helen Elaine 1959(?)- . . . . **CLC 86**

Lee, Julian
See Latham, Jean Lee

Lee, Larry
See Lee, Lawrence

Lee, Lawrence 1941-1990 . . . . **CLC 34**
See also CA 131; CANR 43

Marivaux, Pierre Carlet de Chamblain de 1688-1763 . . . . **LC 4**

Markandaya, Kamala . . . . **CLC 8, 38**
See also Taylor, Kamala (Purnaiya)

Markfield, Wallace 1926- . . . . **CLC 8**
See also CA 69-72; CAAS 3; DLB 2, 28

Markham, Edwin 1852-1940 . . . . . . **TCLC 47**
See also DLB 54

Markham, Robert
See Amis, Kingsley (William)

Marks, J
See Highwater, Jamake (Mamake)

Marks-Highwater, J
See Highwater, Jamake (Mamake)

Markson, David M(errill) 1927- . . . . **CLC 67**
See also CA 49-52; CANR 1

Marley, Bob . . . . **CLC 17**
See also Marley, Robert Nesta

Marley, Robert Nesta 1945-1981
See Marley, Bob
See also CA 107; 103

Marlowe, Christopher 1564-1593 . . . . . **LC 22; DA; DC 1; WLC**
See also CDBLB Before 1660; DLB 62

Marmontel, Jean-Francois 1723-1799 . . . . **LC 2**

Marquand, John P(hillips) 1893-1960 . . . . **CLC 2, 10**
See also CA 85-88; DLB 9, 102

Marquez, Gabriel (Jose) Garcia
See Garcia Marquez, Gabriel (Jose)

Marquis, Don(ald Robert Perry) 1878-1937 . . . . **TCLC 7**
See also CA 104; DLB 11, 25

Marric, J. J.
See Creasey, John

Marrow, Bernard
See Moore, Brian

Marryat, Frederick 1792-1848 . . . . **NCLC 3**
See also DLB 21

Marsden, James
See Creasey, John

Marsh, (Edith) Ngaio 1899-1982 . . . . **CLC 7, 53**
See also CA 9-12R; CANR 6; DLB 77; MTCW

Marshall, Garry 1934- . . . . **CLC 17**
See also AAYA 3; CA 111; SATA 60

Marshall, Paule 1929- . . . . **CLC 27, 72; BLC; SSC 3**
See also BW 2; CA 77-80; CANR 25; DLB 33; MTCW

Marsten, Richard
See Hunter, Evan

Martha, Henry
See Harris, Mark

Martial c. 40-c. 104 . . . . **PC 10**

Martin, Ken
See Hubbard, L(afayette) Ron(ald)

Martin, Richard
See Creasey, John

Martin, Steve 1945- . . . . **CLC 30**
See also CA 97-100; CANR 30; MTCW

Martin, Violet Florence 1862-1915 . . . . **TCLC 51**

Martin, Webber
See Silverberg, Robert

Martindale, Patrick Victor
See White, Patrick (Victor Martindale)

Martin du Gard, Roger 1881-1958 . . . . **TCLC 24**
See also CA 118; DLB 65

Martineau, Harriet 1802-1876. . . . **NCLC 26**
See also DLB 21, 55; YABC 2

Martines, Julia
See O'Faolain, Julia

Martinez, Jacinto Benavente y
See Benavente (y Martinez), Jacinto

Martinez Ruiz, Jose 1873-1967
See Azorin; Ruiz, Jose Martinez
See also CA 93-96; HW

Martinez Sierra, Gregorio 1881-1947 . . . . **TCLC 6**
See also CA 115

Martinez Sierra, Maria (de la O'LeJarraga) 1874-1974 . . . . **TCLC 6**
See also CA 115

Martinsen, Martin
See Follett, Ken(neth Martin)

Martinson, Harry (Edmund) 1904-1978 . . . . **CLC 14**
See also CA 77-80; CANR 34

Marut, Ret
See Traven, B.

Marut, Robert
See Traven, B.

Marvell, Andrew 1621-1678 . . . . . **LC 4; DA; PC 10; WLC**
See also CDBLB 1660-1789; DLB 131

Marx, Karl (Heinrich) 1818-1883 . . . . **NCLC 17**
See also DLB 129

Masaoka Shiki . . . . **TCLC 18**
See also Masaoka Tsunenori

Masaoka Tsunenori 1867-1902
See Masaoka Shiki
See also CA 117

Masefield, John (Edward) 1878-1967 . . . . **CLC 11, 47**
See also CA 19-20; 25-28R; CANR 33; CAP 2; CDBLB 1890-1914; DLB 10, 19; MTCW; SATA 19

Maso, Carole 19(?)- . . . . **CLC 44**

Mason, Bobbie Ann 1940- . . . . **CLC 28, 43, 82; SSC 4**
See also AAYA 5; CA 53-56; CANR 11, 31; DLBY 87; MTCW

Mason, Ernst
See Pohl, Frederik

Mason, Lee W.
See Malzberg, Barry N(athaniel)

Mason, Nick 1945- . . . . **CLC 35**

Mason, Tally
See Derleth, August (William)

Mass, William
See Gibson, William

Masters, Edgar Lee 1868-1950 . . . . . . **TCLC 2, 25; DA; PC 1**
See also CA 104; 133; CDALB 1865-1917; DLB 54; MTCW

Masters, Hilary 1928- . . . . **CLC 48**
See also CA 25-28R; CANR 13, 47

Mastrosimone, William 19(?)- . . . . . . **CLC 36**

Mathe, Albert
See Camus, Albert

Matheson, Richard Burton 1926- . . . **CLC 37**
See also CA 97-100; DLB 8, 44

Mathews, Harry 1930- . . . . **CLC 6, 52**
See also CA 21-24R; CAAS 6; CANR 18, 40

Mathews, John Joseph 1894-1979. . . **CLC 84**
See also CA 19-20; 142; CANR 45; CAP 2; NNAL

Mathias, Roland (Glyn) 1915- . . . . . . **CLC 45**
See also CA 97-100; CANR 19, 41; DLB 27

Matsuo Basho 1644-1694 . . . . **PC 3**

Mattheson, Rodney
See Creasey, John

Matthews, Greg 1949- . . . . **CLC 45**
See also CA 135

Matthews, William 1942- . . . . **CLC 40**
See also CA 29-32R; CAAS 18; CANR 12; DLB 5

Matthias, John (Edward) 1941- . . . . . . **CLC 9**
See also CA 33-36R

Matthiessen, Peter 1927- . . . . **CLC 5, 7, 11, 32, 64**
See also AAYA 6; BEST 90:4; CA 9-12R; CANR 21; DLB 6; MTCW; SATA 27

Maturin, Charles Robert 1780(?)-1824 . . . . **NCLC 6**

Matute (Ausejo), Ana Maria 1925- . . . . **CLC 11**
See also CA 89-92; MTCW

Maugham, W. S.
See Maugham, W(illiam) Somerset

Maugham, W(illiam) Somerset 1874-1965 . . . . . . **CLC 1, 11, 15, 67; DA; SSC 8; WLC**
See also CA 5-8R; 25-28R; CANR 40; CDBLB 1914-1945; DLB 10, 36, 77, 100; MTCW; SATA 54

Maugham, William Somerset
See Maugham, W(illiam) Somerset

Maupassant, (Henri Rene Albert) Guy de 1850-1893 . . . . **NCLC 1, 42; DA; SSC 1; WLC**
See also DLB 123

Maurhut, Richard
See Traven, B.

Mauriac, Claude 1914- . . . . **CLC 9**
See also CA 89-92; DLB 83

Mauriac, Francois (Charles) 1885-1970 . . . . **CLC 4, 9, 56**
See also CA 25-28; CAP 2; DLB 65; MTCW

Mavor, Osborne Henry 1888-1951
See Bridie, James
See also CA 104

Maxwell, William (Keepers, Jr.) 1908- .... **CLC 19**
See also CA 93-96; DLBY 80

May, Elaine 1932- .... **CLC 16**
See also CA 124; 142; DLB 44

Mayakovski, Vladimir (Vladimirovich) 1893-1930 .... **TCLC 4, 18**
See also CA 104

Mayhew, Henry 1812-1887 ...... **NCLC 31**
See also DLB 18, 55

Maynard, Joyce 1953- .... **CLC 23**
See also CA 111; 129

Mayne, William (James Carter) 1928- .... **CLC 12**
See also CA 9-12R; CANR 37; CLR 25; JRDA; MAICYA; SAAS 11; SATA 6, 68

Mayo, Jim
See L'Amour, Louis (Dearborn)

Maysles, Albert 1926- .... **CLC 16**
See also CA 29-32R

Maysles, David 1932- .... **CLC 16**

Mazer, Norma Fox 1931- .... **CLC 26**
See also AAYA 5; CA 69-72; CANR 12, 32; CLR 23; JRDA; MAICYA; SAAS 1; SATA 24, 67

Mazzini, Guiseppe 1805-1872 .... **NCLC 34**

McAuley, James Phillip 1917-1976 .... **CLC 45**
See also CA 97-100

McBain, Ed
See Hunter, Evan

McBrien, William Augustine 1930- .... **CLC 44**
See also CA 107

McCaffrey, Anne (Inez) 1926- ...... **CLC 17**
See also AAYA 6; AITN 2; BEST 89:2; CA 25-28R; CANR 15, 35; DLB 8; JRDA; MAICYA; MTCW; SAAS 11; SATA 8, 70

McCall, Nathan 1955(?)- .... **CLC 86**

McCann, Arthur
See Campbell, John W(ood, Jr.)

McCann, Edson
See Pohl, Frederik

McCarthy, Charles, Jr. 1933-
See McCarthy, Cormac
See also CANR 42

McCarthy, Cormac 1933- ..... **CLC 4, 57, 59**
See also McCarthy, Charles, Jr.
See also DLB 6, 143

McCarthy, Mary (Therese) 1912-1989 ... **CLC 1, 3, 5, 14, 24, 39, 59**
See also CA 5-8R; 129; CANR 16; DLB 2; DLBY 81; MTCW

McCartney, (James) Paul 1942- .... **CLC 12, 35**

McCauley, Stephen (D.) 1955- ..... **CLC 50**
See also CA 141

McClure, Michael (Thomas) 1932- .... **CLC 6, 10**
See also CA 21-24R; CANR 17, 46; DLB 16

McCorkle, Jill (Collins) 1958- ...... **CLC 51**
See also CA 121; DLBY 87

McCourt, James 1941- .... **CLC 5**
See also CA 57-60

McCoy, Horace (Stanley) 1897-1955 .... **TCLC 28**
See also CA 108; DLB 9

McCrae, John 1872-1918 .... **TCLC 12**
See also CA 109; DLB 92

McCreigh, James
See Pohl, Frederik

McCullers, (Lula) Carson (Smith) 1917-1967 .... **CLC 1, 4, 10, 12, 48; DA; SSC 9; WLC**
See also CA 5-8R; 25-28R; CABS 1, 3; CANR 18; CDALB 1941-1968; DLB 2, 7; MTCW; SATA 27

McCulloch, John Tyler
See Burroughs, Edgar Rice

McCullough, Colleen 1938(?)- ...... **CLC 27**
See also CA 81-84; CANR 17, 46; MTCW

McElroy, Joseph 1930- .... **CLC 5, 47**
See also CA 17-20R

McEwan, Ian (Russell) 1948- ... **CLC 13, 66**
See also BEST 90:4; CA 61-64; CANR 14, 41; DLB 14; MTCW

McFadden, David 1940- .... **CLC 48**
See also CA 104; DLB 60

McFarland, Dennis 1950- .... **CLC 65**

McGahern, John 1934- .... **CLC 5, 9, 48; SSC 17**
See also CA 17-20R; CANR 29; DLB 14; MTCW

McGinley, Patrick (Anthony) 1937- .... **CLC 41**
See also CA 120; 127

McGinley, Phyllis 1905-1978 ...... **CLC 14**
See also CA 9-12R; 77-80; CANR 19; DLB 11, 48; SATA 2, 44; SATA-Obit 24

McGinniss, Joe 1942- .... **CLC 32**
See also AITN 2; BEST 89:2; CA 25-28R; CANR 26

McGivern, Maureen Daly
See Daly, Maureen

McGrath, Patrick 1950- .... **CLC 55**
See also CA 136

McGrath, Thomas (Matthew) 1916-1990 .... **CLC 28, 59**
See also CA 9-12R; 132; CANR 6, 33; MTCW; SATA 41; SATA-Obit 66

McGuane, Thomas (Francis III) 1939- .... **CLC 3, 7, 18, 45**
See also AITN 2; CA 49-52; CANR 5, 24; DLB 2; DLBY 80; MTCW

McGuckian, Medbh 1950- .... **CLC 48**
See also CA 143; DLB 40

McHale, Tom 1942(?)-1982 .... **CLC 3, 5**
See also AITN 1; CA 77-80; 106

McIlvanney, William 1936- .... **CLC 42**
See also CA 25-28R; DLB 14

McIlwraith, Maureen Mollie Hunter
See Hunter, Mollie
See also SATA 2

McInerney, Jay 1955- .... **CLC 34**
See also CA 116; 123

McIntyre, Vonda N(eel) 1948- ..... **CLC 18**
See also CA 81-84; CANR 17, 34; MTCW

McKay, Claude ..... **TCLC 7, 41; BLC; PC 2**
See also McKay, Festus Claudius
See also DLB 4, 45, 51, 117

McKay, Festus Claudius 1889-1948
See McKay, Claude
See also BW 1; CA 104; 124; DA; MTCW; WLC

McKuen, Rod 1933- .... **CLC 1, 3**
See also AITN 1; CA 41-44R; CANR 40

McLoughlin, R. B.
See Mencken, H(enry) L(ouis)

McLuhan, (Herbert) Marshall 1911-1980 .... **CLC 37, 83**
See also CA 9-12R; 102; CANR 12, 34; DLB 88; MTCW

McMillan, Terry (L.) 1951- ..... **CLC 50, 61**
See also BW 2; CA 140

McMurtry, Larry (Jeff) 1936- .... **CLC 2, 3, 7, 11, 27, 44**
See also AITN 2; BEST 89:2; CA 5-8R; CANR 19, 43; CDALB 1968-1988; DLB 2, 143; DLBY 80, 87; MTCW

McNally, T. M. 1961- .... **CLC 82**

McNally, Terrence 1939- ...... **CLC 4, 7, 41**
See also CA 45-48; CANR 2; DLB 7

McNamer, Deirdre 1950- .... **CLC 70**

McNeile, Herman Cyril 1888-1937
See Sapper
See also DLB 77

McPhee, John (Angus) 1931- ...... **CLC 36**
See also BEST 90:1; CA 65-68; CANR 20, 46; MTCW

McPherson, James Alan 1943- .... **CLC 19, 77**
See also BW 1; CA 25-28R; CAAS 17; CANR 24; DLB 38; MTCW

McPherson, William (Alexander) 1933- .... **CLC 34**
See also CA 69-72; CANR 28

Mead, Margaret 1901-1978 .... **CLC 37**
See also AITN 1; CA 1-4R; 81-84; CANR 4; MTCW; SATA-Obit 20

Meaker, Marijane (Agnes) 1927-
See Kerr, M. E.
See also CA 107; CANR 37; JRDA; MAICYA; MTCW; SATA 20, 61

Medoff, Mark (Howard) 1940- ... **CLC 6, 23**
See also AITN 1; CA 53-56; CANR 5; DLB 7

Medvedev, P. N.
See Bakhtin, Mikhail Mikhailovich

Meged, Aharon
See Megged, Aharon

Meged, Aron
See Megged, Aharon

Megged, Aharon 1920- .... **CLC 9**
See also CA 49-52; CAAS 13; CANR 1

Mehta, Ved (Parkash) 1934- .... **CLC 37**
See also CA 1-4R; CANR 2, 23; MTCW

Melanter
See Blackmore, R(ichard) D(oddridge)

Melikow, Loris
See Hofmannsthal, Hugo von

Melmoth, Sebastian
See Wilde, Oscar (Fingal O'Flahertie Wills)

Meltzer, Milton 1915- .... **CLC 26**
See also AAYA 8; CA 13-16R; CANR 38; CLR 13; DLB 61; JRDA; MAICYA; SAAS 1; SATA 1, 50, 80

Melville, Herman
1819-1891 .... **NCLC 3, 12, 29, 45; DA; SSC 1, 17; WLC**
See also CDALB 1640-1865; DLB 3, 74; SATA 59

Menander
c. 342B.C.-c. 292B.C. ... **CMLC 9; DC 3**

Mencken, H(enry) L(ouis)
1880-1956 .... **TCLC 13**
See also CA 105; 125; CDALB 1917-1929; DLB 11, 29, 63, 137; MTCW

Mercer, David 1928-1980........... **CLC 5**
See also CA 9-12R; 102; CANR 23; DLB 13; MTCW

Merchant, Paul
See Ellison, Harlan (Jay)

Meredith, George 1828-1909... **TCLC 17, 43**
See also CA 117; CDBLB 1832-1890; DLB 18, 35, 57

Meredith, William (Morris)
1919- .... **CLC 4, 13, 22, 55**
See also CA 9-12R; CAAS 14; CANR 6, 40; DLB 5

Merezhkovsky, Dmitry Sergeyevich
1865-1941 .... **TCLC 29**

Merimee, Prosper
1803-1870 .... **NCLC 6; SSC 7**
See also DLB 119

Merkin, Daphne 1954-............ **CLC 44**
See also CA 123

Merlin, Arthur
See Blish, James (Benjamin)

Merrill, James (Ingram)
1926- .... **CLC 2, 3, 6, 8, 13, 18, 34**
See also CA 13-16R; CANR 10; DLB 5; DLBY 85; MTCW

Merriman, Alex
See Silverberg, Robert

Merritt, E. B.
See Waddington, Miriam

Merton, Thomas
1915-1968 .. **CLC 1, 3, 11, 34, 83; PC 10**
See also CA 5-8R; 25-28R; CANR 22; DLB 48; DLBY 81; MTCW

Merwin, W(illiam) S(tanley)
1927- ... **CLC 1, 2, 3, 5, 8, 13, 18, 45**
See also CA 13-16R; CANR 15; DLB 5; MTCW

Metcalf, John 1938-.............. **CLC 37**
See also CA 113; DLB 60

Metcalf, Suzanne
See Baum, L(yman) Frank

Mew, Charlotte (Mary)
1870-1928 .... **TCLC 8**
See also CA 105; DLB 19, 135

Mewshaw, Michael 1943-........... **CLC 9**
See also CA 53-56; CANR 7, 47; DLBY 80

Meyer, June
See Jordan, June

Meyer, Lynn
See Slavitt, David R(ytman)

Meyer-Meyrink, Gustav 1868-1932
See Meyrink, Gustav
See also CA 117

Meyers, Jeffrey 1939- .... **CLC 39**
See also CA 73-76; DLB 111

Meynell, Alice (Christina Gertrude Thompson)
1847-1922 .... **TCLC 6**
See also CA 104; DLB 19, 98

Meyrink, Gustav .... **TCLC 21**
See also Meyer-Meyrink, Gustav
See also DLB 81

Michaels, Leonard
1933- .... **CLC 6, 25; SSC 16**
See also CA 61-64; CANR 21; DLB 130; MTCW

Michaux, Henri 1899-1984 ...... **CLC 8, 19**
See also CA 85-88; 114

Michelangelo 1475-1564............ **LC 12**

Michelet, Jules 1798-1874....... **NCLC 31**

Michener, James A(lbert)
1907(?)- .... **CLC 1, 5, 11, 29, 60**
See also AITN 1; BEST 90:1; CA 5-8R; CANR 21, 45; DLB 6; MTCW

Mickiewicz, Adam 1798-1855 ..... **NCLC 3**

Middleton, Christopher 1926- ...... **CLC 13**
See also CA 13-16R; CANR 29; DLB 40

Middleton, Richard (Barham)
1882-1911 .... **TCLC 56**

Middleton, Stanley 1919-........ **CLC 7, 38**
See also CA 25-28R; CANR 21, 46; DLB 14

Middleton, Thomas 1580-1627........ **DC 5**
See also DLB 58

Migueis, Jose Rodrigues 1901- ..... **CLC 10**

Mikszath, Kalman 1847-1910 ..... **TCLC 31**

Miles, Josephine
1911-1985 .... **CLC 1, 2, 14, 34, 39**
See also CA 1-4R; 116; CANR 2; DLB 48

Militant
See Sandburg, Carl (August)

Mill, John Stuart 1806-1873 ..... **NCLC 11**
See also CDBLB 1832-1890; DLB 55

Millar, Kenneth 1915-1983 .... **CLC 14**
See also Macdonald, Ross
See also CA 9-12R; 110; CANR 16; DLB 2; DLBD 6; DLBY 83; MTCW

Millay, E. Vincent
See Millay, Edna St. Vincent

Millay, Edna St. Vincent
1892-1950 ...... **TCLC 4, 49; DA; PC 6**
See also CA 104; 130; CDALB 1917-1929; DLB 45; MTCW

Miller, Arthur
1915- .... **CLC 1, 2, 6, 10, 15, 26, 47, 78; DA; DC 1; WLC**
See also AITN 1; CA 1-4R; CABS 3; CANR 2, 30; CDALB 1941-1968; DLB 7; MTCW

Miller, Henry (Valentine)
1891-1980 .... **CLC 1, 2, 4, 9, 14, 43, 84; DA; WLC**
See also CA 9-12R; 97-100; CANR 33; CDALB 1929-1941; DLB 4, 9; DLBY 80; MTCW

Miller, Jason 1939(?)- .... **CLC 2**
See also AITN 1; CA 73-76; DLB 7

Miller, Sue 1943- .... **CLC 44**
See also BEST 90:3; CA 139; DLB 143

Miller, Walter M(ichael, Jr.)
1923- .... **CLC 4, 30**
See also CA 85-88; DLB 8

Millett, Kate 1934-............... **CLC 67**
See also AITN 1; CA 73-76; CANR 32; MTCW

Millhauser, Steven 1943-....... **CLC 21, 54**
See also CA 110; 111; DLB 2

Millin, Sarah Gertrude 1889-1968 .. **CLC 49**
See also CA 102; 93-96

Milne, A(lan) A(lexander)
1882-1956 .... **TCLC 6**
See also CA 104; 133; CLR 1, 26; DLB 10, 77, 100; MAICYA; MTCW; YABC 1

Milner, Ron(ald) 1938-....... **CLC 56; BLC**
See also AITN 1; BW 1; CA 73-76; CANR 24; DLB 38; MTCW

Milosz, Czeslaw
1911- ... **CLC 5, 11, 22, 31, 56, 82; PC 8**
See also CA 81-84; CANR 23; MTCW

Milton, John 1608-1674... **LC 9; DA; WLC**
See also CDBLB 1660-1789; DLB 131

Min, Anchee 1957-............... **CLC 86**

Minehaha, Cornelius
See Wedekind, (Benjamin) Frank(lin)

Miner, Valerie 1947- .... **CLC 40**
See also CA 97-100

Minimo, Duca
See D'Annunzio, Gabriele

Minot, Susan 1956- .... **CLC 44**
See also CA 134

Minus, Ed 1938-................. **CLC 39**

Miranda, Javier
See Bioy Casares, Adolfo

Mirbeau, Octave 1848-1917....... **TCLC 55**
See also DLB 123

Miro (Ferrer), Gabriel (Francisco Victor)
1879-1930 .... **TCLC 5**
See also CA 104

Mishima, Yukio
.... **CLC 2, 4, 6, 9, 27; DC 1; SSC 4**
See also Hiraoka, Kimitake

Mistral, Frederic 1830-1914 ...... **TCLC 51**
See also CA 122

Mistral, Gabriela............ **TCLC 2; HLC**
See also Godoy Alcayaga, Lucila

Mistry, Rohinton 1952-........... **CLC 71**
See also CA 141

Mitchell, Clyde
See Ellison, Harlan (Jay); Silverberg, Robert

Mitchell, James Leslie 1901-1935
See Gibbon, Lewis Grassic
See also CA 104; DLB 15

Morris, Wright 1910- . . . **CLC 1, 3, 7, 18, 37**
See also CA 9-12R; CANR 21; DLB 2; DLBY 81; MTCW

Morrison, Chloe Anthony Wofford
See Morrison, Toni

Morrison, James Douglas 1943-1971
See Morrison, Jim
See also CA 73-76; CANR 40

Morrison, Jim . . . . **CLC 17**
See also Morrison, James Douglas

Morrison, Toni
1931- . . **CLC 4, 10, 22, 55, 81; BLC; DA**
See also AAYA 1; BW 2; CA 29-32R; CANR 27, 42; CDALB 1968-1988; DLB 6, 33, 143; DLBY 81; MTCW; SATA 57

Morrison, Van 1945- . . . . **CLC 21**
See also CA 116

Mortimer, John (Clifford)
1923- . . . . **CLC 28, 43**
See also CA 13-16R; CANR 21; CDBLB 1960 to Present; DLB 13; MTCW

Mortimer, Penelope (Ruth) 1918- . . . . **CLC 5**
See also CA 57-60; CANR 45

Morton, Anthony
See Creasey, John

Mosher, Howard Frank 1943- . . . . . . **CLC 62**
See also CA 139

Mosley, Nicholas 1923- . . . . **CLC 43, 70**
See also CA 69-72; CANR 41; DLB 14

Moss, Howard
1922-1987 . . . . **CLC 7, 14, 45, 50**
See also CA 1-4R; 123; CANR 1, 44; DLB 5

Mossgiel, Rab
See Burns, Robert

Motion, Andrew 1952- . . . . **CLC 47**
See also DLB 40

Motley, Willard (Francis)
1909-1965 . . . . **CLC 18**
See also BW 1; CA 117; 106; DLB 76, 143

Motoori, Norinaga 1730-1801 . . . . **NCLC 45**

Mott, Michael (Charles Alston)
1930- . . . . **CLC 15, 34**
See also CA 5-8R; CAAS 7; CANR 7, 29

Mowat, Farley (McGill) 1921- . . . . . **CLC 26**
See also AAYA 1; CA 1-4R; CANR 4, 24, 42; CLR 20; DLB 68; JRDA; MAICYA; MTCW; SATA 3, 55

Moyers, Bill 1934- . . . . **CLC 74**
See also AITN 2; CA 61-64; CANR 31

Mphahlele, Es'kia
See Mphahlele, Ezekiel
See also DLB 125

Mphahlele, Ezekiel 1919- . . . . . **CLC 25; BLC**
See also Mphahlele, Es'kia
See also BW 2; CA 81-84; CANR 26

Mqhayi, S(amuel) E(dward) K(rune Loliwe)
1875-1945 . . . . **TCLC 25; BLC**

Mr. Martin
See Burroughs, William S(eward)

Mrozek, Slawomir 1930- . . . . **CLC 3, 13**
See also CA 13-16R; CAAS 10; CANR 29; MTCW

Mrs. Belloc-Lowndes
See Lowndes, Marie Adelaide (Belloc)

Mtwa, Percy (?)- . . . . **CLC 47**

Mueller, Lisel 1924- . . . . **CLC 13, 51**
See also CA 93-96; DLB 105

Muir, Edwin 1887-1959 . . . . **TCLC 2**
See also CA 104; DLB 20, 100

Muir, John 1838-1914 . . . . **TCLC 28**

Mujica Lainez, Manuel
1910-1984 . . . . **CLC 31**
See also Lainez, Manuel Mujica
See also CA 81-84; 112; CANR 32; HW

Mukherjee, Bharati 1940- . . . . **CLC 53**
See also BEST 89:2; CA 107; CANR 45; DLB 60; MTCW

Muldoon, Paul 1951- . . . . **CLC 32, 72**
See also CA 113; 129; DLB 40

Mulisch, Harry 1927- . . . . **CLC 42**
See also CA 9-12R; CANR 6, 26

Mull, Martin 1943- . . . . **CLC 17**
See also CA 105

Mulock, Dinah Maria
See Craik, Dinah Maria (Mulock)

Munford, Robert 1737(?)-1783 . . . . **LC 5**
See also DLB 31

Mungo, Raymond 1946- . . . . **CLC 72**
See also CA 49-52; CANR 2

Munro, Alice
1931- . . . . **CLC 6, 10, 19, 50; SSC 3**
See also AITN 2; CA 33-36R; CANR 33; DLB 53; MTCW; SATA 29

Munro, H(ector) H(ugh) 1870-1916
See Saki
See also CA 104; 130; CDBLB 1890-1914; DA; DLB 34; MTCW; WLC

Murasaki, Lady . . . . **CMLC 1**

Murdoch, (Jean) Iris
1919- . . . . . . **CLC 1, 2, 3, 4, 6, 8, 11, 15, 22, 31, 51**
See also CA 13-16R; CANR 8, 43; CDBLB 1960 to Present; DLB 14; MTCW

Murnau, Friedrich Wilhelm
See Plumpe, Friedrich Wilhelm

Murphy, Richard 1927- . . . . **CLC 41**
See also CA 29-32R; DLB 40

Murphy, Sylvia 1937- . . . . **CLC 34**
See also CA 121

Murphy, Thomas (Bernard) 1935- . . . **CLC 51**
See also CA 101

Murray, Albert L. 1916- . . . . **CLC 73**
See also BW 2; CA 49-52; CANR 26; DLB 38

Murray, Les(lie) A(llan) 1938- . . . . . **CLC 40**
See also CA 21-24R; CANR 11, 27

Murry, J. Middleton
See Murry, John Middleton

Murry, John Middleton
1889-1957 . . . . **TCLC 16**
See also CA 118

Musgrave, Susan 1951- . . . . **CLC 13, 54**
See also CA 69-72; CANR 45

Musil, Robert (Edler von)
1880-1942 . . . . **TCLC 12**
See also CA 109; DLB 81, 124

Musset, (Louis Charles) Alfred de
1810-1857 . . . . **NCLC 7**

My Brother's Brother
See Chekhov, Anton (Pavlovich)

Myers, Walter Dean 1937- . . . **CLC 35; BLC**
See also AAYA 4; BW 2; CA 33-36R; CANR 20, 42; CLR 4, 16, 35; DLB 33; JRDA; MAICYA; SAAS 2; SATA 27, 41, 71

Myers, Walter M.
See Myers, Walter Dean

Myles, Symon
See Follett, Ken(neth Martin)

Nabokov, Vladimir (Vladimirovich)
1899-1977 . . . . . **CLC 1, 2, 3, 6, 8, 11, 15, 23, 44, 46, 64; DA; SSC 11; WLC**
See also CA 5-8R; 69-72; CANR 20; CDALB 1941-1968; DLB 2; DLBD 3; DLBY 80, 91; MTCW

Nagai Kafu . . . . **TCLC 51**
See also Nagai Sokichi

Nagai Sokichi 1879-1959
See Nagai Kafu
See also CA 117

Nagy, Laszlo 1925-1978 . . . . **CLC 7**
See also CA 129; 112

Naipaul, Shiva(dhar Srinivasa)
1945-1985 . . . . **CLC 32, 39**
See also CA 110; 112; 116; CANR 33; DLBY 85; MTCW

Naipaul, V(idiadhar) S(urajprasad)
1932- . . . . **CLC 4, 7, 9, 13, 18, 37**
See also CA 1-4R; CANR 1, 33; CDBLB 1960 to Present; DLB 125; DLBY 85; MTCW

Nakos, Lilika 1899(?)- . . . . **CLC 29**

Narayan, R(asipuram) K(rishnaswami)
1906- . . . . **CLC 7, 28, 47**
See also CA 81-84; CANR 33; MTCW; SATA 62

Nash, (Frediric) Ogden 1902-1971 . . **CLC 23**
See also CA 13-14; 29-32R; CANR 34; CAP 1; DLB 11; MAICYA; MTCW; SATA 2, 46

Nathan, Daniel
See Dannay, Frederic

Nathan, George Jean 1882-1958 . . . **TCLC 18**
See also Hatteras, Owen
See also CA 114; DLB 137

Natsume, Kinnosuke 1867-1916
See Natsume, Soseki
See also CA 104

Natsume, Soseki . . . . **TCLC 2, 10**
See also Natsume, Kinnosuke

Natti, (Mary) Lee 1919-
See Kingman, Lee
See also CA 5-8R; CANR 2

Naylor, Gloria
1950- . . . . **CLC 28, 52; BLC; DA**
See also AAYA 6; BW 2; CA 107; CANR 27; MTCW

Peacock, Thomas Love 1785-1866 .... **NCLC 22**
See also DLB 96, 116

Peake, Mervyn 1911-1968 .... **CLC 7, 54**
See also CA 5-8R; 25-28R; CANR 3; DLB 15; MTCW; SATA 23

Pearce, Philippa .... **CLC 21**
See also Christie, (Ann) Philippa
See also CLR 9; MAICYA; SATA 1, 67

Pearl, Eric
See Elman, Richard

Pearson, T(homas) R(eid) 1956- .... **CLC 39**
See also CA 120; 130

Peck, Dale 1968(?)- .... **CLC 81**

Peck, John 1941- .... **CLC 3**
See also CA 49-52; CANR 3

Peck, Richard (Wayne) 1934- ...... **CLC 21**
See also AAYA 1; CA 85-88; CANR 19, 38; CLR 15; JRDA; MAICYA; SAAS 2; SATA 18, 55

Peck, Robert Newton 1928-.... **CLC 17; DA**
See also AAYA 3; CA 81-84; CANR 31; JRDA; MAICYA; SAAS 1; SATA 21, 62

Peckinpah, (David) Sam(uel) 1925-1984 .... **CLC 20**
See also CA 109; 114

Pedersen, Knut 1859-1952
See Hamsun, Knut
See also CA 104; 119; MTCW

Peeslake, Gaffer
See Durrell, Lawrence (George)

Peguy, Charles Pierre 1873-1914 .... **TCLC 10**
See also CA 107

Pena, Ramon del Valle y
See Valle-Inclan, Ramon (Maria) del

Pendennis, Arthur Esquir
See Thackeray, William Makepeace

Penn, William 1644-1718 .... **LC 25**
See also DLB 24

Pepys, Samuel 1633-1703 .... **LC 11; DA; WLC**
See also CDBLB 1660-1789; DLB 101

Percy, Walker 1916-1990 .... **CLC 2, 3, 6, 8, 14, 18, 47, 65**
See also CA 1-4R; 131; CANR 1, 23; DLB 2; DLBY 80, 90; MTCW

Perec, Georges 1936-1982 .... **CLC 56**
See also CA 141; DLB 83

Pereda (y Sanchez de Porrua), Jose Maria de 1833-1906 .... **TCLC 16**
See also CA 117

Pereda y Porrua, Jose Maria de
See Pereda (y Sanchez de Porrua), Jose Maria de

Peregoy, George Weems
See Mencken, H(enry) L(ouis)

Perelman, S(idney) J(oseph) 1904-1979 ... **CLC 3, 5, 9, 15, 23, 44, 49**
See also AITN 1, 2; CA 73-76; 89-92; CANR 18; DLB 11, 44; MTCW

Peret, Benjamin 1899-1959 .... **TCLC 20**
See also CA 117

Peretz, Isaac Loeb 1851(?)-1915 ... **TCLC 16**
See also CA 109

Peretz, Yitzkhok Leibush
See Peretz, Isaac Loeb

Perez Galdos, Benito 1843-1920 ... **TCLC 27**
See also CA 125; HW

Perrault, Charles 1628-1703 .... **LC 2**
See also MAICYA; SATA 25

Perry, Brighton
See Sherwood, Robert E(mmet)

Perse, St.-John .... **CLC 4, 11, 46**
See also Leger, (Marie-Rene Auguste) Alexis Saint-Leger

Peseenz, Tulio F.
See Lopez y Fuentes, Gregorio

Pesetsky, Bette 1932-............. **CLC 28**
See also CA 133; DLB 130

Peshkov, Alexei Maximovich 1868-1936
See Gorky, Maxim
See also CA 105; 141; DA

Pessoa, Fernando (Antonio Nogueira) 1888-1935 .... **TCLC 27; HLC**
See also CA 125

Peterkin, Julia Mood 1880-1961.... **CLC 31**
See also CA 102; DLB 9

Peters, Joan K. 1945-............. **CLC 39**

Peters, Robert L(ouis) 1924-........ **CLC 7**
See also CA 13-16R; CAAS 8; DLB 105

Petofi, Sandor 1823-1849........ **NCLC 21**

Petrakis, Harry Mark 1923-........ **CLC 3**
See also CA 9-12R; CANR 4, 30

Petrarch 1304-1374................. **PC 8**

Petrov, Evgeny .... **TCLC 21**
See also Kataev, Evgeny Petrovich

Petry, Ann (Lane) 1908- ...... **CLC 1, 7, 18**
See also BW 1; CA 5-8R; CAAS 6; CANR 4, 46; CLR 12; DLB 76; JRDA; MAICYA; MTCW; SATA 5

Petursson, Halligrimur 1614-1674 .... **LC 8**

Philipson, Morris H. 1926-........ **CLC 53**
See also CA 1-4R; CANR 4

Phillips, David Graham 1867-1911 .... **TCLC 44**
See also CA 108; DLB 9, 12

Phillips, Jack
See Sandburg, Carl (August)

Phillips, Jayne Anne 1952- .... **CLC 15, 33; SSC 16**
See also CA 101; CANR 24; DLBY 80; MTCW

Phillips, Richard
See Dick, Philip K(indred)

Phillips, Robert (Schaeffer) 1938-... **CLC 28**
See also CA 17-20R; CAAS 13; CANR 8; DLB 105

Phillips, Ward
See Lovecraft, H(oward) P(hillips)

Piccolo, Lucio 1901-1969.......... **CLC 13**
See also CA 97-100; DLB 114

Pickthall, Marjorie L(owry) C(hristie) 1883-1922 .... **TCLC 21**
See also CA 107; DLB 92

Pico della Mirandola, Giovanni 1463-1494 .... **LC 15**

Piercy, Marge 1936- .... **CLC 3, 6, 14, 18, 27, 62**
See also CA 21-24R; CAAS 1; CANR 13, 43; DLB 120; MTCW

Piers, Robert
See Anthony, Piers

Pieyre de Mandiargues, Andre 1909-1991
See Mandiargues, Andre Pieyre de
See also CA 103; 136; CANR 22

Pilnyak, Boris .... **TCLC 23**
See also Vogau, Boris Andreyevich

Pincherle, Alberto 1907-1990 ... **CLC 11, 18**
See also Moravia, Alberto
See also CA 25-28R; 132; CANR 33; MTCW

Pinckney, Darryl 1953-........... **CLC 76**
See also BW 2; CA 143

Pindar 518B.C.-446B.C.......... **CMLC 12**

Pineda, Cecile 1942-.............. **CLC 39**
See also CA 118

Pinero, Arthur Wing 1855-1934 ... **TCLC 32**
See also CA 110; DLB 10

Pinero, Miguel (Antonio Gomez) 1946-1988 .... **CLC 4, 55**
See also CA 61-64; 125; CANR 29; HW

Pinget, Robert 1919- .... **CLC 7, 13, 37**
See also CA 85-88; DLB 83

Pink Floyd
See Barrett, (Roger) Syd; Gilmour, David; Mason, Nick; Waters, Roger; Wright, Rick

Pinkney, Edward 1802-1828 ..... **NCLC 31**

Pinkwater, Daniel Manus 1941-.... **CLC 35**
See also Pinkwater, Manus
See also AAYA 1; CA 29-32R; CANR 12, 38; CLR 4; JRDA; MAICYA; SAAS 3; SATA 46, 76

Pinkwater, Manus
See Pinkwater, Daniel Manus
See also SATA 8

Pinsky, Robert 1940-........ **CLC 9, 19, 38**
See also CA 29-32R; CAAS 4; DLBY 82

Pinta, Harold
See Pinter, Harold

Pinter, Harold 1930- ..... **CLC 1, 3, 6, 9, 11, 15, 27, 58, 73; DA; WLC**
See also CA 5-8R; CANR 33; CDBLB 1960 to Present; DLB 13; MTCW

Pirandello, Luigi 1867-1936 ..... **TCLC 4, 29; DA; DC 5; WLC**
See also CA 104

Pirsig, Robert M(aynard) 1928- .... **CLC 4, 6, 73**
See also CA 53-56; CANR 42; MTCW; SATA 39

Pisarev, Dmitry Ivanovich 1840-1868 .... **NCLC 25**

Pix, Mary (Griffith) 1666-1709....... **LC 8**
See also DLB 80

Pixerecourt, Guilbert de 1773-1844 .... **NCLC 39**

Prokosch, Frederic 1908-1989 . . . . **CLC 4, 48**
See also CA 73-76; 128; DLB 48

Prophet, The
See Dreiser, Theodore (Herman Albert)

Prose, Francine 1947- . . . . **CLC 45**
See also CA 109; 112; CANR 46

Proudhon
See Cunha, Euclides (Rodrigues Pimenta) da

Proulx, E. Annie 1935- . . . . **CLC 81**

Proust, (Valentin-Louis-George-Eugene-) Marcel
1871-1922 . . . **TCLC 7, 13, 33; DA; WLC**
See also CA 104; 120; DLB 65; MTCW

Prowler, Harley
See Masters, Edgar Lee

Prus, Boleslaw 1845-1912 . . . . **TCLC 48**

Pryor, Richard (Franklin Lenox Thomas)
1940- . . . . **CLC 26**
See also CA 122

Przybyszewski, Stanislaw
1868-1927 . . . . **TCLC 36**
See also DLB 66

Pteleon
See Grieve, C(hristopher) M(urray)

Puckett, Lute
See Masters, Edgar Lee

Puig, Manuel
1932-1990 . . . **CLC 3, 5, 10, 28, 65; HLC**
See also CA 45-48; CANR 2, 32; DLB 113; HW; MTCW

Purdy, Al(fred Wellington)
1918- . . . . **CLC 3, 6, 14, 50**
See also CA 81-84; CAAS 17; CANR 42; DLB 88

Purdy, James (Amos)
1923- . . . . **CLC 2, 4, 10, 28, 52**
See also CA 33-36R; CAAS 1; CANR 19; DLB 2; MTCW

Pure, Simon
See Swinnerton, Frank Arthur

Pushkin, Alexander (Sergeyevich)
1799-1837 . . . . **NCLC 3, 27; DA; PC 10; WLC**
See also SATA 61

P'u Sung-ling 1640-1715 . . . . **LC 3**

Putnam, Arthur Lee
See Alger, Horatio, Jr.

Puzo, Mario 1920- . . . . **CLC 1, 2, 6, 36**
See also CA 65-68; CANR 4, 42; DLB 6; MTCW

Pym, Barbara (Mary Crampton)
1913-1980 . . . . **CLC 13, 19, 37**
See also CA 13-14; 97-100; CANR 13, 34; CAP 1; DLB 14; DLBY 87; MTCW

Pynchon, Thomas (Ruggles, Jr.)
1937- . . . . . **CLC 2, 3, 6, 9, 11, 18, 33, 62, 72; DA; SSC 14; WLC**
See also BEST 90:2; CA 17-20R; CANR 22, 46; DLB 2; MTCW

Qian Zhongshu
See Ch'ien Chung-shu

Qroll
See Dagerman, Stig (Halvard)

Quarrington, Paul (Lewis) 1953- . . . . **CLC 65**
See also CA 129

Quasimodo, Salvatore 1901-1968 . . . **CLC 10**
See also CA 13-16; 25-28R; CAP 1; DLB 114; MTCW

Queen, Ellery . . . . **CLC 3, 11**
See also Dannay, Frederic; Davidson, Avram; Lee, Manfred B(ennington); Sturgeon, Theodore (Hamilton); Vance, John Holbrook

Queen, Ellery, Jr.
See Dannay, Frederic; Lee, Manfred B(ennington)

Queneau, Raymond
1903-1976 . . . . **CLC 2, 5, 10, 42**
See also CA 77-80; 69-72; CANR 32; DLB 72; MTCW

Quevedo, Francisco de 1580-1645 . . . . **LC 23**

Quiller-Couch, Arthur Thomas
1863-1944 . . . . **TCLC 53**
See also CA 118; DLB 135

Quin, Ann (Marie) 1936-1973 . . . . **CLC 6**
See also CA 9-12R; 45-48; DLB 14

Quinn, Martin
See Smith, Martin Cruz

Quinn, Simon
See Smith, Martin Cruz

Quiroga, Horacio (Sylvestre)
1878-1937 . . . . **TCLC 20; HLC**
See also CA 117; 131; HW; MTCW

Quoirez, Francoise 1935- . . . . **CLC 9**
See also Sagan, Francoise
See also CA 49-52; CANR 6, 39; MTCW

Raabe, Wilhelm 1831-1910 . . . . **TCLC 45**
See also DLB 129

Rabe, David (William) 1940- . . . **CLC 4, 8, 33**
See also CA 85-88; CABS 3; DLB 7

Rabelais, Francois
1483-1553 . . . . **LC 5; DA; WLC**

Rabinovitch, Sholem 1859-1916
See Aleichem, Sholom
See also CA 104

Radcliffe, Ann (Ward) 1764-1823 . . **NCLC 6**
See also DLB 39

Radiguet, Raymond 1903-1923 . . . . **TCLC 29**
See also DLB 65

Radnoti, Miklos 1909-1944 . . . . **TCLC 16**
See also CA 118

Rado, James 1939- . . . . **CLC 17**
See also CA 105

Radvanyi, Netty 1900-1983
See Seghers, Anna
See also CA 85-88; 110

Rae, Ben
See Griffiths, Trevor

Raeburn, John (Hay) 1941- . . . . **CLC 34**
See also CA 57-60

Ragni, Gerome 1942-1991 . . . . **CLC 17**
See also CA 105; 134

Rahv, Philip 1908-1973 . . . . **CLC 24**
See also Greenberg, Ivan
See also DLB 137

Raine, Craig 1944- . . . . **CLC 32**
See also CA 108; CANR 29; DLB 40

Raine, Kathleen (Jessie) 1908- . . . **CLC 7, 45**
See also CA 85-88; CANR 46; DLB 20; MTCW

Rainis, Janis 1865-1929 . . . . **TCLC 29**

Rakosi, Carl . . . . **CLC 47**
See also Rawley, Callman
See also CAAS 5

Raleigh, Richard
See Lovecraft, H(oward) P(hillips)

Rallentando, H. P.
See Sayers, Dorothy L(eigh)

Ramal, Walter
See de la Mare, Walter (John)

Ramon, Juan
See Jimenez (Mantecon), Juan Ramon

Ramos, Graciliano 1892-1953 . . . . . **TCLC 32**

Rampersad, Arnold 1941- . . . . **CLC 44**
See also BW 2; CA 127; 133; DLB 111

Rampling, Anne
See Rice, Anne

Ramuz, Charles-Ferdinand
1878-1947 . . . . **TCLC 33**

Rand, Ayn
1905-1982 . . . . . . **CLC 3, 30, 44, 79; DA; WLC**
See also AAYA 10; CA 13-16R; 105; CANR 27; MTCW

Randall, Dudley (Felker)
1914- . . . . **CLC 1; BLC**
See also BW 1; CA 25-28R; CANR 23; DLB 41

Randall, Robert
See Silverberg, Robert

Ranger, Ken
See Creasey, John

Ransom, John Crowe
1888-1974 . . . . **CLC 2, 4, 5, 11, 24**
See also CA 5-8R; 49-52; CANR 6, 34; DLB 45, 63; MTCW

Rao, Raja 1909- . . . . **CLC 25, 56**
See also CA 73-76; MTCW

Raphael, Frederic (Michael)
1931- . . . . **CLC 2, 14**
See also CA 1-4R; CANR 1; DLB 14

Ratcliffe, James P.
See Mencken, H(enry) L(ouis)

Rathbone, Julian 1935- . . . . **CLC 41**
See also CA 101; CANR 34

Rattigan, Terence (Mervyn)
1911-1977 . . . . **CLC 7**
See also CA 85-88; 73-76; CDBLB 1945-1960; DLB 13; MTCW

Ratushinskaya, Irina 1954- . . . . **CLC 54**
See also CA 129

Raven, Simon (Arthur Noel)
1927- . . . . **CLC 14**
See also CA 81-84

Rawley, Callman 1903-
See Rakosi, Carl
See also CA 21-24R; CANR 12, 32

Rawlings, Marjorie Kinnan
1896-1953 . . . . **TCLC 4**
See also CA 104; 137; DLB 9, 22, 102; JRDA; MAICYA; YABC 1

Ray, Satyajit 1921-1992........ **CLC 16, 76**
See also CA 114; 137

Read, Herbert Edward 1893-1968.... **CLC 4**
See also CA 85-88; 25-28R; DLB 20

Read, Piers Paul 1941- ...... **CLC 4, 10, 25**
See also CA 21-24R; CANR 38; DLB 14; SATA 21

Reade, Charles 1814-1884........ **NCLC 2**
See also DLB 21

Reade, Hamish
See Gray, Simon (James Holliday)

Reading, Peter 1946- .... **CLC 47**
See also CA 103; CANR 46; DLB 40

Reaney, James 1926- .... **CLC 13**
See also CA 41-44R; CAAS 15; CANR 42; DLB 68; SATA 43

Rebreanu, Liviu 1885-1944 .... **TCLC 28**

Rechy, John (Francisco)
1934- .... **CLC 1, 7, 14, 18; HLC**
See also CA 5-8R; CAAS 4; CANR 6, 32; DLB 122; DLBY 82; HW

Redcam, Tom 1870-1933 .... **TCLC 25**

Reddin, Keith..................... **CLC 67**

Redgrove, Peter (William)
1932- .... **CLC 6, 41**
See also CA 1-4R; CANR 3, 39; DLB 40

Redmon, Anne.................... **CLC 22**
See also Nightingale, Anne Redmon
See also DLBY 86

Reed, Eliot
See Ambler, Eric

Reed, Ishmael
1938- ... **CLC 2, 3, 5, 6, 13, 32, 60; BLC**
See also BW 2; CA 21-24R; CANR 25; DLB 2, 5, 33; DLBD 8; MTCW

Reed, John (Silas) 1887-1920 ...... **TCLC 9**
See also CA 106

Reed, Lou........................ **CLC 21**
See also Firbank, Louis

Reeve, Clara 1729-1807 .... **NCLC 19**
See also DLB 39

Reich, Wilhelm 1897-1957........ **TCLC 57**

Reid, Christopher (John) 1949-..... **CLC 33**
See also CA 140; DLB 40

Reid, Desmond
See Moorcock, Michael (John)

Reid Banks, Lynne 1929-
See Banks, Lynne Reid
See also CA 1-4R; CANR 6, 22, 38; CLR 24; JRDA; MAICYA; SATA 22, 75

Reilly, William K.
See Creasey, John

Reiner, Max
See Caldwell, (Janet Miriam) Taylor (Holland)

Reis, Ricardo
See Pessoa, Fernando (Antonio Nogueira)

Remarque, Erich Maria
1898-1970 .... **CLC 21; DA**
See also CA 77-80; 29-32R; DLB 56; MTCW

Remizov, A.
See Remizov, Aleksei (Mikhailovich)

Remizov, A. M.
See Remizov, Aleksei (Mikhailovich)

Remizov, Aleksei (Mikhailovich)
1877-1957 .... **TCLC 27**
See also CA 125; 133

Renan, Joseph Ernest
1823-1892 .... **NCLC 26**

Renard, Jules 1864-1910 .... **TCLC 17**
See also CA 117

Renault, Mary............... **CLC 3, 11, 17**
See also Challans, Mary
See also DLBY 83

Rendell, Ruth (Barbara) 1930- .. **CLC 28, 48**
See also Vine, Barbara
See also CA 109; CANR 32; DLB 87; MTCW

Renoir, Jean 1894-1979 .... **CLC 20**
See also CA 129; 85-88

Resnais, Alain 1922-.............. **CLC 16**

Reverdy, Pierre 1889-1960 .... **CLC 53**
See also CA 97-100; 89-92

Rexroth, Kenneth
1905-1982 ...... **CLC 1, 2, 6, 11, 22, 49**
See also CA 5-8R; 107; CANR 14, 34; CDALB 1941-1968; DLB 16, 48; DLBY 82; MTCW

Reyes, Alfonso 1889-1959 .... **TCLC 33**
See also CA 131; HW

Reyes y Basoalto, Ricardo Eliecer Neftali
See Neruda, Pablo

Reymont, Wladyslaw (Stanislaw)
1868(?)-1925 .... **TCLC 5**
See also CA 104

Reynolds, Jonathan 1942- .... **CLC 6, 38**
See also CA 65-68; CANR 28

Reynolds, Joshua 1723-1792 .... **LC 15**
See also DLB 104

Reynolds, Michael Shane 1937- .... **CLC 44**
See also CA 65-68; CANR 9

Reznikoff, Charles 1894-1976 .... **CLC 9**
See also CA 33-36; 61-64; CAP 2; DLB 28, 45

Rezzori (d'Arezzo), Gregor von
1914- .... **CLC 25**
See also CA 122; 136

Rhine, Richard
See Silverstein, Alvin

Rhodes, Eugene Manlove
1869-1934 .... **TCLC 53**

R'hoone
See Balzac, Honore de

Rhys, Jean
1890(?)-1979 .... **CLC 2, 4, 6, 14, 19, 51**
See also CA 25-28R; 85-88; CANR 35; CDBLB 1945-1960; DLB 36, 117; MTCW

Ribeiro, Darcy 1922- .... **CLC 34**
See also CA 33-36R

Ribeiro, Joao Ubaldo (Osorio Pimentel)
1941- .... **CLC 10, 67**
See also CA 81-84

Ribman, Ronald (Burt) 1932- .... **CLC 7**
See also CA 21-24R; CANR 46

Ricci, Nino 1959- .... **CLC 70**
See also CA 137

Rice, Anne 1941- .... **CLC 41**
See also AAYA 9; BEST 89:2; CA 65-68; CANR 12, 36

Rice, Elmer (Leopold)
1892-1967 .... **CLC 7, 49**
See also CA 21-22; 25-28R; CAP 2; DLB 4, 7; MTCW

Rice, Tim(othy Miles Bindon)
1944- .... **CLC 21**
See also CA 103; CANR 46

Rich, Adrienne (Cecile)
1929- .... **CLC 3, 6, 7, 11, 18, 36, 73, 76; PC 5**
See also CA 9-12R; CANR 20; DLB 5, 67; MTCW

Rich, Barbara
See Graves, Robert (von Ranke)

Rich, Robert
See Trumbo, Dalton

Richards, David Adams 1950-...... **CLC 59**
See also CA 93-96; DLB 53

Richards, I(vor) A(rmstrong)
1893-1979 .... **CLC 14, 24**
See also CA 41-44R; 89-92; CANR 34; DLB 27

Richardson, Anne
See Roiphe, Anne (Richardson)

Richardson, Dorothy Miller
1873-1957 .... **TCLC 3**
See also CA 104; DLB 36

Richardson, Ethel Florence (Lindesay)
1870-1946
See Richardson, Henry Handel
See also CA 105

Richardson, Henry Handel.......... **TCLC 4**
See also Richardson, Ethel Florence (Lindesay)

Richardson, Samuel
1689-1761 .... **LC 1; DA; WLC**
See also CDBLB 1660-1789; DLB 39

Richler, Mordecai
1931- .... **CLC 3, 5, 9, 13, 18, 46, 70**
See also AITN 1; CA 65-68; CANR 31; CLR 17; DLB 53; MAICYA; MTCW; SATA 27, 44

Richter, Conrad (Michael)
1890-1968 .... **CLC 30**
See also CA 5-8R; 25-28R; CANR 23; DLB 9; MTCW; SATA 3

Riddell, J. H. 1832-1906 .... **TCLC 40**

Riding, Laura.................... **CLC 3, 7**
See also Jackson, Laura (Riding)

Riefenstahl, Berta Helene Amalia 1902-
See Riefenstahl, Leni
See also CA 108

Riefenstahl, Leni.................. **CLC 16**
See also Riefenstahl, Berta Helene Amalia

Riffe, Ernest
See Bergman, (Ernst) Ingmar

Riggs, (Rolla) Lynn 1899-1954 .... **TCLC 56**
See also CA 144; NNAL

Riley, James Whitcomb
1849-1916 .... **TCLC 51**
See also CA 118; 137; MAICYA; SATA 17

Riley, Tex
See Creasey, John

Rilke, Rainer Maria
1875-1926 .... **TCLC 1, 6, 19; PC 2**
See also CA 104; 132; DLB 81; MTCW

Rimbaud, (Jean Nicolas) Arthur
1854-1891 ..... **NCLC 4, 35; DA; PC 3; WLC**

Rinehart, Mary Roberts
1876-1958 .... **TCLC 52**
See also CA 108

Ringmaster, The
See Mencken, H(enry) L(ouis)

Ringwood, Gwen(dolyn Margaret) Pharis
1910-1984 .... **CLC 48**
See also CA 112; DLB 88

Rio, Michel 19(?)-................ **CLC 43**

Ritsos, Giannes
See Ritsos, Yannis

Ritsos, Yannis 1909-1990..... **CLC 6, 13, 31**
See also CA 77-80; 133; CANR 39; MTCW

Ritter, Erika 1948(?)-............. **CLC 52**

Rivera, Jose Eustasio 1889-1928... **TCLC 35**
See also HW

Rivers, Conrad Kent 1933-1968...... **CLC 1**
See also BW 1; CA 85-88; DLB 41

Rivers, Elfrida
See Bradley, Marion Zimmer

Riverside, John
See Heinlein, Robert A(nson)

Rizal, Jose 1861-1896........... **NCLC 27**

Roa Bastos, Augusto (Antonio)
1917- .... **CLC 45; HLC**
See also CA 131; DLB 113; HW

Robbe-Grillet, Alain
1922- ...... **CLC 1, 2, 4, 6, 8, 10, 14, 43**
See also CA 9-12R; CANR 33; DLB 83; MTCW

Robbins, Harold 1916-............. **CLC 5**
See also CA 73-76; CANR 26; MTCW

Robbins, Thomas Eugene 1936-
See Robbins, Tom
See also CA 81-84; CANR 29; MTCW

Robbins, Tom................ **CLC 9, 32, 64**
See also Robbins, Thomas Eugene
See also BEST 90:3; DLBY 80

Robbins, Trina 1938- .... **CLC 21**
See also CA 128

Roberts, Charles G(eorge) D(ouglas)
1860-1943 .... **TCLC 8**
See also CA 105; CLR 33; DLB 92; SATA 29

Roberts, Kate 1891-1985 .... **CLC 15**
See also CA 107; 116

Roberts, Keith (John Kingston)
1935- .... **CLC 14**
See also CA 25-28R; CANR 46

Roberts, Kenneth (Lewis)
1885-1957 .... **TCLC 23**
See also CA 109; DLB 9

Roberts, Michele (B.) 1949-........ **CLC 48**
See also CA 115

Robertson, Ellis
See Ellison, Harlan (Jay); Silverberg, Robert

Robertson, Thomas William
1829-1871 .... **NCLC 35**

Robinson, Edwin Arlington
1869-1935 .... **TCLC 5; DA; PC 1**
See also CA 104; 133; CDALB 1865-1917; DLB 54; MTCW

Robinson, Henry Crabb
1775-1867 .... **NCLC 15**
See also DLB 107

Robinson, Jill 1936-.............. **CLC 10**
See also CA 102

Robinson, Kim Stanley 1952- ...... **CLC 34**
See also CA 126

Robinson, Lloyd
See Silverberg, Robert

Robinson, Marilynne 1944-........ **CLC 25**
See also CA 116

Robinson, Smokey................. **CLC 21**
See also Robinson, William, Jr.

Robinson, William, Jr. 1940-
See Robinson, Smokey
See also CA 116

Robison, Mary 1949- .... **CLC 42**
See also CA 113; 116; DLB 130

Rod, Edouard 1857-1910 .... **TCLC 52**

Roddenberry, Eugene Wesley 1921-1991
See Roddenberry, Gene
See also CA 110; 135; CANR 37; SATA 45; SATA-Obit 69

Roddenberry, Gene .... **CLC 17**
See also Roddenberry, Eugene Wesley
See also AAYA 5; SATA-Obit 69

Rodgers, Mary 1931- .... **CLC 12**
See also CA 49-52; CANR 8; CLR 20; JRDA; MAICYA; SATA 8

Rodgers, W(illiam) R(obert)
1909-1969 .... **CLC 7**
See also CA 85-88; DLB 20

Rodman, Eric
See Silverberg, Robert

Rodman, Howard 1920(?)-1985..... **CLC 65**
See also CA 118

Rodman, Maia
See Wojciechowska, Maia (Teresa)

Rodriguez, Claudio 1934-.......... **CLC 10**
See also DLB 134

Roelvaag, O(le) E(dvart)
1876-1931 .... **TCLC 17**
See also CA 117; DLB 9

Roethke, Theodore (Huebner)
1908-1963 ...... **CLC 1, 3, 8, 11, 19, 46**
See also CA 81-84; CABS 2; CDALB 1941-1968; DLB 5; MTCW

Rogers, Thomas Hunton 1927- ..... **CLC 57**
See also CA 89-92

Rogers, Will(iam Penn Adair)
1879-1935 .... **TCLC 8**
See also CA 105; 144; DLB 11; NNAL

Rogin, Gilbert 1929-............. **CLC 18**
See also CA 65-68; CANR 15

Rohan, Koda .... **TCLC 22**
See also Koda Shigeyuki

Rohmer, Eric..................... **CLC 16**
See also Scherer, Jean-Marie Maurice

Rohmer, Sax .... **TCLC 28**
See also Ward, Arthur Henry Sarsfield
See also DLB 70

Roiphe, Anne (Richardson)
1935- .... **CLC 3, 9**
See also CA 89-92; CANR 45; DLBY 80

Rojas, Fernando de 1465-1541 ...... **LC 23**

Rolfe, Frederick (William Serafino Austin Lewis Mary) 1860-1913...... **TCLC 12**
See also CA 107; DLB 34

Rolland, Romain 1866-1944....... **TCLC 23**
See also CA 118; DLB 65

Rolvaag, O(le) E(dvart)
See Roelvaag, O(le) E(dvart)

Romain Arnaud, Saint
See Aragon, Louis

Romains, Jules 1885-1972 .... **CLC 7**
See also CA 85-88; CANR 34; DLB 65; MTCW

Romero, Jose Ruben 1890-1952 ... **TCLC 14**
See also CA 114; 131; HW

Ronsard, Pierre de
1524-1585 .... **LC 6; PC 11**

Rooke, Leon 1934- .... **CLC 25, 34**
See also CA 25-28R; CANR 23

Roper, William 1498-1578.......... **LC 10**

Roquelaure, A. N.
See Rice, Anne

Rosa, Joao Guimaraes 1908-1967... **CLC 23**
See also CA 89-92; DLB 113

Rose, Wendy 1948-............... **CLC 85**
See also CA 53-56; CANR 5; NNAL; SATA 12

Rosen, Richard (Dean) 1949-....... **CLC 39**
See also CA 77-80

Rosenberg, Isaac 1890-1918....... **TCLC 12**
See also CA 107; DLB 20

Rosenblatt, Joe .... **CLC 15**
See also Rosenblatt, Joseph

Rosenblatt, Joseph 1933-
See Rosenblatt, Joe
See also CA 89-92

Rosenfeld, Samuel 1896-1963
See Tzara, Tristan
See also CA 89-92

Rosenthal, M(acha) L(ouis) 1917-... **CLC 28**
See also CA 1-4R; CAAS 6; CANR 4; DLB 5; SATA 59

Ross, Barnaby
See Dannay, Frederic

Ross, Bernard L.
See Follett, Ken(neth Martin)

Ross, J. H.
See Lawrence, T(homas) E(dward)

Ross, Martin
See Martin, Violet Florence
See also DLB 135

Ross, (James) Sinclair 1908-....... **CLC 13**
See also CA 73-76; DLB 88

Rossetti, Christina (Georgina)
1830-1894 ... **NCLC 2; DA; PC 7; WLC**
See also DLB 35; MAICYA; SATA 20

Salinger, J(erome) D(avid)
1919- . . . . . . **CLC 1, 3, 8, 12, 55, 56; DA; SSC 2; WLC**
See also AAYA 2; CA 5-8R; CANR 39; CDALB 1941-1968; CLR 18; DLB 2, 102; MAICYA; MTCW; SATA 67

Salisbury, John
See Caute, David

Salter, James 1925- . . . . **CLC 7, 52, 59**
See also CA 73-76; DLB 130

Saltus, Edgar (Everton)
1855-1921 . . . . **TCLC 8**
See also CA 105

Saltykov, Mikhail Evgrafovich
1826-1889 . . . . **NCLC 16**

Samarakis, Antonis 1919- . . . . **CLC 5**
See also CA 25-28R; CAAS 16; CANR 36

Sanchez, Florencio 1875-1910 . . . . . **TCLC 37**
See also HW

Sanchez, Luis Rafael 1936- . . . . **CLC 23**
See also CA 128; DLB 145; HW

Sanchez, Sonia 1934- . . . **CLC 5; BLC; PC 9**
See also BW 2; CA 33-36R; CANR 24; CLR 18; DLB 41; DLBD 8; MAICYA; MTCW; SATA 22

Sand, George
1804-1876 . . . . . . **NCLC 2, 42; DA; WLC**
See also DLB 119

Sandburg, Carl (August)
1878-1967 . . . . **CLC 1, 4, 10, 15, 35; DA; PC 2; WLC**
See also CA 5-8R; 25-28R; CANR 35; CDALB 1865-1917; DLB 17, 54; MAICYA; MTCW; SATA 8

Sandburg, Charles
See Sandburg, Carl (August)

Sandburg, Charles A.
See Sandburg, Carl (August)

Sanders, (James) Ed(ward) 1939- . . . **CLC 53**
See also CA 13-16R; CANR 13, 44; DLB 16

Sanders, Lawrence 1920- . . . . **CLC 41**
See also BEST 89:4; CA 81-84; CANR 33; MTCW

Sanders, Noah
See Blount, Roy (Alton), Jr.

Sanders, Winston P.
See Anderson, Poul (William)

Sandoz, Mari(e Susette)
1896-1966 . . . . **CLC 28**
See also CA 1-4R; 25-28R; CANR 17; DLB 9; MTCW; SATA 5

Saner, Reg(inald Anthony) 1931- . . . . **CLC 9**
See also CA 65-68

Sannazaro, Jacopo 1456(?)-1530 . . . . . . **LC 8**

Sansom, William 1912-1976 . . . . **CLC 2, 6**
See also CA 5-8R; 65-68; CANR 42; DLB 139; MTCW

Santayana, George 1863-1952 . . . . . **TCLC 40**
See also CA 115; DLB 54, 71

Santiago, Danny . . . . **CLC 33**
See also James, Daniel (Lewis); James, Daniel (Lewis)
See also DLB 122

Santmyer, Helen Hoover
1895-1986 . . . . **CLC 33**
See also CA 1-4R; 118; CANR 15, 33; DLBY 84; MTCW

Santos, Bienvenido N(uqui) 1911- . . . **CLC 22**
See also CA 101; CANR 19, 46

Sapper . . . . **TCLC 44**
See also McNeile, Herman Cyril

Sappho fl. 6th cent. B.C.- . . . . **CMLC 3; PC 5**

Sarduy, Severo 1937-1993 . . . . **CLC 6**
See also CA 89-92; 142; DLB 113; HW

Sargeson, Frank 1903-1982 . . . . **CLC 31**
See also CA 25-28R; 106; CANR 38

Sarmiento, Felix Ruben Garcia
See Dario, Ruben

Saroyan, William
1908-1981 . . . . . **CLC 1, 8, 10, 29, 34, 56; DA; WLC**
See also CA 5-8R; 103; CANR 30; DLB 7, 9, 86; DLBY 81; MTCW; SATA 23; SATA-Obit 24

Sarraute, Nathalie
1900- . . . . **CLC 1, 2, 4, 8, 10, 31, 80**
See also CA 9-12R; CANR 23; DLB 83; MTCW

Sarton, (Eleanor) May
1912- . . . . **CLC 4, 14, 49**
See also CA 1-4R; CANR 1, 34; DLB 48; DLBY 81; MTCW; SATA 36

Sartre, Jean-Paul
1905-1980 . . . . **CLC 1, 4, 7, 9, 13, 18, 24, 44, 50, 52; DA; DC 3; WLC**
See also CA 9-12R; 97-100; CANR 21; DLB 72; MTCW

Sassoon, Siegfried (Lorraine)
1886-1967 . . . . **CLC 36**
See also CA 104; 25-28R; CANR 36; DLB 20; MTCW

Satterfield, Charles
See Pohl, Frederik

Saul, John (W. III) 1942- . . . . **CLC 46**
See also AAYA 10; BEST 90:4; CA 81-84; CANR 16, 40

Saunders, Caleb
See Heinlein, Robert A(nson)

Saura (Atares), Carlos 1932- . . . . **CLC 20**
See also CA 114; 131; HW

Sauser-Hall, Frederic 1887-1961 . . . . **CLC 18**
See also CA 102; 93-96; CANR 36; MTCW

Saussure, Ferdinand de
1857-1913 . . . . **TCLC 49**

Savage, Catharine
See Brosman, Catharine Savage

Savage, Thomas 1915- . . . . **CLC 40**
See also CA 126; 132; CAAS 15

Savan, Glenn 19(?)- . . . . **CLC 50**

Sayers, Dorothy L(eigh)
1893-1957 . . . . **TCLC 2, 15**
See also CA 104; 119; CDBLB 1914-1945; DLB 10, 36, 77, 100; MTCW

Sayers, Valerie 1952- . . . . **CLC 50**
See also CA 134

Sayles, John (Thomas)
1950- . . . . **CLC 7, 10, 14**
See also CA 57-60; CANR 41; DLB 44

Scammell, Michael . . . . **CLC 34**

Scannell, Vernon 1922- . . . . **CLC 49**
See also CA 5-8R; CANR 8, 24; DLB 27; SATA 59

Scarlett, Susan
See Streatfeild, (Mary) Noel

Schaeffer, Susan Fromberg
1941- . . . . **CLC 6, 11, 22**
See also CA 49-52; CANR 18; DLB 28; MTCW; SATA 22

Schary, Jill
See Robinson, Jill

Schell, Jonathan 1943- . . . . **CLC 35**
See also CA 73-76; CANR 12

Schelling, Friedrich Wilhelm Joseph von
1775-1854 . . . . **NCLC 30**
See also DLB 90

Schendel, Arthur van 1874-1946 . . . **TCLC 56**

Scherer, Jean-Marie Maurice 1920-
See Rohmer, Eric
See also CA 110

Schevill, James (Erwin) 1920- . . . . **CLC 7**
See also CA 5-8R; CAAS 12

Schiller, Friedrich 1759-1805 . . . . **NCLC 39**
See also DLB 94

Schisgal, Murray (Joseph) 1926- . . . . . **CLC 6**
See also CA 21-24R

Schlee, Ann 1934- . . . . **CLC 35**
See also CA 101; CANR 29; SATA 36, 44

Schlegel, August Wilhelm von
1767-1845 . . . . **NCLC 15**
See also DLB 94

Schlegel, Friedrich 1772-1829 . . . . **NCLC 45**
See also DLB 90

Schlegel, Johann Elias (von)
1719(?)-1749 . . . . **LC 5**

Schlesinger, Arthur M(eier), Jr.
1917- . . . . **CLC 84**
See also AITN 1; CA 1-4R; CANR 1, 28; DLB 17; MTCW; SATA 61

Schmidt, Arno (Otto) 1914-1979 . . . . **CLC 56**
See also CA 128; 109; DLB 69

Schmitz, Aron Hector 1861-1928
See Svevo, Italo
See also CA 104; 122; MTCW

Schnackenberg, Gjertrud 1953- . . . . . **CLC 40**
See also CA 116; DLB 120

Schneider, Leonard Alfred 1925-1966
See Bruce, Lenny
See also CA 89-92

Schnitzler, Arthur
1862-1931 . . . . **TCLC 4; SSC 15**
See also CA 104; DLB 81, 118

Schor, Sandra (M.) 1932(?)-1990 . . . **CLC 65**
See also CA 132

Schorer, Mark 1908-1977 . . . . **CLC 9**
See also CA 5-8R; 73-76; CANR 7; DLB 103

Schrader, Paul (Joseph) 1946- . . . . . . **CLC 26**
See also CA 37-40R; CANR 41; DLB 44

Schreiner, Olive (Emilie Albertina)
1855-1920 . . . . **TCLC 9**
See also CA 105; DLB 18

Schulberg, Budd (Wilson) 1914- .... **CLC 7, 48**
See also CA 25-28R; CANR 19; DLB 6, 26, 28; DLBY 81

Schulz, Bruno 1892-1942 .... **TCLC 5, 51; SSC 13**
See also CA 115; 123

Schulz, Charles M(onroe) 1922- .... **CLC 12**
See also CA 9-12R; CANR 6; SATA 10

Schumacher, E(rnst) F(riedrich) 1911-1977 .... **CLC 80**
See also CA 81-84; 73-76; CANR 34

Schuyler, James Marcus 1923-1991 .... **CLC 5, 23**
See also CA 101; 134; DLB 5

Schwartz, Delmore (David) 1913-1966 ...... **CLC 2, 4, 10, 45; PC 8**
See also CA 17-18; 25-28R; CANR 35; CAP 2; DLB 28, 48; MTCW

Schwartz, Ernst
See Ozu, Yasujiro

Schwartz, John Burnham 1965- .... **CLC 59**
See also CA 132

Schwartz, Lynne Sharon 1939- ..... **CLC 31**
See also CA 103; CANR 44

Schwartz, Muriel A.
See Eliot, T(homas) S(tearns)

Schwarz-Bart, Andre 1928- .... **CLC 2, 4**
See also CA 89-92

Schwarz-Bart, Simone 1938- .... **CLC 7**
See also BW 2; CA 97-100

Schwob, (Mayer Andre) Marcel 1867-1905 .... **TCLC 20**
See also CA 117; DLB 123

Sciascia, Leonardo 1921-1989 .... **CLC 8, 9, 41**
See also CA 85-88; 130; CANR 35; MTCW

Scoppettone, Sandra 1936- .... **CLC 26**
See also AAYA 11; CA 5-8R; CANR 41; SATA 9

Scorsese, Martin 1942- .... **CLC 20**
See also CA 110; 114; CANR 46

Scotland, Jay
See Jakes, John (William)

Scott, Duncan Campbell 1862-1947 .... **TCLC 6**
See also CA 104; DLB 92

Scott, Evelyn 1893-1963 .... **CLC 43**
See also CA 104; 112; DLB 9, 48

Scott, F(rancis) R(eginald) 1899-1985 .... **CLC 22**
See also CA 101; 114; DLB 88

Scott, Frank
See Scott, F(rancis) R(eginald)

Scott, Joanna 1960- .... **CLC 50**
See also CA 126

Scott, Paul (Mark) 1920-1978 .... **CLC 9, 60**
See also CA 81-84; 77-80; CANR 33; DLB 14; MTCW

Scott, Walter 1771-1832 .... **NCLC 15; DA; WLC**
See also CDBLB 1789-1832; DLB 93, 107, 116, 144; YABC 2

Scribe, (Augustin) Eugene 1791-1861 .... **NCLC 16; DC 5**

Scrum, R.
See Crumb, R(obert)

Scudery, Madeleine de 1607-1701 ..... **LC 2**

Scum
See Crumb, R(obert)

Scumbag, Little Bobby
See Crumb, R(obert)

Seabrook, John
See Hubbard, L(afayette) Ron(ald)

Sealy, I. Allan 1951- .... **CLC 55**

Search, Alexander
See Pessoa, Fernando (Antonio Nogueira)

Sebastian, Lee
See Silverberg, Robert

Sebastian Owl
See Thompson, Hunter S(tockton)

Sebestyen, Ouida 1924- .... **CLC 30**
See also AAYA 8; CA 107; CANR 40; CLR 17; JRDA; MAICYA; SAAS 10; SATA 39

Secundus, H. Scriblerus
See Fielding, Henry

Sedges, John
See Buck, Pearl S(ydenstricker)

Sedgwick, Catharine Maria 1789-1867 .... **NCLC 19**
See also DLB 1, 74

Seelye, John 1931- .... **CLC 7**

Seferiades, Giorgos Stylianou 1900-1971
See Seferis, George
See also CA 5-8R; 33-36R; CANR 5, 36; MTCW

Seferis, George .... **CLC 5, 11**
See also Seferiades, Giorgos Stylianou

Segal, Erich (Wolf) 1937- .... **CLC 3, 10**
See also BEST 89:1; CA 25-28R; CANR 20, 36; DLBY 86; MTCW

Seger, Bob 1945- .... **CLC 35**

Seghers, Anna .... **CLC 7**
See also Radvanyi, Netty
See also DLB 69

Seidel, Frederick (Lewis) 1936- ..... **CLC 18**
See also CA 13-16R; CANR 8; DLBY 84

Seifert, Jaroslav 1901-1986 ..... **CLC 34, 44**
See also CA 127; MTCW

Sei Shonagon c. 966-1017(?) ...... **CMLC 6**

Selby, Hubert, Jr. 1928- ..... **CLC 1, 2, 4, 8**
See also CA 13-16R; CANR 33; DLB 2

Selzer, Richard 1928- .... **CLC 74**
See also CA 65-68; CANR 14

Sembene, Ousmane
See Ousmane, Sembene

Senancour, Etienne Pivert de 1770-1846 .... **NCLC 16**
See also DLB 119

Sender, Ramon (Jose) 1902-1982 .... **CLC 8; HLC**
See also CA 5-8R; 105; CANR 8; HW; MTCW

Seneca, Lucius Annaeus 4B.C.-65 .... **CMLC 6; DC 5**

Senghor, Leopold Sedar 1906- .... **CLC 54; BLC**
See also BW 2; CA 116; 125; CANR 47; MTCW

Serling, (Edward) Rod(man) 1924-1975 .... **CLC 30**
See also AAYA 14; AITN 1; CA 65-68; 57-60; DLB 26

Serna, Ramon Gomez de la
See Gomez de la Serna, Ramon

Serpieres
See Guillevic, (Eugene)

Service, Robert
See Service, Robert W(illiam)
See also DLB 92

Service, Robert W(illiam) 1874(?)-1958 ...... **TCLC 15; DA; WLC**
See also Service, Robert
See also CA 115; 140; SATA 20

Seth, Vikram 1952- .... **CLC 43**
See also CA 121; 127; DLB 120

Seton, Cynthia Propper 1926-1982 .... **CLC 27**
See also CA 5-8R; 108; CANR 7

Seton, Ernest (Evan) Thompson 1860-1946 .... **TCLC 31**
See also CA 109; DLB 92; JRDA; SATA 18

Seton-Thompson, Ernest
See Seton, Ernest (Evan) Thompson

Settle, Mary Lee 1918- .... **CLC 19, 61**
See also CA 89-92; CAAS 1; CANR 44; DLB 6

Seuphor, Michel
See Arp, Jean

Sevigne, Marie (de Rabutin-Chantal) Marquise de 1626-1696 .... **LC 11**

Sexton, Anne (Harvey) 1928-1974 .... **CLC 2, 4, 6, 8, 10, 15, 53; DA; PC 2; WLC**
See also CA 1-4R; 53-56; CABS 2; CANR 3, 36; CDALB 1941-1968; DLB 5; MTCW; SATA 10

Shaara, Michael (Joseph Jr.) 1929-1988 .... **CLC 15**
See also AITN 1; CA 102; DLBY 83

Shackleton, C. C.
See Aldiss, Brian W(ilson)

Shacochis, Bob .... **CLC 39**
See also Shacochis, Robert G.

Shacochis, Robert G. 1951-
See Shacochis, Bob
See also CA 119; 124

Shaffer, Anthony (Joshua) 1926- .... **CLC 19**
See also CA 110; 116; DLB 13

Shaffer, Peter (Levin) 1926- .... **CLC 5, 14, 18, 37, 60**
See also CA 25-28R; CANR 25, 47; CDBLB 1960 to Present; DLB 13; MTCW

Shakey, Bernard
See Young, Neil

Shalamov, Varlam (Tikhonovich) 1907(?)-1982 .... **CLC 18**
See also CA 129; 105

Shamlu, Ahmad 1925- .... **CLC 10**

Simmons, Charles (Paul) 1924- ..... **CLC 57**
See also CA 89-92

Simmons, Dan 1948- .... **CLC 44**
See also CA 138

Simmons, James (Stewart Alexander)
1933- .... **CLC 43**
See also CA 105; DLB 40

Simms, William Gilmore
1806-1870 .... **NCLC 3**
See also DLB 3, 30, 59, 73

Simon, Carly 1945- .... **CLC 26**
See also CA 105

Simon, Claude 1913- .... **CLC 4, 9, 15, 39**
See also CA 89-92; CANR 33; DLB 83; MTCW

Simon, (Marvin) Neil
1927- .... **CLC 6, 11, 31, 39, 70**
See also AITN 1; CA 21-24R; CANR 26; DLB 7; MTCW

Simon, Paul 1942(?)- .... **CLC 17**
See also CA 116

Simonon, Paul 1956(?)- .... **CLC 30**

Simpson, Harriette
See Arnow, Harriette (Louisa) Simpson

Simpson, Louis (Aston Marantz)
1923- .... **CLC 4, 7, 9, 32**
See also CA 1-4R; CAAS 4; CANR 1; DLB 5; MTCW

Simpson, Mona (Elizabeth) 1957- ... **CLC 44**
See also CA 122; 135

Simpson, N(orman) F(rederick)
1919- .... **CLC 29**
See also CA 13-16R; DLB 13

Sinclair, Andrew (Annandale)
1935- .... **CLC 2, 14**
See also CA 9-12R; CAAS 5; CANR 14, 38; DLB 14; MTCW

Sinclair, Emil
See Hesse, Hermann

Sinclair, Iain 1943- .... **CLC 76**
See also CA 132

Sinclair, Iain MacGregor
See Sinclair, Iain

Sinclair, Mary Amelia St. Clair 1865(?)-1946
See Sinclair, May
See also CA 104

Sinclair, May .... **TCLC 3, 11**
See also Sinclair, Mary Amelia St. Clair
See also DLB 36, 135

Sinclair, Upton (Beall)
1878-1968 ...... **CLC 1, 11, 15, 63; DA; WLC**
See also CA 5-8R; 25-28R; CANR 7; CDALB 1929-1941; DLB 9; MTCW; SATA 9

Singer, Isaac
See Singer, Isaac Bashevis

Singer, Isaac Bashevis
1904-1991 .... **CLC 1, 3, 6, 9, 11, 15, 23, 38, 69; DA; SSC 3; WLC**
See also AITN 1, 2; CA 1-4R; 134; CANR 1, 39; CDALB 1941-1968; CLR 1; DLB 6, 28, 52; DLBY 91; JRDA; MAICYA; MTCW; SATA 3, 27; SATA-Obit 68

Singer, Israel Joshua 1893-1944 ... **TCLC 33**

Singh, Khushwant 1915- .... **CLC 11**
See also CA 9-12R; CAAS 9; CANR 6

Sinjohn, John
See Galsworthy, John

Sinyavsky, Andrei (Donatevich)
1925- .... **CLC 8**
See also CA 85-88

Sirin, V.
See Nabokov, Vladimir (Vladimirovich)

Sissman, L(ouis) E(dward)
1928-1976 .... **CLC 9, 18**
See also CA 21-24R; 65-68; CANR 13; DLB 5

Sisson, C(harles) H(ubert) 1914- ..... **CLC 8**
See also CA 1-4R; CAAS 3; CANR 3; DLB 27

Sitwell, Dame Edith
1887-1964 .... **CLC 2, 9, 67; PC 3**
See also CA 9-12R; CANR 35; CDBLB 1945-1960; DLB 20; MTCW

Sjoewall, Maj 1935- .... **CLC 7**
See also CA 65-68

Sjowall, Maj
See Sjoewall, Maj

Skelton, Robin 1925- .... **CLC 13**
See also AITN 2; CA 5-8R; CAAS 5; CANR 28; DLB 27, 53

Skolimowski, Jerzy 1938- .... **CLC 20**
See also CA 128

Skram, Amalie (Bertha)
1847-1905 .... **TCLC 25**

Skvorecky, Josef (Vaclav)
1924- .... **CLC 15, 39, 69**
See also CA 61-64; CAAS 1; CANR 10, 34; MTCW

Slade, Bernard .... **CLC 11, 46**
See also Newbound, Bernard Slade
See also CAAS 9; DLB 53

Slaughter, Carolyn 1946- .... **CLC 56**
See also CA 85-88

Slaughter, Frank G(ill) 1908- ...... **CLC 29**
See also AITN 2; CA 5-8R; CANR 5

Slavitt, David R(ytman) 1935- .... **CLC 5, 14**
See also CA 21-24R; CAAS 3; CANR 41; DLB 5, 6

Slesinger, Tess 1905-1945 .... **TCLC 10**
See also CA 107; DLB 102

Slessor, Kenneth 1901-1971 .... **CLC 14**
See also CA 102; 89-92

Slowacki, Juliusz 1809-1849 ..... **NCLC 15**

Smart, Christopher 1722-1771 .... **LC 3**
See also DLB 109

Smart, Elizabeth 1913-1986 .... **CLC 54**
See also CA 81-84; 118; DLB 88

Smiley, Jane (Graves) 1949- .... **CLC 53, 76**
See also CA 104; CANR 30

Smith, A(rthur) J(ames) M(arshall)
1902-1980 .... **CLC 15**
See also CA 1-4R; 102; CANR 4; DLB 88

Smith, Anna Deavere 1950- .... **CLC 86**
See also CA 133

Smith, Betty (Wehner) 1896-1972 ... **CLC 19**
See also CA 5-8R; 33-36R; DLBY 82; SATA 6

Smith, Charlotte (Turner)
1749-1806 .... **NCLC 23**
See also DLB 39, 109

Smith, Clark Ashton 1893-1961 .... **CLC 43**
See also CA 143

Smith, Dave .... **CLC 22, 42**
See also Smith, David (Jeddie)
See also CAAS 7; DLB 5

Smith, David (Jeddie) 1942-
See Smith, Dave
See also CA 49-52; CANR 1

Smith, Florence Margaret 1902-1971
See Smith, Stevie
See also CA 17-18; 29-32R; CANR 35; CAP 2; MTCW

Smith, Iain Crichton 1928- .... **CLC 64**
See also CA 21-24R; DLB 40, 139

Smith, John 1580(?)-1631 .... **LC 9**

Smith, Johnston
See Crane, Stephen (Townley)

Smith, Lee 1944- .... **CLC 25, 73**
See also CA 114; 119; CANR 46; DLB 143; DLBY 83

Smith, Martin
See Smith, Martin Cruz

Smith, Martin Cruz 1942- .... **CLC 25**
See also BEST 89:4; CA 85-88; CANR 6, 23, 43; NNAL

Smith, Mary-Ann Tirone 1944- ..... **CLC 39**
See also CA 118; 136

Smith, Patti 1946- .... **CLC 12**
See also CA 93-96

Smith, Pauline (Urmson)
1882-1959 .... **TCLC 25**

Smith, Rosamond
See Oates, Joyce Carol

Smith, Sheila Kaye
See Kaye-Smith, Sheila

Smith, Stevie .... **CLC 3, 8, 25, 44**
See also Smith, Florence Margaret
See also DLB 20

Smith, Wilbur (Addison) 1933- ..... **CLC 33**
See also CA 13-16R; CANR 7, 46, 46; MTCW

Smith, William Jay 1918- .... **CLC 6**
See also CA 5-8R; CANR 44; DLB 5; MAICYA; SATA 2, 68

Smith, Woodrow Wilson
See Kuttner, Henry

Smolenskin, Peretz 1842-1885 .... **NCLC 30**

Smollett, Tobias (George) 1721-1771 .. **LC 2**
See also CDBLB 1660-1789; DLB 39, 104

Snodgrass, W(illiam) D(e Witt)
1926- .... **CLC 2, 6, 10, 18, 68**
See also CA 1-4R; CANR 6, 36; DLB 5; MTCW

Snow, C(harles) P(ercy)
1905-1980 .... **CLC 1, 4, 6, 9, 13, 19**
See also CA 5-8R; 101; CANR 28; CDBLB 1945-1960; DLB 15, 77; MTCW

Snow, Frances Compton
See Adams, Henry (Brooks)

Snyder, Gary (Sherman)
1930- . . . . **CLC 1, 2, 5, 9, 32**
See also CA 17-20R; CANR 30; DLB 5, 16

Snyder, Zilpha Keatley 1927- . . . . . . **CLC 17**
See also CA 9-12R; CANR 38; CLR 31; JRDA; MAICYA; SAAS 2; SATA 1, 28, 75

Soares, Bernardo
See Pessoa, Fernando (Antonio Nogueira)

Sobh, A.
See Shamlu, Ahmad

Sobol, Joshua. . . . . **CLC 60**

Soderberg, Hjalmar 1869-1941 . . . . **TCLC 39**

Sodergran, Edith (Irene)
See Soedergran, Edith (Irene)

Soedergran, Edith (Irene)
1892-1923 . . . . **TCLC 31**

Softly, Edgar
See Lovecraft, H(oward) P(hillips)

Softly, Edward
See Lovecraft, H(oward) P(hillips)

Sokolov, Raymond 1941- . . . . **CLC 7**
See also CA 85-88

Solo, Jay
See Ellison, Harlan (Jay)

Sologub, Fyodor . . . . **TCLC 9**
See also Teternikov, Fyodor Kuzmich

Solomons, Ikey Esquir
See Thackeray, William Makepeace

Solomos, Dionysios 1798-1857 . . . **NCLC 15**

Solwoska, Mara
See French, Marilyn

Solzhenitsyn, Aleksandr I(sayevich)
1918- . . . . . . **CLC 1, 2, 4, 7, 9, 10, 18, 26, 34, 78; DA; WLC**
See also AITN 1; CA 69-72; CANR 40; MTCW

Somers, Jane
See Lessing, Doris (May)

Somerville, Edith 1858-1949 . . . . . . **TCLC 51**
See also DLB 135

Somerville & Ross
See Martin, Violet Florence; Somerville, Edith

Sommer, Scott 1951- . . . . **CLC 25**
See also CA 106

Sondheim, Stephen (Joshua)
1930- . . . . **CLC 30, 39**
See also AAYA 11; CA 103; CANR 47

Sontag, Susan 1933- . . . **CLC 1, 2, 10, 13, 31**
See also CA 17-20R; CANR 25; DLB 2, 67; MTCW

Sophocles
496(?)B.C.-406(?)B.C. . . . . **CMLC 2; DA; DC 1**

Sorel, Julia
See Drexler, Rosalyn

Sorrentino, Gilbert
1929- . . . . **CLC 3, 7, 14, 22, 40**
See also CA 77-80; CANR 14, 33; DLB 5; DLBY 80

Soto, Gary 1952-. . . . . **CLC 32, 80; HLC**
See also AAYA 10; CA 119; 125; DLB 82; HW; JRDA; SATA 80

Soupault, Philippe 1897-1990 . . . . . . **CLC 68**
See also CA 116; 131

Souster, (Holmes) Raymond
1921- . . . . **CLC 5, 14**
See also CA 13-16R; CAAS 14; CANR 13, 29; DLB 88; SATA 63

Southern, Terry 1926- . . . . **CLC 7**
See also CA 1-4R; CANR 1; DLB 2

Southey, Robert 1774-1843 . . . . **NCLC 8**
See also DLB 93, 107, 142; SATA 54

Southworth, Emma Dorothy Eliza Nevitte
1819-1899 . . . . **NCLC 26**

Souza, Ernest
See Scott, Evelyn

Soyinka, Wole
1934- . . . . **CLC 3, 5, 14, 36, 44; BLC; DA; DC 2; WLC**
See also BW 2; CA 13-16R; CANR 27, 39; DLB 125; MTCW

Spackman, W(illiam) M(ode)
1905-1990 . . . . **CLC 46**
See also CA 81-84; 132

Spacks, Barry 1931-. . . . . **CLC 14**
See also CA 29-32R; CANR 33; DLB 105

Spanidou, Irini 1946- . . . . **CLC 44**

Spark, Muriel (Sarah)
1918- . . . . **CLC 2, 3, 5, 8, 13, 18, 40; SSC 10**
See also CA 5-8R; CANR 12, 36; CDBLB 1945-1960; DLB 15, 139; MTCW

Spaulding, Douglas
See Bradbury, Ray (Douglas)

Spaulding, Leonard
See Bradbury, Ray (Douglas)

Spence, J. A. D.
See Eliot, T(homas) S(tearns)

Spencer, Elizabeth 1921- . . . . **CLC 22**
See also CA 13-16R; CANR 32; DLB 6; MTCW; SATA 14

Spencer, Leonard G.
See Silverberg, Robert

Spencer, Scott 1945-. . . . . **CLC 30**
See also CA 113; DLBY 86

Spender, Stephen (Harold)
1909- . . . . **CLC 1, 2, 5, 10, 41**
See also CA 9-12R; CANR 31; CDBLB 1945-1960; DLB 20; MTCW

Spengler, Oswald (Arnold Gottfried)
1880-1936 . . . . **TCLC 25**
See also CA 118

Spenser, Edmund
1552(?)-1599 . . . . **LC 5; DA; PC 8; WLC**
See also CDBLB Before 1660

Spicer, Jack 1925-1965 . . . . . . **CLC 8, 18, 72**
See also CA 85-88; DLB 5, 16

Spiegelman, Art 1948- . . . . **CLC 76**
See also AAYA 10; CA 125; CANR 41

Spielberg, Peter 1929- . . . . **CLC 6**
See also CA 5-8R; CANR 4; DLBY 81

Spielberg, Steven 1947- . . . . **CLC 20**
See also AAYA 8; CA 77-80; CANR 32; SATA 32

Spillane, Frank Morrison 1918-
See Spillane, Mickey
See also CA 25-28R; CANR 28; MTCW; SATA 66

Spillane, Mickey . . . . **CLC 3, 13**
See also Spillane, Frank Morrison

Spinoza, Benedictus de 1632-1677 . . . . **LC 9**

Spinrad, Norman (Richard) 1940- . . . **CLC 46**
See also CA 37-40R; CAAS 19; CANR 20; DLB 8

Spitteler, Carl (Friedrich Georg)
1845-1924 . . . . **TCLC 12**
See also CA 109; DLB 129

Spivack, Kathleen (Romola Drucker)
1938- . . . . **CLC 6**
See also CA 49-52

Spoto, Donald 1941-. . . . . **CLC 39**
See also CA 65-68; CANR 11

Springsteen, Bruce (F.) 1949- . . . . . . **CLC 17**
See also CA 111

Spurling, Hilary 1940-. . . . . **CLC 34**
See also CA 104; CANR 25

Spyker, John Howland
See Elman, Richard

Squires, (James) Radcliffe
1917-1993 . . . . **CLC 51**
See also CA 1-4R; 140; CANR 6, 21

Srivastava, Dhanpat Rai 1880(?)-1936
See Premchand
See also CA 118

Stacy, Donald
See Pohl, Frederik

Stael, Germaine de
See Stael-Holstein, Anne Louise Germaine Necker Baronn
See also DLB 119

Stael-Holstein, Anne Louise Germaine Necker Baronn 1766-1817 . . . . **NCLC 3**
See also Stael, Germaine de

Stafford, Jean 1915-1979 . . . **CLC 4, 7, 19, 68**
See also CA 1-4R; 85-88; CANR 3; DLB 2; MTCW; SATA-Obit 22

Stafford, William (Edgar)
1914-1993 . . . . **CLC 4, 7, 29**
See also CA 5-8R; 142; CAAS 3; CANR 5, 22; DLB 5

Staines, Trevor
See Brunner, John (Kilian Houston)

Stairs, Gordon
See Austin, Mary (Hunter)

Stannard, Martin 1947- . . . . **CLC 44**
See also CA 142

Stanton, Maura 1946- . . . . **CLC 9**
See also CA 89-92; CANR 15; DLB 120

Stanton, Schuyler
See Baum, L(yman) Frank

Stapledon, (William) Olaf
1886-1950 . . . . **TCLC 22**
See also CA 111; DLB 15

Starbuck, George (Edwin) 1931- . . . . **CLC 53**
See also CA 21-24R; CANR 23

Stark, Richard
See Westlake, Donald E(dwin)

Staunton, Schuyler
See Baum, L(yman) Frank

Stead, Christina (Ellen) 1902-1983 .... **CLC 2, 5, 8, 32, 80**
See also CA 13-16R; 109; CANR 33, 40; MTCW

Stead, William Thomas 1849-1912 .... **TCLC 48**

Steele, Richard 1672-1729.......... **LC 18**
See also CDBLB 1660-1789; DLB 84, 101

Steele, Timothy (Reid) 1948-....... **CLC 45**
See also CA 93-96; CANR 16; DLB 120

Steffens, (Joseph) Lincoln 1866-1936 .... **TCLC 20**
See also CA 117

Stegner, Wallace (Earle) 1909-1993 .... **CLC 9, 49, 81**
See also AITN 1; BEST 90:3; CA 1-4R; 141; CAAS 9; CANR 1, 21, 46; DLB 9; DLBY 93; MTCW

Stein, Gertrude 1874-1946 ...... **TCLC 1, 6, 28, 48; DA; WLC**
See also CA 104; 132; CDALB 1917-1929; DLB 4, 54, 86; MTCW

Steinbeck, John (Ernst) 1902-1968 ...... **CLC 1, 5, 9, 13, 21, 34, 45, 75; DA; SSC 11; WLC**
See also AAYA 12; CA 1-4R; 25-28R; CANR 1, 35; CDALB 1929-1941; DLB 7, 9; DLBD 2; MTCW; SATA 9

Steinem, Gloria 1934-............. **CLC 63**
See also CA 53-56; CANR 28; MTCW

Steiner, George 1929-............. **CLC 24**
See also CA 73-76; CANR 31; DLB 67; MTCW; SATA 62

Steiner, K. Leslie
See Delany, Samuel R(ay, Jr.)

Steiner, Rudolf 1861-1925........ **TCLC 13**
See also CA 107

Stendhal 1783-1842 ..... **NCLC 23, 46; DA; WLC**
See also DLB 119

Stephen, Leslie 1832-1904........ **TCLC 23**
See also CA 123; DLB 57, 144

Stephen, Sir Leslie
See Stephen, Leslie

Stephen, Virginia
See Woolf, (Adeline) Virginia

Stephens, James 1882(?)-1950...... **TCLC 4**
See also CA 104; DLB 19

Stephens, Reed
See Donaldson, Stephen R.

Steptoe, Lydia
See Barnes, Djuna

Sterchi, Beat 1949-............... **CLC 65**

Sterling, Brett
See Bradbury, Ray (Douglas); Hamilton, Edmond

Sterling, Bruce 1954-............. **CLC 72**
See also CA 119; CANR 44

Sterling, George 1869-1926 .... **TCLC 20**
See also CA 117; DLB 54

Stern, Gerald 1925- .... **CLC 40**
See also CA 81-84; CANR 28; DLB 105

Stern, Richard (Gustave) 1928-... **CLC 4, 39**
See also CA 1-4R; CANR 1, 25; DLBY 87

Sternberg, Josef von 1894-1969..... **CLC 20**
See also CA 81-84

Sterne, Laurence 1713-1768 .... **LC 2; DA; WLC**
See also CDBLB 1660-1789; DLB 39

Sternheim, (William Adolf) Carl 1878-1942 .... **TCLC 8**
See also CA 105; DLB 56, 118

Stevens, Mark 1951- .... **CLC 34**
See also CA 122

Stevens, Wallace 1879-1955 .... **TCLC 3, 12, 45; DA; PC 6; WLC**
See also CA 104; 124; CDALB 1929-1941; DLB 54; MTCW

Stevenson, Anne (Katharine) 1933- .... **CLC 7, 33**
See also CA 17-20R; CAAS 9; CANR 9, 33; DLB 40; MTCW

Stevenson, Robert Louis (Balfour) 1850-1894 .... **NCLC 5, 14; DA; SSC 11; WLC**
See also CDBLB 1890-1914; CLR 10, 11; DLB 18, 57, 141; JRDA; MAICYA; YABC 2

Stewart, J(ohn) I(nnes) M(ackintosh) 1906- .... **CLC 7, 14, 32**
See also CA 85-88; CAAS 3; CANR 47; MTCW

Stewart, Mary (Florence Elinor) 1916- .... **CLC 7, 35**
See also CA 1-4R; CANR 1; SATA 12

Stewart, Mary Rainbow
See Stewart, Mary (Florence Elinor)

Stifle, June
See Campbell, Maria

Stifter, Adalbert 1805-1868...... **NCLC 41**
See also DLB 133

Still, James 1906-................ **CLC 49**
See also CA 65-68; CAAS 17; CANR 10, 26; DLB 9; SATA 29

Sting
See Sumner, Gordon Matthew

Stirling, Arthur
See Sinclair, Upton (Beall)

Stitt, Milan 1941-................ **CLC 29**
See also CA 69-72

Stockton, Francis Richard 1834-1902
See Stockton, Frank R.
See also CA 108; 137; MAICYA; SATA 44

Stockton, Frank R. .... **TCLC 47**
See also Stockton, Francis Richard
See also DLB 42, 74; SATA 32

Stoddard, Charles
See Kuttner, Henry

Stoker, Abraham 1847-1912
See Stoker, Bram
See also CA 105; DA; SATA 29

Stoker, Bram .... **TCLC 8; WLC**
See also Stoker, Abraham
See also CDBLB 1890-1914; DLB 36, 70

Stolz, Mary (Slattery) 1920-....... **CLC 12**
See also AAYA 8; AITN 1; CA 5-8R; CANR 13, 41; JRDA; MAICYA; SAAS 3; SATA 10, 71

Stone, Irving 1903-1989............ **CLC 7**
See also AITN 1; CA 1-4R; 129; CAAS 3; CANR 1, 23; MTCW; SATA 3; SATA-Obit 64

Stone, Oliver 1946-............... **CLC 73**
See also CA 110

Stone, Robert (Anthony) 1937- .... **CLC 5, 23, 42**
See also CA 85-88; CANR 23; MTCW

Stone, Zachary
See Follett, Ken(neth Martin)

Stoppard, Tom 1937- ...... **CLC 1, 3, 4, 5, 8, 15, 29, 34, 63; DA; WLC**
See also CA 81-84; CANR 39; CDBLB 1960 to Present; DLB 13; DLBY 85; MTCW

Storey, David (Malcolm) 1933- .... **CLC 2, 4, 5, 8**
See also CA 81-84; CANR 36; DLB 13, 14; MTCW

Storm, Hyemeyohsts 1935- .... **CLC 3**
See also CA 81-84; CANR 45; NNAL

Storm, (Hans) Theodor (Woldsen) 1817-1888 .... **NCLC 1**

Storni, Alfonsina 1892-1938 .... **TCLC 5; HLC**
See also CA 104; 131; HW

Stout, Rex (Todhunter) 1886-1975 ... **CLC 3**
See also AITN 2; CA 61-64

Stow, (Julian) Randolph 1935- .. **CLC 23, 48**
See also CA 13-16R; CANR 33; MTCW

Stowe, Harriet (Elizabeth) Beecher 1811-1896 .... **NCLC 3; DA; WLC**
See also CDALB 1865-1917; DLB 1, 12, 42, 74; JRDA; MAICYA; YABC 1

Strachey, (Giles) Lytton 1880-1932 .... **TCLC 12**
See also CA 110; DLBD 10

Strand, Mark 1934- ...... **CLC 6, 18, 41, 71**
See also CA 21-24R; CANR 40; DLB 5; SATA 41

Straub, Peter (Francis) 1943- ...... **CLC 28**
See also BEST 89:1; CA 85-88; CANR 28; DLBY 84; MTCW

Strauss, Botho 1944- .... **CLC 22**
See also DLB 124

Streatfeild, (Mary) Noel 1895(?)-1986 .... **CLC 21**
See also CA 81-84; 120; CANR 31; CLR 17; MAICYA; SATA 20; SATA-Obit 48

Stribling, T(homas) S(igismund) 1881-1965 .... **CLC 23**
See also CA 107; DLB 9

Strindberg, (Johan) August 1849-1912 ...... **TCLC 1, 8, 21, 47; DA; WLC**
See also CA 104; 135

Stringer, Arthur 1874-1950 .... **TCLC 37**
See also DLB 92

Stringer, David
See Roberts, Keith (John Kingston)

Strugatskii, Arkadii (Natanovich)
1925-1991 .... **CLC 27**
See also CA 106; 135

Strugatskii, Boris (Natanovich)
1933- .... **CLC 27**
See also CA 106

Strummer, Joe 1953(?)- .... **CLC 30**

Stuart, Don A.
See Campbell, John W(ood, Jr.)

Stuart, Ian
See MacLean, Alistair (Stuart)

Stuart, Jesse (Hilton)
1906-1984 .... **CLC 1, 8, 11, 14, 34**
See also CA 5-8R; 112; CANR 31; DLB 9, 48, 102; DLBY 84; SATA 2; SATA-Obit 36

Sturgeon, Theodore (Hamilton)
1918-1985 .... **CLC 22, 39**
See also Queen, Ellery
See also CA 81-84; 116; CANR 32; DLB 8; DLBY 85; MTCW

Sturges, Preston 1898-1959 .... **TCLC 48**
See also CA 114; DLB 26

Styron, William
1925- .... **CLC 1, 3, 5, 11, 15, 60**
See also BEST 90:4; CA 5-8R; CANR 6, 33; CDALB 1968-1988; DLB 2, 143; DLBY 80; MTCW

Suarez Lynch, B.
See Bioy Casares, Adolfo; Borges, Jorge Luis

Su Chien 1884-1918
See Su Man-shu
See also CA 123

Sudermann, Hermann 1857-1928 .. **TCLC 15**
See also CA 107; DLB 118

Sue, Eugene 1804-1857 .... **NCLC 1**
See also DLB 119

Sueskind, Patrick 1949- .... **CLC 44**
See also Suskind, Patrick

Sukenick, Ronald 1932- ..... **CLC 3, 4, 6, 48**
See also CA 25-28R; CAAS 8; CANR 32; DLBY 81

Suknaski, Andrew 1942- .... **CLC 19**
See also CA 101; DLB 53

Sullivan, Vernon
See Vian, Boris

Sully Prudhomme 1839-1907 ...... **TCLC 31**

Su Man-shu .... **TCLC 24**
See also Su Chien

Summerforest, Ivy B.
See Kirkup, James

Summers, Andrew James 1942- ..... **CLC 26**

Summers, Andy
See Summers, Andrew James

Summers, Hollis (Spurgeon, Jr.)
1916- .... **CLC 10**
See also CA 5-8R; CANR 3; DLB 6

Summers, (Alphonsus Joseph-Mary Augustus) Montague 1880-1948 .... **TCLC 16**
See also CA 118

Sumner, Gordon Matthew 1951- .... **CLC 26**

Surtees, Robert Smith
1803-1864 .... **NCLC 14**
See also DLB 21

Susann, Jacqueline 1921-1974 .... **CLC 3**
See also AITN 1; CA 65-68; 53-56; MTCW

Suskind, Patrick
See Sueskind, Patrick
See also CA 145

Sutcliff, Rosemary 1920-1992 ...... **CLC 26**
See also AAYA 10; CA 5-8R; 139; CANR 37; CLR 1; JRDA; MAICYA; SATA 6, 44, 78; SATA-Obit 73

Sutro, Alfred 1863-1933 .... **TCLC 6**
See also CA 105; DLB 10

Sutton, Henry
See Slavitt, David R(ytman)

Svevo, Italo .... **TCLC 2, 35**
See also Schmitz, Aron Hector

Swados, Elizabeth 1951- .... **CLC 12**
See also CA 97-100

Swados, Harvey 1920-1972 .... **CLC 5**
See also CA 5-8R; 37-40R; CANR 6; DLB 2

Swan, Gladys 1934- .... **CLC 69**
See also CA 101; CANR 17, 39

Swarthout, Glendon (Fred)
1918-1992 .... **CLC 35**
See also CA 1-4R; 139; CANR 1, 47; SATA 26

Sweet, Sarah C.
See Jewett, (Theodora) Sarah Orne

Swenson, May
1919-1989 .... **CLC 4, 14, 61; DA**
See also CA 5-8R; 130; CANR 36; DLB 5; MTCW; SATA 15

Swift, Augustus
See Lovecraft, H(oward) P(hillips)

Swift, Graham (Colin) 1949- .... **CLC 41**
See also CA 117; 122; CANR 46

Swift, Jonathan
1667-1745 ...... **LC 1; DA; PC 9; WLC**
See also CDBLB 1660-1789; DLB 39, 95, 101; SATA 19

Swinburne, Algernon Charles
1837-1909 ...... **TCLC 8, 36; DA; WLC**
See also CA 105; 140; CDBLB 1832-1890; DLB 35, 57

Swinfen, Ann .... **CLC 34**

Swinnerton, Frank Arthur
1884-1982 .... **CLC 31**
See also CA 108; DLB 34

Swithen, John
See King, Stephen (Edwin)

Sylvia
See Ashton-Warner, Sylvia (Constance)

Symmes, Robert Edward
See Duncan, Robert (Edward)

Symonds, John Addington
1840-1893 .... **NCLC 34**
See also DLB 57, 144

Symons, Arthur 1865-1945 .... **TCLC 11**
See also CA 107; DLB 19, 57

Symons, Julian (Gustave)
1912- .... **CLC 2, 14, 32**
See also CA 49-52; CAAS 3; CANR 3, 33; DLB 87; DLBY 92; MTCW

Synge, (Edmund) J(ohn) M(illington)
1871-1909 .... **TCLC 6, 37; DC 2**
See also CA 104; 141; CDBLB 1890-1914; DLB 10, 19

Syruc, J.
See Milosz, Czeslaw

Szirtes, George 1948- .... **CLC 46**
See also CA 109; CANR 27

Tabori, George 1914- .... **CLC 19**
See also CA 49-52; CANR 4

Tagore, Rabindranath
1861-1941 .... **TCLC 3, 53; PC 8**
See also CA 104; 120; MTCW

Taine, Hippolyte Adolphe
1828-1893 .... **NCLC 15**

Talese, Gay 1932- .... **CLC 37**
See also AITN 1; CA 1-4R; CANR 9; MTCW

Tallent, Elizabeth (Ann) 1954- ..... **CLC 45**
See also CA 117; DLB 130

Tally, Ted 1952- .... **CLC 42**
See also CA 120; 124

Tamayo y Baus, Manuel
1829-1898 .... **NCLC 1**

Tammsaare, A(nton) H(ansen)
1878-1940 .... **TCLC 27**

Tan, Amy 1952- .... **CLC 59**
See also AAYA 9; BEST 89:3; CA 136; SATA 75

Tandem, Felix
See Spitteler, Carl (Friedrich Georg)

Tanizaki, Jun'ichiro
1886-1965 .... **CLC 8, 14, 28**
See also CA 93-96; 25-28R

Tanner, William
See Amis, Kingsley (William)

Tao Lao
See Storni, Alfonsina

Tarassoff, Lev
See Troyat, Henri

Tarbell, Ida M(inerva)
1857-1944 .... **TCLC 40**
See also CA 122; DLB 47

Tarkington, (Newton) Booth
1869-1946 .... **TCLC 9**
See also CA 110; 143; DLB 9, 102; SATA 17

Tarkovsky, Andrei (Arsenyevich)
1932-1986 .... **CLC 75**
See also CA 127

Tartt, Donna 1964(?)- .... **CLC 76**
See also CA 142

Tasso, Torquato 1544-1595 .... **LC 5**

Tate, (John Orley) Allen
1899-1979 .... **CLC 2, 4, 6, 9, 11, 14, 24**
See also CA 5-8R; 85-88; CANR 32; DLB 4, 45, 63; MTCW

Author Index

Tindall, Gillian 1938- .... **CLC 7**
See also CA 21-24R; CANR 11

Tiptree, James, Jr. .... **CLC 48, 50**
See also Sheldon, Alice Hastings Bradley
See also DLB 8

Titmarsh, Michael Angelo
See Thackeray, William Makepeace

Tocqueville, Alexis (Charles Henri Maurice Clerel Comte) 1805-1859..... **NCLC 7**

Tolkien, J(ohn) R(onald) R(euel)
1892-1973 .... **CLC 1, 2, 3, 8, 12, 38; DA; WLC**
See also AAYA 10; AITN 1; CA 17-18; 45-48; CANR 36; CAP 2; CDBLB 1914-1945; DLB 15; JRDA; MAICYA; MTCW; SATA 2, 32; SATA-Obit 24

Toller, Ernst 1893-1939 .... **TCLC 10**
See also CA 107; DLB 124

Tolson, M. B.
See Tolson, Melvin B(eaunorus)

Tolson, Melvin B(eaunorus)
1898(?)-1966 .... **CLC 36; BLC**
See also BW 1; CA 124; 89-92; DLB 48, 76

Tolstoi, Aleksei Nikolaevich
See Tolstoy, Alexey Nikolaevich

Tolstoy, Alexey Nikolaevich
1882-1945 .... **TCLC 18**
See also CA 107

Tolstoy, Count Leo
See Tolstoy, Leo (Nikolaevich)

Tolstoy, Leo (Nikolaevich)
1828-1910 ...... **TCLC 4, 11, 17, 28, 44; DA; SSC 9; WLC**
See also CA 104; 123; SATA 26

Tomasi di Lampedusa, Giuseppe 1896-1957
See Lampedusa, Giuseppe (Tomasi) di
See also CA 111

Tomlin, Lily .... **CLC 17**
See also Tomlin, Mary Jean

Tomlin, Mary Jean 1939(?)-
See Tomlin, Lily
See also CA 117

Tomlinson, (Alfred) Charles
1927- .... **CLC 2, 4, 6, 13, 45**
See also CA 5-8R; CANR 33; DLB 40

Tonson, Jacob
See Bennett, (Enoch) Arnold

Toole, John Kennedy
1937-1969 .... **CLC 19, 64**
See also CA 104; DLBY 81

Toomer, Jean
1894-1967 ...... **CLC 1, 4, 13, 22; BLC; PC 7; SSC 1**
See also BW 1; CA 85-88; CDALB 1917-1929; DLB 45, 51; MTCW

Torley, Luke
See Blish, James (Benjamin)

Tornimparte, Alessandra
See Ginzburg, Natalia

Torre, Raoul della
See Mencken, H(enry) L(ouis)

Torrey, E(dwin) Fuller 1937- .... **CLC 34**
See also CA 119

Torsvan, Ben Traven
See Traven, B.

Torsvan, Benno Traven
See Traven, B.

Torsvan, Berick Traven
See Traven, B.

Torsvan, Berwick Traven
See Traven, B.

Torsvan, Bruno Traven
See Traven, B.

Torsvan, Traven
See Traven, B.

Tournier, Michel (Edouard)
1924- .... **CLC 6, 23, 36**
See also CA 49-52; CANR 3, 36; DLB 83; MTCW; SATA 23

Tournimparte, Alessandra
See Ginzburg, Natalia

Towers, Ivar
See Kornbluth, C(yril) M.

Townsend, Sue 1946- .... **CLC 61**
See also CA 119; 127; MTCW; SATA 48, 55

Townshend, Peter (Dennis Blandford)
1945- .... **CLC 17, 42**
See also CA 107

Tozzi, Federigo 1883-1920 .... **TCLC 31**

Traill, Catharine Parr
1802-1899 .... **NCLC 31**
See also DLB 99

Trakl, Georg 1887-1914 .... **TCLC 5**
See also CA 104

Transtroemer, Tomas (Goesta)
1931- .... **CLC 52, 65**
See also CA 117; 129; CAAS 17

Transtromer, Tomas Gosta
See Transtroemer, Tomas (Goesta)

Traven, B. (?)-1969 .... **CLC 8, 11**
See also CA 19-20; 25-28R; CAP 2; DLB 9, 56; MTCW

Treitel, Jonathan 1959- .... **CLC 70**

Tremain, Rose 1943- .... **CLC 42**
See also CA 97-100; CANR 44; DLB 14

Tremblay, Michel 1942- .... **CLC 29**
See also CA 116; 128; DLB 60; MTCW

Trevanian .... **CLC 29**
See also Whitaker, Rod(ney)

Trevor, Glen
See Hilton, James

Trevor, William
1928- .... **CLC 7, 9, 14, 25, 71**
See also Cox, William Trevor
See also DLB 14, 139

Trifonov, Yuri (Valentinovich)
1925-1981 .... **CLC 45**
See also CA 126; 103; MTCW

Trilling, Lionel 1905-1975 .... **CLC 9, 11, 24**
See also CA 9-12R; 61-64; CANR 10; DLB 28, 63; MTCW

Trimball, W. H.
See Mencken, H(enry) L(ouis)

Tristan
See Gomez de la Serna, Ramon

Tristram
See Housman, A(lfred) E(dward)

Trogdon, William (Lewis) 1939-
See Heat-Moon, William Least
See also CA 115; 119; CANR 47

Trollope, Anthony
1815-1882 ...... **NCLC 6, 33; DA; WLC**
See also CDBLB 1832-1890; DLB 21, 57; SATA 22

Trollope, Frances 1779-1863 ..... **NCLC 30**
See also DLB 21

Trotsky, Leon 1879-1940 .... **TCLC 22**
See also CA 118

Trotter (Cockburn), Catharine
1679-1749 .... **LC 8**
See also DLB 84

Trout, Kilgore
See Farmer, Philip Jose

Trow, George W. S. 1943- .... **CLC 52**
See also CA 126

Troyat, Henri 1911- .... **CLC 23**
See also CA 45-48; CANR 2, 33; MTCW

Trudeau, G(arretson) B(eekman) 1948-
See Trudeau, Garry B.
See also CA 81-84; CANR 31; SATA 35

Trudeau, Garry B. .... **CLC 12**
See also Trudeau, G(arretson) B(eekman)
See also AAYA 10; AITN 2

Truffaut, Francois 1932-1984 .... **CLC 20**
See also CA 81-84; 113; CANR 34

Trumbo, Dalton 1905-1976 .... **CLC 19**
See also CA 21-24R; 69-72; CANR 10; DLB 26

Trumbull, John 1750-1831 .... **NCLC 30**
See also DLB 31

Trundlett, Helen B.
See Eliot, T(homas) S(tearns)

Tryon, Thomas 1926-1991 .... **CLC 3, 11**
See also AITN 1; CA 29-32R; 135; CANR 32; MTCW

Tryon, Tom
See Tryon, Thomas

Ts'ao Hsueh-ch'in 1715(?)-1763 .... **LC 1**

Tsushima, Shuji 1909-1948
See Dazai, Osamu
See also CA 107

Tsvetaeva (Efron), Marina (Ivanovna)
1892-1941 .... **TCLC 7, 35**
See also CA 104; 128; MTCW

Tuck, Lily 1938- .... **CLC 70**
See also CA 139

Tu Fu 712-770 .... **PC 9**

Tunis, John R(oberts) 1889-1975 ... **CLC 12**
See also CA 61-64; DLB 22; JRDA; MAICYA; SATA 30, 37

Tuohy, Frank .... **CLC 37**
See also Tuohy, John Francis
See also DLB 14, 139

Tuohy, John Francis 1925-
See Tuohy, Frank
See also CA 5-8R; CANR 3, 47

Turco, Lewis (Putnam) 1934- ... **CLC 11, 63**
See also CA 13-16R; CANR 24; DLBY 84

Wallace, Irving 1916-1990 .... **CLC 7, 13**
See also AITN 1; CA 1-4R; 132; CAAS 1; CANR 1, 27; MTCW

Wallant, Edward Lewis 1926-1962 .... **CLC 5, 10**
See also CA 1-4R; CANR 22; DLB 2, 28, 143; MTCW

Walpole, Horace 1717-1797 .... **LC 2**
See also DLB 39, 104

Walpole, Hugh (Seymour) 1884-1941 .... **TCLC 5**
See also CA 104; DLB 34

Walser, Martin 1927- .... **CLC 27**
See also CA 57-60; CANR 8, 46, 46; DLB 75, 124

Walser, Robert 1878-1956 .... **TCLC 18**
See also CA 118; DLB 66

Walsh, Jill Paton .... **CLC 35**
See also Paton Walsh, Gillian
See also AAYA 11; CLR 2; SAAS 3

Walter, Villiam Christian
See Andersen, Hans Christian

Wambaugh, Joseph (Aloysius, Jr.) 1937- .... **CLC 3, 18**
See also AITN 1; BEST 89:3; CA 33-36R; CANR 42; DLB 6; DLBY 83; MTCW

Ward, Arthur Henry Sarsfield 1883-1959
See Rohmer, Sax
See also CA 108

Ward, Douglas Turner 1930- .... **CLC 19**
See also BW 1; CA 81-84; CANR 27; DLB 7, 38

Ward, Mary Augusta
See Ward, Mrs. Humphry

Ward, Mrs. Humphry 1851-1920 .... **TCLC 55**
See also DLB 18

Ward, Peter
See Faust, Frederick (Schiller)

Warhol, Andy 1928(?)-1987 .... **CLC 20**
See also AAYA 12; BEST 89:4; CA 89-92; 121; CANR 34

Warner, Francis (Robert le Plastrier) 1937- .... **CLC 14**
See also CA 53-56; CANR 11

Warner, Marina 1946- .... **CLC 59**
See also CA 65-68; CANR 21

Warner, Rex (Ernest) 1905-1986 .... **CLC 45**
See also CA 89-92; 119; DLB 15

Warner, Susan (Bogert) 1819-1885 .... **NCLC 31**
See also DLB 3, 42

Warner, Sylvia (Constance) Ashton
See Ashton-Warner, Sylvia (Constance)

Warner, Sylvia Townsend 1893-1978 .... **CLC 7, 19**
See also CA 61-64; 77-80; CANR 16; DLB 34, 139; MTCW

Warren, Mercy Otis 1728-1814 ... **NCLC 13**
See also DLB 31

Warren, Robert Penn 1905-1989 .... **CLC 1, 4, 6, 8, 10, 13, 18, 39, 53, 59; DA; SSC 4; WLC**
See also AITN 1; CA 13-16R; 129; CANR 10, 47; CDALB 1968-1988; DLB 2, 48; DLBY 80, 89; MTCW; SATA 46; SATA-Obit 63

Warshofsky, Isaac
See Singer, Isaac Bashevis

Warton, Thomas 1728-1790 .... **LC 15**
See also DLB 104, 109

Waruk, Kona
See Harris, (Theodore) Wilson

Warung, Price 1855-1911 .... **TCLC 45**

Warwick, Jarvis
See Garner, Hugh

Washington, Alex
See Harris, Mark

Washington, Booker T(aliaferro) 1856-1915 .... **TCLC 10; BLC**
See also BW 1; CA 114; 125; SATA 28

Washington, George 1732-1799 ...... **LC 25**
See also DLB 31

Wassermann, (Karl) Jakob 1873-1934 .... **TCLC 6**
See also CA 104; DLB 66

Wasserstein, Wendy 1950- .... **CLC 32, 59; DC 4**
See also CA 121; 129; CABS 3

Waterhouse, Keith (Spencer) 1929- .... **CLC 47**
See also CA 5-8R; CANR 38; DLB 13, 15; MTCW

Waters, Roger 1944- .... **CLC 35**

Watkins, Frances Ellen
See Harper, Frances Ellen Watkins

Watkins, Gerrold
See Malzberg, Barry N(athaniel)

Watkins, Paul 1964- .... **CLC 55**
See also CA 132

Watkins, Vernon Phillips 1906-1967 .... **CLC 43**
See also CA 9-10; 25-28R; CAP 1; DLB 20

Watson, Irving S.
See Mencken, H(enry) L(ouis)

Watson, John H.
See Farmer, Philip Jose

Watson, Richard F.
See Silverberg, Robert

Waugh, Auberon (Alexander) 1939- .. **CLC 7**
See also CA 45-48; CANR 6, 22; DLB 14

Waugh, Evelyn (Arthur St. John) 1903-1966 ...... **CLC 1, 3, 8, 13, 19, 27, 44; DA; WLC**
See also CA 85-88; 25-28R; CANR 22; CDBLB 1914-1945; DLB 15; MTCW

Waugh, Harriet 1944- .... **CLC 6**
See also CA 85-88; CANR 22

Ways, C. R.
See Blount, Roy (Alton), Jr.

Waystaff, Simon
See Swift, Jonathan

Webb, (Martha) Beatrice (Potter) 1858-1943 .... **TCLC 22**
See also Potter, Beatrice
See also CA 117

Webb, Charles (Richard) 1939- ...... **CLC 7**
See also CA 25-28R

Webb, James H(enry), Jr. 1946- .... **CLC 22**
See also CA 81-84

Webb, Mary (Gladys Meredith) 1881-1927 .... **TCLC 24**
See also CA 123; DLB 34

Webb, Mrs. Sidney
See Webb, (Martha) Beatrice (Potter)

Webb, Phyllis 1927- .... **CLC 18**
See also CA 104; CANR 23; DLB 53

Webb, Sidney (James) 1859-1947 .... **TCLC 22**
See also CA 117

Webber, Andrew Lloyd .... **CLC 21**
See also Lloyd Webber, Andrew

Weber, Lenora Mattingly 1895-1971 .... **CLC 12**
See also CA 19-20; 29-32R; CAP 1; SATA 2; SATA-Obit 26

Webster, John 1579(?)-1634(?) .... **DC 2**
See also CDBLB Before 1660; DA; DLB 58; WLC

Webster, Noah 1758-1843 .... **NCLC 30**

Wedekind, (Benjamin) Frank(lin) 1864-1918 .... **TCLC 7**
See also CA 104; DLB 118

Weidman, Jerome 1913- .... **CLC 7**
See also AITN 2; CA 1-4R; CANR 1; DLB 28

Weil, Simone (Adolphine) 1909-1943 .... **TCLC 23**
See also CA 117

Weinstein, Nathan
See West, Nathanael

Weinstein, Nathan von Wallenstein
See West, Nathanael

Weir, Peter (Lindsay) 1944- .... **CLC 20**
See also CA 113; 123

Weiss, Peter (Ulrich) 1916-1982 .... **CLC 3, 15, 51**
See also CA 45-48; 106; CANR 3; DLB 69, 124

Weiss, Theodore (Russell) 1916- .... **CLC 3, 8, 14**
See also CA 9-12R; CAAS 2; CANR 46; DLB 5

Welch, (Maurice) Denton 1915-1948 .... **TCLC 22**
See also CA 121

Welch, James 1940- .... **CLC 6, 14, 52**
See also CA 85-88; CANR 42; NNAL

Weldon, Fay 1933- .... **CLC 6, 9, 11, 19, 36, 59**
See also CA 21-24R; CANR 16, 46; CDBLB 1960 to Present; DLB 14; MTCW

Wellek, Rene 1903- .... **CLC 28**
See also CA 5-8R; CAAS 7; CANR 8; DLB 63

Weller, Michael 1942- . . . . **CLC 10, 53**
See also CA 85-88

Weller, Paul 1958- . . . . **CLC 26**

Wellershoff, Dieter 1925- . . . . **CLC 46**
See also CA 89-92; CANR 16, 37

Welles, (George) Orson
1915-1985 . . . . **CLC 20, 80**
See also CA 93-96; 117

Wellman, Mac 1945- . . . . **CLC 65**

Wellman, Manly Wade 1903-1986 . . **CLC 49**
See also CA 1-4R; 118; CANR 6, 16, 44; SATA 6; SATA-Obit 47

Wells, Carolyn 1869(?)-1942 . . . . . . **TCLC 35**
See also CA 113; DLB 11

Wells, H(erbert) G(eorge)
1866-1946 . . . . **TCLC 6, 12, 19; DA; SSC 6; WLC**
See also CA 110; 121; CDBLB 1914-1945; DLB 34, 70; MTCW; SATA 20

Wells, Rosemary 1943- . . . . **CLC 12**
See also AAYA 13; CA 85-88; CLR 16; MAICYA; SAAS 1; SATA 18, 69

Welty, Eudora
1909- . . . . . . **CLC 1, 2, 5, 14, 22, 33; DA; SSC 1; WLC**
See also CA 9-12R; CABS 1; CANR 32; CDALB 1941-1968; DLB 2, 102, 143; DLBD 12; DLBY 87; MTCW

Wen I-to 1899-1946 . . . . **TCLC 28**

Wentworth, Robert
See Hamilton, Edmond

Werfel, Franz (V.) 1890-1945 . . . . . . **TCLC 8**
See also CA 104; DLB 81, 124

Wergeland, Henrik Arnold
1808-1845 . . . . **NCLC 5**

Wersba, Barbara 1932- . . . . **CLC 30**
See also AAYA 2; CA 29-32R; CANR 16, 38; CLR 3; DLB 52; JRDA; MAICYA; SAAS 2; SATA 1, 58

Wertmueller, Lina 1928- . . . . **CLC 16**
See also CA 97-100; CANR 39

Wescott, Glenway 1901-1987 . . . . **CLC 13**
See also CA 13-16R; 121; CANR 23; DLB 4, 9, 102

Wesker, Arnold 1932- . . . . **CLC 3, 5, 42**
See also CA 1-4R; CAAS 7; CANR 1, 33; CDBLB 1960 to Present; DLB 13; MTCW

Wesley, Richard (Errol) 1945- . . . . **CLC 7**
See also BW 1; CA 57-60; CANR 27; DLB 38

Wessel, Johan Herman 1742-1785 . . . . **LC 7**

West, Anthony (Panther)
1914-1987 . . . . **CLC 50**
See also CA 45-48; 124; CANR 3, 19; DLB 15

West, C. P.
See Wodehouse, P(elham) G(renville)

West, (Mary) Jessamyn
1902-1984 . . . . **CLC 7, 17**
See also CA 9-12R; 112; CANR 27; DLB 6; DLBY 84; MTCW; SATA-Obit 37

West, Morris L(anglo) 1916- . . . . . **CLC 6, 33**
See also CA 5-8R; CANR 24; MTCW

West, Nathanael
1903-1940 . . . . . **TCLC 1, 14, 44; SSC 16**
See also CA 104; 125; CDALB 1929-1941; DLB 4, 9, 28; MTCW

West, Owen
See Koontz, Dean R(ay)

West, Paul 1930- . . . . **CLC 7, 14**
See also CA 13-16R; CAAS 7; CANR 22; DLB 14

West, Rebecca 1892-1983 . . **CLC 7, 9, 31, 50**
See also CA 5-8R; 109; CANR 19; DLB 36; DLBY 83; MTCW

Westall, Robert (Atkinson)
1929-1993 . . . . **CLC 17**
See also AAYA 12; CA 69-72; 141; CANR 18; CLR 13; JRDA; MAICYA; SAAS 2; SATA 23, 69; SATA-Obit 75

Westlake, Donald E(dwin)
1933- . . . . **CLC 7, 33**
See also CA 17-20R; CAAS 13; CANR 16, 44

Westmacott, Mary
See Christie, Agatha (Mary Clarissa)

Weston, Allen
See Norton, Andre

Wetcheek, J. L.
See Feuchtwanger, Lion

Wetering, Janwillem van de
See van de Wetering, Janwillem

Wetherell, Elizabeth
See Warner, Susan (Bogert)

Whalen, Philip 1923- . . . . **CLC 6, 29**
See also CA 9-12R; CANR 5, 39; DLB 16

Wharton, Edith (Newbold Jones)
1862-1937 . . . . . . **TCLC 3, 9, 27, 53; DA; SSC 6; WLC**
See also CA 104; 132; CDALB 1865-1917; DLB 4, 9, 12, 78; MTCW

Wharton, James
See Mencken, H(enry) L(ouis)

Wharton, William (a pseudonym)
. . . . **CLC 18, 37**
See also CA 93-96; DLBY 80

Wheatley (Peters), Phillis
1754(?)-1784 . . . . **LC 3; BLC; DA; PC 3; WLC**
See also CDALB 1640-1865; DLB 31, 50

Wheelock, John Hall 1886-1978 . . . . **CLC 14**
See also CA 13-16R; 77-80; CANR 14; DLB 45

White, E(lwyn) B(rooks)
1899-1985 . . . . **CLC 10, 34, 39**
See also AITN 2; CA 13-16R; 116; CANR 16, 37; CLR 1, 21; DLB 11, 22; MAICYA; MTCW; SATA 2, 29; SATA-Obit 44

White, Edmund (Valentine III)
1940- . . . . **CLC 27**
See also AAYA 7; CA 45-48; CANR 3, 19, 36; MTCW

White, Patrick (Victor Martindale)
1912-1990 . . **CLC 3, 4, 5, 7, 9, 18, 65, 69**
See also CA 81-84; 132; CANR 43; MTCW

White, Phyllis Dorothy James 1920-
See James, P. D.
See also CA 21-24R; CANR 17, 43; MTCW

White, T(erence) H(anbury)
1906-1964 . . . . **CLC 30**
See also CA 73-76; CANR 37; JRDA; MAICYA; SATA 12

White, Terence de Vere
1912-1994 . . . . **CLC 49**
See also CA 49-52; 145; CANR 3

White, Walter F(rancis)
1893-1955 . . . . **TCLC 15**
See also White, Walter
See also BW 1; CA 115; 124; DLB 51

White, William Hale 1831-1913
See Rutherford, Mark
See also CA 121

Whitehead, E(dward) A(nthony)
1933- . . . . **CLC 5**
See also CA 65-68

Whitemore, Hugh (John) 1936- . . . . . **CLC 37**
See also CA 132

Whitman, Sarah Helen (Power)
1803-1878 . . . . **NCLC 19**
See also DLB 1

Whitman, Walt(er)
1819-1892 . . . . . **NCLC 4, 31; DA; PC 3; WLC**
See also CDALB 1640-1865; DLB 3, 64; SATA 20

Whitney, Phyllis A(yame) 1903- . . . . **CLC 42**
See also AITN 2; BEST 90:3; CA 1-4R; CANR 3, 25, 38; JRDA; MAICYA; SATA 1, 30

Whittemore, (Edward) Reed (Jr.)
1919- . . . . **CLC 4**
See also CA 9-12R; CAAS 8; CANR 4; DLB 5

Whittier, John Greenleaf
1807-1892 . . . . **NCLC 8**
See also CDALB 1640-1865; DLB 1

Whittlebot, Hernia
See Coward, Noel (Peirce)

Wicker, Thomas Grey 1926-
See Wicker, Tom
See also CA 65-68; CANR 21, 46

Wicker, Tom . . . . **CLC 7**
See also Wicker, Thomas Grey

Wideman, John Edgar
1941- . . . . **CLC 5, 34, 36, 67; BLC**
See also BW 2; CA 85-88; CANR 14, 42; DLB 33, 143

Wiebe, Rudy (Henry) 1934- . . . **CLC 6, 11, 14**
See also CA 37-40R; CANR 42; DLB 60

Wieland, Christoph Martin
1733-1813 . . . . **NCLC 17**
See also DLB 97

Wiene, Robert 1881-1938 . . . . **TCLC 56**

Wieners, John 1934- . . . . **CLC 7**
See also CA 13-16R; DLB 16

Wiesel, Elie(zer)
1928- . . . . **CLC 3, 5, 11, 37; DA**
See also AAYA 7; AITN 1; CA 5-8R; CAAS 4; CANR 8, 40; DLB 83; DLBY 87; MTCW; SATA 56

Wiggins, Marianne 1947- . . . . **CLC 57**
See also BEST 89:3; CA 130

Wight, James Alfred 1916-
See Herriot, James
See also CA 77-80; SATA 44, 55

Wilbur, Richard (Purdy)
1921- .... **CLC 3, 6, 9, 14, 53; DA**
See also CA 1-4R; CABS 2; CANR 2, 29; DLB 5; MTCW; SATA 9

Wild, Peter 1940- .... **CLC 14**
See also CA 37-40R; DLB 5

Wilde, Oscar (Fingal O'Flahertie Wills)
1854(?)-1900 .... **TCLC 1, 8, 23, 41; DA; SSC 11; WLC**
See also CA 104; 119; CDBLB 1890-1914; DLB 10, 19, 34, 57, 141; SATA 24

Wilder, Billy .... **CLC 20**
See also Wilder, Samuel
See also DLB 26

Wilder, Samuel 1906-
See Wilder, Billy
See also CA 89-92

Wilder, Thornton (Niven)
1897-1975 ...... **CLC 1, 5, 6, 10, 15, 35, 82; DA; DC 1; WLC**
See also AITN 2; CA 13-16R; 61-64; CANR 40; DLB 4, 7, 9; MTCW

Wilding, Michael 1942- .... **CLC 73**
See also CA 104; CANR 24

Wiley, Richard 1944- .... **CLC 44**
See also CA 121; 129

Wilhelm, Kate .... **CLC 7**
See also Wilhelm, Katie Gertrude
See also CAAS 5; DLB 8

Wilhelm, Katie Gertrude 1928-
See Wilhelm, Kate
See also CA 37-40R; CANR 17, 36; MTCW

Wilkins, Mary
See Freeman, Mary Eleanor Wilkins

Willard, Nancy 1936- .... **CLC 7, 37**
See also CA 89-92; CANR 10, 39; CLR 5; DLB 5, 52; MAICYA; MTCW; SATA 30, 37, 71

Williams, C(harles) K(enneth)
1936- .... **CLC 33, 56**
See also CA 37-40R; DLB 5

Williams, Charles
See Collier, James L(incoln)

Williams, Charles (Walter Stansby)
1886-1945 .... **TCLC 1, 11**
See also CA 104; DLB 100

Williams, (George) Emlyn
1905-1987 .... **CLC 15**
See also CA 104; 123; CANR 36; DLB 10, 77; MTCW

Williams, Hugo 1942- .... **CLC 42**
See also CA 17-20R; CANR 45; DLB 40

Williams, J. Walker
See Wodehouse, P(elham) G(renville)

Williams, John A(lfred)
1925- .... **CLC 5, 13; BLC**
See also BW 2; CA 53-56; CAAS 3; CANR 6, 26; DLB 2, 33

Williams, Jonathan (Chamberlain)
1929- .... **CLC 13**
See also CA 9-12R; CAAS 12; CANR 8; DLB 5

Williams, Joy 1944- .... **CLC 31**
See also CA 41-44R; CANR 22

Williams, Norman 1952- .... **CLC 39**
See also CA 118

Williams, Tennessee
1911-1983 ..... **CLC 1, 2, 5, 7, 8, 11, 15, 19, 30, 39, 45, 71; DA; DC 4; WLC**
See also AITN 1, 2; CA 5-8R; 108; CABS 3; CANR 31; CDALB 1941-1968; DLB 7; DLBD 4; DLBY 83; MTCW

Williams, Thomas (Alonzo)
1926-1990 .... **CLC 14**
See also CA 1-4R; 132; CANR 2

Williams, William C.
See Williams, William Carlos

Williams, William Carlos
1883-1963 .... **CLC 1, 2, 5, 9, 13, 22, 42, 67; DA; PC 7**
See also CA 89-92; CANR 34; CDALB 1917-1929; DLB 4, 16, 54, 86; MTCW

Williamson, David (Keith) 1942- .... **CLC 56**
See also CA 103; CANR 41

Williamson, Ellen Douglas 1905-1984
See Douglas, Ellen
See also CA 17-20R; 114; CANR 39

Williamson, Jack .... **CLC 29**
See also Williamson, John Stewart
See also CAAS 8; DLB 8

Williamson, John Stewart 1908-
See Williamson, Jack
See also CA 17-20R; CANR 23

Willie, Frederick
See Lovecraft, H(oward) P(hillips)

Willingham, Calder (Baynard, Jr.)
1922- .... **CLC 5, 51**
See also CA 5-8R; CANR 3; DLB 2, 44; MTCW

Willis, Charles
See Clarke, Arthur C(harles)

Willy
See Colette, (Sidonie-Gabrielle)

Willy, Colette
See Colette, (Sidonie-Gabrielle)

Wilson, A(ndrew) N(orman) 1950- .. **CLC 33**
See also CA 112; 122; DLB 14

Wilson, Angus (Frank Johnstone)
1913-1991 .... **CLC 2, 3, 5, 25, 34**
See also CA 5-8R; 134; CANR 21; DLB 15, 139; MTCW

Wilson, August
1945- .. **CLC 39, 50, 63; BLC; DA; DC 2**
See also BW 2; CA 115; 122; CANR 42; MTCW

Wilson, Brian 1942- .... **CLC 12**

Wilson, Colin 1931- .... **CLC 3, 14**
See also CA 1-4R; CAAS 5; CANR 1, 22, 33; DLB 14; MTCW

Wilson, Dirk
See Pohl, Frederik

Wilson, Edmund
1895-1972 .... **CLC 1, 2, 3, 8, 24**
See also CA 1-4R; 37-40R; CANR 1, 46; DLB 63; MTCW

Wilson, Ethel Davis (Bryant)
1888(?)-1980 .... **CLC 13**
See also CA 102; DLB 68; MTCW

Wilson, John 1785-1854 .... **NCLC 5**

Wilson, John (Anthony) Burgess 1917-1993
See Burgess, Anthony
See also CA 1-4R; 143; CANR 2, 46; MTCW

Wilson, Lanford 1937- .... **CLC 7, 14, 36**
See also CA 17-20R; CABS 3; CANR 45; DLB 7

Wilson, Robert M. 1944- .... **CLC 7, 9**
See also CA 49-52; CANR 2, 41; MTCW

Wilson, Robert McLiam 1964- ..... **CLC 59**
See also CA 132

Wilson, Sloan 1920- .... **CLC 32**
See also CA 1-4R; CANR 1, 44

Wilson, Snoo 1948- .... **CLC 33**
See also CA 69-72

Wilson, William S(mith) 1932- ..... **CLC 49**
See also CA 81-84

Winchilsea, Anne (Kingsmill) Finch Counte
1661-1720 .... **LC 3**

Windham, Basil
See Wodehouse, P(elham) G(renville)

Wingrove, David (John) 1954- ...... **CLC 68**
See also CA 133

Winters, Janet Lewis .... **CLC 41**
See also Lewis, Janet
See also DLBY 87

Winters, (Arthur) Yvor
1900-1968 .... **CLC 4, 8, 32**
See also CA 11-12; 25-28R; CAP 1; DLB 48; MTCW

Winterson, Jeanette 1959- .... **CLC 64**
See also CA 136

Wiseman, Frederick 1930- .... **CLC 20**

Wister, Owen 1860-1938 .... **TCLC 21**
See also CA 108; DLB 9, 78; SATA 62

Witkacy
See Witkiewicz, Stanislaw Ignacy

Witkiewicz, Stanislaw Ignacy
1885-1939 .... **TCLC 8**
See also CA 105

Wittig, Monique 1935(?)- .... **CLC 22**
See also CA 116; 135; DLB 83

Wittlin, Jozef 1896-1976 .... **CLC 25**
See also CA 49-52; 65-68; CANR 3

Wodehouse, P(elham) G(renville)
1881-1975 ... **CLC 1, 2, 5, 10, 22; SSC 2**
See also AITN 2; CA 45-48; 57-60; CANR 3, 33; CDBLB 1914-1945; DLB 34; MTCW; SATA 22

Woiwode, L.
See Woiwode, Larry (Alfred)

Woiwode, Larry (Alfred) 1941- ... **CLC 6, 10**
See also CA 73-76; CANR 16; DLB 6

Wojciechowska, Maia (Teresa)
1927- .... **CLC 26**
See also AAYA 8; CA 9-12R; CANR 4, 41; CLR 1; JRDA; MAICYA; SAAS 1; SATA 1, 28

Literary Criticism Series Cumulative Topic Index

This index lists all topic entries in Gale's *Classical and Medieval Literature Criticism, Contemporary Literary Criticism, Literature Criticism from 1400 to 1800, Nineteenth-Century Literature Criticism, and Twentieth-Century Literary Criticism.*

CLC Cumulative Nationality Index

ARGENTINIAN

AUSTRALIAN

AUSTRIAN

BARBADIAN

CLC-86 Title Index

ISBN 0-8103-4996-5
90000
9 780810 349964